CIVIL PROCEDURE

SECOND EDITION

By

LARRY L. TEPLY
Professor of Law, Creighton University

and

RALPH U. WHITTEN
Professor of Law, Creighton University

New York, New York
FOUNDATION PRESS
2000

TEXT IS PRINTED ON 10% POST CONSUMER RECYCLED PAPER

PREFACE

Since the first edition of this textbook was published in 1994, significant developments have occurred in virtually every area of civil procedure. These developments have necessitated a second edition to assure that students and others using the text have available the most up-to-date description and evaluation of procedural topics that is possible in a one volume treatment of the subject. With one exception, we have retained the order of coverage contained in the first edition. The exception is that we have reversed the coverage of Chapters 3 and 4 to place coverage of personal jurisdiction before venue. This change seems more compatible with the coverage of procedural topics in most American Civil Procedure courses. In other respects, the format of the book remains the same.

As was true at the time of the first edition, American courses in civil procedure tend to be protean in nature. This being so, the second edition of the textbook, like the first attempts to remain useful to students regardless of what their law school civil procedure course includes. This produces a somewhat more detailed exposition of each topic in procedure than is found in other ''hornbooks'' on the subject. However, because excessive detail can sometimes overwhelm students of basic civil procedure, each chapter contains illustrations designed to simplify the textual explanations of specific procedural issues. From the standpoint of the beginning student, these illustrations remain one of the most useful aspects of the book.

It is our aim that students be able to use the book as an aid to obtain general background information *or* to assimilate the detail necessary to prepare for the (usually tough) examination that they will encounter at the end of the standard civil procedure course. In addition, we have not ignored the theoretical aspects of procedure. Throughout, we have attempted to provide analysis and critique of the procedures discussed, whether they be derived from court decisions, statutes, or court-made rules such as the Federal Rules of Civil Procedure. Furthermore, because we have continued to include the latest case developments on the most conceptually difficult matters of state and federal practice, we hope that practitioners will also find the book useful and informative.

Each chapter of the second edition contains extensive historical material explaining the evolution of the modern procedural rules and systems that are the main focus of the book. This historical material is essential to provide a complete understanding of current procedural systems. In addition, Chapters 3 and 5 contain historical material based on the original research of the authors. The material in Chapter 3 sheds new light on the development of personal jurisdiction rules in the United States. The material in Chapter 5 presents a nontraditional analysis of the federal courts' source of law authority in the nineteenth century, an analysis that is continually being reinforced by recent scholarship. All historical material is presented in a nonintrusive way. The primary goal throughout is to assure the reader's understanding of modern procedural systems. Increasing activity in the lower federal courts within the topic known as the ''*Erie* doctrine'' (which is the main focus of Chapter 5) has also motivated us to add subsections in all chapters dealing with the Rules of Decision Act and Rules Enabling Act problems that are occupying those courts. The descriptive and analytical help provided students in these subsections is, we believe, unique among civil procedure texts. This new material enhances the value of the text not only to students of Civil Procedure, but also to students of other courses in which the *Erie* doctrine is pertinent, such as Federal Courts and Conflict of Laws.

The second edition retains the first edition's extensive treatment of federal practice. We continue to believe this coverage is justified both because of the ever-increasing importance of the federal courts in the United States and because of the influence of federal practice on the states, particularly through the vehicle of the Federal Rules of Civil Procedure. Up-to-date coverage of federal subject-matter jurisdiction and venue developments constitutes one of the book's most important features. Our coverage includes judicial interpretations (through 1999) of the amendments to Title 28 of the United States Code from 1988 to the present. The case interpretations have been extensive. Among other things, these interpretations indicate how the lower federal courts are resolving the knotty interpretive problems presented by the new supplemental jurisdiction statute, 28 U.S.C. § 1367, as well as by the other 1990 amendments to Title 28. Added to this updated case treatment is a treatment of proposed reform efforts, such as the American Law Institute's Judicial Code Revision Project. Of course, the second edition retains the first edition's complete explanation of the 1993 amendments to the Federal Rules of Civil Procedure, including the revolutionary changes in federal discovery, which are sure to influence state practice in the future, along with pertinent case developments under the rules since 1994. It remains our hope that the extensive treatment of federal materials will also make the book useful to students in courses in Federal Courts and Federal Practice and Procedure.

Even though we extensively discuss federal practice, the second edition preserves the thorough exploration of code and other state procedural practices contained in the first edition. Many state procedural systems still contain significant features of code practice, while being influenced in other respects by the Federal Rules of Civil Procedure. We also treat non-code procedure when relevant. For example, Chapter 2 still contains a discussion of some of the most important theoretical problems of state subject-matter jurisdiction. This discussion provides a useful contrast to the federal subject-matter jurisdiction issues examined in the same chapter. Likewise, Chapter 4 continues to cover, among other discussions of state venue problems, an examination of the newly recommended Uniform Transfer of Litigation Act, which may be widely adopted by the states in the future. In addition, we have added an important section to Chapter 4 on antisuit injunctions, which are becoming increasingly important in both multistate and international litigation.

The U.S. Constitution imposes important limits on the operation of the federal and state procedural systems. We explore these constitutional limits at a number of points in the text. Chapter 3 of the second edition retains an extensive analysis of the federal constitutional limitations on the states' power to assert personal jurisdiction over nonresidents. Chapter 5 examines problems of separation of powers and federalism in the context of federal source-of-law authority in diversity actions. Chapter 6 contains a discussion of the latest U.S. Supreme Court decisions on state power to issue provisional remedies without prior notice and an opportunity to be heard in defense.

We owe a sizeable debt to the persons who supported and encouraged us in the preparation of this edition, as well as those who helped with the original work. Particular mention should be made of the generous research support supplied by Creighton University Law School. This support reflected a faith in the merits of the work by former Dean (now Dean Emeritus) Rodney Shkolnick, former Dean Lawrence Raful, and our current Dean, Patrick Borchers. Thanks are also due to our librarian, Kay Andrus and his extraordinary staff. Throughout the preparation of both editions, Kay and the Creighton library staff have solved our research problems with alacrity. Our students assisted us by cheerfully identifying and bringing to our attention flaws and ambiguities in the original text.

Special contributions were made to the original edition by Rickee Arntz, William Beck, Mary Jo Donahue, Robin Green, Beth Hanson, Sandy Henderson, Lisa Henkel, Karen Kassebaum, Michael Matukewicz, Patricia O'Leary, Angela Smith, and Debra Zorn. In addition, thanks go to Jen Bries, Mark Curran, Laurie Heer-Clark, and Shannon O'Connor for their invaluable proofreading and cite checking of the final draft of the manuscript of the second edition. We also thank Robert Teply for his review of Chapter 1. We also appreciate the efficient and cheerful secretarial assistance provided by Pat Anderson and Joan Hillhouse as well as the excellent copying service provided by Tianne Snell.

We want to express our appreciation to respective spouses, Frances Gayle and Jean, to our children, Ben, Chuck, Matt, and Robert, for their continuing support, understanding, and encouragement.

Larry L. Teply
Ralph U. Whitten
March 2000

SUMMARY OF CONTENTS

TABLE OF CONTENTS

Page

Chapter 6. Pleading and Related Matters—Continued

Chapter 6. Pleading and Related Matters—Continued

Chapter 8. Joinder of Parties—Continued

Chapter 9. Discovery and Pretrial Conferences—Continued

CIVIL PROCEDURE

*

Chapter 1

INTRODUCTION TO CIVIL PROCEDURE AND PRACTICE

Civil Procedure is the body of rules that prescribes the manner of conducting "civil actions." Section A of this chapter discusses the role of civil actions in the administration of justice. Section B examines the important distinction between "substantive" and "procedural" rules that permeates the entire subject of Civil Procedure. Section C discusses the role of the "adversary process" in Anglo-American systems of civil procedure. It also considers various procedural and ethical constraints on the adversary process. Section D examines methods of "alternative dispute resolution" that are becoming increasingly important in the American system of justice. Section E examines the historical evolution of the Anglo-American procedural systems. This historical background will be essential to an understanding of many aspects of modern civil procedure examined in later chapters.

SECTION A. THE ROLE OF CIVIL ACTIONS IN THE ADMINISTRATION OF JUSTICE

In the Anglo-American legal system, three basic types of proceedings are used to resolve disputes, enforce rights, or punish wrongs: civil actions, criminal actions, and administrative actions. Civil actions are governed by noncriminal substantive law and are conducted according to the applicable rules of civil procedure. Criminal and administrative actions are conducted, respectively, according to rules of criminal procedure and administrative procedure. Although civil, criminal, and administrative actions reflect different choices about how substantive legal norms should be enforced, significant overlap and interplay exist among these types of proceedings. Two examples from the familiar area of traffic violations will help illustrate this relationship.

Illustration 1-1. Assume that a police officer issues a traffic citation to a speeding motorist. This traffic citation initiates a minor criminal proceeding under a substantive criminal ordinance or statute. If the motorist pleads guilty or if a court finds the motorist guilty after a hearing, the ordinance or statute will usually provide for a fine. In this situation, society has chosen the criminal law and a criminal proceeding as the exclusive means of assuring compliance with speed limits.

Illustration 1-2. More serious traffic violations may result in both criminal and civil proceedings. For example, killing a pedestrian while driving under the influence of alcohol may result in a charge of motor vehicular homicide. This crime is usually a felony punishable by imprisonment. The deceased pedestrian's estate may also bring a civil wrongful death action against

1

the motorist to recover damages that result from the pedestrian's death. Because a single act can violate both criminal and civil substantive rules, corresponding criminal and civil proceedings may be brought to enforce those rules. The criminal proceeding vindicates the public's interest in deterring drunk driving. The civil proceeding compensates the deceased's survivors for losses they have suffered because of the death. In this way, the dual set of criminal and civil laws and proceedings serves both public and private interests.

* * * * *

Criminal and civil proceedings can interact in complicated ways. For example, in many jurisdictions, a party in a civil action can use a criminal judgment to establish facts that are common to both the criminal and civil proceeding.

Illustration 1-3. The criminal conviction for motor vehicle homicide described in *Illustration 1-2* may be used in a civil proceeding to establish that the defendant was driving while intoxicated. If the defendant has had a full and fair opportunity to litigate the issue in the criminal proceeding, the civil plaintiff will not have to offer evidence on this issue in the civil action. Instead, the plaintiff will be able to show by an appropriate procedure that the issue has been adjudicated in the criminal proceeding. The civil court will then accept the criminal finding as conclusive.[1] This procedure is valuable to the civil plaintiff for at least two reasons. First, it is usually easy for the plaintiff to prove that an issue has been fully and fairly adjudicated in the criminal action. Second, it is less expensive than reproducing all the evidence of the defendant's culpable behavior in the civil proceeding.[2]

* * * * *

Another way in which civil and criminal actions can interact involves the habeas corpus remedy. A person convicted of a criminal offense can sometimes seek a writ of habeas corpus to challenge the validity of the criminal judgment. A habeas corpus proceeding is a civil action in which a person in the custody of another (such as the warden of a prison) seeks to have the custodian justify the confinement. If the justification is an invalid criminal judgment, the confined person can obtain a release or retrial, whichever is appropriate.

Illustration 1-4. Assume that *A* is convicted in a state court and then imprisoned for violating a state criminal statute. Assume further that *A* believes that the state criminal statute violates the U.S. Constitution. After exhausting the remedies available in the state courts—*i.e.,* first presenting the merits of the constitutional claim to the state courts—*A* may petition an appropriate U.S. District Court for a writ of habeas corpus. In the habeas corpus proceeding in federal

---

1. In legal terms, the criminal judgment is "res judicata" and has an "issue preclusion" effect in the civil action. Res judicata and issue preclusion are described more fully in Chapter 13 ("Finality in Litigation") *infra.*

2. Because of special protections afforded to the defendants in criminal cases, it would be impossible to reverse this example and use a finding in the civil proceeding in a later criminal action. The defendant in a criminal case is constitutionally entitled to have the facts of guilt proved beyond a reasonable doubt by the government. In a civil action, however, the plaintiff will usually not have such a stringent burden of proof. Thus, to allow the government to use a civil judgment to establish facts in a criminal action would deprive the criminal defendant of the benefit of the higher burden of proof required in criminal actions. *See* Chapter 13(C)(2)*(d)* ("Differences in the Burden of Proof") *infra.*

court, the court will determine the validity of *A's* constitutional claim. If the claim is meritorious, the court will order *A's* release.[3]

* * * * *

The functions of the criminal law can sometimes be achieved by a civil proceeding. Likewise, criminal proceedings can indirectly support the objectives of civil proceedings.[4]

Illustration 1-5. Assume *B* violated a substantive civil rule of law (*e.g.*, committed an intentional tort) and consequently harmed *A*. In some circumstances, *A* can seek not only compensatory damages, but also punitive damages, in a civil action. Like criminal fines, punitive damages are designed to deter and punish the defendant. In the civil proceeding, *A*, the aggrieved plaintiff, keeps both the compensatory and the punitive damages that the court awards. In contrast, a criminal defendant ordinarily pays a fine to the governmental authority that brought the criminal action. By awarding punitive damages, civil proceedings can fulfill some of the purposes of the criminal law.

Illustration 1-6. In some civil proceedings, courts issue orders to a party that, if disobeyed, can result in both civil and criminal contempt proceedings. Civil contempt proceedings perform the function of assuring future compliance with court orders. Alternatively, a civil contempt fine can be tailored to compensate a party for losses that the party has suffered as a result of a violation of a court order. For example, the court may order a defendant who disobeys an order to pay a civil contempt fine each time the defendant disobeys the order in the future. Criminal contempt proceedings are designed to punish a party for a past violation of a court order. The court may impose a fixed fine or term of imprisonment on a party who disobeys a court order even once. Thus, criminal contempt proceedings also help assure general compliance with civil court orders through the deterrent operation of the criminal law.[5]

* * * * *

Administrative proceedings also interact with civil and criminal proceedings in important ways. In their simplest form, administrative proceedings occur when governmental officials, performing their duties, make preliminary determinations of fact or law. For example, tax assessors value property and set tax rates. Government pension administrators determine the level of benefits that potential beneficiaries are entitled to receive. Police officers make preliminary determinations that motorists have violated the traffic laws and issue traffic

---

3. *See* 28 U.S.C. §§ 2241-2254. The federal habeas corpus action described in this illustration is by no means the criminal defendant's only method of challenging the constitutional validity of the state statute. The state trial court in which the criminal action is pending may invalidate the statute, or a state appellate court may do so after the defendant is convicted. The U.S. Supreme Court has appellate jurisdiction to review the decisions of the state courts when an issue of federal law is involved in the case, such as the constitutional issue in this illustration. *See* 28 U.S.C. § 1257. Thus, a refusal of the state courts to rule favorably on the criminal defendant's constitutional claim could result in review and reversal by the U.S. Supreme Court. All of these possibilities, and perhaps others, may avoid the need for a federal habeas corpus proceeding.

4. Problems can occur when criminal and civil rules of procedure differ and parties attempt to use procedures in a concurrent proceeding, civil or criminal, to accomplish results in the other proceeding that would ordinarily be forbidden. For a discussion of these problems, see David A. Hayman, *When Rules Collide: Procedural Intersection and the Rule of Law*, 71 Tul. L. Rev. 1389 (1997).

5. Criminal and civil contempt are discussed further in Chapter 6(F) (''Provisional Remedies'') *infra*.

citations. In these examples, as well as thousands of others that occur daily, an administrative determination may later be the subject of a civil or criminal judicial proceeding.

Administrative agencies conduct all administrative proceedings. Several kinds of administrative agencies exist. Some agencies are simply departments of the executive branch of government headed by cabinet officers. These agencies help the chief executive officer—for example, the President at the national level—carry out the various constitutional responsibilities of the executive branch.[6] Other administrative agencies also exist within the executive branch, although they do not have "cabinet rank."[7] Finally, some agencies are designated as "independent" of the executive branch for political reasons. Technically, these agencies are arms of the legislative branch of government. They usually have complicated regulatory responsibilities.[8]

Agencies charged with the enforcement of a regulatory scheme perform a variety of functions. Typically, the legislature enacts a statute that directs an agency to accomplish socially desirable objectives in a certain area of concern. The agency then formulates regulations designed to carry out the legislature's directive.[9] The agency may then enforce the regulations in a variety of ways, depending upon the authorizing legislation and other statutes. The legislature may simply authorize the agency to bring civil or criminal court proceedings to enforce the regulatory scheme. Often, however, the legislature may authorize the agency to enforce a regulatory scheme in a specific type of administrative proceeding. In this case, the determination made in the agency proceeding will be subject to judicial review in a civil court proceeding. Usually, a party aggrieved by an agency's action must exhaust administrative remedies before seeking judicial review of the agency's action.[10]

Illustration 1-7. Congress has authorized the National Labor Relations Board (NLRB) to prohibit unfair labor practices by employers engaged in interstate or foreign commerce. To this end, the NLRB may hold administrative hearings to determine whether an employer is engaged in such practices. If the NLRB finds that the employer has engaged in unfair labor practices, the employer may obtain judicial review of the agency's determination in the federal courts. However, prior to seeking judicial review, the employer must exhaust its remedies before the NLRB.[11]

* * * * *

---

6. The Defense, Justice, and State Departments are examples of such agencies. *See* RICHARD J. PIERCE, JR. ET AL., ADMINISTRATIVE LAW AND PROCESS § 4.4.1 (2d ed. 1992).

7. The Environmental Protection Agency is an example of such an agency. *See id.*

8. Examples of such agencies at the national level are the Federal Trade Commission and the Securities and Exchange Commission. *Id.* Independent agencies are often referred to as "regulatory agencies." *See id.* This terminology is somewhat misleading, as it suggests that other kinds of agencies do not perform regulatory functions. However, agencies like the Environmental Protection Agency, an agency attached to the executive branch of government, also perform complicated regulatory functions.

9. *See id.* §§ 1.4.1-1.4.2 (discussing the National Traffic and Motor Vehicle Safety Act).

10. *See id.* § 5.7.2.

11. *See id.* § 5.7.2, at 175 (discussing Myers v. Bethlehem Shipbuilding Corp., 303 U.S. 41, 58 S. Ct. 459, 82 L. Ed. 638 (1938)).

In addition to agency-initiated proceedings, private parties may initiate appropriate proceedings before an agency or a court. In such a proceeding, the private party may seek to prevent a threatened enforcement of an administrative regulation or order.[12] Likewise, in some schemes of administrative adjudication, private parties are both plaintiffs and defendants.

Illustration 1-8. In a typical workers' compensation scheme, workers who are disabled while engaged in job-related activities may institute proceedings before a workers' compensation tribunal. This proceeding determines the facts, the extent of the worker's disability, and the level of appropriate compensation for that disability. In such a proceeding, the defendant will usually be either the worker's employer or the employer's insurer. The losing party may obtain review of the determination of the workers' compensation tribunal in an appropriate court proceeding. Typically, the courts will review whether the tribunal's determinations of law were correct and whether the evidence supported the tribunal's findings of fact.[13]

* * * * *

Although distinct procedures exist for civil, criminal, and administrative actions, all three kinds of adjudication share many common themes. Most importantly, the state and federal constitutions contain due process clauses. Before life, liberty, or property may be taken from individuals, due process clauses require that individuals receive adequate notice of the proceedings and an opportunity to be heard in defense. Due process requirements apply to all civil, criminal, and administrative proceedings.[14] Likewise, many of the same rules of evidence govern civil and criminal proceedings,[15] although special rules apply to criminal proceedings due to constitutional requirements.[16] Ordinary rules of evidence do not usually apply in administrative proceedings. However, some standards in administrative procedural rules are analogous to those in civil and criminal rules of evidence.[17]

---

12. The appropriate kind of proceeding depends on the statutory scheme. *See generally id.* § 5.3.

13. *See, e.g.*, Crowell v. Benson, 285 U.S. 22, 52 S. Ct. 285, 76 L. Ed. 598 (1932) (providing an example and discussion of judicial review in a workers' compensation proceeding).

14. The basic requirements of due process in civil proceedings are discussed in Chapter 3 ("Personal Jurisdiction and Service of Process") and Chapter 6(F) ("Provisional Remedies") *infra*. Due process issues are also discussed in Chapter 8(D)(4) ("Class actions") and Chapter 13(C)(3)*(a)* ("The Mutuality of Estoppel Rule and Traditional Exceptions to the Rule") *infra*.

15. *See, e.g.*, FED. R. EVID. 101, 1101(b).

16. *See, e.g.*, Miranda v. Arizona, 384 U.S. 436, 86 S. Ct. 1602, 16 L. Ed. 2d 694 (1966) (statements from defendants during incommunicado interrogation in police-dominated atmosphere, without full warning of constitutional rights, were inadmissible because they were obtained in violation of constitutional privilege against self-incrimination); Mapp v. Ohio, 367 U.S. 643, 81 S. Ct. 1684, 6 L. Ed. 2d 1081 (1961) (evidence obtained in search violating the Fourth and Fourteenth Amendments inadmissible and vitiated conviction); *cf.* United States v. Leon, 468 U.S. 897, 104 S. Ct. 3405, 82 L. Ed. 2d 677 (1984) (Fourth Amendment did not require exclusion of evidence used in the prosecution's case in chief that had been obtained by officers acting in reasonable reliance on a search warrant issued by a detached and neutral magistrate but ultimately found to be invalid).

17. *Compare* FED. R. EVID. 402 (inadmissibility of irrelevant evidence) *with* 5 U.S.C. § 556(d) (while an agency may receive any oral or documentary evidence, "the agency as a matter of policy shall provide for the exclusion of irrelevant, immaterial, or unduly repetitious evidence").

SECTION B. THE SUBSTANCE-PROCEDURE DISTINCTION

Procedural rules are said to define the form and method by which legal rights are enforced. On the other hand, substantive rules are said to define the legal rights themselves. Thus, procedure is often referred to as "adjective law" because procedural rules function to secure the objectives of the substantive law.

Illustration 1-9. Assume that *B* is driving too fast and hits *A*, a pedestrian. The substantive law of torts contains, *inter alia*, rules that make one person liable to another for negligence. This liability exists when (a) the substantive tort law imposes on a person a duty to exercise due care; (b) that person fails to conform to the duty; (c) a direct causal connection exists between the breach of duty and an injury inflicted on another person; and (d) the injured person actually suffers some damage. *Substantive* tort rules provide that under these circumstances *B* must pay damages to *A*. These rules also govern how *A's* damages should be measured. In contrast, the law of *procedure* establishes, *inter alia*, (a) the method by which the injured party *A* may begin a lawsuit against the tortfeasor, *B*; (b) the degree of detail with which the injured party must describe the "claim" for the court and the opposing party; and (c) the rules governing how the injured party must prove the facts constituting the breach of the duty, the injury, and the other elements of the tort.

* * * * *

Although "pure" substantive rules and "pure" procedural rules exist, many rules are a mixture of both substance and procedure. Some rules that seem to be procedural are adopted for substantive reasons; likewise, some rules that seem to be substantive are adopted for procedural reasons.

Illustration 1-10. *A* and *B* collide in their automobiles. The accident occurred in State *X* where both *A* and *B* live. *A* sues *B* in State *X* to recover damages for personal injuries received in the accident. The law of State *X* establishes the following "burden-of-proof" rule: the plaintiff must bear the burden of proving (a) that *B* was negligent; (b) that *B's* negligence directly caused *A's* injuries; and (c) the extent to which *A* was injured. Lawmakers often establish such rules purely for reasons of procedural policy. The plaintiff normally has the burden of proving these elements simply because the plaintiff is the party requesting relief. Thus, it is both convenient and fair that the plaintiff be required to produce evidence of a particular quality on certain basic elements of the "claim for relief."[18]

Illustration 1-11. In *Illustration 1-10*, suppose that the substantive law of State *X* provides that a plaintiff in a negligence action cannot recover if (a) the plaintiff was contributorily negligent and (b) that negligence contributed to the plaintiff's injuries. Assume that State *X* requires that the defendant prove that the plaintiff was contributorily negligent. Lawmakers sometimes allocate the burden of proof in this fashion because they disfavor the defense of contributory

---

18. *See generally* JOHN W. STRONG ET AL., MCCORMICK ON EVIDENCE § 337 (4th ed. 1992).

negligence.[19] Under such circumstances, lawmakers have arguably adopted the burden-of-proof rule for a substantive reason—even though the rule regulates an aspect of trial procedure. Procedural policies generally involve *efficiency* considerations, which include, but are not limited to, the orderly, speedy, and inexpensive administration of judicial proceedings. Lawmakers are not aiming at efficiency considerations when they create a burden-of-proof rule designed to make it harder for one side to win. Rather, the lawmakers are aiming at achieving a substantive social objective that transcends efficiency in judicial proceedings.

   Illustration 1-12. Statutes of frauds require that certain kinds of contracts be in writing to be enforceable. Oral contracts falling within the scope of a statute of frauds are, therefore, unenforceable. Statutes of frauds are designed, in part, to regulate the out-of-court behavior of parties contemplating the formation of contracts. They are often designed to avoid the difficulties of proof inherent in a civil action in which one party asserts the existence of an oral contract and the other party denies its existence. This requirement is arguably a procedural one because it focuses on the fallibility of the evidentiary process employed in judicial proceedings.[20] However, instead of, or in addition to, this procedural purpose, statutes of frauds are sometimes supported by an "admonitory" or "cautionary" policy. For example, the legislature may want parties to certain contracts to stop and think carefully before entering into the contracts to prevent "ill-considered and impulsive promises."[21] A written document is thought to assure that promises will be carefully considered before being made. This policy is a "substantive" one because it focuses on behavior outside the context of litigation rather than problems that oral contracts would cause in the litigation process.

* * * * *

   Identifying the policy reasons behind various rules provides insight into the extent to which particular rules should be considered "substantive" or "procedural." Legal disputes, however, are not abstract inquiries. In resolving concrete disputes, the policy reasons behind a rule are often not the most significant factors in categorizing a rule as substantive or procedural. Unless one knows why it is important to categorize a rule in the first place, the policies

---

19. *See id.* at 570; *see also* RESTATEMENT (SECOND) OF CONFLICT OF LAWS § 133 illus. 2 (1971).

20. *See* D. Michael Risinger, *"Substance" and "Procedure" Revisited, with Some Afterthoughts on the Constitutional Problems of Irrebuttable Presumptions*, 30 UCLA L. REV. 189, 206-07 (1982); *cf.* RESTATEMENT (SECOND) OF CONFLICT OF LAWS § 141 cmt. b (1971) (discussing whether statutes of frauds should be classified as substantive or procedural for conflict-of-laws purposes).

21. *See* 2 E. ALLAN FARNSWORTH, FARNSWORTH ON CONTRACTS § 6.1, at 97 (2d ed. 1998) (discussing the "cautionary" function of statutes of frauds). It is often impossible to tell whether a particular statute of frauds is supported by evidentiary policies, cautionary policies, or both, simply by reading the statute. Sometimes, however, the policy will be readily apparent. For example, the sales provisions of the Uniform Commercial Code contain a statute of frauds that appears to be supported only by evidentiary policies. U.C.C. § 2-201(1) provides that certain contracts for sales of goods must be in writing. However, U.C.C. § 2-201(3)(b) provides that an oral contract will nevertheless be enforceable "if the party against whom enforcement is sought admits in his pleading, testimony, or otherwise in court that a contract for sale was made." This provision seems directed only at solving evidentiary problems with oral contracts. It cannot be supported by a cautionary function or else oral contracts for sale would not be enforceable at all, even if later admitted. *See also* NATIONAL CONFERENCE OF COMMISSIONERS ON UNIFORM STATE LAWS, REVISION OF UNIFORM COMMERCIAL CODE ARTICLE 2—SALES § 2-201(c)(2) (Discussion Draft Dec. 1999) (revision of § 2-201 retaining and expanding the exception to the statute of frauds).

supporting the rule will give little guidance about whether a particular rule should be considered substantive or procedural.

   Illustration 1-13. Assume that a legislature delegates the power to make rules of civil practice and procedure to one or more courts within a jurisdiction. Assume further, however, that the legislature limits this rulemaking power to rules of practice and procedure that do not "abridge, enlarge, or modify any substantive right."[22] Before one can determine whether a particular rule of practice or procedure is valid or invalid under such a standard, one must know the purpose of this legislative limitation. Assume that the legislative history of such a statute reveals that the legislature did not want the courts to create rules that would affect parties' behavior at the primary stages of activity—*i.e.,* when they are driving automobiles, entering into contracts, etc. Otherwise, the courts are free to create any rules that regulate the judicial process. Once the purpose of this limitation is understood, it is easy to see that the courts could not create a statute of frauds such as the one described in *Illustration 1-12*, even if the exclusive reasons for doing so concerned the fallibility of the evidentiary processes in the trial of contract cases. Statutes of frauds affect a party's behavior at the primary stages of the contract-formation process. Therefore, *within the meaning of the legislative qualification*, the statute of frauds would be substantive even if a court created it purely for procedural reasons. On the other hand, the courts could create a burden-of-proof rule such as the one described in *Illustration 1-11*. Even if a court created the rule to disfavor the defense of contributory negligence, the rule does not affect the decisions of persons at the primary stages of activity (in driving automobiles, etc.). Thus, the rule does not abridge, enlarge, or modify substantive rights *within the meaning of the statutory qualification.*[23]

SECTION C. THE ADVERSARY SYSTEM

1. The Adversary Process

   The Anglo-American legal system relies primarily on the "adversary process" to resolve civil disputes. This process requires the parties to (a) begin the lawsuit, (b) define the issues, (c) develop proof in support of their respective positions, and (d) present that proof to a court. The rules and principles of civil procedure establish the framework that governs this adversary development and case presentation.

   Certain assumptions about the best path to justice and efficiency underlie the "adversary system."[24] These assumptions may or may not be true. For

---

   22. *See, e.g.,* 28 U.S.C. § 2072(b).

   23. When examining whether federal courts are obligated to apply state law in certain federal civil actions, it will be possible to see that application of a federal rather than a state burden-of-proof rule can be considered a substantive act. However, this conclusion will be due to the fact that the reasons for classifying rules as substantive or procedural in that context are different than the reasons for the statutory qualification in this illustration. *See* Chapter 5 ("Sources of Law") *infra.*

   24. *See generally* GEOFFREY C. HAZARD, JR., ETHICS IN THE PRACTICE OF LAW 120-35 (1978); Arthur R. Miller, *The Adversary System: Dinosaur or Phoenix,* 69 MINN. L. REV. 1 (1984).

example, many substantive rules of law are designed to serve broader interests than those of private parties. Often, substantive rules reflect social goals. By placing the primary responsibility on the parties in a controversy to initiate and develop litigation within the adversary process, the adversary system forces the parties to choose whether and to what extent substantive rules of law should be enforced. The system thus assumes that the policies underlying the substantive rules of law will be adequately fulfilled by relying upon the decisions of private parties.

Under the adversary system, the parties try to present their own evidence in the best possible light and the opponent's evidence in the worst possible light. The adversary system assumes that party presentation provides the best chance of finding the truth. The system also assumes that parties will develop and present cases affecting their private interests more efficiently than, for example, a public agency with no direct interest in the outcome. Thus, the system assumes that the parties are in the best position to decide whether a case is worth pursuing. Furthermore, party presentation places the expense of developing and presenting cases on the persons most directly affected rather than on the taxpayers at large.

Under the adversary system, lawyers ordinarily act as advocates for the parties. The idea is that skilled advocates operating on opposite sides of a case will develop and present all aspects of the case completely. Of course, this approach assumes that the lawyers for each side are of relatively equal competence. It also assumes that the financial resources available to each side are relatively equal.

Traditionally, the judge's role in the adversary system is reactive. For example, whether by design or through inadvertence, the parties may fail to present genuine factual or legal issues for decision. Ordinarily, if the parties do not raise such issues, the judge will not raise them. Even under the traditional adversary model, however, exceptions to this reactive role exist. The most notable exception relates to a court's institutional power to act. Even in the absence of the parties raising the issue, a court will raise a lack of subject-matter jurisdiction "on its own motion."[25] Nevertheless, on most matters, the parties are the masters of the case. The judge plays a relatively limited, nonintrusive role in the investigation and presentation of the litigation.

Of course, flaws may exist in the assumptions supporting the use of the adversary system.[26] A party presenting a case may seek to mislead rather than to establish the truth. The plaintiff, who initiates the case, may have every incentive to move it forward efficiently. On the other hand, the defendant may stand to lose a great deal upon completion of the lawsuit. Thus, the defendant may have the incentive to delay. Another inherent problem involves the lawyers' varying levels of competence. Different lawyers are no more of equal competence

---

25. *See* Chapter 2 ("Subject-Matter Jurisdiction") *infra*.

26. *Cf.* JOHN P. FRANK, AMERICAN LAW: THE CASE FOR RADICAL REFORM 126-27 (1969) ("[N]o one else pursuing truth would proceed as do lawyers and judges. The [adversary system] may or may not be a sure way of determining truth, but it is surely the most awkward method ever devised"). *See also* Carrie Menkel-Meadow, *The Trouble with the Adversary System in a Post-Modern, Multi-Cultural World*, 1 J. INST. FOR STUDY LEGAL ETHICS 49 (1996).

than different doctors, engineers, plumbers, or members of any other profession. The financial resources available to the parties may, more often than not, be significantly different. Furthermore, judges are subject to all the biases and prejudices of other human beings and differ widely in their intelligence and temperament.

2. Procedural Constraints

Given these potential flaws, one would expect procedural rules to attempt to mitigate the rigors of a pure adversary system. Indeed, modern civil procedure aims to secure the just, speedy, and inexpensive determination of civil actions.[27] Thus, modern rules of procedure attempt to enhance the strengths of the adversary process and to guard against its weaknesses.[28]

Illustration 1-14. For instance, Rule 11 of the Federal Rules of Civil Procedure prohibits, *inter alia*, presenting to the court pleadings, motions, or other papers "for any improper purpose, such as to harass or to cause unnecessary delay or needless increase in the cost of litigation."[29]

3. Ethical Constraints

In addition to the attempt by modern rules of procedure to mitigate the rigors of a pure adversary system, professional disciplinary rules and ethical considerations place limits on the pursuit of pure party interests in litigation.

Illustration 1-15. Under the Model Rules adopted by the American Bar Association in 1983,[30] lawyers have a duty to use the procedures provided by law "for the fullest benefit of the client's cause." At the same time, lawyers also

---

27. *See* FED. R. CIV. P. 1 (requiring that the Federal Rules of Civil Procedure be construed to secure these goals).

28. For an argument that attorney excesses on behalf of clients have been partially caused by changes in civil procedure, see Jonathan T. Molst, *How Changes in the Legal Profession Reflect Changes in Civil Procedure*, 84 VA. L. REV. 995 (1998).

29. FED. R. CIV. P. 11(b)(1); *see* Chapter 6(E) ("Verification and Good Faith Pleading") *infra*, in which Rule 11 sanctions are discussed fully.

30. The American Bar Association (ABA) has adopted three different sets of ethical rules this century. In 1908, the ABA adopted Canons of Professional Ethics, which contained 32 hortatory statements. In 1969, the ABA replaced the Canons with a much more extensive Code of Professional Responsibility, which consisted of nine Canons (axiomatic norms expressing in general terms the standard of professional conduct expected of lawyers), 138 Ethical Considerations (aspirational objectives toward which every member of the profession should strive), and 41 Disciplinary Rules (the minimum level of conduct below which no lawyer may fall without being subject to disciplinary action such as censure or disbarment). The Code of Professional Responsibility was adopted (with some modifications or omissions) as the basis for professional discipline in every state but California. In 1983, the ABA again revised its standards governing professional conduct in the form of Model Rules of Professional Conduct (consisting of a Terminology section, 52 Model Rules, and explanatory Comments). *See* CHARLES W. WOLFRAM, MODERN LEGAL ETHICS § 2.6 (1986). A majority of the states have now adopted the Model Rules as the basis for professional discipline. *See* 2 GEOFFREY C. HAZARD, JR. & W. WILLIAM HODES, THE LAW OF LAWYERING: A HANDBOOK ON THE MODEL RULES OF PROFESSIONAL CONDUCT 1255, 1269-70 (2d ed. 1998) (Appendix 4) (listing adopting jurisdictions). In May 1998, the American Law Institute approved a comprehensive RESTATEMENT (THIRD) OF THE LAW GOVERNING LAWYERS (Proposed Final Draft 1998).

have an ethical "duty not to abuse legal procedure."[31] Several Model Rules directly apply to civil litigation.

First, the Rules provide that "[a] lawyer shall not bring or defend a proceeding, or assert or controvert an issue therein, unless there is a basis for doing so that is not frivolous, which includes a good faith argument for an extension, modification or reversal of existing law."[32]

Second, the Rules require lawyers to make "reasonable efforts to expedite litigation consistent with the interests of the client."[33]

Third, the Rules prohibit lawyers from knowingly making false statements of material facts or offering false evidence. Lawyers must also disclose any legal authority in the controlling jurisdiction known to be directly adverse to their client's position when opposing counsel has not disclosed that legal authority to the tribunal. Furthermore, lawyers must disclose material facts to the tribunal to prevent assisting a client's criminal or fraudulent act.[34]

Fourth, the Rules prohibit a variety of unfair conduct. Lawyers may not conceal, falsify, or destroy evidence. Nor may they allude in trial to matters that they do not reasonably believe to be relevant.[35]

Fifth, the Rules provide that lawyers shall not improperly seek to influence judges, jurors, or other officials. Nor shall lawyers engage in conduct intended to disrupt a tribunal.[36]

Sixth, the Rules prohibit lawyers from knowingly making false statements of law or material fact to third persons in the course of representing their clients. The Rules also require lawyers to disclose material facts to third persons when that disclosure is necessary to avoid assisting their clients in fraudulent or criminal acts (unless lawyer-client confidentiality limits that disclosure).[37]

Seventh, the Rules prohibit lawyers from directly communicating about the subject of the litigation with a party when they know another lawyer represents that party in the matter (unless the other lawyer has consented or the law otherwise permits the communication).[38]

Eighth, the Rules prohibit lawyers from stating or implying that they are disinterested when dealing on behalf of their clients with persons not represented by counsel.[39]

Ninth, the Rules state that lawyers "shall not use means that have no substantial purpose other than to embarrass, delay, or burden a third person, or use methods of obtaining evidence that violate the legal rights of such a person."[40]

---

31. MODEL RULES OF PROFESSIONAL CONDUCT Rule 3.1 cmt. (1983).
32. *Id.* Rule 3.1.
33. *Id.* Rule 3.2.
34. *Id.* Rule 3.3(a).
35. *Id.* Rule 3.4.
36. *Id.* Rule 3.5.
37. *Id.* Rule 4.1.
38. *Id.* Rule 4.2.
39. *Id.* Rule 4.3.
40. *Id.* Rule 4.4.

4. Litigation Costs

(a) Allocating the Direct Costs of Litigation

Litigation in an adversary system involves costs.[41] Some of the "direct" costs of litigation are the salaries of court employees; janitorial services; the time of the litigants, jurors, and witnesses; investigation expenses; expert witness fees; and the legal fees of the litigants' lawyers.[42] The litigants bear some of these direct costs through filing fees and other expenditures. The taxpayers also bear some of the costs through expenditures of public funds to maintain the court system. How a legal system divides these costs between the litigants and the public affects access to the courts.[43] That division reflects fundamental judgments about the functions of a government.[44]

Furthermore, how a judicial system allocates the costs *among the litigants themselves* may influence the litigants' conduct and even the decision to use the judicial process at all.[45] A judgment in a lawsuit will ordinarily award "costs"

---

41. *See* David M. Trubek et al., *The Costs of Ordinary Litigation*, 31 UCLA L. REV. 72 (1983). Litigation "costs" have been described in various ways. *See, e.g.,* FLEMING JAMES, JR. ET AL., CIVIL PROCEDURE § 6.3, at 298-99 (4th ed. 1992) (cost of litigation includes (1) "opportunity," "uncertainty," and "illiquidity" costs; (2) "information processing" costs; and (3) "psychological" costs (or losses) arising from "worry, loss of sleep, tension, and spasms of rage"); Richard A. Posner, *An Economic Approach to Legal Procedure and Judicial Administration*, 2 J. LEGAL STUD. 399, 400 (1973) ("direct" costs and "error" costs). Widespread concern about litigation costs resulted in a requirement that each federal district court submit a civil justice "expense and delay reduction plan." *See* Civil Justice Reform Act of 1990, Pub. L. No. 101-650, § 103, 104 Stat. 5089, 5090 (codified at 28 U.S.C. § 471). These plans have had considerable impact on federal practice, especially discovery, dispositions prior to trial, and trial. Although such plans promote experimentation at the federal district court level, they will also lessen the uniformity of procedure established by the Federal Rules of Civil Procedure. *See* Linda S. Mullinex, *The Counter-Reformation in Procedural Justice*, 77 MINN. L. REV. 375 (1992); Carl Tobias, *The Transformation of Trans-Substantivity*, 49 WASH. & LEE L. REV. 1501 (1992); *see also* section D ("Alternative Dispute Resolution") *infra* (discussing various methods of alternative dispute resolution that may help reduce the cost of resolving disputes).

42. *See* Richard A. Posner, *An Economic Approach to Legal Procedure and Judicial Administration*, 2 J. LEGAL STUD. 399, 401 (1973). Based on figures for Fiscal Year 1988 supplied by the Clerk's Office for the Southern District of Texas, one judge has calculated the public costs of operating a federal court in that district to be approximately $890 per hour. This amount was calculated by dividing the operating expenses per judge in the Southern District ($1,843,437) by the amount of time the federal courts operate per year (2,080 hours). *See* Seneca Resources Corp. v. Moody, 135 B.R. 260, 261 & n.2 (S.D. Tex. 1991).

43. *See generally* Frank I. Michelman, *The Supreme Court and Litigation Access Fees: The Right to Protect One's Rights*, 1973 DUKE L.J. 1153; John F. Vargo, *The American Rule on Attorney Fee Allocation: The Injured Person's Access to Justice*, 42 AM. U. L. REV. 1567 (1993). Congress has provided for the waiver of filing fees in the federal district courts. *See* 28 U.S.C. § 1915(a) (in forma pauperis); Romualdo P. Eclavea, Annotation, *What Constitutes "Fees" or "Costs" Within Meaning of Federal Statutory Provision (Under 28 USCS § 1915(a) and Similar Predecessor Statutes) Permitting Party to Proceed in Forma Pauperis Without Prepayment of Fees and Costs or Security Therefor*, 20 A.L.R. FED. 274 (1974); *cf.* Boddie v. Connecticut, 401 U.S. 371, 91 S. Ct. 780, 28 L. Ed. 2d 113 (1971) (due process prevents a state from imposing filing, service, and publication fees on welfare recipients seeking divorces).

44. *See generally* Rex E. Lee, *The American Courts as Public Goods: Who Should Pay the Costs of Litigation*, 34 CATH. U. L. REV. 267 (1985); Phillip L. Spector, *Financing the Courts Through Fees: Incentives and Equity in Civil Litigation*, 58 JUDICATURE 330 (1975);

45. *See generally* Thomas D. Rowe, Jr., *The Legal Theory of Attorney Fee Shifting: A Critical Overview*, 1982 DUKE L.J. 651; Thomas D. Rowe, Jr., *Predicting the Effects of Attorney Fee Shifting*, 47 LAW & CONTEMP. PROBS. 139 (1984); Steven Shavell, *Suit, Settlement and Trial: A Theoretical Analysis Under Alternative Methods for the Allocation of Legal Costs*, 11 J. LEGAL STUD. 55, 58-69 (1982); Note, *Use of* to the prevailing party.[46] The law in each jurisdiction defines "taxable" (recoverable) costs. Taxable costs usually are small in comparison to the overall expenses of litigation. Examples of taxable costs in the federal courts include fees of the clerk and marshall, fees of court reporters for the stenographic transcripts obtained for use in the case, and fees for witnesses.[47] Shifts in the liability for costs can be designed to encourage specific policies or actions.

Illustration 1-16. Federal Rule 68 shifts costs to encourage settlement. If the plaintiff rejects an "offer of judgment" and then fails to obtain a more favorable judgment, the plaintiff must pay the "costs" (as defined by law) incurred after the offer was made.[48]

* * * * *

A significant litigation expense is the attorney's fee. However, under the "American Rule," the attorney's fee of the winning party is ordinarily *not* a recoverable cost.[49] Judicially created exceptions to the American Rule include the "common fund" rule,[50] the "substantial benefit" rule,[51] and the "private

---

Taxable Costs to Regulate the Conduct of Litigants, 53 COLUM. L. REV. 78 (1953)

46. *See, e.g.*, FED. R. CIV. P. 54(d); *cf.* D.R. Rimmer, Annotation, *Award of Costs in Appellate Proceedings in Federal Court Under Rule 39 of Federal Rules of Appellate Procedure*, 68 A.L.R. FED. 494 (1984). *See generally* Thomas J. Goger, Annotation, *Who is the "Successful Party" or "Prevailing Party" for Purposes of Awarding Costs Where Both Parties Prevail on Affirmative Claims*, 66 A.L.R.3D 1115 (1975); Thomas J. Goger, Annotation, *Dismissal of Plaintiff's Action as Entitling Defendant to Recover Attorneys' Fees or Costs as "Prevailing Party" or "Successful Party,"* 66 A.L.R.3D 1087 (1975).

47. *See* 28 U.S.C. § 1920; *see also* Kristine C. Karnezis, Annotation, *Propriety Under 28 USCS § 1920 and Rule 54(d) of the Federal Rules of Civil Procedure of Allowing Prevailing Party Costs for Copies of Depositions*, 50 A.L.R. FED. 472 (1980); Annotation, *Compensation of Expert Witness as Costs Recoverable in Federal Civil Action by Prevailing Party Against Party Other Than United States*, 71 A.L.R. FED. 875 (1985); Margaret Shulenberger, Annotation, *Construction and Application of 28 USCS § 1921 Authorizing Fees of United States Marshals to Be Collected and Taxed as Costs*, 14 A.L.R. FED. 901 (1973); Annotation, *Comment Note–Allowance of Costs for Witness' Travel Expenses in Attending Federal Civil Trial for Purposes of Testifying*, 13 L. Ed. 2d 1036 (1965).

48. *See* FED. R. CIV. P. 68; *see also* Chapter 10(F) ("Miscellaneous Methods of Disposing of an Action Without Trial") *infra*, in which Rule 68 is more fully discussed. For an extensive examination of the role of lawyers in influencing settlement, see Rullell Korobkin & Chris Guthril, *Psychology, Economics, and Settlement: A New Look at the Role of the Lawyer*, 76 TEX. L. REV. 27 (1997).

49. *See* Alyeska Pipeline Serv. Co. v. Wilderness Soc'y, 421 U.S. 240, 247, 95 S. Ct. 1612, 1616, 44 L. Ed. 2d 141, 147 (1975) ("In the United States, the prevailing litigant is ordinarily not entitled to collect a reasonable attorney's fee from the loser."); *see also* DAN B. DOBBS, LAW OF REMEDIES § 3.10(1), at 276-77 (2d student ed. 1993) (describing this rule, its development, and its rationales). *See generally* John Leubsdorf, *Recovering Attorney Fees as Damages*, 38 RUTGERS L. REV. 439 (1986); John P. Ludington, Annotation, *Supreme Court's Views as to Requisites for Award of Attorneys' Fees*, 77 L. Ed. 2d 1540 (1985). The "American Rule" contrasts with English practice. In England, the court may include in the judgment a reasonable allowance for attorney's fees to make the prevailing party whole. *See* Marek v. Chesny, 473 U.S. 1, 8, 105 S. Ct. 3012, 3016, 87 L. Ed. 2d 1, 8 (1985) (in contrast to England, "under the 'American Rule,' each party [must] bear its own attorney's fees"); *cf.* Arthur L. Goodhart, *Costs*, 38 YALE L.J. 849, 851-72 (1929) (describing the English practice); Werner Pfennigstorf, *The European Experience with Attorney Fee Shifting*, 47 LAW & CONTEMP. PROBS. 37 (1984). For an examination of whether the "American Rule" or the "English Rule" on attorney's fees better discourages plaintiffs who have a low probability of recovery from suing, see A. Michael Polinsky & Daniel L. Rubenfield, *Does the English Rule Discourage Low-Probability-of-Prevailing Plaintiffs?* 27 J. LEG. STUD. 519 (1998).

50. Persons who share in a fund produced or preserved by a prevailing plaintiff's litigation are responsible for a proportionate part of the costs of the litigation, including the attorney's fee. *See* DAN B. DOBBS, LAW OF REMEDIES § 3.10(2), at 279-81 (2d student ed. 1993). *See generally* John P. Dawson, *Lawyers and Involuntary Clients: Attorney Fees from Funds*, 87 HARV. L. REV. 1597 (1974); Ferdinand S. Tinio, Annotation, *Attorneys' Fees in Class Actions*, 38 A.L.R.3D 1384 (1971).

attorney general'' theory.[52] Statutes likewise establish exceptions to the American Rule.

Illustration 1-17. Examples of federal statutes creating exceptions to the American Rule include the Freedom of Information Act; Securities Act of 1933; Packers and Stockyards Act; Education Amendments of 1972; Truth in Lending Act; Water Pollution Control Act; Clayton Act; and Civil Rights Act of 1964.[53]

Illustration 1-18. The Equal Access to Justice Act (EAJA)[54] provides that a court, unless prohibited by statute, has the *discretion* to award reasonable attorney's fees and expenses to the prevailing party in any civil action brought by or against the U.S. Government.[55] The EAJA also *requires* a court to award attorneys' fees, unless prohibited by statute, to an otherwise eligible prevailing party in such an action when the position of the United States is not ''substantially justified'' or ''special circumstances'' make such an award just.[56]

---

51. This ''substantial benefit'' rule extends the ''common fund'' rule to cases involving non-cash benefits in the context of institutional defendants. DAN B. DOBBS, LAW OF REMEDIES § 3.10(2), at 281-83 (2d student ed. 1993) (discussing this extension and critiquing the restitutionary argument made in such cases); *see* Hall v. Cole, 412 U.S. 1, 93 S. Ct. 1943, 36 L. Ed. 2d 702 (1973) (union defendant liable for plaintiff union member's attorney's fees after establishing free speech rights for the union membership generally); Mills v. Electric Auto-Lite Co., 396 U.S. 375, 90 S. Ct. 616, 24 L. Ed. 2d 593 (1970) (corporate defendant liable for plaintiff shareholder's attorney's fees after plaintiff established intangible rights on behalf of all shareholders).

52. The ''private attorney general'' theory supports the recovery of attorney's fees from the defendant when substantial public benefits have resulted from litigation that otherwise might not be brought. DAN B. DOBBS, LAW OF REMEDIES § 3.10(2), at 283 (2d student ed. 1993). This theory was judicially adopted in Serrano v. Priest, 20 Cal. 3d 25, 569 P.2d 1303, 141 Cal. Rptr. 315 (1977). The *Serrano* result was subsequently codified. *See* CAL. CIV. PROC. CODE § 1021.5 (West Supp. 1999) (fees may be awarded against opposing parties when ''an important right affecting the public interest'' has been enforced and ''(a) a significant benefit, whether pecuniary or nonpecuniary, has been conferred on the general public or a large class of persons, (b) the necessity and financial burden of private enforcement, or of enforcement by one public entity against another public entity, are such as to make the award appropriate, and (c) such fees should not in the interest of justice be paid out of the recovery, if any''). Several courts have refused to adopt this theory. *See* DAN B. DOBBS, LAW OF REMEDIES § 3.10(2), at 283-84 & n.30 (2d student ed. 1993) (citing cases).

53. Other examples include the Longshoremen's and Harbor Workers' Compensation Act; Federal Marine Protection, Research, and Sanctuaries Act of 1972; patent infringement statutes; Trust Indenture Act; Securities Exchange Act of 1934; Servicemen's Readjustment Act; Clean Air Act; Fair Housing Act of 1968; Railway Labor Act; Merchant Marine Act of 1936; Communications Act of 1934; Interstate Commerce Act; Norris-LaGuardia Act; Fair Labor Standards Act; Bankruptcy Act; Perishable Agricultural Commodities Act; Unfair Competition Act; Noise Control Act of 1972; Organized Crime Control Act of 1970; and the Motor Vehicle Information and Cost Savings Act. *See* Alyeska Pipeline Serv. Co. v. Wilderness Soc'y, 421 U.S. 240, 260 n.33, 95 S. Ct. 1612, 1624 n.33, 44 L. Ed. 2d 141, 155 n.33 (1975) (citing the examples in the illustration and this footnote).

54. 28 U.S.C. § 2412.

55. *Id.* § 2412(b) (including U.S. agencies and U.S. officials acting in their official capacity).

56. *Id.* § 2412(d). *See generally* Gregory G. Sarno & Anne M. Payne, Annotation, *Recoupment of Attorney Fees, Under Equal Access to Justice Act (EAJA) (28 U.S.C.A. § 2412), by Litigant Represented by Counsel to Whom No Fee Is Paid by Litigant*, 121 A.L.R. FED. 291 (1994); Ralph V. Seep, Annotation, *Who Is ''Party'' Entitled to Recover Attorneys' Fees Under Equal Access to Justice Act (28 USCS § 2412(d))*, 107 A.L.R. FED. 827 (1992); Gregory G. Sarno, Annotation, *Recoupment by Pro Se Litigant of Attorney's Fees Under Equal Access to Justice Act (28 USCS § 2412)*, 107 A.L.R. FED. 888 (1992); Ralph V. Seep, Annotation, *What Constitutes ''Special Circumstances'' Precluding Award of Attorneys' Fees Under Equal Access to Justice Act (28 USCS § 2412(d))*, 106 A.L.R. FED. 191 (1992); Francis M. Dougherty, Annotation, *Who Is ''Prevailing Party'' so as to Be Entitled to Award of Attorneys' Fees by Court Under Equal Access to Justice Act (28 USCS § 2412(d))*, 105 A.L.R. FED. 110 (1991); Gregory G. Sarno, Annotation, *Recoupment by Alien or Foreign Entity of Attorneys' Fees Under Equal Access to Justice Act (28 USCS § 2412)*, 96 A.L.R. FED. 275 (1990); Kevin W. Brown, Annotation, *What Constitutes Substantial Justification of Government's Position so as to Prohibit*

Procedural rules sometimes also provide exceptions.

Illustration 1-19. Federal Rule 56(g) allows courts to assess costs, including a reasonable attorney's fee, against a party who presents affidavits in bad faith in the context of a summary judgment motion.[57]

(b) "Error" Costs

From an economic viewpoint, legal procedures should attempt to minimize the sum of the (1) "direct" and (2) "error" costs of litigation. Sometimes, the judicial system fails to perform the "allocative or other social functions assigned to it" by mistakenly imposing, or failing to impose, liability.[58] This failure creates error costs. Such costs are just as real as direct costs and cause an inefficient allocation of resources.[59]

Illustration 1-20. Assume that *A's* product causes occasional injuries. Assume also that *A* can buy relatively inexpensive safety devices that could reduce the accident rate significantly. If the substantive (tort) law imposes liability for these accidents and if the law is flawlessly enforced, *A* will be induced to purchase the optimum quantity of safety devices. However, if the law is not perfectly enforced—for example, because of inaccurate determinations in civil proceedings brought to impose liability—*A* will procure a suboptimum quantity of safety devices. This suboptimal procurement will result in a social loss.[60]

Awards of Attorneys' Fees Against Government Under Equal Access to Justice Act (28 USCS § 2412(d)(1)(A)), 69 A.L.R. FED. 130 (1984).

57. *See* FED. R. CIV. P. 56(g); *see also* Chapter 10(C) ("Summary Judgment") *infra*, in which summary judgment practice is more fully discussed; *cf.* 28 U.S.C. § 1447(c) (order remanding a removed case from federal court to state court may require payment of actual expense, including attorney's fees, caused by improper removal); FED. R. CIV. P. 11 (sanctions for instituting or conducting litigation in bad faith or engaging in dilatory or abusive tactics); DAN B. DOBBS, LAW OF REMEDIES § 3.10(3), at 290-91 (2d student ed. 1993) (litigation misconduct and contempt of court); Debra T. Landis, Annotation, *What Conduct Constitutes Multiplying Proceedings Unreasonably and Vexatiously so as to Warrant Imposition of Liability on Counsel Under 28 USCS § 1927 for Excess Costs, Expenses, and Attorney Fees*, 81 A.L.R. FED. 36 (1987); Daniel P. Jones, Annotation, *Attorneys' Fees: Obduracy as Basis for State-Court Award*, 49 A.L.R.4TH 825 (1986); William A. Harrington, Annotation, *Award of Counsel Fees to Prevailing Party Based on Adversary's Bad Faith, Obduracy, or Other Misconduct*, 31 A.L.R. FED. 833 (1977); Annotation, *Construction and Application of State Statute or Rule Subjecting Party Making Untrue Allegations or Denials to Payment of Costs or Attorneys' Fees*, 68 A.L.R.3D 209 (1976); A.S. Klein, Annotation, *Allowance of Attorneys' Fees in Civil Contempt Proceedings*, 43 A.L.R.3D 793 (1972); J.L. Litwin, Annotation, *Attorneys' Fees or Other Expenses of Litigation as Element in Measuring Exemplary or Punitive Damages*, 30 A.L.R.3D 1443 (1970).

58. Richard A. Posner, *An Economic Approach to Legal Procedure and Judicial Administration*, 2 J. LEGAL STUD. 399, 400-01 (1973).

59. *See id.*

60. *Id.* at 402-06 (analyzing in detail error costs in accident cases). One would not, however, "want to increase the direct cost [of litigation] by one dollar in order to [produce more accurate determinations that would] reduce error costs by 50 (or [even] 99) cents." *Id.* at 401.

SECTION D. ALTERNATIVE DISPUTE RESOLUTION

Adjudication of disputes in civil actions is the traditional form of dispute resolution. However, parties to disputes have long had other alternatives available, such as arbitration, mediation, and negotiation. In recent years, concern has mounted about court congestion, spiraling costs, increasing delays, and other negative effects of litigation.[61] These concerns have led to an increased use of these and other means of "alternative dispute resolution" (ADR). Parties often find that these alternatives meet their need for a more satisfactory way of resolving disputes.[62] Federal and state legislation has encouraged this use of ADR.[63] ADR processes can be set in motion through the parties' mutual agreement to undertake them or through court-annexed procedures. Not everyone, however, is convinced that ADR is a panacea.[64] This section provides an overview of the major ADR processes.

1. Negotiation

Negotiation involves consensual bargaining in an attempt to reach a mutually satisfactory settlement of an actual or potential dispute.[65] The autonomy of the parties and the lack of third-party intervention in the process during negotiation distinguish it from other forms of dispute resolution.[66] A negotiated settlement avoids the "winner-take-all" nature and limited scope of most legal

---

61. *See, e.g.,* RICHARD A. POSNER, THE FEDERAL COURTS: CRISIS AND CHALLENGE 53-189 (1996).

62. In 1976, Professor Frank Sander gave impetus to alternative dispute resolution by proposing a "multidoor courthouse." Such an approach would direct disputes to appropriate alternative dispute mechanisms, such as mediation, fact finding, arbitration, ombudsman, or adjudication. *See* Frank Sander, *Varieties of Dispute Processing,* 70 F.R.D. 111, 114-33 (1976).

63. *See, e.g.,* Civil Justice Reform Act of 1990, 28 U.S.C. § 473(a)(6) (civil justice plans may authorize referral of cases "to appropriate alternative dispute resolution programs that–(A) have been designated for use in a district court; or (B) the court may make available, including mediation, minitrial, and summary jury trial").

64. *See, e.g.,* Edward Brunet, *Questioning the Quality of Alternative Dispute Resolution,* 62 TUL. L. REV. 1 (1987); Kim Dayton, *The Myth of Alternative Dispute Resolution in the Federal Courts,* 76 IOWA L. REV. 889 (1991); Richard Delgado et al., *Fairness and Formality: Minimizing the Risk of Prejudice in Alternative Dispute Resolution,* 1985 WIS. L. REV. 1359 (ADR disadvantages for minorities and poor persons); Harry T. Edwards, *Alternative Dispute Resolution: Panacea or Anathema?* 99 HARV. L. REV. 668 (1986); Owen M. Fiss, *Against Settlement,* 93 YALE L.J. 1073 (1984); Owen M. Fiss, *Out of Eden,* 94 YALE L.J. 1669 (1985); Trina Grillo, *The Mediation Alternative: Process Dangers for Women,* 100 YALE L.J. 1545 (1991) (ADR disadvantages for women); Lisa G. Lerman, *Mediation of Wife Abuse Cases: The Adverse Impact of Informal Dispute Resolution on Women,* 7 HARV. WOMEN'S L.J. 57 (1984); Richard A. Posner, *The Summary Jury Trial and Other Methods of Alternative Dispute Resolution: Some Cautionary Observations,* 53 U. CHI. L. REV. 366 (1986).

65. *See generally* ROBERT M. BASTRESS & JOSEPH D. HARBAUGH, INTERVIEWING, COUNSELING, AND NEGOTIATION: SKILLS FOR EFFECTIVE REPRESENTATION 339-522 (1990); ROGER FISHER & WILLIAM URY, GETTING TO YES (1981); DONALD G. GIFFORD, LEGAL NEGOTIATION: THEORY AND APPLICATIONS (1989); LARRY L. TEPLY, LEGAL NEGOTIATION IN A NUTSHELL (1992); WILLIAM URY, GETTING PAST NO: NEGOTIATING WITH DIFFICULT PEOPLE (1991); GERALD R. WILLIAMS, LEGAL NEGOTIATION AND SETTLEMENT (1983); Carrie Menkel-Meadow, *Toward Another View of Legal Negotiation: The Structure of Problem-Solving,* 31 UCLA L. REV. 754 (1984); Gerald R. Williams, *Negotiation as a Healing Process,* 1996 J. DISP. RESOL. 1.

66. *But see* Annette M. Sansone, Annotation, *Imposition of Sanctions by Federal Courts for Failure to Engage in Compromise and Settlement Negotiations,* 104 A.L.R. FED. 461 (1991).

remedies available in court, which allows the parties the opportunity to fashion a package meeting their specific goals and interests. A negotiated settlement avoids the vagaries and uncertainties of trial and appeal. It also avoids the substantial economic, social, and psychological costs of litigation. These costs include the anxiety and stress of trial, possible embarrassment or adverse publicity, and further damage to any relationship between the parties.

2. Mediation

Mediation is a "facilitated negotiation." In a mediation, neutral third parties—mediators—assist the parties or their representatives in resolving their disputes themselves.[67] Mediation is usually a voluntary process. In some jurisdictions, however, statutes, rules, or court orders may mandate participation in mediation.[68] The disputants and their mediator ordinarily control the process. They decide when and where the mediation will occur, who will be involved, how the cost of the mediation will be paid, whether the mediator will meet individually with the disputants, and other details of the mediation process. The mediator assists the settlement process by (1) providing the forum for the parties' negotiations; (2) supervising the exchange of information and the bargaining process; (3) helping the parties find common ground and deal with unrealistic expectations; (4) offering alternatives and creative solutions; and (5) assisting in the drafting of the final settlement.[69]

3. Arbitration

Arbitration involves submitting a dispute to a neutral third person for a decision. Traditionally, the decision to arbitrate is based on a voluntary agreement between the parties. This agreement may be the result of a preexisting contractual provision. It may also be the result of an ad hoc agreement after the dispute has arisen. Such agreements typically provide (1) a mechanism for selecting the arbitrator; (2) the manner in which the arbitral hearing will be held; (3) the procedural and evidentiary rules to be used; and (4) the controlling law.

A party initiates the arbitration process by notifying the other party. Usually, a party makes a written demand for arbitration. Typically, only one

---

67. *See* SUSAN M. LEESON & BRYAN M. JOHNSTON, ENDING IT: DISPUTE RESOLUTION IN AMERICA 133-34 (1988).

68. *See* John F. Wagner, Jr., Annotation, *Validity and Effect of Local District Court Rules Providing for Use of Alternative Dispute Resolution Procedures as Pretrial Settlement Mechanisms*, 86 A.L.R. FED. 211 (1988); *see also* Richard D. English, Annotation, *Alternative Dispute Resolution: Sanctions for Failure to Participate in Good Faith, or Comply with the Agreement Made in, Mediation*, 43 A.L.R.5TH 545 (1996); Craig A. McEwen & Thomas W. Milburn, *Explaining a Paradox of Mediation*, 9 NEGOTIATION J. 23 (1993).

69. *See* JAY E. GRENIG, ALTERNATIVE DISPUTE RESOLUTION WITH FORMS §§ 7.1-7.93 (2d ed. 1997); SUSAN M. LEESON & BRYAN M. JOHNSTON, ENDING IT: DISPUTE RESOLUTION IN AMERICA 133-34 (1988); JACQUELINE M. NOLAN-HALEY, ALTERNATIVE DISPUTE RESOLUTION IN A NUTSHELL 54-118 (1992); NANCY H. ROGERS & CRAIG A. MCEWEN, MEDIATION: LAW, POLICY, PRACTICE (2d ed. 1994); BETTE J. ROTH, RANDALL W. WULFF & CHARLES A. COOPER, THE ALTERNATIVE DISPUTE RESOLUTION PRACTICE GUIDE §§ 23:1 to 35:7 (1998).

arbitrator conducts the arbitration. Some agreements call for a panel of three arbitrators, two of whom are chosen by the parties. The two arbitrators chosen by the parties, in turn, choose a third arbitrator by mutual agreement. The arbitration hearing usually resembles a judicial hearing. The parties make opening and closing statements, present testimony, and offer documentary proof. Typically, arbitrators have wide discretion in admitting evidence and in making decisions. Sometimes, the arbitration agreement will require the arbitrator to choose between "final offers" submitted by the parties. This procedure militates against a possible tendency of the arbitrator to make a compromise decision. It also pressures each party to make a reasonable offer in face of the risk that the arbitrator will accept the other party's offer. Judicial review of the arbitration award is limited.[70]

In contrast to the traditional arbitration model based on a voluntary agreement to arbitrate, compulsory arbitration has been widely adopted for critical public sector employees, such as fire fighters, police, and teachers. Some jurisdictions have also required arbitration of other types of disputes, such as medical malpractice. In addition, "court-annexed" arbitration has become compulsory for certain categories of civil cases in several state and federal district courts. In some jurisdictions, however, court-annexed arbitration is simply offered as an option. The arbitrators in court-annexed arbitrations are usually lawyers or retired judges. In a mandatory court-annexed arbitration, a party dissatisfied with the arbitrator's decision can proceed with a trial *de novo*. Some jurisdictions provide a disincentive to exercising that right. If the dissatisfied party fails to secure a better outcome at trial, that party must pay the arbitrator's fees or court costs.[71]

4. Summary Jury Trial and Early Neutral Evaluation

In a summary jury trial, the litigants' lawyers present a capsulized version of the case to a jury. This presentation usually occurs after the parties have completed discovery and the judge has resolved any pending motions. Particular proceedings vary, but can include voir dire (a preliminary examination to test the qualifications of prospective jurors), opening statements, summarized presentation of admissible evidence, live witness testimony, rebuttal, closing arguments, and jury instruction. The jury then renders a nonbinding, advisory decision. If the jury

---

70. *See generally* FRANK ELKOURI & EDNA ASPER ELKOURI, HOW ARBITRATION WORKS (5th ed. Marlin M. Volz & Edward P. Goggin eds. 1997); DENNIS R. NOLAN, LABOR AND EMPLOYMENT ARBITRATION IN A NUTSHELL (1998); JACQUELINE M. NOLAN-HALEY, ALTERNATIVE DISPUTE RESOLUTION IN A NUTSHELL 119-69 (1992); BETTE J. ROTH, RANDALL W. WULFF & CHARLES A. COOPER, THE ALTERNATIVE DISPUTE RESOLUTION PRACTICE GUIDE §§ 2:1 to 22:29 (1998).

71. *See generally* JACQUELINE M. NOLAN-HALEY, ALTERNATIVE DISPUTE RESOLUTION IN A NUTSHELL 125-30 (1992); Deborah R. Hensler, *What We Know and Don't Know About Court-Administered Arbitration*, 69 JUDICATURE 270 (1986); A. Leo Levin, *Court-Annexed Arbitration*, 16 J.L. REFORM 537 (1983); Edward F. Sherman, *Court-Mandated Alternative Dispute Resolution: What Form of Participation Should Be Required?* 46 SMU L. REV. 1001 (1993); John F. Wagner, Jr., Annotation, *Validity and Effect of Local District Court Rules Providing for Use of Alternative Dispute Resolution Procedures as Pretrial Settlement Mechanisms*, 86 A.L.R. FED. 211 (1988).

is unable to reach a consensus, each juror provides an opinion on liability and damages. Lawyers may question the jurors in a debriefing session. After attending this summary jury trial, the parties then attempt to settle the case.[72]

Another court-annexed dispute resolution is "early neutral evaluation."[73] This evaluation ordinarily occurs after the first status conference. The court chooses a private lawyer who is experienced in the substantive area of the law involved in the dispute. That lawyer then holds a confidential evaluation session. Before the session, the court orders the litigants' lawyers to submit written statements identifying (1) the issues in dispute and (2) the discovery that would be useful in fashioning a settlement. The court also orders the parties to identify the names of any opposing parties whose presence might assist in settling the case. These parties, in turn, are ordered by the court to attend the session. The session typically includes an opening statement by the neutral evaluator and narrative presentations by the litigants' lawyers. The evaluator then identifies areas of agreement. The evaluator assesses the strengths and weaknesses of the parties' positions, estimates the likelihood of liability and dollar range of damages, and may propose stipulations and facilitate the planning for discovery.

5. Mini-Trial and Other Hybrid Dispute Resolution Processes

The "mini-trial" is a hybrid of adversarial case presentation, negotiation, and mediation. A mini-trial consists of a discovery phase, a hearing phase, and a post-hearing settlement discussion between the parties. A mini-trial is initiated by an agreement of the parties on the procedures that will govern the process. Typically, if the agreement requires a neutral adviser, a lawyer or retired judge will be chosen. The agreement will also provide for limited exchanges, such as introductory statements, key exhibits, and summaries of testimony. At the hearing, usually lasting one day, each side's lawyers present a summary of their "best

---

72. *See* JAY E. GRENIG, ALTERNATIVE DISPUTE RESOLUTION WITH FORMS §§ 9.1-9.37 (2d ed. 1997); JACQUELINE M. NOLAN-HALEY, ALTERNATIVE DISPUTE RESOLUTION IN A NUTSHELL 171-79 (1992); Thomas D. Lambros, *Summary Jury Trial–An Alterative Method of Resolving Disputes*, 69 JUDICATURE 286 (1986); Thomas D. Lambros, *The Summary Jury Trial and Other Alternative Methods of Dispute Resolution: A Report to the Judicial Conference of the United States, Committee on the Operation of the Jury System*, 103 F.R.D. 461 (1984); Molly M. McNamara, Note, *Summary Jury Trials: Is There Authority for Federal Judges to Impanel Summary Jurors?* 27 VAL. U. L. REV. 461 (1993); Ann E. Woodley, *Saving the Summary Jury Trial: A Proposal to Halt the Flow of Litigation and End the Uncertainties*, 1995 J. DISP. RESOL. 213; Ann E. Woodley, *Strengthening the Summary Jury Trial: A Proposal to Increase Its Effectiveness and Encourage Uniformity in Its Use*, 12 OHIO ST. J. ON DISP. RESOL. 541 (1997). *But see* Thomas B. Metzloff, *Reconfiguring the Summary Jury Trial*, 41 DUKE L.J. 806 (1992); Richard A. Posner, *The Summary Jury Trial and Other Methods of Alternative Dispute Resolution: Some Cautionary Observations*, 53 U. CHI. L. REV. 366 (1986); Neil Vidmar & Jeffrey Rice, *Jury-Determined Settlements and Summary Jury Trials: Observations About Alternative Dispute Resolution in an Adversary Culture*, 19 FLA. ST. U. L. REV. 89 (1991) (asserting that despite its potential benefits, the summary jury trial largely fails because it is (1) nonbinding and (2) court-instituted and court-controlled); Shirley A. Wiegand, *A New Light Bulb or the Work of the Devil? A Current Assessment of Summary Jury Trials*, 69 OR. L. REV. 87 (1990).

73. *See* JACQUELINE M. NOLAN-HALEY, ALTERNATIVE DISPUTE RESOLUTION IN A NUTSHELL 180-82 (1992); David I. Levine, *Early Neutral Evaluation*, 1989 J. DISP. RESOL. 1; David I. Levine, *Northern District of California Adopts Early Neutral Evaluation to Expedite Dispute Resolution*, 72 JUDICATURE 235 (1989).

cases'' to individuals from each party's organization—ordinarily, senior executives with full settlement authority. The neutral advisor may ask questions, comment on the evidence or arguments, and evaluate the probable outcome of the case. The representatives on the mini-trial panel then enter into post-hearing settlement discussions. The neutral advisor may mediate these discussions.[74]

Other hybrid dispute resolution processes include ''med-arb'' and private judging. In med-arb, the same individual typically serves as both a mediator and then as the arbitrator if the parties do not settle their dispute.[75] Private judging involves the submission of a dispute to a referee, often a retired judge. Its principal advantages are the speed in which a decision is rendered, privacy, ability to select the referee, and the right to a full review of the decision.[76]

SECTION E. THE HISTORICAL EVOLUTION OF CIVIL PROCEDURE

Modern American procedural systems are the products of a long evolutionary process. Some parts of the systems are entirely the result of historical accident, and they can only be understood as such. Other parts represent the cumulative efforts of modern procedural reform to update older procedures to fit modern conditions. Even when a modern rule is the result of a reform process that has largely replaced an older rule, knowing the purpose of the reform is essential to interpreting and applying the modern rule properly.

This section discusses the origins of modern systems of civil procedure in English and early American practice. This history is complex, but only so much is presented here as is necessary to understand the reforms that have produced modern procedural rules (discussed below in the last two subsections).

1. The Common-Law Courts and the Forms of Action

(a) Origin of the Common-Law Courts

The English common law originated in the new procedures and judicial machinery brought to England after the Norman Conquest in 1066. Before the

---

74. *See* JAY E. GRENIG, ALTERNATIVE DISPUTE RESOLUTION WITH FORMS §§ 8.1-8.42 (2d ed. 1997); JACQUELINE M. NOLAN-HALEY, ALTERNATIVE DISPUTE RESOLUTION IN A NUTSHELL 191-99 (1992); Eric D. Green, *Growth of the Mini-Trial*, LITIG., Fall 1982, at 12; Ronald L. Olson, *Dispute Resolution: An Alternative for Large Case Dispute Resolution*, LITIG., Winter 1980, at 22.

75. BETTE J. ROTH, RANDALL W. WULFF & CHARLES A. COOPER, THE ALTERNATIVE DISPUTE RESOLUTION PRACTICE GUIDE §§ 37:1 to 37:15 (1998); Jacqueline M. Nolan-Haley, Alternative Dispute Resolution in a Nutshell 200-01 (1992); Stephen B. Goldberg, *The Mediation of Grievances Under a Collective Bargaining Contract: An Alternative to Arbitration*, 77 NW. U. L. REV. 270 (1982).

76. *See* BETTE J. ROTH, RANDALL W. WULFF & CHARLES A. COOPER, THE ALTERNATIVE DISPUTE RESOLUTION PRACTICE GUIDE §§ 40:1 to 40:5 (1998); JACQUELINE M. NOLAN-HALEY, ALTERNATIVE DISPUTE RESOLUTION IN A NUTSHELL 199-200 (1992); Note, *The California Rent-A-Judge Experiment: Constitutional and Policy Considerations of Pay-as-You-Go Courts*, 94 HARV. L. REV. 1592 (1981).

Conquest, local courts—the Hundred, Shire, and County courts—administered justice based on local customs.[77] After the Conquest, a system of central royal courts—the King's Bench, Exchequer, and Common Pleas—was established.[78] These royal courts did not replace the local courts. Instead, the royal courts heard litigants who were dissatisfied with the quality of justice in the local courts.[79]

(b) Issuance of Writs by the Chancellor and the Initial Development of the Forms of Action

In the system of Norman administration, the chancellor was the king's secretary. The office of chancellor was strictly a household office.[80] The king conducted the administration of the realm by having the chancellor write out and dispatch orders.[81] As each of the three royal common-law courts formed, each court was limited to the business delegated to it by one of these administrative orders. These orders came to be known as *original writs*.[82]

In effect, the original writs were the means by which litigants obtained permission to sue in the royal courts. Litigants purchased these writs from the chancellor. The litigants had to choose the proper writ to recover. If the facts that were ultimately proved fell outside the selected writ ("form of action"), the plaintiff lost—even if the facts proved would have been sufficient to support a recovery under another writ. Thus, the forms of actions embodied in the writs were "pigeon-holes" into which plaintiffs had to fit their cases. If the plaintiffs failed, they could start over—provided a proper form of action covered the situation and they had the wherewithal to do so.[83]

At first, the chancellor awarded these writs "according to the apparent justice and need of the case."[84] The writs came to be granted routinely (called "writs of course") in three basic categories: (1) *real actions* (involving the ownership and possession of land), (2) *ex contractu personal actions* (based on a contract, express or implied), and (3) *ex delicto personal actions* (arising out of or founded upon a wrong or a tort).[85]

(i) Real Actions

Real actions focused on property rights. They were primarily used for the specific recovery of seisin—the possession of a freehold estate in real property.[86]

---

77. *See* JOSEPH H. KOFFLER & ALISON REPPY, HANDBOOK OF COMMON LAW PLEADING § 8, at 32-33 (1969).

78. *See id.* at 33.

79. *See id.*

80. *See* THEODORE F.T. PLUCKNETT, A CONCISE HISTORY OF THE COMMON LAW 695 (5th ed. 1956).

81. *See* JOSEPH H. KOFFLER & ALISON REPPY, HANDBOOK OF COMMON LAW PLEADING § 8, at 33 (1969).

82. *See id.* at 34.

83. FREDERIC W. MAITLAND, THE FORMS OF ACTION AT COMMON LAW 3-4 (1936).

84. BENJAMIN J. SHIPMAN, HANDBOOK OF COMMON-LAW PLEADING § 29, at 59 (3d ed. 1923).

85. *See* JOSEPH H. KOFFLER & ALISON REPPY, HANDBOOK OF COMMON LAW PLEADING § 9 (1969).

86. Real actions included the writ of right, the assize of novel disseisin, and the assize of mort d'ancestor. *See id.* § 10, at 47-53.

Illustration 1-21. Assume that *B* ousted *A* from possession of land on which *A* was living and that *A* wanted to regain possession. *A* would use one of the real actions, most likely one based on a writ of entry. Such a writ came to "lie" (be available) against a person whose possession had been derived from a disseisin.

(ii) Ex Contractu Personal Actions

Ex contractu personal actions focused on contract rights. A writ of *debt* was used when services had been rendered, goods had been sold and delivered, or money lent, but the defendant refused to pay the agreed-upon amount due.[87]

Illustration 1-22. *B* orally promised to buy *A's* horse for $100. *A* gave *B* the horse, but *B* then refused to pay. *A* could use a writ of debt because the transaction was half-completed and the sum due was fixed ($100).

* * * * *

Several variants of debt existed: (1) debt on a specialty, (2) debt on a statute, and (3) debt on a record. *Debt on a specialty* was used when a promise to pay a fixed sum was acknowledged in a sealed instrument—one in which the parties to be bound affixed their name and seal. Such an instrument could be a deed or a bond. The promise was often subject to a "condition subsequent": a fixed sum would become due if the obligor failed to observe a covenant, failed to pay rent, or failed to repay money borrowed.[88] *Debt on a statute* would lie when a statute permitted an injured private party to recover a definite sum as a penalty or forfeiture.[89] Furthermore, if the plaintiff had won an action and the defendant had refused to pay, the plaintiff would ordinarily obtain a writ of execution from the court. This writ would direct the sheriff to seize and sell the defendant's property to satisfy the judgment. After a year and a day from the date of the recovery of a judgment, the courts would no longer issue a writ of execution because the judgment would be presumed to have been satisfied. Thereafter, an action of *debt on a record* was the only means to enforce the judgment. In such an action, the plaintiff did not have to prove the elements of the original claim. Instead, to obtain a new judgment, the plaintiff had to prove the prior judgment was still in force, but still unsatisfied.[90]

Another *ex contractu* personal action was *covenant*. Covenant was used to recover "unliquidated" (unascertained in amount) damages when the promise

---

87. Thus, debt (also called "debt on a simple contract") would only lie to force the defendant to carry out the *half-completed* transaction if the sum due was *fixed*. The theory was that the debtor was holding back something which had been granted and which, therefore, actually belonged to the creditor—not that the debtor was merely under an obligation to pay. *See* BENJAMIN J. SHIPMAN, HANDBOOK OF COMMON-LAW PLEADING §§ 52-53, at 132-35 (3d ed. 1923).

88. *See id.* at 135.

89. For example, assume that a statute provides a monetary penalty for engaging in unauthorized fishing or hunting. *B* was caught fishing on *A's* land. Assuming that the statute provided that the landholder was entitled to the penalty, debt on a statute would be the proper form of action for *A* to recover the penalty. The underlying theory was that, by force of the statute, *B* "owed a debt" to *A. See* JOSEPH H. KOFFLER & ALISON REPPY, HANDBOOK OF COMMON LAW PLEADING § 141, at 295-97 (1969); EDMUND M. MORGAN & FRANCIS X. DWYER, INTRODUCTION TO THE STUDY OF LAW 94 (2d ed. 1948).

90. *See* BENJAMIN J. SHIPMAN, HANDBOOK OF COMMON-LAW PLEADING §§ 52-53, at 136 (3d ed. 1923).

was under seal.[91] Other *ex contractu* personal actions included *detinue* to recover unlawfully detained chattels[92] and *account* used to force fiduciaries to provide an accounting.[93]

Illustration 1-23. *B* promised in writing under seal to buy *A's* horse by paying *A* its "reasonable value." *A* then delivered the horse, but *B* refused to pay. Covenant would be the proper form of action because (1) the promise was under seal and (2) the amount was unliquidated. Debt on a specialty would not lie because the amount was not a specific, fixed amount (but instead the "reasonable value" of the horse).

Illustration 1-24. *A* loaned a horse to *B*. *B* liked it so much that *B* refused to give it back. *A* could sue *B* in detinue when *B*, the bailee, refused to return a specific ascertained chattel (the horse).

(iii) Ex Delicto Personal Actions

The chancellor also issued writs to redress wrongs and to recover personal property. The writ of *trespass* covered injuries committed with actual or implied force. Courts would imply force when the injury was immediate and direct—for example, when the defendant peacefully but wrongfully came onto the plaintiff's land. When an injury to property was involved, the plaintiff had to be in actual or constructive possession of the property at the time of the injury.[94] One writ of trespass in its various forms could cover several wrongs.

Illustration 1-25. A trespass action could include (1) assault and battery; (2) injury to personal property; (3) carrying away of personal property (trespass de bonis asportatis); (4) trespass to real property (trespass quare clausum fregit); (5) false imprisonment; and (6) trespass for a loss of services, as in an action by a husband, father, or master for enticing away, seducing, or debauching his wife, daughter, or servant (trespass per quod servitium amisit).[95] For example, assume that *B* sneaked onto *A's* land and stole *A's* horse from *A's* barn. In this situation, a trespass to real property (trespass quare clausum fregit) and a carrying away of

---

91. Later, covenant could also be used when the amount under seal was liquidated; in that instance, debt on a specialty and covenant were concurrent, provided there was an express covenant (promise) to pay the debt or there were words that could be so construed. *See id.* § 55, at 141-43.

92. At first, detinue and debt were identical actions; as detinue slowly "branched off" from debt, detinue came to lie for the recovery of specific ascertained chattels (such as a specific horse), while debt would lie for a fixed amount of money or for a fixed amount of unascertained chattels (such as fifty bushels of grain). Detinue was initially available to a bailor when the bailee wrongfully detained the bailed goods ("chattels"). It was also available to recover goods lost by the plaintiff when the finder refused to surrender them after a proper demand had been made. In detinue actions, the defendant had the option of returning the chattel or paying its value to the plaintiff. The plaintiff also received damages for wrongful detention of the chattel. *See* EDMUND M. MORGAN & FRANCIS X. DWYER, INTRODUCTION TO THE STUDY OF LAW 97-98 (2d ed. 1948).

93. When a person received property for the use and benefit of other persons (*e.g.*, collected rents or sold goods on their behalf), the law imposed an obligation to account for the proceeds or the property. Account would lie when such a *fiduciary relationship* existed between the parties (one founded upon a trust or confidence) and when the amount due was *uncertain and unliquidated*. If the sum was certain, however, debt would be the proper form. *See* JOSEPH H. KOFFLER & ALISON REPPY, HANDBOOK OF COMMON LAW PLEADING § 154, at 310-11 (1969).

94. *Id.* § 77, at 152.

95. *See* BENJAMIN J. SHIPMAN, HANDBOOK OF COMMON-LAW PLEADING § 35, at 66 (3d ed. 1923).

personal property (trespass de bonis asportatis) have occurred. *A* could use one writ of trespass to recover damages for these harms.

* * * * *

Replevin originated as a form of action to keep "distress" within bounds. A feudal lord could "distrain" (seize) a vassal's chattels when the vassal failed to render feudal services or to pay rent that was due. Distress was also permitted when trespassing animals were causing damage. In these situations, the distressed chattels could be held until the services were rendered, the amount in arrears was paid, the proper compensation was offered, or security was given if the matter was to be taken to court. When a wrongful distraint or an improper refusal to return the distrained chattels had occurred, a replevin action could be brought. If the plaintiff won, the plaintiff not only had the chattels returned, but also recovered damages for their wrongful detention.[96] The theory of replevin was broad enough to cover any case of *wrongful taking*, not merely wrongful distress.[97]

Illustration 1-26. Assume *B* stole *A*'s horse. *A* wanted its return, with damages for its wrongful detention. Replevin came to lie for any wrongful taking from the plaintiff's possession. If *A* posted security, *A* could have the horse returned at the outset of the replevin action. If *A* won the lawsuit, *A* could recover damages arising from *B*'s wrongful detention of the horse. Detinue would not have been the proper form of action under these circumstances because detinue was available only when the defendant acquired possession *lawfully*—for example, when the plaintiff loaned a chattel to the defendant who later refused to return it. In contrast, replevin would be proper because the defendant *unlawfully* obtained possession (by a trespass). *A* would not want to use trespass de bonis asportatis because *A* wanted the horse returned. In trespass, the plaintiff would receive damages (the value of the horse), not the return of the horse.

(c) Subsequent Development of the Forms of Action

At first, the king was interested in only certain types of cases, such as breaches of the king's peace. The standardized forms of the original writs were limited accordingly.[98] Inevitably, as the king's interests expanded, the power of

---

96. EDMUND M. MORGAN & FRANCIS X. DWYER, INTRODUCTION TO THE STUDY OF LAW 90 (2d ed. 1948); *see also* JOSEPH H. KOFFLER & ALISON REPPY, HANDBOOK OF COMMON LAW PLEADING § 127, at 254-55 (1969). The writ directed the sheriff to return the distrained chattels to the plaintiff after pledges were furnished to assure that the action would be prosecuted. To prevent the defendant from being deprived of distress remedy if the plaintiff disposed of the chattels before trial and became insolvent, the Statute of Westminster II, 13 Edw. I, ch. 2 (1285), required the plaintiff to give security for the return of the chattels if the defendant won the suit. EDMUND M. MORGAN & FRANCIS X. DWYER, INTRODUCTION TO THE STUDY OF LAW 89-90 (2d ed. 1948).

97. JOSEPH H. KOFFLER & ALISON REPPY, HANDBOOK OF COMMON LAW PLEADING § 127, at 255 (1969). Late in the fifteenth century, replevin was extended by judicial decision to apply to any wrongful taking. EDMUND H. MORGAN & FRANCIS X. DWYER, INTRODUCTION TO THE STUDY OF LAW 91 (2d ed. 1948).

98. The following is an example of a writ of trespass:

> The King to the Sheriff, &c. If A. shall make you secure, &c. then put by gages and safe pledges B. that he be before us on the morrow of All Souls, wheresoever we shall then be in England, to show wherefore [*ostensurous quare*] with force and arms [*vi et armis*] he made an assault upon him the said A. at N. and beat, wounded and ill treated him, so

the king's courts clashed with the interests of the feudal lords who controlled the local courts. In 1258, the Barons extracted the Provisions of Oxford from Henry III, which forbade the chancellor from framing new writs without permission from the king and the king's council.[99] In 1285, the Statute of Westminster II authorized the chancery clerks to issue new writs in cases similar to (*in consimili casu*), but not quite identical with, those in which writs had been previously granted.[100] Subsequent developments focused on the gradual expansion of the trespass action rather than the issuance of new writs creating entirely new forms of action.[101] The principal "offshoots" from the writ of trespass were the following: (1) trespass on the case, (2) assumpsit, (3) trover, and (4) ejectment. The development of these writs led to the creation of much of England's substantive common law. As discussed below, this development also reflected the plaintiffs' efforts to avoid problems of proof in certain circumstances and to avoid certain modes of trial. It also reflected the plaintiffs' efforts to secure different measures of damages and to secure better remedies.

---

that his life was despaired of, and other enormous things to him did, to the great damage of him the said A. and against our peace [*contra pacem nostram*]: and have there the names of the pledges and this writ. Witness, &c.

1 ANTHONY FITZ-HERBERT, NATURA BREVIUM 86 I (9th ed. 1794), *reprinted in* RICHARD H. FIELD ET AL., MATERIALS FOR A BASIC COURSE IN CIVIL PROCEDURE 397 (7th ed. 1997). This writ reflected the concept of the "king's peace" as the original basis of the royal court's jurisdiction. First, this writ used the term "*vi et armis*" to indicate that an application of force had occurred. Second, it stated not only that A. was damaged, but also that B.'s actions were "against our peace." *See* FREDERIC W. MAITLAND, THE FORMS OF ACTION AT COMMON LAW 39-40 (1936). The writ directed the sheriff to assure the appearance of the defendant "by gages and safe pledges" if the plaintiff gave security to prosecute ("if A. shall make you secure"). This stringent process against defendants made the action very popular with plaintiffs. *See id.*

99. FREDERIC W. MAITLAND, THE FORMS OF ACTION AT COMMON LAW 8 (1936). The Provisions to which Henry III (1216-1272) agreed imposed an oath upon the chancellor that no writs should be granted "excepting Writs of Course without the Commandment of the King and of his Council who shall be present." JOSEPH H. KOFFLER & ALISON REPPY, HANDBOOK OF COMMON LAW PLEADING § 8, at 43 (1969). "Writs of course" referred to writs for which precedent might be found in the form book (Register of Writs) kept in the Chancery. The Provisions of Oxford were annulled five years later, but the chancellor's former power to issue writs appears not to have been restored. ROBERT W. MILLAR, CIVIL PROCEDURE OF THE TRIAL COURT IN HISTORICAL PERSPECTIVE 18 (1952).

100. *See* Statute of Westminster II, 13 Edw. I, ch. 24 (1285).

101. *See* FREDERIC W. MAITLAND, THE FORMS OF ACTION AT COMMON LAW 44 (1936); WILLIAM F. WALSH, A HISTORY OF ANGLO-AMERICAN LAW 70 (2d ed. 1932). Legal scholars differ on the extent of the impact of the Statute of Westminster II on the subsequent development of the forms of action. *See* JOSEPH H. KOFFLER & ALISON REPPY, HANDBOOK OF COMMON LAW PLEADING § 45 (1969) (summarizing the varying views). For example, Millar maintains that this statute had a substantial effect on the subsequent development of the writ system.

Whatever might have been the case had it been given a more liberal construction, this statute mark[ed] a definite check upon the writ-issuing power. Except for the later development under [this] statutory authority which gave us the action of trespass on the case and its derivatives, the tally of writs was complete, the area of common-law justice determined.

ROBERT W. MILLAR, CIVIL PROCEDURE OF THE TRIAL COURT IN HISTORICAL PERSPECTIVE 19 (1952). Although it is debated whether trespass on the case really originated under the Statute of Westminster II, there is no question that subsequent developments of the forms of action focused on the gradual expansion of the trespass action (into trespass on the case, etc.) rather than on the issuance of entirely new writs creating entirely new forms of action.

(i) Trespass on the Case

Trespass covered immediate and direct injuries committed with actual or implied force. When injury to property was involved, the plaintiff must have been in actual or constructive possession of the property at the time of the injury.[102] In contrast, *trespass on the case* (or simply "*case*") covered situations in which the action of trespass did not apply—*i.e.*, indirect or consequential injuries to persons, goods, or lands resulting from the defendant's negligence or wrongful acts.[103]

Illustration 1-27. Assume that a log was thrown onto a highway and hit someone standing in the highway. Trespass would be the proper form of action because the wrong was "immediate." On the other hand, if a log was wrongfully left on a highway and someone later stumbled over it in the dark, trespass on the case would be the proper form because the injury was "consequential."[104]

* * * * *

Over a long period, the courts worked out the distinctions between trespass and trespass on the case. Case is the source of the modern law of negligence and nuisance. It was also the proper form of action to recover for injuries to incorporeal (intangible) rights, such as libel, slander, deceit, malicious prosecution, or improper use of an easement.[105] Furthermore, case was the form of action used to recover for injuries to reversionary interests. Such interests included that of a bailor of a chattel lent for a specific term and that of a landowner whose land was in the possession of a tenant for a term of years.[106]

* * * * *

Like some other forms of action, trespass and case were concurrent in certain situations.[107]

Illustration 1-28. Assume that the defendant negligently drove a vehicle into the plaintiff's vehicle. In situations involving an immediate injury to persons or property attributable to negligence like this one, the courts eventually allowed plaintiffs to sue either in trespass (focusing on the immediate crash as the injury)

---

102. *See* section E(1)*(b)(iii)* ("*Ex Delicto* Personal Actions") *supra.*

103. For a discussion of the development of trespass on the case from trespass, see JOSEPH H. KOFFLER & ALISON REPPY, HANDBOOK OF COMMON LAW PLEADING § 84, at 175-76 (1969).

104. *See* Reynolds v. Clarke, 93 Eng. Rep. 747, 748 (K.B. 1726).

105. JOSEPH H. KOFFLER & ALISON REPPY, HANDBOOK OF COMMON LAW PLEADING § 84, at 174-75 (1969).

106. Assume that *B* wrongfully damaged a dwelling house on land owned by *A*. However, the house was leased for a term of years to *C* when it was injured. *A* could not sue in trespass because *A* was not in possession of the land at the time of the injury. Case was the proper form of action to recover for the injury to *A's* reversionary interest. *C* could sue in trespass and recover damages for the injury to *C's* possessory interest and *A's* reversionary interest, but *C* would be liable to *A* for the portion of the recovery that represented damage to the reversionary interest. *See* EDMUND M. MORGAN & FRANCIS X. DWYER, AN INTRODUCTION TO THE STUDY OF LAW 107 (2d ed. 1948).

107. For example, a husband, master, or father could eventually sue in case for loss of services or society of his wife, servant, or daughter (instead of trespass per quod servitium amisit) by treating the loss as the injury rather than the defendant's implied forceful act of enticing away, seducing, or debauching his wife, servant, or daughter. *See* BENJAMIN J. SHIPMAN, HANDBOOK OF COMMON-LAW PLEADING § 39, at 89 (3d ed. 1923).

or in case (focusing on the negligence of the wrongdoer as the cause of action).[108]

* * * * *

When forms of action were concurrent, some of the peril of choosing the wrong form was removed. Even then, however, the plaintiff was not always free of risk.

Illustration 1-29. In the example of the vehicle crash in *Illustration 1-28*, assume the plaintiff sued in case. If the evidence ultimately showed that the defendant had not been negligent but instead had intentionally hit the plaintiff, the plaintiff would lose because only trespass would lie for intentional injuries. Similarly, assume that a vehicle had been negligently left standing on the highway and it was later hit by another vehicle at night. If the plaintiff sued in trespass, the plaintiff would lose if the court found the injury to be consequential rather than immediate.[109]

(ii) Assumpsit

Debt, covenant, and account would not lie to enforce unsealed, executory promises. During the sixteenth century, assumpsit developed to provide this remedy. Assumpsit originated as a variant of trespass on the case. It covered a defendant's active misfeasance, such as (1) when the defendant undertook (''assumpsit'') to perform some act, but did so negligently or (2) when the defendant undertook through an express promise to care for goods entrusted to the defendant, but did so improperly. Courts then extended assumpsit to situations in which a seller promised to sell goods to a buyer, but instead sold them to someone else. Courts considered the seller's action to be an active misfeasance in breach of the undertaking. Finally, early in the sixteenth century, courts extended assumpsit to a seller's nonfeasance (the refusal to perform the unsealed promise). This form of action was known as *special assumpsit*. It became the basis of modern contract law.[110]

Up to this point, plaintiffs still could not use assumpsit to recover for simple debts arising from the receipt of benefit or value because debt covered such half-completed transactions. Courts viewed the promise to repay the debt as a ''grant,'' and not as an undertaking. The courts began to permit assumpsit actions in this situation when the debtor had made a second promise to pay.[111] In 1602, courts finally held that a second promise would be *implied*. This form of assumpsit, known as *indebitatus* or *general assumpsit*, became concurrent with debt.[112]

---

108. *See* Williams v. Holland, 131 Eng. Rep. 848 (C.P. 1833); *see also* M.J. Prichard, *Trespass, Case and the Rule in* Williams v. Holland, 1964 CAMBRIDGE L.J. 234 (discussing the historical evolution of this rule).

109. *See* JOSEPH H. KOFFLER & ALISON REPPY, HANDBOOK OF COMMON LAW PLEADING § 81, at 165-66 (1969).

110. EDMUND M. MORGAN & FRANCIS X. DWYER, AN INTRODUCTION TO THE STUDY OF LAW 108-09 (2d ed. 1948).

111. *Id.* at 110.

112. *See* Slade's Case, 76 Eng. Rep. 1072 (K.B. 1602); *see also* 1 DAN B. DOBBS, LAW OF REMEDIES § 4.2(3), at 578-79 (2d practitioner ed. 1993).

Courts also extended general assumpsit to cover other situations in which the defendant, in good conscience, was bound to pay the plaintiff.[113]

Illustration 1-30. Assume that the plaintiff rendered services or sold goods with the reasonable expectation of receiving a reasonable value for them. Because the sum (reasonable value) was not fixed, debt could not be brought. Because no express promise to pay had been made, special assumpsit could not be used. Nevertheless, based upon the defendant's conduct creating the belief that reasonable value would be paid, the courts began to imply a promise to pay. When the law implied such a promise, the court referred to this implied obligation as a *quasi-contract*.

* * * * *

Because special and general assumpsit were variants of the same form of action, plaintiffs sometimes used both special and general assumpsit in the same action. For example, plaintiffs often used a count declaring in special assumpsit based upon an express contract and a count in general assumpsit based upon an implied promise to pay the reasonable value of the delivered goods or services. This approach alleviated the risk that the plaintiff might fail to prove that a binding express contract existed in special assumpsit. For example, an express contract might be voidable or the plaintiff might be found not to have substantially performed the contract. Nevertheless, the plaintiff's proof might still reveal the necessary elements for an implied undertaking to pay the reasonable value for the benefits conferred.[114]

Illustration 1-31. Assume that the parties exchanged promises and formed an express contract. When the plaintiff had delivered goods or conveyed a parcel of land as promised, the plaintiff could declare in special assumpsit, based on the express promise. If nothing remained to be performed except for the defendant to pay the price in money, the plaintiff could also add a count in general assumpsit to recover the reasonable value of the benefits received—based on the "debt" arising from the passage of a *quid pro quo*.

(iii) Trover

About the same time that assumpsit split off from trespass on the case, trover also split off from trespass on the case. Trover originally provided an action against the finder of lost goods who used or disposed of the goods instead of returning them. Courts then allowed trover to be used against any person who obtained possession of another's personal property by any means and then (1) sold or used it without the consent of the owner or (2) refused to deliver it when demanded. In trover, the plaintiff recovered as damages the entire value of the chattel at the time and place of the wrongful act of conversion (a substantial interference with the plaintiff's "dominion" over the property). The plaintiff did not recover for the act of taking as in trespass (the actual harm to the chattel and

---

113. *See* DAN B. DOBBS, LAW OF REMEDIES § 4.2(3), at 385-88 (2d student ed. 1993).

114. *See* JOSEPH H. KOFFLER & ALISON REPPY, HANDBOOK OF COMMON LAW PLEADING § 173, at 340 (1969).

loss of its use).[115] When the defendant had satisfied the judgment in trover, the defendant received title to the converted chattel. Trover thus amounted to a "forced sale."[116]

Illustration 1-32. Assume that *B* found *A's* cart on the side of the road and that *B* refused to return it to *A*. *A* could sue in detinue. In detinue, the defendant had the option of returning the cart or paying its value to the plaintiff. Furthermore, in detinue, *A* might have to accept the return of the cart even if it was damaged. More likely, if *A* wanted the cart back, *A* would use replevin.[117] If *A* did not want it back, *A* would sue in trover. In trover, *A* would recover the value of the cart at the time and place of its conversion.

* * * * *

When the defendant secured possession of a chattel by a trespass, the plaintiff could elect between trover and trespass. Furthermore, if the converter had sold the chattel, the plaintiff could *waive the tort* (trespass) and sue in general assumpsit to recover the proceeds of the sale.[118]

Illustration 1-33. Assume that *B* stole *A's* horse, which was worth $100 at that time. Assume that the price of horse then rose and that *B* was able to sell it to *C* for $200. *A* could sue in general assumpsit to recover the entire $200 which, in good conscience, belonged to *A*. *A's* pleading would use the common count of "money had and received."[119]

(iv) Ejectment

About 1500, ejectment branched off from trespass. Ejectment became the common means of establishing title and recovering possession of land. The reasons for its success included the availability of a jury trial and the more efficient procedure offered by the trespass action.[120] Originally, a lessee used ejectment to recover for damages resulting from an ouster from an estate for a term of years. Through an elaborate fiction, courts allowed plaintiffs to use ejectment to recover not only possession of a term, but also to assert the right of possession based upon title to a freehold estate (one for life or in fee simple).

Illustration 1-34. Assume that *B* was in possession of a tract of land and claimed to own it in fee simple. *A* also claimed to own the same land in fee

---

115. *Id.* § 97, at 207.

116. *See* W. PAGE KEETON ET AL., PROSSER AND KEETON ON THE LAW OF TORTS § 15, at 89-90 (5th ed. 1984).

117. *See* section E(1)*(b)(ii)* (discussing detinue) and section E(1)*(b)(iii)* (discussing replevin) *supra.*

118. *See* Lamine v. Dorrell, 92 Eng. Rep. 303 (K.B. 1706) (recognizing waiver of tort and suit in assumpsit); *see also* DAN B. DOBBS, LAW OF REMEDIES § 4.2(3), at 388-90 (2d student ed. 1993); JOSEPH H. KOFFLER & ALISON REPPY, HANDBOOK OF COMMON LAW PLEADING § 176, at 351-52 (1969).

119. For a discussion of the common counts, see Chapter 6(A)(2) ("Stating the Plaintiff's Claim in the Declaration") *infra.*

120. Real actions such as a writ of right, an assize of novel disseisin, and the writ of entry used a "highly technical system of pleading which [set] many traps for the litigant" and were extremely slow. FREDERIC W. MAITLAND, THE FORMS OF ACTION AT COMMON LAW 46 (1936); *see also* JOSEPH H. KOFFLER & ALISON REPPY, HANDBOOK OF COMMON LAW PLEADING § 10, at 47 (1969) (noting that there were about sixty ancient real actions, "the distinction between them being highly technical and refined"); section E(1)*(b)(i)* ("Real Actions") *supra.*

simple. Because ejectment was technically available only to a tenant for a term of years, *A* would pretend that the land had been demised (leased) a few days earlier to John Doe. An action would then be commenced in John Doe's name. Doe's action would allege an entry, lease, and ouster by a fictitious "casual ejector," Richard Roe. *A's* title would also be alleged. Notice would then be given to the actual tenant (*B*) by the casual ejector (the fictitious Richard Roe). This notice offered *B* the opportunity to defend. If *B* wanted to defend, *B* would appear and ask to be substituted.[121] By means of a court rule (the "Common Consent Rule"), *B* would be substituted for Roe only if *B* consented to admit the entry, lease, and ouster. This consent left the issue of title between *A* and *B* as the only issue to be tried.[122] If *B* refused to defend, default would be entered in favor of the fictitious lessee and the plaintiff. The sheriff would then dispossess *B* pursuant to a writ of execution.[123] *B* thus had no practical choice but to enter the suit and defend on the ground that *B*, and not *A*, had title.

(d) Modes of Trial Under the Writ System

Four early modes of trial existed in England: (1) ordeal, (2) battle, (3) wager of law, and (4) jury trial. The Lateran Council abolished trial by ordeal in 1215.[124] The Normans introduced battle as a mode of trial. Trial by battle permitted litigants to challenge adverse witnesses to defend their veracity using combat. Certain witnesses could employ "champions" to represent them. These witnesses included women, infants, and persons over sixty years of age. The power to appoint champions was later extended to able-bodied litigants.[125]

Wager of law (also called "compurgation") required one of the parties to swear a formal oath to the justice or injustice of the opposing party's claim and to produce several "oath helpers," usually twelve. The oath helpers did not swear to the facts. Instead, the oath helpers swore that a party's oath was trustworthy. A party lost if a party was unable to get the required number of oath helpers. A

---

121. The action would be styled *Doe ex dem.* (ex demissione, meaning "upon the demise") *P v. D. See generally* David Mellinkoff, *Who Is "John Doe"?* 12 UCLA L. REV. 79 (1964).

122. JOSEPH H. KOFFLER & ALISON REPPY, HANDBOOK OF COMMON LAW PLEADING § 106, at 229-30 (1969); *see also* FREDERIC W. MAITLAND, THE FORMS OF ACTION AT COMMON LAW 47-48 (1936).

123. A writ of execution evidenced the plaintiff's right to possession of the property and directed the sheriff to put the plaintiff in possession. When the plaintiff secured a money judgment in a common-law action, the writ of execution evidenced the "debt" that the defendant owed to the plaintiff. In that situation, the writ directed the sheriff to seize and sell the defendant's property to satisfy the debt (judgment). *See* BERNARD C. GAVIT, CASES AND MATERIALS ON AN INTRODUCTION TO LAW AND THE JUDICIAL PROCESS 11 (1936).

124. Accused persons who persisted in maintaining their innocence might be bound by a rope and let down into water. If the water accepted them (*i.e.*, they sank), they would be deemed innocent and, ideally, pulled from the water in time to be saved. If the water rejected them (*i.e.*, they floated), they would be deemed guilty. *See* THEODORE F.T. PLUCKNETT, A CONCISE HISTORY OF THE COMMON LAW 114 (5th ed. 1956); *see also* FREDERIC W. MAITLAND, THE FORMS OF ACTION AT COMMON LAW 14 (1936) ("We must not suppose that the unreasonableness of these archaic institutions was suddenly perceived; . . . the remembrance of the ordeal was dear to the people; they would 'swim a witch' long centuries after the Lateran Council . . . .").

125. *See* 1 WILLIAM S. HOLDSWORTH, A HISTORY OF ENGLISH LAW 140-41 (1903).

party also lost if the party or any of the oath helpers made an error in the formal oath.[126]

A legal historian has observed that "if we are to understand the history of the forms of action, we must be mindful of these things; a long chapter that might be entitled 'Dodges to evade Wager of Battle', a still longer chapter, 'Dodges to evade Wager of Law'."[127] Thus, much of the development of the forms of action is attributable to the desire to secure a trial by jury, which was available in trespass and its derivatives. Although the jury trial did not take the form it does today,[128] it nevertheless provided a more rational method of trial.

Illustration 1-35. On the facts of *Illustration 1-32*, detinue and trover were concurrent forms of action. *A* would surely sue in trover because, *inter alia*, wager of law was available in detinue, at the defendant's option. As a derivative of trespass (on the case), trover provided a jury trial.

2. Equity Jurisdiction and Procedure

"Equity" was another important aspect of the traditional English system.[129] Equity jurisdiction and procedure have significantly influenced modern procedural reform. The English chancellor, the king's secretary, prepared and issued the original writs by which actions were commenced in the three royal courts.[130] In this capacity, the chancellor presided over a staff of professional clerks who drafted and issued the writs. This writ-issuing function allowed the chancellor to develop a system of courts (separate from the three royal courts) ultimately known as "equity" courts. Like the development of the common-law forms of action, the development of "equity" courts from "common-law" or "law" courts did not occur in a planned fashion. Rather, a separate equity system emerged as a result of the slow disappearance of "equitable powers" from the common-law courts.

As the practice in the common-law courts became less flexible, the royal courts became unable to supply the quality of relief litigants desired in all cases. Lawyers began to apply to the chancellor for the desired relief. The new procedures and judicial machinery brought to England at the Norman Conquest were, in a sense, thought to be the king's private property. Unlike the preexisting local courts, they were not part of the public machinery of the state to which

---

126. *See id.* at 138; 1 FREDERICK POLLOCK & FREDERIC W. MAITLAND, THE HISTORY OF ENGLISH LAW 38-39 (2d rev. ed. 1968).

127. FREDERIC W. MAITLAND, THE FORMS OF ACTION AT COMMON LAW 14 (1936).

128. *See* Chapter 4(A) ("Transitory and Local Actions") and Chapter 11(C) ("Trial by Jury in Anglo-American Law") *infra.*

129. The term "equity" is used in Anglo-American law in different senses. In a "general juristic" sense, equity is sometimes referred to as the power to do justice in the individual case. In a more technical sense, however, equity refers to the system of law—substantive, remedial, and procedural—that was applied by the English chancery courts and their successors. *See* HENRY L. MCCLINTOCK, HANDBOOK OF THE PRINCIPLES OF EQUITY 1 (2d ed. 1948).

130. *See* section E(1)*(b)* ("Issuance of Writs by the Chancellor and the Initial Development of the Forms of Action") *supra.*

individuals might apply to vindicate their private interests.[131] The procedures were thus available at the king's discretion and applied only to those cases that interested the king.

Linked with the specific procedures and judicial machinery of the royal courts was a particular conception of the king. The king was regarded not only as "the lord paramount of the realm," but also as owing a duty to the country to preserve order and see that justice was done.[132] This duty, coupled with the king's prerogative power, was an early precursor to equity. This early power, however, was originally a part of the ordinary justice provided in the royal courts. All common-law "actions in the eleventh and twelfth centuries . . . began with a petition asking the king to interfere to secure justice where it would not be secured by the ordinary and existing processes of law."[133]

At first, therefore, the chancellor, as the king's delegate, freely issued the writs permitting actions in the royal courts. The courts granted flexible relief–later called "equitable relief" or "specific relief"–suited to the nature of the individual case. This relief included orders compelling the defendant to do or refrain from doing certain acts (in addition to granting money damages, the remedy most often associated with the common-law courts today).[134] As the forms of action developed, however, the common-law system became inflexible. Specific relief (as opposed to money damages) became the exception rather than the rule.[135] In 1258, the Provisions of Oxford exacerbated this lack of flexibility. The Provisions forbade the chancellor from framing new writs without permission from the king and the king's council.[136] In 1285, the Statute of Westminster II somewhat improved the circumstances. It allowed the law to develop through an expansion of the trespass action.[137] Nevertheless, specific relief was largely eliminated from common-law remedies. This development resulted in many cases in which royal courts provided no relief or only ineffective relief.[138] The decay in the equitable powers of the common-law courts was slow and was not complete until after the middle of the fourteenth century.[139]

The inflexibility of the common law prompted lawyers to apply to the "reserve of justice in the king"–*i.e.*, the power to do justice in all cases in which justice was demanded.[140] These applications were made to the king's council,

---

131. *See* George B. Adams, *The Origin of English Equity*, 16 COLUM. L. REV. 87, 89 (1916).

132. *See id.* at 89-91.

133. *Id.* at 91.

134. WILLIAM F. WALSH, A TREATISE ON EQUITY 5-6 (1930). *Compare* George B. Adams, *The Origins of English Equity*, 16 COLUM. L. REV. 87 (1916) *with* William S. Holdsworth, *The Relation of the Equity Administered by the Common Law Judges to the Equity Administered by the Chancellor*, 26 YALE L.J. 1 (1916), George B. Adams, *The Continuity of English Equity*, 26 YALE L.J. 550 (1917) *and* THEODORE F.T. PLUCKNETT, A CONCISE HISTORY OF THE COMMON LAW 681-82 (5th ed. 1956).

135. *See* WILLIAM F. WALSH, A TREATISE ON EQUITY 7-8 (1930).

136. *Id.* at 8; *see* section E(1)*(c)* ("Subsequent Development of the Forms of Action") *supra*.

137. *See* WILLIAM F. WALSH, A HISTORY OF ANGLO-AMERICAN LAW 70 (2d ed. 1932); *see* section E(1)*(c)* ("Subsequent Development of the Forms of Action") *supra*.

138. *See* WILLIAM F. WALSH, A TREATISE ON EQUITY 10 (1930).

139. *See id.*

140. *See* FREDERIC W. MAITLAND, EQUITY 3 (1929); WILLIAM F. WALSH, A TREATISE ON EQUITY 12 (1930).

which was a collection of the officers of the state and other advisers of the king.[141] Because the chancellor was the prime minister and an especially learned member of the council, the chancellor read and considered a large share of the petitions.[142]

About the middle of the fourteenth century, the Chancery was recognized as a separate court. The chancellor, however, was still acting essentially as the representative of the council, not on his own authority.[143] The cases submitted to the Chancery were ones in which the ordinary mechanisms of the common-law courts would not work, so-called cases of "outrage." In these cases, petitioners alleged that they were poor, that their adversaries were rich or powerful, and that their adversaries would intimidate or corrupt the jury.[144]

In the fifteenth century, these cases of outrage continued to occupy a large part of the chancellor's business. They diminished in the latter part of the century "as a more settled state of law and order was established."[145] Moreover, the power of the chancellor to interfere in cases of outrage provoked both the common-law judges and parliament. The chancellor "[was] warned off the field of common law—he [was] not to hear cases which might go to the ordinary courts, he [was] not to make himself a judge of torts and contracts, of property in lands and goods."[146]

The chancellor's power could not be dispensed with entirely, however, because the chancellor had begun to do some valuable things, especially in enforcing uses (trusts).[147] In the fourteenth century, certain landowners had conveyed their lands to friends to hold for their own use and benefit or for some third person.[148] These uses (trusts) were utilized for several reasons. For example, the common law did not permit disposition of land by will at that time. The use or trust could evade this restriction. Legal title could be transferred to a trustee who would hold the title for the benefit of the landowner for a term measured by the landowner's life. Upon the landowner's death, the trustee would transfer the land according to the landowner's will. The same process of transferring title could also be used to avoid creditors or forfeiture.[149]

Such landowners, however, faced a potentially serious problem. If the trustee turned out to be dishonest, the common-law courts would not recognize any rights in the landowner (called the *cestui que use*) because the trustee possessed the legal title. The chancellor protected the *cestui que use* as a matter

---

141. *See* WILLIAM F. WALSH, A TREATISE ON EQUITY 13 (1930).

142. *See* FREDERIC W. MAITLAND, EQUITY 3 (1929).

143. *See* WILLIAM F. WALSH, A TREATISE ON EQUITY 16 (1930).

144. *See* FREDERIC W. MAITLAND, EQUITY 4 (1929); STROUD F.C. MILSOM, HISTORICAL FOUNDATIONS OF THE COMMON LAW 74-75 (1969).

145. WILLIAM F. WALSH, A TREATISE ON EQUITY 18 (1930).

146. FREDERIC W. MAITLAND, EQUITY 6 (1929).

147. *Id.*

148. *See* CORNELIUS J. MOYNIHAN, INTRODUCTION TO THE LAW OF REAL PROPERTY 173 (1962).

149. The ability to avoid forfeiture was particularly important during the War of the Roses. *See* WILLIAM F. WALSH, A HISTORY OF ANGLO-AMERICAN LAW 198-99 (2d ed. 1932). For an excellent treatment of the relationship between law and equity during the Tudor period and a critical examination of the justification by Christopher St. Germain for equitable intervention to mitigate the "rigors" of the common law, see George Behrens, *An Early Tudor Debate on the Relation Between Law and Equity*, 19 J. LEGAL HIST. 143 (1998).

of conscience—because "a man ought to keep his promises, and should not be allowed profit by his own breach of faith."[150] The chancellor's enforcement of uses "assured the development of equity as a separate system outside of the common law."[151]

In addition to enforcing uses, the chancellor acted in other cases in which common-law relief was unavailable or inadequate.

Illustration 1-36. In the fifteenth century, the form of action known as covenant would lie for breach of a contract under seal. Debt would lie if an obligation to pay a specific sum existed. In the absence of a debt for a fixed sum, no remedy existed for breach of a contract not under seal. The chancellor would give relief in such cases either by awarding damages or by decreeing specific performance. In the sixteenth century, the form of action of assumpsit developed in the "law" courts to provide adequate relief by way of damages in simple contract cases. Equity then relinquished its jurisdiction over such matters. Equity retained only such power as was necessary to decree specific performance when damages constituted an inadequate remedy.[152]

* * * * *

Five other principal areas existed in which the chancellor gave relief because of inadequacies in the remedy at law. (1) Equity would provide relief when the owner of chattels sought relief against a person in possession of the chattels and either no relief or inadequate relief at law existed. (2) Equity would provide relief in certain cases involving fraud and mistake. For example, the common-law courts would enforce contracts under seal even when they had been procured by fraud. Equity would provide relief from such contracts. (3) Equity in the fifteenth century granted relief against penalties enforced by the common-law courts. For example, equity would reduce a bond for double the amount of a debt (enforceable at law) to the amount of the debt. (4) Equity would act when the petitioner sought an injunction to restrain waste or some other wrongful act.[153] (5) Equity would also enforce assignments of "choses in action" (the right to sue to recover a debt or claim). Such assignments were not enforceable in the common-law courts.[154] Indeed, during the fifteenth century, equity "interfered to give relief in many other cases where because of technicality of procedure, defective methods of proof, and other shortcomings in the common law, adequate relief could be had only in equity."[155] By the early part of the sixteenth century, the "Chancery had developed into a distinct court, primarily of equity, and equity as administered by this court, had grown to be a great system of law, outside of the common law, competing with it in many ways."[156]

---

150. Cornelius J. Moynihan, Introduction to the Law of Real Property 175 (1962).

151. William F. Walsh, A Treatise on Equity 19 (1930).

152. *See id.* at 23-25.

153. Such cases, though not common, did occur, though equitable relief against torts developed mainly in the eighteenth and nineteenth centuries. *Id.* at 27.

154. *See id.*

155. *Id.*

156. *Id.*

As might be expected, the common-law courts came to resent competition from equity courts. The chancellor had been warned off the field of the common law at one time. Thus, the chancellor's powers had been achieved largely by indirection. The equity courts did not act in direct opposition to the common law. Instead, equity courts enforced their decrees on the defendant's person. This mode of enforcement contrasted sharply with the common-law "in rem" mode of execution against the defendant's property by the sheriff.[157]

This conflict was finally resolved during the reign of James I (1603-1625) in the Coke-Ellesmere dispute (so-named after Chief Justice Coke and Lord Chancellor Ellesmere). The equity courts enjoined the enforcement of the judgments of the common-law courts under certain circumstances—for example, when a judgment had been procured by fraud. Equity courts used their "contempt power" to imprison persons who enforced such common-law judgments. The common-law courts, however, began releasing those persons on habeas corpus.[158] Worse, Chief Justice Coke asserted that petitioners in equity who obtained such injunctions were violating the Statutes of Praemunire. These statutes made it illegal to question the judgments of the king's courts in other courts.[159]

The king appointed Francis Bacon to head a commission to resolve the conflict. The commission approved the traditional formula. The equity courts could enjoin a person from enforcing a common-law judgment, but the action did not affect the judgment itself or act directly against the common-law court that rendered it. This formula effectively resolved the dispute in favor of the equity courts.[160] "From this time forward the Chancery had the upper hand. It did not claim to be superior to the courts of law, but it could prevent men from going to those courts, whereas those courts could not prevent men from going to it."[161]

The victory of the Chancery cleared the way for a highly developed system of equitable relief. Equity built this system upon the foundations laid in the fourteenth and fifteenth centuries. In contrast to the procedure in the common-law courts, the final disposition of an equity case took the form of a *decree* rather than a *judgment*. Ordinarily, the decree ordered the defendant to do or stop doing some specific act. Under the "clean-up" doctrine, equity avoided a multiplicity of suits by awarding money damages that would otherwise have to be recovered in a separate common-law action. As a result, the plaintiff did not have to bring an additional action in the common-law courts.[162] Failure of the defendant to obey an equity decree was punishable by *contempt* (a fine or imprisonment). Thus, the enforcement of equity decrees differed from enforce-

---

157. *See id.*

158. *See, e.g.*, Courtney v. Glanvil, 79 Eng. Rep. 294, 294-95 (K.B. 1615).

159. These statutes had originally been aimed at the Papal curia. FREDERIC W. MAITLAND, EQUITY 10 (1929).

160. The controversy and the judgment of the king are described in 21 Eng. Rep. 576-88. *See generally* HENRY L. MCCLINTOCK, HANDBOOK OF THE PRINCIPLES OF EQUITY 11 (2d ed. 1948).

161. FREDERIC W. MAITLAND, EQUITY 10 (1929).

162. *See* Chapter 7(A) ("Joinder of Claims by Plaintiffs at Common Law and in Equity") and *Illustration 7-6 infra.*

ment of common-law judgments (which were enforced by a writ of execution).[163]

3. Procedure in the American Colonies and After Independence

Compared to the English system, the early history of the American colonies reveals a far less formal approach to litigation. In the earliest stages, the colonies were relatively primitive societies. Consequently, it was difficult for them to incorporate common-law principles of either a substantive or procedural nature except in the most general way. The English common law was a sophisticated body of principles that had evolved with English society. Implementing that body of law required a trained lawyer class as well as the accouterments of that class—law books and institutions suitable for legal training. These were largely absent in the colonies. Indeed, a general hostility existed toward lawyers during the colonial period.

This hostility, coupled with the primitive state of colonial legal institutions, resulted in an attempt to codify the law. The codifications departed from the English common law in many respects. Furthermore, they did not cover every matter that came to be the subject of a dispute. Although the common law was declared to be subsidiary law in cases not covered by local codes, the absence of a trained lawyer class rendered such declarations largely ineffective. As a result, in areas not covered by the codes, the courts had great discretion in supplying a rule that satisfied local conditions. Therefore, while the English common law was sometimes used as a model, it played a relatively minor role in the early administration of colonial justice.[164]

Judicial proceedings were informal during this early period, especially in the "popular courts" that grew up in the colonies. These courts were composed of a relatively large number of judges. Trials resembled a community deliberation. The judges of these courts were not trained professionals. Instead, they were representatives of the community who enforced a popular sense of justice and local custom. In this way, the popular courts were reminiscent of the very early English courts. Pleading was simple compared to the English system. In the popular courts, litigants pleaded their own cases. Although the labels of the English forms of action were often used, the English rigidity of enforcing the forms was absent. In general, the jury system was retained in the colonies, sometimes with modifications.[165]

The administration of equity jurisprudence varied widely. Sometimes, the governor and council of a colony administered it. At other times, the colonial legislatures administered it. Special courts were sometimes given equity powers.

---

163. *See* BERNARD C. GAVIT, CASES AND MATERIALS ON AN INTRODUCTION TO LAW AND THE JUDICIAL PROCESS 9 (1936); CHRISTOPHER C. LANGDELL, A SUMMARY OF EQUITY PLEADING xxii-xxiii (1877).

164. *See* Paul S. Reinsch, *The English Common Law in the Early American Colonies, in* 1 SELECT ESSAYS IN ANGLO-AMERICAN LEGAL HISTORY 367 (1907).

165. *See id.* at 411-12.

At other times, equity powers were delegated to the regular courts. Despite this irregular pattern, the need for Chancery power was recognized. Before the Revolutionary War, courts of equity—or at least courts with equity powers—existed in some form in every colony.[166]

By 1800, the colonies—now states—had reached a more highly developed stage. State legal systems increasingly absorbed common-law institutions at both the substantive and procedural levels. By the nineteenth century, the United States had incorporated much of the technicality of English procedure. Although some procedural reforms had occurred in America, significant reform of the common-law system did not come until the middle of the nineteenth century. In addition, the structure of the state appellate courts did not resemble modern systems (in which a single court of last resort exists whose principal function is to review inferior court decisions).[167] Rather, both "superior" and "inferior" courts were often trial courts. Successive trials whose aim was to reach the single "correct result" were common.[168] In these proceedings, judges, lawyers, and juries all conducted a search for "the true rule of law."[169] Modern hierarchial systems of appellate review were not established until the nineteenth—and in some instances the twentieth—century.[170]

As part of the adoption of English procedure, equity jurisprudence had become a fairly regular feature of American judicial practice.[171] Unlike the English system, however, the same court that exercised common-law power often also exercised equity jurisdiction in America—though the common-law and equity activities of the courts were kept formally distinct.[172] In a few states, law and equity courts were separate. In two, Pennsylvania and Massachusetts, equity did not exist in any ordinary form.[173]

4. The Field Code and the Reform of Procedure in the States

The first significant reform in American procedure came in New York around the middle of the nineteenth century. The New York Constitution of 1846 abolished the New York Court of Chancery.[174] The constitution also directed the Legislature, at its first session after the adoption of the constitution, to appoint

---

166. *See generally* Sydney G. Fisher, *The Administration of Equity Through Common Law Forms*, 1 L.Q. REV. 455 (1885); William F. Walsh, *The Growing Function of Equity in the Development of the Law, in* 3 LAW: A CENTURY OF PROGRESS 139, 145-55 (1937); Solon D. Wilson, *Courts of Chancery in America—Colonial Period*, 18 AM. L. REV. 226 (1884); Edwin H. Woodruff, *Chancery in Massachusetts*, 5 L.Q. REV. 370 (1889).

167. *See* WILFRED J. RITZ, REWRITING THE HISTORY OF THE JUDICIARY ACT OF 1789, at 27-52 (Wythe Holt & J.H. LaRue eds., 1993).

168. *Id.* at 35.

169. *See id.* at 28-30.

170. *See id.* at 41-49. *See generally* ROSCOE POUND, ORGANIZATION OF COURTS (1940).

171. *See* William F. Walsh, *The Growing Function of Equity in the Development of the Law, in* 3 LAW: A CENTURY OF PROGRESS 139, 151 (1937).

172. *See id.*

173. *See* Sydney G. Fisher, *The Administration of Equity Through Common Law Forms*, 1 L.Q. REV. 455 (1885); Edwin H. Woodruff, *Chancery in Massachusetts*, 5 L.Q. REV. 370 (1889).

174. N.Y. CONST. OF 1846, art. VI, § 3.

three commissioners. Their duty ''shall be to revise, reform, simplify, and abridge the rules of practice, pleading, forms, and proceedings of the courts . . . of this State, and to report thereon to the legislature, subject to their adoption and modification from time to time.''[175]

The Legislature appointed the commission,[176] which rendered its report in 1848.[177] In accord with the commissioners' recommendations, the Legislature enacted the *Field Code*, so-named after David Dudley Field, the most prominent commissioner.[178] The Field Code embodied numerous reforms, including (1) the merger of law and equity, (2) the simplification and limitation of the pleading process, (3) the broadening of claim and party joinder, and (4) the liberalization of amendments to pleadings (and the corresponding deemphasis of variances between pleading and proof). By 1900, almost thirty states had adopted some version of the Field Code. More adopted it in the twentieth century.[179]

Despite the laudable aims of the ''codes,'' reform did not, and in certain respects has not yet, come easily. For example, although the codes merged law and equity, troublesome questions remained about the interaction between the rules that were formerly administered in separate systems. Of particular concern was (1) a party's constitutional right to a jury trial in a merged system and (2) the status of rules previously used to determine when a court would grant equitable relief.[180]

5. Development of Federal Procedure and the Federal Rules of Civil Procedure

Article III of the U.S. Constitution vests the judicial power of the federal government in ''one supreme Court, and in such inferior Courts as the Congress may from time to time ordain and establish.''[181] The Constitution extends that power to ''all Cases, in Law and Equity'' within certain limited categories.[182] In 1789, Congress implemented the provisions of Article III by establishing a Supreme Court and a system of circuit and district courts.[183] Congress has always directly regulated many procedural subjects. For example, Congress has always regulated in detail subject-matter jurisdiction and venue, which are treated in Chapters 2 and 3. Of primary interest here, however, is the historical development of the procedural rules of the federal trial courts. These rules govern the manner of conducting the civil actions which Congress has authorized the federal courts to hear.

---

175. *Id.* § 24.

176. Act of Apr. 8, 1847, ch. 59, § 8, 1847 N.Y. Laws 66, 67.

177. FIRST REPORT OF THE NEW YORK COMMISSIONERS ON PRACTICE AND PLEADINGS (1848).

178. Act of Apr. 12, 1848, ch. 379, 1848 N.Y. Laws 497.

179. *See* FLEMING JAMES, JR. ET AL., CIVIL PROCEDURE § 1.7, at 19 (4th ed. 1992); ROBERT W. MILLAR, CIVIL PROCEDURE OF THE TRIAL COURT IN HISTORICAL PERSPECTIVE 54-55 (1952).

180. *See* DAN B. DOBBS, LAW OF REMEDIES § 2.6 (2d student ed. 1993).

181. U.S. CONST. art. III, § 1.

182. *Id.* § 2; *see* Chapter 2(C) (''Subject-Matter Jurisdiction of the Federal Courts'') *infra*.

183. Judiciary Act of 1789, ch. 20, §§ 1-4, 1 Stat. 73, 73-75.

Law and equity were not administered in separate federal courts. Nonetheless, the traditional distinction between equity and common-law jurisdiction was maintained in the federal courts until 1938. The First Process Act (1789) provided

> [t]hat until further provision shall be made . . . the forms of writs and executions, except their style, and modes of process and rates of fees, except fees to judges, in the circuit and district courts, in suits at common law, shall be the same in each state respectively as are now [1789] used or allowed in the supreme courts of the same. And the forms and modes of proceedings in causes of equity . . . shall be according to the course of the civil law.[184]

In 1792, Congress modified this provision. Although the provision remained the same in suits at common law, procedure in equity cases was henceforth declared to be "according to the principles, rules and usages which belong to courts of equity . . . as contra-distinguished from courts of common law."[185] However, Congress made both common-law and equity cases in federal courts subject to a rulemaking power in the U.S. Supreme Court and the lower federal courts.[186]

The result of these process acts was to establish a *static conformity* to state procedure in common-law cases. Thus, the federal courts were obligated to use the procedural law of the state in which they were sitting as the procedural law appeared in 1789. Even though state procedural laws might change, as indeed they did, federal procedure continued to exist as it had in the states in 1789. This arrangement was made even worse because the original process acts did not apply to states admitted to the Union after 1789. Congress partially remedied the latter difficulty by enacting process acts in 1828 and 1842. These acts, however, primarily dealt with the problem of newly admitted states. For the most part, the federal courts in the older states were bound by the 1789 procedures.[187]

The courts could have used their rulemaking power to minimize the difficulties of static conformity, but they did not. In the Conformity Act of 1872, Congress repealed the rulemaking authority and established a *dynamic conformity* to state procedures in common-law actions.[188] Thus, in common-law cases, federal procedure conformed to state procedures that existed at the time the federal court heard the case. This dynamic conformity lasted until the Federal Rules of Civil Procedure were adopted in 1938.

Federal equity procedure was quite different. The process acts did not require conformity, static or otherwise, to state procedure in equity cases. Furthermore, the U.S. Supreme Court showed no reluctance to utilize its rulemaking power for equity cases. The Court promulgated equity rules in 1822, 1842,

---

184. Act of Sept. 29, 1789, ch. 21, § 2, 1 Stat. 93, 93-94.

185. Act of May 8, 1792, ch. 36, § 2, 1 Stat. 275, 276.

186. *See id.; see also* Judiciary Act of 1789, ch. 20, § 17, 1 Stat. 73, 83; Act of Aug. 23, 1842, ch. 188, § 6, 5 Stat. 516, 518.

187. *See* Act of May 19, 1828, ch. 68, 4 Stat. 278; Act of Aug. 1, 1842, ch. 109, 5 Stat. 499.

188. Act of June 1, 1872, ch. 255, § 5, 17 Stat. 196, 197.

and 1912.[189] In 1915, Congress provided that "equitable defenses" could be raised in actions at law. Congress also abolished the objection that a party had brought the suit on the wrong "side" of the court. Prior to this change, the objection would have caused a dismissal of the action.[190] With a few modifications, the 1912 equity rules lasted until the Federal Rules of Civil Procedure merged law and equity in 1938.

Despite dynamic conformity and extensive use of the rulemaking power for equity cases, widespread dissatisfaction with the federal procedural scheme remained. By the twentieth century, most states had established a uniform procedure for law and equity cases. In addition, interpretation of the Conformity Act produced numerous areas in which the federal courts could disregard state procedure in favor of independent federal practices.[191] The result was a system that did not achieve uniformity between state and federal courts in the same state. Nor was there uniformity between federal courts sitting in different states. Under the American Bar Association's leadership, a movement to reform federal procedure finally produced the Rules Enabling Act of 1934:

> [Sec. 1.] . . . [T]he Supreme Court of the United States shall have the power to prescribe, by general rules, for the district courts of the United States and for the courts of the District of Columbia, the forms of process, writs, pleadings, and motions, and the practice and procedure in civil actions at law. Said rules shall neither abridge, enlarge, nor modify the substantive rights of any litigant. They shall take effect six months after their promulgation, and thereafter all laws in conflict therewith shall be of no further force or effect.
>
> Sec. 2. The court may at any time unite the general rules prescribed by it for cases in equity with those in actions at law so as to secure one form of civil action and procedure for both: *Provided, however,* That in such union of rules the right of trial by jury as at common law and declared by the [S]eventh [A]mendment to the Constitution shall be preserved to the parties inviolate. . . .[192]

Pursuant to this authority, the U.S. Supreme Court appointed an Advisory Committee to draft new rules.[193] After the legal profession examined the Committee's proposed rules, some changes were made. The Court approved the Federal Rules of Civil Procedure with the changes. The Rules took effect on September 16, 1938.[194] Since then, the Federal Rules of Civil Procedure have been amended numerous times.

---

189. In 1822, the Court promulgated 33 equity rules. 20 U.S. (7 Wheat.) xvii-xxi (1822). In 1842, the Court replaced the 1822 rules with 92 rules. 42 U.S. (1 How.) xli-lxx (1842). The 1842 rules, in turn, were replaced by 81 rules in 1912. 226 U.S. 627, 649-73 (1912).

190. Law and Equity Act, ch. 90, 38 Stat. 956 (1915).

191. *See* RICHARD H. FALON ET AL., HART & WECHSLER'S THE FEDERAL COURTS AND THE FEDERAL SYSTEM 663 (4th ed. 1996).

192. Rules Enabling Act of 1934, ch. 651, 48 Stat. 1064 (codified as amended at 28 U.S.C. §§ 2072-2074).

193. 295 U.S. 774 (1935).

194. *See* 308 U.S. 645, 645-766 (1937).

The principal purposes of the Federal Rules of Civil Procedure were similar to those of the codes: (1) the merger of law and equity, (2) the simplification and limitation of pleading, (3) the broadening of claim and party joinder, (4) the liberalization of amendments to pleadings, and (5) the deemphasis of variances between pleading and proof. The Federal Rules differ in several important respects from the codes in how they achieve these purposes. In addition, the Federal Rules established comprehensive procedures for "discovery" before trial—a major improvement over the limited discovery provided under the codes.[195] The Federal Rules are designed to be "trans-substantive" in nature: the Rules govern procedures in all civil actions, regardless of the substantive nature of the claims or defenses in the suit.[196]

The influence of the Federal Rules of Civil Procedure has been widespread. Every state has modified its procedure to accord with the Federal Rules in some ways. About half of the states have adopted the Federal Rules almost unchanged.[197] Furthermore, lawyers can use federal precedents as persuasive authority in construing state court rules of procedure modeled on the Federal Rules.[198] The dominance of the Federal Rules in the United States has also influenced the structure and content of the modern Civil Procedure course, which this book is designed to accompany.[199] Consequently, while relevant common-law, equity, and code procedure is examined in later chapters, the Federal Rules constitute the main focus of each procedural topic covered in this book.

---

195. *See* FLEMING JAMES, JR. ET AL., CIVIL PROCEDURE § 1.8, at 22 (4th ed. 1992); Stephen N. Subrin, *How Equity Conquered the Common Law: The Federal Rules of Civil Procedure in Perspective*, 135 U. PA. L. REV. 1873 (1987).

196. *See* Richard L. Marcus, *Of Babies and Bathwater: The Prospects for Procedural Progress*, 59 BROOK. L. REV. 761, 776-79 (1993).

197. *See* CHARLES A. WRIGHT, HANDBOOK OF THE LAW OF FEDERAL COURTS § 62, at 430 (5th ed. 1994); *cf.* John B. Oakley & Arthur F. Coon, *The Federal Rules in State Courts: A Survey of State Court Systems of Civil Procedure*, 61 WASH. L. REV. 1367, 1427 (1986) (finding that 23 jurisdictions have unqualifiedly replicated the Federal Rules of Civil Procedure; under a less restrictive "affinity" test, a substantial majority of state courts follow the Federal Rules of Civil Procedure). Professors Oakley and Coon point out that "[t]wo factors caution . . . against exaggeration of the dominance of the Federal Rules in modern American state courts. First, populous states have proven unusually inert to procedural reforms. Second, the era of an 'accelerating trend' of state court reform of civil procedure in the image of the Federal Rules has ended. The trend continues, albeit slowly, but with ratchet-like effect." *Id.* (footnote omitted). *See generally* Maurice Rosenberg, *Federal Rules of Civil Procedure in Action: Assessing Their Impact*, 137 U. PA. L. REV. 2197 (1989).

198. *See, e.g., Ex parte* Dorsey Trailers, Inc., 397 So. 2d 98, 103 (Ala. 1981) ("cases construing the Federal Rules of Civil Procedure are authority for construction of the Alabama Rules of Civil Procedure").

199. *See* Mary Brigid McMammon, *The History of the Civil Procedure Course: A Study in Evolving Pedagogy*, 30 ARIZ. ST. L.J. 397, 430-33 (1998) (discussing the influence of the Federal Rules on the development of the modern Civil Procedure course).

Chapter 2

SUBJECT-MATTER JURISDICTION

SECTION A. THE NATURE OF SUBJECT-MATTER JURISDICTION

1. Sources and Scope of Subject-Matter Jurisdiction

Subject-matter jurisdiction is the competency of a court to hear and decide particular *categories* of cases. In the United States, constitutional and statutory provisions define and limit the subject-matter jurisdiction of state and federal courts.

Illustration 2-1. H and W are married and live in Arizona. W is considering divorce. The Arizona Constitution would be the starting point for determining which Arizona court has subject-matter jurisdiction over divorce actions. The Arizona Constitution allocates jurisdiction over divorce matters as follows: "The superior court shall have original jurisdiction of . . . [d]ivorce and for annulment of marriage."[1]

* * * * *

State-court subject-matter configurations vary widely. In all states, however, a court of *general jurisdiction* exists to handle all cases not exclusively delegated to another court within the state. Courts of general jurisdiction always possess the broadest subject-matter authority within a state. When no other courts within the system have subject-matter jurisdiction over a particular action, courts of general jurisdiction, as "repository" courts, have subject-matter authority over such actions.

Illustration 2-2. The Arizona Constitution provides that "[t]he superior court shall have original jurisdiction of . . . [c]ases and proceedings in which exclusive jurisdiction is not vested by law in another court" and "[s]pecial cases and proceedings not otherwise provided for, and such other jurisdiction as may be provided by law.[2] Thus, in Arizona, the court of general jurisdiction, the repository court, is the superior court.[3]

* * * * *

---

1. ARIZ. CONST. art. VI, § 14. "Original" jurisdiction means that the action would be initially presented and tried in a superior court. Original jurisdiction contrasts with "appellate" jurisdiction, which relates to the power of a tribunal to correct legal errors made by an inferior tribunal.

2. *Id.*

3. *See id.* The name of the court designated as the court of general jurisdiction varies from state to state. For example, in Illinois, the court of general jurisdiction is called the circuit court. *See* ILL. CONST. art. VI, § 9. In New York, it is the supreme court. N.Y. CONST. art. VI, § 7. In Iowa, it is the district court. *See* IOWA CONST. art. V, § 6.

Typically, each state also has one or more courts of *limited jurisdiction*. The law circumscribes the authority of these courts in a variety of ways. For example, the law may limit the subject-matter jurisdiction of a court according to amount in controversy or geographical area. Likewise, the law may prohibit a court from hearing cases involving certain subjects, such as title to land. In addition, a court may possess *concurrent* or *exclusive* subject-matter jurisdiction over certain kinds of cases. If the court has exclusive jurisdiction over a class of cases, no other court within the system has authority to hear cases within that class. If the court has concurrent jurisdiction, at least one other court in the state may also hear cases within the class. If concurrent jurisdiction exists, the plaintiff will be able to decide in which court to commence the action. A court of limited jurisdiction may also possess exclusive jurisdiction over certain classes of cases.

Illustration 2-3. In Nebraska, the district court is the court of general jurisdiction. County courts are courts of limited jurisdiction. The district court has "general, original and appellate jurisdiction in all matters, both civil and criminal, except where otherwise provided."[4] On the other hand, the county court exercises exclusive jurisdiction in certain types of cases, such as decedents' estates.[5] In other types of cases, the county court exercises concurrent jurisdiction with the district court—for example, "in all civil actions of any type when the amount in controversy does not exceed fifteen thousand dollars."[6] In the latter category of cases, the plaintiff may sue in either a district or county court.

2. The "No-Waiver, No-Consent" Rule

The parties to an action cannot consent to allow a court to hear a case beyond its subject-matter competence as defined by the relevant constitutional and statutory provisions. Under conventional rules, a party also cannot waive an objection to subject-matter jurisdiction.[7] As a result, a party may successfully object to subject-matter jurisdiction at late stages of a proceeding or sometimes in wholly separate proceedings.[8] Furthermore, a court of original jurisdiction must raise the lack of subject-matter jurisdiction on its own initiative (*sua sponte*), even when the parties do not. Likewise, in reviewing a lower court judgment, an appellate court must raise objections to the subject-matter jurisdiction of the lower court even if neither the lower court nor the parties have objected.[9]

---

4. NEB. REV. STAT. § 24-302 (1995).

5. *Id.* § 24-517(1).

6. *Id.* § 24-517(4).

7. *See, e.g.*, State Farm Mut. Auto. Ins. Co. v. Marshall, 618 So. 2d 1377, 1381 (Fla. Dist. Ct. App. 1993); Springfield City Sch. Support Personnel v. State Employment Relations Bd., 84 Ohio App. 3d 294, 616 N.E.2d 983 (1992).

8. *See* FED. R. CIV. P. 12(h)(3). The ability to attack a judgment in a subsequent proceeding because of a lack of subject-matter jurisdiction is discussed in Chapter 13(E) ("Claim and Issue Preclusion on Questions of Subject-Matter and Personal Jurisdiction") *infra*.

9. *See, e.g.*, Louisville & Nashville R.R. Co. v. Mottley, 211 U.S. 149, 151, 29 S. Ct. 42, 43, 53 L. Ed. 126, 127 (1908); International Longshoremen's Ass'n v. Davis, 470 So. 2d 1215, 1216 (Ala. 1985); Lockamy v. Lockamy, 111 N.C. App. 260, 261, 432 S.E.2d 176, 177 (1993); Riden v. Snider, 832 S.W.2d 341, 343 (Tenn. Ct. App. 1991); Texas Ass'n of Bus. v. Texas Air Control Bd., 852 S.W.2d 440, 443-44 (Tex. 1993).

This strict *no-waiver, no-consent rule* for subject-matter jurisdiction originated in English common-law practice. It arose out of a conflict between the king's courts and various other courts of limited jurisdiction. Three superior royal courts evolved through a process of delegation and specialization: the Court of Exchequer for revenue matters; the Court of Common Pleas for ordinary civil litigation; and the Court of King's Bench for criminal matters and wrongs done *vi et armis* (by force of arms). By the time of Edward I (1272-1307), these three royal courts "had become in one way or another courts of first instance for almost all litigation."[10] However, a few kinds of cases were not within the jurisdiction of the three superior royal courts. For example, the ecclesiastical courts handled certain types of cases. Other minor courts existed, including the Court of the Marshalsea, the court of the king's household.

In the leading *Case of the Marshalsea*,[11] Richard Hall was imprisoned for three months pursuant to process issued by the Marshalsea Court. The Court of the King's Bench permitted Hall to bring a trespass action for false imprisonment against (1) the party who had sued him in the Marshalsea Court, (2) the marshal who directed the execution of the process, and (3) the officer who executed it. The King's Bench held that the Marshalsea Court lacked jurisdiction over the case because neither the plaintiff nor the defendant was of the king's household. The marshal and officer defended by asserting that they had acted in good faith pursuant to the process issued. The King's Bench stated that if the Marshalsea Court would have had jurisdiction over the "cause" (which is referred to today as the "subject matter") and had merely proceeded "erroneously," no action would lie against them. However, because the Marshalsea Court did not have jurisdiction over the action, the whole proceeding was *coram non judice* (not before a judge) and absolutely void. Acting in good faith pursuant to process was not a defense in such a void action.[12]

Although England subsequently limited the no-waiver, no-consent rule, the United States accepted the rule as part of the jurisprudence inherited from England. The rule fit well with the allocation of authority among the three branches of the federal government. It also fit well with the division of authority between federal and state court systems in the U.S. Constitution.[13]

---

10. FREDERIC W. MAITLAND, THE CONSTITUTIONAL HISTORY OF ENGLAND 114 (1908); *see* Chapter 1(E)(1)*(a)* ("Origin of the Common-Law Courts") *supra.*

11. 77 Eng. Rep. 1027 (K.B. 1613).

12. *Id.* at 1038-40; *see* Dan B. Dobbs, *The Decline of Jurisdiction by Consent,* 40 N.C. L. REV. 49, 67-68 (1961) (discussing the *Marshalsea* decision). The same rule was applied in English law when the plaintiff sought prohibition (a writ prohibiting an inferior court from acting outside its jurisdiction). For example, the common-law courts issued writs of prohibition to the ecclesiastical courts, even after a defendant had been forced to admit jurisdiction and judgment had been entered. Dan B. Dobbs, *The Decline of Jurisdiction by Consent,* 40 N.C. L. REV. 49, 66-67 (1961).

13. *See* Dan B. Dobbs, *The Decline of Jurisdiction by Consent,* 40 N.C. L. REV. 49, 77-78 (1961). For a more complete discussion of the limitations of and exceptions to the no-waiver, no-consent rule, see Dan B. Dobbs, *The Validation of Void Judgments: The Bootstrap Principle* (pts. 1 & 2), 53 VA. L. REV. 1003, 1241 (1967); Dan B. Dobbs, *Beyond Bootstrap: Foreclosing the Issue of Subject-Matter Jurisdiction Before Final Judgment,* 51 MINN. L. REV. 491 (1967); *see also* section B ("Subject-Matter Jurisdiction of the State Courts") *infra.*

Given the significance of subject-matter jurisdiction in American judicial systems, it follows that courts should ordinarily consider and dispose of objections based on subject-matter jurisdiction *before* considering other issues in a case. Two recent U.S. Supreme Court decisions illustrate the considerations involved in determining whether subject-matter jurisdiction objections should be given priority.

    Illustration 2-4. In *Steel Co. v. Citizens for a Better Environment*,[14] the Supreme Court held that federal district courts must first decide whether they have subject-matter jurisdiction before deciding whether an action should be dismissed on the ground that the complaint fails to state a claim upon which relief can be granted—even though the failure-to-state-a-claim issue might be easier to decide under available authorities.[15] In addition to the high importance of subject-matter jurisdiction, this priority is also justified by the potential operation of issue preclusion in a subsequent action on the failure-to-state-a-claim issue. If a federal court could dismiss on the ground of failure to state a claim without first considering whether it has subject-matter jurisdiction, one of two unfortunate consequences might follow. Either the plaintiff would be prevented by the doctrine of issue preclusion from commencing a second action on the same complaint in another court,[16] or the second court would have to disregard the first dismissal as "void" because the first court did not have subject-matter jurisdiction to make the dismissal.[17] In the latter case, the second court, which might be a state court, would find itself in the awkward position of determining whether the federal court lacked subject-matter jurisdiction over the action, when the federal court is in a better position to determine that question for itself.[18]

    Illustration 2-5. In *Ruhrgas AG v. Marathon Oil Co.*,[19] the Supreme Court distinguished *Steel Co.* by holding that in removed actions,[20] no absolute

---

   14. 523 U.S. 83, 118 S. Ct. 1003, 140 L. Ed. 2d 210 (1998).

   15. *Id.* at __, 118 S. Ct. at 1011-16, 140 L. Ed. 2d at __. Note that because a dismissal on subject-matter jurisdiction grounds is not "on the merits," the plaintiff would also not be prevented from bringing the second action by the doctrine of "claim preclusion," which only precludes a suit on the same claim when a prior judgment in an action on the claim is "on the merits" or "with prejudice." *See* FED. R. CIV. P. 41(b); Chapter 13(B) *infra* (discussing the doctrine of claim preclusion).

   16. This result would occur because the judgment of dismissal in the first federal action might be held to preclude relitigation of the failure to state a claim issue in a subsequent action in another court. *See* Chapter 13(B)(2) *infra* (discussing the doctrine of direct estoppel).

   17. *See* Chapter 13(E) *infra* (discussing exceptions to preclusion when the court in an initial action lacked subject-matter jurisdiction).

   18. *See also* Hernandez v. Conriv Realty Assocs., 182 F.3d 121 (2d Cir. 1999) (dismissal with prejudice as a procedural sanction is improper when court lacks subject-matter jurisdiction); University of S. Ala. v. American Tobacco Co., 168 F.3d 405 (11th Cir. 1999) (although voluntary dismissal may normally precede any analysis of subject-matter jurisdiction because voluntary dismissal is self-executing and moots all pending motions, district court must nevertheless reach subject-matter jurisdiction issues first when ruling on the notice of dismissal requires court to reach complex, important questions of state substantive law).

   19. 526 U.S. 574, 119 S. Ct. 1563, 143 L. Ed. 2d 760 (1999); *see also* Ortiz v. Fibreboard Corp., __ U.S. __, 119 S. Ct. 2295, 144 L. Ed. 2d 715 (1999) (Rule 23 class certification issues are logically antecedent to Article III standing issues and themselves pertain to statutory standing, which may properly be treated before Article III standing; therefore, class certification issues would be treated first). *Steel Co.*, *Ruhrgas*, and *Ortiz* are discussed in Richard D. Freer, *Observations on the Scope of the Supreme Court's Rejection of "Hypothetical Jurisdiction,"* 8 FED. LITIG. GUIDE REP. 247 (1999).

   20. *See* section (C)(5) *infra* (discussing removal jurisdiction).

bar exists to considering and disposing of personal jurisdiction[21] issues before taking up questions of subject-matter jurisdiction. Although the Court stated that a federal court customarily resolves issues of subject-matter jurisdiction before questions on the merits (such as failure of the complaint to state a claim on which relief can be granted), no absolute necessity existed for the courts to give priority to subject-matter jurisdiction questions over personal jurisdiction questions. Unlike subject-matter jurisdiction, personal jurisdiction is a "waivable" defect, but it is still an essential element of a court's power to proceed to an adjudication on the merits. When an inquiry into subject-matter jurisdiction would involve a difficult and novel question, but the federal district court is faced with a straightforward issue of personal jurisdiction involving no complex questions of state law, the court may, in its discretion, resolve the personal jurisdiction issue first.[22]

3. The Mandatory Nature of Subject-Matter Jurisdiction

Courts in the United States consider it obligatory to hear cases within their grants of constitutional and legislative subject-matter jurisdiction. This obligation is the product of principles of legislative supremacy embedded in the separation-of-powers doctrine. The courts disregard this obligation only for the most compelling reasons.[23]

If a dismissal results from a court's refusal to hear a case within its subject-matter jurisdiction, the proper course is an appeal.[24] If a judge refuses to schedule a case for trial or to render a decision, the proper course is to seek a writ of mandamus from a superior court.[25] The court of superior jurisdiction will command the inferior court to exercise its authority. The counterpart to a writ of mandamus is a writ of prohibition. A writ of prohibition directs the judge and the parties to a suit in an inferior court to cease litigating matters outside the inferior court's jurisdictional authority.

In some instances, the U.S. Constitution imposes an obligation on state courts to hear cases.

Illustration 2-6. In *Hughes v. Fetter,*[26] an administrator commenced an action in a Wisconsin state court to recover damages for the death of a decedent who was fatally injured in an automobile accident in Illinois. The action was based on the Illinois wrongful death statute. The Wisconsin trial court dismissed

---

21. *See* Chapter 3 *infra* (discussing personal jurisdiction).

22. 526 U.S. at __, 119 S. Ct. at 1569-71, 143 L. Ed. 2d at __. Nevertheless, the Court's decision leaves troubling questions. If the plaintiff recommences the dismissed action in a state court in the same state, will the state court be permitted to second guess the personal jurisdiction determination if it finds that the federal court acted without subject-matter jurisdiction, or will it be prevented from doing so on the ground that issue preclusion prevents reconsideration of the federal court's dismissal? *See* Chapter 13(E) *infra* (discussing claim and issue preclusion on questions of subject-matter and personal jurisdiction).

23. *But see* David L. Shapiro, *Jurisdiction and Discretion,* 60 N.Y.U. L. REV. 543 (1985).

24. *See, e.g.,* Buckman v. United Mine Workers, 80 Wyo. 199, 339 P.2d 398 (1959).

25. *See, e.g.,* Lyons v. Westinghouse Elec. Corp., 222 F.2d 184 (2d Cir.), *cert. denied,* 350 U.S. 825, 76 S. Ct. 52, 100 L. Ed. 737 (1955).

26. 341 U.S. 609, 71 S. Ct. 980, 95 L. Ed. 1212 (1951).

the complaint. The court found that a Wisconsin statute created a right of action for death caused in Wisconsin and established a local policy against Wisconsin courts entertaining suits brought under the wrongful death acts of other states. On appeal, the U.S. Supreme Court held that "Wisconsin cannot escape [this] constitutional obligation to enforce rights and duties validly created under the laws of other states by the simple device of removing jurisdiction from courts otherwise competent."[27] The Court explained that Wisconsin had no public policy against wrongful death actions because it had a wrongful death statute of its own. Wisconsin had no other legitimate reason for dismissing the action, such as a lack of any connection between the state and the case. Consequently, the Court concluded that the Full Faith and Credit Clause obligated the Wisconsin state court to hear the action.[28]

   Illustration 2-7. In *McKnett v. St. Louis & San Francisco Railway Co.,*[29] a resident of Tennessee commenced an action in an Alabama state court. The plaintiff sued a railroad for injuries occurring in Tennessee. The plaintiff based the case on a right of action created by the Federal Employers' Liability Act. That Act is the federal workers' compensation law covering employees of railroads engaged in interstate and foreign commerce. The Alabama court dismissed this action. No Alabama court had jurisdiction of any suit against a foreign corporation (in this instance, a railroad incorporated outside of Alabama) unless the cause of action had arisen in Alabama. The Alabama Supreme Court affirmed. The court held that the Alabama Legislature had modified this rule only to the extent of allowing plaintiffs to bring actions based on the common law or the statutes of another *state* in Alabama, not those arising under *federal* law. On certiorari, the U.S. Supreme Court reversed. The Supreme Court pointed out that the Alabama court would have had jurisdiction if the accident had occurred in Alabama or the plaintiff had sued under Tennessee law. Under these circumstances, the U.S. Constitution prohibited Alabama from discriminating against rights created by federal law.[30]

---

27. *Id.* at 611, 71 S. Ct. at 982, 95 L. Ed. at 1216.

28. *Id.* at 612-13, 71 S. Ct. at 982-83, 95 L. Ed. at 1216-17. The Full Faith and Credit Clause requires, *inter alia*, that "[f]ull faith and credit shall be given in each State to the public Acts . . . of every other State." U.S. CONST. art. IV, § 1. For criticism of the result in *Hughes,* see RUSSELL J. WEINTRAUB, COMMENTARY ON THE CONFLICT OF LAWS 556-57 (3d ed. 1986). The Court's reference to dismissal because of lack of connections between Wisconsin and the case was part of a discussion of the doctrine of forum non conveniens, which is examined in Chapter 4(D) ("Forum Non Conveniens and Change of Venue") *infra.* The Full Faith and Credit Clause is discussed further in conjunction with the doctrine of personal jurisdiction in Chapter 3(A)(1)*(c)-(e) infra.*

29. 292 U.S. 230, 54 S. Ct. 690, 78 L. Ed. 1227 (1934).

30. Specifically, the Court stated that the U.S. Constitution forbids

> state courts of general jurisdiction from refusing to [hear actions] solely because the suit is brought under a federal law. The denial of jurisdiction by the Alabama court is based solely upon the source of law sought to be enforced. The plaintiff is cast out because he is suing to enforce a federal act. A state may not discriminate against rights arising under federal laws.

Id. at 233-34, 54 S. Ct. at 692, 78 L. Ed. at 1229.

SECTION B. SUBJECT-MATTER JURISDICTION OF THE STATE COURTS

Subject-matter jurisdiction of the state and federal courts share many common characteristics. For example, the no-waiver, no-consent rule operates in both sets of courts.[31] However, the existence of courts of both limited and general jurisdiction within the states create some conceptual problems. These problems do not exist at the federal level, where all courts are of limited jurisdiction. Furthermore, because the states have courts of both general and limited jurisdiction, they have been able to avoid the inconvenience and inefficiency of dismissing cases erroneously commenced in courts lacking jurisdiction. Instead, many states allow actions to be transferred to courts possessing jurisdiction. These transfer statutes are an important feature of state jurisprudence.

1. Presumptions in Favor of and Against Jurisdiction

It is commonly said that the subject-matter jurisdiction of a court of general jurisdiction is presumed to exist, but that the subject-matter jurisdiction of a court of limited jurisdiction is presumed not to exist and must be demonstrated.[32] If this statement were literally true, the no-waiver, no-consent rule, as a universal proposition, would only apply to courts of limited jurisdiction. The "presumption" in favor of the subject-matter jurisdiction of courts of general jurisdiction would supply authority when none actually existed.[33] In reality, of course, these presumptions do not limit the no-waiver, no-consent rule in courts of general jurisdiction. Rather than being true presumptions, they actually express other differences between the subject-matter authority of courts of general and limited jurisdiction. Some of those differences are valid elements of practice today while others are now obsolete.

Plaintiffs in courts of limited jurisdiction must ordinarily demonstrate the basis for the court's subject-matter jurisdiction.[34] Even if subject-matter

---

31. *See* section A(2) ("The 'No-Waiver, No-Consent' Rule") *supra.*

32. *See, e.g.,* 13 CHARLES A. WRIGHT ET AL., FEDERAL PRACTICE AND PROCEDURE: JURISDICTION AND RELATED MATTERS § 3522, at 60-63 (2d ed. 1984).

33. For example, assume the plaintiff commences an action in a court of general jurisdiction. Assume also, however, that the action actually belongs to the exclusive jurisdiction of another court within the state. If the defendant does not raise the issue of subject-matter jurisdiction and come forward with sufficient evidence to destroy the presumption, the court of general jurisdiction might enter a valid judgment against the defendant. Presumptions normally operate in this way. *See* Chapter 11(H)(3) ("Presumptions") *infra.* The court of general jurisdiction could rely on the presumption to provide it with subject-matter jurisdiction instead of being required by the no-waiver, no-consent rule to raise the objection to subject-matter jurisdiction on its own motion. Moreover, an appellate court would not be able to reverse the judgment for lack of jurisdiction. The presumption would provide the necessary jurisdictional predicate for the lower court's action.

34. *See, e.g.,* State *ex rel.* Smilack v. Bushong, 93 Ohio App. 201, 209-10, 112 N.E.2d 675, 680 (1952); State v. Vijil, 784 P.2d 1130, 1133 (Utah 1989). The cases usually state that the "record" must affirmatively demonstrate the jurisdiction of the court. *See, e.g.,* Hall v. Franklin County, 184 Miss. 77, 86-87, 185 So. 591, 594-95 (1939); Colagrovanni v. District Ct., 47 R.I. 323, 324, 133 A. 1, 2 (1926). Thus, if the action moves past the pleading stage—for example, if a judgment is rendered which is then appealed—the court may rely on jurisdiction actually exists under the existing facts, the failure to demonstrate the jurisdictional basis of the action will result in dismissal or transfer. In contrast, plaintiffs in courts of general jurisdiction do not ordinarily have to affirmatively demonstrate the existence of subject-matter jurisdiction.[35] However, even if a plaintiff demonstrates jurisdiction by a statement in the complaint, a court of limited jurisdiction will be required by the no-waiver, no-consent rule to dismiss the action if facts come to light showing that no subject-matter jurisdiction actually exists. Similarly, the presumption of subject-matter jurisdiction in courts of general jurisdiction does not eliminate the court's obligation to question subject-matter jurisdiction on its own initiative if it appears affirmatively that jurisdiction may be lacking.[36]

Illustration 2-8 Assume that the county court in State X is a court of limited jurisdiction. State X law authorizes county courts to adjudicate actions in which the amount in controversy is not less than $500 and not more than $2,000. A sues B in the county court for property damage arising from an automobile accident. A's complaint does not contain a jurisdictional statement or demonstrate in any other way the amount in controversy. A is actually seeking $900 in damages, an amount within the jurisdiction of the court. B does not object to subject-matter jurisdiction. The usual rules governing the authority of courts of limited jurisdiction do not authorize the county court to adjudicate the action. A must include a jurisdictional statement in a pleading or make some other appropriate demonstration of the amount in controversy. Even though B has not objected to the court's jurisdiction, the court should raise the jurisdictional objection on its own motion.

Illustration 2-9. On the facts of *Illustration 2-8*, assume that A's complaint does contain a jurisdictional statement. A alleges that the amount in controversy is not less than $500 and does not exceed $2,000. Under the usual rules governing the authority of courts of limited jurisdiction, this statement satisfies the special jurisdictional pleading requirements applicable to those courts. However, assume that A is actually seeking only $200 in damages from B. This fact becomes clear during the trial. B again does not object to the court's subject-matter jurisdiction. Despite the jurisdictional statement in A's initial pleading, the court should raise the issue of subject-matter jurisdiction on its own motion and take appropriate action to dismiss or transfer the action, whichever the state's statutes require.

---

the entire record to establish the necessary jurisdictional facts. However, at the commencement of the action, the plaintiff's initial pleading is, of necessity, the only vehicle for demonstrating jurisdiction. *See* Blount County Bank v. Barnes, 218 Ala. 230, 232, 118 So. 460, 461 (1928).

35. *See, e.g.,* Broom v. Board of Supervisors, 171 Miss. 586, 593, 158 So. 344, 345 (1934); Dougherty v. Matthews, 35 Mo. 520 (1865); State *ex rel.* Smilack v. Bushong, 93 Ohio App. 201, 112 N.E.2d 675 (1952); Peek v. Equipment Serv. Co., 779 S.W.2d 802 (Tex. 1989); State v. Vijil, 784 P.2d 1130 (Utah 1989); Slater v. Melton, 119 W. Va. 259, 262, 193 S.E. 185, 186 (1937).

36. *Compare* Richardson v. First Nat'l Life Ins. Co., 419 S.W.2d 836 (Tex. 1967) (specific pleading controls over general pleading for determining jurisdiction) *with* Peek v. Equipment Serv. Co., 779 S.W.2d 802, 804 (Tex. 1989) (liberal construction of pleadings appropriate; lack of allegation of jurisdictional amount cured at trial).

Illustration 2-10. Assume that the superior court is the court of general jurisdiction in State *Y*. Assume that *A* sues *B* for patent infringement in the superior court. Patent infringement actions are within the exclusive jurisdiction of the federal courts.[37] *B* does not object to the court's subject-matter jurisdiction. The superior court should raise the objection to its subject-matter jurisdiction on its own motion and dismiss the action. If the superior court fails to do so and the judgment is appealed, the appellate court should raise the objection on its own motion if the parties fail to do so. In this situation, the action will have to be dismissed. State courts cannot transfer cases to federal courts.

* * * * *

At one time, the traditional presumptions concerning courts of general and limited jurisdiction produced another distinction. This distinction concerned challenges to the validity of judgments of the two kinds of courts in subsequent proceedings, as opposed to challenges raised in the original proceeding in which the judgment was rendered (such as by appeal). Traditionally, the presumption in favor of the jurisdiction of courts of general jurisdiction prevented a party from attacking the judgment of such a court in a later action on the ground of lack of subject-matter jurisdiction. However, the judgments of courts of limited jurisdiction, not having the benefit of the presumption, could be "impeached" for lack of subject-matter jurisdiction in a subsequent action.[38] Today, however, no such distinction is drawn.[39]

Illustration 2-11. Assume that the State *Y* superior court is the court of general jurisdiction in the state. State *Y* statutes expressly forbid the superior court from adjudicating automobile accident cases. State *Y* has exclusively allocated those actions to the jurisdiction of a special automobile claims court. *A* sues *B* in the superior court for $100,000 in damages for personal injuries received in an automobile accident. Neither the court nor the parties raise an issue of subject-matter jurisdiction. After a trial, the court enters judgment for *A* on an express finding that *B's* negligence caused *A's* injuries. Subsequently, *C* sues *B* for personal injuries received in the same accident. *C's* action is brought in the special automobile claims court in State *Y*. To establish *B's* negligence in *C* v. *B*, *C* wishes to use the finding of *B's* negligence in *A* v. *B* against *B*. *C* can use the judgment to establish *B's* negligence only if it is immune from attack on subject-matter jurisdiction grounds. In determining whether the judgment is immune from attack today, it would be irrelevant that a court of general jurisdiction rendered the judgment.[40]

---

37. *See* 28 U.S.C. § 1338(a). Because the federal courts are provided by statute with exclusive jurisdiction over patent infringement actions, if any such action is commenced in the state courts, it appears affirmatively in the record that the state court lacks jurisdiction.

38. *See* RESTATEMENT (SECOND) OF JUDGMENTS § 12 cmt. e (1982).

39. *See id.*

40. *See id.* Under modern rules governing the ability to attack judgments on subject-matter jurisdiction grounds in later actions, the judgment in *A* v. *B* would probably be invalid because the subject-matter of the action was so plainly beyond the superior court's jurisdiction that entertaining the action in that court was a "manifest abuse of authority." *See id.* § 12(1); *see also* Chapter 13(E) ("Claim and Issue Preclusion on Questions of Subject-Matter and Personal Jurisdiction") *infra*, which fully discusses the grounds for attacking a judgment for lack of subject-matter jurisdiction in a subsequent action.

2. Transfer to Cure Subject-Matter Jurisdiction Deficiencies

Except in rare instances, when a federal court lacks subject-matter jurisdiction, the court must dismiss the action.[41] In the states, statutes often authorize transfer from a court without subject-matter jurisdiction to a court possessing subject-matter jurisdiction. While transfer schemes avoid the inconvenience of dismissal, they sometimes produce their own special complications.[42]

Transfer issues often arise in the context of an action properly commenced in a court of limited jurisdiction when the defendant asserts a counterclaim that is beyond the court's jurisdiction—or would have been if the counterclaim had been asserted as an original claim in the same court. Under these circumstances, several procedural interests may compete with each other. One such interest is the plaintiff's interest in choosing the forum. The plaintiff may prefer the court of limited jurisdiction to prosecute the action. If a counterclaim beyond the jurisdiction of the court results in transfer of the case to a different court, the transfer will deprive the plaintiff of the natural forum preference that plaintiffs ordinarily possess.[43] In addition, if the state permits transfer upon the assertion of counterclaims that are factually unrelated to the plaintiff's claim,[44] the transfer will undermine the plaintiff's forum preference for reasons having little to do with the convenient resolution of claims in the same proceeding. Indeed, in the latter situation, the defendant may have asserted the factually unrelated claim purely as a forum shopping tactic rather than as a result of considerations of procedural convenience.

Countervailing considerations exist for the defendant. When the plaintiff's claim factually relates to the defendant's counterclaim, the plaintiff may have consciously engaged in a "race to the courthouse" to trap the defendant in the court of the plaintiff's choosing—at least in those states that do not permit transfer

---

41. *See* 28 U.S.C. § 1631 (providing for transfers in limited circumstances, such as transfers from U.S. District Courts to the U.S. Claims Court); Kier Bros. Invs., Inc. v. White, 943 F. Supp. 1, 4 (D.D.C. 1996) (dismissal only appropriate remedy when court lacks subject-matter jurisdiction in a diversity case; section 1631 does not allow a federal court to transfer actions to state courts); Jeffrey W. Tayson, *The Federal Transfer Statute: 28 U.S.C. § 1631*, 29 S. TEX. L. REV. 189 (1987); section C ("Subject-Matter Jurisdiction of the Federal Courts") *infra*.

42. For a discussion of the transfer systems in two states, see Joseph M. Lynch, *Lack of Jurisdiction of the Subject Matter in the New Jersey Courts: Application of N.J.R. 1:13-4, the Transfer of Causes Rule*, 6 SETON HALL L. REV. 1 (1974); Lee Blalack, Comment, *Civil Procedure*—Flowers v. Dyer County: *The Death of the Motion to Dismiss for Lack of Subject Matter Jurisdiction*, 23 MEMPHIS ST. U. L. REV. 409 (1993). For a discussion of additional jurisdictional and other problems related to the state courts, see Edson R. Sunderland, *Problems Connected with the Operation of a State Court System*, 1950 WIS. L. REV. 585.

43. Of course, the plaintiff may have brought the claim in the court of limited jurisdiction because it was the only court with subject-matter jurisdiction over the claim. In such circumstances, it is unrealistic to speak of the plaintiff having a forum choice. Nevertheless, even if the plaintiff does not have a forum choice, the plaintiff may still have a forum preference for the court in which the action was commenced. Furthermore, in some cases the plaintiff *can* frame the claim for relief so that it fits within the jurisdiction of one court rather than another.

44. This type of counterclaim would normally be classified as a permissive counterclaim under state procedural rules patterned on the Federal Rules of Civil Procedure. *See* FED. R. CIV. P. 13(b).

to another court on the basis of the counterclaim. If the action is not transferred, but the defendant is required to assert the claim in a separate action, other difficulties may result. Procedural inconvenience may result from having to litigate factually related claims in different proceedings. Additionally, the doctrine of issue preclusion may preclude certain factual or legal matters determined against the defendant in the court of limited jurisdiction from relitigation in the action on the defendant's claim in another court. Furthermore, even if the defendant's counterclaim is not factually or legally related to the plaintiff's claim, many procedural systems permit the assertion of the counterclaim on the assumption that it may be convenient for parties to resolve all claims existing between them in a single action.[45] To require the defendant to assert the counter-claim in a separate proceeding would deprive the defendant of this potential procedural convenience.

The manner in which any given procedural system resolves transfer issues depends upon how it balances this complex mix of factors. No single solution is inherently better than another. The following illustrations demonstrate some possible solutions.

Illustration 2-12. A sued B in a magistrate court in State X for $1,016.79. State X law limits the jurisdiction of the magistrate court to actions in which the sum demanded does not exceed $1,500. *B's* answer contained a counterclaim for $7,308.13 arising out of the same facts as the plaintiff's claim. After serving the answer containing the counterclaim, B sought a mandatory injunction from the circuit court to prevent the magistrate court from proceeding with the action. The circuit court issued an injunction restraining the magistrate court from proceeding and ordered the case to be certified to the circuit court for decision. On appeal, the court of appeals reversed. The court of appeals held that asserting a counter-claim in excess of the jurisdictional amount did not deprive the magistrate court of jurisdiction, even though the magistrate court had no power to enter judgment in favor of B for an amount in excess of $1,500.[46] The court of appeals noted that the magistrate court could enter judgment for B in an amount that did not exceed the jurisdictional amount. The court also noted that B could pursue the claim in a separate action in the circuit court. In a separate action, the doctrine of claim preclusion would not prevent B from asserting the claim, although the doctrine of issue preclusion could result in B being bound in the circuit court action by findings made against B in the magistrate court.[47] By resolving the

---

45. State procedural systems based on the Federal Rules of Civil Procedure permit unlimited joinder of claims at the pleading stage of the litigation; they provide other procedural mechanisms for separating and resolving the claims at later stages of the litigation if it turns out that the hoped-for procedural convenience is not actually present. *See* Chapter 7(F) ("Counterclaims and Cross-Claims Under the Federal Rules") *infra*.

46. *See* State *ex rel.* St. Louis Boiler & Equip. Co. v. Gabbert, 241 S.W.2d 79, 82 (Mo. Ct. App. 1951).

47. *See id.* at 81-82. The court did not indicate whether the doctrine of claim preclusion would allow the defendant to assert part of the claim in the magistrate court and the excess in the circuit court. However, in Brother Int'l Corp. v. Southeastern Sales Co., 234 S.C. 573, 109 S.E.2d 444 (1959), the court indicated that the defendant could assert the counterclaim in the court of limited jurisdiction and waive the amount in excess of the jurisdictional limit or assert the entire claim in a separate action. *See id.* at 575, 109 S.E.2d at 445. This approach is consistent with the modern law of claim preclusion. *See* Chapter 13(B) ("Claim Preclusion") *infra*. However, in McDaneld v. Lynn Hickey Dodge, Inc., 1999 OK 30, 979 P.2d 252, the Oklahoma Supreme Court held that when a defendant who is sued in a small claims court possesses a compulsory counterclaim in excess transfer issue in this manner, the court of appeals in State X weighed the inefficiencies of resolving factually related claims and counterclaims in separate proceedings as less than depriving the plaintiff of a possible forum preference for the magistrate court. In addition, it gave little weight to the danger of forum shopping by the plaintiff through a "race to the courthouse" and the potential difficulties posed for the defendant by the operation of the doctrine of issue preclusion.

Illustration 2-13. Assume that county courts in State Y are authorized to hear any case involving amounts up to $5,000. A sued B in a county court of State Y to recover $2,000 on a promissory note B gave to A. B's answer contained defenses to A's claim. B's answer also contained a counterclaim for $7,000 based on an alleged conversion of B's property by A. B then sought a transfer of the action to a circuit court in State Y. The county court reasoned that only compulsory counterclaims exceeding the jurisdictional limit required transfer of the action; B's claim was a permissive counterclaim because it was unrelated to A's claim. Thus, the county court concluded that the action need not be transferred and that the counterclaim could not be asserted in the county court because it was beyond the jurisdiction of the county court. The court of appeals in State Y granted a writ of prohibition to prevent the county court from exercising jurisdiction in the action. The appellate court interpreted the transfer provision in State Y as requiring transfer of an action when either a compulsory or a permissive counterclaim exceeded the jurisdictional amount limit of the county court.[48] In contrast to the case described in *Illustration 2-12*, the court of appeals in State Y has given great weight to the convenience of resolving even factually unrelated claims in the same proceeding and more weight to the defendant's interests than to the plaintiff's forum preference.

SECTION C. SUBJECT-MATTER JURISDICTION OF THE FEDERAL COURTS

Article III, § 1 of the U.S. Constitution provides that the judicial power of the United States "shall be vested" in a Supreme Court "and in such inferior Courts as the Congress may from time to time ordain and establish."[49] This language has been interpreted as requiring Congress to establish a Supreme Court, but giving Congress the discretion to create inferior courts.[50] Section 2 of Article III limits the judicial power to specific classes of cases:

> The judicial Power shall extend to all Cases, in Law and Equity,
> arising under this Constitution, the Laws of the United States,

---

of the court's jurisdictional competence, the defendant must plead the counterclaim and seek transfer of the action to a court that possesses subject-matter jurisdiction. Failure to plead the counterclaim and seek transfer will result in preclusion of a separate action on the claim.

48. *See* State *ex rel.* Rosenfeld v. Boyer, 145 So. 2d 547, 549 (Fla. Dist. Ct. App. 1962); *see also* Elliott v. Roach, 409 N.E.2d 661, 669 (Ind. Ct. App. 1980); State *ex rel.* Moore v. Morrison, 1964 OK 154, ¶ 10, 401 P.2d 484, 486.

49. U.S. CONST. art. III, § 1.

50. *See, e.g.*, CHARLES A. WRIGHT, THE LAW OF FEDERAL COURTS § 4, at 13 (5th ed. 1994).

and Treaties made, or which shall be made, under their Authority;—to all Cases affecting Ambassadors, other public Ministers
and Consuls;—to all Cases of admiralty and maritime Jurisdiction;—to Controversies to which the United States shall be a
Party;—to Controversies between two or more States;—between a
State and Citizens of another State;—between Citizens of different
States;—between Citizens of the same State claiming Lands under
Grants of different States, and between a State, or the Citizens
thereof, and foreign States, Citizens or Subjects.[51]

This section further provides that

[i]n all Cases affecting Ambassadors, other public Ministers and
Consuls, and those in which a State shall be Party, the supreme
Court shall have original Jurisdiction. In all the other Cases
before mentioned, the supreme Court shall have appellate Jurisdiction, both as to Law and Fact, with such Exceptions, and
under such Regulations as the Congress shall make.[52]

It is generally agreed that this latter part of § 2 prevents Congress from depriving
the Supreme Court of its original jurisdiction in any of the cases listed. However,
disagreement exists about the extent to which Congress can limit the Court's
appellate jurisdiction through "exceptions and regulations."[53]

In the Judiciary Act of 1789, Congress created inferior federal courts, but
Congress did not vest them with the full jurisdiction that Article III allows.
Congress has greatly expanded the jurisdiction of the lower federal courts over
the years, but Congress has never conferred upon them the full scope of Article
III jurisdiction. Today, the principal trial courts in the federal system are the U.S.
District Courts, which are located in "judicial districts" throughout the United
States. Each state has at least one judicial district, and some states have more than
one. With one unimportant exception,[54] the district lines do not extend across
state lines.[55]

---

51. U.S. CONST. art. III, § 2.

52. *Id.*

53. *See* 13 CHARLES A. WRIGHT ET AL., FEDERAL PRACTICE AND PROCEDURE: JURISDICTION AND RELATED
MATTERS § 3525, at 216, 221-27, § 3526, at 230-41 (2d ed. 1984); 15 MARTIN H. REDISH, MOORE'S FEDERAL
PRACTICE § 100App.01, at 4 & n.13 (3d ed. 1999). Although the accepted view of the power of Congress over
the original jurisdiction is as stated in the text, recent reexamination of the text and history of Article III has led
one commentator to conclude that Congress can deprive the Supreme Court of some of the original jurisdiction
authorized by Article III, § 2. Professor Akhil Reed Amar has offered the opinion that Congress may not deprive
the Court of original jurisdiction over cases affecting ambassadors, other public ministers and consuls, but that
it can deprive the Court of original jurisdiction over controversies in which a state is a party. *See* Akhil Reed
Amar, Marbury, *Section 13, and the Original Jurisdiction of the Supreme Court*, 56 U. CHI. L. REV. 443, 478-98
(1989). This theory is part of a broader theory of the structure of Article III. *See* Akhil Reed Amar, *A Neo-
Federalist View of Article III: Separating the Two Tiers of Federal Jurisdiction*, 65 B.U. L. REV. 205 (1985).
For a critique and discussion of Amar's theory, along with a citation of additional criticisms, see RICHARD H.
FALLON ET AL., HART & WECHSLER'S THE FEDERAL COURTS AND THE FEDERAL SYSTEM 362, 370-73 (4th ed.
1996).

54. *See* 28 U.S.C. § 131 (establishing the district lines for the U.S. District Court of Wyoming).

55. The number and exact boundaries of districts within a particular state are set out in §§ 81-131 of Title
28 of the *United States Code. See, e.g.,* 28 U.S.C. § 84 (dividing California into four judicial districts to be
known as the Northern, Eastern, Central, and Southern Districts of California). In addition, these sections

Much of the jurisdiction of the federal district courts is concurrent with that of the state courts. For example, two important branches of district court jurisdiction are *diversity jurisdiction* (when a suit is between citizens of different states and the amount in controversy exceeds $75,000, exclusive of interest and costs)[56] and general *federal question jurisdiction* (when a case arises "under the Constitution, laws, or treaties of the United States").[57] The plaintiff may bring cases falling within these grants of jurisdiction in either state or federal court. When the plaintiff chooses a state court, the Judicial Code may allow the defendant to "remove" the case to the federal district court.[58] If the plaintiff properly files suit in federal court in the first instance, the option to move the case to state court does not exist.[59]

In addition to concurrent jurisdiction with the state courts, a certain portion of the jurisdiction of the federal district courts is exclusive of the state courts. When federal jurisdiction is exclusive, the state courts may not hear cases included within the exclusive grant. Any such actions commenced in state courts must be dismissed for lack of subject-matter jurisdiction. However, because Congress excludes the state courts from hearing cases within the federal judicial power only for compelling reasons, exclusive federal jurisdiction is the exception rather than the rule. Usually, those reasons involve a perceived need for an unbiased or uniform interpretation of some federal law of great national importance.

Illustration 2-14. Federal courts have exclusive jurisdiction over admiralty, patent, and copyright cases.[60]

* * * * *

In contrast with the organization of the state courts, all federal courts are courts of limited jurisdiction. As a result, restrictive rules exist in the federal system concerning how federal subject-matter jurisdiction must be pleaded and established. For example, a plaintiff who wants to invoke some branch of federal jurisdiction must plead its existence in the complaint.

Illustration 2-15. Federal Rule 8(a)(1) requires that a complaint contain a short and plain statement of the grounds upon which the jurisdiction of the court depends. The first paragraph of the complaint usually sets forth this statement. The following two allegations illustrate how federal subject-matter jurisdiction is typically pleaded:

---

indicate where court will be held within the district. *See, e.g., id.* (stating that the Northern District of California comprises the counties of Alameda, Contra Costa, Del Norte, Humboldt, Lake Marin, Mendocino, Monterey, Napa, San Benito, Santa Cruz, San Francisco, San Mateo, and Sonoma; and designating that court for the Northern District shall be held at Eureka, Oakland, San Francisco, and San Jose).

56. *See* U.S. CONST. art. III, § 2; 28 U.S.C. § 1332(a).

57. *See* U.S. CONST. art. III, § 2; 28 U.S.C. § 1331.

58. "Removal" jurisdiction is discussed in subsection 5 ("Removal Jurisdiction") *infra.*

59. *But see* 42 PA. CONS. STAT. ANN. § 5103(b) (Supp. 1999) (authorizing a party in a dismissed federal action to transfer the action to a state court).

60. *See* 28 U.S.C. §§ 1333, 1338.

(a) "This claim arises under the United States Copyright Act, United States Code, Title 17, §§ 101 *et seq.*, and this court has jurisdiction of this claim pursuant to *United States Code*, Title 28, § 1338(a)."[61]

(b) "Plaintiff *A* is a citizen of the State of Ohio, plaintiff *B* is a citizen of the State of Florida, defendant *C* is a citizen of the State of New York, defendant *D* is a citizen of the State of California, and defendant *E* is a citizen of the State of Arkansas. The amount in controversy exceeds, exclusive of interest and costs, the sum of seventy-five thousand dollars ($75,000)." This allegation pleads jurisdiction over the action based on diversity of citizenship involving multiple natural persons.[62]

* * * * *

If federal subject-matter jurisdiction is not pleaded properly, the district court must dismiss the case on its own motion without waiting for the defendant to object.[63] If the defendant objects to subject-matter jurisdiction, the plaintiff has the burden of proving its existence, even if the plaintiff has properly pleaded it.[64] Even when no objection to subject-matter jurisdiction occurs at the district court level and the case proceeds to judgment, the federal appellate courts must raise any apparent objections to the district court's or their own subject-matter jurisdiction. Thus, an action can be fully tried and judgment rendered without anyone objecting to subject-matter jurisdiction, but the case may be reversed on appeal when the appellate court or a party objects to subject-matter jurisdiction.[65]

The following subsections introduce the jurisdiction of the federal district courts (1) in cases arising under federal law; (2) in actions in which the United States is a party; (3) in controversies between citizens of different states; (4) pursuant to "supplemental" jurisdiction; and (5) in cases removed from state to federal court.

1. Cases Arising Under the Constitution and Laws of the United States

The Judiciary Act of 1789 created federal trial courts. At an early date, Congress conferred subject-matter jurisdiction in those courts over particular

---

61. *Cf.* Form 2(b) ("Jurisdiction founded on the existence of a Federal question") in the Appendix of Forms following the Federal Rules of Civil Procedure. Section 1338 authorizes copyright claims to be brought in federal court. *See* 28 U.S.C. § 1338(a).

62. *Cf.* Form 2(a) ("Jurisdiction founded on diversity of citizenship and amount") in the Appendix of Forms following the Federal Rules of Civil Procedure.

63. Jurisdictional defects have long been raised by federal courts on their own motion. *See, e.g.,* Capron v. Van Noorden, 6 U.S. (2 Cranch) 126, 2 L. Ed. 229 (1804).

64. Assume that the plaintiff's diversity allegation in *Illustration 2-15* inadvertently stated that each of the parties was a "resident" rather than a "citizen" of each of the states listed. Rule 15 of the Federal Rules of Civil Procedure permits amendments either as of right or by leave of the district court. Thus, the plaintiff ordinarily has the opportunity to amend a defective allegation of jurisdiction prior to a complete dismissal of the claim. Section 1653 of Title 28 also specifically provides that "[d]efective allegations of jurisdiction may be amended, upon terms, in the trial or appellate courts." 28 U.S.C. § 1653. *See* subsection *3(h)* ("Correcting Defects in Diversity Jurisdiction and Adjudicating Disputes Over Diversity") *infra.*

65. *See* Louisville & Nashville R.R. Co. v. Mottley, 211 U.S. 149, 29 S. Ct. 42, 53 L. Ed. 126 (1908).

matters arising under federal statutes through specific statutory grants. For example, Congress specifically conferred federal question jurisdiction over actions for patent infringement.[66] However, Congress did not give those courts subject-matter jurisdiction over all cases arising under the Constitution, laws, or treaties of the United States (general federal question jurisdiction) until 1875.[67] Today, the general federal question statute confers on the district courts "original jurisdiction of all civil actions arising under the Constitution, laws, or treaties of the United States.'"[68] This general federal question jurisdiction is concurrent with the state courts.

The conventional justification for conferring general federal question jurisdiction on the federal district courts, rather than leaving cases arising under federal law to the state courts, is that the federal courts will provide a more expert, more uniform, and more sympathetic interpretation of federal law than the state courts.[69] Several empirically unsupported assumptions underlie this conventional justification. Furthermore, the structure of Article III and the Supremacy Clause of the Constitution undermine the justification.[70] The Supremacy Clause assumes that state courts are fully competent to deal with matters of federal law; and they are bound to uphold the supremacy and validity of that law, notwithstanding anything to the contrary that may exist in their own constitutions and laws.[71] In addition, even if all assumptions supporting conferral of the federal question jurisdiction on the district courts are valid, the achievement of an expert, uniform, and sympathetic interpretation of federal law is left to the discretion of the parties in most cases because of the concurrent nature of much of the jurisdiction.

(a) The Constitutional Scope of Federal Question Jurisdiction

The seminal U.S. Supreme Court decision defining the scope of Congress' power to create federal question jurisdiction is *Osborn v. Bank of the United States*.[72] In an opinion written by Chief Justice Marshall, the Supreme Court interpreted Article III to allow Congress to confer jurisdiction on the federal

---

66. *See* Root v. Railway Co., 105 U.S. 189, 28 L. Ed. 975 (1881).

67. Act of Mar. 3, 1875, ch. 137, § 1, 18 Stat. 470, 470. Originally, this grant of jurisdiction was subject to a jurisdictional amount requirement, but that requirement no longer exists. *See* 28 U.S.C. § 1331.

68. 28 U.S.C. § 1331.

69. *See* ALI STUDY OF THE DIVISION OF JURISDICTION BETWEEN STATE AND FEDERAL COURTS 164-68 (1969); ERWIN CHEMERINSKY, FEDERAL JURISDICTION § 5.2.1, at 252 (3d ed. 1999); Paul M. Bator, *The State Courts and Federal Constitutional Litigation*, 22 WM. & MARY L. REV. 605, 607, 623 (1981).

70. *See* U.S. CONST. art. III, VI.

71. *See* THE FEDERALIST No. 82 (Alexander Hamilton) (Jacob E. Cooke ed., 1961); Paul M. Bator, *The State Courts and Federal Constitutional Litigation*, 22 WM. & MARY L. REV. 605, 606, 624, 627-29 (1981). The question whether the state courts are, in fact, in parity with federal courts in the enforcement of federal rights is hotly contested. *See, e.g.*, Burt Neuborne, *The Myth of Parity*, 90 HARV. L. REV. 1105 (1977). For a summary of the debate on this issue, *see* ERWIN CHEMERINSKY, FEDERAL JURISDICTION § 1.5, at 33-37 (3d ed. 1999).

72. 22 U.S. (9 Wheat.) 738, 6 L. Ed. 204 (1824); *see* ERWIN CHEMERINSKY, FEDERAL JURISDICTION § 5.2.2, at 267 (3d ed. 1999). *See generally* Annotation, *Supreme Court's Views as to Scope of "Arising Under" Clause of Article III, § 2, Clause 1 of Federal Constitution*, 76 L. Ed. 2d 831 (1985).

courts whenever federal law forms some ingredient in the case, even if no actual issue of federal law exists in the case and even if no federal law confers the basic right of action. The *Osborn* case contained a federal question because the Bank of the United States relied on the U.S. Constitution to invalidate a state law that had levied a tax on the Bank.[73] However, the opinion in *Osborn* supported a much broader theory. According to Chief Justice Marshall, the federal act incorporating the Bank formed an original "ingredient" in every case in which the Bank was a party, even if no question of the interpretation or validity of the act was ever raised in the case.[74]

The *Osborn* ingredient theory has sometimes been viewed as a kind of "but for" test. "But for" the federal act creating the Bank, the Bank could not legitimately engage in any transactions or sue or be sued. However, under this view, it is sometimes questionably asserted that the *Osborn* decision authorizes Congress to confer jurisdiction over cases in which federal law is a less active ingredient than was the act incorporating the Bank.

Illustration 2-16. Osborn is sometimes said to authorize Congress to create federal question jurisdiction over virtually every case involving the title to land in the western states because title to land in those states originated in a grant from the United States.[75] This view assumes that the *Osborn* holding extends to any situation in which a right originated remotely in a law of the United States, even if the federal law has exhausted its original force and has no current effect or operation. In other words, "but for" the original grant of land, the current title would not exist. However, in *Osborn*, the act incorporating the Bank was an essential part of the Bank's daily ability to operate. If the act had ceased to exist, the Bank would have ceased to exist. In contrast, after the passage of sufficient time, the original federal law under which a title was granted ceases to have any current force or effect, and the title depends entirely on state law for its current viability.[76] Thus, suppose the United States invalidly conveys title to *A* when *D*

---

73. *See* CHARLES A. WRIGHT, THE LAW OF FEDERAL COURTS § 17, at 101 (5th ed. 1994). It is sometimes asserted that the Bank was asserting a "claim under the federal Constitution." *See id.* However, this assertion is incorrect on the facts of the case. Technically, the Bank's claim was an injunction against trespass. The defense asserted to the claim was that official authority under the state statute authorized the levy of the tax. In effect, the federal constitutional issue came into the action as a reply to this defense, not as a part of the plaintiff's "claim," which arose under state law. *See* 22 U.S. at 836-37, 6 L. Ed. at 833. Nevertheless, a *case* still arises under the laws of the United States for purposes of Article III when the federal issue in the case comes into the action as a defense or a reply to a defense. *See* section C(1)*(b)(ii) infra* (discussing the well-pleaded complaint rule). For a discussion of the nature of trespass, see Chapter 1(E)(1) ("The Common-Law Courts and the Forms of Action") *supra*.

74. *See* 22 U.S. (9 Wheat.) at 823-24, 6 L. Ed. at 820; *see also* CHARLES A. WRIGHT, THE LAW OF FEDERAL COURTS § 17, at 102 (5th ed. 1994). The Act incorporating the Bank was the only basis for federal jurisdiction in Bank of the United States v. Planters Bank, 22 U.S. (9 Wheat.) 904, 6 L. Ed. 244 (1824), in which no issues of federal law were involved in the case.

75. *See* CHARLES A. WRIGHT, THE LAW OF FEDERAL COURTS § 17, at 102 (5th ed. 1994); *see also* Shulthis v. McDougal, 225 U.S. 561, 569-70, 32 S. Ct. 704, 706, 56 L. Ed. 1205, 1211 (1912); Shoshone Mining Co. v. Rutter, 177 U.S. 505, 507, 20 S. Ct. 726, 726, 44 L. Ed. 864, 865 (1900), which discuss why the title-to-western-land cases do not fit within the statutory federal question jurisdiction.

76. Ordinarily, when a title is granted by the United States, the incidents of the title are not thereafter forever controlled by federal law. Instead, state law controls subsequent transfers of title as well as other rights to hold and enjoy peaceable possession. Thus, even if a defect existed in the original title that could be challenged by someone at the time the title had been granted to the original purchaser, state adverse possession is actually entitled to receive title under federal law. *A* then enters the land and conveys to *B*. *B* lives on the land for eighty years and dies. *B* bequeaths the land to *C*, who lives on the land another fifty years. Under these circumstances, state limitations law will preclude *D's* heirs from challenging *C's* title based on title defects in the original grant to *A* under federal law. For Congress to have the power to grant federal question jurisdiction in a case between *C* and *D's* heirs, *Osborn* would have to be extended beyond its facts to circumstances in which federal law could not possibly have any current force. This example demonstrates that if Article III is interpreted to establish a "but for" test of Congress' power to establish federal question jurisdiction, the holding of *Osborn* cannot be its basis.

* * * * *

Whatever the scope of the *Osborn* holding, the decision permits Congress to create federal question jurisdiction in cases in which a federally chartered corporation is a party.

Illustration 2-17. In *American National Red Cross v. S.G.*,[77] a blood recipient sued the Red Cross, a federally chartered corporation, in state court. The recipient alleged that blood supplied by the Red Cross had caused the recipient to contract AIDS. The Red Cross removed the action to a U.S. District Court on the basis of federal question jurisdiction. The district court upheld jurisdiction based on a provision in the Red Cross charter authorizing the Red Cross "to sue and be sued in courts of law and equity, State or Federal, within the jurisdiction of the United States." The U.S. Court of Appeals reversed. It held that Congress did not intend the "sue and be sued" provision of the charter to be a grant of subject-matter jurisdiction. The U.S. Supreme Court granted certiorari and reversed the court of appeals. Relying on *Osborn* and other decisions, the Court held the "sue and be sued" provision granted federal question jurisdiction within Article III of the Constitution. The Court interpreted its prior decisions as establishing the rule that a congressional charter's "sue and be sued" provision may be read to confer federal jurisdiction "if, but only if, it specifically mentions the federal courts."[78]

(b) The Scope of the Statutory Grant of Federal Question Jurisdiction

Osborn (discussed in the preceding subsection) establishes how far Congress may go in creating jurisdiction for cases arising under Article III. The rule established by *Osborn* must be distinguished from the rules that apply to the

---

statutes operating on the title would, after the passage of sufficient time, eliminate the ability to assert a valid challenge to the title based on "federal" defects. Thus, the force of federal law would be eliminated from any dispute about the title.

77. 505 U.S. 247, 112 S. Ct. 2465, 120 L. Ed. 2d 201 (1992).

78. *Id.* at 255, 112 S. Ct. at 2471, 120 L. Ed. 2d at 211. In most cases involving congressionally chartered corporations, federal jurisdiction has been limited by statute to corporations in which the United States owns more than one-half the capital stock. *See* 28 U.S.C. § 1349. However, the Court held that the Red Cross charter conferred jurisdiction independently of this statutory restriction. *See* 505 U.S. at 251 n.3, 112 S. Ct. 2469 n.3, 120 L. Ed. 2d 209 n.3.

statutory grant of general federal question jurisdiction in 28 U.S.C. § 1331. Because the language of the general federal question statute is substantially the same as the language of the Constitution, one might think that Congress has conferred on the district courts the full scope of the "federal question" jurisdiction permitted under Article III. However, Congress need not confer the full scope of the jurisdiction authorized by any clause of Article III on the inferior federal courts. In fact, the constitutional scope of federal question jurisdiction has always been much broader than the jurisdiction conferred by the general federal question statute. This difference means, *inter alia*, that Congress has a significant repository of power to draw upon in expanding the statutory jurisdiction to meet future requirements in the administration of federal law.

The U.S. Supreme Court has interpreted the statutory grant of general federal question jurisdiction much more narrowly than the constitutional grant to prevent "a flood of litigation" based on some remote federal "ingredient" in the cases.[79] This restrictive interpretation of the general federal question statute has given rise to a set of complex rules for determining whether a case arises under federal law for purposes of jurisdiction in the federal district courts.[80] The following subsections explore (1) the analytical categories of cases in which federal question jurisdiction has been found to exist, (2) a frequently stated test for federal question jurisdiction called the *well-pleaded complaint rule*, and (3) special problems of determining whether federal question jurisdiction exists in actions seeking the remedy of declaratory judgment.

---

79. CHARLES A. WRIGHT, THE LAW OF FEDERAL COURTS § 17, at 102 (5th ed. 1994); *see also* ERWIN CHEMERINSKY, FEDERAL JURISDICTION § 5.2.2, at 269 (3d ed. 1999); 15 MARTIN H. REDISH, MOORE'S FEDERAL PRACTICE § 103.30 (3d ed. 1999). Professor Wright has explained the reason for the differing interpretation of the Constitution and the statute:

> What . . . had not always been kept in mind . . . is that there is a difference between construing the Constitution, as Marshall was obliged to do in *Osborn*, and construing a statute. The very expansive reading Marshall gave to the "cases arising under" language of the Constitution is appropriate in dealing with a constitution. It leaves room for Congress to grant such particular jurisdiction as may in the future be seen to be necessary. But to hold that [§ 1331] gives federal jurisdiction wherever some element of federal law is an "ingredient" of the cause of action would mean, for example, that virtually every case involving the title to land in the western states, where title descends from a grant from the United States, could be litigated in federal court. If Congress in fact meant to open the door of the federal courthouse to such a flood of litigation, the *Osborn* case shows that it had the power to do so. Actually both the language of [§ 1331], following so closely the constitutional language, and such skimpy legislative history as exists, do support the view that Congress meant to give all the jurisdiction it could constitutionally confer, but this is not an inevitable conclusion, and the courts acted understandably in giving a restrictive reading to the statute.

CHARLES A. WRIGHT, THE LAW OF FEDERAL COURTS § 17, at 102-03 (5th ed. 1994) (footnotes omitted). Although these conclusions about the western land title cases has been questioned in the preceding subsection, Professor Wright is nevertheless correct that interpreting 28 U.S.C. § 1331 to confer the full scope of the constitutionally permissible jurisdiction would undoubtedly open the doors of the federal courts to an excess of litigation only remotely related to substantial federal interests.

80. The classic works on federal question jurisdiction are James H. Chadbourn & A. Leo Levin, *Original Jurisdiction of Federal Questions*, 90 U. PA. L. REV. 639 (1942); William Cohen, *The Broken Compass: The Requirement That a Case Arise "Directly" Under Federal Law*, 115 U. PA. L. REV. 890 (1967); Paul J. Mishkin, *The Federal "Question" in the District Courts*, 53 COLUM. L. REV. 157 (1953).

(i) The Categories of Cases That Arise Under Federal Law Within the Meaning of 28 U.S.C. § 1331

Section 1331 has been read to grant jurisdiction in three general categories of cases. First, § 1331 grants jurisdiction when *federal law expressly creates a remedy*.[81]

Illustration 2-18. Civil rights actions under 42 U.S.C. § 1983 vindicate infringements of constitutional rights by persons acting under color of state law. Section 1983 expressly authorizes legal and equitable remedies when a person's federal constitutional rights have been deprived.[82]

* * * * *

Second, § 1331 grants jurisdiction when *federal law imposes a duty from which a remedy may be implied*.[83]

Illustration 2-19. Assume that a federal official violates the plaintiff's right not to be subjected to unreasonable searches and seizures under the Fourth Amendment to the U.S. Constitution. No federal law expressly creates a remedy for a Fourth Amendment violation. Rather, federal law in the form of the Fourth Amendment imposes a duty upon the federal official. The U.S. Supreme Court has implied the remedy of damages from that duty.[84]

* * * * *

These first two categories of federal question jurisdiction are sometimes subsumed under a single rule: A case "arises under" federal law for purposes of the general federal question statute "if the plaintiff asserts a federally created cause of action."[85] This statement is accurate and can be relied on without harm, provided it is recognized that not every federal "duty" is of the sort that is appropriate for the implication of a remedy that will produce a federal "cause of action."[86]

Third, § 1331 grants jurisdiction when *state law creates both the right and the remedy, but an important question of federal law is an essential element*

---

81. *See* 13B CHARLES A. WRIGHT ET AL., FEDERAL PRACTICE AND PROCEDURE: JURISDICTION § 3562, at 40 (2d ed. 1984).

82. *But see* International Science & Tech. Instit. Inc. v. Inacom Communication, Inc., 106 F.3d 1146 (4th Cir. 1997), in which Congress enacted a statute creating a private right of action for damages and injunctive relief for violation of the statute. However, Congress further provided that plaintiffs could file suit under the statute "if otherwise permitted by the laws or rules of court of a State . . . in an appropriate court of that State." The court held that no federal question jurisdiction existed under the statute. The court reasoned that a permissive authorization of jurisdiction extends only to a court of general jurisdiction; it is inadequate to confer jurisdiction on a court of limited jurisdiction, such as a federal court, because courts of limited jurisdiction "are competent to hear only those cases specifically authorized." *Id.* at 1151-52.

83. *See* 13B CHARLES A. WRIGHT ET AL., FEDERAL PRACTICE AND PROCEDURE: JURISDICTION § 3562, at 40 (2d ed. 1984).

84. *See* Bivens v. Six Unknown Named Agents of Fed. Bureau of Narcotics, 403 U.S. 388, 91 S. Ct. 1999, 29 L. Ed. 2d 619 (1971). *See generally* John E. Theuman, Annotation, *When Will Private Right of Action for Damages ("Bivens Action") Be Implied from Provision of Federal Constitution–Supreme Court Cases*, 127 L. Ed. 2d 715 (1998).

85. RICHARD H. FALLON ET AL., HART & WECHSLER'S THE FEDERAL COURTS AND THE FEDERAL SYSTEM 926 (4th ed. 1996); *see also* ERWIN CHEMERINSKY, FEDERAL JURISDICTION § 5.2.3 (3d ed. 1999).

86. *See generally* RICHARD H. FALLON ET AL., HART & WECHSLER'S THE FEDERAL COURTS AND THE FEDERAL SYSTEM 866-77 (4th ed. 1996).

in the plaintiff's case.[87] This category may seem quite broad. In fact, however, it is seldom the basis for federal question jurisdiction. The case authority supporting this basis for jurisdiction is narrow. Most likely, it may be used to establish jurisdiction only in cases in which (1) the federal interest in the action is sufficiently substantial to justify the exercise of federal jurisdiction and (2) when both state and federal law significantly contribute to the existence of the plaintiff's claim.

Illustration 2-20. In *Smith v. Kansas City Title & Trust Co.*,[88] state law prohibited the directors of a corporation from investing in illegally issued securities and provided shareholders a remedy against the directors for breach of this duty. The U.S. Supreme Court found that federal question jurisdiction existed because the directors wanted to invest in securities that had allegedly been issued in violation of federal law. In this case, state law created the plaintiff's basic right of action—the right to sue to prevent directors from investing in illegal securities. However, federal law was essential to the existence of this right because federal law made the issuance of the securities illegal. In addition, the question of federal law in the case was an important one: the constitutionality of a federal statute authorizing the issuance of the securities that the plaintiff alleged were illegally issued. In this situation, the impact of an erroneous state court decision on the question of federal law was potentially severe. If a state court incorrectly decided that the statute was unconstitutional, all the federal securities issued under the statute would, as a practical matter, become unmarketable until the state court decision was corrected on appeal. Thus, not only was federal law essential to the plaintiff's claim, the federal interest in a correct decision was great. As stated earlier, the justification for conferring federal question jurisdiction on the district courts is that those courts will provide a more expert, sympathetic, and uniform interpretation of federal law than the state courts. If so, the federal interest in such an interpretation in *Smith* clearly justified the exercise of jurisdiction.

Illustration 2-21. In *Merrell Dow Pharmaceuticals Inc. v. Thompson*,[89] the U.S. Supreme Court held federal jurisdiction improper when the federal interest in the case was not as strong as in the *Smith* case. In *Merrell Dow*, the plaintiffs sought damages for the birth of deformed children that resulted from the mothers' ingestion during pregnancy of a drug manufactured by the defendant. Five of six counts in each complaint were based entirely on state law. One count, however, alleged that the drug had been misbranded in violation of the Federal Food, Drug, and Cosmetic Act (FDCA).[90] If this allegation proved to be correct, a rebuttable presumption would arise under state law that the defendant had been negligent. Thus, a federal law would contribute to the plaintiffs' state claims for negligence. However, the Court held that the failure of Congress to create a federal right of action in damages for violation of the FDCA made the exercise of federal jurisdiction improper. In effect, the Court held that since Congress

---

87. *See* 13B CHARLES A. WRIGHT ET AL., FEDERAL PRACTICE AND PROCEDURE: JURISDICTION AND RELATED MATTERS § 3562, at 41-48 (2d ed. 1984 & 1999 Supp.).
88. 255 U.S. 180, 41 S. Ct. 243, 65 L. Ed. 577 (1921).
89. 478 U.S. 804, 106 S. Ct. 3229, 92 L. Ed. 2d 650 (1986).
90. 21 U.S.C. §§ 301-393.

failed to provide a remedy for the violation of the FDCA, the federal interest in the case was too weak to justify the exercise of federal question jurisdiction.[91]

* * * * *

Merrell Dow should not be read to mean that whenever Congress fails to provide a remedy, the strength of the federal interest is too weak to justify the exercise of federal jurisdiction. If so, *Smith*, which involved no congressionally created right of action, would no longer be good law. Yet, the Court cited and discussed *Smith* with approval in *Merrell Dow*.[92] Fortunately, the facts of *Merrell Dow* and *Smith*, when read in conjunction, suggest an alternative rationale. The Court could have reached the same result without placing such emphasis on the failure of Congress to provide a right of action in damages under the FDCA.

In *Merrell Dow*, the Court explicitly rejected the view that federal question jurisdiction was improper because the plaintiff could also recover on the exclusively state-law claims.[93] Thus, the fact that in *Smith* federal law was the only basis upon which the plaintiff could win will not be a viable distinction. Nevertheless, violation of federal law would have produced only a rebuttable presumption of negligence in *Merrell Dow*. In contrast, violation of federal law in *Smith* would have produced *automatic* victory. Therefore, the contribution of federal law in *Smith* was, in a sense, more important than in *Merrell Dow*. In addition, the court in *Merrell Dow* distinguished *Smith* by observing: "In *Smith* . . . the issue was the constitutionality of an important federal statute."[94] This observation suggests either that federal question jurisdiction will exist (1) when a federal constitutional question contributes to a state right of action, (2) when an "important" federal statute contributes to the state right of action, or (3) when the state claim involves the federal constitutionality of an important federal statute.

A more satisfactory distinction would focus on the degree of impact that an erroneous state-court decision might have on the enforcement of federal law. In *Merrell Dow*, the impact of an erroneous decision on the federal issue was not nearly as severe as in *Smith*. If a state court erroneously decided that the defendant's drug had been mislabeled in violation of the FDCA, the erroneous decision might result in the defendant and others similarly situated having to exercise more care than the FDCA really requires during the time necessary to overturn the state decision on appeal. However, a defendant who exercises more care than legally required does not really undermine the purpose of the FDCA, which requires care in labelling to protect consumers. On the other hand, if a state court erroneously determined that the defendant's drug was *not* misbranded in violation of federal law, the decision would not bind the Federal Food and Drug Administration. The law could still be enforced against the defendant independently of the state court decision. Thus, *Merrell Dow* was an easy case in which

---

91. *See Merrell Dow*, 478 U.S. at 814-17, 106 S. Ct. at 3235-36, 92 L. Ed. 2d at 662-64.

92. *See* 478 U.S. at 814 n.12, 106 S. Ct. at 3235 n.12, 92 L. Ed. 2d at 662 n.12.

93. *See id.* at 817 n.15, 106 S. Ct. at 3236 n.15, 92 L. Ed. 2d at 664 n.15.

94. *See id.* at 814 n.12, 106 S. Ct. at 3235 n.12, 92 L. Ed. 2d at 662 n.12.

the federal issue was neither an essential component of the state claim nor important enough to warrant the exercise of federal jurisdiction.[95]

To clarify the *Merrell Dow* test, the Court needs to establish what weight federal courts should give to (1) the importance of the contribution made by federal law to the state claim, (2) the significance of a federal constitutional contribution to the state claim (or of inclusion in the state claim of the federal constitutionality of an important federal statute), and (3) the danger to the administration of federal law of an erroneous state-court decision.[96] Because of the existing ambiguities of the test, the lower federal courts have applied it in divergent ways. Some illustrative cases follow.

Illustration 2-22. In *Guardian National Acceptance Corp. v. Swartzlander Motors, Inc.,*[97] an automobile finance company accepted an assignment from an automobile dealer of a contract with a car buyer. The car buyer sued the dealer and the finance company under the contract. The buyer claimed that the dealer violated the Truth in Lending Act, a federal statute. The finance company was dismissed from the action because it was not a "creditor" within the meaning of the Truth in Lending Act, and the Act was therefore not applicable to the company. The action against the dealer was settled without determining whether the dealer had violated the Act. The finance company then sued the dealer in federal court. The finance company claimed that the dealer breached its warranties in the assignment contract by violating the Act and sought indemnification for the costs of defending the suit by the buyer. Although the action was based on state contract law, the finance company would have to prove a violation of the Truth

---

95. For a complete discussion and criticism of *Merrell Dow*, see Note, *The Supreme Court, 1985 Term—Leading Cases,* 100 HARV. L. REV. 100, 230-40 (1986).

96. Future clarification of the *Smith-Merrell Dow* test will determine the continuing vitality of some arcane precedents involving mixed state-federal claims. For example, it has been held that federal question jurisdiction exists in an action to remove a cloud on the title to land, but not in a action to quiet title to land because allegations as to the (federal) nature of the cloud are proper in the first kind of action, but not in the second. *Compare* Hopkins v. Walker, 244 U.S. 486, 37 S. Ct. 711, 61 L. Ed. 1270 (1917) *with* Shulthis v. McDougal, 225 U.S. 561, 32 S. Ct. 704, 56 L. Ed. 1205 (1912). For a discussion of these and similar distinctions, see ALI STUDY OF THE DIVISION OF JURISDICTION BETWEEN STATE AND FEDERAL COURTS 169-70 (1969). In Christianson v. Colt Industries Operating Corp., 486 U.S. 800, 108 S. Ct. 2166, 100 L. Ed. 2d 811 (1998), plaintiffs sued Colt in U.S. District Court for violation of the antitrust laws, a federal claim, and for tortious interference with business relationships. Colt's defense to the latter claim produced a motion for summary judgment by plaintiffs. The plaintiffs contended that certain patents on which Colt's defense was based were invalid. The district court granted summary judgment for plaintiffs, invalidating a number of Colt's patents in the process. Colt appealed to Court of Appeals for the Federal Circuit, which had jurisdiction of the appeal only if the case was one "arising under any Act of Congress relating to patents" within the meaning of 28 U.S.C. § 1338. The "arising under" language in § 1338 is interpreted essentially the same as the identical language in § 1331. Thus, although federal question jurisdiction clearly existed at the district court level because of the federal antitrust claim, the question of appellate jurisdiction seemed to raise a *Merrell Dow* issue: Did the federal patent laws contribute to the plaintiff's claims in a way that would produce original federal question jurisdiction under § 1338? Curiously, the U.S. Supreme Court, in holding that there was no case arising under the patent laws, ignored *Merrell Dow*. Some commentators have suggested that *Christianson* might represent a retreat from the restrictive approach of *Merrell Dow*. *See* 15 MARTIN H. REDISH, MOORE'S FEDERAL PRACTICE § 103.31[5][b] (3d ed. 1999). However, such a retreat seems unlikely given the confused procedural posture of the case and the distinct probability that the patent laws in no way contributed to any of the plaintiff's *claims*, but instead were injected into the case as replies to defenses raised by Colt. *Cf. id.* (case appears not to have been construed as a retreat from *Merrell Dow*).

97. 962 F. Supp. 1137 (N.D. Ind. 1997).

in Lending Act to win. The district court sustained federal question jurisdiction. The court held that this federal contribution to the state claim was sufficient.[98]

Illustration 2-23. The Family and Medical Leave Act (FMLA)[99] applies only to employers who employ fifty or more people at one site. An employer who employed only twenty-nine people voluntarily adopted many of the policies of the FMLA in formulating its own family and medical leave policy. Subsequently, the employer violated the voluntarily adopted policies. An employee sued in state court for violation of the Act and the employer removed the action to federal court. In *Douglas v. E.G. Baldwin & Associates*,[100] the Sixth Circuit Court of Appeals held that violation of the policies did not produce a case arising under federal law for purposes of 28 U.S.C. § 1331.[101]

Illustration 2-24. In *Torres v. Southern Peru Copper Corp.*,[102] the plaintiffs, Peruvian citizens, sued the copper company, a mining corporation incorporated in Delaware with its principal place of business in Peru. The action was commenced in state court based on state law claims. The defendant removed the action to federal court. The Peruvian Government protested the lawsuit by filing a letter with the U.S. State Department and a friend-of-the-court brief in the litigation. The Peruvian Government maintained "that the litigation implicates some of its most vital interests and, hence, will affect relations with the United States."[103] The Fifth Circuit Court of Appeals found federal question jurisdiction appropriate on the ground that "the action . . . strikes not only at vital economic interests but also at Peru's sovereign interests by seeking damages for activities and policies in which the government actively has been engaged."[104] Thus, the court concluded that "plaintiff's complaint raises substantial questions of federal common law by implicating important foreign policy concerns."[105]

---

98. Note that the violation of the federal Truth in Lending Act was the only basis upon which the plaintiff could win on the state contract claim, and violation of the federal Act would produce automatic victory for the plaintiff.

99. 29 U.S.C. § 2601 *et seq.*

100. 150 F.3d 604 (6th Cir. 1998).

101. The court stated that "[t]he fact that the parties contracted to incorporate the terms and responsibilities of the FMLA into their employment relationship does not bring them within the Act itself. Parties cannot create subject[-]matter jurisdiction by contract where none exists . . . ." *Id.* at 608.

102. 113 F.3d 540 (5th Cir. 1997).

103. *Id.* at 542.

104. *Id.* at 543; *see also* Berg v. Leason, 32 F.3d 422 (9th Cir. 1994) (suit in federal court on a state claim for malicious civil prosecution, contending that a prior federal action based on federal law that was dismissed on summary judgment was brought without probable cause; thus, although the right of action was created by state law, the court would have to analyze federal law to determine whether probable cause existed; no federal question jurisdiction). In Pineville Real Estate Operation Corp. v. Michael, 32 F.3d 88 (4th Cir. 1994), *cert. denied*, 513 U.S. 1127, 115 S. Ct. 935, 130 L. Ed. 2d 880 (1995), *B* obtained a judgment against *C* in a U.S. District Court based on a claim under a federal statute; as permitted by the law of the state where the federal judgment was rendered, *B* recorded the judgment in the local land records as a lien on *C's* property; later, *C* sold the property to *A*, who brought an action in U.S. District Court to enjoin enforcement of the lien, claiming that the federal judgment in *B v. C* was not final under Federal Rule 54(b), which, if true, would render the lien ineffective under state law; the court held that federal question jurisdiction did not exist because (1) the Federal Rules of Civil Procedure are not "laws" within the meaning of § 1331 and (2) Federal Rules of Civil Procedure cannot be the basis of subject-matter jurisdiction because they are forbidden to expand jurisdiction.

105. 113 F.3d at 543. For a discussion of federal common law, see Chapter 5(I) *infra*.

The court, however, never identified the precise way in which federal law contributed to the plaintiff's claim.

(ii) The Well-Pleaded Complaint Rule

In each category of cases in which jurisdiction is appropriate under § 1331, the focus is on the plaintiff's claim for relief. This focus has resulted in a "well pleaded complaint" test for jurisdiction under the statute. This test is often stated separately from the tests described in the preceding subsection, but it is actually complementary to them: in all situations in which jurisdiction is based on § 1331, the federal question must appear on the face of the plaintiff's *well-pleaded complaint*.[106] In other words, federal law must contribute to the plaintiff's original claim. The basis of federal jurisdiction may not be federal defenses, even if the federal defenses are the only important issues in the case and the plaintiff correctly anticipates in the complaint that the defendant will raise them. Nor may federal question jurisdiction be based on federal laws that would negate a defense.

Illustration 2-25. In *Louisville & Nashville Railroad Co. v. Mottley*,[107] the Louisville & Nashville Railroad settled a personal injury claim by agreeing to issue passes for free transportation on the railroad as long as E.L. Mottley and his wife lived. In 1906, Congress passed a law prohibiting railroads from giving free transportation or passes.[108] The railroad issued the Mottleys their passes and renewed them annually from 1871 until 1907, but then refused to renew the passes. The Mottleys sued in federal court to compel the railroad's performance of its contract. They alleged that the railroad's refusal to renew the passes was based solely on the Act of Congress. They maintained that the Act did not prohibit the railroad from issuing passes under the circumstances of their case, but if it did, the Act deprived them of their property without due process of law in violation of the Fifth Amendment. The U.S. Supreme Court held that the Mottleys' action did not fit within the federal question jurisdiction. The Mottleys' claim was a state breach of contract claim. The Act of Congress was a defense that the railroad might be expected to raise to this state breach of contract claim. The question of the Act's constitutionality was a reply to this defense that the Mottleys might raise. It was not part of the Mottleys' original claim for relief. Thus, no federal issue contributed in any way to the Mottleys' original claim, and federal question jurisdiction was lacking.[109]

---

106. For a criticism of the "well-pleaded complaint rule," see Donald L. Doernberg, *There's No Reason For It; It's Just Our Policy: Why the Well-Pleaded Complaint Rule Sabotages the Purposes of Federal Question Jurisdiction*, 38 HASTINGS L.J. 597 (1987). For a summary of the criticisms and justifications for the well-pleaded complaint rule (which amount to criticisms and justifications for requiring the federal question to be a part of the plaintiff's claim), see ERWIN CHEMERINSKY, FEDERAL JURISDICTION § 5.2.3, at 274-75 (3d ed. 1999).

107. 211 U.S. 149, 29 S. Ct. 42, 53 L. Ed. 126 (1908).

108. *See* Act of June 29, 1906, ch. 3591, 34 Stat. 584.

109. *Mottley*, 211 U.S. at 152, 29 S. Ct. at 43, 53 L. Ed. at 127-28. In rejecting the Mottleys' action, the Court stated that:

> [i]t is the settled interpretation of these words, as used in this statute, conferring [general federal question] jurisdiction, that a suit arises under the Constitution and laws of the

Illustration 2-26. In *Federated Department Stores v. Moitie*,[110] the U.S. Supreme Court permitted federal question jurisdiction in a case in which the only apparent federal question was a defense based on a plea of res judicata under a prior federal judgment. This decision led many lower federal courts to sustain removal jurisdiction predicated on res judicata defenses based on prior federal judgments. However, in *Rivet v. Regions Bank*,[111] the Court has now directly held that a res judicata defense based on a prior federal judgment does not provide a proper basis for federal question jurisdiction under the *Mottley* principle.[112]

Illustration 2-27. To further illustrate how the well-pleaded complaint rule operates, consider the following pleadings:

(a) Form 16 in the Appendix of Forms to the Federal Rules of Civil Procedure illustrates a complaint for infringement of a patent. Paragraph 1 of the complaint (alleging subject-matter jurisdiction) would state that the action arises under 35 U.S.C. §§ 1-376 (the patent laws). This allegation, however, does not alone satisfy the well-pleaded complaint rule. It must appear from the body of the complaint that the plaintiff's right of action is the sort conferred by the federal patent laws. Paragraphs 2, 3, and 4 of the complaint reveal that this complaint, in fact, alleges a right of action authorized by the federal patent laws; however, it is possible to reach this conclusion only *if one possesses some knowledge of the patent laws and, therefore, of the kinds of actions that they authorize.*

(b) Form 3 in the Appendix of Forms to the Federal Rules of Civil Procedure illustrates a complaint on a promissory note. By reading Form 3 *and by possessing the knowledge that the laws generally governing promissory notes are state (not federal) laws*, one can see that the plaintiff's action arises under state law and does not come within federal court jurisdiction under 28 U.S.C. § 1331.

United States only when the plaintiff's statement of his own cause of action shows that it is based upon those laws or that Constitution. It is not enough that the plaintiff alleges some anticipated defense to his cause of action and asserts that the defense is invalidated by some provision of the Constitution of the United States. Although such allegations show that very likely, in the course of the litigation, a question under the Constitution would arise, they do not show that the suit, that is, the plaintiff's original cause of action, arises under the Constitution.

Id.

110. 452 U.S. 394, 397 n.2, 101 S. Ct. 2424, 2427 n.2, 69 L. Ed. 2d 103, 108 n.2 (1981).

111. 522 U.S. 470, 118 S. Ct. 921, 139 L. Ed. 2d 912 (1998); *see* Arthur R. Miller, *Artful Pleading: A Doctrine in Search of Definition*, 76 TEX. L. REV. 1781 (1998).

112. Subsequent to *Rivet*, the U.S. Court of Appeals for the Eighth Circuit considered a case removed from state to federal court by a defendant; after removal, the defendant moved to dismiss the action on the basis that it was precluded under a prior federal judgment, a consent decree. The court acknowledged that *Rivet* precluded removal based on the res judicata effect of the prior federal judgment. However, the court held that removal was proper under 28 U.S.C. § 1651(a), the "All Writs Act." This Act authorizes federal courts to "issue all writs necessary or appropriate in aid of their respective jurisdictions and agreeable to the usages and principles of law." The court reasoned that the All Writs Act authorized removal based on the district court's continuing supervisory power over the consent decree. However, other courts have held removal of similar cases improper under the All Writs Act. *See, e.g.,* Hillman v. Webley, 115 F.3d 1461 (10th Cir. 1997); *cf.* 28 U.S.C. § 2283 (precluding federal injunctions against state-court proceedings except, *inter alia*, "to protect or effectuate [their] judgments"). For further discussion of the circumstances under which federal injunctions are appropriate against state proceedings, see CHARLES A. WRIGHT, LAW OF FEDERAL COURTS § 46 (5th ed. 1994).

(c) Suppose, however, that a plaintiff filed the following complaint in a U.S. District Court:

1. The action arises under 51 U.S.C. § 1 [a hypothetical federal statute] and the Fifth Amendment to the U.S. Constitution, as hereinafter more fully appears.

2. Defendant on or about [date], executed and delivered to plaintiff a promissory note, a copy of which is hereto attached as Exhibit A, whereby defendant promised to pay to plaintiff or order on [date], the sum of $100,000 with interest thereon at the rate of eighteen percent per annum.

3. Defendant refused to pay the amount of said note or interest when due, asserting as an excuse for nonpayment that 51 U.S.C. § 1 nullified defendant's obligation to pay because the interest rate charged by the note exceeded the legally permitted maximum rate of twelve percent per annum.

4. Plaintiff alleges that the defendant's interpretation of 51 U.S.C. § 1 is erroneous in the following respects:

a. 51 U.S.C. § 1 is inapplicable to the note made by defendant because the statute applies only to notes given as part of a transaction in interstate commerce, and the note made by defendant was given in payment for a transaction wholly intrastate in nature.

b. Even if 51 U.S.C. § 1 is applicable to the note made by defendant, it does not wholly nullify the defendant's obligation to pay principal and interest. At most, it nullifies the defendant's obligation to pay amounts of interest in excess of twelve percent per annum.

5. Alternatively, plaintiff alleges that if 51 U.S.C. § 1 is applicable to the note made by defendant and if the statute wholly nullifies defendant's obligation to pay principal and interest, the statute violates the Fifth Amendment of the U.S. Constitution by depriving plaintiff of property without due process of law.

6. Therefore, defendant owes to plaintiff the principal amount of said note and interest.

Wherefore plaintiff demands judgment against defendant for the sum of $118,000.00, interest, and costs.

This complaint violates the well-pleaded complaint rule. To state a claim for relief, all the plaintiff had to allege was the facts in paragraph 2, paragraph 6, and the introductory clause of the sentence that makes up paragraph 3. The remainder of the complaint attempts to anticipate certain defenses under federal law that defendant will raise to plaintiff's action and to counter those defenses. Assuming, therefore, that the hypothetical federal statute (51 U.S.C. § 1) and the Fifth Amendment do not confer a right of action on plaintiff for the amount of the note—an eventuality unlikely in the extreme given the structure of the complaint—the only pertinent federal law in the case will come up by way of defenses or counters to defenses.

* * * * *

The well-pleaded complaint rule will be satisfied whenever the action fits within any of the categories of cases discussed in the preceding subsection that are appropriate for jurisdiction under § 1331. Analytically, if one determines that an action fits one of the categories, one need not separately consider whether the well-pleaded complaint rule is satisfied. In this sense, the rule is a superfluity.

Often, however, the courts apply the rule without specific analytical reference to any one of the situations in which § 1331 jurisdiction is proper. Sometimes, courts intertwine the rule with the analysis of the jurisdictional category in such a fashion as to be inseparable from it. Ordinarily, this approach will cause no harm. However, considering the well-pleaded complaint rule without specific reference to the analytical categories in which federal question jurisdiction is proper does pose some danger of confusion.

Illustration 2-28. The plaintiffs' statement of their claim in the *Merrell Dow* case, discussed in *Illustration 2-21*, above, seems to satisfy the well-pleaded complaint rule; the plaintiffs did allege a violation of federal law as an element contributing to their claim. Yet the Court held jurisdiction improper in *Merrell Dow* because the federal interest was not sufficiently substantial to justify exercising jurisdiction. Thus, the well-pleaded complaint rule cannot be safely applied to determine the propriety of jurisdiction without referring to the analytical categories of cases in which the Court has held jurisdiction to be proper under § 1331.[113]

(iii) Determining Federal Question Jurisdiction in Declaratory Judgment Actions

When the plaintiff seeks a declaratory judgment, special problems arise in determining federal question jurisdiction. A declaratory judgment action seeks a judicial declaration of the rights and liabilities of the parties to a dispute. Declaratory judgments cannot be executed against a party's person or property. They are useful when the parties to a transaction are involved in a dispute over their legal rights and need an authoritative statement from a court about the nature and extent of those rights. In declaratory judgment actions, parties will usually obey court decrees voluntarily, so no need exists for a decree that can be executed against the loser.[114] In federal courts, declaratory judgments are authorized by 28 U.S.C. §§ 2201-2202. A precondition of such an action is an actual controversy within the subject-matter jurisdiction of a federal court.[115] When enacting these provisions, however, Congress did not intend for them to have a "jurisdictional effect."[116]

A person who might have been a defendant in an action for some other kind of remedy may bring a declaratory judgment action as a plaintiff. In that situation, the declaratory plaintiff's complaint may state a dispute or controversy about a proposition of federal law. Such a statement would seem to satisfy the well-pleaded complaint rule; in order to state a claim for declaratory relief, a

---

113. For a useful examination of the bases of "arising under" jurisdiction discussed in this section, see John B. Oakley, *Federal Jurisdiction and the Problem of the Litigative Unit: When Does What "Arise Under" Federal Law*, 76 TEX. L. REV. 1829 (1998).

114. *See* EDWIN BORCHARD, DECLARATORY JUDGMENTS 4, 13, 25-28 (2d ed. 1941). Of course, if a declaratory judgment is not voluntarily obeyed, the party obtaining the judgment can seek other remedies based on the judgment. *See id.* at 13-14.

115. *See* 28 U.S.C. § 2201(a).

116. *See* Skelly Oil Co. v. Phillips Petroleum Co., 339 U.S. 667, 671, 70 S. Ct. 876, 879, 94 L. Ed. 1194, 1199 (1950).

plaintiff must describe some sort of dispute or controversy that a declaratory judgment will serve a useful purpose in resolving.[117] If the only dispute or controversy in the case is over a proposition of federal law, then the declaratory plaintiff's proper statement of the claim for declaratory relief will necessarily contain a federal question. The difficulty is, of course, that if an action had been brought for some other kind of relief, the defendant in the declaratory judgment action often would have brought it rather than the declaratory plaintiff, and the action would not have involved a claim based on federal law at all. Instead, the federal question would have been a matter of defense or, perhaps, a reply to a defense.

The U.S. Supreme Court has addressed the problem of federal question jurisdiction in the context of declaratory judgment actions several times. In determining how the well-pleaded complaint rule should be applied, the Court has focused on the relationship between the declaratory action and the action that would have been brought had the declaratory judgment action not been brought. In essence, the Court has held that an action for declaratory relief may not be brought within the federal question jurisdiction unless one of the parties to the action could have brought an action as a plaintiff for some other kind of relief in federal court.[118] However, the facts of the cases decided by the Court in this area may support a broader rule. Thus, the Court may some day reinterpret its decisions to allow more declaratory actions than have yet been permitted. The following illustrations examine the operation of the well-pleaded complaint rule in declaratory judgment actions and discuss the broader rule that may be derived from the Court's decisions.

Illustration 2-29. (a) Two individuals, *A* and *B*, enter into a contract that requires each individual to perform at different times. Before the time arrives for *B* to perform, *A* and *B* dispute the validity of the contract. *B* contends that the contract is void, and *A* contends that it is valid. *A* threatens to sue *B* for damages if, at the time performance is due, *B* refuses to perform. Obviously, if the threatened suit were actually brought, *A* would be the plaintiff and *B* would be the defendant. Assume that *B* relies on federal law to support *B's* view that the contract is void. *A* relies on state law to support *A's* claim. *A* also disputes *B's* view of federal law. *A's* threatened action would not be within the federal question jurisdiction of the federal district courts. The action is, in all respects, like *Louisville & Nashville Railroad v. Mottley*, discussed in *Illustration 2-25*. The well-pleaded complaint rule prevents *A*, who is suing on a state breach of contract

---

117. UNIF. DECLARATORY JUDGMENTS ACT § 6, 12A U.L.A. 302 (1996) provides as follows: "The court may refuse to render or enter a declaratory judgment or decree where such judgment or decree, if rendered or entered, would not terminate the uncertainty or controversy giving rise to the proceeding." In effect, this standard is often said to involve a determination whether a declaratory judgment will serve a "useful purpose" in resolving the controversy between the parties. *See* EDWIN BORCHARD, DECLARATORY JUDGMENTS 293 (2d ed. 1941); Edwin Borchard, *Discretion to Refuse Jurisdiction of Actions for Declaratory Judgments*, 26 MINN. L. REV. 677, 678 (1942).

118. The decisions discussed below have, in effect, adopted the rule advocated in *Developments in the Law: Declaratory Judgments—1941-1949*, 62 HARV. L. REV. 787, 802-03 (1949); *see also* Commercial Union Ins. Co. v. United States, 999 F.2d 581 (D.C. Cir. 1993) (federal question jurisdiction in declaratory judgment and interpleader actions determined in the same way).

claim, from anticipating the issue of federal law that is the basis of *B's* defense. Thus, no federal question jurisdiction exists because the federal question would not appear as part of the plaintiff's well-pleaded complaint.

(b) Assume that in the above situation, *A* sought a declaratory judgment to resolve the dispute instead of waiting to sue for breach of contract after *B* refused to perform. Such a judgment would seek to establish the validity of *A's* state claim and the invalidity of *B's* federal defense. In this situation, when the plaintiff in the declaratory judgment action also would have been the plaintiff in the action for a nondeclaratory remedy, the Supreme Court has clearly indicated that no jurisdiction exists under § 2201 because no jurisdiction would have existed in the action for the nondeclaratory remedy (see (a) above).[119]

Illustration 2-30. (a) Assume that *A* is threatening to sue *B* for patent infringement, an action over which the federal courts would have exclusive jurisdiction.[120] Assume that instead of waiting for *A* to sue, *B* sues in federal court for a declaratory judgment that *A's* patent is invalid—an issue that would have been raised as a defense in *A's* infringement suit. In this situation, federal question jurisdiction under § 2201 *exists* because the *declaratory defendant*, *A*, could have sued as a plaintiff in federal court within the federal question jurisdiction to obtain nondeclaratory relief.[121] The difference between this situation and that in *Illustration 2-29* is that here one of the parties—*A*, the declaratory judgment defendant—could have litigated the action in a federal court action for a nondeclaratory remedy. In the example in *Illustration 2-29, neither* party could have sued within the federal question jurisdiction for a nondeclaratory remedy.

(b) A qualification must be added. Not all suits in which the declaratory judgment defendant could have sued in federal court for a nondeclaratory remedy will fit within the federal question jurisdiction. In *Franchise Tax Board v. Construction Laborers Vacation Trust,*[122] the Supreme Court held that the declaratory judgment plaintiff also must have "a clear interest" in a swift *federal* resolution of the issue of federal law upon which the parties disagree.[123] A clear interest exists in the patent case discussed in (a), above, because the alleged patent infringer, who is suing for federal declaratory relief, will be liable for damages if it turns out the patent is being infringed, and also because the alleged infringer's contractual relations with other parties may be disrupted by the allega-

---

119. *See* Skelly Oil Co. v. Phillips Petroleum Co., 339 U.S. 667, 70 S. Ct. 876, 94 L. Ed. 1194 (1950). However, the well-pleaded complaint rule, applied in a straightforward manner to the plaintiff's complaint, would seem to be satisfied. To state a claim for declaratory relief, the plaintiff must describe a live dispute or controversy with the defendant. When the plaintiff describes such a controversy here, the plaintiff describes a dispute or controversy over federal law.

120. *See* 28 U.S.C. § 1338.

121. 13B CHARLES A. WRIGHT ET AL., FEDERAL PRACTICE AND PROCEDURE: JURISDICTION AND RELATED MATTERS § 3566, at 93-94 (2d ed. 1984).

122. 463 U.S. 1, 103 S. Ct. 2841, 77 L. Ed. 2d 420 (1983). *See generally* Kevin W. Brown, Annotation, *Federal Question Jurisdiction in Declaratory Judgment Suit Challenging State Statute or Regulation on Grounds of Federal Pre-Emption,* 69 A.L.R. FED. 753 (1984).

123. *See Franchise Tax Bd.*, 463 U.S. at 20, 21 n.23, 103 S. Ct. at 2851-52 n.23, 77 L. Ed. 2d at 437-38 n.23.

tions of infringement.[124] However, in *Franchise Tax Board*, the Court held that a suit by a state to declare that the defendant has no valid federal claim against the enforcement of the state's tax laws is not within the federal question jurisdiction—even though the declaratory judgment defendant could have sued for an injunction against enforcement of the tax laws in federal court within the federal question jurisdiction. The Court reasoned that the interests of the state in a swift resolution of the question of federal law were not sufficient to support federal question jurisdiction.[125]

Illustration 2-31. (a) Assume again the basic facts of *Illustration 2-29*, in which *A* and *B* entered into a contract that required future performance. Recall that before the time for performance arrived, *B* claimed that the contract was void under federal law. If *B* refused to perform at the appointed time, *A* could attempt to sue for breach of contract under state law. However, *A* could not sue for breach of contract or for a declaratory judgment in federal court because *A*'s claim was based on state law. The only federal issue in the case would be *B*'s federal defense, and the well-pleaded complaint rule would preclude jurisdiction based on a federal defense. What would happen if *B*, instead of *A*, brought an action for a declaratory judgment on the ground that federal law rendered the contract void? If *B* is the plaintiff, the entire basis of *B*'s claim for the declaratory judgment is based upon federal law. Should the court apply the well-pleaded complaint rule in a straightforward fashion and conclude that federal jurisdiction exists on the theory that *B* only has to plead the dispute over federal law to state a claim for declaratory relief? Or should the court instead conclude that to allow the action to be brought in federal court would result in an *expansion* of the federal question jurisdiction, something that is not supposed to result from the enactment of the declaratory judgment statute? Extensive dicta in U.S. Supreme Court cases indicate that no federal question jurisdiction would exist over *B*'s declaratory judgment action against *A*.[126]

(b) However, the Court has never directly held that *B*'s suit is not a proper case for federal question jurisdiction. The Court indicated in the *Franchise Tax Board* case that "[p]arties subject to conflicting state and federal regulatory

---

124. *See id.* at 21 n.23, 103 S. Ct. at 2852 n.23, 77 L. Ed. 2d at 438 n.23.

125. *Id.* at 21, 103 S. Ct. at 2852, 77 L. Ed. 2d at 438. The Supreme Court explained that
> [s]tates are not significantly prejudiced by an inability to come to federal court for a declaratory judgment in advance of a possible injunctive suit by a person subject to federal regulation. They have a variety of means by which they can enforce their own laws in their own courts, and they do not suffer if the [preemption] questions such enforcement may raise are tested there.

Id.

126. For example, the Court has stated that
> [i]f the cause of action, which the declaratory defendant threatens to assert, does not itself involve a claim under federal law, it is doubtful if a federal court may entertain an action for a declaratory judgment establishing a defense to that claim. This is dubious even though the declaratory complaint sets forth a claim of federal right, if that right is in reality in the nature of a defense to a threatened cause of action.

Public Serv. Comm'n v. Wycoff Co., 344 U.S. 237, 248, 73 S. Ct. 236, 242-43, 97 L. Ed. 291, 298 (1952); *see also* Skelly Oil Co. v. Phillips Petroleum Co., 339 U.S. 667, 673-74, 70 S. Ct. 876, 880, 94 L. Ed. 1194, 1199-1200 (1950); *cf.* Franchise Tax Bd. v. Construction Laborers Vacation Trust, 463 U.S. 1, 19, 103 S. Ct. 2841, 2851, 77 L. Ed. 2d 420, 437 (1983).

schemes . . . have a clear interest in sorting out the scope of each government's authority, especially [when] they face a threat of liability if the application of federal law is not quickly made clear."[127] *B* is precisely in this situation. Therefore, although the *Franchise Tax Board* decision applied the "clear interest" test to *exclude* from federal court a case that would have fallen within the federal question jurisdiction under the test described in *Illustration 2-30(a)*, the "clear interest" test could conceivably be applied affirmatively in the future to *allow* a case such as *B's* to be brought in federal court. If the Court adopts this approach, the "clear interest" test of *Franchise Tax Board* would become the exclusive test for federal questions in declaratory judgment actions.[128]

* * * * *

One question about the *Franchise Tax Board* "clear interest" test is whether it is the same as the test used in *Merrell Dow*[129] to determine the substantiality of the federal interest necessary to confer federal question jurisdiction in cases in which federal law contributes to a state claim for relief. *Merrell Dow* was decided after *Franchise Tax Board*, and the Court in the former case cited and discussed the latter one with approval.[130] However, the Court did not state in *Merrell Dow* that the "federal interest" tests were identical. Rather, it cited *Franchise Tax Board* for the more general proposition that, in areas of "uncertain jurisdiction," there was a "need for careful judgments about the exercise of federal judicial power."[131] Furthermore, while the "federal interest" test of each case has been used to *exclude* actions from federal court that involve contributions of federal law that would otherwise make federal question jurisdiction appropriate, the focus of the two tests is very different. The *Merrell Dow* test seems designed to vindicate the general policies of § 1331, which are aimed not merely at party protection, but also at the proper administration of federal law in the national interest. In contrast, the *Franchise Tax Board* test seems to focus on the need of the party seeking declaratory relief for a swift federal adjudication of the issue of federal law upon which the controversy depends. So focused, the test appears to focus primarily, if not exclusively, upon party protection.[132]

If, indeed, the *Franchise Tax Board* and *Merrell Dow* cases are different, there may be cases in which each test must be applied separately to determine whether a case is appropriate for federal question jurisdiction.

Illustration 2-32. Reconsider *Illustration 2-20*, above, which examined the exercise of federal question jurisdiction in the case of *Smith v. Kansas City Title & Trust Co.* Assume that instead of suing the bank and its directors for an injunction to prevent them from investing in the (allegedly) unconstitutionally

---

127. 463 U.S. at 21 n.21, 103 S. Ct. at 2852 n.21, 77 L. Ed. 2d at 438 n.21.

128. Concededly, however, the test has been used thus far only to exclude cases from federal jurisdiction that would otherwise be appropriate. *See* the discussion below.

129. The *Merrell Dow* test is discussed in subsection *(b)(i), supra.*

130. *See* 478 U.S. at 813-14, 106 S. Ct. at 3234-35, 92 L. Ed. 2d at 661-62.

131. *Id.* at 814, 106 S. Ct. at 3235, 92 L. Ed. 2d at 662.

132. As noted below, the *Franchise Tax Board* test seems to be no more than a recasting into a jurisdictional rule of the usual standard for whether declaratory judgment complaint states a claim upon which relief can be granted.

issued federal securities, the shareholders simply threaten to sue. The directors then sue the shareholders for a declaratory judgment that the federal securities are valid. Assuming, as discussed above, that *Smith* is still good law after *Merrell Dow*, the first step in determining the existence of federal question jurisdiction in declaratory judgment cases is satisfied. The shareholders could sue for nondeclaratory relief (an injunction) within the federal question jurisdiction because they would be asserting a state claim for relief to which federal law made an essential and important contribution. In such an action, the federal interest would be sufficiently substantial under the *Smith-Merrell Dow* cases to justify the exercise of federal question jurisdiction.

However, it is more problematic whether the "clear interest" test of *Franchise Tax Board* would be satisfied. The bank and its directors, who would be the defendants in an injunction suit, are not precisely in the same position as the alleged patent infringer, who could demonstrate the necessary interest to justify federal declaratory judgment jurisdiction. The alleged patent infringer is subject to conflicting state and federal regulatory schemes and may incur a damage judgment if it continues to manufacture the allegedly infringing product. The alleged infringer will also lose profits if it stops manufacturing the product in response to threats of an infringement action. It is far from clear that the bank or its directors are subject to the same peril. They face no threat of a damages judgment. There could, of course, be adverse consequences to the bank if it invested in securities that were later determined to be illegal. However, these consequences are produced by the constitutional doubt that exists about the validity of the securities issue. This doubt would exist even if there had been no threat of an injunction suit by the shareholder. The bank is not committed to a single course of investment and can, therefore, dispel the doubt by buying different securities. It is, therefore, unclear whether the bank can demonstrate a sufficient interest to justify the exercise of federal declaratory judgment jurisdiction under the *Franchise Tax Board* test.[133]

* * * * *

Apart from the problem of coordinating *Merrell Dow* and *Franchise Tax Board*, additional, unnecessary confusion exists in the Supreme Court's decisions on federal question jurisdiction in declaratory judgment actions. First, the Court

---

133. The bank's dilemma in this illustration should not be confused with the problem of whether the mere existence of a *penal* or *regulatory* statute should enable a party subject to the statute to obtain a declaratory judgment of its validity in a suit against the person charged with its administration in the absence of a threat of enforcement. *See* Edwin Borchard, *Challenging "Penal" Statutes by Declaratory Action*, 52 YALE L.J. 445, 459, 467-75 (1943); Note, *Developments in the Law-Declaratory Judgments* 1941-1949, 62 HARV. L. REV. 787, 870-71 (1949); Note, *Official Threat of Enforcement as a Requisite of Justiciability in Declaratory Judgment Actions*, 50 YALE L.J. 1278 (1941). In such cases, the peril and insecurity arising from the mere existence of a statute applicable to the declaratory judgment plaintiff's activities should be sufficient to justify the issuance of the remedy against the statute's administrator. *See* Ralph U. Whitten, *Federal Declaratory and Injunctive Interference with State Court Proceedings: The Supreme Court and the Limits of Judicial Discretion*, 53 N.C. L. REV. 591, 618-19 (1975) (and authorities there cited). The bank's situation is different in the above illustration. It is not compelled to invest in the questionable securities. To be entitled to a federal declaratory remedy, the *Franchise Tax Board* test would have to be extended to cases of lesser peril than that of the alleged patent infringer, which parallels that of the person whose ongoing activities are potentially subject to as yet unenforced the penal or regulatory statute.

may be correct that the Federal Declaratory Judgment Act was not designed to expand the jurisdiction of the federal courts.[134] However, allowing a declaratory judgment action in federal court that could not be brought there by one of the parties for nondeclaratory relief should not be considered a ''jurisdictional'' expansion. For example, the Federal Rules of Civil Procedure are also not supposed to have a jurisdictional effect.[135] Yet, no one supposes that federal jurisdiction has been expanded by those rules because it is possible under the liberalized pleading standards of Rule 8 to bring an action in federal court that could not have been brought there under the more restrictive pleading standards that existed prior to the advent of the Rules. The Court has never adequately explained why a simple increase in the number of cases that can be brought within the federal question jurisdiction should be considered an expansion of federal jurisdiction when the standards for determining jurisdiction have remained constant. Indeed, the better argument would be that there is no jurisdictional effect as long as the rules of jurisdiction, applied to declaratory judgment actions straightforwardly, have not changed. Instead, all that has happened is that the old jurisdictional rules are operating within a new procedural context.[136]

Second, even accepting the premise that allowing additional cases into federal court constitutes an expansion of the federal question jurisdiction, the Court's approach is internally inconsistent. *Illustration 2-30(a)* demonstrates that when a person is threatened with a nondeclaratory action in federal court, the Court allows that person to sue for a declaratory judgment that the threatened claim in the federal action is invalid under federal law. In the Court's view, such an action does not constitute an expansion of jurisdiction because the declaratory judgment defendant could bring an action for nondeclaratory relief in federal court. Thus, no additional case is being allowed within federal jurisdiction because the declaratory judgment defendant could have sued within the federal question jurisdiction.

This position, however, is flawed. Absent the declaratory judgment remedy, the declaratory judgment plaintiff would have had no access to federal court at all. Indeed, the declaratory judgment plaintiff would not have a remedy in any court, unless a state-created right of action happened to exist for the threats to sue being made by the opposing party in the case.[137] Furthermore, no guarantee exists that the declaratory judgment defendant would ever have brought the threatened federal action. A threat to sue is not, after all, a suit. By analyzing the jurisdictional question hypothetically, the Court is allowing the declaratory judgment statute to have a jurisdictional impact under the very test it has embraced.[138]

---

134. *But see* Paul J. Mishkin, *The Federal ''Question'' in the District Courts*, 53 COLUM. L. REV. 157, 178 n.99 (1953).

135. *See* FED. R. CIV. P. 82.

136. *See* Paul J. Mishkin, *The Federal ''Question'' in the District Courts*, 53 COLUM. L. REV. 157, 178 (1953).

137. *See* American Well Works Co. v. Layne & Bowler Co., 241 U.S. 257, 36 S. Ct. 585, 60 L. Ed. 987 (1916).

138. *Cf.* Paul J. Mishkin, *The Federal ''Question'' in the District Courts*, 53 COLUM. L. REV. 157, 181 (1953).

Illustration 2-33. *A* believes that *B* is infringing *A's* patent by manufacturing and selling an item covered by the patent without permission. *B* believes that *A's* patent is invalid. *A* threatens to sue *B* and all persons purchasing the item from *B* for patent infringement in federal court. Without waiting for *A* to sue, *B* commences an action in federal court for slander of title to the item in question. *B's* action seeks an injunction to prevent *A* from threatening *B* and *B's* customers with suit and damages for the past injuries caused by the threats. Prior to the enactment of the Federal Declaratory Judgment Act, the Supreme Court held that *B's* action could not be brought in federal court because slander of title is a claim arising wholly under state law, even though the only significant issue in the action is the validity of *A's* patent.[139] This situation is very similar to that in *Illustration 2-30.* That illustration demonstrated that today, after the enactment of the Federal Declaratory Judgment Act, *B* could bring an action for a declaratory judgment against *A* in federal court to determine the issue of patent validity. Under the modern doctrine of supplemental jurisdiction, discussed in subsection 4, below, *B* could join the state slander of title claim with the federal declaratory judgment claim and have both claims decided by the federal court. Thus, the Supreme Court precedents that allowed *B* to sue *A* for a federal declaratory judgment can result in a claim being brought in federal court (the state slander of title claim) that could not be brought there in the absence of the declaratory judgment remedy.

* * * * *

Finally, the Court's latest attempt to restrict federal question jurisdiction in declaratory judgment actions is unnecessarily vague. In *Franchise Tax Board*, the Court held that even if an action for declaratory judgment was otherwise appropriate for federal question jurisdiction, if the declaratory plaintiff could not demonstrate a clear interest in a swift federal resolution of the issue of federal law, the declaratory judgment action may be disqualified from federal jurisdiction. Although delineating the categories of cases in which the federal courts will exercise discretion to decline jurisdiction is arguably both desirable and inevitable,[140] the way in which the Court delineates those discretionary categories is important. In *Franchise Tax Board*, the Court seemingly did no more than adopt as a jurisdictional rule the usual standard for determining whether the plaintiff's complaint for a declaratory judgment states a claim for relief, with the qualification that the demonstration must include a showing that relief is necessary from a *federal* court. This rule, however, gives no clear guidance to the district courts about how strong the plaintiff's interest in *federal* relief must be before federal jurisdiction is appropriate. It therefore violates one of the cardinal principles of procedure—that jurisdictional rules should be as clear as possible to avoid the

---

139. *See* American Well Works Co. v. Layne & Bowler Co., 241 U.S. 257, 36 S. Ct. 585, 60 L. Ed. 987 (1916).

140. *See* David L. Shapiro, *Jurisdiction and Discretion*, 60 N.Y.U. L. Rev. 543 (1985).

waste of time and energy that results when they are not.[141] Furthermore, as noted in *Illustration 2-31(b)*, the *Franchise Tax Board* standard could logically produce an expansion of federal question jurisdiction in situations that the Court has indicated in dictum to be inappropriate for jurisdiction. The overall picture is, therefore, one of unfortunate and unnecessary confusion that a clearer standard would avoid.[142]

2. Civil Actions to Which the United States is a Party

Federal courts have subject-matter jurisdiction over civil actions in which the United States Government is a party.[143] Section 1345 of Title 28 grants the district courts original jurisdiction, except as otherwise provided, over all civil actions commenced by the United States, its agencies, and officers expressly authorized by Congress to sue.[144] In such cases, the district courts usually have concurrent jurisdiction with the state courts. The federal courts, however, have exclusive jurisdiction over suits involving seizures, recovery of fines, penalties, and forfeitures incurred under acts of Congress.[145] The federal district courts also have jurisdiction when the United States is named as a party defendant.[146] The most notable precondition to such actions is that the federal government must have waived its sovereign immunity to suit.[147]

3. Diversity and Alienage Jurisdiction

Article III of the U.S. Constitution authorizes jurisdiction in "Controversies . . . between citizens of different States" and "between a State, or the

---

141. *See* ZECHARIAH CHAFEE, JR., SOME PROBLEMS OF EQUITY 311-12 (1950). When jurisdictional rules are not clear, some cases in which the trial courts have subject-matter jurisdiction will be erroneously dismissed, and the dismissal will be reversed on appeal after much expense and waste of time. Other cases in which the trial courts do not have subject-matter jurisdiction will be erroneously retained, with the result that a dismissal on appeal will produce even more waste. In the latter situation, the action will have to be tried over again in a proceeding commenced in a court that possesses subject-matter jurisdiction.

142. Another difficult problem of determining the existence of federal question jurisdiction occurs in cases in which federal law has preempted the operation of state law. This problem is discussed in subsection 5 on removal jurisdiction *infra*.

143. Article III of the Constitution extends the judicial power to "Controversies to which the United States shall be a party." U.S. CONST. art. III, § 2.

144. *See* 28 U.S.C. § 1345.

145. *See* 28 U.S.C. §§ 1355, 1356.

146. Over one-third of the civil cases filed in the federal district courts involved the United States either as a party plaintiff or defendant, which makes the United States the most frequent litigant in those courts. For the year ending September 30, 1992, for example, out of 230,509 cases filed, 35,453 were commenced by the United States. The United States was named as a party defendant in 27,147 cases. CHARLES A. WRIGHT, THE LAW OF FEDERAL COURTS § 22, at 126 n.2 (5th ed. 1994).

147. *See* 28 U.S.C. § 1346. Section 1346(a)(1) permits suits to recover internal revenue taxes. Section 1346(a)(2) lists several situations in which the federal government has consented to suit (derived from the 1855 Act creating the Court of Claims and the 1887 Tucker Act). Section 1346(b) is the jurisdictional grant for the Federal Tort Claims Act, which was enacted in 1946.

Citizens thereof, and foreign States, Citizens, or Subjects.''[148] Congress gave the lower federal courts jurisdiction of actions between citizens of different states and between citizens of a state and citizens or subjects of a foreign state—so-called diversity jurisdiction and alienage jurisdiction—in the Judiciary Act of 1789.[149] Since then, diversity and alienage jurisdiction have continued in varying forms. The existing grant of diversity jurisdiction is found in § 1332 of Title 28 of the *United States Code*. Diversity jurisdiction is concurrent with the state courts.

The historical justification for conferring diversity jurisdiction on the federal district courts was the fear of prejudice in state courts against citizens of other states—prejudice which would manifest itself against out-of-staters in state court proceedings.[150] The continuing vitality of this justification has been questioned today.[151] Indeed, it has been questioned whether significant prejudice against out-of-state citizens in state courts ever really existed.[152] However, repeated attempts to abolish or significantly curtail diversity jurisdiction have failed.[153]

(a) Complete Diversity Requirement

Like the grant of general federal question jurisdiction, the general diversity statute does not confer the full scope of diversity jurisdiction permissible under the Constitution. For one thing, courts have always interpreted the general diversity statute to require complete diversity of citizenship between the adverse

---

148. U.S. CONST. art. III, § 2.

149. *See* Act of Sept. 24, 1789, § 11, 1 Stat. 73, 78-79.

150. *See* ALI STUDY OF THE DIVISION OF JURISDICTION BETWEEN STATE AND FEDERAL COURTS 101 (1969). The actual statement of the traditional justification is somewhat more complex than mere fear of prejudice against out-of-state citizens:

> On a broader theory, potential deterrence to free movement and business activity throughout the several states lay in the risk, or the fear of the risk, that the courts of the states other than one's own could not be relied upon to render adequate justice. On this view, the possible reasons for concern included protracted delay, inefficient or untrained personnel, and procedural complexities and restrictions, as well as prejudice against strangers. From either aspect, the availability of a federal forum away from home for litigation with strangers served to provide a guarantee of efficient, competent, and disinterested justice that, by its reassurance to one considering movement or business in another state, contributed to the expansion of trade and intercourse throughout the nation.

Id.

151. *See id.* at 106. *See generally* ERWIN CHEMERINSKY, FEDERAL JURISDICTION § 5.3.2 (3d ed. 1999).

152. *See* Henry J. Friendly, *The Historic Basis of Diversity Jurisdiction*, 41 HARV. L. REV. 483, 493 (1928). In addition, the diversity jurisdiction is configured more broadly than necessary to prevent bias or prejudice against out-of-state citizens. A plaintiff who is a citizen of the forum state may commence a diversity action in a federal court within the plaintiff's "home" state. The American Law Institute has recommended that this possibility be eliminated. *See* ALI STUDY OF THE DIVISION OF JURISDICTION BETWEEN STATE AND FEDERAL COURTS § 1302(a) (1969).

153. *See* 13B CHARLES A. WRIGHT ET AL., FEDERAL PRACTICE AND PROCEDURE: JURISDICTION AND RELATED MATTERS § 3601, at 346-63 (2d ed. 1984) and authorities there cited and discussed; 15 MARTIN H. REDISH, MOORE'S FEDERAL PRACTICE § 102App.03 (3d ed. 1999); *see also* Thomas D. Rowe, Jr., *Abolishing Diversity Jurisdiction: Positive Side Effects and Potential for Further Reforms*, 92 HARV. L. REV. 963 (1979). The latest recommendation to limit the diversity jurisdiction has not been implemented by Congress. *See* REPORT OF THE FEDERAL COURTS STUDY COMMITTEE 38-43 (1990); 1 FEDERAL COURTS STUDY COMMITTEE WORKING PAPERS AND SUBCOMMITTEE REPORTS 418-67 (1990).

parties to the suit. This "complete diversity" requirement means that all the persons who join as plaintiffs must not have any overlapping citizenship with the persons joined as defendants.[154] This restriction on the exercise of diversity jurisdiction may result in the very kind of bias or prejudice in state court that the jurisdiction was designed to guard against.

Illustration 2-34. A (a citizen of Vermont), *B* (a citizen of Kentucky), and *C* (a citizen of Alabama) sue *D* (a citizen of California), *E* (a citizen of Florida), and *F* (a citizen of Kentucky) in a U.S. District Court for $500,000. Complete diversity does not exist because a citizen of Kentucky is present on both sides of the lawsuit. Thus, if all of the plaintiffs are going to bring the action against all of the defendants, the plaintiffs will have bring the action in a state court. However, if the plaintiffs bring the action in a state court, bias and prejudice against out-of-state citizens might operate in a variety of ways. Assume that *A*, *B*, and *C* are suing *D*, *E*, and *F* on claims in the alternative for personal injuries arising from an automobile accident. A trier of fact could find any combination of *D*, *E*, and *F*, or only one of them, liable to *A*, *B*, and *C* for their injuries. If the plaintiffs bring the action in a Kentucky state court, a Kentucky trier of fact might find in favor of *A*, *B*, and *C* and against *D* or *E*, but exonerate *F* (the defendant from Kentucky) from liability. If the plaintiffs bring the action in a Vermont state court, a Vermont trier of fact could find in favor of *A*, the Vermont plaintiff, and against one or more of the out-of-state defendants, even if the defendants had strong, but not conclusive, factual defenses against *A*, such as contributory negligence. Thus, if bias or prejudice actually exists against out-of-staters, the complete diversity rule may allow that bias or prejudice to operate in many cases.[155]

(b) Determination of State Citizenship

Diversity of citizenship must exist at the time that the action is commenced.[156] Two general requirements must be met for a person to be a citizen of a state within the meaning of 28 U.S.C. § 1332. First, a person must be a citizen of the United States. Second, the person must be "domiciled" within some state.[157] Domicile is a common-law concept drawn from the subject of conflict of laws. To acquire a domicile within a state, one must be physically present within the state. Simultaneous with this physical presence, one must

---

154. *Compare* Strawbridge v. Curtiss, 7 U.S. (3 Cranch) 267, 2 L. Ed. 435 (1806) ("complete diversity" required under statutory grant of jurisdiction) *with* State Farm Fire & Cas. Co. v. Tashire, 386 U.S. 523, 87 S. Ct. 1199, 18 L. Ed. 2d 270 (1967) ("incomplete diversity" permitted by the Constitution). *See generally* ERWIN CHEMERINSKY, FEDERAL JURISDICTION § 5.3.3, at 281 n.37 (3d ed. 1999).

155. *See* David P. Currie, *The Federal Courts and the American Law Institute* (pt. 1), 36 U. CHI. L. REV. 1, 18-19 (1968).

156. *See* ERWIN CHEMERINSKY, FEDERAL JURISDICTION § 5.3.3, at 298 (3d ed. 1999); 13B CHARLES A. WRIGHT ET AL., FEDERAL PRACTICE AND PROCEDURE: JURISDICTION AND RELATED MATTERS § 3608, at 448 (2d ed. 1984).

157. *See* RICHARD H. FALLON ET AL., HART & WECHSLER'S THE FEDERAL COURTS AND THE FEDERAL SYSTEM 1524 (4th ed. 1996).

intend to remain in the state indefinitely or permanently or to make the state one's home.[158] Everyone has a domicile, and no one has more than one.

Illustration 2-35. A person's "domicile of origin" is the domicile that the person has at birth.[159] The domicile of a child is that of the parent with whom the child lives. If the domicile of the parent changes, the domicile of the minor also changes.[160]

* * * * *

Once a person has acquired a domicile, that domicile continues until the person acquires a new one.

Illustration 2-36. If an adult's domicile is in Texas, that domicile continues in Texas until the adult acquires a new "domicile of choice" by being physically present within the borders of another state and possessing the intent to remain in the new state indefinitely or permanently.[161]

* * * * *

The domicile requirement produces several difficulties in determining state citizenship for purposes of the diversity statute. If a party's domicile is disputed, the main problem arises in determining whether that party really intends to make a particular state that party's home. Two common situations present this question. One situation exists when a party moves from one state to another, and the issue is whether the party really intends to make the new state home. The other situation exists when a party has substantial day-to-day relationships with more than one state, and a court must determine which state is the party's domicile. No mathematical formula exists to resolve the domicile issue. Courts consider a variety of factors in each situation that bear on the party's intent to make one or another state home. The totality of the facts must be taken into account.

Illustration 2-37. *A*'s domicile of origin is Massachusetts. *A* moved from Massachusetts to Nebraska to attend law school. *A* lived in Nebraska only during the school year. Each summer, *A* returned to Massachusetts. While in Massachusetts during the summer after *A*'s second year of law school, *B* allegedly assaulted *A*. *B* is a citizen of Massachusetts. *A* sued *B* in a U.S. District Court to recover damages for the assault. The jurisdictional statement in *A*'s complaint alleged that *A* was a citizen of Nebraska and that *B* was a citizen of Massachusetts. *B* moved to dismiss the action for lack of subject-matter jurisdiction on the ground that *A* was really a citizen of Massachusetts. On similar facts, a federal district court agreed with *B* and dismissed the action. In addition to returning to Massachusetts each summer to work, *A* had retained a Massachusetts driver's license, had never obtained a Nebraska automobile registration, and had never registered to vote in Nebraska. The totality of the circumstances indicated that *A*'s domicile had never

---

158. *See* RESTATEMENT (SECOND) OF CONFLICT OF LAWS §§ 15-18 (1971).

159. *See id.* § 14.

160. *See id.* § 22.

161. *See id.* §§ 11-23; *cf.* Annotation, *Domicil of Prisoner for Purposes of Federal Diversity Jurisdiction (28 USCS Sec. 1332)*, 23 A.L.R. FED. 611 (1975); G.B. Cook, Annotation, *Change of Domicil of Mental Incompetent*, 96 A.L.R.2D 1236 (1964).

shifted from Massachusetts to Nebraska. Therefore, no diversity of citizenship was present between the parties.[162]

Illustration 2-38. *A* sued *B* for libel in a U.S. District Court in Nevada. The jurisdictional statement in *A's* complaint alleged that *A* was a citizen of California and that *B* was a citizen of Nevada. *B* moved to dismiss the action on the ground that *A* was really a citizen of Nevada and, therefore, diversity of citizenship was lacking. The facts developed at an evidentiary hearing on the jurisdictional issue indicated that *A* had maintained a residence in California about fifteen miles from the Nevada border. *A* lived in this residence with *A's* spouse and children for eight years before commencement of the lawsuit. After commencement of the action, the IRS seized the residence, and it later burned. However, *A* was licensed to practice law in Nevada, and *A's* law practice had always been based there. *A* also maintained an apartment in the same building in Nevada where *A* practiced law. *A's* automobiles had Nevada registrations. *A* possessed a Nevada driver's license, banked exclusively in Nevada, and listed a Nevada mailing address on federal income tax returns. *A* never filed a California income tax return. Although *A* registered to vote in California, *A* never actually voted there. *A* had voted in at least one presidential election in Nevada. On these facts, a federal district court held that *A* was domiciled in California and that diversity of citizenship existed. The court emphasized that *A* and *A's* family had lived at the California address for eight years before the action was commenced and had considered the residence to be their home.[163]

* * * * *

A United States citizen can be domiciled abroad. As a result, it is possible for a United States citizen to have no state citizenship for diversity purposes.[164]

Illustration 2-39. *A* was born in Virginia. *A* abandons *A's* home in Virginia and travels to Paris, France. *A* intends to remain there permanently. However, *A* does not become a naturalized citizen of France, but retains U.S. citizenship. *A* cannot sue or be sued in federal court based upon diversity jurisdiction. *A* is a citizen of the United States. However, because *A* is not domiciled within any *state*, *A* cannot be a citizen of a state. In any suit *A* brings against a citizen of a state as well as in any suit brought against *A* by a citizen of a state, the action would not be "between citizens of different states."[165]

* * * * *

Few problems exist with determining whether a party is physically present in a state. However, in rare circumstances, the physical presence requirement and

---

162. *See* Murphy v. Newport Waterfront Landing, Inc., 806 F. Supp. 322 (D.R.I. 1992); *see also* Las Vistas Villas, S.A. v. Petersen, 778 F. Supp. 1202 (M.D. Fla. 1991); Bevilaqua v. Bernstein, 642 F. Supp. 1072 (S.D.N.Y. 1986).

163. *See* Abbott v. United Venture Capital, Inc., 718 F. Supp. 823 (D. Nev. 1988).

164. *See, e.g.,* Newman-Green, Inc. v. Alfonzo-Larrain, 490 U.S. 826, 828, 109 S. Ct. 2218, 2220-21, 104 L. Ed. 2d 893, 899 (1989); Sadat v. Mertes, 615 F.2d 1176 (7th Cir. 1980). *See generally* Martin M. Heit, Annotation, *When is a Citizen of United States Who Resides in Foreign Country a Citizen of a Particular State for Purposes of 28 USCS Sec. 1332(a)(1), Granting Federal District Courts Jurisdiction of Certain Actions Between Citizens of Different States*, 54 A.L.R. Fed. 422 (1981).

165. Nor, since *A* retained United States citizenship, could there be a suit between a citizen of a state and a citizen or subject of a foreign state. *See* 28 U.S.C. § 1332(a)(2); subsection (d) *infra*.

the rule that diversity is determined at the commencement of the action can combine to create or defeat diversity.

     Illustration 2-40. *B's* domicile is Michigan. *B* abandons that domicile, moves to Pennsylvania, and intends to make Pennsylvania *B's* permanent home. However, after *B* left Michigan but before *B* arrived in Pennsylvania, *A* sued *B* in a U.S. District Court for breach of contract. *A* is a citizen of Michigan. *B* moved to dismiss on the ground that no diversity of citizenship existed. On the facts, a federal district court agreed and dismissed the action. *B* had not arrived in Pennsylvania on the date the action was commenced. Thus, *B* still retained *B's* Michigan domicile. Diversity of citizenship did not exist even though *B* intended to make Pennsylvania home.[166] If a citizen of any state other than Michigan, including Pennsylvania, had sued *B*, diversity would have existed. After *A's* action is dismissed, *A* may commence a new action in federal court based on diversity of citizenship. Assuming that *B* has reached Pennsylvania in the interim and thus established a new domicile, diversity of citizenship would exist in the new action.[167] If a citizen of Pennsylvania had sued *B* before *B* reached Pennsylvania, *B's* arrival in Pennsylvania and shift of domicile to that state would not destroy jurisdiction. This result is attributable to the rule that federal jurisdiction, once it has attached, will not be ousted by subsequent events.[168]

(c) Citizenship of Corporations and Associations

     The general diversity statute confers multiple citizenship upon corporations.[169] Except in direct actions against liability insurers,[170] a corporation is a citizen of any state where it is incorporated *and* the state where it has its principal place of business.[171] Corporations are sometimes incorporated in more

---

    166. *See* Albert Trostel & Sons v. Valentine, No. 1:93:CV:108, 1993 U.S. Dist. LEXIS 6863 (W.D. Mich. Mar. 24, 1993); Linardos v. Fortuna, 157 F.3d 945 (2d Cir. 1998) (district court erred in concluding that the plaintiff's domicile changed as soon as the plaintiff formed the intent to move from one state to the other, but before the plaintiff actually moved and was physically present in the new state).

    167. Of course, other obstacles may arise to prevent *A* from successfully maintaining the action, such as the running of the relevant statute of limitations before the second action is commenced.

    168. *See* RICHARD H. FALLON ET AL., HART & WECHSLER'S THE FEDERAL COURTS AND THE FEDERAL SYSTEM 1527 (4th ed. 1996).

    169. *See* 28 U.S.C. § 1332(c)(1). The diversity statute has not always explicitly conferred citizenship on corporations. For the history of the development of corporate citizenship under earlier statutes, see 13B CHARLES A. WRIGHT ET AL., FEDERAL PRACTICE AND PROCEDURE: JURISDICTION AND RELATED MATTERS § 3623 (2d ed. 1984).

    170. As amended in 1964, § 1332(c)(1) provides a special rule for a direct action against an insurer when the insured has not been joined as a party defendant. Besides being deemed a citizen of any state where the insurer is incorporated as well as the state where it has its principal place of business, a liability insurer is also deemed to be a citizen of the state where the insured is a citizen. *See* 28 U.S.C. § 1332(c)(1). *See generally* Russel J. Davis, Annotation, *Applicability of Proviso in 28 USCS § 1332(c), Pertaining to Citizenship of Insurer for Diversity Jurisdiction Purposes, to Direct Action Brought by Liability Insurer*, 56 A.L.R. FED. 613 (1982); Walter W. Jones, Jr., Annotation, *What Constitutes "Direct Action" Within Proviso to 28 USCS § 1332(c) that for Purposes of Diversity Jurisdiction in Direct Action Against Liability Insurer in Which Insured Is Not Joined as a Party Defendant, Insurer Shall Be Deemed Citizen of State of Which Insured Is a Citizen*, 13 A.L.R. FED. 398 (1972).

    171. *See generally* ERWIN CHEMERINSKY, FEDERAL JURISDICTION § 5.3.3, at 295 (3d ed. 1999).

than one state,[172] but a corporation can have only one principal place of business. This multiple citizenship limits diversity jurisdiction to cases in which no party opposing a corporation is a citizen of any state in which the corporation is incorporated or has its principal place of business.

Illustration 2-41. A, a citizen of Utah, sues *B Corporation. B* is incorporated in Delaware and has its principal place of business in Utah. Under the prevailing view of § 1332(c)(1), complete diversity is not present. *A* cannot allege only *B's* state of incorporation to establish diversity. *B* is a citizen of Delaware *and* Utah. Thus, the overlap with *A's* Utah citizenship is fatal to diversity jurisdiction.[173]

*   *   *   *   *

The location of the principal place of business of a corporation is a question of fact determined by the "total activities" of the corporation.[174] Under this test, a corporation's principal place of business is the state where the "bulk of the corporate activity" occurs.[175] If the activities are "dispersed among several states and no one state clearly predominates," the location of the corporation's home office, or "nerve center," is considered to be its principal place of business.[176] The "total activities" test is consistent with the purposes of the diversity jurisdiction. A corporation with substantial operations in a state is not likely to encounter the kind of bias or prejudice against out-of-state citizens that the diversity jurisdiction was designed to eliminate.[177]

Illustration 2-42. A Corporation is incorporated in Illinois. Its sole manufacturing plant is in Mississippi. *A* sued *B*, a citizen of Mississippi, in a U.S. District Court in Mississippi. *B* moved to dismiss the action on the ground that diversity of citizenship was lacking. *B* contended that *A's* principal place of

---

172. *See, e.g.*, Bell v. United Cities Gas Co., No. 90-0479-R, 1991 U.S. Dist. LEXIS 15811 (W.D. Va. Apr. 26, 1991).

173. *See* 13B CHARLES A. WRIGHT ET AL., FEDERAL PRACTICE AND PROCEDURE: JURISDICTION § 3624, at 609-10 (2d ed. 1984). For a discussion of how to determine whether diversity exists in cases in which a corporation is incorporated in more than one state, see ERWIN CHEMERINSKY, FEDERAL JURISDICTION § 5.3.3, at 295 (3d ed. 1999); T.W. Cousens, Annotation, *Federal Diversity of Citizenship Jurisdiction Where One of the States in Which Multistate Corporation Party Litigant Is Alleged to Be Incorporated Is Also State of Citizenship of Opponent*, 27 A.L.R.2D 745 (1953); *cf.* CHARLES A. WRIGHT, THE LAW OF FEDERAL COURTS § 27, at 167-68 (5th ed. 1994).

174. *See generally* 13B CHARLES A. WRIGHT ET AL., FEDERAL PRACTICE AND PROCEDURE: JURISDICTION AND RELATED MATTERS § 3625 (2d ed. 1984).

175. CHARLES A. WRIGHT, THE LAW OF FEDERAL COURTS § 27, at 168 (5th ed. 1994).

176. *Id.*; *see also* ERWIN CHEMERINSKY, FEDERAL JURISDICTION § 5.3.3, at 296 (3d ed. 1999); 15 MARTIN H. REDISH, MOORE'S FEDERAL PRACTICE § 102.54 (3d ed. 1999); 13B CHARLES A. WRIGHT ET AL., FEDERAL PRACTICE AND PROCEDURE: JURISDICTION § 3625, at 625-35 (2d ed. 1984); Jeffrey F. Ghent, Annotation, *Determination of Corporation's Principal Place of Business for Purposes of Diversity Jurisdiction Under 28 U.S.C. § 1332(c)*, 6 A.L.R. FED. 436 (1971).

177. *See* Note, *A Corporation's Principal Place of Business for Purposes of Diversity Jurisdiction*, 44 MINN. L. REV. 308, 321-14, 320 (1959); *see also* High Ridge Park Assocs. v. Nycom Info. Servs., Inc., 821 F. Supp. 835, 837 (D. Conn. 1993). The American Law Institute has recommended that businesses, including corporations, which have maintained a local establishment in a state for more than two years, should not be able to invoke the diversity jurisdiction originally or on removal in any action arising out of the activities of the business. This recommendation, which has much to commend it, is based on the theory that such business enterprises are not likely to be subjected to the kind of bias or prejudice that the diversity jurisdiction was designed to guard against. *See* ALI STUDY OF THE DIVISION OF JURISDICTION BETWEEN STATE AND FEDERAL COURTS § 1302(b), commentary at 126 (1969).

business was in Mississippi. *A* argued that its principal place of business should be considered to be Illinois because its executive offices were located in Illinois. On these facts, the federal district court agreed with *B* that under the "total activity" test, *A's* principal place of business was Mississippi. Therefore, diversity of citizenship was absent, and the court would have to dismiss the action.[178]

Illustration 2-43. *A*, a citizen of Kentucky, sued *B Corporation* in a state court in Kentucky. *B* is incorporated in New York. *B* removed the action to a U.S. District Court in Kentucky.[179] *A* moved to remand the action to the Kentucky state court on the ground that diversity jurisdiction was lacking. *A* contended that *B* was a citizen of Kentucky because its principal place of business was in Kentucky. *B's* plant in Kentucky employed over 9,000 employees. The federal district court, however, found that *B's* activities were spread over several states. Furthermore, some of *B's* operations in other states generated more income for *B* than its Kentucky operations. Thus, the court concluded that *B's* principal place of business was New York, the state in which basic corporate and personnel records were maintained (*i.e.*, home office or "nerve center" test).[180]

* * * * *

Unlike corporations, unincorporated associations do not have artificial citizenship under the general diversity statute. Thus, labor unions, partnerships, joint stock companies, trade groups, governing boards of institutions, societies, and other unincorporated associations are deemed, for diversity purposes, to be citizens of *each* state where one of their members is a citizen.[181]

Illustration 2-44. *F* fraternal society, an unincorporated association, has members in all fifty states. Thus, *F* cannot sue or be sued in federal court within

---

178. *See* J.A. Olson Co. v. City of Winona, 818 F.2d 401 (5th Cir. 1987).

179. Removal jurisdiction is discussed in subsection 5 *infra*.

180. *See e.g.*, Breitman v. May Co. Cal., 37 F.2d 562 (9th Cir. 1994); Gafford v. General Elec. Co., 997 F.2d 150 (6th Cir. 1993); *see also* Peterson v. Cooley, 142 F.3d 181 (4th Cir. 1998) (where corporation was a passive investment vehicle that was engaged primarily in the ownership and management of investment assets in the form of notes secured by property located in states where the obligors of the notes lived, the home office or "nerve center" test should be used to determine principle place of business). A corporation's principal place of business can change. *See* Athena Automotive, Inc. v. DiGregorio, 166 F.3d 288 (4th Cir. 1999) (corporation's principal place of business was at one time in Maryland, but had ceased activity there and corporation had activity only in Georgia and Virginia; therefore, diversity existed between corporation and citizens of Maryland); *see also* Dawn Levy, *Where Do Dead Corporations Live? Determining the Citizenship of Inactive Corporations for Diversity Jurisdiction Purposes,* 62 BROOK. L. REV. 663 (1996). Federally chartered corporations whose activities are limited to one state are citizens of that state, but if their activities are spread over more than one state, it has been held that they are national citizens only and not citizens of any state, with the result that they cannot sue or be sued within the diversity jurisdiction. *See* Little League Baseball, Inc. v. Welsh Publ'g Group, Inc., 874 F. Supp. 648 (M.D. Pa. 1995).

181. *See* Carden v. Arkoma Assocs., 494 U.S 185, 110 S. Ct. 1015, 108 L. Ed. 2d 157 (1990); United Steelworkers of Am. v. R.H. Bouligny, Inc., 382 U.S. 145, 86 S. Ct. 272, 15 L. Ed. 2d 217 (1965); 13B CHARLES A. WRIGHT ET AL., FEDERAL PRACTICE AND PROCEDURE: JURISDICTION AND RELATED MATTERS § 3630 (2d ed. 1984); ERWIN CHEMERINSKY, FEDERAL JURISDICTION § 5.3.3, at 296-97 (3d ed. 1999); Sara L. Johnson, Annotation, *Determination of Citizenship of Partnership, for Purposes of Diversity Jurisdiction Under 28 USCS § 1332(a),* 83 A.L.R. FED. 136 (1987); Walter W. Jones, Jr., Annotation, *Determination of Citizenship of Unincorporated Associations, for Federal Diversity of Citizenship Purposes, in Actions by or Against Such Associations,* 14 A.L.R. FED. 849 (1973).

the diversity jurisdiction by another U.S. citizen because complete diversity can never exist.[182]

(d) Alienage Jurisdiction

The general diversity statute includes within its scope more than jurisdiction of suits between citizens of different states. Section 1332(a) also allows jurisdiction of suits between (a) citizens of a state and citizens or subjects of a foreign state, (b) citizens of different states in which citizens or subjects of a foreign state are additional parties, and (c) a foreign state as plaintiff and citizens of a state or of different states.[183]

Illustration 2-45. A, a citizen of Texas, U.S.A., sues *B*, a citizen of France. This action can be brought in a U.S. District Court under 28 U.S.C. § 1332(a)(2), which permits suits between citizens of a state and citizens or subjects of a foreign state.[184]

Illustration 2-46. A, a citizen of Florida, U.S.A., and *B*, a citizen of Canada, sue *C*, a citizen of Oregon, U.S.A. This action can be brought in a U.S. District Court under 28 U.S.C. § 1332(a)(3), which permits suits between "citizens of different states and in which citizens or subjects of a foreign state are additional parties."[185]

* * * * *

In some instances, a person will possess dual United States and foreign citizenship. When confronted with this situation, most courts only recognize the U.S. nationality of the party.[186] This approach will result in a denial of jurisdiction when the party possessing dual citizenship is domiciled within a state and the opposing party is a citizen of the same state. This result probably coincides with the purposes of the alienage jurisdiction. No bias or prejudice will be likely against the party with dual citizenship in a state court where the party is

---

182. It is sometimes possible for an unincorporated association to sue or be sued as a class. *See* FED. R. CIV. P. 23.2. When the prerequisites for a class action have been met, only the citizenship of the named representative of the class is taken into account in determining diversity of citizenship. *See, e.g.*, Deloitte Noraudit A/S v. Deloitte Haskins & Sells, 148 F.R.D. 523 (S.D.N.Y. 1993). Diversity requirements in class actions are discussed in Chapter 8(D)(4) ("Class Actions") *infra*.

183. 28 U.S.C. § 1332(a)(2)-(4).

184. The use of the expression "citizens of a state" does not mean that all of the domestic parties in the action must be citizens of the same state. *See* Iraola & CIA, SA v. Kimberly-Clark Corp., 31 F. Supp. 2d 1378 (N.D. Ga. 1998).

185. *See, e.g.*, Zurich Ins. Co. v. Sigourney, 278 F.2d 826 (9th Cir. 1960); Hunter v. Shell Oil Co., 198 F.2d 485 (5th Cir. 1952). Under 28 U.S.C. § 1332(a)(2) and (3), suits in which an alien and a citizen of a state are on one side and an alien is on the other are usually held beyond the jurisdiction of the district courts. *See, e.g.*, Ed & Fred, Inc. v. Puritan Marine Ins. Underwriters Corp., 506 F.2d 757 (5th Cir. 1975); Engstrom v. Hornseth, 959 F. Supp. 545 (D.P.R. 1997). However, actions may fit within 28 U.S.C. § 1332(a)(3) when citizens of different states are plaintiff and defendant and aliens are also joined on both sides of the suit. *See* Dresser Indus., Inc. v. Underwriters at Lloyd's, 106 F.3d 494 (3d Cir. 1997). *See generally* 13B CHARLES A. WRIGHT ET AL., FEDERAL PRACTICE AND PROCEDURE: JURISDICTION AND RELATED MATTERS § 3604, at 389-391 (2d ed. 1984).

186. *See* Mutuelles Unies v. Kroll & Linstrom, 957 F.2d 707 (9th Cir. 1992); Action S.A. v. Marc Rich & Co., 951 F.2d 504 (2d Cir. 1991); Sadat v. Mertes, 615 F.2d 1176 (7th Cir. 1980). *But see* Aguirre v. Nagel, 270 F. Supp. 535 (E.D. Mich. 1967).

domiciled. In addition, the foreign state is not likely to be affronted by the treatment of its citizen in state court because its citizen is also a citizen of the United States.[187]

Illustration 2-47. *A*, a citizen of the United States, also possesses Swiss citizenship. *A* is domiciled in California. *B* is a citizen of California. *A* cannot sue *B* in a U.S. District Court because *A* is considered to be a citizen of California, not Switzerland. Consequently, no diversity of citizenship exists between *A* and *B*.

* * * * *

In 1988, Congress modified the "alienage" jurisdiction authorized by § 1332. Section 1332(a) now provides that "an alien admitted to the United States for permanent residence shall be deemed a citizen of the State in which such alien is domiciled."[188] This amendment destroys jurisdiction between citizens of states who sue or are sued by aliens domiciled in the same state.

One other potential effect of the amendment is to create jurisdiction between an alien admitted to permanent residence within the United States who is domiciled within a state and another alien not domiciled within the state. Although Congress may not have intended this effect, it is a possible result under the wording of the amendment. Such a result may be unconstitutional because Article III of the Constitution does not authorize jurisdiction over suits between two aliens.[189] However, Congress has conferred artificial state citizenship on corporations in § 1332(c) as well as on citizens of territories, the District of Columbia, and Puerto Rico in § 1332(d). This conferral of artificial state citizenship has been upheld as valid.[190] These analogies may sustain the validity of jurisdiction in a suit between two aliens under the amendment,[191] but there

---

187. *See* 13B CHARLES A. WRIGHT ET AL., FEDERAL PRACTICE AND PROCEDURE: JURISDICTION AND RELATED MATTERS § 3621, at 582 (2d ed. 1984).

188. Judicial Improvements and Access to Justice Act of 1988, Pub. L. No. 100-702, § 203, 102 Stat. 4642, 4646 (codified at 28 U.S.C. § 1332(a)). For an alien to be admitted to the United States for permanent residence, the alien must be admitted to permanent residence under the immigration laws—*i.e.*, have a "green card." Thus, if the alien has simply lived in the United States for a number of years on a temporary work permit without being formally admitted to permanent status, the alien retains his or her status as a citizen or subject of a foreign state for purposes of the alienage jurisdiction. *See* Fay v. Schantz, Sebatzman & Aaronson, P.A., 108 F.3d 1347 (11th Cir. 1997) (jurisdiction sustained). Given the fact that federal subject-matter jurisdiction must be affirmatively alleged, one might think that the "permanent resident alien" provision would now require plaintiffs to allege that any foreign citizens are *not* permanent resident aliens domiciled in a state where any opposing party is a citizen, but at least one court has refused to impose such a requirement. *See* Karazanos v. Madison Two Assocs., 147 F.3d 624 (7th Cir. 1998).

189. *See* Larry Kramer, *Diversity Jurisdiction*, 1990 B.Y.U. L. REV. 97, 122; John B. Oakley, *Recent Statutory Changes in the Law of Federal Jurisdiction and Venue*, 24 U.C. DAVIS L. REV. 735, 745 (1991); David D. Siegel, *Changes in Federal Jurisdiction and Practice Under the New Judicial Improvements and Access to Justice Act*, 123 F.R.D. 399, 408-09 (1989).

190. On corporations, see 15 MARTIN H. REDISH, MOORE'S FEDERAL PRACTICE § 102.50 (3d ed. 1999); 13B CHARLES A. WRIGHT ET AL., FEDERAL PRACTICE AND PROCEDURE: JURISDICTION AND RELATED MATTERS §§ 3623-24 (2d ed. 1984). On citizens of the District of Columbia, see National Mut. Ins. Co. v. Tidewater Transfer Co., 337 U.S. 582, 69 S. Ct. 1173, 93 L. Ed. 1556 (1949); ERWIN CHEMERINSKY, FEDERAL JURISDICTION § 5.3.3, at 294 (3d ed. 1999).

191. *See* William VanDercreek, *From the Judiciary Act of 1789 to the Judicial Improvements Act of 1989—Two Hundred Years of Non-Inferior "Inferior Courts,"* 14 OKLA. CITY U. L. REV. 565, 595-97 (1989); *cf.* 13B CHARLES A. WRIGHT ET AL., FEDERAL PRACTICE AND PROCEDURE: JURISDICTION AND RELATED MATTERS § 3621, at 581 (2d ed. 1984) (discussing these analogies as applied to stateless aliens).

are significant differences between the situations described and the 1988 alienage amendment.

Corporations are associations of individuals that are treated as artificial persons for several practical reasons other than citizenship for diversity jurisdiction. This tradition of treating corporations as artificial persons for other purposes may justify their treatment as state citizens for purposes of the diversity jurisdiction. No analogous tradition exists with regard to aliens. Furthermore, Congress arguably may have gone beyond the limits of the Constitution in opening the diversity jurisdiction to suits by and against citizens of the territories, the District of Columbia, and Puerto Rico, even though it has technically been upheld in so doing.[192]

To be constitutional, the grant of jurisdiction to the district courts of suits between two aliens must be a necessary and proper[193] incident of the power of Congress to regulate the jurisdiction of the lower federal courts under Article III of the Constitution. Arguably, Congress must have a certain amount of discretion to define state citizenship as a necessary and proper incident of its authority to regulate the diversity jurisdiction. The examples of corporate citizenship and artificial state citizenship for citizens of the District of Columbia, Puerto Rico, and the territories may be considered situations in which this discretion has been exercised. As long as Congress has a legitimate purpose for such jurisdictional regulations (grounded in established policies supporting federal subject-matter jurisdiction), there is no danger of an illegitimate expansion of the diversity jurisdiction beyond the limits of Article III. The discrimination that the alienage jurisdiction was designed to guard against can occur in an action between an alien domiciled within a state and another alien. An alien domiciled within the state may, as a practical matter, be viewed as a state citizen by other domicilaries of the state who may serve as triers of fact in a state action between the parties. If so, discrimination in state court fact finding may result in favor of the alien domiciliary and against the nonresident alien. To prevent this evil, Congress arguably should have the power to treat the alien domiciliary as a state citizen for purposes of the diversity jurisdiction.

Despite this argument, however, the better result would be for the courts to construe the 1988 amendment as intended only to limit the alienage jurisdiction, not to create jurisdiction in suits between two aliens.[194] As noted earlier, this result would be consistent with legislative intent because Congress probably did not intend to expand federal jurisdiction to actions between two aliens. Furthermore, in the past, courts have subjected similarly worded jurisdictional provisions to a narrowing construction to avoid the kinds of difficult constitu-

---

192. In National Mutual Insurance Co. v. Tidewater Transfer Co., 337 U.S. 582, 69 S. Ct. 1173, 93 L. Ed. 1556 (1949), a majority of the Supreme Court rejected all the possible constitutional grounds under which Congress might have conferred state citizenship on citizens of the District of Columbia. However, different minorities of the Court, acting under different constitutional theories, sustained the constitutionality of Congress' action. *See* RICHARD H. FALLON ET AL., HART & WECHSLER'S THE FEDERAL COURTS AND THE FEDERAL SYSTEM 441-44 (4th ed. 1996).

193. *See* U.S. CONST. art. I, § 8, cl. 18.

194. Several courts have so held. *See, e.g.,* Saadeh v. Farouki, 107 F.3d 52 (D.C. Cir. 1997); Engstrom v. Hornseth, 959 F. Supp. 545 (D.P.R. 1997); Arai v. Tachibana, 778 F. Supp. 1535 (D. Haw. 1991).

tional questions the 1988 amendment raises.[195] Until Congress makes it clear that it is departing from the longstanding limits of the alienage jurisdiction, these past precedents should control the interpretation of the 1988 amendment. Nevertheless, some courts have read the amendment literally. They have concluded that the 1988 amendment expands as well as contracts the diversity jurisdiction.[196]

Illustration 2-48. *A*, a citizen of Nevada, and *B*, a citizen of Canada admitted to the United States for permanent residence and domiciled in Nevada, have an automobile accident in Nevada. Prior to the 1988 amendment to § 1332, *A* could sue *B* in a U.S. District Court under 28 U.S.C § 1332(a)(2), which permits actions between citizens of a state (*A*) and citizens or subjects of a foreign state (*B*).[197] After the 1988 amendment, *A* cannot sue *B* in federal court within the alienage jurisdiction because both parties would be considered citizens of Nevada.

Illustration 2-49. *A*, a citizen of France admitted to permanent residence in the United States and domiciled in Texas, is involved in an automobile accident in Texas with *B*, a citizen of Great Britain domiciled in Great Britain. On the face of the 1988 amendment to § 1332, *A* could sue *B* in a U.S. District Court within the alienage jurisdiction. Under the wording of the amendment, *A* is treated as a citizen of Texas, and *B* is a subject of Great Britain. Thus, jurisdiction appears to exist under 1332(a)(2), because the action is between a citizen of a state and a subject of a foreign state. To avoid the constitutional difficulties this result would present, however, courts should construe the 1988 amendment to § 1332 to be inapplicable to this case. Thus, the suit should be considered to be between two aliens and not within the subject-matter jurisdiction of the U.S. District Courts.

* * * * *

The 1988 amendment's use of the term "alien" presents another difficulty. The general diversity statute confers jurisdiction in certain controversies

---

195. *See* Hodgson v. Bowerbank, 9 U.S. (5 Cranch) 303, 3 L. Ed. 108 (1809); *see also* Dennis J. Mahoney, *A Historical Note on* Hodgson v. Bowerbank, 49 U. Chi. L. Rev. 725 (1982).

196. *See, e.g.,* Singh v. Damler-Benz AG, 9 F.3d 303 (3d Cir. 1993) (action by alien plaintiff admitted for permanent residence and domiciled in Virginia against Delaware-New Jersey corporation and German corporation; holding jurisdiction exists under 28 U.S.C. § 1332); Iscar, Ltd. v. Katy, 743 F. Supp. 339 (D.N.J. 1990) (action by Israeli plaintiff against a New Jersey corporation and an Israeli defendant admitted to permanent residence in U.S. and domiciled in state; holding 1988 amendment is retroactive and cures defect in diversity jurisdiction existing at commencement of action); D'Arbois v. Sommelier's Cellars, 741 F. Supp. 489 (S.D.N.Y. 1990) (action by French plaintiff against French defendant admitted to permanent residence in the U.S. and domiciled in a state and another citizen of a state; holding 1988 amendment not retroactive and therefore cannot cure defect in jurisdiction existing at commencement of action). None of these cases involved a constitutional difficulty because they all had at least one citizen of a state present in the action in addition to two aliens.

197. Unlike the requirement of state citizenship for diversity purposes—*i.e.,* that a person be (1) a citizen of the United States *and* (2) domiciled within some state to be a citizen of a state—a party did not have to be domiciled in a foreign state to be considered a citizen or subject of the foreign state for purposes of the alienage jurisdiction. This absence of a domicile requirement is still true, except when the alien in question is admitted to the United States for permanent residence and is domiciled within a state. Thus, a citizen of France domiciled in England is still considered a citizen of France for purposes of the alienage jurisdiction, even after the 1988 amendment to 28 U.S.C. § 1332.

involving "citizens or subjects of a foreign state." However, the 1988 amendment speaks of "an alien admitted to the United States for permanent residence" who is domiciled within a state. Before the amendment, rare cases arose that involved persons who were "stateless aliens"–persons who were not citizens or subjects of any foreign state because they had lost their national citizenship.[198] For the most part, the federal courts declined jurisdiction over actions involving stateless aliens because they were not "citizens or subjects of a foreign state."[199] The amendment might be read as conferring state citizenship upon stateless aliens admitted to the United States for permanent residence and domiciled within a state. Although they are not "citizens or subjects of a foreign state," they are "aliens." Thus, the amendment might apply to them. Nevertheless, Congress no more intended this result than it intended to authorize actions between two parties who are citizens of foreign states. Therefore, courts should not interpret the amendment to confer state citizenship on stateless aliens.

Illustration 2-50. *A* is a Cuban refugee who is no longer a citizen of Cuba. However, *A* has not acquired any other national citizenship. *A* has been admitted to permanent residence in the United States and is domiciled in Florida. Before the 1988 amendment, most decisions held that *A* could not sue or be sued within the diversity or alienage jurisdiction. Because *A* was not a citizen of the United States, *A* was not a citizen of a state within the meaning of the diversity statute. Because *A* possessed no national citizenship, *A* was also not a citizen or subject of a foreign state within the meaning of the statute. The same result should occur after the 1988 amendment because the word "alien" in that amendment should be read to mean "citizen or subject of a foreign state."[200]

---

198. Unlike domicile, national citizenship can be lost without acquiring new national citizenship.

199. *See* 13B CHARLES A. WRIGHT ET AL., FEDERAL PRACTICE AND PROCEDURE: JURISDICTION AND RELATED MATTERS § 3621, at 579-81 (2d ed. 1984).

200. A similar interpretive problem exists in determining the citizenship of "alien" corporations because of the wording of 28 U.S.C. § 1332(c)(1). That section provides that a corporation shall be deemed a citizen of any "State" by which it has been incorporated and the "State" where it has its principal place of business. The use of the word "State" in the statute has led some courts to conclude that it does not apply to a corporation incorporated in the United States with its principal place of business in a foreign country or to a corporation incorporated in a foreign country with its principal place of business in a state of the United States. *See, e.g.,* Torres v. Southern Peru Copper Corp., 113 F.3d 540 (5th Cir. 1997). However, a majority of the U.S. Courts of Appeals have held that 28 U.S.C. § 1332(c)(1) confers dual citizenship on all corporations. *See, e.g.,* Danjaq, S.A. v. Pathe Communications Corp., 979 F.2d 772 (9th Cir. 1992); Cabalceta v. Standard Fruit Co., 883 F.2d 1553 (11th Cir. 1989); Jerguson v. Blue Dot Inv., Inc., 659 F.2d 31 (5th Cir. Unit B Oct. 1981), *cert. denied,* 456 U.S. 946, 102 S. Ct. 2013, 72 L. Ed. 2d 469 (1982). This interpretation accords with the American Law Institute's recommendations for revision of the diversity jurisdiction statute. *See* ALI STUDY OF THE DIVISION OF JURISDICTION BETWEEN STATE AND FEDERAL COURTS § 1301(b)(1) (1969). Note, however, that corporations organized under the laws of countries that the United States does not formally recognize may not be considered citizens of a "foreign state" within the meaning of § 1332(a)(2). *See* Matimak Trading Co. v. Khalily, 118 F.3d 76 (2d Cir. 1997), *cert. denied,* 525 U.S. 1091, 118 S. Ct. 883, 139 L. Ed. 2d 871 (1998); *cf.* Klein v. Marriott Int'l, Inc., 34 F. Supp. 2d 176 (S.D.N.Y. 1999) (Bermuda corporation is not a citizen or subject of a foreign state under § 1332 because Bermuda is not a foreign state, but a Dependent Territory of the United Kingdom not formally recognized as an independent sovereign state by the U.S. State Department). Note also that even if alien corporations can have dual citizenship, there will be the same problems with determining their principal place of business as exist with domestic corporations. *See* Bel-Bel Int'l Corp. v. Community Bank, 162 F.3d 1101 (11th Cir. 1998) (corporation incorporated in Panama had its only investment in Florida where it also had a bank account and attorneys and was designed as an investment vehicle whereby Venezuelan citizens could make loans to a Florida tomato farm; all shareholders of corporation were Venezuelan citizens;

(e) Amount-in-Controversy Requirement

The diversity jurisdiction has always been subject to an amount-in-controversy requirement.[201] Congress has raised the amount in controversy from time to time in an attempt to reduce the volume of diversity actions in federal court. In 1996, Congress raised the amount from more than $50,000 to its current level of more than $75,000.[202] Even though the dollar amount has changed, however, the rules for determining the amount in controversy remain unchanged.

(i) Single Plaintiff with a Single Claim or Multiple Claims Against a Single Defendant

In actions for damages, when a single plaintiff asserts a single claim against a single defendant, the amount claimed by the plaintiff controls—if it is apparently made in good faith. It must appear to a legal certainty that the plaintiff cannot recover more than $75,000 before a court can dismiss the case.[203] However, only the "direct effect" of the judgment will be considered, not collateral effects that the judgment may have by way of res judicata or stare decisis.[204] Interests and costs are excluded in calculating the amount in controversy.

Illustration 2-51. A, a citizen of State *X*, sues *B Bank*, a corporation incorporated and with its principal place of business in State *Y*, in a U.S. District Court. *A* seeks damages of $137,000 from *B* for negligent failure to pay a check. *A* alleges that *B* negligently failed to credit *A's* account for $37,000, the amount of a check that *A* had deposited with *B*. *A* also seeks $100,000 in punitive damages. Assume that the substantive law applicable to the case prohibits the recovery of punitive damages under the allegations in *A's* complaint. Thus, it appears to a legal certainty that *A* cannot recover more than $37,000. As a result, the court should dismiss *A's* complaint.[205]

Illustration 2-52. A, a citizen of State *X*, sues *B*, a citizen of State *Y*, in a U.S. District Court. *A* seeks damages for the conversion of a negotiable

---

the corporation's principal place of business was in Venezuela).

201. 15 Martin H. Redish, Moore's Federal Practice § 102.100 (3d ed. 1999); 14B Charles A. Wright et al., Federal Practice and Procedure: Jurisdiction and Related Matters § 3701 (3d ed. 1998). Other provisions of the Judicial Code have also been subject to an amount-in-controversy requirement. The general federal question jurisdiction was subject to a jurisdictional amount until 1980, when Congress eliminated the requirement. *See* Act of Dec. 1, 1980, Pub. L. No. 96-486, 94 Stat. 2396. For a nondiversity statute containing an amount-in-controversy requirement in the current Judicial Code, see 28 U.S.C. § 1346(a)(2).

202. *See* Federal Courts Improvement Act of 1996, Pub. L. No. 104-317, § 205, 110 Stat. 3847, 3850 (codified at 28 U.S.C. § 1332(a)). The Judiciary Act of 1789 set the amount at $500. Congress raised it to $2,000 in 1887, to $3,000 in 1911, to $10,000 in 1958, and to $50,000 in 1988. *See* Richard H. Fallon et al., Hart & Wechsler's The Federal Courts and the Federal System 1542 (4th ed. 1996).

203. *See* St. Paul Mercury Indem. Co. v. Red Cab Co., 303 U.S. 283, 58 S. Ct. 586, 82 L. Ed. 845 (1938).

204. *See* Healy v. Ratta, 292 U.S. 263, 54 S. Ct. 700, 78 L. Ed. 1248 (1934); Richard H. Fallon et al., Hart & Wechsler's The Federal Courts and the Federal System 1547 (4th ed. 1996); 14B Charles A. Wright et al., Federal Practice and Procedure: Jurisdiction and Related Matters § 3702, at 77-81 (3d ed. 1998).

205. *See* D'Amato v. Rhode Island Hosp. Trust Nat'l Bank, 772 F. Supp. 1322 (D.R.I. 1991).

instrument with a face value of $75,000, interest at the legal rate, attorney's fees, and costs. Assume that the substantive law applicable to the action does not allow the recovery of attorney's fees. Under the express prohibition in 28 U.S.C. § 1332, costs are not a permissible element in calculating the jurisdictional amount. In addition, interest may not be included in calculating the jurisdictional amount when interest is simply the result of delay in payment, as it appears to be from *A's* claim for relief.[206] The face amount of the negotiable instrument ($75,000) is the only permissible element of damages. This amount fails to meet the amount-in-controversy requirement. Section 1332 requires that *more than* $75,000 be in controversy. Thus, the court should dismiss *A's* action for failure to meet the jurisdictional amount.[207]

Illustration 2-53. *A*, a citizen of State *X*, sues *B*, a citizen of State *Y*, in a U.S. District Court. *A* seeks damages for personal injuries received in an automobile accident. *A's* only injury in the accident was a broken thumb. *A* claimed $1,026 in lost wages and medical expenses. *A* also claimed $80,000 for pain and suffering. On similar facts, a federal district court dismissed *A's* action. The court held that it appeared to a legal certainty that *A's* claim did not meet the amount-in-controversy requirement because if a jury had awarded damages that met the amount requirement, the trial judge would have been bound to set the award aside as excessive.[208]

* * * * *

The rules governing the determination of the amount in controversy in single-plaintiff, single-defendant damage actions may seem straightforward enough, but there is still uncertainty in the area. The uncertainty is produced by the interaction of a number of subsidiary rules governing amount-in-controversy disputes and the failure of the courts to recognize that they are violating these

---

206. When interest is simply the result of delay in payment, such as when a statute provides for the recovery of interest at a certain rate from the date a claim matures, it is not permissible to take it into account in calculating the jurisdictional amount. However, when interest is an essential element of the claim for relief, it may be taken into account. Thus, in the illustration, if *A* had claimed $80,000, which included $75,000 in principal and $5,000 in interest that were both part of the face amount of the note due at maturity, the amount-in-controversy requirement would have been met. The purpose of this distinction is to prevent plaintiffs from delaying suit in order to inflate the claim above the amount in controversy by interest that accrues after the claim matures. *See* 14B CHARLES A. WRIGHT ET AL., FEDERAL PRACTICE AND PROCEDURE: JURISDICTION AND RELATED MATTERS 3712, at 279-84 (3d ed. 1998).

207. *See* Bradford Nat'l Life Ins. Co. v. Union State Bank, 794 F. Supp. 296 (E.D. Wis. 1992); *see also* Gardynski-Leschuck v. Ford Motor Co., 142 F.3d 955 (7th Cir. 1998), in which the plaintiff claimed $51,000 in damages plus $25,000 in attorney's fees, the fees representing the plaintiff's estimate of the amount the attorney would have to be paid after full litigation of the suit. The court of appeals held that the amount-in-controversy requirement had been violated. Even if attorney's fees were recoverable under the applicable substantive law, the amount in controversy had to be calculated as of the commencement of the action. At that time, the fees had not been incurred and might not be. For example, the fees might be avoided by the defendant's prompt payment or settlement of the plaintiff's claim.

208. *See* Burns v. Anderson, 502 F.2d 970 (5th Cir. 1974). The *Burns* approach represents a trend in which the lower federal courts have been willing to scrutinize cases involving unliquidated damages more carefully than in earlier cases in which the plaintiff's claim was virtually conclusive on the question. *See, e.g.,* Deutsch v. Hewes St. Realty Corp., 359 F.2d 96 (2d Cir. 1966). *See generally* RICHARD H. FALLON ET AL., HART AND WECHSLER'S THE FEDERAL COURTS AND THE FEDERAL SYSTEM 1545 (4th ed. 1996); W.E. Shipley, Annotation, *Criteria of Jurisdictional Amount in Tort Action for Unliquidated Damages in Federal Court*, 47 A.L.R.2D 651 (1956).

rules, or some of them, in the very cases in which they purport to be applying them.

First, it is settled that the amount in controversy is determined as of the commencement of the action.[209] A second rule follows from the first: if the proper amount in controversy exists at the commencement of the action, subsequent events may not oust the jurisdiction by reducing the amount below its level at commencement.[210] For example, the plaintiff may not reduce the amount in controversy after commencement to defeat federal jurisdiction (as, for example, in a case removed by the defendant from state to federal court).[211] Nor may a valid defense to part or all of the claim defeat jurisdiction.[212] The difficulty in administering these rules can be illustrated by some recent decisions in the U.S. Courts of Appeals.

In *Tongkook America, Inc. v. Shipton Sportswear Co.*,[213] the plaintiff sued the defendant for $117,621.05, plus interest, for breach of contract. The amount represented a balance that both parties believed was due on a sale of goods by the plaintiff to the defendant. During discovery, the parties learned that the plaintiff had, prior to commencement of the action, drawn $80,760.00 on a letter of credit that had been provided by the defendant to the plaintiff. As a result, the actual amount of the plaintiff's claim at commencement was $36,861.05, which was below the amount-in-controversy requirement of $50,000 existing at the time of the action. The defendant amended its answer to raise the defense of partial payment. After the district court raised the issue of jurisdictional amount, the defendant sought dismissal for lack of subject-matter jurisdiction. However, the district court retained jurisdiction and ultimately entered judgment for the plaintiff in the amount of $38,861.05.

The Second Circuit Court of Appeals reversed. The court held that the "good-faith, legal-certainty" rule, discussed above, had been violated. The court's opinion acknowledged (1) the rule that the amount in controversy is determined as of commencement; (2) the rule that events subsequent to commencement cannot defeat jurisdiction; and (3) the rule that valid defenses cannot defeat jurisdiction. Nevertheless, the court held that record demonstrated to a legal certainty that the requisite amount in controversy *never* existed.

The problem with the court's conclusion is that payment is a defense.[214] It is clear, therefore, that the court allowed the assertion of a valid defense to defeat jurisdiction. It has been observed that "[c]ourts have distinguished between subsequent events that cannot destroy subject-matter jurisdiction, and subsequent events that require the case's dismissal because they reveal that the necessary dollar amount was not actually in controversy at the commencement of the

---

209. *See* 14B CHARLES A. WRIGHT ET AL., FEDERAL PRACTICE AND PROCEDURE: JURISDICTION AND RELATED MATTERS § 3712, at 62 (3d ed. 1998).

210. *See id.* at 64.

211. *See* St. Paul Mercury Indem. Co. v. Red Cab Co., 303 U.S. 283, 58 S. Ct. 586, 82 L. Ed. 843 (1938).

212. *See* 308 U.S. at 289, 58 S. Ct. at 590, 82 L. Ed. at 848; 14B CHARLES A. WRIGHT ET AL., FEDERAL PRACTICE AND PROCEDURE: JURISDICTION AND RELATED MATTERS § 3712, at 74-77 (3d ed. 1998).

213. 14 F.3d 781 (2d Cir. 1994).

214. *See* FED. R. CIV. P. 8(c) (listing payment as one of a number of affirmative defenses).

action."[215] However, this distinction cannot realistically be viewed as consistent with the subsidiary rules governing jurisdictional amount when the subsequent event in question is the revelation of a valid defense during the discovery stage of litigation.

Furthermore, there are cases that do not follow the "never-in-controversy" rule. For example, in *Coventry Sewage Associates v. Dworkin Realty Co.*,[216] a mistaken calculation by a third party upon whom the parties had no choice but to rely resulted in the inflation of the amount in controversy above the required minimum. In effect, as in *Tongkook*, the objective facts existing at commencement demonstrated that the required amount in controversy *never* existed. Nevertheless, the First Circuit Court of Appeals upheld jurisdiction. The court distinguished *Tongkook* on the ground that the plaintiff in *Tongkook* should have discovered that its claim did not meet the amount-in-controversy requirement. On the other hand, the third-party's error in *Coventry Sewage* was not obvious, and the parties could not have discovered it prior to commencement. Nevertheless, if the prevailing theory is that discovery of objective facts after commencement can reveal that the required amount at commencement *never* existed, *Coventry Sewage* is both wrong *and* inconsistent with *Tongkook*.

Tongkook, *Coventry Sewage*, and other cases administering the amount-in-controversy requirement[217] cannot be reconciled with each other under the rules they purport to apply. Nevertheless, the results of the cases may be justifiable according to a rule not yet fully articulated by the courts. The cases discussed above, as well as others,[218] seem to be aimed at preventing the negligent or manipulative creation of federal jurisdiction through inflation of the amount in controversy. If the plaintiff has not conducted a reasonable investigation that would have uncovered facts prior to commencement showing the amount-in-controversy requirement was not met, jurisdiction should be declined. Conversely, if a reasonable pre-commencement investigation could not have uncovered the relevant facts bearing on jurisdictional amount, discovery of those facts after

---

215. 14B CHARLES A. WRIGHT ET AL., FEDERAL PRACTICE AND PROCEDURE: JURISDICTION AND RELATED MATTERS § 3712, at 71 (3d ed. 1998) (citing authorities).

216. 71 F.3d 1 (1st Cir. 1995).

217. *See e.g.*, Wolde v. Vocational Instruction Project Community Servs., Inc., 166 F.3d 59 (2d Cir. 1999), in which Second Circuit upheld jurisdiction after the amount in controversy was reduced below the required level by a grant of summary judgment produced by the addition to the case of certain legal defenses by the defendant and the inability of the plaintiff to adduce evidence to establish the claim. The court distinguished *Tongkook* on the ground that the partial payment in that case meant the requisite amount in controversy never existed. The problem is that a grant of summary judgment can only occur when there is no genuine issue of material fact and the moving party is entitled to judgment as a matter of law. The inability of the plaintiff to produce evidence in support of his claim would seem to mean that it was invalid on the objective facts as of commencement. *Accord* Herremans v. Carrera Designs, Inc., 157 F.3d 1118 (7th Cir. 1998) (claims eliminated by summary judgment did not defeat jurisdiction); *see also* McNulty v. Travel Park, 853 F. Supp. 144 (E.D. Pa. 1994) (during discovery, plaintiff's attorney concluded on the basis of certain medical information that the plaintiffs could not recover an amount sufficient to meet the amount in controversy and moved to dismiss; the court refused, holding that jurisdiction had to be determined without regard to success on the merits).

218. Of course, not *all* cases in this area can be reconciled on the basis of the policies discussed in the text. However, a large number of cases can be understood if the rules the courts purport to be enforcing are ignored and one focuses instead on whether there is a danger of negligent or manipulative creation of jurisdiction.

commencement should not defeat jurisdiction. This approach reconciles *Tongkook* and *Coventry Sewage*.[219]

The same approach should be taken when there is a danger that the amount in controversy has been intentionally inflated or otherwise illegitimately manipulated to meet the amount-in-controversy requirement.

Illustration 2-54. In *Indiana Hi-Rail Corp. v. Decatur Junction Railway Co.*,[220] the plaintiff sued the defendant in U.S. District Court for the conversion of a locomotive. Under the applicable substantive law of conversion, the plaintiff was entitled to recover damages measured by the value of the locomotive at the time of the conversion, which exceeded the amount-in-controversy requirement. However, if the property converted had been returned, the plaintiff's damages were limited to any amount the plaintiff had lost by reason of the detention of the property. Despite the fact that the locomotive had been returned before commencement of the federal action, the plaintiff sought damages measured by the value of the locomotive at the time of conversion. The Seventh Circuit Court of Appeals held that the amount-in-controversy requirement was not met, even though the plaintiff did not have to say anything in the complaint about failure to return the locomotive to state a claim for relief and the issue of return was thus clearly a defense to be pleaded by the defendant. To allow the plaintiff to claim an amount to which it clearly was not entitled under clear and knowable substantive rules would be to allow the manipulative creation of federal jurisdiction because of the fortuitous allocation of the burden of pleading under state law. Note that if the locomotive had been returned *after* the commencement of the federal action, the result should be different. The plaintiff would then have been suing for an amount to which it was entitled under the applicable substantive law, and return of the locomotive by the defendant after commencement should not be allowed to defeat federal jurisdiction.

* * * * *

It should be understood that the guidelines discussed above concerning negligent and manipulative creation of jurisdiction are designed only for cases in which matters come to light after commencement that bear directly upon the amount in controversy, as opposed to the underlying substantive validity of the

---

219. In *Tongkook* there was no excuse for the plaintiff's failure to learn about the partial payment before commencement, and jurisdiction was properly declined. However, in *Coventry Sewage* there was no realistic way that either party could have learned of the miscomputation by the third party prior to commencement, and jurisdiction was properly upheld. *See also* McNulty v. Travel Park, 853 F. Supp. 144 (E.D. Pa. 1994), in which plaintiff discovered medical information that appeared to be inaccessible prior to commencement and that demonstrated the plaintiff could not recover the required amount. Jurisdiction was upheld. Cases that superficially appear inconsistent with the approach suggested in the text can often be reconciled with it. For example, in Zacharia v. Harbor Island Spa, Inc., 684 F.2d 199 (2d Cir. 1982), the court held it was error for the district court to dismiss the plaintiff's action against a hotel for lack of proper jurisdictional amount based on the hotel's defense under an applicable statute limiting its liability to $1,000 for loss of a guest's valuables. Parts of the court's opinion spoke in absolute terms about the impermissibility of taking defenses into account. However, throughout the opinion, the court discussed facts indicating that there was real doubt about whether the defense was valid on the facts. Therefore, there was no certainty at the time of commencement that the plaintiff was not entitled to recover the amount requested and no danger of negligent or manipulative creation of jurisdiction as a result.

220. 37 F.3d 363 (7th Cir. 1994).

plaintiff's claim. Jurisdiction should never be defeated by elimination of an entire claim due to the inability of the plaintiff to establish an essential element of the claim or because of a valid substantive defense asserted by the defendant not bearing specifically on the amount of the claim. It would be administratively complex and wasteful to extend the negligent and manipulative creation of jurisdiction policies to all substantive disposition of claims. There are other effective tools available to the federal courts with which to discourage frivolous factual and legal presentations on the merits of claims.[221] The case law generally, though not explicitly, embraces this distinction.

Illustration 2-55. *A*, a citizen of State *X*, sues *B*, a citizen of State *Y*, in a U.S. District Court in State *Y*. *A* seeks $100,000 in damages for breach of an oral contract. *B's* answer contains a defense that *A's* claim for relief is barred under the applicable statute of frauds. If this defense is valid, *A's* action should be dismissed on the merits. It should not be dismissed for lack of jurisdiction, even though the validity of the statute of frauds defense means that, on the objective facts existing at the time of commencement, the plaintiff was entitled to recover nothing. The statute-of-frauds defense addresses the substantive merits of the plaintiff's claim, not the ability of the plaintiff to recover the amount of damages requested, or any portion of it. To permit dismissal for lack of the proper jurisdictional amount whenever a defendant raises a valid affirmative defense directed to the merits of the plaintiff's claim rather than the amount requested would result in many jurisdictional dismissals at late stages of federal actions. Such a result would be wasteful and would not directly address the problem of illegitimate inflation of the amount in controversy to create federal jurisdiction. If *A* has frivolously resisted *B's* statute-of-frauds defense, the district court has power to impose appropriate sanctions on *A*.[222]

Illustration 2-56. *A*, a citizen of State *X*, sues *B*, a citizen of State *Y*, in a U.S. District Court in State *Y*. *A* seeks $1,000,000 in damages due to the exposure of *A* to an asbestos product manufactured by *B*. After a full opportunity for discovery, *A* is unable to develop any proof that the product to which *A* was exposed belonged to *B*, which is an essential element that *A* must prove to establish the claim. *B* moves for summary judgment. To defeat *B's* motion, *A* must come forward with some evidence to show that *B* manufactured the product to which *A* was exposed. If *A* cannot do so, the court should grant summary judgment.[223] However, *A's* action should not be dismissed for lack of jurisdiction, even though the objective facts available after full opportunity for discovery indicate that *A* is entitled to recover nothing. For the same reasons given in *Illustration 2-55*, it would be wasteful to dismiss actions like *A's* for lack of jurisdiction. Furthermore, it would not directly address the problem of illegitimate inflation of the amount-in-controversy requirement. If *A* has asserted a claim for relief against *B* without proper precommencement investigation of the facts, the

---

221. *See* Chapter 6(E)(2) *infra* (discussing Federal Rule 11).

222. *See id.*

223. *See* the discussion of *Celotex v. Catrett* in *Illustration 10-12* in Chapter 10(C)(2) ("Applying the Summary Judgment Standard") *infra*.

district court has the power to impose an appropriate sanction on *A* or *A's* attorney.[224]

* * * * *

When the benefit to the plaintiff of the relief requested has a different value than the cost that the relief will impose on the defendant—for example, as in some injunction suits—a split of authority exists about how to determine whether the amount in controversy has been satisfied. The cases variously hold that (1) the value to the plaintiff, (2) the value to the defendant, (3) the value to either plaintiff or defendant if one or the other, but not both, satisfies the amount-in-controversy requirement, or (4) the value to the person who invokes federal jurisdiction (the plaintiff in an original action or the defendant in an action removed from state court) controls.[225]

Illustration 2-57. *A*, a citizen of State *X*, seeks an injunction in federal court requiring *B*, a citizen of State *Y*, to remove a building partially constructed on *A's* land. Assume that the encroachment decreases the value of *A's* land by $5,000. Removing the encroaching part of the building would cost *B* over $100,000. Courts following the "value to the plaintiff" rule or the "person who invokes jurisdiction" rule would hold that the amount-in-controversy requirement is not satisfied. On the other hand, courts following the "value to the defendant" rule or the "value to either" rule would allow the action to proceed.

* * * * *

When a single plaintiff sues a single defendant on two or more claims, the plaintiff may aggregate the plaintiff's claims to meet the requirement, no matter how unrelated the claims are.[226]

Illustration 2-58. Assume that *A* has three unrelated claims against *B*. The first is for negligence for $30,000. The second is for breach of contract for $35,000. The third is for slander for $25,000. *A* may join all three claims in a single action against *B*. Because a total of $90,000 is sought, the amount in controversy is satisfied.

---

224. *See* FED. R. CIV. P. 11(b)(2), (3); Chapter 6(E)(2) ("Good Faith Pleading: Rule 11") *infra.*

225. *See, e.g.,* Ericsson GE Mobile Communications v. Motorola Communications, Inc., 120 F.3d 216 (11th Cir. 1997) (plaintiff's viewpoint controls; no jurisdiction); Hoffman v. Vulcan Materials Co., 19 F. Supp. 2d 475, 481-82 (M.D.N.C. 1998) ("flexible approach" that takes into account defendant's viewpoint applied; jurisdiction upheld); Crawford v. American Bankers Ins. Co., 987 F. Supp. 1408 (M.D. Ala. 1997) (plaintiff's viewpoint must be used in injunction case); *cf.* Grinnell Mut. Reins Co. v. Shierk, 121 F.3d 1114 (7th Cir. 1997) (insured sued in state court for damages "in excess of $15,000"; insurance company brings a federal diversity action for a declaration that it is not obligated to defend or indemnify the insured in the state action under a policy with a limit of $100,000; later, judgment was rendered in the state action against the insured for $14,045; court of appeals reverses district court's dismissal for lack of jurisdiction, holding that at commencement of the federal action, the company could have incurred liability of up to $100,000; the subsequent event of the state judgment did not destroy jurisdiction); Guardian Life Ins. Co. of Am. v. Muniz, 101 F.3d 93 (11th Cir. 1996) (amount in controversy met in action by an insurance company to cancel a life insurance policy of $100,000, even though the insured party was still alive). *See generally* ERWIN CHEMERINSKY, FEDERAL JURISDICTION § 5.3.4, at 304-05 (3d ed. 1999); 15 MARTIN H. REDISH, MOORE'S FEDERAL PRACTICE § 102.109 (3d ed. 1999); 14B CHARLES A. WRIGHT ET AL., FEDERAL PRACTICE AND PROCEDURE: JURISDICTION AND RELATED MATTERS § 3703 (3d ed. 1998); C.T. Drechsler, Annotation, *Criterion of Jurisdictional Amount to Vest Jurisdiction of Federal Court Where Injunction Is Sought,* 30 A.L.R.2D 602 (1953).

226. *See, e.g.,* Bullard v. City of Cisco, 290 U.S. 179, 54 S. Ct. 177, 78 L. Ed. 254 (1933).

(ii) Aggregation of Claims with Multiple Parties: The "Common and Undivided Interest" Test

Multiple parties may aggregate claims to satisfy the amount-in-controversy requirement only "if the several parties have a common undivided interest and a single title or right is involved."[227] This test requires much more than simply a legal and factual relationship between the claims.

Illustration 2-59. Assume that two plaintiffs, *A* and *B*, each have a $56,000 claim for personal injuries arising out of the same automobile accident. Because the plaintiffs' claims involve injuries to rights possessed separately by each plaintiff, the plaintiffs may not aggregate their claims against a defendant to meet the amount-in-controversy requirement.

* * * * *

When would the "common and undivided interest" test be satisfied? A comparison of two cases will illustrate how difficult this question is to answer. In *Manufacturers Casualty Insurance Co. v. Coker,*[228] the Fourth Circuit held that a common and undivided interest was present when an insurance company sued for a declaratory judgment asserting that it was not liable under an insurance policy to several persons who had obtained judgments against the insured party. The aggregate amount of the judgments was more than the required jurisdictional amount, but no single judgment exceeded that amount. The parties who had obtained the judgments were held to have a common and undivided interest against the insurance company arising out of the policy of insurance.

On the other hand, in *Aetna Insurance Co. v. Chicago, Rock Island & Pacific Railroad Co.,*[229] the Tenth Circuit held that no common and undivided interest was present when forty-seven insurance companies had joined in issuing a single policy of insurance to a railroad and sued for a declaration that a certain loss suffered by the railroad was not covered by the policy. The court in *Aetna* stated that:

> [h]ere the claims of the plaintiffs are common in the sense of a community of interest in the rights asserted, but they are not undivided in the sense that they "constitute in their totality an integrated right." Instead they are separate and distinct having only a common basis of fact and law arising from a single instrument.[230]

---

227. CHARLES A. WRIGHT, THE LAW OF FEDERAL COURTS § 36, at 211 (5th ed. 1994); *see also* Snyder v. Harris, 394 U.S. 332, 89 S. Ct. 1053, 22 L. Ed. 2d 319 (1969); 15 MARTIN H. REDISH, MOORE'S FEDERAL PRACTICE § 102.108 (3d ed. 1999). *See generally* S.R. Shapiro, Annotation, *Right to Aggregate Multiple Claims or Interests in Order to Satisfy Minimum Jurisdictional Amount Requirement in Federal District Court,* 2 A.L.R. FED. 18 (1969).

228. 219 F.2d 631 (4th Cir. 1955).

229. 229 F.2d 584 (10th Cir. 1956).

230. *Id.* at 586. The *Aetna* and *Coker* cases are discussed in CHARLES A. WRIGHT, THE LAW OF FEDERAL COURTS § 36, at 212-13 (5th ed. 1994); 14B CHARLES A. WRIGHT ET AL., FEDERAL PRACTICE AND PROCEDURE: JURISDICTION AND RELATED MATTERS § 3704, at 151-52 (3d ed. 1998). For a discussion of additional cases applying the aggregation rule, *see* 14B CHARLES A. WRIGHT ET AL., FEDERAL PRACTICE AND PROCEDURE: JURISDICTION AND RELATED MATTERS § 3704 (3d ed. 1998).

There has been vigorous criticism of applying the "common and undivided interest" test in a modern procedural context in which joinder of parties and claims is permitted much more liberally than when the test originated over one hundred fifty years ago. Nevertheless, recent U.S. Supreme Court decisions indicate that the test will continue to govern aggregation in the absence of congressional action to modify it.[231] As the discussion of the *Aetna* and *Coker* cases indicates, no single approach to administering the test will reconcile all the decisions. For example, if the *Aetna* view had been applied to the *Coker* facts, the result in the latter case would have differed.

To simplify the test, the following question should be asked: Must the parties sue or be sued together to obtain the relief sought in the action? If they must, courts should permit aggregation. If separate actions might have been brought by or against the parties, courts should still permit aggregation if the amount in controversy would be the same in either a single or multiple party action. This situation will sometimes occur when the relief given to one plaintiff or against one defendant will, as a practical matter, result in relief to the other plaintiff(s) or against the other defendant(s). However, courts should not permit aggregation merely because the relief requested for or against one party will result in relief for or against another. Rather, an action by or against one of the multiple parties must involve the same amount in controversy as a multiple party action. Thus, courts should not permit aggregation when separate actions might have been brought by or against the multiple parties and the jurisdictional amount would not be the same in the (hypothetical) separate action(s) and the multiple party action.

Illustration 2-60. *D*, a citizen of State *X*, sold land to *C*, a citizen of State *Y*. *D* took two separate notes, each for $40,000, in return for the land. *D* also reserved a vendor's lien on the land. Subsequently, *D* validly assigned one of the notes to *A* and the other to *B*. *A* and *B* are also citizens of State *X*. When the notes matured, *C* failed to pay them. *A* and *B* sued *C* in a U.S. District Court to enforce the vendor's lien. *A* and *B* may aggregate the amount of the notes to meet the amount-in-controversy requirement. Although their claims on the notes are

---

231. *See* Zahn v. International Paper Co., 414 U.S. 291, 94 S. Ct. 505, 38 L. Ed. 2d 511 (1973); Snyder v. Harris, 394 U.S. 332, 89 S. Ct. 1053, 22 L. Ed. 2d 319 (1969); *cf.* Crawford v. American Bankers Ins. Co., 987 F. Supp. 1408 (M.D. Ala. 1997) (common and undivided interest test satisfied in injunction action in which an injunction would prevent defendant from engaging in a certain form of business and the injunction had no separable value to each member of the class); 14B CHARLES A. WRIGHT ET AL., FEDERAL PRACTICE AND PROCEDURE: JURISDICTION AND RELATED MATTERS § 3704, at 160-67 (3d ed. 1998). Recent decisions in the lower federal courts have divided on the issue of whether, in a class action in which none of the individual claimants have compensatory damages claims that meet the amount-in-controversy requirement, the class may use a punitive damages claim to meet the requirement on the theory that each class member has an undivided interest in the punitive damages. *Compare* Ard v. Transcontinental Gas Pipe Line Corp., 138 F.3d 596 (5th Cir. 1998) (claims cannot be aggregated), Gilman v. BHC Sec., Inc., 104 F.3d 1418 (2d Cir. 1997) (no aggregation unless underlying claim is common and undivided), *and* Johnson v. Gerber Prods. Co., 949 F. Supp. 327 (E.D. Pa. 1996) (no aggregation) *with* Tapscott v. MS Dealer Serv. Corp., 77 F.3d 1353 (11th Cir. 1996); Allen v. R & H Oil & Gas Co., 63 F.3d 1326 (5th Cir. 1995) *and* Sharrow v. General Motors Acceptance Corp., 938 F. Supp. 518 (C.D. Ill. 1996) (punitive damages may be taken into account, but punitive damages are not recoverable in the particular case). *See generally* Christopher J. Willis, *Aggregation of Punitive Damages in Class Action Cases: Will the Real Amount in Controversy Please Stand Up?* 30 LOY. L.A. L. REV. 775 (1997).

"separate and distinct," their claim under the vendor's lien is "common and undivided." The lien is common security for the payment of both notes, and neither *A* nor *B* could sue to enforce the lien without joining the other.[232]

Illustration 2-61. *D*, a citizen of State *Y*, died. *D's* will provided that a certain amount of *D's* personal estate should be held in trust by the *C Bank*, a corporation incorporated and with its principal place of business in State *Y*. The beneficiaries of the trust were *D's* children, *A* and *B*, both citizens of State *X*. *A* and *B* sue *C* in a U.S. District Court. *A* and *B* claimed that the bank breached its fiduciary duty through improper investments. As a result, *C* lost $80,000 of the estate funds. *A* and *B* seek to have *C* restore the $80,000 to the trust. Assume that either *A* or *B* could have brought this action without joining the other. Under these circumstances, the amount-in-controversy requirement is satisfied. In this situation, relief granted to one beneficiary will result in relief to the other, but the amount-in-controversy requirement is not satisfied for this reason. The requirement is satisfied because, even if a single trust beneficiary had sued, the amount in controversy would have been the same as in a multiple plaintiff action. A single plaintiff action would seek to have the principal amount of $80,000 restored to the trust by *C*.[233]

Illustration 2-62. *C*, a citizen of State *Y*, operates a manufacturing plant in State *X*. The plant emits fumes that are damaging separate parcels of land owned by *A* and *B*, both citizens of State *X*. This "nuisance" is reducing the value of *A's* land by $40,000 and of *B's* land by the same amount. If *A* and *B* join in an action against *C* in a U.S. District Court to have the nuisance abated, the amount-in-controversy requirement will not be met. Either *A* or *B* could sue separately to abate the nuisance. If that suit were successful, the relief granted to one plaintiff would also result in relief to the other. However, the amount in controversy in a suit by only one of the plaintiffs would be $40,000, the amount by which that plaintiff's land is being reduced in value by the nuisance.[234]

Illustration 2-63. *C* is *D's* executor. Both *C* and *D* are citizens of State *Y*. *D's* will provided bequests for all of *D's* children except *A* and *B*. *A* and *B* are citizens of State *X*. *A* and *B* sue *C* in a U.S. District Court to set aside *D's* will. They claim that they were omitted from the will by mistake. If this claim is correct, *A* and *B* will each be entitled to a share in *D's* estate in the amount they would have received if *D* had died intestate (without a will)–$40,000 each. However, *A* and *B* may not aggregate their claims to meet the amount-in-controversy requirement. The question whether one child has been omitted from a will by mistake is entirely distinct from the question whether the other has been omitted by mistake. For example, the testator could have mistakenly omitted *A*

---

232. *See* Troy Bank v. G.A. Whitehead & Co., 222 U.S. 39, 41, 32 S. Ct. 9, 9-10, 56 L. Ed. 81, 82-83 (1911).

233. *See* Hyde v. First & Merchants Nat'l Bank, 41 F.R.D. 527 (W.D. Va. 1967); *cf.* Packard v. Provident Nat'l Bank, 994 F.2d 1039 (3d Cir. 1993) (jurisdictional amount not satisfied in suit by beneficiaries of separate trusts managed by trustee).

234. This conclusion is based on the assumption that the amount in controversy is measured from the plaintiff's viewpoint. If the amount is measured from the defendant's viewpoint, and if the cost of abating the nuisance to the defendant exceeds $75,000, the amount-in-controversy requirement would be met in either a single or a multiple party action.

and intentionally omitted *B*. *A* and *B* may assert their claims in separate actions. They need not join in a single suit. In the separate actions, however, the amount in controversy would only be $40,000, and thus they would not be within the diversity jurisdiction.[235]

(iii) The Effect of Counterclaims on the Amount in Controversy

When a counterclaim is involved in the action, the question arises whether the amount of the counterclaim can be aggregated with the plaintiff's claim to meet the amount-in-controversy requirement. This question arises when the plaintiff sues for $75,000 or less, but the defendant possesses a counterclaim that exceeds $75,000. It also arises when the plaintiff sues for $75,000 or less and the defendant possesses a counterclaim that is also less than $75,000, but the plaintiff's claim combined with the defendant's counterclaim exceed $75,000. Because of a peculiar U.S. Supreme Court decision, doubt exists about the extent to which counterclaims can be taken into account in satisfying the jurisdictional amount requirement.[236] This matter is discussed in Chapter 7.[237]

(f) Creating and Destroying Diversity of Citizenship

Because diversity of citizenship is determined in part by reference to an individual's domicile, an individual can change home states to create or destroy diversity of citizenship with a potential adversary. In addition, diversity jurisdiction may be created or destroyed in other ways. For example, a claim owned by one person may be "assigned" to another person to create or destroy diversity. Likewise, the representative of a deceased person's estate may be selected because of the representative's citizenship to create or destroy diversity. To what extent should such attempts to create or destroy diversity be successful?

When creation of diversity is at issue, 28 U.S.C. § 1359 must be considered. Section 1359 deprives federal district courts of subject-matter jurisdiction whenever "any party, by assignment or otherwise, has been improperly or collusively made or joined to invoke the jurisdiction of such court."[238] Acting under this section, the U.S. Supreme Court has concluded that a colorable rather than a real assignment will not result in the creation of diversity jurisdiction.[239] Some federal courts have also held that if the motive for making

---

235. *See* Pinel v. Pinel, 240 U.S. 594, 36 S. Ct. 416, 60 L. Ed. 817 (1916).

236. *See* Horton v. Liberty Mut. Ins. Co., 367 U.S. 348, 81 S. Ct. 1570, 6 L. Ed. 2d 890 (1961). A full understanding of the problem requires a familiarity with federal pleading, motion practice, and counterclaim rules.

237. *See* Chapter 7(F)(2)*(d)* ("Effect of a Counterclaims on the Amount in Controversy") *infra*.

238. 28 U.S.C. § 1359.

239. *See* Kramer v. Caribbean Mills, Inc., 394 U.S. 823, 89 S. Ct. 1487, 23 L. Ed. 2d 9 (1969).

the assignment is primarily to create diversity, this motive can be taken into account as a negative factor in determining whether jurisdiction exists.[240]

Illustration 2-64. A Corp. is incorporated and has its principal place of business in State *X. B Corp.* is a wholly owned subsidiary of *A. B* is incorporated with its principal place of business in State *Y. A* possesses a claim against *C*, a citizen of State *X*, for $100,000. *A* assigns the claim to *B. B* sues *C* in a diversity action in a U.S. District Court. Under these circumstances, a court will presume that the assignment was improper and made primarily to create diversity jurisdiction. Unless *B* can show that the assignment was made for legitimate business purposes, the court will dismiss the action.[241]

* * * * *

In determining whether appointment of a representative will be allowed to create diversity jurisdiction, the federal courts have examined (1) the nature of the representative's duties, (2) the relationship of the representative to the parties being represented, (3) the existence of alternative representatives who are not of diverse citizenship, (4) whether the motive for selecting the representative was the creation of diversity jurisdiction, and (5) other similar factors.[242] In the Judicial Improvements and Access to Justice Act of 1988, Congress amended § 1332 to deal directly with appointments of representatives creating diversity.[243] Section 1332(c)(2) provides that "the legal representative of the estate of a decedent shall be deemed to be a citizen only of the same State as the decedent, and the legal representative of an infant or incompetent shall be deemed to be a citizen only of the same State as the infant or incompetent."[244] Thus, § 1332 now prevents appointments that create diversity jurisdiction in the classes of cases covered by the amendment. It is, therefore, no longer necessary to refer to the factors developed under § 1359 to evaluate the legitimacy of such appointments.[245]

---

240. *See* 15 MARTIN H. REDISH, MOORE'S FEDERAL PRACTICE § 102.19[4] (3d ed. 1999); 6A CHARLES A. WRIGHT ET AL., FEDERAL PRACTICE AND PROCEDURE: CIVIL § 1557 (2d ed. 1990); 14 CHARLES A. WRIGHT ET AL., FEDERAL PRACTICE AND PROCEDURE: JURISDICTION AND RELATED MATTERS § 3639 (3d ed. 1998).

241. *See* Prudential Oil Corp. v. Phillips Petroleum Co., 546 F.2d 469 (2d Cir. 1976).

242. *See, e.g.*, Bianca v. Parke-Davis Pharm. Div., 723 F.2d 392 (5th Cir. 1984); Vaughan v. Southern Ry., 542 F.2d 641 (4th Cir. 1976); Groh v. Brooks, 421 F.2d 589, 595 (3d Cir. 1970).

243. Judicial Improvements and Access to Justice Act of 1988, Pub. L. No. 100-702, § 202, 102 Stat. 4642, 4646 (codified at 28 U.S.C. § 1332(c)(2)).

244. 28 U.S.C. § 1332(c)(2).

245. In addition to the provisions discussed in the text, one other provision of the Judicial Code will influence whether diversity exists in certain actions against insurance companies. Section 1332(c)(1) of Title 28 provides that in a direct action against an insurer to which the insured is not joined as a party defendant, the insurer will be considered a citizen of the state of which the insured is a citizen, as well as any state by which the insurer is incorporated and the state where it has its principal place of business. Thus, if *A*, a citizen of State *X*, is injured in an automobile accident with *B*, a citizen of State *X*, but sues *B's* insurance company, which is incorporated and has its principal place of business in State *Y*, there would be no diversity of citizenship in the action. However, not every action against an insurance company is a direct action within the meaning of § 1332(c)(1). For example, an action by an insured party against the party's own insurer for bad faith refusal of the insurer to indemnify the insured is not a direct action. *See, e.g.,* Searles v. Cincinnati Ins. Co., 998 F.2d 728 (9th Cir. 1993); Warth v. State Farm Fire & Cas. Co., 792 F. Supp. 101 (M.D. Fla. 1992); Kelly v. State Farm Mut. Auto. Ins. Co., 764 F. Supp. 1337 (S.D. Iowa 1991); Kimball Small Properties v. American Nat'l Fire Ins. Co., 755 F. Supp. 1465 (N.D. Cal. 1991); *see also* Rosa v. Allstate Ins. Co., 981 F.2d 669 (2d Cir. 1992) (action by passenger against driver's insurance company not a direct action because no-fault laws prevented driver from being sued directly); *but cf.* Boston v. Titan Indem. Co., 34 F. Supp. 2d 419, 423-24

Amended § 1332(c)(2), however, has not solved all problems related to creation of diversity jurisdiction by appointment of representatives. First, appointments of representatives who are not representatives of estates, infants, or incompetents are not covered by the amendment and will continue to be governed by § 1359. Second, there is some question about who qualifies as the "legal representative of the estate of a decedent" within the meaning of the statute. Third, the normal rules governing pleading and proof of federal subject-matter jurisdiction may cause problems in some cases for the representatives of decedents estates when they are unable to establish the citizenship of decedents. Finally, there is a split of authority over the ability of the representative of an incompetent to change the domicile of the incompetent in a way that creates diversity jurisdiction.[246]

Illustration 2-65. S, a citizen of North Carolina, was electrocuted while working for *D Corp.*, which is incorporated and has its principal place of business in North Carolina. *P* is incorporated and has its principal place of business in Pennsylvania. *P* manufactured a crane upon which *S* was working when *S* was electrocuted. *M*, a citizen of Louisiana, is *S's* mother. *M* was appointed *S's* personal representative. *M* sued *D* and *P* in a U.S. District Court to recover for the wrongful death of *S*. On these facts, a federal district court held that *M* had to be deemed a citizen of North Carolina under 28 U.S.C. § 1332(c)(2). Therefore, diversity of citizenship did not exist between *M* and D.[247]

Illustration 2-66. M is *S's* mother. *M* and *S* are citizens of Minnesota. *F*, a citizen of Illinois, is *S's* father. *S* was killed in an automobile accident with *B*, a citizen of Minnesota. *F* was appointed trustee for *S's* next of kin under the Minnesota wrongful death statute. *F* sued *B* for the wrongful death of *S* in a U.S. District Court, invoking the diversity jurisdiction. *F* claimed to be suing as the trustee of an express trust, not as the legal representative of the estate of a decedent. Thus, *F* contended that *F's* Illinois citizenship, rather than *S's* citizenship, should control in determining diversity of citizenship. A federal district court rejected this argument and held § 1332(c)(2) applied to *F*. As a result, diversity of citizenship did not exist.[248]

(N.D. Mass. 1999) (holding a garnishment proceeding by a judgment creditor to obtain the proceeds of an insurance policy owned by the judgment debtor to be a direct action within the meaning of § 1332(c)(1)).

246. This problem is discussed in Chapter 8(C)*(2)(b)* ("Subject-Matter Jurisdiction Problems in Administering Rule 17(b)") *infra.*

247. *See* Janeau v. Pitman Mfg. Co., No. 92-1923, 1993 WL 280354, 1993 U.S. App. LEXIS 19646 (4th Cir. July 27, 1993) (unpublished opinion); *see also* Fox v. Mandelbaum, No. 92-1352-FGT, 1993 WL 338728, 1993 U.S. Dist. LEXIS 12091 (D. Kan. July 12, 1993); Tilyou v. Carroll, No. CV-92-0750 (CPS), 1992 WL 170916, 1992 U.S. Dist. LEXIS 10204 (E.D.N.Y. July 2, 1992); Koss v. Metropolitan Ins. & Annuity Co., No. 1: CV-92-0177, 1992 U.S. Dist. LEXIS 8534 (M.D. Pa. June 8, 1992); Warth v. State Farm Fire & Cas. Co., 792 F. Supp. 101 (M.D. Fla. 1992); Snyder v. Pleasant Valley Finishing Co., 756 F. Supp. 725 (S.D.N.Y. 1990).

248. *See* Green v. Lake of the Woods County, 815 F. Supp. 305 (D. Minn. 1993). Other problems of interpretation are presented by the use of the word "State" in § 1332(c)(2) when the administrator of the decedent's estate is an alien. At least one court has held that § 1332(c)(2) applies to alien administrators. *See* Geler v. National Westminster Bank USA, 763 F. Supp. 722 (S.D.N.Y. 1991). A parallel problem exists when the decedent is an alien and the administrator is a citizen of a state. One court has also applied § 1322(c)(2) to this situation. *See* Nolan v. Boeing Co., 736 F. Supp. 120 (E.D. La. 1990); *cf.* Jones v. Petty-Ray Geophysical Geosource, Inc., 954 F.2d 1061 (5th Cir.) (holding that the plaintiff, a Texas administrator, could not defeat diversity by using § 1332(c)(2) to assume the citizenship of the decedent, a subject of Great Britain, because

Illustration 2-67. In *Tank v. Chronister*,[249] the Tenth Circuit Court of Appeals held that § 1332(c)(2) does not apply to a person who is authorized by a wrongful death statute to sue for damages, but who is not a representative of the decedent's estate bringing the action for the benefit of the estate. Other federal courts have reached similar results.[250]

Illustration 2-68. R, the representative of the estate of a decedent, D, commences an action against B, a citizen of State Y, on behalf of the estate. R's complaint alleges that D was a citizen of State X. B moves to dismiss on the ground that D was not a citizen of State X. In this situation, at least one federal court has held that the action must be dismissed if R cannot prove that D was a citizen of State X, even if there is no indication that D was a citizen of the same state as B.[251]

* * * * *

When a person changes domiciles to create diversity, it is strained to conclude that someone has been "improperly or collusively made or joined" to create subject-matter jurisdiction within the meaning of 28 U.S.C. § 1359. Generally, if one of the motives for the change of domicile, even the predominant motive, is to create diversity jurisdiction, that motive will not destroy subject-matter jurisdiction as long as the change of domicile is otherwise genuine. In other words, if the party invoking federal jurisdiction actually intends to remain in the new state indefinitely or permanently, subject-matter jurisdiction should exist. However, the fact that the change was made to create diversity can be considered as evidence indicating that the change of domicile is not real—that the party did not intend to remain in the new state indefinitely or permanently. Thus, motive will be examined along with all other factors tending to indicate whether there has been a real, or only pretended, change of domicile.[252]

No statute like 28 U.S.C. § 1359 prohibits parties from destroying diversity jurisdiction by assigning claims. The only formal word from the Supreme Court indicates that devices destroying diversity will be effective.[253] However, some federal courts have reasoned that modern Supreme Court cases

---

the action was filed prior to the effective date of § 1332(c)(2)), *cert. denied*, 506 U.S. 867, 113 S. Ct. 193, 121 L. Ed. 2d 136 (1992).

249. 160 F.3d 597 (10th Cir. 1998).

250. *See, e.g.,* Webb v. Banquer, 19 F. Supp. 2d 649, 652 (S.D. Miss. 1998) (when wrongful death action is brought by beneficiary of the action rather than the court-appointed representative of the estate, § 1332(c)(2) is inapplicable and the relevant citizenship is that of the beneficiary); Winn v. Panolce-Harrison Elec. Coop., Inc., 40 F. Supp. 2d 850 (E.D. Tex. 1997) ("plain language" of § 1332(c)(2) refers to claims under a survival statute, which is created in favor of heirs, legal representative, and estate of a decedent, not a claim under a wrongful death statute for the benefit of survivors).

251. *See* Davis v. Morganti Nat'l, Inc., No. 2:95-CV256, 1997 U.S. Dist. LEXIS 5014 (W.D.N.C. Jan. 27, 1997).

252. *See, e.g.,* Korn v. Korn, 398 F.2d 689 (3d Cir. 1968); O'Brien v. Delta Gas, Inc., 486 F. Supp. 810 (E.D. La. 1980). *See generally* James O. Pearson, Jr., Annotation, *What Constitutes Improper or Collusive Making or Joining of Parties, Under 28 USCS § 1359, for Purpose of Invoking Federal District Court Jurisdiction*, 67 A.L.R. FED. 463 (1984).

253. *See* Mecom v. Fitzsimmons Drilling Co., 284 U.S. 183, 52 S. Ct. 84, 76 L. Ed. 233 (1931). However, *Mecom* involved an appointment to destroy diversity rather than an assignment. Appointments are now largely controlled by 28 U.S.C. § 1332(c)(2). *See Illustrations 2-65* and *2-66 supra.* There is no direct Supreme Court authority on assignments to destroy diversity.

under § 1359 have rendered this traditional view obsolete. These courts have begun to evaluate attempts to destroy diversity of citizenship in the same way they evaluate attempts to create it.[254] If this approach prevails, a court will not give effect to devices used to destroy diversity when the real controversy in a case is between citizens of different states.[255]

In addition, the 1988 amendment to § 1332 discussed earlier will probably prevent the destruction of diversity jurisdiction by the appointment of a nondiverse representative of an estate, an infant, or an incompetent person. On its face, the amendment does not distinguish between appointments designed to create diversity and those designed to destroy diversity. Furthermore, the wording of the amendment has its roots in a 1969 recommendation made by the American Law Institute. That recommendation was explicitly designed to prevent the destruction, as well as the creation, of diversity jurisdiction.[256]

(g) *Judicial Exceptions to Diversity Jurisdiction*

Two judicially created exceptions to diversity jurisdiction exist. The federal courts will not take jurisdiction in suits between citizens of different states involving (1) domestic relations and (2) probate matters. The courts created these exceptions when the statute conferring diversity jurisdiction on the federal courts granted jurisdiction over civil suits ''in law or in equity.'' Because the federal courts believed that the English ecclesiastical courts, rather than the common-law and equity courts, handled domestic relations and probate matters, the federal courts read the statute as excluding these subject areas. Although 28 U.S.C. § 1332(a) now extends diversity jurisdiction to all civil actions, courts have nevertheless continued to read these exceptions into the current statute.[257]

In *Ankenbrandt v. Richards*,[258] the Supreme Court held that the domestic relations exception is only an interpretation of the general diversity statute, not an exception compelled by Article III of the Constitution.[259] However, the Court also held that the exception is limited to actions seeking to grant or modify a divorce, alimony, or child custody decree.[260]

Illustration 2-69. *M* is the mother of *A* and *B*. *M*, *A*, and *B* are all citizens of State *X*. *F*, a citizen of State *Y*, is the father of *A* and *B* and the former spouse of *M*. *M*, acting as the representative of *A* and *B*, sued *F* in a U.S. District

---

254. *See, e.g.*, Miller v. Perry, 456 F.2d 63 (4th Cir. 1972).

255. *See generally* Jerald J. Director, Annotation, *Validity and Effect of Plaintiff's Assignment of Claim or Part Thereof to Prevent Removal of Action from State Court to Federal District Court on Ground of Diversity of Citizenship*, 8 A.L.R. FED. 845 (1971).

256. *See* ALI STUDY OF THE DIVISION OF JURISDICTION BETWEEN STATE AND FEDERAL COURTS § 1301(b)(4), commentary at 117 (1969).

257. *See* ERWIN CHEMERINSKY, FEDERAL JURISDICTION § 5.3.3, at 300-01 (3d ed. 1999); 13B CHARLES A. WRIGHT ET AL., FEDERAL PRACTICE AND PROCEDURE: JURISDICTION AND RELATED MATTERS § 3609, at 462-63 (2d ed. 1984); *see also* Francis M. Dougherty, Annotation, *''Domestic Relations'' Exception to Jurisdiction of Federal Courts Under Diversity of Citizenship Provisions of 28 USCS § 1332(a)*, 100 A.L.R. FED. 700 (1990).

258. 504 U.S. 689, 112 S. Ct. 2206, 119 L. Ed. 2d 468 (1992).

259. *Id.* at 695-96, 112 S. Ct. at 2210-11, 119 L. Ed. 2d at 477.

260. *Id.* at 701-04, 112 S. Ct. at 2213-15, 119 L. Ed. 2d at 481-83.

Court for $100,000 in damages. *M* alleged that *F* physically and sexually abused *A* and *B* while they were in *F's* custody under an order of a state court granting *F* visitation rights with *A* and *B*. The federal district courts have diversity jurisdiction over this action because the action does not seek the granting or modification of a divorce, alimony, or custody decree.[261]

Illustration 2-70. A, a citizen of State *X*, sued *B*, a citizen of State *Y*, in a U.S. District Court seeking enforcement of the judgment of a state court ordering *B* to pay alimony to *A*. *A* seeks payment of $80,000 of back alimony awarded but unpaid under the state judgment. The U.S. District Court has diversity jurisdiction over this action. The domestic relations exception does not apply because the action does not seek an award of alimony or a modification of the state alimony decree. Instead, it seeks enforcement of the state judgment that awarded the alimony.[262]

* * * * *

Under the probate exception to the diversity jurisdiction, the U.S. District Courts cannot probate a will or administer an estate.[263] However, like the domestic relations exception, the district courts do not lack jurisdiction over every action that somehow involves a decedent's estate. The district courts may entertain actions that involve estates as long as the actions do not interfere with state probate proceedings or assume "general jurisdiction of the probate or control of property in a state court's custody."[264] Unfortunately, this rule produces some subtle distinctions between the kinds of relief that courts can and cannot award against executors and administrators.

Illustration 2-71. A, a citizen of State *X*, sued *B*, a citizen of State *Y*, in U.S. District Court. *B* is the executor of *T's* will. *T* is a citizen of State *Y*. *A's* action sought a declaration that certain gifts under *T's* will had lapsed and that *A* was the sole party entitled to share in *T's* residuary estate. In addition, *A* sought

---

261. *See generally id.* at 704, 112 S. Ct. at 2215, 119 L. Ed. 2d at 482; *see also* Stone v. Wall, 135 F.3d 1438 (11th Cir. 1998) (diversity action by father and minor daughter against daughter's maternal grandmother, aunt, and their attorney to recover damages for interference with father's custody of daughter not within domestic relations exception). In United States v. Johnson, 114 F.3d 476 (4th Cir. 1997), the court held in a federal question criminal prosecution that the domestic relations exception is only a judicially implied limit on diversity jurisdiction, but the exception did not limit the federal question jurisdiction. In *Johnson*, the prosecution was under the federal Child Support Recovery Act, 18 U.S.C. § 228.

262. *See* Barber v. Barber, 62 U.S. (21 How.) 582, 16 L. Ed. 226 (1859). *Barber* was cited and discussed with approval in *Ankenbrandt*. *See* 504 U.S. at 693-703, 112 S. Ct. at 2209-14, 119 L. Ed. 2d at 475-82. In two recent cases, federal courts of appeals have allowed parties to use federal declaratory judgment proceedings to adjudicate the federal constitutional validity of prior state divorce judgments. Both opinions rejected the application of the domestic relations exception to the case. *See* Rash v. Rash, 173 F.3d 1376 (11th Cir. 1999); Caty v. Chalker, 142 F.3d 279 (6th Cir. 1998). These cases pose the danger that the declaratory judgment procedure could undermine the policy supporting exclusion of divorce cases from federal jurisdiction.

263. *See* 13B CHARLES A. WRIGHT ET AL., FEDERAL PRACTICE AND PROCEDURE: JURISDICTION AND RELATED MATTERS § 3610, at 480 (2d ed. 1984).

264. *Id.* at 484-87. In some cases, the existence of federal jurisdiction depends on state practice. For example, the probate exception generally applies to disallow federal jurisdiction over actions to set aside a will, but if the state where the will is being probated has given its own courts of general jurisdiction authority over such actions, the federal courts may also entertain them under the diversity jurisdiction. *See id.* at 499-500; Rienhardt v. Kelly, 164 F.3d 1296 (10th Cir. 1999) (standard for determining whether probate exception applies is whether the claim in question could be adjudicated under state law only in state probate court; if so, the exception applies; if not, the exception is inapplicable); *see also Illustration 2-63 supra.*

to obtain an accounting for all the decedent's assets coming into *B's* hands as well as the amount of the residuary estate. *A's* claims under the will exceed $90,000. The district court has jurisdiction to determine whether the gifts have lapsed. The court also has jurisdiction to determine whether *A* is the sole party entitled to the residuary estate under the will. These determinations will bind the executor in the state probate proceeding. However, the district court does not have the power to order an accounting because such an order would directly interfere with an exclusive function of the state probate court.[265]

Illustration 2-72. *A*, a citizen of State *X*, suffered personal injuries in an automobile accident with *C*, a citizen of State *Y*. *C* was killed in the accident. *B*, a citizen of State *Y*, was appointed administrator of *C's* estate. *A* sues *B* in a U.S. District Court to recover $100,000 for the personal injuries *A* received in the accident. The district court has diversity jurisdiction over this action. The action does not directly affect any probate proceeding being conducted for the purposes of distributing *C's* estate. If *A* wins the action, *B* will be bound in *B's* capacity as administrator to pay the judgment out of the proceeds of *C's* estate.

* * * * *

Further exploration of the domestic relations and probate exceptions would not be profitable in this work. Accordingly, the reader is referred to more complete works on federal court procedure for a thorough discussion of the exceptions.[266] Suffice it here to say that the historical foundation for the original exceptions has been seriously questioned,[267] and the current statutory language no longer supports their existence.[268] A suggested modern justification for these exceptions is that domestic relations and probate are matters of peculiar state interest and competence.[269] Some federal practitioners, however, believe that the exceptions continue because federal judges do not like to deal with domestic relations and probate matters.

(h) Correcting Defects in Diversity Jurisdiction and Adjudicating Disputes Over Diversity Jurisdiction

Section 1653 of Title 28 states that "[d]efective allegations of jurisdiction may be amended, upon terms, in the trial or appellate courts."[270] Thus, if the plaintiff makes a mistake in pleading jurisdictional facts, § 1653 allows the

---

265. *See* Waterman v. Canal-Louisiana Bank & Trust Co., 215 U.S. 33, 44-46, 30 S. Ct. 10, 12-13, 54 L. Ed. 80, 84-85 (1909).

266. *See* 13B CHARLES A. WRIGHT ET AL., FEDERAL PRACTICE AND PROCEDURE: JURISDICTION AND RELATED MATTERS §§ 3609-3610 (2d ed. 1984); John F. Winkler, *The Probate Jurisdiction of the Federal Courts*, 14 PROB. L.J. 77, 137-52 (1997); *see also* Ronald I. Mirvis, Annotation, *Modern Status of Jurisdiction of Federal Courts, Under 28 U.S.C.S. § 1332(A), of Diversity Actions Affecting Probate or Other Matters Concerning Administration of Decedents's Estates*, 61 A.L.R. FED. 536 (1983).

267. *See* Spindel v. Spindel, 283 F. Supp. 797 (E.D.N.Y. 1968).

268. *See* Ankenbrandt v. Richards, 504 U.S. 689, 706, 112 S. Ct. 2206, 2217, 119 L. Ed. 2d 468, 485 (1992) (Blackmun, J., concurring).

269. *See* 13B CHARLES A. WRIGHT ET AL. FEDERAL PRACTICE AND PROCEDURE: JURISDICTION AND RELATED MATTERS § 3609, at 461 & n.4 (2d ed. 1984).

270. 28 U.S.C. § 1653.

plaintiff to amend the complaint to allege the facts correctly. However, § 1653 only applies to defective allegations of jurisdiction. The statute does not apply when, under the objective facts, diversity jurisdiction does not actually exist.[271] Under these circumstances, when complete diversity of citizenship does not exist between all the parties to the action, a U.S. District Court can employ Federal Rule 21 to drop a nondiverse party.[272] The U.S. Supreme Court has also held that the courts of appeals may use Rule 21 to drop nondiverse parties. However, the court of appeals may drop such a party only if dismissing the nondiverse party will not prejudice the remaining parties to the action.[273]

Illustration 2-73. *A*, a citizen of State *X*, commences an action in U.S. District Court against *B*, a citizen of State *Y*. *A's* complaint alleges that *B* is a "resident" of State *Y*. This allegation is defective because it alleges *B's* residence, but not *B's* citizenship. Section 1653 of Title 28 authorizes *A* to amend the complaint to allege that *B* is a "citizen of State *Y*." The amendment may be permitted by the U.S. District Court or, if the case reaches the appellate stage before anyone recognizes the defect, by the U.S. Court of Appeals.

Illustration 2-74. *A*, a citizen of State *X*, sues *B*, a citizen of State *Y*, and *C*, a citizen of State *X*, in a U.S. District Court. No diversity jurisdiction exists. Citizens of State *X* are on both sides of the action. This problem cannot be corrected under the authority of 28 U.S.C. § 1653. That statute applies only to defective allegations of jurisdiction. On these facts, no allegation of jurisdiction can save the case. Instead, the district court must drop *C* from the action under Federal Rule 21. If the action reaches the appellate stage before the jurisdictional defect is recognized, the court of appeals must take that action.

*   *   *   *   *

Like all other defects in federal jurisdiction, defects in diversity jurisdiction are raised by the parties or the court on its own motion. However, the procedures employed to determine the existence of diversity can be more elaborate than the procedures employed in other kinds of cases in which federal jurisdiction is questioned.[274] Questions such as the determination of the domicile of an individual or the principal place of business of a corporation cannot be resolved on the face of the pleadings. In determining such questions, the U.S. District Courts have broad discretion over the procedures they employ.

Illustration 2-75. Assume that (a) the plaintiff's complaint alleges diversity of citizenship between plaintiff and defendant; (b) the defendant believes

---

271. *See* Newman-Green, Inc. v. Alfonzo-Larrain, 490 U.S. 826, 109 S. Ct. 2218, 104 L. Ed. 2d 893 (1989).

272. Rule 21 states that "[p]arties may be dropped or added by order of the court on motion of any party or of its own initiative at any stage of the action and on such terms as are just." FED. R. CIV. P. 21. For a party to be dropped, the party must not be indispensable under Rule 19. *See* FED. R. CIV. P. 19; Chapter 8(C)(3) ("Joinder of Persons Needed for Just Adjudication") *infra* for a discussion of Rule 19.

273. *See* Newman-Green, Inc. v. Alfonzo-Larrain, 490 U.S. 826, 832-38, 109 S. Ct. 2218, 2223-26, 104 L. Ed. 2d 893, 902-06 (1989).

274. For instance, in federal question cases, it is usually apparent from the face of the plaintiff's complaint whether an action fits within one of the appropriate categories of cases in which an action will be deemed to arise under federal law. Likewise, in diversity actions, it will be readily apparent when an allegation of diversity jurisdiction is defective or missing from the complaint.

that the plaintiff's allegation of citizenship is incorrect because the plaintiff and defendant are both U.S. citizens domiciled in the same state; and thus (c) no diversity jurisdiction exists. Typically, the plaintiff's allegation of diversity jurisdiction will be put in issue by either a preanswer motion pursuant to Federal Rule 12(b)(1) or a challenge to jurisdiction in the defendant's answer.[275] However, if the lack of diversity should come to the attention of the district court in any other way, the court must raise the issue of subject-matter jurisdiction on its own motion. The court has broad discretion over the manner in which it determines the issue of citizenship. For example, the district judge may decide the question based on the pleadings, affidavits of the parties, and available depositions. The court may hold a full-scale evidentiary hearing or, at its discretion, submit the issue to a jury.[276]

4. Supplemental Jurisdiction

The doctrines of "pendent" and "ancillary" jurisdiction traditionally allowed federal courts to hear claims that were not otherwise within the original jurisdiction of those courts. This expansion of federal jurisdiction occurred only when (1) the pendent or ancillary claims were asserted in an action containing other claims over which the federal courts had original jurisdiction (freestanding claims); and (2) a close factual relationship existed between the freestanding claims and the pendent or ancillary claims.

In 1990, Congress codified and expanded the doctrines of pendent and ancillary jurisdiction. In the Judicial Improvements Act of 1990,[277] Congress added a new § 1367 to Title 28 of the *United States Code*.[278] This new section substitutes the term "supplemental jurisdiction" for the terms "pendent" and "ancillary" jurisdiction. Supplemental jurisdiction has raised several new and difficult interpretative issues for the federal courts. In order to understand these issues and the operation of supplemental jurisdiction statute, it is first necessary to examine the general nature of pendent and ancillary jurisdiction as well as the constitutional and statutory bases of these doctrines. With this background, supplemental jurisdiction as authorized by § 1367 will then be examined in detail.

---

275. *See* Form 19 ("Motion to Dismiss, Presenting Defenses of Failure to State a Claim, of Lack of Service of Process, of Improper Venue, and of Lack of Jurisdiction under Rule 12(b)") and Form 20 ("Answer Presenting Defenses under Rule 12(b)") in the Appendix of Forms following the Federal Rules of Civil Procedure. *See* Chapter 6(D)(3) ("Responding to the Complaint") *infra*.

276. *See* 13B CHARLES A. WRIGHT ET AL., FEDERAL PRACTICE AND PROCEDURE: JURISDICTION AND RELATED MATTERS) § 3612, at 540-41, n.50, 543-44 (2d ed. 1984). In determining whether diversity of citizenship exists in an action, the court must also employ the doctrine of "realignment." This doctrine simply provides that the parties to an action, regardless of how they are aligned in the pleadings, must be arranged according to their true interests in the action. Realignment can result in diversity being preserved where it appears to be absent on the face of the pleadings or destroyed where it appears to be present. Realignment is discussed in Chapter 8(C)(3)*(c) infra* ("Problems of Subject-Matter Jurisdiction, Personal Jurisdiction, and Venue Under Rule 19") in conjunction with practice under Federal Rule 19.

277. Pub. L. No. 101-650, 104 Stat. 5089.

278. *See id.* § 310, 104 Stat. 5089, 5113-14.

(a) The General Nature of Pendent
and Ancillary Jurisdiction

The doctrine of *pendent jurisdiction* applied only to federal question cases. Furthermore, it applied only to original claims asserted by plaintiff(s) against defendant(s) in an action.[279] For example, if a U.S. District Court had federal question jurisdiction over a plaintiff's claim, the doctrine of pendent jurisdiction would allow the court to exercise jurisdiction over all state claims originally asserted by the plaintiff which were *factually related* to the federal claim. Thus, without a federal claim in an action, pendent jurisdiction would not allow a federal court to obtain jurisdiction over a nondiverse party. Jurisdiction over a nondiverse party was restricted by the rule requiring complete diversity of citizenship between the parties under 28 U.S.C. § 1332.[280] Likewise, when diversity of citizenship between the parties was the exclusive basis for jurisdiction, pendent jurisdiction did not allow a federal court to obtain jurisdiction over claims that did not independently meet the jurisdictional amount requirement of § 1332. Jurisdiction over such claims had to be determined by reference to the aggregation rules developed under § 1332.[281] The term "pendent jurisdiction" was thus properly applied only to cases under 28 U.S.C. § 1331 (and other federal question statutes) in which state claims could be asserted because they arose out of the same facts as the federal question claim that conferred subject-matter jurisdiction.

Illustration 2-76. *A*, a citizen of State *X*, sued *B*, also a citizen of State *X*, in a U.S. District Court in State *X*. Assume that *A* asserted two claims against *B*, one under a federal statute and the other based on the same facts, but arising under state law. Because no diversity of citizenship existed between the parties, the district court had no independent basis for exercising subject-matter jurisdiction over the state claim. Nevertheless, because the state and federal claims arose from the same facts, the district court was said to have "pendent jurisdiction" over the state claim—which simply meant that the court's unquestioned jurisdiction over the federal claim under 28 U.S.C. § 1331 gave the federal district court authority to adjudicate the state claim as well.

Illustration 2-77. *A*, a citizen of State *X*, sued *B*, a citizen of State *Y*, and *C*, a citizen of State *X*, in a U.S. District Court in State *X*. *A's* claims arose under state law and were for $1,000,000 in the alternative against *B* and *C*.[282] The

---

279. *Cf.* ERWIN CHEMERINSKY, FEDERAL JURISDICTION § 5.4, at 329 (3d ed. 1999); 1 FEDERAL COURTS STUDY COMMITTEE WORKING PAPERS AND SUBCOMMITTEE REPORTS 546 (1990). The definitions of "pendent" and "ancillary" jurisdiction in the text are generally accurate for the federal courts. However, state courts may use the terms in a different manner. *See* Energy Miss., Inc. v. Burdette Gin Co., 726 So. 2d 1202 (Miss. 1998) (using the term "pendent" jurisdiction to apply to a third-party claim in which a person not originally a party is brought into the action by the defendant).

280. *See* Owen Equip. & Erection Co. v. Kroger, 437 U.S. 365, 98 S. Ct. 2396, 57 L. Ed. 2d 274 (1978).

281. *See* Zahn v. International Paper Co., 414 U.S. 291, 94 S. Ct. 505, 38 L. Ed. 2d 511 (1973); Snyder v. Harris, 394 U.S. 332, 89 S. Ct. 1053, 22 L. Ed. 2d 319 (1969); section C(3)*(e)(ii)* ("Aggregation of Claims with Multiple Parties: the 'Common and Undivided Interest' Test") *supra*.

282. A claim in the alternative asserts that either *B* or *C* is liable to *A* for a specific amount of damages. As long as the specific amount claimed exceeds $75,000, claims in the alternative satisfy the amount-in-controversy requirement.

doctrine of pendent jurisdiction did not allow *A* to join *C* in the action. Pendent jurisdiction applied only to federal question cases. Jurisdiction in *A's* action against *B* and *C* was based solely on diversity of citizenship. Consequently, the complete diversity rule of 28 U.S.C. § 1332 barred jurisdiction over the action. However, if *B* and *C* both had been citizens of State *Y* and *A* had asserted alternative claims against them arising out of the same automobile accident, the complete diversity rule and the amount-in-controversy requirement would have been satisfied. On the other hand, if, instead of asserting claims in the alternative, *A's* claim against *B* was for $80,000 and *A's* claim against *C* was for only $10,000, *A* could not join *C*. The aggregation rules of 28 U.S.C. § 1332 would not allow *C's* claim to be added to *B's* claim to satisfy the jurisdictional amount requirement.[283]

* * * * *

The doctrine of *ancillary jurisdiction* applied to both federal question and diversity actions. However, it applied only to claims coming into an action *after* the plaintiff's original claims, not to those original claims themselves.[284] Thus, ancillary jurisdiction enabled a federal court to exercise subject-matter jurisdiction over claims asserted by the defendant that were closely related to the principal claim in the action, even if no independent subject-matter jurisdiction existed over the claims.

Illustration 2-78. *A*, a citizen of State *X*, sued *B*, a citizen of State *Y*, in a U.S. District Court in State *Y*. *A* asserted a claim against *B* arising under state law for $80,000. *B's* answer contained a compulsory counterclaim against *A* for $1,000, which also arose under state law. The counterclaim did not meet the amount-in-controversy requirement of § 1332, and no other basis for federal subject-matter jurisdiction existed over the claim. Nevertheless, the federal district court could adjudicate the counterclaim. By definition, a compulsory counterclaim arises out of the same transaction or occurrence as the opposing party's claim.[285] Thus, because of the close factual relationship between the plaintiff's claim and the defendant's counterclaim, the court had ''ancillary jurisdiction'' over the counterclaim.

(b) The Constitutional Basis of Pendent and Ancillary Jurisdiction

Pendent and ancillary jurisdiction share a common constitutional basis. When Article III of the Constitution authorized Congress to give federal courts jurisdiction over cases enumerated in § 2 of that Article, it authorized Congress

---

283. Under these circumstances, the ''common and undivided interest'' test is not satisfied because *A* is claiming that *B* damaged *A* in the amount of $80,000 and that *C* inflicted separate damage in the amount of $10,000. Neither defendant is liable for the damage inflicted by the other. *See* subsection *3(e)(ii) supra.*

284. *See* ERWIN CHEMERINSKY, FEDERAL JURISDICTION § 5.4, at 329 (3d ed. 1999); 1 FEDERAL COURTS STUDY COMMITTEE WORKING PAPERS AND SUBCOMMITTEE REPORTS 546 (1990).

285. *See* FED. R. CIV. P. 13(a).

to confer jurisdiction over *entire* cases, not just the "federal" parts of the cases.[286] Therefore, in the case of pendent jurisdiction, when the events giving rise to a federal claim over which the federal district courts have independent subject-matter jurisdiction also give rise to a claim under state law, both claims are considered to be a part of the same case for purposes of Article III.[287] This same theory provides the constitutional basis of ancillary jurisdiction. For example, when a defendant possesses a counterclaim arising out of the same facts as the plaintiff's claim, both claims are considered to be a part of the same case or controversy under Article III of the Constitution.

In *United Mine Workers v. Gibbs*[288] and later cases,[289] the U.S. Supreme Court strongly suggested in dicta that Article III of the Constitution not only permits, but requires, the federal and nonfederal claims to be *factually related—i.e.*, to arise from a "common nucleus of operative fact." These Supreme Court dicta[290] have led to a general belief that federal and nonfederal claims *must* be factually related to satisfy Article III.[291] Nevertheless, caution would seem in order on this question. Nothing in the language of Article III explicitly requires that the scope of a "case" or "controversy" be defined by reference to the factual relationship between the joined claims, as opposed to, for example, the entire relationship between the parties to an action, which may include factually unrelated claims. Furthermore, the history of joinder-of-claims practice supports the theory that a single case may include factually unrelated claims.[292]

---

286. This theory is derived from *Osborn v. Bank of the United States*, discussed in subsection 1*(a)*, *supra*. *See generally* Finley v. United States, 490 U.S. 545, 109 S. Ct. 2003, 104 L. Ed. 2d 593 (1989); ERWIN CHEMERINSKY, FEDERAL JURISDICTION § 5.4, at 327 (3d ed. 1999).

287. *See* United Mine Workers v. Gibbs, 383 U.S. 715, 725, 86 S. Ct. 1130, 1138, 16 L. Ed. 2d 218, 227-28 (1966); Osborn v. Bank of the United States, 22 U.S. (9 Wheat.) 738, 6 L. Ed. 204 (1824).

288. *See* United Mine Workers v. Gibbs, 383 U.S. 715, 725, 86 S. Ct. 1130, 1138, 16 L. Ed. 2d 218, 227-28 (1966).

289. *See, e.g.*, Finley v. United States, 490 U.S. 545, 548, 109 S. Ct. 2003, 2006, 104 L. Ed. 2d 593, 601 (1989) (interpreting *Gibbs* as extending pendent jurisdiction as far as the Constitution permits—*i.e.*, to state claims that arise out of the same facts as federal claims).

290. In United Mine Workers v. Gibbs, 383 U.S. 715, 86 S. Ct. 1130, 16 L. Ed. 2d 218 (1966), the Court held that federal and nonfederal claims arising from the same facts were part of the same Article III case or controversy. However, the Court did not have before it a case in which factually unrelated federal and state claims had been joined. Therefore, the Court's references to Article III of the Constitution technically cannot be read as holding that factually unrelated federal and state claims can never be part of the same case or controversy. In Finley v. United States, 490 U.S. 545, 548, 109 S. Ct. 2003, 2006, 104 L. Ed. 2d 593, 601 (1989), the Court stated that *Gibbs* had extended pendent claim jurisdiction "to the full extent permitted by the Constitution." This statement was also unnecessary to the decision of that case, which, again, did not involve factually unrelated claims. Thus, there is technically no direct authority that Congress lacks the power in an appropriate case to provide for pendent jurisdiction over factually unrelated state claims in a federal question case. Nevertheless, the strong statement in *Finley* may well indicate the Court's current view of the scope of Article III.

291. *See, e.g.*, ERWIN CHEMERINSKY, FEDERAL JURISDICTION § 5.4, at 327 (3d ed. 1999); CHARLES A. WRIGHT, THE LAW OF FEDERAL COURTS § 39, at 239 n.33 (5th ed. 1994) (discussing the constitutionality of removing factually unrelated federal and state claims under 28 U.S.C. § 1441(c)); *see also* 16 MARTIN H. REDISH, MOORE'S FEDERAL PRACTICE §106.21[1] (3d ed. 1999); 13B CHARLES A. WRIGHT ET AL., FEDERAL PRACTICE AND PROCEDURE: JURISDICTION AND RELATED MATTERS § 3567, at 116 (2d ed. 1984).

292. At common law, it was possible to join factually unrelated claims as long as the claims fell within the same form of action. *See* Chapter 7(A) ("Joinder of Claims by Plaintiffs at Common Law and in Equity") *infra*. Equity courts would permit a defendant to set off a claim arising out of a different transaction or occurrence than the plaintiff's claim, and this equitable practice was later extended to the common-law courts by statute.

Historical practice aside, sound reasons may sometimes exist for defining the scope of a case or controversy to include unrelated claims—reasons grounded in policies designed to protect or enhance the operation of federal subject-matter jurisdiction. When such policies can be seen to support a statute, a conferral of jurisdiction over factually unrelated federal and state claims arguably should be held to be within the power of Congress under Article III of the Constitution and the Necessary and Proper Clause.[293] This interpretation of Article III conforms to the flexible approach that the U.S. Supreme Court has traditionally taken to Congress' power to confer jurisdiction on the federal courts.[294]

Illustration 2-79. *A*, a citizen of State *X*, sues *B*, a citizen of State *X*, in a State *X* court. *A* asserts against *B* a claim arising under a federal statute. *A* joins with this federal claim a factually unrelated claim under state law, as permitted by State *X* joinder of claim rules.[295] Congress might wish to allow *B* to "remove"[296] this entire case to federal district court, both to protect the policies supporting the grant of removal jurisdiction under 28 U.S.C. § 1441 *and* to protect the plaintiff, *A*. If *B* is not allowed to remove at least the federal claim, *A* can "trap" *B* in state court by joining a factually unrelated state claim solely to prevent removal under the general removal statutes.[297] If *B* is permitted to remove only the federal claim to federal court, *A* may be treated unfairly. The liberal State *X* joinder of claim rules may be based on a policy of allowing A to adjudicate factually unrelated claims in the same action when it will be convenient for *A* to do so. Thus, *A* may have sound reasons of convenience for joining the unrelated claims and may not be joining them simply to prevent removal by *B*. By permitting *B* to remove the entire case, perhaps with discretion in the district court to remand the state claim if *A* does not have good convenience-based reasons for joining it, the policies of removal jurisdiction in federal question cases can be protected while also avoiding unfairness to the plaintiff.[298]

See Chapter 7(D) ("Joinder of Claims by Defendants at Common Law and in Equity") *infra*. The federal courts have actually entertained set-off claims. *See* Richard A. Matasar, *Rediscovering "One Constitutional Case": Procedural Rules and the Rejection of the* Gibbs *Test for Supplemental Jurisdiction*, 71 CAL. L. REV. 1399, 1474-75 (1983). Under the codes, joinder of factually unrelated claims by the plaintiff is permitted when the claims fall within certain legal categories. *See* Chapter 7(B) ("Joinder of Claims by Plaintiffs under the Codes") *infra*. Similarly, code counterclaim joinder practice permits joinder of factually unrelated contract counterclaims in actions in which the plaintiff's claim is also based on contract. *See* Chapter 7(E) ("Counterclaims and Cross-Claims Under the Codes") *infra*. Early federal joinder-of-claims practice in common-law cases was governed by the conformity acts, which would have incorporated common-law and code joinder rules prevalent in the states. *See* Chapter 1(E)(5) ("Development of Federal Procedure and the Federal Rules of Civil Procedure") *supra*. Furthermore, the Federal Equity Rules specifically recognized the practice of equitable set off. *See* Chapter 7(F) ("Counterclaims and Cross-Claims Under the Federal Rules") *infra*.

    293. *See* U.S. CONST. art. I, § 8, cl. 18.

    294. *See* section C(1)*(a) supra*, where the "ingredient theory" propounded by Chief Justice Marshall in Osborn v. Bank of the United States, 22 U.S. (9 Wheat.) 738, 6 L. Ed. 204 (1824), is discussed; *see also* State Farm Fire & Cas. Co. v. Tashire, 386 U.S. 523, 87 S. Ct. 1199, 18 L. Ed. 2d 270 (1967) (incomplete diversity permitted by the U.S. Constitution).

    295. *Cf.* FED. R. CIV. P. 18.

    296. Removal is discussed in subsection 5 *infra*.

    297. *See* 28 U.S.C. § 1441(a) & (b). These statutes are discussed in subsection 5 *infra*.

    298. *See* 28 U.S.C. § 1441(c). As discussed in subsection 5, *infra*, the policies described in this illustration may, in fact, be the policies that support "separate and independent" claim removal under 28 U.S.C. § 1441(c).

Illustration 2-80. *A*, a citizen of State *X*, sues *B*, a citizen of State *X*, in a federal district court in State *X*. *A* asserts a claim for damages against *B* under a federal statute. *B* possesses a permissive counterclaim against *A* arising under state law. By definition, a permissive counterclaim is one that does not arise out of the same facts as the opposing party's claims.[299] Congress might wish to allow *B* to assert this permissive counterclaim in the action against *A* to avoid potential unfairness to *B*. For example, if *A* is insolvent, refusing to allow *B* to assert *B's* state claim in *A's* federal action might, as a practical matter, mean that *B* will never be able to collect the state claim. Delays in the state courts may mean that *A's* claim will be adjudicated in federal court long before *B's* claim is adjudicated in state court. Furthermore, if *A* wins in federal court and collects a judgment from *B*, the funds collected under the federal judgment may be dissipated before *B* wins a judgment against *A* in state court and can collect it. Allowing *B* to join the permissive counterclaim will thus prevent the exercise of federal jurisdiction over *B* from working an unfairness—a purpose that is arguably a necessary and proper incident of establishing federal jurisdiction.

* * * * *

Because Congress might have legitimate policy reasons for conferring pendent or ancillary jurisdiction over factually unrelated nonfederal claims, it is unwise to conclude that the scope of an Article III "case or controversy" can never be extended to such claims. Instead, the determination whether Congress has such power should await each specific instance in which the issue is directly presented. As discussed in subsections (4)*(d)* and (5), below, the statutory scheme of supplemental and removal jurisdiction may someday present this question directly.

(c) The Statutory Basis of Pendent and Ancillary Jurisdiction

The U.S. Supreme Court has made it clear that the exercise of pendent jurisdiction requires a statutory basis as well as a constitutional one.[300] The Court's earliest modern decisions seemed to stand for the proposition that federal jurisdictional statutes would be presumed to allow the assertion of pendent or ancillary jurisdiction.[301] Although some decisions allowed this presumption to be rebutted,[302] the burden seemed to rest on the party opposing pendent or ancillary jurisdiction to demonstrate that an affirmative statutory policy against the exercise of jurisdiction existed.[303] In *Finley v. United States*,[304] the Court

---

299. *See* FED. R. CIV. P. 13(b).

300. *See* Finley v. United States, 490 U.S. 545, 109 S. Ct. 2003, 104 L. Ed. 2d 593 (1989); Owen Equip. & Erection Co. v. Kroger, 437 U.S. 365, 98 S. Ct. 2396, 57 L. Ed. 2d 274 (1978); Aldinger v. Howard, 427 U.S. 1, 96 S. Ct. 2413, 49 L. Ed. 2d 276 (1976).

301. *See, e.g.,* United Mine Workers v. Gibbs, 383 U.S. 715, 86 S. Ct. 1130, 16 L. Ed. 2d 218 (1966); 1 FEDERAL COURTS STUDY COMMITTEE WORKING PAPERS AND SUBCOMMITTEE REPORTS 549-52 (1990).

302. *See* Owen Equip. & Erection Co. v. Kroger, 437 U.S. 365, 98 S. Ct. 2396, 57 L. Ed. 2d 274 (1978); Aldinger v. Howard, 427 U.S. 1, 96 S. Ct. 2413, 49 L. Ed. 2d 276 (1976).

303. *See* 1 FEDERAL COURTS STUDY COMMITTEE WORKING PAPERS AND SUBCOMMITTEE REPORTS 549-52 (1990).

reversed this burden and required the demonstration of the existence of an affirmative statutory grant of pendent or ancillary jurisdiction before such jurisdiction could be exercised.[305]

Finley involved "pendent party" jurisdiction—*i.e.*, jurisdiction that would, if valid, allow the plaintiff to join a federal claim against one defendant with a factually related state claim in which a separate, nondiverse party is a defendant. While indicating that pendent party jurisdiction would be improper in the absence of an affirmative grant of authority from Congress, the Court in *Finley* did not disturb its previous decisions approving pendent and ancillary claim jurisdiction.[306] Thus, after *Finley*, pendent and ancillary claim jurisdiction was still proper under the general statutory grants of subject-matter jurisdiction in § 1331 and § 1332, even before the recent codification of those doctrines in § 1367.[307]

Illustration 2-81. *A*, a citizen of State *X*, sues *B*, a citizen of State *X*, asserting a claim against *B* under a federal statute. *A* also joins *C*, a citizen of State *X*, in the action. *A* asserts a state claim against *C* arising out of the same facts as *A's* federal claim against *B*. Under *Finley*, this assertion of pendent party jurisdiction over *C* is invalid unless Congress has affirmatively granted authority to the federal courts to hear the claim in the statute that confers federal jurisdiction over *A's* claim against *B*. If the jurisdiction is based on 28 U.S.C. § 1331, the assertion of pendent party jurisdiction is invalid, because § 1331 does not affirmatively authorize pendent party jurisdiction.

Illustration 2-82. On the facts of *Illustration 2-81*, if *A* asserted a state claim against *B* alone arising out of the same facts as *A's* federal claim against *B*, the assertion of pendent jurisdiction over the state claim would be proper, even after *Finley*.

* * * * *

At the statutory level, the policy reasons supporting the doctrine of pendent jurisdiction are different from those supporting ancillary jurisdiction. Pendent jurisdiction is based largely on the fear that if the plaintiff is unable to assert a factually related state claim in a federal question case, the plaintiff might be deterred from asserting the federal claim in federal court.[308] The inability to sue on both claims in federal court would leave the plaintiff with several unacceptable choices. The plaintiff might bring two actions, one in federal court on the federal claim and one in state court on the state claim—with the wasteful

---

304. 490 U.S. 545, 109 S. Ct. 2003, 104 L. Ed. 2d 593 (1989).

305. *See id.*; 1 FEDERAL COURTS STUDY COMMITTEE WORKING PAPERS AND SUBCOMMITTEE REPORTS 552-53 (1990).

306. *See* 1 FEDERAL COURTS STUDY COMMITTEE WORKING PAPERS AND SUBCOMMITTEE REPORTS 553 (1990). The Court's decision in *Finley* also casts doubt upon ancillary *party* jurisdiction because such jurisdiction is not explicitly authorized by § 1331 and § 1332 of Title 28. *See id.* at 554-55. However, given that the Court drew an explicit distinction between "pendent claim" and "pendent party" jurisdiction, it seems far fetched to assert, as some have, that *Finley* also casts doubt on pendent and ancillary claim jurisdiction. *See id.* at 555-56.

307. As discussed in subsection C(4)*(d) infra*, the primary purpose of 28 U.S.C. § 1367 was to overrule *Finley* and thereby render pendent and ancillary party jurisdiction proper.

308. *See, e.g.*, ALI STUDY OF THE DIVISION OF JURISDICTION BETWEEN STATE AND FEDERAL COURTS 209 (1969).

duplication of effort and the danger of issue preclusion[309] that dual proceedings entail.[310]

Alternatively, the plaintiff might choose to bring both claims in state court to avoid the perils and burdens of dual federal and state proceedings. The result of this choice would be that the policies supporting the creation of subject-matter jurisdiction over federal claims would be undermined by the lack of authority in the federal courts to hear the factually related state claim. If the federal courts have exclusive jurisdiction over the federal claim, the plaintiff might even be induced by the inconvenience of dual actions to abandon the federal claim and sue only on the state claim in state court.[311] Such difficulties have traditionally been thought to justify the exercise of pendent jurisdiction over factually related state claims in federal question cases.

In cases originally brought in federal court, the policies supporting ancillary jurisdiction are different than the policies supporting pendent jurisdiction. By definition, ancillary jurisdiction applies only to claims coming into an action after the plaintiff's original claim. Therefore, there will normally be no danger that anyone will be deterred from resorting to federal court by a denial of ancillary jurisdiction in an original action commenced in federal court. For example, in *Illustration 2-78*, above, if ancillary jurisdiction were denied over the defendant's compulsory counterclaim, no one would be deterred from resorting to federal court. The plaintiff who invoked jurisdiction would be delighted that the defendant could not assert the counterclaim and might even file in federal court to obtain the benefit of a denial of ancillary jurisdiction. The defendant has no choice but to be in federal court and can do nothing to get the case to a state court to have both claims tried there.[312]

In cases originally commenced in federal district court, ancillary jurisdiction must be based on policies of fairness to the party asserting the ancillary claim. Again, to use the example of ancillary jurisdiction over compulsory counterclaims in *Illustration 2-78*, if jurisdiction were denied over the counterclaim, the defendant would be subjected to substantial burdens by having to try two

---

309. The danger of issue preclusion exists because the federal and state claims are factually related. Under these circumstances, issues of fact may be adjudicated in the first action that proceeds to judgment. That adjudication also effectively terminates the other action because the losing party will be precluded from relitigating the facts in the second action. Issue preclusion is fully discussed in Chapter 13(C) ("Issue Preclusion") *infra*.

310. *See* ALI STUDY OF THE DIVISION OF JURISDICTION BETWEEN STATE AND FEDERAL COURTS 209 (1969).

311. *Cf. id.* at 209-10; 1 FEDERAL COURTS STUDY COMMITTEE WORKING PAPERS AND SUBCOMMITTEE REPORTS 556-58 (1990).

312. In the discussion of removal jurisdiction in subsection C(5), *infra*, it will be seen that if a defendant is sued in a state court action that the plaintiff could have brought in federal court, the defendant can sometimes remove the action. In cases in which removal is possible, a denial of ancillary jurisdiction to the defendant might deter the defendant from resorting to the right of removal. Thus, in removal cases, the policies supporting pendent and ancillary jurisdiction may conform more closely to each other. However, they do not so conform in actions originally filed in federal court.

actions arising out of the same facts when one would suffice.[313] It is legitimate to interpret the grants of general federal question and diversity jurisdiction to avoid these burdens on the defendant, who, after all, has not chosen the federal forum.

The differing policy bases of pendent and ancillary jurisdiction may make no difference in the way in which the two doctrines operate.[314] However, when interpreting federal jurisdictional grants, it is important to recognize the limits on the kinds of evils that can be prevented by interpreting the grants one way or the other. It is also important to understand the kinds of policies that support pendent and ancillary jurisdiction, to judge whether Congress has legitimate reasons for expanding those doctrines to new kinds of cases.

(d) The Codification of Pendent and Ancillary Jurisdiction

In the Judicial Improvements and Access to Justice Act of 1988, Congress established the Federal Courts Study Committee to study and recommend possible reforms in federal court jurisdiction.[315] In 1990, the Committee published its study, which recommended extensive revisions of federal jurisdiction.[316] The Committee recommended that Congress specifically authorize federal courts "to hear any claim arising out of the same 'transaction or occurrence' as a claim within federal jurisdiction, including claims within federal question jurisdiction, that require the joinder of additional parties, namely, defendants against whom . . . plaintiff has a closely related state claim."[317] In addition to codifying the doctrines of pendent and ancillary claim jurisdiction, this recommendation was designed to overrule the Supreme Court's decision in *Finley v. United States*[318] and thus allow the federal courts to exercise pendent party jurisdiction.[319]

In the Judicial Improvements Act of 1990, Congress responded to the Committee's recommendation by enacting 28 U.S.C. § 1367.[320] Section 1367 combines both pendent and ancillary jurisdiction under the label "supplemental

---

313. In Owen Equip. & Erection Co. v. Kroger, 437 U.S. 365, 376, 98 S. Ct. 2396, 2404, 57 L. Ed. 2d 274, 284 (1978), the Supreme Court hinted at this policy of fairness when it stated that ancillary jurisdiction "typically involves claims by a defending party haled into court against his will, or by another person whose rights might be irretrievably lost unless he could assert them in an ongoing action in federal court."

314. Indeed, it has been said that "the distinction between ancillary and pendent jurisdiction has no functional significance and merely confuses matters." 1 FEDERAL COURTS STUDY COMMITTEE WORKING PAPERS AND SUBCOMMITTEE REPORTS 546 (1990). It would seem wise, however, to bear in mind the different policy bases when legislating in the area, so that a grant or restriction of pendent or ancillary authority will be based on policies designed to support or enhance the operation of the basic grants of federal subject-matter jurisdiction.

315. *See* Judicial Improvements and Access to Justice Act of 1988, Pub. L. No. 100-702, §§ 101-109, 102 Stat. 4642, 4644-45.

316. *See generally* REPORT OF THE FEDERAL COURTS STUDY COMMITTEE (1990).

317. *Id.* at 47; *see also* 1 FEDERAL COURTS STUDY COMMITTEE WORKING PAPERS AND SUBCOMMITTEE REPORTS 559-68 (1990).

318. 490 U.S. 545, 109 S. Ct. 2003, 104 L. Ed. 2d 593 (1989).

319. *Finley* and "pendent party" jurisdiction were discussed briefly in subsection C(4)*(c)*, *supra*. They are also discussed in Chapter 8(C)(4) ("Permissive Joinder of Parties") *infra*.

320. *See* Pub. L. No. 101-650, § 310, 104 Stat. 5089, 5113-14 (codified at 28 U.S.C. § 1367).

jurisdiction." This approach reflects the Federal Courts Study Committee's belief that no functional difference exists between the two doctrines.[321] The Federal Courts Study Committee recommended that Congress provide for supplemental jurisdiction over any claim arising out of the same transaction or occurrence as a claim within federal jurisdiction.[322] However, Congress did not use that recommended language. Instead, Congress enacted the following provision:

> (a) Except as provided in subsections (b) and (c) or as expressly provided otherwise by Federal statute, in any *civil action* of which the district courts have *original jurisdiction*, the district courts shall have *supplemental jurisdiction over all other claims that* are so related to claims in the action within such original jurisdiction that they *form part of the same case or controversy under Article III of the United States Constitution.* Such supplemental jurisdiction shall include claims that involve the joinder or intervention of additional parties.[323]

The failure of Congress to use the language recommended by the Federal Courts Study Committee in § 1367(a) has produced difficult interpretative problems.[324] In addition, serious interpretive problems also exist with both

---

321. *See* 1 FEDERAL COURTS STUDY COMMITTEE WORKING PAPERS AND SUBCOMMITTEE REPORTS 546 (1990).

322. *See* REPORT OF THE FEDERAL COURTS STUDY COMMITTEE 47 (1990). In fact, the working papers of the Committee contained a recommendation as to the precise statutory language that Congress should use:

> (a) Except as provided in subsections (b) and (c) or in another provision of this Title,
> in any civil action on a claim for which jurisdiction is provided, the district court shall
> have jurisdiction over all other claims arising out of the same transaction or occurrence,
> including claims that require the joinder of additional parties.

1 FEDERAL COURTS STUDY COMMITTEE WORKING PAPERS AND SUBCOMMITTEE REPORTS 567 (1990).

323. *See* Judicial Improvements Act of 1990, Pub. L. No. 101-650, § 310, 104 Stat. 5089, 5113-14 (codified at 28 U.S.C. § 1367) (emphasis added). The legislative history of the statute can be found in H.R. REP. NO. 734, 101st Cong., 2d Sess. 27-30 (1990); *Hearing Before the Subcommittee on Courts, Intellectual Property, and the Administration of Justice of the Committee on the Judiciary House of Representatives on H.R. 5381 to Implement Certain Proposals of the Federal Courts Study Committee, and for Other Purposes and H.R. 3898 Civil Justice Reform Act of 1990,* 101st Cong., 2d Sess. 28-32, 87, 92-96, 102, 147, 155-56, 185, 201, 216-17, 224-28, 686-722, 735-36 (1990).

324. The literature on § 1367 is already extensive and reflects the controversy surrounding the drafting and interpretation of the statute. Two early articles discussing the enactment and scope of § 1367 are Thomas M. Mengler et al., *Congress Accepts Supreme Court's Invitation to Codify Supplemental Jurisdiction,* 74 JUDICATURE 213 (1991); David D. Siegel, *Changes in Federal Jurisdiction and Practice Under the New (Dec. 1, 1990) Judicial Improvements Act,* 133 F.R.D. 61, 62-69 (1991); *see also* David D. Siegel, *Practice Commentary,* 28 U.S.C.A. § 1367 (Supp. 1992). Criticism and defense of the new statute erupted in full, but bitter, flower in the pages of the *Emory Law Journal. See* Richard D. Freer, *Compounding Confusion and Hampering Diversity: Life After* Finley *and the Supplemental Jurisdiction Statute,* 40 EMORY L.J. 445 (1991); Thomas D. Rowe, Jr. et al., *Compounding or Creating Confusion About Supplemental Jurisdiction? A Reply to Professor Freer,* 40 EMORY L.J. 943 (1991); Thomas C. Arthur & Richard D. Freer, *Grasping at Burnt Straws: The Disaster of the Supplemental Jurisdiction Statute,* 40 EMORY L.J. 963 (1991); Thomas D. Rowe, Jr. et al., *A Coda on Supplemental Jurisdiction,* 40 EMORY L.J. 992 (1991); Thomas C. Arthur & Richard D. Freer, *Close Enough for Government Work: What Happens When Congress Doesn't Do Its Job,* 40 EMORY L.J. 1007 (1991). Although the primary antagonists in the debate were Professors Arthur and Freer (for the prosecution) and Professors Burbank, Mengler, and Rowe (for the defense), other voices were soon heard. *See* Erwin Chemerinsky, *Rationalizing Jurisdiction,* 41 EMORY L.J. 3 (1992); Rochelle Cooper Dreyfuss, *The Debate Over § 1367: Defining the Power to Define Federal Judicial Power,* 41 EMORY L.J. 13 (1992); Karen Nelson Moore, *The Supplemental Jurisdiction Statute: An Important But Controversial Supplement to Federal Jurisdiction,* 41 EMORY L.J. 31 (1992); Joan Steinman, *Section 1367—Another Party Heard From,* 41 EMORY L.J. 85 (1992).

§ 1367(b), which contains provisions designed to preserve the policies of the diversity jurisdiction, and § 1367(c), which is designed to guide the district court's discretion in retaining and dismissing supplemental claims. The remainder of this subsection explores these problems. This subsection also discusses the American Law Institute's proposed revision of § 1367.

(i) The Scope of Supplemental Jurisdiction: Section 1367(a)

Section 1367 states that "in any civil action of which the district courts have original jurisdiction," the federal district courts shall also have supplemental jurisdiction over "all other claims that are so related to claims in the action within such original jurisdiction" that they form part of the same case or controversy under Article III.[325] This wording suggests an "action-specific" interpretation of § 1367(a).[326] That is, it suggests that before supplemental jurisdiction will be proper, there must *first* be a "civil action"—as opposed to simply a "claim for relief"—within the original jurisdiction of the district courts. Section 1367(a) does not itself confer jurisdiction over the "civil action" that its language seems to require as a prerequisite to supplemental jurisdiction. One must thus refer outside the statute to other jurisdictional provisions, such as 28 U.S.C. § 1331, to satisfy the "action-specific" prerequisite.

This approach seems straightforward enough until one realizes that the *Finley* interpretation governs statutes such as 28 U.S.C. § 1331. *Finley* holds that jurisdictional provisions must explicitly authorize pendent party jurisdiction before such jurisdiction may be permissibly exercised under the provisions.[327] Because § 1331 does not explicitly authorize pendent party jurisdiction, a civil action commenced under § 1331 by a plaintiff who asserts a federal claim against one nondiverse party and a state claim against another nondiverse party is not within the original jurisdiction of the district courts. Thus, if the courts applied the language of § 1367(a) literally, it would defeat the main purpose of the statute—overruling *Finley*.[328]

Useful analyses apart from the immediate combat are found in Marilyn J. Ireland, *Supplemental Jurisdiction Over Claims in Intervention*, 23 N.M. L. Rev. 57 (1993); Denis F. McLaughlin, *The Federal Supplemental Jurisdiction Statute—A Constitutional and Statutory Analysis*, 24 Ariz. St. L.J. 849 (1992); John B. Oakley, *Recent Statutory Changes in the Law of Federal Jurisdiction and Venue: The Judicial Improvements Acts of 1988 and 1990*, 24 U.C. Davis L. Rev. 735 (1991); Joan Steinman, *Supplemental Jurisdiction in § 1441 Removed Cases: An Unsurveyed Frontier of Congress' Handiwork*, 35 Ariz. L. Rev. 305 (1993).

325. 28 U.S.C. § 1367(a).

326. The expressions "action-specific" and "claim-specific" used in the discussion that follows have been adapted from terminology used by Professor John Oakey, the Reporter for the American Law Institute's Federal Judicial Code Revision Project. *See, e.g.*, ALI Federal Judicial Code Revision Project at 51-79 (Council Draft No. 1 1996). The ALI's proposed revision is discussed later in this subsection.

327. *See* the discussion of *Finley* in subsection 4(c) *supra*.

328. Several commentators have expressed fear that § 1367 may be interpreted in accord with its "plain language." *See* Thomas C. Arthur & Richard D. Freer, *Grasping at Burnt Straws: The Disaster of the Supplemental Jurisdiction Statute*, 40 Emory L.J. 963, 986 (1991); Denis F. McLaughlin, *The Federal Supplemental Jurisdiction Statute—A Constitutional and Statutory Analysis*, 24 Ariz. St. L.J. 849, 942 n.480, 973 (1992). However, the statute in its totality cannot be given a "plain meaning" interpretation. Section 1367(a)'s "plain meaning" (as explained above in the text) is that plaintiffs may not join a federal claim against one party with a related state claim against a separate, nondiverse party within the supplemental jurisdiction. Yet,

Illustration 2-83. *A*, a citizen of State *X*, sues *B*, a citizen of State *X*, and *C*, a citizen of State *X*, in a U.S. District Court. *A* asserts a claim against *B* under a federal statute and a factually related claim against *C* under state law. This case is thus like *Finley v. United States*, which 28 U.S.C. § 1367(a) was designed to overrule. However, the wording of § 1367(a), read literally, would not provide for jurisdiction over this action. As a prerequisite to supplemental jurisdiction, § 1367(a) seems to require that there be a "civil action" over which there is original jurisdiction under some provision of the Judicial Code other than § 1367. The action of *A v. B & C* is a "civil action," but no original jurisdiction exists over this civil action under other provisions of the Judicial Code, such as 28 U.S.C. § 1331, because those other provisions do not explicitly authorize pendent party jurisdiction.[329]

* * * * *

Even under a literal interpretation of its language, however, § 1367(a) would not be meaningless. Rather, a literal interpretation would result in a codification of the doctrine of ancillary jurisdiction (including ancillary party jurisdiction). The wording of the statute suggests that once a civil action has been commenced over which there is original jurisdiction, supplemental claims that are sufficiently related to the civil action can then be *added* to the action. The doctrine of ancillary jurisdiction precisely encompassed this situation prior to the enactment of § 1367.[330]

Illustration 2-84. *A*, a citizen of State *X*, sues *B*, a citizen of State *X*, in a U.S. District Court. *A* asserts a claim against *B* under a federal statute. *B's* answer contains a state counterclaim arising out of the same facts as *A's* federal claim. *B* joins *C*, a citizen of State *X*, as an additional party on the state counterclaim as permitted by Federal Rules 13(h) and 20. Under a literal reading of § 1367(a), supplemental jurisdiction would exist over *B's* counterclaim. *A v. B* is a civil action over which there is original jurisdiction under 28 U.S.C. § 1331. Once such an action exists, the last clause of § 1367(a)'s first sentence allows the assertion of an additional claim (*B's* counterclaim) that is part of the same Article III case or controversy as the civil action over which there is original jurisdiction.[331] The second sentence of § 1367(a) permits the joinder of

---

as demonstrated in subsection 4*(d)(ii) infra*, § 1367(b) is specifically aimed at exempting from § 1367(a) multiple claims by plaintiffs against nondiverse parties in diversity actions. If § 1367(a) does not confer supplemental jurisdiction over such claims, § 1367(b) is unnecessary.

329. There is, of course, a claim for relief in the action over which the district courts would have original jurisdiction if the claim were asserted alone—the claim by *A* against *B*. However, the language of § 1367, read literally, would not allow supplemental jurisdiction simply because there is a claim in the case over which the district courts would have original jurisdiction. Rather, the language literally requires a "civil action" over which there is original jurisdiction. The action by *A v. B & C* does not qualify as such a civil action. Thus, the initial prerequisite for the operation of § 1367(a) does not seem to be present. *See* James E. Pfander, *Supplemental Jurisdiction and Section 1367: The Case for a Sympathetic Textualism*, 148 U. PA. L. REV. 109, 142 (1999) (agreeing with this text that a literal reading of § 1367 would not overrule *Finley*).

330. In subsection 4*(a)*, *supra*, ancillary jurisdiction was described as encompassing claims that come into the action after the plaintiff's original claim or claims.

331. The relevant language of the sentence confers supplemental jurisdiction "over all other claims that are so related to claims in the action within such original jurisdiction that they form part of the same case or controversy under Article III of the United States Constitution." 28 U.S.C. § 1367(a).

C as an additional party on the supplemental claim.[332] Thus, § 1367(a), read literally, would codify and preserve ancillary party jurisdiction.[333]

* * * * *

Furthermore, the doctrine of pendent claim jurisdiction would continue to operate as an interpretation of statutes such as 28 U.S.C. § 1331, because *Finley* did not purport to disturb the interpretation of statutes permitting pendent claim jurisdiction.

Illustration 2-85. *A*, a citizen of State *X*, sues *B*, a citizen of State *X*, in a U.S. District Court. *A* asserts a claim against *B* under a federal statute and a factually related state claim. Pendent claim jurisdiction exists over *A's* state claim against *B* under 28 U.S.C. § 1331 without the need to resort to 28 U.S.C. § 1367(a). As discussed in subsection 4*(c)*, above, *Finley* does not affect the validity of pendent *claim* jurisdiction.

* * * * *

Because a literal interpretation of 28 U.S.C. § 1367(a) would defeat the primary purpose of the statute, which was to overrule *Finley v. United States* and authorize pendent party jurisdiction, the statute should not be read literally. Instead, it should be interpreted as if it read ''in any civil action in which a claim is asserted over which the district courts would have original jurisdiction if that claim were asserted alone, the district courts shall have supplemental jurisdiction over all other claims that are so related to claims within the original jurisdiction that they form part of the same case or controversy under Article III.'' This interpretation conforms to the legislative history of the statute, even though it does not conform to its wording.[334]

Since the enactment of § 1367, the vast majority of federal courts have interpreted § 1367(a) in this ''claim specific'' fashion.[335] In *City of Chicago v.*

---

332. The second sentence provides that ''[s]uch supplemental jurisdiction shall include claims that involve the joinder or intervention of additional parties.'' *Id.*

333. The language of § 1367(a) would technically apply to a case in which the plaintiff first commenced a ''civil action'' against one nondiverse defendant on a federal claim and then later amended the complaint to add a factually related state claim against another nondiverse defendant. There would be original jurisdiction over the first ''civil action'' under 28 U.S.C. § 1331, and the later state claim would then be added to the action in a manner similar to an ancillary claim. However, in this kind of situation the courts have traditionally insisted that the amended complaint satisfy the same jurisdictional standards as the original complaint. To do otherwise would be to invite evasion of jurisdictional requirements by the simple expedient of amendments adding new defendants to an action. *See, e.g.,* Sta-Rite Indus., Inc. v. Allstate Ins. Co., 96 F.3d 281 (7th Cir. 1996); Wellness Community-Nat'l v. Wellness House, 70 F.3d 46 (7th Cir. 1996); *cf.* R.F. Barron Corp. v. Nuclear Fields (Austl.) Pty. Ltd., No. 91 C 7610, 1992 U.S. Dist. LEXIS 9612 (N.D. Ill. July 6, 1992) (diversity jurisdiction cannot be created where there is none by the simple expedient of amendments adding nondiverse defendants to the action).

334. *See* H.R. REP. NO. 734, 101st Cong., 2d Sess. 28-29 (1990) (''[Section 1367(a)] generally authorizes the district court to exercise jurisdiction over a supplemental claim whenever it forms part of the same constitutional case or controversy as the claim or claims that provide the basis of the district court's original jurisdiction'').

335. Many courts simply transform the language of § 1367(a) to eliminate the expression ''civil action'' and substitute the term ''claim'' or an equivalent expression. *See, e.g.,* Detroit Edison Co. v. Mich. Dep't of Envtl. Quality, 29 F. Supp. 2d 786 (E.D. Mich. 1998) (once district court has original jurisdiction over a claim, it may exercise supplemental jurisdiction over all other claims that are so related to that claim as to form part of the same case or controversy under Article III); Miller Parts Co. v. Joe Self Chevrolet, Inc., No. 93-1035-PFK, 1993 WL 246071, 1993 U.S. Dist. LEXIS 9700 (D. Kan. June 14, 1993) (§ 1367 gives district courts

International College of Surgeons,[336] The U.S. Supreme Court indirectly endorsed this view. In *City of Chicago*, the defendants removed state actions to federal court in which the plaintiffs were seeking judicial review of decisions made by the Chicago Landmark Commission. The actions contained claims that certain city ordinances violated the federal and state constitutions and also sought judicial review of the Landmarks Commission's decisions under the ordinances on the record of the Commission, a type of review known as "deferential review." The U.S. District Court to which the action was removed ruled in favor of the City, but the Seventh Circuit reversed.

The Seventh Circuit held that the district court did not have subject-matter jurisdiction over an action for deferential review of a state agency decision. The Seventh Circuit reasoned that such review involved an appellate function that is inconsistent with the function of a court of original jurisdiction. Thus, the action was not a "civil action" within the district court's "original jurisdiction" under the removal statute, 28 U.S.C. § 1441(a). The U.S. Supreme Court reversed. It held that the district court had original jurisdiction over the federal claims and could exercise supplemental jurisdiction over the state claims under § 1367(a). The Court's language seemed to adopt the claim-specific interpretation of § 1367(a) described above:

> [O]nce the case was removed, the District Court had original jurisdiction over ICS's claim arising under federal law, and thus could exercise supplemental jurisdiction over the accompanying state law claims so long as those claims constitute "other claims that . . . form part of the same case or controversy." 28 U.S.C. § 1367(a), we think it's clear that they do.[337]

Despite the suggestive language of the *City of Chicago* opinion, it would be premature to conclude that the court has adopted a "claim-specific" interpretation of § 1367(a). *City of Chicago* was essentially a pendent-claim case.[338] As noted above,[339] § 1367(a) did not alter the status of pendent claim

---

supplemental jurisdiction over all state claims which are related to claims over which the court has original jurisdiction); Leith v. Lufthansa German Airlines, 793 F. Supp. 808 (N.D. Ill. 1992) (once jurisdiction over the main claim is established, the statute mandates that the district court shall have supplemental jurisdiction over all other claims that are so related to claims in the action within such original jurisdiction as to form part of same case or controversy under Article III); *see also* David D. Siegel, *Changes in Federal Jurisdiction and Practice Under the New (Dec. 1, 1990) Judicial Improvements Act*, 133 F.R.D. 61, 65 (1991) (under § 1367(a), as long as a district court has original jurisdiction of a claim, it shall have supplemental jurisdiction over the related claims). Other courts simply ignore the significance of the phrase "civil action" and interpret the statute in a claim-specific fashion. *See, e.g.*, Stromberg Metal Works, Inc. v. Press Mechanical, Inc., 77 F.3d 928 (7th Cir. 1996) (§ 1367(a) provides that district courts shall have supplemental jurisdiction over all other claims that are so related to claims in the action within such original jurisdiction that they form part of the same case or controversy within Article III); Free v. Abbott Labs., 51 F.3d 524 (5th Cir. 1995) (§ 1367 grants district courts jurisdiction over related claims generally).

   336. 522 U.S. 156, 118 S. Ct. 523, 139 L. Ed. 2d 525 (1997).

   337. *Id.* at 165, 118 S. Ct. at 530, 139 L. Ed. 2d at 535-36.

   338. Although there were two plaintiffs and multiple defendants in the case, which involved several consolidated actions, the plaintiffs were asserting the same federal and state claims in both actions, and the court treated the defendants as a single entity, designating them "the City." *See id.* at 161, 118 S. Ct. at 527, 139 L. Ed. 2d at 533. Thus, the case is indistinguishable from a single-plaintiff, single-defendant case.

   339. *See* subsection 4(d) *supra*.

jurisdiction, which operates the same way after its codification in § 1367(a) as it did before codification. Putting it differently, in simple pendent-claim cases, there is a "claim" within the jurisdiction of the district courts under § 1331, and there is also a "civil action" within federal jurisdiction under § 1331. Therefore, whether a "claim-specific" or "action-specific" interpretation of § 1367 is adopted, supplemental jurisdiction exists in pendent-claim cases.

Illustration 2-86. *A*, a citizen of State *X*, sues *B*, a citizen of State *X*, in a U.S. District Court of State *X*. *A* asserts a claim for relief under a federal statute and a factually related claim for relief under state law. *A's* action against *B* is an example of pendent-claim jurisdiction. If § 1367(a) requires the entire "civil action" that *A* has commenced against *B* to be within the original jurisdiction of the district court under some provision of the Judicial Code other than § 1367(a), the requirement is satisfied. Under the Supreme Court's interpretation of 28 U.S.C. § 1331 existing before § 1367(a) was enacted, there is original jurisdiction over *A's* entire action.[340] Of course, if § 1367(a) only requires a federal claim over which there would be original jurisdiction in order to confer supplemental jurisdiction over *A's* related state claim against *B*, that requirement is also satisfied: *A's* federal claim would be within the original jurisdiction of the district court under 28 U.S.C. § 1331 if were asserted alone.

* * * * *

A truly authoritative determination of whether § 1367(a) embodies an "action-specific" or a "claim-specific" interpretation will have to await a pendent-party jurisdiction case. As noted above,[341] § 1367(a) was specifically designed to overrule *Finley v. United States*. The *Finley* rule governs the exercise of pendent party jurisdiction under § 1331 and other federal question jurisdiction statutes.[342] Therefore, pendent party cases directly present the "action-specific-claim-specific" question.

Thus far, only a few federal courts have noted that § 1367's language requires original jurisdiction over a "civil action" as a prerequisite to the exercise of supplemental jurisdiction, and, for the most part, those cases have not recognized the full implications of the statute's wording.[343] Furthermore, many cases in which the interpretive issue might have been raised have simply ignored the significance of the "civil action" language of the statute.[344] A notable

---

340. *See* subsection 4*(c)*, *Illustration 2-82, supra.*

341. *See* subsection 4*(d)*, text preceding subsection 4*(d)(i), supra.*

342. *See Illustration 2-81, supra.*

343. *See* Moore v. Rosenthal & Schanfield, P.C., No. 92 C 7460, 1992 WL 346422, 1992 U.S. Dist. LEXIS 17874 (N.D. Ill. Nov. 19, 1992) ("By its own terms the statute applies only 'in any civil action of which the district courts have original jurisdiction' and only then may the case-or-controversy claims be added in the action"); ZB Holdings, Inc. v. White, 144 F.R.D. 42, 47 (S.D.N.Y. 1992) ("The fundamental question for this [c]ourt to resolve is what the term 'original jurisdiction' means in . . . this statute. . . . This [c]ourt understands 'original jurisdiction' to mean jurisdiction in the first instance over a viable lawsuit, without regard to parties to be joined later. Stated differently, the term 'original jurisdiction' presupposes a viable lawsuit"); *cf.* Noble v. White, 996 F.2d 797, 799 (5th Cir. 1993) (district court has supplemental jurisdiction over state claims that are part of the same case or controversy over which the district court has original jurisdiction).

344. The interpretive issue would be central to the typical pendent parties jurisdiction case. *See, e.g.,* Stromberg Metal Works, Inc. v. Press Mechanical, Inc., 77 F.3d 928 (7th Cir. 1996); Free v. Abbott Labs., 51 F.3d 524 (5th Cir. 1995); Godfrey v. Perkin-Elmer Corp., 794 F. Supp. 1179 (D.N.H. 1992); Arnold v.

exception is the decision of the Tenth Circuit in *Leonhardt v. Western Sugar Co.*[345] In *Leonhardt*, the Tenth Circuit was reacting to certain decisions of the Fifth and Seventh Circuits under Federal Rule 23 and 28 U.S.C. § 1367(b), discussed in subsection *(ii)* and Chapter 8, below.[346] These decisions interpreted § 1367(b) expansively, but ignored the wording of § 1367(a). The Tenth Circuit responded, as follows:

> In our view, a literal and textually faithful reading of § 1367(a) leads to the opposite conclusion from that of the Fifth and Seventh Circuits. Section 1367(a) specifically addresses "any civil action of which the district courts have *original jurisdiction.*" . . . It then provides for *supplemental jurisdiction* over transactionally related claims. Section 1332 is what confers original jurisdiction over diversity cases and it expressly requires that the "matter in controversy exceed[] the sum or value of $75,000." . . . Thus, Congress in § 1367(a) expressly excepted claims brought under § 1332 and its well-understood definition of "matter in controversy." . . .[347]

The court's literal reading of § 1367(a) corresponds closely to the literal reading described in the text, above. Furthermore, because *Leonhardt* was decided after the U.S. Supreme Court's decision in *Steel Co.*, it is authority for the proposition that an action-specific interpretation of § 1367(a) is still viable in pendent-party cases. However, neither the Tenth Circuit in *Leonhardt* nor any other federal decision has yet acknowledged that a literal interpretation of § 1367(a) would undermine the central purpose of the statute to overrule the Supreme Court's *Finley* decision and codify the doctrine of pendent-party jurisdiction.[348]

Kimberly Quality Care Nursing Serv., 762 F. Supp. 1182 (M.D. Pa. 1991).

345. 160 F.3d 631 (10th Cir. 1998).

346. *See* Stromberg Metal Works, Inc. v. Press Mechanical, Inc., 77 F.3d 928 (7th Cir. 1996); Free v. Abbott Labs., 51 F.3d 524 (5th Cir. 1995); Chapter 8(D) ("Special Joinder Devices") *infra*.

347. 160 F.3d at 640. Out of caution, the court went on to examine the legislative history of § 1367, which it found to support the same result produced by its textual analysis. *Leonhardt* was followed by the Third Circuit Court of Appeals in Meritcare, Inc. v. St. Paul Mercury Ins. Co., 166 F.3d 214 (3d Cir. 1999); *see also* City of San Francisco v. Hartford Life Ins. Co., No. C99-0225 CRB ARB, 1999 WL 354522 (N.D. Cal. May 17, 1999).

348. Likewise, a literal interpretation of § 1367(a) would collide with the language of § 1367(b). This point is explored in subsection *(ii)*, *infra*, and in Chapter 8 in conjunction with an examination of jurisdictional problems under the multiple-party joinder provisions of the Federal Rules of Civil Procedure. Even though the federal courts have generally interpreted § 1367(a) in a nonliteral, or "claim-specific," fashion, they have not altogether ignored the phrases "in any civil action" and "in the action" in the statute. They have universally insisted that supplemental jurisdiction can only be exercised over state claims joined in the same action with federal claims, as opposed to state claims that are factually related to federal claims, but which are asserted in a completely separate state proceeding that the defendant is trying to remove to federal court. *See, e.g.,* Orltof v. Silver Bar Mines, 111 F.3d 85 (9th Cir. 1997); Ahern v. Charter Township, 100 F.3d 451 (6th Cir. 1996); George v. Borden Chems. & Plastics Operating Ltd. Partnership, 960 F. Supp. 92 (M.D. La. 1997); Emerson Power Transmission Corp. v. Roller Bearing Co. of Am., 922 F. Supp. 1306 (N.D. Ind. 1996); *In re* Estate of Tabas, 879 F. Supp. 464 (E.D. Pa. 1995); Veeder v. Omaha Tribe, 864 F. Supp. 889 (N.D. Iowa 1994); Halt v. Lockheed Support Sys., Inc., 835 F. Supp. 325 (W.D. La. 1993); Zewe v. Law Firm of Adams & Reese, 852 F. Supp. 516 (E.D. La. 1993).

It is possible that Congress may again address the question of supplemental jurisdiction and resolve the "claim-specific-action-specific" dilemma. The American Law Institute has proposed a revision of § 1367 that would explicitly make the supplemental jurisdiction statute "claim-specific":

§ 1367. Supplemental jurisdiction

(a) *Definitions*. As used in this section:

(1) A "freestanding" claim means a claim for relief that is within the original jurisdiction of the district courts independently of this section.

(2) A "supplemental" claim means a claim for relief, not itself freestanding, that is part of the same case or controversy under Article III of the Constitution as a freestanding claim that is asserted in the same civil action.

. . . .

(b) *General grant of supplemental jurisdiction.* Except as provided by subsection (c) or as otherwise expressly provided by statute, a district court shall have original jurisdiction of all supplemental claims, including claims that involve the joinder or intervention of additional claiming or defending parties.[349]

If Congress follows the ALI's recommendation and adopts this revision, § 1367(a) would, through introduction of the concept of a freestanding claim, make the operation of supplemental jurisdiction depend explicitly on the presence in a federal action of a claim over which the federal courts would have subject-matter jurisdiction independently of § 1367. Supplemental claims would, by definition, be claims asserted in the same civil action as a freestanding claim, but over which the district courts would not have subject-matter jurisdiction independently of § 1367—*i.e.*, under some other provision of the Judicial Code. If these supplemental claims are part of the same Article III case or controversy as a freestanding claim, § 1367(b) would confer jurisdiction over them. This revision would thus confirm the approach of a majority of federal courts, discussed above, which have read current § 1367(a) as "claim-specific."[350]

In addition to the question whether § 1367(a) should be read literally or in a claim-specific fashion, the language in the statute providing for supplemental jurisdiction over claims that fall within "the same case or controversy under Article III of the Constitution" may cause practical difficulties. Congress believed that the "same transaction or occurrence" test proposed by the Federal Courts Study Committee was coextensive with the scope of an Article III case or controversy. The portion of the House Report explaining 28 U.S.C. § 1367 stated:

---

349. ALI FEDERAL JUDICIAL CODE REVISION PROJECT 1-2 (Tent. Draft No. 2 1998).

350. The ALI has made other suggestions for improvements in § 1367. These will be discussed as they become pertinent, *infra. See also* Symposium, *A Reappraisal of the Supplemental Jurisdiction Statute: Title 28 U.S.C. § 1367*, 74 IND. L.J. 1 (1998). One contributor to the symposium has objected to the process whereby § 1367 and other jurisdictional statutes are being made longer and more complex; instead, he argues that the statute should be simplified and the federal courts given more discretion to determine whether supplemental claims should be adjudicated. *See* David L. Shapiro, *Supplemental Jurisdiction: A Confession, An Avoidance, and a Proposal,* 74 IND. L.J. 211 (1998).

This section [28 U.S.C. § 1367] implements a recommendation of the Federal Courts Study Committee . . . . The doctrines
of pendent and ancillary jurisdiction, in this section jointly
labeled supplemental jurisdiction, refer to the authority of the
federal courts to adjudicate, without an independent basis of
subject matter jurisdiction, claims that are so related to other
claims within the district court's original jurisdiction that they
form part of the same case or controversy under Article III of the
United States Constitution.[351]

Federal and nonfederal claims arising from the same transaction or
occurrence *are* unquestionably part of the same Article III case or controversy.
It also *may be* true that the scope of an Article III case or controversy extends no
further than freestanding and supplemental claims arising out of the same transaction or occurrence. Subsection 4*(b)*, above, discussed U.S. Supreme Court
decisions containing pronouncements to this effect. However, subsection 4*(b)* also
noted that (1) no U.S. Supreme Court decision has ever directly *held* that
factually unrelated federal and nonfederal claims fall outside the same Article III
case or controversy; (2) Article III of the Constitution does not contain any
explicit direction that the scope of a constitutional case or controversy be defined
by reference to the factual relatedness of the claims asserted in the action; (3) the
history of joinder-of-claims practice at common law, in equity, and under the
Codes supported the theory that unrelated claims can be part of the same case;
and (4) Congress might have good reasons, linked to policies designed to protect
or enhance the operation of basic federal subject-matter jurisdiction grants, to
define the scope of a case or controversy to include factually unrelated claims.
These reasons suggest that Article III and the Necessary and Proper Clause should
be interpreted to allow Congress to provide for jurisdiction over nonfederal claims
joined with factually unrelated federal claims in some cases.[352]

Ironically, if the constitutional power does exist to provide for jurisdiction
over factually unrelated federal and state claims, § 1367(a), read literally, would
constitute an exercise of that power. The language of the statute would allow a
plaintiff asserting a federal claim in an action to join a factually unrelated state
claim against the same party, even in the absence of diversity of citizenship, and
even, perhaps, if the state claim required the joinder of additional nondiverse
parties as defendants. Likewise, a defendant sued on a federal claim could assert
a factually unrelated counterclaim against the plaintiff arising under state law,
even in the absence of diversity of citizenship, and even, perhaps, if the
counterclaim required the joinder of additional nondiverse parties.

---

351. H.R. Rep. No. 734, 101st Cong., 2d Sess. 27-28 (1990). In a later passage the Report stated that
§ 1367(a) "generally authorizes the district court to exercise jurisdiction over a supplemental claim whenever
it forms part of the same constitutional case or controversy as the claim or claims that provide the basis of the
district court's original jurisdiction." *Id.* at 28-29. In a footnote appended to this sentence, the Report added:
"In so doing, subsection (a) codifies the scope of supplemental jurisdiction first articulated by the Supreme
Court in *United Mine Workers v. Gibbs* . . . ." *See id.* at 29 n.15.

352. *See* subsection (4)*(b)* & *Illustrations 2-79* and *2-80, supra.*

Nevertheless, the legislative history of § 1367 demonstrates that Congress did not intend to authorize jurisdiction over factually unrelated claims when it used the same Article III case or controversy language in 28 U.S.C. § 1367(a). Instead, Congress was under the (probably) mistaken impression that Article III requires a factual relationship between claims before they may be deemed part of the same case or controversy. The question now is whether there is any reasonable way to interpret the statute to prevent the results described. One way would be for the Supreme Court to simply recognize that while Article III sometimes permits Congress to provide for jurisdiction over factually unrelated federal and nonfederal claims, Congress did not actually intend to do so in § 1367(a). Rather, Congress intended to provide for supplemental jurisdiction only over claims that arise out of the same transaction or occurrence as the claims in the action that are within original federal jurisdiction. The only real issue is whether the courts should disregard the clear language of the statute in favor of a construction based on legislative intent.[353]

Fortunately, a time-honored practice of disregarding both the language and legislative history of jurisdictional provisions exists when otherwise "inconvenient" results would occur. As noted earlier, the language of the general federal question statute seems to confer the full scope of the federal question jurisdiction permitted by Article III of the Constitution. However, the Supreme Court has never interpreted the language of the statute this broadly because of the enormous amount of litigation that such an interpretation would produce in the federal courts.[354] Furthermore, in the case of the general federal question statute, the legislative history indicates that Congress intended to confer the full scope of the federal question jurisdiction permissible under Article III.[355] In contrast, the language and legislative history of 28 U.S.C. § 1367(a) point in different directions. Therefore, it is even more justifiable for the courts to disregard the language of § 1367(a) than it has been for them to disregard the language of 28 U.S.C. § 1331(a).[356]

In fact, the existing court decisions under § 1367 almost all agree that a factual relationship between claims is essential for supplemental jurisdiction to exist.[357] The decisions do not always reveal whether the courts believe this

---

353. Unfortunately, the American Law Institute's proposed revision of § 1367 will not, even if adopted by Congress, solve this problem. The revision continues to use the "Article III case or controversy" language, rather than specifying the degree of factual relationship that must exist between freestanding and supplemental claims.

354. *See* subsection 1 ("Cases Arising Under the Constitution and Laws of the United States") *supra.*

355. *See* CHARLES A. WRIGHT, THE LAW OF FEDERAL COURTS § 17, at 102-03 (5th ed. 1994); Ray Forrester, *Federal Question Jurisdiction and Section 5*, 18 TUL. L. REV. 263, 276-78 (1943).

356. In addition, as later discussed in subsection 5, *infra*, this construction of § 1367(a) solves a knotty problem that Congress created when it enacted that section and simultaneously amended 28 U.S.C. § 1441(c)–the separate and independent claim removal provision–to apply only in federal question cases.

357. At this writing, only one case has indicated that factually unrelated claims will be within the district courts' supplemental jurisdiction under § 1367(a). *See* Wesley v. General Motors Acceptance Corp., No. 91 C 3368, 1991 WL 169204, 1991 U.S. Dist. LEXIS 11745 (N.D. Ill. Aug. 20, 1991) (permissive counterclaim not arising out of the same transaction or occurrence as plaintiff's claim is within supplemental jurisdiction); *cf.* Winn v. North Am. Philips Corp., 826 F. Supp. 1424 (S.D. Fla. 1993) (court assumes that common nucleus of operative fact test and § 1367(a) test are different). Numerous courts have dismissed claims that they perceived to be lacking the necessary factual relationship with claims within the original jurisdiction. *See, e.g.*, Hudson result is compelled by the Constitution or only the statute. However, they appear to be premised on the U.S. Supreme Court dicta discussed earlier, which stated that a factual relationship between federal and nonfederal claims is necessary to satisfy Article III.[358] Therefore, until the Supreme Court reviews a case in which the Article III and statutory issues are directly presented, the prevailing view will be, contrary to this text, that both the Constitution and the statute necessitate a factual relationship.

Assuming that the Supreme Court concludes that some factual relationship between freestanding and supplemental claims is necessary to satisfy Article III (or § 1367(a)), how close must the factual relationship be? Many federal courts have held a "loose" factual relationship between the federal and nonfederal claims to be sufficient to satisfy the "common nucleus of operative fact" test of the *Gibbs* case.[359] However, other courts have required a closer factual relationship, rejecting supplemental jurisdiction over state claims simply because they arise out of the same employer-employee relationship when they involve no overlapping facts.[360] They have also rejected supplemental jurisdiction over non-overlapping state claims that are part of a continuing, festering dispute between the parties.[361] A few cases have even rejected supplemental jurisdiction when some facts overlap between the federal and state claims and the claims arise out of the same events.

Illustration 2-87. In *Doe v. Neal*,[362] a police officer kidnapped and raped the plaintiff in a parking lot. The plaintiff sued the city and a number of

---

v. Delta Airlines, Inc., 90 F.3d 451 (11th Cir. 1996), *cert. denied*, 519 U.S. 1149, 117 S. Ct. 1082, 137 L. Ed. 2d 217 (1997) (state breach of contract claim arising out of same employer-employee relationship not part of same case or controversy as federal ERISA claim when contract was not part of ERISA plan and was administered by different department of employer); Lyon v. Whisman, 45 F.3d 758 (3d Cir. 1995) (federal Fair Labor Standards Act claim against employer for failure to pay overtime not part of same case or controversy as state tort claim for failure to pay employee a bonus); Hunt v. Up North Plastics, Inc., 980 F. Supp. 1042 (D. Minn. 1998) (no supplemental jurisdiction when no overlapping facts); Bullock v. Barham, 957 F. Supp. 154 (N.D. Ill. 1997) (federal and state claims cannot simply arise from same event, but must arise from a common nucleus of operative fact; no jurisdiction where plaintiff's federal claim against one defendant shares no overlapping facts with state claims against other defendant); Ginsberg, D.O. v. Valhalla Anesthesia Assocs., P.C., 971 F. Supp. 144 (S.D.N.Y. 1997) (no supplemental jurisdiction over counterclaim when its only relationship with principal claim is that it arose out of same employer-employee relationship); *see also In re* Prudential Ins. Co. of Am. Sales Practices Litig. Agent Actions, 148 F.3d 283 (3d Cir. 1998) (district court may not assert supplemental jurisdiction over state claims that are totally unrelated to the federal claims that form the bases of the court's jurisdiction, citing *Lyon*, but necessary relationship satisfied here by common scheme to defraud class); Axel Johnson, Inc. v. Carroll Carolina Oil Co., 145 E.3d 660 (4th Cir. 1998) (plaintiff, in arguing for Federal Rule 54(b) certification, contended federal claims were factually distinct from dismissed state claims; court of appeals used this argument against plaintiff in holding claims were not part of the same case or controversy).

358. Numerous decisions explicitly rely on the Supreme Court dicta discussed earlier. *See, e.g.*, Rolex Watch, U.S.A., Inc. v. Bulova Watch Co., 820 F. Supp. 60 (E.D.N.Y. 1993); Carlucci v. United States, 793 F. Supp. 482 (S.D.N.Y. 1992).

359. *See* 13B CHARLES A. WRIGHT, ET AL., FEDERAL PRACTICE AND PROCEDURE: JURISDICTION AND RELATED MATTERS § 3567.1, at 117 (2d Ed. 1984) (and authorities there cited).

360. *See, e.g.,* Hudson v. Delta Airlines, Inc., 90 F.3d 451 (11th Cir. 1996), *cert. denied*, 519 U.S. 1149, 117 S. Ct. 1082, 137 L. Ed. 2d 217 (1997); Lyon v. Whisman, 45 F.3d 758 (3d Cir. 1995); Ginsberg, D.O. v. Valhalla Anesthesia Assocs., P.C., 971 F. Supp. 144 (S.D.N.Y. 1997).

361. *See, e.g.*, Council of Unit Owners of Wisp Condo., Inc. v. Recreational Indus., Inc., 793 F. Supp. 120 (D. Md. 1992).

362. No. 94-4294, 1994 WL 702876, 1994 U.S. Dist. LEXIS 177 46 (E.D. Pa. Dec. 12, 1994).

city officials. The plaintiff asserted federal claims against the defendants under the civil rights laws for the policeman's actions. The plaintiff also joined the owner of the parking lot as a defendant. The plaintiff asserted a state claim against the owner for negligently failing to secure the parking lot from trespassers. Despite the fact that the federal and state claims all originated in the rape committed by the police officer, the court held that the claims did not arise from a "common nucleus of operative fact."

Illustration 2-88. In *Obendorfer v. Gitano Group, Inc.,*[363] the plaintiff sued the company for which she worked in U.S. District Court. The plaintiff asserted federal sex harassment and sex discrimination claims against the company arising out of the behavior of her supervisor toward her. The plaintiff's fiancé, a lawyer, joined with her as a plaintiff in the federal action. He asserted a state claim for slander against the supervisor. The slander claim was based on remarks the supervisor made to the plaintiff to the effect that her fiancé was a cheat and a liar, like all lawyers. Despite the fact that the allegedly slanderous remarks were part of the ongoing harassment of the plaintiff, the court held that the slander claim was insufficiently related to the federal claim to be part of the same case or controversy.

* * * * *

Even if Article III requires some kind of factual relationship between federal and nonfederal claims, the cases requiring more than a loose factual relationship between federal and state claims seem wrong. There is no basis in the text or history of Article III that justifies the decisions, and they impose an inflexible barrier to the power of Congress to define the scope of a case in a reasonable way. Their rationale should be rejected by the Supreme Court in an appropriate case.

(ii) Exceptions to the Scope of Supplemental Jurisdiction in Diversity Cases: Section 1367(b)

In 28 U.S.C. § 1367(b), Congress attempted to limit the operation of supplemental jurisdiction. Congress provided that supplemental jurisdiction must be exercised consistently with the requirements of 28 U.S.C. § 1332, the general diversity statute. Section 1367(b) provides:

> (b) In any civil action of which the district courts have original jurisdiction founded solely on section 1332 of this title, the district courts shall not have supplemental jurisdiction under subsection (a) over claims by plaintiffs against persons made parties under Rule 14, 19, 20, or 24 of the Federal Rules of Civil Procedure, or over claims by persons proposed to be joined as plaintiffs under Rule 19 of such rules, or seeking to intervene as plaintiffs under Rule 24 of such rules, when exercising supple-

---

363. 838 F. Supp. 950 (D.N.J. 1993).

mental jurisdiction over such claims would be inconsistent with the jurisdictional requirements of section 1332.[364]

The clear import of this provision is to prevent plaintiffs invoking diversity jurisdiction from evading the restrictions of 28 U.S.C. § 1332. The House Report confirms this interpretation. The Report explained the purpose of § 1367(b) as follows:

> In diversity-only actions the district courts may not hear plaintiffs' supplemental claims when exercising supplemental jurisdiction would encourage plaintiffs to evade the jurisdictional requirement of 28 U.S.C. § 1332 by the simple expedient of naming initially only those defendants whose joinder satisfies section 1332's requirements and later adding claims not within original federal jurisdiction against other defendants who have intervened or been joined on a supplemental basis. In accord with case law, the subsection also prevents the joinder or intervention of persons [as] plaintiffs if adding them is inconsistent with section 1332's requirements.[365]

Section 1367(b) restricts supplemental jurisdiction more than the Federal Courts Study Committee recommended. The statutory language proposed in the Committee's working papers only prohibited supplemental jurisdiction as to parties joined under Rules 14 and 19 of the Federal Rules of Civil Procedure and as to claims by parties who intervened permissively under Federal Rule 24(b).[366] In addition, the Committee proposed that, even as to parties joined under Federal Rules 14, 19, and 24(b), the federal courts be permitted to exercise supplemental jurisdiction when "necessary to prevent substantial prejudice to a party or third party."[367] In contrast, § 1367(b) precludes supplemental jurisdiction over claims asserted against persons joined under Rules 14, 19, 20, or 24(a) *or* (b) of the Federal Rules. Furthermore, § 1367(b) also precludes supplemental jurisdiction over claims asserted *by* persons who are joined and aligned as plaintiffs under Federal Rule 19[368] and *by* persons who intervene on the plaintiff's side of the

---

364. Judicial Improvements Act of 1990, Pub. L. No. 101-650, § 310, 104 Stat. 5089, 5113-14 (codified at 28 U.S.C. § 1367(b)).

365. H.R. REP. NO. 734, 101st Cong., 2d Sess. 29 (1990).

366. *See* 1 FEDERAL COURTS STUDY COMMITTEE WORKING PAPERS AND SUBCOMMITTEE REPORTS 567-68 (1990).

367. *Id.* at 568.

368. The language of § 1367(b) precludes supplemental jurisdiction "over claims by persons proposed to be joined as plaintiffs under [Federal] Rule 19." This wording is peculiar, since as demonstrated in Chapter 8(C)(3)*(c)*, the standard procedure in cases under Rule 19 is to join a party whose joinder is necessary for just adjudication as a defendant and then, if necessary, to realign the party for jurisdictional purposes. Except in rare cases within the "involuntary plaintiff" clause of the rule, Rule 19 parties are not "joined as plaintiffs." The best interpretation of the phrase "persons . . . joined as plaintiffs" in § 1367(b), therefore, would seem to be "persons . . . joined as defendants under Rule 19 and realigned as plaintiffs for jurisdictional purposes." The peculiar wording of § 1367(b) may have been derived from a portion of the Federal Study Committee's working papers in which the case of Acton Co. v. Bachman Foods, Inc., 668 F.2d 76 (1st Cir. 1982), was discussed in terms of joinder of a Rule 19 party as a plaintiff. *See* 1 FEDERAL COURTS STUDY COMMITTEE WORKING PAPERS AND SUBCOMMITTEE REPORTS 564 (1990). The *Acton* case, however, spoke in very conventional terms of defendant joinder and realignment. *See Acton*, 668 F.2d at 79.

litigation under Federal Rule 24. Section 1367(b) also eliminates the recommended discretion to exercise supplemental jurisdiction to prevent injustice.[369]

The interpretive problems with § 1367(b) cannot be fully understood apart from joinder of claims and parties practice under the Federal Rules of Civil Procedure. Therefore, a complete discussion of this section of the statute will be deferred until Chapters 7 and 8, where federal claim and party joinder are examined. As seen in those chapters, drafting mistakes have produced a number of serious interpretive issues under § 1367(b). These issues will either have to be resolved by the Supreme Court or by Congress.

One proposal to cure the problem with § 1367(b) has been made by the American Law Institute. The ALI's proposal to reform § 1367(a) was discussed above.[370] The ALI also proposes to reform § 1367(b) by substituting for it the following provision:

> (c) *Restriction of supplemental jurisdiction in diversity litigation.* When the jurisdiction of a district court over a supplemental claim depends upon a freestanding claim that is asserted in the same pleading and that qualifies as a freestanding claim solely on the basis of the jurisdiction conferred by section 1332 of this title, the court shall have jurisdiction of the supplemental claim only if it—
>
> (1) is asserted representatively by or against a class of additional unnamed parties; or
>
> (2) would be a freestanding claim on the basis of section 1332 of this title but for the value of the claim; or
>
> (3) has been joined to the action by the intervention of a party whose joinder is not indispensable to the litigation of the action.[371]

When examining the interpretive problems that have arisen under § 1367(b) in Chapters 7 and 8, below, it will be useful to return to this proposed reform to determine how it addresses the problems. For now, it is sufficient to note that the language of the subsection is framed in the same "claim-specific" manner as the ALI's proposed revisions to § 1367(a).

(iii) The Discretion to Decline Supplemental Jurisdiction: Section 1367(c)

Under both the pendent and the ancillary jurisdiction doctrines, courts had a certain amount of discretion to decline to exercise jurisdiction over pendent and ancillary claims—even though the courts had the *power* to exercise jurisdic-

---

369. *See* 28 U.S.C. § 1367(b).

370. *See* subsection *(d)(i), supra.*

371. ALI FEDERAL JUDICIAL CODE REVISION PROJECT § 1367(c) (Tent. Draft No. 2 1998). The ALI's amendment of § 1367(b) is found in subsection (c) of the proposed revision because the revision of current § 1367(a) now occupies two subsections of the proposed new statute, (a) and (b).

tion.[372] The Supreme Court articulated the factors that should guide a district court's discretion in deciding whether to retain or dismiss a pendent state claim in federal question cases in *United Mine Workers v. Gibbs*.[373] The Court listed five considerations that would point toward dismissal of the state claim: (1) the absence of judicial economy, convenience, and fairness to litigants; (2) the avoidance of needless decisions of state law; (3) the dismissal of federal claims before trial; (4) the predominance of state issues in terms of proof, scope of the issues raised, or comprehensiveness of the remedy sought; and (5) the likelihood of jury confusion in treating divergent legal theories.[374] In addition, the Court stated that if the state claim is closely tied to federal policy, retaining jurisdiction over the claim would be justifiable.[375]

In 28 U.S.C. § 1367(c), Congress attempted to codify the factors that the Supreme Court had previously recognized as legitimate bases for declining to exercise "supplemental jurisdiction":

(c) The district courts may decline to exercise supplemental jurisdiction over a claim under subsection (a) if—

(1) the claim raises a novel or complex issue of state law,

(2) the claim substantially predominates over the claim or claims over which the district court has original jurisdiction,

(3) the district court has dismissed all claims over which it has original jurisdiction, or

(4) in exceptional circumstances, there are other compelling reasons for declining jurisdiction.[376]

On the face of the statute, the factors in subsection (c) apply to all exercises of "supplemental jurisdiction," including those that would formerly have been covered by the doctrine of "pendent jurisdiction" and those that would have been covered by the doctrine of "ancillary jurisdiction." However, before § 1367 was enacted, the federal courts did not exercise their discretion exactly the same in pendent and ancillary jurisdiction cases. Dismissal of the action prior to trial based on a lack of subject-matter jurisdiction would result in dismissal of both pendent and ancillary claims in the vast majority of cases.[377] Likewise, under both pendent and ancillary jurisdiction, the district courts had discretion to dismiss or retain pendent and ancillary claims when the jurisdiction conferring,

---

372. *See* 13B CHARLES A. WRIGHT ET AL., FEDERAL PRACTICE AND PROCEDURE: JURISDICTION AND RELATED MATTERS § 3523, at 105 (2d ed. 1984); 13B *id.* § 3567.1, at 122-23.

373. 383 U.S. 715, 86 S. Ct. 1130, 16 L. Ed. 2d 218 (1966).

374. *See id.* at 726-27; 86 S. Ct. at 1139, 16 L. Ed. 2d at 228.

375. *See id.* at 727, 86 S. Ct. at 1139, 16 L. Ed.2d at 228.

376. 28 U.S.C. § 1367(c); *see* H.R. REP. NO. 734, 101st Cong., 2d Sess. 29 (1990).

377. *Compare* 13 CHARLES A. WRIGHT ET. AL., FEDERAL PRACTICE AND PROCEDURE: JURISDICTION AND RELATED MATTERS § 3523, at 105-06 (2d ed. 1984) *with* 13B *id.* § 3567.1, at 114-15. *But cf. id.* § 3567.1, at 136-37 (discretionary whether to proceed with state claim after dismissal of federal claim on grounds of mootness); Rosado v. Wyman, 397 U.S. 397, 90 S. Ct. 1207, 25 L. Ed. 2d 442 (1970).

or freestanding, claim was dismissed, even when it was dismissed prior to trial on the merits.[378]

However, dismissal of a state claim because it raises a novel or complex issue of state law[379] or because it substantially predominates over the jurisdiction conferring claim[380] are grounds of dismissal that are applicable only to certain situations: (1) those formerly covered by the doctrine of pendent jurisdiction; and (2) perhaps to ancillary jurisdiction cases in which the basis of federal jurisdiction is a claim arising under federal law.[381] It would be highly improper to dismiss a state claim in a pure diversity case on the grounds that "it predominates" or "raises a novel or complex issue of state law." As discussed in Chapter 5, most diversity actions involve *only* issues of state law. Therefore, it would constitute a serious abdication of the district courts' responsibility in diversity actions to allow dismissal on the grounds listed in § 1367(c)(1) & (2).[382] Rather than apply the factors in § 1367(c) blindly to all cases of supplemental jurisdiction, courts should therefore interpret § 1367(c) with an eye toward the prior operation of the doctrines of pendent and ancillary jurisdiction.[383]

Since the enactment of § 1367(c), the vast majority of dismissals have occurred under § 1367(c)(3) after the claims conferring federal jurisdiction have been eliminated from the action.[384] However, the courts do not always dismiss the supplemental claims when the jurisdiction conferring claims go out of the case. Courts have retained supplemental claims in the following situations: when a large amount of effort has already gone into the case and it is almost ready for trial;[385] when extensive discovery has been completed on the state claims and they can be disposed of on summary judgment along with the federal claims;[386] when it is clear that the state claim lacks merit or its proper disposition is

---

378. *See* Scarfo v. Ginsberg, 175 F.3d 957 (11th Cir. 1999) (federal courts of appeals uniformly agree state claims should be dismissed when federal claims dismissed for lack of jurisdiction); 13 CHARLES A. WRIGHT ET AL., FEDERAL PRACTICE AND PROCEDURE: JURISDICTION AND RELATED MATTERS § 3523, at 105-06 (2d ed. 1984) and authorities there cited; 13B *id.* § 3567.1, at 133-37, and authorities there cited.

379. *See* 28 U.S.C. § 1367(c)(1).

380. *See* 28 U.S.C. § 1367(c)(2).

381. *See* United Mine Workers v. Gibbs, 383 U.S. 715, 725-27, 86 S. Ct. 1130, 1138-39, 16 L. Ed. 2d 218, 227-28 (1966); 13B CHARLES A. WRIGHT ET AL., FEDERAL PRACTICE AND PROCEDURE: JURISDICTION AND RELATED MATTERS § 3567.1, at 138-39 (2d ed. 1984); *cf.* 13 *id.* § 3523, at 105-06.

382. Only one court seems to have applied § 1367(c) in a diversity action to dismiss a state-law claim. In Crown Life Ins. Co. v. Harris Bank Hinsdale, No. 91 C 4222, 1992 WL 3699, 1992 U.S. Dist. LEXIS 31 (N.D. Ill. Jan. 2, 1992), the court dismissed a third-party claim in a diversity action because state law predominated. However, the third-party claim was probably not proper under Federal Rule 14 because it did not assert liability against the third-party defendant that was dependent on the defendant/third-party-plaintiff's liability to the plaintiff. Third-party claims are discussed in Chapter 8(D)(1) ("Impleader") *infra*.

383. There seems no problem with applying 28 U.S.C. § 1367(c)(3) and (4) to all cases of supplemental jurisdiction.

384. *See, e.g.,* Price v. FCC Nat'l Bank, 4 F.3d 472 (7th Cir. 1993); Noble v. White, 996 F.2d 797 (5th Cir. 1993); Packett v. Stenberg, 969 F.2d 721 (8th Cir. 1992); Ashland Oil, Inc. v. Sonford Prods. Corp., 810 F. Supp. 1057 (D. Minn. 1993); ZB Holdings, Inc. v. White, 144 F.R.D. 42 (S.D.N.Y. 1992); Procopio v. Johnson, 785 F. Supp. 1317 (N.D. Ill. 1992).

385. *See, e.g.,* Nowak v. Ironworkers Local 6 Pension Fund, 81 F.3d 1182 (2d Cir. 1996) (state claim properly retained when federal claim dismissed only nine days before trial; Roche v. John Hancock Mut. Life Ins. Co., 81 F.3d 249 (1st Cir. 1996) (litigation had matured beyond discovery stages).

386. *See, e.g.,* Roche v. John Hancock Mut. Life Ins. Co., 81 F.3d 249 (1st Cir. 1996).

otherwise clear;[387] and when retaining jurisdiction over the supplemental claims would be efficient and would preserve the resources of the litigants and the court system.[388]

When the district courts dismiss under § 1367(c)(1) on the ground that novel and complex issues of state law exist in the action, often it is because no authoritative state precedents exist on the state-law issues involved in the case.[389] It is more difficult to generalize about dismissals under § 1367(c)(2) on the ground that state law predominates. Sometimes, the sheer number of the state issues in comparison to the federal issues will lead the courts to conclude that state law predominates.[390] In other instances, discovery reveals that the state-law issues are the true focus of the case, and the federal issues are secondary.[391] However, some district courts, in clearly improper actions, have dismissed entire cases, including federal claims, because state law predominated.[392] The explicit terms of § 1367(c) only permit the district courts to dismiss "a claim under subsection (a)," if one or more of the factors under § 1367(c) is present. Section 1367(c) does not authorize the courts to dismiss the entire case. Furthermore,

---

387. *See, e.g.,* Rothman v. Emory Univ., 123 F.3d 446 (7th Cir. 1997) (decisions on federal claim also dispositive of state counterclaim); Korzen v. Local Union 705, Int'l Bhd. of Teamsters, 75 F.3d 285 (7th Cir. 1996) (state claim plainly without merit); Wright v. Associated Ins. Cos., 29 F.3d 1244 (7th Cir. 1994) (correct disposition of state claims is clear).

388. *See* Rothman v. Emory Univ., 123 F.3d 446 (7th Cir. 1997) (decisions on federal claim also dispositive of state counterclaim); Roche v. John Hancock Mut. Life Ins. Co., 81 F.3d 249 (1st Cir. 1996) (action had matured beyond discovery stage, summary judgment record was complete, and federal and state claims were intertwined); Parks v. Hayward's Pit, Inc., No. 93-2387-JWL, 1993 WL 545231, 1993 U.S. Dist. LEXIS 18529 (D. Kan. Dec. 21, 1993) (state claim against one defendant had evidentiary overlap with federal claim against another defendant); Daniels v. Board of Trustees of the Herington Mun. Hosp., 841 F. Supp. 363 (D. Kan 1993) (retention of jurisdiction because of time expended by parties on issue).

389. *See, e.g.,* Women Prisoners of D.C. Dep't of Corrections v. District of Columbia, 93 F.3d 910 (D.C. Cir. 1996); Winn v. North Am. Philips Corp., 826 F. Supp. 1424 (S.D. Fla. 1993); Schwartz v. System Software Assocs., Inc., 813 F. Supp. 1364 (N.D. Ill. 1993); Support Ministries for Persons with AIDS, Inc. v. Village of Waterford, 799 F. Supp. 272 (N.D.N.Y. 1992); *see also* Seabrook v. Jacobson, 153 F.3d 70 (2d Cir. 1998) (state issue not only undecided, but depended on balancing of important state policies; if federal courts decide issue, their decision might soon be replaced by state adjudication); O'Connor v. Nevada, 27 F.3d 357 (9th Cir. 1994) (difficult issue of state constitutional law); Lane v. Calhoun-Liberty County Hosp. Ass'n, 846 F. Supp. 1543 (N.D. Fla. 1993) (new state statutory cause of action presents novel issue); Mars Inc. v. Nippon Conlux Kabushiki-Kaisha, 825 F. Supp. 73 (D. Del. 1993) (claims presenting complex issues of Japanese law dismissed); *cf.* Salt v. Wen Lung Yu, No. 92-55430, 1993 WL 306153, 1993 U.S. App. LEXIS 20636 (9th Cir. Aug. 11, 1993) (unpublished opinion) (dismissal refused because California law settled); Atkinson v. B.C.C. Assocs., Inc., No. 91 Civ. 4443 (MBM), 1992 WL 51568, 1992 U.S. Dist. LEXIS 2824, (S.D.N.Y. Mar. 9, 1992) (remand on grounds of complex and unsettled issues of state law refused when plaintiff admits there is direct authority on state issues from state supreme court).

390. *See, e.g.,* Town of Jaffrey v. Town of Fitzwilliam, 846 F. Supp. 3 (D.N.H. 1994); James v. Sun Glass Hut, Inc., 799 F. Supp. 1083 (D. Colo. 1992); Anspec Co. v. Johnson Controls, Inc., 788 F. Supp. 951 (E.D. Mich. 1992).

391. *See* Freer v. Mayer, 796 F. Supp. 89 (S.D.N.Y. 1992); Elb-Mattison, Inc. v. M/V Kosciuszko, No. 91 C 5449, 1992 WL 132538, 1992 U.S. Dist. LEXIS 7992 (N.D. Ill. June 8, 1992); *see also* Lassiter v. Kulp, No. 93-1176, 1993 WL 364694, 1993 U.S. Dist. LEXIS 12720 (E.D. Pa. Sept. 13, 1993) (state claims involving entirely different threshold issues, burdens of proof, and evidentiary proffers).

392. *See, e.g., In re* City of Mobile, 75 F.3d 605 (11th Cir. 1996); Borough of W. Mifflin v. Lancaster, 45 F.3d 780 (3d Cir. 1995); Bodenner v. Graves, 828 F. Supp. 516 (W.D. Mich. 1993). The *Bodenner* court cited a decision of another district court involving remand of a removed case to state court when state issues predominated. As subsection 5 *infra* on removal will demonstrate, remand of an entire removed case on these grounds is also improper.

dismissal of federal as well as state claims deprives the plaintiff of the congress-ionally granted privilege of suing on the federal claims in federal court. When state issues predominate, the plaintiff may have a difficult choice if the district court dismisses the plaintiff's state claims. Nevertheless, the choice to keep the federal claim in federal court, take it to state court, or drop either the federal or state claims should always reside with the plaintiff.

One issue that has split the courts of appeals under § 1367(c) is the extent to which the statute is intended to confine the open-ended discretion of the Supreme Court's *Gibbs* decision, discussed above. In *Executive Software North America, Inc. v. United States District Court*,[393] the Ninth Circuit held that the factors listed in § 1367(c) were the exclusive bases for discretionary dismissals of supplemental claims:

> It is clear that, once it is determined that the assertion of supplemental jurisdiction is permissible under sections 1367(a) and (b), section 1367(c) provides the only valid basis upon which the district court may decline jurisdiction . . . . Moreover, we conclude that although subsections (c)(1)-(3) appear to codify most preexisting applications of the *Gibbs* doctrine, subsection (c)(4), which also permits a court to decline jurisdiction when, "in exceptional circumstances, there are other compelling rea-sons," channels the district court's discretion to identify new grounds for declining jurisdiction more particularly than did preexisting doctrine. Accordingly, we conclude that the district court erred to the extent that it relied on a basis for [declining jurisdiction over] pendent claims not permitted under section 1367(c).[394]

Other courts of appeals have disagreed with the *Executive Software* approach and concluded that the *Gibbs* open-ended discretionary approach has survived the codification of the factors in § 1367(c).[395]

The American Law Institute's proposed revision of § 1367(c), addresses some of the questions that have arisen under the existing statute:

> (d) *Discretion to decline to exercise jurisdiction.* This section does not permit a district court to decline to exercise jurisdiction of any freestanding claim except as provided by subsection (e). A district court may decline to exercise jurisdiction of a supple-mental claim if—
>
> (1) all freestanding claims that are the basis for its jurisdiction of a supplemental claim have been dismissed before trial of that claim;

---

393. 24 F.3d 1545 (9th Cir. 1994).

394. *Id.* at 1551-52; *see also* McLaurin v. Prater, 30 F.3d 982 (8th Cir. 1994) (§ 1367(a) is mandatory unless § 1367(b) or (c) apply).

395. *See* Edmondson & Gallagher v. Alban Towers Tenants Ass'n, 48 F.3d 1260 (D.C. Cir. 1995) (*Gibbs* determines the framework within which § 1367 factors are to be considered); Diven v. Amalgamated Transit Union Int'l, 38 F.3d 598 (D.C. Cir. 1994) (statute fairly exudes discretion under the exceptions in § 1367(c)).

(2) the supplemental claim raises a novel or complex issue of State law that the district court need not otherwise decide; or

(3) the exercise of supplemental jurisdiction would substantially alter the character of the litigation; or

(4) in exceptional circumstances, there are other compelling reasons for declining supplemental jurisdiction.[396]

The first sentence of this proposal would clarify that the district courts do not ordinarily have discretion to dismiss federal claims when they exercise their discretion to dismiss supplemental state claims.[397] In addition, the proposal reorders and, in some respects, reframes the existing § 1367(c) factors. The reordering is designed to reflect "the increasingly subjective nature of each ground for declining supplemental jurisdiction."[398] In addition, the terms of subsections (d)(1)-(3) of the statute have narrowed the degree to which the district courts may exercise discretion to dismiss supplemental claims. New subsection (d)(1) only permits dismissal of supplemental claims when the freestanding claim that is the basis of jurisdiction has been dismissed "before trial," as opposed to existing subsection (c)(3), which does not contain this restriction.[399]

Proposed § 1367(d)(2) incorporates a restriction not contained in existing § 1367(c)(1) to which it corresponds: declining supplemental jurisdiction over novel or complex issues of state law is impermissible unless it would avoid the need to decide the novel or complex issue of state law. This provision is designed primarily to prevent the district courts from declining jurisdiction over state issues in diversity actions that they would still have to decide as to freestanding claims.[400] However, as indicated above, it is still not clear that it is ever justifiable for a district court to refuse to decide a novel and complex issue of state law in a diversity case, and it might have been better for the ALI to forbid this ground of dismissal altogether except in federal question cases.

Proposed subsection (d)(3) corresponds with existing § 1367(c)(2), but has been reformulated to narrow the permissible grounds for dismissal. The supplemental claims would have to "predominate" by "substantially" altering the character of the litigation.

> The gist of [the *Gibbs'*] reasoning is not, as present § 1367(c)(2) would suggest, that a district court should attempt to weigh the "relative importance" or compare the number of supplemental and freestanding *claims* that must be determined in order to render judgment. Even though a supplemental claim is based on state law, its adjudication may require reference to

---

396. ALI FEDERAL JUDICIAL CODE REVISION PROJECT § 1367(d) (Tent. Draft No. 2 1998). The ALI revision is designated subsection (d) because the revisions of § 1367(a) and (b) occupy subsections (a)-(c) in the proposal.

397. The reference to subsection (e) in this opening sentence deals with certain problems involving joinder of additional defendants whose presence would otherwise destroy diversity and are within the prohibition of subsection (c) of the proposal, discussed in subsection *(d)(ii) supra*. Subsection (e) of the ALI proposal is discussed in subsection *5(a) infra*.

398. ALI FEDERAL JUDICIAL CODE REVISION PROJECT § 1367(d), at 7, expl. note (Tent. Draft No. 2 1998).

399. *See id.* at 87-88, *cmt. d-6.*

400. *See id.* at 88, *cmt. d-7.*

federal law, or may require resolution of substantially the same disputed facts as must be determined incident to adjudicating freestanding claims. Thus, new § 1367(d)(3) is articulated in terms of the effect of exercising supplemental jurisdiction on "the character of the litigation" that the district court has no discretion to decline.[401]

Finally, proposed § 1367(d)(4), while differing only slightly from existing § 1367(c)(4), makes it clear that "compelling reasons" and "exceptional circumstances" can only justify declining supplemental jurisdiction, not jurisdiction over freestanding claims.[402] The overall effect of the ALI's proposal would be to create a "modestly more restrictive" provision than existing § 1367(c).[403]

(iv) Tolling of Limitations for Dismissed Claims: Section 1367(d)

Section 1367(d) provides a tolling period for any statute of limitations that might apply to claims dismissed under § 1367:

(d) The period of limitations for any claim asserted under subsection (a), and for any other claim in the same action that is voluntarily dismissed at the same time as or after the dismissal of the claim under subsection (a), shall be tolled while the claim is pending and for a period of 30 days after it is dismissed unless State law provides for a longer tolling period.[404]

This provision protects parties who choose to assert supplemental claims in federal court from finding that state statutes of limitation bar their claims if the claims are dismissed or if the parties choose to dismiss other claims voluntarily after dismissal of their supplemental claims. In the absence of § 1367(d), a party might find that state law would not toll the applicable statute of limitations as to a dismissed supplemental claim or as to a voluntarily dismissed claim over which original jurisdiction existed. Thus, § 1367(d) is a valuable provision because it prevents injustice to parties asserting supplemental claims.[405]

Illustration 2-89. A, a citizen of State *X*, sues *B*, a citizen of State *X*, in U.S. District Court. *A* asserts a federal claim against *B* and joins a factually related state law claim. After the lapse of a substantial period of time within which the parties and the court are occupied with various pretrial matters, the

---

401. *Id.* at 91, *cmt. d-7; see generally id.* at 88-92, *cmt. d-7.*

402. *See id.* at 92, *cmt. d-9.*

403. *See id. cmt. d-10.*

404. 28 U.S.C. § 1367(d).

405. Section 1367(d) appears to have been patterned after § 1386(b) of the American Law Institute's 1969 proposals. *See* ALI STUDY OF THE DIVISION OF JURISDICTION BETWEEN STATE AND FEDERAL COURTS 651 (1969). The constitutionality of provisions like § 1367(d) are discussed in *id.* at 453-57; *see also* Denis F. McLaughlin, *The Federal Supplemental Jurisdiction Statute—A Constitutional and Statutory Analysis*, 24 ARIZ. ST. L.J. 849, 985-89 (1992). For an article arguing that § 1367(d) is unconstitutional, *see* Brian A. Beckom, *Pushing the Limits of the Judicial Power: Tolling State Statutes of Limitation Under 28 U.S.C. § 1367(d)*, 77 TEX. L. REV. 1049 (1999).

court dismisses *A's* state claim under 28 U.S.C. § 1367(c)(1) because it raises a novel and complex issue of state law. The state statute of limitations applicable to the dismissed claim expired after commencement of the federal action, but before dismissal of the state claim. Assume that under state law, the statute would not be considered tolled by the pendency of the federal action. By virtue of 28 U.S.C. § 1367(d), however, the state period of limitations was tolled during the pendency of the federal action. *A* has thirty days after dismissal to commence an action on the state claim in state court.[406]

Illustration 2-90. In *Illustration 2-89*, assume that after dismissal of the state claim, *A* wishes also to dismiss the federal claim voluntarily to pursue both claims in state court. The statute of limitations applicable to the federal claim would also be considered tolled under 28 U.S.C. § 1367(d) during the pendency of the federal action and for a period of thirty days after the voluntary dismissal of the federal claim.[407]

Illustration 2-91. In both *Illustrations 2-89* and *2-90*, if state law provides a longer tolling period than thirty days, *A* will have the benefit of the longer tolling period under state law in which to commence a state action on the federal and state claims.[408]

* * * * *

The American Law Institute's proposed revision of § 1367(d) would clarify and somewhat expand the provisions of the existing statute.[409]

---

406. *See* H.R. Rep. No. 734, 101st Cong., 2d Sess. 30 (1990).

407. *See id.*

408. For a discussion of various minor issues of interpretation under § 1367(d), see Denis F. McLaughlin, *The Federal Supplemental Jurisdiction Statute–A Constitutional and Statutory Analysis,* 24 Ariz. St. L.J. 849, 984-85 (1992). In Kolani v. Gluska, 64 Cal. App. 4th 402, 75 Cal. Rptr. 2d 257 (1998), the California Court of Appeals, in a curious opinion, considered what § 1367(d) means by "tolled while the claim is pending" plus 30 days. The state statute of limitations was two years. The plaintiff commenced a federal action on the claim, as a supplemental claim, after one year. Two years later, the federal court dismissed the federal action under § 1367(c). One issue considered by the court of appeals was whether the plaintiff had one year and thirty days after the federal dismissal to commence an action in state court in these circumstances. The issue is presented because, literally, "tolled while the action is pending" can be read to mean "stops running while the action is pending." This reading would, again literally, give the plaintiff the one-year remaining on the state statute of limitations plus the additional 30 days provided by § 1367(d). The Court of Appeals correctly rejected this interpretation of § 1367(d) as unreasonable.

409. ALI Federal Judicial Code Revision Project § 1367(f) (Tent. Draft No. 2 1998):

> *(f) Disposition of supplemental claims; tolling of limitations period.* When a district court lacks or declines to exercise supplemental jurisdiction, the court shall dismiss the supplemental claim unless it was joined before removal of the action, in which case the district court shall remand the claim to the State court from which it was removed. The period of limitations for the following claims shall be tolled until 30 days after their dismissal becomes final, unless the applicable law provides for a longer tolling period:
>
> (1) any supplemental claim dismissed because the district court lacks or declines to exercise supplemental jurisdiction; and
>
> (2) any other claim in the same civil action that is voluntarily dismissed as the result of a notice or stipulation of dismissal, or motion for order of dismissal, filed within 30 days after—
>
> (A) the dismissal or remand of a supplemental claim because the district court lacks or declines to exercise supplemental jurisdiction; or
>
> (B) the court's decision under subsection (e) to refuse to permit the joinder of a supplemental claim against an additional defendant.

See also id. at 98-100, cmts. f-1 to f-3.

5. Removal Jurisdiction

In the first Judiciary Act, Congress gave defendants a limited right to "remove" cases from state to federal court. Congress has steadily expanded this right.[410] Today, the general removal statute is 28 U.S.C. § 1441. Section 1441(a) sets out the general rule on removal jurisdiction. Section 1441(b) and (c) describe exceptions to the general rule.[411] Several other statutes provide for removal of specific kinds of cases from state to federal court.[412] Section 1445 of Title 28 sets out certain cases that are not removable, even if they fall within the terms of one of the removal statutes.[413] Finally, §§ 1446-1450 deal with the procedures for removal and the procedures after removal, including remand of improperly removed cases.[414] The following subsections discuss removal under 28 U.S.C. § 1441, the procedures governing removal, and remand.

(a) General Rule of Removal Jurisdiction: Section 1441(a)

Section 1441(a) states the general rule of removal jurisdiction for the U.S. District Courts. A civil action may be removed from a state court to a U.S. District Court whenever the U.S. District Court would have original jurisdiction of the action. Removal under § 1441 is limited to defendants.[415] Usually, in

---

410. *See* CHARLES A. WRIGHT, THE LAW OF FEDERAL COURTS § 38, at 223-24 (5th ed. 1994).

411. 28 U.S.C. § 1441(a)-(c).

412. *See, e.g.,* 28 U.S.C. § 1442 (involving federal officers or agencies sued or prosecuted), § 1442a (involving members of armed forces sued or prosecuted), § 1443 (civil rights cases), § 1444 (foreclosure actions against the United States), § 1452 (involving claims related to bankruptcy cases).

413. 28 U.S.C. § 1445 (involving certain civil actions against railroads or carriers; claims arising under state workers' compensation laws; and civil actions based on the Violence Against Women Act of 1994).

414. 28 U.S.C. § 1446 ("Procedure for removal"), § 1447 ("Procedure after removal generally"), § 1448 ("Process after removal"), § 1449 (state court record for use in removed action), § 1450 (status of attachments, injunctions, orders, bonds issued prior to removal).

415. *See* Shamrock Oil & Gas Corp. v. Sheets, 313 U.S. 100, 61 S. Ct. 868, 85 L. Ed. 1214 (1941) (plaintiff may not remove on the basis of defendant's counterclaim). The *Shamrock* case was a diversity action, but it has also been held applicable to federal question counterclaims. *See* General Elec. Capital Auto Lease, Inc. v. Mires, 788 F. Supp. 948 (E.D. Mich. 1992). In its proposed revision of the Judicial Code, the American Law Institute retains these basic rules in revised language:

§ 1441. Right of removal of civil actions—in general

(a) Basic right of removal.

(1) Except as provided in subsection (f), for purposes of this section a removable claim is any claim that is within the subject-matter jurisdiction of the district courts.

(2) Except as otherwise expressly provided by Act of Congress, a civil action brought in a State court may be removed by the defendant or defendants to the district court of the United States for the district in which the civil action is pending if every claim asserted in the complaint or other initial pleading is a removable claim, disregarding any claim against a party not properly joined or aligned as a defendant with respect to that claim.

ALI FEDERAL JUDICIAL CODE REVISION PROJECT § 1441, at 1 (Tent. Draft No. 3 1999). In contrast to the claim-specific nature of the ALI's proposed revision of the supplemental jurisdiction statute, discussed in subsection 4 *supra*, the removal provision remains action-specific as it is under current law. However, a claim-specific analysis must precede the determination whether the entire action is removable. *See id.* at 21-23 (commentary). Thus, for a civil action to be removable under proposed § 1441(a), every claim in the action must be within the subject-matter jurisdiction of the district courts.

actions involving multiple defendants, all defendants must be willing to remove, or removal will not be allowed.[416]

Illustration 2-92. A, a citizen of California, sues *B*, a citizen of New Jersey, and *C*, a citizen of New York, in a New York state court on a claim based on federal law. *B* and *C* can remove the case to a New York federal district court. Removal jurisdiction exists because the federal district courts would have original jurisdiction of the action as a case arising under federal law pursuant to 28 U.S.C. § 1331.[417]

* * * * *

Because removal jurisdiction is generally based on the existence of original jurisdiction in the district courts, the well-pleaded complaint rule also applies when a case is removed from state to federal court on the basis of federal question jurisdiction. Thus, removal ordinarily cannot be based on a federal defense to a state claim for relief even if the plaintiff anticipates the federal defense in the complaint. An exception to this rule exists when federal law has completely preempted state law within an area. When state law has been completely preempted, any claim purportedly based on the preempted state law is considered federal from its inception. Therefore, the claim arises under federal law for purposes of removal even if the complaint does not in any way rely on federal law. However, when federal law does not completely preempt an area of state law, but leaves the plaintiff a choice whether to base the claim on federal or state law, the plaintiff can prevent removal from state court by simply pleading a claim for relief based on state law alone.[418]

In determining whether the so-called "complete preemption" doctrine allows removal of an action commenced in state court, it is important to determine whether federal law simply negates the plaintiff's state claims for relief. If it does, preemption is only a defense, and the action is not removable. On the other hand, if federal law occupies the field so as to create a federal claim for relief that displaces state remedies, the action is removable.

Illustration 2-93. U, a labor union, enters into a collective bargaining agreement with *E*, a corporation. Subsequently, *P*, an employee of *E*, brings an action in state court against *E* to recover damages for rights allegedly violated by

---

416. *See* 14C CHARLES A. WRIGHT ET AL., FEDERAL PRACTICE AND PROCEDURE: JURISDICTION AND RELATED MATTERS § 3731, at 258 (3d ed. 1998). An exception to this rule exists when a case is removed under 28 U.S.C. § 1441(c), discussed below. In § 1441(c) cases, only the defendant against whom the removable claim is asserted need seek removal. *See id.* at 267. Another exception exists when removal is based on diversity of citizenship and it is alleged and proved that the plaintiff has "fraudulently joined" a resident defendant to prevent removal. Under such circumstances, the nonresident defendant alone can remove upon a proper allegation and proof of the fraudulent joinder. *See, e.g.*, Wilson v. Republic Iron & Steel Co., 257 U.S. 92, 42 S. Ct. 35, 66 L. Ed. 144 (1921); Green v. Amerada Hess Corp., 707 F.2d 201 (5th Cir. 1983), *cert. denied*, 464 U.S. 1039, 104 S. Ct. 701, 79 L. Ed. 2d 166 (1984). Fraudulent joinder is discussed in 14B CHARLES A. WRIGHT ET AL., FEDERAL PRACTICE AND PROCEDURE: JURISDICTION AND RELATED MATTERS § 3723, at 625-58 (3d ed. 1998).

417. Cases involving federal claims and supplemental state claims within the district court's original jurisdiction under § 1367 are, of course, also removable. For an excellent discussion of problems involving the interplay of § 1367 and removal, see Joan Steinman, *Crosscurrents: Supplemental Jurisdiction, Removal, and the ALI Revision Project*, 74 IND. L.J. 75 (1998).

418. *See* Caterpillar Inc. v. Williams, 482 U.S. 386, 107 S. Ct. 2425, 96 L. Ed. 2d 318 (1987); Metropolitan Life Ins. Co. v. Taylor, 481 U.S. 58, 107 S. Ct. 1542, 95 L. Ed. 2d 55 (1987).

E under the agreement. *E* files a timely notice of removal to federal court. Even though *P's* complaint does not rely explicitly on federal law, the action is removable. The U.S. Supreme Court has held that when a state complaint relies on the provisions of a collective bargaining agreement, the complaint arises under federal law. The federal labor laws have entirely preempted state law as a source of private rights to enforce collective bargaining agreements.[419]

Illustration 2-94. If, in *Illustration 2-93*, *P* had brought a state action to enforce an individual employment contract with *E*, rather than to enforce the provisions of a collective bargaining agreement, the action could be brought under state law and would be nonremovable. The federal labor laws only preempt state remedies for violations of collective bargaining agreements. Even if *P* also possesses substantial rights under the collective bargaining agreement, *P* can choose not to rely on that agreement in framing the complaint. In that event, *P* may prevent removal because the complaint will be based entirely on state law.[420]

*   *   *   *   *

Removal under § 1441(a) is of "civil actions." Recall from subsection 4(d)(i), above, that in *City of Chicago v. International College of Surgeons*,[421] the U.S. Supreme Court held that a state action for deferential judicial review of a state agency's action was a "civil action" within the meaning of § 1441(a). The Court reached this conclusion because (1) there were federal claims within the original jurisdiction of the district courts present in the action and (2) § 1367 provided supplemental jurisdiction over the state claims in the action. In *Wisconsin Department of Corrections v. Schacht*,[422] the Court sustained removal jurisdiction over a case in which claims barred by the Eleventh Amendment[423] to the U.S. Constitution were joined with claims not barred by the Amendment. Citing the *City of Chicago* case, the Court held that the presence of even one federal claim over which there is original jurisdiction suffices to make the action a "civil action . . . of which the district courts . . . have original jurisdiction" within the meaning of § 1441(a). The Court distinguished diversity removal cases in which nondiverse defendants had been joined on the ground that the complete diversity rule of § 1332 cannot be waived, while the Eleventh Amendment defense can be.[424]

When removal is based on diversity of citizenship, diversity must exist at the time the action was commenced in state court as well as when the petition for removal is filed. Thus, a nondiverse defendant cannot change domiciles after

---

419. *See* Avco Corp. v. Aero Lodge No. 735, 390 U.S. 557, 88 S. Ct. 1235, 20 L. Ed. 2d 126 (1968).

420. *See* Caterpillar Inc. v. Williams, 482 U.S. 386, 107 S. Ct. 2425, 96 L. Ed. 2d 318 (1987); *see also* Jacob v. SmithKline Beecham, 824 F. Supp. 552 (E.D. Pa. 1993) (ERISA did not completely preempt plaintiff's contract claim). *See generally* Karen A. Jordan, *The Complete Preemption Dilemma: A Legal Process Perspective*, 31 WAKE FOREST L. REV. 927 (1996).

421. 522 U.S. 156, 118 S. Ct. 523, 139 L. Ed. 2d 525 (1997).

422. 524 U.S. 381, 118 S. Ct. 2047, 141 L. Ed. 2d 364 (1998).

423. U.S. Const. amend. XI.

424. 524 U.S. at __, 118 S. Ct. at 2053, 141 L. Ed. 2d at __.

commencement to create diversity and make the action removable.[425] If a non-diverse defendant is eliminated by voluntary action of the plaintiff, however, the remaining defendant(s) can remove.[426]

Congress has also provided that the citizenship of defendants sued under fictitious names shall be disregarded for purposes of removal.[427] If, after removal, the plaintiff seeks to join additional defendants whose joinder would destroy subject-matter jurisdiction, the court has discretion to deny the joinder or to allow it and remand the case to the state court.[428] The purpose of the latter provision is to give the district court flexibility when a party must be joined under Federal Rule 19 after removal. It permits joinder and remand, instead of only dismissal or denial of joinder, when the party to be joined would destroy diversity.[429]

In addition, if a plaintiff "fraudulently joins" a nondiverse defendant with a diverse defendant to prevent removal, the diverse defendant will be

---

425. *See, e.g.,* Kellam v. Keith, 144 U.S. 568, 12 S. Ct. 922, 36 L. Ed. 544 (1892); Kanzelberger v. Kanzelberger, 782 F.2d 774 (7th Cir. 1986); *see also* 16 GEORGINE VARIO, MOORE'S FEDERAL PRACTICE § 107.14[2][h][ii] (3d ed. 1999); 14B CHARLES A. WRIGHT ET AL., FEDERAL PRACTICE AND PROCEDURE: JURISDICTION AND RELATED MATTERS § 3723, at 574 (3d ed. 1998).

426. *See* 14B CHARLES A. WRIGHT ET AL., FEDERAL PRACTICE AND PROCEDURE: JURISDICTION AND RELATED MATTERS § 3723, at 574-83 (3d ed. 1998). If a nondiverse defendant is dropped by order of the court, rather than by voluntary action by the plaintiff, the cases are divided on whether the action can be removed. The best result is that the case should not be considered removable. The "distinction [between voluntary action by the plaintiff making an action removable and action by the court that does not make the action removable has] merit in that it prevent[s] removal when the nondiverse party [is] eliminated by a court order that might be [subject to] revers[al] on appeal." *Id.* at 581-82; *see also* ERWIN CHEMERINSKY, FEDERAL JURISDICTION § 5.5, at 342 (3d ed. 1999). The American law Institute's proposed revisions of the Judicial Code would essentially preserve this rule in its proposed § 1446(b)(2). This proposal would allow removal of actions not removable at commencement only when they have become removable by the "voluntary act of the plaintiff or plaintiffs." *See* ALI FEDERAL JUDICIAL CODE REVISION PROJECT § 1446(b)(2) (Tent. Draft No. 3 1999). The reporter has acknowledged that this provision might permit removal if the plaintiff changes citizenship to create diversity after commencement of the state action. *See id.* at 41 (commentary). However, this result could only occur if the defendant is not a citizen of the state in which the action is brought. *See id.* § 1441(b)(2); subsection *(b)* *infra.* Thus, the situations in which a change of domicile by the plaintiff would create removal jurisdiction would be rare.

427. *See* The Judicial Improvements and Access to Justice Act of 1988, Pub. L. No. 100-702, § 1016(a), 102 Stat. 4642, 4669 (codified at 28 U.S.C. § 1441(a)). This amendment was intended to overrule the Ninth Circuit's decision in Bryant v. Ford Motor Co., 832 F.2d 1080 (9th Cir. 1987). *Bryant* held that naming fictitious defendants under California law destroys diversity jurisdiction and thus the ability to remove to federal court. The American Law Institute would preserve this rule under its proposed revision of § 1441. *See* ALI FEDERAL JUDICIAL CODE REVISION PROJECT § 1441(b)(1) (Tent. Draft No. 3 1999). *See generally* David M. Epstein, Annotation, *Propriety of Use of Fictitious Name of Defendant in Federal Court,* 139 A.L.R. FED. 553 (1997).

428. *See* The Judicial Improvements and Access to Justice Act of 1988, Pub. L. No. 100-702, § 1016(e), 102 Stat. 4642, 4669 (codified at 28 U.S.C. § 1447(e)).

429. *See* H.R. REP. No. 889, 100th Cong., 2d Sess. 72-73, *reprinted in* 1988 U.S.C.C.A.N. 5982, 6033; *see also* Yniques v. Cabral, 985 F.2d 1031 (9th Cir. 1993) (Rule 19 and § 1447(e) give district courts three options: (1) deny joinder, conclude the nonjoined party is indispensable, and dismiss; (2) deny joinder, conclude the nonjoined party is not indispensable, and allow the action to continue; or (3) allow joinder and remand) (the district court may *not* permit joinder and *dismiss*). If a district court does allow joinder of such a party and then adjudicates the action, the court of appeals may be able to cure the error by allowing a nondiverse, nonindispensable party to be dismissed at the appellate level. *See* Ingram v. CSX Transp., Inc., 146 F.3d 858 (11th Cir. 1998). In its proposed revision of the Judicial Code, the American Law Institute would also give district courts the option of retaining the action and exercising supplemental jurisdiction over the claim against the newly joined nondiverse defendant. *See* ALI FEDERAL JUDICIAL CODE REVISION PROJECT § 1367(e) (Tent. Draft No. 2 1998); *Id.* § 1447[e] (Tent. Draft No. 3 1999).

permitted to remove and the fraudulently joined defendant will be dismissed[430] A defendant is fraudulently joined when a plaintiff ''has not or cannot'' state a claim for relief against that defendant,[431] although some courts have recognized other grounds for fraudulent joinder.[432]

Before 1986, a strange rule in the area of removal provided that removal jurisdiction was ''derivative.'' If the state court in which the action had been commenced had no jurisdiction over the case, the federal court to which removal was sought had no jurisdiction either because the federal court's jurisdiction was derived from that of the state court. Thus, curious as it may seem, if the federal courts had exclusive subject-matter jurisdiction of a case and the case was erroneously commenced in state court, it could not be removed to federal court. In such a situation, the state court had no jurisdiction because of the grant of exclusive jurisdiction to the federal courts. Because the state court had no jurisdiction and the federal court's removal jurisdiction was derivative, the case could not be removed.[433]

In 1986, Congress abolished the derivative jurisdiction rule by adding subsection (e) to 28 U.S.C. § 1441: ''The court to which such civil action is removed is not precluded from hearing and determining any claim in such civil action because the State court from which such civil action is removed did not have jurisdiction over that claim.''[434]

Illustration 2-95. *A* sues *B* in a Massachusetts state court for treble damages under the federal antitrust laws based upon an alleged scheme to fix the price of dynamite sold in interstate and foreign commerce with the United States. Prior to 1986, *B* could not remove the action to a Massachusetts federal district court because of the derivative-jurisdiction rule. The Massachusetts state court

---

430. *See* 14B CHARLES A. WRIGHT, ET AL., FEDERAL PRACTICE AND PROCEDURE: JURISDICTION AND RELATED MATTERS § 3523, at 625-58 (3d ed. 1998).

431. *See id.* at 631.

432. *See id.* at 631-58 (plaintiff does not intend to obtain a judgment against the defendant; procedural misjoinder).

433. *See* RICHARD H. FALLON ET AL., HART & WECHSLER'S THE FEDERAL COURTS AND THE FEDERAL SYSTEM 1622 (4th ed. 1996).

434. 28 U.S.C. § 1441(e). Today, therefore, the district courts may hear removed cases over which they have exclusive jurisdiction as well as other cases properly falling within subsections (a)-(d) of 28 U.S.C. § 1441 that have been commenced in a state court lacking subject-matter jurisdiction as a matter of state law. However, state-court jurisdiction will not always be irrelevant to the right to remove. In Sheppard v. Exxon Co. U.S.A., 760 F. Supp. 92 (M.D. La. 1990), the court held that an action could not be removed from state court on the basis that original jurisdiction existed under 28 U.S.C. § 1332, because the amount-in-controversy requirement of that statute was not satisfied. Plaintiff had filed suit in a state court that had a statutory jurisdictional amount limitation of $10,000. Thus, even though the plaintiff was seeking punitive damages, the amount in controversy could not exceed $10,000, because that was the largest amount for which the state court could render a judgment. Furthermore, a number of cases have held that the abolition of the derivative jurisdiction rule only applies to cases removed under § 1441 and that jurisdiction is still derivative under other removal statutes. *See, e.g.,* Elko County Grand Jury v. Siminoe, 109 F.3d 554 (9th Cir. 1997) (removal under § 1442); Edwards v. United States Dep't of Justice, 43 F.3d 312 (7th Cir. 1994) (removal under § 1442). *But see* North Dakota v. Fredericks, 940 F.2d 333 (8th Cir. 1991) (removal under § 1444; although derivative jurisdiction rule has explicitly been abolished only in § 1441 removal cases, rule is judicially abolished in all other cases). The American Law Institute's proposed revision of § 1441 would clarify that the derivative jurisdiction rule is abolished in all cases. *See* ALI FEDERAL JUDICIAL CODE REVISION PROJECT § 1441(e) (Tent. Draft. No. 3 1999).

lacked jurisdiction because Congress has vested exclusive authority to hear federal antitrust claims in federal district courts. Instead, *B* could have had the state court action dismissed for lack of subject-matter jurisdiction. Today, however, *B* may remove the case.

* * * * *

The defendant may waive the right to remove by taking substantial defensive action in the state court, such as the filing of an answer on the merits.[435] Given the thirty-day time limit that exists on removal (discussed in subsection *(d)*, below), the waiver doctrine is of minor significance today.[436] A party will seldom be able to take substantial defensive action in a state court before the thirty-day time limit for removing the action expires.[437] Waiver of the right to remove may also occur by entering into a valid forum selection clause.[438]

Illustration 2-96. *A*, a citizen of State *X*, contracts with *B*, a citizen of State *Y*. The contract contains a forum selection clause in which *B* agrees to submit to a forum selected by *A*. The clause also prohibits *B* from removing the action to federal court. Subsequently, *A* sues *B* in a state court in State *X*. *B* removes the action to federal court. The action should be remanded. *B* has waived the right to remove by entering into a valid forum selection clause.[439]

(b) Exception to the General Rule of Removal Jurisdiction in Diversity Cases: Section 1441(b)

Section 1441(b) excepts certain diversity cases from the removal jurisdiction conferred by § 1441(a). When removal is based entirely on diversity of citizenship, a case may not be removed if *any* of the defendants is a citizen of the state in which the action is brought. This restriction reflects the policies of the diversity jurisdiction. If a state court is satisfactory to a noncitizen plaintiff, the defendant may not remove because no danger of bias or prejudice exists against the defendant as an outsider in the courts of the defendant's own state.[440]

---

435. *See* 14B CHARLES A. WRIGHT ET AL., FEDERAL PRACTICE AND PROCEDURE: JURISDICTION AND RELATED MATTERS AND RELATED MATTERS § 3721, at 363-68 (3d ed. 1998). *But cf.* Aqualon Co. v. MAC Equip., Inc., 149 F.3d 262 (4th Cir. 1998) (no waiver by conduct when defendant filed motion for judgment against third party the same day notice of removal filed because waiver by conduct does not occur when removal precedes any action by the state court).

436. *See* RICHARD H. FALLON ET AL., HART & WECHSLER'S THE FEDERAL COURTS AND THE FEDERAL SYSTEM 1625 (4th ed. 1996).

437. *But see* Scholz v. RDV Sports, Inc., 821 F. Supp. 1469 (M.D. Fla. 1993).

438. *See, e.g.,* Snapper, Inc. v. Redan, 171 F.3d 1249 (11th Cir. 1999); Excell, Inc. v. Sterling Boiler & Mechanical, Inc., 106 F.3d 318 (10th Cir. 1997); Travelers Ins. Co. v. Keeling, 996 F.2d 1485 (2d Cir. 1993).

439. *See, e.g.,* Foster v. Chesapeake Ins. Co., 933 F.2d 1207 (3d Cir. 1991).

440. The American Law Institute's proposed revision of § 1441 retains this restriction, but it broadens the language of the restriction to make it clear that it applies to defendants who have voluntarily appeared without being served with process and to plaintiffs who have been realigned as defendants. (The doctrine of realignment is examined in Chapter 8(C)(3)*(c) infra.) See* ALI FEDERAL JUDICIAL CODE REVISION PROJECT § 1441(b)(2) (Tent. Draft No. 3 1999); *id.* at 40-41 (commentary).

However, § 1441(b) creates a curious imbalance between original jurisdiction and removal jurisdiction in diversity cases. A plaintiff who is a citizen of the state in which the action is brought may sue an out-of-state citizen within the diversity jurisdiction under 28 U.S.C. § 1332, but a defendant who is a citizen of the state in which the action is brought may not remove an action brought in state court by an out-of-state citizen. Furthermore, in multiple defendant actions in which only one of the defendants is a citizen of the state in which the action is brought, the restriction on removal in § 1441(b) can potentially result in the out-of-state defendant being subjected to the kind of bias or prejudice that the diversity jurisdiction was designed to guard against. In this respect, however, § 1441(b) is no worse that the rule requiring complete diversity of citizenship for original (and removal) jurisdiction. As indicated in subsection 3*(a)*, above, that rule can also result in the operation of bias or prejudice against noncitizens.[441]

Illustration 2-97. *A*, a citizen of State *X*, sues *B*, a citizen of State *Y*, for $500,000 in a State *Y* state court. *A's* claim arises under state law. *B* may not remove the action to a U.S. District Court in State *Y* because of the restriction in § 1441(b) on removal jurisdiction. *B* is a citizen of the state in which the action is brought and the claim is based entirely on state law. However, if a citizen of the forum state possesses a claim for relief against a noncitizen meeting the amount-in-controversy requirement, the citizen can sue the noncitizen in a U.S. District Court in the forum state notwithstanding the fact that the plaintiff is a citizen of the state in which the action is brought.[442]

Illustration 2-98. In *Illustration 2-97*, if *A's* claim had been based on federal law, the § 1441(b) restriction would not prevent removal. Section 1441(b) provides that when removal is based on a claim arising under federal law, the action can be removed without regard to the citizenship of the parties.

Illustration 2-99. *A*, a citizen of State *X*, sues *B*, a citizen of State *Y*, and *C*, a citizen of State *Z*, in a state court in State *Y*. *A* asserts a state claim in the alternative for $500,000 against *B* and *C* arising out of an automobile accident. The action cannot be removed even though a U.S. District Court would have had original jurisdiction over the action. *B* is a citizen of State *Y*. Thus, § 1441(b) prevents removal. Note that the State *Y* trier of fact may find in favor of *A* and against *C* while exonerating *B*, the State *Y* citizen, on the basis of bias or prejudice. *C's* position is different from *A's*. If a State *Y* trier of fact discriminates against *A*, it is because *A* did not sue in a U.S. District Court in State *Y* where the bias or prejudice is (presumably) absent or can be controlled. However, because of *B's* presence in the action, *C* may not remove to a federal forum. *C* is thus deprived of a choice by § 1441(b) that *A* possessed, but chose to relinquish.

---

441. *See Illustration 2-34* and accompanying text *supra.*

442. If, after *A* sues *B* in the state court, *B* asserts a counterclaim against *A*, *A* cannot remove to federal court; only defendants can remove and *A* is a plaintiff. *See* Shamrock Oil & Gas Corp. v. Sheets, 313 U.S. 100, 61 S. Ct. 868, 85 L. Ed. 1214 (1941).

(c) Removal of Separate and Independent Claims: Section 1441(c)

Section 1441(c) provides for removal of a category of cases over which no original jurisdiction exists in the district courts. Thus, § 1441(c) encompasses certain cases that are not removable under § 1441(a). Generally, § 1441(c) provides for removal of civil actions in which a claim is asserted within 28 U.S.C. § 1331 (the general federal question statute) when those actions also contain nonfederal claims that are factually unrelated to the federal claim in the action. Actions containing factually related federal and nonfederal claims are removable under § 1441(a) & (b), because they are within the original jurisdiction of the district courts under § 1331 and § 1367 (the supplemental jurisdiction statute). Consequently, § 1441(c) provides for removal of federal question cases containing state claims that are too unrelated to the federal claims in the action to fall within the supplemental jurisdiction of the district courts. When a claim is removable under § 1441(c), only the defendant against whom the removable claim is asserted must seek removal. This result is contrary to the usual rule that all defendants must agree to remove the action.[443]

Before 1990, 28 U.S.C. § 1441(c) provided that when a "separate and independent" claim or cause of action, which would be removable if sued on alone, was joined with a nonremovable claim, the entire action could be removed to federal court.[444] In the Judicial Improvements Act of 1990, § 1441(c) was amended to eliminate its application to diversity actions.[445] Section 1441(c) now reads:

> (c) Whenever a separate and independent claim or cause of action within the jurisdiction conferred by section 1331 of this title is joined with one or more otherwise non-removable claims or causes of action, the entire case may be removed and the district court may determine all issues therein, or, in its discretion, may remand all matters in which State law predominates.[446]

The stated purpose of the 1990 amendment was to implement, "in modified form," a recommendation of the Federal Courts Study Committee.[447] However, the Federal Courts Study Committee had recommended outright repeal of § 1441(c).[448] The Committee recognized that the principal purpose of § 1441(c) was to prevent a defendant's right of removal from being defeated by the joinder of an unrelated nonremovable claim[449] and that most § 1441(c)

---

443. *See* 14C CHARLES A. WRIGHT ET AL., FEDERAL PRACTICE AND PROCEDURE: JURISDICTION AND RELATED MATTERS § 3731, at 267-68 (3d ed. 1998).

444. *See generally* William T. Goglia, Annotation, *What Is "A Separate and Independent Claim or Cause of Action" Within 28 U.S.C.S. § 1441(c) Which Permits Nonresident Codefendant to Remove Case From State to Federal Court,* 58 A.L.R. FED. 458 (1982).

445. Pub. L. No. 101-650, § 312, 104 Stat. 5089, 5114 (codified at 28 U.S.C. § 1441(c)).

446. *Id.*

447. *See* H.R. REP. NO. 734, 101st Cong., 2d Sess. 22 (1990).

448. *See* REPORT OF THE FEDERAL COURTS STUDY COMMITTEE 94-95 (1990).

449. *See id.* at 94.

applications occurred in diversity actions.[450] The Committee felt that the statute caused "much litigation apart from the merits as defendants try and mostly fail to qualify for separate claim removal."[451] The Committee's only reference to federal question cases was the following passage:

> In the small number of federal question cases in which the statute might apply . . . it can work fairly well as a backstop to the general removal provisions (§§ 1441(a) & (b)). Hence we recommend its repeal only if Congress retains the general diversity jurisdiction, in which most of the difficulties with § 1441(c) arise.[452]

Congress did retain the general diversity jurisdiction. So why was § 1441(c) modified and not repealed as the Committee recommended? The House Report accompanying the amendment § 1441(c) explained:

> The amendment would . . . retain the opportunity for removal in the one situation in which it seems clearly desirable. The joinder rules of many states permit a plaintiff to join completely unrelated claims in a single action. The plaintiff could easily bring a single action on a federal claim and a completely unrelated state claim. The reasons for permitting removal of federal question cases [apply] with full force. In addition, the amended provision could actually simplify determination of removability. In many cases the federal and state claims will be related in such a way as to establish pendant [sic] jurisdiction over the state claim. Removal of such cases is possible under Sec. 1441(a). *The amended provision would establish a basis for removal that would avoid the need to decide whether there is pendant [sic] jurisdiction.*[453]

---

450. *See id.* at 94-95.

451. *Id.* at 95.

452. *Id.*

453. H.R REP. NO. 734, 101st Cong., 2d Sess. 23 (1990) (emphasis added). The legislative history in the Senate is similar, but contains a reference to the need to remand "state claims" that do not form part of the same case or controversy as federal claims with which they are joined:

> The amendment would . . . retain the opportunity for removal in the one situation in which it seems clearly desirable. The joinder rules of many states permit a plaintiff to join completely unrelated claims in a single action. The plaintiff could easily bring a single action on a federal claim and a completely unrelated state claim. The reasons for permitting removal of federal question cases applies with full force. In addition, the amended provision could actually simplify determinations of removability. In many cases the federal and state claims will be related in such a way as to establish pendant [sic] jurisdiction over the state claim. Removal of such cases is possible under 28 U.S.C. § 1441(a).
>
> The further amendment to 28 U.S.C. § 1441(c) that would permit remand of all matters in which state law predominates also should simplify administration of the separate and independent claim removal. Of course, a district court must remand state claims that are so unrelated to the federal claim that they do not form part of the same Article III case or controversy.

136 CONG. REC. 517, 581 (Oct. 27, 1990) (statement of Sen. Grassley). The Senate history thus eliminates a reference in the House Report that indicates § 1441(c) would avoid the need to determine whether there is pendant jurisdiction. The Senate history then adds a sentence (in the second paragraph quoted above) indicating

Numerous and severe problems exist with the text of § 1441(c). Problems also exist with the explanation given in the legislative history of the 1990 amendment to the section. These problems are explored below. Specifically, three issues of interpretation will be discussed: (1) when claims should be considered "separate and independent" within the meaning of § 1441(c); (2) how § 1367 and § 1441(c) can be reconciled with each other and the Constitution; and (3) the scope of the remand provision of § 1441(c).

(i) The Meaning of "Separate and Independent"

Before the 1990 amendment, it was not entirely clear what kinds of cases were removable under the statute. In *American Fire & Casualty Co. v. Finn*,[454] the U.S. Supreme Court held that when the plaintiff sought to recover for a single wrong resulting from an interlocked series of transactions, no separate and independent claims existed under § 1441(c).

Illustration 2-100. A, a citizen of Texas, sued *B Insurance Corp.*, a corporation incorporated and with its principal place of business in Indiana, and *B's* agent *C*, a citizen of Texas, in a state court in Texas. *A* sought to recover for a fire loss allegedly covered by *B. A's* complaint sought recovery in the alternative against *B* and *C*. The claim against *B* was under a policy of insurance issued by *B*. The claim against *C* alleged that if recovery under the policy was impossible because the policy had lapsed, *C* was liable to *A* for the amount of the loss because *C* had a duty to notify *A* of any cancellation or expiration of the policy and did not do so. Under these circumstances, the action would not be removable to federal court under former § 1441(c). The claim against *B* was a claim which would be removable if sued on alone because it was within the diversity jurisdiction, and, before the 1990 amendment, § 1441(c) applied to diversity cases. In addition, the removable diversity claim was joined with a nonremovable claim, the claim against *C*. However, *Finn* held that claims are not separate and independent within the meaning of § 1441(c) when the plaintiff seeks a recovery for a single loss against multiple defendants based on a single event.

* * * * *

---

that state claims which are not part of the bases for removal would have to be remanded. One commentator has read this change as specific evidence that "Congress" chose to address the constitutional difficulties with § 1441(c) (discussed in subsection *(ii), infra*) by "counting on federal courts to use the power of remand." *See* Edward Hartnett, *A New Trick From An Old and Abused Dog: Section 1441(c) Lives and Now Permits the Remand of Federal Question Cases*, 63 FORDHAM L. REV. 1099, 1150 (1995). This conclusion, however, ignores the fact that amended § 1441(c) only provides for remand of state claims when they "predominate." In any event, the reference by Senator Grassley to remand of "state claims" does not support Professor Hartnett's position that § 1441(c) permits the remand of entire cases. Indeed, remand of federal claims as well as state claims would gut the central purpose of removal under § 1441(c), something that the legislative history in both the House and Senate indicated as applying in "full force." *See* subsection (iii) *infra*; *see also* REED DICKERSON, THE INTERPRETATION AND APPLICATION OF STATUTES 154-59 (1975) (discussing the lack of reliability of floor statements when compared with committee reports).

454. 341 U.S. 6, 14, 71 S. Ct. 534, 540, 95 L. Ed. 702, 708-09 (1951). *See generally* ERWIN CHEMERINSKY, FEDERAL JURISDICTION § 5.5, at 344 (3d ed. 1999).

Finn was the only Supreme Court decision directly construing § 1441(c) before the 1990 amendment. However, in *Carnegie-Mellon University v. Cohill*,[455] the Supreme Court stated in dictum that § 1441(c) "is not directly applicable to suits involving pendent [today supplemental] claims, because pendent claims are not 'separate and independent' within the meaning of the removal statute."[456] This statement confirms the strong impression left by *Finn* and the language of § 1441(c) that separate and independent claims must be factually unrelated. Factually related claims always fit within the scope of pendent (today supplemental) jurisdiction. Furthermore, if the federal and state claims do not arise out of the same facts, they will surely seek separate recoveries. Taking *Finn* and *Carnegie-Mellon* together, therefore, claims would be "separate" when separate recoveries are sought and "independent" when the claims arise from different facts.

Illustration 2-101. Assume that *A*, a citizen of State *X*, sues *B*, also a citizen of State *X*, in a State *X* state court. *A's* suit consists of two claims, one arising under federal law for $500,000 and one arising under state law for $30,000. The claims seek separate recoveries and are unrelated, factually and legally. Thus, they are "separate and independent." The claim arising under federal law would be removable if sued upon alone. The state claim would not be removable if sued upon alone. Thus, the entire case is removable both under the language of § 1441(c) and the precedents interpreting it.

* * * * *

Nevertheless, a difficult question of interpretation existed under former § 1441(c) involving cases falling between those exemplified by *Illustrations 2-100* and *2-101*. In particular, when a plaintiff sues multiple defendants for multiple losses (rather than a single recovery) arising from the same or a related set of facts, or multiple plaintiffs seek recoveries against a single defendant for losses arising from a single or related set of facts, are the claims asserted "separate and independent" within the meaning of § 1441(c)? *Finn* and *Carnegie-Mellon* suggest not. However, some lower federal court decisions before the amendment of § 1441(c) permitted removal in these kinds of cases despite the Supreme Court's suggestion that removal was improper.[457]

Illustration 2-102. *A*, a citizen of State *X*, and *B*, a citizen of State *Y*, sued *C Airline*, a corporation incorporated and with its principal place of business in State *Y*. *A* and *B* brought the action in a state court in State *X*. *A* sought $100,000 in damages for personal injuries resulting from the crash of a *C* airliner. *B* also sought $100,000 in damages for personal injuries received in the same crash. Before the 1990 amendment of § 1441(c), some lower federal courts

---

455. 484 U.S. 343, 108 S. Ct. 614, 98 L. Ed. 2d 720 (1988).

456. *Id.* at 354, 108 S. Ct. at 621, 98 L. Ed. 2d at 732.

457. *See, e.g.*, Twentieth Century-Fox Film Corp. v. Taylor, 239 F. Supp. 913 (S.D.N.Y. 1965) (action against Richard Burton and Elizabeth Taylor for breach of their employment contracts during the filming of the movie "Cleopatra") (disapproved in Gardner & Florence Call Cowles Found. v. Empire Inc., 754 F.2d 478, 482 n.5 (2d Cir. 1985)); Herrmann v. Braniff Airways, Inc., 308 F. Supp. 1094 (S.D.N.Y. 1969) (action by multiple plaintiffs arising from a single aircraft accident). For additional cases, see 16 GEORGINE VARIO, MOORE'S FEDERAL PRACTICE § 107.14[6][a] (3d ed. 1999); 14C CHARLES A WRIGHT ET AL., FEDERAL PRACTICE AND PROCEDURE: JURISDICTION AND RELATED MATTERS § 3724, at 36-39 (3d ed. 1998).

permitted *C* to remove this action under the section. *A's* claim would be removable if sued on alone. *B's* claim was not removable if sued on alone. Even though the claims arose from the same event, the courts that permitted removal considered the claims to be both separate and independent because separate recoveries were sought.

* * * * *

The structure and probable purpose of § 1441(c), together with the legislative history of the 1990 amendment to the section, should dispel any doubt about the meaning of the terms "separate and independent." Only claims that arise from entirely unrelated facts and seek separate recoveries should be removable under the section. In deciphering the statute, several questions should be considered: (1) Why did Congress make removability contingent upon the joined claims being sufficiently unrelated to each other? (2) When the claims meet the relationship test of the statute, why is the entire action, as opposed to only the claim over which the district court has original jurisdiction, made removable? (3) Once the action has been removed, why was the district court given discretion to keep the entire case or to remand the nonremovable claim before 1990?

Focusing first on the requirement that the joined claims must be unrelated, note that even prior to the 1990 amendment to § 1441(c), Congress was probably attempting to prevent the joinder of removable and nonremovable claims in state court simply for the purpose of preventing removal by the defendant. This danger is greatest in that category of cases in which joinder by the plaintiff is least likely to be for legitimate procedural reasons—cases in which the claims are factually and legally unrelated to each other. In other cases, when some factual relationship exists between the claims, plaintiffs are less likely to join claims simply to prevent removal.[458]

Nevertheless, some plaintiffs may join factually unrelated claims for legitimate reasons. In joinder systems patterned on Federal Rule 18, unlimited joinder of claims is permitted even if no factual or legal relationship exists between the claims. The theory of this kind of system is that no harm results from unlimited joinder of claims at the pleading stage of the litigation, but only, sometimes, by trying unrelated claims together. However, if inconvenience will result from trying unrelated claims together, the inconvenience can be dealt with under provisions, such as Federal Rule 42(b), which allow separate trials of the claims to be ordered.[459] Thus, the policy of modern unlimited joinder practice

---

458. The textual discussion is applicable only to situations in which joinder of the claims in question is not "fraudulent." Whenever a plaintiff collusively or fraudulently joins a claim against a resident defendant in a diversity action to prevent removal, the nonresident defendant may remove by alleging and proving the fraudulent joinder. Thus, the textual discussion here is limited to cases in which the joinder does not meet the fraudulent joinder standards, but may be primarily intended to defeat removal nonetheless. Fraudulent joinder is discussed in 14B CHARLES A. WRIGHT ET AL., FEDERAL PRACTICE AND PROCEDURE: JURISDICTION AND RELATED MATTERS § 3723, at 625-58 (3d ed. 1998). The most common situation in which fraudulent joinder is found is when the plaintiff has failed to state a claim for relief against a nondiverse defendant. *See id.* at 630-31; Green v. Amerada Hess Corp., 707 F.2d 201 (5th Cir. 1983), *cert. denied*, 464 U.S. 1039, 104 S. Ct. 701, 79 L. Ed. 2d 166 (1984).

459. 6A CHARLES A. WRIGHT ET AL., FEDERAL PRACTICE AND PROCEDURE: CIVIL § 1586 (2d ed. 1990).

is to leave to the plaintiff in the first instance the decision whether it will be convenient to resolve all claims the plaintiff possesses against the defendant in one proceeding, subject to later discretion in the court to sever the claims for trial.

The original § 1441(c) drafters' decision can, therefore, be seen as an attempt to accommodate the policy of unlimited joinder of claims that is found in many modern procedural systems with the policy of avoiding the joinder of unrelated claims simply to prevent removal. Limiting removal to situations in which wholly unrelated claims were joined protected against joinder designed to prevent removal. Plaintiffs are less likely to join completely unrelated claims for reasons of litigational convenience than they are to join related claims for these same reasons. Allowing removal of the entire case, rather than only the removable claim, accommodated the policy of unlimited joinder that is found in modern procedural systems. Finally, giving discretion to the district court to remand the nonremovable claim allowed the court to determine whether the plaintiff's reasons for joinder were legitimate or whether joinder was effectuated simply to prevent removal. Therefore, before the 1990 amendment, to conform removal to both the language and the structure of the statute, the courts should have limited the application of § 1441(c) to cases in which no factual relationship existed between the claims.[460]

The legislative history of the 1990 amendment to the statute should resolve any doubt about the kinds of cases that are removable under § 1441(c). That history confirms that the words "separate and independent" require factually unrelated claims seeking separate recoveries. The House Report explains that Congress retained separate and independent claim removal to prevent the defendant's right of removal from being destroyed when the plaintiff joins federal and state claims that are completely unrelated to each other, factually and legally.[461]

Unfortunately, the court decisions construing § 1441(c) since the 1990 amendment do not entirely dispel the pre-1990 confusion about the statute's interpretation. Several decisions since the amendment have allowed removal of factually related federal and state claims. A few of these decisions seem to confuse the relationship between § 1441(a), § 1441(c), and § 1367 of Title 28. Some courts combine the different statutes, despite their language, to allow

---

460. Unfortunately, the legislative history of the statute prior to 1990 adds little to the understanding of the meaning of the words "separate and independent." *See* RICHARD H. FALLON ET AL., HART & WECHSLER'S THE FEDERAL COURTS AND THE FEDERAL SYSTEM 1625-26 (4th ed. 1996). However, candor requires the admission that the history of the statute, to the extent it adds anything, works against the interpretation in the text. Under the textual interpretation, few diversity actions would be removable. *Cf.* CHARLES A. WRIGHT, THE LAW OF FEDERAL COURTS § 39, at 236 (5th ed. 1994). Thus, the section had its primary value in federal question cases. Yet it may be that in the 1948 revision of the Judicial Code, Congress did not think that § 1441(c) would be applicable to federal question cases. *See* 1 FEDERAL COURTS STUDY COMMITTEE WORKING PAPERS AND SUBCOMMITTEE REPORTS 534 (1990), and authorities there discussed in note 59; *see also* CHARLES A. WRIGHT, THE LAW OF FEDERAL COURTS § 39, at 237 (5th ed. 1994).

461. Recall that the House Report accompanying the amendment to § 1441(c) stated that when, as permitted by joinder rules like Federal Rule 18, the plaintiff joined a federal claim "and a completely unrelated state claim," "[t]he reasons for permitting removal of federal question cases [apply] with full force." H.R. REP. NO. 734, 101st Cong., 2d Sess. 23 (1990). The legislative history in the Senate was identical on this point. *See* 136 Cong. Rec. at 5.17,581 (Oct. 27, 1990) (statement of Sen. Grassley).

removal of factually related claims.[462] Nevertheless, courts that show an awareness of the proper differences between the statutes also allow removal of factually related claims seeking separate recoveries.[463]

Illustration 2-103. *A*, a citizen of State *X*, had a flat tire and sought the assistance of *B*, a police officer and citizen of State *X*. *B* called an agent of *C*, a corporation incorporated and with its principal place of business in State *X*, to assist *A*. After *C's* agent had changed *A's* flat tire, the agent demanded payment in cash. When *A* could not pay, the agent called *B*, who arrested *A*. *A* sued *B* and *C* in a state court of State *X*. *A* asserted a claim against *B* under 42 U.S.C. § 1983, the Civil Rights Act of 1871. *A* asserted only a state-law claim against *C* for unfair and deceptive trade practices. *B* attempted to remove the action to a U.S. District Court in State *X* under § 1441(c). Because *B* alone sought removal, § 1441(a) and (b), which require all defendants to seek removal, could not be used. On these facts, a federal district court allowed removal under § 1441(c). The court stated that the harm allegedly caused by *C* was separate and distinct from the harm caused by *B*. The court's opinion was based on the fact that separate recoveries were sought on the claims against *B* and *C*. However, the claims arose from the same facts and would have been within the supplemental jurisdiction of the district court under § 1367. Therefore, had both defendants joined in seeking removal of the action, jurisdiction would have been proper under § 1441(a). Under the pre-1990 U.S. Supreme Court precedents interpreting § 1441(c), and given the probable purposes of the statute and the legislative history of the 1990 amendment, it is highly unlikely that the action was properly removed.[464]

* * * * *

Despite the persistence of decisions allowing removal under § 1441(c) when joined federal and state claims are factually related, the overwhelming majority of decisions after 1990 hold that removal under § 1441(c) requires factually unrelated claims. Under this view, which accords with the language, structure, and the 1990 legislative history of § 1441(c), few cases will be removable under the statute. Thus, most decisions deny removal because the

---

462. *See, e.g.,* Newton v. Coca-Cola Bottling Co. Consol., 958 F. Supp. 248 (W.D.N.C. 1997) (Title VII claim that plaintiff fired in retaliation for complaining about sexual violence committed against her by former employee and nonremovable Violence Against Women Act claim against employee are separate and independent); Richmond v. American Sys. Corp., 792 F. Supp. 449 (E.D. Va. 1992); *see also* Scranna *ex rel.* Urso v. Furlong, 56 F. Supp. 1000 (N.D. Ill. 1999) (stating that "[i]t is not the facts that the court focuses upon to determine whether the claims are separate and independent," but rather the legal rights involved (citing *Finn* as authority)!); Dobiecki v. Chicago Osteopathic Hosps., 829 F. Supp. (N.D. Ill. 1993) (describing § 1441(c) and § 1367(c) as alternative provisions allowing removal whenever there is a federal question in the case).

463. *See* Alexander v. Goldome Credit Corp., 772 F. Supp. 1217 (M.D. Ala. 1991) (separate recoveries, related facts); Rey v. Classic Cars, 762 F. Supp. 421 (D. Mass. 1991); *see also* Moore v. DeBiase, 766 F. Supp. 1311, 1318-19 n.13 (D.N.J. 1991) (separate recoveries, related facts; action removed under §§ 1441(a) & (b), remanded under § 1441(c); court stated that § 1441(c) allows removal of federal question cases in which state claims are somewhat related to federal claims, but not sufficiently related to be within pendent jurisdiction); *see also* Joan Steinman, *Supplemental Jurisdiction in § 1441 Removed Cases: An Unsurveyed Frontier of Congress' Handwork*, 35 ARIZ. L. REV. 305 (1993).

464. *Cf.* Rey v. Classic Cars, 762 F. Supp. 421 (D. Mass. 1991) (facts simplified for purposes of illustration).

federal and state claims are factually related.[465] Only a few cases have allowed removal on the basis that the federal and state claims were unrelated, and the courts in those cases may have mistakenly perceived that the federal and state claims were sufficiently disassociated to be ''separate and independent'' within the meaning of § 1441(c).[466]

Illustration 2-104. *A,* a citizen of State *X,* sued *B,* a citizen of State *X* who was *A's* former employer, in a state court of State *X.* *A* asserted two claims against *B.* One claim was a federal claim for failure to pay *A* overtime for certain work performed by *A* while *A* was employed by *B.* The second claim was a state-law claim for breach of an implied contract of employment when *B* fired *A.* *A* did not allege that the firing was related to *A's* complaints about *B's* failure to pay overtime. *B* removed the action under § 1441(c). In allowing removal, the district court reasoned that *A's* federal claim would turn on whether *A* had devoted more than half *A's* time to supervisory duties when employed by *B,* while the second claim would depend on establishing an implied contract of employment and its breach. Because proving one claim would be of no assistance in proving the other, the court considered the claims separate and independent. However, although *A* sought separate recoveries from *B,* the federal and state claims were probably not sufficiently disassociated to be separate and independent. Both claims arose out of the same employment relationship between *A* and *B.* The claims were thus sufficiently related to justify removal on the basis of supplemental jurisdiction under 28 U.S.C. § 1367 and § 1441(a).[467] Under the pre-1990 U.S. Supreme Court precedents construing § 1441(c), claims sufficiently related to fall within supplemental jurisdiction are not separate and independent.

---

465. *See, e.g.,* Mullins v. Hinkle, 953 F. Supp. 744 (S.D. W. Va. 1997); Texas Hosp. Ass'n v. National Heritage Ins. Co., 802 F. Supp. 1507 (W.D. Tex. 1992); Lang v. American Elec. Power Co., 785 F. Supp. 1331 (N.D. Ind. 1992); Allsup v. Liberty Mut. Ins. Co., 782 F. Supp. 325 (N.D. Tex. 1991); Sullivan v. Leaf River Forest Prods., Inc., 791 F. Supp. 627 (S.D. Miss. 1991); *cf.* Borough of W. Mifflin v. Lancaster, 45 F.3d 780 (3d Cir. 1995) (district court had pendent jurisdiction under § 1367; therefore, claims could not be separate and independent and could not be remanded under § 1441(c)).

466. *See, e.g.,* Moralez v. Meat Cutters Local 539, 778 F. Supp. 368 (E.D. Mich. 1991); Nesbitt v. Bun Basket, Inc., 780 F. Supp. 1151 (W.D. Mich. 1991).

467. *See* Nesbitt v. Bun Basket, Inc., 780 F. Supp. 1151, 1152 (W.D. Mich. 1991). In subsection 4*(d)(i),* it was suggested that only a loose factual relationship is necessary to satisfy the requirements for pendent jurisdiction. *See* 13B CHARLES A. WRIGHT ET AL., FEDERAL PRACTICE AND PROCEDURE: JURISDICTION AND RELATED MATTERS § 3567.1, at 117 (2d ed. 1984). Note, however, that if the cases hold something more than a ''loose factual relationship'' necessary to bring federal and state claims within the scope of the same case, two possibilities for the interpretation of § 1441(c) arise. One possibility, supported by the pre-amendment interpretation of § 1441(c) by the U.S. Supreme Court and by the legislative history of amended § 1441(c), is that complete factual disassociation between the removable and nonremovable claims will be required. Thus, there could be federal removable claims joined with claims that would be nonremovable under §§ 1367(a) and 1441(a) because they were only ''loosely'' related to the federal claim, but which would be too closely related to the federal claims to be removable under § 1441(c). *See* CHARLES A. WRIGHT, LAW OF FEDERAL COURTS § 39, at 238 (5th ed. 1994) (discussing this possibility under the pre-1990 version of the statute). The second possibility, which would contradict the U.S. Supreme Court's interpretation of the statute and the legislative history of the 1990 amendment, would treat claims as separate and independent if they are ''loosely'' related *or* totally unrelated. This approach would allow removal under § 1441(c) of all cases in which the federal removable claims and the nonremovable claims are not closely enough related to fit within the supplemental jurisdiction conferred by § 1367(a). This approach would, of course, be subject to the constitutional restrictions discussed in subsection *(ii) infra.*

Illustration 2-105. *A*, a citizen of State *X*, is a merchant. *A* was assaulted by *B*, a police officer who is also a citizen of State *X*. The assault occurred when *B* stopped *A's* automobile for speeding. Several months before the assault, *B* had purchased goods on a time payment plan from *A's* store. The entire transaction had been handled by one of *A's* sales representatives, and *B* did not even know the store was owned by *A*. Later, *B* stopped making payments on the goods. The assault had nothing to do with the sale of goods or *B's* failure to make payments. *A* sued *B* in a State *X* court. *A* asserted a federal civil rights claim against *B* and a state-law claim for breach of the contract for sale of goods. This kind of action is one in which removal would be proper under § 1441(c). *A* asserts claims that seek separate recoveries and are factually unrelated in time, space, origin, and motivation.

Illustration 2-106. On the facts of *Illustration 2-105*, assume that *A* was assaulted by *B* and *C*. Both *B* and *C* are police officers and citizens of State *X*. All other facts remain the same. *A* sues *B* and *C* in a state court of State *X*. *A* asserts federal civil rights claims against both *B* and *C*. *A* joins with these claims the state-law claim against *B* for breach of the contract to sell goods.[468] This action is also removable under § 1441(c). The civil rights claims are within the jurisdiction conferred by 28 U.S.C. § 1331. They are separate and independent from the breach of contract claim on the facts described.

(ii) The Relationship Between Supplemental Jurisdiction and Separate and Independent Claim Removal

In retaining separate and independent claim removal for federal question cases, Congress overlooked a problem created by the interaction of § 1441(c) and § 1367 of the Judicial Code dealing with supplemental jurisdiction.[469] Recall from subsection *4(d)*, above, that Congress provided for "supplemental jurisdiction" over claims that are joined in a federal action when those claims "are so related" to claims over which the district court has original jurisdiction as to "form part of the same case or controversy under Article III of the United States Constitution."[470] This language (from 28 U.S.C. § 1367(a)) produces an immediate difficulty. If wholly unrelated federal and state claims are within the same constitutional case or controversy, original jurisdiction exists over such claims under 28 U.S.C. § 1331 (the general federal question statute) and

---

468. Under joinder of claims and parties rules like Rules 18 and 20 of the Federal Rules of Civil Procedure, these claims would be properly joined. *See* Chapter 8(C)(4) ("Permissive Joinder of Parties") *infra*.

469. Some commentators have argued that the legislative history of § 1441(c) in the Senate indicates that "Congress" intended to handle the constitutional problems with § 1441(c) by remand. *See* Edward Hartnett, *A New Trick From An Old and Abused Dog: Section 1441(c) Lives and Now Permits the Demand of Federal Question Cases*, 63 FORDHAM L. REV. 1099, 1150 (1995). However, the House and Senate history is contradictory on this point. *See* subsection *(c)(i)* and accompanying notes *supra*. Furthermore, if Congress intended to require remand in cases of constitutional difficulty under § 1441(c), "why does the text of § 1441(c) speak only of 'discretion' to remand?" RICHARD H. FALLON ET AL., HART AND WECHSLER'S THE FEDERAL COURTS AND THE FEDERAL SYSTEM 1628 (4th ed. 1996).

470. *See* Judicial Improvements Act of 1990, Pub. L. No. 101-650, § 310, 104 Stat. 5089, 5113-14 (codified at 28 U.S.C. § 1367(a)).

§ 1367(a)—with the result that a case involving such claims is removable under 28 U.S.C. § 1441(a) and (b). In this event, 28 U.S.C. § 1441(c) is superfluous. On the other hand, if joined federal and state claims must arise from the same facts to be within the same constitutional case or controversy, amended § 1441(c) can have no constitutional applications.[471]

This dilemma can be avoided if the courts interpret the scope of a constitutional case or controversy and the scope of 28 U.S.C. § 1367(a) as this text recommends. Subsection 4*(b)*, above, asserted that Article III should be interpreted to permit joinder of factually unrelated federal and state claims when Congress has a legitimate reason for authorizing such joinder linked to policies designed to protect or enhance the operation of federal jurisdictional grants within Article III. Congress has such legitimate purposes in precisely the situation now governed by 28 U.S.C. § 1441(c).[472] In addition, subsection 4*(d)(i)* asserted that, despite the Article III case or controversy language found in 28 U.S.C. § 1367(a), Congress did not mean to extend jurisdiction under that section to factually unrelated claims. Rather, Congress intended only to provide for "supplemental jurisdiction" over cases in which the federal and nonfederal claims arise out of the same facts.[473] If § 1367(a) is limited in its operation to factually related claims, and if Article III of the Constitution is interpreted to permit jurisdiction over factually unrelated claims in the situation now covered by 28 U.S.C. § 1441(c), the latter section will be neither superfluous nor unconstitutional.

Another way to solve the problems of interaction between § 1367 and § 1441(c) would be for Congress to revise one or both statutes. The American Law Institute has proposed that Congress do just that by amending § 1441(c). The ALI's proposal would allow removal of entire actions containing removable and nonremovable claims that are not part of the same Article III case, but would require remand of the nonremovable claim.[474]

---

471. At least two federal district courts have held § 1441(c) unconstitutional to the extent that it permits removal of factually unrelated federal and state claims. *See* Fullin v. Martin, 34 F. Supp. 2d 726 (E.D. Wis. 1999); Salei v. Boardwalk Regency Corp., 913 F. Supp. 993 (E.D. Mich. 1996); *cf.* 1 FEDERAL COURTS STUDY COMMITTEE WORKING PAPERS AND SUBCOMMITTEE REPORTS 537 (1990); CHARLES A. WRIGHT, THE LAW OF FEDERAL COURTS § 39, at 238-39 (5th ed. 1994). Recall that the House Report accompanying the amendment to 28 U.S.C. § 1441(c) stated that "[t]he amended provision would establish a basis for removal that would avoid the need to decide whether there is pendent [sic] jurisdiction." H.R. REP. NO. 734, 101st Cong., 2d Sess. 23 (1990). This statement is clearly not true if the "constitutional case or controversy" language in 28 U.S.C. § 1367(a) means what it says. For in every case brought to federal court, originally or by removal, the courts are obligated to determine whether the jurisdiction conferred by Congress is constitutional. Therefore, in every federal question case involving joined claims, the courts must determine whether the joined claims fit within the same case or controversy under Article III of the Constitution.

472. *See* subsection 4*(b)*, *Illustration 2-79 supra*. The argument in favor of interpreting Article III to permit joinder of some factually unrelated federal and state claims conforms to the reasons, discussed above, why Congress decided to retain separate and independent claim removal in federal question cases, rather than to repeal § 1441(c) as recommended by the Federal Courts Study Committee.

473. Furthermore, only a "loose" factual relationship should be required by the statute. *See* subsection 4*(d)(i)* and accompanying notes *supra*.

474. ALI FEDERAL JUDICIAL CODE REVISION PROJECT § 1441(c) (Tent. Draft No. 3 1999);

(c) *Removal of claim arising under federal law when joined to unrelated, nonremovable claim.* If a civil action is not removable under subsection (a) solely because a claim that is removable on the basis of the jurisdiction conferred by section 1331 of this title has

(iii) Remand Under Section 1441(c)

Section 1441(c) contains its own remand provision. Before the 1990 amendment to § 1441(c), this section simply provided that the district court might "remand all matters not otherwise within its original jurisdiction." Under the 1990 amendment, the district courts are authorized to "remand all matters in which state law predominates."[475] Several problems of interpretation exist with this change in wording.

Early commentary suggested that this new wording might now justify remand of an entire case in which the state claim(s) predominate over the federal claim(s).[476] Despite the lack of support for this position in the legislative history of the statute[477] and only the barest justification in the statutory language,[478] several courts have followed this suggestion and remanded entire cases in which they perceived that state law predominated over federal law.[479] However, permitting the remand of an entire case risks undermining the primary purpose of § 1441(c). The statute was designed to prevent defendants against whom federal claims were asserted from being trapped in federal court by having an unrelated state claim joined against them. Allowing remand of both federal and state claims undermines this purpose anytime the plaintiff can join an unrelated state claim that somehow "predominates" over the federal claim. The better, and majority, interpretation of § 1441(c) is that only nonremovable claim(s) can be remanded.[480]

---

been joined to a nonremovable claim that is not part of the same case under Article III of the Constitution, any such nonremovable claim shall be disregarded and the entire action may be removed as provided by subsection (a). Upon such removal the district court shall sever from the action all claims that are not part of the same case as the claim that is removable under section 1331, and shall remand the severed claims to the State court from which the action was removed.

475. *See* 28 U.S.C. § 1441(c).

476. *See* EDWARD HARTNETT, *A New Trick From An Old and Abused Dog: Section 1441(c) Lives and Now Permits Remand of Federal Question Cases*, 63 FORDHAM L. REV. 1099 (1995); David D. Siegel, *Changes in Federal Jurisdiction and Practice Under the New (Dec. 1, 1990) Judicial Improvements Act*, 133 F.R.D. 61, 78 (1991).

477. *See* H.R. REP. NO. 734, 101st Cong., 2d Sess. 23 (1990) (which simply states that the new wording should simplify administration of separate and independent claim removal); 136 CONG. REC. 517, 581 (Oct. 27 1990) (statement of Sen. Grassley) (indicating that district courts must remand state "claims" that are so unrelated to the federal claim that they do not form part of the same case or controversy).

478. The entire position depends upon the interpretation of the word "matters" in the statute to include entire "cases." However, the word "matters" was also used in the pre-1990 version of the statute and it did not include entire "cases" then.

479. *See, e.g.,* Cotton v. South Dakota *ex rel.* South Dakota Dep't of Soc. Servs., 843 F. Supp. 564 (D.S.D. 1994) (dictum); Administaff, Inc. v. Kaster, 799 F. Supp. 685 (W.D. Tex. 1992); Alexander v. Goldome Credit Corp., 772 F. Supp. 1217 (M.D. Ala. 1991); Moore v. DeBiase, 766 F. Supp. 1311 (D.N.J. 1991); Martin v. Drummond Coal Co., 756 F. Supp. 524 (N.D. Ala. 1991); Holland v. World Omni Leasing, Inc., 764 F. Supp. 1442 (N.D. Ala. 1991).

480. *See, e.g.,* Eastus v. Blue Bell Creameries, 97 F.3d 100 (5th Cir. 1996); Brockman v. Merabank, 40 F.3d 1013 (9th Cir. 1994); Burks v. Amerada Hess Corp., 8 F.3d 301 (5th Cir. 1993); Buckner v. FDIC, 981 F.2d 816, 820 (5th Cir. 1993); Hickerson v. City of New York, 932 F. Supp. 550 (S.D.N.Y. 1996); Williams v. Huron Valley Sch. Dist., 858 F. Supp. 97 (E.D. Mich. 1994); Kabealo v. Davis, 829 F. Supp. 923 (S.D. Ohio 1993).

Some courts have also applied the remand provision of § 1441(c) to cases that were removed under § 1441(a) and (b).[481] This approach is improper. The remand provision of § 1441(c) was not designed to provide additional remand authority to the district courts in non-§ 1441(c) cases. Furthermore, no support in the language or legislative history exists for this interpretation of § 1441(c). Fortunately, most courts have rejected this view.[482]

The 1990 change in § 1441(c)'s wording can also be interpreted to mean that no discretion exists to remand state claims that do not "predominate," even if the district court finds that those claims were joined solely to prevent removal. Likewise, the language, though discretionary, can be read to encourage the district courts to remand state claims that do "predominate," even if the remand will cause substantial inconvenience to a plaintiff who joined them in good faith. However, this reading is not inevitable. It would be better for the courts to exercise the discretion to remand with a careful eye on the reasons why the plaintiff joined wholly unrelated federal and state claims in the state action.

Illustration 2-107. *A*, a citizen of State *X*, sues *B*, a citizen of State *X*, in a state court in State *X*. *A* asserts a claim against *B* under a federal statute and a factually and legally unrelated claim under state law. The claims are not properly joined under state law. State joinder law requires either that claims be factually related or that they fall within the same legal category, such as contract, tort, etc.[483] Instead of objecting to joinder in the state court, *B* removes the entire action to a U.S. District Court in State *X* under § 1441(c). The state claim does not predominate over the federal claim and is, in fact, relatively minor in terms of the complexity of the issues and the relief sought. Nevertheless, the district court should have the discretion to remand the state claim under § 1441(c) if the state and federal claims do not form a convenient trial unit.[484]

---

481. *See, e.g.,* Weird v. County of Ingham, No. 5:94-CV-28, 1994 U.S. Dist. LEXIS 8612 (W.D. Mich. Apr. 25, 1994); Land & Lakes Co. v. Henderson, No. 94 C 1815, 1994 WL 124876, 1994 U.S. Dist. LEXIS 4514 (N.D.Ill. Apr. 11, 1994); Neal v. Fairman, No. 92 C 6785, 1992 U.S. Dist. LEXIS 18540 (N.D. Ill. Dec. 1, 1992); Moore v. DeBiase, 766 F. Supp. 1311 (D.N.J. 1991).

482. *See, e.g.,* Borough of W. Mifflin v. Lancaster, 45 F.3d 780 (3d Cir. 1995); John G. & Marie Stella Kennedy Mem. Found. v. Mauro, 21 F.3d 667 (5th Cir.), *cert. denied,* 513 U.S. 1016, 115 S. Ct. 577, 130 L. Ed. 2d 493 (1994); Surprise v. GTE Serv. Corp., 47 F. Supp. 2d 240 (D. Conn. 1999); Thatton v. International Bhd. of Painters, 933 F. Supp. 560 (S.D.W. Va. 1996); McGilvray v. Hallmark Fin. Group, Inc., 891 F. Supp. 265 (E.D. Va. 1995). Of course, remand of state claims is permitted in cases removed under § 1367 and § 1441(a) after the federal claims have been dismissed, but otherwise remand of the entire case, including the federal claims, is not proper. *See, e.g.,* Williams v. Ragnone, 147 F.3d 700 (8th Cir. 1998) (district court has no power to remand case removed under §§ 1331, 1367(a), and 1441(a)); Choice Hotels Int'l, Inc. v. Bonham, No. 96-2717, 1997 WL 600061, 1997 U.S. App. LEXIS (4th Cir. Sept. 30, 1997) (unpublished opinion) (*Carnegie Mellon* permits remand of state claims after federal claims dismissed).

483. Joinder-of-claims provisions in code pleading states often contain provisions restricting joinder in the manner described in this illustration. *See* Chapter 7(B) ("Joinder of Claims by Plaintiffs Under the Codes") *infra.* Some courts have held that procedural misjoinder of certain kinds constitutes "fraudulent joinder," which would allow removal without regard to the misjoined claim. *See* 14B CHARLES A. WRIGHT, FEDERAL PRACTICE AND PROCEDURE: JURISDICTION AND RELATED MATTERS § 3723, at 656-58 (3d ed. 1998). If this doctrine extends to the facts of this illustration, there would be no need to resort to the remand provisions of § 1441(c).

484. Practice under § 1441(c) has given rise to a number of problems other than the major ones discussed in the text. For example, the courts are split on the question whether third-party defendants joined under Federal Rule 14 can remove under § 1441(c). *Compare, e.g.,* Jones v. Petty-Ray Geophysical Geosource, Inc., 954 F.2d 1061, 1066 (5th Cir.), *cert. denied,* 506 U.S. 867, 113 S. Ct. 193, 121 L. Ed. 2d 136 (1992); Hayduk v. United

(d) Removal Procedure

Under 28 U.S.C. § 1446(a), a case is removed by filing a notice of removal signed pursuant to Federal Rule 11. The notice must contain a short and plain statement of the grounds for removal, together with a copy of all process, pleadings, and orders that have been served upon the defendant in the state action.[485] After 1988, a removal bond is no longer required.[486] The notice must be filed within thirty days of the defendant's receipt of the initial pleading, or within thirty days after service of summons if the initial pleading is filed in court but not required to be served on the defendants, whichever period is shorter.[487] In *Murphy Bros. v. Michetti Pipe Stringing, Inc.*,[488] the U.S. Supreme Court held that the 30-day removal period is triggered either by simultaneous

---

Parcel Serv., 930 F. Supp. 584 (S.D. Fla. 1996) *with* Monmouth-Ocean Collection Serv., Inc. v. Klor, 46 F. Supp. 2d 385 (D.N.J. 1999) (third-party defendants may not remove under § 1441(c), but third-party claim is not separate and independent in any event); Galen-Med, Inc. v. Owens, 41 F. Supp. 2d 611 (W.D. Va. 1999) (third-party defendant may not remove under either §§ 1441(a) or 1441(c)); Lane v. Mitchell, Civ. No. 1:97CV278, 1997 U.S. Dist. LEXIS 20853 (W.D.N.C. Dec. 1, 1997) (no removal on basis of third-party claim); Rosario v. Witchin Co., No. Civ. A. 97-702, 1997 WL 313221 (E.D. La. June 5, 1997) (third-party claim not removable because not separate and independent); New Venture Gear, Inc. v. Fonehouse, 982 F. Supp. 892 (N.D.N.Y. 1997) (third-party claim involves overlapping facts, so not separate and independent). Also, the Fifth Circuit Court of Appeals allowed a party to remove under § 1441(c) who had been added to a case as an additional party to a federal counterclaim against the original plaintiffs. *See* Texas *ex rel.* Board of Regents v. Walker, 142 F.3d 813 (5th Cir. 1998). In addition to the question whether the additional party qualifies for removal at all, there was a question whether the federal counterclaim and state claims were separate and independent, because they both arose from the same general, festering dispute between the parties, even though they did not involve common elements of proof. At least one court has allowed removal under § 1441(c) by a codefendant based on a cross-claim for indemnity asserted by another codefendant. *See* Acme Brick Co. v. Agrupacion Exportadora de Maqumaria Ceramica, 855 F. Supp. 163 (N.D. Tex. 1994). But note that cross-claims, by definition, must arise out of the same transaction or occurrence as the subject matter of the original action or a counterclaim therein. FED. R. CIV. P. 13(g). How can they possibly be ''separate and independent'' under such circumstances? *See generally* Michael C. Massengale, *Riotous Uncertainty: A Quarrel with the ''Commentators Rule'' Against Section 1441(c) Removal for Counterclaim, Cross-Claim, and Third-Party Defendants*, 75 TEX. L. REV. 659 (1997).

485. *See* 28 U.S.C. § 1446(a). In the Judicial Improvements and Access to Justice Act of 1988, Congress amended 28 U.S.C. § 1446(a) to provide for a notice of removal signed pursuant to Rule 11 rather than the verified petition for removal required under the former version of the statute. *See* Judicial Improvements and Access to Justice Act of 1988, Pub. L. No. 100-702, § 1016(b), 102 Stat. 4642, 4669 (codified at 28 U.S.C. § 1446(a)).

486. Section 1446(d) formerly required that the defendant file a bond to assure that the defendant would pay all costs incurred by the removal proceedings if they are later determined to be improper. In 1988, Congress eliminated subsection (d) and, thus, eliminated the bond requirement. *See* The Judicial Improvements and Access to Justice Act of 1988, Pub. L. No. 100-702, § 1016(b)(3), 102 Stat. 4642, 4670. Subsections (e) and (f) of § 1446 were relettered (d) and (e), respectively. *See id.* (codified at 28 U.S.C. § 1446). However, new § 1446(d) continues to refer to a bond. Doubtless, the continued reference was an oversight by Congress and should not be interpreted to preserve the bond requirement.

487. *See* 28 U.S.C. § 1446(b); McKinney v. Board of Trustees, 955 F.2d 924 (4th Cir. 1992) (when multiple defendants served on different dates, each defendant has thirty days from date of service to join otherwise valid petition for removal).

488. 520 U.S. 344, 119 S. Ct. 1322, 143 L. Ed. 2d 448 (1999). The American Law Institute has proposed a revisions of § 1446 that would require the notice of removal to be filed within 30 days after receipt or possession by a defendant of a copy of the complaint ''at or after the time of service or waiver of effective summons of that defendant'' or ''after the service of effective summons upon a defendant'' if the complaint has been filed in state court and is not required to be served. *See* ALI FEDERAL JUDICIAL CODE REVISION PROJECT § 1446(b)(1) (Tent. Draft No. 3 1999).

service of the summons and complaint or by receipt of the complaint after and apart from service of the summons. The Court made it clear that mere receipt of the complaint without any formal service would not trigger the removal period. This decision resolved a dispute among the lower federal courts about whether a receipt of a "courtesy copy" of the complaint before service could start the 30-day period.[489]

"Promptly" after filing the notice of removal, the defendant is directed to give written notice to all adverse parties and to file a copy of the notice with the state court clerk. This action effects removal, and the state court is directed to proceed no further in the action.[490]

Even if the case stated by the initial pleading is not removable, the defendant still may remove within thirty days after receipt of an amended pleading (or other paper) from which it can first be ascertained that the case is removable.[491] In 1988, Congress provided that when removal is based on diversity of citizenship, a case may not be removed more than one year after commencement of the action.[492] This provision may provide unscrupulous plaintiffs with a weapon with which to prevent the removal of some diversity actions. A plaintiff who can manipulate joinder of parties or the jurisdictional amount to prevent the existence of diversity jurisdiction for more than a year can effectively thwart removal of the action.

Illustration 2-108. A, a citizen of State *X*, sues *B*, a citizen of State *Y*, and *C*, a citizen of State *X*, in a state court in State *X*. *A* asserts claims in the alternative against *B* and *C* for $1,000,000 arising out of an automobile accident. One year and a day after *A* commenced the action, *A* voluntarily dismisses *C* from the action. Under the time limit for removal established in 1988, *B* may not remove the action.

* * * * *

Fortunately, the U.S. Courts of Appeals, led by the Ninth Circuit, have begun to limit some of the more absurd applications of the one-year provision. In *Ritchey v. Upjohn Drug Co.*,[493] the plaintiff joined three defendants in a state action, two of whom were nondiverse to the plaintiff. The plaintiff did not serve or notify the defendants of the state action until more than a year had passed and previously commenced federal litigation had been resolved against the plaintiff.

---

489. *See generally* Robert P. Faulkner, *The Courtesy Copy Trap: Untimely Removal from State to Federal Court*, 52 MO. L. REV. 374 (1993); Donna Rohwer, *The Forty-Year Dispute: What Triggers the Start of the Remand Period Under 28 U.S.C. § 1441(b)?* 61 UMKC L. REV. 359 (1992); Jean F. Rydstrom, Annotation, *When Period for Filing Petition for Removal of Civil Action From State to Federal District Court Begins to Run Under 28 U.S.C.S. § 1446(b)*, 16 A.L.R. FED. 287 (1973); Jean F. Rydstrom, Annotation, *What Constitutes "Initial Pleading" for Purposes of Computing Time for Removal of Civil Action from State to Federal Court Under 28 U.S.C.S. § 1446(b)*, 15 A.L.R. FED. 733 (1973).

490. *See* 28 U.S.C. § 1446(d); *see also* ALI FEDERAL JUDICIAL CODE REVISION PROJECT § 1446 (Tent. Draft No. 3 1999) (clarifying and revising § 1446).

491. *See* 28 U.S.C. § 1446(b); *see also* ALI FEDERAL JUDICIAL CODE REVISION PROJECT § 1446(b)(2) (Tent. Draft No. 3 1999) (clarifying existing § 1446(b) by, for example, making it clear that the receipt must occur "at or after service" or waiver of service).

492. *See* The Judicial Improvements and Access to Justice Act of 1988, Pub. L. No. 100-702, § 1016(b)(2)(B), 102 Stat. 4642, 4669 (codified at 28 U.S.C. § 1446(b)).

493. 139 F.3d 1313 (9th Cir. 1998).

When notified of the action, the diverse defendant removed the action. The diverse defendant contended that the two nondiverse defendants had been fraudulently joined. The plaintiff invoked the one-year limit, but the court of appeals held the limit applicable only to cases that are not removable from the outset. Because the two nondiverse defendants were fraudulently joined, the action was removable at commencement. Thus, the diverse defendant had 30-days after receiving a copy of the initial pleading within which to remove,[494] even though receipt occurred more than a year after commencement.

The result in the *Ritchey* case is clearly correct and, at this writing, has uniformly been followed by the other U.S. Courts of Appeals.[495] Other solutions to manipulation of the one-year limit that have been suggested by the lower federal courts are more problematic. For example, in *Norman v. Sundance Spas, Inc.*,[496] the plaintiff had joined one nondiverse defendant with several diverse defendants. Some of the diverse defendants had been joined at the commencement of the action, but some were added to the action by amendment one month after commencement. The nondiverse defendant was eliminated from the action over a year after commencement (along with some of the diverse defendants), leaving two diverse defendants, one of whom had been joined at commencement and one of whom had been added a month after commencement. The defendants removed within thirty days after the elimination of the nondiverse defendant, and the plaintiff moved to remand on the basis of the one year limit. The district court ordered the case remanded, even though one defendant was seeking removal within a year of being added to the action. The presence of the diverse defendant who had been joined at commencement prevented removal, because that defendant was seeking removal more than one year after commencement.

The court expressed concern that plaintiffs might delay removal beyond the one-year period by manipulating the liberal joinder and amendment provisions of the Federal Rules of Civil Procedure. However, the court suggested that the federal courts might develop fraudulent delay in joinder rules that were analogous to the fraudulent joinder doctrine already existing in removal cases. However, it is not apparent, given the unclear boundaries of the fraudulent joinder doctrine itself,[497] that a "fraudulent delay in joinder" doctrine would be a useful solution to the problem of later-joined defendants. A simpler and better solution might be to measure both the 30-day period for removal and the one-year period from the date that the last diverse defendant is joined in the state action.[498]

---

494. *See* 28 U.S.C. § 1446(b) (first paragraph).

495. *See* Brierly v. Alusiusse Flexible Packaging, Inc., 170 F.3d 583 (6th Cir. 1999) (one-year limit applies only to cases not originally removable); New York Life Ins. Co. v. Deshotel, 142 F.3d 873 (5th Cir. 1998) (one-year limit applies only to cases not originally removable).

496. 844 F. Supp. 355 (W.D. Ky. 1994).

497. *See* 14B CHARLES A. WRIGHT ET AL., FEDERAL PRACTICE AND PROCEDURE: JURISDICTION AND RELATED MATTERS § 3723, at 623-658 (3d ed. 1998) (discussing the variations in the fraudulent joinder doctrine); subsection 5(a), *supra*.

498. *See* 14C CHARLES A. WRIGHT ET AL., FEDERAL PRACTICE AND PROCEDURE: JURISDICTION AND RELATED MATTERS § 3732, at 336-40 (3d ed. 1998) (discussing the fairness of this rule in the context of the 30-day time limit).   Plaintiffs also attempt to manipulate the amount in controversy to prevent removal, and sometimes, even in the absence of manipulation, it is difficult to determine the amount in controversy because some state pleading rules do not require or allow the amount of damages requested to be set out by the plaintiff.

The American Law Institute's recommendation may represent the best overall solution to the problems produced by the one-year limit. The ALI proposes to confer discretion on the U.S. District Courts to remand diversity actions removed after one year "in the interest of justice."[499] Although the "interest of justice" standard "clearly invites the district court to weigh the equities when deciding whether to exercise this special remand power, [the preconditions built into the statute] substantially curtail the scope of this discretionary power."[500]

(e) Remand of Removed Cases

The district court must remand any case removed without jurisdiction prior to final judgment in the case.[501] In 1988, Congress provided that a motion to remand a case to state court based on a defect in removal procedure, as opposed to a defect of jurisdiction, must be made within thirty days after filing the notice of removal.[502] In 1996, the language of § 1447(c) was amended

---

The result is a large number of federal decisions dealing with how to cope with these problems in various contexts. *See, e.g.,* Singer v. State Farm Mut. Auto. Ins. Co., 116 F.3d 373 (9th Cir. 1997) (state law prohibited plaintiffs from setting out a monetary amount of damages, but plaintiff's admission before the federal court that the case was worth considerably more than the amount in controversy established that the requirement was satisfied); Sheppard v. Exxon Co., U.S.A., 760 F. Supp. 92 (M.D. La. 1990) (action in a state court with a jurisdictional limit of $10,000; amount-in-controversy requirement not satisfied because court could not render judgment for more than $10,000); Jock E. Karns, *Removal to Federal Court and the Jurisdictional Amount in Controversy Pursuant to State Statutory Limitations on Pleading Damage Claims,* 29 Creighton L. Rev. 1091 (1996); Alice M. Noble-Allgire, *Removal of Diversity Actions When the Amount in Controversy Cannot Be Determined From the Face of the Plaintiff's Complaint: The Need for Judicial and Statutory Reform to Preserve Defendant's Equal Access to Federal Courts,* 62 Mo. L. Rev. 681 (1997); *see also* Benson v. SI Handing Sys., Inc., 188 F.3d 780 (7th Cir. 1999) (case removed and remanded because defendant failed to show amount in controversy met; after developing information during discovery showing the amount requirement met, defendant removed again, but the district court held that successive removal is not permissible; court of appeals disagreed and reversed).

499. ALI Federal Judicial Code Revision Project § 1447(b) (Tent. Draft No. 3 1999):

    (b) *Remand in interest of justice.* If a civil action has been removed under sections 1441(a) and 1446(b)(2) of this chapter more than one year after the commencement of the action, and if the sole basis for removal is the jurisdiction conferred by sections 1332 or 1367 of this title, the district court may in the interest of justice remand the action to the State court from which it was removed. No such remand shall be ordered except upon motion of a party filed within the time permitted for a motion to remand under subsection (c)(1).

500. *Id.* at 158 (commentary on § 1447). Note that under the current statute the courts are split over whether, if the one-year limit is violated, they may nevertheless employ "equitable considerations" in determining whether to remand. *Compare* Jenkins v. Sandoz Pharm. Corp., 965 F. Supp. 861 (N.D. Miss. 1997) (impermissible to employ equitable considerations) *with* Ferguson v. Security Life Ins. Co., 996 F. Supp. 597 (N.D. Tex. 1998) (equitable principles may be employed), Kinabrew v. Emco-Wheaton, Inc., 936 F. Supp. 351 (M.D. La. 1996) (equitable principles employed), *and* Morrison v. National Benefit Life Ins. Co., 889 F. Supp. 945 (S.D. Miss. 1995) (equitable principles employed).

501. *See* 28 U.S.C. § 1447(c).

502. *See* Judicial Improvements and Access to Justice Act of 1988, Pub. L. No. 100-702, § 1016(c), 102 Stat. 4262, 4670 (codified at 28 U.S.C. § 1447(c)); *see also* Snapper, Inc. v. Redan, 171 F.3d 1249 (11th Cir. 1999) (remand on basis of forum selection clause not jurisdictional; clause constitutes absolute waiver of right to remove); Ragas v. Tennessee Gas Pipeline Co., 136 F.3d 455 (5th Cir. 1998) (limitation on removal jurisdiction waived by not moving to remand within thirty days as long as district court would have had original jurisdiction over case); Archuleta v. Lacuesta, 131 F.3d 1359 (10th Cir. 1997) (removal statutes do not set forth again, this time to provide that "[a] motion to remand the case on the basis of any defect other than lack of subject-matter jurisdiction" must be made within 30 days after the notice of removal is filed.[503] These various changes in language are obviously designed to distinguish between defects in "subject-matter" jurisdiction and lesser "procedural" defects. Nevertheless, Congress has not been notably successful in clarifying what it considers to be a "defect . . . of subject-matter jurisdiction." The most likely meaning of "subject-matter jurisdiction" in § 1447(c) is "original subject-matter" jurisdiction, such as that conferred by provisions of the Judicial Code such as §§ 1331 and 1332. Other limitations on removal, such as those found in § 1446, would not be considered jurisdictional.[504]

Illustration 2-109. *A*, a citizen of State *X*, sues *B*, a citizen of State *Y*, and *C*, a citizen of State *Y*, in a state court in State *X*. *A* asserts claims in the alternative against *B* and *C* for $1,000,000 arising out of an automobile accident. *B* files a timely notice of removal, but *C* does not join in the removal notice. Subsequently, *C* also files a notice of removal, but *C's* notice is not timely under 28 U.S.C § 1446(b). Sixty days after *B's* notice of removal is filed, *A* moves to remand the action because both defendants did not join in removing the action in a timely fashion. This defect in removal procedure cannot be asserted as the basis of remand more than thirty days after the notice of removal is filed.[505]

* * * * *

The problem with this view is that it would treat as nonjurisdictional some important limitations on removal. For example, the restrictions in § 1441(b) on the ability of citizens of the forum state to remove is not a limit on the federal courts original diversity jurisdiction. Likewise, the one-year limit on removal in diversity cases in § 1446(b) is also not a limit on original federal jurisdiction. Furthermore, 28 U.S.C. § 1445, entitled "Nonremovable Actions," contains a whole list of cases that Congress has declared nonremovable, but which can be brought originally in federal court. It is not clear from the text of § 1447(c) whether Congress really wishes to treat all of these limitations on removal as "nonjurisdictional."[506]

If a case is removed in a procedurally proper and timely fashion, but without jurisdiction under the removal statute, situations exist in which it will not have to be remanded. If "after removal a case is tried on the merits without objection and the federal court enters judgment, the issue . . . on appeal is not

---

principles of subject-matter jurisdiction); Harmon v. OKI Sys., 115 F.3d 477 (7th Cir. 1997) (failure of defendant to allege basis for subject-matter jurisdiction in notice of removal is procedural, not jurisdictional).

503. Pub. L. No. 104-219, § 1, 110 Stat. 3022 (1996) (codified at 28 U.S.C. § 1447(c)).

504. *See, e.g.,* Ragas v. Tennessee Gas Pipeline Co., 136 F.3d 455 (5th Cir. 1998); Baris v. Sulpicio Lines, Inc., 932 F.2d 1540, 1544-45 (5th Cir.), *cert. denied,* 502 U.S. 963, 112 S. Ct. 430, 116 L. Ed. 2d 449 (1991).

505. *See* Miller v. National Brokerage Servs., Inc., 782 F. Supp. 1440 (D. Nev. 1991).

506. *See* ALI FEDERAL JUDICIAL CODE REVISION PROJECT at 195, rptr's notes (Tent. Draft No. 3 1999) (discussing statutory restrictions on the right of removal and the distinctions between "procedural" and "jurisdictional" defects in removal). The American Law Institute's proposed revision of § 1447 would retain the procedural-jurisdictional distinction of current § 1447(c) and would clarify that, indeed, "restriction[s] on the right of removal" and "procedure[s] for exercising" the right of removal are waivable unless made the subject of a motion to remand within 30 days after removal. *See id.* § 1447(c)(1)(3).

whether the case was properly removed, but whether the federal district court would have had original jurisdiction of the case had it been filed in that court."[507]

Illustration 2-110. *A*, a citizen of State *X*, sues *B*, a citizen of State *Y*, and *C*, a citizen of State *Z*, in a state court in State *Z*. *A* asserts claims in the alternative against *B* and *C* for $1,000,0000 arising out of an automobile accident. *B* and *C* remove the action to a U.S. District Court in State *Z*. Neither the court nor the parties realize that the action is not removable because *C* is a citizen of the state in which the action is brought. Therefore, no one objects to removal and the action is tried on the merits. A judgment is rendered for *A* against *C* but in favor of *B*. *C* appeals, raising as error that the case was not removable under § 1441(b). The case before the district court was one over which it would have had original jurisdiction had it been initially commenced in that court. Thus, *C's* objection will not prevail because it is untimely.[508]

* * * * *

In *Caterpillar Inc. v. Lewis*,[509] a state court defendant removed an action to federal court, even though there was another nondiverse defendant joined in the action. The district court erroneously refused to remand on plaintiff's motion, but the nondiverse defendant was dismissed prior to trial, thus making diversity of citizenship complete. The Supreme Court held that the district court's error was not fatal to the validity of the judgment because diversity existed at the time judgment was rendered. This holding considerably extends the principle exemplified by the case described in *Illustration 2-110*. There, neither the parties nor the court recognized the absence of removal authority under § 1441(b). In *Caterpillar*, there was an absence of original jurisdiction under § 1332 at the time of removal, the parties and the district court recognized the lack of jurisdiction, the court and defendant improperly ignored it, and the plaintiff challenged jurisdiction at the district court level and on appeal. Thus, in the absence of some clarification by the court, *Caterpillar* contains the seeds for wholesale evasion of jurisdictional restrictions in removal cases.[510]

Except in removal of civil rights cases under 28 U.S.C. § 1443, an order remanding a case to the state court from which it was removed is not reviewable on appeal or otherwise.[511] However, this limitation on the reviewability of remand orders applies only if the remand is on a ground specified in 28 U.S.C. § 1447(c), which covers remand based on defects in removal procedure and lack

---

507. *See* Grubbs v. General Elec. Credit Corp., 405 U.S. 699, 702, 92 S. Ct. 1344, 1347, 31 L. Ed. 2d 612, 617 (1972).

508. It has been held that removal of a case over which there is original jurisdiction under 28 U.S.C. § 1332, but in which one of the defendants is a citizen of the state in which the action is brought, is a defect in removal procedure under 28 U.S.C. § 1447(c) that must be raised within thirty days after the notice of removal is filed. *See In re* Shell Oil Co., 932 F.2d 1518 (5th Cir. 1991), *cert. denied*, 502 U.S. 1049, 112 S. Ct. 914, 116 L. Ed. 2d 814 (1992). Under this holding, an objection to removal would be untimely in the illustration long before judgment was rendered at the district court level.

509. 519 U.S. 61, 117 S. Ct. 467, 136 L. Ed. 2d 437 (1996).

510. *But see* Huffman v. Saul Holdings Ltd. Partnership, 194 F.3d 1072 (10th Cir. 1999) (untimely notice of removal, in itself, does not warrant appellate order to remand, but when district court's granting of summary judgment is reversed leaving no judgment on the merits, remand would be ordered).

511. *See* 28 U.S.C. § 1447(d).

of jurisdiction.[512] If the remand is for any other reason, the remand order may be reviewed by a writ of mandamus.[513]

Illustration 2-111. *A*, a citizen of State *X*, sues *B*, a citizen of State *Y*, in a state court of State *X*. *A* asserts a claim for $1,000,000 against *B* based on state law. *B* removes the action to the U.S. District Court for State *X* under 28 U.S.C. § 1441(a) & (b). The district judge remands the action because the docket of the court is too crowded. The order of remand is reviewable by a writ of mandamus in the court of appeals.[514]

* * * * *

Even though express authorization does not exist in 28 U.S.C. § 1447(c), the U.S. Supreme Court has held that the district courts may remand state claims that have been removed on the basis of pendent (today supplemental) jurisdiction when the federal claims that are the source of jurisdiction over the action have been dismissed from the case.[515] Under these circumstances, remand is more efficient than dismissal, which would be the appropriate procedure in a case originally commenced in federal court on the basis of supplemental jurisdiction. This power to remand state claims removed on the basis of supplemental jurisdiction has survived the enactment of 28 U.S.C. § 1367.[516] However, some courts have remanded entire cases under the authority of § 1367(c), including the federal claims in the cases.[517] Such remands are improper. As noted in subsection *4(d)(iii)* above, 28 U.S.C. § 1367(c) only permits dismissal of supplemental claims, not entire cases. The power to remand should not be broader than the power to dismiss under the statute. Furthermore, remand of an entire action unjustifiably deprives the defendant of the right to a federal forum on the federal claim. For these reasons, the better rule is that an entire case can be remanded only when the federal claims have first been dismissed, leaving the case comprised entirely of state claims.[518]

---

512. *See In re* Shell Oil Co., 932 F.2d 1518 (5th Cir. 1991), *cert. denied*, 502 U.S. 1049, 112 S. Ct. 914, 116 L. Ed. 2d 814 (1992); *cf.* Hamilton v. Aetna Life & Cas. Co., 5 F.3d 642 (2d Cir. 1993) (order remanding case removed by *plaintiff* construed as based on procedural reasons; order reviewed and affirmed; no federal subject-matter jurisdiction existed!).

513. *See* Thermtron Prods., Inc. v. Hermansdorfer, 423 U.S. 336, 96 S. Ct. 584, 46 L. Ed. 2d 542 (1976). *See generally* Michael E. Solimine, *Removal, Remands, and Reforming Federal Appellate Procedure*, 58 MO. L. REV. 287 (1993).

514. Review by writ of mandamus is discussed in Chapter 12(B)(3) ("The Final Judgment Rule and Its Exceptions") *infra*.

515. *See* Carnegie-Mellon Univ. v. Cohill, 484 U.S. 343, 108 S. Ct. 614, 98 L. Ed. 2d 720 (1988). This remand is not on the ground of a "defect in removal procedure" within the meaning of 28 U.S.C. § 1447(c); *see also* David D. Siegel, *Commentary on 1988 Revision*, 28 U.S.C.A. § 1447 (West 1993 Supp. at 61-62).

516. *See, e.g.,* Noble v. White, 996 F.2d 797 (5th Cir. 1993); Doe *ex rel.* Doe v. Abbott Labs., No. 93 C 0500, 1993 WL 278458, 1993 U.S. Dist. LEXIS 9850 (N.D. Ill. July 20, 1993); Jones v. Montgomery Hosp., No. 92-6809, 1993 WL 12836, 1993 U.S. Dist. LEXIS 448 (E.D. Pa. Jan. 15, 1993).

517. *See, e.g.,* Administaff, Inc. v. Kaster, 799 F. Supp. 685 (W.D. Tex. 1992); 14C CHARLES A. WRIGHT, ET AL., FEDERAL PRACTICE AND PROCEDURE: JURISDICTION AND RELATED MATTERS § 3739, at 503-04 (3d ed. 1998).

518. *See, e.g.,* Williams v. Ragnone, 147 F.3d 700 (8th Cir. 1998) (no power to remand entire case removed under §§ 1331, 1367 and 1441(a)); Kabealo v. Davis, 829 F. Supp. 923 (S.D. Ohio 1993) (§ 1367 does not permit remand of federal claims); *cf.* Bradgate Assocs., Inc. v. Fellows, Read & Assocs., Inc., 999 F.2d 745 (3d Cir. 1993) (removed case consolidated with one originally filed in federal court; later determined court had no jurisdiction over removed case; remand of case originally filed in federal court with removed case improper).

Chapter 3

PERSONAL JURISDICTION AND
SERVICE OF PROCESS

Personal jurisdiction is the power of a court to impose its decisions on the particular parties in a lawsuit. In modern procedural systems, personal jurisdiction is acquired over defendants by serving them with "process." This service also provides the defendant with notice of the lawsuit. The notice contained in the process directs the defendant to appear and defend the suit or else the court will enter a "default judgment" against the defendant. Rules of personal jurisdiction determine when service of process can authorize a court to enter a *valid* judgment against the defendant.

In the United States, modern rules of personal jurisdiction are the end product of an evolutionary process that stretches over more than two centuries. Today, the landscape of personal jurisdiction is dominated by rules derived from provisions of the U.S. Constitution that restrict the authority of the state and federal governments to adjudicate cases against nonresidents. Originally, these restrictions were based on the concept that governments had *territorial* power over persons and things within their boundaries.

Under this territorial theory, the courts of a state could not constitutionally secure personal jurisdiction over defendants if they (1) were not present within the state when served with process, (2) did not consent to suit there, or (3) did not own property there. The first two bases allowed the sovereign to exercise what is known as *in personam* jurisdiction. The third basis allowed the sovereign to exercise what is known as *in rem* jurisdiction. The territorial rules functioned to protect sovereignty—the characteristic of governments which distinguish and preserve their power and independence from other governments.

Today, courts have relaxed the traditional territorial restrictions on acquiring personal jurisdiction over nonresident defendants. States may constitutionally compel nonresidents to defend suits in the state if they have relationships with the state that make the assertion of jurisdiction "reasonable." The underlying focus of these rules is on the protection of individuals from overreaching by governments—the restriction of the power to enter judgments against persons unless an adequate opportunity to be heard in defense is first afforded to them.

The traditional territorial rules, however, have not been entirely abandoned. Furthermore, sovereignty-oriented policies have been so strong that they have received explicit recognition in some modern cases interpreting the Due Process Clause of the Fourteenth Amendment, a provision undeniably aimed at protection of individuals from state governmental power. This chapter discusses the basic rules of personal jurisdiction, their evolution over time, and modern procedures for serving process.

SECTION A. DEVELOPMENT OF TERRITORIAL RULES OF PERSONAL JURISDICTION

1. Personal Jurisdiction Restrictions Prior to the Adoption of the Fourteenth Amendment

(a) The Forms of Action in Suits on Foreign Judgments and the "International" Rules of Jurisdiction

At the time the U.S. Constitution was ratified, the method for enforcing a judgment that was not capable of direct execution was to bring an action of debt on a record.[1]

Illustration 3-1. Assume that *A* sued *B* in an English common-law court and recovered a judgment for money. By means of a writ of execution, *A* could have *B's* property sold to satisfy the judgment. Under the law of England, however, the plaintiff's right to have the judgment directly executed (by obtaining a writ of execution) ceased if the judgment had not been executed within a year and a day of its recovery. After that time, the plaintiff had to commence a new action using the form of action known as debt on a record. In this new action, the plaintiff did not have to prove the original claim again. The domestic judgment (one rendered by a court of record in England) was res judicata. Thus, the plaintiff had only to plead and prove the prior judgment to win. Similarly, if the defendant in the original action won and the plaintiff attempted to sue the defendant again on the same claim, the defendant could plead the original judgment in defense as res judicata.[2]

* * * * *

When a judgment of a court of a foreign country was involved, debt on a record was not the proper form of action. The judgment of a foreign court was not considered to be a "record" because the judgment had not been rendered by a court deriving its authority from the same sovereign as the judgment-enforcing court. Thus, the plaintiff had to employ either debt on a simple contract or general assumpsit, rather than debt on a record.[3] Furthermore, the foreign judgment was not res judicata because it was not a record. Rather, it was only prima facie evidence of the debt being sued on, and the defendant could rebut it.[4]

---

1. *See generally* Ralph U. Whitten, *The Constitutional Limitations on State-Court Jurisdiction: A Historical Interpretative Reexamination of the Full Faith and Credit and Due Process Clauses* (pt. 1), 14 CREIGHTON L. REV. 499, 509-14 (1981).

2. *See* JOSEPH H. KOFFLER & ALISON REPPY, HANDBOOK OF COMMON LAW PLEADING § 142, at 297-99 (1969); Chapter 1(E)(1)*(b)(ii)* ("*Ex Contractu* Personal Actions") *supra*.

3. *See* Gage v. Bulkeley, 27 Eng. Rep. 824 (Ch. 1744); Chapter 1(E)(1)*(b)(ii)* ("*Ex Contractu* Personal Actions") & Chapter 1(E)(1)*(c)(ii)* ("Assumpsit") *supra*. *See generally* Ralph U. Whitten, *The Constitutional Limitations on State-Court Jurisdiction: A Historical Interpretative Reexamination of the Full Faith and Credit and Due Process Clauses* (pt. 1), 14 CREIGHTON L. REV. 499, 511-14 (1981).

4. *See* Gage v. Bulkeley, 27 Eng. Rep. 824 (Ch. 1744); Walker v. Witter, 99 Eng. Rep. 1 (K.B. 1778); Galbraith v. Neville, 99 Eng. Rep. 5 (K.B. 1789) (*Galbraith* appears as a note to *Walker v. Witter*).

The English decisions eventually evolved away from this prima facie evidence rule. In the earliest stages of the evolutionary process, the English courts drew a distinction between foreign judgments sued on affirmatively and those pleaded defensively. Foreign judgments sued on affirmatively were treated as prima facie evidence. Foreign judgments pleaded defensively were given a res judicata (conclusive) effect.[5] Later, the English rule evolved into its modern form, in which all foreign judgments rendered with jurisdiction are given a res judicata effect.[6] However, the important point is that at the time the U.S. Constitution was framed and ratified, and for some time before, foreign judgments were *not* treated the same as domestic judgments in English and American law.

To be given any effect, a foreign judgment had to have been rendered in compliance with certain "international" rules of jurisdiction.[7] These rules were part of a larger body of common-law rules known as private international law. As such, they governed the relations between the courts of separate sovereigns.[8] Three bases for international judicial jurisdiction were traditionally recognized: (1) presence of the person within the territory of the sovereign; (2) consent by the person to the jurisdiction of the courts of a sovereign; and (3) presence of something belonging to the person within the territory of the sovereign.[9]

Illustration 3-2. If a court in France obtained jurisdiction over an English citizen in compliance with the international rules of jurisdiction, the judgment of the French court would be enforceable in an English court. Thus, the French plaintiff only had to sue on the judgment in England. Today, such a judgment will be given a "res judicata" effect by the English courts—even if the French court committed nonjurisdictional errors of fact or law in the case.[10] On the other hand, if no jurisdiction in the "international sense" exists, the French judgment will be considered void and unenforceable in England—even if the French court accurately determined the merits of the case and the French plaintiff

---

5. *See* Geyer v. Aguilar, 101 Eng. Rep. 1196, 1205 (K.B. 1789); Phillips v. Hunter, 126 Eng. Rep. 618, 622 (C.P. 1795) (Eyre, C.J. dissenting).

6. *See* P.M. NORTH & J.J. FAWCETT, CHESHIRE AND NORTH'S PRIVATE INTERNATIONAL LAW 346 (12th ed. 1992) and authorities there cited.

7. *See id.* at 348.

8. In the United States, private international law rules are usually referred to as conflict-of-law or choice-of-law rules. Today, the rules of jurisdiction that govern the power of courts in different nations to adjudicate cases that affect the interests of other nations are considered to be part of customary international law, while the rules that govern the power of state courts of the United States to adjudicate cases that affect the interests of other states are part of the national law of the United States. *See* RESTATEMENT (THIRD) OF THE FOREIGN RELATIONS LAW OF THE UNITED STATES 304 (1987); RESTATEMENT (SECOND) OF CONFLICT OF LAWS §§ 24-79 (1971 & Supp. 1988).

9. The grounds stated in the text are the traditional grounds recognized in English and early American practice. Today, the recognized bases for jurisdiction to adjudicate in international law are more numerous. *See* RESTATEMENT (THIRD) OF THE FOREIGN RELATIONS LAW OF THE UNITED STATES § 421 (1987). Furthermore, the modern international rules governing jurisdiction to adjudicate differ in important respects from the traditional bases and from some of the modern American bases. Notably, the modern international rules do not recognize jurisdiction based on transient presence or on the presence of property unconnected with the claim, whereas the traditional rules did recognize these bases, and modern American law still recognizes transient presence as a proper basis for asserting personal jurisdiction. *See id.* § 421(2)(a), (k).

10. *See* P.M. NORTH & J.J. FAWCETT, CHESHIRE AND NORTH'S PRIVATE INTERNATIONAL LAW 368 (12th ed. 1992).

complied with all the French domestic rules governing service of process and acquisition of personal jurisdiction.[11]

Illustration 3-3. B, a citizen of Belgium, punched *A*, a citizen of England, in the nose. The punch occurred in Germany while *A* and *B* were in Germany on vacation. *A* sued *B* in an English court by serving *B* with process in England while *B* was traveling there. Under the presence theory, the English court acquired in personam jurisdiction in compliance with the international rules of personal jurisdiction by the service of process on *B* while *B* was in England. Thus, even if *B* left England and did not defend the action, the English court could enter a judgment against *B* that would be recognized and enforced by courts in other nations. Under the presence theory, it was irrelevant whether the event that was the subject of the action occurred in the country where process was served on the defendant. Although it is fairer to require a more substantial connection between the country where the action is brought and the subject matter of the action or the parties, the presence theory did not require anything more than transient presence of the defendant when process was served.[12] However, even when a ground such as transient presence was recognized as a valid basis for jurisdiction in the international sense, a country might have certain domestic rules, such as the doctrine of forum non conveniens,[13] which would produce dismissal of an action that was only remotely connected with the country.

(b) Colonial Developments and the Articles of Confederation

Several American colonies statutorily dealt with judgments of other colonies. The statutes seemed primarily aimed at problems of authentication and proof, rather than the effect to be given to a judgment of another colony. Only one colony, Massachusetts, seems to have elevated the judgments of other colonies to a higher level than foreign judgments.[14] Thus, as far as can be determined from these statutes, the colonies considered themselves to be independent sovereigns in relation to other colonies.

The Articles of Confederation contained a Full Faith and Credit Clause stating that "[f]ull faith and credit shall be given in each of these states to the records, acts, and judicial proceedings of the courts and magistrates of every other State."[15] Unlike the later Full Faith and Credit Clause of the U.S. Constitution,

---

11. *Cf.* Restatement (Third) of the Foreign Relations Law of the United States § 421 (Jurisdiction to Adjudicate), § 481 (Recognition and Enforcement of Foreign Judgments), § 482 (Grounds for Nonrecognition of Foreign Judgments) (1987).

12. The tenuous connection upon which the "presence" theory allows the forum country to exercise jurisdiction makes the theory controversial. *See* P.M. North & J.J. Fawcett, Cheshire and North's Private International Law 349-50 (12 ed. 1992). As a result, the theory has been generally discarded as a basis of jurisdiction to adjudicate in modern international law. *See* Restatement (Third) of the Foreign Relations Law of the United States § 421(2)(a) (1987); *see also* Unif. Foreign Money-Judgments Recognition Act § 5 (1962), 13 U.L.A. 272 (1986).

13. *See* Chapter 4(D) ("Forum Non Conveniens and Change of Venue") *infra*.

14. *See generally* Ralph U. Whitten, *The Constitutional Limitations on State Court-Jurisdiction: A Historical-Interpretative Reexamination of the Full Faith and Credit and Due Process Clauses* (pt. 1), 14 Creighton L. Rev. 499, 527-35 (1981).

15. Arts. of Confed. art. IV.

this provision did not contain any requirement that the "public acts" of other states be given full faith and credit; nor did it authorize the Continental Congress to prescribe rules of authentication or the effect of state judgments. The history of the framing and interpretation of this Clause adds little to the understanding of how the expression "full faith and credit shall be given" should be understood.[16] However, at least one decision rejected an argument that the Full Faith and Credit Clause of the Articles of Confederation required a conclusive effect to be given to the judgments of other states. Instead, the court held that the Clause only required the states to receive the judgments of other states into evidence as "full evidence of . . . such judicial proceedings"—*i.e.*, as conclusive proof that the proceeding embodied in the judgment occurred and adjudicated the matters described in the judgment.[17] If the states viewed the judgments of other states as "foreign judgments," the international rules of jurisdiction would have controlled the validity of the judgments in courts of other states.

(c) The Full Faith and Credit Clause of the U.S. Constitution

When the United States was formed, the states were essentially considered to possess the status of independent sovereigns. When they ratified the U.S. Constitution, the states ceded some of their sovereignty to the federal government. This relationship created two potential sources of restrictions on state-court jurisdiction. First, each state still might create "local" or "domestic" restrictions on the power of its courts to render valid judgments against residents and nonresidents of the state.[18] In theory, these domestic restrictions might appear in statutory, constitutional, or common-law form. Second, the U.S. Constitution itself might provide direct restrictions on state-court jurisdiction or authorize Congress to create such restrictions.[19]

In the original Constitution, the provision having the most direct bearing on the obligation of a state court to enforce the judgments of other states was the Full Faith and Credit Clause of Article IV, § 1: "Full Faith and Credit shall be given in each State to the public Acts, Records, and judicial Proceedings of every other State. And the Congress may by general Laws prescribe the Manner in which such Acts, Records and Proceedings shall be proved and the Effect thereof."[20] Like the identical language in the Articles of Confederation, the expression "full faith and credit" originated in English evidence law. The expression was interpreted to mean simply that each state was obliged, when

---

16. *See* Ralph U. Whitten, *The Constitutional Limitations on State-Court Jurisdiction: A Historical Interpretative Reexamination of the Full Faith and Credit and Due Process Clauses* (pt. 1), 14 CREIGHTON L. REV. 499, 523-27, 535-41 (1981).

17. *See* James v. Allen, 1 Dall. 188, 190 (Pa. 1786).

18. For example, "local" or "domestic" rules of personal jurisdiction would include rules governing the procedures for issuing summons, subpoenas, and writs of attachment.

19. *See generally* Ralph U. Whitten, *The Constitutional Limitations on State-Court Jurisdiction: A Historical Interpretative Reexamination of the Full Faith and Credit and Due Process Clauses* (pt. 1), 14 CREIGHTON L. REV. 499, 542-46 (1981); Ralph U. Whitten, *The Constitutional Limitations on State Choice of Law: Full Faith and Credit*, 12 MEM. ST. U. L. REV. 1 (1981).

20. U.S. CONST. art. IV, § 1.

asked to enforce a judgment rendered by a court in another state, to admit the judgment into evidence as conclusive proof that the judgment had been rendered and the court had adjudicated the matters described in the judgment.[21] In other words, the Full Faith and Credit Clause did not require directly that one state give a res judicata effect to the judgments of other states rendered with jurisdiction.[22] Similarly, the Full Faith and Credit Clause did not limit the power of states to choose their own law over the law of other states. As far as state statutes were concerned, all the Clause required was that the states admit properly authenticated "public acts" of other states into evidence as conclusive proof of their existence and contents.[23]

Illustration 3-4. Assume that *A* sued *B* in State *X* and recovered a judgment against *B*. Assume further that *A* was forced to take the judgment rendered in State *X* to another state to enforce it. *A* would do so by commencing an action on the judgment in the other state. In the suit to enforce the judgment, the first sentence of the Full Faith and Credit Clause would require of its own force that the enforcing state admit the judgment into evidence to prove that it had been rendered and had adjudicated the matters described in the judgment record. However, as originally understood, the Clause did not require that the court give the judgment a res judicata effect. In the absence of a statute enacted by Congress or the judgment-enforcing state requiring a greater effect, the result would be that the enforcing state would treat the judgment as a "foreign" judgment and give the judgment an effect only as rebuttable evidence of the plaintiff's claim. This result did not follow from the Full Faith and Credit Clause itself, but from the common-law rules derived from English practice that applied to the judgments of foreign nations.[24]

(d) The 1790 Implementing Statute

The Full Faith and Credit Clause granted Congress the power to declare the "effect" that state judgments and statutes would have in other states.[25] Thus,

---

21. Many historical sources indicate that the words "faith" and "credit" in English law were evidentiary terms. *See generally* Ralph U. Whitten, *The Constitutional Limitations on State-Court Jurisdiction: A Historical Interpretative Reexamination of the Full Faith and Credit and Due Process Clauses* (pt. 1), 14 CREIGHTON L. REV. 499, 508-23 (1981). The words were flexible enough to mean, standing alone, that a conclusive effect should be given to some item of evidence, or that some effect less than a conclusive effect should be given to the item. Likewise, when the words were modified with a term such as "full," "entire," or "implicit," they were usually meant to convey that a conclusive effect should be given to a piece of evidence. *See id.* at 519.

22. *See id.* at 508-55.

23. *See generally* Ralph U. Whitten, *The Original Understanding of the Full Faith and Credit Clause and the Defense of Marriage Act*, 32 CREIGHTON L. REV. 255 (1998); Ralph U. Whitten, *The Constitutional Limitations on State Choice of Law: Full Faith and Credit*, 12 MEM. ST. U. L. REV. 1 (1981).

24. *See* Ralph U. Whitten, *The Constitutional Limitations on State-Court Jurisdiction: A Historical Interpretative Reexamination of the Full Faith and Credit and Due Process Clauses* (pt. 1), 14 CREIGHTON L. REV. 499, 508-55 (1981).

25. When the Full Faith and Credit Clause of the Constitution was being framed, a clause was reported to the constitutional convention which provided that "[f]ull faith and credit ought to be given in each State to the public acts, records, and Judicial proceedings of every other State, and the Legislature shall by general laws prescribe the manner in which such acts, Records & proceedings shall be proved, and the effect which Judgments obtained in one State, shall have in another." 2 THE RECORDS OF THE FEDERAL CONVENTION OF

Congress has the authority to promulgate both nationwide conflict-of-laws rules and interstate jurisdictional standards to determine the effect of state-court judgments. In 1790, pursuant to this authority, the first Congress passed "An Act to prescribe the mode in which the public Acts, Records, and Judicial Proceedings in each State shall be authenticated so as to take effect in every other state."[26] This "implementing" statute provided:

> That the acts of the legislatures of the several states shall be authenticated by having the seal of their respective states affixed thereto: That the records and judicial proceedings of the courts of any state, shall be proved or admitted in any other court within the United States, by the attestation of the clerk, and the seal of the court annexed, if there be a seal, together with a certificate of the judge, chief justice, or presiding magistrate, as the case may be, that the said attestation is in due form. And the said records and judicial proceedings authenticated as aforesaid, shall have such faith and credit given to them in every court within the United States, as they have by law or usage in the courts of the state from whence the said records are or shall be taken.[27]

Several things should be noted about this statute. First, its title does not say that its purpose is to *declare* the effect that the records and judicial proceedings of one state should have when taken to another state. Instead, the title indicates that the Act prescribes the mode by which state statutes, records, and judicial proceedings shall be authenticated "so as to take effect" in other states. Thus, the Act is a provision that will allow state acts, records, and judgments to be authenticated so as to take effect in accordance with some set of rules outside the statute.[28] Second, Congress used the faith-and-credit language of the Constitution to provide that "such faith and credit" should be given to state records and judicial proceedings as they would have in the courts of the state from which they were taken. If this language was intended to prescribe an effect, why did Congress not use the word "effect"? Alternatively, if the language of the Constitution prescribes an effect, why was it necessary to duplicate the language in the implementing statute?

1787, at 485 (Max Farrand ed. 1911). In the debate over this clause, it was moved that the power of Congress be expanded, so that it would have the authority to declare the effect of public acts and records as well as judicial proceedings. *See id.* at 488. One delegate objected to this motion. James Wilson replied "that if the Legislature were not allowed to *declare the effect* the provision would amount to nothing more than what now takes place among all Independent Nations." *Id.* Wilson's remark indicates as clearly as any evidence available that the expression "full faith and credit shall be given" was not being used to give direct commands to the states about conflict of laws or jurisdictional matters. If the "full faith and credit" language of the Constitution had no greater effect "than what now takes place among independent nations," it could not be elevating state judgments to a higher level than foreign nation judgments or supplanting state conflict-of-laws doctrine with a constitutional command. Rather, Wilson's statement indicates that the important authority under the clause was being given to Congress through the power to declare the "effect" of public acts, records, and judicial proceedings.

26. Act of May 26, 1790, ch. 11, 1 Stat. 122 (now codified as 28 U.S.C. § 1738).

27. *Id.*

28. *See* Ralph U. Whitten, *The Constitutional Limitations on State-Court Jurisdiction: A Historical Interpretative Reexamination of the Full Faith and Credit and Due Process Clauses* (pt. 1), 14 CREIGHTON L. REV. 499, 556 (1981).

The debate in the early decisions over the interpretation of the implementing statute concerned the "such faith and credit" language of the Act. Some courts held that Congress had intended to declare the effect that the judgments of one state should have when taken to another state by using the "such faith and credit" language. Other courts disagreed. They believed that the terms "faith" and "credit" in the Constitution prescribed only an evidentiary (or admissibility) effect, not a res judicata effect. Thus, it was unreasonable to suppose that Congress had used the words in the statute in a different sense than it had used them in the Constitution.[29]

Significantly, however, even when the courts construed the Act as prescribing a non-evidentiary effect for state judgments and records, they sometimes agreed that the language of the Constitution was *not* designed, of its own force, to give more than an evidentiary command. Thus, in *Green v. Sarmiento*,[30] Justice Washington, sitting as a circuit judge, interpreted the "such faith and credit" language of the statute as designed to declare the effect of the judgments of a state court in other states. However, throughout the opinion, Washington was careful to distinguish between the use of the "faith and credit" language in the Constitution and its use in the statute.[31] In *Peck v. Williamson*,[32] Chief Justice Marshall, sitting as a circuit judge, interpreted the implementing statute contrary to Justice Washington's interpretation in *Green*.

---

29. *See generally id.* at 559-70.

30. 10 F. Cas. 1117 (C.C.D. Pa. 1810) (No. 5760).

31. At one point, Justice Washington stated that the Full Faith and Credit Clause of the Constitution had three objectives: (1) to declare that faith and credit should be given in each state to the public acts, records, and judicial proceedings of other states; (2) to provide a method of authenticating the acts, records, and proceedings of the states; and (3) to declare the effect of acts, records, and judicial proceedings of the state courts in other states. The first objective, stated Washington, "is declared and established by the Constitution itself, and was to receive no aid." *Id.* at 1118. However, "the second and third objects of the section, were expressly referred to the legislature of the Union, to carry them into effect in such manner, as to that body might seem right." *Id.* Washington also drew a distinction between "full faith and credit" and effect when commenting on the differences between the Full Faith and Credit Clauses of the Articles of Confederation and the Constitution. The Articles of Confederation clause "goes no farther than to declare that 'full faith and credit shall be given in each state, to the records, acts, and judicial proceedings of the courts and magistrates of every other state;' whereas the constitution proceeds to add, that congress may declare . . . the effect of such records, acts, and judicial proceedings." *Id.* at 1118-19. Thus, Washington viewed the direct effect of the Constitution's language, which was basically the same as the language of the Full Faith and Credit Clause of the Articles of Confederation, as relatively unimportant. What was important was the power that had been given to Congress under the Constitution. Finally, Washington answered an argument that the language of the implementing statute was designed only to mean "no more than that full faith and credit shall be given to the record, so authenticated; as evidence, that such proceedings were had, and such judgment rendered, as the record imports." *Id.* at 1119. "But the sentence does not go so far as this; for it does not give full faith and credit, but such faith and credit as the record has in the state from whence it is taken." *Id.* Washington was here arguing that the Constitution already provided full faith and credit "as a matter of evidence" and Congress could not qualify that command. Thus, Congress had to be declaring "effect" in the "same faith and credit" language of the statute. *See id.* This conclusion, however, seems questionable. An evidentiary effect is still an effect. Therefore, it seems clear that Congress had the right in the "effects" clause to declare evidentiary as well as other effects. As demonstrated *infra*, this is likely what Congress was really attempting to do in the statute. Thus, while Washington's opinion is a good indication that the direct effect of the Full Faith and Credit Clause was to impose only a limited rule of evidence, it is not a sound guide to the scope of the powers of Congress under the clause. Nevertheless, Washington's opinion is a very clear statement that the constitutional language was understood as evidentiary language and that evidentiary effects were distinguished from other kinds of effects.

32. 19 F. Cas. 85 (C.C.D.N.C. 1813) (No. 10,896).

Importantly, however, Chief Justice Marshall agreed with Justice Washington on the evidentiary character of the Constitution's language. To Marshall, it appeared "very clear" that the Constitution made "a pointed distinction between the faith and credit, and the effect, of a record in one state when exhibited in evidence in another."[33]

In 1813, in *Mills v. Duryee*,[34] the U.S. Supreme Court interpreted the last sentence of the implementing statute to be an attempt by Congress to declare the effect state-court judgments should have in other states. In *Mills*, an action of debt was brought in the U.S. Circuit Court for the District of Columbia on the judgment of a New York state court. The defendant pleaded *nul tiel record*, which denies the existence of the record and was the proper defensive plea in an action of debt on a record. The issue in the case turned on whether this plea was proper, or whether a plea of *nil debet*, the proper plea in an action on a foreign judgment, was the proper plea.[35] The resolution of the pleading issue depended on whether the implementing statute had elevated the status of state judgments to domestic judgments in other states.[36] The U.S. Supreme Court held that it had.[37] Thus, according to *Mills*, if a judgment would be given a res judicata effect by the judgment-rendering state, the judgment would have to be given a res judicata effect by other states as well.

Illustration 3-5. Assume that *A* obtained a judgment against *B* for $100,000 from a State *X* court that possessed no personal jurisdiction under State *X* law and thus was void in State *X*. Under the 1790 implementing statute, as interpreted in *Mills*, the judgment would be entitled to no effect in State *Y* if *A* attempted to enforce the judgment there against *B*. This conclusion followed under the *Mills* interpretation of the statute because State *X* itself would give no effect to the judgment. Since State *Y* was required only to give the same effect to the judgment that State *X* would give it, State *Y* also would treat the judgment

---

33. Chief Justice Marshall stated that "[u]nless Congress had prescribed its effect, it should be allowed only such as it possesses on common-law principles. In our opinion, Congress have not prescribed its effect. To suppose that they have is to believe that they use the words "faith and credit" in a sense different from that which they have in the clause of the constitution upon which they were legislating." *Id.* For other decisions also interpreting the Constitution as Marshall interpreted it in *Peck*, see Bartlett v. Knight, 1 Mass. 401, 404-05, 405-07, 409 (1805); Hitchcock v. Aiken, 1 Cai. R. 460, 475-77, 479-81, 483 (N.Y. Sup. Ct. 1803); Wright v. Tower, Browne's R. App. i, x-xii (Pa. 1801) (Court of Common Pleas of Luzerne County, Third Judicial District); Hammond v. Smith, 2 S.C.L. (2 Bay) 52, 54 (1802). For a discussion of these cases, as well as the minority of decisions reaching the opposite conclusion before 1813 when the Supreme Court resolved the issue, see Ralph U. Whitten, *The Original Understanding of the Full Faith and Credit Clause and the Defense of Marriage Act*, 32 CREIGHTON L. REV. 255, 297-327 (1998); Ralph U. Whitten, *The Constitutional Limitations on State-Court Jurisdiction: A Historical Interpretative Reexamination of the Full Faith and Credit and Due Process Clauses* (pt. 1), 14 CREIGHTON L. REV. 499, 559-64 (1981); Ralph U. Whitten, *The Constitutional Limitations on State Choice of Law: Full Faith and Credit*, 12 MEM. ST. U. L. REV. 1, 41-49 (1981).

34. 11 U.S. (7 Cranch) 481, 3 L. Ed. 411 (1813).

35. *See* Chapter 6(A)(3)(f) ("The General Issue") *infra*.

36. Recall the discussion of the forms of action appropriate to actions on domestic and foreign judgments in subsection *(a)*, *supra*.

37. Justice Johnson dissented on the ground that the statute had not elevated the judgments of one state to the status of records in another. He observed that faith and credit were terms strictly applicable to evidence. *See* 11 U.S. (7 Cranch) at 304-05, 3 L. Ed. at 413-14.

as void. Therefore, a violation of the judgment-rendering state's *domestic rules of jurisdiction* could render a judgment unenforceable in other states.

* * * * *

The U.S. Supreme Court's incorrect[38] interpretation of the implementing statute in *Mills* caused no appreciable problems in the enforcement of state judgments in other states. Making a judgment's enforceability in another state depend upon its enforceability in the state where it was rendered is a sensible rule, with few complicating features.[39] However, the *Mills* interpretation has produced two other problems.

First, many years after *Mills* was decided and the dispute over the meaning of the implementing statute and the Constitution had been forgotten, the Supreme Court utilized *Mills* as authority for construing the Full Faith and Credit Clause to contain a command to the states that they apply the law of other states under certain circumstances. In *Chicago & Alton Railroad v. Wiggins Ferry Co.*,[40] Chief Justice Waite stated:

> Without doubt the constitutional requirement, Art. IV, § 1, that "full faith and credit shall be given in each state to the public acts, records, and judicial proceedings of every other state,"

---

38. The *Mills'* interpretation of the statute was surely incorrect. As Chief Justice Marshall had written in *Peck v. Williamson*, 19 F. Cas. 85 (C.C.D.N.C. 1813) (No. 10,896), to suppose that Congress was trying to declare the effect of a judgment rendered in one state when taken to another was to suppose that it had used the terms "faith and credit" in the statute differently than they had been used in the Constitution. It is more likely that Congress was also giving a kind of evidentiary command in the statute to deal with a rather obvious problem that would be produced by the language of the Constitution. There were courts within the states that were courts of inferior jurisdiction. These courts were not courts of record, and their judgments would probably not be admitted into evidence in the other courts of the same state, much less given a res judicata effect. However, the unadulterated language of the Full Faith and Credit Clause would have commanded the courts of other states to admit the judgments of these inferior courts into evidence as conclusive proof that they had been rendered and adjudicated the matters described in the judgment. To prevent the anomaly of a judgment inadmissible in the state where it was rendered from having to be admitted in the courts of other states because of the Full Faith and Credit Clause, Congress provided in the implementing statute that the admissibility of state judgments would depend upon their admissibility in the state from which they were taken. *See* Ralph U. Whitten, *The Original Understanding of the Full Faith and Credit Clause and the Defense of Marriage Act*, 32 CREIGHTON L. REV. 255, 330-32 (1998); Ralph U. Whitten, *The Constitutional Limitations on State-Court Jurisdiction: A Historical Interpretative Reexamination of the Full Faith and Credit and Due Process Clauses* (pt. 1), 14 CREIGHTON L. REV. 499, 557-59 (1981); Ralph U. Whitten, *The Constitutional Limitations of State Choice of Law: Full Faith and Credit*, 12 MEM. ST. U. L. REV. 1, 52-53 (1981). This reading also explains the absence from the statute of a command that the public acts of one state be given "such faith and credit" as they would have in the state from which they were taken. There would have been no problem of statutory admissibility under the Full Faith and Credit Clause that would parallel the potential problems with judgments and records. Domestic statutes did not have to be proved to courts in the state where the statute was enacted. The courts of the enacting state would take judicial notice of the statutes of their own states. Statutes only had to be proved when they were brought into issue in the courts of other states. Thus, the command of the Full Faith and Credit Clause produced no anomaly in the case of statutes. There would never be a case in which the Clause commanded a state to admit a statute of another state into evidence when the statute would not be admitted into evidence in the state where it was enacted. The implementing statute thus provided how to authenticate statutes so they could be admitted in other states, but it was unnecessary for Congress to limit their admissibility in the "such faith and credit" passage. *See id.* at 53.

39. The question whether the *Mills* interpretation of the statute eliminated the ability to refuse enforcement of a judgment that violated the international rules of jurisdiction is discussed in the next subsection. Other issues under the statute are discussed in Chapter 13(F)(1) ("Enforcement of State Judgments") *infra*.

40. 119 U.S. 615, 7 S. Ct. 398, 30 L. Ed. 519 (1887).

implies that the *public acts* of every state shall be given the same effect by the courts of another state that they have by law and usage at home. This is clearly the logical result of the principles announced as early as 1813 in *Mills v. Duryee . . .* and steadily adhered to ever since.[41]

In this passage, Chief Justice Waite failed to appreciate the nature of the controversy over the implementing statute. Waite concluded that because the language of the statute and the Constitution were the same, they must mean the same thing. This conclusion was correct as an original matter because both the language of the statute and of the Constitution had been intended to give limited evidentiary commands. However, Chief Justice Waite failed to realize that *Mills* interpreted the language of the implementing statute to mean something *different* than the language of the Constitution. This misunderstanding led to a more expansive view of the Full Faith and Credit Clause of the Constitution than was justifiable under its language and history.[42] Worse, it seemed to establish a constitutional rule that, had it persisted, would have been insensible.[43]

Illustration 3-6. If the *Mills* interpretation of the "faith and credit" language is read into the Full Faith and Credit Clause of the Constitution, that interpretation would require that each state apply the law of some other state instead of its own in multistate disputes. Thus, assume that *A*, a citizen of State *X*, has an automobile accident in State *Y* with *B*, a citizen of State *Y*, and is killed. States *X* and *Y* both have wrongful death statutes with limits on the amount that can be recovered, but the limit in each state is different. The *Mills* rule, applied to public acts, would seem to require State *X* to apply the wrongful death limit of State *Y* if the suit is commenced in State *X*. Similarly, it would seem to require State *Y* to apply the wrongful death limit of State *X* if the suit is commenced in State *Y*. This is the logical result of commanding each state to give the same effect to the statutes of another state that the statute would have in the state that enacted it.[44]

* * * * *

Second, in 1948, Congress for the first time added "public acts" to the faith and credit command of the implementing statute.[45] The only explanation

---

41. *Id.* at 622, 7 S. Ct. at 401-02, 30 L. Ed. at 522 (emphasis added).

42. *See* Ralph U. Whitten, *The Constitutional Limitations on State Choice of Law: Full Faith and Credit*, 12 MEM. ST. U. L. REV. 1, 4-5, 55-56 (1981).

43. Chief Justice Waite's understanding of the constitutional rule did not persist, probably because it became apparent that it would produce an unintelligible constitutional command. *See Illustration 3-6 infra.* However, an expansive view of the Full Faith and Credit Clause as applied to choice-of-law matters did persist. *See* Ralph U. Whitten, *The Constitutional Limitations on State Choice of Law: Full Faith and Credit*, 12 MEM. ST. U. L. REV. 1, 4-11 (1981).

44. *Cf.* Ralph U. Whitten, *The Constitutional Limitations on State Choice of Law: Full Faith and Credit*, 12 MEM. ST. U. L. REV. 1, 61-62 (1981) (discussing the modern implementing statute).

45. The 1948 language has been retained to the present. After providing for the authentication of public acts, records, and judicial proceedings, the statute reads:

> Such *Acts*, records and judicial proceedings or copies thereof, so authenticated, shall have the same full faith and credit in every court within the United States and its Territories and Possessions as they have by law or usage in the courts of such State, Territory, or Possession from which they are taken.

for this change in the statute's language was found in the Revisers' Notes, which stated that public acts were added to follow the language of the Constitution.[46] The difficulty is, of course, that the *Mills* interpretation of the statute would now apply to public acts in addition to records and judicial proceedings. The revisers obviously did not grasp the implications of such an application, nor of the fact that *Mills* had interpreted the "faith and credit" language of the statute to mean something different than the same language in the Constitution. The result is that, as with Chief Justice Waite's mistaken reliance on *Mills* as an interpretation of the constitutional Clause, the modern implementing statute gives an unintelligible command with regard to public acts.[47]

Illustration 3-7. On the facts of *Illustration 3-6*, the implementing statute appears to require (1) State *X* to apply the wrongful death limit of the "public act" of State *Y* if the suit is commenced in State *X* and (2) State *Y* to apply the wrongful death limit of the "public act" of State *X* if the suit is commenced in State *Y*.

* * * * *

Properly, however, the U.S. Supreme Court has ignored the requirement of full faith and credit to public acts in the statute,[48] although the Court has incorporated limited choice-of-law commands to the states through the first sentence of the Full Faith and Credit Clause.[49]

(e) The Status of the Territorial Rules of Jurisdiction Under the Full Faith and Credit Clause and the Implementing Statute

After *Mills*, the status of the territorial "international" rules of jurisdiction was still in doubt. The *Mills* interpretation of the statute required a reference to the domestic jurisdictional rules of the judgment-rendering state to determine the effect that the state-court judgment should have. Did either the Constitution or the implementing statute require, permit, or forbid an additional reference to the territorial rules of jurisdiction to determine the effect that the judgments of one state should have in another?

In 1851, the Supreme Court answered this question in *D'Arcy v. Ketchum*.[50] In *D'Arcy*, the Court held that neither the Constitution nor the implementing statute dealt with the territorial jurisdictional rules. Instead, those rules of jurisdiction remained as they were in 1789–although Congress had the power to modify them under the Full Faith and Credit Clause if Congress decided to do so. This conclusion had been drawn by the state courts both before and after

---

28 U.S.C. § 1738 (emphasis added).

46. *See* Ralph U. Whitten, *The Constitutional Limitations on State Choice of Law: Full Faith and Credit*, 12 MEM. ST. U. L. REV. 1, 60-61 (1981).

47. There is general agreement on this point. *See id.* at 61-62.

48. *See id.* at 62.

49. *See id.* at 4-5, 55-56.

50. 52 U.S. (11 How.) 165, 174, 13 L. Ed. 648, 652 (1851).

Mills v. Duryee.[51] The Court's reasoning in *D'Arcy* explains the relationship between the Constitution and implementing statute on the one hand, and the territorial jurisdictional rules on the other:

> In construing the Act of 1790, the law as it stood when the act was passed must enter into that construction; so that the existing defect in the old law may be seen, and its remedy by the act of Congress comprehended. Now it was most reasonable, on general principles of comity and justice, that, among States and their citizens united as ours are, judgments rendered in one should bind citizens of other States, where defendants had been served with process, or voluntarily made defence.
>
> As these judgments, however, were only *prima facie* evidence, and subject to be inquired into by plea when sued on in another State, Congress saw proper to remedy the evil, and to provide that such inquiry and double defence should not be allowed. To this extent, it is declared in the case of *Mills v. Duryee*, Congress has gone in altering the old rule. Nothing more was required.
>
> On the other hand, the international law as it existed among the States in 1790 was, that a judgment rendered in one State, assuming to bind the person of a citizen of another, was void within the foreign State, when the defendant had not been served with process or voluntarily made defence, because neither the legislative jurisdiction, nor that of courts of justice, had binding force.
>
> Subject to this established principle, Congress also legislated; and the question is, whether it was intended to overthrow this principle, and to declare a new rule, which would bind the citizens of one State to the laws of another; as must be the case if the laws of New York bind this defendant in Louisiana. There was no evil in this part of the existing law, and no remedy called for, and in our opinion Congress did not intend to overthrow the old rule by the enactment that such faith and credit should be given to records of judgments as they had in the State where made.[52]

Thus, neither the U.S. Constitution nor the implementing statute touched the preexisting customary international territorial rules of jurisdiction.[53] Furthermore, the Supreme Court did not describe the international territorial rules as

---

51. *See, e.g.*, Bissell v. Briggs, 9 Mass. 462, 466-67 (1813); Ralph U. Whitten, *The Constitutional Limitations on State-Court Jurisdiction: A Historical Interpretative Reexamination of the Full Faith and Credit and Due Process Clauses* (pt. 1), 14 CREIGHTON L. REV. 499, 571-72, 578 (1981).

52. 52 U.S. (11 How.) at 175-76, 13 L. Ed. at 653.

53. Today, the recognized bases for jurisdiction to adjudicate in international law are more numerous. *See* RESTATEMENT (THIRD) OF THE FOREIGN RELATIONS LAW OF THE UNITED STATES § 421 (1987). For excellent discussions of the territorial nature of jurisdictional rules in the early nineteenth century, see Michael M. O'Hear, *"Some of the Most Embarrassing Questions": Extraterritorial Divorces and the Problem of Jurisdiction Before Pennoyer*, 104 YALE L.J. 1507 (1995); James Weinstein, *The Early American Origins of Territoriality in Judicial Jurisdiction*, 37 ST. LOUIS L.J. 1 (1992).

constitutional rules. Instead, the Court referred to the rules as based on international law as it existed among the States in 1790.[54] Some of the state courts that had adopted an interpretation of the implementing statute identical to that in *Mills* had also stated explicitly that neither the Constitution nor the implementing statute had incorporated or otherwise touched the preexisting jurisdictional rules.[55]

Illustration 3-8. Assume that *A*, a citizen and resident of State *X*, sued *B*, a citizen and resident of State *Y*, in a State *X* court. *A* seeks to recover $100,000. *B* was served with process in State *Y* under a State *X* statute allowing mail service on nonresidents outside State *X*. *B* did not appear and defend. The State *X* court then entered a default judgment against *B* for $100,000. Assume that State *X* would consider this judgment valid and binding under its domestic law. Nevertheless, the courts of State *Y*, or of any other state, would refuse to enforce the State *X* judgment on the ground that the judgment was rendered in violation of the international territorial rules of jurisdiction. Those rules were not satisfied. *B* was not served with process while physically present in State *X*, *B* did not consent to suit there, and *B* owned no property there. Neither the Full Faith and Credit Clause of the Constitution nor its implementing statute altered or incorporated the international jurisdictional rules. Consequently, they operated after the formation of the Constitution in the same way that they had operated before.

---

54. Nevertheless, despite this evidence, some commentators have argued that the Clause incorporated the international territorial rules of jurisdiction as constitutional commands to the states, the violation of which would invalidate state-court judgments under the Clause. *See* FLEMING JAMES, JR. ET AL., CIVIL PROCEDURE § 2.4, at 57 (4th ed. 1992); Geoffrey C. Hazard, Jr., *A General Theory of State-Court Jurisdiction*, 1965 SUP. CT. REV. 241. For a view of the historical record that is contrary to the view presented in this section, see also Douglas Laycock, *Equal Citizens of Equal and Territorial States: The Constitutional Foundations of Choice of Law*, 92 COLUM. L. REV. 249, 295-305 (1992). *But see* Ralph U. Whitten, *The Original Understanding of the Full Faith and Credit Clause and the Defense of Marriage Act*, 32 CREIGHTON L. REV. 255, 346-72 (1998) (disputing Laycock's interpretation).

55. For example, in Bissell v. Briggs, 9 Mass. 462 (1813), the Supreme Judicial Court of Massachusetts held that the implementing statute required a res judicata effect to be given to the judgments of other states, and then stated:

> But neither . . . the federal constitution, nor the act of Congress, had any intention of enlarging, restraining, or in any manner operating upon, the jurisdiction of the legislatures, or of the courts of any of the *United States*. The jurisdiction remains as it was before; and the public acts, records, and judicial proceedings contemplated, and to which full faith and credit are to be given, are such as were within the jurisdiction of the state whence they shall be taken. Whenever, therefore, a record of a judgment of any court of any state is produced as conclusive evidence, the jurisdiction of the court rendering it is open to inquiry; and if it should appear that the court had no jurisdiction of the cause, no faith or credit whatever will be given to the judgment.

Id. at 466-67. Given the explicit statements about the nonconstitutional nature of the international rules of jurisdiction, it is difficult to see how anyone can interpret the case law as holding that the constitutional clause incorporated the rules, but some commentators have tried. *See* Douglas Laycock, *Equal Citizens of Equal and Territorial States: The Constitutional Foundations of Choice of Law*, 92 COLUM. L. REV. 249, 298-301 (1992). *But see* Ralph U. Whitten, *The Original Understanding of the Full Faith and Credit Clause and the Defense of Marriage Act*, 32 CREIGHTON L. REV. 255, 346-72 (1998) (disputing Laycock's interpretation).

2. Territorial Rules and the Due Process Clause of the Fourteenth Amendment of the U.S. Constitution

(a) Interpretation of State Due Process Clauses Prior to the Fourteenth Amendment

The states could impose restrictions on the jurisdictional reach of their *own* courts, either by common-law, statutory, or constitutional rules. Each state had adopted a due process clause or its equivalent, even before the Fourteenth Amendment imposed a federal due process requirement on the states.[56] Because the federal Due Process Clause has been so important in limiting the jurisdictional authority of state courts after 1868, it is important to consider whether the *state* due process clauses were interpreted to impose domestic restrictions on the states' own courts prior to the Fourteenth Amendment. The interpretation of the state due process clauses before the Civil War constitutes a significant source of evidence about how the Due Process Clause of the Fourteenth Amendment would have been understood.

The evidence indicates that prior to the adoption of the Fourteenth Amendment the requirement of "due process" was interpreted to require that persons had to be provided a judicial proceeding with an adequate opportunity to defend before they could be deprived of life, liberty, or property. Also, it was thought that due process required the proceeding to be a "regular" proceeding with "regular allegations, opportunity to answer, and a trial according to some settled course of judicial proceedings."[57] Nevertheless, Congress and the state legislatures were thought to have wide latitude to dispense with "ordinary" judicial proceedings.[58]

Embodied in the basic concept of a "regular" judicial proceeding was the opportunity to be heard in defense before a state could take life, liberty, or property. Several pre-Fourteenth Amendment cases dealt with an essential precondition of the opportunity-to-be-heard principle: notice of the pending action. These decisions revealed a broad power in the legislative branches of the state and federal governments to dispense with personal notice to a defendant by in-hand service of process. The cases approved *constructive notice*–by publication of notice of the suit in a newspaper instead of in-hand service. The cases indicated that the choice of a particular form of notice by the legislature would be upheld

---

56. *See generally* Ralph U. Whitten, *The Constitutional Limitations on State-Court Jurisdiction: A Historical Interpretative Reexamination of the Full Faith and Credit and Due Process Clauses* (pt. 2), 14 CREIGHTON L. REV. 735 (1981); *see also* Ralph U. Whitten, *The Constitutional Limitations on State Choice of Law: Due Process*, 9 HASTINGS CONST. L.Q. 851 (1982).

57. *See* Murray's Lessee v. Hoboken Land & Improvement Co., 59 U.S. (18 How.) 272, 280, 15 L. Ed. 372, 376 (1856).

58. *See* Ralph U. Whitten, *The Constitutional Limitations on State-Court Jurisdiction: A Historical Interpretative Reexamination of the Full Faith and Credit and Due Process Clauses* (pt. 2), 14 CREIGHTON L. REV. 735, 796-98 (1981) (summary proceedings approved in tax cases and other situations).

unless the legislature had provided for a type of proceeding in which it was not plausible to believe that notice would reach the defendant.[59]

　　　The due process rules concerning notice and an opportunity to defend should be contrasted with the international territorial rules of jurisdiction. The latter rules reflected traditional notions of the territorial authority of a sovereign to control persons or property within its borders.[59] Such sovereignty-oriented rules were not related to the traditional due process concept of an opportunity to be heard in defense, although rules requiring adequate notice to the defendant obviously relate to a fair opportunity to defend. For example, a state could not, under the international rules, compel a defendant outside the state to appear when the defendant did not own property within the state and could not be served with process in the state. Under those circumstances, the state could not render a judgment against the defendant enforceable in another state. This result would follow even if the forum state was a perfectly convenient place of trial for the defendant and would not adversely affect the defendant's opportunity to be heard. Conversely, if a defendant were served with process while temporarily in a state, the state could enter a judgment against the defendant that would be enforceable in other states under the international rules. This result would follow even if the judgment-rendering state was so inconvenient a place to maintain the action that the defendant literally could not afford to defend the suit there. Therefore, before the Fourteenth Amendment, it is not surprising that the due process clauses of the state constitutions usually were *not* interpreted to require the states to follow the international rules of jurisdiction, but they *were* interpreted to require adequate notice.[60]

(b) Incorporation of the Territorial Rules into the Due Process Clause of the Fourteenth Amendment

Pennoyer v. Neff[61] was the first decision of the U.S. Supreme Court to

---

59. *See, e.g.*, Mason v. Messenger & May, 17 Iowa 261 (1864), *error dismissed*, 77 U.S. (10 Wall.) 507, 19 L. Ed. 1028 (1871); United States Trust Co. v. United States Fire Ins. Co., 18 N.Y. 199 (1858); *see also* Davidson v. Farrell, 8 Minn. 258 (1863); Jack v. Thompson, 41 Miss. 49 (1866).

59. For an excellent discussion of sovereignty in the law of the personal jurisdiction before the Fourteenth Amendment, see Michael M. O'Hear, *"Some of the Most Embarrassing Questions": Extraterritorial Divorces and the Problem of Jurisdiction Before* Pennoyer, 104 YALE L.J. 1507, 1534-35 (1995).

60. *See generally* Ralph U. Whitten, *The Constitutional Limitations on State-Court Jurisdiction: A Historical Interpretative Reexamination of the Full Faith and Credit and Due Process Clauses* (pt. 2), 14 CREIGHTON L. REV. 735, 774-804 (1981). It is, of course, true that the states usually did follow the traditional rules because they were the accepted common-law procedures of the day. *See, e.g.*, JOSEPH STORY, COMMENTARIES ON THE CONFLICT OF LAWS § 554 (1834).

61. 95 U.S. 714, 24 L. Ed. 565 (1878). For an excellent analysis of *Pennoyer*, see Patrick J. Borchers, *The Death of the Constitutional Law of Personal Jurisdiction: From* Pennoyer *to* Burnham *and Back Again*, 24 U.C. DAVIS L. REV. 19 (1990). For a spirited debate provoked by Professor Borchers' article, see Patrick J. Borchers, *Jurisdictional Pragmatism: International Shoe's Half-Buried Legacy*, 28 U.C. DAVIS L. REV. 561 (1995); John B. Oakley, *The Pitfalls of "Hint and Run" History: A Critique of Professor Borchers' "Limited View" of* Pennoyer v. Neff, 28 U.C. DAVIS L. REV. 591 (1995); Patrick J. Borchers, Pennoyer's *Limited Legacy: A Reply to Professor Oakley*, 29 U.C. DAVIS L. REV. 115 (1995); *see also* Harold L. Korn, *Rethinking Personal Jurisdiction and Choice of Law in Multistate Torts*, 97 COLUM. L. REV. 2183, 2190-93 (1997); Wendy Collins Perdue, *Sin, Scandal, and Substantive Due Process: Personal Jurisdiction and* Pennoyer *Reconsidered*, 62 indicate that the Due Process Clause of the Fourteenth Amendment limited the power of the states to adjudicate cases involving nonresident defendants. The significance of *Pennoyer* was that a case decided by a state court in excess of its jurisdiction could be reviewed directly by the Supreme Court on the ground that the state-court judgment violated due process.[62] As noted in section A(1), before the ratification of the Fourteenth Amendment and *Pennoyer's* interpretation of it, a state judgment rendered without jurisdiction under the international territorial rules could be invalidated only when the judgment was taken to the courts of another state or to the federal courts for enforcement. Ironically, although *Pennoyer* established that the Due Process Clause of the Fourteenth Amendment limited state-court jurisdiction over nonresidents, the Due Process Clause was not the basis of the Court's holding in the case.

In *Pennoyer*, Neff claimed a tract of land in Oregon under a "land patent" issued to him by the United States in 1866. Pennoyer claimed the land by virtue of an execution sale made by a local sheriff pursuant to a judgment of an Oregon state court rendered in 1866. Neff was a nonresident defendant in the state action leading to the sheriff's sale. He had been served with process in the state action by publication of notice in a newspaper, as provided for by Oregon law. Neff brought an action against Pennoyer in the U.S. Circuit Court in Oregon to recover possession of the land. In that action, he attacked the validity of the Oregon state judgment, but not on federal due process grounds.[63] The U.S. Circuit Court held the state judgment invalid because of certain defects in an affidavit that was necessary under state law to obtain the service by publication. However, the U.S. Supreme Court did not regard the defects in the affidavit found by the circuit court to be the kind of error that could be raised in a subsequent proceeding brought to attack the judgment. Rather, such errors could be raised only on appeal of the state judgment to a higher Oregon state court.[64] Nevertheless, the Supreme Court affirmed the judgment of the circuit court on other grounds.

The Court held that the state judgment was void because the defendant had not been personally served with process while present in Oregon and the property which was the subject of the action had not been seized prior to judgment. Thus, the state judgment violated the international rules of jurisdiction. Under well-settled principles, no other state or federal court had to give effect to

---

WASH. L. REV. 479 (1987).

    62. *See* Philip B. Kurland, *The Supreme Court, The Due Process Clause and the In Personam Jurisdiction of State Courts—From* Pennoyer *to* Denckla: *A Review*, 25 U. CHI. L. REV. 569, 585 (1958). The availability of direct review on due process grounds assumes that the state possesses a "special appearance" procedure or its equivalent that allows nonresident defendants to challenge a court's assertion of personal jurisdiction over them. Special appearance procedures are discussed in subsection B(3) *infra.*

    63. No due process argument was made or discussed in the lower federal court that decided *Pennoyer. See* Neff v. Pennoyer, 17 F. Cas. 1279 (C.C.D. Or. 1875) (No. 10,083), *aff'd,* 95 U.S. 714, 24 L. Ed. 565 (1878). Furthermore, no due process argument appears in the appellate brief of Neff, the defendant in error, who would have been the party to raise it, nor anywhere else in the record on appeal. *See generally* Brief for Defendant in Error, Pennoyer v. Neff, 95 U.S. 714, 24 L. Ed. 565 (1878); Transcript of Record, *id.; see also* Ralph U. Whitten, *The Constitutional Limitations on State-Court Jurisdiction: A Historical Interpretative Reexamination of the Full Faith and Credit and Due Process Clauses* (pt. 2), 14 CREIGHTON L. REV. 735, 821 (1981).

    64. *See* Pennoyer v. Neff, 95 U.S. at 720-21, 24 L. Ed. at 567-68.

the judgment under the full-faith-and-credit implementing statute. In addition, the Court, in an extended dictum,[65] indicated that the violation of the international rules of jurisdiction would produce a due process violation in the future:

> Since the adoption of the Fourteenth Amendment to the Federal Constitution, the validity of such judgments [judgments rendered in violation of the international rules] may be directly questioned, and their enforcement in the State resisted, on the ground that proceedings in a court of justice to determine the personal rights and obligations of parties over whom that court has no jurisdiction do not constitute due process of law. Whatever difficulty may be experienced in giving to those terms a definition which will embrace every permissible exertion of power affecting private rights, and exclude such as is forbidden, there can be no doubt of their meaning when applied to judicial proceedings. They mean a course of legal proceedings according to those rules and principles which have been established in our systems of jurisprudence for the protection and enforcement of private rights. To give such proceedings any validity, there must be a tribunal competent by its constitution—that is by the law of its creation—to pass upon the subject-matter of the suit; and, if that involves merely a determination of the personal liability of the defendant, he must be brought within its jurisdiction by service of process within the State, or his voluntary appearance.[66]

The Court was erroneous in at least two important respects. First, in order to invalidate the Oregon judgment, the Court had to conclude that the international rules of jurisdiction had been violated. The Court reasoned that the defendant either had to be served with process personally while present within the state or, if the presence of property was to be the basis of a court's jurisdiction, the property had to be brought under the control of the court by seizure of the property *before* judgment.[67] However, a requirement of seizure before judgment was not a part of the international rules before *Pennoyer*.[68] Thus, prejudgment seizure of the property as the basis for the court's power should have been considered merely a matter of municipal choice by the state.

---

65. The due process portion of the Supreme Court's opinion in *Pennoyer* could not have been part of the Court's holding. The state judgment under consideration in *Pennoyer* had been rendered in 1866. The Fourteenth Amendment was not ratified until 1868. Thus, the Fourteenth Amendment could not have been the basis for voiding the judgment. *See* Ralph U. Whitten, *The Constitutional Limitations on State-Court Jurisdiction: A Historical Interpretative Reexamination of the Full Faith and Credit and Due Process Clauses* (pt. 1), 14 CREIGHTON L. REV. 499, 504-05 (1981); *id.* (pt. 2) at 821.

66. Pennoyer v. Neff, 95 U.S. at 733, 24 L. Ed. at 572.

67. *See id.* at 727-28, 24 L. Ed. at 570-71.

68. *See* Adrian M. Tocklin, Pennoyer v. Neff: *The Hidden Agenda of Stephen J. Field*, 28 SETON HALL L. REV. 75 (1997); Ralph U. Whitten, *The Constitutional Limitations on State-Court Jurisdiction: A Historical Interpretative Reexamination of the Full Faith and Credit and Due Process Clauses* (pt. 1), 14 CREIGHTON L. REV. 499, 507 n.30 (1981); *id.* (pt. 2) at 826. The lack of authority for this part of the opinion was noted by Justice Hunt in dissent. *See* Pennoyer v. Neff, 95 U.S. at 736-48, 24 L. Ed. at 573-78; *see also* Cooper v. Reynolds, 77 U.S. (10 Wall.) 308, 19 L. Ed. 931 (1870); Cleland v. Tavernier, 11 Minn. 194 (1866).

Second, the Court erroneously concluded that a violation of the international rules per se was a violation of the Due Process Clause of the Fourteenth Amendment. Violation of the international territorial rules had not generally been considered to be a violation of the due process clauses of the states prior to the ratification of the Fourteenth Amendment. Thus, violation of such rules would not void a judgment *within* a state, even though other states would not recognize or enforce a judgment rendered without jurisdiction in the "international sense."[69]

Despite these errors, the *Pennoyer* opinion became the basis for the development of the modern law of personal jurisdiction. As later sections will demonstrate, the Supreme Court has moved away from the international territorial rules of personal jurisdiction embraced by *Pennoyer* to more justifiable rules of due process that focus on the burdens placed on the defendant by a state's assertion of personal jurisdiction. However, all vestiges of *Pennoyer's* territorialism have not been eliminated from the Due Process Clause.

SECTION B. THE OPERATION OF THE TERRITORIAL RULES

As indicated in the preceding section, the territorial rules of jurisdiction contained two basic grounds upon which in personam jurisdiction could be exercised—physical presence of the person within the borders of the sovereign and consent. In addition, the international rules recognized the presence of property or the alteration of an inhabitant's status as valid grounds for the exercise of in rem (or quasi in rem) jurisdiction.[70] After the incorporation of these rules into

---

69. *See generally* Ralph U. Whitten, *The Constitutional Limitations on State-Court Jurisdiction: A Historical Interpretative Reexamination of the Full Faith and Credit and Due Process Clauses* (pt. 2), 14 CREIGHTON L. REV. 735 (1981). Although the territorial rules were not suited to the protection of the defendant's opportunity to be heard in defense, compliance with the rules would have been deemed consistent with the due process clauses of the states prior to the Fourteenth Amendment. For example, if a state asserted jurisdiction over a defendant by serving the defendant with process while the defendant was temporarily within the state, or attaching the defendant's property within the state, the resulting judgment would be valid both in the judgment-rendering state and elsewhere. *See, e.g.,* RESTATEMENT (FIRST) OF CONFLICT OF LAWS §§ 77-84 (1934); JOSEPH STORY, COMMENTARIES ON THE CONFLICT OF LAWS §§ 539, 543, 554 (1834). Yet such assertions of jurisdiction are inconsistent with the opportunity-to-be-heard principle of the due process clauses, in that they allow defendants to be subjected to jurisdiction in cases in which the claim has nothing to do with the state and it would be terribly burdensome for the defendant to defend within the state. The deeply rooted acceptance of the territorial rules at common law, together with the inability to acquire personal jurisdiction over absent defendants by other procedural means, probably obscured the impropriety of the rules in a due process sense. Nevertheless, *Pennoyer's* incorporation of the international rules into the Due Process Clause of the Fourteenth Amendment has been defended on the ground that "the restriction on state sovereign power [imposed on the states by *Pennoyer*] is a function of the individual liberty interest preserved by the due process clause." John N. Drobak, *The Federalism Theme in Personal Jurisdiction*, 68 IOWA L. REV. 1015, 1033 (1983). However justifiable it may be to impose some due process limitations on the sovereignty of the states to protect individual liberty interests, it was not justifiable to incorporate the international rules into the clause for that purpose because the international rules permit much more infringement of individual liberty interests than they prohibit.

70. "Pure" in rem jurisdiction should be distinguished from a kind of jurisdiction that has come to be known as *quasi in rem* jurisdiction. Quasi in rem jurisdiction involves the seizure of property as a means of compelling the appearance of the defendant to litigate a dispute that does not concern the property. *See* LUTHER L. McDOUGAL III ET AL., AMERICAN CONFLICTS LAW ch. 3 (5th ed. 2000) (discussing, *inter alia*, the traditional the Due Process Clause in *Pennoyer*, their evolution continued. In addition, a peculiarly American rule permitting a sovereign to exercise jurisdiction over its absent citizens or domiciliaries also evolved.

1. In Rem Jurisdiction

After *Pennoyer v. Neff*, the Supreme Court developed important principles governing in rem jurisdiction. On the affirmative side, *Pennoyer's* conception of state power allowed a state to exercise control over property located within the state. On the restrictive side, *Pennoyer* prevented states from directly exercising power over property located in other states. In addition, the problems posed for defendants whose property was attached by a state court in a quasi in rem proceeding caused some states to authorize ''limited appearance'' procedures.

(a) *Affirmative Principles of In Rem Jurisdiction*

On the affirmative side of *Pennoyer*, the most important problem concerned the location, or *situs*, of intangible property. One issue concerned the location of a debt for purposes of seizure of the debt through attachment or garnishment procedures. In *Harris v. Balk*,[71] Harris, a North Carolina resident, owed a debt of $180 to Balk, also a North Carolina resident. Epstein, a Maryland resident, asserted Balk owed him over $300. On August 6th, Epstein garnished the debt owed by Harris to Balk while Harris was in Maryland on business. Harris consented to garnishment of the $180 debt and paid Epstein $180 on August 11th.

On the same day, Balk sued Harris in North Carolina state court. Harris' defense was the payment of the Maryland judgment. The lower North Carolina court and the North Carolina Supreme Court rejected this defense. The North Carolina courts maintained that the Maryland court lacked jurisdiction to attach or garnish the debt due from Harris to Balk because Harris was only temporarily in Maryland and the situs of the debt was in North Carolina. The North Carolina courts reasoned that the situs of a debt is at the domicile of either the creditor or debtor. Thus, the debt did not follow the debtor, Harris, into Maryland on his temporary visit. Therefore, there was no ''property'' in Maryland that could be attached or garnished.[72]

The U.S. Supreme Court reversed. The Court held that the Maryland judgment was valid and had to be given effect in North Carolina. The Court explained that attachment (and presumably other methods of seizing property) was a matter of local law. As long as state law provided for seizure of the debt based on personal service of process on the debtor within the state, the state court could validly acquire in rem jurisdiction. The debt followed the debtor, even on

---

types of jurisdiction, including quasi in rem). Quasi in rem jurisdiction is a term that is also used to describe jurisdiction in an action that seeks to determine the interest of particular persons, as opposed to the entire world, in a thing. *See id.* This form of quasi in rem jurisdiction is, so far as American jurisdictional theory is concerned, identical to pure in rem jurisdiction.

　71. 198 U.S. 215, 25 S. Ct. 625, 49 L. Ed. 1023 (1905).

　72. *See id.* at 216-17, 25 S. Ct. at 626, 49 L. Ed. at 1023-24.

temporary visits to other states. As long as the debtor could be sued by the creditor in the state, which was beyond dispute in *Harris*, the creditor's creditor (Epstein) could garnish the debt. The garnishee (Harris) could thus set up the Maryland judgment as a defense, provided proper notice of the garnishment proceeding had been given to the garnishee's creditor (Balk). Such notice had indisputably been given in the case. Furthermore, the Court noted that Balk had a year and a day after entry of judgment in the Maryland proceeding to litigate the question of his liability to Epstein in the Maryland courts, but had not done so.[73]

The decision in *Harris v. Balk*, like that in *Pennoyer v. Neff*, was heavily dependent upon the distinction between in rem and in personam proceedings. The force of this distinction became evident in the Supreme Court's decision in *New York Life Insurance Co. v. Dunlevy*,[74] decided nine years after *Harris v. Balk*. In 1907, Boggs & Buhl recovered a valid personal judgment against Dunlevy in a Pennsylvania Court of Common Pleas. In 1909, New York Life Insurance Co. became liable to Gould, Dunlevy's father, for $2,479.70 under a life insurance policy held by Gould. Dunlevy claimed that Gould had assigned the proceeds of the policy to her, but the validity of the assignment was disputed by Gould. In November, 1909, Boggs & Buhl garnished the debt allegedly owed by New York Life to Dunlevy in an action in the Pennsylvania Court of Common Pleas. Both Gould and New York Life were summoned as garnishees.

In January, 1910, Dunlevy sued New York Life and Gould in California. Both New York Life and Gould were served properly with process in that state. In February, 1910, New York Life answered Boggs & Buhl's garnishment process in Pennsylvania by setting up the conflicting claims and requesting interpleader. Pursuant to this answer, New York Life admitted the debt and paid the money into the court. Notice was given to Dunlevy in California, but she did not appear or plead in the Pennsylvania interpleader proceeding. The Pennsylvania jury found that the assignment was invalid, and the proceeds were paid to Gould.

New York Life then set up the Pennsylvania judgment as a bar to Dunlevy's action in California. The California court rejected this defense. The court found the assignment to be valid and awarded the proceeds to Dunlevy. On appeal to the U.S. Supreme Court, the Court held that California did not have to give effect to the Pennsylvania judgment:

> Beyond doubt, without the necessity of further personal service of process upon Mrs. Dunlevy, the Court of Common Pleas at Pittsburgh had ample power through garnishment proceedings to inquire whether she held a valid claim against the insurance company and if found to exist then to condemn and appropriate it so far as necessary to discharge the original judgment. Although herself outside the limits of the State, such disposition of the property would have been binding on her [citing *Harris v. Balk*]. But the interpleader initiated by the com-

---

73. *See id.* at 222-23, 227-28, 25 S. Ct. at 626-29, 49 L. Ed. at 1027-29.
74. 241 U.S. 518, 36 S. Ct. 613, 60 L. Ed. 1140 (1916).

pany was an altogether different matter. This was an attempt to bring about a final and conclusive adjudication of her personal rights, not merely to discover property and apply it to debts. And unless in contemplation of law she was before the court and required to respond to that issue, its orders and judgments in respect thereto were not binding on her. . . .

. . . .

The established general rule is that any personal judgment which a state court may render against one who did not voluntarily submit to its jurisdiction, and who is not a citizen of the State, nor served with process within its borders, no matter what the mode of service, is void, because the court had no jurisdiction over his person.[75]

The result of cases like *Harris* and *Dunlevy* was that litigants had to exercise extreme care in determining the proper categorization of the different kinds of proceedings they wished to bring and the effect of the procedural steps they took within them. In *Dunlevy*, had New York Life simply allowed itself to be garnished in aid of execution of the original judgment that Boggs & Buhl had obtained against Dunlevy in 1907, there would, under the Court's opinion, have apparently been no difficulty. The Supreme Court would have considered the garnishment to be a continuation of the original proceeding against Dunlevy, in which in personam jurisdiction had already been validly acquired over her. Alternatively, the garnishment could have been considered a valid exercise of in rem jurisdiction over property located within the state. In either case, Mrs. Dunlevy would have been bound by the garnishment,[76] which also would have bound Gould because he had been summoned as a garnishee in aid of execution. The Court, however, conceptualized New York Life's petition for interpleader as "collateral" to the original proceeding and not supported by the original acquisition of personal jurisdiction over Dunlevy.[77] As a result, because interpleader was considered an "in personam" action, it required a new acquisition of personal jurisdiction over Dunlevy, who could no longer be served with process because she had left Pennsylvania. Thus, even though the practical effect of the interpleader proceeding on Dunlevy's rights was no different than the practical effect of garnishment in aid of execution, the Court held the interpleader proceeding to be void.[78]

---

75. *Id.* at 520, 522-23, 36 S. Ct. at 613-14, 60 L. Ed. at 1142-43.

76. This point is indicated by the Court's statement that the Pennsylvania court had "ample power through garnishment proceedings" to determine the ownership of the policy proceeds and, if the court determined Mrs. Dunlevy to be the owner, "to condemn and appropriate [the proceeds of the policy] so far as necessary to discharge the original judgment." Even though Mrs. Dunlevy was "outside the limits of the State," the Court indicated that "such disposition of the property would have been binding on her." *See id.* at 520, 36 S. Ct. at 613-14, 60 L. Ed. at 1142-43.

77. *See id.* at 521-22, 36 S. Ct. at 614, 60 L. Ed. at 1142.

78. The difficulty that the *Dunlevy* decision produced for insurance companies caused Congress to enact a federal interpleader statute, which, among other things, authorized federal courts in cases within the subject-matter jurisdiction provisions of the statute to exercise nationwide personal jurisdiction over rival claimants to insurance policies. *See* 7 CHARLES A. WRIGHT ET AL., FEDERAL PRACTICE AND PROCEDURE: CIVIL § 1701, at 485-87 (2d ed. 1986). Interpleader at both the state and federal level is discussed in Chapter 8(D)(2)

(b) Restrictive Principles of In Rem Jurisdiction

On the restrictive side of the in rem jurisdiction concept, the U.S. Supreme Court recognized the rule that only the state where land was located had jurisdiction to deal directly with the title to the land. Again, however, this principle was dramatically affected by the distinction between in personam and in rem jurisdiction.

In *Fall v. Eastin*,[79] a Washington state court awarded real property located in Nebraska to a wife in a divorce action. The husband refused to execute a deed to her. The court subsequently appointed a commissioner to issue a deed to the wife, as authorized by a Washington state statute. The wife went into possession of the Nebraska land under the commissioner's deed. Subsequently, the husband conveyed the same land to his sister (Eastin) in repayment of a debt. After the conveyance, the wife brought a quiet title action in Nebraska. The issue was whether the commissioner's deed had to be recognized by the Nebraska courts. Emphasizing Nebraska's sovereignty over real property located in Nebraska, the U.S. Supreme Court held that the attempt by the Washington state court to transfer title to the land directly to the wife by the commissioner's deed was ineffective and that the Full Faith and Credit Clause did not require Nebraska to accept it.[80]

If a court, such as the Washington court in *Fall v. Eastin*, had in personam jurisdiction over the defendant, the court could order the defendant to convey land located in another state by a deed that would be recognized there. If the defendant refused to convey the land, the defendant could be held in contempt and jailed, if necessary, to obtain compliance with the court's decree. What a court could not do was affect the title to the foreign land *directly* by its judgment—for example, under a statute authorizing the court to transfer title from *A* to *B* by decree or under a statute such as the one in *Fall* that authorized the appointment of an official to transfer title from *A* to *B*. The court's action in the contempt example was conceptually viewed to be limited to the defendant's person, even though it effectively resulted in transfer of title. However, the court's action in the examples involving direct transfer by decree or appointment was viewed as operating directly on the property. Thus, it was thought to violate the exclusive jurisdiction over the land possessed by the courts of the situs state.[81]

Illustration 3-9. A, a citizen of State *X*, enters into a contract with *B*, a citizen of State *X* to purchase land owned by *B* located in State *Y*. When the time for performance arrives, *B* refuses to convey the land. *A* sues *B* in a state court

---

("Interpleader") *infra.*

79. 215 U.S. 1, 30 S. Ct. 3, 54 L. Ed. 65 (1909).

80. *Id.; see also* Durfee v. Duke, 375 U.S. 106, 84 S. Ct. 242, 11 L. Ed. 2d 186 (1963); Clarke v. Clarke, 178 U.S. 186, 20 S. Ct. 873, 44 L. Ed. 1028 (1900); Carpenter v. Strange, 141 U.S. 87, 11 S. Ct. 960, 35 L. Ed. 640 (1891).

81. *See* DAN B. DOBBS, THE LAW OF REMEDIES § 2.7, at 128-29 (2d student ed. 1993); *see also* ALBERT A. EHRENZWEIG, A TREATISE ON THE CONFLICT OF LAWS 209-13 (1962); RUSSELL J. WEINTRAUB, COMMENTARY ON THE CONFLICT OF LAWS § 8.4 (3d ed. 1986).

of State *X*. *A* seeks a decree of specific performance to force *B* to convey the land. *B* is personally served with process in this action in State *X*. The State *X* court issues a decree of specific performance ordering *B* to convey the land in accordance with the contract. *B* refuses. The court holds *B* in contempt. The court then orders *B* placed in jail until *B* complies with the decree of specific performance. After spending some time in jail, *B* complies with the court's order and executes a deed to the land sufficient under the law of State *Y* to convey ownership to *A*. *A* has obtained good title to the land. *A* may record the deed in the land records of the county in State *Y* where the land is located. No due process or full faith and credit problems existed with this procedure because the court did not act directly on the land with its decree. However, if State *X* had possessed a statute allowing the State *X* courts to directly decree the title to the land out of *B* and into *A*, that procedure could not validly have been employed under *Fall v. Eastin*. The court's decree would have been considered as operating directly on the land. Thus, the court's decree would have been invalid.

* * * * *

It is important to appreciate that *Fall v. Eastin* appeared to establish a due process restriction on the power of the state courts even though the Court never mentioned the Due Process Clause. Before *Pennoyer*, the objection to the Washington court's judgment would have been made under the international rules of jurisdiction. Those rules were specifically framed in terms of state territorial sovereignty. The objection would have been available only on collateral attack of the Washington court's judgment when the judgment was taken to Nebraska for enforcement, as in *Fall* itself. After *Pennoyer*, the international rules were incorporated into the Fourteenth Amendment as due process restrictions on the power of the states. The effect of this incorporation was to render the judgment void in the state where it was rendered as a matter of due process as well as void in other states on collateral attack of the judgment. Presumably, therefore, if a state such as Washington had an appropriate procedure for raising jurisdictional objections of the *Fall v. Eastin* sort, the objection could have been raised in the original Washington proceeding. If the Washington courts denied the objection, an appeal might ultimately be taken to the U.S. Supreme Court. Thus, after *Pennoyer* and *Fall*, there appeared to exist the possibility of attacking state judgments affecting foreign land titles directly as well as collaterally (in the state where the land is located).[82]

Nevertheless, great doubt exists about whether (1) the restrictive principles of in rem jurisdiction are due process principles and (2) whether such principles can be used as the basis of direct attack on a judgment involving the title to land located elsewhere. The doubt is created in part because the U.S. Supreme Court has described the restrictive principles of in rem jurisdiction as *subject-matter jurisdiction* principles.[83] It is not clear whether a lack of subject-matter jurisdiction of this sort in a state court ought to be considered a violation

---

82. *Cf.* Eckard v. Eckard, 333 Md. 531, 636 A.2d 531 (1994) (appeal from a civil contempt order on ground that the court had no jurisdiction to enter an order affecting realty outside the state).

83. *See, e.g.,* Durfee v. Duke, 375 U.S. 106, 84 S. Ct. 242, 11 L. Ed. 2d 186 (1963).

of due process. Recall that in *Pennoyer v. Neff,* the Supreme Court stated in dictum that due process required ''a tribunal competent by its constitution —that is by the law of its creation–to pass upon the subject-matter of the suit.''[84] This statement seems to require only that state courts have subject-matter jurisdiction as a matter of their own law to satisfy the Due Process Clause of the Fourteenth Amendment.[85] If so, a lack of ''territorial subject-matter jurisdiction'' would not constitute a violation of the Due Process Clause of the Fourteenth Amendment. Thus, unless *Pennoyer's* incorporation of the traditional territorial rules of jurisdiction into the Due Process Clause encompasses the restrictive in rem principles, no other apparent source of federal law would obligate the states to follow them.[86] The possibility that the rules still may be enforced as nonfederal, sovereignty-based rules is explained below.[87]

In the preceding subsection, it was observed in conjunction with the *Dunlevy* case that the practical effect of the interpleader action was no different than the practical effect of the garnishment in aid of execution. However, it is possible to envision some practical difficulties for the state where land is located if other states are allowed to adjudicate title issues. In *Fall,* the Nebraska Supreme Court had identified a potential practical problem for purchasers of Nebraska land that might be caused by the Washington judgment:

> If the Washington decree bound the conscience of [the husband], so that when he left the jurisdiction of that state any deed that he might make would be absolutely void, and had he sold the land to an innocent purchaser, who had inspected the records and found that [the husband was the owner of the land], such purchaser, though relying on the laws of this state for his protection, would receive no title. . . . [I]f this is correct, the action of the court of another state directly interferes with the operation of the laws of this state over lands within its sovereignty.[88]

The practical difficulties identified by the Nebraska Supreme Court can be eliminated if the plaintiff who obtains title to land through a proceeding in a nonsitus state is required to follow a specific procedure. The plaintiff would have

---

84. 95 U.S. at 733, 24 L. Ed. at 572; *see* section (A)(2)(*b*), *supra.*

85. Even this subject-matter jurisdiction requirement is open to question today. There is no apparent reason why a state should not be able to limit a defendant's objections to its courts' subject-matter jurisdiction to direct attack or make them waivable objections. *See* Chapter 13(E) *infra.* If this can be done, however, it is difficult to see how subject-matter jurisdiction deficiencies rise to the level of a federal due process concern.

86. Recall from section A(1)(*e*), *supra,* that the traditional territorial rules were, prior to the Fourteenth Amendment, considered to be ''international'' rules that operated between independent sovereigns. They were not incorporated either in the Full Faith and Credit Clause or its implementing statute as commands against the states, although the Constitution and statute, in failing to touch or otherwise modify the rules, allowed the states to refuse enforcement to the judgments of other states that violated the rules. However, *Pennoyer* purported to base its holding on ''two principles of public law,'' one of which was ''that no State can exercise direct jurisdiction and authority over persons and property without its territory.'' 95 U.S. at 722, 24 L. Ed. at 568. This principle, of course, encompasses the restrictive principles of in rem jurisdiction and may have been incorporated with the Due Process Clause by the *Pennoyer* dictum.

87. *See* section G(3) (''Sovereignty-Based Restrictions on State-Court Jurisdiction'') *infra.*

88. Fall v. Fall, 75 Neb. 104, 133, 113 N.W. 175, 180 (1905).

to institute a proceeding in the situs state based upon the judgment of the nonsitus court and obtain a judgment of the situs court confirming the plaintiff's title.[89] Once a judgment of the situs court is obtained by the plaintiff, the situs court judgment can be recorded in the land records to protect bona fide purchasers of the land. If the plaintiff is required to follow such a procedure, no serious practical problems would be created for the situs state or people in the situs state resulting from a nonsitus judgment affecting the land. Consequently, all legitimate sovereignty-based interests of the situs state would be protected.

    Illustration 3-10. *A*, a citizen of State *X*, enters into a contract with *B*, a citizen of State *Y*, to purchase land owned by *B* and located in State *Y*. When *B* refuses to perform the contract, *A* sues *B* in a state court in State *X* to obtain specific performance of the contract. The State *X* court renders judgment for *A*. Under a statute of State *X*, the court is allowed to directly convey the land from *B* to *A* in the decree, instead of relying on the contempt proceeding described in *Illustration 3-9*, above. The State *X* court employs this procedure. *A* takes the State *X* decree to State *Y* and there commences an action on the decree to quiet title to the land. *A* requests the State *Y* court to give a res judicata effect to the State *X* judgment transferring title to *A*. No legitimate practical concerns on the part of State *Y* appear to exist if this procedure is followed. State *Y* cannot complain that subsequent purchasers of the land in State *Y* will be misled into believing that *B* has good title to the land. The familiar procedure of filing a notice of lis pendens prevents any such deception. No other considerations appear to justify preventing State *X* from transferring the title to the land located in State *Y* to *A*.[90]

* * * * *

    Despite the fact that following an appropriate procedure would eliminate any legitimate objections that the situs state could have to a nonsitus proceeding, it is doubtful whether the U.S. Supreme Court in the era of *Pennoyer v. Neff* would have agreed.[91] In effect, therefore, *Fall v. Eastin* and similar decisions may have elevated a venue rule known as "the local action rule" into a

---

  89. *See* RUSSELL J. WEINTRAUB, COMMENTARY ON THE CONFLICT OF LAWS § 8.4, at 420 (3d ed. 1986).

  90. Although the specific performance example does not involve any interpretation of State *Y* land title law by the State *X* court, if such an interpretation were required, no significant practical difficulties would exist that would justify refusing enforcement of the State *X* judgment. The courts of State *Y* are not bound, as a matter of stare decisis, to follow the interpretation of State *Y* law by the State *X* court. The decision of the State *X* court, if erroneous, may create some difficulties for persons in State *Y* who wish to engage in similar transactions, but no more so than an erroneous decision on an issue of State *Y* real property law by an inferior court in State *Y* that is not appealed. In either case, the erroneous precedent will have to be clarified by the highest court of State *Y* in a later case. Thus, in both instances the direct effect of the decision is exhausted on the parties, just as in non-land title cases. *But see* Clarke v. Clarke, 178 U.S. 186, 20 S. Ct. 873, 44 L. Ed. 1028 (1900); Carpenter v. Strange, 141 U.S. 87, 11 S. Ct. 960, 35 L. Ed. 640 (1891). Both *Clarke* and *Carpenter* were fully litigated probate cases involving the title to land located in other states. The U.S. Supreme Court appeared to declare flatly that the courts of the non-situs state had no jurisdiction to directly affect the title to land located elsewhere. Passages in both opinions can be read as stating that the situs state is entitled to the opportunity to apply its own law to the title question. *See Clarke*, 178 U.S. at 194-95, 20 S. Ct. at 876, 44 L. Ed. 2d at 1032-33; *Carpenter*, 141 U.S. at 105-06, 11 S. Ct. at 966, 35 L. Ed. 2d at 647-48. This reading flows from the Court's position, discussed in the text, *supra*, that a court in one state has no *subject-matter jurisdiction* over the title to land located in another state.

  91. *See* RUSSELL J. WEINTRAUB, COMMENTARY ON THE CONFLICT OF LAWS § 8A, at 420 (3d ed. 1986).

constitutional limitation under the Due Process Clause of the Fourteenth Amendment, when the "local action" involved an adjudication of the title to land (as opposed, for example, to an request for damages to land located in another state).[92] In later sections, it will be important to determine whether the *Fall* rule has survived the modern decisions articulating due process limits on the power of state courts to assert personal jurisdiction over nonresidents.[93]

(c) Limited Appearance Procedures

A dilemma existed for defendants whose property was attached or garnished in a quasi in rem proceeding brought to satisfy a claim unrelated to the property. If the defendant appeared in the action to defend the property, the appearance would constitute a "general appearance" that would allow the court to enter judgment against the defendant for an amount in excess of the value of the property. On the other hand, if the defendant did not appear, a default judgment would be entered against the defendant and the property would be sold to satisfy the judgment, as in *Pennoyer v. Neff.*

To alleviate this dilemma, some states recognized a device known as the *limited appearance*. In a limited appearance, defendants appeared in the action and defended on the merits. However, the appearance for this purpose did not constitute a *general appearance* that would allow the court to render a judgment against the defendant for an amount in excess of the property attached. Rather, the judgment had a limited effect—if the defendant lost, the plaintiff was able to execute the judgment on the property seized, but if the plaintiff's claim exceeded the amount of the property, the remainder had to be satisfied by a subsequent suit against the defendant in which the plaintiff would again have to prove the claim on the merits.[94] This subsequent proceeding would have to be brought in a state where personal jurisdiction could be obtained over the defendant (or where the defendant owned additional property). Not all courts recognized the limited appearance procedure, but in those that did, the rigors of quasi in rem jurisdiction were mitigated.[95]

2. In Personam Jurisdiction: Physical Presence

Under *Pennoyer*, jurisdiction based upon a person's presence within the sovereign's territorial limits could be achieved by service of process within the

---

92. *See* Chapter 4(A) ("Transitory and Local Actions") *infra.*

93. *See* sections E(1) ("Quasi in Rem and Related Jurisdictional Doctrines") & G(3) ("Sovereignty-Based Restrictions on State-Court Jurisdiction") *infra.*

94. *See* Cheshire Nat'l Bank v. Jaynes, 224 Mass. 14, 112 N.E. 500 (1916); RESTATEMENT (FIRST) OF JUDGMENTS § 40 cmt. a (1942).

95. Whether a state permits limited appearances is less important today than it was prior to 1977. The limited appearance procedure is primarily valuable to defendants in quasi in rem actions, when property located within the state is seized as a means of compelling the defendant's appearance in a proceeding brought to adjudicate a claim unrelated to the property. As discussed in a later section, this type of jurisdiction was held unconstitutional by the U.S. Supreme Court in *Shaffer v. Heitner*, 433 U.S. 186, 97 S. Ct. 2569, 53 L. Ed. 2d 683 (1977). After *Shaffer*, the need for the limited appearance procedure has virtually been eliminated.

state. No other connection between the state, the defendant, and the claim was required. The mere transient presence of the defendant within the state, plus service on the defendant while the presence continued, was sufficient to sustain jurisdiction.[96]

However, two self-imposed limitations on this manner of acquiring jurisdiction should be noted.[97] First, a state may immunize nonresidents from service when they voluntarily enter the state to attend litigation. Under this rule, a nonresident party, that party's counsel, and witnesses are immune from service when they are present in the forum to attend litigation and for a reasonable time in transit.[98] Second, if someone is brought into the state by fraud or unlawful force for the purpose of service of process, a state may not, as a matter of its own domestic law, exercise jurisdiction over the person.[99]

(a) Immunity from Service of Process

The usual justification for granting immunity to nonresident parties, attorneys, and witnesses is that the administration of justice requires the grant of immunity.[100] To encourage the attendance of these nonresidents at judicial proceedings pending within the state, they are granted immunity from service of process in other actions that might be brought against them while they are present to attend the litigation and for a reasonable time to travel to and from the litigation.[101] However, the justification for a grant of immunity to serve the

---

96. In Grace v. MacArthur, 170 F. Supp. 442 (E.D. Ark. 1959), for example, personal jurisdiction was held to have been properly acquired over a defendant by serving the defendant with process over the Eastern District of Arkansas on a nonstop flight from Memphis, Tennessee, to Dallas, Texas. *Cf.* Darrah v. Watson, 36 Iowa 116 (1873) (personal jurisdiction validly acquired after in-hand service of process on the defendant, even though the defendant was in the state only for a few hours on business). This basis of acquiring jurisdiction has been recognized by the RESTATEMENT (SECOND) OF CONFLICT OF LAWS § 28 (1971) ("A state has power to exercise judicial jurisdiction over an individual who is present within its territory, whether permanently or temporarily."). However, developments in the law of personal jurisdiction, discussed later in this chapter, seemed to undermine the physical presence basis of jurisdiction, leading the authors of the *Restatement (Second)* to propose a modification of the presence test: "A state has power to exercise judicial jurisdiction over an individual who is present within its territory unless the individual's relationship to the state is so attenuated as to make the exercise of such jurisdiction unreasonable." *Id.* (Supp. 1988). Section E(2) *infra* discusses the Supreme Court's decision in Burnham v. Superior Court, 495 U.S. 604, 110 S. Ct. 2105, 109 L. Ed. 2d 631 (1990). *Burnham* revives the physical presence test as a valid basis for acquiring jurisdiction over nonresident defendants independent of the developments in the law of personal jurisdiction that caused the *Restatement's* drafters to impose a "reasonableness" limitation on the test. Thus, the modern utility of the self-imposed limitations discussed in the text *infra* must be evaluated in light of *Burnham*.

97. These limitations are not constitutional requirements; a state may decide to exercise jurisdiction in these circumstances if it so desires. If a state chooses not to follow these rules or to limit or qualify their application, its judgments must be recognized and given effect in other states. *See* RESTATEMENT (SECOND) OF CONFLICT OF LAWS § 82 cmt. f, § 83 cmt. b (1971).

98. *See id.* § 83 cmt. b.

99. *See id.* § 82; *see also* RESTATEMENT (SECOND) OF JUDGMENTS § 4(1)(b) (1982).

100. *See* RESTATEMENT (SECOND) OF CONFLICT OF LAWS § 83 (1971). Many of the other reasons often given for granting immunity are far less persuasive than the "needs of judicial administration rationale." *See generally* Arthur J. Keefe & John J. Roscia, *Immunity and Sentimentality,* 32 CORNELL L.Q. 471 (1947); Note, *Immunity of Non-Resident Participants in a Judicial Proceeding From Service of Process—A Proposal for Renovation,* 26 IND. L.J. 459 (1951).

101. *See* RESTATEMENT (SECOND) OF CONFLICT OF LAWS § 83 cmt. b (1971).

needs of judicial administration will vary, depending upon whether the immunity is being granted to a nonresident plaintiff, a nonresident defendant, a witness, or an attorney.

For a nonresident plaintiff to be granted immunity to serve the needs of judicial administration, it must be assumed that the nonresident would not physically attend litigation within the state for fear that process would be served on the plaintiff in an unrelated[102] action. However, if the plaintiff's attendance at discovery proceedings or trial is necessary to the litigation that the plaintiff has commenced, the court has ample power to compel that attendance by forbidding the plaintiff from prosecuting the claim if the plaintiff does not attend. Similarly, if a nonresident defendant refuses to attend proceedings within the state that have been validly commenced against the defendant, a default judgment can be rendered against the defendant which can be enforced in another state under the full faith and credit implementing statute.[103] Thus, the needs of judicial administration do not require a grant of immunity to a nonresident defendant over whom personal jurisdiction has been properly acquired. For a grant of immunity to be justified in the case of either a nonresident plaintiff or defendant, therefore, a justification other than the needs of judicial administration, such as fairness to the plaintiff or defendant, must support the grant. However, the traditional justification for immunity is only the needs of judicial administration, not fairness to the party immunized.[104]

Immunity for nonresident witnesses and attorneys is more justifiable than immunity for parties. If a party to pending litigation within the state cannot persuade a nonresident witness to attend the litigation, the ability of the party to prosecute a claim or defense may be impaired. Similarly, if a party cannot freely choose counsel of the party's choice to prosecute or defend an action within the state, the party's ability to conduct the litigation successfully may also be impaired. Because nonresident witnesses and attorneys are not parties to the case pending within the state, the court does not possess the same coercive powers to compel their attendance at litigation within the state that it possesses over parties. As a result, a grant of immunity may be necessary to prevent witnesses and attorneys from being deterred from entering the state by the fear that litigation will be commenced against them while they are present there. On the other hand, modern procedural rules may be able to alleviate the absence of a witness by

---

102. It must be assumed that the threatened service is in an unrelated action, since under modern procedural rules, related claims can be asserted in a variety of ways against the plaintiff in the action that the plaintiff has commenced within the state. Thus, the defendant can assert both related and unrelated counterclaims against the plaintiff in the action commenced by the plaintiff. *See* Chapter 7(E) (''Counterclaims and Cross-Claims Under the Codes'') & Chapter 7(F) (''Counterclaims and Cross-Claims Under the Federal Rules'') *infra*. Similarly, third parties who may wish to become defendants to defend against the plaintiff's claims and assert counterclaims against the plaintiff may be able to intervene in the action. *See* Chapter 8(D)(3) (''Intervention'') *infra*; *see also* Adam v. Saenger, 303 U.S. 59, 58 S. Ct. 454, 82 L. Ed. 649 (1938). In any event, the convenience of resolving all related matters in a single proceeding may outweigh the needs of judicial administration in cases where related actions are commenced against the plaintiff in the state that could be consolidated with the plaintiff's action.

103. *See* 28 U.S.C. § 1738; section A(1)(*d*) (discussing the implementing statute) *supra*.

104. *See* RESTATEMENT (SECOND) OF CONFLICT OF LAWS § 83 (1971).

devices such as videotape depositions.[105] To the extent that such devices are available under the state's procedural rules, it may be unjustifiable to grant a witness immunity from process to attend trial within the state.

Illustration 3-11. *A*, a citizen of State *X*, commences an action against *B*, a citizen of State *Y*, in a state court in State *Y*. *A* seeks damages from *B* for personal injuries received in an automobile accident in State *Y*. While *A* is attending pretrial proceedings in State *Y*, *A* is served with process by *C*, a citizen of State *Y*, in an action for breach of a contract made and to be performed in State *X*. Traditionally, *A* could plead immunity from process in the action by *C* and have the action dismissed. However, it is highly questionable whether the needs of judicial administration in the action by *A* justify the grant of immunity. *A* can be compelled to attend the proceedings in *A v. B* in State *Y* on pain of losing the claim for relief if *A* does not attend. The situation would not differ if *B* were the nonresident who was served in the unrelated action. By hypothesis, *B* has been validly subjected to personal jurisdiction in State *Y*. Therefore, if *B* does not participate in the litigation as needed, the court can render a default judgment against *B* that will be enforceable in other states.

Illustration 3-12. On the facts of *Illustration 3-11*, assume that *A*, *B*, and *C* are all citizens and residents of State *Y*. However, *B* wants to summon *W*, a citizen of State *X*, as a witness in the action. Assume that *C's* breach of contract claim is against *W*, rather than *A* or *B*. If the court cannot compensate for *W's* absence under its procedural rules through some device such as a videotape deposition, *W* should be granted immunity in any action brought by *C* while *W* is in State *Y* to attend the litigation between *A* and *B* and for a reasonable period to travel to and from the litigation.

Illustration 3-13. On the facts of *Illustration 3-12*, assume that *C* possesses the breach of contract claim against *L*, a lawyer who is a citizen of State *X*. *B* wishes to hire *L* to defend the action by *A*. *L* should be granted immunity from process in the action by *C* for the period of time *L* is in State *Y* to participate in the litigation and for a reasonable period to travel to and from the litigation. If *L* is not immunized from process and is deterred from representing *B* as a result, no procedural rule can compensate for *L's* absence and the deprivation of *B's* freedom to choose counsel.

Illustration 3-14. On the facts of *Illustration 3-13*, assume that after *L* successfully represents *B*, *L* does not leave State *Y* with reasonable dispatch, but remains in the state to attend a football game that is played two days after the action between *A* and *B* is completed. During the football game, *C* has *L* served with process in the breach of contract action. *L* is not immune from process because *L* did not leave State *Y* within a reasonable period of time.

* * * * *

The immunity rules described above depend on the need to serve a defendant with process while the defendant is physically present within the state. As discussed below, modern due process restrictions on personal jurisdiction permit nonresidents to be summoned to defend actions based on their relationships

---

105. *See* Chapter 9(E) ("Oral Depositions") *infra.*

with the forum state. Such assertions of jurisdiction are accomplished under state "long-arm" statutes.[106] To the extent that the defendant can be validly summoned under modern standards, service of process within the state is irrelevant. Therefore, it would be unjustifiable to grant immunity to a nonresident who is constitutionally subject to personal jurisdiction under a state long-arm statute.

(b) Acquisition of Jurisdiction by Fraud or Unlawful Force

The rule prohibiting the acquisition of jurisdiction by fraud or unlawful force is based on the policy of preventing a plaintiff from profiting by inequitable conduct.[107] Like the immunity rules, this rule is premised on the need to serve the defendant while the defendant is physically present within the state. If another basis exists for acquiring jurisdiction over the defendant, the fraud and force rule becomes irrelevant.

Illustration 3-15. Assume that *B* is a resident of State *X* and that *A* is a resident of State *Y*. *A* and *B* have had a meretricious relationship for several years. *A* writes *B* that *A* is leaving the country to go to *A's* dying mother in Ireland and that *A* will not return. *A* professes undying love for *B* and entreats *B* to come to State *Y* for one last visit. Upon *B's* arrival at an airport in State *Y*, *B* is served with process by *A* in a State *Y* action for money loaned and for seduction under promise to marry. *B* does not appear in the State *Y* action. The court then enters a default judgment against *B*. In an action brought on the State *Y* default judgment in State *X*, the State *X* court should determine whether the law of State *Y* would make the default judgment void because *B* was induced to enter State *Y* by *A's* misrepresentations.[108] If so, the judgment should be held to be unenforceable in State *X*.[109] If *B* were subject to personal jurisdiction on some other basis than service while physically present in State *Y*, *A* would use that basis to acquire jurisdiction and would not need to trick *B* into entering the state.

3. In Personam Jurisdiction: Consent, Appearance, and Waiver

As observed in the earlier discussion of the international rules of jurisdiction, individuals may consent to the jurisdiction of a sovereign's courts, even though they could not validly be subjected to a suit in the state absent their consent. A person may manifest consent by (1) agreeing to jurisdiction in a contract prior to suit, (2) accepting or waiving service of process with the intent to consent to jurisdiction, even though the acceptance or waiver occurs outside

---

106. *See* section F *infra* (discussing modern long-arm statutes).

107. *See* RESTATEMENT (SECOND) OF CONFLICT OF LAWS § 82 cmt. a. (1971).

108. *See* Wyman v. Newhouse, 93 F.2d 313 (2d Cir. 1937), *cert. denied*, 303 U.S. 664, 58 S. Ct. 834, 82 L. Ed. 1122 (1938).

109. The rule against acquiring jurisdiction by fraud and force can be contrasted with the duty of persons voluntarily present within the jurisdiction to submit to service. In the latter instance, the courts will permit a process server to engage in subterfuge to accomplish service. *See* Gumperz v. Hofmann, 245 A.D. 622, 283 N.Y.S. 823 (1935), *aff'd*, 271 N.Y. 544, 2 N.E.2d 687 (1936).

the state, or (3) designating an agent within the state to receive service of process.[110]

Closely related to jurisdiction by consent is jurisdiction conferred by appearance. Defendants who voluntarily appear in an action, even though they are not compelled to do so, consent in a real sense to the jurisdiction of the court over them. However, even if the defendant's appearance in the action is not "voluntary" in this sense, the appearance still may confer jurisdiction on the court. Defendants wanting to object to a court's assertion of personal jurisdiction over them traditionally had to make what is called a *special appearance* in the action—an appearance made for the *sole* purpose of objecting to personal jurisdiction. If the defendant made such a special appearance, and if the court had no jurisdiction over the defendant, the court would dismiss the action.[111]

The procedures for making special appearances were strictly circumscribed. If a defendant "either enters an appearance in an action without limiting the purpose for which he appears or . . . asks for relief which the court may give only if it has jurisdiction over him," the defendant makes what is known as a *general appearance*.[112] A general appearance conferred jurisdiction on the court. Thus, if defendants did not carefully follow the procedures set out in a state for making a special appearance to challenge jurisdiction, they could find that they had appeared generally and conferred jurisdiction on the court.[113]

The U.S. Supreme Court has held that a state is not constitutionally required to provide a method, such as a special appearance procedure, by which the defendant may raise objections to the state's assertion of jurisdiction. The defendant's ability to ignore the assertion of jurisdiction and challenge the validity of a default judgment on jurisdictional grounds when the plaintiff seeks to enforce the judgment against the defendant in another state—to *collaterally attack* the judgment—is considered constitutionally sufficient.[114]

This holding presents no problem today because every state now provides for a special appearance procedure or its equivalent. Before these procedures existed in all the states, however, defendants could be placed in an uncomfortable position. If a defendant failed to appear and litigate the action in a state that did not provide for a special appearance, a default judgment would be rendered. When the plaintiff sought to enforce the default judgment against the defendant in another state, the defendant could challenge the validity of the judgment on the ground that it had been rendered without jurisdiction. But if the defendant's juris-

---

110. *See* RESTATEMENT (SECOND) OF CONFLICT OF LAWS § 32 cmts. a, d, e & f (1971).

111. *See id.* § 81.

112. *Id.* § 33 cmt. d.

113. The same result can occur today under procedural systems governed by the Federal Rules of Civil Procedure, which provide for challenges to personal jurisdiction by motion, rather than by special appearance. If the procedure prescribed by the Federal Rules is not followed exactly, the defendant will have "waived" the objection to the court's jurisdiction. *See* FED. R. CIV. P. 12(g) & (h). "Waiver" and "general appearance" are equivalent expressions which signify that the defendant has submitted to the court's jurisdiction, whether or not the defendant intended to do so. Waiver under the Federal Rules is discussed more fully in Chapter 6(D)(3)*(g)* ("Consolidation and Waiver of Defenses") *infra.* Because some states still have the old special appearance schemes, while others follow the more modern Federal Rules motion scheme, practitioners must examine the law of the state in which they are challenging jurisdiction carefully to determine which procedure is appropriate.

114. *See* York v. Texas, 137 U.S. 15, 11 S. Ct. 9, 34 L. Ed. 604 (1890).

dictional objection was invalid, the default judgment would be valid and enforceable against the defendant, even though the defendant had never litigated the merits of the case.[115]

A scheme of special appearances would not help the defendant in quasi in rem or in rem cases, in which the court's power was based on the presence of property owned by the defendant within the state. Under the rule of *Pennoyer v. Neff*, a state could validly acquire jurisdiction to adjudicate up to the limits of the property if the property had been properly seized. A special appearance would fail if the property was attached in the manner prescribed in *Pennoyer* and later cases. As a practical matter, therefore, the attachment of property might compel the defendant to enter a general appearance to defend the property from loss. Unless the state provided for the kind of limited appearance discussed in section B(1)*(c)*, above, a defendant was posed with an even greater dilemma than in an in personam action. If the defendant did not appear and defend on the merits, the defendant would lose the property attached. However, if the defendant did appear and defend, the defendant made a general appearance that might result in a binding judgment for an amount far in excess of the value of the property—a judgment that could be enforced against the defendant in another state.

4. In Personam Jurisdiction: Domicile

Substantial doubt exists whether either nationality or domicile traditionally constituted a sufficient basis for jurisdiction in private international law. The theory that nationality is a sufficient basis is predicated on the notion that a citizen of a nation is bound to obey the commands of that citizen's sovereign and

---

115. Though this dilemma is eased for the defendant when a state provides a special appearance procedure or its equivalent, it may not be eliminated entirely. If a defendant specially appears to challenge the jurisdiction of the court, the court may overrule the objection. At that point, the defendant may or may not be able to appeal the jurisdictional determination of the trial court, depending on whether the state permits interlocutory appeals. If the state does not permit the defendant to appeal immediately, the defendant will have to defend the action on the merits. The defendant may not refuse to defend further, allow a default judgment to be entered, and defend on jurisdictional grounds when the default judgment is enforced in another state. The determination of the jurisdictional issue against the defendant in the special appearance procedure will be res judicata in the subsequent action on the default judgment, and again the defendant will have lost the ability to defend on the merits. Thus, the defendant's only alternative is to defend on the merits and if the defendant loses, appeal, raising the objection to the court's jurisdiction along with any errors allegedly occurring in the trial of the merits. *See* RESTATEMENT (SECOND) OF JUDGMENTS § 10(2) cmt. d (1982). This *direct attack* on the judgment will preserve the jurisdictional objection, but the defendant may encounter substantial inconvenience in trying the merits before obtaining appellate review on the jurisdictional point. Yet this pattern of review is followed in most states and the federal courts. *See* RESTATEMENT (SECOND) OF CONFLICT OF LAWS § 81 cmt. c (1971); Harkness v. Hyde, 98 U.S. 476, 25 L. Ed. 237 (1879). Even if a state permits interlocutory appeals from adverse jurisdictional determinations in special appearance proceedings, all of the defendant's difficulties may not be eliminated. A problem may arise if the state *requires* defendants to appeal the jurisdictional question before litigating the merits of the case. *See* RESTATEMENT (SECOND) OF CONFLICT OF LAWS § 81 cmt. c (1971). Under this approach, a failure to take an interlocutory appeal will result in loss of the right to litigate the jurisdictional question later in the proceedings. The interlocutory appeal on the jurisdictional issue may fail, however, and the defendant will be forced to litigate the merits of the case in the state. This process may produce wasted expense for the defendant, but the problems of a plaintiff faced with an unscrupulous defendant who uses the interlocutory appeal only for purposes of delay may be worse.

thus the judgments of the courts of that sovereign.[116] However, it does not necessarily follow that other sovereigns ought to enforce a judgment rendered on the basis of nationality.[117] Furthermore, strong support still exists for the proposition that domicile is not a ground of jurisdiction recognized at the international level.[118]

Nevertheless, after *Pennoyer v. Neff*, the U.S. Supreme Court recognized that nationality and domicile were bases for the exercise of in personam jurisdiction that would not violate the Due Process Clauses of the U.S. Constitution. In *Blackmer v. United States*,[119] the Court held that service of a subpoena on an American citizen abroad as authorized by a federal statute was consistent with the Due Process Clause of the Fifth Amendment. The Court stated the underlying principle for the exercise of state-court jurisdiction based on a person's domicile in *Milliken v. Meyer*[120]: "[T]he authority of a state over one of its citizens is not terminated by the mere fact of his absence from the state. The state which accords him privileges and affords protection to him and his property by virtue of his domicile may also exact reciprocal duties."[121]

Domicile has never been a common-law basis of jurisdiction. In other words, unlike presence and consent, a specific statutory authorization had to exist before a court would assert jurisdiction over a nonresident domiciliary of the state.[122] For example, in *Milliken*, the Court upheld jurisdiction acquired under a Wyoming statute that provided for service by publication in actions when resident defendants had departed from the county of their residence with the intent to delay or defraud their creditors or to avoid service of a summons. The defendant had been personally served with process outside the state pursuant to another provision of the Wyoming statutes that allowed such service in all cases in which service could be made by publication. Because jurisdiction had been acquired properly, the Court required other states to give effect to the judgment entered pursuant to these statutes.[123]

In private international law, the absence of domicile as a recognized ground of international jurisdiction means that a judgment rendered by a United States court under the *Blackmer* and *Milliken* principles might not be enforceable in the courts of a foreign country. This result is unexceptional in international practice. It has long been recognized that the courts of one country may render judgments that comply with their own domestic rules, but which are unenforceable in foreign courts because they are not based on an accepted ground of

---

116. *See* P.M. NORTH & J.J. FAWCETT, CHESHIRE AND NORTH'S PRIVATE INTERNATIONAL LAW 359-60 (12th ed. 1992).

117. *See id.*

118. *See id.* at 360. *But see* Note, *Developments in the Law—State-Court Jurisdiction*, 73 HARV. L. REV. 909, 913 (1960); RESTATEMENT (THIRD) OF THE FOREIGN RELATIONS LAW OF THE UNITED STATES § 421(2)(b) (1987); UNIF. FOREIGN MONEY-JUDGMENTS RECOGNITION ACT § 5(4) (1962), 13 U.L.A. 272 (1986).

119. 284 U.S. 421, 52 S. Ct. 252, 76 L. Ed. 375 (1932).

120. 311 U.S. 457, 61 S. Ct. 339, 85 L. Ed. 278 (1940).

121. *Id.* at 463, 61 S. Ct. at 343, 85 L. Ed. at 283.

122. *See* RESTATEMENT (SECOND) OF CONFLICT OF LAWS § 29 cmt. d (Supp. 1988).

123. *Milliken*, 311 U.S. at 458-63, 61 S. Ct. at 340-43, 85 L. Ed. at 281-83.

international jurisdiction.[124] Thus, federal and state statutes authorizing jurisdiction based on nationality and domicile are domestic rules of the United States, not necessarily binding in international practice, even though the statutes comply with the Due Process Clauses of the U.S. Constitution.

The unusual feature of American jurisprudence produced by *Pennoyer v. Neff* is that a judgment rendered by one state based on the domicile of the defendant *must be* recognized and enforced by other states. This conclusion results because (1) *Pennoyer* incorporated the international rules of jurisdiction into the Due Process Clause as constitutional rules; (2) after *Pennoyer*, the jurisdictional rules that operated through the Due Process Clause and in full-faith-and-credit cases came to be viewed as identical; and (3) the Court treated domicile as a sufficient basis of jurisdiction under the Due Process Clause, making it also a sufficient basis in cases in which a judgment rendered by one state is taken for enforcement to another state under the full-faith-and-credit implementing statute.

Illustration 3-16. B, who is domiciled in State *X*, departed from State *X* to roam the world. *B* never returned to State *X*, but *B* also never acquired a new domicile by being physically present in any other state or country and having the intention to make that state or country *B's* home indefinitely or permanently. Consequently, under the rules of domicile traditionally applied in the United States, *B* technically retained a domicile in State *X*. *A*, who is also domiciled in State *X*, sued *B* in a State *X* court to recover damages for personal injuries received in an automobile accident with *B* in State *Y*, where *A* and *B* were temporarily present. *B* was served with process in State *Z*, where *B* was temporarily present, under a statute of State *X* authorizing State *X* to assert personal jurisdiction over nonresident domiciliaries of State *X* who are absent from the state. Under the rules that evolved in the United States after *Pennoyer v. Neff*, State *X* could validly assert personal jurisdiction over *B* based on *B's* technical domicile in State *X*.

* * * * *

To this point, domicile has been spoken of as a basis of jurisdiction over an individual who is absent from the state. However, domicile in the United States also became an important prerequisite for jurisdiction to alter status under certain circumstances. The best example of this basis of jurisdiction occurs in divorce cases. A state has jurisdiction to divorce a married couple if either or both spouses are domiciled within the state.[125] Traditionally, this rule was, like jurisdiction over property, a species of in rem jurisdiction over status.[126]

---

124. *See* P.M. NORTH & J.J. FAWCETT, CHESHIRE AND NORTH'S PRIVATE INTERNATIONAL LAW 348 (12th ed. 1992).

125. *See* RESTATEMENT (SECOND) OF CONFLICT OF LAWS §§ 70-71 (1971).

126. *See* RESTATEMENT (FIRST) OF CONFLICT OF LAWS § 110 cmt. a (1934). The in rem theory of status resembled in many ways the theory propounded by the Court in *Harris v. Balk*, discussed in section B(1)*(a) supra*. Recall that the presence of a person within the state gave power to the state to garnish a debt owed by the person to another nonresident. The theory was that the debt followed the debtor wherever the debtor went. In the divorce cases, the status follows the person and is treated as modifiable wherever the person is domiciled. The only difference is that in the divorce cases, a more substantial relationship between the state and the plaintiff is required—domicile rather than mere presence.

However, the portion of the rule allowing divorce based on the domicile of only one spouse is of relatively recent origin. The traditional approach was that the domicile of a single spouse was insufficient, without more, to satisfy due process in a divorce case.[127]

Illustration 3-17. *H* and *W* are a married couple who have lived all their lives in State *X*. *H* abandons *W* and travels to State *Y*, where *H* establishes a new domicile. *H* sues *W* for divorce in a State *Y* court. Under the domicile rule that evolved in the United States after *Pennoyer v. Neff*, the State *Y* court could constitutionally divorce *H* and *W*, even though *W* has never been near State *Y* and *W* does not appear and defend the divorce action. If the State *Y* judgment is later attacked in a proceeding in State *X* or another state, it must be given effect insofar as it changes the marital status of *H* and *W*. However, *W* can resist enforcement of the divorce decree on the ground that *H* did not acquire a legitimate domicile in State *Y* and that, as a result, State Y did not have jurisdiction to grant the divorce.

SECTION C. FICTIONAL EVOLUTION OF THE PRESENCE AND CONSENT TESTS FOR PERSONAL JURISDICTION

1. Jurisdiction over Corporations

The preceding section only discussed jurisdiction over nonresident individuals. But much of the law of personal jurisdiction after *Pennoyer* developed in cases in which corporations were defendants. One of the theories used to justify state-court jurisdiction over corporations–the implied consent theory–was then adapted to certain kinds of actions over individuals. The landmark Supreme Court decision[128] establishing the modern test governing state-court jurisdiction under the Fourteenth Amendment was a reaction to the fictional adaptations of the presence and consent theories to actions against corporate and individual defendants. Thus, a brief discussion of the development of the *Pennoyer* doctrines in these cases will be useful in understanding modern theories of state-court jurisdiction.

A corporation, like an individual, could consent to suit in a forum where it would otherwise not have been amenable to suit. In the absence of *actual* consent, the traditional rule was that a corporation could not be sued outside the

---

127. *See* RESTATEMENT (FIRST) OF CONFLICT OF LAWS § 71 cmt. a (1934); Michael M. O'Hear, *"Some of the Most Embarrassing Questions": Extraterritorial Divorces and the Problems of Jurisdiction Before Pennoyer*, 104 YALE L.J. 1507, 1525-34 (1995). *Compare* Haddock v. Haddock, 201 U.S. 562, 26 S. Ct. 525, 50 L. Ed. 867 (1906) *with* Williams v. North Carolina, 317 U.S. 287, 63 S. Ct. 207, 87 L. Ed. 279 (1942). *See also* RESTATEMENT (THIRD) OF THE FOREIGN RELATIONS LAW OF THE UNITED STATES § 484 (1987) (providing that U.S. courts will recognize foreign divorce decrees of a state where both parties were domiciled and may, but need not, recognize foreign divorce decrees of states where only one party was domiciled).

128. *See* the discussion of the *International Shoe* decision in section D *infra*.

state that chartered it.[129] To circumvent this rule, states began to require that a *foreign* corporation—one incorporated in another state—appoint an agent upon whom service could be made as a condition of conducting local business of the corporation in the state. If the corporation did not make an actual appointment, the state statutes generally provided for service upon the secretary of state, another public official, or an agent of the corporation in the state. A state could require such an appointment on the theory that the state had the sovereign authority to exclude a foreign corporation from doing local (as opposed to interstate) business altogether. Thus, the state could condition its permission to do local business on the foreign corporation's consent to the appointment of an agent to receive process.[130]

When a foreign corporation conducted only interstate commerce within the state, for example by shipping goods into the state, the state could not exclude the foreign corporation from transacting that interstate commerce. Thus, the consent theory would not work. To subject foreign corporations to jurisdiction under these circumstances, the courts resorted to the presence theory: "A foreign corporation is amenable to process to enforce a personal liability, in the absence of consent, only if it is doing business within the State in such a manner and to such extent as to warrant the inference that it is present there."[131] In the absence of corporate "presence," service on a corporate agent was deemed to be ineffective.[132]

Under either theory—consent or presence—the foreign corporation had to be "doing business." Therefore, the central question in each case became whether, in fact, it was doing such business as would subject it to jurisdiction under the theory upon which the state's assertion of jurisdiction was based.[133] A large body of case law grew up on the question of what constituted "doing

---

129. St. Clair v. Cox, 106 U.S. 350, 354, 1 S. Ct. 354, 358, 27 L. Ed. 222, 224 (1882) ("[A] foreign corporation could not be sued in an action for the recovery of a personal demand outside of the State by which it was chartered. The principle that a corporation must dwell in the place of its creation, and cannot . . . migrate to another sovereignty, coupled with the doctrine that an officer of the corporation does not carry his functions with him when he leaves his State, prevented the maintenance of personal actions against it. There was no mode of compelling its appearance in the foreign jurisdiction. Legal proceedings there against it were, therefore, necessarily confined to the disposition of such property belonging to it as could be there found; and to authorize them legislation was necessary"); *see also* Bank of Augusta v. Earle, 38 U.S. (13 Pet.) 519, 588, 10 L. Ed. 274, 308 (1839).

130. Even before *Pennoyer*, this manipulation of the concept of consent had been approved by the Supreme Court in Lafayette Insurance Co. v. French, 59 U.S. (18 How.) 404, 407, 15 L. Ed. 451, 452-53 (1856).

131. Philadelphia & Reading Ry. v. McKibbin, 243 U.S. 264, 265, 37 S. Ct. 280, 280, 61 L. Ed. 710, 711-12 (1917). The presence theory offered a loophole through which a corporation could escape jurisdiction. If the claim against the corporation arose out of its activities within the state, it could still avoid jurisdiction by ceasing to do business within the state before an action was commenced. Under such circumstances, it would cease to be "present" within the state. *See* Robert Mitchell Furniture Co. v. Selden Breck Constr. Co., 257 U.S. 213, 42 S. Ct. 84, 66 L. Ed. 201 (1921). However, if the corporation was found to have consented to jurisdiction, ceasing business prior to suit would not vitiate the consent. *See* Washington *ex rel.* Bond & Goodwin & Tucker, Inc. v. Superior Ct., 289 U.S. 361, 53 S. Ct. 624, 77 L. Ed. 1256 (1933).

132. *See, e.g.*, Riverside & Dan River Cotton Mills v. Menefee, 237 U.S. 189, 35 S. Ct. 579, 59 L. Ed. 910 (1915) (a state cannot acquire jurisdiction over a corporation by in-hand service on one of the corporate directors residing in the state when the corporation had no other connection with that state).

133. *See* Philip B. Kurland, *The Supreme Court, The Due Process Clause and the In Personam Jurisdiction of State Courts—From* Pennoyer *to* Denckla: *A Review*, 25 U. CHI. L. REV. 569, 584 (1958).

business'' for jurisdictional purposes. The cases drew distinctions that tended to focus on the quantity or level of activity without focusing on practical considerations, such as the burden on the defendant of suit in a particular state or the need for adjudication there.[134]

Although an individual who was present within a state could be served with process and subjected to jurisdiction even in cases in which the claim arose outside the state, it was unclear whether a corporation could likewise be subjected to jurisdiction based on presence when the claim arose elsewhere. Some cases denied jurisdiction. Others upheld jurisdiction when the claim did not arise out of the activities of the corporation in the state. The distinction between the decisions may have turned upon the level of corporate activity within the state, with ''continuous and systematic'' activity resulting in jurisdiction over cases involving claims unrelated to the state.[135]

2. Implied Consent Extended Beyond Corporations

In addition to employing implied consent as a means of establishing jurisdiction over foreign corporations, the states utilized the implied consent theory to gain personal jurisdiction over individual nonresidents under certain circumstances.

Illustration 3-18. In *Hess v. Pawloski*,[136] the Supreme Court upheld a Massachusetts statute deeming the use of the state's highways by nonresident motorists to be equivalent to an appointment by them of the registrar of motor vehicles as their agent upon whom process could be served in any action arising out of an accident on the state's highways. The statute conditioned the sufficiency of service upon the nonresident motorists' actual receipt of process by registered mail and the granting of continuances to afford them a reasonable opportunity to

---

134. *See id.*; *see also Developments in the Law–State-Court Jurisdiction*, 73 HARV. L. REV. 909, 922-23 (1960).

135. *Compare* Simon v. Southern Ry., 236 U.S. 115, 35 S. Ct. 255, 59 L. Ed. 492 (1915) (jurisdiction denied), Louisville & Nashville R.R. v. Chatters, 279 U.S. 320, 328, 49 S. Ct. 329, 331-32, 73 L. Ed. 711, 717-18 (1929) (jurisdiction denied; dictum) *and* Takacs v. Philadelphia & Reading Ry., 228 F. 728 (S.D.N.Y. 1915) *with* Atchison, Topeka & Santa Fe Ry. v. Weeks, 248 F. 970, 979 (W.D. Tex. 1918) (jurisdiction upheld) *and* Tauza v. Susquehanna Coal Co., 220 N.Y. 259, 115 N.E. 915 (1917) (jurisdiction upheld) (Cardozo, J.). An anomalous result occurred under the consent theory because the courts applied the theory both when the corporation actually appointed an agent to receive service of process as required by statute and when the corporation violated the statute by not appointing an agent. When the corporation actually appointed an agent as required by statute, the cases held that it had consented to suit both as to claims arising from its activities within the state and as to claims arising outside the state. *See* Pennsylvania Fire Ins. Co. v. Gold Issue Mining & Milling Co., 243 U.S. 93, 37 S. Ct. 344, 61 L. Ed. 610 (1917). However, even if the corporation did not comply with a state statute requiring it to appoint an agent to receive service, the courts concluded it had consented to suits arising from its activities within the state by doing business within the state. ''The rationale of the latter result was that a corporation which did not appoint an agent but did business within the state should not be in a better position than one which complied with the statute.'' *Developments in the Law–State-Court Jurisdiction*, 73 HARV. L. REV. 909, 920 (1960). Nevertheless, an advantage still accrued to the noncomplying corporation because the courts held that such a corporation only consented as to claims that arose out of its activities within the state. *See* Simon v. Southern Ry., 236 U.S. 115, 35 S. Ct. 255, 59 L. Ed. 492 (1915).

136. 274 U.S. 352, 47 S. Ct. 632, 71 L. Ed. 1091 (1927).

defend.[137] Because the state had the power to regulate use of its highways, the state could exclude nonresidents from operating motor vehicles on its highways unless an appointment of an agent to receive process had been made. In the absence of a formal appointment, one could be implied by the Massachusetts Legislature from a nonresident's decision to use its highways.[138]

* * * * *

The implied consent theory was sufficiently broad to allow the states to imply the consent of an individual to suit any time the state possessed the power to regulate, and thus place conditions on, the defendant's activity within the state. For example, the states were held to have the power to make the use, ownership, or possession of real estate situated in the state by a nonresident a ground for exercising personal jurisdiction over the nonresident on claims arising out of such use, ownership, or possession.[139] Thus, a jurisdictional theory that had been stretched to fit corporations was stretched even further to fit actions against individuals. The result was a morass of fictional rules that were ill-suited to the society that had evolved in the United States by the middle of the twentieth century.[140]

SECTION D. THE DEVELOPMENT OF MODERN RESTRICTIONS ON STATE-COURT JURISDICTION: THE MINIMUM CONTACTS TEST

In *International Shoe Co. v. Washington*,[141] the U.S. Supreme Court began to evolve a new test for determining personal jurisdiction over foreign

---

137. *Id.* at 354, 47 S. Ct. at 632-33, 71 L. Ed. at 1093-94.

138. *Id.* at 356-57, 47 S. Ct. at 633-34, 71 L. Ed. at 1094-95.

139. *See* Dubin v. City of Philadelphia, 34 D. & C. 61 (C.P. Phila. Co. 1938); RESTATEMENT (SECOND) OF CONFLICT OF LAWS § 38(1) (1971). There was some indication that the question whether a state had power to adjudicate based on the implied consent theory depended on whether the state had manifested its interest in the subject matter in a formalized way. In *Dubin*, above, the rules of liability were common law in nature, but the state had a specific long-arm statute by which it manifested its interest in the subject of nonresident owners and users of real estate. In Flexner v. Farson, 248 U.S. 289, 39 S. Ct. 97, 63 L. Ed. 250 (1919), the Court invalidated an assertion of jurisdiction over a partnership in a suit for breach of contract to sell bonds. The state did not regulate the securities business, and jurisdiction was asserted under a general "doing business" long-arm statute. However, in Henry L. Doherty & Co. v. Goodman, 294 U.S. 623, 55 S. Ct. 553, 79 L. Ed. 1097 (1935), the Supreme Court sustained jurisdiction over a nonresident individual in a suit for damages arising out of a stock sale. The state regulated the securities business extensively by statute, although jurisdiction was again asserted under a general long-arm statute. Assuming the validity of the assertion of jurisdiction in *Dubin*, the cases might be read as standing for the proposition that the state must either have a specific long-arm statute or a specific regulatory scheme expressing its formalized interest in the case before the implied consent theory would work. This possible reading is important in light of the Court's emphasis on the "state's interest" as a factor militating in favor of jurisdiction in modern cases and the view that interest can be enhanced by a formalized statutory expression of the interest. *See* sections G(2)*(b)(iv)* ("The Reasonableness Test") *infra*.

140. *See* Philip B. Kurland, *The Supreme Court, The Due Process Clause and the In Personam Jurisdiction of State Courts—From* Pennoyer *to* Denckla: *A Review*, 25 U. CHI. L. REV. 569, 585-86 (1958).

141. 326 U.S. 310, 66 S. Ct. 154, 90 L. Ed. 95 (1945). The approach adopted in *International Shoe* was essentially that articulated by Judge Learned Hand in Hutchinson v. Chase & Gilbert, Inc., 45 F.2d 139 (2d Cir. 1930). *See* Philip B. Kurland, *The Supreme Court, the Due Process Clause and the In Personam Jurisdiction of State Courts—From* Pennoyer *to* Denckla: *A Review*, 25 U. CHI. L. REV. 569, 579-80, 583-84 (1958).

corporations and other defendants: the *minimum contacts* test. International Shoe was a Delaware corporation having its principal place of business in St. Louis, Missouri. International Shoe manufactured and sold shoes and other footwear. The business conducted by International Shoe in Washington was purely interstate commerce. However, to conduct this business, International Shoe employed salesmen who resided and worked within the state. As a result, Washington assessed International Shoe for contributions to the state unemployment compensation fund. International Shoe was properly notified of the administrative proceeding brought to assess the tax against it and specially appeared to challenge Washington's authority to assert personal jurisdiction over it. The Washington administrative agency before which the proceeding was pending and the Washington courts reviewing the agency's action all rejected this challenge.[142]

On appeal to the U.S. Supreme Court, International Shoe relied on cases in which it had been held that the mere solicitation of orders for the purchase of goods within a state, to be accepted outside the state and filled by shipment of the purchased goods interstate, did not render the corporate seller amenable to suit within the state. International Shoe also argued that "since it was not present within the state, it [was] a denial of due process to subject [the company] to taxation or other money exaction."[143] The Court rejected International Shoe's contentions.

Although it might have sustained Washington's assertion of jurisdiction over International Shoe under the presence test,[144] the Court instead chose to articulate a new test for personal jurisdiction. The Court stated that the presence test as applied to corporations was merely "symbolic" of the activities within the state that would be deemed sufficient under the Due Process Clause to allow the state to subject the corporation to jurisdiction.[145] To satisfy the demands of due process, the corporation must have such "contacts" with the forum state "as make it reasonable, in the context of our federal system of government, to require the corporation to defend the particular suit which is brought there."[146] This "minimum contacts" test would be satisfied when the "quality and nature of the activity" of the defendant within the state was sufficient "in relation to the orderly administration of the laws that it was the purpose of the [D]ue [P]rocess [C]lause to insure."[147] The Due Process Clause would not permit an assertion of jurisdiction "against an individual or corporate defendant with which the state has no contacts, ties, or relations."[148] In applying the test, "[a]n 'estimate of

---

142. *See International Shoe*, 326 U.S. at 313-15, 66 S. Ct. at 156-57, 90 L. Ed. at 100-01.

143. *Id.* at 315-16, 66 S. Ct. at 158, 90 L. Ed. at 101.

144. In its analysis, the Court cited and discussed its prior decisions under the presence and consent tests that would have sustained jurisdiction over International Shoe. *See id.* at 317-19, 66 S. Ct. at 159, 90 L. Ed. at 102-03.

145. *See id.* at 316-17, 66 S. Ct. at 158, 90 L. Ed. at 102.

146. *Id.* at 317, 66 S. Ct. at 158, 90 L. Ed. at 102. The Court had earlier stated that "due process requires only that in order to subject a defendant to a judgment *in personam*, if he be not present within the territory of the forum, he have certain minimum contacts with it such that the maintenance of the suit does not offend 'traditional notions of fair play and substantial justice.' " *Id.* at 316, 66 S. Ct. at 158, 90 L. Ed. at 102 (citations omitted).

147. *Id.* at 319, 66 S. Ct. at 160, 90 L. Ed. at 104.

148. *Id.*

the inconveniences' which would result to the corporation from a trial away from its 'home' or principal place of business is relevant.''[149]

Since the decision in *International Shoe*, the minimum contacts test has dominated the landscape of personal jurisdiction in the United States. However, in addition to being ambiguous on several points, the Court's decision left several issues for resolution in the future. The following five sections explore the development and application of the minimum contacts test in the more than half-century since the Court decided *International Shoe*. Specifically, those sections will explore (1) the status of the territorial rules of *Pennoyer v. Neff* after the advent of the minimum contacts test; (2) the enactment by the states of new "long-arm" statutes in reaction to the minimum contacts test; (3) the content of the minimum contacts test; (4) the application of the minimum contacts test in particular categories of cases; and (5) the possible development of a concept of "jurisdiction by necessity." The final three sections of the chapter will examine (1) the due process requirement of notice, which is a separate requirement from the minimum contacts test; (2) the mechanics of service of process in state and federal courts; and (3) special problems of amenability to process in federal courts.

SECTION E. THE STATUS OF THE TERRITORIAL RULES OF JURISDICTION AFTER *INTERNATIONAL SHOE*

The effect of the Court's decision in *International Shoe* on the territorial rules of *Pennoyer v. Neff* was not immediately apparent. On one hand, as indicated above, the Court could have decided the case under the old presence test. The fact that the Court went out of its way to develop a new test might have meant that the new test replaced the old tests used under *Pennoyer*. This interpretation of the case was reinforced by the derogatory way in which the Court described the presence and consent tests in its opinion.[150] Furthermore, the new test focused on contacts between the defendant and the forum. The Court's statement about an "estimate of the inconveniences" of a trial in the forum being relevant to the administration of the test seemed to indicate that the new test replaced the territorial rules of *Pennoyer*. As observed in the earlier discussion of those rules, the territorial rules did not aim at preserving, as due process rules arguably should, an effective opportunity to be heard for the defendant. The new minimum contacts test, however, did seem to be aimed at this goal.

---

149. *Id.* at 317, 66 S. Ct. at 158, 90 L. Ed. at 102.

150. The Court stated that to say a corporation is present in a state "is to beg the question to be decided" and that the terms "present" or "presence" are used merely to symbolize the activities of the corporation within the state that will justify an assertion of jurisdiction over the corporation under the Due Process Clause of the Fourteenth Amendment. *See International Shoe*, 326 U.S. at 316-17, 66 S. Ct. at 158, 90 L. Ed. at 102. In addition, the Court described its decisions subjecting the corporation to suit base on consent as based on a "legal fiction." *See id.* at 318, 66 S. Ct. at 159, 90 L. Ed. at 103.

On the other hand, the tone of the Court's opinion in *International Shoe* was expansive. The minimum contacts test seemed to afford the states more leeway in asserting jurisdiction over nonresidents than the old territorial rules, even as those rules had evolved under the fictional presence and consent tests. Thus, it was possible to read *International Shoe* as if the minimum contacts test constituted an additional justification for an assertion of jurisdiction over nonresidents when the territorial rules could not be used to acquire jurisdiction over a defendant. This reading of the Court's opinion was reinforced by its statement that due process would be satisfied by an assertion of jurisdiction over a defendant who had minimum contacts with the state "if he be not present within the territory of the forum."[151]

Finally, the Court took care to analyze its prior decisions to indicate the consistency of their results with the new minimum contacts approach. Thus, while the new test was replacing *Pennoyer's* territorial analysis, it could mean that the results under the new test would be the same as under the old territorial rules. Under this reading of the opinion, the minimum contacts test would be neither expansive nor contractive. Rather, it would simply represent a more rational, nonfictional way of analyzing the due process validity of a state's assertion of jurisdiction over nonresidents.

Amazingly, in the more than fifty years since *International Shoe* was decided, the Supreme Court has not completely resolved the status of the territorial rules. In 1977, the Court appeared to say that the territorial rules were no longer valid bases for state-court jurisdiction. However, a Supreme Court decision in 1990 again threw doubt on the issue.

1. Quasi In Rem and Related Jurisdictional Doctrines

In *Shaffer v. Heitner*,[152] the Supreme Court appeared to clarify the respective roles of the minimum contacts test of *International Shoe* and the territorial rules of *Pennoyer*. In *Shaffer*, the plaintiff was the owner of one share of stock in the Greyhound Corporation. The plaintiff sued Greyhound and twenty-eight present or former officers of Greyhound in a Delaware state court. The plaintiff alleged that the individual defendants had violated their duties to Greyhound by causing the company to engage in actions that resulted in it being held liable for substantial antitrust damages and criminal contempt fines. The actions that allegedly led to the damages and contempt fines occurred in Oregon. Greyhound was a Delaware corporation. However, both the plaintiff and the individual defendants were nonresidents of Delaware.[153]

At the time the plaintiff filed the complaint, the plaintiff sequestered the property of the individual defendants, which constituted a substantial number of shares of stock and stock options. The sequestration was accomplished pursuant to a Delaware statute by placing "stop transfer" orders on the books of the

---

151. *Id.* at 316, 66 S. Ct. at 158, 90 L. Ed. at 102.
152. 433 U.S. 186, 97 S. Ct. 2569, 53 L. Ed. 2d 683 (1977).
153. *See id.* at 189-91, 97 S. Ct. at 2572-73, 53 L. Ed. 2d at 688-90.

Greyhound Corporation. The stock and options were not physically present in Delaware. However, the stock was considered to be subject to seizure in the state because of a Delaware statute that made Delaware the situs of ownership of all stock in Delaware corporations. In effect, the Delaware sequestration procedure was the equivalent of the garnishment to achieve quasi in rem jurisdiction that had occurred in *Harris v. Balk*, discussed above.[154]

The defendants entered a special appearance to challenge Delaware's assertion of quasi in rem jurisdiction over them. The defendants asserted that they lacked sufficient contacts with the state to sustain jurisdiction under the minimum contacts test of *International Shoe*. The Delaware trial court rejected this jurisdictional challenge. The Delaware Supreme Court affirmed the judgment of the trial court on the ground that an assertion of quasi in rem jurisdiction was not subject to the limitations of the minimum contacts test.[155]

The U.S. Supreme Court reversed the judgment of the Delaware Supreme Court. The Court held "that all assertions of state-court jurisdiction must be evaluated according to the standards set forth in *International Shoe* and its progeny."[156] The extension of the *International Shoe* standards to "all" assertions of state-court jurisdiction logically seemed to invalidate more than simply quasi in rem jurisdiction of the *Harris v. Balk* variety. Also placed in jeopardy by this part of the Court's opinion were the traditional rules permitting jurisdiction based on (1) service of process on a defendant who is only transitorily present in the state, (2) the domicile of the defendant, when the domicile is only "technical" and the defendant no longer has a substantial relationship with the state, and (3) the domicile of the plaintiff in ex parte divorce cases, even though the defendant has no contacts with the state.

In a cryptic footnote in *Shaffer*, however, the Court created doubt whether it really meant to subject "all" assertions of state-court jurisdiction to the minimum contacts test: "We do not suggest that jurisdictional doctrines other than those discussed in [the] text, such as the particularized rules governing the adjudications of status, are inconsistent with the [*International Shoe*] standard of fairness."[157] This statement appears to be a direct reference to ex parte divorce cases, in which the states are allowed to divorce two parties based on the domicile of only the plaintiff in the state.[158] The *International Shoe* test focused on the fairness of the jurisdictional assertion to the defendant. Thus, it was not immediately apparent how the ex parte divorce jurisdiction could be consistent with the test. In ex parte divorce cases, the defendant often has no contact at all with the forum state. In addition, the forum state would usually also be a burdensome place for the defendant to litigate.

---

154. *See id.* at 190-92, 97 S. Ct. at 2572-73, 53 L. Ed. 2d at 688-90. *Harris v. Balk* is discussed in section B(1)*(a)* ("Affirmative Principles of In Rem Jurisdiction") *supra.*

155. *See Shaffer*, 433 U.S. at 190-95, 97 S. Ct. at 2572-75, 53 L. Ed. 2d at 689-92.

156. *Id.* at 212, 97 S. Ct. at 2584, 53 L. Ed. 2d at 703.

157. *Id.* at 208 n.30, 97 S. Ct. at 2582 n.30, 53 L. Ed. 2d at 700 n.30.

158. *See, e.g.*, Williams v. North Carolina, 317 U.S. 287, 63 S. Ct. 207, 87 L. Ed. 279 (1942) (*Williams I*); Williams v. North Carolina, 325 U.S. 226, 65 S. Ct. 1092, 89 L. Ed. 1577 (1945) (*Williams II*); *see also* E. Roy Hawkens, *The Impact of* Shaffer v. Heitner *on the Jurisdictional Standard in Ex Parte Divorces*, 18 FAM. L.Q. 311 (1984).

The explanation for the Court's footnote may lie in the substantive nature of most ex parte divorce proceedings. If a plaintiff commences an ex parte divorce action in a state with a no fault divorce law, there is realistically no defense to the action. Because the Due Process Clause is designed to insure the defendant an adequate opportunity to be heard in defense, it is possible to reason that when no defense exists under the applicable substantive law, the defendant is not deprived of anything by the state's assertion of jurisdiction. A problem exists, of course, if the forum state has a no fault divorce law that it will apply to the action, while the state of the marital domicile has a fault divorce law that would prevent the plaintiff from obtaining the divorce. But this problem should not be addressed through due process limits on the state's ability to assert personal jurisdiction. Instead, it is a problem of determining whether the state should be permitted to apply its substantive divorce law to dissolve a marriage between a domiciliary of the state and a nonresident who has no connections with the state.

Illustration 3-19. *H* and *W* are a husband and wife who are domiciled in State *X*. *H* abandons *W* and travels to State *Y*, where *H* establishes a new domicile. After acquiring a domicile in State *Y*, *H* commences a divorce action in a State *Y* court under the State *Y* no fault divorce law. *W* is served with mail process in this action in State *X*. *W*, who has never been near State *Y*, does not appear and defend the action. The court then enters a default judgment granting the divorce. The State *Y* judgment is arguably valid under the minimum contacts test. The minimum contacts test is designed to assure that the defendant has an adequate opportunity to be heard in defense before life, liberty, or property is taken from the defendant. Because there is no defense to the State *Y* divorce action, there is nothing for *W* to be heard about in the proceeding. Therefore, the Due Process Clause arguably does not protect *W* against an assertion of no-fault divorce jurisdiction by State *Y*. However, if State *X* is a "fault" divorce state, *W* may possess a valid constitutional objection to the *State Y's* application of its divorce law to the action.[159]

* * * * *

The impact of ex parte divorce jurisdiction on the defendant has been mitigated by the concept of "divisible divorce" developed by the U.S. Supreme Court. Under the divisible divorce concept, the right of a defendant spouse to support or alimony cannot be cut off by a judgment of divorce unless the state

---

159. Recent Supreme Court decisions under the Full Faith and Credit Clause and the Due Process Clause have held that a state must have a significant contact with a case that creates a legitimate interest on the part of a state in applying its law. *See* Allstate Ins. Co. v. Hague, 449 U.S. 302, 101 S. Ct. 633, 66 L. Ed. 2d 521 (1981). However, long established and still subsisting conflict-of-laws practices do not violate either the Full Faith and Credit Clause or the Due Process Clause. *See* Sun Oil Co. v. Wortman, 486 U.S. 717, 108 S. Ct. 2117, 100 L. Ed. 2d 743 (1988). Under either of these standards, the state of the plaintiff's domicile may be able to apply its divorce law constitutionally to the case described in this illustration. Nevertheless, there is reason to believe that the Due Process Clause should be interpreted to prohibit the application by a state of its law that will unfairly surprise the defendant. *See* Ralph U. Whitten, *The Constitutional Limitations on State Choice of Law: Due Process*, 9 HAST. CONST. L.Q. 851 (1982). Under an unfair surprise standard, the defendant in an ex parte divorce proceeding might have a valid constitutional objection to the application by the forum state of its no-fault divorce law, if the defendant lives in a fault-based divorce state.

where the divorce proceeding is pending has personal jurisdiction consistent with the minimum contacts test over the defendant.[160] Thus, while the domicile of the plaintiff alone will suffice to permit a state to terminate the marital status of the plaintiff and the defendant, domicile of the plaintiff alone will not allow the state to cut off the personal rights of the defendant to support or alimony.[161]

Although the Court in *Shaffer* clearly indicated that traditional in rem jurisdiction based on property within the state would be subject to the *International Shoe* standard, the Court carefully pointed out that nothing precluded the state where property was located from asserting jurisdiction to adjudicate claims directly related to the property, as opposed to claims such as the one in *Shaffer* that were unrelated to the property.[162]

Illustration 3-20. *A*, a citizen of State *X*, sues *B*, a citizen of State *Y*, in a state court in State *X*. *A* seeks to quiet title to land located in State *X*. *B* has no contacts with State *X* other than a claim to the ownership of the land. Under *Shaffer*, the location of the land in the state is sufficient contact for the state to assert jurisdiction over *B* to adjudicate the title to the land consistent with due process.

* * * * *

Interestingly, the concept of divisible divorce has recently collided with the language in *Shaffer* indicating that the states have the constitutional power to adjudicate claims to property located within the state. In *Abernathy v. Abernathy*,[163] a husband and wife were married in Florida and resided in Louisiana until their separation. Upon separation, the husband moved to Georgia and purchased real property there, apparently with assets accumulated during the marriage and taken by the husband from Louisiana to Georgia. After about a year, the husband commenced a divorce proceeding against the wife in Georgia. As part of the divorce proceeding, the husband requested that the property located in Georgia be awarded to him. The wife objected to personal jurisdiction, but the Georgia trial court asserted jurisdiction over the "res of the marital relationship" and "in rem jurisdiction with respect to [the] property located within this state."[164]

The Georgia Supreme Court affirmed. According to the court, the Georgia courts had jurisdiction to divorce based on the plaintiff's domicile in Georgia. The assertion of in rem jurisdiction to dispose of the property did not violate the minimum contacts test of *International Shoe*. The language in *Shaffer* preserved the jurisdiction of state courts to adjudicate claims to property within the state.

---

160. *See* Vanderbilt v. Vanderbilt, 354 U.S. 416, 77 S. Ct. 1360, 1 L. Ed. 2d 1456 (1957); Estin v. Estin, 334 U.S. 541, 68 S. Ct. 1213, 92 L. Ed. 1561 (1948).

161. *See* RUSSELL J. WEINTRAUB, COMMENTARY ON THE CONFLICT OF LAWS § 5.2E2 (3d ed. 1986); *see also* David E. Seidelson, *Jurisdictional Reach and Choice-of-Law Determinations in Divorce*, 6 WIDENER J. PUB. L. 423 (1997). However, the divisible divorce concept does not protect all personal rights of the defendant spouse. For example, the Supreme Court has held that a husband's ex parte divorce can terminate a wife's dower rights in the husband's estate. *See* Simons v. Miami Beach First Nat'l Bank, 381 U.S. 81, 85 S. Ct. 1315, 14 L. Ed. 2d 232 (1965).

162. *See Shaffer*, 433 U.S. at 207-08, 97 S. Ct. at 2581-82, 53 L. Ed. 2d at 699-700.

163. 267 Ga. 815, 482 S.E.2d 265 (1997).

164. *Id.* at 816, 482 S.E.2d at 266.

Presiding Justice Fletcher dissented on the ground that the divisible divorce concept compelled the opposite conclusion:

> The majority's opinion opens the doors of Georgia's courts to any citizen of this country who wants to divorce and to obtain an unfair advantage over his or her spouse in the division of marital property. All any citizen need do is leave his or her marital home, take any or all assets of the couple, move to Georgia and file for divorce . . . . The non-resident spouse is then forced to litigate his or her claim to those marital assets in a foreign jurisdiction.[165]

Also in dissent, Justice Sears observed that the Georgia Legislature had, in the Georgia long-arm statute, specifically required personal jurisdiction over a non-resident spouse in actions for division of marital property.[166] In the alternative, Justice Sears argued that the minimum contacts test was violated by Georgia's assertion of jurisdiction over the wife. He observed that the U.S. Supreme Court had, in *Shaffer*, also given an example of when property located within the state would *not* support jurisdiction to adjudicate a claim to the property. That example was taken from comment c of the *Restatement (Second) of Conflict of Laws* § 60.[167] The example provided that a state will not *usually* exercise jurisdiction over personal property brought into its territory without the owner's consent.[168]

The debate between the majority and the dissenters in *Abernathy* may have a broad impact on cases in which personal property is brought into a state without the consent of all the persons who claim the property. The citation by the U.S. Supreme Court in *Shaffer* of the *Restatement (Second) of Conflict of Laws* § 60 is ambiguous: Section 60 deals with the personal-property equivalent of the rules governing the acquisition of jurisdiction by fraud or force over persons.[169] Thus, the citation could simply be an innocuous reference to nonconstitutional fraud-and-force rules. Alternatively, it could be a suggestion by the Supreme Court that the fraud-and-force rules as applied to property will have constitutional status, at least in some circumstances.[170] What is clear is that *Abernathy* has brought to the forefront a latent problem with the U.S. Supreme Court's dictum in *Shaffer*. The solution to that problem depends upon whether the Court interprets the minimum contacts test as applicable to the kind of claim in

---

165. *Id.* at 819, 482 S.E.2d at 269.

166. *See id.* at 821-22, 482 S.E.2d at 270-71. The majority had held the Georgia long-arm statute irrelevant because the trial court was exercising in rem jurisdiction over the property.

167. RESTATEMENT (SECOND) OF CONFLICT OF LAWS § 60, cmt c (1971).

168. *See id.*

169. *See id.* cmts c, d (stating that the limits are not based on "any principle of jurisdiction"; *cf.* section B(2)(*b*), *supra* (discussing the nonjurisdictional limits on state jurisdiction acquired by fraud or force).

170. *See* RESTATEMENT (SECOND) OF CONFLICT OF LAWS § 60, cmt. a (1971) (stating that, while a state "may exercise judicial jurisdiction" to affect interests in a chattel within its territory, if the chattel is situated in a state that has no relation to the parties or the occurrence in question, the assertion of jurisdiction "might be thought inconsistent with the basic principle of reasonableness which underlies the field of judicial jurisdiction"). The reference to reasonableness is clearly a reference to the *International Shoe* standard, and the RESTATEMENT (SECOND) cited § 24 and § 56 as references to the reasonableness principle. These sections are based on the minimum contacts test. *See id.* § 24 cmt. b, § 56 cmt. c.

Abernathy, as well as to other claims involving personalty brought into a state without the consent of all claimant's to the property.

As discussed earlier,[171] traditional notions of state control over property involved not only affirmative powers to deal with property located within the state, but also restrictions on the ability of states to deal with land located in other states. The Court's statement in *Shaffer* that all assertions of state-court jurisdiction would be governed by *International Shoe* suggested that a state with sufficient contacts to make it fair to assert jurisdiction over the defendant could render a judgment that directly affects the title to land located in another state. However, this position was contradicted by the Court's footnote aimed at preserving traditional ex parte divorce jurisdiction. It was also contradicted by later statements in the opinion focusing on the importance of the state's interest in the minimum contacts analysis.[172] The requirement that the state have a sufficient interest in adjudicating a particular dispute might result in the preservation of the exclusive jurisdiction of the state where land is located over matters that directly affect the title to the land.

Before *Shaffer*, some states, following the lead of *Seider v. Roth*,[173] had approved of a form of quasi in rem jurisdiction in automobile accident cases against insured defendants. In these cases, the plaintiff would garnish the obligation of the defendant's insurance company to defend and indemnify the defendant. In this way, the plaintiff could bring the action in any state where the insurance company was doing business and thus subject to personal jurisdiction. The theory of these actions was obviously based on *Harris v. Balk*, which the states had assumed survived the decision in *International Shoe*.[174]

After *Shaffer*, there was reason to believe that the form of quasi in rem jurisdiction exercised in *Seider v. Roth* would still be valid. *Seider* jurisdiction had been limited in important ways to assure fairness to both the insurer and the insured. Specifically, the judgment in a *Seider* action was limited to the face amount of the insurance policy, the defendant had the right to a limited appearance,[175] and the plaintiff either had to reside in the forum state or the claim had to arise there.[176] These protections made the *Seider* jurisdiction appear much like a direct action against the insurance company, which some states authorize

---

171. *See* section B(1)*(b)* ("Restrictive Principles of In Rem Jurisdiction") *supra*.

172. In responding to an argument by the plaintiff, the Court stated that the defendants' positions as officers and directors of Greyhound did not, of itself, give Delaware a sufficient "interest" in asserting jurisdiction in the case. *See Shaffer*, 433 U.S. at 214-15, 97 S. Ct. at 2585, 53 L. Ed. at 704. The role of the state's interest in the minimum contacts analysis is discussed further in section G(2)*(b)(iv)* *infra*.

173. 17 N.Y.2d 111, 216 N.E.2d 312, 269 N.Y.S.2d 99 (1966).

174. *See, e.g.*, Minichiello v. Rosenberg, 410 F.2d 106 (2d Cir.), *aff'd on rehearing en banc*, 410 F.2d 117 (2d Cir. 1968), *cert. denied*, 396 U.S. 844, 90 S. Ct. 69, 24 L. Ed. 2d 94 (1969).

175. Limited appearance is discussed in section B(1)*(c)* ("Limited Appearance Procedures") *supra*.

176. *See, e.g.*, O'Connor v. Lee-Hy Paving Corp., 579 F.2d 194, 200-02 (2d Cir. 1978), *cert. denied*, 439 U.S. 1034, 99 S. Ct. 638, 58 L. Ed. 2d 696 (1978); Minichiello v. Rosenberg, 410 F.2d 106 (2d Cir.), *aff'd on rehearing en banc*, 410 F.2d 117 (2d Cir. 1968), *cert. denied*, 396 U.S. 844, 90 S. Ct. 69, 24 L. Ed. 2d 67 (1969); Simpson v. Loehmann, 21 N.Y.2d 305, 234 N.E.2d 669, 287 N.Y.S.2d 633 (1967). *See generally* Napoleon B. Williams, Jr., *The Validity of Assuming Jurisdiction by the Attachment of Automobile Liability Insurance Obligations: The Impact of* Shaffer v. Heitner *Upon* Seider v. Roth, 9 RUT.-CAM. L.J. 241 (1977).

by statute. Nevertheless, in 1980, the Supreme Court invalidated *Seider* jurisdiction in *Rush v. Savchuk.*[177]

In *Rush*, the Supreme Court stated that *Seider* actions were not the equivalent of direct actions against the insurer. The Court held that the state's ability to assert power over the insured was "analytically prerequisite" to the insurer's entry into the case.[178] Furthermore, the Court held that the "assumption" that the insured party had no real stake in the litigation was "far from self-evident."[179] In support of this last conclusion, the Court cited (1) the potential economic impact on the insured when multiple plaintiffs sued in different states for an aggregate amount in excess of the policy limits; (2) the potential that an adverse decision might affect the defendant's insurability; and (3) the potential noneconomic impact that might occur in professional malpractice actions, in which the insured's professional competence and integrity are questioned.[180] Finally, the Court stated that it was improper to attribute the insurer's contacts to the insured to satisfy the minimum contacts test because "[t]he requirements of *International Shoe . . .* must be met as to each defendant over whom a state court exercises jurisdiction."[181]

Rush casts substantial doubt on the constitutionality of direct action statutes. Those statutes possess many of the same flaws that the Court deemed present in *Seider* quasi in rem jurisdiction. Specifically, the hypothetical adverse effects on the insured party that the Court said were involved in *Seider* cases are seemingly also present in direct actions.[182] Nevertheless, the Court's statement that *Seider* jurisdiction is not the equivalent of a direct action against the insurer may save the constitutionality of direct action statutes.[183] Of greater concern is the Court's exaltation of form over substance in *Rush*. For example, although the Court stated that jurisdiction over the insured was an analytical prerequisite to jurisdiction over the insurer, it gave no persuasive reason for this conclusion. Given the protections that had evolved in *Seider* actions to assure fairness to both the insured and the insurer, no significant due process problem seemed to exist with the jurisdiction.

---

177. 444 U.S. 320, 100 S. Ct. 571, 62 L. Ed. 2d 516 (1980).

178. *See id.* at 330-31, 100 S. Ct. at 578, 62 L. Ed. 2d at 526.

179. *Id.* at 331, 100 S. Ct. at 579, 62 L. Ed. 2d at 527.

180. *See id.* at 331 n.20, 100 S. Ct. at 579 n.20, 62 L. Ed. 2d at 527 n.20. None of these factors was actually present in the *Rush* case itself, raising the question whether the Court should have invalidated *Seider* jurisdiction in a case in which no adverse effects on the actual insured involved in the case could be identified.

181. *Id.* at 332, 100 S. Ct. at 579, 62 L. Ed. 2d at 527.

182. *See id.* at 331 n.20, 100 S. Ct. at 579 n.20, 62 L. Ed. 2d at 527 n.20.

183. *Cf.* APC Commodity Corp. v. Ram Dis Ticaret A.S., 965 F. Supp. 461 (S.D.N.Y. 1997) (district court held that quasi in rem jurisdiction existed over funds held by an importer-defendant's New York bank where the funds were related to contracts between the plaintiff and defendant that called for a series of exchanges in New York City, which gave rise to a reason why the defendant should have been expected to be sued in New York; however, the court had previously held the defendant subject to personal jurisdiction in New York under the New York long-arm statute. Under such circumstances, there was no real reason to sustain jurisdiction on a quasi in rem theory).

2. Transient Presence Jurisdiction

As discussed above, the Court's apparent willingness in *Shaffer* to preserve ex parte divorce jurisdiction from attack under the *International Shoe* standard also raised questions about whether the Court would be willing to preserve other traditional grounds of jurisdiction, such as transient presence, from attack. Only one Supreme Court decision since *Shaffer* has addressed the status of the other traditional territorial rules of jurisdiction. In *Burnham v. Superior Court*,[184] the Court unanimously sustained the rule permitting jurisdiction to be acquired over a defendant who is temporarily within the state when served with process. Although the Court was unanimous in upholding transient presence as a basis of jurisdiction, a majority could not agree on why the rule of transient presence is valid. The *Burnham* decision is, therefore, of limited value in predicting the Court's approach to the validity of other features of the territorial system. The primary value of the case lies in what it reveals about the divisions among the members of the Court (as then constituted) over the philosophy of interpretation that should govern applications of the Due Process Clause to questions of personal jurisdiction.

Burnham involved a divorce action in California. The Burnhams were married in 1976 in West Virginia. They later moved to New Jersey, where their two children were born. They separated in 1987. At the time of the separation, they agreed that the wife would take custody of the children and move to California, while the husband would remain in New Jersey. The plan was for the wife to file suit for divorce on the ground of irreconcilable differences. After the wife moved, the husband commenced a divorce action in New Jersey on the ground of desertion, but the wife was never served in this action.

In 1988, after the husband refused to abide by the agreement to submit to an irreconcilable differences divorce, the wife commenced a divorce action in California. Shortly after the wife commenced the action, the husband was served with process while he was temporarily present in California on business and was visiting his children. The husband specially appeared to object to personal jurisdiction in this action on the ground that he did not have sufficient contacts with California to justify an assertion of jurisdiction under the Due Process Clause.[185] The California Superior Court denied the husband's motion to quash the service of process. The California Court of Appeal denied a writ of mandamus on the ground that service while physically present within the state was a valid

---

184. 495 U.S. 604, 110 S. Ct. 2105, 109 L. Ed. 2d 631 (1990).

185. The significance of this objection was not directed to the ability of the wife to obtain a California divorce. Recall from the discussion of *Shaffer* that the Court, in footnote 30 of that decision, appeared to preserve the validity of traditional ex parte divorce jurisdiction in cases in which the defendant has no contacts at all with the forum state. *See* Shaffer v. Heitner, 433 U.S. 186, 208 n.30, 97 S. Ct. 2569, 2582 n.30, 53 L. Ed. 2d 683, 700 n.30 (1977). Rather, the significance of the defendant's challenge to California's assertion of jurisdiction must be seen as relevant to issues of support and alimony, which require valid personal jurisdiction over the defendant. *See* the discussion of "divisible divorce" in the text accompanying the discussion of *Shaffer v. Heitner* in section E(1) ("Quasi in Rem and Related Jurisdictional Doctrines") *supra*.

basis for asserting personal jurisdiction under the Due Process Clause. The U.S. Supreme Court granted certiorari and affirmed.[186]

All nine Justices of the Court agreed that California's assertion of personal jurisdiction over the husband was valid. However, they disagreed concerning the proper standard for judging the validity of the jurisdictional assertion. Writing for four members of the Court,[187] Justice Scalia distinguished between the Due Process Clause as a limitation on the introduction of "novel procedures" and as a limitation on traditionally accepted procedures.[188] Essentially, the opinion stated that the minimum contacts test of *International Shoe* is a standard designed to measure the due process validity of assertions of state-court jurisdiction over defendants who are not served while physically present within the state.[189] According to Justice Scalia, the minimum contacts test does not apply to a traditionally accepted method of obtaining personal jurisdiction.

But what of *Shaffer v. Heitner*, in which the minimum contacts test had been used to invalidate a traditional method of acquiring jurisdiction to adjudicate? Justice Scalia's opinion attempted to distinguish *Shaffer* on the ground that *Shaffer* recognized that quasi in rem jurisdiction was really a fictional way of acquiring in personam jurisdiction over a defendant who is *absent* from the state.[190] Thus, *Shaffer* simply placed "all suits against absent nonresidents on the same constitutional footing, regardless of whether a separate Latin label is attached to one particular basis of contact."[191] Perhaps uneasy with this ground of distinction, Justice Scalia added that the plurality's basic approach to the Due Process Clause in *Burnham* was different than in *Shaffer*. In *Burnham*, the plurality refused to make an independent inquiry into the fairness of the transient presence rule, while in *Shaffer* just such an inquiry was used to invalidate quasi in rem jurisdiction. Furthermore, under the plurality's approach in *Burnham*, the application of the minimum contacts test would be reserved to judge the constitutionality of "new procedures hitherto unknown," while doctrines accepted when the Due Process Clause was adopted and still generally observed would automatically satisfy due process.[192]

---

186. *Burnham*, 495 U.S. at 608, 110 S. Ct. at 2109, 109 L. Ed. 2d at 638.

187. Justice White concurred in those portions of Justice Scalia's opinion that articulated the standard by which the constitutionality of the traditional territorial rules should be measured under the Due Process Clause. Along with Justice Scalia, the Chief Justice, and Justice Kennedy, Justice White made up the four-member plurality in favor of that standard. Justice White did not concur in sections II-D or III of Justice Scalia's opinion, however. Section II-D of the opinion attempted to distinguish *Shaffer v. Heitner*. Section III responded to Justice Brennan's concurring opinion. Justice White also filed a separate concurring opinion. *See id.* at 626-27, 110 S. Ct. at 2119, 109 L. Ed. 2d at 650. Justice White's concurrence is discussed in the text *infra*.

188. *Id.* at 619, 110 S. Ct. at 2115, 109 L. Ed. 2d at 644-45.

189. *See id.* at 618, 110 S. Ct. at 2114, 109 L. Ed. 2d at 644.

190. *Id.* at 620-21, 110 S. Ct. at 2115-16, 109 L. Ed. 2d at 645-46.

191. *Id.* at 621, 110 S. Ct. at 2116, 109 L. Ed. 2d at 646.

192. *Id.* at 622, 110 S. Ct. at 2116-17, 109 L. Ed. 2d at 646-67 (footnote omitted). In a footnote, Justice Scalia suggested that *Shaffer* may have involved a unique state procedure, in that Delaware was the only state that treated the place of incorporation as the situs of corporate stock. *See id.* at 622, n.4, 110 S. Ct. at 2116, n.4, 109 L. Ed. 2d at 646, n.4. This fact may be true, but it is certainly disingenuous. Quasi in rem jurisdiction based solely on the attachment of property located in the state was a widespread feature of American jurisprudence when the Fourteenth Amendment was adopted *and* when *Shaffer* was decided. Yet *Shaffer* appeared to invalidate

Justice White, who concurred in most of Justice Scalia's opinion, filed a separate opinion.[193] While agreeing that jurisdiction based on physical presence was and is too well accepted to be invalid, Justice White nevertheless indicated that "the Court has the authority under the [Fourteenth Amendment] to examine even traditionally accepted procedures and declare them invalid."[194] However, Justice White was unwilling to invalidate the transient presence rule because no showing had been made "that as a general proposition the rule is so arbitrary and lacking in common sense in so many instances that it should be held violative of Due Process in every case."[195] Until such a general showing is made, Justice White indicated that "claims in individual cases that the rule would operate unfairly as applied to the particular nonresident involved need not be entertained."[196]

Justice Brennan filed a concurring opinion, in which Justices Marshall, Blackmun, and O'Connor joined.[197] While the concurring Justices believed that tradition was relevant to the due process inquiry, they did not deem it to be dispositive.[198] Rather, they argued that the minimum contacts test of *International Shoe* should be applied to every case, even those involving traditional methods of acquiring jurisdiction over nonresidents.[199] However, in applying the minimum contacts test to the facts of the case, the concurring Justices felt that the test was satisfied for several reasons. First, "[t]he transient rule is consistent with reasonable expectations and is entitled to a strong presumption that it comports with due process"[200] because when individuals visit another state, they knowingly assume the risks that the state will exercise some power over their person or property while they are there.[201] The presence of the individual in a state enhances the foreseeability of suit there.[202] Second, by visiting a state, individuals avail themselves of "significant benefits" provided by the state, including police, fire, emergency medical services, freedom of travel on the state's roads and waterways, and the "fruits of the state's economy."[203] Finally, the concur-

---

quasi in rem jurisdiction as practiced in all states, not just in its Delaware form.

193. *See id.* at 628, 110 S. Ct. at 2119, 109 L. Ed. 2d at 650.

194. *See id.*

195. *Id.* at 628, 110 S. Ct. at 2119-20, 109 L. Ed. 2d at 650.

196. *Id.* at 628, 110 S. Ct. at 2120, 109 L. Ed. 2d at 650. It is mystifying, to say the least, how a showing that the rule operates unfairly in "so many instances" could be made in the course of litigation without reference to the specific facts of the case under adjudication, which Justice White said need not be considered in any event.

197. *See id.*

198. *See id.* at 629-34, 110 S. Ct. at 2120-22, 109 L. Ed. 2d at 650-53.

199. *See id.* at 630-32, 110 S. Ct. at 2121-22, 109 L. Ed. 2d at 651-53. Justice Brennan's opinion also questioned the historical pedigree of the transient presence rule, which Justice Scalia had accepted. *See id.* at 633-37, 110 S. Ct. at 2122-24, 109 L. Ed. 2d at 653-56.

200. *Id.* at 636, 110 S. Ct. at 2124, 109 L. Ed. 2d at 656.

201. *See id.*

202. *See id.*

203. *See id.* at 637-38, 110 S. Ct. at 2124-25, 109 L. Ed. 2d at 656-57. Justice Brennan added that without transient presence jurisdiction, "an asymmetry would arise" because nonresidents could sue as plaintiffs within the state while remaining immune from suit as defendants. *See id.* at 638, 110 S. Ct. at 2125, 109 L. Ed. 2d at 657 (citing Earl M. Maltz, *Sovereign Authority, Fairness, and Personal Jurisdiction: The Case for the Doctrine of Transient Jurisdiction*, 66 WASH. U. L.Q. 671, 698-99 (1988)). However, there is symmetry in the fact that all nonresidents can sue in the courts of all residents' states while remaining immune from jurisdiction within ring Justices argued that the burdens on the transient defendant were slight because of modern means of transportation and communication and the availability of procedural devices with which to mitigate inconvenience.[204] Moreover, the fact that the defendant has journeyed once to the forum is itself an indication that suit in the forum would not be prohibitively inconvenient.[205]

The effect of *Burnham* on other "traditional" rules is made especially unclear by Justice Stevens' concurrence. As indicated above, four Justices were willing to rely on the historical pedigree of a rule in sustaining its validity, while four others believed traditional rules must, like others, be justified under the *International Shoe* test. Justice Stevens refused to join in any of the other opinions. However, Justice Stevens agreed that the considerations articulated in all other opinions justified affirmance of the California judgment.[206]

The task now confronting practitioners and scholars of civil procedure is to decipher the meaning of *Burnham* for other cases.[207] It is difficult to determine which opinion will prevail due to Justice Stevens' concurrence. Furthermore, the Court's due process methodology outside the personal jurisdiction area has been inconsistent.[208] If Justice Brennan's approach prevails, the validity of the other traditional grounds for and limits on personal jurisdiction

---

the state. Thus, California residents can sue New York residents in New York, while remaining immune from suit in New York (unless they have minimum contacts with New York) and New York residents can sue California residents in California while remaining immune from suit in California (unless they have minimum contacts with California). What is "asymmetrical" about this? Even if it is "asymmetrical," the Due Process Clause guarantees an adequate opportunity to be heard in defense before life, liberty, or property is taken from someone. It doesn't guarantee "symmetry."

204. *See Burnham*, 495 U.S. at 638, 110 S. Ct. at 2125, 109 L. Ed. 2d at 657.

205. *See id.* at 639, 110 S. Ct. at 2125, 109 L. Ed. 2d at 657.

206. *See id.* at 640, 110 S. Ct. at 2126, 109 L. Ed. 2d at 658. In *Shaffer*, Justice Stevens had concurred on the ground that the Due Process Clause should be interpreted to require not only adequate notice of the existence of the action, but also fair warning that a particular kind of activity might subject the defendant to the jurisdiction of "a foreign sovereign." *See* Shaffer v. Heitner, 433 U.S. 186, 218, 97 S. Ct. 2569, 2587, 53 L. Ed. 2d 683, 706 (1977) (Stevens, J., concurring). Because such fair warning was, in his view, absent in *Shaffer*, Justice Stevens concurred in the judgment. *See id.* at 218-19, 97 S. Ct. at 2587, 53 L. Ed. 2d at 706-07. However, Justice Stevens agreed with Justice Powell that the Court's opinion should not be read to invalidate quasi in rem jurisdiction when real estate is involved. *See id.* at 219, 97 S. Ct. at 2587, 53 L. Ed. 2d at 707. Justice Stevens also stated that he would not invalidate other long-established methods of acquiring jurisdiction over persons with notice that their local activities might subject them to suit. *See id.* One may extrapolate from Justice Stevens' opinion in *Shaffer*, then, that he agrees with the four members of the Court led by Justice Brennan that transient presence provides adequate foreseeability that the defendant may be sued within the state without more, even if the claim arises outside the state. If the defendant's activities within the state give rise to the claim, transient presence is unnecessary. The defendant can be served outside the state, if necessary, and subjected to jurisdiction consistent with the Due Process Clause under the *International Shoe* test.

207. For an excellent article suggesting that the Supreme Court get out of the business of using the Due Process Clause to restrict state court jurisdiction, see Patrick J. Borchers, *The Death of the Constitutional Law of Personal Jurisdiction: From* Pennoyer *to* Burnham *and Back Again*, 24 U.C. DAVIS L. REV. 19 (1990).

208. In Sun Oil Co. v. Wortman, 486 U.S. 717, 108 S. Ct. 2117, 100 L. Ed. 2d 743 (1988), a majority of the Court, in an opinion by Justice Scalia, validated a traditional conflict-of-laws rule on the grounds that it was accepted at the time the Fourteenth Amendment was adopted and its acceptance had continued into the present. However, in Pacific Mutual Life Insurance Co. v. Haslip, 499 U.S. 1, 111 S. Ct. 1032, 113 L. Ed. 2d 1 (1991), the Court, in validating the common-law method of assessing punitive damages, gave the historical pedigree of the rule substantial weight, but refused to consider it conclusive. Justice Scalia protested this methodology. *See id.* at 24-40, 111 S. Ct. at 1046-54, 113 L. Ed. 2d at 24-34 (Scalia, J., concurring). *Haslip* was decided after *Burnham* and may indicate that Justice Scalia's opinion will not command a majority of the Court in the future.

would remain in doubt. The main problem in that event would be sorting out how the different Justices would choose to apply the minimum contacts test to particular facts—a daunting task, given that the concurring Justices in *Burnham* were willing to validate transient presence under the test.

If Justice Scalia's position ultimately prevails, there would be different problems. The question in each instance would be (1) whether a traditional ground of jurisdiction existed that was sufficiently accepted at the time the Due Process Clause was formed and (2) whether the states have continued to follow that ground. "Technical domicile"[209] might survive under this test, for example, if it is found that domicile was recognized as a basis of jurisdiction by a sufficient number of states at the time the Fourteenth Amendment was ratified for it to be considered a valid historical basis of asserting jurisdiction—as long as, of course, the states have continued to recognize it. On the other hand, technical domicile does involve an attempt to acquire jurisdiction over a defendant who is absent from the state, a basis that Justice Scalia relied on for distinguishing *Shaffer* from *Burnham*. Furthermore, the Court's decisions recognizing domicile as a valid basis of jurisdiction were not decided until after the Fourteenth Amendment was ratified,[210] giving rise to the possibility that the rule's historical pedigree would not be found adequate under Justice Scalia's approach.[211]

SECTION F. THE REACTION OF THE STATES TO THE MINIMUM CONTACTS TEST: LONG-ARM STATUTES

After *International Shoe* was decided, the states reacted to the new minimum contacts jurisprudence by enacting statutes to extend the reach of their jurisdiction over nonresidents. Just as the "long-arm" statutes enacted by the states between *Pennoyer* and *International Shoe* had relied for their structure on the territorial theories of the former case—notably on the implied consent theory—so did the statutes enacted after *International Shoe* begin to generalize the grounds upon which the states could assert jurisdiction over nonresident defendants under the minimum contacts theory. The first of these generalized long-arm statutes was enacted by Illinois in 1955. The Illinois Act provided that the courts of the state could assert jurisdiction over a nonresident defendant on a "cause of action" arising from any one of four kinds of acts performed in the

---

209. "Technical domicile" is domicile that continues because the defendant has not acquired a new domicile, even though the defendant has left the domiciliary state and no longer has substantial connections with the state. Technical domicile should be distinguished from domicile that is accompanied by substantial connections with the state, such as when the defendant continues to reside in the domiciliary state.

210. *See* section B(4) ("In Personam Jurisdiction: Domicile") *supra*.

211. Similarly, if a state attempted to depart from the restrictive in rem principles of jurisdiction discussed in section B(1)*(b) supra*, it might be considered a novel assertion of personal jurisdiction to be judged by reference to the minimum contacts test assuming that, as "subject-matter jurisdiction" limits, these restrictions were incorporated into the Due Process Clause by *Pennoyer*. Thus, despite the long historical pedigree of the restrictions, they could be supplanted by a minimum contacts analysis. On the other hand, in rem restrictions might be considered valid, traditional bases upon which the situs state might refuse to enforce the judgment of another state directly affecting the title to land.

state: (1) transacting any business within the state; (2) committing a tortious act within the state; (3) owning, using, or possessing any real estate in the state; or (4) contracting to insure any person, property or risk located within the state at the time of the contract was made.[212] When jurisdiction was based on this Act, only causes of action enumerated in the statute could be asserted against the defendant in the action.[213] The Act authorized process to be served on the defendant personally outside the state.[214]

In addition to the issues of constitutional validity that arise whenever any long-arm statute is applied to the facts of a specific case, there also exist questions of statutory applicability that must be worked out on a case-by-case basis. The Illinois statute was designed to extend the reach of Illinois state-court jurisdiction to the limits permitted by *International Shoe*.[215] However, at the time the Illinois statute was enacted, the limited experience with the minimum contacts test had not necessarily revealed the full range of situations in which the Due Process Clause would permit a state to exercise jurisdiction. As a result, the courts had to interpret the statutory language based on what they perceived *International Shoe* would permit.

The statutory requirement that the "commission of a tortious act [be] within this state" presented one such interpretative problem. In *Gray v. American Radiator & Standard Sanitary Corp.*,[216] a hot water heater had been purchased in the ordinary course of commerce. The hot water heater exploded in Illinois. The injured plaintiff commenced an action in Illinois against the Pennsylvania manufacturer of the hot water heater and one of its suppliers. The plaintiff alleged that the supplier negligently constructed the safety valve of the heater in Ohio and sold it to the manufacturer. The supplier objected to jurisdiction on the ground that it had not committed a tortious act within the state of Illinois. The supplier claimed that whatever negligent acts were performed by it occurred in Ohio. In response, the Illinois Supreme Court relied on the legislative intent as well as the general purpose and effect of the long-arm statute rather than the "technicalities" of the definition of a "tortious act." The court concluded that the alleged negligence in manufacturing could not be separated from the resulting injury in Illinois. Thus, a tortious act had been committed within Illinois within the meaning of the statute.[217]

---

212. 1955 Ill. Laws 2283, § 1. The current version of this statute is found in ILL. COMP. STAT. ANN. ch. 735, § 5/2-209 (West 1992).

213. 1955 Ill. Laws 2283, § 3.

214. *Id.* § 2.

215. *See* Baltimore & Ohio R.R. v. Mosele, 67 Ill. 2d 321, 328, 368 N.E.2d 88, 91 (1977) (Illinois expanded the in personam jurisdiction of its courts to what was in 1955 understood to be the limits permitted under the Due Process Clause of the Fourteenth Amendment).

216. 22 Ill. 2d 432, 176 N.E.2d 761 (1961).

217. *Id.* at 435-36, 176 N.E.2d at 762-63; *see also* Vlasak v. Rapid Collection Sys., Inc., 962 F. Supp. 1096 (N.D. Ill. 1997) (telephone calls and letters from Arizona to Illinois that violated Fair Debt Collections Practices Act constituted commission of a "tortious act" in Illinois); Rivera v. Bank One, 145 F.R.D. 614, 619-21 (D.P.R. 1993) (Puerto Rican long-arm statute authorizing jurisdiction over a person who "[p]articipated in tortious acts within Puerto Rico" interpreted to apply to defendant who committed tortious acts outside Puerto Rico that had an effect in the jurisdiction); Green v. USF & G Corp., 772 F. Supp. 1258 (S.D. Fla. 1991) (Florida long-arm statute authorizing jurisdiction over a defendant who commits tortious acts within the state applicable to

In *Gray*, the court held that a reasonable inference could be drawn from the supplier's general commercial transactions that the substantial use and consumption of its valves in Illinois satisfied *International Shoe's* requirement of "minimum contacts" with the state. When the defendant had made no sales or deliveries in the state and had no agent or office there, the complaint had to show affirmatively that the defendant's distribution pattern or volume was such that a reasonable inference could be drawn that the defendant had chosen to operate in national channels of commerce.[218] However, once a showing of contact had been made and a cause of action in tort had been stated in the complaint, the defendant could not demand proof of all the facts necessary to establish ultimate liability in tort in order for the court to have jurisdiction. Otherwise, it was feared, a preliminary hearing on jurisdictional issues would involve a "full-dress" trial on the merits.[219]

Seven years after the enactment of the Illinois long-arm statute, the National Conference of Commissioners on Uniform State Laws approved a Uniform Long-Arm Act. Several states have adopted this Uniform Act. The Act attempts to solve some of the problems of interpretation involved in the Illinois statute. Section 1.03 provided:

(a) A court may exercise personal jurisdiction over a person, who acts directly or by an agent, as to a [cause of action] [claim for relief] arising from the person's

(1) transacting any business in this state;

(2) contracting to supply services or things in this state;

(3) causing [a] tortious injury by an act or omission in this state;

(4) causing [a] tortious injury in this state by an act or omission outside this state if he regularly does or solicits business, or engages in any other persistent course of conduct, or derives substantial revenue from goods used or consumed or services rendered, in this state; [or]

(5) having an interest in, using, or possessing real property in this state [; or

(6) contracting to insure any person, property, or risk located within this state at the time of contracting].[220]

Subsections (a)(3) and (4) of this Act separate tortious acts committed entirely within the state from tortious acts committed outside the state that have an impact within the state. The latter situations require greater activity on the part of the defendant within the state to permit an assertion of jurisdiction. Obviously,

---

defendant who made slanderous remarks over the telephone in Maryland to a person in Florida). Not all "tortious act" provisions have been given the broad interpretation found in *Gray* and the cases cited above in this note. *See* Bensusan Restaurant Corp. v. King, 126 F.3d 25 (2d Cir. 1997) (interpreting, on the basis of prior authority, New York's tortious act provision to require physical activities in New York by defendant).

218. Keckler v. Brookwood Country Club, 248 F. Supp. 645 (N.D. Ill. 1965).

219. Nelson v. Miller, 11 Ill. 2d 378, 143 N.E.2d 673 (1957).

220. UNIF. INTERSTATE & INTERNATIONAL PROCEDURE ACT § 1.03 (1962), 13 U.L.A. 361-62 (1986) (Personal Jurisdiction Based upon Conduct); *see also* N.Y. C.P.L.R. § 302 (Consol. 1990).

the Act was drafted under the impression that tortious acts committed outside the state would require greater contact to satisfy the *International Shoe* test.[221]

In contrast to the approach of the Illinois and Uniform Acts, which establish specific categories of cases over which the state's courts may exercise jurisdiction, California has simply authorized its courts to "exercise jurisdiction on any basis not inconsistent with the Constitution of this state or of the United States."[222] California also provides for service of process outside the state in cases in which jurisdiction is asserted pursuant to this statute.[223] A provision like the California statute eliminates questions of statutory construction that may arise under the Illinois and Uniform Acts. The inquiry in each case becomes whether an assertion of jurisdiction by the state satisfies the minimum contacts test.[224]

These approaches illustrate the most common ways in which the states have responded to the *International Shoe* test. However, they do not exhaust the responses of the states to long-arm jurisdiction. There are many variations. Cases presenting specific kinds of substantive problems are often treated individually by the state legislatures rather than being left to resolution under a general long-arm statute. Therefore, the statutes of each state must be consulted to determine how personal jurisdiction issues have been addressed.

Illustration 3-21. *B*, a citizen of State *Y*, contracted with *A*, a citizen of State *X*, to purchase four boat engines from *A*. The engines were to be shipped by *A* from State *X* to *B* in State *Y*. *A* subsequently sued *B* in a state court of State *X*. *A* alleged that *B* had failed to fulfill *B's* obligations under the contract. *B* was served with process under a provision of the State *X* long-arm statute, which authorized personal jurisdiction over nonresidents in any action which "[r]elates to goods, documents of title, or other things of value shipped from this state by the plaintiff to the defendant on the defendant's order or direction." In *Riggs Marine Service, Inc. v. McCann*,[225] the court held that the contract between *A* and *B* was precisely the kind of transaction covered by the long-arm statute.

* * * * *

In addition, the advent of modern long-arm statutes that generalize the bases for asserting jurisdiction over nonresident defendants has not necessarily eliminated the possibility of asserting jurisdiction under one of the pre-*International Shoe* methods. For example, in *State ex rel. K-Mart Corp. v. Holliger*,[226]

---

221. *But cf.* Crane v. Carr, 814 F.2d 758, 762 (D.C. Cir. 1987) (Ginsburg, Cir. J.) (subsection (a)(4) may stop short of outer constitutional limits); Fogle v. Ramsey Winch Co., 774 F. Supp. 19, 23 (D.D.C. 1991) (subsection (a)(4) is more restrictive than the Due Process Clause). *See also* Bensusan Restaurant Corp. v. King, 126 F.3d 25 (2d Cir. 1999) (interpreting an identical provision of New York's long-arm statute as inapplicable to actions by a Missouri defendant that may have had an impact in New York because the Missouri defendant did not apparently derive substantial revenue from interstate commerce).

222. CAL. CIV. PROC. CODE § 410.10 (West 1973).

223. *See* CAL. CIV. PROC. CODE § 415.40 (West Supp. 1999).

224. However, the U.S. Supreme Court has indicated that a particularized statutory declaration of interest may strengthen the case for jurisdiction. *See, e.g.,* Keeton v. Hustler Magazine, Inc., 465 U.S. 770, 775-77, 104 S. Ct. 1473, 1479, 79 L. Ed. 2d 790, 798-99 (1984); Shaffer v. Heitner, 433 U.S. 186, 214-15, 97 S. Ct. 2569, 2585, 53 L. Ed. 2d 683, 704 (1977); *see* section G(2)*(b)(iv)* ("The Reasonableness Test") *infra.*

225. 160 Wis. 2d 846, 467 N.W.2d 155 (1991).

226. 986 S.W.2d 165 (Mo. 1999).

the defendant was served in Missouri through its registered agent there. The defendant conceded that it was doing substantial and continuous business in the state. However, the defendant objected to personal jurisdiction on the ground that the action did not fit within any of the categories in the Missouri long-arm statute. The Missouri Supreme Court rejected this argument. The court held that the long-arm statute applied only when service outside the state was necessary.[227] The enactment of the long-arm statute did not preclude assertion of jurisdiction under one of the pre-*International Shoe* forms, as long as the minimum contacts test was satisfied.[228]

SECTION G. THE CONTENT OF THE MINIMUM CONTACTS TEST

Since *International Shoe*, the U.S. Supreme Court has decided a significant number of cases that attempt to define the content of the minimum contacts test. The approach of these cases has not always been consistent, as the discussion of the *Shaffer* and *Burnham* cases in section E, above, has indicated. However, the decisions do articulate the factors that will determine the constitutionality of a state's assertion of jurisdiction over nonresidents under the minimum contacts test. This section examines the content of the minimum contacts test as it has evolved since *International Shoe*. The next section then examines the application of the test to specific categories of cases.

1. Cases to Which the Minimum Contacts Test Applies

Because of the *Burnham* decision, discussed in section E, above, evaluations of a state's assertion of jurisdiction over a nonresident must first consider whether the state is applying a traditional or novel rule of personal jurisdiction. If the state is applying a traditional rule, one must consider whether, under Justice Scalia's opinion in *Burnham*, the historical pedigree of the rule and its continuing acceptance by the states are sufficient to make it constitutional.[229] However, because there was no majority opinion in *Burnham*, it cannot be certain that Justice Scalia's test will be used to determine the validity of even traditional rules in the future. Consequently, until the Court provides further guidance on this question, an alternative analysis under the minimum contacts test must be employed to determine whether the assertion of jurisdiction will satisfy that test. If the assertion passes muster under both the historical and minimum contacts tests, there is obviously no difficulty. However, if the tests point in different directions on the constitutional issue, the Court will have to make a difficult decision about which test is controlling.

---

227. *See id.* at 168.

228. *See id.* at 168-69.

229. *See* William M. Richman, *Understanding Personal Jurisdiction*, 25 ARIZ. ST. L.J. 599, 638, 641 (1993).

Fortunately, the circumstances in which *Burnham* is likely to cause difficulties are few. *Burnham* did not purport to disturb *Shaffer's* holding that quasi in rem jurisdiction is unconstitutional.[230] Furthermore, *Burnham* itself upheld the constitutionality of transient presence jurisdiction under both the historical and minimum contacts tests. *Shaffer* stated that the state where property is located will have sufficient contacts to adjudicate claims directly involving the property.[231] However, this statement must be qualified because of the problem raised by the *Abernathy* case, discussed in section E(1), above: if property is brought within the state without the consent of the claimants to the property, it is unclear whether the state will have jurisdiction to adjudicate claims to the property consistent with due process.

The only traditional rules upon which the Court has not generally pronounced are consent, domicile, and the rule restricting states from directly affecting the title to land located in other states. Undoubtedly, the Court would not constitutionally invalidate consent as a basis of jurisdiction under any test—whether it is true consent or consent by appearance or waiver.[232] *Shaffer* preserved domicile of the plaintiff in ex parte divorce actions from attack under the minimum contacts test. For the reasons given in section E(1), above, this conclusion does not seem to be vulnerable to reversal. Domicile of the defendant will never be an unconstitutional basis for asserting jurisdiction if the defendant actually resides in the state of domicile or has other substantial relations with the state. The problem case will be that of the nonresident domiciliary who no longer has any substantial contacts with the state, but who has not acquired a domicile in another state or nation. Such cases of "technical domicile" will be rare, if not nonexistent. Finally, the restriction on the power of states to directly affect the title to land located in other states will rarely be a problem either. Venue rules in the forum state will often preclude the state from adjudicating such actions apart from constitutional restrictions.[233] State forum non conveniens doctrines may also produce the dismissal of many such cases. Consequently, while the distinction between traditional and novel assertions of jurisdiction must be addressed when relevant, it seems unlikely to be of great significance in the jurisprudence of state-court jurisdiction.

---

230. In a footnote, Justice Scalia suggested that *Shaffer* might be distinguished from other quasi in rem cases because the Delaware statute declaring the situs of corporate stock to be in the state of incorporation was unique. This observation may indicate that some members of the Court are prepared to uphold other kinds of quasi in rem jurisdiction that are more "traditional." *See Burnham*, 495 U.S. at 622, n.4, 110 S. Ct. at 2116, n.4, 109 L. Ed. 2d at 646, n.4. In addition, Justice Stevens had indicated in *Shaffer* that the decision should not be read to invalidate quasi in rem jurisdiction when real estate was the property involved. *See Shaffer*, 433 U.S. at 218, 97 S. Ct. at 2587, 53 L. Ed. 2d at 706 (Stevens, J., concurring).

231. *See Shaffer*, 433 U.S. at 207-08, 97 S. Ct. at 2581-82, 53 L. Ed. 2d at 699-700.

232. The Court's recent decisions on the validity of jurisdiction acquired under forum selection clauses suggest that something less than true consent will suffice to satisfy constitutional standards. *See* Chapter 4(C)(12) ("Raising and Waiving Federal Venue Objections") *infra*.

233. *See* Chapter 4(A) *infra* (discussing the local action rule).

2. General and Specific Jurisdiction

In a path-breaking article, Professors Von Mehren and Trautman argued that the traditional terminology used to discuss multistate personal jurisdiction was not helpful.[234] They recommended that the expression ''jurisdiction to adjudicate'' be substituted for the traditional categories of jurisdiction.[235] They suggested the term ''specific jurisdiction'' to describe power to adjudicate issues arising out of ''the very controversy that establishes jurisdiction to adjudicate.''[236] They suggested the term ''general jurisdiction'' to describe ''power to adjudicate any kind of controversy when jurisdiction is based on relationships, direct or indirect, between the forum and the person or persons whose legal rights are to be affected.''[237] U.S. Supreme Court decisions have adopted this terminology.[238]

The distinction between general and specific jurisdiction must be addressed at the threshold of the minimum contacts analysis because the validity of each kind of jurisdiction is determined differently under the Supreme Court's decisions. Subsection *(a)* will discuss general jurisdiction and the standards that apply to determine its validity. Subsection *(b)* will similarly discuss specific jurisdiction. Subsection *(c)* will examine recent decisions indicating confusion about the distinction between general and specific jurisdictions. It will also examine cases suggesting that the general and specific jurisdiction doctrines may be converging. Subsection *(d)* will then question why the two kinds of jurisdiction should be analyzed differently and suggest a common test for both.

---

234. *See* Arthur T. Von Mehren & Donald T. Trautman, *Jurisdiction to Adjudicate: A Suggested Analysis*, 79 HARV. L. REV. 1121, 1135 (1966).

235. *See id.* at 1135-36.

236. *See id.* at 1136.

237. *See id.*

238. The first decision to adopt the terminology explicitly was Helicopteros Nacionales de Colombia, S.A. v. Hall, 466 U.S. 408, 414 nn.8-9, 104 S. Ct. 1868, 1872 nn.8-9, 80 L. Ed. 2d 404, 411 nn.8-9 (1984). The Court's definition of the terms specific and general jurisdiction was somewhat different than that of Professors Von Mehren and Trautman. The Court defined specific jurisdiction as an exercise of personal jurisdiction ''over a defendant in a suit arising out of or related to the defendant's contacts with the forum.'' *Id.* at n.8, 104 S. Ct. at 1872 n.8, 80 L. Ed. 2d at 411 n.8. It defined general jurisdiction as the exercise of jurisdiction ''over a defendant in a suit not arising out of or related to the defendant's contacts with the forum.'' *Id.* at n.9, 104 S. Ct. at 1872 n.9, 80 L. Ed. 2d at 411 n.9. *Hall* involved an attempt by Texas to exercise general jurisdiction because the assertion of jurisdiction was to adjudicate a claim arising out of events that occurred outside Texas. Thus, in the Court's definition, the suit did not arise out of the defendant's contacts with Texas, but with the defendant's contacts with Peru. In Von Mehren and Trautman's definition, Texas was attempting to assert jurisdiction based on the relationship between the defendant and the state, not the relationship between the controversy and the state. *Hall* is discussed in the text *infra*. For recent commentary on the scope of general and specific jurisdiction, see Robert Banks, Jr., *The Future of General Jurisdiction in Tennessee*, 27 U. MEM. L. REV. 559 (1997); Mary Twitchell, *The Myth of General Jurisdiction*, 101 HARV. L. REV. 610 (1988); Lea Brilmayer, *Related Contacts and Personal Jurisdiction*, 101 HARV. L. REV. 1444 (1988); Mary Twitchell, *A Rejoinder to Professor Brilmayer*, 101 HARV. L. REV. 1465 (1988).

(a) General Jurisdiction

The U.S. Supreme Court has decided only two cases involving general jurisdiction since *International Shoe*. The first, *Perkins v. Benguet Consolidated Mining Co.*,[239] was decided before the Court had divided the universe under the Due Process Clause into "general" and "specific" jurisdiction cases. The second, *Helicopteros Nacionales de Colombia, S.A. v. Hall*,[240] was the decision

---

239. 342 U.S. 437, 72 S. Ct. 413, 96 L. Ed. 485 (1952). In *Perkins*, the plaintiff sued a Philippine corporation in an Ohio state court. The plaintiff sought to recover $68,400 in dividends and $2,500,000 in damages due to the failure of the corporation to issue certain shares of stock to her. The corporation was served with process by service of a summons on its president in Ohio. The U.S. Supreme Court held that "no requirement of federal due process . . . either *prohibits* Ohio from opening its courts to the cause of action . . . presented or *compels* Ohio to do so." 342 U.S at 446, 72 S. Ct. at 418, 96 L. Ed. at 493. The Court characterized the activities of the corporation in Ohio as "continuous and systematic." *See id.* at 445, 72 S. Ct. at 418, 96 L. Ed. at 492. This level of activities made it valid under the minimum contacts test for Ohio to assert jurisdiction over the corporation, even though the claim against the corporation did not arise out of the corporation's activities within the state. *See id.* at 445-46, 72 S. Ct. at 418, 96 L. Ed. at 492-93; *see also id.* at 447-48, 72 S. Ct. at 419-20, 96 L. Ed. at 493-94 (describing the activities of the corporation within Ohio). *International Shoe* had recognized that foreign corporations could be sued on claims arising outside the state if the activities of the corporations were "continuous" and sufficiently "substantial." *See International Shoe*, 326 U.S. at 318, 66 S. Ct. at 159, 90 L. Ed. at 103. Nothing in the Court's opinion in *International Shoe* had cast doubt on the states' continuing ability to summon foreign corporations to defend suits on this basis. *See* Philip B. Kurland, *The Supreme Court, the Due Process Clause, and the In Personam Jurisdiction of State Courts—From* Pennoyer *to* Denckla: *A Review*, 25 U. CHI. L. REV. 569, 601 (1958). Therefore, it was unsurprising to find jurisdiction sustained in *Perkins*, given the substantial nature of the corporate activity in Ohio. However, the Court's application of the minimum contacts test to the facts in *Perkins* did nothing to clarify how the test would be applied in future cases. After indicating that corporations conducting systematic and continuous activities within a state could be sued there on claims arising outside the state, the Court simply recited the activities of the defendant in *Perkins* and stated that they were sufficient to sustain an assertion of jurisdiction against a due process challenge. *See id.* at 447-48, 72 S. Ct. at 419-20, 96 L. Ed. at 493-94. The Court gave no indication how low the level of corporate activity might fall before an exercise of jurisdiction to adjudicate a claim arising outside the state would be considered invalid.

240. 466 U.S. 408, 104 S. Ct. 1868, 80 L. Ed. 2d 404 (1984). *Hall* was a wrongful death action brought in a Texas state court. Hall sued Helicol, Bell Helicopter, and Consorcio to recover for the death of her husband that occurred in a helicopter crash in the Peruvian jungle. Helicol was a Colombian corporation with its principal place of business in Bogota, Colombia. Helicol provided helicopter transportation for oil and construction companies in South America. It purchased $4,000,000 worth of helicopters, spare parts, and accessories from Bell Helicopter in Fort Worth, Texas from 1970-77. During the same period, its pilots were also trained by Bell in Fort Worth and ferried helicopters from Fort Worth to Colombia. Bell also trained Helicol management and maintenance personnel from 1970-77. Consorcio was the Peruvian alter-ego of a joint venture among Williams International Sudamericana, Ltd., a Delaware Corporation, Sedco Construction Corporation, a Texas corporation, and Horn International, Inc., a Texas corporation. The purpose of the joint venture was to construct an oil pipeline from the interior of Peru to the Pacific Ocean. Consorcio was formed because Peruvian law forbade construction of the pipeline by a non-Peruvian entity. Consorcio, in turn, contracted with Helicol to obtain helicopter transportation for the construction project. The claim arose when a helicopter owned by Helicol crashed in Peru, killing, among others, four United States citizens. None of the four was a citizen of Texas, though all were hired by Consorcio in Houston to work on the pipeline project. The claim asserted against Helicol was negligence in the form of pilot error. In addition to the contacts already mentioned, Helicol had sent its chief executive officer to Houston for a contract negotiating session with Consorcio and accepted payments into its New York and Florida bank accounts from Consorcio drawn upon Consorcio's Houston bank. Helicol challenged the jurisdiction of the Texas state courts, but its challenge was overruled at the trial-court level. A verdict was directed in favor of Bell Helicopter and Consorcio, but a general jury verdict of $1,141,200 was entered against Helicol. Consorcio also obtained judgment on a cross-claim against Helicol for $70,000. The Texas Supreme Court ultimately sustained jurisdiction over Helicol and affirmed, construing its long-arm statute to extend as far as due process permits. The U.S. Supreme Court granted certiorari and reversed. *See Hall*, 466 U.S. at 409-13, 104 S. Ct. at 1869-72, 80 L. Ed. 2d at 408-10. In evaluating the case, the Court placed primary emphasis in which the Court adopted the terms "general" and "specific" jurisdiction. Both cases applied the same test to determine the validity of an assertion of general jurisdiction–the "systematic and continuous contacts" test. Like *Perkins*, however, *Hall* provided little guidance about how to determine whether the level of contacts in a case is "systematic and continuous" or something less. All that is clear is that the systematic and continuous contacts test for general jurisdiction requires a higher overall level of contacts than the test for specific jurisdiction.

In both *Perkins* and *Hall*, the defendants were corporations. One question that arises after the *Burnham* decision discussed in section E(2), above, is whether the concept of general jurisdiction has any meaningful application to individual defendants. Justice Scalia's opinion in *Burnham* suggested that the systematic and continuous contacts test might be applicable only to corporate defendants.[241] It is difficult to see what purpose the rule serves in cases in which individual defendants are being sued on claims arising outside the state. Presumably individuals who are currently engaging in systematic activities within the state can easily be served personally inside the state while they are there conducting those activities. Personal service on an individual defendant in the state validly subjects the defendant to jurisdiction under the Due Process Clause without regard to the level of the defendant's activities within the state.[242]

The only situation in which the systematic-and-continuous-activities test might be relevant to suits against individuals is when an individual is alerted to the possibility of an action within the state and ceases the activities or otherwise remains outside the state. In that situation, the plaintiff would have to use a long-arm statute to serve the defendant, giving rise to a possible challenge on ground that the defendant's (former) activities are insufficient to justify suit on a claim arising outside the state.

However, it is unclear from the reported decisions whether general jurisdiction may be asserted over a defendant whose activities within the state have ceased by the time the action has been commenced. Furthermore, even if systematic and continuous contacts may be established by past activities, it is not clear how far in the past a court may reach to determine whether systematic and continuous activities exist. For example, in *Serafini v. Superior Court of El Dorado County*,[243] the California Court of Appeals held an assertion of general jurisdiction over an individual defendant invalid. The court's opinion linked the general jurisdiction concept as applied to both corporate and individual defendants

---

on two prior decisions: *Perkins* and *Rosenberg Bros. & Co. v. Curtis Brown Co.*, 260 U.S. 516, 43 S. Ct. 170, 67 L. Ed. 372 (1923), the latter of which antedated *International Shoe*. The Court first compared the defendant's contacts with those of the defendant in the *Perkins* case to determine whether the contacts in Hall were of the "systematic and continuous" sort that sustained jurisdiction in *Perkins*. The Court concluded that they were not. *See Hall*, 466 U.S. at 414-17, 104 S. Ct. at 1872-74, 80 L. Ed. 2d at 410-13. The Court relied on *Rosenberg* for the proposition that purchases and related trips are not sufficient to sustain jurisdiction to adjudicate an action based on a claim arising outside the state. *See id.* at 417-18, 104 S. Ct. at 1873-74, 80 L. Ed. 2d at 413.

241. *See Burnham*, 495 U.S. at 610 n.1, 110 S. Ct. at 2110 n.1, 109 L. Ed. 2d at 639 n.1.

242. Presumably, this will be true not only under Justice Scalia's historical analysis, but also under the minimum contacts test, which the concurring Justices found satisfied by the transient presence of the defendant in *Burnham*.

243. 68 Cal. App. 4th 70, 80 Cal. Rptr. 2d 159 (Cal. Ct. App. 1998).

to the old "presence" test of jurisdiction that was used prior to *International Shoe*.[244] Under that test, cessation of activities destroyed the basis for jurisdiction.[245] In this regard, *Serafini* is clearly wrong. Even though general jurisdiction was originally based on the theory that a corporation "doing business" in the state was "present" there,[246] that is no longer the basis of the doctrine after *International Shoe*. Today, general jurisdiction is justified on the basis that a defendant's systematic and continuous contacts with the state makes an assertion of jurisdiction "reasonable" in terms of the burdens imposed on the defendant by suit on an unrelated claim.[247]

A more justifiable approach was taken by the Second Circuit in *Metropolitan Life Insurance Co. v. Robertson-Ceco Corp.*[248] In *Met Life*, the court considered whether an assertion of general jurisdiction over a corporate defendant would be proper. Although the Second Circuit ultimately held that general jurisdiction would be improper on the facts of the case,[249] it indicated that the appropriate procedure was to "examine a defendant's contacts with the forum state over a period that is reasonable under the circumstances–up to and including the date the suit was filed–to assess whether they satisfy the 'continuous and systematic' standard."[250] Implicit in the court's holding is the notion that systematic and continuous contacts can be based on past activities that have now ceased, as long as they have not ceased so long in the past as to make an assertion of jurisdiction based on them "unreasonable."

(b) Specific Jurisdiction

(i) Claims Arising Out of or Related to the Defendant's Contacts with the State

In determining whether a case involves general or specific jurisdiction, it is obviously important to determine whether the defendant's actions in the state gave rise to the claim for relief. If the claim arose from the defendant's contacts with the state, the case is one of specific jurisdiction. However, even if the claim arose out of the defendant's activities in another state, the case still may be a specific jurisdiction case, which requires something less than "systematic and continuous" contacts by the defendant to justify the state's assertion of jurisdiction. A case may be deemed a specific jurisdiction case even though the claim technically arose elsewhere if the claim is "related to" the defendant's activities within the forum state.

---

244. *Id.* at 79-80, 80 Cal. Rptr. 2d at 165.
245. *See id.*
246. *See* section C(1) ("Jurisdiction over Corporations") *supra.*
247. *See* subsection *(c) infra.*
248. 84 F.3d 560 (2d Cir. 1996).
249. This aspect of the decision is discussed in subsection *(c) infra.*
250. 84 F.3d at 569-70. The court drew strength for its holding from the fact that the U.S. Supreme Court, in *Helicopteros*, had evaluated the defendant's contacts over a seven-year period. *See id.* at 569.

The Court originally suggested in *Hall* that there might be a distinction drawn between controversies that arise out of the defendant's contacts with the state and controversies that are merely related to the defendant's contacts with the state.[251] However, the Court refused to address the distinction because it had not been raised or briefed in the case.[252] In a decision after *Hall*, the Court stated that "specific jurisdiction" involves "injuries that 'arise out of or relate to' " the defendant's activities within the forum state,[253] while general jurisdiction involves an exercise of "personal jurisdiction over a defendant in a suit not arising out of or related to the defendant's contacts with the forum."[254] This statement indicates that a claim arising out of the defendant's activities in another state but related to the activities in the forum state will indeed present a case of specific jurisdiction. As yet, the Court has not defined what it means for a claim to be "related to" the defendant's contacts with the forum.

A proper determination of when a claim is "related to" the defendant's contacts with the forum can only be made in conjunction with the test employed by the Court for specific jurisdiction and the purposes of that test. The specific jurisdiction test will be discussed fully in subsections *(b)(ii)-(iv)*, below. However, only the first step in the specific jurisdiction test appears to be relevant to the question whether a claim arising outside the forum state should be considered "related to" the defendant's contacts with the forum. The Supreme Court has indicated that the first step in analyzing specific jurisdiction is to determine whether the defendant's contacts with the state have been "purposeful."[255] The requirement of purposeful contacts is designed to fulfill the objective of the Due Process Clause. That objective is to protect the defendant's individual liberty

---

251. This distinction was initially raised by Justice Brennan in dissent and then answered by the majority. Justice Brennan objected to the majority's refusal "to consider any distinction between controversies that 'relate to' a defendant's contacts with the forum and causes of action that 'arise out of' such contacts . . . ." *Hall*, 466 U.S at 420, 104 S. Ct. at 1875, 80 L. Ed. 2d at 415 (Brennan, J., dissenting). Justice Brennan was actually objecting to the implication, which he saw in the majority opinion, that a distinction might be drawn between controversies "related to" the defendant's contacts with the state and causes of action "arising out" of the defendant's contacts with the state. His fear was that the Court would approve of specific jurisdiction only in cases in which the controversy arose out of the defendant's contacts with the state and would require the level of contacts necessary to sustain *general* jurisdiction in cases in which the controversy was only "related to" the defendant's contacts with the state. *See id.* Justice Brennan viewed Helicol's contacts with Texas to be related to its activities within the state because the plaintiff claimed that Helicol was legally responsible for the pilot's negligence, and Helicol had negotiated the contract to provide transportation services in Texas, had purchased the helicopter involved in the crash in Texas, and had the pilot trained in Texas. *See id.* at 425-26, 104 S. Ct. at 1877-78, 80 L. Ed. 2d at 418-19. To Justice Brennan, these factors made the Texas contacts directly related to the negligence that caused the accident and also should have made it foreseeable to Helicol that it could be sued in Texas. *See id.* at 426, 104 S. Ct. at 1878, 80 L. Ed. 2d at 418-19.

252. Thus, the Court withheld decision on whether the expressions "arising out of" and "related to" describe different connections between the claim and the state. It also reserved judgment on what kind of relationship between the defendant and the state would determine whether either connection exists. Likewise, the Court refused to determine whether cases involving claims "related to" the defendant's contacts with the state should be analyzed as specific or general jurisdiction cases, assuming that "arising out of" and "related to" describe different relationships with the state. *Id.* at 415-16 n.10, 104 S. Ct. at 1872-73 n.10, 80 L. Ed. 2d at 411-12 n.10.

253. Burger King Corp. v. Rudzewicz, 471 U.S. 462, 472, 105 S. Ct. 2174, 2182, 85 L. Ed. 2d 528, 540-41 (1985).

254. *Id.* at 473, n.15, 105 S. Ct. at 2182, n.15, 85 L. Ed. 2d at 541, n.15.

255. *See id.* at 471-72, 105 S. Ct. at 2181-82, 85 L. Ed. 2d at 540.

interest by assuring that the defendant has fair warning that the activity being conducted within the state can subject the defendant to suit there. This fair warning gives the legal system a degree of predictability that allows potential defendants to structure their activity with some minimum assurance as to where it may subject them to suit. Defendants possessing this knowledge can protect themselves by (1) ceasing the jurisdiction-producing activity, or (2) if this is not possible, taking steps such as purchasing insurance to defray the burdens of suit that the activity may produce.[256]

Under the purposeful contacts step, the most important factor in determining whether a claim is "related to" the defendant's activities within the forum state is the notice-giving quality of the activities. If the activities are such that the defendant can expect lawsuits within the forum based on its activities, and if preparation for the lawsuits that might arise from the defendant's forum activity would also protect the defendant from lawsuits based on the claim actually sued on, the claim should be considered "related to" the defendant's contacts with the state. On the other hand, if the defendant's activities in the forum state would not enable the defendant to protect against an action brought by the plaintiff on a claim arising elsewhere, the claim should be considered "unrelated to" the defendant's contacts with the forum. Under the latter circumstances, the assertion of jurisdiction should be considered general, with the corresponding necessity that a higher level of contacts with the state should be required to satisfy due process.

With this understanding of when a claim should be considered "related to" the defendant's contacts with the state, it is possible to make some critical judgments about the kinds of facts that will produce a specific jurisdiction case when the claim arises outside the forum state. In his dissent in *Hall*, Justice Brennan argued that a claim should be considered "related to" the defendant's activities within the state when the defendant has engaged in some acts within the state in preparation for later activities outside the state that give rise to the claim for relief. Under these circumstances, the state where the preparatory acts occurred could validly assert jurisdiction to adjudicate the claim, even if none of the preparatory acts made up an element of the claim.[257]

The problem with this position is that if the activity being conducted by the defendant in the state is not of the sort that would give rise to some kind of liability, the activity may not give sufficient notice to the defendant to allow the defendant to defray the burdens of a suit within the state. Therefore, if the goal of the purposeful contacts step in the jurisdictional test is to be fulfilled, "related to" must be given a meaning that will allow the defendant to avoid or defray the

---

256. *See id.* at 471-76, 105 S. Ct. at 2181-84, 85 L. Ed. 2d at 540-43.

257. *See Hall*, 466 U.S. at 427, 104 S. Ct. at 1879, 80 L. Ed. 2d at 419. The quoted passage thus argues that specific jurisdiction ought to be valid based on nonliability-producing acts of the sort that are connected with the liability-producing acts that occur outside the state in a rather loose chain of events.

burdens of suit within the state. Thus, the defendant's activities in the forum will normally have to be of a liability-producing sort.[258]

The most likely situation in which a claim can properly be considered related to the defendant's contacts with the state is when the defendant is engaging in activity within the forum that is similar or identical to liability-producing conduct that the defendant conducts elsewhere. The conduct within the state may be of the sort that should alert the defendant to the possibility of a suit within the state based on the conduct. Furthermore, the defense of a suit based in the state arising from liability-producing activities occurring outside the state may be no more burdensome than defense of a suit arising from the defendant's conduct within the state. This will be so when, if the defendant had done those things necessary to protect itself against a suit in the state based on its conduct within the state, it would also have protected itself against the suit brought based on its conduct elsewhere.[259] Under these circumstances, an assertion of jurisdiction over the defendant to adjudicate the claim arising outside the state should be sustained.

Illustration 3-22. Assume that *B Co.* manufactures products *Q* and *R*, which are similar, but not identical. *A* purchases product *Q* in State *X*, where it explodes and injures *A*. Subsequently, *A* moves to State *Y*. *B* does not sell product *Q* in State *Y*, but does sell product *R* there. *A* sues *B* in State *Y* for the personal injuries that *A* received in State *X* due to the explosion of product *Q* in State *X*. As long as the court in State *Y* can see that the sales of product *R* in State *Y* should have led to preparations by *B* to defend the sort of suit brought by *A*, the court should sustain jurisdiction to adjudicate over *B*. Those preparations assure that *B* will not be deprived of an adequate opportunity to be heard in defense in State *Y*, even though *A's* claim is based entirely on events occurring in State *X*. *B's* preparations for potential lawsuits over sales of product *R* in *Y* should defray the burdens of *A's* suit based on the sales of product *Q* in State *X*.

* * * * *

---

258. In Aylward v. Fleet Bank, 122 F.3d 616 (8th Cir. 1997), the court held that the defendant's contacts were related to the activity about which the plaintiff was complaining; nevertheless, they were insufficient to establish jurisdiction because they were not liability producing. However, the court did not identify how the contacts were related in order to determine whether the case was one of specific or general jurisdiction; instead, they were part of a three-factor test for personal jurisdiction that did not correspond to the Supreme Court's decisions on specific and general jurisdiction. In addition, note that the court's conclusion does *not* conform to the analysis recommended in the text, *supra.* After the claim has arisen (by definition in another state), acts that are "related to" the claim will always be non-liability producing. The recommendation in the text is that, viewed as of the time the "related to" acts are conducted, they must have the possibility of producing liability of some sort. If they do, they may, depending on the circumstances, have the capacity to give the quality of warning to the defendant that due process requires.

259. Thus, Justice Brennan's argument in *Hall* should be effective only if it can be seen that Helicol's activity in Texas was of the sort that might produce liability in itself. If the activity was potentially liability producing, Helicol should have taken steps to defray the burdens of suit that the activity might produce. If the preparation for suit that Helicol should have undertaken would also have defrayed the burdens of the suit that was actually brought against Helicol, the claim should be considered "related to" Helicol's activity within the state, and Texas' assertion of jurisdiction should be considered specific. For example, if Helicol's activities in Texas would ordinarily lead a prudent business to purchase liability insurance providing for the defense of actions based on activities and events within and outside of Texas, the claim against Helicol, though technically arising in Peru, should be considered related to the Texas activities.

In administering the specific jurisdiction test, the courts must remember that the test is not simply designed to allow the defendant to defray the burdens of suit within a state, but also to avoid jurisdiction altogether by ceasing the jurisdiction-producing activity within the state. Thus, the mere fact that the defendant is conducting some kind of activity within the state should not lead to the conclusion that a claim arising outside the state is related to that activity—even if the activity within the forum would normally cause the defendant to take steps, such as purchasing insurance, that would defray the burdens of any kind of suit within the state. As long as the U.S. Supreme Court maintains that the defendant is entitled to avoid the jurisdiction of a state by ceasing jurisdiction-producing activities within the state, it will be necessary to inquire whether the defendant has reasonably taken steps to do so.[260]

Illustration 3-23. *A*, a State *X* corporation, and *B*, a Scottish corporation, had enjoyed a long-term relationship in which *A* sold engine parts from time to time to *B*. The parts were shipped from State *X* to wherever *B* wanted. *B* notified *A* that *C*, another Scottish corporation, had engines to sell that *A* might want to buy for resale in the U.S. *A* negotiated a contract with *C* to buy the engines. Subsequently, *A* and *B* agreed that *B* would obtain the engines from *C*, take certain parts off the engines that *B* wanted for itself, and then send the engines to *A* in State *Y*, where *A* intended to store them. During the shipments of the engines to State *Y*, two of the engines broke loose and were damaged, allegedly because *B* had improperly packed them. *A* sued *B* in State *X*. *A* asserted personal jurisdiction over *B* under the State *X* long-arm statute, which extends as far as the Due Process Clause permits. In *RAR, Inc. v. Turner Diesel, Ltd.*,[261] the Seventh Circuit held that *B*'s contacts with State *X* did not give rise to an assertion of specific jurisdiction. The court held that the prior contacts between the parties had nothing to do with the specific contract for shipment of the engines.[262] Because that specific contract had no relationship to State *X* other than the fact that it arose out of the general business relationship between the parties, it could not give rise to an assertion of specific jurisdiction.[263] The court was concerned that

---

260. For other discussion of the "related contacts" requirement including the application of a "but for" test and a test requiring the forum contacts to have "substantive relevance" to the cause of action, see Lea Brilmayer, *Related Contacts and Personal Jurisdiction*, 101 HARV. L. REV. 1444 (1988); Mark M. Maloney, Note, *Specific Jurisdiction and the "Arise from or Related to" Requirement . . . What Does It Mean?* 50 WASH. & LEE L. REV. 1265 (1993); Lea Brilmayer, *How Contacts Count: Due Process Limitations on State Court Jurisdiction*, 1980 SUP. CT. REV. 77; William M. Richman, *Casad's Jurisdiction in Civil Actions* (pt. 1), *A Sliding Scale to Supplement the Distinction Between General and Specific Jurisdiction* (pt. 2), 72 CAL. L. REV. 1328, 1338 (1984). In subsection *(d)*, below, the possibility of establishing a unified test for general and specific jurisdiction is discussed. Under a unified test, there will be some cases in which jurisdiction is valid, even though the defendant has done nothing at all within the state, because the defendant will not be able to demonstrate significantly greater burdens of suit within the state than exist elsewhere. Thus, the discussion in the text is premised on the retention by the U.S. Supreme Court of the existing analysis of state-court jurisdiction problems under the Due Process Clause.

261. 107 F.3d 1272 (7th Cir. 1997).

262. *See id.* at 1278-80.

263. *See id.* at 1278. The court stated:

Admittedly, [*A*'s] suit is, in a certain sense, related to [*B*'s] contacts with [State *X*], if only because [*B*] never would have come to handle the engines in Scotland had it not previously dealt with [*A*] in [State *X*]. We do not think, however, that using such a loose a less-restrictive standard for specific jurisdiction would leave potential defendants "uncertain as to what causal connections courts might draw between past conduct and current litigation."[264] To avoid unfair surprise, therefore, the court indicated that "[u]nless their contacts are continuous and systematic enough to rise to the level of general jurisdiction, individuals and corporations must be able to conduct interstate business confident that transactions in one context will not come back unexpectedly to haunt them in another."[265]

Illustration 3-24. In *Von Cos. v. Seabest Foods, Inc.*,[266] a franchiser sued a meat supplier in California state court for selling the franchiser contaminated meat. The meat supplier, in turn, asserted claims against nonresident franchisees. The supplier alleged that the nonresident franchisee's failure to cook the meat properly caused the plaintiff's harm. The California Supreme Court held that an assertion of specific jurisdiction over the franchisees was appropriate because the meat supplier's claim against them was related to their franchise arrangements with the California franchiser. The court held that it was sufficient that the plaintiff's claim had a substantial connection with the franchisee's business contacts with California. The court observed that specific jurisdiction would exist in a suit by the franchiser against the franchisee for any liability that the franchiser suffered as a result of the franchisee's undercooking of the meat because the franchise agreement provided that the franchisees would prepare their products in conformance with the franchiser's regulations. Failure to do so would produce a breach of contract claim that would arise from the franchisee's contacts with California.[267] Under these circumstances, the court was correct to conclude that the franchisee's contacts with California were sufficiently related to the meat

---

> causal connection between a suit and a defendant's forum contacts as the basis for personal jurisdiction comports with fair play and substantial justice. . . . [S]pecific jurisdiction is not appropriate "merely because a plaintiff's cause of action arose out of the general relationship between the parties; rather, the action must directly arise out of the specific contacts between the defendant and the forum state."

Id. at 1278 (citing and quoting Sawtelle v. Farrell, 70 F.3d 1381, 1389 (1st Cir. 1995)). Because the plaintiff did not allege systematic and continuous contacts with State *X*, the court held that it had "waived any general jurisdiction argument." 107 F.3d at 1277.

264. *Id.* at 1278-79.

265. *Id.* at 1278. The court's test, while not precisely like the test stated in the text, *supra*, is very close. Note that the nature of shipment contract between *A* and *B* was different than the nature of their prior contracts. Therefore, preparation to defray the burden of suits in State *X* on those prior contracts would not necessarily have defrayed the burdens of suit on the particular contract involved in the suit. Likewise, the court seems correct that the defendant should be able to avoid suit in State *X* unless its activities are so substantial as to alert it that it can be sued in State *X* for anything. *Cf.* African Dev. Co. v. Keene Eng'g, Inc., 963 F. Supp. 522 (E.D. Va. 1997) (specific jurisdiction proper over seller in breach of contract action, where seller shipped defective mining dredges from California to Virginia; court emphasized that, in addition to shipping the dredges into Virginia, the defendant had engaged in extensive telephone negotiations and had solicited the plaintiff's business by mailing catalogues to plaintiff). It has been suggested that provisions in long-arm statutes authorizing personal jurisdiction over defendants who cause tortious injury in a state by an act or omission outside the state if the defendants regularly do or solicit business in the state or engage in any other persistent cause of conduct in the state authorize a kind of hybrid jurisdiction that is neither "general" or "specific." *See* Linda Sandstrom Simard, *Hybrid Personal Jurisdiction: It's Not General Jurisdiction, or Specific Jurisdiction, But Is It Constitutional?* 48 CASE W. RES. L. REV. 559 (1998).

266. 14 Cal. 4th 434, 926 P.2d 1085, 58 Cal. Rptr. 899 (1996).

267. *See id.* at 451, 926 P.2d at 1095-96, 58 Cal. Rptr. 2d at 909; *see also* the discussion of *Burger King Corp. v. Rudzewicz*, in subsection *(ii)* and section H(2), *infra*.

supplier's claim against them to sustain an assertion of specific jurisdiction. The franchisee's could not claim a lack of fair warning that they might be sued in California based on their activities outside the state. Nor had they attempted to structure their activities so as to avoid the jurisdiction of California's courts on claims that would be virtually identical to the ones asserted against them.

(ii) The Two-Step Test for the Validity of Specific Jurisdiction

The test currently employed by the U.S. Supreme Court for specific jurisdiction is the product of an evolutionary process. During most of that process, the Court took a very loose, unstructured approach to determining whether "minimum contacts" existed between the defendant and the forum. In *Burger King Corp. v. Rudzewicz*,[268] the Court began to add structure to the specific jurisdiction part of the minimum contacts test.[269] Specifically, the Court stated that when the forum is asserting specific jurisdiction, a two step analysis is necessary to determine the validity of the jurisdictional assertion. As noted in subsection *(b)*(i), above, the first step in the analysis requires the court to determine whether the defendant has conducted purposeful activities within the forum state. Even if purposeful contacts are found present in a case, however, jurisdiction can still be defeated under the second step in the test.

The second step in the analysis involves a balancing test, referred to as the "reasonableness" test. This step requires the court to take into account (1) the burdens on the defendant of a suit within the forum (2) the forum state's interest in adjudicating the dispute, (3) the plaintiff's interest in obtaining convenient and effective relief, (4) the interstate judicial system's interest in the most efficient resolution of controversies, and (5) the shared interests of the several states in furthering fundamental substantive social policies.[270] However, the Court has made it clear that once purposeful contacts are established between the defendant and the forum, there will be a heavy burden imposed on the defendant to defeat

---

268. 471 U.S. 462, 105 S. Ct. 2174, 85 L. Ed. 2d 528 (1985).

269. The test articulated in *Burger King* was actually created in World-Wide Volkswagen Corp. v. Woodson, 444 U.S. 286, 100 S. Ct. 559, 62 L. Ed. 2d 490 (1980). However, after using the test in *World-Wide Volkswagen*, the Court's next several decisions did not apply it, but returned to the loose analysis of prior cases. *See* Calder v. Jones, 465 U.S. 783, 104 S. Ct. 1482, 79 L. Ed. 2d 804 (1984); Keeton v. Hustler Magazine, Inc., 465 U.S. 770, 104 S. Ct. 1473, 79 L. Ed. 2d 790 (1984); *see also* Rush v. Savchuk, 444 U.S. 320, 100 S. Ct. 571, 62 L. Ed. 2d 516 (1980) (decided the same day as *World-Wide Volkswagen*, in which the Court also did not apply the *World-Wide Volkswagen* test). For cases prior to *World-Wide Volkswagen* employing the unstructured approach to the minimum contacts test described in the text, see McGee v. International Life Ins. Co., 355 U.S. 220, 78 S. Ct. 199, 2 L. Ed. 2d 223 (1957); Mullane v. Central Hanover Bank & Trust Co., 339 U.S. 306, 70 S. Ct. 652, 94 L. Ed. 865 (1950). Three cases suggest a more structured approach to minimum contacts, although not the one ultimately adopted by the Court: *Burger King*, are Kulko v. Superior Court, 436 U.S. 84, 98 S. Ct. 1690, 56 L. Ed. 2d 132 (1978); Shaffer v. Heitner, 433 U.S. 186, 97 S. Ct. 2569, 53 L. Ed. 2d 683 (1977) (discussed above); and Hanson v. Denckla, 357 U.S. 235, 78 S. Ct. 1228, 2 L. Ed. 2d 1283 (1958). For a discussion of the analysis in *Kulko* and *Shaffer*, see Catherine T. Dixon, Note, *Constitutional Law—Jurisdiction—A New Minimum Contacts Analysis*—Kulko v. Superior Court, *98 S. Ct. 1690 (1978)*, 12 CREIGHTON L. REV. 905 (1979). The cases cited in this footnote are discussed *infra* in conjunction with specific topics in this section and in the next section on the application of the minimum contacts test to specific cases.

270. *See Burger King*, 471 U.S. at 476-77, 105 S. Ct. at 2184-85, 85 L. Ed. 2d at 543-44.

the state's assertion of jurisdiction with the reasonableness test.[271] In *Burger King*, the Court also indicated that the reasonableness test may be used "to establish the reasonableness of jurisdiction upon a lesser showing of minimum contacts than would otherwise be required."[272]

To understand the operation of the two-step test, it will be useful to examine each step and element of the test separately. Many of the Supreme Court cases applying the different elements of the test were decided before *Burger King*. However, these cases are still good authority for the purpose of determining how these elements should be applied today. After examining the operation of the test, an evaluation can then be made of whether the Court's approach to either general or specific jurisdiction cases properly addresses the concerns of the Due Process Clause of the Fourteenth Amendment.

(iii) *The Purposeful Contacts Test*

The first U.S. Supreme Court decision to emphasize that the defendant must engage in purposeful activities within the state was *Hanson v. Denckla*.[273] In *Hanson*, a Pennsylvania settlor established a trust in Delaware and later moved to Florida. The settlor executed a will in Florida and died there in 1952. However, at the time the will was executed, the settlor also executed two appointments from the Delaware trust to certain legatees. In the Florida proceeding brought to probate the settlor's will, the Florida court held these powers of appointment void. The U.S. Supreme Court held the Florida probate judgment invalid because the Florida court did not have personal jurisdiction over the Delaware trustee and certain other Delaware defendants consistent with the Due Process Clause. The Court stated that "[t]he unilateral activity of those who claim some relationship with a nonresident defendant cannot satisfy the requirement of contact with the forum [s]tate." Rather, the minimum required before a state might exercise jurisdiction over a nonresident defendant was that "there be some act by which the defendant purposefully avails itself of the privilege of conducting activities within the forum State, thus invoking the benefits and protections of its laws."[274] Because the Delaware defendants had been essentially passive in the relationships and transactions leading to the controversy, there was no activity that would satisfy the purposeful contact requirement.

In *Shaffer v. Heitner*,[275] the Court indicated that the purposeful contacts test was linked to the foreseeability of suit within the state. In addition, the Court indicated that a properly framed state long-arm statute might enhance that

---

271. *See id.* at 476-78, 105 S. Ct. at 2184-85, 85 L. Ed. 2d at 543-44.

272. *Id.* at 477, 105 S. Ct. at 2184, 85 L. Ed. 2d at 543-44. The Court cited Keeton v. Hustler Magazine, Inc., 465 U.S. 770, 104 S. Ct. 1473, 79 L. Ed. 2d 790 (1984) and McGee v. International Life Insurance Co., 355 U.S. 220, 78 S. Ct. 199, 2 L. Ed. 2d 223 (1957), in conjunction with this statement. As discussed in the next section, these cases both emphasized the state's interest in asserting jurisdiction, indicating that it will be the most important factor in enhancing jurisdiction under the *Burger King* analysis.

273. 357 U.S. 235, 78 S. Ct. 1228, 2 L. Ed. 2d 1283 (1958).

274. *Id.* at 253, 78 S. Ct. at 1239-40, 3 L. Ed. 2d at 1298.

275. 433 U.S. 186, 97 S. Ct. 2569, 53 L. Ed. 2d 683 (1977).

foreseeability.[276] The Court then observed that Delaware had not enacted a statute treating the acceptance of a directorship in a Delaware corporation as consent to jurisdiction in the state.[277] This statement suggested that a properly framed long-arm statute could, by alerting the defendants that their actions would subject them to suit within the state, satisfy the purposeful contact component of the Due Process Clause.[278]

In *World-Wide Volkswagen Corp. v. Woodson*,[279] the Court addressed the operation of the purposeful contacts test in the context of a products liability action. The issue before the Court was whether Oklahoma could properly exercise personal jurisdiction over a nonresident automobile retailer and its wholesale distributor whose only connection with the state was that an automobile sold in New York to New York residents became involved in an accident in Oklahoma. The Court held that the necessary purposeful contact was not present under these circumstances. The Court found that the dispute was based on one isolated occurrence, which fortuitously occurred in Oklahoma. It rejected the argument that because an automobile is mobile by its very design and purpose, it was "foreseeable" that it would cause injury in Oklahoma. Rather, the Court stated that foreseeability alone had never been sufficient to satisfy the Due Process Clause.[280] The kind of foreseeability that is relevant to the due process analysis is the kind which assures that "the defendant's conduct and connection with the forum State are such that he should reasonably anticipate being haled into court there."[281] This kind of foreseeability is important because it "gives a degree

---

276. In *Shaffer*, the Court held that Delaware could not assert personal jurisdiction over the nonresident directors and officers of a Delaware corporation in a shareholders' derivative action. Among other reasons, the Court stated that the defendants, who had no contacts with Delaware other than the acceptance of positions as officers and directors in the corporation, had not, by their actions, established the purposeful contacts with the state required by *Hanson*. See *Shaffer*, 433 U.S. at 216, 97 S. Ct. at 2586, 53 L. Ed. 2d at 705.

277. See *id.* at 416, 97 S. Ct at 2586, 53 L. Ed. 2d at 705. In addition, the Court stated that the absence of a specific expression of statutory interest on the part of Delaware in the kind of action brought in *Shaffer* rendered the state's interest in maintaining the action in Delaware weak. The state's interest factor is now employed in the second step of the due process analysis—the reasonableness test. This aspect of *Shaffer* is discussed in subsection *(iv) infra*.

278. This suggestion was promptly followed by the Delaware legislature. See DEL. CODE ANN. tit. 10, § 3114 (Supp. 1998) (effective Sept. 1, 1977). The constitutionality of the statute was upheld in Armstrong v. Pomerance, 423 A.2d 174, 176-79 (Del. 1980). See Susan Stuckert, Note, *A Constitutional Analysis of the New Delaware Director-Consent-to-Service Statute*, 70 GEO. L.J. 1209 (1982); see also David L. Ratner & Donald E. Schwartz, *The Impact of* Shaffer v. Heitner *on the Substantive Law of Corporations*, 45 BROOK. L. REV. 641 (1979). However, it is difficult to accept that a state long-arm statute alone will be sufficient to provide the purposeful contacts required by the minimum contacts test, where, as in *Shaffer,* the defendants "have simply had nothing to do with the state" asserting jurisdiction. See *Shaffer*, 433 U.S. at 216, 97 S. Ct. at 2586, 53 L. Ed. 2d at 705. As discussed below, the purposeful contacts test, as it has evolved, insures that the defendant will have fair warning that the defendant's *conduct* may produce an assertion of jurisdiction by the state. It is the notice-giving quality of the conduct that provides the defendant with the opportunity to avoid the state's jurisdiction or to defray the burdens of a suit within the state. A long-arm statute detached from conduct will not necessarily give the requisite fair warning to the defendant. Thus, it seems safer to read *Shaffer* as saying that a long-arm statute can buttress the case for jurisdiction in marginal cases in which the defendant's conduct alone is almost, but not quite, sufficient to provide the necessary fair warning that a suit might be brought within the state.

279. 444 U.S. 286, 100 S. Ct. 559, 62 L. Ed. 2d 490 (1980).

280. See *id.* at 295-96, 100 S. Ct. at 566-67, 62 L. Ed. 2d at 500-01.

281. *Id.* at 297, 100 S. Ct. at 567, 62 L. Ed. 2d at 501.

of predictability to the legal system that allows potential defendants to structure their primary conduct with some minimum assurance as to where that conduct will and will not render them liable to suit.''[282]

Significantly, the Court distinguished the situation of the local retailer and regional distributor from that of the manufacturer and importer of the automobile, who were also defendants in the action. The manufacturer and importer purposefully availed themselves of the privilege of conducting activities in the forum by attempting to serve the national market. This attempt to serve the national market was relevant because a state does not violate the Due Process Clause if it asserts ''personal jurisdiction over a corporation that delivers its products into the stream of commerce with the expectation that they will be purchased by consumers in the forum [s]tate.''[283] In contrast, the Court noted that the retailer's sales were made in Massena, New York, and that the regional distributor's market, although substantially larger, was limited to dealers in New York, New Jersey, and Connecticut. Thus, while it might be foreseeable that the purchasers of automobiles sold by the distributor and the retailer would take them to Oklahoma, ''the mere 'unilateral activity of those who claim some relationship with a nonresident defendant cannot satisfy the requirement of contact with the forum state' [citing *Hanson v. Denckla*].''[284]

Illustration 3-25. *B*, a citizen of State *Y*, is in the business of selling tires from a retail outlet located adjacent to an interstate highway in State *Y*. *A*, a citizen of State *X*, is vacationing in State *Y* when two of *A's* tires require replacement. *A* purchases two tires from *B*, who installs them on *A's* automobile. *B* is aware that *A* is from State *X* and will drive back to State *X* in the automobile. After *A* returns to State *X*, *A* is seriously injured in an accident due to defects in the tires sold and installed by *B*. *A* sues *B* in a state court of State *X*. *A* asserts jurisdiction over *B* under the State *X* long-arm statute that extends as far as the U.S. Constitution permits. If *B* objects to State *X's* assertion of personal jurisdiction over *B*, the court should dismiss the action. *B* lacks the purposeful contact with State *X* required by the minimum contacts test. Even though *B* knew that *A* was from State *X* and was returning there, *B* was not attempting to serve the market encompassed by State *X*. *B's* activities were entirely local to State *Y*.[285]

* * * * *

---

282. *Id.*

283. *Id.* at 298, 100 S. Ct. at 567, 62 L. Ed. 2d at 502 (citing Gray v. American Radiator & Standard Sanitary Corp., 22 Ill. 2d 432, 176 N.E.2d 761 (1961)).

284. *Id.* at 298, 100 S. Ct. at 567, 62 L. Ed. 2d at 502. The Court also rejected the argument that jurisdiction could be supported by the fact that petitioners earned substantial revenue from goods used in Oklahoma. The Court noted that ''[t]his argument seems to make the point that the purchase of automobiles in New York, from which the petitioners earn substantial revenue, would not occur *but for* the fact that the automobiles are capable of use in distant States like Oklahoma.'' *Id.* at 298, 100 S. Ct. at 568, 62 L. Ed. 2d at 502. The Court, however, found that ''whatever marginal revenues'' Seaway and World-Wide may have received by virtue of the fact that their products were capable of use in Oklahoma was ''far too attenuated a contact to justify that [s]tate's exercise of *in personam* jurisdiction over them.'' *Id.* at 299, 100 S. Ct. at 568, 62 L. Ed. 2d at 502.

285. *See id.* at 296, 100 S. Ct. at 566, 62 L. Ed. at 500-01; *see also* Erlanger Mills, Inc. v. Cohoes Fibre Mills, Inc., 239 F.2d 502, 507 (4th Cir. 1956).

Despite the Court's apparent approval of a "stream of commerce" test to establish purposeful contacts with the state in *World-Wide Volkswagen*,[286] doubt remains about the degree of contact that is necessary to subject a manufacturer to jurisdiction under such a test. In *Asahi Metal Industry Co. v. Superior Court*,[287] four Justices indicated that placing a product into the stream of commerce alone would not be sufficient to satisfy the purposeful contact portion of the minimum contacts test.[288] To satisfy that part of the test, "additional conduct" of the defendant would have to indicate an "intent or purpose" to serve the market in the forum state. Such additional conduct could include designing the product for the market in the forum state, advertising in the forum state, establishing channels for providing regular advice to customers in the forum state, or selling the product through a distributor who has agreed to be a sales agent in the forum state. However, merely placing the product in the stream of commerce with the awareness that it would wind up in the forum state would not alone satisfy the purposeful contact requirement.[289]

Four other Justices disagreed with this conclusion.[290] Instead, they concluded that placing a product into the stream of commerce alone was sufficient to satisfy the purposeful contact portion of the test. In addition, Justice Stevens, joined by Justices White and Blackmun, stated that even under the plurality's theory, the "stream of commerce plus" test had been satisfied, though they also indicated that it was unnecessary to formulate the theory for this case.[291] While

---

286. In *World-Wide Volkswagen*, the Court cited Gray v. American Radiator & Standard Sanitary Corp., 22 Ill. 2d 432, 176 N.E.2d 761 (1961), with seeming approval at the end of its statement about the stream of commerce, quoted above. *See* 444 U.S. at 297-98, 100 S. Ct. at 567, 62 L. Ed. 2d at 501-02. *Gray* involved the explosion of a water heater due to a defective component part. Jurisdiction was sustained in the case over the component part manufacturer that had sold the part to the manufacturer outside the forum state. *Gray* is discussed in section F ("The Reaction of the States to the Minimum Contacts Test: Long-Arm Statutes") *supra*.

287. 480 U.S. 102, 107 S. Ct. 1026, 94 L. Ed. 2d 92 (1987). The *Asahi* case arose out of a California motorcycle accident in which the driver of a Honda motorcycle collided with a tractor when one of the tires on the motorcycle exploded. The motorcycle driver commenced a products liability action in a California state court against the Taiwanese tire manufacturer, among others. The tire manufacturer sought indemnity from its codefendants and from Asahi Metal Industry Co., a Japanese corporation that manufactured the valve stem for the tire. Asahi was served with process pursuant to California's long-arm statute, which authorizes jurisdiction on any basis that is not inconsistent with the U.S. Constitution. Ultimately, the motorcycle driver settled with all of the original defendants, leaving only the indemnity claim between the tire manufacturer and Asahi still pending. *See id.* at 105-06, 101 S. Ct. at 1029-30, 94 L. Ed. 2d at 100, 100-01. Asahi asserted that California could not exercise jurisdiction over it consistent with the Due Process Clause of the Fourteenth Amendment. Based on information that Asahi's valve stems were incorporated extensively in the manufacturer's tires and distributed throughout the United States with Asahi's knowledge, the California trial court sustained jurisdiction. The California Court of Appeal ordered the service quashed. It believed that it would be unreasonable for Asahi to have to defend an action in California based simply on the foreseeability that its product would wind up there. The California Supreme Court reversed the Court of Appeal, holding that Asahi's act of placing its product into the stream of commerce with knowledge of distribution in California was sufficient to satisfy the Fourteenth Amendment. The U.S. Supreme Court granted certiorari and reversed. *See id.* at 106-08, 101 S. Ct. at 1029-31, 94 L. Ed. 2d at 100-02.

288. Justices O'Connor, Powell, Scalia, and Chief Justice Rehnquist agreed that placing a product in the stream of commerce alone is not enough to satisfy the purposeful contacts portion of the test. *See Asahi*, 480 U.S. at 105, 109-13, 101 S. Ct. at 1029, 1031-33, 94 L. Ed. 2d at 100, 102-05.

289. *See id.* at 112, 101 S. Ct. at 1033, 94 L. Ed. 2d at 104.

290. *See id.* at 116-21, 101 S. Ct. at 1035-38, 94 L. Ed. 2d at 107-10 (Brennan, J., with whom White, J., Marshall, J., and Blackmun, J. joined, concurring).

291. *See id.* at 121-22, 101 S. Ct. at 1038, 94 L. Ed. 2d at 100, 110-11.

the plurality would require something more than a significant quantity of sales of the product in the forum state, these Justices took the view that "a regular course of dealing that results in deliveries of over 100,000 units annually over a period of several years would constitute 'purposeful availment' even though the item delivered to the forum State was a standard product marketed throughout the world."[292] Thus, even if the "stream of commerce plus" theory receives majority approval in the future, the Justices may disagree on how it should be applied to particular facts.[293]

Most of the decisions applying the purposeful contact requirement discussed thus far found jurisdiction to be lacking under the test. The only case explicitly finding the test satisfied was *Burger King.*[294] *Burger King* was a diversity action in the U.S. District Court for the Southern District of Florida. In this action, Burger King sought damages and injunctive relief against two individual defendants. Burger King alleged that the defendants had failed to make certain payments under a franchise agreement to Burger King in Florida. Burger King also asserted that the defendants were infringing its trademarks by continuing to operate as a Burger King franchise. The defendants were Michigan residents operating the Burger King franchise in Michigan.[295] Jurisdiction was

---

292. *Id.* at 122, 101 S. Ct. at 1038, 94 L. Ed. 2d at 111. However, eight Justices in *Asahi* agreed that on the facts of the case the reasonableness test would defeat the state's assertion of jurisdiction. Only Justice Scalia did not join in the Court's opinion on the reasonableness test. *See id.* at 105, 101 S. Ct. at 1029, 94 L. Ed. 2d at 100. In addition, three Justices indicated that it was unnecessary to examine whether purposeful contacts existed in the case when it could be seen that the reasonableness test would defeat jurisdiction. Thus, these Justices would not require that the purposeful contacts analysis precede the reasonableness analysis. *See id.* at 121-22, 101 S. Ct. at 1038, 94 L. Ed. 2d at 100, 110-11 (Stevens, J., with whom White, J. and Blackmun, J. joined, concurring).

293. The plurality's "stream of commerce plus" requirement seems at odds with the Court's reasons for requiring purposeful contact under the Due Process Clause. In *World-Wide Volkswagen*, the Court had carefully explained why the purposeful contact component was essential to protect the defendant from unreasonable burdens of suit in the forum: "When a corporation 'purposefully avails itself of the privilege of conducting activities within the forum State' . . . it has clear notice that it is subject to suit there, and can act to alleviate the risk of burdensome litigation by procuring insurance, passing the expected costs on to customers, or, if the risks are too great, severing its connection with the State." *See* 444 U.S. at 297, 100 S. Ct. at 567, 62 L. Ed. 2d at 501 (1980); *see also Asahi*, 480 U.S. at 119, 101 S. Ct. at 1036, 94 L. Ed. 2d at 108-09 (Brennan, J., concurring). This description certainly fits a component parts manufacturer like Asahi. It is difficult to see why it is unfair to subject a defendant to suit in a state where the defendant knows its product will be distributed and may cause harm, given the options available to alleviate the burdens of suit in the state. As discussed in subsection *(b)(iv)*, *infra*, it is likely that if the injured plaintiff had sued Asahi directly, jurisdiction could not have been defeated under the reasonableness test. Therefore, because there are circumstances under which Asahi could clearly be sued within the state, it should have anticipated and prepared for litigation in California. If it had done so, it would probably have defrayed the burdens of the actual indemnity action brought against it in the case, as well as the burdens of a direct action against it by the plaintiff. Under these circumstances, it would seem clear that placing a product into the stream of commerce without more gives a manufacturer all the warning that due process requires to protect it from the burdens of suit within a state.

294. Numerous other cases exist in which the Court found jurisdiction to be constitutional but did not explicitly discuss the purposeful contact requirement. These cases are consistent with the test. They will be discussed in section H ("Application of the Minimum Contacts Test to Specific Cases") *infra*.

295. Burger King was a Florida corporation with its principal place of business in Florida. *See* 471 U.S. at 464, 105 S. Ct. at 2178, 85 L. Ed. 2d at 535. The controversy leading to the action arose out of a franchise granted by Burger King to the defendants in Michigan. The defendants had jointly applied to Burger King's Birmingham, Michigan, office for the franchise in 1978. That office forwarded the application to Burger King's Miami office. Extensive negotiations ensued, leading to the execution of a franchise agreement between the parties and the commencement of the franchise operation in 1979. Although the franchise enjoyed early success, asserted over them under a provision of Florida's long-arm statute. That provision authorized jurisdiction over anyone who breaches a contract in Florida by failing to perform acts required by the contract in the state, provided the cause of action arises from the alleged contract breach.[296]

In evaluating the district court's assertion of jurisdiction over the defendants, the Court found that purposeful contacts existed between the defendants and Florida. The Court recognized that the existence of a contract with a resident of the forum state alone cannot automatically satisfy the purposeful contact requirement. Nevertheless, a combination of factors, such as prior negotiations, contemplated future consequences, the terms of the contract, and the parties actual course of dealing, can establish purposeful contacts.[297] Thus, the fact that the defendants had voluntarily reached out beyond their home state of Michigan to negotiate a franchise arrangement with a Florida corporation produced the necessary purposeful conduct.[298] The Court emphasized that the contract documents and the parties' actual course of dealing should have indicated to the defendants that ultimate decision-making authority was vested in Burger King's Miami office. Consequently, it was foreseeable that an action might be brought there to enforce the agreement.[299]

Illustration 3-26. M Manufacturing Co. is incorporated with its sole place of business in State *X*. *M* manufactures various types of springs to the special order of its customers. *D Manufacturing Co.* is incorporated with its sole place of business in State *Y*. *D* is contacted by a sales representative of *M* about the possibility of placing an order for springs from *M*. After negotiations with *M*, all of which took place by telephone between States *X* and *Y*, *D* entered into a contract with *M*. The contract provided that *M* would manufacture an order of springs for *D* according to *D's* specifications. The contract contained a choice-of-law clause providing that the law of State *X* would govern the contract. After the springs were manufactured and shipped, *D* refused to pay for them because they

---

a recession in 1979 curtailed its business, with the result that the defendants fell behind in payments that they had agreed to make under the franchise agreement. After notices of default from the Florida office and extensive, but unsuccessful, negotiations between that office and the defendants, Burger King terminated the franchise and ordered the defendants to vacate the premises of the franchise location. They refused and continued to operate the facility as a Burger King franchise, whereupon Burger King commenced the Florida action. *See id.* at 464-68, 105 S. Ct. at 2178-80, 85 L. Ed. 2d at 535-38.

296. *See id.* at 463-64, 468-69, 105 S. Ct. at 2177, 2180, 85 L. Ed. 2d at 535, 538. Jurisdiction was asserted over the trademark infringement claim under the tortious act provisions of the Florida long-arm statute, but this assertion of jurisdiction was not before the Supreme Court because the trademark claim was the subject of a compromise, which resulted in waiver of the right to appeal the claim. Thus, the Supreme Court reserved the question whether the tortious act provision of the Florida statute could extend to out-of-state trademark infringements. *See id.* at 469 n.11, 105 S. Ct. at 2180 n.11, 85 L. Ed. 2d at 539 n.11.

297. *See id.* at 478-79, 105 S. Ct. at 2185, 85 L. Ed. 2d at 544-45.

298. *See id.* at 480, 105 S. Ct. at 2186, 85 L. Ed. 2d at 545-46.

299. *See id.* at 480-81, 105 S. Ct. at 2186-87, 85 L. Ed. 2d at 545-46. Furthermore, the contract itself provided that it would be governed by Florida substantive law and permitted Burger King to bring suit either in Florida or elsewhere in controversies arising out of the agreement. Although the Court had indicated in prior cases that the ability of a state to apply its law to a controversy did not automatically establish personal jurisdiction, the Court held in *Burger King* that the fact that a contract contained a choice-of-law provision could, when combined with other factors, help establish that a defendant possesses purposeful contact with the state. *See id.* at 481-82, 105 S. Ct. at 2187, 85 L. Ed. 2d at 546-47.

were allegedly defective. *M* sued *D* in a state court of State *X*. *M* asserted jurisdiction over *D* under a provision of the State *X* long-arm statute that permits jurisdiction to be asserted over defendants who enter into contracts to be performed in whole or part in State *X*. The assertion of jurisdiction over *D* satisfies the purposeful contact requirement. *D* negotiated a contract with a resident of State *X*. The contract was to be performed in part in State *X*. The contract also contained a choice-of-law clause providing that the law of State *X* would govern the contract. Under the *Burger King* test, it was foreseeable to *D* that an action might be brought in State *X* to enforce the contract.[300]

* * * * *

The purposeful contact requirement has evolved into a major protection for defendants under the minimum contacts analysis. Nevertheless, the purposeful contact requirement does not seem indispensable to protect the defendant's opportunity to be heard. As discussed in subsection *(c)*, below, it may be possible to develop a unified test for jurisdiction in both general and specific jurisdiction cases. Under this test, it will be important to inquire whether the defendant's conduct would cause a reasonable person to take steps to defray the kinds of burdens that will be imposed on the defendant by a state's assertion of jurisdiction. It is possible that these burdens may reasonably be defrayed in some cases even though the defendant has never engaged in the kind of purposeful activity that the Court has thus far required under the Due Process Clause of the Fourteenth Amendment. Under such circumstances, the absence of purposeful contacts should not defeat jurisdiction.

(iv) The Reasonableness Test

The Court has only applied the reasonableness test once to defeat a state's assertion of jurisdiction under the minimum contacts test. Furthermore, the Court has never explicitly used the test to create jurisdiction when the purposeful contacts requirement has not been satisfied. Despite the sparse use of the test, however, it is possible to make some general observations about how the factors in the test should operate based on the Court's decisions.

The single decision in which the Court has used the reasonableness test to defeat jurisdiction is *Asahi Metal Industry Co. v. Superior Court*.[301] As noted in subsection *(b)(iii)*, above, majority support for reversing the judgment of the California Supreme Court existed in *Asahi* only because eight members of the Court agreed that the reasonableness portion of the specific jurisdiction test defeated jurisdiction. Justice O'Connor's opinion for these members of the Court emphasized the burdens that would be placed upon Asahi by the action in California. These burdens included not only the distance from Japan to California, but also the fact that the dispute between the foreign tire manufacturer and Asahi would be adjudicated by "a foreign nation's judicial system."[302]

---

300. *See* Springmasters, Inc. v. D & M Mfg., 303 S.C. 528, 402 S.E.2d 192 (1991).
301. 480 U.S 102, 107 S. Ct. 1026, 94 L. Ed. 2d 92 (1987).
302. *Id.* at 114, 107 S. Ct. at 1034, 94 L. Ed. 2d at 105.

The other elements in the reasonableness test were not sufficient to overcome these burdens. The tire manufacturer's interest in litigating its indemnity claim in California was considered slight. The transaction that was the basis of the claim occurred in Taiwan, and the tire valves had been shipped from Japan to Taiwan.[303] Finally, the Court addressed the shared interests of the several states in efficient procedural resolution of the controversy and in furthering fundamental substantive social policies. On the facts of the case, this factor required consideration of "the procedural and substantive policies of other nations" affected by California's assertion of jurisdiction. The Court concluded that these interests, as well as the foreign-relations interests of the United States, would be "best served by an inquiry into the reasonableness of the assertion of jurisdiction in the particular case, and an unwillingness to find serious burdens on an alien defendant outweighed by minimal interests on the part of the plaintiff or the forum State."[304]

The result in *Asahi* was a product, in part, of the peculiar procedural posture of the case. A change in that posture would likely produce a different result under the reasonableness test. Under the Court's analysis, if Asahi had been sued directly by the California motorcycle driver, both California and the plaintiff would probably have sufficiently strong interests in the case to counterbalance the burdens that a suit in California would impose on Asahi. In addition, if Asahi had been one of a number of defendants sued by the driver, it would be procedurally efficient to resolve the relative liabilities of all of the multiple defendants in the California proceeding. Furthermore, it would arguably be in the interests of the interstate and international community to assure that substantive tort liability was imposed on the correct party through proceedings in California. Thus, in a changed procedural context, the Court would probably not be able to justify dismissing Asahi under the reasonableness test.

Illustration 3-27. *A*, a citizen of State *X*, sues *B*, a citizen of State *X*, and *C*, a citizen of State *Y*, in a state court in State *X*. *A* asserts a claim in the alternative against *B* and *C* in tort. *A* was injured when a machine manufactured by *C* exploded in State *X*. *B* is the doctor who treated *A* for *A's* injuries. *A* asserts that the negligence of either *B* or *C* or both contributed to certain permanent injuries received by *A*. *B* and *C* are not indispensable parties to the action. Thus, *A* could sue *B* in State *X* and *C* in State *Y*. However, if *A* sued *C* in State *Y*, *B* could not be subjected to jurisdiction in State *Y* because all of *B's* actions occurred in State *X*. If *A* is forced to bring separate actions against *B* in State *X*

---

303. *See id.* California's interest in entertaining the indemnity claim in its courts was also weak, because none of the parties to the indemnity claim was a resident of California. Although the California Supreme Court had argued that California had an interest in protecting its consumers by assuring that foreign manufacturers complied with the state's safety standards, the U.S. Supreme Court held that, for several reasons, this definition of the state's interest was overly broad. The dispute was mainly about indemnity, not safety standards. It was also unclear whether it was appropriate for California law to govern an indemnity claim between two foreign manufacturers based on a foreign transaction. Furthermore, while the possibility of a suit in California might create some additional deterrence, the Court felt that Asahi would receive similar pressures from the manufacturers who incorporated its products into their tires as long as those manufacturers were subject to California tort law. *See id.* at 114-15, 101 S. Ct. at 1034, 94 L. Ed. 2d at 100, 105-06.

304. *See id.* at 115, 107 S. Ct. at 1034-35, 94 L. Ed. 2d at 106.

and *C* in State *Y*, each defendant may defend on the ground that the other defendant is exclusively liable for *A*'s permanent injuries. A trier of fact in State *X* might find in favor of *B* on the ground that *C* was exclusively responsible for *A*'s injuries, and a trier of fact in State *Y* might find that *B* was exclusively responsible for *A*'s injuries. Thus, two triers of fact would have agreed that one of the defendants was liable for *A*'s permanent injuries, but *A* would not recover from either defendant. Under these circumstances, the state's and plaintiff's interests in conducting the action in State *X*, the only state where both defendants can possibly be joined, are strong. Likewise, it will be procedurally more efficient to resolve the relative liability of *B* and *C* in the State X proceeding than to conduct separate actions for this purpose. Finally, the interstate system has an interest in assuring that tort liability is not avoided by the parties through inconsistent judgments.

* * * * *

Further examination of how the elements of the reasonableness test operate will be reserved until section H, below, where the test will be applied to specific categories of cases. However, one aspect of the test is important enough to explore briefly here. In *Shaffer v. Heitner*,[305] the Supreme Court rejected an argument that the state's interest in adjudicating the suit was high. In so doing, the Court stated that the argument was "undercut by the failure of the [state legislature] to assert the state interest [plaintiff] finds so compelling."[306] Thus, the Court suggested that the state's interest could be enhanced by the enactment of a particularized long-arm statute, as opposed to the general kind of statute involved in *Shaffer*.[307] Since *Shaffer*, the Court has explicitly addressed enhancement of the state's interest by statute only once. In *Keeton v. Hustler Magazine, Inc.*,[308] a libel action, the Court found the state's interest enhanced by two features of the statutory scheme. First, the state had not limited its criminal defamation statute to libels aimed at the state's residents. Second, the state had amended its long-arm statute to eliminate a requirement that torts falling within the statute be committed against residents of the state. These statutory features were said to constitute a clear expression of the state's interest in protecting nonresident victims of libel.[309]

Shaffer and *Keeton*, taken together, do not provide adequate guidance to the states about the kinds of statutes that will enhance their interests for purposes of the reasonableness test. *Keeton* has a particularly clouding effect. In that

---

305. 433 U.S. 186, 97 S. Ct. 2569, 53 L. Ed. 2d 683 (1977).

306. *Id.* at 214, 97 S. Ct. 2585, 53 L. Ed. 2d at 704. The Court added that "[i]f Delaware perceived its interest in securing jurisdiction over corporate fiduciaries to be as great as [plaintiff] suggests, we would expect it to have enacted a statute more clearly designed to protect that interest." *Id.* at 214-15, 97 S. Ct. at 2585, 53 L. Ed. 2d 704.

307. Recall that the statute in *Shaffer* was a generalized sequestration statute applicable to many kinds of cases. The Court also indicated that the foreseeability of suit within the state was adversely affected by the absence of a statute treating acceptance of a directorship in a Delaware corporation as consent to jurisdiction. *See* section G(2)*(b)(iii)* ("The Purposeful Contacts Test") *supra*. Thus, the presence of a focused long-arm statute can enhance both the likelihood of purposeful contacts with the state and the state's interest in adjudicating the action.

308. 465 U.S. 770, 104 S. Ct. 1473, 79 L. Ed. 2d 790 (1984).

309. *See id.* at 777, 104 S. Ct. at 1479, 79 L. Ed. 2d at 799.

decision, the criminal defamation statute said to be a "clear" expression of the state's interest was inapplicable to the case before the Court. In addition, the expression of the state's interest was discovered in an omission of a limitation from the statute. Furthermore, the amendment of the state's long-arm statute eliminated a restriction on suits by nonresidents in *all* tort cases, not just in libel cases. *Keeton* thus raises the interesting prospect that a state's interest can be increased by (1) the absence of limitations in inapplicable statutes or (2) amendments to long-arm statutes that eliminate restrictions that are applicable to broad categories of cases. The philosophy of *Keeton* thus seems to be at odds with the insistence in *Shaffer* on a rather precise declaration of the state's interest by means of a tightly focused long-arm statute. Because of the apparent inconsistency in the approach of the two cases, therefore, clarification of the precise way in which a state's interest may be enhanced by statute will obviously have to await future decisions.[310]

In addition, *Keeton* described the state interest factor of the reasonableness test as a "surrogate" for other factors in the due process analysis.[311] This description clouds the operation of the reasonableness test even further by suggesting that a high state interest in adjudicating a dispute may, by itself, justify an assertion of specific jurisdiction. The Supreme Court has not returned to this suggestion since reviving the two-step test for the validity of specific jurisdiction in *Burger King*. However, at least one lower federal court has held that if the forum state has "an appreciable interest in the litigation" because issues in the litigation either would be affected by or would impact on policies expressed in the state's "substantive, procedural, or remedial laws," an assertion of jurisdiction by the state is "prima facie constitutional,"[312] even if there is no territorial connection between the state and the events giving rise to suit.[313] Only a demonstration of an inability by the defendant to "mount a defense in the state without suffering relatively substantial hardship" can defeat this prima facie case.[314]

(c) Confusion and Possible Convergence

Not all cases in the state and lower federal courts have fully appreciated the U.S. Supreme Court's distinction between general and specific jurisdiction or applied it in a sensible fashion. For example, in *Roxas v. Marcos*,[315] the

---

310. One of the interesting questions about statutory enhancement is whether a statute such as the Uniform Interstate and International Procedure Act, discussed *supra* section F, contains sufficiently precise categories of jurisdiction to give the state's interest a boost. Presumably, a general long-arm statute of the California variety, discussed *supra* section F, will not enhance the state's interest. However, such a statute apparently will not detract from the state's interest if it is otherwise sufficient. In Calder v. Jones, 465 U.S. 783, 104 S. Ct. 1482, 79 L. Ed. 2d 804, another libel case decided the same day as *Keeton*, the Court sustained an exercise of jurisdiction by California under its general long-arm statute without discussing the state's interest or the absence of a precise long-arm statute. *Keeton* and *Calder* are discussed further *infra* in section H(1) ("Tort Cases").

311. *See* Keeton, 465 U.S. at 776, 104 S. Ct. at 1479, 79 L. Ed. 2d at 798.

312. *In re* DES Cases, 789 F. Supp. 552, 587 (E.D.N.Y. 1992).

313. *See id.* at 577-87.

314. *Id.* at 587.

315. 89 Haw. 91, 969 P.2d 1209 (1998).

plaintiff, a Philippine national, sued former President of the Philippines Ferdinand Marcos and his wife in Hawaii state court for conversion. In determining whether Marcos, who had died during the pendency of the action, was subject to personal jurisdiction in Hawaii, the Hawaii Supreme Court indicated that, although Marcos had not established a domicile in Hawaii, he had lived there for 3½ years and had thus purposely availed himself of the forum. It is clear that the assertion of jurisdiction over Marcos was "general" in the case. The court did not rely on the existence of any traditional territorial rule, such as presence or domicile. Furthermore, the claim clearly "arose" in the Philippines and did not "relate to" anything Marcos had done in Hawaii. Yet the court did not consider whether the assertion of jurisdiction was "general" or "specific" and applied the "purposeful availment" step of the specific jurisdiction test, but not the "reasonableness" analysis.

Cases such as *Roxas* are unfortunately sloppy, but they do not necessarily reach incorrect results.[316] It is not uncommon to see courts ignore the issue whether an assertion of jurisdiction is general or specific, or apply only the first step in the specific jurisdiction analysis.[317] Sometimes, when jurisdiction is asserted under a state long-arm statute that requires the claim to arise out of a particular kind of activity conducted within the state, it will be completely justifiable for a court to treat the general jurisdiction category as irrelevant.[318] However, when a state has a long-arm statute that, explicitly or as construed, extends jurisdiction as far as the U.S. Constitution permits, it is analytically preferable for the courts to first determine whether the assertion of jurisdiction is "general" or "specific" before proceeding to determine whether it is valid.[319]

Furthermore, in any case involving an assertion of specific jurisdiction, the courts should address the reasonableness factors. When purposeful contacts have been established, the courts should at least comment on whether the defendant has met its burden of overcoming the presumption of validity established by the purposeful contacts.[320] If purposeful contacts have not been

---

316. Under the authority of the *Burnham* decision, discussed in section E(2), *supra*, the court could have exercised jurisdiction based on Marcos' physical presence in Hawaii. Likewise, if general jurisdiction is a category applicable to individuals, *see* section G(2)*(a) supra*, it could have been sustained based on Marcos' 3½ year residence in Hawaii, even if Marcos had not established a domicile there. *Cf.* RESTATEMENT (SECOND) OF CONFLICT OF LAWS § 30 (1971) (state has power to exercise jurisdiction over an individual who is a resident unless the individual's relationship is so attenuated as to make the exercise of jurisdiction unreasonable).

317. *See, e.g.,* Northwest Airlines, Inc. v. Astraea Aviation Servs., Inc., 111 F.3d 1386 (8th Cir. 1997); Generadora de Electricidad del Caribe v. Foster-Wheeler Corp., 30 F. Supp. 2d 196 (D.P.R. 1998).

318. Thus, in the *Generadora* case, cited in the preceding note, jurisdiction was asserted under a provision of the Puerto Rican long-arm statute allowing "personal jurisdiction over nonresident defendants . . . when the litigation arises out of transactions in Puerto Rico." 30 F. Supp. 2d at 199.

319. Thus, in Northwest Airlines, Inc. v. Astraea Aviation Services, Inc., 111 F.3d 1386 (8th Cir. 1997), the court observed that Minnesota's long-arm statute "is applied to the fullest extent permitted under the [D]ue [P]rocess [C]lause of the [F]ourteenth [A]mendment." *Id.* at 1390. The court did not directly consider whether the assertion of jurisdiction was general or specific, but at one point in its opinion it did identify several contacts with Minnesota "which related to the disputed contracts under which [the plaintiff] brought its breach of contract claims." *Id.* at 1391. Nevertheless, it is unclear from the opinion whether the court was made this reference to establish the assertion of jurisdiction as specific or as the first step in the test for determining validity—*i.e.,* the purposeful contacts test. *See id.* at 1391-92.

320. *See* section G(2)*(b)(ii)* ("The Two-Step Test for the Validity of Specific Jurisdiction") *supra*.

established, the court should at least briefly discuss whether the plaintiff has overcome the lack of purposeful contacts by the reasonableness factors.[321] Only by addressing the elements of the jurisdictional tests in a systematic way can the courts hope to clarify their operation over time.

A separate question that has arisen in recent years is the role of the "reasonableness factors" in assessing the validity of an assertion of general jurisdiction. As the discussion in preceding subsections has demonstrated, the U.S. Supreme Court has thus far addressed the reasonableness factors only in specific jurisdiction cases. By implication, this suggests that it is not proper to employ those factors to defeat an assertion of general jurisdiction when systematic and continuous contacts have been established, or to enhance the validity of an assertion of general jurisdiction when the defendant's contacts with the forum are less than systematic and continuous. Nevertheless, some courts have considered the reasonableness factors to be relevant to assertions of general jurisdiction.

The leading case is *Metropolitan Life Insurance Co. v. Robertson-Ceco Corp.*[322] In *Met Life*, an insurance company sued a manufacturer of building materials in the U.S. District Court for the District of Vermont. The claim was based on breach of contract and negligence in conjunction with materials supplied for the construction of a building owned by the insurance company in Miami, Florida. The defendant moved to dismiss the action for lack of personal jurisdiction. The district court dismissed the action. The court found that the activities of the defendant in Vermont did not rise to the "systematic and continuous" level necessary to sustain an assertion of general jurisdiction. The district court also applied the "reasonableness test" of the Supreme Court's specific jurisdiction cases and stated that even if systematic and continuous contacts had been established, that test would make the assertion of jurisdiction over the defendant unreasonable.[323]

On appeal, the Second Circuit disagreed with the conclusion of the district court that the defendant did not have systematic and continuous contacts with Vermont.[324] However, the Second Circuit agreed with the district court that the "reasonableness factors" could be used to test the validity of general jurisdiction and that those factors defeated jurisdiction on the facts of the case.[325] Although the Second Circuit acknowledged that the Supreme Court had not specifically applied the reasonableness test to general jurisdiction cases,[326] it felt justified in doing so by the uniform view of other courts of appeals,[327] as well as by the absence of any indication from the Supreme Court that the reasonableness inquiry

---

321. *See id.* (discussing the statement in *Burger King* indicating that the reasonableness factors can be used to sustain jurisdiction upon a lesser showing of "minimum contacts" than would otherwise be required).

322. 84 F.3d 560 (2d Cir. 1996), *cert. denied*, 519 U.S. 1006, 117 S. Ct. 508, 136 L. Ed. 2d 398 (1996). *Metropolitan Life* was also discussed in section G(2)*(a)* ("General Jurisdiction") *supra*.

323. *See id.* at 566.

324. *See id.* at 570-73.

325. *See id.* at 573-76.

326. *See id.* at 573.

327. *See id.* (citing and discussing Donatelli v. National Hockey League, 893 F.2d 459, 465 (1st Cir. 1990) and Bearry v. Beech Aircraft Corp., 818 F.2d 370, 377 (5th Cir. 1987)).

is inappropriate in general jurisdiction cases.[328] In evaluating the factors, the court found that the "burden on the defendant" factor cut "slightly" in favor of the defendant on the facts,[329] but that Vermont had no interest in the suit,[330] the plaintiff's interest in suing in Vermont was weak,[331] no witnesses or evidence were located in Vermont,[332] and no "shared interests of the several states" or "substantive social policies" had been shown by the plaintiff to exist in favor of Vermont as a forum.[333] Thus, the Second Circuit found that the first factor weighed slightly against jurisdiction, while the second through fourth factors weighed heavily against it, in combination defeating jurisdiction.[334]

The majority's approach in *Met Life* provoked a strong dissent from Judge Walker.[335] The dissenting opinion canvassed many of the Supreme Court's decisions discussed in this text in preceding and following sections. It provides an admirable summary and evaluation of the minimum contacts test as well as the confusion it has produced in the lower federal and state courts.[336] As to the use of the reasonableness test in general jurisdiction cases, Judge Walker stated:

> In the wake of *Burger King* and *Asahi*, we are bound to adhere to the Supreme Court's adoption of a reasonableness inquiry in the specific jurisdiction context. In the general jurisdiction context, however, we are not so bound . . . . Unless

---

328. *See Met Life*, 84 F.3d at 573.

329. *See id.* at 573-74.

330. *See id.*

331. The plaintiff had sued in Vermont because it had a long statute of limitations. The court, on the authority of Keeton v. Hustler Magazine, Inc., 465 U.S. 770, 778, 104 S. Ct. 1473, 1480, 79 L. Ed. 2d 790, 799 (1984), discussed in section H(1) *infra*, considered this fact irrelevant. *See Met Life*, 84 F.3d at 574.

332. *See id.* at 574-75.

333. *See id.* at 575.

334. *See id.*

335. *See id.* at 576 (Walker, J., dissenting).

336. Judge Walker provided the following summary:

> The Supreme Court's opinion in *International Shoe*, which implicated only the interests of the defendant and not the interests of the plaintiff or of the forum state, made it clear that whether due process is satisfied turns exclusively on the fairness to the defendant in being made to defend a suit in a particular forum.
>
> The majority's holding is, in part, an accommodation of the Supreme Court's more recent jurisprudence which reconfigures the jurisdictional underpinning of *International Shoe*. Thirty-five years after the Supreme Court hailed "minimum contacts" as the constitutional touchstone of the due process analysis, it espoused, albeit in dicta, an additional due process consideration concerning the protection of interstate federalism. *World-Wide Volkswagen* . . . . This supplemental function of due process is the precursor to the majority's "reasonableness" inquiry in the present case. Only two years later, however, in *Insurance Corp. of Ireland* . . . , the Supreme Court reaffirmed its earlier course, recognizing that the personal jurisdiction requirement "represents a restriction on judicial power not as a matter of sovereignty, but as a matter of individual liberty" . . . .
> In spite of this reassertion, in *Burger King* . . . and later in *Asahi* . . . the Supreme Court doubled-back to its holding in *World-Wide Volkswagen* by defining the test for specific jurisdiction to include both a "minimum contacts" and a "reasonableness" component. In other words, the concept of "traditional notions of fair play and substantive justice," which was defined in *International Shoe* only by the "contacts" of the defendant with the forum state, has been transformed into the notion of reasonableness apart from the contacts.

Id. at 577.

and until the Supreme Court instructs us in a general jurisdiction case that interests other than those of the defendant are implicated by due process in the personal jurisdiction analysis, we should not rush to make them so. I believe that these ancillary interests, which have nothing to do with whether it is fair and just for a foreign defendant to be haled into an out-of-state court, are properly accounted for under the doctrine of forum non conveniens.

The fact that other circuits have chosen the course embarked on by the majority, if anything, reinforces my concerns. The sprouting like weeds of multi-pronged tests for the reasonableness inquiry in the circuits in both specific and general jurisdiction cases has left this legal garden in disarray.[337]

The majority's approach in *Met Life* represents a strong trend.[338] Nevertheless, the dissent has by far the better case. As discussed in the next subsection, there are great difficulties with the minimum contacts test as it has evolved in U.S. Supreme Court decisions. Although a unified test for general and specific jurisdiction cases is desirable, it cannot be coherently formulated by grafting the reasonableness factors onto the general jurisdiction test. To mention but one problem, it is impossible to see how a defendant who has systematic and continuous contacts with a state should ever be able to complain that the state is such a burdensome place to adjudicate any claim as to deprive the defendant of due process. Judge Walker was entirely correct in arguing that residual problems of inconvenience that may exist in such cases should be dealt with through transfers of venue or discretionary dismissal on forum non conveniens grounds.

(d) Toward a Unified Test for General and
Specific Jurisdiction

Serious difficulties exist with the minimum contacts analysis evolved by the U.S. Supreme Court. The Court has never explained why a different standard is applied to general and specific jurisdiction cases. In other words, why is the validity of general jurisdiction judged by whether ''systematic and continuous'' contacts with the forum exist, while specific jurisdiction is judged initially by

---

337. *Id.* The doctrine of forum non conveniens mentioned in Judge Walker's dissent, as well as the related problem of transfer of venue in federal court under 28 U.S.C. § 1404(a), are discussed in Chapter 4(D) (''Forum Non Conveniens and Change of Venue'') *infra*. The role of sovereignty interests in the Supreme Court's decisions and in jurisdictional analysis move generally is discussed in section G(3) (''Sovereignty-Based Restrictions on State-Court Jurisdiction'') *infra*.

338. In addition to the cases cited and discussed by the majority, *supra*, see *Ex parte* United Bhd. of Carpenters of Am., 688 So. 2d 246 (Ala.), *cert. denied*, 521 U.S. 1118, 117 S. Ct. 2509, 138 L. Ed. 2d 1012 (1997) (after systematic and continuous contacts established, reasonableness test applied to sustain jurisdiction); Transportes Aereos de Coahiula, S.A. v. Falcon, 5 S.W.3d 712 (Tex. Ct. App. 1999); *see also* Shannon McGhee-Hernandez, *Civil-Procedure-Metropolitan Life Insurance Co. v. Robertson-Ceco Corp.: The Reasonableness Inquiry in the Context of General Jurisdiction*, 27 U. MEM. L. REV. 723 (1997); Note, *Civil Procedure-Personal Jurisdiction-Second Circuit Applies ''Reasonableness'' Test for General Personal Jurisdiction-Metropolitan Life Ins. Co. v. Robertson Ceco Corp.*, 84 F.3d 560 (2d Cir.), *cert. denied*, 519 U.S. 1006, 117 S. Ct. 508, 136 L. Ed. 2d 398 (1996), 110 HARV. L. REV. 1328 (1997).

whether "purposeful contacts" between the defendant and the forum state exist that are not outweighed by reasonableness factors? Why does the Court not use the two-tiered approach to jurisdiction in both general and specific jurisdiction cases as suggested by the *Met Life* case discussed in the preceding subsection. Alternatively, why is a territorial nexus necessarily required between the claim or the defendant at all?

The separate tests used in general and specific jurisdiction cases seem to be aimed at achieving the same goal. The objective of the Due Process Clause is to assure an adequate opportunity to be heard in defense before a valid judgment may be entered against the defendant. Jurisdictional tests that restrict the location of suit serve this purpose by assuring that the defendant may not be subjected to an unreasonably burdensome place of suit. By requiring that systematic and continuous contacts exist between the defendant and the forum when the claim does not arise out of or relate to the defendant's forum activities, the Court may be trying to assure that the forum will not be unreasonably burdensome. When a defendant's forum activities are "systematic and continuous," the defendant cannot be heard to complain that any suit brought against the defendant in the forum is so burdensome that it violates due process. A helpful illustration is the case of an action brought in the state of the defendant's domicile on a claim arising outside the state. If the domicile is substantial, rather than technical, the defendant can hardly complain that the plaintiff has chosen to sue the defendant at the defendant's home rather than in a distant forum where the claim arose. To be sure, there may be inconvenience in a trial at the defendant's domicile if important witnesses and evidence are located where the claim arose. However, any such inconvenience does not rise to the level of a due process violation and can often be accommodated by a forum non conveniens dismissal, a transfer of the litigation, or other procedural means.[339]

Similarly, in specific jurisdiction cases, the requirement of purposeful contacts is aimed at protecting the defendant from unreasonable burdens that might be imposed by a suit in a particular state. By assuring that the defendant can predict where its activities may result in a suit, the purposeful contacts test assures that the defendant can avoid jurisdiction-producing activities in states where the burdens of suit will be too great, or take steps to defray the burdens with insurance or other measures. A test that allowed the defendant to object to the burdens of suit in a state even when the defendant might have avoided or defrayed the burdens would be unjustifiable. Insistence on reasonable efforts to anticipate the consequences of one's forum-related activity are not unjust under the Due Process Clause, given the options open to potential defendants to avoid or alleviate the burdens of suit.[340]

---

339. *See* Chapter 4(D) ("Forum Non Conveniens and Change of Venue") *infra.*

340. While the purposeful contacts test reasonably accommodates the competing interests of the defendant, the forum, and the plaintiff, it is difficult to say the same about the reasonableness test. The reasonableness test allows a defendant to defeat jurisdiction when, by definition, the defendant has had an opportunity to anticipate a suit in the state and avoid or defray its burdens. If the defendant has had an adequate ability to predict a suit based on the defendant's activities within the state, the defendant should take the steps available to defray or avoid the burdens the suit would impose. If the defendant does not do so, the reasonableness test suggests that there will be cases, however rare, in which the defendant can still defeat jurisdiction by demonstrating significant

Because the goal of the general and specific jurisdiction tests is the same, the Court can, by returning to first principles, create a unified test for the two kinds of jurisdiction. The Court could focus in each case on the function of the Due Process Clause to ensure an adequate opportunity to be heard in defense. Under such an approach, a state would always be allowed to exercise jurisdiction over a defendant unless it could be demonstrated that the objective burdens of defending the action within the state are so great that the defendant would, as a practical matter, have to relinquish the opportunity to be heard rather than incur the burdens. A defendant who engages in activity within the state of the sort that should alert the defendant of the possibility of a suit within the state could never make the required demonstration because such a defendant should act to defray the burdens of the suit before the suit occurs. In addition, a defendant should never be allowed to defeat a state's assertion of jurisdiction if it can be seen that the forum is no more burdensome to the defendant as a practical matter than some other state in which the defendant concededly might be sued. Under this approach, the state's interest, the plaintiff's interest, and other interests would be adequately accommodated without the necessity of emphasizing them separately as part of a vague reasonableness test.

Furthermore, the suggested approach, although it might expand the reach of state-court jurisdiction somewhat, would do so while retaining the focus on the defendant's right to an adequate opportunity to be heard that it is the purpose of the Due Process Clause to assure. Any additional protections for the defendant that are necessary should be imposed through due process limitations on the ability of a state to apply its substantive law in a manner that produces unfair surprise,[341] or by self-imposed limits on a state-court's jurisdiction under doctrines such as forum non conveniens.[342]

---

objective burdens coupled with, for example, weak state and plaintiff interests in maintaining the suit in the forum. However, if a defendant has failed to take the steps necessary to protect itself, it is difficult to see why weak state and plaintiff interests should allow the defendant to escape jurisdiction. Why not afford the defendant an adequate opportunity to predict the suit and alleviate its burdens and let the state and the plaintiff be the judge of their own interests? The jurisdiction-enhancing function of the reasonableness test is even more questionable. If a defendant's activities are not sufficiently purposeful to provide warning that the defendant can be subjected to suit within the state, it is difficult to understand how it can possibly be "fair" to subject the defendant to a suit within the state if the burdens of suit are significant. Furthermore, as noted in section G(2)*(b)(iv)*, *supra*, many Supreme Court decisions suggest that the state interest factor may be the most important jurisdiction-enhancing element in the reasonableness test. *See, e.g.*, Burger King Corp. v. Rudzewicz, 471 U.S. 462, 477, 105 S. Ct. 2174, 2184, 85 L. Ed. 2d 528, 543 (1985); Keeton v. Hustler Magazine, Inc., 465 U.S. 770, 104 S. Ct. 1473, 79 L. Ed. 2d 790 (1984); McGee v. International Life Ins. Co., 355 U.S. 220, 78 S. Ct. 199, 2 L. Ed. 2d 223 (1957). This emphasis is especially objectionable because the state's interest seems to have nothing to do with the core objective of the Due Process Clause, which is to provide defendants with an adequate opportunity to be heard in defense. If defendant's activities are not such as to provide fair warning of the possibility of a suit within the state, and if the burdens of suit are substantial, it would seem that due process should protect the defendant from jurisdiction no matter how high the state's interest happens to be.

341. *See* Ralph U. Whitten, *The Constitutional Limitations on State Choice of Law: Due Process*, 9 HASTINGS CONST. L.Q. 851, 913, 917 (1982).

342. *See* Chapter 4(D) ("Forum Non Conveniens and Change of Venue") *infra*. The standard recommended should also not preclude the development of reasonable modern sovereignty-based restrictions on the enforcement of sister-state judgments to replace the sovereignty-oriented "international" rules that existed prior to *Pennoyer v. Neff* and which were eliminated with the development of the minimum contacts test of *International Shoe*. A judgment should not necessarily have to be enforced by another state simply because the

Illustration 3-28. *B*, a citizen of Texas, collides with *A*, a citizen of Omaha, Nebraska, in Council Bluffs, Iowa, which is a city separated from Omaha by the Missouri River. *A* sues *B* in a Nebraska state court in Omaha. *B* is served with process in Texas under a Nebraska long-arm statute extending the jurisdiction of Nebraska courts as far as the U.S. Constitution will permit. *B* should have no valid due process objection to an action in Omaha because Omaha is no more burdensome a forum than would be a court in Council Bluffs, where the accident occurred. The absence of a due process objection to jurisdiction does not preclude *B* from objecting on due process grounds to the application of Nebraska substantive law to the accident, if such an application would produce unfair surprise to *B*. Nor does it preclude *B* from moving to dismiss the action under the doctrine of forum non conveniens.

3. Sovereignty-Based Restrictions on State-Court Jurisdiction

When *Pennoyer v. Neff* incorporated the international rules of jurisdiction into the Due Process Clause of the Fourteenth Amendment, the Supreme Court's decision effectively constitutionalized rules that previously had not been constitutional rules. As noted in the discussion of *Pennoyer*,[343] these rules were not suitable due process rules because they did not focus on the effectuation of the defendant's opportunity to be heard in defense. Instead, the rules reflected the authority of the states as independent sovereigns, at least as this authority was understood at the time the Constitution was formed. However, although the international rules were not appropriate due process rules, *Pennoyer's* incorporation of them into the Due Process Clause did nothing to impair their value as safeguards of state sovereign interests. After *Pennoyer* but before *International Shoe*, therefore, a judgment that violated the state sovereignty interests reflected in the rules was unenforceable both in the state where it was rendered and in other states.

When *International Shoe* began replacing the territorial rules with the minimum contacts test, especially after *Shaffer* indicated that the latter test would govern all assertions of state-court jurisdiction, it was not recognized that this

---

judgment does not offend the Due Process Clause or domestic rules of the judgment-rendering state. The development of sovereignty-based restrictions is discussed subsection 3, *infra*. *See also* Stephen B. Burbank, *Jurisdiction to Adjudicate: End of the Century or Beginning of the Millennium*, 7 TUL. J. INT'L & COMP. L. 111 (1999) (discussing personal jurisdiction in the United States in a historical and comparative context); Robert C. Casad, *Jurisdiction in Civil Actions at the End of the Twentieth Century: Forum Conveniens and Forum Non Conveniens*, 7 TUL. J. INT'L & COMP. L. 91 (1999) (making suggestions for how the law of personal jurisdiction should develop in the twenty-first century); Kevin C. McMunigal, *Desert, Utility, and Minimum Contacts: Toward a Mixed Theory of Personal Jurisdiction*, 108 YALE L.J. 189 (1998) (discussing how the Supreme Court might make better use of the ingredients it has identified as relevant under the minimum contacts analysis by developing a "mixed" theory of personal jurisdiction that blends notions of desert, utility, and proportionality); Michael E. Solimine, *The Quiet Revolution in Personal Jurisdiction*, 73 TUL. L. REV. 1 (1988) (empirically examining whether federal and state courts have responded differently to the Supreme Court's personal jurisdiction decisions and how often plaintiffs leave their home states to shop for more favorable fora).

343. *See* section A(2)*(b)* ("Incorporation of the Territorial Rules into the Due Process Clause of the Fourteenth Amendment") *supra*.

replacement might obliterate the protection that the territorial rules had afforded to state sovereignty interests. While the minimum contacts test, with its focus on fairness to the defendant, was certainly a better due process test than the territorial rules, the minimum contacts test was not concerned with safeguarding state sovereign prerogatives.[344] Thus, the combined effect of *Pennoyer* and *International Shoe* is that a judgment that satisfies the minimum contacts test must be enforced in other states under the full-faith-and-credit implementing statute. There is apparently no room for a state to refuse enforcement of another state's judgment on the ground that it violates the sovereignty of the judgment-enforcing state as long as the judgment satisfies due process.

In *World-Wide Volkswagen Corp. v. Woodson,*[345] the Supreme Court appeared ready to restore some protection for state sovereign interests under the minimum contacts test. On review of an Oklahoma decision, the Court stated that

> [t]he concept of minimum contacts . . . can be seen to perform two related, but distinguishable functions. It protects the defendant against the burdens of litigating in a distant or inconvenient forum. And it acts to ensure that the States through their courts, do not reach out beyond the limits imposed by their status as coequal sovereigns in a federal system.[346]

In *World-Wide Volkswagen,* the Court indicated that the sovereignty component of the minimum contacts test was an independent standard that had to be met in addition to a "convenience" or burdens component (based upon a balancing of the interests of the defendant, the plaintiff, the state asserting jurisdiction, and other factors). Thus, the first step in the minimum contacts analysis was to determine whether the state asserting jurisdiction possessed the sovereign power to do so by estimating whether the defendant had engaged in activity that was sufficiently "purposeful."[347]

Two years after *World-Wide Volkswagen,* the Court reversed course and held that the minimum contacts test was not, in fact, designed to perform a sovereignty-protection role. In *Insurance Corp. of Ireland, Ltd. v. Compagnie des Bauxites de Guinee,*[348] the defendant refused to cooperate in discovery proceedings aimed at determining whether the necessary minimum contacts with the state existed to satisfy due process. As a sanction for the defendant's failure to make discovery, the district court imposed a finding under Federal Rule of Civil Procedure 37(b)(2)(A) that minimum contacts existed. The defendant contended that

---

344. *Burnham's* potential preservation of the validity of some territorial rules did not restore the sovereign authority of the states as it had existed under *Pennoyer.* All *Burnham* suggested was that an assertion of jurisdiction under (some) traditional rules would not *violate* due process. "Novel" assertions of state-court jurisdiction that would have violated state sovereign interests under *Pennoyer* and earlier decisions are still governed by the minimum contacts test after *Burnham.*

345. 444 U.S. 286, 100 S. Ct. 559, 62 L. Ed. 2d 490 (1980).

346. *Id.* at 291-92, 100 S. Ct. at 564, 62 L. Ed. 2d at 498; *see also id.* at 293, 100 S. Ct. at 565, 62 L. Ed. 2d at 497-98, in which the Court stated that the framers had intended for the states to retain many of the attributes of independent sovereigns and that sovereign limits on the power of state courts was inherent both in the plan of the original Constitution and the Fourteenth Amendment.

347. *See id.* at 293-99, 100 S. Ct. at 565-68, 62 L. Ed. 2d at 498-502.

348. 456 U.S. 694, 102 S. Ct. 2099, 72 L. Ed. 2d 492 (1982).

it was impermissible to apply Rule 37(b)(2)(A) to jurisdictional facts because to do so might establish judicial power when such power did not exist in fact.[349]

In rejecting this argument, the Supreme Court distinguished between objections based on subject-matter and personal jurisdiction. The Court described federal subject-matter jurisdiction limits as sovereignty-based separation-of-powers restrictions, but stated that the "personal jurisdiction requirement . . . represents a restriction on judicial power not as a matter of sovereignty, but as a matter of individual liberty."[350] In discussing *World-Wide Volkswagen*, the Court stated:

> The restriction on state sovereign power described in *World-Wide Volkswagen Corp.* . . . must be seen as ultimately a function of the individual liberty interest preserved by the Due Process Clause. That clause is the only source of the personal jurisdiction requirement and the Clause itself makes no mention of federalism concerns. Furthermore, if the federalism concept operated as an independent restriction on the sovereign power of the court, it would not be possible to waive the personal jurisdiction requirement: Individual actions cannot change the powers of sovereignty, although the individual can subject himself to powers from which he may otherwise be protected.[351]

Thus, as quickly as the Court had brought the state sovereignty function of the minimum contacts test into existence, the Court eliminated it. After *Insurance Corp. of Ireland*, the only components of the minimum contacts test that may function to protect state sovereignty are found in the reasonableness test. The state's interest, the interstate judicial system's interest in the most efficient resolution of controversies, and the shared interests of the several states in furthering fundamental substantive social policy may afford some protection to state sovereign interests. However, these components are, at best, indirect and inefficient standards with which to protect state sovereignty.

A better approach would be for the Supreme Court to recognize directly that protection for state sovereign interests has been undermined radically by the *International Shoe* test. The Court should hold that a judgment which satisfies the Due Process Clause does not, for that reason alone, deserve enforcement in another state. Instead, the states should be able to employ reasonable sovereignty-based jurisdictional restrictions to refuse enforcement to the judgments of other states. The Court can, as it did prior to the Fourteenth Amendment, supervise the states' administration of sovereignty-based jurisdictional restrictions through the use of its appellate jurisdiction over the state courts. A refusal to enforce a judgment of another state presents a federal question under the full-faith-and-credit implementing statute, even if the refusal is based on the violation of a nonconstitutional sovereignty-based rule. In cases within the appellate jurisdiction

---

349. *See id.* at 696-701, 102 S. Ct. at 2101-03, 72 L. Ed. 2d at 497-500.

350. *Id.* at 702, 102 S. Ct. at 2104, 72 L. Ed. 2d at 501.

351. *Id.* at 702-03 n.10, 102 S. Ct. at 2104 n.10, 72 L. Ed. 2d at 501 n.10.

on these grounds, the Court has the authority to assure that the reasons given by the state courts are justifiable.[352]

   If the Court were to adopt this approach, modern sovereignty-based rules would have to be developed. How often would the states be able to refuse the enforcement of other states' judgments under those rules? Sensible restrictions on the development of modern sovereignty-based rules can readily be envisioned. One restriction should be that a state could never refuse enforcement of another state's judgment on the ground that the judgment was rendered in violation of a nonconstitutional jurisdictional rule if the judgment-enforcing state would itself exercise jurisdiction under the same circumstances. Given the existence of broad long-arm statutes in virtually every state, this restriction alone would prevent wholesale refusals by the states to enforce the judgments of other states. A second, complementary restriction should be that a state could not refuse enforcement to another state's judgment if the refusal does not accord with generally accepted jurisdictional principles. Thus, even if a state has a very narrow long-arm statute, it could not refuse enforcement to the judgments of other states if the jurisdictional rule on which it relied was not generally accepted throughout the states. This last restriction parallels pre-Fourteenth Amendment practice under the full-faith-and-credit implementing statute, when the international rules used to determine the validity of state judgments were the restrictions on state sovereign power that were generally accepted at the time.

   Given the restrictions that would necessarily attend the development and administration of modern sovereignty-based rules of jurisdiction, only one situation is immediately apparent in which the states would justifiably be able to refuse enforcement to other states' judgments. If a state judgment directly affects the title to land located in another state, the situs state should be able to refuse enforcement of the judgment, even if no due process defect exists in the judgment. Even if no practical problems would be created for the situs state or its citizens, the situs state should still be able to refuse enforcement of the judgment. Although no rational basis exists for preventing states from directly affecting the title to land located in other states if no practical problems would be created by the adjudication, the tradition is still strong in the United States that such adjudications infringe the sovereignty of the situs state.[353] A jurisdictional rule so firmly established in the states constitutes a justifiable basis for refusing enforcement of a judgment. When nonconstitutional sovereignty-based rules are at issue, the states must ultimately be the judges of their own interests.

   Illustration 3-29. *A* and *B* are citizens of State *X*. They both claim title to the same plot of land in State *Y*. *A* sues *B* in a state court of State *X* to quiet the title to the land in State *Y*. Although *B* is personally served with process in

---

   352. *See* Ralph U. Whitten, *The Constitutional Limitations on State-Court Jurisdiction: A Historical-Interpretative Reexamination of the Full Faith and Credit and Due Process Clauses* (pt. 1), 14 CREIGHTON L. REV. 499, 596-99 (1981) (discussing the Court's exercise of appellate jurisdiction in implementing act cases prior to the Fourteenth Amendment and the concept of "jurisdiction of" the common law).

   353. *See* sections B(1)*(b)* ("Restrictive Principles of In Rem Jurisdiction") & H(3) ("Property Cases"), *infra*. As discussed, in the latter section, however, this jurisdictional restriction must be limited by the Supreme Court's holdings on raising and foreclosure of jurisdictional questions.

this action in State *X*, *B* fails to appear and defend the action. The court enters a default judgment quieting the title to the land located in State *Y*. This procedure should not be deemed to violate the Due Process Clause because all necessary protections under that Clause have been afforded to the defendant, *B*.

  Illustration 3-30. On the facts of *Illustration 3-29*, if *A* sues on the State *X* judgment in State *Y* to establish title, no apparent practical problems would be created for the situs state or its citizens. The State *Y* court in which the action is brought can investigate any matters that would render the judgment void under State *X* law before enforcing the judgment. Once a State *Y* judgment has been rendered in favor of *A*, that judgment can be recorded in the land records in the county of State *Y* where the land is located. A State *Y* judgment appearing in the land records will not cause any greater practical problems in this kind of case than in a purely domestic land title action in State *Y* in which a judgment is rendered. Nevertheless, State *Y* should still be able to refuse enforcement to the judgment because of the strong tradition against such judgments in the United States. The tradition gives rise to a legitimate sovereignty-based limitation on State *X's* jurisdiction, even though the rule may make no practical sense.

  Illustration 3-31. On the facts of *Illustration 3-30*, if *B* appears in the State *X* action and litigates the title issue on the merits, *B* should be foreclosed from raising the issue of jurisdiction in accordance with the ordinary rules governing the raising and foreclosure of jurisdictional issues examined in section B(3), above, and section H(3) and Chapter 13(E), below, as long as the State *X* court applies State *Y* substantive land title law to resolve the dispute. However, if State *X* applies its own substantive title law to resolve the dispute, the State *Y* court should be able to disregard the State *X* judgment, whether or not *B* objected to State *X's* lack of jurisdiction to adjudicate the issue under State *X* law. This result also accords with the Supreme Court's modern decisions on raising and foreclosure of jurisdictional issues.

SECTION H. APPLICATION OF THE MINIMUM CONTACTS TEST TO SPECIFIC CASES

  Many of the Supreme Court's decisions applying the minimum contacts test were decided before the *Burger King* decision had established the two-step analysis for specific jurisdiction cases. Nevertheless, these cases remain good authority for determining the due process validity of state-court jurisdiction in particular categories of cases. By examining the situations in which the Court has approved and disapproved of jurisdictional assertions by the states, it will be possible to obtain a better picture of how the minimum contacts test should be applied to future cases. The discussion that follows will describe the results in the categories of cases thus far addressed by the Court and also analyze whether the results are still justified under the *Burger King* test. When pertinent, the discussion will also address whether jurisdiction would be justified under the unified test for jurisdiction recommended in section G(2)*(d)* or the modern sovereignty-based restrictions discussed in section G(3), above.

One word of caution is in order about the following discussion. The discussion assumes in the situations examined that it is appropriate to apply the minimum contacts analysis. It does not address the question whether jurisdiction can be exercised based on one of the traditional territorial rules of *Pennoyer v. Neff*. The possibility that one of the traditional rules will provide a valid basis of jurisdiction must be left open after *Burnham v. Superior Court*, discussed in sections E(2) and G(1), above. Thus, one of the threshold inquiries in every case today must be whether the state is exercising jurisdiction under a "traditional" or "novel" rule. If under a "traditional" rule, the disagreement among the members of the Supreme Court about the proper mode of analysis must be confronted and resolved.

1. Tort Cases

Section C(2), above, discussed the extension of state implied consent statutes beyond corporations to individuals under the doctrine of *Pennoyer v. Neff*. In that section it was observed that the states had asserted jurisdiction over nonresident motorists under statutes implying the consent of the motorists to suit in the state by the act of driving an automobile within the state. These assertions of jurisdiction were upheld by the Supreme Court under the Due Process Clause of the Fourteenth Amendment. Nothing in *International Shoe* or the later evolution of the minimum contacts test casts doubt on the ability of the states to assert jurisdiction in this kind of case today. A person who drives an automobile into another state engages in the kind of purposeful conduct required under *Burger King* to give fair warning that litigation in the state may result if the motorist has an accident there. The motorist should take steps either to protect against the burdens of suit by purchasing insurance or by not driving in the state. Any objective burdens on a nonresident motorist forced to litigate within the state will always be outweighed by the other factors in the reasonableness test, particularly the interest of the state in providing a forum for its injured resident and the interest of the injured plaintiff in litigating within the state. It is, of course, also likely that the state of the accident will often be a convenient place to resolve the dispute because of the location of witnesses and evidence there.

The case of a nonresident motorist sued in the state of the accident must be carefully distinguished from the case in which a defendant is sued based on a claim arising outside the state, as in *Helicopteros Nacionales de Colombia, S.A. v. Hall*, discussed in section G(2)*(a)*, above. In such cases, if the defendant has no activities within the forum that can be considered "related to" the activities outside the state that gave rise to the claim,[354] the state will be asserting general jurisdiction over the defendant and "systematic and continuous" contacts will be

---

354. *See* section (G)(2)*(b)(i)* ("Claims Arising Out of or Related to the Defendant's Contacts with the State") *supra*. It must be kept in mind that a threshold inquiry in every case in which a defendant is sued on a claim arising outside the state is whether the defendant is engaging in activities related to the claim within the state. If related activities exist, the case is one of specific jurisdiction, which requires application of the purposeful contacts-reasonableness test analysis of *Burger King*. *See* section (G)(2)*(b)(ii)-(iv) supra*.

required under *Hall*. If the defendant's contacts with the forum are "related to" the activity giving rise to the claim outside the state, the state will be asserting specific jurisdiction, and the analysis in the preceding paragraph will be applicable.

Illustration 3-32. *B*, a citizen and resident of State *Y*, operates a delivery service. The service delivers packages to customers in States *Y*, *X*, and *Z*. While driving a delivery truck in State *Z*, *B* collided with *A*, a citizen and resident of State *X*. *A* sued *B* in a state court of State *X* to recover damages for personal injuries received in the accident. *B* was served under the State *X* long-arm statute, which extends jurisdiction of the State *X* courts as far as the Due Process Clause permits. *B* specially appears and objects that State *X's* assertion of personal jurisdiction violates the Due Process Clause of the Fourteenth Amendment. If *B's* activities in State *X* are not considered "related to" the activities that gave rise to the claim in State *Z*, State *X's* assertion of jurisdiction is general. Thus, *B's* activities in State *X* must be of a "systematic and continuous" nature for jurisdiction to be valid. If *B's* activities in State *X* are considered "related to" the activities in State *Z* that gave rise to the claim, State *X's* assertion of jurisdiction is specific. Under the latter circumstances, *B's* action in purposefully operating a delivery truck in State *X* should give fair warning to *B* that a suit might result in the state if an accident occurs there. *B* should purchase insurance or take other action to defray the burdens of suit in State *X*. If *B* has taken such action, it will defray the burden of suit on the claim arising in State *Z*. If *B* has not taken action to defray the burdens of suit, *B* should not be excused from jurisdiction on the ground that the burdens of suit are heavy in State *X* and the state and plaintiff interests are less than they would be if the accident had actually occurred in State *X*.[355]

* * * * *

In two decisions after *International Shoe*, the Supreme Court sustained exercises of state-court jurisdiction over nonresident defendants in libel actions. In *Keeton v. Hustler Magazine, Inc.*,[356] the Court sustained an exercise of jurisdiction by New Hampshire over a publisher who had committed a nationwide libel. Jurisdiction was proper not only for that part of the claim arising from the distribution of the defendant's magazines in New Hampshire, but also for that part

---

355. Depending on the facts, the objective burdens of a suit in State *X* may be no greater than the objective burdens of a suit in State *Z*, where the accident occurred. For example, States *X*, *Y*, and *Z* may be adjacent states. It may be as easy for *B* to defend a suit in State *X* as in State *Z*. Under these circumstances, whether the assertion of jurisdiction is general or specific would be irrelevant if the test suggested in section (G)(2)*(c)* ("Toward a Unified Test for General and Specific Jurisdiction") *supra* is adopted. Under that test, a defendant would never be able to object to an assertion of jurisdiction on due process grounds if the objective burdens of suit are no greater in the forum than they would be in some other state where the defendant could concededly be sued. *But cf.* Felch v. Transportes Lar-Mex SA de CV, 92 F.3d 320 (5th Cir. 1996), in which the plaintiff sued the defendant, a Mexican corporation, in Texas for the wrongful death of the plaintiff's mother in an automobile accident in Mexico. The defendant transports cargo in Mexico to Nuevo Laredo, a city on the Mexican side of the Texas-Mexico border. Normally, the defendant drops the cargo off on the Mexican side and has others to deliver the cargo into Texas. Occasionally, but rarely, the defendant delivers the cargo into Texas. Under these circumstances, the Fifth Circuit held that the defendant's contacts with Texas were insufficient to establish either specific or general jurisdiction.

356. 465 U.S. 770, 104 S. Ct. 1473, 79 L. Ed. 2d 790 (1984).

of the claim resulting from distribution in other states. The Court did not use the two-step test for jurisdiction established later in *Burger King*. However, the elements of that test would seem to be satisfied on the facts of *Keeton*. The defendant's actions in distributing magazines in New Hampshire were purposeful and gave clear warning that a suit might result in New Hampshire based on the activities.[357] In addition, the activities conducted in other states would seem to fit the definition of activities that are "related to" the defendant's contacts with New Hampshire—publication and distribution of the same libellous article. Consequently, New Hampshire's assertion of jurisdiction is properly classified as specific as to the entire claim, and the first step in the specific jurisdiction analysis is satisfied.

Furthermore, the elements of the reasonableness test would not allow the defendant to defeat jurisdiction on the facts of *Keeton*. Even if the objective burdens of suit are great in New Hampshire, the state had compensatory and deterrent interests in providing a forum for the plaintiff, even though she was a nonresident.[358] In addition, the plaintiff sued under the "single publication rule." This rule allowed recovery for the damages done to the plaintiff nationwide by the libel in a single forum. The interstate judicial system's interests in efficiently resolving the claim for libel in a single action, rather than multiple actions, weighs in favor of the validity of jurisdiction in cases like *Keeton*.[359] Similarly, the shared interests of the several states in furthering fundamental substantive social policy was furthered in *Keeton* by an action in New Hampshire in which damages for the nationwide libel could be recovered.[360]

A second libel case was decided the same day as *Keeton*. In *Calder v. Jones*,[361] Shirley Jones commenced a libel action in a California state court against the *National Enquirer*, the California distributor of the *National Enquirer*, Calder (the president and editor of the *Enquirer*), and South (a reporter for the *Enquirer*). The *Enquirer* and the local distributor appeared and answered the complaint, but Calder and South, both residents of Florida, objected to the court's assertion of personal jurisdiction over them. Calder's contacts with California consisted of two trips to California, one for pleasure and one to testify in an unrelated case. As president and editor, Calder supervised all the functions of the *Enquirer*. Calder reviewed and approved the subject of the article about Jones,

---

357. In *Keeton*, the Court stated that Hustler, because of its continuous and deliberate exploitation of the New Hampshire market, and because it could "be charged with knowledge of 'the single publication rule,' " (described in the text *infra*) should reasonably have anticipated being haled into court within the state. *See id.* at 781, 104 S. Ct. at 1481-82, 79 L. Ed. 2d at 801-02.

358. In *Keeton*, the Court concluded that New Hampshire's interest was strong in part because the libel was committed partly within New Hampshire. This fact gave the state deterrent and compensatory interests in awarding damages to protect both the nonresident "subject of the falsehood" and its own citizens who were deceived by the libel. *See id.* at 776-77, 104 S. Ct. at 1479, 79 L. Ed. 2d at 799.

359. On the facts of *Keeton*, there could be only one action because the statutes of limitation of all other states had run. However, in this class of cases, the single publication rule clearly affords the possibility of an efficient single-suit recovery that will avoid a multiplicity of suits even when other fora are available.

360. The Court observed that New Hampshire had an interest in cooperating with other states through the single publication rule to provide an efficient forum in which to litigate interstate libel cases. *See id.* at 777-78, 104 S. Ct. at 1480, 79 L. Ed. 2d at 799.

361. 465 U.S. 783, 104 S. Ct. 1482, 79 L. Ed. 2d 804 (1984).

edited the article in its final form, and declined a request by Jones to print a retraction. South frequently traveled to California on business, but did most, if not all, of the research on the Jones article from Florida by phone.

The Court concluded that the relationship between the defendants, the state, and the litigation was sufficient to sustain California's assertion of jurisdiction under the minimum contacts test. Particularly important in *Calder* was the fact that California was the focal point of the allegedly libelous article as well as the location of the harm suffered. For this reason, the Court was easily able to sustain jurisdiction in California because of the effects that the article had caused there.[362] The Court also rejected an argument that special First Amendment jurisdictional limitations should be placed on libel cases. Because special substantive First Amendment limits were already placed on the ability of a plaintiff to recover in libel cases, the Court felt that additional jurisdictional limits for such cases would be a form of "double counting."[363]

Calder is arguably good authority for asserting jurisdiction in any case in which the defendant commits an intentional wrong against a citizen of the forum state.[364] Thus, *Calder* has been cited as authority for assertions of jurisdiction in trademark infringement actions[365] and antitrust cases,[366] among others.[367] However, some courts have considered even intentional torts committed against a resident of the forum state inadequate to sustain jurisdiction when the facts of

---

362. *See id.* at 788-89, 104 S. Ct. at 1485, 79 L. Ed. 2d at 810. In one of the more ironic arguments to be made in American jurisprudence, the editor and reporter of the National Enquirer likened themselves to boiler workers who had worked on a boiler in Florida which later exploded in California due to the workers' negligence. Their notion was that while it might be fair to subject the manufacturer of the boiler to jurisdiction in California in such a case, it would not be appropriate to subject the workers to jurisdiction there because of their lack of control over the distribution of the boiler and the absence of any benefit to them from its distribution in the state. *See id.* at 789, 104 S. Ct. at 1487, 79 L. Ed. 2d at 812. The Supreme Court rejected this argument. Unlike the hypothetical boiler workers, the editor and reporter were not charged with "untargeted negligence," but rather with an intentional tort whose focal point was California. *See id.* at 789-90, 104 S. Ct. at 1487, 79 L. Ed. 2d at 812-13.

363. *See id.* at 790-91, 104 S. Ct. at 1487-88, 79 L. Ed. 2d at 813.

364. *See, e.g.,* Blue Compass Corp. v. Polish Masters of Am., 777 F. Supp. 4 (D. Vt. 1991) (jurisdiction to adjudicate claims of copyright infringement and unfair competition existed in Vermont based on advertisement in national magazine that produced several inquiries from Vermont and one Vermont customer). *But cf.* Chaiken v. VV Publ'g Corp., 119 F.3d 1018 (2d Cir. 1997) (personal jurisdiction did not exist in Massachusetts over New York resident who acted as reporter for Israeli newspaper or over newspaper in suit by former residents of Massachusetts for defamation; Massachusetts long-arm statute did not apply to reporter and assertion of jurisdiction over newspaper would violate due process because only four copies of the newspaper containing defamatory article reached Massachusetts would not create sufficient contacts to sustain jurisdiction).

365. *See* Dakota Indus., Inc. v. Dakota Sportswear, Inc., 946 F.2d 1384 (8th Cir. 1991) (trademark infringement in which defendant's actions were "uniquely" aimed at the forum state).

366. VDI Techs. v. Price, 781 F. Supp. 85 (D.N.H. 1991) (antitrust and unfair competition claims; jurisdiction sustained on authority of *Calder* because New Hampshire was location of injury).

367. *See* Rothstein v. Carriere, 41 F. Supp. 2d 381 (E.D.N.Y. 1999) (jurisdiction appropriate in New York in action for malicious prosecution and intentional infliction of emotional distress against defendant who made false statements outside the forum resulting in a criminal prosecution of the plaintiff outside the forum, because plaintiff was located in the forum at the time of the statements and thus harm was caused there and was a foreseeable consequence of defendant's actions); Lowry v. Owens, 621 So. 2d 1262 (Ala. 1993) (nonresident automobile dealer and salesman fraudulently sold used automobile as new to a resident of the state; dealer advertised extensively in the state and solicited business there, even though sale did not occur in the state).

the case revealed a more passive relationship between the defendants and the forum than was present in *Calder*.[368]

Illustration 3-33. *A*, a citizen and resident of State *X*, is a collector of Civil War memorabilia. *A* purchased a rare Confederate battle flag from *C*, a citizen and resident of State *Z*, in State *Z*. Subsequently, *B*, a citizen of State *Y*, asserted that the flag had belonged to *B* and was stolen from *B* at a date long prior to the time that *A* had purchased it from *C*. *C's* assertions were made outside State *X* to a number of collectors attending events on Civil War antiques. However, some collectors in State *X* also learned of the assertions indirectly. *A* contends that the assertions are false and that *B* sold the flag along with a number of other Civil War artifacts to a person unknown, who later sold them to *C*. *A* commences an action against *B* in State *X*. *A* seeks damages for slander of *A's* title to the flag. *B* is served with process in State *Y* under the provisions of the State *X* long-arm statute, which extends jurisdiction as far as permitted by the U.S. Constitution. *Calder* supports the State *X* assertion of jurisdiction because *B* made the assertions in question knowing of *A's* possession of the flag in State *X* and claims of ownership to it. Thus, *B* could reasonably foresee the impact of the assertions on *A* in State *X*. Nevertheless, *Calder* is distinguishable from this case, in that *B* did not make the assertions in State *X*. Furthermore, the assertions were only indirectly learned of by collectors in State *X*. Thus, *B's* contact with State *X* is less direct and immediate than the contact of the defendants in *Calder* and might be considered too tenuous to satisfy the purposeful contact test. If the foreseeability of the impact on *A's* title in State *X* is sufficient to produce the conclusion that *B* has engaged in purposeful conduct with regard to State *X*, *Keeton* is authority that *A* can sue *B* in State *X* for damages incurred throughout the United States produced by the assertions.[369]

* * * * *

The Supreme Court has dealt with products liability cases twice since *International Shoe*. In both cases, the Court invalidated state-court assertions of jurisdiction. As discussed in section G(2)*(b)(iii)*, above, the important issue in this kind of case will be whether placing a product into the stream of commerce alone is enough to satisfy the purposeful contacts portion of the due process test, as suggested in *World-Wide Volkswagen Corp. v. Woodson*, or whether stream of commerce activity "plus" other actions by the defendant will be necessary, as suggested by the plurality opinion in *Asahi Metal Industry Co. v. Superior Court*. Regardless of which position is adopted, however, clear cases at each extreme exist in which jurisdiction can easily be judged valid or invalid.

Illustration 3-34. *B Corp.* is incorporated and has its principal place of business in State *Y*. *B* manufactures machine tools and sells the tools nationwide

---

368. *See* Green v. USF & G Corp., 772 F. Supp. 1258 (S.D. Fla. 1991) (slanderous telephone calls from Maryland to Florida not sufficient to justify assertion of jurisdiction under the Due Process Clause).

369. *See also* IMO Indus., Inc. v. Kiekert AG, 155 F.3d 254 (3d Cir. 1998) (intentional tort having impact in forum does not justify assertion of jurisdiction over defendant when tort was not specifically directed at forum); Noonan v. Wintston Co., 135 F.3d 85 (1st Cir. 1998) (inadvertent tort committed through an advertisement that included a picture of plaintiff without permission; tort had impact on forum, but was not specifically directed at forum and did not, as a consequence, justify jurisdiction).

through distributors in each of the fifty states. *B* also advertises extensively in trade magazines circulated in each state and by direct mail sent to companies in each state known to be potential purchasers of the kind of machine tools that *B* manufactures. *B* has also established a toll-free number for purchasers of its products to call for technical advice on the operation of its products. For problems that cannot be efficiently addressed over the telephone, *B* has established a practice of sending engineers to the plants of any customers encountering problems with its products. Through the distribution process described above, *B* sells approximately $9,000,000 worth of machine tools each year in State *X*. *C Corp.* is incorporated with its principal place of business in State *X*. *C* purchased a number of machine tools from *B*. One of the machines malfunctioned, seriously injuring *A*, an employee of *C*. *A* sued *B* in a state court of State *X* to recover damages for the personal injuries received in the accident. *B* was served with process under the State *X* long-arm statute, which extends jurisdiction as far as permitted by the U.S. Constitution. The assertion of jurisdiction is valid under the Constitution. Even under the ''stream of commerce plus'' theory of *Asahi*, the defendant has engaged in the kind of purposeful contacts with the forum that justify an assertion of state-court jurisdiction. In addition to placing its products into the stream of commerce, *B* has advertised in the forum state, established regular channels for providing advice to customers in the forum state, and marketed its products through distributors in the forum state who have agreed to serve *B's* sales agents there. These are all actions that *Asahi* indicated would sufficiently indicate a purpose to serve the market encompassed by the forum state.[370] In addition, jurisdiction cannot be defeated through use of the reasonableness test, as in *Asahi*. Whatever the burdens on the defendant of a suit in the forum, the state's interest in providing a forum for its injured resident and the plaintiff's interest in suing at home are strong in this case because the plaintiff is suing the defendant directly. The defendant is not, as in *Asahi*, being pulled into the case by the action of another defendant asserting an indemnity claim.

   Illustration 3-35. *A*, a citizen and resident of State *X*, is vacationing by automobile in State *Y* when *A* stops at a roadside store operated by *B*, a citizen and resident of State *Y*. *A* purchases a canned soft drink. When the sale is made, *B* knows that *A* is from State *X* and is returning there by automobile. *A* does not immediately open the soft drink, but places it in a cooler and resumes the trip. After returning to State *X*, *A* removes the soft drink from the cooler and drinks it, ingesting a decomposed mouse in the process. *A* sues *B* in a state court of State *X* to recover damages for the injuries received when *A* ingested the mouse. *B* is served with process under the State *X* long-arm statute, which extends as far as the U.S. Constitution permits. The assertion of jurisdiction is invalid because *B* has not engaged in purposeful contact with State *X*. *B's* activities are entirely localized. *B* in no way attempts to serve the market encompassed by State *X*.

---

370. *See Asahi*, 480 U.S. 102, 112, 107 S. Ct. 1026, 1033, 94 L. Ed. 2d 92, 104 (1987).

Even if a simple stream of commerce test is ultimately adopted by the Supreme Court, therefore, *B* could not be subjected to jurisdiction in State *X*.[371]

* * * * *

In categories of tort actions not directly addressed by the Supreme Court, the state courts and lower federal courts must, of necessity, evaluate particular cases under the tests for general and specific jurisdiction established in the Supreme Court's decisions. Most cases present straightforward problems that can easily be solved by the courts. As the minimum contacts test continues to evolve, however, difficult problems will often be presented about the analysis that is appropriate in different fact situations.

Illustration 3-36. B, a physician, is a citizen and resident of State *Y*. *B* owns a clinic that is located in State *Y*. *B's* practice is territorially limited to State *Y*. However, *B* advertises in a newspaper published in State *Y*, but circulated in states adjoining State *Y*, including State *X*. The newspaper advertisements include a toll-free number for prospective patients to call in order to make appointments at *B's* clinic. *A*, a citizen of State *X*, read an advertisement by *B* printed in one of the editions of the newspaper published in State *Y*, but circulated in State *X*. *A* called the toll-free number and made an appointment at *B's* clinic in State *Y*. Subsequently, *B* treated *A* on several occasions at the clinic in State *Y*. *A* contends that this treatment was negligent and caused *A* permanent injuries. *A* sued *B* in a state court of State *X* to recover for the injuries inflicted on *A* by *B's* malpractice. *B* was served with process in this action under the State *X* long-arm statute, which extends jurisdiction as far as permitted under the U.S. Constitution. The claim arose from *B's* activities in State *Y*. The advertisements in State *X* might be classified as activities "related to" *B's* actions in State *X* giving rise to the claim, but this classification is uncertain. If the advertisements are not "related to" *B's* claim-producing conduct in State *Y*, the case is one of general jurisdiction, which will require "systematic and continuous" contacts between *B* and State *X*. Whether such contacts exist will depend on the extent of the solicitation of patients through advertising that *B* does in State *X*. If *B's* advertising in State *X* is considered "related to" *B's* claim-producing activity in State *Y*, which seems appropriate, the assertion of jurisdiction will be specific. In this event, the solicitation of patients through advertising in State *X* will have to constitute "purposeful contact" with State *X*. If purposeful contacts exist, jurisdiction will only be defeated if the burdens of suit in State *X* outweigh State *X's* interest in providing a forum for *A*, *A's* interest in suing in State *X*, the interstate judicial system's interest in the most efficient resolution of controversies, and the shared interest of the several states in furthering fundamental substantive social policies. At least one court has viewed this kind of case as

---

371. *See World-Wide Volkswagen*, 444 U.S. 286, 296, 100 S. Ct. 559, 566, 62 L. Ed. 2d 490, 500-01 (1980); *see also* Uppgren v. Executive Aviation Servs., Inc., 304 F. Supp. 165, 170-71 (D. Minn. 1969).

involving an assertion of specific jurisdiction by State X that is valid under the Due Process Clause.[372]

* * * * *

Mass tort cases arising out of the national or international marketing of a product can produce special jurisdictional problems. Although the Supreme Court has not yet addressed the appropriate due process standards in such cases, at least one U.S. District Court has done so. In the *DES Cases*,[373] Judge Weinstein noted that the due process standards developed by the Supreme Court to control state personal jurisdiction had been developed in cases "almost all of which involved one or a few parties on each side."[374] Accordingly, Judge Weinstein asserted that those standards were inapt for mass tort cases. Judge Weinstein argued that a "territorial nexus" requirement "is arguably least pressing in mass torts [and] the continued reliance on such protections creates significant obstacles to their resolution."[375] Instead, Judge Weinstein substituted a two-step test. In the first step, the court must determine whether the forum state has an "appreciable interest" in the litigation.[376] This inquiry focuses on whether the "litigation raises issues whose resolution would be affected by, or have a probable impact on the vindication of, policies expressed in the substantive, procedural, or remedial laws of the forum."[377] If an "appreciable state interest" is established, the assertion of jurisdiction is "prima facie constitutional." It will be considered valid unless "given the actual circumstances of the case, the defendant is unable to mount a defense in the forum."[378] Evidence bearing on the latter question includes (1) the defendant's available assets; (2) whether the defendant has or is engaged in substantial interstate commerce; (3) whether the defendant is being represented by an indemnitor or is sharing the cost of defense with someone else; (4) the comparative hardship the

---

372. *See* Sanders v. Hunter, 253 N.J. Super. 666, 602 A.2d 809 (Law Div. 1991). The court clearly viewed the defendant's actions in soliciting patients through advertising within the state as purposeful. This seems correct. The solicitation should have given the defendant fair warning that an action might be brought by a disgruntled patient from another state. However, the effect of advertising in establishing purposeful contacts is currently the subject of controversy in the lower federal and state courts. *Compare* Nowak v. Tak How Invs., Ltd., 94 F.3d 708 (1st Cir. 1996), *cert. denied*, 520 U.S. 1155, 117 S. Ct. 1333, 137 L. Ed. 2d 493 (1997) (business sends representatives to Hong Kong regularly; on one trip an executive negotiates special rates with hotel for business's executives in future; hotel then sends information about special corporate rates and other promotional literature to the business in the forum; based on the information received, one of business's executives makes reservations for himself and wife at hotel; wife killed in drowning accident; contacts of hotel with forum are sufficient to sustain specific jurisdiction over hotel in forum) *with* Lott v. J.W. O'Connor & Co., 991 F. Supp. 785 (N.D. Miss. 1998) (no general jurisdiction in forum over a shopping mall in another state where plaintiff was injured; jurisdictional assertion based on general, untargeted advertising in other state that reaches consumers in forum). *See generally* Keith H. Beyler, *Personal Jurisdiction Based on Advertising: The First Amendment and Federal Liberty Issues*, 61 Mo. L. Rev. 61 (1996). Special problems of jurisdiction based on internet activities are discussed in section H(7), *infra*.

373. *In re* DES Cases, 789 F. Supp. 552 (E.D.N.Y. 1992).

374. *Id.* at 585.

375. *Id.* at 586.

376. *Id.* at 587.

377. Id. "The notion that a forum state ought to have an interest in litigation before asserting jurisdiction over the parties is based on the idea that a state may not impose obligations on nonresidents without a reason." *Id.* at 585.

378. *Id.* at 587.

defendant will incur in defending the suit in a different forum; and (5) the comparative hardship to the plaintiff if the action is dismissed.[379]

Whether Judge Weinstein's standards can be squared with cases like *Asahi* is doubtful. Whether the Supreme Court will adopt this analysis for mass tort cases only time will tell. What is clear, in mass torts and elsewhere, is that more workable standards than those yet developed under *International Shoe* are greatly to be desired.

2. Contract Cases

The Supreme Court has decided two significant contract cases under the minimum contacts test since *International Shoe*. One of these, *Burger King Corp. v. Rudzewicz*, was discussed in section G(2)*(b)(ii)* and *(iii)*, above. *Burger King* established the two-step analysis that must now be applied to all cases of specific jurisdiction. The other decision, *McGee v. International Life Insurance Co.*,[380] was one of the early decisions under the minimum contacts test. Taken together, *McGee* and *Burger King* provide general guidance about the kinds of situations in which states may validly assert jurisdiction in contract cases.[381]

In *McGee*, a resident of California purchased an insurance policy from an Arizona insurance corporation in 1944. In 1946, the defendant, a Texas corporation, assumed all of the Arizona company's insurance obligations. The defendant mailed a reinsurance certificate to the California insured, offering to reinsure him in accordance with the policy he held with the Arizona corporation. This offer was accepted. The insured paid premiums on the policy by mailing the premiums from California to Texas until his death in 1950. Other than this contact with California, there was no evidence that either the defendant or the Arizona insurance company had any offices or agents in California or had ever done any other insurance business there. The defendant refused to pay the proceeds of the policy to the beneficiary upon the insured's death, claiming the insured had committed suicide. The beneficiary sued in a California court, asserting jurisdiction under a California statute subjecting foreign insurance companies to suit in California on insurance contracts with residents of California, even though the companies could not be served within the state. A default judgment was ultimately entered against the defendant. The plaintiff sued on the judgment in Texas to enforce it there. The defendant challenged the validity of the judgment on the ground that California's assertion of jurisdiction violated the Due Process Clause of the Fourteenth Amendment.

The U.S. Supreme Court sustained the validity of the California judgment. The Court stated that it was "sufficient for purposes of due process that the suit was based on a contract which had substantial connection with [California]."[382]

---

379. *Id.*

380. 355 U.S. 220, 78 S. Ct. 199, 2 L. Ed. 2d 223 (1957).

381. For a comprehensive evaluation of personal jurisdiction in contracts cases, see Martin B. Louis, *Jurisdiction Over Those Who Breach Their Contracts: The Lessons of* Burger King, 72 N.C. L. Rev. 55 (1993).

382. *Id.* at 223, 78 S. Ct. at 201, 2 L. Ed. 2d at 226.

The Court emphasized that modern means of transportation and communication made it much less burdensome for a party to defend an action where the party engages in economic activity.[383] The Court also stated that "California [had] a manifest interest in providing effective means of redress for its residents," who "would be at a severe disadvantage if they were forced to follow the insurance company to a distant State in order to hold it accountable."[384]

Applying the two-step *Burger King* analysis to the facts of *McGee* produces the conclusion that California's assertion of jurisdiction was proper. The defendant's solicitation of an insurance contract with the plaintiff and acceptance of premiums constitutes purposeful contacts with the state, even if the insurance agreement is the only one ever solicited in the state. For the reasons given by the Court, it would seem impossible to defeat jurisdiction with the reasonableness test. The burdens on the defendant of a suit in California are probably not great and should, in any event, have been taken into account before the defendant entered into business in the state. The state's and plaintiff's interests in maintaining the action in California are strong. Furthermore, it would seem more efficient to resolve the dispute in California than anywhere else, because the witnesses and evidence pertinent to determine whether the insured committed suicide are most likely present there. Finally, if shared interests of the several states in furthering fundamental substantive social policies exist, they must surely focus on assuring that interstate insurance companies meet their obligations to the people that they insure in the state where they insure them.

Given the clear propriety of jurisdiction in *McGee* under the two-step test, it is curious that the Supreme Court cited *McGee* in *Burger King* as an example of a situation in which the reasonableness test might *create* jurisdiction even in the face of less than optimal purposeful contacts between the defendant and the forum state.[385] The citation of *McGee* for this proposition suggests that it was a case in which the defendant did not have "adequate" purposeful contacts with the state, which seems clearly wrong. The better interpretation is that the Court was simply illustrating the kind of state and plaintiff interests that would serve to enhance jurisdiction if purposeful contacts are absent, without meaning to suggest that they were actually absent in *McGee*.

Burger King itself made it clear that an extensive course of negotiations by the defendant with a plaintiff located in the forum state will help establish the kinds of purposeful contacts that are necessary to sustain jurisdiction under the Due Process Clause. In *Burger King*, extensive negotiations led to a contract that was to be performed in part in the forum state and that contained a choice-of-law clause stating that the forum state's law would be applied to resolve disputes under the contract. Taken together, these factors established the kind of fair warning necessary under the Due Process Clause that an action on the contract might be brought in the forum.[386] The Court made it clear that when these kinds

---

383. *See id.* at 222-23, 78 S. Ct. at 200, 2 L. Ed. 2d at 226.

384. *Id.* at 223, 78 S. Ct. at 201, 2 L. Ed. 2d at 226; *see also* Traveler's Health Ass'n v. Virginia, 339 U.S. 643, 648-49, 70 S. Ct. 927, 929-30, 94 L. Ed. 1154, 1161-62 (1950) (dictum).

385. *See Burger King*, 471 U.S at 476, 105 S. Ct. at 2184, 85 L. Ed. 2d at 543.

386. *See id.* at 478-82, 105 S. Ct. at 2185-87, 85 L. Ed. 2d at 544-47.

of factors are present, the fact that the defendant never entered the forum state will be irrelevant.[387] Furthermore, the reasonableness test could not be used to defeat jurisdiction. The state and plaintiff's interests in maintaining the action in the forum were strong, and the burdens on the defendant could be addressed short of a jurisdictional dismissal, through procedural means such as a change of venue.[388]

Taken together, *McGee* and *Burger King* seem to establish that an assertion of jurisdiction to adjudicate a contract case will always be valid if the defendant has taken an active role in forming a contract to be performed, at least in part, in the forum. In cases in which the defendant is an interstate business, such as an insurance company, it may be sufficient that the company enters into a contract to be performed in the forum without more.[389] For example, in *McGee*, if the plaintiff had purchased the insurance in Texas without a prior solicitation from the defendant, but at the time of contracting the defendant had knowingly undertaken to insure a risk in California and accepted premiums from the plaintiff in that state over a number of years, it would seem that the purposeful contact portion of the minimum contacts test would still be satisfied. Other situations in which the defendant is only tenuously connected with the state will present greater difficulties.

Illustration 3-37. B Corp. is a large catalog order business that sells popular electronic products and novelty items to consumers. *B* obtains the names of potential customers by purchasing mailing lists from other catalog companies. It then mails catalogs unsolicited to the potential customers, who are located in all fifty states. *B* is incorporated with its principal place of business in State *Y*. *B* obtains *A*'s name as a potential customer from a mailing list. *A* is a citizen and resident of State *X*. *B* mailed a copy of one of its catalogs to *A* in State *X*. *A* subsequently purchased an expensive electronic item from *B* by mail. When the product arrived, it did not function properly. *B* refused to accept a return of the product or to return *A*'s money. *A* sued *B* in a state court of State *X* for breach of contract. *B* was served under the State *X* long-arm statute, which extends jurisdiction as far as permitted by the U.S. Constitution. State *X* should be able to assert jurisdiction over *B* in the breach of contract action. *B*'s action in mailing the catalog to *A* and shipping goods to *A* in State *X* was purposeful contact of the sort sufficient under *McGee* and *Burger King* to establish jurisdiction over *B*. Even if the burdens of litigating in State *X* are substantial, the state and plaintiff's interests are strong in maintaining the action in State *X* to protect consumers in *A*'s position, and the shared interests of the several states in furthering fundamental substantive social policy are arguably implicated by the need to provide

---

387. *See id.* at 476, 105 S. Ct. at 2184, 85 L. Ed. 2d at 543.

388. *See id.* at 482-84, 105 S. Ct. at 2187-88, 85 L. Ed. 2d at 547-48.

389. *But cf.* OMI Holdings, Inc. v. Royal Ins. Co. of Can., 149 F.3d 1086 (10th Cir. 1998) (defendant insurers agreed to defend the plaintiff whenever it was sued, but declined to defend action in Kansas on the ground that it was not covered by the policy; after losing in Kansas, plaintiff sued defendants there to recover attorneys fees and costs incurred in defending the suit; court held that the agreement to defend the plaintiff anywhere satisfied the purposeful contacts portion of the specific jurisdiction test, but that the burden of litigating in Kansas made the assertion of jurisdiction unreasonable).

consumers throughout the states with protection from mail order products that turn out not to be as advertised. The fact that the defendant has no sales representatives in the state and maintains no sales outlets in the state is irrelevant.[390]

Illustration 3-38. Assume the facts of *Illustration 3-37*, except that after *B* extends credit to *A* and ships the product to *A* in State *X*, *A* refuses to pay for it. *B* sues *A* in a state court of State *Y* to recover the purchase price of the product. *A* is served under the State *Y* long-arm statute, which extends jurisdiction as far as permitted by the U.S. Constitution. State *Y's* assertion of jurisdiction should be considered invalid. Even if *A's* action in ordering the product from *B* in State *Y* and agreeing to pay *B* for the product there is purposeful contact of the sort necessary to satisfy the first step in the minimum contacts analysis, the reasonableness test should defeat jurisdiction in this case. The burdens of litigating in State *Y* will be substantial for *A*, and the countervailing interests are not strong. *B* can protect itself by requiring credit card payment at the time the order is placed or by arranging for c.o.d. payment. Given the means available to *B* to structure its business in a way as to protect itself in case of disputes with its customers, *B* should not be allowed to sue *A* in State *Y*.

3. Property Cases

The Supreme Court's position on jurisdiction to adjudicate property cases is derived from *Shaffer v. Heitner*, discussed in section E(1), above. *Shaffer* made it clear that the presence of property within the state could not be used as the basis for adjudicating a claim having nothing to do with the property. However, the Court also made it clear that the states have power consistent with the Due Process Clause to adjudicate disputes over the ownership of property located in the state. As indicated in the discussion of *Abernathy v. Abernathy* in section E(1), above, questions still exists about the power of the states to adjudicate claims to property brought into the state without the consent of the property's owner.[391] Another important issue remaining open under the Court's decisions is whether a state will have jurisdiction under the Due Process Clause to directly affect the title to land located in another state. The resolution of this issue may

---

390. *See* Quill Corp. v. North Dakota *ex rel.* Heitkamp, 504 U.S. 298, 112 S. Ct. 1904, 119 L. Ed. 2d 91 (1992), discussed in subsection 6 ("State Tax Cases"), *infra*; *see also* Leventhal v. Harrelson, 723 So. 2d 566 (Ala. 1998) (plaintiffs, Alabama citizens, were trustees of a pension plan who sued a Georgia resident who had influenced their decision to invest in a limited partnership in investment property in Georgia; plaintiffs travelled to Georgia to discuss the investment with defendant; defendant's partner recommended the investment to the plaintiffs, and defendant sent a letter agreement to Alabama to dispel misgivings the plaintiffs had about the investment, but never entered Alabama; jurisdiction in Alabama upheld); Spectrum Pool Prods., Inc. v. MW Golden, Inc., 1998 Mont. 283, 968 P.2d 728 (contract negotiated by phone between Colorado swimming pool installation contractor and Montana swimming pool component manufacturer for Montana party to provide component for pool in Colorado; all contacts and correspondence initiated by Colorado party; contract provided for manufacture of component in Montana, shipping to Colorado, and, later, repair of product in Montana; when full payment was not made, Montana party sued Colorado party in Montana; defendant's contacts with Montana held to be purposeful and jurisdiction upheld).

391. *See* section E(1) ("Quasi In Rem and Related Jurisdictional Doctrines") *supra*.

depend on how the dispute between different minorities of the Court in *Burnham v. Superior Court*, discussed in section E(2), above, is resolved. If Justice Scalia's view of the Due Process Clause prevails, and if the restriction on state jurisdiction to affect the title to land located elsewhere is classified as a traditional rule, only the situs state will be able to deal directly with the title to land. If Justice Brennan's view prevails, the minimum contacts test will be applied to determine the validity of a state's assertion of jurisdiction to adjudicate title to land located elsewhere. This issue has been adequately discussed elsewhere and need not be treated further here.[392]

If the restrictive principles of in rem jurisdiction persist, either as due process, full faith and credit, or common-law sovereignty restrictions, they should be subject to the ordinary rules developed by the U.S. Supreme Court to govern raising and foreclosure of jurisdictional issues. Recall from section B(1)*(b)*, above, that the Supreme Court has characterized these restrictive principles as subject-matter jurisdiction restrictions.[393] Nevertheless, it is clear from the Court's decisions that even subject-matter jurisdiction limitations can be foreclosed from consideration if they are raised and determined against the losing party in an initial proceeding, and even if they are not raised at all in a fully litigated action. In *Durfee v. Duke*,[394] the defendant in a Nebraska state action fully litigated the issue of whether land claimed by the defendant was located in Nebraska or Missouri. The Nebraska courts determined that the land was located in Nebraska, and the defendant lost. Subsequently, the defendant in the Nebraska proceeding commenced an action in Missouri to quiet title to the same land. The U.S. Supreme Court held that, despite the fact that Nebraska only had power to determine the merits of an action if it had subject-matter jurisdiction over the land, the question of subject-matter jurisdiction itself was foreclosed by prior litigation of the issue in Nebraska. In *Chicot County Drainage District v. Baxter State Bank*,[395] the Court had previously held that an issue of subject-matter jurisdiction could be foreclosed if not raised in a fully litigated action.[396] Taken together, these decisions should preclude relitigation of subject-matter jurisdiction issues concerning the power of courts over extrastate land that have been fully and fairly litigated in an initial action. They should also preclude, in most cases, litigation of subject-matter jurisdiction issues concerning the power of courts over extrastate land when those issues are not raised in an initial action that is otherwise fully litigated on the merits.[397]

---

392. *See* section G(1) ("Cases to Which the Minimum Contacts Test Applies") *supra.*

393. *See* section B(1)*(b)* ("Restrictive Principles of In Rem Jurisdiction") *supra.*

394. 375 U.S. 106, 84 S. Ct. 242, 11 L. Ed. 2d 686 (1963).

395. 308 U.S. 371, 60 S. Ct. 317, 84 L.Ed 329 (1941) *Chicot*, however, did not involve a question of jurisdiction over land.

396. Foreclosure of subject-matter jurisdiction questions in fully litigated proceedings should be distinguished from foreclosure of such issues in cases in which the defendant defaults. In Thompson v. Whitman, 85 U.S. (18 Wall.) 457, 21 L. Ed. 897 (1873), the Court allowed an issue of subject-matter jurisdiction to be raised in a section action when the defendant had not appeared in the first proceeding.

397. Foreclosure of subject-matter jurisdiction and personal jurisdiction by the doctrines of claim and issue preclusion are discussed fully in Chapter 13(E) *infra.* While the same rules of preclusion normally apply to both personal and subject-matter jurisdiction questions, there are some exceptions to preclusion in the case of subject-matter jurisdiction questions. *See* RESTATEMENT (SECOND) OF JUDGMENTS § 12 (1982).

Unfortunately, not all courts have recognized the significance for land cases of the Supreme Court's modern decisions on foreclosure of subject-matter jurisdiction issues. For example, in the case of *In re Estate of Hannan v. Glover*,[398] a Virginia domiciliary died leaving as part of her residual estate land located in Nebraska, which she devised to her surviving children and the "issue" of her children per stirpes. The decedent's will was probated in Virginia. The Virginia Supreme Court held that under Virginia law the word "issue" did not include adopted children. In an ancillary probate proceeding in Nebraska, the adopted child of one of the decedent's deceased children attempted successfully to relitigate the question whether "issue" included adopted children under Nebraska law. Ultimately, the Nebraska Supreme Court applied Nebraska law to this question and held that the word "issue" included adopted children. The court did not discuss the effect of the judgment in the Virginia probate proceeding, in which the adopted child had participated, noting simply that Nebraska followed the conflict-of-law rule that the law of the state where real property is located governs devises of such property by will.[399] However, the Nebraska Court of Appeals had discussed the effect of the Virginia proceeding.[400] Relying on the old U.S. Supreme Court decision of *Clarke v. Clarke*,[401] the Nebraska Court of Appeals held that the Virginia courts did not have jurisdiction to control the devolution of real property located in another state.[402] Therefore, the Virginia probate judgment was not entitled to full faith and credit in Nebraska.

Standing alone, the *Clarke* decision would indeed support denial of full faith and credit to the Virginia judgment in *Hannan*. In *Clarke*, the South Carolina courts, in a litigated proceeding, held that a will had worked an "equitable conversion" of real property located in Connecticut into personal property. This conversion allowed the courts to determine how the property should pass under the will because it was no longer realty; instead it was personality over which the courts in the decedent's domicile had "jurisdiction."[403] In a subsequent proceeding in Connecticut, the South Carolina judgment was denied full faith and credit. The U.S. Supreme Court affirmed. The Court held that the South Carolina courts did not have subject-matter jurisdiction over the Connecticut land. Thus, *Clarke* parallels in many respects the facts of *Hannan*. The difficulty is that the holding of *Clarke* has arguably been modified by the Court's later decisions in *Durfee* and *Chicot County*, discussed above. If a question concerning the title to land is fully litigated on the merits in a nonsitus forum without anyone raising the question of the forum's subject-matter jurisdiction, it is difficult to see why the situs state should be permitted to deny effect to the nonsitus state's judgment. Similarly, if an issue of subject-matter jurisdiction is actually litigated and determined in the nonsitus state, there is no

---

398. 246 Neb. 828, 523 N.W.2d 672 (1994).

399. *Id.* at 831, 523 N.W.2d at 674.

400. *See In re* Estate of Hannan v. Glover, 2 Neb. Ct. App. 636, 513 N.W.2d 339 (1994).

401. 178 U.S. 186, 20 S. Ct. 873, 44 L. Ed. 1028 (1900).

402. 2 Neb. Ct. App. at 642, 513 N.W.2d at 344.

403. *See* LUTHER L. MCDOUGAL III ET AL., AMERICAN CONFLICTS LAW ch. 17 (5th ed. 2000) (discussing, *inter alia*, conflicts-of-laws issues concerning equitable conversion).

apparent reason why relitigation of the issue should be permitted, at least in the absence of a gross disregard of the interests of the situs.[404] In both instances, the policies supporting finality in litigation support foreclosure of the jurisdictional issue, as well as issues concerning the merits.[405]

In general, the *Shaffer* decision controls the jurisdiction of the states to adjudicate disputes in which either real or personal property is involved. *Shaffer* itself involved the seizure of personal property in an attempt to obtain jurisdiction to adjudicate a dispute having nothing to do with the property. However, there is one major difference between jurisdiction over personal and real property. Even assuming that there are constitutional restrictions on the power of states to adjudicate disputes involving the title to land located in other states, there have never been comparable restrictions on the power to adjudicate the title to personalty located elsewhere. Similarly, there are no sufficient sovereign interests to justify a refusal to enforce the judgment of another state's courts adjudicating the title to personalty in which the judgment-enforcing state has an interest. Therefore, if a state can acquire jurisdiction over the defendant under conventional standards, the state will be able to adjudicate an action validly even though it involves the title to personalty located elsewhere.

Illustration 3-39. A, a citizen and resident of State *X*, claims ownership of a valuable painting in the possession of *B*, a citizen and resident of State *Y*. *B* also claims ownership of the painting. *B* is temporarily present in State *X* when *A* has *B* personally served with process in an action in a State *X* court for a declaratory judgment that *A* is the true owner of the painting. Assuming that the personal service on *B* is valid under the *Burnham* decision discussed in section E(2), above, or that jurisdiction can validly be asserted against *B* under the minimum contacts test, State *X* may enter a valid judgment determining the ownership of the painting, even though the painting is located in State *Y*. If the judgment determines that *A* owns the painting, a State *Y* court will be obligated to enforce the judgment under the implementing statute to the Full Faith and Credit Clause.[406]

---

404. In modern practice, an exception exists to issue preclusion on questions of subject-matter jurisdiction when "[t]he subject-matter of the action was so plainly beyond the court's jurisdiction that . . . entertaining the action was a manifest abuse of authority." RESTATEMENT (SECOND) OF JUDGMENTS § 12(1) (1982). Thus, one might draw a distinction between cases like *Durfee*, which involved questions of fact concerning the physical location of land, and cases like *Clarke* and *Hannan*, which involved conceded applications of the nonsitus states substantive law to determine a question involving devolution of land elsewhere. The difficulty is that, while there are cases in which it is so clear that the situs states substantive law should be applied to a title question that failure to do so might constitute "manifest abuse of authority," of which *Clarke* may be one, *Hannan* does not seem to involve such a situation. Indeed, in *Hannan*, the Nebraska Court of Appeals held that, in determining the intent of a nonresident testator as to a term in a will, Nebraska should follow the law of the testator's domicile as to devises of both real and personal property and that it did not violate Nebraska's public policy to do so in the case. *See Hannan*, 2 Neb. Ct. App. at 644-49, 513 N.W.2d at 345-47; *see also* Chapter 13(E) ("Claim and Issue Preclusion on Questions of Subject-Matter and Personal Jurisdiction"), *infra*; *cf. Illustrations 3-29 to 3-31* in section G(3), *supra*.

405. *See* Chapter 13 ("FINALITY IN LITIGATION").

406. Of course, if other claimants to the painting are "indispensable parties" to the action and are not subject to the jurisdiction of the court, the action might not be maintainable for that reason. *See* Chapter 8(C)(3) ("Joinder of persons Needed for Just Adjudication") *infra*.

4. Trust and Estate Cases

The U.S. Supreme Court has adjudicated two cases involving trust assets. In *Hanson v. Denckla*,[407] discussed in section G(2)*(b)(iii)* above, the Court held that a state had no authority to adjudicate the interests of nonresidents in trust assets located in another state when the nonresidents did not have minimum contacts with the state. *Hanson* was based on the absence of purposeful contacts between the defendants and the forum state. The defendants were essentially passive with regard to the forum and could not have anticipated and defrayed the burdens of a suit there. Furthermore, there was an alternate forum where the action could be conveniently adjudicated against all parties.

The other trust case was *Mullane v. Central Hanover Bank & Trust Co.*[408] In *Mullane*, New York enacted "common trust fund" legislation, which permitted numerous small trust estates to be pooled in a single fund for purposes of investment administration. Provisions were made for accountings twelve to fifteen months after a bank had established such a fund and triennially thereafter. In such accounting proceedings, the judicial decree was made binding and conclusive upon all persons having any interest in the common fund or any participating estate, trust, or fund. Central Hanover Bank & Trust established such a common trust fund in January, 1946. In March, 1947, the bank petitioned the New York Surrogate's Court for settlement of its first account as common trustee. In this accounting proceeding, the power of the state of New York to adjudicate as to nonresident beneficiaries of the trust was raised. The argument was made that the New York court did not have power to adjudicate the interests of nonresident beneficiaries without personal service of process on them within the state. The authority for this argument was, of course, *Pennoyer v. Neff*.[409] The U.S. Supreme Court stated that whether the proceedings were classified by the New York court as in rem or in personam, the state had the power to adjudicate the interests of the nonresidents due to its strong interests in providing means to close trusts that are established under its laws and are administered under the supervision of its courts.[410]

Mullane was decided prior to *Shaffer v. Heitner* and *Burger King Corp. v. Rudzewicz*, at a time when the minimum contacts test was still maturing. Therefore, with the exception of the Court's emphasis on the state's interest, *Mullane* did not apply any element of the modern two-step minimum contacts analysis. However, the modern analysis also supports the result in *Mullane*. *Shaffer* confirmed that a state has power to adjudicate claims to property located within the state. Therefore, the location of the trust assets in New York provides ample basis for New York to assert jurisdiction over nonresident beneficiaries of the trust.

---

407. 357 U.S. 235, 78 S. Ct. 1228, 2 L. Ed. 2d 1283 (1958).
408. 339 U.S. 306, 70 S. Ct. 652, 94 L. Ed. 865 (1950).
409. *See id.* at 311-12, 70 S. Ct. at 655-56, 94 L. Ed. at 871-72.
410. *Id.* at 313, 70 S. Ct. at 656, 94 L. Ed. at 872.

In addition, the nonresident beneficiaries' claims to the trust assets present a case of specific jurisdiction. Under a specific jurisdiction analysis, the possibility of litigation in the state to supervise the administration of the trust was foreseeable to the party investing in the common trust. However, the original investors in the common trust would not always, or even often, have been the beneficiaries of the trust whose interests were being affected by the adjudication. It may be, therefore, that the beneficiaries of the trust would not have been in a position to foresee and, therefore, to protect themselves from the burdens of litigation in New York. Nevertheless, even if the beneficiaries could do nothing to defray the burdens of suit within the state, it would seem that New York was the most convenient location in which an action for an accounting by the trustee might be brought, thus enhancing the case for personal jurisdiction under the *Burger King* reasonableness test. The Court in *Mullane* emphasized the strong state interest in supervising trusts established under its laws. In addition, no other state could probably assert jurisdiction over all the nonresident beneficiaries, thus creating strong plaintiff's interests in a suit in New York because of the absence of a convenient alternative forum. The prevention of multiple suits in different states also creates an interest on the part of the interstate judicial system in having the action adjudicated in New York. Furthermore, New York had established a procedure in which a representative was appointed to safeguard the interests of the nonresident beneficiaries of the trust. Finally, it would seem that states share a substantive interest in establishing procedures whereby trustees will be required to account for their management of trust assets. The state where the trust is established and the assets are managed would seem to be the most logical place to conduct such an accounting.[411]

Hanson and *Mullane* taken together may indicate a preference by the Supreme Court for an action in the state where the trust is established and the assets are located, if a single action in that state is feasible between the contestants. However, it is also arguable that *Hanson* was wrongly decided under the modern due process analysis. In *Hanson*, Florida asserted jurisdiction over the nonresident defendants in a proceeding to probate the will of a deceased domiciliary of the state. The state where a decedent is domiciled at death certainly has an interest in probating the will and disposing of the estate's assets in an efficient manner. Furthermore, Florida seems as logical a forum to settle all claims pertaining to the decedent's assets as Delaware. It was no more inconvenient for the Delaware parties to litigate in Florida than it was for the Florida parties to litigate in Delaware.

Under the Court's holding in *Hanson*, it will be necessary for an executor or administrator of an estate to bring ancillary proceedings in every state where personal property of the decedent is located when residents of the situs state assert claims to the property and lack purposeful contacts with the state where the probate proceeding is being conducted. Separate proceedings will result in the

---

411. *Mullane* is also a possible example of a case in which, even if ordinary due process standards are not satisfied, the doctrine of ''jurisdiction by necessity'' may allow a state such as New York to assert jurisdiction. *See* section I (''Jurisdiction by Necessity'') *infra*.

possibility of conflicting holdings on matters of fact and applicable law that may impede the process of administration.[412] It seems no more necessary or desirable to require multiple proceedings to protect nonresident beneficiaries of an estate than it would be to insist on separate accounting proceedings in each state where the beneficiary of a trust is located. Given these problems with *Hanson*, it would seem desirable to limit the holding of the case as much as possible.

Illustration 3-40. *R*, a citizen and resident of State *X*, is the representative of the employees of certain motion picture and record companies. *R* sues *T*, a citizen and resident of State *Y*. *T* is the trustee of a trust established to receive payment of certain royalties from the employers of the employees that *R* represents. The action is brought in a state court of State *X*. The action seeks to invalidate collective bargaining and related trust agreements between the employers and the employee's union. The allegation is that the union violated its duty as the employee's collective bargaining agent by agreeing with the employers that the royalty payments should be paid into the trust rather than to the employees as wages. *R* seeks a declaratory judgment of the invalidity of the agreement, the appointment of a receiver to collect future royalty payments, and preliminary injunctive relief against payment of further royalties to the trust by the employers. In *Atkinson v. Superior Court*,[413] jurisdiction was sustained over the nonresident trustee in an action of this sort after *Hanson* was decided, and the U.S. Supreme Court denied certiorari to review the state-court decision.

Hanson and *Atkinson* can be distinguished on several grounds. First, the trustee in *Atkinson* had established a continuing relationship with nonresidents in which the assets of the trust were constantly being enhanced by payments from out of state. In contrast, *Hanson* involved a continuing relationship in which the corpus of the trust was not being enhanced by the settlor, but the Delaware trustee was instead paying amounts to the settlor from time to time in Florida. Second, the nonresident trustee in *Atkinson* established a relationship with residents of a state who remained residents of the same state. That state turned out to be the forum. In *Hanson*, the settlor of the trust was a resident of Pennsylvania when she established the trust and later moved to Florida. Thus, the trustee in *Atkinson* could anticipate litigation in the state where the employees lived at the time the trust was formed, while the trustee in *Hanson* could not anticipate litigation in Florida when the trust was formed. Finally, the action in *Atkinson* sought in part to prevent the future transfer of assets out of the forum to the trustee. Surely the forum had jurisdiction to grant this relief based on the presence of the property (wages) in the state. Under these circumstances, combining the other relief against the trustee with this relief against the employers seems to be an efficient and convenient litigation package.

---

412. *See, e.g., In re* Estate of Crichton, 20 N.Y.2d 124, 228 N.E.2d 799, 281 N.Y.S.2d 811 (1967).
413. 49 Cal. 2d 338, 316 P.2d 960 (1957), *cert. denied*, 357 U.S. 569, 78 S. Ct. 1381, 2 L. Ed. 2d 1546 (1958).

5. Domestic Relations Cases

As discussed in section E(1), above, *Shaffer v. Heitner* preserved ex parte interstate divorce jurisdiction from attack under the minimum contacts test. However, the Supreme Court did not explain how the ex parte divorce cases could be justified under the test. A possible explanation, also offered in section E(1), is that in a no fault divorce action, the defendant has no substantive rights that the Due Process Clause can effectively protect through the imposition of location-of-suit rules. However, it must be remembered that this rationale applies only to claims for divorce. Under the concept of "divisible divorce," a nonresident spouse's rights to support and alimony cannot be cut off without minimum contacts between the defendant and the forum.[414] Since *Shaffer*, the Supreme Court has decided only two domestic relations cases under the minimum contacts test: *Kulko v. Superior Court*[415] and *Burnham v. Superior Court*.[416] These cases illustrate the operation of the test in domestic relations cases well.

In *Kulko v. Superior Court*,[417] the Court invalidated an assertion of personal jurisdiction by California over a nonresident father who was sued for increased child support. The jurisdictional assertion was defective because of the absence of purposeful contact between the father and California. The fact that the father, who had custody of the children in New York, allowed them to go to California to live permanently with their mother was not sufficient to establish purposeful contacts with the forum.[418]

---

414. *See* Vanderbilt v. Vanderbilt, 354 U.S. 416, 77 S. Ct. 1360, 1 L. Ed. 2d 1456 (1957); Estin v. Estin, 334 U.S. 541, 68 S. Ct. 1213, 92 L. Ed. 1561 (1948); RUSSELL J. WEINTRAUB, COMMENTARY ON THE CONFLICT OF LAWS § 5.2E2 (3d ed. 1986).

415. 436 U.S. 84, 98 S. Ct. 1690, 56 L. Ed. 2d 132 (1978).

416. 495 U.S. 604, 110 S. Ct. 2105, 109 L. Ed. 2d 631 (1990).

417. 436 U.S. 84, 98 S. Ct. 1690, 56 L. Ed. 2d 132 (1978).

418. In *Kulko*, a married couple domiciled in New York decided to divorce. The couple entered into a separation agreement which provided that the couple's two children would reside with the husband in New York during the school year, but would spend Christmas, Easter, and summer vacations with the wife. The wife waived any claim for her own support, but the agreement provided that the husband was to pay $3,000 per year in child support for the periods that the children resided with the wife. The wife then obtained a Haitian divorce that incorporated the terms of the separation agreement. Subsequently, each of the children expressed a desire to live permanently with the wife in California, and the husband permitted them to do so. After the children had taken up residence in California, the wife instituted a California proceeding to establish the Haitian divorce as a California judgment, to modify the judgment to award her permanent custody of the children, and to increase the support obligations of the father. The husband was served with long-arm process in this action under the general California long-arm statute, providing that the state's courts could exercise jurisdiction on any basis not inconsistent with the Constitution. The husband specially appeared to challenge the jurisdiction of the California courts over him under the Due Process Clause. The California courts held that due process was not violated by the state's assertion of jurisdiction. The California Supreme Court concluded that jurisdiction was proper because the husband had caused an "effect" in California by purposely sending at least one of the children to live with the wife. *See id.* at 86-90, 98 S. Ct. at 1694-95, 56 L. Ed. 2d at 138-40. The U.S. Supreme Court reversed the California judgment. The Court held that the mere act of sending a child to live with his or her mother did not demonstrate an intent to obtain nor an expectancy of receiving a corresponding benefit from the state that would make it fair to assert jurisdiction over the husband. *See id.* at 92-94, 98 S. Ct. at 1696-98, 56 L. Ed. 2d at 141-43. After determining that there was no "purposeful act" by the defendant that would sustain an exercise of jurisdiction by California, the Court weighed California's interest in adjudicating the action in its courts against the burdens that would be imposed on the husband by litigation in California and concluded under this balancing process that California was not a fair forum. *See id.* at 92-97,

In *Burnham v. Superior Court*,[419] discussed in section E(2), above, the Court sustained an assertion of jurisdiction by California over a nonresident husband-father for divorce, custody, and alimony. Jurisdiction was sustained on the basis that the husband-father was personally served within the state while temporarily present there. This "transient presence" jurisdiction was obviously not relevant to the ability of the plaintiff-wife to obtain a divorce, which could have been granted ex parte on the basis of *Shaffer*. Rather, the jurisdictional assertion enabled California to make support and alimony awards that would not otherwise have been possible in the absence of minimum contacts between the husband-father and the state.

In *Burnham*, the plaintiff did not attempt to obtain jurisdiction over the defendant under the California long-arm statute. An obvious obstacle to asserting jurisdiction over the defendant under a long-arm statute was *Kulko*. However, it is interesting to consider whether the facts in *Kulko* and *Burnham* are sufficiently distinguishable to allow a valid assertion of jurisdiction under the minimum contacts test in the latter case. In *Burnham*, the couple was residing in New Jersey at the time of their separation. They agreed that the wife would take the two children and move to California while the husband would remain in New Jersey. In addition, they agreed that the wife would commence an action in California for divorce based on irreconcilable differences and that the husband would submit to this proceeding. However, after the wife and children moved to California, the husband not only refused to submit to the California divorce proceeding, but also commenced a New Jersey divorce proceeding on grounds of desertion.

In contrast, the wife and husband in *Kulko* entered into a separation agreement providing for custody of the children in the husband and for payment of limited support amounts by the husband during short periods when the children resided with the mother in California. The husband complied fully with the terms of this agreement. Although the husband later allowed the children to go to California to live with the mother permanently, he did not, as did the father in *Burnham*, contrive to send the entire family to California to live in the first instance and then breach an agreement that he had made with the wife to submit to proceedings in California.

These factual differences between *Kulko* and *Burnham* seem significant in light of the goal of the minimum contacts test. That test is structured to allow a defendant to anticipate litigation in a distant state in order to either avoid jurisdiction-conferring actions or defray the burdens of a suit away from home. The husband in *Kulko* cooperated in a plan that resulted in divorce, custody, and support awards without litigation in a distant forum. Indeed, it is difficult to see

---

98-101, 98 S. Ct. at 1696-99, 1700-01, 56 L. Ed. 2d at 141-45, 145-47. This two-step process resembles the analysis established in *Burger King*. Under *Burger King*, the absence of purposeful contacts will defeat jurisdiction, unless the reasonableness test can be used to enhance the case for jurisdiction. As discussed in subsection G(2)*(b)(iv)* ("The Reasonableness Test"), *supra*, the factor in the reasonableness test that appears to be most important in enhancing the case for jurisdiction is the state's interest in adjudicating the action in its courts. Assuming that *Kulko* was anticipating the *Burger King* decision, therefore, it can be read as a case in which the state's interest was inadequate to overcome the absence of purposeful contacts.

419. 495 U.S. 604, 110 S. Ct. 2105, 109 L. Ed. 2d 631 (1990).

what else the husband could have done to protect himself from distant litigation, except to prevent the children from migrating to live with their mother, an action that seems extreme under the circumstances of the case. Given that he acted prior to the action to avoid burdensome litigation and complied with all obligations assumed in the agreement he entered into, it would seem unjustified to subject him to jurisdiction in California. In contrast, the husband in *Burnham* contrived to send his entire family to California to live and, rather than forming an agreement with the wife that would have protected him from distant litigation, actively breached an agreement to submit to divorce jurisdiction in California. These actions seem sufficiently purposeful to justify an assertion of jurisdiction over the husband-father under a long-arm statute.

If this distinction between *Kulko* and *Burnham* is valid, the wife could have asserted jurisdiction over the husband-father in the latter case under California's long-arm statute. There was thus no need to establish transient presence jurisdiction over the defendant to award support and alimony. Minimum contacts were satisfied not, as Justice Brennan argued, because of the defendant's transient presence in the state, but because of the defendant's prior actions in sending the family to live in California and breaching an agreement with the plaintiff that would have resulted in jurisdiction over the defendant in California.

6. State Tax Cases

International Shoe itself involved an assertion of jurisdiction by Washington to impose a tax on the defendant. The Supreme Court's decision in the case thus stands for the proposition that a state can subject a nonresident defendant to jurisdiction in order to collect taxes levied on the basis of the defendant's activities within the state. In *International Shoe*, the defendant had sales representatives within the state and maintained both temporary and permanent outlets within the state where samples of its merchandise could be viewed. All of its business, however, was interstate commerce because all sales of its goods were made on the basis of orders sent by the sales representatives to the defendant in St. Louis, Missouri, and the goods were shipped from that location to Washington.

More recently, in *Quill Corp. v. North Dakota ex rel. Heitkamp*,[420] the Supreme Court considered the power of North Dakota to require an out-of-state retailer to collect a state use tax from its customers within the state. Unlike the defendant in *International Shoe*, the retailer in *Quill* maintained no outlets or sales representatives within the state. All of its sales were made through catalogs, flyers, advertisements in national publications, and telephone calls. Through these processes, the defendant sold approximately $1,000,000 worth of goods annually in North Dakota. The Supreme Court held that the Due Process Clause did not restrict North Dakota's power to collect the use tax from the defendant, although the Court also held that the Commerce Clause of the Constitution did prohibit the

---

420. 504 U.S. 298, 112 S. Ct. 1904, 119 L. Ed. 2d 91 (1992).

tax. The due process holding was predicated on the Court's analysis in judicial jurisdiction cases.[421] The Court stated that "there is no question that Quill has purposefully directed its activities at North Dakota residents, that the magnitude of those contacts are more than sufficient for due process purposes, and that the use tax is related to the benefits that Quill receives from access to the State."[422] Under these circumstances, it is irrelevant that the defendant had no physical presence in the state.

Because of the Court's reliance on the judicial jurisdiction cases, *Quill* stands for the proposition that the state has power to subject a nonresident defendant to jurisdiction to adjudicate the validity of a tax, as well as for the proposition that the Due Process Clause imposes no obstacle to the state's power to levy the tax. In addition, it is arguable that *Quill* is also authority for the proposition that a defendant such as Quill can be subjected to jurisdiction within the state by one of its customers in a breach of contract action. The activity of the defendant is no less purposeful in such a case than in the case of the state's power to tax. Thus, the fact that the defendant has no physical presence in the state should not matter.[423]

7. Internet Activities

In recent years, the rise of internet activities has produced difficult issues of personal jurisdiction. The U.S. Supreme Court has not yet addressed these issues, but internet activities have produced significant litigation in other courts. They have also spawned an extensive academic literature.[424] In general, the decided cases have struggled, with only limited success, to fit internet activities within the models supplied by the U.S. Supreme Court for other cases. This subsection will illustrate the problems involved through a discussion of several lower federal court decisions that have dealt with the issues in different factual contexts.

---

421. *See id.* at 306-08, 112 S. Ct. at 1910-11, 119 L. Ed. 2d at 103-04.

422. *Id.* at 308, 112 S. Ct. at 1911, 119 L. Ed. 2d at 104.

423. *Cf. Illustrations 3-37* and *3-38, supra.*

424. *See, e.g.,* Corey B. Ackerman, World-Wide Volkswagen, *Meet the World-Wide Web: An Examination of Personal Jurisdiction Applied to a New World,* 71 ST. JOHN'S L. REV. 403 (1997); Lori Irish Bauman, *Personal Jurisdiction and Internet Advertising,* 14 COMPUTER LAW. 1 (1997); Charles H. Fleisher, *Will the Internet Abrogate Territorial Limits on Personal Jurisdiction?* 33 TORT & INS. L.J. 107 (1997); Jack L. Goldsmith, *Against Cyberanarchy,* 65 U. CHI. L. REV. 1199 (1998); Christopher W. Meyer, *World Wide Web Advertising: Personal Jurisdiction Around the Whole Wide World?* 54 WASH. & LEE L. REV. 1269 (1997); Joseph S. Pevsner & Gregory W. Curry, *Down the Block But Outside Jurisdiction: Personal Jurisdiction in a Modern World,* 29 TEX. TECH. L. REV. 977 (1998); Martin H. Redish, *Of New Wine and Old Bottles: Personal Jurisdiction, the Internet, and Constitutional Evolution,* 38 JURIMETRICS J. 575 (1998); Richard Phillip Rolls, *The Morass of Internet Personal Jurisdiction: It Is Time for a Paradigm Shift,* 51 FLA. L. REV. 667 (1999); Katherine C. Sheehan, *Predicting the Future: Personal Jurisdiction for the Twenty-First Century,* 66 U. CIN. L. REV. 385 (1998); David L. Statl, *Personal Jurisdiction in Cyberspace: The Constitutional Boundary of Minimum Contacts Limited to a Web Site,* 25 J. COMP. & INT'L L. 819 (1997); Howard B. Stravitz, *Personal Jurisdiction in Cyberspace: Something More Is Required on the Electronic Stream of Commerce,* 49 S.C. L. REV. 925 (1998); David Wille, *Personal Jurisdiction and the Internet—Proposed Limits on State Jurisdiction Over Data Communications in Tort Cases,* 87 KY. L.J. 95 (1998); Ryan Yagura, *Does Cyberspace Expand the Boundaries of Personal Jurisdiction?* 38 IDEA 301 (1998).

One of the leading decisions in the area is *Compuserve, Inc. v. Patterson*.[425] In *Compuserve*, a Texas resident subscribed to a network service based in Ohio. He also entered into a separate agreement with the service to sell his software over the internet. He regularly sent software to the service in Ohio and advertised the software through the service. Later, he claimed the service, by marketing a similar software product, had infringed his trademarks and engaged in deceptive trade practices. After he demanded $100,000 to settle his claims, the service sued him in Ohio. The service sought a declaratory judgment that it had not infringed his trademarks or engaged in deceptive trade practices.

The U.S. District Court in which the action was brought dismissed it for lack of personal jurisdiction, but the Sixth Circuit reversed. Because the service had based its action on the behavior of the defendant in sending his software to Ohio for sale on the service, the Sixth Circuit considered the case one of specific jurisdiction.[426] It also concluded that the purposeful contact requirement of the specific jurisdiction test was satisfied by the user's behavior in subscribing to the service and entering into an agreement designed to market his software through the service in other states (which contained a choice-of-law clause providing that Ohio law would govern the agreement). The court emphasized that the defendant *both* formed a contract with the plaintiff *and* placed a product into the stream of commerce. The court held that entering into this ongoing relationship with the service provided adequate notice that he could be sued in Ohio. Applying the reasonableness step of the specific jurisdiction test, the court found that the defendant could not overcome the presumption of jurisdiction raised by the existence of purposeful contacts, largely because the state and plaintiff's interests were high in maintaining the suit in Ohio.

There are many similarities between *Compuserve* and *Burger King*. In particular, the Sixth Circuit seemed influenced by the entrepreneurial nature of the defendant's activities,[427] as well as the fact that the defendant had initiated an ongoing relationship with the service.[428] Although the court did not draw the parallel explicitly, the defendant's activities in *Compuserve* are very similar to those of the Michigan franchisees in *Burger King*.[429] This analogy breaks down somewhat, however, because of the procedural posture of the case. In *Burger King,* the franchisor was suing for breach of a franchise agreement into which the nonresident defendants had entered. In *Compuserve*, the affirmative claims for relief were possessed by the nonresident defendant, and the plaintiff had anticipated the claims by a declaratory judgment action in Ohio. *Burger King*

---

425. 89 F.3d 1257 (6th Cir. 1996); *see* Michael J. Sikora III, *Beam Me Into Your Jurisdiction: Establishing Personal Jurisdiction Via Electronic Contacts in Light of the Sixth Circuit's Decision in* Compuserve, Inc. v. Patterson, 27 CAP. U. L. REV. 163 (1998); David D. Tyler, Case Note, *Personal Jurisdiction Via E-Mail: Has Personal Jurisdiction Changed in the Wake of* Compuserve, Inc. v. Patterson, 51 ARK. L. REV. 429 (1998).

426. The court considered the contacts of the defendant described in the text to be "related to" the claims of trademark infringement and deceptive trade practices that he asserted. *See* 89 F.3d at 1267. His action in threatening to sue for an injunction and damages also gave rise, in part, to the service's declaratory judgment claim. *See id.*

427. *See id.* at 1268.

428. *See id.* at 1266-67.

429. *See* section G(2)*(b)(iii)* & H(2) *supra* (discussing *Burger King*).

would be on all fours with *Compuserve* if the franchisees in the former case had entrusted property (*e.g.*, recipes for a new food product) to Burger King in Florida, Burger King had allegedly misappropriated the property, and, when the franchisees threatened to sue in Michigan, Burger King had sought a declaratory judgment in Florida that the property had not been misappropriated. Even in the face of an ongoing franchise relationship, an assertion of jurisdiction over the Michigan franchisees would be troublesome in such a case.

One dispute that has arisen in the decisions in whether a so-called "passive" website in one state can justify an assertion of jurisdiction over the owner of the site in a distant state where the site has caused damage to a plaintiff. The cases are split. In *Cybersell, Inc. v. Cybersell, Inc.*,[430] an Arizona corporation sued a Florida corporation for trademark infringement in Arizona. The Arizona corporation alleged that it had been damaged by the defendant's use of its mark on the defendant's home page in Florida. The Ninth Circuit held that the actions of the Florida corporation were not sufficient to establish personal jurisdiction over it in Arizona. The court acknowledged that the Florida home page could be accessed by anyone in the world, but opined that posting "an essentially passive home page on the web" was insufficient to establish the purposeful contacts that were necessary to validate an assertion of specific jurisdiction.[431] The court also noted that there was no evidence that any part of the defendant's business had occurred in Arizona or with people from Arizona.[432]

In contrast to *Cybersell*, the U.S. District Court for the Eastern District of Missouri rejected the notion that a "passive" website could not create jurisdiction. In *Maritz, Inc. v. CyberGold, Inc.*,[433] a trademark infringement action was brought in Missouri against a California corporation. As in *Cybersell*, the claim was based on a website maintained by the defendant in another state, California. The district court concluded that the defendant was subject to jurisdiction under Missouri's "tortious act" provision of its long-arm statute. The court held this assertion of jurisdiction constitutional:

---

430. 130 F.3d 414 (9th Cir. 1997).

431. *See id.* at 419. The plaintiff had conceded that the plaintiff did not "exist" in Arizona, so only specific jurisdiction was appropriate. *See id.* at 416. However, when a party establishes a website with the knowledge, and probably the desire, that it be accessed by persons everywhere, there is a sense in which it is conducting activities wherever other parties are located who access it. This "general jurisdiction" possibility has yet to be sufficiently explored in the decisions. Among other problems, it raises the question whether access by a third party—*i.e.*, a "hit"—from a distant state should be considered activity of the defendant "in" that state based on the knowledge and desire of the defendant that the hit, and many others like it, would take place.

432. *See id.* at 419; *see also* Panavision Int'l, L.P. v. Toeppen, 141 F.3d 1316 (9th Cir. 1998) (simply registering another party's trademark as a domain name and posting a website on the internet is not sufficient to subject a nonresident to jurisdiction sustained because defendant's actions were in pursuit of a scheme to extract money from plaintiff that the defendant knew would adversely affect plaintiff in the forum); Millennium Enterprises, Inc. v. Millennium Music, L.P., 33 F. Supp. 2d 907 (Ore. 1999) (for an interactive website to provide a basis for jurisdiction defendant must engage in deliberate action within the forum through the site or purposefully direct its activities at forum residents; fact that someone accessing the site could buy a product not enough; action was trademark infringement action in which there had been only one sale of a product to a forum resident).

433. 947 F. Supp. 1328 (1996); *see* Brian K. Epps, Recent Developments, Martz, Inc. v. CyberGold, Inc.: *The Expansion of Personal Jurisdiction in the Modern Age of Internet Advertising*, 32 GA. L. REV. 237 (1997).

Although CyberGold characterizes its activity as merely maintaining a "passive website," its intent is to reach all internet users regardless of geographic location. Defendant's characterization of its activity as passive is not completely accurate . . . . With CyberGold's website, CyberGold automatically and indiscriminately responds to each and every internet user who accesses its website. Through its website, CyberGold has consciously decided to transmit advertising information to all internet users, knowing that such information will be transmitted globally. Thus, CyberGold's contacts are of such a quality and nature, albeit a very new quality and nature for personal jurisdiction, that they favor the exercise of personal jurisdiction over the defendant.[434]

The court in *Maritz* correctly rejected the notion that a "passive" website cannot result in personal jurisdiction in another state. However, it cannot be said that the case otherwise established a workable test for distinguishing between internet activities that should, and those that should not, result in jurisdiction. One possible distinction between *Maritz* and *Cybersell* is that, in the latter case, there was no past or apparent future commercial benefit to the defendant in the forum resulting from the nonforum website, while in *Maritz* there had been 131 out-of-state "hits" from Missouri on the defendant's out-of-state website.[435] Although the website had not yet become operational, and thus there had been no actual commercial benefit to the defendant from these hits, the plaintiff was seeking injunctive relief to prevent the future damage to its interests that the defendant's activities would cause. No similar evidence, even of future harm, appeared to exist in *Cybersell.*

Whatever course the decisions take in the future, one sound result would be to deny jurisdiction over nonforum websites that are advertising for purely local commercial benefits. For example, in *Bensusan Restaurant Corp. v. King,*[436] the defendant was an operator of a small club in Columbia, Missouri. He established a local website to advertise the club. The plaintiff, who operated a club with an identical name in New York, sued the defendant in the U.S. District Court for the Southern District of New York for trademark infringement. The district court dismissed the action for lack of personal jurisdiction. The court held that jurisdiction did not exist under New York's long-arm statute. It also held that even if jurisdiction existed under the statute, it would violate due process.[437] The court was correct, given the localized nature of the defendant's activities and the fact that benefits from the website advertising would result to the defendant, if at all, in Missouri. As the court observed:

---

434. 947 F. Supp. at 1333.

435. *See id.* at 1333; *see also* Gary Scott Int'l, Inc. v. Baroudi, 981 F. Supp. 714 (D. Mass. 1997) (personal jurisdiction for trademark infringement claim sustained in Massachusetts over California seller who advertised over internet nationwide and intended to sell large amounts of product—cigar humidors—in Massachusetts, even though only 12 humidors had actually been sold there).

436. 937 F. Supp. 295 (S.D.N.Y. 1996), *aff'd*, 126 F.3d 25 (2d Cir. 1997).

437. The Second Circuit Court of Appeals affirmed only on the long-arm statute issue. *See* 126 F.3d at 26-29.

There are no allegations that [the defendant] actively sought to encourage New Yorkers to access his site, or that he conducted any business—let alone a continuous and systematic part of its business—in New York. There is in fact no suggestion that [the defendant] has any presence of any kind in New York other than the website that can be accessed worldwide. [The plaintiff's] argument that [the defendant] should have foreseen that users could access the site and be confused as to the relationship of the two . . . clubs is insufficient to satisfy due process.[438]

It is difficult to determine what course the decisions will take in cases involving internet activities. One perceptive suggestion is that the "reasonableness" test may offer the best solution to "cases involving electronic contacts as the Internet gives individuals who would not have the financial ability or business experience to engage in traditional commerce with other states and countries [the capacity] to distribute documents and other electronic products worldwide."[439] The reasonableness test may indeed be the most feasible means of resolving the myriad of factually diverse states involving internet activities. However, the downside of this suggestion is that the degree of judicial discretion involved in applying the reasonableness test does not offer the prospect of significant certainty and predictability.

SECTION I. JURISDICTION BY NECESSITY

U.S. Supreme Court decisions under the Due Process Clause suggest that there may be a doctrine of "jurisdiction by necessity." The basic notion supporting jurisdiction by necessity is that there must be at least one forum somewhere with power to adjudicate every case. Within this notion, however, there are at least two distinguishable kinds of jurisdiction by necessity cases.[440] One kind of case is represented by *Mullane v. Central Hanover Bank & Trust Co.*, discussed in section H(4), above. In the *Mullane* kind of "jurisdiction by necessity" case, strong practical considerations point to a particular state as the only realistic forum in which to settle a dispute. The second kind of jurisdiction by necessity case is one in which no forum possesses the necessary relationships with all of the defendants to assert jurisdiction under conventional due process standards. In this kind of "jurisdiction by necessity" case, the forum selected by the plaintiff would be allowed to exercise jurisdiction over the defendants simply because there is no other available forum that is any better.

There is little difficulty with the doctrine of jurisdiction by necessity when dealing with examples like the absent beneficiaries of the trust in the *Mullane* case or a dispute involving conflicting claims to land located within a

---

438. 937 F. Supp. at 301.

439. 4 CHARLES R. WRIGHT ET AL., FEDERAL PRACTICE AND PROCEDURE § 1067, at 77 (2d ed. Supp. 1999).

440. *See* Arthur T. Von Mehren & Donald T. Trautman, *Jurisdiction to Adjudicate: A Suggested Analysis*, 79 HARV. L. REV. 1121, 1173-74 (1966); *see also* George B. Fraser, Jr., *Jurisdiction By Necessity—An Analysis of the* Mullane *Case*, 100 U. PA. L. REV. 305 (1951).

state. In such cases, strong practical considerations dictate that defendants who do not have contacts with the state be subject to the jurisdiction of the state for purposes of settling their claims. Otherwise, absent defendants could, simply by refusing to consent to the jurisdiction of the state's courts, paralyze the ability of others also interested in the subject matter of the suit to settle their own claims to the property or assets located within the state. It would be no answer to require a suit in an absent defendant's home state to settle the defendant's claim. For such an approach would require actions in every state where potential claimants resided, with the attendant danger of conflicting judgments to the property or assets that would bind no other claimant. Under these circumstances, the state where the subject matter of the suit is located is simply the most convenient place to settle the dispute.

Thus, even if these kinds of cases are viewed as ones in which the "conventional standards" of the minimum contacts test are not met, jurisdiction by necessity would seem to be a justifiable concept to prevent the burdens of multiple suits and attendant dangers of substantive paralysis that might follow. However, as discussed in section H(4) in conjunction with the *Mullane* decision, the application of the modern minimum contacts analysis does seem to justify the result in the case. Specifically, even if the purposeful contacts portion of the test is not satisfied in a case like *Mullane* because of the inability of the trust beneficiaries to anticipate and defray the burdens of litigation in New York, the *Burger King* reasonableness test applied to the facts enhances the case for jurisdiction sufficiently to satisfy due process. Therefore, it would seem unnecessary to resort to a doctrine of jurisdiction by necessity in this kind of case, because "conventional standards" sustain jurisdiction to adjudicate.

Much more difficult is the notion that the doctrine of jurisdiction by necessity should be extended to situations in which there are multiple defendants, but no conflicting claims to property or assets located within the state. This concept of jurisdiction by necessity receives some support from recent Supreme Court decisions. In *Shaffer v. Heitner*, the Court reserved decision on whether jurisdiction would exist in the state where the defendant owned property, if no other forum were available to the plaintiff. This statement cannot sensibly be read as a reference to the power of a state court to settle claims to the property itself, a power which the Court made it clear elsewhere in the *Shaffer* opinion the states possess.[441] Rather, it must be read as a reference to the potential power of the states to exercise jurisdiction to adjudicate claims that have nothing to do with the property when the defendant lacks minimum contacts with the state and cannot be sued elsewhere. It is, however, difficult to imagine such a case. If the claim arose elsewhere, why can the defendant not be sued where the claim arose or where the defendant resides?[442]

It is possible that the Court had in mind cases in which the only alternate forum is in a foreign country. However, in *Helicopteros Nacionales de Colombia v. Hall*, discussed in section G(2)*(a)*, above, the Court stated:

---

441. *See* Shaffer v. Heitner, 433 U.S. 186, 207-08, 97 S. Ct. 2569, 2581, 53 L. Ed. 2d 683, 700 (1977).
442. Or, after *Burnham*, discussed in sections E(2) and H(5) *supra*, where the defendant can be served.

As an alternative to traditional minimum-contacts analysis, respondents suggest that the Court hold that the State of Texas had personal jurisdiction over Helicol under a doctrine of "jurisdiction by necessity" [citing footnote 37 in *Shaffer v. Heitner*]. We conclude, however, that respondents failed to carry their burden of showing that all three defendants could not be sued together in a single forum. It is not clear from the record, for example, whether suit could have been brought against all three defendants in either Colombia or Peru.[443]

Based on this passage, if all defendants could be sued in Columbia or Peru, it would be inappropriate for Texas to exercise jurisdiction by necessity. Thus, if the availability of a forum in a foreign nation defeats jurisdiction by necessity, the statement in *Shaffer* remains cryptic. However, the statement in *Hall* of the possible parameters of a doctrine of jurisdiction by necessity also raises other problems. If the plaintiff in *Hall* had demonstrated that it was impossible to sue all defendants in a single foreign court, the statement suggests that it *might* have been appropriate for Texas to exercise jurisdiction by necessity. This suggestion raises troubling questions of its own.

First, why should jurisdiction by necessity extend to this fact situation at all? Even if the defendants cannot be sued together in a single foreign forum, they can surely be sued individually in separate actions. True, such multiple actions would involve the danger of conflicting judgments, but the problem here is not as grave as the situation discussed above in which a court needs to settle conflicting claims to property or assets located within the state. In the latter situation, an individual suit against a claimant will not bind the other claimants if they do not participate in the action. The result is that unless all claimants are brought together in a single proceeding (or unless separate suits against each claimant happen, fortuitously, to result in judgments in one claimant's favor), the title to the property or assets subject to the conflicting claims may effectively be clouded forever. In the *Hall* situation, however, individual actions against multiple defendants in different courts will settle the dispute one way or the other. Of course, the plaintiff is at a tactical disadvantage if multiple actions must be brought because each defendant may successfully convince a trier of fact that one of the absent defendants is the party actually responsible for the plaintiff's injuries. But the result is simply that the plaintiff will not recover. This result is unfortunate if the plaintiff might have won a judgment by bringing all defendants together in a single proceeding. However, unfortunate or not, the dispute will be settled by the multiple judgments. The question is why a tactical disadvantage to the plaintiff should outweigh the defendants' ordinary due process rights to a reasonably nonburdensome forum?

A second question is, why Texas? Even assuming that jurisdiction by necessity extends to the *Hall* facts, how does one determine which of all the places in the universe of fora gets to exercise jurisdiction under the doctrine? In

---

443. Helicopteros Nacionales de Colombia, S.A. v. Hall, 466 U.S. 408, 419 n.13, 104 S. Ct. 1868, 1874 n.13, 80 L. Ed. 2d 404, 414 n.13 (1984).

Hall itself, there were present factors that probably made Texas the most logical state of the United States in which to bring an action. Bell Helicopter was one of the defendants and was located in Fort Worth. The decedents in the crash had been hired in Texas by another of the defendants, even though the decedents and their survivors were not residents of Texas, and so forth.[444] Thus, if jurisdiction by necessity is a viable doctrine, the plaintiff may have to bear the burden of selecting the most logical forum of all those possessing contacts with the parties and the transaction. But at this juncture, the Court's skimpy references to the doctrine have provided little guidance on this and other questions.[445]

    Illustration 3-41. *A*, a citizen and resident of State *X*, sues *B*, a citizen of a foreign nation, in State *Y*, by attaching property located in State *Y* owned by *B*. Other than the ownership of the property, *B* has no contacts with State *Y*. *A's* claim is based on an automobile accident that occurred in Canada between *A* and *B*. *B* has returned to *B's* home country, which would not permit its courts to entertain an action by *A* and would not enforce a judgment against *B* obtained in any court of the United States or any court of any other nation. These facts may represent a valid case for jurisdiction by necessity in State *Y*. If *A* is not allowed to assert the claim in State *Y* and use the property owned by *B* there as a means of satisfying a judgment obtained against *B*, *A* will, practically speaking, be deprived of *A's* claim for relief. It would be senseless to require *A* to proceed first in a Canadian court to obtain a judgment against *B* and then enforce the judgment against the land located in State *Y*. In addition to posing risks to *A* that *B* will dispose of the property in State *Y* to avoid the potential Canadian judgment, there is no reason to believe that proceeding first in Canada to obtain a judgment would place fewer burdens on *B* than would a suit in State *Y*.[446]

---

444. *See id.* at 409-12, 104 S. Ct. at 1869-71, 80 L. Ed. 2d at 408-10.

445. Another case that may have jurisdiction-by-necessity implications is Phillips Petroleum Co. v. Shutts, 472 U.S. 797, 105 S. Ct. 2965, 86 L. Ed. 2d 628 (1985). *Phillips* was a class action brought to recover interest on certain royalty payments withheld from the plaintiff class members. The defendants objected that the Kansas courts did not have sufficient contacts with nonresident members of the plaintiff's class to justify adjudicating their claims as part of the class action. The Supreme Court rejected this contention. The Court held that absent members of a plaintiff class did not face the same burdens as nonresident defendants given the protections afforded to the class by the Kansas class action rules. The reason *Phillips* may be an example of jurisdiction by necessity is that the claims of each individual member of the class were so small as to make pursuit of the claims in individual actions by the class members uneconomical. Unless a state that does not have contacts with all the class members can entertain the class action, often no action at all may be possible to vindicate the plaintiffs' claims. Another twist to the jurisdiction-by-necessity doctrine concerns the kinds of factors that will legitimately render a forum the only logical, available one. In *Keeton v. Hustler Magazine, Inc.*, 465 U.S. 770, 104 S. Ct. 1473, 79 L. Ed. 2d 790 (1984), New Hampshire was selected as the forum because the statutes of limitation of all other states had run. Likewise, in the *Phillips* litigation, the Supreme Court in a later decision held that it was constitutional for Kansas to apply its longer statute of limitations to interest claims that had arisen in other states and were barred by the statutes of limitation of the claim states. *See* Sun Oil Co. v. Wortman, 486 U.S. 717, 108 S. Ct. 2117, 100 L. Ed. 2d 743 (1988). In both *Keeton* and *Sun Oil*, the states asserting jurisdiction had some contact with the events giving rise to suit. The question is, would a state be allowed to assert jurisdiction by necessity if it had no contacts with the parties or the event giving rise to suit merely because it is the only state whose statute of limitations has not run? For an argument that it should not be able to do so, see Lea Brilmayer, An Introduction to Jurisdiction in the American Federal System 36 (1986).

446. The same would be true if the accident had occurred in another state of the United States and the question is whether to make *A* proceed in the state of the accident first.

Illustration 3-42. On the facts of *Illustration 3-41*, but assuming that *B* is a citizen of Great Britain, a proper case of jurisdiction by necessity would not seem to be presented under the *Hall* dictum. *A* can either sue *B* in Great Britain or in Canada and obtain an enforceable judgment. There is no justification for *A* to use the presence of property in State *Y* as the basis of jurisdiction under these circumstances.

Illustration 3-43. *A*, a citizen of State *X*, sues *B*, a citizen of State *X*, and *C*, a citizen of State *Y*, in a state court of State *X*. *B* has no contacts, ties, or relations with State *Y* and *C* has no contacts, ties, or relations with State *X*. Neither *B* nor *C* has any contacts, ties, or relations with a state where the other party has contacts, ties, or relations. Neither *B* nor *C* owns property outside the states where they are citizens. *B* and *C* are indispensable parties to an action against either of them. Because *B* and *C* are indispensable, *A* may not prosecute separate actions against *B* in State *X* and *C* in State *Y*.[447] These facts may present a jurisdiction-by-necessity case. To deny *A* the right to sue both parties in either State *X* or State *Y* will effectively deny *A* the right to recover on *A's* claim. However, to give *A* the right to suit will deprive either *B* or *C* the conventional protections afforded to defendants by the Due Process Clause. It is not clear why the rights of *A*, the plaintiff, should be preferred to the rights of either *B* or *C* in this situation under a doctrine of jurisdiction by necessity.

Illustration 3-44. On the facts of *Illustration 3-43*, but assuming that *B* and *C* are not indispensable parties to actions against the other, a jurisdiction-by-necessity case would not seem to be present. *A* can pursue separate actions against *B* in State *X* and *C* in State *Y*. Although *A* may encounter tactical problems in maintaining separate actions against *B* and *C*, especially if *A* is asserting claims in the alternative against the two defendants,[448] those tactical problems are not sufficient to justify depriving one of the defendants of the conventional due process protections afforded by the minimum contacts test.

SECTION J. NOTICE

Due process has always been seen as a guarantee to the defendant of an opportunity to be heard in defense before the defendant's life, liberty, or property may be taken. The minimum contacts test discussed in the preceding sections supports this opportunity-to-be-heard principle by securing a reasonably nonburdensome place of trial for the defendant. Obviously, if the location of trial places great burdens of expense or inconvenience on defendants, they might well relinquish their opportunity to be heard rather than incur those burdens. However, as the earlier discussion indicated, due process restrictions on the permissible

---

447. The indispensable party doctrine is discussed in Chapter 8(C)(3) ("Joinder of Persons Needed for Just Adjudication") *infra*.

448. When claims in the alternative are asserted, each defendant may defend by pointing the finger at the other defendant. Triers of fact in separate actions may absolve the defendant before them on the theory that the other defendant is responsible for the plaintiff's injuries. Therefore, two triers of fact in different actions may conclude that someone is liable to the plaintiff, but the plaintiff will not recover. *Cf. Illustration 3-27 supra*.

locations of suit are an innovation that occurred subsequent to the adoption of the Fourteenth Amendment. Far older is the due process requirement that the defendant receive adequate notice that an action has been commenced. Indeed, the notice requirement is not only older, but more basic, than the location-of-suit restrictions of the Due Process Clause. Obviously, even if litigation is conducted in the most convenient possible location from the defendant's point of view, the defendant will not be able to defend the action adequately if no notice is provided that the action has been commenced.[449]

In addition to being older and more fundamental than the location-of-suit rules imposed under the rubric of the minimum contacts test, the notice requirements of the Due Process Clause are simpler and more consistent. Recall from section A(2)*(a)*, above, that the pre-Fourteenth Amendment due process decisions of the state courts established that state legislatures had wide latitude to dispense with personal service of process as a form of notice and to provide alternate forms of notice. The decisions indicated that the form of notice chosen by the legislature would be upheld unless it was not plausible to believe that the form would reach the defendant. In effect, given the options available, the legislature had to choose a form of notice that was reasonably likely to reach the defendant. Often, this standard allowed the legislature to choose notice by publication in a newspaper because under the relatively crude conditions existing in most of the country, notice by publication was as likely to reach the defendant as an alternate form of notice.

The modern due process notice decisions by the Supreme Court follow the same fundamental principle as the pre-Fourteenth Amendment decisions of the state courts under their own due process clauses. Although the modern Fourteenth Amendment notice requirements may superficially appear inconsistent with early due process jurisprudence, they in fact apply the same rule: the form of notice provided must, given the options available to the legislature, be a form that is reasonably likely to provide the defendant with actual notice of the action.

Recall that in *Mullane v. Central Hanover Bank & Trust Co.*,[450] discussed in section H(4), above, the Supreme Court sustained the power of New York to settle a trust account with regard to nonresident beneficiaries of the trust. The *Mullane* case also contained an important holding on the quality of notice that had to be provided to the beneficiaries of the trust. In *Mullane*, the only notice that had been given to beneficiaries of the trust account was notice by publication in a newspaper, as provided by statute. The Supreme Court held this notice to be inadequate under the Due Process Clause as to beneficiaries whose whereabouts were known, although it was adequate as to beneficiaries whose interests or whereabouts could not be ascertained.[451] As to known, present beneficiaries, the Court stated that mail notice was the least form of notice

---

449. Certain other rules, concerning the opportunity to be heard in defense before a person's property may be taken by a provisional remedy such as attachment or garnishment, are examined in Chapter 6(F) ("Provisional Remedies"). These rules concern the timing of the opportunity to be heard, which does not always have to be provided prior to the taking that is the subject of the due process challenge.

450. 339 U.S. 306, 70 S. Ct. 652, 94 L. Ed. 865 (1950).

451. *See id.* at 317-18, 70 S. Ct. at 658-59, 94 L. Ed. at 875.

permissible under the Due Process Clause.[452] The general standard the Court articulated for notice under that Clause was a form of notice which "within the limits of practicability" was "reasonably calculated to reach interested parties."[453]

In *Pennoyer v. Neff*,[454] the Supreme Court had, in part, connected a requirement of seizure of the property before judgment to the due process requirement of notice. The Court conditioned the sufficiency of notice by publication upon the seizure of the property or some other equivalent act.[455] A passage in *Mullane* seemed to indicate that this part of *Pennoyer* was still good law.[456] Subsequent decisions have, however, confirmed that even in actions concerning property within the state, the *Mullane* decision requires the best form of notice that is practicable under the circumstances. This standard will usually require at least mail notice to interested persons whose whereabouts are known or reasonably ascertainable.[457]

The *Mullane* standard thus governs all attempts by the legislative branch of government to provide notice to defendants in civil actions. The standard is connected in a straight line with the pre-Fourteenth Amendment decisions of the state courts governing notice restrictions under their own due process clauses.[458] Compared with the complexities of the minimum contacts test of *International Shoe*, the standard is simple and easy to apply.

---

452. *Id.* at 318, 70 S. Ct. at 659, 94 L. Ed. at 875-76.

453. *Id.; see also id.* at 314-20, 70 S. Ct. at 657-60, 94 L. Ed. at 873-77. For an argument that due process is satisfied by internet service of process, see Rachel Cantor, Comment, *Internet Service of Process: A Constitutionally Adequate Alternative*, 66 U. CHI. L. REV. 943 (1999).

454. 95 U.S. 714, 24 L. Ed. 565 (1878).

455. *See id.* at 727, 24 L. Ed. at 570. For a criticism of this portion of Justice Field's opinion for the Court in *Pennoyer*, see Ralph U. Whitten, *The Constitutional Limitations on State-Court Jurisdiction: A Historical-Interpretative Reexamination of the Full Faith and Credit and Due Process Clauses* (pt. 2), 14 CREIGHTON L. REV. 735, 828-35 (1981).

456. *See Mullane*, 339 U.S. at 316, 70 S. Ct. at 658, 94 L. Ed. at 874.

457. *See, e.g.*, Mennonite Bd. of Missions v. Adams, 462 U.S. 791, 103 S. Ct. 2706, 77 L. Ed. 2d 180 (1983); Walker v. City of Hutchinson, 352 U.S. 112, 77 S. Ct. 200, 1 L. Ed. 2d 178 (1956); *see also* Tulsa Prof'l Collection Servs., Inc. v. Pope, 485 U.S. 478, 108 S. Ct. 1340, 99 L. Ed. 2d 565 (1988); W.S. Frey Co. v. Heath, 729 A.2d 1037 (N.J. 1999) (acknowledging that due process does not require actual notice, but holding the mail notice used in the case inadequate under the circumstances; the notice violated the Virginia long-arm statute under which it was sent because it was not sent to the defendant's lᴀst known address, which was easily determinable). *But see* Miserandino v. Resort Properties, Inc., 345 Md. 43, 691 A.2d 208 (Md. Ct. App.), *cert. denied*, 522 U.S. 963, 118 S. Ct. 397, 139 L. Ed. 2d 310 (1997) (first-class mail notice permitted by Virginia statute on Maryland defendants violates due process). *See also* Dispensa v. University State Bank, 987 S.W.2d 923 (Tex. Ct. App. 1999) (default judgment against nonresident who was not served was not void under Due Process Clause, when nonresident learned of judgment in time to take remedial measures under forum law, such as file a motion for new trial, but did not do so and when, also, the nonresident had minimum contacts with the state).

458. It has sometimes been stated that the *Mullane* decision "radically modified" the traditional notice requirements. *See* RESTATEMENT (SECOND) OF JUDGMENTS at 27 (1982). This statement is based on *Mullane's* rejection of notice by publication, which had been traditionally approved under the Due Process Clause. However, rejection of notice by publication in *Mullane* was based on the availability of better forms of notice at the time the case was decided. At the time of the pre-Fourteenth Amendment decisions, notice by publication may well have been the best available form in most situations. Thus, the principle enforced in *Mullane* arguably was the same principle being enforced in the earlier cases.

Illustration 3-45. *A* possesses a claim against *B* for money lent to *B*. *B* refuses to pay. *A* sues *B* in a state court of proper subject-matter jurisdiction and venue in the state where the parties reside. The statutes in the state where the action is brought provide that the normal method of serving process on a defendant in a civil action is by delivering a copy of the summons and complaint to the defendant. This method is unsuccessful in *A v. B*, because *B*, having become aware that *A* has commenced the action, successfully evades numerous attempts at service. A statute of the state authorizes service of process on defendants by publication of a notice in a newspaper for several successive weeks when ordinary means of serving process on the defendant fail or the plaintiff is able to demonstrate that the whereabouts of the defendant are unknown. *A* uses this statute to serve *B* by publication. After notice has been published for the necessary statutory period, *A* obtains a default judgment against *B*. The judgment is valid under the *Mullane* test. The statutory forms of notice provided by the state are the best that are practicable under the circumstances. They are reasonably calculated to provide actual notice of the action to *B* and no better forms of notice are available.

* * * * *

Sometimes a lack of notice to a person can be overcome if the person's interests are adequately represented in an action, such as a class action, or there is a special substantive relationship between the parties to the actions—often called a "privity" relationship—that justifies binding the unnotified party's interests.[459]

However, the U.S. Supreme Court has made it clear that actions in which the interests of outsiders are alleged to have been represented will be scrutinized closely to assure that the representation actually occurred and was adequate. For example, in *Richards v. Jefferson County*,[460] plaintiffs sued in Alabama state court to challenge the federal constitutionality of a state tax. The Alabama courts held the suit precluded by the judgment in a prior action. The plaintiffs were not parties to the prior action and had not received any notice that an action was pending in which their rights would be adjudicated.[461] Nevertheless, the Alabama Supreme Court held that the judgment bound the plaintiffs because their interests were adequately represented by the plaintiffs in the prior action.

The U.S. Supreme Court reversed. The Court held that there was insufficient indication that the court in the prior action had taken care to protect the plaintiffs' interests. There was no "privity" between the parties, the first action was not brought as a class action, and the plaintiffs in that action showed no intent to represent the interests of outsiders or awareness that they were doing so. In addition, the judgment in the prior action did not purport to bind any nonparties.[462] Under these circumstances, the Supreme Court was unable to conclude that the plaintiffs in the prior action provided "representation sufficient to make up for the fact that [plaintiffs in the second suit] neither participated

---

459. Privity is discussed in Chapter 13(D)(1)*(b)* ("Substantive Relationships Binding Nonparties") *infra*.
460. 517 U.S. 793, 116 S. Ct. 1761, 135 L. Ed. 2d 76 (1996).
461. *See id.* at 799, 116 S. Ct. at 1766, 135 L. Ed. 2d at 84.
462. *See id.* at 801-02, 116 S. Ct. at 1767-68, 135 L. Ed. 2d at 86.

in . . . nor had the opportunity to participate in, the [prior] action. Accordingly, due process prevents [plaintiffs] from being bound by the . . . judgment.''[463]

Richards indicates that to bind nonparties on the theory that their interests are adequately represented in an action, the ''representatives'' in the first action, as well as the court, must be aware of the representative nature of the proceeding and take steps to assure that the nonparties' interests are adequately protected. However, the case does not specify further the kinds of protections, including possible notice to the nonparties, that must be afforded to satisfy due process in a representational proceeding. These issues are examined in Chapter 8(D)(4), dealing with ''class actions,'' below.

SECTION K. SERVICE OF PROCESS

1. Service of Process in English and Early United States Practice

One of the functions of the original writ at common law was to order the sheriff to compel the defendant's appearance. The appearance of the defendant was essential to further proceedings. The plaintiff did not have to appear or plead until the defendant had appeared, nor could there be a trial or judgment.[464] Under this system, the means available to compel the defendant to appear were of great importance.

At a relatively early date,[465] statutes authorized writs of *capias ad respondendum* to be issued in almost all actions at law.[466] Pursuant to these writs, the sheriff was commanded to arrest the defendant and to hold the defendant until either security for the defendant's appearance (''safe pledges'')

---

463. *Id.* at 802, 116 S. Ct. at 1768, 135 L. Ed. 2d at 86; *see also* South Cent. Bell Tel. Co. v. Alabama, 526 U.S. 160, 119 S. Ct. 1180, 143 L. Ed. 2d 258 (1999). In *South Central Bell*, corporations had sued to challenge the constitutionality of an Alabama tax under the Commerce Clause. After this suit was commenced, other corporations instituted an action to challenge the tax on the same grounds, but for additional tax years. The first action resulted in a holding that the tax was constitutional, whereupon the trial court in the second action appeared to hold that action barred by the res judicata effect of the judgment in the first. The U.S. Supreme Court found the case indistinguishable from *Richards*, even though the plaintiffs in the second action were aware of the first action, one of their lawyers was representing the plaintiffs in the first action, and they had requested their action to be held in abeyance until the first action was decided. The plaintiffs in the second action were still strangers to the first action, the first action was not a class action in which the interests of the plaintiffs in the second action were being represented, and there was no special relationship that would create ''privity'' between the parties.

464. ROBERT W. MILLAR, CIVIL PROCEDURE OF THE TRIAL COURT IN HISTORICAL PERSPECTIVE 74 (1952).

465. At common law, the first process for the purpose of securing the defendant's appearance was the summons, which was simply a warning to the defendant to appear. If a defendant failed to appear in response to the summons or offer any excuse (''essoin'') for nonappearance, other means were used to compel appearance. In the earliest times, these means involved a lengthy series of ever more serious penalties, including seizure of the defendant's land, seizure of the defendant's body, seizure of the defendant's goods, and outlawry. As Pollock and Maitland state, this ''mesne process'' ''[v]ery slowly . . . turn[ed] the screw which [brought] pressure to bear upon . . . defendant[s].'' 2 FREDERICK POLLOCK & FREDERIC W. MAITLAND, THE HISTORY OF ENGLISH LAW 591 (2d ed. 1968).

466. ROBERT W. MILLAR, CIVIL PROCEDURE OF THE TRIAL COURT IN HISTORICAL PERSPECTIVE 75-76 (1952) (Statute of Marlbridge (1267), Statute of Westminster (1285), and others).

was provided or the date for appearance arrived. This process worked if the defendant was subject to arrest. If the defendant was not subject to arrest—for instance, when the defendant was absent from the country—a writ of attachment commanding the seizure of the defendant's property was available to compel appearance.[467]

Appearance of the defendant was as necessary in equity as in common-law actions. However, the procedure for compelling appearance of the defendant was different. An equity proceeding was commenced by a bill, which was the initial pleading in the action. In form, this bill was a prayer for a *subpoena ad respondendum* to issue to compel the defendant's appearance.[468] The subpoena served the same function as the summons at common law: to notify the defendant of the action and compel the defendant to appear or suffer a penalty.[469] The form of the subpoena differed from the summons because a subpoena was directed to the defendant rather than an officer of the court. If the defendant failed to appear in response to the subpoena, the court considered the defendant in contempt of court and issued a writ of attachment.

Early United States procedures for service of process and commencement of common-law actions did not follow a uniform pattern. Some states, such as New York, used the *capias ad respondendum* as the usual method of commencing personal (principally contract and tort) actions. The initial process in other states was a summons, often combined with an attachment of property. In equity cases, the states generally followed the method used in English chancery actions. Suits were normally commenced by filing a bill and issuing a subpoena.[470]

In the later English and early American practice, actual appearance of the defendant was not required. Instead, if the defendant failed to appear after being properly served with a summons in a common-law action or a subpoena in an equity action, a "default" would be entered, and the case would proceed to judgment against the defendant.[471] The default judgment could then be enforced like a judgment entered after an appearance by the defendant.

2. Modern Methods of Serving Process

Under modern systems of procedure, the process for notifying the defendant of the action and securing jurisdiction to adjudicate the proceeding is the service of a summons, whether the suit was formerly one at law or in equity. The subpoena is the name given to the process to compel the attendance of witnesses at trial and pretrial proceedings. The content of the summons is

---

467. *See* JOSEPH H. KOFFLER & ALISON REPPY, HANDBOOK OF COMMON LAW PLEADING § 16, at 73-74 (1969).

468. *See* ROBERT W. MILLAR, CIVIL PROCEDURE OF THE TRIAL COURT IN HISTORICAL PERSPECTIVE 78 (1952).

469. The subpoena was also used in the common-law courts to compel the attendance of witnesses and was probably introduced into equity from the common-law practice. *See* JOSEPH STORY, COMMENTARIES ON EQUITY PLEADINGS § 45 (9th ed. 1879).

470. *See* ROBERT W. MILLAR, CIVIL PROCEDURE OF THE TRIAL COURT IN HISTORICAL PERSPECTIVE 74-84 (1952).

471. *See id.* at 82-84.

regulated by statute or by rule,[472] as is the time and method of its proof,[473] by whom the summons may be served,[474] upon whom it may be served,[475] and so forth.

Methods of serving process in the states vary widely, but include the traditional methods of service already discussed in earlier sections, such as in-hand service, service by leaving a copy of the process at the defendant's home, usual residence, or place of business, and service by publication under circumstances where other methods fail or are unavailable. Rule 4 of the Federal Rules of Civil Procedure prescribes the requirements of service of process for the federal courts and states operating under provisions identical to the Federal Rules. An examination of Rule 4 will provide a good illustration of the technical aspects of service of process rules in both federal and state courts.

Rule 4 has been amended several times since it first became effective in 1938. In particular, amendments of Rule 4 in 1983 and 1993 made extensive changes in the operation and structure of the rule in the federal courts. Before 1993, Rule 4 governed not only service of the summons, but also service of certain other kinds of process. The 1993 amendments to Rule 4 restrict its application to service of the summons.[476] A new rule, Rule 4.1, was created in 1993 to govern service of process other than the summons or a subpoena.[477] Service of a subpoena is governed by Federal Rule 45. In addition, Federal Rule 5 governs service of pleadings and papers other than process.

(a) Form of the Summons

Rule 4(a)[478] provides that the summons must be signed by the clerk, bear the seal of the court, identify the court and the parties, be directed to the defendant, and state either the name and address of the plaintiff's attorney or of an unrepresented plaintiff. The summons must also state the time within which the defendant must appear and defend and notify the defendant that failure to do

---

472. *See, e.g.*, CAL. CIV. PROC. CODE § 412.20 (West Supp. 1999).

473. *See, e.g.*, FED. R. CIV. P. 4(*l*); CAL. CIV. PROC. CODE § 417.10 (West Supp. 1999).

474. *See, e.g.*, CAL. CIV. PROC. CODE § 414.10 (West 1973).

475. *See, e.g.*, FED. R. CIV. P. 4(*l*).

476. For a general review of amended Rule 4, see Kent Sinclair, *Service of Process: Amended Rule 4 a nd the Presumption of Jurisdiction*, 14 REV. LITIG. 159 (1994).

477. For example, Federal Rule 69(a) states that "[p]rocess to enforce a judgment for the payment of money shall be a writ of execution, unless the court directs otherwise." FED. R. CIV. P. 69(a). After the 1993 amendments to the Federal Rules, it would appear that service of a writ of execution will be governed by Federal Rule 4.1. *But see* Apostolic Pentecostal Church v. Colbert, 169 F.3d 409 (6th Cir. 1999) (service of writ of garnishment pursuant to state law valid; Rule 69 governs, not Rule 4.1(a)). Rule 4.1(a) provides that process other than a summons or subpoena shall be served by a U.S. marshal, deputy marshal, or a person specially appointed to serve process. The person serving process under Rule 4.1 must make proof of service as provided in Rule 4(*l*). Proof of service under Rule 4(*l*) is discussed in the text *infra*. Process under Rule 4.1 may be served anywhere within the territorial limits of the state in which the district court is located, or beyond the limits of the state when authorized by a federal statute. Rule 4.1(b) provides for service of orders of commitment for civil contempt. *See* FED. R. CIV. P. 4.1.

478. Prior to 1993, Rule 4(a) governed the issuance of the summons and Rule 4(b) governed the form of the summons. These provisions were switched in the 1993 amendments to Rule 4. *See* FED. R. CIV. P. 4 advisory committee's note to the 1993 amendment.

so will result in a default judgment for the relief demanded in the complaint. The 1993 amendments to Rule 4 eliminated a requirement that a federal summons conform as nearly as possible to the form required by state law when state law was utilized under other provisions of Rule 4 to serve process. The change was designed to make the form of a federal court summons uniform in all cases.[479] If the content of the summons does not conform to the requirements of Rule 4(a), the defendant may object pursuant to Rule 12(b)(4) based on insufficiency of process. However, the last sentence of Rule 4(a) provides that the court may allow the summons to be amended.

Illustration 3-46. *A* commences an action against *B* in a U.S. District Court. *A* presents a summons to the clerk as required by Rule 4(b).[480] The clerk signs, seals, and issues the summons. However, the summons is defective because it fails to state the time within which the defendant must appear and defend the action. Under Federal Rule 12(b), *B* may move to dismiss the action for insufficiency of process. Alternatively, *B* may make an insufficiency of process objection in *B's* answer, as permitted by Rule 12(b).[481] However, the court may permit *A* to amend the summons under Rule 4(a).[482]

(b) Issuance of the Summons

Rule 4(b) provides that on or after the complaint is filed, the plaintiff may present a summons to the clerk for the signature and seal required by Rule 4(a). If the summons is in the form prescribed by Rule 4(a), the clerk must sign, seal, and issue it to the plaintiff for service on the defendant. If there are multiple defendants, a separate summons or a copy of an original summons must be issued for each defendant. The 1993 amendments to the rule provided that it is the plaintiff's responsibility to fill in the summons, not the responsibility of the clerk.[483]

(c) What Must Be Served with the Summons and Who May Serve the Summons

Rule 4(c)(1) requires that a copy of the complaint be served with the summons. The plaintiff must serve the summons and complaint within the time allowed by Rule 4(m). The plaintiff must also furnish the process server with the necessary copies of the summons and complaint. Rule 4(c)(2) states that service may be effected by any person who is not a party and who is at least 18 years of age. However, Rule 4(c)(2) also provides that, under certain circumstances, the court may direct that service be made by a U.S. marshal or other person specially appointed by the court.

---

479. *See id.*
480. Rule 4(b) is discussed in the text *infra.*
481. Federal Rule 12(b) is discussed in Chapter 6(D)(3)*(d)* (''Motions to Dismiss'') *infra.*
482. *See* FED. R. CIV. P. 4(a).
483. *See id.* advisory committee's note to the 1993 amendment.

Before 1983, Rule 4(a) directed the clerk to deliver the summons to the marshal or to anyone else authorized by Rule 4 to serve process. Rule 4, in turn, provided for service by the marshal, by some person specially appointed by the court to serve process, or by anyone authorized to serve process in an action brought in the courts of general jurisdiction of the state in which the district court is held. The 1983 amendments to Rule 4 relieved marshals of most of the duty of serving process in civil litigation.[484] After 1983, Rule 4 placed the primary responsibility for securing service on the plaintiff or the plaintiff's attorney. The 1993 amendments to Rule 4 continued the trend of the 1983 amendments by further reducing the obligations of the marshal to serve process in actions in which the United States is seeking service. Like other litigants, the United States may now employ any nonparty who is 18 years of age to serve process. Service by the marshal or other specially appointed process server is today mandatory only in situations in which the plaintiff is authorized to proceed in forma pauperis under 28 U.S.C. § 1915 or as a seaman under 28 U.S.C. § 1916.[485]

(d) Waiver of Service of Process

Rule 4(d) contains the most important portion of the 1993 amendments to Rule 4. Rule 4(d) is designed to reduce the costs of service of process by encouraging certain classes of defendants to waive the service of the summons.[486] The waiver provisions of Rule 4(d) are only applicable to defendants who are competent, adult individuals, or corporations, partnerships, or unincorporated associations.[487] The waiver provisions are not applicable to individual defendants who are infants or incompetent persons, to the United States, its agencies, corporations, or officers, or to foreign, state, or local governments. Rule 4(g), (i), and (j) contain provisions prescribing the manner in which the latter classes of defendants must be served.

With regard to the classes of defendants governed by Rule 4(d), the rule provides that the plaintiff may notify the defendant in writing that the action has been commenced and request that the defendant waive the service of a

---

484. The 1983 amendment to Rule 4 was not accomplished in the ordinary fashion by promulgation under the Rules Enabling Act by the Supreme Court. *See* Chapter 1(E)(5) ("Development of Federal Procedure and the Federal Rules of Civil Procedure") *supra* (describing the rulemaking process under the Rules Enabling Act); *see also* Chapter 5(F) ("The Evolution of the *Erie* Doctrine: Conflicts Between State Law and Federal Rules of Civil Procedure") *infra*. Rather, Congress, dissatisfied with changes in the rule proposed by the Advisory Committee and adopted by the Supreme Court, acted directly to amend the rule into its 1983 form. *See* 4 CHARLES A. WRIGHT & ARTHUR R. MILLER, FEDERAL PRACTICE AND PROCEDURE: CIVIL § 1061, at 220 (2d ed. 1987).

485. *See* FED. R. CIV. P. 4(c)(2); *see also* FED. R. CIV. P. 4 advisory committee's note to the 1993 amendment. Lawyers must take care when hiring private process servers in some jurisdictions. For example, in New York, it has been held that if a lawyer hires a private process server and the process server negligently fails to serve the defendant before the statute of limitations runs, the lawyer can be held vicariously liable to the client for the negligence of the process server. *See* Kleeman v. Rheingold, 81 N.Y.2d 270, 614 N.E.2d 712, 598 N.Y.S.2d 149 (1993).

486. The text of Rule 4(d) is new, but was substantially derived from the provisions of former Federal Rule 4(c)(2)(C) & (D). *See* FED. R. CIV. P. 4 advisory committee's note to the 1993 amendment.

487. *See* FED. R. CIV. P. 4(d)(2), (e), (f) & (h).

summons.[488] The notice and request must be addressed directly to individual defendants.[489] If the defendant is a corporation, partnership, or unincorporated association, the notice and request must be addressed to an officer, a managing or general agent, or an agent otherwise authorized by appointment or law to receive service of process.[490] The notice and request must be sent by first-class mail or "other reliable means." They also must be accompanied by a copy of the complaint and identify the court in which the action has been filed.[491] The notice and request must correspond to Form 1A in the Appendix of Approved Forms to the Federal Rules of Civil Procedure.[492] That form requests the defendant to return a waiver of service of summons.[493] The form must be enclosed with the notice and request.[494] The form also notifies the defendant that return of the waiver will mean that the summons will not be served on the defendant and the action will proceed as if the defendant had been served on the date that the waiver is filed with the court by the plaintiff.[495] The defendant must be given a reasonable time to return the waiver. The amount of time cannot be less than 30 days from the date on which the request is sent, or 60 days if the defendant is served outside the United States.[496]

If the defendant returns the waiver of service as requested, the normal 20 day period within which to answer the complaint after normal service of a summons is extended to 60 days or to 90 days if the defendant is outside the United States.[497] If the defendant does not waive service, the notice and request inform the defendant that service will be effectuated in another manner authorized by the Federal Rules of Civil Procedure and that the plaintiff will request the court to impose the full costs of the alternative service on the defendant.[498] The rule provides that the court must impose costs on a defendant located within the United States unless the defendant shows good cause for the failure to return the waiver.[499] These costs include not only the expenses incurred in effecting

---

488. *See* FED. R. CIV. P. 4(d)(2).

489. In D'Orange v. Feely, No. 95-7904, 1996 WL 446254, 1996 U.S. App. LEXIS 20495 (2d Cir. Aug. 8, 1996) (unpublished opinion), the plaintiff sent a notice and request for waiver to the defendant's attorney in a related action. The attorney refused to accept the waiver for the defendant, but the defendant was aware of the service on the attorney, obtained the waiver, and returned within 30 days from the date it was sent to the attorney. However, the plaintiff, instead of directing a new waiver to the defendant, had the defendant served with a summons and complaint. The defendant did not answer the complaint within 20 days of this latter service as required by Rule 12(a), and a default was entered against the defendant. The defendant moved to set aside the default, claiming that the return of the waiver meant there was 60 days in which to answer. The district court refused to set aside the default, and entered a default judgment. The court of appeals affirmed on the ground that the defendant had not shown good cause for the default.

490. *See* FED. R. CIV. P. 4(d)(2)(A).

491. *See* FED. R. CIV. P. 4(d)(2)(B)-(C).

492. *See* FED. R. CIV. P. 4(d)(2)(D).

493. *See* Form 1B in the Appendix of Forms following the Federal Rules of Civil Procedure.

494. *See* FED. R. CIV. P. 4(d)(2)(G) (providing that the defendant must be provided with an extra copy of the notice and request and a prepaid means of compliance in writing).

495. *See* FED. R. CIV. P. 4(d)(4).

496. *See* FED. R. CIV. P. 4(d)(2)(F).

497. *See* FED. R. CIV. P. 4(d)(3), 12(a)(B)(1).

498. *See* Form 1A in the Appendix of Forms following the Federal Rules of Civil Procedure.

499. *See* FED. R. CIV. P. 4(d)(2) (the last paragraph applies the cost shifting provision only to defendants located within the United States); *see also* FED. R. CIV. P. 4 advisory committee's note to the 1993 amendment.

service under Rule 4(e), (f), or (h), but also a reasonable attorney's fee for any motion that must be filed to collect the fee.[500] Rule 4(d) thus imposes a duty on the defendant to avoid unnecessary costs of serving the summons.[501] However, the rule explicitly provides that the waiver of a service of summons does not thereby waive any objection that the defendant has to venue or personal jurisdiction.[502]

Illustration 3-47. *A*, a citizen of State *X*, sues *B*, a citizen of State *Y*, in a U.S. District Court in State *X* for $500,000. *A's* claim is for personal injuries received in an automobile accident with *B* in State *Z*. *B* has no contacts, ties, or relations with State *X*. After commencement of the action, *A's* attorney sends the notice and request prescribed by Rule 4(d) to *B*. After consulting an attorney, *B* returns the form waiving service of a summons, and the waiver is filed with the U.S. District Court in State *X*. Subsequently, *B* moves under Federal Rule 12(b)(2) and (3) to dismiss the action for lack of personal jurisdiction and improper venue. *B's* motion should be granted. The return of the waiver of service of summons pursuant to Rule 4(d) does not waive *B's* personal jurisdiction and venue objections, which are valid on the facts of this illustration.

Illustration 3-48. Assume on the facts of *Illustration 3-47* that after returning the waiver of service, *B* does not appear further in the action and a default judgment is rendered against *B*. When *A* attempts to enforce the judgment against *B* in State *Y*, *B* may resist the enforcement of the judgment on the ground that it is void because the U.S. District Court in State *X* did not have personal jurisdiction over *B*.[503]

Illustration 3-49. Assume on the facts of *Illustration 3-47* that *B* does not return the waiver of service as requested. Subsequently, *A* has *B* personally served with the summons and complaint under the law of State *Y* where *B* resides, as authorized by Rule 4(e)(1). *A* then moves to have *B* pay the costs of service, as required by Rule 4(d). The court orders *B* to show cause why the costs of the alternative service should not be imposed on *B*. *B* argues that personal jurisdiction and venue were plainly improper and that the failure to return the waiver was justified as a consequence. The fact that jurisdiction and venue were lacking is not good cause for the failure to return the waiver and will not exempt *B* from having to pay the costs of service.[504] However, the fact that personal jurisdiction and venue were clearly improper may give *B* the right to move for sanctions against *A* under Federal Rule 11 at some point in the action.[505]

Illustration 3-50. Assume on the facts of *Illustration 3-49* that *B* argues that the cost of having process personally served on *B* in State *Y* where *B* lives

---

500. *See* FED. R. CIV. P. 4(d)(5); Double "S" Truck Line, Inc. v. Frozen Food Express, 171 F.R.D. 251 (D. Minn. 1997).

501. *See* FED. R. CIV. P. 4(d)(2).

502. *See* FED. R. CIV. P. 4(d)(1).

503. *See* FED. R. CIV. P. 4 advisory committee's note to the 1993 amendment.

504. *See id.*

505. Rule 11 is discussed in Chapter 6(E)(2) ("Good Faith Pleading: Rule 11") *infra.* It is also not a sufficient excuse for failure to return the waiver that the plaintiff's complaint is baseless. *See* Morales v. SI Diamond Tech, No. 98-CIV.-8309 CSH, 1999 WL 144469, 1999 U.S. Dist. LEXIS 2964 (S.D.N.Y. Mar. 17, 1999).

is unjustified because *A* had less expensive ways of effectuating service on *B* and instead employed the more expensive method of personal service under the law of the state where *B* resides. Specifically, *B* points to the State *X* long-arm statute, which authorizes service on *B* by first class mail and which was available to *A* under Rule 4(e)(1). Neither the text of Rule 4 nor the accompanying Advisory Committee's note indicate whether *A* is obligated to employ the least expensive form of alternative service when *B* refuses to return the waiver of service of summons. However, it is arguable that the use of a more expensive form of notice than was necessary under the circumstances should be taken into account in determining the costs that *B* must pay under Rule 4(d). *A* should be required to show why the more expensive form of notice was used. If *A* cannot offer a reasonable explanation for use of the more expensive form, *B* should not have to pay more than the costs of the least expensive form of notice.

   Illustration 3-51. Assume on the facts of *Illustration 3-47* that the statute of limitations of State *X* where the action is commenced requires that an action be commenced by personal service of summons on the defendant within the statutory period. At the time *B* receives the notice and request for waiver of service of summons, the statute has not yet run. However, by the time that *B* returns the waiver and it is filed by *A*, the statute has run. *B* answers the complaint in the action in part by asserting the affirmative defense of the statute of limitations. *B's* defense is good, and the action should be dismissed. Rule 4(d)(4) makes it clear that upon the filing of the waiver with the court by *A*, "the action shall proceed . . . as if a summons and complaint had been served at the time of filing the waiver."[506] Thus, the State *X* statute of limitations was not tolled by the receipt of the notice and request by *B*. Obviously, if *B* had not returned the waiver at all, the same result would follow if *A* were unable to have *B* personally served before the expiration of the statute of limitations. If an applicable statute of limitations is about to run, a plaintiff must attempt to serve process in a way that will toll the statute effectively. The notice and request for waiver cannot safely be used when the applicable statute of limitations does not toll upon receipt by the defendant of notice of the action.[507]

(e) Manner of Service

   Assuming that a defendant does not waive service of process or that the defendant is a member of one of the classes to which waiver does not apply, Rule 4(e)-(j) provide the manner in which service must be made on the defendant. A few examples will suffice to indicate how the rule operates. If service is to be made on a competent, adult individual located within the United States,[508] Rule

---

506. *See* FED. R. CIV. P. 4(d)(4); *see also* FED. R. CIV. P. 4 advisory committee's note to the 1993 amendment.

507. The interaction between state statutes of limitation and federal procedural rules is discussed in Chapter 5(E) ("The Evolution of the *Erie* Doctrine: Applicability of State "Substantive Law" Under the Rules of Decision Act") *infra.*

508. For provisions governing service on competent adults located outside the United States, see FED. R. CIV. P. 4(f).

4(e) provides several methods of service. The defendant may be served pursuant to the law of the state in which the district court is located or pursuant to the law of the state in which service is made.[509] However, the state law in question must be that applicable to the service of a summons in the state's courts of general jurisdiction.[510] In addition, Rule 4(e)(2) provides that the defendant may be served (1) by delivering a copy of the summons and complaint to the defendant personally;[511] (2) by leaving a copy of the summons and complaint at the defendant's dwelling house or usual place of abode with someone of suitable age and discretion residing there;[512] or (3) by delivering a copy of the summons and complaint to an agent authorized by appointment or law to receive service. Rule 4(e) provides that service may be made in any judicial district of the United States. However, mere service does not establish personal jurisdiction. Whether service establishes personal jurisdiction is governed by Rule 4(k), discussed below.[513] Service on individuals who are infants or incompetent persons located in the United States is made in the manner prescribed by the law governing service of a summons on those categories of individuals in the courts of general jurisdiction in the state where service is made.[514]

Domestic or foreign corporations, partnerships, and unincorporated associations not waiving service are served within the United States (1) in the manner prescribed by state law for service of the summons in the courts of general jurisdiction of the state or (2) by delivering a copy of the summons and complaint to an officer, a managing or general agent, or any other agent authorized by appointment or law to receive service. If service is made on an agent authorized by statute to receive service, a copy of the summons and complaint must also be mailed to the defendant if the statute so requires.[515]

---

509. Williams v. Moody, No. Civ. A. 98-1211, 1999 WL 79535 (E.D. Pa. Jan. 22, 1999) (defendant, a member of U.S. Navy stationed in Spain, was involved n an auto accident in Sicily; process served by mailing a copy of the complaint to defendant in care of the Navy Department in Washington, D.C., on the theory, under Pennsylvania law, that was defendant's usual place of business; service improper; because defendant is not a resident of any judicial district, Rule 4(f) must be used).

510. *See* FED. R. CIV. P. 4(e)(1).

511. When a rule such as Rule 4(e) provides for delivery to an individual personally, there is the possibility of differences of opinion over the meaning of ''personally.'' In particular, does ''personally'' mean that process must actually be handed to the defendant, or, under appropriate circumstances, may it be left somewhere in the defendant's vicinity. *See, e.g.,* CRB v. Wyoming Dep't of Family Servs., 974 P.2d 931 (Wyo. 1999) (sufficient to deposit process in mailbox outside defendant's apartment after process server phoned defendant while outside defendant's apartment and defendant refused to open door); Freund Equip., Inc. v. Fox, 301 Ill. App. 3d 163, 703 N.E.2d 542 (1998) (placing the process in the general vicinity of defendant and announcing the nature of the papers was sufficient).

512. *See* Stars' Desert Inn Hotel & Country Club, Inc. v. Hwang, 105 F.3d 521 (9th Cir. 1997) (defendant, a citizen of Taiwan, was residing in a state of the U.S. when process served at his U.S. residence by leaving the process with a security guard; service proper; defendant did not have to be served pursuant to Rule 4(f) because he was not a citizen of the U.S.).

513. *See* FED. R. CIV. P. 4 advisory committee's note to the 1993 amendment.

514. *See* FED. R. CIV. P. 4(g). An infant or incompetent person located outside the United States is served pursuant to the provisions of Federal Rule 4(f)(2)(A) or (B), or in a manner directed by the court. *See id.*

515. *See* FED. R. CIV. P. 4(h)(1); Ayres v. Jacobs & Crumplar, P.A., 99 F.3d 565 (3d Cir. 1996) (service on office manager not authorized by appointment or by law was improper); Baade v. Price, 175 F.R.D. 403 (D.D.C. 1997) (service on receptionist of individual codefendant was not service on university when receptionist not an agent by appointment or by law).

Service on these same categories of defendants outside the United States is made in the manner prescribed for service on individuals outside the United States under Rule 4(f), except that corporations, partnerships, and unincorporated associations may not be served by personal delivery pursuant to Rule 4(f)(2)(C)(i).[516]

Failure to follow the provisions governing manner of service in Rule 4(e)-(j) can be raised as an insufficiency of service of process objection under Federal Rule 12(b)(5).

Illustration 3-52. *A* sues *B*, a competent adult, in a U.S. District Court. *A* has *B* served under Rule 4(e)(2), but the process server leaves a copy of the summons and complaint at *B's* home with *B's* child, who is four years old. *B* may move to dismiss the complaint under Federal Rule 12(b)(5) for insufficiency of service of process because process was not left with someone of "suitable age and discretion" as required by Rule 4(e)(2).

(f) Territorial Limits of Effective Service

Rule 4(k)(1) provides that service of a summons or waiver of service is effective to establish personal jurisdiction over a defendant (1) who could be subjected to the jurisdiction of a court of general jurisdiction in the state in which the district court is located, (2) who is a party joined under Rule 14 or 19 and is served at a place within a judicial district of the United States that is not more than 100 miles from the place where the summons issues, (3) who is subject to the federal interpleader jurisdiction under 28 U.S.C. § 1335, or (4) who is subject to jurisdiction under a statute of the United States. The provision authorizing personal jurisdiction over a defendant who is subject to jurisdiction under state law, when combined with the manner of service provisions found in Rule 4(e)-(j), allows the federal courts to use state long-arm statutes to acquire personal jurisdiction over nonresident defendants. However, as discussed in section L, below, the federal courts adhere to the Fourteenth Amendment limitations on the power of state courts when asserting personal jurisdiction under state law. Therefore, the due process restrictions of the minimum contacts test discussed in earlier sections of this chapter are applicable to cases in which state long-arm statutes are used to acquire personal jurisdiction over nonresidents in federal actions.

Rule 4(k)(2) is an independent "federal long-arm rule" added by the 1993 amendments to Rule 4.[517] Rule 4(k)(2) provides that service of the summons or filing a waiver of service will be effective to establish personal

---

516. *See* FED. R. CIV. P. 4(h)(2); *see also* Hunter Douglas Metals v. Aluminio Conesa, S.A. de C.V., No. 96 C 6853, 1997 WL 282880, 1997 U.S. Dist. LEXIS 7344 (N.D. Ill. May 16, 1997) (service on alien corporation in foreign country by registered mail under Rule 4 invalid if foreign country does not recognize service by registered mail). *But see* Dee-K Enters., Inc. v. Heveafil Sdn. Bhd., 174 F.R.D. 376 (E.D. Va. 1997) (fact that the form of service employed is not authorized by foreign law does not mean that it is "prohibited" by foreign law within the meaning of Rule 4(f)(2)(C)).

517. *See generally* Gary B. Born & Andrew M. Vollmer, *The Effect of the Revised Federal Rules of Civil Procedure on Personal Jurisdiction, Service, and Discovery in International Cases*, 149 F.R.D. 221, 222-29 (1993).

jurisdiction over a defendant "with respect to claims arising under federal law" when the defendant is not subject to personal jurisdiction of the courts of general jurisdiction of any state and the assertion of jurisdiction will not violate the Constitution or laws of the United States. This rule was added to close a gap in the ability to obtain personal jurisdiction when the defendant is a nonresident of the United States who has sufficient contacts with the United States to justify an assertion of personal jurisdiction under the Constitution, but lacks sufficient contacts with any single state to meet the requirements of the Fourteenth Amendment.[518]

The Advisory Committee on the Federal Rules of Civil Procedure had doubts about the validity of Rule 4(k)(2). In a special note, the Advisory Committee called the attention of the Supreme Court and Congress to Rule 4(k)(2). In doing so, the Committee cited only its concerns that the rule might be invalid under the Rules Enabling Act, 28 U.S.C. § 2072.[519] The Committee's only constitutional concerns were addressed to the limitations that may exist on the territorial reach of the federal court's jurisdiction under the Due Process Clause of the Fifth Amendment.[520] As discussed in Chapter 5, however, a Federal Rule of Civil Procedure extending the territorial reach of the district courts' jurisdiction probably does not violate the Rules Enabling Act, the Advisory Committee's concerns notwithstanding.[521] Nevertheless, even though such a rule does not violate the Rules Enabling Act, a strong argument can be made that it violates separation of powers restrictions on judicial rulemaking.[522]

Illustration 3-53. A, a citizen of State *X*, sues *B*, a citizen of France, in a U.S. District Court in State *X* for $10,000 on a claim arising under a federal statute. The events giving rise to the claim occurred in State *Z*. After commencement of the action, *A* sends *B* the notice and request for waiver of service prescribed by Rule 4(f). *B* returns the waiver, and *A* files it with the court. Subsequently, *B* appears and moves to dismiss the action for lack of personal jurisdiction. Rule 4(k)(2) does not afford a basis for personal jurisdiction over *B*,

---

518. *See* FED. R. CIV. P. 4 advisory committee's note to the 1993 amendment; *see also* Omni Capital Int'l, Ltd. v. Rudolf Wolff & Co., 484 U.S. 97, 108 S. Ct. 404, 98 L. Ed. 2d 415 (1987). Of course, in the situations covered by Rule 4(k)(2), there is also no federal long-arm statute in existence that would authorize the federal courts to assert jurisdiction over the nonresident. If such a long-arm statute existed and could be applied consistently with the Constitution, Rule 4(k)(1)(D) would authorize the use of the federal statute and use of Rule 4(k)(2) would be unnecessary.

519. *See* FED. R. CIV. P. 4(k)(2) special advisory committee's note. The Rules Enabling Act is discussed in Chapter 1(E)(5) ("Development of Federal Procedure and the Federal Rules of Civil Procedure") *supra* and in Chapter 5(F) ("The Evolution of the *Erie* Doctrine: Conflicts Between State Law and Federal Rules of Civil Procedure") *infra*.

520. *See* FED. R. CIV. P. 4 advisory committee's note to the 1993 amendments. The Fifth Amendment limitations on the territorial reach of federal process are discussed in section L ("Special Problems of Amenability to Process in Federal Court") *infra*.

521. *But see* Stephen B. Burbank, *The World in Our Courts*, 89 MICH. L. REV. 1456, 1484 n.164 (1991) (reviewing GARY B. BORN & DAVID WESTIN, INTERNATIONAL CIVIL LITIGATION IN UNITED STATES COURTS: COMMENTARY AND MATERIALS (1989)).

522. *See* Ralph U. Whitten, *Separation of Powers Restrictions on Judicial Rulemaking: A Case Study of Federal Rule 4*, 40 ME. L. REV. 41, 103-06 (1988). For further discussion of the validity of Rule 4(k)(2) under the Rules Enabling Act and the separation-of-powers doctrine, see Chapter 5 *infra*, where the subject can be placed in the context of a full discussion of the Supreme Court's rulemaking authority.

even assuming that the Due Process Clause of the Fifth Amendment would not be violated by an assertion of jurisdiction in State X on the facts of this illustration. Rule 4(k)(2) is inapplicable if the defendant in an action is subject to personal jurisdiction in the courts of general jurisdiction in any state. Here, B would surely be subject to personal jurisdiction in State Z, where the events giving rise to the suit occurred.

(g) Proof of Service

As provided by Rule 4(l), proof of service must be made by the person making the service. When that person is someone other than a U.S. marshal or deputy marshal, the proof of service must be made by affidavit. When service is made outside the United States by internationally agreed means calculated to give notice, as authorized by Rule 4(f)(1), proof of service must be made pursuant to the treaty or international convention under which service is authorized. When service outside the United States is made under other provisions of Rule 4(f), proof of service must include a receipt signed by the addressee or other evidence of delivery to the addressee that is satisfactory to the court. Failure to make proof of service does not invalidate the service, and the court may allow proof of service to be amended under Rule 4(l).

(h) Time Limits on Effectuating Service

Pursuant to Rule 4(m), if service is not made within 120 days after the filing of the complaint, the court may, on motion or on its own initiative and after notice to the plaintiff, dismiss the action without prejudice as to any defendant not served. Alternatively, the court may order that service be effectuated within a specified time. If the plaintiff shows good cause for failing to make service within the 120 day period, the court must extend the time for "an appropriate period." However, it is not good cause for failure to serve the defendant within the time limits that the plaintiff mailed the defendant a proper request for waiver and the defendant did not return it.[523] The time limits do not apply to service in a foreign country under Rule 4(f).

Illustration 3-54. A, a citizen of State X, sues B, a citizen of State Y, in a U.S. District Court for $500,000. *A's* claim is for personal injuries received in an automobile accident with B in State X. The State X statute of limitations applicable to *A's* claim will run 20 days after commencement of the action. The statute requires that an action such as *A's* be commenced by personal service of process on the defendant within the statutory period. Under these circumstances, A should not use the notice and request for waiver of service provisions of Rule 4(d), but should, with celerity, have B served personally in State Y before the

---

523. *See* Troxell v. Fedders of N. Am., Inc., 160 F.3d 381 (7th Cir. 1998). An objection that service is untimely under Rule 4(m) is an insufficiency of process objection under Rule 12(b)(5) which can be waived under Rule 12(h)(1) if not included in a preanswer motion. *See* McCurdy v. American Bd. of Plastic Surgery, 157 F.3d 191 (3d Cir. 1998); *see also* City of Merced v. Fields, 997 F. Supp. 1326 (E.D. Cal. 1998) (new time period to serve begins for defendants added to the action after 120 days).

statutory time period runs. Rule 4(d)(2)(F) requires that a defendant be given at least 30 days from the date on which the request is sent to return the waiver. Thus, a severe danger exists that the statute of limitations will have run before *B* returns the waiver and *A* files it with the court.

(i) In Rem and Quasi in Rem Jurisdiction

Rule 4(n) is a curious provision that authorizes the assertion of in rem and quasi in rem jurisdiction in the federal courts. Rule 4(n)(1) states that the court can assert jurisdiction over property if authorized by a statute of the United States. When such jurisdiction is exercised, notice must be sent to claimants of the property either in the manner authorized by the statute or by service of a summons under Rule 4. Section 1655 of Title 28 provides for nationwide long-arm jurisdiction in actions in the district courts to enforce liens upon or claims to, or to remove encumbrances or liens or clouds upon, the title to real and personal property within the district. Section 1655 is the kind of statute incorporated by reference in Rule 4(n).[524] Any constitutional issues concerning the application of this federal statute would be determined by reference to the Fifth Amendment due process limits on the power of Congress.[525] However, under *Shaffer v. Heitner*, discussed in section E(1), above, an assertion of jurisdiction by a court where property is located to adjudicate a matter directly concerning the property does not violate the Due Process Clause of the Fourteenth Amendment. Because the Fifth Amendment due process restrictions on the power of Congress are not narrower than the Fourteenth Amendment due process restrictions on the power of the states, there should be no constitutional difficulties with the application of § 1655 or similar statutes under Rule 4(n)(1).

More troublesome is the authorization of quasi in rem jurisdiction in Rule 4(n)(2). Rule 4(n)(2) states that a district court may exercise jurisdiction over a defendant's assets located within the district by seizing the assets under the circumstances and in the manner authorized by the law of the state in which the district court is located. The only qualification of this authority in the text of Rule 4(n) is that there must be a showing that personal jurisdiction cannot be obtained over the defendant in the district where the action is brought "with reasonable efforts by service of summons in any manner authorized by this rule." Thus, the rule appears to authorize the acquisition of jurisdiction based on the presence of property alone, without regard to whether the defendant can be constitutionally subjected to personal jurisdiction within the state under the minimum contacts test.

The Advisory Committee's note to this portion of Rule 4 states that it is, indeed, the intention of Rule 4(n)(2) to authorize quasi in rem jurisdiction, but only under "exigent circumstances." The Committee's note also states that the occasion to use quasi in rem jurisdiction of this sort should be rare, such as when

---

524. *See* FED. R. CIV. P. 4 advisory committee's note to the 1993 amendment.

525. *See* the discussion of the Fifth Amendment limits on federal jurisdiction in section L ("Special Problems of Amenability to Process in Federal Court") *infra*.

the defendant is a fugitive or the assets are in imminent danger of disappearing.[526] This statement appears to suggest that seizure of property under the rule can only occur in accord with the accepted constitutional restrictions on the use of state provisional remedies.[527] If this is the meaning of Rule 4(n)(2), the rule does not really constitute an attempt to authorize the acquisition of jurisdiction based only on property contrary to *Shaffer v. Heitner*. However, the text of the rule does not contain this limitation. It is bothersome that the Advisory Committee has placed such an important qualification of the rule in its note rather than in the text itself. In several instances, the Supreme Court has insisted on interpreting Federal Rules of Civil Procedure in accordance with their "plain language," even when this approach has produced a seemingly unreasonable result.[528] Under the plain text of Rule 4(n)(2), quasi in rem jurisdiction of the sort outlawed by *Shaffer* seems to be authorized. Therefore, the rule, as phrased, raises unfortunate constitutional questions.

    Illustration 3-55. *A*, a citizen of State *X*, sues *B*, a citizen of State *Y*, in a U.S. District Court in State *X* for $500,000. *A's* claim is based on an automobile accident that occurred between *A* and *B* in State *Z*. *B* owns a parcel of land in State *X* worth $1,000,000, but has no other contacts with State *X*. *A* has no evidence that *B* is about to dispose of the land. Assume that State *X* has a statute allowing property owned by a nonresident defendant to be attached merely *because* the defendant is a nonresident. Rule 4(n)(2) would seem to allow *A* to institute a quasi in rem action against *B* in State *X* by attaching the land owned by *B* under the State *X* statute. However, if the U.S. District Court follows the usual approach of the federal courts to personal jurisdiction acquired pursuant to state law, the court would enforce the Fourteenth Amendment limitations on the ability to utilize quasi in rem jurisdiction announced by *Shaffer v. Heitner*. These limitations would require the court to dismiss *A's* action on *B's* motion. Rule 4(n) should not be read to override the normal constitutional restrictions on personal jurisdiction that would be enforced in diversity actions. To do so would require that the court treat Rule 4(n) as a kind of federal long-arm rule of procedure, whose validity would have to be evaluated under the Due Process Clause of the Fifth Amendment and the separation of powers restrictions on judicial rulemaking referred to above. The text and Advisory Committee note do not clearly indicate that Rule 4(n)(2) was intended to operate this broadly.

SECTION L. SPECIAL PROBLEMS OF AMENABILITY TO PROCESS IN FEDERAL COURT

    In determining whether a defendant can be subjected to personal jurisdiction by a federal court, one must confront two separate sets of problems.

---

    526. *See* FED. R. CIV. P. 4 advisory committee's note to the 1993 amendment.

    527. These restrictions are discussed in Chapter 6(F)(5) ("Constitutional Limitations on Provisional Remedies") *infra*.

    528. *See, e.g.*, Delta Air Lines, Inc. v. August, 450 U.S. 346, 101 S. Ct. 1146, 67 L. Ed. 2d 287 (1981). *Delta Air Lines* is discussed in Chapter 10(F)(2) ("Settlement: Rule 68") *infra*.

First, there exists a question about the proper constitutional standard to apply to assertions of long-arm jurisdiction under federal statutes. Second, there exists a question about the proper constitutional standard to use when the federal courts assert jurisdiction under a state long-arm statute. The Supreme Court has never authoritatively resolved these questions. Furthermore, general agreement among the federal courts exists on only a few of the questions.

1. The Constitutional Standard Under Federal Long-Arm Statutes and Rules

There is universal agreement that the Due Process Clause of the Fifth Amendment limits the power of Congress to enact federal long-arm statutes, while the Due Process Clause of the Fourteenth Amendment limits the power of the state legislatures to enact state long-arm statutes. As demonstrated in earlier sections of this chapter, when the constitutionality of applying a state long-arm statute is in issue, the minimum contacts test of *International Shoe v. Washington* is applied.

When Congress enacts a long-arm statute that allows the federal courts to serve process nationwide, what standard does the Fifth Amendment impose on the power to apply the statute to nonresidents of the district or state in which the action is brought? The traditional assumption has been that Congress has absolute power to extend long-arm jurisdiction throughout the United States without restriction by the Due Process Clause of the Fifth Amendment.[529] This traditional view evolved when *Pennoyer v. Neff's* territorial understanding of the Fourteenth Amendment's due process restrictions on state court jurisdiction prevailed.[530] Under *Pennoyer*, the Due Process Clause of the Fourteenth Amendment only limited the power of the states to assert personal jurisdiction when the states reached outside their borders. Applied to the Due Process Clause of the Fifth Amendment, this theory would only limit the power of federal courts to assert personal jurisdiction when those courts are authorized to reach outside the borders of the United States. Thus, Congress might authorize a district court to assert jurisdiction over any defendant within the country, despite the lack of any contact between the defendant and the particular place within the country where the district court is located.[531] Such a conferral of long-arm jurisdiction

---

529. *See* ALI STUDY OF THE DIVISION OF JURISDICTION BETWEEN STATE AND FEDERAL COURTS 437 (1969); RICHARD H. FALLON ET AL., HART & WECHSLER'S THE FEDERAL COURTS AND THE FEDERAL SYSTEM 1587-88 (4th ed. 1996). Numerous cases have stated in dictum that Congress' power to provide for nationwide long-arm jurisdiction is absolute. *See, e.g.*, Mississippi Publ'g Corp. v. Murphree, 326 U.S. 438, 442, 66 S. Ct. 242, 245, 90 L. Ed. 185, 190 (1946); Robertson v. Railroad Labor Bd., 268 U.S. 619, 622, 45 S. Ct. 621, 622, 69 L. Ed. 1119, 1121 (1925); United States v. Union Pac. R.R., 98 U.S. 569, 603-04, 25 L. Ed. 143, 151 (1879); Toland v. Sprague, 37 U.S. (12 Pet.) 300, 328, 9 L. Ed. 1093, 1105 (1838).

530. *See* RICHARD H. FALLON ET AL., HART & WECHSLER'S THE FEDERAL COURTS AND THE FEDERAL SYSTEM 1587-88 (4th ed. 1996).

531. Under the influence of the minimum contacts test of *International Shoe*, federal courts operating under the traditional view often state that minimum contacts with the United States are required for an assertion of jurisdiction under a federal long-arm statute to be valid. *See, e.g.*, Lorelei Corp. v. County of Guadalupe, 940 F.2d 717, 720 (1st Cir. 1991); New Eng. Health Care Employees Union, Dist. 1199 v. Fall River Nursing Home, Inc., 802 F. Supp. 674, 677 (D.R.I. 1992); Duckworth v. Medical Electro-Therapeutics, Inc., 768 F. Supp. 822, 826 (S.D. Ga. 1991); *see also* Dakota Indus., Inc. v. Dakota Sportswear, Inc., 946 F.2d 1384 (8th Cir. 1991).

would be valid because Congress would not be extending the reach of process beyond the territorial limits of the United States.

    Illustration 3-56. *A*, a citizen of State *X*, and *B*, a citizen of State *Y*, collide in their automobiles in State *Z*. State *X* is a state on the East Coast of the United States. State *Y* is a state on the West Coast of the United States. State *Z* is a state in the Mid-West. *B* has no contacts with State *X*. Under the traditional view of Congress' power under the Due Process Clause of the Fifth Amendment, Congress may validly authorize a U.S. District Court in State *X* to assert jurisdiction over *B* to adjudicate a claim for personal injuries by *A* arising out of the automobile accident, despite the fact that *B* has no contacts with State *X* and defending the action there would be very burdensome.[532]

* * * * *

    The traditional view of Congress' power under the Due Process Clause of the Fifth Amendment is at odds with the purposes of the minimum contacts test of the Fourteenth Amendment. The latter test seeks to preserve the defendant's opportunity to be heard in defense by allowing the defendant to anticipate the burdens of suit in a particular location and avoid or defray those burdens. Even if the defendant has "purposeful contacts" with the forum, the defendant is still allowed to show that the burdens of suit are unreasonable under the *Burger King* reasonableness test. It makes no sense to suppose that the Fourteenth Amendment imposes restrictions on the power of the states designed to protect defendants from unreasonably burdensome places of trial, but the Fifth Amendment allows Congress to impose such burdens without restraint. Perhaps for this reason, it has been suggested that the Fifth Amendment restrictions on the power of Congress may contain restrictions similar to those imposed on the states under the Fourteenth Amendment.[533]

    Some lower federal courts have agreed that the Fifth Amendment must be read to contain standards protecting the defendant from burdensome litigation similar to those contained in the Fourteenth Amendment. For example, in *Republic of Panama v. BCCI Holdings (Luxembourg) S.A.*,[534] the court held that the Fifth Amendment standard governing federal long-arm service over a domestic defendant included the same reasonableness standards as the Fourteenth Amendment and allowed defendants to demonstrate that a forum is excessively burdensome. Although the Fifth Amendment standard required evaluation of the

---

    532. In this illustration, venue would not be proper under 28 U.S.C. § 1391(a). Thus, it must be assumed that Congress, in addition to authorizing personal jurisdiction in the district court for State *X*, also authorizes venue there. Furthermore, under 28 U.S.C. § 1404(a), *B* could move for a transfer of venue for the convenience of the parties and witnesses and in the interests of justice, and a transfer would surely be granted. Under the *Burger King* decision, discussed in section (G)(2)*(b)(ii)* ("The Two-Step Test for the Validity of Specific Jurisdiction") *supra*, the availability of transfer could be taken into account in evaluating the due process validity of an assertion of jurisdiction under the minimum contacts test of the Fourteenth Amendment. Thus, Congress might also have to repeal § 1404(a) to present a pure case under the Fifth Amendment.

    533. *See* FED. R. CIV. P. 4(k)(2) advisory committee's note to the 1993 amendment; *see also* Maryellen Fullerton, *Constitutional Limits on Nationwide Personal Jurisdiction in the Federal Courts*, 79 NW. U. L. REV. 1, 39-60 (1984); Ralph U. Whitten, *The Constitutional Limitations on State-Court Jurisdiction: A Historical-Interpretative Reexamination of the Full Faith and Credit and Due Process Clauses* (pt. 2), 14 CREIGHTON L. REV. 735, 850 (1981).

    534. 119 F.3d 935 (11th Cir. 1997).

defendant's contacts with the United States, those contacts would not automatically satisfy due process. The defendant was entitled to demonstrate that an assertion of jurisdiction in the forum will make litigation so gravely difficult that the defendant is at a severe disadvantage in comparison to the plaintiff. Once this showing is made, due process will only be satisfied if the federal interest in having the action litigated in the forum outweighs the burdens on the defendant.[535]

When a defendant must be served outside the United States, similar issues exist. Some federal courts hold that national, rather than state, contacts are relevant to the due process inquiry.[536] Other cases seem more willing to use standards closer to the Fourteenth Amendment restrictions on state-court jurisdiction.[537]

The Supreme Court has not directly confronted the question of the power of Congress to confer long-arm jurisdiction on the federal courts since *International Shoe* was decided.[538] Given the view articulated in the Court's decisions under the Fourteenth Amendment, however, it is difficult to believe that the Court will allow Congress to confer long-arm jurisdiction on the federal courts without restriction. The case of *Insurance Corp. of Ireland v. Compagnie des Bauxites de Guinee*, discussed in section G(3), above, presents a strong argument against the traditional view.[539] *Insurance Corp. of Ireland* emphasized that the purpose of the Due Process Clause of the Fourteenth Amendment is to protect the defendant's individual liberty interest in civil actions. If the Due Process Clause

---

535. *See also* ESAB Group, Inc. v. Centricut, Inc., 126 F.3d 617 (4th Cir. 1997), *cert. denied*, 523 U.S. 1048, 118 S. Ct. 1364, 140 L. Ed. 2d 513 (1998) (following *Republic of Panama*, but stating that when defendants are located within the United States, they must look primarily to federal venue requirements for protection from onerous litigation).

536. *See, e.g.*, Szafarowicz v. Gotterup, No. 98-40023-NMG, 1999 WL 782028, 1999 U.S. Dist. LEXIS 14988 (D. Mass. Sept. 24, 1999); SEC v. Carrillo, 115 F.3d 1540 (11th Cir. 1997); Miller Pipeline Corp. v. British Gas PLC, 901 F. Supp. 1416 (S.D. Ind. 1995).

537. *See, e.g.*, Chew v. Dietrich, 137 F.3d 748 (2d Cir. 1998) (jurisdiction proper under Rule 4(k)(2) in Rhode Island where defendant assembled crew in Rhode Island for round trip yacht voyage to Bermuda and plaintiff's decedent killed on return leg; contacts with Rhode Island "related to" claim and satisfied Fifth Amendment); Doe v. Unocal Corp., 27 F. Supp. 2d 1174 (C.D. Cal. 1998) (jurisdiction asserted under Rule 4(k)(2) over French corporation invalid, *inter alia*, because contract with California citizen inadequate by itself under *Burger King* to establish purposeful contacts and reasonableness test need not be reached); Nissho Iwai Corp. v. M/V Star Sapphire, No. Civ. A. H-94-1599, 1995 WL 847172, 1995 U.S. Dist. LEXIS 21443 (S.D. Tex. Aug. 24, 1995) (claim arising outside U.S. requires systematic and continuous contacts with U.S. as a whole to satisfy assertion of federal long-arm jurisdiction).

538. For discussions of Fifth Amendment restrictions on assertions of jurisdiction by federal courts, see Robert C. Casad, *Personal Jurisdiction in Federal Question Cases*, 70 TEX. L. REV. 1589 (1992); Maryellen Fullerton, *Constitutional Limits on Nationwide Personal Jurisdiction in the Federal Courts*, 79 NW. U. L. REV. 1 (1984); Irene D. Sann, *Personal Jurisdiction in Federal Question Suits: Toward a Unified and Rational Theory for Personal Jurisdiction Over Non-Domiciliary and Alien Defendants*, 16 PAC. L.J. 1 (1984); David E. Seidelson, *The Jurisdictional Reach of a Federal Court Hearing a Federal Cause of Action: A Path Through the Maze*, 23 DUQ. L. REV. 323 (1985); Pamela J. Stephens, *The Federal Court Across the Street: Constitutional Limits on Federal Court Assertions of Personal Jurisdiction*, 18 U. RICH. L. REV. 697 (1984); *see also* Gerald Abraham, *Constitutional Limitations Upon the Territorial Reach of Federal Process*, 8 VILL. L. REV. 520 (1963).

539. *Cf.* Robert C. Casad, *Personal Jurisdiction in Federal Question Cases*, 70 TEX. L. REV. 1589, 1602 (1992) (discussing commentators and authorities relying on *Insurance Corp. of Ireland* to stand for the proposition that a basic fairness test, rather than simply a "national contacts test" should be applied under the Fifth Amendment).

of the Fourteenth Amendment is designed for that purpose, it is difficult to understand how the Fifth Amendment cannot be aimed at the same goal. Under this reasoning, surely the traditional view of Congress' power must give way to a test that focuses on the burdens that the forum places on the defendant's opportunity to be heard.

Nevertheless, a contrary inference about the content of the Fifth Amendment can be derived from *Burnham v. Superior Court*, discussed in section E(2), above. In *Burnham*, the Court indicated that the assertion by the states of transient presence jurisdiction would not violate the Due Process Clause of the Fourteenth Amendment. The plurality opinion by Justice Scalia relied on the basis of the historical pedigree of the transient presence rule and its continuing acceptance in the states rather than under the minimum contacts test. If a majority of the Court adopts Justice Scalia's view of due process, the Court might also hold that the Due Process Clause of the Fifth Amendment is not violated whenever a defendant can be served with process within the United States.[540] Thus, the resolution of questions about the scope of Congress' power to confer nationwide long-arm jurisdiction on the federal courts may depend on whether the philosophy of *Insurance Corp. of Ireland* or the philosophy of *Burnham* will control the application of the Fifth Amendment.

2. Restrictions on Federal Jurisdiction to Adjudicate Imposed by Use of State Long-Arm Statutes and Other Methods of Service

The number of federal long-arm statutes is limited. In most cases in federal court, the courts utilize state long-arm statutes to assert jurisdiction over nonresidents under the authority provided in Federal Rule 4.[541] In addition, federal courts can acquire jurisdiction to adjudicate if a defendant is served personally with process within the state where the district court is located. When federal courts utilize state long-arm statutes to assert jurisdiction, or when the defendant is served personally with process in the state where the district court is located, what constitutional standard do the federal courts use to determine the validity of the jurisdictional assertion?

After the discussion in the preceding subsection, one might think that the answer to this question would be easy. The reach of federal jurisdiction to adjudicate should be judged by reference to the standards of the Fifth Amendment. Whatever the standards of the Fifth Amendment turn out to be, the federal courts should apply them to determine whether they may exercise jurisdiction under state long-arm statutes or in any other circumstances. Fortunately or

---

540. *See id.* at 1605.

541. After the 1993 amendments to Rule 4, discussed in section K(2) ("Modern Methods of Serving Process") *supra*, this authority will exist, for example, with regard to competent, adult individuals under Rule 4(e)(1). Before the 1993 amendments, the provisions of Rule 4(e) authorized service on all nonresidents "under the circumstances and in the manner" provided by state law.

unfortunately, this simple answer is not the one that the courts have given to amenability questions in either federal question or diversity cases.

(a) Service Pursuant to State Long-Arm Statutes

Before 1993, Federal Rule 4(e) authorized the federal courts to use state long-arm statutes to acquire jurisdiction over nonresidents. However, Rule 4(e) only authorized service to be made under state long-arm statutes ''under the circumstances and in the manner prescribed by the statute.''[542] This language clearly limited the use of state long-arm statutes to the situations described in the statutes. However, the language of the rule said nothing about the constitutional standards that would limit the application of the statutes. Nevertheless, given the tendency of the states to enact statutes that, either explicitly or as construed, extend state court jurisdiction as far as the Fourteenth Amendment permits, it is understandable that the federal courts have held that they may apply state long-arm statutes only as far as the Fourteenth Amendment would permit state courts to apply them. Thus, whether the case is based on federal question or diversity jurisdiction, when a federal court used a state long-arm statute, the court is confined in its application of the statute by the minimum contacts test of *International Shoe.*[543]

In the 1993 amendments to Federal Rule 4, Rule 4(e) was repealed and other provisions substituted for it. However, under the current provisions of Rule 4, the federal courts will still be confined by the Fourteenth Amendment limitations on state-court jurisdiction when exercising authority under state long-arm provisions.[544] Thus, while other provisions of amended Rule 4 may widen the federal court's ability to assert long-arm jurisdiction, the preexisting practice under state long-arm statutes should remain unaffected under the new rule.

(b) Service Under Rule 4 when the State Courts Would Not Assert Jurisdiction: Federally Created Rights Cases

More difficult questions are presented when federal process is served on a defendant within the state where the federal action is pending, but the state courts would not assert jurisdiction over the defendant. Before 1993, this problem

---

542. *See* 146 F.R.D. 550 (1993) (amendment eliminating former Rule 4(e)).

543. *See, e.g.*, Dakota Indus., Inc. v. Dakota Sportswear, Inc., 946 F.2d 1384 (8th Cir. 1991); Lorelei Corp. v. County of Guadalupe, 940 F.2d 717 (1st Cir. 1991); United Elec. Workers of Am. v. 163 Pleasant St. Corp., 960 F.2d 1080 (1st Cir. 1992); New Eng. Health Care Employees Union, Dist. 1199 v. Fall River Nursing Home, Inc., 802 F. Supp. 674 (D.R.I. 1992); *see also* Robert C. Casad, *Personal Jurisdiction in Federal Question Cases*, 70 Tex. L. Rev. 1589, 1594-95 (1992).

544. For example, Federal Rule 4(e)(1) provides that service on a competent, adult individual may be made ''pursuant to the law of the state in which the district court is located, or in which service is effected.'' Federal Rule 4(k)(1)(A), in turn, states that service of a summons or filing a waiver of service will be effective to establish personal jurisdiction over a defendant ''who could be subjected to the jurisdiction of a court of general jurisdiction in the state in which the district court is located.'' Putting these two provisions together, if a defendant is served under the circumstances and in the manner provided by a state long-arm statute, as authorized by Federal Rule 4(e)(1), the defendant can be subjected to jurisdiction if the courts of the state would be able to do so under the Fourteenth Amendment, as stated in Federal Rule 4(k)(1)(A).

arose because of the interaction of Federal Rule 4(d) and (f). Before 1993, Rule 4(d) prescribed the manner in which process could be served on a defendant who was an inhabitant of or found within the state. Rule 4(f) provided that process could be served anywhere within the territorial limits of the state in which the district court was held. Thus, the question arose whether the federal courts could acquire jurisdiction by serving the defendant within the state, as prescribed in Rule 4(f), in a manner prescribed by Rule 4(d), even though no federal statute authorized the court to assert *jurisdiction* over the defendant, and even though the state courts of the state in which the district court is held would refuse to exercise *jurisdiction* over the defendant. Depending on whether the plaintiff's claim was created by federal or state law, the answer differed.

When the plaintiff was suing on a federally created right, the cases generally agreed that a federal amenability standard should limit the reach of personal jurisdiction under Rule 4.[545] Disagreement existed, however, about the proper content of the federal standard. Some cases attempted to measure whether the defendant had minimum contacts with the state in which the district court was sitting, thus applying the Fourteenth Amendment due process restrictions on the power of the states as the federal test of amenability.[546] Other cases stated that the Due Process Clause of the Fifth Amendment should determine the content of the federal standard. Under this standard, the test was stated to be whether the defendant had minimum contacts with the United States.[547] Finally, some cases applied a *state* standard of amenability even in cases where the plaintiff's action was based on a federally created right, when service was made under former Rule

---

545. *See, e.g.*, Fraley v. Chesapeake & Ohio Ry., 397 F.2d 1 (3d Cir. 1968); Volkswagen Interamericana, S.A. v. Rohlsen, 360 F.2d 437 (1st Cir.), *cert. denied*, 385 U.S. 919, 87 S. Ct. 230, 17 L. Ed. 2d 143 (1966); *see also* 4 CHARLES A. WRIGHT & ARTHUR R. MILLER, FEDERAL PRACTICE AND PROCEDURE: CIVIL § 1075, at 480 (2d ed. 1987).

546. *See, e.g.*, Fraley v. Chesapeake & Ohio Ry., 397 F.2d 1 (3d Cir. 1968); PPS, Inc. v. Jewelry Sales Representatives, Inc., 392 F. Supp. 375 (S.D.N.Y. 1975); Goldberg v. Mutual Readers League, Inc., 195 F. Supp. 778 (E.D. Pa. 1961).

547. *See* Volkswagen Interamericana, S.A. v. Rohlsen, 360 F.2d 437 (1st Cir.), *cert. denied*, 385 U.S. 919, 87 S. Ct. 230, 17 L. Ed. 2d 143 (1966); Holt v. Klosters Rederi A/S, 355 F. Supp. 354 (W.D. Mich. 1973); Edward J. Moriarty & Co. v. General Tire & Rubber Co., 289 F. Supp. 381 (S.D. Ohio 1967). These cases seemed to assume that the standards under the Fifth and Fourteenth Amendments were identical. *See, e.g.*, Holt v. Klosters Rederi A/S, 355 F. Supp. 354 (W.D. Mich. 1973). That is, the assumption seemed to be that due process limits are *only* a product of territorial limitations on the power of a government, so that minimum contacts with the relevant government's territory (the state's in the case of the Fourteenth Amendment and the United States' in the case of the Fifth) is all that is necessary to satisfy due process. This approach rejected the view, discussed in subsection 1, above, that the minimum contacts test serves the function of protecting the defendant's individual liberty interest by assuring the defendant a reasonably nonburdensome place of trial. If the Supreme Court should someday hold that the Due Process Clause of the Fifth Amendment contains protections for the defendant's individual liberty interest, the federal courts holding the contrary view would have to alter the results of their decisions accordingly. *Cf.* Goldberg v. Mutual Readers League, Inc., 195 F. Supp. 778 (E.D. Pa. 1961). *See generally* Gerald Abraham, *Constitutional Limitations Upon the Territorial Reach of Federal Process*, 8 VILL. L. REV. 520 (1963); Pamela J. Stephens, *The Federal Court Across the Street: Constitutional Limits on Federal Court Assertions of Personal Jurisdiction*, 18 U. RICH. L. REV. 697 (1984). However, as also noted in the previous subsection, the *Burnham* decision might be applied by the Court to validate federal power to extend jurisdiction nationwide, regardless of the burdens that may be imposed on the defendants thereby.

4 in a *manner* prescribed by state law.[548] The principle of latter cases did not permit the federal courts to assert jurisdiction when the courts of the state in which the district court was held would not assert jurisdiction over the defendant.

The use of a federal amenability standard in federally created rights cases means that there were situations in which federal courts would assert personal jurisdiction over defendants pursuant to Rule 4(d) and (f), even though the state courts would not have asserted jurisdiction over the defendant as a matter of state law. Furthermore, before the federal courts could apply a federal amenability standard, there had to be some federal statute, state statute, or Federal Rule of Civil Procedure that authorized service of process on the defendant. The Supreme Court made it clear that federal courts do not have the power to create common-law service of process rules.[549] However, in the cases discussed thus far, Rule 4 provided authority to serve the defendant. The question was, once served, could the defendant be subjected to jurisdiction.

After 1993, the question of what amenability standard to apply in federally created right cases will arise under amended Rule 4. The former provisions of Rule 4(d) and (f) have been reorganized and supplemented with new provisions governing the manner of service and the territorial reach of the district courts' jurisdiction. Whether it was intended or not by the drafters, these new provisions can be read to prohibit the use of a federal "common-law" amenability standard in the situations described above. Before 1993, Rule 4(d) and (f) did not specifically address problems of amenability. Instead, Rule 4(d) provided for the manner of service on different categories of defendants, while Rule 4(f) simply provided where process might be served. Neither provision specifically attempted to authorize jurisdiction to be asserted over the different categories of defendants to be served. Left with this ambiguity, the courts evolved amenability standards such as those discussed in the text above to govern questions of personal jurisdiction under Rule 4(d) and (f).

After 1993, Rule 4(e)-(j) govern the manner of serving process on different categories of defendants. Like the pre-1993 Rule 4(d), these provisions do not establish personal jurisdiction over defendants. Instead, they merely provide for the manner of service on particular kinds of defendants.[550] However, unlike former Rule 4(f), which was silent on questions of amenability, Rule 4(k) now specifically addresses these questions. Rule 4(k)(1) begins by stating that service of a summons or filing a waiver of service "is effective to establish jurisdiction over the person of a defendant" under the circumstances described in the rule. Rule 4(k)(1) then follows with four situations in which jurisdiction will be established: (1) when the defendant could be subjected to personal

---

548. *See* Gkiafis v. S.S. Yiosonas, 342 F.2d 546 (4th Cir. 1965); Scott Paper Co. v. Scott's Liquid Gold, Inc., 374 F. Supp. 184 (D. Del. 1974).

549. *See* Omni Capital Int'l, Ltd. v. Rudolf Wolff & Co., 484 U.S. 97, 108 S. Ct. 404, 98 L. Ed. 2d 415 (1987).

550. For example, Federal Rule 4(e) now provides for service on competent, adult individuals. In its comments on Rule 4(e), the Advisory Committee stated: "Service of the summons under this subdivision does not conclusively establish the jurisdiction of the court over the person of the defendant. A defendant may assert the territorial limits of the court's reach set forth in subdivision (k) . . . ." FED. R. CIV. P. 4(e) advisory committee's note to the 1993 amendment.

jurisdiction of a court of general jurisdiction in the state where the district court is located; (2) when a Rule 14 or 19 party is served within 100 miles of the place from which the summons issues; (3) when the defendant is subject to the federal interpleader jurisdiction under 28 U.S.C. § 1335; or (4) when a federal long-arm statute authorizes jurisdiction over the defendant. In addition, Rule 4(k)(2) explicitly creates a narrow federal long-arm rule applicable to cases involving claims based on federal law.[551]

The specific reference by Rule 4(k) to questions of personal jurisdiction gives rise to a strong inference that Rule 4(k) articulates the exclusive standards for determining the territorial reach of the district courts' jurisdiction. If this interpretation of Rule 4(k) is correct, the courts can no longer create or apply federal amenability standards that do not exist in Rule 4(k).

Illustration 3-57. *A*, a citizen of State *X*, is an employee of *B Corp.*, a corporation incorporated with its principal place of business in State *X*. *A* is injured while working for *B* in State *X*. Subsequently, *A* moves to State *Z*, where *A* commences an action against *B* to recover damages for the injuries received while working for *B*. *A's* claim is based on a federal statute and is commenced in a U.S. District Court in State *Z*. *B* is served with process under Federal Rule 4(h)(1) by delivering a copy of the summons and complaint to an officer of *B Corp.* in State *Z*. No federal long-arm statute authorizes the federal courts to assume personal jurisdiction over *B* under the circumstances described. The courts of State *Z* would not, as a matter of their own law, assert jurisdiction over *B* under these circumstances. Before the 1993 amendments to Rule 4, whether *B* could be subjected to personal jurisdiction in State *Z* would be determined by a federal amenability standard of the sort described in the text, above. After the 1993 amendments to Rule 4, it may not be possible to use a federal amenability standard to justify an assertion of jurisdiction. Rule 4(k)(1)(A) does not allow an assertion of jurisdiction unless the defendant is subject to jurisdiction in the courts of general jurisdiction in the state where the action is brought, which is not possible here. Rule 4(k)(1)(B) only applies to cases in which Rule 14 or 19 parties are served within 100 miles from the place where the summons was issued. *B* is not a Rule 14 or 19 party. Rule 4(k)(1)(C) only applies to interpleader cases, and this is not an interpleader case. Rule 4(k)(1)(D) only applies to cases in which a federal statute authorizes jurisdiction over the defendant, which is not true here. Rule 4(k)(2) only applies to actions in which the defendant is not subject to personal jurisdiction in the courts of general jurisdiction of any state.

---

551. *See generally* Dora A. Corby, *Putting Personal Jurisdiction Within Reach: Just What Has Rule 4(k)(2) Done for the Personal Jurisdiction of Federal Courts*, 30 MCGEORGE L. REV. 167 (1998). Several federal courts have held that admiralty law is "federal" law for purposes of Rule 4(k)(2). *See* World Tanker Carriers Corp. v. M/V Ya Mawlaya, 99 F.3d 717 (5th Cir. 1996); West Afr. Trading & Shipping Co. v. London Int'l Group, 968 F. Supp. 996 (D.N.J. 1997); Western Equities, Ltd. v. Hanseatic, Ltd., 956 F. Supp. 1232 (D.V.I. 1997); Sarah S. Nickerson, World Tanker Carriers Corp. v. M/V Ya Mawlaya: *The Fifth Circuit Finds Rule 4(k)(2) Applicable to Admiralty Claims,* 72 TUL. L. REV. 1047 (1997). This conclusion is interesting, given that the U.S. Supreme Court has held that admiralty law is not federal law for purposes of federal question jurisdiction under 28 U.S.C. § 1331. *See* Romero v. International Terminal Operating Co., 358 U.S. 354, 79 S. Ct. 468, 3 L. Ed. 2d 368 (1959).

B could be sued in State *X*. Therefore, if the provisions of Rule 4(k) are given their natural meaning, *A's* action must be dismissed.[552]

* * * * *

It is unclear whether the drafters of the 1993 amendments to Rule 4 intended to prevent the creation and application of federal amenability standards beyond the circumstances described in Rule 4(k). The Advisory Committee's note to the 1993 amendments to Rule 4 does not directly address this question. It does seem strange that the drafters of the rule would produce such a significant result without explanatory commentary. Nevertheless, the text of Rule 4(k) is compelling and should not be departed from lightly. Unless the courts identify ambiguities in the rule that would justify the creation of federal amenability standards, Rule 4(k) should be treated as excluding the creation of federal amenability standards beyond the circumstances described in the text of the rule.

A separate question is who bears the burden of showing whether the criteria of Rule 4(k)(2) are met. In *United States v. Swiss American Bank, Ltd.*,[553] the First Circuit held that a plaintiff who seeks to invoke Rule 4(k)(2) must make a prima facie case for the applicability of the rule by showing that (1) the claim arises under federal law; (2) personal jurisdiction is not available under any federal statute; and (3) the defendant's contacts with the United States are sufficient to satisfy the Constitution. In addition, the plaintiff must certify that, based on the information readily available to the plaintiff and the plaintiff's attorney, the defendant is not subject to personal jurisdiction in any state. Upon making this showing, the burden shifts to the defendant to produce evidence which would either show that the defendant is subject to personal jurisdiction in one or more specific states, or that its contacts with the United States are constitutionally insufficient.[554]

(c) Service Under Rule 4 when the State Courts Would Not Assert Jurisdiction: Diversity Actions

Before 1993, when the jurisdiction of a federal court was based solely on diversity of citizenship, the appellate cases unanimously held that a state, rather than a federal, standard of amenability should be applied when service was effectuated under Rule 4 on a defendant within the state.[555] Thus, if the state in which the district court was held would not assert jurisdiction over the defendant, even if it could do so under the Fourteenth Amendment, the federal court would not assert jurisdiction through the use of former Federal Rule 4(d)

---

552. Of course, when jurisdiction is asserted under Federal Rule 4(k)(2), the Fifth Amendment Due Process Standards will have to be satisfied. *See* section L(1), *supra*, for a discussion of these standards.

553. 191 F.3d 30 (1st Cir. 1999).

554. *Id.* at 41. If the defendant successfully shows that it is subject to personal jurisdiction in one or more states, the plaintiff may (a) move for a transfer to one of those states; (b) discontinue the action and refile it in one of those states; or (c) contest the defendant's evidence, in which case the defendant will be deemed to waived any contention that it is subject to personal jurisdiction in a state other than the ones the defendant has identified. *Id.* at 42.

555. *See* 4 Charles A. Wright & Arthur R. Miller, Federal Practice and Procedure: Civil § 1075, at 489, n.32 (2d ed. 1987) and authorities there cited.

and (f). This result was the product of Judge Friendly's opinion for the Second Circuit Court of Appeals in *Arrowsmith v. United Press International.*[556]

In *Arrowsmith*, a citizen of Maryland sued United Press International, a New York corporation, in the U.S. District Court for Vermont. The plaintiff asserted a claim for libel based on a U.P.I. story about the dynamiting of a synagogue in Atlanta, Georgia. Apparently, the action was brought in Vermont because Vermont had a longer statute of limitations than other states on libel claims. The defendant was served with process under Federal Rule 4(d)(3) by serving the manager of the defendant's Montpelier news bureau in Vermont. The defendant moved to dismiss the action under Federal Rule 12(b) for lack of personal jurisdiction, improper venue, and failure to state a claim upon which relief could be granted.

The district court dismissed on the latter ground, and the plaintiff appealed. The Second Circuit Court of Appeals held that the district court erred in dismissing for failure to state a claim upon which relief could be granted without first considering the issue of personal jurisdiction. The court thus vacated the district court's judgment of dismissal and remanded for consideration of the jurisdictional question. In so doing, the court considered it necessary to decide what standard should govern the district court's determination of the jurisdictional issue.

The Second Circuit held that when the subject-matter jurisdiction of a federal court is based solely on diversity of citizenship, the court cannot acquire personal jurisdiction pursuant to Rule 4(d) and (f) when the state in which the district court is held would not assert jurisdiction over the defendant. The court based its decision in part on the failure of Rule 4 to address questions of amenability to suit, as opposed to manner of service. In addition, the court refused to read into the statutes conferring diversity jurisdiction a congressional mandate to disregard state jurisdictional restrictions.[557]

The *Arrowsmith* rule seems secure after the 1993 amendments to Rule 4. Rule 4(k)(1)(A) now specifically states that service of a summons under Rule 4 will establish personal jurisdiction over a defendant "who could be subjected to the jurisdiction of a court of general jurisdiction in the state in which the district court is located." The remaining provisions of Rule 4(k) authorize jurisdiction over defendants in special situations and do not contradict the *Arrowsmith* rule. Therefore, it would seem that in diversity actions in which no state or federal long-arm statute authorizes jurisdiction over a defendant, amenability to process will be determined by reference to the ability of the forum state to assert jurisdiction, just as before 1993.

(d) Amenability Questions Under the 100-Mile Bulge Rule

In addition to the amenability questions that existed when process is served pursuant to Rule 4(d) and (f) within the state in which the federal district

---

556. 320 F.2d 219 (2d Cir. 1963).

557. *See id.* at 225-27.

court sits, a similar amenability problem existed under the so-called 100-mile bulge provision of Rule 4. Rule 4(f) was amended in 1963 to allow federal process to be served outside the territorial limits of the state, but within the United States, at any place that was not more than 100 miles from the place in which the action is commenced, or to which it is assigned or transferred for trial. This 100-mile bulge rule only applied when (1) process is being served on a person who is being brought in as a party under Rule 14, (2) process is being served on a person who is being brought in as an additional party to a pending action or a counterclaim or cross-claim therein pursuant to Rule 19, or (3) process is being served on a person required to respond to an order of commitment for civil contempt.

In explaining the purpose of the 100-mile provision, the Advisory Committee stated:

> The bringing in of parties under the 100-mile provision in the limited situations enumerated is designed to promote the objective of enabling the court to determine entire controversies. In the light of present-day facilities for communication and travel, the territorial range of the service allowed . . . can hardly work hardship on the parties summoned. The provision will be especially useful in metropolitan areas spanning more than one State. Any requirements of subject-matter jurisdiction and venue will still have to be satisfied as to the parties brought in. . . .[558]

Although the Advisory Committee's note implied that anyone who was served with federal process within the 100-mile area would be subjected to the personal jurisdiction of the district court, the courts did not reach this result under Rule 4(f). Like defendants served within the state pursuant to Rule 4(d) and (f), restrictive amenability standards were also read into the 100-mile provision. Generally, the courts insisted that for personal jurisdiction to exist, the party served with process had to have minimum contacts with the bulge area.[559] Most courts holding that minimum contacts had to exist with the "bulge" area seem to be adopting a suggestion by Professor Kaplan that the 100-mile provision should be interpreted to contain such a limitation on amenability—an interpretation that, in effect, incorporated the Fourteenth Amendment minimum contacts test as

---

558. FED. R. CIV. P. 4(f) advisory committee's note to the 1963 amendment.

559. *See* Sprow v. Hartford Ins. Co., 594 F.2d 412, 416 (5th Cir. 1979); Drames v. Melgreva Co. Maritima, S.A., 571 Supp. 737, 738-39 (E.D. Pa. 1983); Jacobs v. Flight Extenders, Inc., 90 F.R.D. 676, 679 (E.D. Pa. 1981) (minimum contacts with either forum state or bulge must exist; here contacts with bulge existed); Paxton v. Southern Pa. Bank, 93 F.R.D. 503, 505 (D. Md. 1982); School Dist. v. Missouri, 460 F. Supp. 421, 436 (W.D. Mo. 1978); Lee v. Ohio Cas. Ins. Co., 445 F. Supp. 189, 193-94 (D. Del. 1978) (court need not determine whether amenability by law of forum or only contacts with bulge necessary, since both are present); Pillsbury Co. v. Delta Boat & Barge Rental, Inc., 72 F.R.D. 630, 632 (E.D. La. 1976); McGonigle v. Penn-Central Transp. Co., 49 F.R.D. 58, 62-63 (D. Md. 1969). *But see* Coleman v. American Export Isbrandtsen Lines, Inc., 405 F.2d 250, 252 (2d Cir. 1968) (process can be validly served in bulge only on persons over whom bulge state has jurisdiction and, very likely, only on persons over whom it has chosen to exercise jurisdiction); Spearing v. Manhattan Oil Transp. Corp., 375 F. Supp. 764, 771 (S.D.N.Y. 1974) (jurisdiction can only be asserted over persons over whom the bulge state has chosen to exercise jurisdiction).

part of the rule.[560] Some courts, however, concluded that the "minimum contacts" amenability standard of the 100-mile provision was compelled by the Constitution. Of these courts, some indicated that it was the Due Process Clause of the Fourteenth Amendment that compelled the result.[561] This conclusion is clearly wrong because the Fourteenth Amendment limits state-court jurisdiction, not federal-court jurisdiction. Other courts cited the Fifth Amendment Due Process Clause as the source of the amenability restriction.[562]

After the 1993 amendment to Rule 4, the amenability problems discussed in the previous paragraph have probably been eliminated. Rule 4(k)(1)(B) now contains the 100-mile bulge provision. However, as noted in subsection (2)(b), above, Rule 4(k) now specifically addresses questions of personal jurisdiction. The rule provides that service of a summons is effective to establish personal jurisdiction over a defendant "who is a party joined under Rule 14 or Rule 19 and is served at a place within a judicial district of the United States and not more than 100 miles from the place from which the summons issues."[563] Thus, the rule now explicitly provides that personal jurisdiction is acquired by simple service of process within the "bulge" area.

Illustration 3-58. *A*, a citizen of State *X*, sues *B*, a citizen of State *Y*, in a U.S. District Court for the Western District of State *Y*, where *B* resides. *A's* claim is for personal injuries received in an automobile accident in State *R*. The accident was caused when *C*, who was *B's* employee, driving *B's* truck on *B's* business, collided with *A* in State *R*. *B* asserts that if *B* is liable to *A*, *C* is liable to *B* for any damages that *B* must pay to *A*. *C* is a citizen of State *Z* who resides in the Southern District of State *Z*. The Southern District of State *Z* abuts the northern side of the Western District of State *Y*. However, *C* lives more than 100 miles from the city in the Southern District of State *Y* where the action is pending and the summons was issued. Thus, *C* cannot be served with process in State *Z*. However, *B* has *C* served with a summons and third-party complaint under Rule 14 while *C* is passing through the Eastern District of State *Q*, which abuts the western side of the Western District of State *Y*. *C* is served 30 miles from the city in the Western District of State *Y* where the action is pending and the summons was issued. Under the terms of Rule 4(k)(1)(B), the U.S. District Court in the Western District of State *Y* acquires personal jurisdiction over *C* by the service of process on *C* in the Eastern District of State *Q*.

* * * * *

---

560. *See* Benjamin Kaplan, *Amendments of the Federal Rules of Civil Procedure, 1961-1963 (I)*, 77 HARV. L. REV. 601, 632-33 (1964).

561. *See* Paxton v. Southern Pa. Bank, 93 F.R.D. 503, 505 (D. Md. 1982); McGonigle v. Penn-Central Transp. Co., 49 F.R.D. 58, 63 (D. Md. 1969).

562. *See* Jacobs v. Flight Extenders, Inc., 90 F.R.D. 676, 679 (E.D. Pa. 1981).

563. FED. R. CIV. P. 4(k)(1)(B).

Chapter 4

VENUE

Venue rules determine the location where the action will be conducted. Legislatures establish venue rules primarily for the *convenience* of the parties.[1] The rules define those places where the legislature believes the parties can try certain categories of cases most fairly and efficiently. Frequently, a procedural system will allow a change of venue for the convenience of the parties or witnesses. Unlike subject-matter jurisdiction,[2] defendants may waive venue objections by not raising them promptly in the manner prescribed by individual procedural systems.[3]

Personal jurisdiction also limits the geographical areas in which civil actions may be brought to assure a nonburdensome place of adjudication for the defendant. Obviously, venue restrictions overlap with personal jurisdiction restrictions. However, venue is different from personal jurisdiction in two important respects. First, venue either is or is not proper in the court in which an action is commenced. In contrast, personal jurisdiction, even if proper, still must be acquired by the action of service of process on the defendant. Second, venue restrictions do not ordinarily render judgments void and subject to collateral attack in subsequent proceedings; in contrast, exceeding the limits on the reach of a court's personal jurisdiction can void a judgment.[4] Thus, if an action is commenced in an improper venue within a state against a nonresident defendant, the defendant may not default and collaterally attack the judgment in another state for lack of proper venue.[5]

The first section of this chapter discusses a historical distinction between "local" and "transitory" actions. This distinction remains important today in most jurisdictions. The next two sections discuss modern venue rules in state and federal courts. The next section examines the doctrine of "forum non conveniens" and transfers of venue. The last section examines injunctions prohibiting extrastate litigation and other devices for controlling the location of litigation.

---

1. In contrast, subject-matter jurisdiction rules are supported by separation-of-powers considerations. *See* Chapter 2(A)(2) ("The 'No-Waiver, No-Consent' Rule") *supra*.

2. Subject-matter jurisdiction may not be waived or conferred on a court by consent of the parties. *See id.*

3. *See, e.g.*, FED. R. CIV. P. 12(h)(1) (waiver of venue under the Federal Rules).

4. *See* Chapter 3(B)(3) ("In Personam Jurisdiction: Consent, Appearance, and Waiver") *supra* (discussing the option of collaterally attacking a judgment for lack of personal jurisdiction).

5. This result is the byproduct of the fact that a judgment rendered by a court with improper venue is not void within the state where the judgment is rendered. Therefore, it must, under the full-faith-and-credit implementing statute 28 U.S.C. § 1738, be enforced by all other states. *See* Chapter 3(A)(1)*(d)* ("The 1790 Implementing Statute") *supra* & Chapter 13(E) ("Claim and Issue Preclusion on Questions of Subject-Matter and Personal Jurisdiction") *infra* (both discussing the effect of the judgment-rendering state's rules governing the validity of judgments on the enforceability of the judgments elsewhere).

SECTION A. TRANSITORY AND LOCAL ACTIONS

The most important venue concept produced by English law was the distinction between *local* and *transitory* actions. If the events giving rise to the action could have occurred only in a particular place, the courts characterized the action as local. Examples include actions for the recovery of land or for damages for injury to land. Transitory actions were actions based on events that could have occurred anywhere. Examples include actions to recover damages for slander or assault and battery.[6] Local actions always have something to do with land, but not all actions having to do with land are local actions.

The distinction between local and transitory actions remains important today. However, understanding the distinction requires some historical background. The distinction is a product of the evolution of trial by jury in England. The Norman kings began to allow juries to decide cases in the king's courts. Before the fifteenth century, however, these juries based their decisions chiefly on their own knowledge of the case. The jurors acquired this knowledge as neighbors of the litigants or by searching out evidence before trial.[7]

Illustration 4-1. The court of the mesne lord[8] normally tried the question of ownership of land. The usual method of trial was battle.[9] The Grand Assize, enacted during the reign of Henry II (1154-1189), gave the defendant the option to refuse battle. Instead, the defendant could remove the action to the king's court. The court then tried the case through the oath of twelve neighbors who "knew by their own eyes and ears" who had the better title.[10] Similarly, a plaintiff could use the writ of novel disseisin to determine the immediate right to possession of land.[11] This writ required the sheriff to obtain "twelve men of the neighborhood to view the land."[12] They then had "to attend the king's court at a day named, prepared to deliver their verdict."[13] In the field of criminal law, oaths of neighbors formed the basis of indictments for robberies and other violent misdeeds.[14]

* * * * *

The courts considered these situations (as well as others) to be "local" in nature because the jurors would ordinarily have to be from the vicinity where the events or misdeeds at issue actually occurred. This need to secure a local jury prompted the courts to require the parties to allege with great particularity the location where the events giving rise to the suit had occurred. When factual issues

---

6. *See* JOSEPH H. KOFFLER & ALISON REPPY, HANDBOOK OF COMMON LAW PLEADING § 29, at 103-04 (1969).

7. *See* W.H. Wicker, *The Development of the Distinction Between Local and Transitory Actions*, 4 TENN. L. REV. 55 (1926).

8. A mesne lord was an intermediate lord who stood between the tenant and a superior lord.

9. *See* 1 WILLIAM S. HOLDSWORTH, A HISTORY OF ENGLISH LAW 140-41 (1903); *see also* Chapter 1(E)(1)*(d)* ("Modes of Trial Under the Writ System") *supra*.

10. ALBERT T. CARTER, A HISTORY OF THE ENGLISH COURTS 29-30 (5th ed. 1927).

11. *See* Chapter 1(E)(1)*(b)(i)* ("Real Actions") *supra*.

12. WILLIAM F. WALSH, A HISTORY OF ANGLO-AMERICAN LAW 60 (2d ed. 1932).

13. *Id.*

14. FREDERIC W. MAITLAND, THE CONSTITUTIONAL HISTORY OF ENGLAND 108-09 (1908).

existed, the court could then summon jurors from that location to Westminster to decide them.[15] English courts could not try an action arising outside of England because it was impossible to secure a jury with knowledge of the facts.[16]

In the thirteenth century, the common-law courts began to sit en banc at Westminster during four terms each year (the Easter, Trinity, Michaelmas, and Hilary terms, each of which lasted only a few weeks). Individual judges on circuit held jury trials away from the courts at Westminster.[17] The judge did not enter judgment on a jury verdict immediately. Instead, judgment was delayed until after commencement of the next term—at which time the losing party could present motions designed to prevent entry of the judgment. Under this *nisi prius* system, an allegation of venue thus determined the place of trial. It also determined the location from which the jury was selected.[18]

The jury's function ultimately evolved into judging the truth of testimony presented at trial. Because personal knowledge of the jurors was no longer needed to determine the facts, the reason for requiring a local jury ceased. As a result, the courts gradually relaxed venue rules.[19] In most actions, the courts permitted plaintiffs to state the county where the action arose in the margin of the declaration. The courts selected the jury based on this *marginal venue*. The courts held that this allegation of venue was not material. Thus, the defendant could not dispute ("traverse") it in most personal actions.[20] One commentator has suggested, however, that the courts "innate conservatism" may have been the reason why the courts did not apply this view to actions involving real estate.[21]

As the law developed, local actions became those that sought one of the following: (1) the recovery of land—for example, ejectment actions; (2) the establishment or enforcement of a right arising out of land—for example, enforcement of covenants running with the land based upon privity of estate; or (3) the recovery of damages for injury to land—for example, trespass or nuisance actions for damage to real estate.[22] The plaintiff had to try these actions where the land was located.[23]

In contrast, other common-law actions became transitory. When the plaintiff brought a transitory action in a place where the events giving rise to the

---

15. W.H. Wicker, *The Development of the Distinction Between Local and Transitory Actions*, 4 TENN. L. REV. 55, 59 (1926); *see* 5 WILLIAM S. HOLDSWORTH, A HISTORY OF ENGLISH LAW 117 (1924).

16. W.H. Wicker, *The Development of the Distinction Between Local and Transitory Actions*, 4 TENN. L. REV. 55, 59 (1926).

17. *Id.* at 61.

18. *Id.* at 60.

19. *Id.*

20. *Id.* at 61; *see also* Chapter 6(A)(3)*(d)* ("Traverses") and Chapter 6(A)(6) ("Relation of Pleading to Proof at Trial") *infra.*

21. W.H. Wicker, *The Development of the Distinction Between Local and Transitory Actions*, 4 TENN. L. REV. 55, 60-62 (1926) (the old precedents caused the courts "to refuse to swallow the fiction that land was situated somewhere other than where it was in fact").

22. *See, e.g.,* L.S. Rogers, Annotation, *Venue of Action for the Cutting, Destruction, or Damage of Standing Timber or Trees*, 65 A.L.R.2D 1268 (1959); F.T. Woods, Annotation, *Venue of Suit to Enjoin Nuisance*, 7 A.L.R.2D 481 (1949).

23. If the plaintiff alleged a false location to gain a favorable venue and the defendant showed the land to be located elsewhere, the court could dismiss the action. JOSEPH H. KOFFLER & ALISON REPPY, HANDBOOK OF COMMON LAW PLEADING § 29, at 103-05 (1969).

action had not occurred, the courts permitted the plaintiff, after stating the true venue, to use a *videlicet* (viz. or to wit) to allege a place within the court's jurisdiction.[24] In this way, the courts were able to maintain in England actions arising outside of England if they were not "local" in nature.[25] Thus, in *Doulson v. Matthews*,[26] Justice Buller of the Court of King's Bench stated that:

> [i]t is now too late for us to inquire whether it were wise or politic to make a distinction between transitory and local actions: it is sufficient for the Courts that the law has settled the distinction, and that an action [for trespass] *quare clausum fregit* is local. We may try actions here which are in their nature transitory, though arising out of a transaction abroad, but not such as are in their nature local.[27]

Equity courts did not use jurors. Equity courts ordinarily based their jurisdiction on the defendant's presence before the court. Therefore, plaintiffs did not have to bring equity suits in particular counties. When an equity court ordered a change of possession of land located in England, the court could assist the plaintiff by issuing a writ. Such a writ directed the sheriff of the county where the land was located to help the plaintiff take possession.[28] When the defendant was before the court but the land was located abroad, the court had to rely upon contempt and other measures to enforce its decree.[29]

State venue rules in the United States commonly preserve the distinction between local and transitory actions.

Illustration 4-2. Section 103 of the Field Code of 1848, for example, provided as follows:

> § 103. Actions for the following causes, must be tried in the county where the cause or some part thereof arose, or in which the subject of the action or some part thereof is situated, subject to the power of the court to change the place of trial, in the cases provided by statute.
>
> 1. For the recovery of real property or of an estate or interest therein, or for the determination, in any form, of such right or interest, and for injuries to real property;
>
> 2. For the partition of real property;
>
> 3. For the foreclosure of a mortgage of real property.[30]

This section classified actions for injuries to real property as local in nature. It required that they be brought in the county where the land was located.

---

24. *Id.* at 106; *see also* Chapter 6(A)(6) ("Relation of Pleading to Proof at Trial") *infra*.

25. W.H. Wicker, *The Development of the Distinction Between Local and Transitory Actions*, 4 TENN. L. REV. 55, 61-62 (1926).

26. 100 Eng. Rep. 1143 (K.B. 1792).

27. *Id.* at 1144 (dismissing trespass action in England for money damages for entering plaintiff's dwelling house in Canada and expelling the plaintiff); *see also* Chapter 1(E)(1)*(b)(iii)* ("*Ex Delicto* Personal Actions") *supra*.

28. William W. Blume, *Place of Trial of Civil Cases*, 48 MICH. L. REV. 1, 27 (1949).

29. *Id.* at 27-28; *see* Penn v. Baltimore, 27 Eng. Rep. 1132 (Ch. 1750) (holding specific performance decree proper for land outside England).

30. Act of Apr. 12, 1848, ch. 379, § 103, 1848 N.Y. Laws 497, 517.

The current New York statute eliminates specific reference to actions for injuries to real property:

> § 507. Real Property actions.
>
> The place of trial of an action in which the judgment demanded would affect the title to, or the possession, use or enjoyment of, real property shall be in the county in which any part of the subject of the action is situated.[31]

The New York courts could have interpreted this statute as eliminating a local action venue requirement in actions for trespass to land. However, New York decisions continue to classify actions involving injury to land as local in nature.[32] These decisions demonstrate the resiliency of the local action rule, even in a time when the premises of the rule have come into question.[33]

* * * * *

A few courts have discarded the local action rule when a statute does not compel its application.

Illustration 4-3. In *Reasor-Hill Corp. v. Harrison*,[34] for example, the Arkansas Supreme Court held that the Arkansas courts could entertain a suit for injuries to real property located in Missouri. The court examined the reasons given in support of the local action rule and found them unpersuasive. It concluded that the local action rule, as applied to the case before it, had ''no basis in logic or equity and rests solely upon English cases that were decided before America was discovered and in circumstances that are not even comparable to those existing in our Union.''[35]

* * * * *

The courts have abandoned the local action rule mainly in actions seeking to recover damages for injuries to real property located outside the state.[36] In actions directly involving the title to land located outside the state, courts apparently have not relaxed the rule.[37] Likewise, with regard to land located

---

31. N.Y. C.P.L.R. § 507 (McKinney 1976).

32. *See, e.g.*, Town of Hempstead v. City of New York, 88 Misc. 2d 366, 388 N.Y.S.2d 78 (Sup. Ct. 1976); Geidel v. Niagara Mohawk Power Corp., 46 Misc. 2d 990, 261 N.Y.S.2d 379 (Sup. Ct. 1965).

33. *See, e.g.*, Brainerd Currie, *The Constitution and the "Transitory" Cause of Action*, 73 HARV. L. REV. 36, 67-69 (1959).

34. 220 Ark. 521, 249 S.W.2d 994 (1952).

35. *Id.* at 525, 249 S.W.2d at 996.

36. *See, e.g.*, Reasor-Hill Corp. v. Harrison, 220 Ark. 521, 249 S.W.2d 994 (1952); Little v. Chicago St. Paul, Minneapolis & Omaha Ry., 65 Minn. 48, 67 N.W. 846 (1896); Ingram v. Great Lakes Pipe Line Co., 153 S.W.2d 547 (Mo. Ct. App. 1941); M.O. Regensteiner, Annotation, *Jurisdiction of Action at Law for Damages for Tort Concerning Real Property in Another State or Country*, 30 A.L.R.2D 1219 (1953). New York has abolished the local action rule by statute in actions to recover damages for injury to land located outside the state and in actions for breach of contract or covenants relating to land outside the state. *See* N.Y. REAL PROP. ACTS. § 121 (1989). Most states have retained the local action rule in this category of cases. *See* RUSSELL J. WEINTRAUB, COMMENTARY ON THE CONFLICT OF LAWS § 4.39 (3d ed. 1986).

37. *See* RUSSELL J. WEINTRAUB, COMMENTARY ON THE CONFLICT OF LAWS §§ 8.4-8.5 (3d ed. 1986). As discussed in Chapter 3, *supra*, and in the text, *infra*, this situation may involve due process restrictions on the power of courts to affect the title to land located outside the state. *See* Chapter 3(B)(1)*(b)* (''Restrictive Principles of In Rem Jurisdiction'') *supra*.

within the state, most states have retained the local action rule as it traditionally operated.[38] The justifications for retaining the rule include the following:

> [T]he court of the county in which the res, which is the subject matter of the suit, is located is best able to deal with the problem. The local sheriff can attach, deliver, or execute upon the property. The local clerk can make the necessary entries with a minimum of red tape where title to land is affected. Trial convenience is served where "a view" is necessary or of value in reaching a determination. Third parties can readily ascertain, at a logical point of inquiry, the status of a res in which they may be interested.
>
> . . . [T]hese factors are of sufficient importance in this type of case to outweigh other considerations such as convenience of parties or witnesses in the selection of place of trial. Consequently, in actions of the type generally referred to as local, venue based upon where the subject of action or part thereof is situated makes sense and should be preserved.[39]

Regardless whether these justifications made sense in the past, they do not make sense today. Local officials can attach, deliver, or execute upon land based on the judgment of a court located in another county, if the law authorizes them to do so. There should be few administrative problems involved if the clerk in the county where land is located is authorized to make entries concerning the title based on an action pending in some other county. A view of property is seldom necessary, even when land is the subject of the action. When a view is necessary, the court can transfer the action under an appropriate statute to the county where the land is located.[40] In addition, other kinds of actions exist in which a view is sometimes necessary, but those actions are not, as a consequence, classified as local actions.[41] Finally, third parties can still ascertain the status of land in which they are interested in the county where the land is located, even if actions concerning the land are allowed in other counties. For example, a notice of lis pendens can be entered in the records of the county where the land is located based on an action concerning the land in another county, as long as the law authorizes such an entry.

For these reasons, retention of the local action rule is questionable today. Nevertheless, as noted in *Illustration 4-2*, above, the rule has shown great resilience. Furthermore, no strong nationwide legislative movement is afoot today to abolish the rule.

---

38. *See, e.g.*, S.D. CODIFIED LAWS ANN. §§ 15-5-1(1) to (3) (action for recovery of realty, partition of realty, foreclosure of mortgage on realty, and damages for injury to realty must be brought in county where subject of the action, or some part thereof, is situated), § 15-5-8 (action for damages to property may, at plaintiff's option be brought in county where damages were inflicted or cause of action arose) (1984); *cf.* SDDS, Inc. v. State, 502 N.W.2d 852 (S.D. 1993) (action by solid waste developer challenging initiative and referendum resulting in denial of permit was not a suit in which the subject of action was land).

39. George N. Stevens, *Venue Statutes: Diagnosis and Proposed Cure*, 49 MICH. L. REV. 307, 310 (1951).

40. *See* section D ("Forum Non Conveniens and Change of Venue") *infra*.

41. *See* RUSSELL J. WEINTRAUB, COMMENTARY ON THE CONFLICT OF LAWS § 4.39, at 229 (3d ed. 1986).

One issue concerning the local action rule is whether the courts should treat it as a rule of venue or subject-matter jurisdiction. Some courts consider the local action objection to be waivable like other venue objections.[42] However, other courts, sometimes influenced by state constitutional provisions classifying certain actions as local, consider the objection to be jurisdictional in nature.[43] Absent a specific legislative or constitutional classification recognizing that a case is beyond a court's subject-matter jurisdiction when it is brought somewhere other than where land is situated, little justification exists for considering the objection to be jurisdictional in nature.

Chapter 3 discussed decisions of the U.S. Supreme Court holding that states do not have subject-matter jurisdiction to entertain actions that directly affect the title to land located in other states.[44] As there discussed, it is clear that this restrictive principle of jurisdiction was not, prior to the Fourteenth Amendment, considered a matter of constitutional law. Rather, the principle was one of a number of sovereignty-based rules of international law that the states were entitled to enforce in order to protect their prerogatives from the encroachment of other states.[45] After the adoption of the Fourteenth Amendment, the status of these rules as "constitutional" rules or "nonconstitutional" sovereignty-based rules is unclear.[46] However, the Supreme Court has continued to enforce them.

For purposes of this chapter, it is important to note that some local actions in state courts will, and some will not, overlap with the principle prohibiting actions that directly affect the title to land located elsewhere. For example, actions to recover damages for trespass to land located in another state will surely not be held to "directly" affect the title to the land in a way that would entitle the situs state to refuse to enforce the forum's judgment.[47] Note,

---

42. *See, e.g.,* Cirillo Bros. Petroleum Co. v. Kyne Realty Corp., 30 Misc. 2d 702, 216 N.Y.S.2d 269 (City Ct. 1961).

43. *Compare* Maguire v. Cunningham, 64 Cal. App. 536, 222 P. 838 (1923) *with* Childs v. Eltinge, 29 Cal. App. 3d 843, 851, 105 Cal. Rptr. 864, 869 (1973).

44. *See* Chapter 3(B)(1)*(b)* ("Restrictive Principles of In Rem Jurisdiction") & Chapter 3(H)(3) ("Property cases") *supra.*

45. *See* Chapter 3(A)(1) ("Personal Jurisdiction Restrictions Prior to the Adoption of the Fourteenth Amendment") *supra.*

46. *See* Chapter 3(B)(1)*(b)* ("Restrictive Principles of In Rem Jurisdiction") *supra; see also* Chapter 3(G)(3) ("Sovereignty-Based Restrictions on State-Court Jurisdiction") *supra.*

47. In addition, the states may issue equitable decrees such as injunction or decrees of specific performance against defendants over whom they have personal jurisdiction, even though the injunction or decree will affect foreign land. The reason is that these kinds of decrees act "in personam," that is, on the person of the defendant instead of "directly" on the land. *See* the discussion of the equity courts power in the text, *supra.* Actions seeking such orders have traditionally not been considered "local" in nature; nor were they restricted by the traditional, territorial, international rules. *Cf.* RESTATEMENT (SECOND) OF CONFLICT OF LAWS § 55 (1971) (court has power to order a person subject to its jurisdiction to do an act in the state, even if carrying out the order will affect a thing in another state). There may, of course, be actions in between the situations described in the text that the Supreme Court will have to determine as either being within the "direct effect on title" principle or not. *See, e.g.,* Farha v. Signal Cos., 216 Kan. 471, 532 P.2d 1330 (1975), in which the Kansas Supreme Court permitted the adjudication of an action for damages in Kansas for the use and occupation of land in Texas. The action involved an issue of adverse possession to the Texas land, which one would think would "directly affect" the title. Nevertheless, the court held that an action for damages for use and occupation of the land was "transitory" in nature and that the Kansas courts had jurisdiction to adjudicate the issue of title by adverse possession as an incidental matter. It is interesting to speculate whether a Texas court should be permitted to deny issue preclusion effect to the adverse possession determination in a subsequent action in Texas where the however, that if the forum state not only classifies such an action as "local," but treats the local action rule as a subject-matter jurisdiction restriction, the same result would follow as if the restriction were encompassed in the rules enforced by the Supreme Court in land title cases. The situs state could refuse enforcement to the judgment under the latter circumstances because it would be void under the law of the state where it was rendered and, therefore, entitled to no effect under the full-faith-and-credit implementing statute.[48] Thus, when dealing with actions concerning land located in other states, litigants must be alert to the nature and scope of the forum's local action rule. In addition, they must be alert to principles that the U.S. Supreme Court has allowed the situs state to enforce apart from the forum's own rules.[49]

The federal courts have traditionally observed the distinction between local and transitory actions. Although federal statutes make only oblique references to the local action concept,[50] judicial interpretation has settled that the local action rule exists in the federal courts.[51] A split of authority exists in the federal courts about whether the defendant can waive a local action defect. Although the better view is that a local action objection should be waivable like other venue defects, some cases treat such an objection as nonwaivable, like a subject-matter jurisdiction deficiency.[52] Other federal venue defects, however, are uniformly considered waivable.[53]

---

title was directly involved. Note that this sort of issue can also come up in the trespass to land case, if lack of title in the plaintiff is asserted as a defense.

48. *See* Chapter 3(A)(1)*(d)* ("The 1790 Implementing Statute") *supra* & Chapter 13(E) ("Claim and Issue Preclusion on Questions of Subject-Matter and Personal Jurisdiction") *infra.*

49. It should also be noted that, in theory, the states possess power to extend their local action rules to encompass any kind of civil action, whether or not the action involves land. As long as the local action designation is a restriction that the state would be imposing on its own authority, no federal constitutional objection exists, whether the state designates the restriction as one of venue or as a subject-matter jurisdiction limit. However, a state cannot necessarily bind other states to adhere to novel forms of local actions that would preclude them from adjudicating actions if the actions are otherwise within the scope of the subject-matter and personal jurisdiction authority of the other states. Other states may honor such restrictions on their authority as a matter of comity, but they would not be obligated to do so. For example, in Wilson v. Celestral Greetings, Inc., 896 S.W.2d 759 (Mo. Ct. App. 1995), a shareholder of a Delaware corporation dissented from a merger decision and commenced an action in Missouri state court under Delaware statutory law to have her shares appraised and to obtain compensation. The Missouri Court of Appeals held that the action was a local action that could only be brought in Delaware. The court agreed that the action was basically a contract action that would be transitory in nature, but it interpreted the Delaware statutes as requiring that the action be brought in Delaware. Clearly, even if the court's interpretation of Delaware law is correct, Delaware has no power by classifying an action as local to *force* other states to dismiss the action. Thus, unless the court of appeals decision is viewed as based on comity with Delaware, it is incorrect. Only if an action classified as "local" fits within constitutional or other rules that restrict state power can the states be forced to refuse jurisdiction of the action.

50. *See* 28 U.S.C. § 1392.

51. *See, e.g.,* Livingston v. Jefferson, 15 F. Cas. 660 (C.C.D. Va. 1811) (No. 8411).

52. *See* 15 CHARLES A. WRIGHT ET AL., FEDERAL PRACTICE AND PROCEDURE: JURISDICTION AND RELATED MATTERS (VENUE) § 3822, at 206-07 (2d ed. 1986). Some federal courts have also considered the local action question as controlled by the law of the state in which the federal court sits. *See, e.g.,* Trust Co. Bank v. United States Gypsum Co., 950 F.2d 1144 (5th Cir. 1992). However, this view is almost certainly incorrect. *See* 15 CHARLES A. WRIGHT ET AL., FEDERAL PRACTICE AND PROCEDURE: JURISDICTION AND RELATED MATTERS (VENUE) § 3822, at 208 (2d ed. 1986).

53. *See* FED. R. CIV. P. 12(h)(1). The details of the federal waiver process are discussed in Chapter 6(D)(3)*(g)* ("Consolidation and Waiver of Defenses") *infra.*

As discussed in section C(4)*(c)*, below, there is a possibility that recent amendments to the federal venue statutes have eliminated the local action rule in federal court. However, the statutes still refer to the rule, and there has not been any direct holding on this question.

SECTION B. VENUE IN STATE COURTS

In areas that do not concern local actions, state venue schemes vary widely. They reflect "historical developments and piecemeal legislative tinkering."[54] Proper venue in a particular state will depend on one or more of the following factors: (1) the theory of the claim; (2) the subject matter of the claim; and (3) the parties involved. Most states provide the plaintiff with a narrower range of venue choices than the English common law did in transitory actions. These choices typically include: (1) where the cause of action arose or accrued;[55] (2) where the defendant resides; (3) where the plaintiff resides; (4) where the defendant is doing business; (5) where the defendant has an office or a place of business or where one of its agents or officers resides; (6) where the defendant may be found; (7) where the defendant may be summoned or served; and (8) where the seat of government is located.[56]

When a venue statute allows the plaintiff to bring an action in the county "where the cause of action arose" or "where the damages were sustained," a conceptual problem may exist. This problem may arise when time and space separate the defendant's actions from the ultimate injury suffered by the plaintiff.

Illustration 4-4. P_1 and P_2 are the parents of C. P_1, P_2, and C reside in County X. D is a doctor who resides and practices medicine in County Y. P_1 and P_2 take C to County Y, where D negligently treats C. P_1, P_2, and C return to County X. C then dies due to the negligent treatment. P_1 and P_2 sue D in a court in County X. The venue statutes provide that a plaintiff may bring an action for wrongful death in the county "where the damages were sustained." On similar facts, the Louisiana Court of Appeal held venue improper in County X.[57] The court stated that C, the patient, sustained the damages where the negligent treatment occurred, not where C died.[58]

---

54. George N. Stevens, *Venue Statutes: Diagnosis and Proposed Cure*, 49 MICH. L. REV. 307, 307 (1951).

55. *See* Jay M. Zitter, Annotation, *Place Where Claim or Cause of Action "Arose" Under State Venue Statute*, 53 A.L.R.4TH 1104 (1987).

56. *See* George N. Stevens, *Venue Statutes: Diagnosis and Proposed Cure*, 49 MICH. L. REV. 307, 309-16 (1951).

57. Keele v. Knecht, 621 So. 2d 106 (La. Ct. App. 1993) (statute provided for venue in parish where wrongful conduct occurred or where the damages were sustained; if any damage occurs in same parish where wrongful conduct occurred, that parish is the only proper venue).

58. This construction is, of course, far from inevitable. The situation in this illustration is a variation of the problem discussed in section C(3), *infra*, under the former language of 28 U.S.C. § 1391 providing for venue where the "cause of action arose." The language suggests the cause of action can arise in only one place. Under the state statute in *Keele*, the language suggests that the damages can occur in only one county, though the court did not hold this construction to be true in every case. In products liability actions in which the wrongful conduct and damages usually occur in entirely different counties, venue would be proper where the damages occur. *See* 621 So. 2d at 110-11.

Illustration 4-5. Assume that *B* injures *A* in a construction accident in County *X*, where both *A* and *B* reside. *A* sues *B* in County *X* to recover for *A's* personal injuries. After *A* commences this action, *A* has an automobile accident in County *Y* with *C*, a resident of County *Y*. After this accident with *C*, *A* amends the complaint in *A's* action against *B* in County *X*. *A's* amended complaint adds *C* as a defendant in that action. The amended complaint alleges that *C's* negligence caused the automobile accident and aggravated injuries suffered by *A* in the construction accident. Assume that the venue statute allows the plaintiff to sue in the county of residence ''of any defendant who is joined in good faith and with probable cause for the purpose of obtaining a judgment against the defendant and not solely for the purpose of fixing venue in that county.'' On similar facts, the Illinois Appellate Court held venue proper in County *X*.[59] *A* did not join *C* merely to establish venue in County *X*. *A's* action against *B* and *C* in County *X* sought a correct apportionment of damages between the two defendants.[60]

SECTION C. VENUE IN FEDERAL COURTS

The general federal venue provisions are found in 28 U.S.C. §§ 1391-1407. These sections reveal the basic pattern of federal venue.

1. Plaintiff's Residence as Proper Venue

Before 1990, the federal venue statutes contained several peculiarities. Congress addressed many of these peculiarities in the Judicial Improvements Act of 1990.[61] Before the 1990 amendments, Congress allowed actions based on diversity of citizenship to be brought only in the district (1) where all the plaintiffs resided, (2) where all the defendants resided, or (3) where the claim arose.[62] However, when jurisdiction was based in part on the existence of a federal question in the action, venue was proper only in either the district (1) where all the defendants resided or (2) where the claim arose.[63] No defensible reason existed for this difference.[64]

In 1990, the Federal Courts Study Committee recommended extensive changes in the general venue statute.[65] One of these recommendations was that ''Congress [should] eliminate the century-old anomaly . . . providing for venue in diversity but not federal question cases 'in the judicial district where all plaintiffs . . . reside.' ''[66] Following a 1969 recommendation of the American

---

59. Hall v. Keating, 246 Ill. App. 3d 538, 616 N.E.2d 683 (1993).

60. *Id.* at 539, 616 N.E.2d at 684.

61. *See* Pub. L. No. 101-650, § 311, 104 Stat. 5089, 5114.

62. This standard was found in former 28 U.S.C. § 1391(a).

63. This standard was found in former 28 U.S.C. § 1391(b).

64. *See* 15 CHARLES A. WRIGHT ET AL., FEDERAL PRACTICE AND PROCEDURE: JURISDICTION AND RELATED MATTERS (VENUE) § 3802, at 9, n.10 (2d ed. 1986).

65. *See* REPORT OF THE FEDERAL COURTS STUDY COMMITTEE 94 (1990).

66. *Id.*

Law Institute,[67] the Committee recommended[68] and Congress enacted[69] amendments to 28 U.S.C. § 1391(a) & (b). These amendments eliminated plaintiff's residence as a basis for venue in diversity actions.

2. Defendants' Residence as Proper Venue

The Judicial Improvements Act of 1990 provided for venue in both federal questions and diversity cases in "a judicial district where any defendant resides, if all defendants reside in the same *state*."[70] These amendments may appear to have expanded the permissible locations for suit based on defendants' residence. As noted in the preceding subsection, before 1990, § 1391(a) & (b) provided for venue at defendants' residence only when all the defendants resided in the same *district*. However, even before the 1990 amendments, § 1392(a) of Title 28 allowed plaintiffs to bring nonlocal actions against defendants residing in different districts in the same state "in any of such districts."[71] For a time, Congress did not repeal or amend § 1392(a) to conform to the 1990 amendments of § 1391(a) & (b). Thus, two separate statutes made venue proper in a district within a state in which "any defendant resides" as long as "all defendants reside in the same state." However, it was clear that the amendments to § 1391(a) & (b) made 28 U.S.C. § 1392(a) superfluous, and the section was repealed in 1996.[72]

Illustration 4-6. A, a citizen of State *X*, wishes to sue *B* and *C* for $500,000 in damages resulting from an automobile accident. *B* and *C* are both citizens of State *Y*. However, *B* resides in the Northern District and *C* resides in the Southern District of State *Y*. Before 1990, *A* could sue *B* and *C* in either the Northern or Southern District of State *Y* by virtue of § 1392(a). After 1990, both § 1391(a)(1) and § 1392(a) authorized suit by *A* against *B* and *C* in either the Northern or Southern District of State *Y*. After 1996, § 1391(a)(1), only, authorizes this result.

Illustration 4-7. A, a citizen of State *X*, wishes to sue *B* and *C* in a federal diversity action for $500,000 in damages resulting from an automobile accident. *B* is a citizen of State *Y* who resides in the Northern District of State *Y*. *C* is a citizen of State *Z* who resides in the Northern District of State *Z*. Before 1990, *A* could not base federal venue on the defendants' residence. Nor can *A* do so today. The defendants live in different districts in different states. The Judicial Code does not authorize venue based on the defendants' residence when the defendants reside in different districts in different states.[73] Thus, *A* will have to

---

67. *See* ALI STUDY OF THE DIVISION OF JURISDICTION BETWEEN STATE AND FEDERAL COURTS §§ 1303(a)(2), 1314(a)(2) (1969).

68. *See* REPORT OF THE FEDERAL COURTS STUDY COMMITTEE 94 (1990).

69. Judicial Improvements Act of 1990, Pub. L. No. 101-650, § 311, 104 Stat. 5089, 5114 (codified at 28 U.S.C. §§ 1391(a)(1) & (b)(1)).

70. *See id.* (emphasis added).

71. 28 U.S.C. § 1392(a).

72. *See* Act of Oct. 1, 1996, Pub. L. No. 104-220, 110 Stat. 3023.

73. Even if *A* had a transitory federal question claim, the same would be true. *See* 28 U.S.C. §§ 1391(b)(1) & 1392(a).

establish venue on some other basis than defendants' residence, such as where the events giving rise to suit occurred.

* * * * *

One question that sometimes arises under the "defendant's residence" provisions is whether a defendant who resides in the state and district in which the action is brought can raise a venue objection for a nonresident as to whom venue is improper. The language of the venue statute literally makes venue improper in such cases, and it might be reasoned that any defendant should be able to raise the defect. However, some courts have held that resident defendants cannot raise venue objections for nonresidents.[74] This result seems correct. Venue is a defense personal to the party to whom it applies and can be waived,[75] just like a personal jurisdiction objection. Thus, if one defendant resides in a district and state and another does not, the nonresident should be able to legitimize venue that would otherwise be defective by either consenting to suit within the district or waiving the venue objection, just as would be the case with personal jurisdiction.

3. Venue Proper Where Events Giving Rise to Suit Occur

Before 1963, Congress based federal venue under the general venue statutes wholly on the residence of the parties.[76] In 1963, Congress added a special venue provision for "tort claims arising out of the manufacture, assembly, repair, ownership, maintenance, use, or operation of an automobile."[77] In such civil actions, Congress permitted venue in the district where the act or omission occurred.[78] In 1966, Congress repealed this provision.[79] Instead, Congress provided for venue in the district where "the claim arose" in both diversity and federal question cases.[80] The "claim arose" language of § 1391 seemed to assume that a claim could arise in only one district. In some cases, this language presented no problem.

Illustration 4-8. Assume that *A* and *B* are involved in an automobile accident. *A* claims that *A* was injured as a result of *B's* negligent operation of a

---

74. *See* Gerety v. Sunrise Express, Inc., 95 Civ. 2090 (NB), 1996 WL 19047, 96 U.S. Dist. LEXIS 378 (S.D.N.Y. Jan. 18, 1996); Prath v. Rowland, 769 F. Supp. 1128 (N.D. Cal. 1991), *rev'd on other grounds*, 65 F.3d 802 (9th Cir. 1995).

75. However, note that at least one federal court, incorrectly, thinks venue is an objection that can be raised by the court on its own motion. *See, e.g.,* California Advocates for Nursing Home Reform v. Creekside Care Convalescent Hosp., Inc., No. C-94-3519-VRW, 1994 WL 589459, 1994 U.S. Dist. LEXIS 14761 (N.D. Cal. Oct. 6, 1994). *But see* Woodke v. Dahm, 70 F.3d 983 (8th Cir. 1995) (no rule requires district court to dismiss defendant sua sponte to preserve venue).

76. *See* 15 CHARLES A. WRIGHT ET AL., FEDERAL PRACTICE AND PROCEDURE: JURISDICTION AND RELATED MATTERS (VENUE) § 3806, at 41 (2d ed. 1986).

77. Act of Dec. 23, 1963, Pub. L. No. 88-234, 77 Stat. 473 (adding subsection (f) to 28 U.S.C. § 1391).

78. *Id.*

79. Act of Nov. 2, 1966, Pub. L. No. 89-714, 80 Stat. 1111.

80. *See* 15 CHARLES A. WRIGHT ET AL., FEDERAL PRACTICE AND PROCEDURE: JURISDICTION AND RELATED MATTERS (VENUE) § 3806, at 42 (2d ed. 1986).

motor vehicle. This claim clearly arises in the district where the accident occurred and *A* was injured.[81]

* * * * *

When the transaction or event that was the subject of the action had connections with more than one district, the issue was whether the claim could be deemed to arise in more than one district. If so, the plaintiff would have a choice among several districts having connections with the claim. The U.S. Supreme Court never resolved this issue. However, in *Leroy v. Great Western United Corp.*,[82] the Court did indicate that if the plaintiff had such a choice, it would be limited to those "districts that with approximately equal plausibility—in terms of the availability of witnesses, the accessibility of other relevant evidence, and the convenience of the defendant (but *not* [the convenience] of the plaintiff)—may be assigned as locus of the claim."[83]

In 1990, the Federal Courts Study Committee recommended replacing "the claim arose" language. The Committee proposed permitting venue in "any judicial district in which a substantial part of the events or omissions giving rise to the claim occurred, or a substantial part of [the] property that is the subject of the action is situated."[84] The Committee patterned its recommendation on a 1969 proposal of the American Law Institute.[85] Congress followed this recommendation in the Judicial Improvements Act of 1990.[86] Congress thus eliminated the interpretive difficulties of the "claim arose" language. Today, in both diversity and federal question cases, the plaintiff may bring a civil action in any district "in which a substantial part of the events or omissions giving rise to the claim occurred, or a substantial part of property that is the subject of the action is situated."[87]

Nevertheless, some commentators have suggested that the 1990 amendments to the venue statute will result in as much litigation as the previous "claim arose" language.[88] One difficulty lies in developing a test to determine whether the events or omissions occurring within a district are "substantial." If all of the events giving rise to the claim occur in one district, the events are obviously substantial and venue is proper in the district.[89] Similarly, if no events giving rise to the claim occur within a district, the plaintiff obviously cannot

---

81. *See* Annotation, *What Is the Judicial District "In Which the Claim Arose" for Venue Purposes Under 28 U.S.C. § 1391(a) and (b)*, 59 A.L.R. FED. 320, 324 (1982).

82. 443 U.S. 173, 99 S. Ct. 2710, 61 L. Ed. 2d 464 (1979).

83. *Id.* at 185, 99 S. Ct. at 2717, 61 L. Ed. 2d at 475 (emphasis added).

84. *See* REPORT OF THE FEDERAL COURTS STUDY COMMITTEE 94 (1990).

85. *See* ALI STUDY OF THE DIVISION OF JURISDICTION BETWEEN STATE AND FEDERAL COURTS §§ 1303(a)(1), 1314(a)(1) (1969).

86. *See* Pub. L. No. 101-650, § 311, 104 Stat. 5089, 5114 (codified at 28 U.S.C. § 1391(a)(2) & (b)(2)).

87. *See id.*

88. *See* John B. Oakley, *Recent Statutory Changes in the Law of Federal Jurisdiction and Venue: The Judicial Improvements Acts of 1988 and 1990*, 24 U.C. DAVIS L. REV. 735, 775 (1991); David D. Siegel, *Changes in Federal Jurisdiction and Practice Under the New (Dec. 1, 1990) Judicial Improvements Act*, 133 F.R.D. 61, 72 (1991).

89. *See, e.g.*, Ward v. Hampton Psychiatric Hosp., No. 92-CV-4392, 1993 WL 419143, 1993 U.S. Dist. LEXIS 14725 (E.D. Pa. Oct. 19, 1993); Baker v. Coughlin, No. 1084 (RSW), 1993 WL 356852, 1993 U.S. Dist. LEXIS 12445 (S.D.N.Y. Sept. 9, 1993); Paradis v. Dooley, 774 F. Supp. 79 (D.R.I. 1991).

predicate venue in the district on § 1391(a)(2) or (b)(2).[90] Presumably, also, if the plaintiff brings an action in a district where a majority (over 50%) of the events or omissions giving rise to suit occurred, no one would disagree that the events in the district are substantial.

The problem cases will be those in which the plaintiff brings the action in a district in which some, but less than a majority, of the events or omissions giving rise to the suit occurred. Both the language and the legislative history of § 1391(a)(2) and (b)(2) indicate that a substantial part of the events giving rise to the suit can occur in more than one district.[91] Therefore, the test established cannot make venue proper only where most (*i.e.*, 51% or more) of the events occurred.[92] Nor can venue be made proper only where the largest portion of the events occurred (*e.g.*, 34% in the proper district as opposed to 33% and 33% in each of two other districts).[93]

(a) Fixed Minimum Percentage Test

One approach to creating a workable test would be to establish a fixed minimum percentage of the events or omissions that must occur within the district before venue is proper. Under this type of test, if the percentage dropped below the minimum level, the plaintiff could not base venue in the district. The difficulty in formulating such a test is setting the appropriate percentage of events. In some actions, a large number of events in a district could constitute a relatively small percentage of the total activity giving rise to suit. Therefore, establishing a minimum percentage risks eliminating as proper venues districts where a considerable amount of activity took place and where no substantial inconve-

---

90. Numerous cases have dismissed or transferred actions that were commenced in a district where none of the events giving rise to suit occurred and where venue was not proper on the basis of the defendants' residence. *See, e.g.*, Krain v. Devich, No. 91-15758, 1992 WL 129195, 1992 U.S. App. LEXIS 1354 (9th Cir. June 4, 1992) (unpublished opinion); Banque de la Mediterranee-France, S.A. v. Thergen, Inc., 780 F. Supp. 92 (D.R.I. 1992); Berube v. Brister, 140 F.R.D. 258 (D.R.I. 1992); Lahm v. Wagner, 776 F. Supp. 114 (E.D.N.Y. 1991); Sani-Dairy v. Yeutter, 782 F. Supp. 1060 (W.D. Pa. 1991).

91. *See* H.R. REP. NO. 734, 101st Cong., 2d Sess. 23 (1990) (language "avoids the problem created by the frequent cases in which substantial parts of the underlying events have occurred in several districts"). *See* Bates v. C & S Adjusters, Inc., 980 F.2d 865, 867 (2d Cir. 1992); Baker v. Coughlin, No. 93 Civ. 1084 (RWS), 1993 WL 356852, 1993 U.S. Dist. LEXIS 12445 (S.D.N.Y. Sept. 9, 1993); Miller v. Meadowlands Car Imports, Inc., 822 F. Supp. 61, 64 (D. Conn. 1993); VDI Techs. v. Price, 781 F. Supp. 85 (D.N.H. 1991).

92. *See* First of Mich. Corp. v. Bramlet, 141 F.3d 260 (6th Cir. 1998) (majority of events need not take place in district to be substantial).

93. *See, e.g.*, Timberline Indus., Inc. v. Frame Indus. Suppliers, Inc., No. 93-735-FR, 1993 WL 393031, 1993 U.S. Dist. LEXIS 13815 (D. Or. Sept. 29, 1993) (events in both Texas and Oregon; activities in both substantial); Brimmer v. May Dep't Stores Co., No. 93-0838 (CRR), 1993 WL 267437, 1993 U.S. Dist. LEXIS 9576 (D.D.C. July 8, 1993) (some events in Virginia, but actions in District of Columbia are substantial, so venue proper in D.C.); Merchants Nat'l Bank v. SafraBank, 776 F. Supp. 538, 541 (D. Kan. 1991) (events in Kansas substantial, even though most events took place in California). *But see* MacGuire v. Gary, No. 93-0037, 1993 WL 393057, 1993 U.S. Dist. LEXIS 13662 (W.D. Va. Sept. 24, 1993) (greater and substantial part of events occurred in another district, so venue improper); Eastman v. Initial Invs., Inc., 827 F. Supp. 336 (E.D. Pa. 1993) (court finds the contacts with Texas outweigh the contacts with Pennsylvania, so venue improper in Pennsylvania under § 1391(b)(2)); Sedio v. Bell, No. 91 C 3691, 1992 WL 182209, 1992 U.S. Dist. LEXIS 874 (N.D. Ill. Jan. 28, 1992) (one of three investments took place in Illinois; if other two investments took place in the same district, it would detract from Illinois as a place where a substantial part of the events took place).

nience would result in conducting the action. When the total activity is large but only a small percentage of the activity occurred in any one district, establishing a fixed minimum could also mean that venue would not be proper anywhere based on a substantial part of the events or omissions. Thus, courts should reject this approach.[94]

Illustration 4-9. *A*, a citizen and resident of the Southern District of State *X*, sues *B*, a citizen of State *Y*, seeking damages for trademark infringement under federal law. *A* brought this action in the U.S. District Court for the Southern District of State *X*. *B's* infringing activity occurred in the form of sales of a product throughout the United States. The total sales of the product were $500,000,000. The sales in the Southern District of State *X* were $4,000,000. The largest amount of sales in any district was $15,000,000. If the court establishes a fixed minimum percentage, venue might not be proper in the Southern District of State *X*. The activity in State *X* is less than 1% of the total. Indeed, if courts establish a fixed percentage without regard to the facts of different cases, venue might not be proper in this case in any district under § 1391(b)(2). For example, if the fixed minimum is established as 33%, under § 1391(b)(2) venue would not be proper anywhere. The largest amount of infringing activity occurring in any district is only 3% ($15,000,000).[95]

(b) Relative Activity Test

An alternative approach would apply a "relative activity" test under § 1391(a)(2) & (b)(2). This approach would not fix a minimum percentage that all cases must meet. Instead, it would permit venue in districts in which a relatively small, but significant, amount of activity had occurred. However, this approach fails to establish clear guidelines for determining what part of the events or omissions are substantial. Thus, such a test would breed litigation. In many cases, the defendant could legitimately dispute whether a "substantial part" of the events or omissions had occurred in the district.[96]

---

94. *See* Imagineering, Inc. v. Lukingbeal, No. 94 Civ. 2589 (RLC), 1996 WL 148431, 1996 U.S. Dist. LEXIS 3939 (S.D.N.Y. Apr. 1, 1996) (no minimum percentage necessary).

95. *See* Alcoholics Anonymous World Servs., Inc. v. Friedman, No. 91 Civ. 8741 (RLC), 1992 WL 150633, 1992 U.S. Dist. LEXIS 8939 (S.D.N.Y. June 17, 1992) (holding that less than 1% of the defendant's nationwide sales was not a substantial amount, but the court failed to examine sales in other districts; no fixed minimum percentage established); *cf.* Time Prods., PLC v. J. Tiras Classic Handbags, Inc., No. 93 CIV. 7856 (RWS), 1997 WL 139525 (S.D.N.Y. Mar. 26, 1997) (2.52% of defendant's sales constituted a substantial part of the events); Halsoprodukter Labs Karnerud Ab. v. Gero Vita Int'l, No. 93 C 2129, 1993 WL 384525, 1993 U.S. Dist. LEXIS 13519 (N.D. Ill. Sept. 28, 1993) (3% of sales and 5% of advertising in state sufficient to constitute substantial part of events). At this writing, no case has attempted to establish a fixed minimum percentage requirement under the statute. *But cf.* Telamerica Media, Inc. v. AMN Television Mktg., No. 99-25-72, 1999 WL 124423, 1999 U.S. Dist. LEXIS 19423 (E.D. Pa. Dec. 21, 1999) (events so spread out across U.S. that no district contained substantial part; because multiple defendants residing in different states were involved, fallback provision of § 1391 applicable).

96. This approach is consistent with most of the opinions interpreting § 1391(a)(2) & (b)(2). The courts tend to approach the statute generally, without attempting to establish any fixed minimum percentage of events or omissions that will be required to make venue proper in a district. *See, e.g.*, Miller v. Meadowlands Car Imports, Inc., 822 F. Supp. 61 (D. Conn. 1993).

One case rejecting a relative activity approach is *Joint Stock Society "Trade House of Descendants of Peter Smirnoff" v. Heublin, Inc.*[97] The court refused to measure "substantial activity" by examining the percentage of the defendant's national sales that took place in the district, Delaware, because this approach would understate the effect of the products in question on Delaware consumers due to the fact that Delaware is a small state. Instead, the court examined other factors, such as the revenue from Delaware, the number of products sold in Delaware, and the use of sales agents in Delaware. Although the defendants' Delaware sales only amounted to 113th of 1% of its national sales, annual sales of the product (vodka) in Delaware totaled $1,000,000, and the defendants had two distributors and six sales representatives serving the state. On the basis of these factors, the court concluded that a substantial part of the sales giving rise to the claim occurred in Delaware.[98]

(c) Linking the Test to Minimum Contacts

Another approach would link the definition of a substantial part of the events or omissions to the minimum contacts test for personal jurisdiction.[99] This test would regard the events or omissions giving rise to the claim to be "substantial" for venue purposes any time they are sufficient to permit long-arm jurisdiction over the defendant consistent with the Due Process Clause of the Fourteenth Amendment. Personal jurisdiction consistent with the Constitution must exist in every case. Otherwise, the court, on the defendant's motion, will dismiss the action. In many cases, the plaintiff will establish personal jurisdiction in a federal court through the use of a state long-arm statute based on the defendant's claim-producing activities within the state.[100] Thus, the inquiry into personal jurisdiction would also determine whether venue was proper under § 1391(a)(2) & (b)(2).

A venue test linked to personal jurisdiction offers substantial advantages. The substantial events or omissions rule for venue and the minimum contacts test for personal jurisdiction involve similar inquiries.[101] In addition, both venue and

---

97. 936 F. Supp. 177 (D. Del. 1996).

98. *See also* Lumpkin v. Land, CV No. 1:97CV00753, 1997 U.S. Dist. LEXIS 20846 (M.D.N.C. Nov. 5, 1997) (1/3 of events in district were not substantial because they were tangential to the dispute).

99. The minimum contacts test is discussed in Chapter 3(D) & (G) *supra.*

100. *See* Chapter 3(L) ("Special Problems of Amenability to Process in Federal Court") *supra.*

101. Only one court has explicitly rejected a test for substantial activities linked to the minimum contacts test. *See* Ware v. Hedges, Nos. 4:92:CV:98 & 4:93:CV:21, 1993 U.S. Dist. LEXIS 11830 (W.D. Mich. July 12, 1993). In *Ware*, the court relied on a statement from Shapiro v. Republic of Bolivia, 930 F.2d 1013, 1019 (2d Cir. 1991), interpreting the term "substantial contact" in the Foreign Sovereign Immunities Act, 28 U.S.C. § 1603(e). *Shapiro* stated that "substantial contact" meant more than minimum contacts. However, the "substantial contact" language of the Foreign Sovereign Immunities Act is used to define when a foreign state can be sued within the "commercial activity" exception to the rule of sovereign immunity. *See* 28 U.S.C. § 1605(a)(2). This objective is far different than the one that supports the "substantial events" language of § 1391(a)(2) & (b)(2). Additionally, the *Ware* opinion appears to be based on a verbal confusion. The fact that "minimum contacts" are required to satisfy the Due Process Clause of the Fourteenth Amendment does not mean that the requisite contacts will not be "substantial." The minimum contacts label is a term of art that encompasses the whole inquiry whether a nonresident's relationship with a state is sufficient to satisfy the Due Process Clause.

personal jurisdiction requirements are meant to assure that the action will be conducted in a reasonably convenient place. Furthermore, while satisfying personal jurisdiction requirements will not always result in satisfying venue rules, this result will occur in a significant number of cases. Therefore, courts could reasonably deem that the events or omissions giving rise to the claim to be substantial anytime personal jurisdiction over the defendant is obtained.[102]

Illustration 4-10. A, a citizen and resident of State *X*, sued *B*, a citizen and resident of State *Y*. *A* seeks $2,000,000 damages resulting from a libel of *A* in a national magazine published by *B*. *A* brought the action in a U.S. District Court in State *Z*, a single district state. *A* sued in State *Z* because it was the only state whose statute of limitations had not run on *A's* claim. *A* seeks damages from *B* for the harm caused throughout the United States by the publication of the article. *B* sells 10,000 to 15,000 copies of the magazine per month in State *Z*, but sells many more copies elsewhere. Under these circumstances, courts may constitutionally assert personal jurisdiction over *B* in State *Z* based on *B's* activity in State *Z*.[103] Under § 1391(a)(2), venue should be deemed proper because a substantial part of the events giving rise to the claim occurred in State *Z*.

Illustration 4-11. A, a citizen of State *X* residing in the Central District of State *X*, sued *B*, a citizen of State *Y*, in the U.S. District Court for the Central District of State *X*. *A* seeks to recover on a life insurance policy issued to *A's* spouse by *B*. *A's* spouse originally purchased the policy from *C*, a citizen of State *Z*. Later, *C* sold the insurance business to *B*. *B* sent a reinsurance notice to *A's* spouse in the Central District of State *X* offering to reinsure the spouse in accordance with the policy previously held with *C*. *A's* spouse signed this agreement and subsequently sent premiums to *B* in State *Y* until the spouse died. *B* refused to pay the insurance benefits to *A*. *B* asserted that *A's* spouse had committed suicide. *B's* actions in sending the reinsurance agreement to *A's* spouse and accepting premiums are sufficient to subject *B* to personal jurisdiction in State *X*.[104] Therefore, venue should be considered proper in the Central District

---

102. Several courts have either explicitly linked the personal jurisdiction test discussed in the text with the venue rule in § 1391(a) & (b), or found personal jurisdiction and venue to be proper because of the same activities within the district. *See, e.g.,* Alternative Pioneering Sys., Inc. v. Direct Innovative Prods., Inc., No. 4-92-278, 1992 WL 510190, 1992 U.S. Dist. LEXIS 21762 (D. Minn. Aug. 20, 1992) (amenability to long-arm jurisdiction in district satisfies substantial events test); Gould, Inc. v. Alter Metals Co., No. 91 C 20371, 1992 WL 170567, 1992 U.S. Dist. LEXIS 10483 (N.D. Ill. July 16, 1992) (defendant shipped hazardous materials to plaintiff in state; personal jurisdiction proper; venue proper under § 1391(b)(2) because personal jurisdiction proper); Fogle v. Ramsey Winch Co., 774 F. Supp. 19 (D.D.C. 1991) (injury within district from product sold by out-of-state defendant sustains personal jurisdiction and venue under § 1391(a)(2)); Sidco Indus., Inc. v. Wimar Tahoe Corp., 768 F. Supp. 1343 (D. Or. 1991) (trademark infringement action in which personal jurisdiction and venue under § 1391(b)(2) established by same action of defendant sending brochures into state); *see also* Magic Toyota, Inc. v. Southeast Toyota Distribs., Inc., 784 F. Supp. 306 (D.S.C. 1992) (personal jurisdiction and venue improper because of lack of contacts between defendants and forum). The test proposed in the text is similar to the statutorily imposed test for a corporate defendant's residence under 28 U.S.C. § 1391(c), discussed in subsection 6, *infra*.

103. *See* Keeton v. Hustler Magazine, Inc., 465 U.S. 770, 104 S. Ct. 1473, 79 L. Ed. 2d 790 (1984). *Keeton* is discussed in Chapter 3(H)(1) ("Tort Cases") *supra*.

104. *See* McGee v. International Life Ins. Co., 355 U.S. 220, 78 S. Ct. 199, 2 L. Ed. 2d 223 (1957). *McGee* is discussed in Chapter 3(H)(2) ("Contract Cases") *supra*.

of State X under § 1391(a)(2) on the ground that a substantial part of the events giving rise to the claim occurred there.

* * * * *

A venue test linked with personal jurisdiction would have to avoid several pitfalls. First, as Chapter 3 discusses, the plaintiff can establish personal jurisdiction over a defendant without regard to the defendant's claim-producing activities within the state. For example, the plaintiff can establish personal jurisdiction by personally serving the defendant within the state, even when the events giving rise to suit occurred outside the state. Similarly, the plaintiff can sometimes base personal jurisdiction on a high level of the defendant's general activities within the state, even when the event giving rise to the claim occurred elsewhere. Sections 1391(a)(2) & (b)(2), however, require that venue be based on claim-producing activities within the district. Therefore, when personal jurisdiction is based on something other than the defendant's claim-producing activities, a court would have to make a separate venue inquiry. This inquiry would have to assure that sufficient claim-producing events or omissions occurred within the district where the action is commenced to sustain venue.[105]

Illustration 4-12. A, a citizen and resident of the Northern District of State X, sues B, a citizen and resident of the Southern District of State Y. A commences this action in the U.S. District Court for the Northern District of State X. A's action seeks $500,000 in damages against B for personal injuries received in an automobile accident in State Z. The plaintiff acquires personal jurisdiction over B in the Northern District of State X by personally serving B with process while B is present in the Northern District. The basis of personal jurisdiction is not B's claim-producing activities. In fact, no claim-producing events or omissions occurred in the Northern District. Thus, despite the existence of valid personal jurisdiction over B, venue is not proper under § 1391(a)(2).

* * * * *

Second, when the plaintiff bases personal jurisdiction on the claim-producing activities of the defendant within the state, the activities within the *entire state* are relevant to the jurisdictional inquiry. However, § 1391(a)(2) & (b)(2) require substantial claim-producing events or omissions within the *district* where the action is brought. In multiple district states, the activities of the defendant giving rise to the claim can occur entirely within one district. If the plaintiff commences an action in a district within the state in which none of the claim-producing activities occur, venue will obviously not be proper in that district. If the defendant's claim-producing activities occur in more than one district within the state, the court in the district where the action is commenced will have to inquire whether the amount of those activities occurring within that

---

105. In Lohman v. Township of Oxford, No. 91-7037, 1992 WL 95914, 1992 U.S. Dist. LEXIS 5276 (E.D. Pa. Apr. 22, 1992), the court viewed the defendants' activities alternatively as forum related and non-forum related, and sustained personal jurisdiction under both viewpoints. The court then went on to state that venue was proper under § 1391(b)(2): "As can be seen from the personal jurisdiction analysis above, a sufficiently substantial part of the events in this case occurred in the Eastern District of Pennsylvania." It is unclear whether the court believed that forum activity by the defendant that was not claim producing, but which satisfied personal jurisdiction standards, would satisfy the venue test under § 1391(b)(2).

district would have sustained personal jurisdiction over the defendant. The activities in the other districts within the state are irrelevant to this inquiry.

Illustration 4-13. A, a citizen of State X residing in the Western District of State X, sues B, a citizen and resident of State Y. A's claim is for damages under the Fair Debt Collection Practices Act, a federal statute.[106] The action is brought in the Western District of State X. A had incurred a debt while residing in the Western District of State Y. A's creditor referred the debt for collection to B. Meanwhile, A had moved to the Western District of State X. B mailed a collection notice to A at A's former address in the Western District of State Y. The U.S. Postal Service forwarded the collection notice to A in the Western District of State X. A's claim is based on the contents of this collection notice. Assume that placing the collection notice in the mail without an instruction to the Postal Service not to forward the notice, together with A's actual receipt of the notice, are sufficient to subject B to personal jurisdiction in the Western District of State X. Under such circumstances, venue should be considered proper under § 1391(b)(2) on the basis that substantial events giving rise to the claim occurred in the Western District of State X.[107]

On the other hand, if these acts are insufficient in themselves to sustain personal jurisdiction over B, venue should be deemed improper under § 1391(b)(2), even if personal jurisdiction is acquired over B on some other basis. For example, B might waive any personal jurisdiction objection that B possesses. Likewise, B's general level of activities in State X, apart from the sending and receipt of the notice, might be sufficiently high to sustain jurisdiction over B on any claim. Nonetheless, even if personal jurisdiction is asserted over B on some basis other than the acts giving rise to the claim, the court should not *assume* that venue is improper under § 1391(b)(2). Instead, the court should make an independent inquiry to determine whether the nature and quality of B's actions in the district would be sufficient to sustain personal jurisdiction over B.[108]

---

106. 15 U.S.C. §§ 1692-1692o.

107. *Cf.* Bates v. C & S Adjusters, Inc., 980 F.2d 865 (2d Cir. 1992). In *Bates*, the court held venue proper under § 1391(b)(2) on these facts. The defendant did not challenge personal jurisdiction, so it is impossible to know what the court would have held if such a challenge had been raised. However, there is reason to believe that the sending and receiving of the collection notice would have been sufficient to sustain personal jurisdiction. *Cf.* Calder v. Jones, 465 U.S. 783, 104 S. Ct. 1482, 79 L. Ed. 2d 804 (1984) (sustaining jurisdiction over nonresident defendants in a libel action on the basis that the tort was intentionally directed at the defendant in the forum state).

108. *But cf.* United Liberty Life Ins. Co. v. Pinnacle W. Capital Corp., 149 F.R.D. 558 (S.D. Ohio 1993) (substantial events occurred where misleading financial statements created, not where they were received). As in determining a corporate defendant's residence under 28 U.S.C. § 1391(c), discussed *infra* section 6, it is theoretically possible for the defendant's claim-producing activities to be spread thinly across several districts of a multiple district state. Thus, it might be feared that while the total activities in the state are sufficient to sustain personal jurisdiction, the activities within any one district would not be sufficient to do so. However, given the structure of the minimum contacts test, such a case is not likely to occur. When the defendant's activities within the district give rise to part of the claim, it is highly likely that the contacts with the district will be sufficient to sustain personal jurisdiction. *See* Chapter 3(G)(2)*(b)* ("Specific Jurisdiction") *supra; cf.* Keeton v. Hustler Magazine, Inc., 465 U.S. 770, 104 S. Ct. 1473, 79 L. Ed. 2d 790 (1984); *Illustration 4-10 supra.*

(d) When Do Events Give Rise to the Claim?

For venue to be proper under § 1391(a)(2) or (b)(2), the "substantial" events occurring within a district must give rise to the claim. Literally, therefore, non-claim producing activities are irrelevant to the inquiry under the statute. As a result, the district courts must engage in careful analysis. For example, in *Daleus v. Kovelesky*,[109] the plaintiff, a citizen of New York, sued the defendant, a citizen of New Jersey, in a U.S. District Court in New York. *A* sought damages for personal injuries received in an automobile accident in New Jersey. The plaintiff contended that venue was proper in the Southern District of New York because the medical care and treatment the plaintiff received in New York after the accident were substantial events occurring in New York. The district court held that these events were not sufficient to make venue proper because they did not give rise to the claim. The court stated that "[t]he subsequent remedial actions taken in New York may have contributed to the amount of damages, but can in no meaningful way be said to have given rise to the claim itself."[110] Although this common-sense result prevents manipulation of the venue statutes, it is not literally true that damages are not part of the claim itself. The medical expenses did accrue in New York; consequently, they were, in a sense, partially involved in "giving rise to the claim." Thus, a literal interpretation of the venue statutes might produce a different result.

Another difficulty exists in multiple defendant cases when the events giving rise to the claim against some defendants occur in the district and the events giving rise to claims against other defendants occur entirely outside the district. In *Kaplan v. Reed*,[111] the district court held that venue was improper as to the defendants whose acts occurred entirely outside the district. Note, however, that if a combination of events by some defendants in the district and by some outside are sufficient to produce personal jurisdiction over all defendants in the district, venue could be considered proper under the test suggested in subsection *(c)*, above. Under the test for specific jurisdiction discussed in Chapter 3, a defendant neither has to act within the state nor ever enter the state to be subject to personal jurisdiction. Unlike the situation discussed in subsection *(c)*, above, concerning general jurisdiction, the impact of the defendant's activities in the district, especially if they are part of a combined course of action with other defendants who have acted within the district, may be enough to sustain both personal jurisdiction and venue.[112]

---

109. No. 98 Civ. 9628 (JSR), 1998 WL 856077, 1998 U.S. Dist. LEXIS 19331 (S.D.N.Y. Dec. 7, 1998).

110. *Id.* at *1, 1998 U.S. Dist. LEXIS at *2; *accord* Labranche v. Embassy Suites, Inc., No. Civ. A. 97-3721, 1999 WL 58841, 1999 U.S. Dist. LEXIS 1495 (E.D. La. Feb. 3, 1999) (plaintiff injured in defendant's hotel in Iowa received medical treatment that contributed to his damages in Louisiana, his home state; the court held that the medical treatment did not give rise to the claim).

111. 28 F. Supp. 2d 1191 (D. Colo. 1998).

112. *Cf.* Schomann Int'l Corp. v. Northern Wireless, Ltd., 35 F. Supp. 2d 205 (N.D.N.Y. 1999) (both personal jurisdiction and substantial events venue proper over nonresident defendant who entered into contract to be performed outside the forum, where contract required defendant to maintain regular communication with plaintiff's forum office and plaintiff received purchase orders in and made regular payments from the district; contract negotiated by phone and fax and defendants representatives never entered forum).

(e) Miscellaneous Issues

Several federal courts in New York have held that if venue is proper in a district where all of the defendants reside under 28 U.S.C. § 1391(b)(1), the plaintiff cannot sue in another district where a substantial part of the events giving rise to the claim occurred under § 1391(b)(2).[113] This position is based on pre-1990 authority interpreting the "claim arose" language of old § 1391(b) in cases in which the court was struggling to apply the U.S. Supreme Court's decision in *Leroy v. Great Western United Corp.*, discussed in the introduction to this section.[114] However, *Leroy* and the pre-1990 New York authority interpreting it were attempting to determine when it was appropriate to allow an action to be brought in a district where some, or some parts of, but not all, the claim(s) arose at a time when § 1391 appeared to assume that a claim could only arise in one place. The rationale of the New York cases is that the 1966 amendment inserting the "claim arose" language into the old § 1391 was only intended to close venue gaps and should not be read more broadly than necessary to do so. Because there is no venue gap when venue can be predicated upon defendants' residence, the plaintiff should not have the option to choose an alternative forum under such circumstances.[115] In the view of these courts, the 1990 amendment was simply a "revision" of this original gap-closing measure and did not alter the rationale of pre-1990 authorities.[116]

Whatever may be said for the rationale of the pre-1990 New York cases, and much may be said against it, the rationale cannot survive the 1990 amendments to § 1391(a) & (b). As can be seen from the wording of the "fallback" provisions, § 1391(a)(3) & (b)(3) discussed in subsection 5, below, when Congress wanted to make the applicability of one subsection of the venue statute depend on the inapplicability of another, it knew how to do so. Yet the terms of the statute do not make either § 1391(a)(2) or § 1391(b)(2) dependent on the inapplicability of § 1391(a)(1) or (b)(1), respectively.

4. Presence of Property As a Basis of Venue

Sections 1391(a)(2) & (b)(2) also provide that venue is proper in a district where "a substantial part of the property that is the subject of the action is situated." Like venue based on the occurrence of substantial events or omissions, these provisions pose several problems of interpretation.

---

113. *See* Dashman v. Peter Letterese & Assocs., Inc., 999 F. Supp. 553 (S.D.N.Y. 1998); Cobra Partners L.P. v. Liegl, 990 F. Supp. 332 (S.D.N.Y. 1998); Welch Foods, Inc. v. Packer, 93-CV-0811E(F), 1994 WL 665399, 1994 U.S. Dist. LEXIS 16974 (W.D.N.Y. Nov. 22, 1994).

114. *See* Canaday v. Kotch, 598 F. Supp. 1139 (E.D.N.Y. 1984).

115. *See, e.g.,* Welch Foods, Inc. v. Packer, 93-CV-0811E(F), 1994 WL 665399 at *2, 1994 U.S. Dist. LEXIS 16974 at *6 (W.D.N.Y. Nov. 22, 1994).

116. *See id.* at *3, 1994 U.S. Dist. LEXIS at *7. *But see* Gregory v. Pocono Grow Fertilizer Corp., 35 F. Supp. 2d 295 (W.D.N.Y. 1999) (rejecting the view described in the text and holding that §§ 1391(a)(1) & (2) and (b)(1) & (2) are alternatives to each other).

(a) When Property Should Be Considered to Be the "Subject of the Action"

An issue of interpretation that has already arisen under the location-of-property provisions is when property should be considered to be "the subject of the action." The language of the statute was drawn from a 1969 American Law Institute proposal.[117] However, the commentary to the proposal gives no clue about how to determine when property is "the subject of the action."[118] The legislative history of § 1391(a)(2) & (b)(2) is also silent on this question.[119]

(i) Ownership of Property Directly at Issue

The property must be directly, rather than tangentially, involved in the action to satisfy "the subject of action" requirement.[120] This requirement will surely be met when the controversy directly concerns the ownership of specific property.

(ii) Actions for Damages for Injury to Land or to Prevent Future Harm to Land

The "subject of the action" requirement will also probably be met when the action seeks to recover damages for injury to land or to prevent future harm to land.[121]

Illustration 4-14. A, a citizen and resident of State *X*, sues *B*, a citizen and resident of State *Y*. *A* seeks to obtain specific performance of a contract between *A* and *B* to convey land worth $2,000,000. The action is brought in the

---

117. *See* ALI STUDY OF THE DIVISION OF JURISDICTION BETWEEN STATE AND FEDERAL COURTS §§ 1303(a)(1), 1314(a)(1).

118. *See id.* at 135-37, 216.

119. *See* H.R. REP. NO. 734, 101st Cong., 2d Sess. 23 (1990).

120. *See* United States v. Selland, No. 93-1719, 1993 WL 347187, 1993 U.S. App. LEXIS 23396 (8th Cir. Sept. 14, 1993) (unpublished opinion) (action to foreclose on property is proper in district where property is located); *cf.* Anderson v. FDIC, 1996 U.S. Dist. LEXIS 19907 (E.D. Mich. Nov. 25, 1996), in which the F.D.I.C. denied applications for deposit insurance sent to Washington, D.C., and Chicago, Illinois. The plaintiffs sued in the Eastern District of Michigan on the theory that the bank in question would have been located in Pontiac, Michigan, in the Eastern District. Thus, the "property" that was the "subject of the action" was arguably located in the Eastern District. However, the court held that property was not the subject of the action. *See also* Pfeiffer v. Insty Prints, No. 93 C 2937, 1993 WL 443403, 1993 U.S. Dist. LEXIS 15317 (N.D. Ill. Oct. 29, 1993) (action for breach of contract to produce play did not involve ownership of play; therefore, property not the subject of the action).

One question that has not yet directly arisen is whether, and if so how, §§ 1391(a)(2) & (b)(2) will apply to intangible property, such as the debt in *Harris v. Balk*, discussed in Chapter 3(B)(1)*(a)* ("Affirmative Principles of In Rem Jurisdictions"), *supra*. At least one court has raised the possibility that such property may not be included within the statute at all. *See* Pfeiffer v. Insty Prints, No. 93 C 2937, 1993 WL 443403, n.4, 1993 U.S. Dist. LEXIS 15317, n.4 (N.D. Ill. Oct. 29, 1993). Thus, venue would have to be predicated on defendant's residence or the events giving rise to suit. If intangible property is included within the statute, the courts will have to struggle with the situs of such property, as in *Harris*.

121. When the claim is for damages to land or to prevent future harm to land, venue will usually also be proper on the basis that a substantial part of the events giving rise to the claim occurred in the district where the land is located.

Western District of State *Z*, where the land is located. The land is clearly property that is "the subject of the action." Venue is, therefore, proper in the Western District.

Illustration 4-15. *A*, a citizen and resident of State *X*, sues *B*, a citizen and resident of State *Y*. *A* seeks to recover $80,000 damages for injuries to land owned by *A*. The action is brought in the Southern District of State *Z*, where the land is located. In an action for injury to land, the land is central to the action and should be considered "the subject of the action." Thus, the court should consider venue to be proper in the Southern District.[122]

Illustration 4-16. *A*, a citizen and resident of State *X*, sues *B*, a citizen and resident of State *Y*. *A* seeks to force *B* to abate a nuisance. *A* claims that the nuisance is reducing the value of *A's* land in the Eastern District of State *Z* by $1,000,000. The source of the nuisance is a manufacturing plant that emits noxious fumes. The plant is located in State *Y*, which is adjacent to the border of State *Z*. In an action to abate a nuisance that decreases the value of land, the land being harmed is central to the action. The court should consider it to be "the subject of the action." Thus, the court should rule venue to be proper in the Eastern District.[123]

(iii) Damages for Injury to Specific Personal Property

Actions seeking damages for injury to specific personal property must be approached more cautiously. The mobility of personal property presents the danger that the property might be located in a district that has no relationship to the focus of the action brought. In addition, a danger exists that the plaintiff might attempt to manipulate the venue of the action by removing the property to a district where venue would otherwise be improper. When administering the statute, courts should prevent such manipulation.

Illustration 4-17. *A*, a citizen of State *X*, sues *B*, a citizen of State *Y*. *A* seeks to recover $100,000 for property damage to *A's* truck in an accident between *A* and *B*. *A* has brought the action in the Northern District of State *X*, where the truck is located and where *A* resides. The accident occurred in the Southern District of State *Z*. The truck was then towed to a repair shop in the Northern District of State *X* and has been located there ever since. Venue should not be considered proper in the Northern District of State *X*. Although the action seeks to recover damage to a truck, which is technically "property," the court should not regard the truck as "the subject of the action" and allow venue to be established in the district of *A's* residence. The 1990 amendments to § 1391(a) specifically repealed plaintiff's residence as a proper venue. The district of the plaintiff's residence has no connection with the events or omissions giving rise to the claim.

---

122. Venue would also be proper here on the ground that the events giving rise to the claim occurred in the Southern District.

123. Because the impact of the nuisance occurs in the district where the land is located, venue would also be proper because a substantial part of the events giving rise to the claim occurred there.

(iv) Money

Money is property, but the courts should not consider all cases involving money to be ones in which property is the "subject of the action."[124] Instead, courts should consider money to be property that is the subject of the action only when the claim relates to a specific fund or source of money within the district.[125]

Illustration 4-18. Assume the same facts as in *Illustration 4-17*, except that *A* seeks to recover $100,000 in damages for personal injuries received in the accident. *A* brings the action in the Western District of State *Q*, where *B* has a $100,000 bank account. *A* contends that venue is proper because the bank account is property that *A* seeks to recover in the action and is, therefore, the "subject of the action." The court should not consider venue to be proper in the Western District. *A* has no specific claim to the money in the bank account, as opposed to $100,000 of *B's* general assets. The court should not permit *A* to use the property-as-subject-of-the-action provision to establish venue in a district that has nothing to do with the central focus of the action, the accident between *A* and *B*.

Illustration 4-19. *A*, a citizen and resident of State *X*, sues *B*, a citizen and resident of State *Y*. *A* seeks to recover $85,000 from *B* for breach of *B's* fiduciary duty in managing a trust of money. *A* is the beneficiary of the trust, and B is the trustee of the trust. The action is brought in the Northern District of State Z, where the trust assets are deposited in a bank. Venue should be considered proper in the Northern District of State Z because the property that is the subject of the action is located there. The action directly concerns a specific fund of money located within the district.[126]

Illustration 4-20. *A*, a citizen and resident of State *X*, sues *B*, a citizen and resident of State *Y*. *A* seeks to recover rents in the amount of $650,000. *B* assigned the rents to *A* as security for a mortgage and promissory note that *B* had given to *A*. The land that *B* mortgaged to *A* is located in the Eastern District of State Z. *A* has brought the action in that district. Venue is proper in the Eastern District of State Z for two reasons. First, the mortgaged property is located there and is properly considered the "subject of the action." Second, even if no mortgage existed, the property is the source of the assigned rents.[127]

---

124. *See* David D. Siegel, *Changes in Federal Jurisdiction and Practice Under the New (Dec. 1, 1990) Judicial Improvements Act*, 133 F.R.D. 61, 72 (1991).

125. *See* Jackson Nat'l Life Ins. Co. v. Stillman Land Co., No. 5:92-CV-66, 1993 U.S. Dist. LEXIS 14218 (W.D. Mich. Sept. 22, 1993) (suit on an insurance claim does not involve property as subject of the action; suit is not for a specific fund; contrary ruling would mean any suit for damages would be one in which property would be the subject of the action).

126. *See* Brady v. Capital Group, Inc., No. CIV.A.91-3873, 1992 WL 46337, 1992 U.S. Dist. LEXIS 2478 (E.D. La. Mar. 4, 1992).

127. *See* Travelers Ins. Co. v. Swolsky, No. CIV.A.91-7537, 1992 WL 150698, 1992 U.S. Dist. LEXIS 8408 (E.D. Pa. June 17, 1992).

(v) Other Cases

Other cases will, of necessity, depend on whether property is central to the controversy or only remotely involved. No mechanical test will resolve all the cases.

Illustration 4-21. A, a citizen of State *X*, sues *B*, a citizen of State *Y. A* seeks $10,000,000 for common-law fraud. *A* brings the action in the Western District of State *Z. A* bases the claim on a transaction between *A* and *B* in which *B* sold a manufacturing plant located in the Western District to *A*. As part of the transaction, *B* provided *A* with an affidavit stating that no hazardous wastes had been stored on the plant site and no hazardous substances had been released in violation of the law. *A* asserts that this affidavit was false. *A* also asserts that *A* will incur $10,000,000 in clean-up costs. Venue is proper in the Western District of State *Z*. The action seeks to recover the costs of cleaning a contaminated plant located within the district. The plant, which is property, is correctly considered the "subject of the action," even though the claim is for common-law fraud.[128]

Illustration 4-22. A, a citizen of State *X*, sued *B*, a citizen of State *Y*, in the U.S. District Court for State *X. A's* claim is for $1,000,000 for fraud and negligent misrepresentation. *A's* claim arose out of the sale of an apartment complex located in the District of State *X. A* sold the complex to *C*, a citizen of State *Y. B* is an accountant who prepared *C's* financial statement. *A* alleges that the financial statement contained false statements. *B* sent the financial statement to *D* in State *Q* to obtain *D's* consent to the sale. *D* is a mortgagee of the apartment complex. *B* performed all services in State *Y. A* never saw the financial statement or knew about the misrepresentations in it until after the sale. It is questionable whether venue is proper in the District of State *X* on the ground that the apartment complex is located there. In *Illustration 4-21*, the plaintiff sought to recover the expenses that the plaintiff would incur to clean up specific property located within the district. In this illustration, the defendant's alleged fraud is more remote from the property. On these facts, one court has held venue to be improper in the district where the apartment complex was located because the complex was not "the subject of the action."[129]

(b) When a "Substantial Part" of the Property Should Be Considered Located Within the District

When property is concededly the "subject of the action," problems may arise in determining when a "substantial part" of the property is located within the district. As in venue based on events or omissions within the district, § 1391(a)(2) & (b)(2) provide for venue in more than one district when the amount of property located in multiple districts is "substantial." If the amount

---

128. *See* Samuel G. Keywell Co. v. Weinstein, No. CIV.A.HAR-91-659, 1991 WL 149894, 1991 U.S. Dist. LEXIS 10570 (D. Md. July 31, 1991).

129. *See* Monarch Normandy Square Partners v. Normandy Square Assocs., 817 F. Supp. 896 (D. Kan. 1993).

of property located in a given district is not "substantial," however, venue cannot be proper in that district based on the location of property.

Obviously, if no property is located within the district, the amount is not substantial. Conversely, if all the property is located within a district, the amount of property is substantial. Furthermore, if more than half the property is located in a district, the amount of property is substantial. Therefore, as in venue based on events and omissions giving rise to the claim, the problem case concerns situations in which less than half of the property is located in a district.

As with events-based venue, it is inappropriate to establish an irreducible minimum percentage of property that must be present in the district to support venue. A large amount of property located within a district might be only a small percentage of the total amount of property involved in the action. Yet no inconvenience may occur in basing venue on the location of the small percentage of property.

Illustration 4-23. *A*, a citizen and resident of State *X*, sues *B*, a citizen and resident of State *Y*. *A* seeks specific performance of a contract to convey land located in the Southern District of State *Z* and the Northern District of State *Q*. *A* has brought the action in the Northern District of State *Q*. Ninety-five thousand acres of the land are located in the Southern District of State *Z* and five thousand acres of the land are located in the Northern District of State *Q*. Even though the amount of land located in the Northern District of State *Q* is only 5% of the total amount, the court should not disqualify the Northern District as a proper venue based on the amount of property located there.

* * * * *

With respect to events-based venue, it was suggested that a test linked to the minimum contacts test for personal jurisdiction would be the best approach to determine when events or omissions within the district were substantial. In the context of venue based on the location of property, however, a test linked to whether the presence of a certain amount of property within the district would sustain personal jurisdiction is not appropriate. If a claim directly concerns property, personal jurisdiction will often exist regardless of how little property is located in the district.[130] However, § 1391(a)(2) & (b)(2) envision that the amount of property located within a district can be too insubstantial to support venue. Thus, when property is involved, a venue test linked to personal jurisdiction should not be adopted because such a test might result in finding

---

130. Recall from Chapter 3 that in Shaffer v. Heitner, 433 U.S. 186, 97 S. Ct. 2569, 53 L. Ed. 2d 683 (1977), the Supreme Court held that the presence of property unrelated to the claim would not, of itself, sustain personal jurisdiction. This sort of case presents no problem under the venue statutes, since property that is unrelated to the claim will not be "the subject of the action." However, *Shaffer* made it clear that when a claim directly concerns property located within the state, the state will be able to assert jurisdiction to adjudicate the claim, at least if the property has not been brought within the state without the consent of all the claimants. *See Shaffer*, 433 U.S. at 207-08, 97 S. Ct. at 2581-82, 53 L. Ed. 2d at 699-700; *see also* Chapter 3(E)(1) ("Quasi in Rem and Related Jurisdictional Doctrines") *supra*.

venue proper regardless of how small the amount of property within the district might be.[131]

Thus, in the case of property-based venue, there seems to be no escape from a fluid test for substantiality that will depend on the facts of particular cases. Nevertheless, since the venue statutes are designed to provide convenient locations for trial, courts should consider whether the particular district chosen by the plaintiff is substantially less convenient than other districts in which the property is also located.

Illustration 4-24. In *Illustration 4-23*, the court should not consider a substantial amount of property to be located in the Northern District of State *Q* if that district is substantially less convenient than the Southern District of State *Z*.[132]

(c) Effect on the Local Action Rule

Another problem of interpretation concerns the interaction of § 1391(a)(2) & (b)(2) with § 1392(b) of Title 28. Section 1392(b) deals with local actions involving property located in different districts in the same state. Section 1392(b) allows the plaintiff to bring such a local action in any of the districts where the property is located.[133] Like § 1392(a), discussed in subsection 2, above, Congress did not repeal or amend § 1392(b) when it enacted the amendments to § 1391(a) & (b). The retention of § 1392(b) thus gives rise to a problem of construction. Should § 1391(a)(2) and (b)(2) be read as overriding § 1392(b)? Indeed, should § 1391(a)(2) and (b)(2) be read as repealing the local action rule altogether? Alternatively, should the courts attempt to reconcile § 1391(a)(2) & (b)(2) with § 1392(b)?

The language of § 1391(a)(2) and (b)(2) was drawn from a 1969 American Law Institute (ALI) proposal. The ALI did not suggest that the language of its proposal would definitely have the effect of eliminating the local action rule. However, it did state its hope that the removal of all references to local actions in its proposal would "contribute to a fresh appraisal of the problems."[134] Furthermore, in a section of the proposal *not* enacted by Congress in 1990, the American Law Institute did deal with one particularly troublesome local action problem: actions for trespass to land.[135] The unenacted ALI proposal provided that plaintiffs could bring such actions in any of the districts that were

---

131. In contrast, under the substantial events test of § 1391(a)(2) & (b)(2) and the minimum contacts test for personal jurisdiction, a defendant's activities within the state can be too tenuous to support personal jurisdiction and, therefore, venue.

132. Even if this test is not adopted by the courts, an action brought in a proper, but substantially inconvenient, venue can be transferred to a more convenient venue under 28 U.S.C. § 1404(a). Transfer under § 1404(a) is discussed in section D(2)*(a)* ("Section 1404(a) Transfers") *infra*.

133. *See* 28 U.S.C. § 1392(b).

134. *See* ALI STUDY OF THE DIVISION OF JURISDICTION BETWEEN STATE AND FEDERAL COURTS 139-40 (1969).

135. *See id.* § 1303(c).

appropriate in its general venue proposal. Thus, the proposal made actions for trespass to land transitory.[136]

In contrast to the ALI proposal, Congress did not remove all references to local actions from the existing venue statutes. Specifically, § 1392(b) continues to refer to the local action concept.[137] Furthermore, Congress did not, as the ALI proposed, convert actions for trespass to land into transitory actions. These omissions suggest that the court should read the venue statutes as leaving the local action rule in full force. However, the intent of Congress is unclear on this question. Thus, the courts may fulfill the ALI's hope for a fresh appraisal of the problems of local actions.[138]

Illustration 4-25. *A*, a citizen and resident of the Southern District of State *X*, sues *B*, a citizen and resident of State *Y*. *A* seeks to quiet the title to land worth $80,000 located in the Northern District of State *X*. *A* has brought the action in the District of State *Y*. If § 1391(a)(2) is read as impliedly repealing the local action rule, venue is proper in the District of State *Y* because under § 1391(a)(1), the defendant resides in the district. If the local action rule still exists, venue is proper only in the Northern District of State *X* because *A's* action is local and that is where the land is located.

* * * * *

If § 1391(a)(2) & (b)(2) have not impliedly repealed the local action rule, then the courts will have to address the interaction of those sections with § 1392(b). One possible interpretation would emphasize that § 1391(a)(2) & (b)(2) were enacted after § 1392(b). Even though the local action rule continues to exist, when a plaintiff has brought a local action involving property located in different districts in the same state, § 1391(a)(2) & (b)(2), as the later enacted provisions, could be read to modify § 1392(b) by implication. Under this interpretation, the local action could not be brought in a district where part of the property was located unless the amount of the property within the district is "substantial," as required by § 1391(a)(2) & (b)(2).

Illustration 4-26. *A*, a citizen and resident of State *X*, sues *B*, a citizen and resident of State *Y*. *A* seeks to quiet title to land located in the Northern and Southern Districts of State *Z*. Fifty thousand acres are located in the Northern District and one acre is located in the Southern District. *A* has brought the action in the Southern District. If § 1391(a)(2) & (b)(2) are interpreted to override § 1392(b), venue in the Southern District will be held improper on the ground that a substantial part of the property that is the subject of the action is not located in the district.

* * * * *

---

136. *See id.*

137. Until 1996, § 1392(a) & (b) both referred to local actions. In 1996, Congress repealed § 1392(a), but left § 1392(b), which now comprises the entirety of the statute, intact, including the reference to the local action concept. *See* Act of Oct. 1, 1996, Pub. L. No. 104-220, 110 Stat. 3023.

138. *Cf.* New York Trap Rock Corp. v. Rankin County Econ. Dev. Dist., 158 B.R. 642 (S.D.N.Y. 1993) (the notion of a local action appears eclipsed by the general language enacted in 1990); *see also* Aguinda v. Texaco, Inc., 93 Civ. 7527 (VLB), 1994 WL 142006, 1994 U.S. Dist. LEXIS 4718 (S.D.N.Y. Apr. 11, 1994) (suggesting, but not holding, that the local action rule may have been abrogated by the 1990 amendments to § 1391).

An alternative interpretation of § 1391(a)(2) & (b)(2) and § 1392(b) would give effect to both statutes. Section 1392(b) specifically applies to local actions in which the property is located in "different districts in the same state." In contrast, § 1391(a)(2) & (b)(2) are not limited to actions in which the property is located in different districts in the same state. Therefore, one way to reconcile the statutes would be to hold that § 1391(a)(2) & (b)(2) apply to local actions involving property located in different districts in different states. On the other hand, the more specific language of § 1392(b) would control local actions in which the property is located in different districts in the same state.

A problem with this interpretation exists, however. As noted in section A, above, the Constitution may prohibit actions having a direct effect on the title to land located in another state. Therefore, in any such action, the federal courts might not be able to exercise jurisdiction to adjudicate the title to land located in another district in another state because there would be no "subject-matter jurisdiction" over such land. Thus, § 1391(a)(2) & (b)(2) would govern only local actions not directly affecting the title to land located in different districts in different states. As a practical matter, this interpretation might limit those sections to actions for damages for injury to land, the category of cases in which the local action rule is most under attack. Any such cases involving land that is located in different districts in different states would be rare, if not nonexistent, rendering § 1391(a)(2) & (b)(2) virtually irrelevant to multidistrict local actions.[139]

Illustration 4-27. On the facts of *Illustration 4-26*, if § 1391(a)(2) and (b)(2) are interpreted to apply only to local actions involving property located in different districts in different states, § 1392(b) would control. The land that is the subject of the action is located in different districts in the same state, State *Z*. Therefore, venue would be proper in the Southern District of State *Z*. Section 1392(b) does not require that a substantial amount of the property be located in a district for venue to be proper.

Illustration 4-28. On the facts of *Illustration 4-26*, assume that fifty thousand acres of the land are located in the Eastern District of State *Z* and one acre is located in the Western District of State *Q*. Section 1392(b) is inapplicable by its terms to this action. If § 1391(a)(2) & (b)(2) apply only to local actions involving property located in different districts in different states, venue may not be proper in the Western District of State *Q* on the ground that a substantial part of the land is not located there. However, an action in either district where the land is located may not be able to adjudicate the title to land located in the other district due to jurisdictional restrictions on the power of the federal courts to directly affect the title to land located in other states.[140] In that event, the plaintiff would have to bring two actions to quiet the title to the land, one in each state where the land is located.

* * * * *

---

139. *Cf.* Raphael J. Musicus, Inc. v. Safeway Stores, Inc., 743 F.2d 503 (7th Cir. 1984) (action for breach of leases to land located in Nebraska and Montana; court recognizes that if this is a local action, there is a gap in the venue statutes; classifies action as transitory).

140. *Cf.* Kavouras v. Fernandez, 737 F. Supp. 477 (N.D. Ill. 1989) (action to foreclose mortgage on property in another state is a local action not within the jurisdiction of the federal courts).

One final problem of interpretation of § 1391(a)(2) & (b)(2) and § 1392(b) should be considered. Sections 1391(a)(2) & (b)(2) do not refer to the local action concept at all. In contrast, § 1392(b) explicitly applies only to local actions. It is therefore possible to interpret § 1391(a)(2) & (b)(2) as applicable only to nonlocal actions involving property. Under this interpretation, local actions involving property located in only one district would have to be brought in the district where the land is located, just as before the 1990 amendments to the venue statutes. Local actions involving land located in different districts in the same state would be controlled by the explicit terms of § 1392(b). The problem with this interpretation is that the courts have always read the local action rule into the general venue statutes without explicit textual authorization. There seems to be no reason not to do the same with § 1391(a)(2) & (b)(2).

In truth, none of the interpretations discussed above have much to commend them except a complete reconsideration of the local action rule. The best solution would be for Congress to abolish the local action rule explicitly. Short of such an abolition, the courts should take up the suggestion of the ALI and reconsider the rule on their own initiative. If Congress does not like the result, Congress can change it.

5. The "Fallback" Provisions of § 1391

In addition to the amendments to § 1391(a) & (b) discussed above, Congress added two other provisions to the statute in 1990. Section 1391(a) provides for venue in actions in which jurisdiction is based only on diversity of citizenship. In that provision, Congress originally provided that venue would be proper in "a judicial district in which the defendants are subject to personal jurisdiction at the time the action is commenced."[141] This addition seemed to be patterned after a 1988 amendment to 28 U.S.C. § 1391(c), discussed below, which deals with venue when corporations are defendants. However, the amendment was curious for several reasons. First, unlike the two previous amendments discussed above, the Federal Courts Study Committee had not recommended it.[142] Second, this provision seemed to make the other provisions of 28 U.S.C. § 1391(a) superfluous. As demonstrated in Chapter 3, it is always necessary to obtain personal jurisdiction over the defendants in an action. If venue is proper whenever personal jurisdiction can be obtained, it is unnecessary to provide for venue on any other basis, such as defendants' residence. Conversely, in the unlikely event that personal jurisdiction could not be obtained over the defendants—for example, in the district where one of them resided or in the district where a substantial part of the events giving rise to the claim occurred—then the fact that venue was proper in those districts would be irrelevant.

---

141. Judicial Improvements Act of 1990, Pub. L. No. 101-650, § 311(1), 104 Stat. 5089, 5114 (codified at 28 U.S.C. § 1391(a)(3)).

142. *See* REPORT OF THE FEDERAL COURTS STUDY COMMITTEE 94 (1990).

The legislative history of § 1391(a)(3) indicates that Congress intended the amendment to be a "fallback" provision. It was to apply only when § 1391(a)(1) & (2) were inapplicable.[143] In other words, § 1391(a)(3) would apply only to actions in which no substantial part of the events giving rise to the claim occurred in the United States and the defendants resided in different districts in different states. Because the language of the statute did not restrict venue to fallback cases, however, some district courts interpreted the provision to apply to any action in which plaintiffs could obtain personal jurisdiction over the defendants.[144] In 1992, Congress amended § 1391(a)(3) to make it clear that the provision is indeed a fallback provision.[145] Thus, after the amendment, § 1391(a)(3) provided that venue is proper in "a judicial district in which the defendants are subject to personal jurisdiction at the time the action is commenced, if there is no district in which the action may otherwise be brought."[146]

In 1995, § 1391(a)(3) was again amended to provide that venue would be proper in a district in which "any defendant" is subject to personal jurisdiction at the time the action is commenced.[147] This amendment made it clear that only one defendant must be subject to personal jurisdiction at commencement for venue to be proper, as is the case with § 1391(b)(3), discussed below.[148]

Illustration 4-29. *A*, a citizen and resident of State *X*, *B*, a citizen and resident of State *Y*, and *C*, a citizen and resident of State *Z*, collide in automobiles they are driving in France. *A* brings an action for $500,000 to recover for personal injuries received in the accident. *A* brings the action in a U.S. District Court for the District of State *Y* against *B* and *C*. *B* is subject to personal jurisdiction in State *Y* because it is *B's* domicile. *C* is subject to personal jurisdiction in State *Y* because *C* conducts substantial activities within the state. Under these circumstances, venue is proper in the District of State *Y* under § 1391(a)(3).

Illustration 4-30. On the facts of *Illustration 4-29*, assume that *C* is not subject to personal jurisdiction in the District of State *Y* when *A* commences the action because *C* is not present in the district and has never conducted any

---

143. H.R. REP. NO. 734, 101st Cong., 2d Sess. 23 (1990) stated:

> Subsection 3 is meant to cover the cases in which no substantial part of the events happened in the United States and in which all the defendants do not reside in the same state. This provision would act as a safety net by allowing venue in a "judicial district in which the defendants are subject to personal jurisdiction at the time the action is commenced.["] If personal jurisdiction cannot be brought in a single federal court, this proposal does not create any new basis for personal jurisdiction. Instead two actions must be brought in separate courts.

144. *See, e.g.*, Bartle v. Capy, No. 91-2308, 1991 WL 152955, 1991 U.S. Dist. LEXIS 10954 (E.D. Pa. Aug. 6, 1991); Siemion v. USX Corp., No. 90 C 7092, 1991 WL 125933, 1991 U.S. Dist. LEXIS 8669 (N.D. Ill. June 27, 1991).

145. Federal Courts Administration Act of 1992, Pub. L. No. 102-572, § 504, 106 Stat. 4506, 4513 (codified at 28 U.S.C. § 1391(a)(3)).

146. 28 U.S.C. § 1391(a)(3).

147. *See* Act of Oct. 3, 1995, Pub. L. 104-34, § 1, 109 Stat. 293, 293.

148. However, as discussed below, other differences in language between § 1391(a)(3) and (b)(3) were, mysteriously given the criticism of the statute that had already occurred, not eliminated.

activities there. After commencement of the action, however, *C* is served with process while passing through the district. Venue is still proper under these circumstances, though it would not have been before 1995. After the 1995 amendment to the statute, only one defendant need be subject to personal jurisdiction at the commencement of the action (here *B*) for venue to be proper.

* * * * *

In 1990, Congress also added a fallback provision to § 1391(b), which governs actions in which jurisdiction is not based entirely on diversity of citizenship. In § 1391(b)(3), Congress provided that venue would be proper in "a judicial district in which any defendant may be found, if there is no district in which the action may otherwise be brought."[149] Again, the Federal Courts Study Committee made no such recommendation,[150] and, unless the legislative history accompanying the amendment to § 1391(a)(3) is also applicable to this amendment, there is no explanation at all in the legislative history as to why Congress added the provision.[151] However, the language of the provision is similar to the language of a 1969 American Law Institute (ALI) proposal.[152] The ALI's explanation for its recommendation parallels the explanation in the House Report for the amendment to § 1391(a)(3): "In the rare case where the events occurred outside the United States, and there is a defendant not resident within the United States, venue may be laid where any defendant may be found . . . ."[153]

The difficulty is that while the venue portion of the ALI proposal did not attempt to make personal jurisdiction and venue coextensive, a separate subsection of the ALI proposal did authorize nationwide long-arm jurisdiction in federal question cases.[154] Thus, under the ALI proposal, in a case where the events giving rise to suit occurred outside the United States but the defendants were scattered throughout the United States, venue would be proper where any defendant could be "found." Personal jurisdiction could then be asserted over the remaining defendants in that district under the nationwide long-arm provision. In effect, therefore, because personal jurisdiction could be obtained over all the defendants in any district (so long as they could be served somewhere in the United States), venue and personal jurisdiction were coextensive under the ALI proposal.

Under the amendment to 28 U.S.C. § 1391(b)(3), however, this is not the case. As discussed in Chapter 3, it may be possible to obtain personal jurisdiction over a defendant wherever the defendant is found. However, if other defendants in the action cannot be subjected to personal jurisdiction in the district where the

---

149. Judicial Improvements Act of 1990, Pub. L. No. 101-650, § 311, 104 Stat. 5089, 5114 (codified at 28 U.S.C. § 1391(b)(3)).

150. *See* REPORT OF THE FEDERAL COURTS STUDY COMMITTEE 94 (1990).

151. *See* H.R. REP. NO. 734, 101st Cong., 2d Sess. 23 (1990).

152. *See* ALI STUDY OF THE DIVISION OF JURISDICTION BETWEEN STATE AND FEDERAL COURTS § 1314(a)(3) (1969). The language of the ALI proposal provided for venue in a district in which "any defendant may be found, if there is no district within the United States in which the action may otherwise be brought under this subsection." *Id.*

153. *See id.* at 31, reporter's note to § 1314(a)(3); *see also id.* at 218-19.

154. *See id.* § 1314(d).

action is brought, venue will be proper under the wording of § 1391(b)(3), but the action will still have to be dismissed as to the defendants not subject to personal jurisdiction.

The central question about § 1391(a)(3) & (b)(3) is why Congress worded the two provisions differently. That is, why does § 1391(a)(3) make venue proper in a district in which any defendant "is subject to personal jurisdiction" at the commencement of the action, while § 1391(b)(3) makes venue proper in a district in which any defendant "may be found"? The difference in language holds the potential for different results under the two subsections. For example, under the language of § 1391(a)(3) venue would be proper in a district where one of several nonresident defendants is subject to personal jurisdiction at commencement because the defendant has minimum contacts with the state in which the action was brought. However, § 1391(b)(3)'s use of the phrase "may be found" suggests that the defendant must be physically present within the jurisdiction, not subject to personal jurisdiction under a long-arm statute. On the other hand, § 1391(b)(3) does not require that the defendant be "found" within the district at commencement. Thus, under that subsection, if a defendant can be served within the district *after* commencement, the court would have personal jurisdiction over the defendant and venue would be proper, but the same would not be true under § 1391(a)(3).

There is no apparent reason why Congress would want to treat venue differently under § 1391(a)(3) & (b)(3). Thus, the difference in wording appears to be a byproduct of extremely poor drafting. The best result would be for the courts to interpret the two provisions as if they both read like § 1391(a)(3).

Illustration 4-31. *A*, a citizen and resident of State *X*, sues *B*, a citizen and resident of State *X*, and *C*, a citizen and resident of State *Y*, in a U.S. District Court in State *X*. *A's* claim is based on a federal statute. The events giving rise to the claim occurred outside the United States. *B* is personally served with process in State *X*, where *B* is domiciled. *C* is not subject to personal jurisdiction in State *X*. Venue is proper in State *X* under the wording of § 1391(b)(3), which provides that venue is proper in a district in which "any defendant may be found" if there is no other district in which the action may be brought. However, *C* will have to be dismissed from the action because there is no personal jurisdiction over *C*. If § 1391(b)(3) is construed as identical with § 1391(a)(3), *A* may be able to bring the action in another federal court, if *A* can find a district somewhere in which either *B* or *C* are subject to personal jurisdiction at the commencement of the action. However, the action would still have to be dismissed against the other defendant unless personal jurisdiction could also be acquired over that defendant. If the courts literally construe the word "found" in § 1391(b)(3), personal jurisdiction over at least one of the defendants will have to be based on service of process on the defendant while the defendant is physically present within the state, rather than on the defendant's contacts with the state. There is no apparent reason why Congress would have wanted to produce this result. Therefore, § 1391(b)(3) should be interpreted as if it provided for proper venue when any defendant is subject to personal jurisdiction, just like § 1391(a)(3).

6. Residence of Corporations and Associations

Before 1988, another peculiarity of the venue statute was found in 28 U.S.C. § 1391(c). This subsection defined venue for suits against corporations. It provided that "[a] corporation may be sued in any judicial district in which it is incorporated or licensed to do business or is doing business, and such judicial district shall be regarded as the residence of such corporation for venue purposes." The language "and such judicial district shall be regarded as the residence of such corporation for venue purposes" might have been read as making the section applicable to the venue of corporate plaintiffs as well as corporate defendants. However, even before 1988, it was generally settled that this section was intended only to broaden venue for suits against corporate defendants and did not fix venue for corporate plaintiffs. Before 1990, a corporation predicating venue on the plaintiff's residence had to sue where it was incorporated.[155] After 1990, the plaintiff's residence is no longer a proper venue under either 28 U.S.C. § 1391(a) or (b).

In 1988, § 1391(c) was amended and now expressly applies to only corporate defendants.[156] In addition, § 1391(c) now provides that a corporate defendant "shall be deemed to reside in any judicial district in which it is subject to personal jurisdiction at the time the action is commenced."[157] In states containing more than one judicial district, however, corporate defendants may be sued only in those judicial districts in which their activities would be sufficient to subject them to personal jurisdiction if the districts were separate states.[158] This restriction is designed to protect corporations that conduct activities primarily

---

155. *See* 15 CHARLES A. WRIGHT ET AL., FEDERAL PRACTICE AND PROCEDURE: JURISDICTION AND RELATED MATTERS (VENUE) § 3811, at 108-09 (2d ed. 1986).

156. *See* Judicial Improvements and Access to Justice Act of 1988, Pub. L. No. 100-702, § 1013, 102 Stat. 4642, 4669 (codified at 28 U.S.C. § 1391(c)). Section 1391(c) defines residence of a corporate defendant "[f]or purposes of venue under this chapter," which means that the definition of a corporate defendant's residence applies not only for purposes of venue under §§ 1391(a)(1) & (b)(1), but also for purposes of any venue statute in Chapter 87 of Title 28 that provides for proper venue at defendant's residence. *See, e.g., In re* Regents of the Univ. of Cal., 964 F.2d 1128 (Fed. Cir. 1992) (patent infringement); Dakota Indus., Inc. v. Dakota Sportswear, Inc., 946 F.2d 1384 (8th Cir. 1991) (trademark infringement); Milwaukee Concrete Studios, Ltd. v. Fjeld Mfg. Co., 795 F. Supp. 277 (E.D. Wis. 1992) (copyright infringement); *see also* Bass v. Energy Transp. Corp., 787 F. Supp. 530 (D. Md. 1992) (definition of corporate residence applied to venue under the Jones Act, 46 U.S.C § 688).

157. *See* 28 U.S.C. § 1391(c). This portion of § 1391(c) is straightforward and poses no special difficulties of administration apart from, perhaps, a complicated inquiry into whether personal jurisdiction is proper in a given case. *See* Dakota Indus., Inc. v. Dakota Sportswear, Inc., 946 F.2d 1384 (8th Cir. 1991). *But see* Davies Precision Machining, Inc. v. Defense Logistics Agency, 825 F. Supp. 105 (E.D. Pa. 1993) (Defense Logistics Agency, a federal agency, is not a corporation for purposes of § 1391(c)); Variable-Parameter Fixture Dev. Corp. v. Morpheus Lights Co., 832 F. Supp. 643 (S.D.N.Y. 1993) (venue proper as to majority shareholders of corporation in district where corporation is subject to personal jurisdiction).

158. *See* 28 U.S.C. § 1391(c). Under this portion of the statute, a court must focus on the contacts with the district, not simply on contacts with the state. *See* Bicicletas Windsor, S.A. v. Bicycle Corp. of Am., 783 F. Supp. 781 (S.D.N.Y. 1992) (focusing on contacts with the entire state for purposes of personal jurisdiction, but focusing on contacts with the district for purposes of venue). Some courts, however, have simply assumed that contacts with a state sufficient to confer personal jurisdiction automatically satisfy the venue test. *See, e.g.,* Kaufman v. First Wachovia Corp., No. C-91-4456 MHP ARB, 1992 U.S. Dist. LEXIS 5617 (N.D. Cal. Apr. 3, 1992) (contacts with California sustain personal jurisdiction; these contacts simultaneously created venue in the district).

or exclusively in only one district of a state from being sued in another district in the state with which they have little or no contact, unless venue would be proper in that other district on a different basis than defendant's residence.[159] In addition, § 1391(c) now provides that if there is no district, evaluated as a separate state, in which a corporate defendant has sufficient contacts to subject it to personal jurisdiction, the corporation may be sued in the district "within which it has the most significant contacts."[160] This unwieldy provision seems designed to take care of the following rare case: A corporate defendant might have sufficient contacts with an entire state to subject it to personal jurisdiction within the state, but might lack sufficient contacts with any one of the federal districts in that state to subject it to personal jurisdiction within a particular district.

Illustration 4-32. *A*, a citizen and resident of State *X*, sued *B Corporation*, a corporation incorporated and with its principal place of business in State *Y*. *A* brings the action in a U.S. District Court for the Northern District of State *Z*. *A* asserts a claim based on state law for $500,000. The events giving rise to the claim occurred in State *Q*. *B* does extensive business in the Southern District of State *Z* and is subject to personal jurisdiction in State *Z* as a result. *B* conducts no activities in the Northern District of State *Z*. Venue is, therefore, improper in the Northern District of State *Z*. In multiple district states, § 1391(c) requires that the activities of a corporate defendant be evaluated with regard to each district in order to determine corporate residence. If the activities in one district would be sufficient to subject the defendant to personal jurisdiction if that district were a separate state, the defendant is deemed to reside there for purposes of § 1391(a)(1) & (b)(1). However, if the defendant's activities in a district would not be sufficient to subject it to personal jurisdiction if that district were a separate state, the defendant does not reside there under § 1391(c). Here, *B* conducts no activities in the Northern District of State *Z* and, therefore, that district cannot be deemed to be its residence.

Illustration 4-33. On the facts of *Illustration 4-32*, assume that *A* brought the action against both *B Corporation* and *C*, a citizen of State *Z* who resides in the Northern District of State *Z*. Under these circumstances, venue is proper in the Northern District of State *Z* under § 1391(a)(1). Because of its activities in the Southern District of State *Z*, *B* is deemed to reside there under § 1391(c). *C* is a resident of the Northern District of State *Z*. Therefore, the action is against multiple defendants who reside in different districts in the same state. Section 1391(a)(1) provides that, under these circumstances, venue is proper in a district where any defendant resides.

---

159. *See* H.R. Rep. No. 889, 100th Cong., 2d Sess. 70, *reprinted in* 1988 U.S.C.C.A.N. 5982, 6031. Thus, because personal jurisdiction is measured by reference to the contacts between the defendant and an entire state, the general language of the amendment to § 1391(c) would have subjected a corporation conducting activities only in the southern district of a state to suit in the northern district. The qualification in § 1391(c) prevents this result unless venue is proper on other grounds, such as when the northern district is the place where the events giving rise to the action occurred. *See id.*

160. *See* Judicial Improvements and Access to Justice Act of 1988, Pub. L. No. 100-702, § 1013, 102 Stat. 4642, 4669 (codified at 28 U.S.C. § 1391(c)).

Illustration 4-34. *A*, a citizen of State *X*, sues *B Corp.*, a corporation incorporated and with its principal place of business in State *Y*, in a U.S. District Court for the Northern District of State *Z*. *A* asserts a claim based on state law for $500,000. The events giving rise to the claim occurred entirely in State *Q*. *B* does sufficient business in State *Z* to subject it to personal jurisdiction there, but its activities are spread over the Northern and Southern Districts of State *Z*. The activities in each district, viewed alone, would not be sufficient to subject *B* to personal jurisdiction in either of the districts if they were separate states. Whether the venue is proper in the Northern District of State *Z* depends upon whether *B's* activities there are more significant than its activities in the Southern District.[161]

* * * * *

The unwieldy hypothetical inquiry required by § 1391(c) means that the district courts will, in some cases, have to go through specific and general jurisdiction analyses with regard to activities of a corporate defendant within the district, even though it is clear that the corporation's activities would be subject to personal jurisdiction within the state where the district is located. Although the problem has seldom arisen, the cases thus far have not reached results that would command unanimous agreement.[162] It is hard to believe that transfer to another district in the same state, which will often be the result of an inquiry under this part of the statute, is worth in convenience to defendants the costs it will impose in judicial administration.

One other question has arisen under § 1391 because of the interaction of § 1391(c) with the language of § 1391(a)(1) & (b)(1). It is clear that a corporate defendant will often ''reside'' in multiple districts in multiple states. When a corporate defendant is joined with an individual defendant, § 1391(a)(1) & (b)(1) can literally be read to permit venue in a district in which the corporate defendant resides, even though the individual defendant does not reside in the same state, as long as the corporate and individual defendants both ''reside'' in some other state. Such a reading was clearly not the intent of Congress in § 1391(a)(1) & (b)(1), however, and the cases have, thus far, unanimously rejected this reasoning.

---

161. Some courts evaluating venue under § 1391(c) have erroneously focused on the defendant's activities in the state, rather than the district. *See, e.g.*, Halsoprodukter Labs. Karnerud Ab. v. Gero Vita Int'l, No. 93 C 2129, 1993 WL 384525, 1993 U.S. Dist. LEXIS 13519 (N.D. Ill. Sept. 27, 1993).

162. *See* Zinn v. Gichner Sys. Group, Civ. No. 93-5817, 1994 WL 116014, 1994 U.S. Dist. LEXIS 4076 (E.D. Pa. Apr. 5, 1994), in which the corporation, which had ample activities to subject it to jurisdiction in Pennsylvania under both the general and specific jurisdiction doctrines, was sued in the Eastern District on a claim arising in the Middle District. After employing general jurisdiction analysis to the corporation's activities in the Eastern District, the court concluded that it would not be able to assert general jurisdiction if the district were a separate state. The court did not employ a specific jurisdiction analysis because the claim for personal injuries clearly ''arose'' in the Middle District. However, the court failed to consider whether the defendants activities in the Eastern District ''related to'' the claim. *See* Chapter 3(G)(2)*(b)(i)* (''Claims Arising Out of or Related to the Defendant's Contacts with the State'') *supra*; *see also* Sanders v. Seal Fleet, Inc., 998 F. Supp. 729 (E.D. Tex. 1998) (insufficient to show that a corporation is incorporated in a district of a multidistrict state; defendant must have sufficient contacts with district in which the action is brought). *But see* Lisseveld v. Marcus, 173 F.R.D. 689 (M.D. Fla. 1997) (defendant's contacts with Middle District of Florida sufficient to subject defendant to personal jurisdiction because, although the defendants products were sold in South Florida, defendant expected the products to enter the stream of commerce of the entire state).

Illustration 4-35. Assume that *A,* a citizen and resident of the Northern
District of State *X,* sues *B Corp.,* which is incorporated and has its principal place
of business in State *Y,* and *C,* a citizen and resident of the Northern District of
State *Z.* The action is brought in the Northern District of State *X,* where *B* does
sufficient business to subject it to personal jurisdiction. *A* contends that venue is
proper because *B* also does sufficient business in the Southern District of State
Z. Thus, A argues that the action has, within the meaning of § 1391(a)(1), been
brought in "any district where one of the defendants resides," because *B* resides
in the Northern District of *X* under § 1391(c). Likewise, *A* contends that the
remainder of § 1391(a)(1) is satisfied because both *B* and *C* "reside in the same
state," State *Z.* The courts have correctly rejected arguments like *A's,* because it
is clear that when venue is based on § 1391(a)(1) or (b)(1) in multiple defendant
cases, Congress intended that venue would be proper only in a state where both
defendants reside.[163]

* * * * *

In 1967, the U.S. Supreme Court held that unincorporated associations
could be sued wherever they were doing business.[164] No statute dictated this
result.[165] Instead, the Court reached the result by analogy to corporate venue in
the old version of § 1391(c).[166] Now that corporate defendants are deemed to
reside in any district in which they are subject to personal jurisdiction, unincorporated associations may also be deemed to reside in any district in which personal jurisdiction can be obtained over the association. At least one lower federal
court has drawn this conclusion.[167]

7. Venue in Actions Involving Aliens

Section 1391(d) states that an "alien may be sued in any district."[168]
Thus, when an alien is a defendant, venue is proper anywhere. The alien can be
sued wherever personal jurisdiction can be obtained. The 1988 amendment to 28
U.S.C. § 1332(a), discussed in Chapter 2, does not alter this rule.[169] That
amendment provided that an alien admitted to permanent residence in the United
States would be considered a citizen of the state in which the alien is

---

163. *See* Schomann Int'l Corp. v. Northern Wireless, Ltd., 35 F. Supp. 2d 205 (N.D.N.Y. 1999); Madotto
v. Rosman, No. Civ. A. 98-3221, 1998 WL 961390, 1998 U.S. Dist. LEXIS 20025 (E.D. Pa. Dec. 10, 1998);
DiFillipo v. Sherenian, Civ. No. 95-4445, 1996 WL 58255, 1996 U.S. Dist. LEXIS 1372 (E.D. Pa. Feb. 9,
1996); Gerety v. Sunrise Express, Inc., 95 Civ. 2090 (HB), 1996 WL 19047, 1996 U.S. Dist. LEXIS 378
(S.D.N.Y. Jan. 18, 1996).

164. *See* Denver & Rio Grande W. R.R. Co. v. Brotherhood of R.R. Trainmen, 387 U.S. 556, 87 S. Ct.
1746, 18 L. Ed. 2d 954 (1967).

165. *See* 15 CHARLES A. WRIGHT ET AL., FEDERAL PRACTICE AND PROCEDURE: JURISDICTION AND
RELATED MATTERS (VENUE) § 3812, at 134 (2d ed. 1986).

166. *See id.* at 135.

167. Graf v. Tastemaker, 907 F. Supp. 1473 (D. Colo. 1995).

168. 28 U.S.C. § 1391(d).

169. *See* Chapter 2(C)(3)*(d)* ("Alienage Jurisdiction") *supra.*

domiciled.[170] However, this provision is expressly applicable only to §§ 1332, 1335, and 1441. Therefore, it is inapplicable to the venue statutes.

Illustration 4-36. A, a citizen and resident of State *X*, sues *B*, a citizen of France admitted to permanent residence in the United States and domiciled in State *Y*, in a U.S. District Court in State *X. A's* claim is for $500,000 and is based on state law. The events giving rise to the claim occurred entirely in State *Q*. Venue is proper in State *X*. Section 1391(d) provides that an alien can be sued in any district. *B* is an alien for purposes of the venue statutes. Therefore, *A* should be able to sue *B* in the District of State *X* if personal jurisdiction can be obtained over *B* there.

8. Venue in Removed Actions

Section 1441(a) of Title 28 provides that civil actions can be removed "to the district court of the United States for the district and division embracing the place where [the state] action is pending."[171] This language has always been understood as establishing special venue for removed actions.[172] Therefore, even if an action is brought in a state court within a district where venue would have been improper if the action had been commenced in the U.S. District Court, venue will be proper in the district if the action is removed to the district court.[173]

Illustration 4-37. A, a citizen and resident of State *X*, sues *B*, a citizen and resident of State *Y*, in a state court in State *X. A's* claim is for $500,000 and is based on state law. The events giving rise to the claim occurred entirely in State *Q. B* removes the action to the U.S. District Court for the District of State *X*. Even though venue would not have been proper if the action had been commenced in the U.S. District Court for the District of State *X* originally, venue is proper over the removed action by virtue of § 1441(a).

9. Divisional Venue

Before 1988, 28 U.S.C. § 1393(a) required nonlocal actions against a single defendant in districts with more than one division to be brought in the division where the defendant resided. Under § 1393(b), nonlocal actions against multiple defendants residing in different divisions of the same district could be

---

170. *See* 28 U.S.C. § 1332(a).

171. *See* 28 U.S.C. § 1441(a).

172. *See* 15 CHARLES A. WRIGHT ET AL., FEDERAL PRACTICE AND PROCEDURE: JURISDICTION AND RELATED MATTERS (VENUE) § 3804, at 28-29 (2d ed. 1986).

173. *Id.; see also* Peterson v. BMI Refractories, 124 F.3d 1386 (11th Cir. 1997) (if action is removed to a district court in *wrong district* in a state, the defect is procedural only, not one of subject-matter jurisdiction, and concerns venue; venue is waivable and was waived by *plaintiff* in the action).

brought in any of the divisions.[174] In 1988, § 1393 was repealed. Thus, divisional venue in civil cases was eliminated.[175]

10. Special Venue Provisions

Special federal venue provisions also exist. These special provisions are sometimes contained in separate statutes[176] or in the statutes that create the right to sue.[177] In some instances, these special federal venue provisions have been interpreted to displace the general federal venue provisions.[178] Usually, the special provisions broaden the choice of venue available under the general venue provisions.[179] In some instances, however, the choice is narrowed.[180]

---

174. *See* Judicial Improvements and Access to Justice Act of 1988, Pub. L. No. 100-702, § 1001, 102 Stat. 4642, 4664.

175. *See* H.R. REP. NO. 889, 100th Cong., 2d Sess. 66-67, *reprinted in* 1988 U.S.C.C.A.N. 5982, 6027. However, as noted in the preceding subsection, 28 U.S.C. § 1441(a), which provides for removal of civil actions from state to federal court, continues to require removal "to the district court of the United States for the district *and division* embracing the place where such action is pending." *See* 28 U.S.C. § 1441(a) (emphasis added). The failure to amend § 1441 to eliminate divisional venue in removed cases was probably inadvertent. Nevertheless, the presence of the quoted language may result in divisional venue being retained for such cases. Furthermore, as noted in subsection 4(c), *supra*, the general federal venue statutes may still be interpreted to incorporate the concept of local actions. If so, despite the repeal of divisional venue generally, the local action rule might still be applied to require an action to be brought in the division where property is located in a multi-division district. Such a result would be unfortunate. The better view is that the repeal of § 1393 should allow a local action to be brought in any division within the district where the property is located. The American Law Institute has proposed to reform the general removal provision to make it clear that divisional venue is also abolished in removed cases. *See* ALI FEDERAL JUDICIAL CODE REVISION PROJECT § 1441(a)(2) (Tent. Draft No. 3 1999) (making civil actions removable "to the district court of the United States for the district in which the civil action is pending").

176. *See, e.g.,* 28 U.S.C. § 1400 (patent and copyright suits).

177. *See, e.g.,* 46 U.S.C. § 688 (allowing seamen who are injured in the course of their employment to sue for damages for the negligence of the owner, master, or fellow crew members). Special venue statutes can be found by using the subject index to the *United States Code*.

178. *Compare* 28 U.S.C. § 1391(e) (special venue provision controls actions against officers, employees, or agencies of the federal government) *and* Jean F. Rydstrom, Annotation, *Construction and Application of 28 USC § 1391(e) Providing for Venue and Process in Civil Actions Against Federal Officers, Employees, or Agencies*, 9 A.L.R. FED. 719 (1971) *with* 45 U.S.C. § 56 (general venue provisions render largely superfluous the special venue provision for Federal Employer's Liability Act cases governing railroad employees engaged in interstate and foreign commerce); *see also* Sunbelt Corp. v. Noble, Denton & Assocs. Inc., 5 F.3d 28 (3d Cir. 1993) (admiralty cases not governed by 28 U.S.C. § 1391). *See generally* 15 CHARLES A. WRIGHT ET AL., FEDERAL PRACTICE AND PROCEDURE: JURISDICTION AND RELATED MATTERS (VENUE) § 3803, at 10-11 (2d ed. 1986) (special venue statutes that expressly cover a particular kind of action "will control over general venue statutes"; however, the general venue statutes will be "read as supplementing the special statute in absence of contrary restrictive indications in the special statute").

179. *See, e.g.,* 15 U.S.C. §§ 15, 22 (allowing antitrust suits to be brought wherever the defendant "resides or is found or has an agent").

180. *See, e.g.,* 12 U.S.C. § 94 (allowing suits against national banks to be brought only in the district where the banks' principal office and place of business are located, as specified in their certificates); Richard Cordero, Annotation, *Venue Provisions of National Bank Act (12 USCS § 94), as Affected by Other Federal Venue Provisions and Doctrines*, 111 A.L.R. FED. 235 (1993).

11. Interaction of Venue, Subject-Matter Jurisdiction and Personal Jurisdiction Rules

The inability to satisfy the requirements of the federal venue provisions may mean that a suit must be brought in a state court. Furthermore, interaction of the venue requirements with the requirements of subject-matter jurisdiction and jurisdiction over the person also may mean at times that an action cannot be brought in any federal court.

Illustration 4-38. *A* suffered personal injuries in a four-car automobile accident involving drivers *B*, *C*, and *D*. *A* is a citizen and resident of State *X*; *B* is a citizen and resident of State *Y*; *C* is a citizen and resident of State *Z*; and *D* is a citizen and resident of State *X*. The accident occurred on a highway in England. If *A* wishes to sue *B*, *C*, and *D* in a single federal court action, *A* may not do so. A suit joining *D* as a defendant would violate the complete diversity requirement because *A* and *D* are both citizens of State *X*.

If *A* wishes to join only *B* and *C* in a federal court action for *A's* injuries, *A* likewise may not do so if a proper objection is made. Complete diversity of citizenship, and therefore subject-matter jurisdiction, would exist in such a case. However, in an action against *B* and *C*, venue (and personal jurisdiction) would probably not be proper anywhere. *B* and *C* do not live in the same state, so venue could not be predicated on the defendants' residence under 28 U.S.C. § 1391(a)(1). The events giving rise to the action occurred outside the United States, so venue could not be predicated on 28 U.S.C. § 1391(a)(2). Because personal jurisdiction can be obtained over *B* and *C* individually in the districts in which they live, venue will be proper under 28 U.S.C. § 1391(a)(3) in those districts in an action against both defendants. However, for the action to proceed against the other defendant, personal jurisdiction would also have to be obtained over that defendant in the forum. Even if *A* sued only *B* in a federal diversity action in the District of State *Y*, where subject-matter jurisdiction, venue, and personal jurisdiction would be proper, *B* might be able to obtain a dismissal under the doctrine of forum non conveniens, discussed in the next section. And the same might be true of a diversity action against *C* in the District of State *Z*.

12. Raising and Waiving Federal Venue Objections

In contrast to actions at common law in which venue had to be alleged in the declaration (the plaintiff's initial pleading), venue need not be alleged in a complaint filed in federal court. Under the Federal Rules of Civil Procedure, improper venue is a matter of *defense* which the defendant must raise.[181] If the

---

181. *See* Notes to Form 2 ("Allegation of Jurisdiction") in the Appendix of Forms following the Federal Rules of Civil Procedure.

defendant fails to object to the venue in a timely and proper fashion, venue objections are waived.[182]

Waiver can also occur through contractual provisions entered into before a dispute arises. Many contracts include a "forum selection" clause. A forum selection clause will usually provide that suit on the contract may be brought only in the courts in a particular place. Courts generally enforce forum selection clauses unless they are deemed unreasonable in themselves or in the effects that they have on the rights of the litigants.[183]

The U.S. Supreme Court has held a forum selection clause in a contract of adhesion (an unbargained for contract in which one of the parties is an unsophisticated consumer not in bargaining parity with the party who drafted the contract) to be enforceable. In *Carnival Cruise Lines, Inc. v. Shute*,[184] a Washington State couple purchased tickets on a cruise ship operated by Carnival Cruise Lines. The tickets contained a forum selection clause requiring that all disputes be litigated in Florida. While on the cruise, one of the plaintiffs suffered personal injuries on the ship. The plaintiffs sued Carnival Cruise Lines in the U.S. District Court for the Western District of Washington. The district court dismissed the action for lack of personal jurisdiction. The Ninth Circuit reversed, holding that Carnival Cruise Lines had sufficient contacts with Washington to sustain personal jurisdiction. In addition, the Ninth Circuit held that the forum selection clause was unenforceable because it was not freely bargained for and operated to deny the plaintiffs their day in court. The Supreme Court reversed, holding the forum selection clause enforceable.

The Court found it irrelevant that the forum selection clause was not negotiated between the parties. Rather, the Court held it reasonable, given the business context involved in the case, that (1) the forum selection clause would be included in a form contract (the ticket); (2) the clause would not be the subject of negotiation between the parties; and (3) the purchaser would not have bargaining parity with the cruise line. The Court noted that the forum selection clause served several important purposes: (1) limiting the fora in which the cruise line, which carries passengers from many locales, can be sued; (2) dispelling confusion about where actions arising from the contract may be brought, thus

---

182. *See* FED. R. CIV. P. 12(h)(1); Annotation, *Comment Note—What Conduct Constitutes Waiver of Venue Privilege—Federal Cases*, 5 L. Ed. 2d 546 (1961). The precise mechanics of waiver under the Federal Rules of Civil Procedure are discussed in Chapter 6(D)(3)*(g)* ("Consolidation and Waiver of Defenses") *infra*.

183. *See, e.g.*, M/S Bremen v. Zapata Off-Shore Co., 407 U.S. 1, 12-19, 92 S. Ct. 1907, 1914-18, 32 L. Ed. 2d 513, 521-26 (1972) (contractual forum selection designating disputes to be brought only before the High Court of Justice in London, England, enforced; no compelling, countervailing reason making enforcement unreasonable); National Equip. Rental, Ltd. v. Szukhent, 375 U.S. 311, 315-16, 84 S. Ct. 411, 415, 11 L. Ed. 2d 354, 357 (1964) (diversity action upholding appointment of an agent for service of process); Durdahl v. National Safety Assocs., Inc., 988 P.2d 525 (Wyo. 1999) (forum selection clauses prima facie valid). *See generally* 15 CHARLES A. WRIGHT ET AL., FEDERAL PRACTICE AND PROCEDURE: JURISDICTION AND RELATED MATTERS (VENUE) § 3803.1 (2d ed. 1986); Francis M. Dougherty, Annotation, *Validity of Contractual Provision Limiting Place or Court in Which Action May Be Brought*, 31 A.L.R.4TH 404 (1984). *But see, e.g.,* Omne Fin., Inc. v. Shacks, Inc., 226 Mich. App. 397, 573 N.W.2d 641 (1997) (contract agreeing to venue in a specific court is unenforceable because legislature has not approved such a rule; allowing parties to contract around venue statutes would undermine the power of the legislature, and contract agreeing to venue would conflict with court rules allowing trial court to change venue).

184. 499 U.S. 585, 111 S. Ct. 1522, 113 L. Ed. 2d 622 (1991).

saving litigants the time and expense of pretrial motions to determine the correct forum and conserving the judicial resources that would be devoted to that subject; and (3) reducing the fares charged to passengers because of the savings that the cruise line enjoys by limiting where it can be sued.[185]

After *Carnival Cruise Lines*, a forum selection clause controlled by federal law[186] will not be held unenforceable simply because it appears in a contract of adhesion.[187] Instead, a forum selection clause of which the plaintiff has adequate notice[188] will be valid if sufficient reasons can be given for including the clause in the contract.

The reasons given in *Carnival Cruise* for holding the forum selection clause enforceable have been criticized as imposing no real limitations on the enforcement of such clauses.[189] However, the result in the *Carnival Cruise Lines*, as well as the value of forum selection clauses generally, has also been well defended. "A healthy but not blind deference to forum selection clauses can serve the values of enhancing the parties' contractual expectations, reducing

---

185. *See id.* at 593, 111 S. Ct. at 1527, 113 L. Ed. 2d at 633.

186. *Carnival Cruise Lines* was an admiralty case, in which federal law controlled the enforceability of the forum selection clause. *See id.* at 589, 111 S. Ct. at 1525, 113 L. Ed. 2d at 630-31. In Schaff v. Sun Line Cruises, Inc., 999 F. Supp. 924 (S.D. Tex. 1998), the court invalidated a forum selection clause in a cruise ticket. The court distinguished *Carnival Cruise Lines* on the grounds that the ticket in *Schaff* required litigation in a foreign country, the ticket was nonrefundable, and the plaintiff did not have an adequate option to reject the contract.

187. Congress has overruled *Carnival Cruise Lines* on its facts by amending 46 U.S.C. app. § 183c. *See* Oceans Act of 1992, Pub. L. No. 102-587, § 3006, 106 Stat. 5039, 5068. Section 183c now makes it "unlawful" for any operator of a vessel transporting passengers between ports of the United States or between ports of the United States and foreign ports to insert "any provision or limitation" into a transportation agreement "purporting . . . to lessen, weaken, or avoid the right of any claimant to a trial by *any* court of competent jurisdiction on the question of liability for . . . loss or injury." The legislative history of the amendment indicates that it was "needed because of the Supreme Court ruling in *Carnival Cruise Lines* . . . . The amendment . . . would overturn the result in *Carnival*." 138 CONG. REC. H11,785 (daily ed. Oct. 5, 1992) (statement of Rep. Studds). In other areas controlled by federal law, the reasoning of *Carnival Cruise Lines* will control.

188. It was conceded in *Carnival Cruise Lines* that the plaintiffs had notice of the forum selection clause in the ticket. The Court's discussion of this point suggested that it might have been significant if the plaintiffs had no notice of the clause. *See* 499 U.S. at 589-90, 111 S. Ct. at 1525-26, 113 L. Ed. 2d at 631. For a criticism of the Court's reasoning on the notice issue, see Patrick J. Borchers, *Forum Selection Agreements in the Federal Courts After* Carnival Cruise*: A Proposal for Congressional Reform*, 67 WASH. L. REV. 55, 75-77 (1992); *see also* Edward A. Purcell, Jr., *Geography as a Litigation Weapon: Consumers Forum-Selection Clauses and the Rehnquist Court*, 40 UCLA L. REV. 423 (1992); David H. Taylor, *The Forum Selection Clause: A Tale of Two Concepts*, 66 TEMPLE L.Q. 785 (1993). For a proposal for a federal statute to insure the enforcement in federal and state courts of forum selection clauses that select a foreign nation's forum, see Young Lee, Note, *Forum Selection Clauses: Problems of Enforcement in Diversity Cases and State Courts*, 35 COLUM. J. TRANSNAT'L L. 663 (1997).

189. Professor Richman has suggested that the reasoning of *Carnival Cruise* may be limited to situations where the drafter of the clause faces a threat of multiple litigation in many different fora, while also suggesting that this limit may not be significant, since many interstate and international commercial enterprises face such a threat. *See* William M. Richman, Carnival Cruise Lines: *Forum Selection Clauses in Adhesion Contracts*, 40 AM. J. COMP. L. 977, 983 (1992). Professor Richman argues that the remainder of the reasons given by the Court were flawed. *See id.* 983-84. Professor Borchers argues that the reasons given by the Court amount to no real limitation on enforcement of forum selection clauses and agrees with Professor Richman that the multiple suits threat is something suffered by every large enterprise. *See* Patrick J. Borchers, *Forum Selection Agreements in the Federal Courts After* Carnival Cruise*: A Proposal for Congressional Reform*, 67 WASH. L. REV. 55, 74 (1992).

litigation over jurisdictional issues, and of respecting procedural due-process protections.''[190] In addition, one feature of *Carnival Cruise Lines*, not mentioned by the Court, deserves emphasis. The contract in which the forum selection clause appeared was a contract for a luxury, not a contract for a necessity of life. It may well be that this aspect of the case will impose an important limitation on the future application of the *Carnival Cruise Lines* principles.[191]

SECTION D. FORUM NON CONVENIENS AND CHANGE OF VENUE

Even if the plaintiff commences a civil action in a court of proper venue, conducting the action elsewhere may be desirable. A more desirable venue may be in (1) another court within the judicial system in which the plaintiff originally commenced the action or (2) a court in a different judicial system. When the more desirable venue is within the same judicial system, statutes often provide for transfer to that venue. The basis for such a transfer is usually for the convenience of the parties and witnesses or for the interests of justice.[192] Traditionally, if the more desirable venue is in a court of a different judicial system, transfer has not been possible. Instead, a common-law doctrine known as forum non conveniens allows a court to dismiss an action in its discretion when a court in another judicial system would provide a more appropriate forum.[193] After dismissal under the doctrine of forum non conveniens, the plaintiff commences a new action in the courts of the more convenient judicial system.

As applied to American courts, this structure produces varying results: (1) statutes or common-law rules often authorize a state court to transfer a case to another court in the same state where the action can be more conveniently conducted;[194] (2) state courts using the doctrine of forum non conveniens will

---

190. Michael E. Solimine, *Forum-Selection Clauses and the Privatization of Procedure*, 25 CORNELL INT'L L.J. 51, 101 (1992); *see id.* at 81-85, for a defense of the result in *Carnival Cruise Lines*.

191. The effect of forum selection clauses in cases in which a transfer of venue is sought from one federal court to another under 28 U.S.C. § 1404(a) is discussed in section D(2)(a) *infra*.

192. *See, e.g.*, NEB. REV. STAT. § 25-410 (1995).

193. For an argument that properly conducted personal jurisdiction and choice of law inquiries eliminate the need for forum non conveniens doctrine, see Margaret G. Stewart, *Forum Non Conveniens: A Doctrine in Search of a Role*, 74 CAL. L. REV. 1259 (1986). For an argument that the doctrine of forum non conveniens provides a mechanism for courts to reach desirable forum selection results without distorting the doctrine of personal jurisdiction, see Alex W. Albright, *In Personam Jurisdiction: A Confused and Inappropriate Substitute for Forum Non Conveniens*, 71 TEX. L. REV. 351 (1992).

194. *See* State *ex rel.* Riffle v. Ranson, 195 W. Va. 121, 464 S.E.2d 763 (1995) (transfer statute is exclusive authority for intrastate transfers). *But see* Perle v. Skelgas, Inc., 163 Ill. 2d 323, 645 N.E.2d 184 (1994) (recognizing common-law doctrine of intrastate forum non conveniens); Stevens v. Blevins, 1995 OK 6, 890 P.2d 936 (same). In Beaven v. McAnulty, 980 S.W.2d 284 (Ky. 1998), the Kentucky Supreme Court reviewed a case in which the trial court had transferred an action to a court in another county under the common-law doctrine of forum non conveniens. Although the court recognized that Oklahoma and Illinois had adopted an intrastate forum non conveniens doctrine, it held that the power to transfer must be conferred by statute. Forum non conveniens, in contrast, only permits courts to dismiss or stay an action. However, the court did not hold that forum non conveniens only applies when the alternative forum is in another state or in a foreign country, leaving open the possibility that an intrastate case might be dismissed or stayed under the dismiss an action when it can be conducted in a substantially more convenient court in another state or a foreign country; (3) federal statutes authorize the federal courts to transfer actions to other federal courts where they might have been brought for the convenience of parties and witnesses and in the interests of justice; and (4) the federal courts dismiss actions under the doctrine of forum non conveniens when the action can be conducted in a substantially more convenient court in a foreign country.

When an action is commenced in an improper venue, statutes in both state and federal courts authorize dismissal or transfer to a proper venue within the respective systems. State courts may not transfer cases to federal courts. Federal courts may not transfer cases to state courts. Traditionally, state courts could not transfer cases to the courts of other states. However, the Uniform Transfer of Litigation Act, proposed by the National Conference of Commissioners on Uniform State Laws, will allow adopting states to transfer litigation to courts in other states instead of dismissing them under the doctrine of forum non conveniens.

The following subsections discuss the forum non conveniens doctrine and transfer of venue. The first subsection discusses the forum non conveniens doctrine as it operates in both state and federal courts. In addition, it discusses the uniform legislation referred to in the preceding paragraph. Although this legislation would authorize transfer between the courts of different states, it is properly discussed in conjunction with the doctrine of forum non conveniens because it would replace that doctrine in the state courts when the more convenient forum is a court of another state. The second subsection then discusses transfer of venue in the federal courts.

1. Forum Non Conveniens and the Uniform Transfer of Litigation Act

(a) Forum Non Conveniens

In general, the defendant may invoke the doctrine of forum non conveniens when the action in question has little or no connection with the place where the plaintiff has commenced the action.[195] Under such circumstances, the burden on the judicial system in which the plaintiff originally commenced the

---

doctrine in an appropriate situation.

195. The historical pedigree of the doctrine of forum non conveniens is the subject of scholarly dispute. The original American treatment of the doctrine is Paxton Blair, *The Doctrine of Forum Non Conveniens in Anglo-American Law*, 29 COLUM. L. REV. 1, 2 (1929). Blair's historical view generally accords with Robert Braucher, *The Inconvenient Federal Forum*, 60 HARV. L. REV. 908, 909-18, 920-21 (1947). The Paxton-Braucher view is disputed in David W. Robertson & Paula K. Speck, *Access to State Courts in Transnational Personal Injury Cases: Forum Non Conveniens and Antisuit Injunctions*, 68 TEX. L. REV. 937, 948 n.68 (1990); Allan R. Stein, *Forum Non Conveniens and the Redundancy of Court-Access Doctrine*, 133 U. PA. L. REV. 781, 796-99 (1985); *see also* Ann Alexander, *Forum Non Conveniens in the Absence of an Alternative Forum*, 86 COLUM. L. REV. 1000, 1001-02 (1986); Russell J. Weintraub, *International Litigation and Forum Non Conveniens*, 29 TEX. INT'L L.J. 321 (1994).

action and the inconvenience to the parties and witnesses of the trial in that system may dictate that the action be dismissed and tried elsewhere.[196]

The doctrine of forum non conveniens presupposes that the plaintiff can bring the action in another forum.[197] The courts often condition a forum non conveniens dismissal on the defendant submitting to personal jurisdiction in the alternative forum or waiving other obstacles to suit there, such as the statute of limitations.[198] Dismissing an action on the ground of forum non conveniens would be unfair to the plaintiff if no other forum existed in which the defendant could be sued.[199] As discussed below, however, certain aspects of this "alternative forum doctrine" may actually be a disguised preference that forum law be applied to the plaintiff's claim.

Forum non conveniens is a discretionary doctrine.[200] In exercising this discretion, courts consider several factors. These factors focus on the convenience of the parties and the public interest in having the action tried elsewhere. In *Gulf Oil Corp. v. Gilbert*,[201] the U.S. Supreme Court summarized these factors. The Court first addressed the private interests of the litigants:

> An interest to be considered, and the one likely to be most pressed, is the private interest of the litigant. Important considerations are the relative ease of access to sources of proof; availability of compulsory process for attendance of unwilling, and the cost of obtaining attendance of willing, witnesses; possibility of view of premises, if view would be appropriate to the action; and all other practical problems that make trial of a case easy, expeditious and inexpensive. There may also be questions as to the enforceability of a judgment if one is obtained. The court will weigh relative advantages and obstacles to fair trial. It is often said that the plaintiff may not, by choice of an inconvenient forum, "vex," "harass," or "oppress" the defendant by inflicting upon him expense or trouble not

---

196. *See, e.g.,* Wayne F. Foster, Annotation, *Doctrine of Forum Non Conveniens: Assumption or Denial of Jurisdiction in Action Between Nonresident Individuals Based Upon Tort Occurring Within Forum State*, 92 A.L.R.3D 797 (1979); E.L. Strobin, Annotation, *Doctrine of Forum Non Conveniens: Assumption or Denial of Jurisdiction of Action in Matrimonial Disputes*, 9 A.L.R.3D 545 (1966); J.C. Vance, Annotation, *Doctrine of Forum Non Conveniens: Assumption or Denial of Jurisdiction of Contract Action Involving Foreign Elements*, 90 A.L.R.2D 1109 (1963). *See generally* Gary Knapp, Annotation, *Forum Non Conveniens in Products Liability Cases*, 76 A.L.R.4TH 22 (1990).

197. *See* Note, *Requirement of a Second Forum for Application of Forum Non Conveniens*, 43 MINN. L. REV. 1199 (1959); Martin J. McMahon, Annotation, *Forum Non Conveniens Doctrine in State Court as Affected by Availability of Alternative Forum*, 57 A.L.R.4TH 973 (1987). *But see* Ann Alexander, *Forum Non Conveniens in the Absence of an Alternative Forum*, 86 COLUM. L. REV. 1000 (1986) (arguing for dismissal on forum non conveniens grounds in the absence of an alternative forum in some circumstances).

198. *See, e.g.,* Abbott v. Owens-Corning Fiberglass Corp., 191 W. Va. 198, 444 S.E.2d 285 (1994); Tim A. Thomas, Annotation, *Validity and Propriety of Conditions Imposed Upon Proceeding in Foreign Forum by Federal Court in Dismissing Action Under Forum Non Conveniens*, 89 A.L.R. FED. 238 (1988).

199. *See, e.g.,* William L. Reynolds, *The Proper Forum for a Suit: Transnational Forum Non Conveniens and Counter-Suit Injunctions in the Federal Courts*, 70 TEX. L. REV. 1663, 1666 (1992).

200. *See* David W. Robertson, *The Federal Doctrine of Forum Non Conveniens: "An Object Lesson in Uncontrolled Discretion,"* 29 TEX. INT'L L.J. 353 (1994).

201. 330 U.S. 501, 67 S. Ct. 839, 91 L. Ed. 1055 (1947).

necessary to his own right to pursue his remedy. But unless the balance is strongly in favor of the defendant, the plaintiff's choice of forum should rarely be disturbed.[202]

The Supreme Court then addressed the factors relating to the public interest:

> Factors of public interest also have [a] place in applying the doctrine. Administrative difficulties follow for courts when litigation is piled up in congested centers instead of being handled at its origin. Jury duty is a burden that ought not to be imposed upon the people of a community which has no relation to the litigation. In cases which touch the affairs of many persons, there is reason for holding the trial in their view and reach rather than in remote parts of the country where they can learn of it by report only. There is a local interest in having localized controversies decided at home. There is an appropriateness, too, in having the trial of a diversity case in a forum that is at home with the state law that must govern the case, rather than having a court in some other forum untangle problems in conflict of laws, and in law foreign to itself.[203]

In evaluating the private interest factors described in *Gulf Oil Corp. v. Gilbert*, the courts usually give the plaintiff's interest great weight. However, in *Piper Aircraft Co. v. Reyno*,[204] the U.S. Supreme Court held that a distinction should be drawn between plaintiffs who have chosen their home forums and foreign plaintiffs. When a plaintiff chooses a home forum, it is reasonable to assume the choice is convenient. Thus, the courts should give the plaintiff's choice deference unless the balance of convenience is heavily in favor of the alternative forum. On the other hand, when the plaintiff is foreign, it is much less reasonable to assume that the plaintiff has chosen a convenient forum. In such circumstances, the courts may give the plaintiff's choice less weight in the balancing process.[205]

Illustration 4-39. *A*, a citizen of Scotland, is the administrator of the estate of *D*, also a citizen of Scotland. *D* died in an aircraft crash in Scotland. *A* sues *B Corp.*, a corporation incorporated and with its principal place of business in State *X* of the United States, in a U.S. District Court for the District of State

---

202. *Id.* at 508, 67 S. Ct. at 843, 91 L. Ed. at 1062 (footnote omitted).

203. *Id.* at 508-09, 67 S. Ct. at 843, 91 L. Ed. at 1062-63.

204. 454 U.S. 235, 102 S. Ct. 252, 70 L. Ed. 2d 419 (1981). For an excellent discussion of the forum non conveniens analysis in *Piper Aircraft* and its development over the decade following the decision, see William L. Reynolds, *The Proper Forum for a Suit: Transnational Forum Non Conveniens and Counter-Suit Injunctions in the Federal Courts*, 70 TEX. L. REV. 1663 (1992).

205. *See* 454 U.S. at 255-56, 102 S. Ct. at 266, 70 L. Ed. 2d at 436; David J. Dorward, Comment, *The Forum Non Conveniens Doctrine and the Judicial Protection of Multinational Corporations from Forum Shopping Plaintiffs*, 19 U. PA. J. INT'L ECON. L. 141 (1998); Douglas W. Dunham & Eric F. Gladboch, *Forum Non Conveniens and Foreign Plaintiffs in the 1990s*, 24 BROOKLYN J. INT'L L. 665 (1999); Anne McGinness Kearse, *Forfeiting the Home-Court Advantage: The Federal Doctrine of Forum Non Conveniens*, 49 S.C.L. REV. 1303 (1998). Not all courts give plaintiffs' choice less weight when the plaintiffs are foreign nationals. *See, e.g.,* Ison v. E.I. DuPont de Nemours & Co., 729 A.2d 832 (Del. 1999) (fact that plaintiffs are foreign nationals does not deprive them of the presumption that their choice of forum should be respected).

X. A seeks $1,000,000 in damages for the wrongful death of *D. B* is the manufacturer of the aircraft in which *D* was a passenger at the time of the crash. If *B* moves for dismissal on grounds of forum non conveniens, *A's* choice of forum is due less deference that it would be if *A* had chosen *A's* home forum.

* * * * *

When a court dismisses an action on the ground of forum non conveniens and the plaintiff recommences the action in a new forum, the substantive law applied to resolve the dispute will often change. The courts of the new forum will apply their own conflict-of-laws rules to select the applicable law. A defendant will seldom move for a forum non conveniens dismissal if the dismissal will result in a disadvantageous substantive law being applied to the defendant. Thus, any change in applicable substantive law will usually be to the plaintiff's disadvantage. In fact, a plaintiff's initial choice of forum often will be motivated by an advantage in the substantive law that will be applied to the action. Should a change in the applicable substantive law affect the court's decision whether to dismiss the action on forum non conveniens grounds?

In *Piper Aircraft Co. v. Reyno*, discussed above, the U.S. Supreme Court held that the possibility of an unfavorable change in the substantive law applicable to the plaintiff's claim "should ordinarily not be given conclusive or even substantial weight in the forum non conveniens inquiry."[206] However, the Court left open the possibility that a change in law that would deprive the plaintiff of a remedy altogether, rather than simply making it harder to win, could be given substantial weight.[207] The latter possibility is an aspect of the policy that a forum non conveniens dismissal is inappropriate unless an alternative forum exists in which the action can be conducted.[208] However, this aspect of the alternative forum doctrine may simply be a disguised preference for applying the forum state's substantive law to resolve the dispute. If the plaintiff's home nation would not provide the plaintiff with a remedy, the plaintiff should arguably be made to live with that result. On the other hand, the forum state's substantive law permitting recovery may be supported by policies that would be furthered if the defendant is held liable, even to an undeserving plaintiff.

Illustration 4-40. On the facts of *Illustration 4-39*, assume that if the action remained in a federal court of State *X*, the substantive law of State *X* would be applied to resolve the dispute under State *X* conflict-of-laws rules.[209] State *X* follows a strict liability theory in this kind of case. Thus, for *A* to recover, *A* would only have to prove that a defect in the aircraft caused the crash. *A* would not have to prove that the defect was the result of the negligence of *B*. If the action is dismissed on the ground of forum non conveniens in favor of a court in Scotland, the Scottish courts would apply Scottish substantive law to resolve the

---

206. *See* 454 U.S. at 247, 102 S. Ct. at 261, 70 L. Ed. 2d at 430 (emphasis deleted).

207. *See* 454 U.S. at 254-55, 102 S. Ct. at 265, 70 L. Ed. 2d at 435.

208. *See* 454 U.S. at 254 n.22, 102 S. Ct. at 265 n.22, 70 L. Ed. 2d at 435 n.22; William L. Reynolds, *The Proper Forum for a Suit: Transnational Forum Non Conveniens and Counter-Suit Injunctions in the Federal Courts*, 70 Tex. L. Rev. 1663, 1670 (1992).

209. As Chapter 5 discusses, the federal court in State *X* would be obligated, in this kind of case, to apply the conflict-of-laws rules of State *X* to select the substantive law that would be applied to the dispute.

action. Scottish substantive law would require *A* to prove that the crash was the result of *B's* negligence. Under *Piper Aircraft*, the federal court cannot refuse to dismiss the action on forum non conveniens grounds because the dismissal would result in an unfavorable change in law to the plaintiff. Furthermore, in evaluating whether to dismiss, the federal court may not even give substantial weight to the fact that a change in the applicable substantive law would occur if the action is dismissed.

Illustration 4-41. On the facts of *Illustration 4-39*, assume that the alternative forum is in a foreign country that does not recognize the action for wrongful death and would apply its own substantive law to the dispute. If the action remains in the federal court in State *X*, the federal court in State *X* would apply State *X* substantive law. State *X* recognizes the right to recover for wrongful death. Furthermore, State *X* would apply strict liability principles to the plaintiff's claim and allow recovery based on proof that a defect in the aircraft caused the crash. Under these circumstances, the federal court in State *X* may give substantial weight to the fact that the plaintiff would have no remedy at all if the action is dismissed. Based on this factor, the action should probably not be dismissed. It would not be unfair to the plaintiff to dismiss the action and leave the plaintiff without a remedy because the plaintiff's home nation would not provide a remedy. Furthermore, the policies of State *X's* strict liability rule may be furthered by holding the defendant liable. If State *X's* law is meant to deter manufacturers from producing and selling defective products, that policy will be furthered by holding the defendant liable. To the extent that State *X* manufacturers exercise greater care in manufacturing products, the citizens of State *X*, as well as citizens of other states and nations, will benefit.[210]

* * * * *

If a legitimate preference for the application of the forum state's law is indeed the basis for part or all of the alternative forum doctrine, it would be desirable for the courts to recognize the preference openly as part of the forum non conveniens inquiry. However, in *Piper Aircraft*, the Supreme Court actually discouraged forum non conveniens analysis that involved complex choice-of-law inquiries. The Court stated that if the possibility of a change in law were given substantial weight in the inquiry, the trial court would have to make a comparative appraisal of the law that would be applied by the chosen forum and the alternative forum. It would also have to evaluate the rights, remedies, and procedures available in each forum. In the Court's view, "[t]he doctrine of forum non conveniens . . . is designed in part to help courts avoid conducting complex exercises in comparative law."[211]

Yet, despite the Court's discouragement of a choice-of-law analysis, such an analysis is inevitable. A choice-of-law inquiry is, by the Court's own admission, relevant to determine whether the plaintiff would be left with any

---

210. *Cf.* Kamel v. Hill-Rom Co., 108 F.3d 799 (7th Cir. 1997) (permissible to dismiss on the ground of forum non conveniens if the alternative forum provides some remedies for plaintiff's loss, but not the complete range of remedies as the forum); Burke v. Quartey, 969 F. Supp. 921 (D.N.J. 1997) (burden on defendant to show that potential alternative fora permit recovery by plaintiff).

211. 454 U.S. at 251, 102 S. Ct. at 263, 70 L. Ed. 2d at 433 (emphasis deleted).

remedy in the alternative forum if dismissal is granted. In addition, when evaluating the public interest factors of *Gulf Oil Corp. v. Gilbert*, it is relevant to inquire whether the chosen forum will have to apply foreign law if a dismissal is not granted and whether the foreign court will have to apply American law if a dismissal is granted.[212] Therefore, since choice-of-law analysis is an inevitable part of every forum non conveniens determination, the courts should make certain that preferences for the application of forum law are openly stated as part of their evaluative process.

Forum non conveniens determinations are committed to the discretion of the trial court. Therefore, an appellate court should not reverse a decision to dismiss an action on forum non conveniens grounds unless the trial court has abused its discretion. This standard limits the appellate court to a review of whether the trial court's analysis of the forum non conveniens factors was reasonable. The appellate court may not substitute its own judgment for that of the trial court by independently weighing each of the factors that are relevant to the analysis.[213]

(b) The Uniform Transfer of Litigation Act

Forum non conveniens dismissals have traditionally been used when there is a substantially more convenient forum in another judicial system. Transfer between different judicial systems has not been possible because no law existed authorizing such transfers. This situation may change with regard to actions commenced in state courts when a substantially more convenient forum exists in a court of another state. In 1991, the National Conference of Commissioners on Uniform State Laws approved the Uniform Transfer of Litigation Act,[214] which would, if adopted by the states, permit transfers between state courts in different states.[215] One of the explicit rationales for the Act is to provide a "better remedy" for actions commenced in inconvenient fora than the traditional doctrine of forum non conveniens.[216]

The Uniform Act permits designated state courts to transfer all or part of an action to a court in another state that consents to the transfer and that can exercise jurisdiction over the matters transferred.[217] The transferring court need not have subject-matter or personal jurisdiction to order a transfer.[218] A transfer may be ordered "to serve the fair, effective, and efficient administration of justice

---

212. *See* William L. Reynolds, *The Proper Forum for a Suit: Transnational Forum Non Conveniens and Counter-Suit Injunctions in the Federal Courts*, 70 TEX. L. REV. 1663, 1671, 1677-79 (1992).

213. *See Piper Aircraft*, 454 U.S. at 257-61, 102 S. Ct. at 266-68, 70 L. Ed. 2d at 436-38.

214. 14 U.L.A. 189 (Supp. 1999).

215. For a brief history and general discussion of the Uniform Act, see Thomas D. Rowe, Jr., *Jurisdictional and Transfer Proposals for Complex Litigation*, 10 REV. LITIG. 325, 354-58 (1991).

216. *See* 14 U.L.A. at 189, pref. note (Supp. 1999).

217. *See id.* §§ 101-103 at 191-94.

218. *See id.* §§ 102-103, at 192, 194. The stated rationale for allowing a court without jurisdiction to order a transfer is that even though a court lacks jurisdiction, it possesses other powers, such as power to order discovery on the jurisdictional issue, to adjudicate jurisdictional issues in a way that will be binding under the doctrine of issue preclusion, and so forth. "The power to transfer to a court that does have personal jurisdiction is properly added to this list." *Id.* § 103 cmt., at 92.

and the convenience of the parties and witnesses'' after the court considers ''all relevant factors, including the interest of each plaintiff in selecting a forum and the public interest in securing a single litigation and disposition of related matters.''[219] A transfer may be ordered on motion of a party or on the court's own initiative after notice and an opportunity to be heard.[220] The transfer order must state the reasons for the transfer.[221] If only part of an action is ordered transferred, the transfer order must identify that part as a term of the transfer. The transfer order may state other terms of the transfer.[222] The transfer order may be filed in the receiving court by the transferring court or a party.[223] The transfer is effective when an order accepting the transfer is filed in the transferring court.[224]

  An order granting or refusing a transfer is made reviewable only by extraordinary writ or permissive interlocutory appeal at the time the order is entered. If an order is not reviewed prior to transfer, it is not reviewable in the transferring state except as to matters returned or transferred back by the receiving court.[225] In addition, an order transferring a case is not reviewable in the receiving state by ''appeal or otherwise.''[226] However, an order accepting a transfer, refusing to accept a transfer, granting a return, or refusing to grant a return is reviewable in the receiving state, but only by extraordinary writ or permissive interlocutory appeal at the time the order is entered.[227] All other orders or rulings made by the receiving court may be reviewed in the receiving state. The receiving state may also review all orders and rulings of the transferring court not reviewed before the transfer took place, except the order granting the transfer.[228]

  The Act authorizes state courts with subject-matter and personal jurisdiction to accept transfers from other states, even if the transferring court does not have subject-matter or personal jurisdiction.[229] In addition, a receiving court that possesses subject-matter jurisdiction but lacks personal jurisdiction is authorized to exercise personal jurisdiction if the transferring court had both subject-matter and personal jurisdiction.[230] The rationale for the latter power is that ''a court with personal jurisdiction [the transferring court] should be able to exercise sufficient control over a case to determine that the litigation is better handled in a court that could not command personal jurisdiction over all parties had the action first been brought there.''[231] Furthermore, although the receiving

---

219. *Id.* § 104, at 194.
220. *Id.* § 105, at 196.
221. *Id.*
222. *Id.*
223. *Id.*
224. *Id.* § 105, at 196; § 206, at 202; *see also id.* §§ 106 (Transmitting Record), 107 (Pending Proceedings), at 197.
225. *Id.* § 109, at 198.
226. *Id.* § 218, at 208.
227. *Id.*
228. *Id.*
229. *Id.* §§ 201-202, at 200.
230. *Id.* § 203, at 201.
231. *Id.* § 102 cmt., at 192.

court cannot exercise personal jurisdiction "beyond the limits of due process or other constitutional constraints," application "of the underlying constitutional concepts may be affected by the transfer process."[232] Especially important in this regard is the fact that the receiving court must consent to the transfer, which "affords strong protection against the danger of improvident or unfair transfer."[233]

A receiving court can refuse a transfer for any reason, but must state its reasons.[234] After transfer, if the receiving court determines that it lacks jurisdiction of all or part of the matters transferred, it may return the matters over which it lacks jurisdiction and any additional matters to the transferring court.[235] In addition, the receiving court may return any transferred matter pursuant to the terms of the transferring order.[236] A return order is effective when filed by the receiving court or the parties with the transferring court.[237]

As noted above, a transfer order can state the terms of transfer. However, the receiving court can depart from the terms stated in the transfer order "for good cause."[238] This power is necessary because, as the case develops, the receiving court will ultimately be in a better position to know whether the terms of the order are still justified.[239]

One question under the Act concerns choice-of-law decisions after transfer. The Act contains several provisions that dictate the applicable law on specific subjects. Section 209 states that the receiving court may not dismiss a matter based on the statute of limitations if the matter would not be barred by limitations in the transferring state, as long as the transferring court possessed subject-matter and personal jurisdiction.[240] Section 211 states that a proceeding pending at the time of transfer must be completed by the receiving court according to the procedural rules of the transferring court, "measuring applicable time limits as if the proceeding had been initiated ten days after the transfer took effect, unless otherwise ordered by the transferring court or the receiving court."[241] Section 213 provides that the law that would be applied by the

---

232. *Id.* Under the modern due process test for personal jurisdiction, one of the factors taken into account is "the interstate judicial system's interest in the most efficient resolution of controversies." Under this factor, mechanisms such as the Uniform Act can be taken into account in evaluating whether due process is violated. *See* Chapter 3(G)(2)*(b)* ("Specific Jurisdiction") *supra*.

233. 14 U.L.A. § 102 cmt., at 193 (Supp. 1999).

234. *Id.* § 204, at 201.

235. *Id.* § 214, at 206.

236. *Id.* § 215, at 207.

237. *Id.* § 216, at 207.

238. *Id.* § 208.

239. *Id.* cmt. The Act contains several provisions regulating proceedings after transfer. Under § 210 the receiving court is to treat the matters transferred as if they were initially filed on the date of filing in the transferring court. Section 211 provides that a proceeding completed in the transferring court will have the same "effect" in the receiving court as in the transferring court unless the receiving court otherwise orders. Section 212 provides that an injunction or other order in effect at the time of transfer will remain in effect until vacated or amended by the receiving court. Section 213 states that the receiving court should permit counsel of record in the transferring court to appear, but may require local counsel to appear also if necessary to ensure the orderly disposition of the transferred matters.

240. 14 U.L.A. § 209, at 203 (Supp. 1999).

241. *Id.* § 211, at 204.

transferring court governs contracts between clients and counsel who appeared in the transferring court. It also applies to any ground advanced to disqualify counsel who appeared in the transferring court.[242]

Beyond the sections dealing with choice of law on specific subjects, no provision dictates how the receiving court should determine the applicable law. Nevertheless, the commentary to the Act suggests that the drafters anticipated the transfer order would often control such decisions. The commentary to § 208 states that "the terms of transfer . . . might include such matters as . . . a designation of the law to be applied to the dispute."[243] However, § 208 provides that the receiving court may depart from the terms of the transfer order for good cause, and the commentary states that "[a]s the case unfolds in the receiving court, it may turn out that . . . a different choice of law is fairer."[244]

Given the ability to depart from the terms of the transfer order, the receiving courts may often end up making independent choice-of-law decisions, rather than applying the law designated by the transfer order. Furthermore, the Act does not directly indicate what the receiving court should do in the absence of a term in the transfer order dictating the applicable law. However, the Act is intended to replace the doctrine of forum non conveniens when the alternative forum is the court of another state. When a forum non conveniens dismissal occurs, the alternative forum always makes its own choice-of-law decisions. The same will likely remain true under the Act in the absence of a term in the transfer order designating the applicable law. Thus, unlike choice of law in federal transfer cases, discussed in the next subsection, a receiving court under the Act will not likely feel bound by the conflict-of-laws rules of the transferring state.

2. Transfer of Venue Between Federal Courts

(a) Section 1404(a) Transfers

In the 1948 revision of the Judicial Code, Congress largely replaced the doctrine of forum non conveniens in the federal courts. Section 1404(a) provides for a change of venue "[f]or the convenience of parties and witnesses, in the interest of justice" to "any other district or division" where the action "might have been brought."[245] In *Hoffman v. Blaski*,[246] the Supreme Court held that the "where it might have been brought" language of the statute prevents transfer

---

242. *Id.* § 213, at 205.

243. *Id.* § 208 cmt., at 203.

244. *Id.*

245. *See* 28 U.S.C. § 1404(a). *See generally* Stowell R. Kelner, Note, *"Adrift on an Uncharted Sea": A Survey of Section 1404(a) Transfer in the Federal System,* 67 N.Y.U. L. REV. 612 (1992); Edmund Kitch, *Section 1404(a) of the Judicial Code: In the Interests of Justice or Injustice?* 40 IND. L.J. 99 (1965); David E. Steinberg, *The Motion to Transfer and the Interests of Justice,* 66 NOTRE DAME L. REV. 443 (1990); C.P. Jhong, Annotation, *Construction and Application of Change of Venue or Transfer Provision of Judicial Code (28 USC § 1404(a)), Apart from Questions of Convenience and Justice of Transfer,* 7 A.L.R. FED. 9 (1971); Annotation, *Questions as to Convenience and Justice of Transfer Under Forum Non Conveniens Provision of Judicial Code (28 U.S.C. § 1404(a)),* 1 A.L.R. FED. 15 (1969).

246. 363 U.S. 335, 80 S. Ct. 1084, 4 L. Ed. 2d 1254 (1960).

to a district where venue or personal jurisdiction would have been improper as an original matter. *Hoffman* means that if the defendant moves for a change of venue under § 1404(a) to a location where venue or personal jurisdiction would have been improper, the defendant cannot be deemed to have "consented" or "waived" the venue or personal jurisdiction objections. In effect, this holding treats the "where it might have been brought" language as jurisdictional.[247]

After the enactment of § 1404(a), transfer to another federal district court under the terms of this section is the appropriate mode of disposition in a case where the other federal district court is more suitable for the trial of the case. Thus, today, dismissal on forum non conveniens grounds is appropriate only in rare instances where the alternative forum is a state court or the court of a foreign country, both instances in which § 1404(a), by its terms, is inoperative.[248] Dismissal on forum non conveniens grounds in preference of a state court in another location will rarely be appropriate, considering that transfer to another federal court in the same location will usually be possible. As a practical matter, therefore, the federal doctrine of forum non conveniens is limited to dismissal in favor of foreign nation tribunals.[249]

Transfer under § 1404(a) presents some complicated choice-of-law problems. In *Van Dusen v. Barrack*,[250] the Supreme Court held that after a transfer granted on the defendant's motion, the transferee district court must apply the same substantive law that the transferor district court would have applied. In *Ferens v. John Deere Co.*,[251] the Court held that the same rule would be applied to a transfer granted on motion of the plaintiff. In *Ferens*, the Court also indicated in a dictum that the *Van Dusen* rule would be applied to transfers when (1) both the defendant and the plaintiff move for transfer; (2) a district court grants a transfer on its own initiative; (3) the plaintiff moves for transfer after the defendant removes an action from state to federal court; (4) only one of several plaintiffs moves for transfer; or (5) through no fault of the plaintiff, circumstances change, making a once desirable forum inconvenient.[252]

Illustration 4-42. *A*, a citizen and resident of State *X*, is injured in State *X* when a machine manufactured by the *B Corp.* malfunctions. *B* is incorporated with its principal place of business in State *Y*. *A* waits too long to commence an action for damages in State *X*, and the statute of limitations runs. *A* commences an action for personal injuries against *B* in a U.S. District Court for the District of State *Z*, where the statute of limitations has not run. *B* does extensive business in State *Z* and is, therefore, subject to personal jurisdiction there. Federal venue

---

247. For a criticism of the result in *Hoffman* and a recommendation that transfers be permitted when the moving party could have sued the non-moving party in the transferee district, see Michael J. Waggoner, *Section 1404(a), "Where It Might Have Been Brought": Brought by Whom?* 1988 B.Y.U. L. REV. 67.

248. 15 CHARLES A. WRIGHT ET AL., FEDERAL PRACTICE AND PROCEDURE: JURISDICTION AND RELATED MATTERS (VENUE) § 3828, at 279-80 (2d ed. 1986).

249. *See* C.P. Jhong, Annotation, *Application of Common-Law Doctrine of Forum Non Conveniens in Federal Courts After Enactment of 28 USC § 1404(a) Authorizing Transfer to Another District*, 10 A.L.R. FED. 352 (1972).

250. 376 U.S. 612, 84 S. Ct. 805, 11 L. Ed. 2d 945 (1964).

251. 494 U.S. 516, 110 S. Ct. 1274, 108 L. Ed. 2d 443 (1990).

252. *See id.* at 529, 110 S. Ct. at 1283, 108 L. Ed. 2d at 456.

is also proper in State *Z* under 28 U.S.C. § 1391(a)(1) & (c) because *B* is subject to personal jurisdiction in State *Z*. After commencing the action, *A* moves to transfer the case to the District of State *X* under § 1404(a). The district court in State *Z* grants the motion. After transfer, the district court in State *X* must apply the State *Z* statute of limitations and consider the action timely.

* * * * *

Van Dusen removed an incentive for defendants to use § 1404(a) to obtain a different applicable substantive law, rather than simply a more convenient forum. As *Illustration 4-42* demonstrates, under *Ferens*, the existence of § 1404(a) constitutes an incentive for a plaintiff to engage in interstate forum shopping for a federal court to obtain, first, a desirable substantive law, and, subsequently, a convenient place of trial. The *Ferens* result might be justified if it were based on important policies supporting the exercise of federal jurisdiction. In fact, both *Van Dusen* and *Ferens* purported to be based on such policies—the limits on the power of federal courts to make law in diversity cases. These policies will be discussed in Chapter 5. There, it will be demonstrated that *Van Dusen* articulated a rule correctly based on the policies limiting federal court lawmaking, but *Ferens* did not.[253]

The factors taken into account in determining whether to transfer a case under § 1404(a) are generally the same as are taken into account in determining whether a forum non conveniens dismissal is appropriate. However, because transfer of an action is not as harsh to the plaintiff as dismissal under the doctrine of forum non conveniens, the discretion of the district courts to transfer under the statute is broader than the discretion to dismiss under the common-law doctrine.[254] In *Stewart Organization, Inc. v. Ricoh Corp.*,[255] the Supreme Court held that the existence of a forum selection clause would not absolutely control the question whether a case should be transferred under § 1404(a). Rather, a forum selection clause is simply one factor to be weighed in the balance to determine whether a transfer is appropriate.[256]

Under *Van Dusen*, discussed above, the Supreme Court has held that the district court where the action is commenced should consider the effect of the law that will be applied after transfer on the convenience of the parties and

---

253. *See* Chapter 5(D)(2)*(b)* ("Special *Erie* Doctrine Problems in Cases of Transfer Under 28 U.S.C. § 1404(a)") *infra.* However, even if plaintiffs are able to obtain a choice-of-law advantage by selecting an inconvenient (though proper) forum in which to commence an action, there is empirical evidence that transfer counterbalances the forum shopping and diminishes the plaintiff's chances of winning the action. Thus, some or all of the burden of pretrial litigation over transfer motions may be outweighed by the diminution of inaccurate results that transfer produces. *See* Kevin M. Clermont & Theodore Eisenberg, *Exorcising the Evil of Forum-Shopping,* 80 CORNELL L. REV. 1507 (1995). For a defense of forum shopping in various forms, see Mary Garvey Algero, *In Defense of Forum Shopping: A Realistic Look at Selecting Venue,* 78 NEB. L. REV. 79 (1999).

254. *See* Norwood v. Kirkpatrick, 349 U.S. 29, 32, 75 S. Ct. 544, 546-47, 99 L. Ed. 789, 793 (1955); *see also* Piper Aircraft Co. v. Reyno, 454 U.S. 235, 253, 258 n.26, 102 S. Ct. 252, 264-65, 267 n.26, 70 L. Ed. 2d 419, 434, 437 n.26 (1981). For a complete discussion of the cases applying the factors under § 1404(a), see 15 CHARLES A. WRIGHT ET AL., FEDERAL PRACTICE AND PROCEDURE: JURISDICTION AND RELATED MATTERS (VENUE) §§ 3847-54 (2d ed. 1986).

255. 487 U.S. 22, 108 S. Ct. 2239, 101 L. Ed. 2d 22 (1988).

256. *See id.* at 29-30, 108 S. Ct. 2239, 2244, 101 L. Ed. 2d 22, 31 (1988).

witnesses.[257] Under the *Van Dusen* rule, the transferee district court must apply the law that the transferor district court would have applied. Thus, if the transferor court determines that it would apply the substantive law of the state in which it is sitting under that state's conflict-of-laws rules, the transferee district court will have to do likewise. If the laws of the transferor state involve complexities that will cause inconvenience to the transferee court, then, under *Van Dusen*, that is one factor militating against transfer. Conversely, if the transferor district court determines that the conflict-of-laws rules of the transferor state require application of the transferee state's substantive law, no inconvenience would occur after transfer in administering the applicable substantive law. Even if inconvenience would result after transfer due to the applicable law, other factors bearing on the convenience of the parties and witnesses and the interests of justice may still justify the transfer.[258]

One other question that has arisen under § 1404(a) is whether the *Van Dusen-Ferens* rule governs in cases where federal law supplies the rule of decision. The issue arises because until the U.S. Supreme Court resolves disputed issues of federal law, conflicts can exist among different federal circuits about the meaning and application of that law. Thus, if an action is commenced in a U.S. District Court with proper venue and personal jurisdiction and transferred to a district court in another circuit under § 1404(a), the issue would be whether the transferee district court should follow the view of its own circuit about the content of federal law or that of the transferor circuit, assuming that the two differ.[259]

As discussed in Chapter 5,[260] below, the *Van Dusen-Ferens* rule is based in part on the obligations of federal courts in diversity actions to follow state law under the *Erie* doctrine. The *Erie* doctrine has no application where federal substantive law governs the case. Rather, federal law is, in theory, uniform and supreme throughout the entire country. Although there may be temporary disagreement about the content of federal law among the circuits, there is, in theory, only one correct answer to the issue of its meaning. In contrast, under state law, the meaning of even identically worded statutes may permissibly differ from state to state. Thus, federal courts should attempt in every case to resolve issues of federal law as they should be resolved, instead of applying the view of some other federal court.[261] In addition, it is important to note that application

---

257. *See Van Dusen*, 376 U.S. at 643-46, 84 S. Ct. at 823-24, 11 L. Ed. 2d at 965-67.

258. *Cf.* Houk v. Kimberly-Clark Corp., 613 F. Supp. 923 (W.D. Mo. 1985) (fact that forum will have to apply foreign law given little weight in determining whether to grant transfer where foreign law is uncomplicated).

259. For a discussion of this problem, *see, e.g., In re* Korean Airlines Disaster, 829 F.2d 1171 (D.C. Cir. 1987) (Ginsburg, J.), *aff'd on other grounds sub nom.* Chan v. Korean Airlines, Ltd., 490 U.S. 122, 109 S. Ct. 1676, 104 L. Ed. 2d 113 (1989); Richard L. Marcus, *Conflict Among Circuits and Transfers Within the Federal Judicial System*, 93 YALE L.J. 677, 721 (1984); Joan E. Schaffer, *Federal Circuit "Choice of Law":* Erie *Through the Looking Glass*, 81 IOWA L. REV. 1173 (1996); Joan Steinman, *Law of the Case: A Judicial Puzzle in Consolidated and Transferred Cases and in Multidistrict Litigation*, 135 U. PA. L. REV. 595, 662-706 (1987).

260. *See* Chapter 5(D)(2)*(b)* ("Special *Erie* Doctrine Problems in Cases of Transfer Under 28 U.S.C. § 1404(a)") *infra*.

261. The vast majority of federal courts and commentators take this approach. *See, e.g., In re* Korean Airlines Disaster, 829 F.2d 1171 (D.C. Cir. 1987) (Ginsburg, J.), *aff'd on other grounds sub nom.* Chan v. Korean Airlines, Ltd., 490 U.S. 122, 109 S. Ct. 1676, 104 L. Ed. 2d 113 (1989); Richard L. Marcus, *Conflict* of the transferor circuit's view of federal law would produce a different interpretation of federal substantive rights to different litigants in the transferee circuit, depending on whether an action is commenced in the circuit or transferred there.[262] This problem was not present in *Van Dusen* and *Ferens*. Under those cases, the transferee court will apply the view of the highest authority in the transferor state about the meaning of the transferor state's law.[263] Similarly, if an action is originally commenced in the transferee state and that state selects another state's law as applicable to the case, it will apply the view of the highest authority in the other state to determine the meaning of that law.

(b) Section 1406 Transfers

Transfer under § 1404(a) is possible only if venue is proper in the district in which the action is originally brought.[264] If venue is improper in the district where the action is brought, transfer is controlled by § 1406. Section 1406 provides that in such circumstances, the district court "shall dismiss, or if it be in the interest of justice, transfer such case to any district or division in which it could have been brought."[265] Transfer is possible under § 1406 even if personal jurisdiction over the defendant is also lacking in the transferor district.[266] Like transfers under § 1404(a), transfer under § 1406 must be to a district where venue would be proper and personal jurisdiction would be obtainable over the defendant.[267]

Among Circuits and Transfers Within the Federal Judicial System, 93 YALE L.J. 677, 721 (1984); Joan E. Schaffer, *Federal Circuit "Choice of Law"*: Erie *Through the Looking Glass*, 81 IOWA L. REV. 1173 (1996); Joan Steinman, *Law of the Case: A Judicial Puzzle in Consolidated and Transferred Cases and in Multidistrict Litigation*, 135 U. PA. L. REV. 595, 662-706 (1987); 15 CHARLES A. WRIGHT ET AL., FEDERAL PRACTICE AND PROCEDURE: JURISDICTION AND RELATED MATTERS § 3846, at 67-68, and authorities there cited in n.34 (2d ed. 1999 Supp.); for contrary authority *see id.* at 68 n.35.

262.   *See In re* Korean Airlines Disaster, 829 F.2d 1171, 1175 (D.C. Cir. 1987), *aff'd on other grounds sub nom.* Chan v. Korean Airlines, Ltd., 490 U.S. 122, 109 S. Ct. 1676, 104 L. Ed. 2d 113 (1989).

263.   *See Korean Airlines*, 828 F.2d at 1174-75. In some federal question cases, the *Van Dusen-Ferens* rule should control. For example, Congress sometimes enacts statutes creating federal claims, but does not provide a statute of limitations to govern such claims. In such cases, the federal courts apply the state statute of limitations that is most analogous to the federal claim. Thus, this situation is indistinguishable from the one in *Ferens*, in which the limitations periods of the transferor and transferee state differed. *See generally* Kimberly Jade Norwood, *Double Forum Shopping and the Extension of* Ferens *to Federal Claims that Borrow State Limitations Periods*, 44 EMORY L.J. 501 (1995).

264.   *See* 15 CHARLES A. WRIGHT ET AL., FEDERAL PRACTICE AND PROCEDURE: JURISDICTION AND RELATED MATTERS (VENUE) § 3844, at 332 (2d ed. 1986), and cases there cited. However, numerous cases hold that if venue is proper, but personal jurisdiction is lacking in the district where the action is originally commenced, the action may be transferred under § 1404(a). *See id.* at 333 and cases there cited in note 12.

265.   28 U.S.C. § 1406(a). *See generally* C.P. Jhoma, Annotation, *Construction and Application of Federal Statute (28 U.S.C. § 1406) Providing for Dismissal or Transfer of Cases for Improper Venue*, 3 A.L.R. FED. 467 (1970). Chapter 5 discusses complicated questions of the applicable law in § 1404 and § 1406 transfer cases.

266.   *See* Goldlawr, Inc. v. Heiman, 369 U.S. 463, 82 S. Ct. 913, 8 L. Ed. 2d 39 (1962). Some courts have held that if venue is proper and personal jurisdiction is lacking, transfer is still appropriate under § 1406(a). *See* 15 CHARLES A. WRIGHT ET AL., FEDERAL PRACTICE AND PROCEDURE: JURISDICTION AND RELATED MATTERS (VENUE) § 3827, at 264-65 (2d ed. 1986) and cases there cited in note 11 (1986). Other cases hold transfer proper in these circumstances under § 1404(a). *See id.* § 3844, at 333 and cases there cited in note 12.

267.   *See* 15 CHARLES A. WRIGHT ET AL., FEDERAL PRACTICE AND PROCEDURE: JURISDICTION AND RELATED MATTERS (VENUE) § 3827, at 274 (2d ed. 1986).

The Supreme Court's decision in *Stewart Organization* (examined in subsection *(a)* above) did not discuss whether an action brought in a statutorily proper venue, but in contravention of a forum selection clause, should be treated as one in which venue is proper or improper. Yet this question has an important bearing on whether transfer should be under § 1404(a) or § 1406. It also has a bearing on whether the transferor or transferee's law should be applied after transfer (discussed below). It is actually arguable that neither § 1404(a), nor § 1406 was applicable to the issue in *Stewart Organization*.[268] The question may be foreclosed by stare decisis in § 1404(a) transfer cases due to the Supreme Court's holding in the case. However, it has not been deemed foreclosed in § 1406 transfer cases, where forum selection clauses, if otherwise enforceable, have controlled.[269]

In cases in which venue is improper and the action is transferred under § 1406, the *Van Dusen-Ferens* rule is inapplicable. After transfer, the law of the transferee state governs in such cases.[270] It would be unconscionable to allow a plaintiff to fix the applicable law by initially selecting an improper forum in which to sue.

(c) Section 1407 Transfers

Another transfer provision, 28 U.S.C. § 1407, authorizes the transfer of civil actions pending in different districts "to *any* district for coordinated or consolidated *pretrial* proceedings."[271] Section 1407 also establishes a Judicial Panel on Multidistrict Litigation.[272] For transfer, the actions must involve "one or more common questions of fact."[273] Also, the panel must determine that the

---

268. *See* Richard D. Freer, *Erie's Mid-Life Crises*, 63 TUL. L. REV. 1087, 1117-21 (1989); Walter L. Heiser, *Forum Selection Clauses in Federal Courts: Limitations on Enforcement After* Stewart Organization *and* Carnival Cruise, 45 FLA. L. REV. 553, 590-95 (1993); Allen R. Stein, *Erie and Court Access*, 100 YALE L.J. 1935, 1961-65 (1991).

269. *See, e.g.,* International Software Sys., Inc. v. Amplicon, Inc., 77 F.3d 112 (5th Cir. 1996) (*Stewart Organization* does not control in cases involving motions to dismiss based on forum selection clauses; uniform approach among circuits discussed); *cf.* Amermed Corp. v. Disetronic Holding AG, 6 F. Supp. 2d 1371 (N.D. Ga. 1998) (provision governing dismissal for improper venue, § 1406, is silent as to dismissal on any ground other than statutorily deficient venue).

270. *See* Adam v. J.B. Hunt Transp., Inc., 130 F.3d 219, 230 (6th Cir. 1997) (transferee state's law applies after § 1406 transfer); Wisland v. Admiral Beverage Corp., 119 F.3d 733 (8th Cir. 1997), *cert. denied*, 522 U.S. 1112, 118 S. Ct. 1043, 140 L. Ed. 2d 108 (1998) (law of transferee state applies after a § 1406 transfer).

271. 28 U.S.C. § 1407(a) (emphasis added); *see* George T. Conway III, Note, *The Consolidation of Multistate Litigation in State Courts*, 96 YALE L.J. 1099 (1987) (proposing that Congress confer upon the Judicial Panel the power to direct litigation to and from the state courts as well). *See generally* 15 CHARLES A. WRIGHT ET AL., FEDERAL PRACTICE AND PROCEDURE: JURISDICTION AND RELATED MATTERS (VENUE) §§ 3861-3868 (2d ed. 1986); Wilson W. Herdon & Ernest R. Higginbotham, *Complex Multidistrict Litigation—An Overview of 28 U.S.C.A. § 1407*, 31 BAYLOR L. REV. 33 (1979); Note, *The Judicial Panel and the Conduct of Multidistrict Litigation*, 87 HARV. L. REV. 1001 (1974).

272. 28 U.S.C. § 1407(d). The panel is appointed by the Chief Justice of the United States. The panel consists of seven circuit or district judges. No more than one judge from a circuit may be appointed. *Id.* Upon its own motion or on motion by any party involved in one of the actions sought to be consolidated, the panel determines whether a transfer should be made, which district should be the transferee forum, and who should preside as the transferee judge. 28 U.S.C. § 1407(c). The concurrence of four of the seven members of the panel is required for any action to be taken. 28 U.S.C. § 1407(d).

273. 28 U.S.C. § 1407(a).

transfer ''will be for the convenience of parties and witnesses and will promote the just and efficient conduct of such actions.''[274] Generally speaking, the kind of case transferred involves complex litigation, such as antitrust or securities actions. After the pretrial proceedings have been completed, the actions are then remanded back to the districts from which they were transferred.[275] In *Lexecon, Inc. v. Milberg Weiss Beishad Hynes & Lerach*,[276] the Supreme Court held that after transfer of a case under § 1407 for pretrial proceedings, the transferee court could not permanently transfer the case to itself under § 1404(a) for trial.[277]

SECTION E. INJUNCTIONS AGAINST EXTRASTATE LITIGATION AND OTHER DEVICES FOR CONTROLLING THE LOCATION OF SUIT

In addition to the methods discussed in earlier sections for controlling the location of suit, it is sometimes possible, when multiple actions have been commenced (or are threatened) in different states or countries concerning the same subject matter, to obtain an injunction in one forum preventing litigation in another or a stay of proceedings in one court in deference to the other. In effect, these devices, when available, allow litigants to limit the venue of an action to a single forum.

1. Injunctions Against Suit

The general rule is that parallel actions in different jurisdictions are allowed to proceed until a judgment is reached in one jurisdiction that can be pleaded as res judicata in the other.[278] However, under appropriate circumstances, injunctions against foreign litigation, which were prohibited in some early decisions, are now widely considered to be proper.[279] An injunction

---

274. *Id.* Even if these requirements are met, transfer is not automatic. *See, e.g., In re* Truck Accident Near Alamagordo, 387 F. Supp. 732 (J.P.M.L. 1975).

275. 28 U.S.C. § 1407(a). By consent of the parties or by use of § 1404(a), however, a consolidated trial may take place in the transferee court. *See also* Menowitz v. Brown, 991 F.2d 36 (2d Cir. 1993) (*Van Dusen-Ferens* rule, discussed *supra* and in Chapter 5(D)(2)*(b)* (''Special *Erie* Doctrine Problems in Cases of Transfer Under 28 U.S.C. § 1404(a)'') *infra*, not applicable in a § 1407 transfer cased based on federal question jurisdiction). *See generally* ALI COMPLEX LITIGATION: STATUTORY RECOMMENDATIONS AND ANALYSIS WITH REPORTER'S STUDY ch. 3 (1994) (discussing federal intrasystem consolidation).

276. 523 U.S. 26, 118 S. Ct. 956, 140 L. Ed. 2d 62 (1998).

277. It has been held that, after a transfer under § 1407, a district court should apply the law of the state that would have been applied to the individual cases if they had not been transferred. *See In re* Temporomandibular Joint (TMJ) Implants Prods. Liab. Litig., 97 F.3d 1050 (8th Cir. 1996).

278. *See, e.g.,* Gau Shan Co. v. Bankers Trust Co., 956 F.2d 1349, 1352 (6th Cir. 1992); Golden Rule Ins. Co. v. Harper, 925 S.W.2d 649, 651 (Tex. 1996); Margarita Trevino de Coale, *Stay, Dimiss, Enjoin, or Abstain?: A Survey of Foreign Parallel Litigation in the Federal Courts of the United States*, 17 B.U. INT'L L.J. 79, 80-81 (1999).

279. *See* Annotation, *Injunction by State Court Against Action in Court of Another State*, 6 A.L.R.2d 896, 899 (1949); *see also* Robin Cheryl Miller, Annotation, *Propriety of Federal Court Injunction Against Suit in Foreign Country*, 78 A.L.R. FED. 831 (1986); Milton Roberts, Annotation, *Propriety of Injunction by Federal* against prosecuting or commencing an action in another jurisdiction is not directed against the court in the other state or nation, but against the party who brought, or is threatening to bring, the foreign action.[280]

There are two general approaches to injunctions against foreign litigation.[281] The "restrictive" approach only permits injunctions to protect the jurisdiction of the forum court or to prevent evasion of important public policies of the forum.[282] Protection of the forum's jurisdiction by an injunction against a foreign suit is most justified in cases in which jurisdiction is based on the presence of property within the court's jurisdictional boundaries–*i.e.,* in in-rem or quasi-in-rem actions. In that situation, concurrent proceedings in a foreign jurisdiction pose "the danger that the foreign court will order the transfer of the property out of the jurisdictional boundaries of the first court, thus depriving it of jurisdiction over the matter."[283] When the proceedings are in personam, as opposed to in rem or quasi in rem, an injunction against a foreign suit will be justifiable when the foreign court is attempting to assert exclusive jurisdiction over an action. Under such circumstances, the foreign proceeding is not merely following a "parallel track," but threatens to deprive the forum proceeding of validity.[284] In addition, it seems settled that once the forum has rendered a judgment on the merits of an action, a parallel proceeding in another jurisdiction dealing with the same claim may be enjoined to prevent "evasion of the judgment through vexatious or oppressive relitigation."[285] The latter circumstance, however, should be limited to relitigation in the courts of foreign countries, because within the states of the United States, a plea of res judicata in the "foreign" court will preclude the action under the full-faith-and-credit implementing statute, 28 U.S.C. § 1738.[286]

The ability to issue an injunction to protect important public policies of the forum may seem broad enough to undermine completely the principle allowing parallel proceedings in different jurisdictions. However, courts following the "restrictive" view do not enforce the "public policy" rule simply to prevent

---

Court in Civil Action Restraining Prosecution of Later Civil Action in Another Federal Court Where One or More Parties or Issues Are, or Allegedly Are, Same, 42 A.L.R. FED. 592 (1979).

280. *See* Annotation, *Injunction By State Court Against Action in Another State,* 6 A.L.R.2D 896, 899 (1949); In Baker *ex rel.* Thomas v. General Motors Corp., 522 U.S. 222, 118 S. Ct. 657, 139 L. Ed. 2d 580 (1998), the Supreme Court held that full faith and credit did not require Missouri to give effect to a Michigan injunction restraining a former employee of G.M. from testifying as an expert witness against G.M. However, the case appears merely to confirm the settled proposition that a state judgment may not ordinarily bind nonparties to the judgment; and the Court indicated that the judgment would be preclusive between the employee and G.M., who were parties. Thus, *Baker* appears not to undermine the results of the cases discussed in this subsection.

281. *See, e.g.,* Gau Shan Co. v. Bankers Trust Co., 956 F.2d 1349, 1353-54 (6th Cir. 1992) (discussing the different standards applied in the U.S. Courts of Appeals).

282. *See id.* at 1353; Sea Containers Ltd. v. Stena AB, 890 F.2d 1205 (D.C. Cir. 1989); China Trade & Dev. Corp. v. M.V. Choong Yong, 837 F.2d 33 (2d Cir. 1987); Laker Airways Ltd. v. Sabena, Belgian World Airlines, 731 F.2d 909 (D.C. Cir. 1984).

283. Gau Shan Co. v. Bankers Trust Co., 956 F.2d 1349, 1356 (6th Cir. 1992); *see also* China Trade & Dev. Corp. v. M.V. Choong Yong, 837 F.2d 33 (2d Cir. 1987).

284. *See* Laker Airways Ltd. v. Sabena, Belgian World Airlines, 731 F.2d 909, 929-30 (D.C. Cir. 1984).

285. *Id.* at 928.

286. *See* Chapter 13(F)(1) ("Enforcement of State Judgments") *infra.*

duplicative foreign litigation involving the same parties and issues.[287] Indeed, one federal court has indicated that a simple "advantage in law" in the forum suit will not warrant invoking the public policy justification for an injunction,[288] and that while "evasion of an important national policy might outweigh certain principles of international comity," it is questionable "whether the public policy of one state could ever outweigh those principles."[289]

Some courts have articulated a more liberal standard for granting injunctions against foreign litigation than the "restrictive" view described above. In addition to the "protection of jurisdiction" and "public policy" justifications, these courts add two additional rationales for such injunctions: (1) prevention of vexation and oppression; and (2) prevention of prejudice to "other equitable considerations."[290] In effect, decisions by these courts seem to stand for the proposition that a duplication of parties and issues alone is sufficient to justify an injunction against foreign litigation.[291] However, not all courts articulating this "liberal" view of foreign antisuit injunctions apply the standards broadly. For example, in *Golden Rule Insurance Co. v. Harper*,[292] the Texas Supreme Court stated that an antisuit injunction is appropriate in the four circumstances encompassed by the "liberal" view.[293] However, the court then reversed the judgment of a lower court granting an injunction against parallel litigation in another state. The court stated:

> [W]e have never accepted the notion that a mirror image proceeding is sufficiently different from an ordinary single parallel proceeding to justify an injunction. We reject the implicit distinction of the court below between single parallel proceedings and mirror image proceedings . . . . This approach fails to give adequate weight to the principle of comity and threatens to allow the exception to swallow the rule.[294]

Golden Rule thus suggests that courts articulating the "liberal" standard for foreign antisuit injunctions may actually administer the standard in a way that

---

287. *See* Gau Shan Co. v. Bankers Trust Co., 956 F.2d 1349, 1357 (6th Cir. 1992).

288. *Id.* at 1357.

289. *Id.* at 1358. This statement implies that injunctions against litigation in foreign nations may be controlled by "federal common law" in diversity and alienage actions. *See* Chapter 5(I) ("Federal Common Law") *infra*.

290. *See, e.g.,* Kaepa, Inc. v. Achilles Corp., 76 F.3d 624 (5th Cir. 1996); Seattle Totems Hockey Club, Inc. v. National Hockey League, 652 F.2d 852, 855 (9th Cir. 1981); *In re* Unterweser Reederei, 428 F.2d 888, 890 (5th Cir. 1970); Golden Rule Ins. Co. v. Harper, 925 S.W.2d 649 (Tex. 1996).

291. *See* Gau Shan Co. v. Bankers Trust Co., 956 F.2d 1349, 1352-53 (6th Cir. 1992) (describing the views of the Fifth and Ninth Circuits in this way).

292. 925 S.W.2d 649 (Tex. 1996); *see also* Allendale Mut. Ins. Co. v. Bull Data Sys., Inc., 10 F.3d 425 (7th Cir. 1993) (Posner, J.) ("lax" standard takes account of international comity, but requires some tangible evidence that it will be impaired before injunction will be refused).

293. *See Golden Rule*, 925 S.W.2d at 651.

294. *Id.* The "mirror image" proceeding the court referenced was a declaratory judgment action brought in Illinois that "mirrored" an action for damages brought in Texas.

is nearer to the restrictive standard. If so, mere duplicative parallel proceedings in another jurisdiction will seldom justify an injunction.[295]

2. Stays of Forum Proceedings in Deference to Out-of-State Litigation

Many state courts follow a rule that they will abate a proceeding involving the same parties and subject matter in favor of a prior pending action in the same state.[296] If the prior pending action is in a different venue within the same state, the plea of prior pending action gives a litigant some control over the venue of the action. However, the abatement of a proceeding in favor of a prior pending action does not extend to proceedings in other states.[297]

Some courts will exercise discretion to stay (as opposed to abate or dismiss) an action in favor of an action in another jurisdiction. The principal reason for granting such a stay is to prevent vexation of the defendant when there is no apparent reason for the plaintiff to bring the same suit in two different states, though other reasons are sometimes also given.[298] When an action in the forum is stayed in favor of an action in another state, a judgment on the merits in the other state will control the forum proceeding under the ordinary principles of res judicata. Under the full-faith-and-credit implementing statute, 28 U.S.C. § 1738, the states are obligated to give the same effect to the judgments of other states as they would receive in the state where the judgments are rendered.[299] When the judgment is rendered by the courts of a foreign nation, however, neither the Full Faith and Credit Clause nor its implementing statute require United States Courts to enforce the judgment.[300] Nevertheless, most state courts today give the same effect to foreign nation judgments as they give to judgments of other states.[301]

---

295. Many articles discuss the use of injunctions against suit in international litigation. *See, e.g.,* George A. Berman, *The Use of Anti-Suit Injunctions in International Litigation,* 28 COLUM. J. TRANSNAT'L L. 589 (1990); Trevor C. Hartley, *Comity and the Use of Antisuit Injunctions in International Litigation,* 35 AM. J. COMP. L. 487 (1987); Markus Lenebach, *Antisuit Injunctions in England, Germany and the United States: Their Treatment Under European Civil Procedure and the Hague Convention,* 20 LOY. L.A. INT'L & COMP. L.J. 257 (1998); Haig Najarian, Note, *Granting Comity Its Due: A Proposal to Revise the Comity-Based Approach to Transnational Antisuit Injunctions,* 68 ST. JOHN'S L. REV. 861 (1994); Eric Roberson, Comment, *Comity Be Damned: The Use of Antisuit Injunctions Against the Courts of a Foreign Nation,* 147 U. PA. L. REV. 409 (1998); Steven R. Swanson, *The Veratiousness of a Vexation Rule: International Comity and Antisuit Injunctions,* 30 GEO. WASH. J. INT'L L. & ECON. 1 (1996). For an English decision in which the House of Lords reversed an injunction against Texas litigation on the ground that the English forum did not have a sufficient interest to justify interference with the litigation in Texas, see Airbus Industrie GIE v. Patel, 2 All Eng. Rep. 257 (H.L. 1998); *see also* Kent Anderson, Comment Abstract, *What Can the United States Learn from English Antisuit Injunctions? An American Perspective on* Airbus Industrie GIE v. Patel, 25 YALE J. INT'L L. 195 (2000).

296. *See* Annotation, *Stay of Civil Proceedings Pending Determination of Action in Another State or Country,* 19 A.L.R.2D 301, 305-06 (1951).

297. *See id.* at 305-06.

298. *See id.* at 306; *see also* RUSSELL J. WEINTRAUB, COMMENTARY ON THE CONFLICT OF LAWS § 4.28, at 228 (3d ed. 1986).

299. *See* Chapter 13(F)(1) ("Enforcement of State Judgments") *infra.*

300. *See* Chapter 13(F)(3) ("Enforcement of Foreign Judgments") *infra.*

301. *See id.*

Chapter 5

SOURCES OF LAW

As discussed in the previous three chapters, lawyers must select a court that possesses subject-matter jurisdiction, venue, and personal jurisdiction before commencing an action. In addition, before selecting a court, lawyers must consider what rules of law a court will apply to resolve the dispute between the parties. However, predicting what law courts will apply can be a difficult task. If the legal system has never confronted and directly resolved a dispute like the one presented in the case, no rule of law may exist that exactly fits the circumstances of the dispute. Under such conditions, lawyers will have to predict whether the courts will (1) extend a rule of law previously applied in a similar, but not identical, case to the facts of the present one or (2) create an entirely new rule. Even when prior decisions have "settled" the law, lawyers must consider whether those prior decisions remain on a sound footing or whether they are subject to attack. Changed conditions may convince an appellate court to overrule even settled decisions.[1]

In the United States, two structural features of the legal system complicate the task of predicting or determining the applicable law. First, the doctrine of separation of powers allocates primary lawmaking authority to the legislative branches of government. It also restrains the power of the courts to make and revise the law. Second, the existence of the federal system complicates the selection of the applicable rules of law. Each of the fifty states and the national government possess lawmaking power within a limited sphere of authority. In actions based on events that occur in more than one state, or in actions involving parties from more than one state, lawyers must determine which state's law the court will select to resolve the dispute. Furthermore, there is an ever-present need to determine whether the national government has promulgated rules that preempt state law and thereby control the outcome of the case.

Many problems of legal interpretation concern the respective lawmaking roles of the legislative and judicial branches of government. Section A briefly examines these "separation of powers" problems. Section B introduces some basic problems of selecting the applicable law in multistate disputes. The remaining sections are devoted to a special source-of-law problem created by the existence of separate state and national courts within each state that possess concurrent authority to adjudicate some of the same disputes.[2]

---

1. Difficult questions of applicable law are not only presented to plaintiffs trying to decide whether to commence an action. The same questions exist on the defendant's side of the case and bear on whether settlement or litigation is the most viable option.

2. Recall the discussion in Chapter 2(C) of the concurrent subject-matter jurisdiction of federal and state courts in diversity and federal question cases, *supra*.

SECTION A. THE SEPARATION-OF-POWERS DOCTRINE

Ideally, the rule of law presupposes the traditional doctrine of separation of powers. Separation of powers limits each branch of government to its appropriate function. The legislative branch must enact only general laws and not acts of attainder or retroactive laws. The executive must act only with the approval of the judiciary in enforcing the laws against individuals. The courts are not to make law, but only to "find" it.[3]

This ideal rule of law is only an "approximation" of what actually occurs.[4] In reality, courts perform lawmaking functions, but their lawmaking authority is not as broad as that of the legislature. While judges inevitably create law when they articulate the rules of law applicable to the dispute before them, simple fairness dictates that judges limit their lawmaking. Courts should not unfairly surprise the parties to a dispute by applying rules of decision that did not exist, at least in an inchoate form, when the parties engaged in their primary behavior. In addition, limitations on the judicial lawmaking authority perform broader political functions. Fundamental policy issues should be reserved for determination by the legislative branch of government. Courts should refrain from taking sides on partisan political issues. The administration of law by the courts should "exhibit coherence of principle" and should not be a process of ad hoc decisionmaking. Values transcending partisan political differences should be recognized in a society's laws. Although these principles potentially conflict, they can be reconciled by maintaining the distinction between legislative and judicial powers. Thus, while judges will inevitably make law when engaged in the process of adjudication, they should take care to make it only interstitially.[5]

Within an individual state, making law "only interstitially" depends on the source of the law. When the courts enforce a constitutional provision, they should be bound by the intention and purposes of the framers and ratifiers of the provision. When enforcing a statute, the courts must determine the meaning communicated by, and objectives of, the legislators. Difficult problems of "interstitial" lawmaking also are posed when the courts enforce common-law principles. It is tempting to conclude that the lawmaking constraints on courts are fewer, or perhaps nonexistent, when courts apply common-law rules. After all, the rules originated with the courts in the first instance. Thus, perhaps they should be subject to repeal or modification by the courts in a policy-oriented fashion. In addition to the serious problems of unfair surprise to the parties such a process would entail, this view oversimplifies the origins of common-law rules and the role of the courts in enforcing those rules in a modern society.

In its earliest stages, English law was customary in nature. The oldest customs were not handed down from central institutions to individuals and local communities. Instead, they originated in the localities and "reflected not different

---

3. *See* John R. Lucas, The Principles of Politics 113-14 (1966).

4. *See id.*

5. *See* Neil MacCormick, Legal Reasoning and Legal Theory 187-88 (1978).

answers to the same problem but different ways of life.''[6] After the Norman Conquest, this system of local customary institutions was taken over by the Conqueror. The product of the centralization of justice that took place after the Conquest with the rise of the king's court became known as the "common law.''[7]

As the common law developed, the courts limited the operation of local custom.[8] The courts placed a "heavy burden of proof" upon persons who contended that local custom should control instead of common-law rules. In effect, the proponents of local custom had to establish the existence of a local custom that favored their side of the dispute. They also had to demonstrate that the custom "has borne fruit in actual practice and governed the decisions of the local courts.''[9] The process of identifying the existence and extent of a local custom was similar to fact finding today.[10] This fact-finding process was not limited to the establishment of local custom that would control instead of a common-law rule. It was also used when local custom was incorporated into the common law as the national rule of decision.

Illustration 5-1. (a) An illustration of how the common-law processes operated in conjunction with local custom is found in the history of the "law merchant" or "mercantile law." The information in this illustration is also relevant to an understanding of the doctrine of *Swift v. Tyson*, discussed in section C, below. The law merchant originated in the local customs of particular places where substantial commercial activity occurred.[11] Despite its character as local custom, the law merchant was conceived of as international in scope and "known to merchants throughout Christendom.''[12] Indeed, long before the English common law incorporated it, the law merchant existed not only at the local level in England, but also as European local custom.[13]

(b) Much of the law merchant was customary maritime law, spread by seaborne commerce along shipping routes.[14] Indeed, the bodies of law that came to be separately known as "Admiralty" and "Commercial Law" were not originally distinguished from each other.[15] "The custom of merchants on land [in Europe] seems to have been more varied [than in the seaport towns]. Every town tended to develop a more or less comprehensive body of merchant custom . . . . Divergences in detail are very numerous, but even here attempts

---

6. S.F.C. MILSOM, HISTORICAL FOUNDATIONS OF THE COMMON LAW 1 (1969).

7. *Id.* "The custom of the king's court is the custom of England and becomes the common law." 1 FREDERICK POLLOCK & FREDERIC W. MAITLAND, THE HISTORY OF ENGLISH LAW 184 (2d ed. 1968).

8. *See* 1 FREDERICK POLLOCK & FREDERIC W. MAITLAND, THE HISTORY OF ENGLISH LAW 184 (2d ed. 1968).

9. *Id.* at 184-85.

10. *See* RANDALL BRIDWELL & RALPH U. WHITTEN, THE CONSTITUTION AND THE COMMON LAW: THE DECLINE OF THE DOCTRINES OF SEPARATION OF POWERS AND FEDERALISM 14 (1977).

11. *See* THEODORE F.T. PLUCKNETT, A CONCISE HISTORY OF THE COMMON LAW 314, 657 (5th ed. 1956).

12. 1 FREDERICK POLLOCK & FREDERIC W. MAITLAND, THE HISTORY OF ENGLISH LAW 467 (2d ed. 1968).

13. *See* THEODORE F.T. PLUCKNETT, A CONCISE HISTORY OF THE COMMON LAW 657-58 (5th ed. 1956).

14. *See id.*

15. *See* GRANT GILMORE & CHARLES L. BLACK, THE LAW OF ADMIRALTY § 1-3, at 5 n.13 and accompanying text (2d ed. 1975); Thomas E. Scrutton, *General Survey of the History of the Law Merchant, in* 3 SELECT ESSAYS IN ANGLO-AMERICAN LEGAL HISTORY 7, 11-12 (1909).

were made to achieve some sort of uniformity.''[16] The ''international character of commerce'' that brought merchants from different countries into contact with each other promoted deliberate attempts to make the mercantile law uniform.[17]

(c) Both on the continent and in England, local maritime tribunals and merchants' courts enforced the law merchant.[18] In England, the inland courts were called ''piepowder'' courts, so named because of the dusty feet of the wandering merchants who used them.[19] English seaport towns had their own maritime courts.[20] Later, the central admiralty courts took over the administration of the law merchant from the local maritime courts. In the fourteenth century, statutory ''courts of the staple'' were set up in competition with the piepowder courts.[21] Later, the common-law courts took over the administration of the law merchant.

(d) When the common-law courts first began to incorporate the law merchant into the common law, a jury of merchants had to establish the alleged existence of a commercial custom in each case.[22] However, ''by the close of the seventeenth century the constant repetition of finding mercantile custom in each case that arose was seen to be unnecessary, and the courts began to take notice of some of the more notable mercantile customs without requiring proof of them, and this policy was finally adopted as a general practice by Lord Mansfield [in the eighteenth century].''[23]

(e) Incorporating the law merchant into the common law subjected the commercial law to the common-law process of analogical reasoning. This process was, of course, the familiar one of arguing ''from one case to another case which is similar though not precisely similar.''[24] Taking judicial notice of a mercantile custom resembled a fact-finding task in many respects, as judicial notice does today, while the analogical reasoning process resembled more what would be called lawmaking today, though it was not so considered in the eighteenth and nineteenth centuries.

(f) When custom was used as a source of law, the particular rules of law that formed the content of the custom were not created by the courts that enforced it. Instead, the rules were created by the interaction of private parties to suit the needs of the parties. As a consequence, when a court enforced a particular rule, no legislative-like policy choice was made—whether the decision about the content of the rule was made by judicial notice or by allegation and proof to a jury. If any policy choice was involved, the choice was to follow custom in the first place. Thus, when the common-law courts decided to incorporate the law merchant as national common law, the courts may have been making a significant

---

16. THEODORE F.T. PLUCKNETT, A CONCISE HISTORY OF THE COMMON LAW 658 (5th ed. 1956).

17. *See id.* at 659.

18. *See* GRANT GILMORE & CHARLES L. BLACK, THE LAW OF ADMIRALTY § 1-3, at 5 (2d ed. 1975); THEODORE F.T. PLUCKNETT, A CONCISE HISTORY OF THE COMMON LAW 660 (5th ed. 1956).

19. *See* THEODORE F.T. PLUCKNETT, A CONCISE HISTORY OF THE COMMON LAW 660 (5th ed. 1956).

20. *Id.*

21. *See id.*

22. *See id.* at 663.

23. *Id.* at 664.

24. 1 FREDERICK POLLOCK & FREDERIC W. MAITLAND, THE HISTORY OF ENGLISH LAW 183 (2d ed. 1968).

policy choice. Thereafter, when they engaged in the process of establishing what the particular rules of the law merchant were, they were merely engaged in fact finding, not in creation of the particular rule for legislative-like policy reasons.

(g) When custom was enforced as law, an important policy underlying the separation-of-powers restriction on lawmaking by judges was preserved. The parties to the dispute were not unfairly surprised by the creation and retroactive application of a legal rule that did not exist when they engaged in the transaction that gave rise to the dispute. Thus, if the court performed the fact-finding task accurately and identified the custom correctly, the rule applied to resolve the dispute was, by definition, the one in existence when the parties entered into their transaction.

(h) When courts properly applied the analogical reasoning process of the common-law method, the courts observed the same separation-of-powers policy. The analogical reasoning process permitted the application of legal rules to disputes only when the disputes had features in common with past applications of the rules that made them substantially identical to the situations giving rise to those applications. This process prevented unfair surprise to the parties because, by hypothesis, the parties ought to have been aware of the similarities between their transaction and the substantially identical transaction to which the legal rule had been applied in the past.

(i) The description in this illustration involves planned transactions, as opposed to unplanned events such as torts. Unfair surprise is often absent in tort cases when common-law rules are extended to new situations because the parties relied on no legal rule in formulating their behavior. Because the tort was not planned or anticipated, the application of one legal rule rather than another defeated no one's expectations. This premise should not be *assumed*, however, because parties may rely on tort rules as well as commercial rules. For example, a charity may rely on a rule of charitable immunity by not purchasing insurance to indemnify itself against tort liability. To avoid unfair surprise in unplanned situations, a court must examine the facts of each case.[25]

* * * * *

When the doctrine of separation of powers was formalized in the state and national constitutions in the United States, the common-law method or process described in *Illustration 5-1* represented an accepted feature of "judicial power." The combined processes of fact-finding, judicial notice, and analogical reasoning that had allowed the English courts to develop and adapt the common law to new situations also satisfied separation-of-powers restrictions on judicial lawmaking by limiting the policy choices of judges and preventing the creation of rules that unfairly surprised the parties to a dispute.[26]

Even in today's substantially different legal system, arguments derived from analogy and preexisting principle are considered vital to the proper performance of the judicial function in a system of separation of powers.

---

25. *See* A.W.B. Simpson, *The Common Law and Legal Theory, in* OXFORD ESSAYS IN JURISPRUDENCE (SECOND SERIES) 77 (A.W.B. Simpson ed. 1973).

26. *See* RANDALL BRIDWELL & RALPH U. WHITTEN, THE CONSTITUTION AND THE COMMON LAW: THE DECLINE OF THE DOCTRINES OF SEPARATION OF POWERS AND FEDERALISM 21 (1977).

Arguments from analogy and preexisting principle permit judges to make law only "interstitially."[27] Thus, while a judge's lawmaking power is more readily conceded today than in the eighteenth and nineteenth centuries, judges are still obligated to avoid encroachment on legislative prerogatives by keeping their lawmaking activities within appropriate boundaries.

Nevertheless, the legitimate scope of the lawmaking power of the courts is disputed today. The lawmaking power of courts has expanded from the narrow scope permissible under the traditional common-law process accepted in the eighteenth and nineteenth centuries. This expansion raises serious, complex questions about the nature and extent of the separation of powers between the legislative and judicial branches of government today. No mathematical formula exists by which proper judicial lawmaking can be distinguished from improper judicial "legislation." The task requires a sensitivity both to historical form and the function of courts in a modern political democracy. For the time being, it is sufficient to note that because a legal rule is "common law," rather than statutory or constitutional in nature, judges are not completely free from constraints on their lawmaking power.

SECTION B. CONFLICT-OF-LAWS PROBLEMS IN A FEDERAL SYSTEM

As described in section A, above, the task of staying within proper lawmaking limits is difficult, even when the courts are only concerned with determining the content of the law of their own government. The task can become much more complex when the judges must determine whether to apply the law of some other government to a dispute, and if so, what that law is. Such cases commonly are said to present "conflict-of-laws" problems.

Illustration 5-2. Assume that *A*, a citizen of State *X*, is injured in an automobile accident in State *X* with *B*, a citizen of State *Y*. Pursuant to a proper long-arm statute, State *X* obtains jurisdiction over *B* in a suit brought by *A*. Should a court in State *X* apply the law of State *X*, of State *Y*, or some other state? If the issue is whether *B* has violated the rules of the road in producing *A's* injuries, the answer will probably be the law of State *X*, which is where the accident occurred. The "conflict of laws" or "choice-of-law" rules of State *X* and most other states would point to *X's* substantive rules under such circumstances. Suppose, however, that State *X* has a guest statute that bars recovery by a guest-passenger in an automobile driven by a host-driver unless gross negligence can be established. Suppose further that *A* was a guest-passenger in a car

---

27.   [T]here must be criterion for distinguishing interstitial from architectural legislation. One
       possible criterion is that either a relevant analogy or an established principle is a necessary
       element of justification of an innovative decision. So if we seek a reason why arguments
       from analogy or from principle have the force they have in legal argument, the answer
       is the existence of a highly desirable conventional rule conferring power on judges to
       extend the law to cover circumstances not directly or unambiguously governed by
       established mandatory rules, but imposing limits on the extent of that power.
NEIL MACCORMICK, LEGAL REASONING AND LEGAL THEORY 188 (1978).

driven by B, that the trip originated and was to end in State Y, and that State Y has no guest statute. Suddenly, the considerations relevant to a determination of the conflict-of-laws problem have multiplied. The substantive law of State X no longer clearly applies to the guest-host relationship formed in another state between a resident host and a foreign guest.

* * * * *

The conflict-of-laws problem described in *Illustration 5-2* is typical of the kinds of problems that can arise in a federal system. A detailed examination of such problems must be reserved for treatises on Conflict of Laws.[28] However, one kind of choice of law problem is directly relevant to Civil Procedure. What law should a federal court apply in cases in which the court's subject-matter jurisdiction is based on diversity of citizenship between the parties? Section 34 of the Judiciary Act of 1789 (the Rules of Decision Act) provided "[t]hat the law of the several states, except where the Constitution, treaties, or statutes of the United States shall otherwise require or provide, shall be regarded as rules of decision in trials at common law in the Courts of the United States, in cases where they apply."[29] Over the two hundred years it has existed, the Rules of Decision Act has undergone differing interpretations. The next three sections of this chapter examine these interpretations.

SECTION C. THE DOCTRINE OF *SWIFT V. TYSON*

The modern interpretation of the Rules of Decision Act is embodied in the *Erie* doctrine—so named for the case of *Erie Railroad v. Tompkins*[30] decided by the U.S. Supreme Court in 1938. To understand the Rules of Decision Act and the *Erie* decision, however, one must begin at a much earlier date, with the decision in *Swift v. Tyson*,[31] decided by the Supreme Court in 1842. That decision is the source of the "*Swift*" doctrine.

1. The *Swift* Decision

The *Swift* case involved a suit on a negotiable instrument brought within the diversity jurisdiction of the federal courts.[32] Two individuals, Norton and Keith, represented themselves to be the owners of land in Maine. Tyson contracted with them to purchase the land. As part of the consideration for the purchase, Norton drew a bill of exchange on Tyson, which Tyson accepted in

---

28. *See, e.g.,* LUTHER L. MCDOUGAL, III ET AL., AMERICAN CONFLICTS LAW (5th ed. 2000); RUSSELL J. WEINTRAUB, COMMENTARY ON THE CONFLICT OF LAWS (3d ed. 1986).

29. § 34, 1 Stat. 73, 92. The current version of the Rules of Decision Act is found in 28 U.S.C. § 1652.

30. 304 U.S. 64, 58 S. Ct. 817, 82 L. Ed. 1188 (1938).

31. 41 U.S. (16 Pet.) 1, 10 L. Ed. 865 (1842).

32. For an excellent discussion of the negotiable instruments aspects of *Swift*, as well as the view of law embodied in the case, see William P. LaPiana, Swift v. Tyson *and the Brooding Omnipresence in the Sky: An Investigation of the Idea of Law in Antebellum America*, 20 SUFFOLK U.L. REV. 771 (1986).

New York.[33] Norton endorsed the bill to Swift in return for Swift's cancellation of a preexisting debt. When the bill became due, Tyson refused to pay Swift because Norton and Keith had fraudulently represented that they owned the land in Maine. Swift sued Tyson in the U.S. Circuit Court for the Southern District of New York to collect the amount of the bill. Tyson attempted to raise the defense that there was fraud in the original transaction between Tyson and Norton and Keith. Swift objected that this defense was not valid as to him because he was a bona fide purchaser for value (today, a holder in due course) of the bill and thus immune from defenses between the original parties. There was no question that Swift had taken the bill before it became due with no knowledge of the fraud practiced by Norton and Keith in the original transaction with Tyson. However, the judges of the circuit court divided on another question. Did cancellation of a preexisting debt constitute valuable consideration for the transfer of the bill of exchange? If it did, Swift was a bona fide purchaser for value. If it did not, Swift was not a bona fide purchaser and was subject to the defenses that would have existed in a suit by Norton and Keith against Tyson.

The circuit court judges certified the question of negotiable instruments law to the U.S. Supreme Court. In his opinion for the Court, Justice Joseph Story first addressed Tyson's contention that because the bill of exchange was accepted in New York, it was a New York contract and thus controlled by the laws of New York. Under the New York decisions, Tyson contended, a preexisting debt did not constitute valuable consideration for the transfer of a negotiable instrument. Story first examined the New York decisions and concluded that they were unsettled on the question certified.[34] Then, in a memorable and often misunderstood passage, Justice Story held for a unanimous Court[35] that even if the New York decisions had been settled, those decisions would not control the case.

To reach this conclusion, Justice Story had to interpret § 34 of the Judiciary Act of 1789—the Rules of Decision Act. Significantly, Story first observed that the "Courts of New York" were not basing their decisions on any local law, but were attempting to "deduce the doctrine from the general principles of commercial law."[36] Nevertheless, it had been argued that the Rules of Decision

---

33. A bill of exchange is a written order from one person directing another person to pay a sum of money to a specified third person, to the drawer of the instrument, or to the bearer of the instrument. If the bill is accepted by the person ordered to pay, it becomes a valid obligation owed by the acceptor. If, as is normally the case, the bill is framed so as to be negotiable, the drawer of the bill can then transfer it to a third party in accord with the rules governing negotiable instruments, and the acceptor of the bill will have to pay the amount owed to the transferee of the bill when it becomes due.

34. *See Swift*, 41 U.S. (16 Pet.) at 16-18, 10 L. Ed. at 870-71.

35. Despite later criticism of Story's opinion in *Swift*, it is significant that on the point of interpretation of the Rules of Decision Act for which *Swift* became famous, the Court was unanimous. Justice Catron concurred, objecting to a dictum by Story on a point of negotiable instruments law not before the Court, *see* 41 U.S. (16 Pet.) at 23-24, 10 L. Ed. at 872. However, no Justice objected to Story's interpretation of the Rules of Decision Act, which, as is demonstrated below, had long been accepted by the time *Swift* was decided.

36. But, admitting the doctrine to be fully settled in New York, it remains to be considered, whether it is obligatory upon this Court, if it differs from the principles established in the general commercial law. It is observable that the Courts of New York do not found their decisions upon this point upon any local statute, or positive, fixed, or ancient local usage: but they deduce the doctrine from the general principles of commercial law.

41 U.S. at 18, 10 L. Ed. at 871.

Act required the federal courts to follow the decisions of the state courts "in all cases to which they apply."[37] This argument was based on an interpretation of the word "laws" in the Rules of Decision Act as including state court decisions.[38] Story rejected this interpretation. The Court held that the word "laws" did not, "[i]n the ordinary use of language," include court decisions.[39] However, his opinion stated that the "laws of a state" were usually understood to include statutes and long-established local customs having the force of law. The Rules of Decision Act, said Story, had been uniformly interpreted to apply only to state laws of a local nature, such as statutes "and the construction thereof adopted by the local tribunals, and to rights and titles to things having a permanent locality, such as the rights and titles to real estate, and other matters immovable and intraterritorial in their nature and character," but not to "questions of a more general nature," such as questions of general commercial law.[40]

The statement that the Rules of Decision Act includes court decisions construing statutes (and other local laws), but not court decisions on matters of general commercial law seems contradictory. It would appear that court decisions should either constitute laws within the meaning of the Rules of Decision Act or they should not. As discussed below, however, the statements are not contradictory when read in the full context of the jurisprudence of the time. A significant factor in explaining the statements is Story's further explanation that when determining questions of general commercial law, "the state tribunals are called upon to perform the like functions as ourselves, that is, to ascertain upon general reasoning and legal analogies . . . what is the just rule furnished by the principles of commercial law to govern the case."[41]

Critics of *Swift* have focused on Story's view of the nature of law expressed in the decision. In particular, Justice Story has been criticized for his view that court decisions were not law and that general commercial law transcended the authority of any specific government. Nevertheless, the best historical scholarship has confirmed that Story's view of law was widely shared

---

37. *See id.*

38. *See id.*

39. In order to maintain the argument, it is essential, therefore, to hold, that the word "laws," in this section, includes within the scope of its meaning the decisions of the local tribunals. In the ordinary use of language it will hardly be contended that the decisions of Courts constitute laws. They are, at most, only evidence of what the laws are; and are not of themselves laws. They are often reexamined, reversed, and qualified by the Courts themselves, whenever they are found to be either defective, or ill-founded, or otherwise incorrect.

41 U.S. at 18, 10 L. Ed. at 871.

40. *See* 41 U.S (16 Pet.) at 18-19, 10 L. Ed. at 871.

41. 41 U.S.(16 Pet.) at 19, 10 L. Ed. at 871. Having reasoned that the U.S. Supreme Court was entitled to make an independent judgment on the content of the general commercial law, Justice Story then concluded that the cancellation of a preexisting debt did constitute valuable consideration for the transfer of a negotiable instrument. *See id.* at 19-22, 10 L. Ed. at 871-72.

at the time *Swift* was decided.[42] In the discussion that follows, it will be demonstrated that the *Swift* decision was fully compatible with principles of separation of powers and federalism. The discussion will necessarily be far ranging because the *Swift* decision was only a component of a larger body of jurisprudence in the federal courts. In understanding that jurisprudence, it is important to keep in mind two aspects of the *Swift* decision. First, at the beginning of the discussion of the Rules of Decision Act, Justice Story pointed out that the New York decisions were not founded on any local rule of common law, but were attempts to deduce the correct principle of general commercial law. In other words, New York courts themselves agreed that cases like *Swift* should be governed by something called *general commercial law*. Second, Justice Story did not say federal courts would never treat state court decisions as binding. Rather, Story said the federal courts would not be bound by such decisions on matters of general law, as opposed to local law. When these two aspects of the opinion are combined with a number of well-accepted principles drawn from the jurisprudence of the time, the *Swift* decision will be seen to be a rather ordinary example of antebellum jurisprudence, acceptable under all potentially applicable constitutional doctrines.

2. The *Swift* Doctrine

The doctrine that has taken its name from *Swift v. Tyson* was, in fact, a complex body of rules governing all aspects of the power of the federal courts to administer law. What became known as the *Swift* doctrine was, in reality, a mixture or interaction of principles derived from at least four different sources: (1) the concepts of sovereignty that governed the power of the states relative to each other and to the federal government during the early nineteenth century; (2) the doctrine of stare decisis, which governed the precedential value of the decisions of courts in a common-law system; (3) the concept of separation of powers between the legislative and judicial branches of the federal government that prevailed in the early nineteenth century; and (4) the early nineteenth-century understanding of the purposes of the diversity jurisdiction exercised by the federal courts.

Once one understands the interaction of the principles derived from these sources, Justice Story's opinion in *Swift* becomes more comprehensible. It also becomes possible to understand how many critics of the *Swift* doctrine have been misled by the opinion. These critics failed to read the opinion in the context of the nineteenth century, law-administering power of the federal courts. Others also failed to recognize that the *Swift* doctrine did not remain static over time, but began to change radically in the latter part of the nineteenth century. The later expansion of the law-administering power of the federal courts, which modern

---

42. *See, e.g.*, WILFRED J. RITZ, REWRITING THE HISTORY OF THE JUDICIARY ACT OF 1789, at 28-30 (Wythe Holt & L.H. LaRue eds., 1989) (discussing the eighteenth century function of judges to "find" law); William P. LaPiana, Swift v. Tyson *and the Brooding Omnipresence in the Sky: An Investigation of the Idea of Law in Antebellum America*, 20 SUFFOLK U.L. REV. 771 (1986); *see also* William A. Fletcher, *The General Common Law and Section 34 of the Judiciary Act of 1789: The Example of Marine Insurance*, 97 HARV. L. REV. 1513 (1984) (finding the *Swift* holding to be a restatement of settled law).

courts and commentators have found objectionable, was not a part of the original *Swift* approach.

(a) Sovereignty

By the time *Swift v. Tyson* was decided, it had long been established that § 34 of the Judiciary Act of 1789 was a conflict-of-laws directive to the federal courts. The portion of § 34 that produced this directive was the Act's "in cases where they apply" language.[43] In this regard, a warning is in order to those reading the modern commentaries on the Rules of Decision Act. Some commentators who attempt to read the Act without benefit of historical research into how it was originally interpreted become befuddled by the "in cases where they apply" language.[44] Specifically, the "in cases where they apply" language directed the federal courts to make an independent conflict-of-laws decision about which state's law was applicable when no federal statutory, constitutional, or treaty provision existed to control the case before the court. However, the Supreme Court also had made it clear that § 34 was merely declarative of the rule that would have been followed even if the section had never been included as part of the original Judiciary Act.[45] Thus, even in the absence of § 34, it would have been implied from the grant of diversity jurisdiction that (1) federal courts were required to administer state law when no controlling federal law existed and (2) because diversity cases by definition involved disputes between citizens of different states, the federal courts were obligated as a matter of necessity to choose which state's law "applied." The rules by which this independent conflict-of-laws decision were to be made were the accepted "territorial" conflict-of-laws rules

---

43. *See* Hawkins v. Barney's Lessee, 30 U.S. (5 Pet.) 457, 464, 8 L. Ed. 190, 192-93 (1831); Society for the Propagation of Gospel v. Wheeler, 22 F. Cas. 756, 767 (C.C.D.N.H. 1814) (No. 13,156) (Story, J.); Van Reimsdyk v. Kane, 28 F. Cas. 1062, 1065 (C.C.D.R.I. 1812) (No. 16,871), *rev'd on other grounds sub nom.* Clark's Ex'rs v. Van Riemsdyk, 13 U.S. (9 Cranch) 153, 3 L. Ed. 688 (1815); RANDALL BRIDWELL & RALPH U. WHITTEN, THE CONSTITUTION AND THE COMMON LAW: THE DECLINE OF THE DOCTRINES OF SEPARATION OF POWERS AND FEDERALISM 110-11 (1977); 2 WILLIAM W. CROSSKEY, POLITICS AND THE CONSTITUTION IN THE HISTORY OF THE UNITED STATES 832-34, 867 (1953); William F. Baxter, *Choice of Law and the Federal System*, 16 STAN. L. REV. 1, 41 (1963).

44. Consider, for example, the following excerpt from MARTIN REDISH, FEDERAL JURISDICTION: TENSIONS IN THE ALLOCATION OF JUDICIAL POWER 121 (2d ed. 1990): "[T]he Act's language contains within it a circularity which renders it all but useless. To say that state laws shall serve as the rules of decision 'in cases where they apply' ultimately fails to tell us to which cases state laws specifically 'apply.' "; *see also* Note, *The Federal Common Law*, 82 HARV. L. REV. 1512, 1515 (1969).

45. *See, e.g.,* Hawkins v. Barney's Lessee, 30 U.S. (5 Pet.) 457, 464, 8 L. Ed. 190, 193 (1831). Recent research by the late Professor Wilfred J. Ritz into the history of the Judiciary Act of 1789 has indicated that *Swift* may have misinterpreted § 34 of the Act. Specifically, Professor Ritz argues that § 34 was probably a temporary measure designed to provide an applicable American law for national prosecutions brought in federal courts before Congress enacted statutory criminal provisions. The historical proof of Professor Ritz's thesis is complex and includes the position of § 34 in the Judiciary Act of 1789, the use of the wording "laws of the several states" instead of "laws of the respective states," and other evidence. *See* WILFRED J. RITZ, REWRITING THE HISTORY OF THE JUDICIARY ACT OF 1789, at 126-48, 149-163 (Wythe Holt & L.H. LaRue eds., 1989). If Professor Ritz is correct, the Supreme Court was incorrect in *Swift* and other cases to read § 34 as a requirement that state local law be applied in diversity actions. However, this does not mean that *Swift* and other decisions were incorrect in their results. As *Hawkins, supra,* and the text indicate, the same results would have been reached by the federal courts in diversity actions even if § 34 had not existed.

of the time, which incorporated the nineteenth century notions of the power of respective sovereigns to control various events with their laws.

As discussed in Chapter 3(A)(1)*(c)*, the international rules of jurisdiction governing the enforceability of the judgments of the courts of one nation in other nations remained in effect after the formation of the U.S. Constitution. By entering into the constitutional system, the states ceded a certain portion of their sovereignty to the national government. However, the states otherwise retained their status as independent sovereigns. Consequently, the international rules of jurisdiction continued in existence. The body of "private international law" containing the rules of jurisdiction also contained conflict-of-laws rules dictating when the courts of one sovereign would apply the substantive law of another sovereign. Like the jurisdictional rules, these conflict-of-laws rules were "territorial" in nature. They focused upon some event occurring, or object or person located, within the borders of a state or nation as the significant indicator of which state or nation's substantive law should be applied. The existence of the territorial conflict-of-laws rules governing the relations of independent sovereigns explains how the federal courts arrived at the independent conflict-of-laws decisions they were obligated to make by the "in cases where they apply" language of the Rules of Decision Act. Those courts simply followed the generally accepted, international territorial rules of conflict of laws that governed the relations between independent sovereigns. The "in cases where they apply" language implied that the conflict-of-laws decision required by the language would be made in accord with those principles that governed the relationships between independent governments. At the time, those principles were the territorial rules.

In *Swift v. Tyson*, the territorial conflict-of-laws rule governing contract cases like *Swift* was that the substantive law of the place where the contract was made governed the rights and obligations of the parties under the contract.[46] Because the bill of exchange had been accepted in New York, the contract was considered to have been "made" there. Under this rule, all other states and nations at that time would have applied New York substantive law to resolve any dispute that arose under the contract. New York followed the general commercial law in *Swift*, so other states and nations would apply the general commercial law to resolve disputes under the contract—exactly what the Supreme Court did in *Swift*. Had the New York courts refused to follow the general commercial law and instead grounded their decisions on the issue in question on some rule of local law, the federal courts would have been obliged to do likewise. This conclusion is implied in *Swift* by Justice Story's observation that the New York courts were basing their decisions in the area on general commercial law rather than local custom. The point that has confused modern readers of *Swift* is Justice Story's refusal to consider the federal courts bound by state court *decisions* on general commercial law matters, as opposed to local matters. This result, however, was

---

46. Professor Ritz has argued that the prevailing conflict-of-laws rule required Maine law to apply in *Swift*. *See* WILFRED J. RITZ, REWRITING THE JUDICIARY ACT OF 1789, at 158 (Wythe Holt & L.H. LaRue eds. 1989). However, his argument appears to be incorrect in so far as the state of the law at the time *Swift* was decided is concerned. *See id.* at 158 n.42 (editors' note).

dictated by the nature of the sovereign choice that New York had made in deciding to follow general commercial law rather than local law.

Recall *Illustration 5-1* in section A, above. There, the law merchant, or general commercial law, was described as a body of worldwide customary rules. When a state decided to apply the general commercial law, the state elected to follow rules that were not uniquely local, but were considered to be the law of the entire civilized world. Thus, once a state had decided to apply the general commercial law, federal courts were not obligated to follow state decisions absolutely because the state had, in fact, made a sovereign decision to apply a body of uniform international custom also followed by all, or most, other states. As part of this decision, the state voluntarily relinquished a certain amount of control over the content of the commercial law that it had decided to enforce. While the state retained the right to determine for itself the content of the general commercial law administered in its own courts, the state's decision to adhere to general commercial law also meant that the courts of all other sovereigns would reserve the right to do likewise in their own courts. Had New York in *Swift v. Tyson* chosen to administer a body of *local* commercial law, whether statutory or common law, the federal courts, New Jersey courts, Maine courts, and all other courts would have considered themselves bound by New York's decisions on the content of that local law. As a result, they would have applied the New York local commercial rule whenever international conflict-of-laws rules would permit New York as a sovereign to control the transaction that gave rise to the dispute.

By deciding to follow the general commercial law instead of a local commercial rule and by deciding that the relevant commercial rule was that a preexisting debt did not constitute valuable consideration, New York sent essentially two messages to the courts of other sovereigns: (1) New York wished to follow the general commercial law, and (2) New York believed the general commercial law to be that a preexisting debt did not constitute valuable consideration. If the courts of other sovereigns saw the second message as incorrect, they were faced with a dilemma—should they disregard the first message and conclude that New York did not wish to follow general commercial law due to its "incorrect" understanding of the content of that law? Alternatively, should they accept the first message and disregard the second, on the assumption that New York really did wish to adhere to the general commercial law, but had (temporarily) misunderstood its content?

In fact, the dilemma was easily resolved because the first message was vastly more important from a policy standpoint. Consequently, the U.S. Supreme Court applied the general commercial law in *Swift* as New York indicated it wished to do. However, the Court made its own independent determination of the content of that law, as New York's decision to follow the general commercial law had given all courts the right to do. By adopting this approach, the U.S. Supreme Court gave New York's sovereignty and the principle of federalism all the respect they were due.

Illustration 5-3. Assume that during the *Swift* era New York enacted a statute providing that cancellation of a preexisting debt would not constitute valuable consideration for the transfer of a bill of exchange. Thereafter, *B*, a citizen of New York, accepts a bill of exchange in New York City drawn by *C*, a citizen of Maine, on *B*. The bill is given in payment for lands located in Maine sold by *C* to *B*. Subsequently, *C* endorses the bill to *A*, a citizen of Maine, in Portland, Maine. In return, *A* cancels a preexisting debt that *C* owes to *A*. When the bill of exchange comes due, *B* refuses to pay it on the ground that the original transaction between *B* and *C* was fraudulent, in that *C* did not have title to the Maine lands that *C* purported to sell to *B*. *A* sues *B* in a federal court in New York to recover the amount of the bill of exchange, jurisdiction being based on diversity of citizenship. *B* defends on the ground that there was fraud in the original transaction. *A* contends that *B*'s defense is invalid, because *A* is a bona fide purchaser for value of the bill of exchange. *A*'s claim should fail. The only difference between facts of this illustration and the facts of *Swift v. Tyson* is that here New York has "localized" its rule of commercial law by enacting a statute. Because the bill of exchange was accepted in New York, the contract was "made" there, and thus New York had the right to control the transaction with its law under the traditional territorial conflict-of-laws rules. Here, unlike *Swift*, New York law is local, and the federal courts, as well as all other courts, would have been obliged to apply it.

    Illustration 5-4. Assume the same facts as in *Illustration 5-3*, except that the bill of exchange was accepted by *B* in Maine. Assume further that Maine decisions indicate that Maine follows the general commercial law. However, the Maine decisions also indicate that the Maine courts believe that the correct general commercial law rule is that cancellation of a preexisting debt does not constitute valuable consideration for the transfer of a bill of exchange. In the federal action in New York, the court should apply general commercial law, but should make an independent judgment about what the correct rule of general commercial law is. Because the bill of exchange was accepted in Maine, Maine had the power to control the transaction with its substantive law under the prevailing territorial conflict-of-laws rules. Maine follows the general commercial law. Therefore, the federal court in New York is obligated to apply the general commercial law also, the New York statute notwithstanding. However, Maine's decision to follow the general commercial law gave authority to any court that was adjudicating a case under Maine law to make an independent judgment about what the correct rule of general commercial law was. Because there was broad agreement that cancellation of a preexisting debt did constitute valuable consideration for the transfer of a bill of exchange under the general commercial law, *A* would win on the facts of this illustration.

(b) Stare Decisis

    In *Swift*, Justice Story interpreted the word "laws" in the Rules of Decision Act as not including court decisions—a pronouncement that led later commentators, such as Professor John Chipman Gray, to ridicule Story's opinion.[47] Gray and others who have examined *Swift* were confused because they neglected to take account of how the doctrine of stare decisis interacted with principles of sovereignty and the Rules of Decision Act to produce different degrees of respect owed to state-court decisions by federal courts and other state courts.

The best explanation of this interaction appears in the case of *Carroll v. Carroll's Lessee.*[48] In *Carroll*, Michael B. Carroll executed a will on September 10, 1837, disposing of his real and personal property. Subsequently, he acquired land in Maryland that he had not owned on the date the will was executed. The Maryland Legislature then enacted a statute providing that wills should be construed to speak and take effect as of the date of the testator's death. The statute altered the Maryland common-law rule that a will could not devise property acquired after the date of the will's execution. However, the statute was to take effect on June 1, 1850. It was not to apply to wills executed before its enactment unless it appeared from the will that the testator intended it to speak as of the date of his death. The issue was whether the statute applied to Carroll's will.

When the case reached the U.S. Supreme Court, the Court determined that the statute did not apply to Carroll's will. In reaching this decision, the Court had to consider the force that should be given to a decision of the Maryland Court of Appeals adjudicating the effect of the same will. The U.S. Supreme Court stated:

> If the Court of Appeals had found it necessary to construe a statute of that State in order to decide upon the rights of parties subject to its judicial control, such a decision, deliberately made, might have been taken by this [C]ourt as a basis on which to rest our judgment. But it must be remembered that we are bound to decide a question of local law, upon which the rights of parties

---

47.   Among the causes which led to the decision in *Swift v. Tyson*, the chief seems to have been the character and position of [Justice] Story. He was then by far the oldest judge in commission on the bench; he was a man of great learning, and of reputation for learning greater even than the learning itself; he was occupied at the time in writing a book on bills of exchange, which would, of itself, lead him to dogmatize on the subject; he had had great success in extending the jurisdiction of the Admiralty; he was fond of glittering generalities; and he was possessed by a restless vanity. All these things conspired to produce the result.

. . . .

If "the laws of a State" in the 34th section of the Judiciary Act mean its statutes only, then the decisions of the State courts should stand alike, and none of them should have the binding weight that is now given to some of them. If, on the other hand, "the laws" are to include "decisions," the Judiciary Act would allow no difference between them and statutes. On the general question, therefore, whether decisions are sources of the law, the doctrine of the Supreme Court of the United States in *Swift v. Tyson* throws no light. If they are sources of Law, they should be followed even when dealing with non-statutory commercial matters. If they are not, then they are not binding when dealing with real estate or the construction of statutes. The doctrine of *Swift v. Tyson* is an anomaly, and does not lend a support to either theory.

JOHN C. GRAY, THE NATURE AND SOURCES OF THE LAW 253, 255 (2d rev. ed. 1921; Peter Smith reprint 1972).
   48.   57 U.S. (16 How.) 275, 14 L. Ed. 936 (1854).

depend, as well as every other question, as we find it ought to be
decided. In making the examination preparatory to this finding,
this [C]ourt has followed two rules, one of which belongs to the
common law, and the other is a part of our peculiar judicial
system. The first is the maxim of the common law, stare decisis.
The second grows out of the thirty-fourth section of the Judiciary
Act, . . . which makes the laws of the several States the rules of
decision in trials at the common law; and inasmuch as the States
have committed to their respective judiciaries the power to
construe and fix the meaning of the statutes passed by their
legislatures, this [C]ourt has taken such constructions as part of
the law of the State, and has administered the law as thus
construed. But this rule has grown up and been held with
constant reference to the other rule, stare decisis; and it is only
so far and in such cases as this latter rule can operate, that the
other has any effect.[49]

Based on basic principles of stare decisis, the Court then explained that the
Maryland decision would not be given effect because it was dictum on the point
in question.[50]

As far as the general commercial law is concerned, the important aspect
of this passage is the Court's statement that, because the states had committed to
their respective judiciaries the power to fix the meaning of the statutes passed by
their legislatures, "this court has taken such constructions as part of the law of
the state, and has administered the law as thus construed." This statement meant
that federal courts would be *bound* by settled state decisions interpreting state
statutes.

Likewise, as Justice Story had indicated in *Swift*, the settled decisions of
the state courts on *local* common-law issues bound the federal courts. Justice
Story's opinion carefully pointed out that on the issue involved in *Swift*, the New
York courts did not base their decisions on "any local statute, or positive, fixed
or ancient local usage."[51] The reason that the state decisions were considered
binding on "local" matters was simply that the state decisions were the highest
evidence of the meaning and content of local law because the states had
committed final authority to "fix" the meaning of local law to their courts.

However, the states could not confer authority on their courts to "fix"
the content of the general commercial law in a way that bound other states. The
general commercial law was, by definition, a body of world-wide custom. A state
choosing to follow the general commercial law was, therefore, choosing to follow
law whose content had been "fixed" over centuries by the practices of merchants
trading internationally. Therefore, the task for the state courts in general
commercial law cases was one of identifying the worldwide custom. A single
state's opinion on a general commercial law matter could not bind all other states

---

49. *Id.* at 286, 14 L. Ed. at 285.
50. *Id.* at 286-87, 14 L. Ed. at 285.
51. *See Swift*, 41 U.S. (16 Pet.) at 18, 10 L. Ed. at 871.

and nations, for a single state had no sovereign authority to fix the content of world custom "finally" as it did to fix the content of local law "finally." As Justice Story observed in *Swift*, on general commercial law matters, "the State tribunals are called upon to perform the like functions as ourselves, that is, to ascertain upon general reasoning and legal analogies, what is the . . . just rule furnished by the principles of commercial law to govern the case."[52]

This scheme honored all relevant principles of federalism. On those issues (of local law) over which the state had the ultimate sovereign power, the federal courts considered themselves *bound* to follow settled state decisions on the content of the law. When the state did not have absolute sovereign power (on issues of the content of general commercial law), however, the federal courts were not bound by state-court decisions in determining the law. The state's sovereign authority was respected fully by the federal court's absolute adherence to whatever decision the state had made about *whether* to follow the general commercial law. If the state chose to do so, as in *Swift*, the federal courts would respect the state's decision.

It is important to understand a second aspect of the doctrine of stare decisis, involved in both *Swift* and *Carroll*. In *Swift*, Justice Story indicated two reasons why the federal courts were not bound by New York decisions on the issue of substantive law disputed in the case. One reason, the one for which *Swift* is famous, was that federal courts were *not bound* by state decisions on issues of general commercial law. The other reason was that the New York decisions on the substantive issue were "unsettled." Thus, even if New York had indicated that it did *not* follow the general commercial law and, therefore, that the substantive issue was controlled by New York local law (either statutory or common law), the federal courts would not have been bound by the unsettled New York decisions on the point of local law.

The reasons for this conclusion were explained in *Carroll*. Recall that the Court there stated that state decisions were binding only to the extent that they were given force by the common-law doctrine of stare decisis. When state-court opinions on a point of law were either contradictory (as in *Swift*) or dictum (as in *Carroll*), the doctrine of stare decisis did not give the opinions binding force. As the Supreme Court observed in *Carroll*, "this [C]ourt and other courts organized under the common law" would not be bound by decisions except in accord with the common-law principles of stare decisis.[53]

This approach did not violate principles of federalism. The state courts, like the federal courts, were "organized under the common law." Consequently, the state courts did not hold themselves obligated to follow their own decisions when those decisions were not rendered binding by traditional principles of stare decisis. Thus, even if a point of local law had been in dispute in *Swift*, the New York courts might not have considered themselves bound to follow the previous New York decisions on the point because those decisions were contradictory.

---

52. *Id.* at 19, 10 L. Ed. at 16.
53. *Carroll*, 57 U.S. (16 How.) at 287, 14 L. Ed. at 287.

Likewise, in *Carroll*, the Maryland Court of Appeals decision would not have been considered binding by Maryland's own courts because the opinion on the relevant substantive point was dictum. Why should the federal courts have considered themselves bound by state decisions that would not be considered binding in the state's own courts? The answer is that the federal courts should not have considered, and did not consider, themselves bound by such decisions.[54]

When were state decisions considered unsettled? In *Swift* itself, the decisions were contradictory and the contradictions had not been resolved clearly by the state courts. Therefore, state law was unsettled. In *Carroll v. Carroll's Lessee*, the state decision was not on point. Consequently, state law was considered to be unsettled. State law also could be unsettled if there were no state cases dealing with the issue in question.[55] Finally, if the state decisions were by a court, such as an inferior state court, without authority finally to "fix" the meaning of state law, state law might be considered unsettled.[56]

Illustration 5-5. In 1789, State *X* had a system of trial courts with general original jurisdiction to determine all civil actions. State *X* did not have an appellate system organized along modern lines. Instead, the trial judges in the state would get together from time to time to consider questions appropriate for decision by a tribunal exercising the functions of appellate review.[57] If the trial judges exercising their appellate function decided a matter of local state law, it would be binding on the federal courts—assuming that the decision was necessary

---

54. Some glaring mistakes have been made by commentators on the *Swift* doctrine who have incorrectly read U.S. Supreme Court decisions refusing to follow *unsettled* state authorities as decisions *overriding settled* state authorities. *Compare, e.g.*, 2 WILLIAM W. CROSSKEY, POLITICS AND THE CONSTITUTION IN THE HISTORY OF THE UNITED STATES 719-53 (1953) (analyzing Huidekoper's Lessee v. Douglass, 7 U.S. (3 Cranch) 1, 2 L. Ed. 347 (1805)) *with* RANDALL BRIDWELL & RALPH U. WHITTEN, THE CONSTITUTION AND THE COMMON LAW: THE DECLINE OF THE DOCTRINES OF SEPARATION OF POWERS AND FEDERALISM 101-05 (1977) (disputing Crosskey's interpretation of *Huidekoper's Lessee*).

55. *See* Wilson v. Mason, 5 U.S. (1 Cranch) 45, 2 L. Ed. 29 (1801); RANDALL BRIDWELL & RALPH U. WHITTEN, THE CONSTITUTION AND THE COMMON LAW: THE DECLINE OF THE DOCTRINES OF SEPARATION OF POWERS AND FEDERALISM 101 (1977).

56. *Cf.* Huidekoper's Lessee v. Douglass, 7 U.S. (3 Cranch) 1, 2 L. Ed. 347 (1805); RANDALL BRIDWELL & RALPH U. WHITTEN, THE CONSTITUTION AND THE COMMON LAW: THE DECLINE OF THE DOCTRINES OF SEPARATION OF POWERS AND FEDERALISM 104-05 (1977). Professor Ritz's excellent work on the Judiciary Act of 1789 has pointed out that most states in the eighteenth century did not have modern systems of appellate review with a single court of last resort charged with the responsibility of fixing the meaning of state law. *See* WILFRED J. RITZ, REWRITING THE JUDICIARY ACT OF 1789, at 27, 35-49 (Wythe Holt & L.H. LaRue eds., 1989). To the extent that a state did not have a modern system of appellate review, the federal courts obviously could not refuse to follow state court decisions that were properly "settled" under the system that the state did have. However, one must approach Professor Ritz's findings with caution. The fact that a state had not established a "pure" system of appellate review along modern lines does not mean that the state did not have a court with final authority to fix the meaning of state law. For example, Professor Ritz points out that Maryland authorized a modern court of appeals in 1776, but did not establish that the Maryland Court of Appeals was to have appellate jurisdiction until 1851. *See id.* at 36, 43-44, 45. This obviously does not mean that, as in *Carroll*, the Maryland Court of Appeals, when it was exercising appellate functions before 1851, would not have been treated as authoritative by the federal courts.

57. *Cf.* WILFRED J. RITZ, REWRITING THE JUDICIARY ACT OF 1789, at 43 (Wythe Holt & L.H. LaRue eds., 1989) (discussing the early judicial systems of North and South Carolina).

to the decision of a case in the common-law sense and that the decision was published in a reliable form available to the federal courts.[58]

Illustration 5-6. *A*, a citizen of State *X*, sued *B*, a citizen of State *Y*, in a federal court in State *X*. *A* sought to quiet title to land located in State *X*. The issue in the case concerned the method by which title to land could be acquired by adverse possession in State *X*. The highest court in State *X* had rendered several decisions on the issue in the case. However, the decisions were conflicting. The latest statement on the issue was contained in a case in which it was unnecessary to the decision. The issue in the action is an issue of local law on which the federal courts under *Swift* were bound to follow the decisions of the state courts. Nevertheless, the federal court would have had to make its own independent determination of the adverse possession issue because the decisions in State *X* on the issue were unsettled.

(c) Separation of Powers

The doctrine of *Swift v. Tyson* has often been criticized as a violation of principles of federalism.[59] The preceding discussion of the concepts of sovereignty and stare decisis prevailing in the early nineteenth century has demonstrated that the *Swift* decision itself involved no such difficulties. In addition to federalism restrictions, however, the Constitution also contains separation-of-powers restrictions. As noted in section A, the traditional doctrine of separation of powers presupposes that the courts' lawmaking activities will be limited. While couched in federalism terms, much of the modern criticism of *Swift* really appears to be based on the theory that the Court was making law in too broad a fashion, thus violating implicit separation-of-powers restrictions on its authority. If the basic lawmaking powers in a case like *Swift* resided either in the sovereign state of New York or in Congress, where did the Supreme Court get the authority in *Swift* to enforce a rule prescribed by neither of those bodies?

The flaw in this criticism lies in a misperception of what the courts were doing when they administered the general commercial law. The most important feature of that law in terms of separation-of-powers principles was its characteristic as a body of private international *custom*. As custom, the commercial law had not been "created" by any one sovereign—*i.e.*, no institution within a government had made a conscious policy choice to make up particular rules for the convenience of its merchants. Rather, general commercial custom originated in the behavior of individuals—merchants—trading among seafaring nations. Indeed, the separate bodies of law now referred to as admiralty and commercial law were at

---

58. *See id.* at 46-48 (discussing the dates that modern systems of law reporting were established and the relationship between courts of appellate review and modern systems of law reporting).

59. *See, e.g.*, the discussion of *Erie Railroad v. Tompkins* in section D, *infra.*

one time a single body of "private international law" and only later separated into distinct subject areas.[60]

Substantively, therefore, the important policy choice involved when a state or nation decided to follow general commercial law was the choice to follow it, not the sovereign's approval or creation of the law's content, which had already been established by the interaction of private individuals. This "legislative" policy choice was respected in cases like *Swift* by the federal courts' adherence to whatever decision the relevant sovereign had made about *whether* to follow the general commercial law; and, of course, which sovereign was the "relevant" one to make the policy choice was determined by the international conflict-of-laws rules enforced under the "in cases where they apply" language of the Rules of Decision Act.

The content that needed to be added to the relatively mature body of commercial law rules in existence by the time of the *Swift* decision was added through the processes of analogical reasoning familiar to the common law and would be called today (as discussed in section A above) "interstitial lawmaking," which involved no separation-of-powers violation. Nevertheless, the separation-of-powers doctrine did impose limitations on the federal courts' ability to administer common-law rules. A comparison of the most important situation in which these limitations were present with cases in which separation of powers was not an obstacle to administration of common-law principles will further illustrate why the *Swift* decision did not involve proscribed lawmaking.

Early cases dealing with the common law of crimes and civil admiralty best illustrate how the separation-of-powers doctrine affected the common-law authority of the federal courts. Section 9 of the Judiciary Act of 1789 conferred exclusive subject-matter jurisdiction on the federal courts over federal crimes. Section 11 of the Act conferred exclusive jurisdiction of civil admiralty cases. Yet in the area of criminal jurisdiction, the Supreme Court refused to permit the administration of a common law of crimes, while in the area of admiralty the courts always and without question have applied "common-law" rules of admiralty.[61]

The distinction between these two kinds of cases was rooted in the separation-of-powers doctrine, which dictated that only the primary lawmaking branch of the government could decide whether a particular act was a crime and affix a punishment to it.[62] Such a fundamental policy choice was beyond the scope of the judicial power because of the nature of the choices that the judiciary would have had to make in adopting common-law crimes as "federal" crimes.

---

60. *See* RANDALL BRIDWELL & RALPH U. WHITTEN, THE CONSTITUTION AND THE COMMON LAW: THE DECLINE OF THE DOCTRINES OF SEPARATION OF POWERS AND FEDERALISM 61 (1977); *see also* GRANT GILMORE & CHARLES L. BLACK, THE LAW OF ADMIRALTY § 1-3, at 5 (2d ed. 1975); THEODORE F.T. PLUCKNETT, A CONCISE HISTORY OF THE COMMON LAW ch. 5 (5th ed. 1956); Thomas E. Scrutton, *General Survey of the History of the Law Merchant, in* 3 SELECT ESSAYS IN ANGLO-AMERICAN LEGAL HISTORY 7, 11-12 (1909).

61. *See generally* RANDALL BRIDWELL & RALPH U. WHITTEN, THE CONSTITUTION AND THE COMMON LAW: THE DECLINE OF THE DOCTRINES OF SEPARATION OF POWERS AND FEDERALISM ch. 3 (1977).

62. *See* United States v. Hudson & Goodwin, 11 U.S. (7 Cranch) 32, 33-34, 3 L. Ed. 259, 260 (1812); United States v. Coolidge, 14 U.S. (1 Wheat.) 415, 4 L. Ed. 124 (1816); JOHN M. GOODENOW, HISTORICAL SKETCHES OF THE PRINCIPLES AND MAXIMS OF AMERICAN JURISPRUDENCE 32 (Arno ed. 1972).

Although there were many acts that constituted crimes in the English common law and the common law of the states, it was inconceivable that *all* such acts would be adopted as federal crimes, given the limited power of the federal government. Yet if some, but not all, common-law crimes were to be adopted as "federal" crimes, how would the courts make the selection? It was apparent to the judges of the time that any process of picking and choosing among common-law crimes would amount to the kind of policy-making that was reserved to Congress. As Justice Johnson explained in the *Trial of William Butler for Piracy*:[63]

> [I]f the courts of the United States are to be at liberty to select such parts [of the common-law of crimes] as in their judgment are applicable, what is this but giving as much force to one part as to another? By what rule or principle are they to be governed in the selection? I know of none; and the consequence is, either that they find the whole system in force, or what is worse, erect themselves into legislators in the selection.[64]

The distinction between the common law of crimes and the civil admiralty was clear. It was not at all ridiculous to suppose that the whole body of "common-law" principle composing admiralty and maritime jurisprudence should be enforced by the federal courts within the exclusive grant of subject-matter jurisdiction to them. The constitutional and statutory grants of subject-matter jurisdiction in admiralty and maritime cases presupposed the existence of a body of rules that the courts would enforce within the jurisdictional grants.[65] As noted earlier, admiralty and maritime rules were private international customary rules that predated the Constitution. These rules were not created by any sovereign, in the first instance, but by seafaring merchants. The grant of admiralty jurisdiction presupposed that the federal courts would administer the whole body of these private rules *without* needing to make any legislative selection of which rules would be enforced. Of course, the question *whether* the United States should enforce the traditional admiralty principles did involve a legislative-like policy choice, but that choice had been made by the constitutional and statutory authorization of admiralty subject-matter jurisdiction itself. The *administration* of the rules of admiralty jurisprudence within the jurisdictional grant did not involve any additional policy choices forbidden to the judges, as would an enforcement of a federal common law of crimes. Moreover, the admiralty and maritime rules remained customary rules, created by private parties; whereas adoption of a common law of crimes would have amounted to a sovereign policy choice to create distinctly federal law, a prerogative reserved to Congress.[66]

---

63. This case is an unreported pamphlet decision of a special circuit court for the trial of crimes against the United States.

64. *See also* JOHN M. GOODENOW, HISTORICAL SKETCHES OF THE PRINCIPLES AND MAXIMS OF AMERICAN JURISPRUDENCE 21 (Arno ed. 1972).

65. *Cf.* GRANT GILMORE & CHARLES L. BLACK, THE LAW OF ADMIRALTY § 1-16, at 45 (2d ed. 1975); DAVID W. ROBERTSON, ADMIRALTY AND FEDERALISM 148 (1970).

66. *Cf.* DAVID W. ROBERTSON, ADMIRALTY AND FEDERALISM 148 (1970); GRANT GILMORE & CHARLES L. BLACK, THE LAW OF ADMIRALTY § 6-58, at 456 (2d ed. 1975).

No separation-of-powers problem was involved when the federal courts administered general commercial law. Like admiralty, general commercial law was a private international body of customary rules. The adoption of the diversity jurisdiction coupled with the decision by an individual state to follow general commercial principles exhausted the legislative-like policy choices that were involved in the administration of commercial rules. Thus, the federal courts were able to enforce general commercial rules, when appropriate, without violating the principles of separation of powers.

Indeed, refusal to enforce the general commercial-law rules would, in its own right, have amounted to a violation of the separation-of-powers doctrine. Grants of subject-matter jurisdiction are not simply authorizations that allow the courts to exercise authority when and if they choose. They are, to an extent at least, legislative commands to exercise jurisdiction in the categories of cases included within the grant.[67] Take, for example, diversity jurisdiction. The purpose of the legislative authorization traditionally has been understood to be the protection of noncitizens from the bias or prejudice that they might encounter in state courts. This purpose would have been undermined if, each time a case involving general commercial law was instituted within the diversity jurisdiction, the federal courts had dismissed the case or adhered to the view of the states in which they were sitting about the content of the law. In either instance, the parties to the action would have been deprived of the benefits Congress had elected to give them. Had there been a dismissal, the parties would have been deprived completely of a federal court; and had the federal court retained jurisdiction but followed state decisions on the content of general commercial law, the parties would have been deprived of the independent judgment of a court about the content of the legal principles controlling their transaction—something they would have had in any other court and which is, arguably, an essential ingredient of judicial power.[68]

(d) The Functions of the Diversity Jurisdiction

One aspect of the law-administering power of the federal courts under *Swift* that has sometimes appeared to violate principles of federalism is the power, under certain circumstances, to disregard *settled* state decisions on *local* matters to preserve the integrity of the congressional grant of diversity jurisdiction. Such decisions were disregarded when the application of the settled state decisions posed a danger that state-court bias in lawmaking would adversely and retroactively affect noncitizens of the state. The principle is illustrated by a line of cases from Mississippi.

The Mississippi Constitution of 1832 declared that ''[t]he introduction of slaves into this state, as merchandise, or for sale, shall be prohibited, from and after the first day of May, eighteen hundred and thirty-three.'' Despite this

---

67. *See* Chapter 2(A)(3) (''The Mandatory Nature of Subject-Matter Jurisdiction'') *supra.*

68. Recall the statement in *Carroll v. Carroll's Lessee*, above, that the Supreme Court was ''bound to decide . . . every . . . question, as we find it ought to be decided.''

provision, a noncitizen of Mississippi imported slaves in 1835 and 1836 and sold them, taking a note in exchange for the slaves. The note was not paid when due, and the holder instituted an action in the U.S. Circuit Court for the District of Louisiana. The sole defense was the illegality of consideration for the note under the Mississippi constitutional provision. The plaintiff won a judgment, and the defendant brought the case to the U.S. Supreme Court. In *Groves v. Slaughter*,[69] the Supreme Court held that the consideration was not illegal because the Mississippi constitutional provision was not self-executing and no legislation had been enacted to make it effective. There were certain Mississippi decisions dealing with the construction of the constitutional provision, but the Court did not consider them binding because all discussion of the issue had been dicta and the state judges had disagreed among themselves about the proper interpretation of the constitutional provision.[70]

After the Supreme Court's decision in *Groves*, the Mississippi Supreme Court held that the constitutional provision in question was self-executing and rendered all sales of slaves made after May 1, 1833, void. An action was then brought in the U.S. Circuit Court for the District of Mississippi to recover on a note given for the purchase of slaves sold in 1836. Under instructions from the circuit court that the note was void if given for slaves imported after May 1, 1833, the jury found for the defendant. Plaintiff brought the case to the U.S. Supreme Court. In *Rowan v. Runnels*,[71] the Court reversed. The Court held that it would give full effect to the Mississippi decision from the time it was made, but would not give it retroactive effect. To do so, said the Court, might render "utterly useless and nugatory" that provision of the U.S. Constitution "which secures to the citizens of another state the right to sue in the courts of the United States."[72]

The Court's concern in *Rowan* was to prevent the operation of possible state-court bias in lawmaking against noncitizens, who had the most to lose from the Mississippi court's interpretation of its constitution. That possible state-court bias in lawmaking was the limit of the doctrine can be seen by a comparison of *Rowan* with *Nesmith v. Sheldon*.[73] In *Nesmith*, the dispute involved a Michigan constitutional provision that required a two-thirds vote of each house of the state legislature to pass any act of incorporation. The Michigan Legislature enacted two statutes that authorized persons to form banking associations in corporate form and made the stockholders of the corporations liable for the debts the corporations incurred. The U.S. Circuit Court for the District of Michigan held these legislative acts valid. However, the Michigan Supreme Court later declared them invalid under the constitutional provision described above.

---

69. 40 U.S. (15 Pet.) 449, 10 L. Ed. 800 (1841).

70. *See id.*; RANDALL BRIDWELL & RALPH U. WHITTEN, THE CONSTITUTION AND THE COMMON LAW: THE DECLINE OF THE DOCTRINES OF SEPARATION OF POWERS AND FEDERALISM 74 (1977).

71. 46 U.S. (5 How.) 134, 12 L. Ed. 85 (1847).

72. *Id.* at 139, 12 L. Ed. at 87; *see* RANDALL BRIDWELL & RALPH U. WHITTEN, THE CONSTITUTION AND THE COMMON LAW: THE DECLINE OF THE DOCTRINES OF SEPARATION OF POWERS AND FEDERALISM 74-75 (1977).

73. 48 U.S. (7 How.) 812, 12 L. Ed. 925 (1849).

The U.S. Supreme Court followed the state court's interpretation of the Michigan Constitution without question. The Court stated that *Groves* and *Rowan* "in relation to the construction of the constitution of Mississippi, stand on very different grounds, as will be seen by a reference to the cases."[74] The difference between cases was that in *Rowan*, the state interpretation would primarily have harmed noncitizens, who were the largest class of importers and sellers of slaves. In *Nesmith*, however, the state decision would harm equally both citizens and noncitizens of Michigan. The suit in *Nesmith* was brought to hold stockholders of a banking corporation liable for its debts. There was no reason to believe that more stockholders were noncitizens than citizens of Michigan.

Thus, despite broad interpretations of the *Rowan* decision as a case permitting "state precedents interpretative of state written law to be disregarded, in the national courts, when necessary 'to establish justice,' "[75] the operative principle was much narrower. Federal courts could refuse to give a *retroactive* effect to state decisions when it appeared that there was a potential for the state decisions to operate more harshly against noncitizens than against citizens of the state. The justification for the principle was the function of the federal courts in suits between citizens of different states to prevent state bias from operating against noncitizens.[76]

In addition to the *Rowan* principle, the U.S. Supreme Court also refused to allow state laws to limit noncitizens' access to federal courts.[77] One case applying this principle, but which has, at times, been read incorrectly to permit the federal courts to disregard state attempts to "localize" the general commercial law, is *Watson v. Tarpley*.[78] In *Watson*, an action was brought on a bill of exchange by a citizen of Tennessee against a citizen of Mississippi in a Mississippi federal court. The trial court instructed the jury that even after presentment of the bill for acceptance, regular protest, and notice of nonacceptance, an action could not be maintained until after the maturity of the bill. Acting under the lower court's instruction, which appeared to be required by a Mississippi statute, the jury gave a verdict for the defendant. The U.S. Supreme

---

74. *Id.* at 818, 12 L. Ed. at 928.

75. *See, e.g.,* 2 WILLIAM W. CROSSKEY, POLITICS AND THE CONSTITUTION IN THE HISTORY OF THE UNITED STATES 862 (1953).

76. *See* RANDALL BRIDWELL & RALPH U. WHITTEN, THE CONSTITUTION AND THE COMMON LAW: THE DECLINE OF THE DOCTRINES OF SEPARATION OF POWERS AND FEDERALISM 73-76 (1977). It is, of course, possible to disagree with the principle announced in *Rowan*. For example, it is possible to reason that the principle was unnecessary to protect noncitizens from bias within the diversity jurisdiction, or that even if it did afford them important protections, the cost of the principle in terms of encroachment on state lawmaking prerogatives was too great. However, disagreement with the necessity or utility of the principle should not be extended to a distortion of the principle itself. It was a highly limited one and did not represent some vast repository of power in the federal courts to disregard state-court decisions with which the federal courts disagreed.

77. *See* Union Bank v. Jolly's Adm'rs, 59 U.S. (18 How.) 503, 507, 15 L. Ed. 472, 474 (1856); RANDALL BRIDWELL & RALPH U. WHITTEN, THE CONSTITUTION AND THE COMMON LAW: THE DECLINE OF THE DOCTRINES OF SEPARATION OF POWERS AND FEDERALISM 76 (1977).

78. 59 U.S. (18 How.) 517, 15 L. Ed. 509 (1856); *see* 2 WILLIAM W. CROSSKEY, POLITICS AND THE CONSTITUTION IN THE HISTORY OF THE UNITED STATES 861-62 (1953); TONY A. FREYER, HARMONY & DISSONANCE: THE *Swift* & *Erie* CASES IN AMERICAN FEDERALISM 51-55 (1981); MORTON J. HORWITZ, THE TRANSFORMATION OF AMERICAN LAW, 1780-1860, at 225 (1977).

Court held the instruction to be erroneous. At one point in its opinion, the Court stated that the Mississippi statute was a "violation of the general commercial law, which a state would have no power to impose, and which the courts of the United States would be bound to disregard."[79] This passage, however, does not mean that the states could not "localize" rules of commercial law. There was no doubt that general commercial law would determine the primary rights and liabilities of the parties in *Watson*. The Mississippi statute thus did not alter the substantive right to recover on the bill of exchange, but only the time when the action could be brought. It was to this impairment of the right to resort to the diversity jurisdiction to which the Court objected.

The Court stated that while "the laws of the several states are of binding authority upon their domestic tribunals," they could not "affect, either by enlargement or diminution, the jurisdiction of the courts of the United States . . . nor destroy or control the rights of parties litigant to whom the right of resort to these courts has been secured by the laws and [C]onstitution."[80] Because the Constitution and the Judiciary Act of 1789 had given noncitizens "the power or privilege of litigating and enforcing their rights acquired under and defined by [the] general commercial law before the judicial tribunals of the United States," the Court concluded that state laws, "the effect of which would be to impair the rights thus secured, or to divest the federal courts of cognizance thereof, in their fullest acceptation under the commercial law, must be nugatory and unavailing."[81] Despite some broad language in *Watson*, therefore, the decision appears consistent with the much narrower principle that state laws will not be permitted to impair a suitor's access to the federal courts.[82]

(e) Equity and Admiralty Cases

Until 1948, the Rules of Decision Act prescribed that state laws were to be regarded as rules of decision only in "trials at common law."[83] Thus, at the time *Swift* was decided, equity and admiralty cases were excluded from the Act's coverage. As noted in the earlier discussion of the separation-of-powers doctrine, the federal courts were granted exclusive jurisdiction over admiralty cases by the first Judiciary Act. When acting within that grant of jurisdiction, the courts applied general maritime law.[84] In equity cases, the pattern was more complex.

---

79. *Watson*, 59 U.S. (18 How.) at 521, 15 L. Ed. at 511.

80. *Id.* at 520, 15 L. Ed. at 511.

81. *Id.* at 521, 15 L. Ed. at 511. *See* RANDALL BRIDWELL & RALPH U. WHITTEN, THE CONSTITUTION AND THE COMMON LAW: THE DECLINE OF THE DOCTRINES OF SEPARATION OF POWERS AND FEDERALISM 77-78 (1977). As in *Rowan*, this result may have been, on balance, unnecessary to protect the policies supporting the diversity jurisdiction. However, as discussed above, like the *Rowan* principle, disagreement with the principle should not be extended to distortion of it.

82. *See* RANDALL BRIDWELL & RALPH U. WHITTEN, THE CONSTITUTION AND THE COMMON LAW: THE DECLINE OF THE DOCTRINES OF SEPARATION OF POWERS AND FEDERALISM 70 (1977).

83. In the 1948 revision of the Judicial Code, the Act was amended to apply to all "civil actions." *See* 28 U.S.C. § 1652.

84. *See* GRANT GILMORE & CHARLES L. BLACK, THE LAW OF ADMIRALTY § 1-16, at 45 (2d ed. 1975); DAVID W. ROBERTSON, ADMIRALTY AND FEDERALISM 148 (1970).

In common-law cases in the federal courts, a "static conformity" to state procedure was required from 1789 to 1872. Then a "dynamic conformity" was required from 1872 to 1938, when the Federal Rules of Civil Procedure were adopted.[85] However, in equity cases, conformity to state procedure was not required. The Supreme Court from time to time prescribed equity rules to govern the practice and procedure in equity cases. Taken together with the omission of equity cases from the coverage of the Rules of Decision Act, it might appear that the federal courts were free in all equitable proceedings to follow their own procedural and substantive rules. Nonetheless, the federal courts were not entirely free to do so.

The independent federal equity power was necessary because some states did not have equity courts.[86] In such states, there might be no equity procedures that federal courts could follow, making procedural conformity impossible. Similarly, because equity contained remedial "rules of decision," there might be an absence of equitable "rules of decision" in states without equity courts, making it necessary to omit equity cases from the Rules of Decision Act to ensure that the grant of jurisdiction to the federal courts in "law and equity" cases would be effective. Nevertheless, by providing effective remedies, equity often operated on "legal" rights when the remedies at law were inadequate. Thus, the federal courts could not disregard state law entirely just because they were sitting in equity. In fact, they did not do so.

Federal courts sitting in equity enforced primary rights defined by state law. The only effect of the independent federal equity power was that the states would not be allowed to destroy the division between law and equity that existed in the federal courts by (1) enacting laws that enlarged or limited the powers of those courts or (2) providing forms of remedies enforceable in federal equity proceedings that were inconsistent with traditional equitable principles. Nor could state-court decisions bind federal courts on matters of general equity jurisprudence.[87] The overall result was that the federal courts in both law and equity cases generally followed state-court decisions defining local primary rights, but not on issues of general commercial law. In addition, the federal courts conformed to state procedure in common-law cases. However, the federal courts had an independent federal equity procedure and independent federal equity remedial power. That power could sometimes override state "substantive" law when necessary for the effective exercise or integrity of the independent equity power.

Illustration 5-7. State *X* and State *Y* settled a boundary dispute between the two states by compact. The compact stated that land titles granted previous to the compact by either state would be as secure as in the state that granted them and not be affected by the compact. After the compact had settled the two states'

---

85. *See* Chapter 1(E)(5) ("Development of Federal Procedure and the Federal Rules of Civil Procedure") *supra.*

86. CHARLES A. WRIGHT, HANDBOOK OF THE LAW OF FEDERAL COURTS § 54, at 374 (5th ed. 1994).

87. *See* RANDALL BRIDWELL & RALPH U. WHITTEN, THE CONSTITUTION AND THE COMMON LAW: THE DECLINE OF THE DOCTRINES OF SEPARATION OF POWERS AND FEDERALISM 172-73 n.46, 186-87 n.43 (1977) (citing cases).

boundaries, certain land that formerly had been in State X fell in State Y. A, a citizen of State X, claims title to this land under the law of State X. B, a citizen of State Y, also claims title to this land under the law of State X. A sues B in a federal court in State Y to eject B from the land. A's claim in the action is based on legal title, while B's claim is based on equitable title. Under the procedures followed by State X courts, an equitable title cannot be set up as sufficient in an action at law, such as ejectment, but must be established in a separate equitable proceeding. Under the procedures followed by the State Y courts, an equitable title can be set up as a defense in an action at law for ejectment. Under the procedures followed by the federal courts, an equitable title could not be set up in an action at law. On facts similar to these, the U.S. Supreme Court held that B could not set up the equitable title in the federal action in State Y.[88] However, under the traditional practice governing separate actions at law and equity, defenses that were recognized exclusively in equity were sometimes made into legal defenses by statute and thereafter recognized by the common-law courts.[89] Even if the State Y procedures are based on statutes in State Y converting the equitable title into legal title, they would not be recognized by the federal courts on these facts, because the law controlling the title dispute is State X law by virtue of the compact. However, the Supreme Court made it clear that, on a matter that State Y law controlled, statutes converting an equitable title into a legal title would be recognized as fully in federal courts as in the courts of the state.[90]

(f) The Swift *Doctrine Changes*

The doctrine taking its name from *Swift v. Tyson* changed radically in the latter part of the nineteenth century. The changes that occurred in the doctrine transformed the power of the federal courts in ways that violated both separation-of-powers and federalism restrictions in the U.S. Constitution. These later alterations in the *Swift* doctrine, not the manner in which the doctrine had operated in the early nineteenth century, produced major objections by courts and commentators and the eventual transformation of the federal courts' source-of-law authority in *Erie Railroad v. Tompkins*.[91]

The transformation of *Swift* was complex and touched many kinds of cases. Two of the earliest, and most grievous, departures from the original *Swift* doctrine occurred in cases involving municipal bonds and torts. From the previous discussion of the *Swift* doctrine, two propositions should be clear. First, the states were not obligated to follow the general commercial law. Instead, they were free to "localize" their commercial law, for example, by enacting statutes to govern commercial transactions. If a state did so, and if under the prevailing territorial conflict-of-law rules the state had the authority to control a dispute with its law,

---

88. *See* Robinson v. Campbell, 16 U.S. (3 Wheat.) 212, 4 L. Ed. 372 (1818).

89. *See* Chapter 7(D)(2) *infra* (discussing the recognition of "set-off" in equity courts, the subsequent enactment of "set-off" statutes, and the recognition of set-off thereafter in the common-law courts).

90. *See* Robinson v. Campbell, 16 U.S. (3 Wheat.) 212, 223, 4 L. Ed. 372, 376 (1818).

91. 304 U.S. 64, 58 S. Ct. 817, 82 L. Ed. 1188 (1938).

the federal courts had no authority to apply general commercial law instead of the local law. The *Swift* decision itself implied as much.

Second, distinct limits to "general" law existed. There was a "general commercial law" and "general admiralty law" because those bodies of law were comprised of international customary rules. However, all property law was local to the sovereign where the property was located. Likewise, all tort law was local to the sovereign where the alleged tort was committed.

In municipal bond cases, the U.S. Supreme Court departed from *Swift* by disregarding explicit state statutory limitations on the power of localities to issue negotiable bonds.[92] Yet nothing could have been clearer under *Swift* than a state's right to limit negotiable transactions by statute. All who engaged in such transactions within the state were bound to know whatever limitations the state had imposed, at their peril.[93] Thus, the Court was making law in disregard of the sovereign rights of the states to control transactions within their borders.

In tort cases, the Court departed from *Swift* by the applying a "general" law of torts.[94] Quite clearly there was no international body of customary tort law that deserved the label "general." The Court simply made the "general tort law" up as it went along. This approach violated restrictions (observed under *Swift*) on its lawmaking authority. It also violated the sovereign right of the states to impose their own tort law in cases arising within their borders.[95]

SECTION D. THE *ERIE* DOCTRINE

Incursions upon the prerogatives of Congress and the states such as those in the municipal bond and tort cases produced the reaction known today as the "*Erie* doctrine"—so named after *Erie Railroad v. Tompkins*.[96] In *Erie*, the U.S. Supreme Court reinterpreted the Rules of Decision Act to require that the federal courts follow state-court decisions on all matters of state law.[97] The Court overruled *Swift* and eradicated the distinction drawn under the *Swift* doctrine between matters of local and general law. The Court in *Erie* established a new distinction between substantive matters, upon which the federal courts were bound to follow state decisions if no controlling federal statute existed, and procedural matters, which could be controlled by federal decisions.[98] In addition, after *Erie*, the federal courts were empowered to fashion federal substantive common-law

---

92. *See, e.g.,* Board of Comm'rs v. Aspinwall, 62 U.S. (21 How.) 539, 16 L. Ed. 208 (1859).

93. *See* RANDALL BRIDWELL & RALPH U. WHITTEN, THE CONSTITUTION AND THE COMMON LAW: THE DECLINE OF THE DOCTRINES OF SEPARATION OF POWERS AND FEDERALISM 116-19 (1977).

94. *See id.* 199-222.

95. Compare the discussion above of the Court's decisions in the common law of crimes and civil admiralty areas during the early nineteenth century. *See also* TONY A. FREYER, HARMONY & DISSONANCE: THE *SWIFT* & *ERIE* CASES IN AMERICAN FEDERALISM ch. III (1981); RICHARD H. FALLON ET AL., HART & WECHSLER'S THE FEDERAL COURTS AND THE FEDERAL SYSTEM 683-87 (4th ed. 1996).

96. 304 U.S. 64, 58 S. Ct. 817, 82 L. Ed. 1188 (1938).

97. *See* Ralph U. Whitten, Erie *and the Federal Rules: A Review and Reappraisal After* Burlington Northern Railroad v. Woods, 21 CREIGHTON L. REV. 1, 2 (1987).

98. *See id.* at 1-4.

rules on some matters that would control the outcome of cases in both federal and state courts.

1. The *Erie* Decision

In *Erie*, the plaintiff, Tompkins, a citizen of Pennsylvania, was walking along a railroad right of way in Pennsylvania. Tompkins was struck by something protruding from the car of one of the defendant's trains. Tompkins sued the Erie Railroad in a federal district court in New York. Tompkins alleged that Erie's negligence caused the accident. Erie's defense was that under Pennsylvania law, its duty to Tompkins was no greater than that owed to a trespasser. Under Pennsylvania law, unless its negligence were wilful or wanton, it could not be held liable. The district judge refused to instruct the jury that the applicable law precluded recovery. The jury brought in a verdict for Tompkins. On appeal, the Second Circuit held that it was unnecessary to consider whether the law of Pennsylvania required wilful or wanton negligence because the question was one of general law upon which the federal courts could make an independent judgment. Under this "general tort law," the Second Circuit held that the railroad could be held liable for ordinary negligence. The U.S. Supreme Court granted certiorari and reversed.[99]

Despite the fact that no one had argued that *Swift* should be over-ruled,[100] the opening sentence of Justice Brandeis' opinion for the Court stated: "The question for decision is whether the oft-challenged doctrine of *Swift v. Tyson* shall now be disapproved."[101] The Court seemed to treat the problem created by the *Swift* doctrine as exclusively one of federalism.[102] The Court also asserted that the *Swift* doctrine created a problem of forum shopping. According to the Court, the diversity jurisdiction was designed to provide a nondis-criminatory forum for the noncitizen.[103] The *Swift* doctrine, however, had resulted in discrimination by noncitizens against citizens. Because noncitizens were able to choose either state or federal court, they were able to survey the state and federal decisions on the substantive matters at issue in the case and select the court that would apply the most favorable substantive law.[104] Howev-

---

99. *See Erie*, 304 U.S. at 69-70, 58 S. Ct. at 818, 82 L. Ed. at 1189-90.

100. *See id.* at 66 (argument for petitioner did not question the finality of the doctrine of *Swift v. Tyson*; petitioner argued that state decisions were controlling if "sufficiently established"); *id.* at 68 (argument for respondent contending that the question was one of general law and that there was no doctrine that a matter was one of local law if "sufficiently established" in local decisions).

101. 304 U.S. at 69, 58 S. Ct. at 818, 82 L. Ed. at 1189.

102. "The federal courts assumed in the broad field of 'general law,' the power to declare rules of decision which Congress was confessedly without power to enact as statutes." *Id.* at 72-73, 58 S. Ct. at 819, 82 L. Ed. at 1191 (footnotes omitted).

103. *See id.* at 74, 58 S. Ct. at 820, 82 L. Ed. at 1192.

104. *See id.* at 74-75, 58 S. Ct. at 820-21, 82 L. Ed. at 1192. The reason that the noncitizen has the choice of forum, of course, is due to the configuration of the diversity and removal jurisdiction. Recall from Chapter 2(C)(5) ("Removal Jurisdiction") that the noncitizen plaintiff can choose to sue in either federal or state court. If the noncitizen plaintiff chooses federal court, the citizen defendant is obligated to defend there. However, if the noncitizen plaintiff chooses state court, the citizen defendant must defend there if diversity of citizenship is the only basis of federal jurisdiction, because a citizen of the state in which the action is brought may not er, the Court indicated that the forum shopping problem would not, in itself, have caused *Swift* to be overruled if the issue were merely one of a longstanding misconstruction of the Rules of Decision Act. Rather, the Court was compelled to overrule *Swift* because "the unconstitutionality of the course pursued" had become clear to it.[105]

The result in *Erie* was undoubtedly correct for at least two reasons. First, the dispute was controlled by substantive tort principles. As noted in section C(2)(f), above, the Court had distorted the *Swift* doctrine when it concluded that there existed a general law of torts upon which the federal courts had a right, in diversity cases, to make a judgment independent of state decisions. All tort law should have been considered local in nature. Second, by the time *Erie* was decided, it was probably true that there was not anything that could reasonably be labeled "general" law in any area, even the commercial law area. The notion of a customary law whose content transcended the control of any given government while being accepted by all (or most) governments had been discarded.[106] In its place, American courts had generally accepted the notion that all law, from the general corpus of a subject area (such as torts or contracts) to the content of the individual rules within the area, must be the product of some sovereign's will. Under this view, judges were seen as active participants in the policy-making processes of lawmaking. They did not "find" law even in the limited sense described and accepted in *Swift*. If this attitude about law had not been entirely accepted by the time *Erie* was decided, at least its acceptance was well underway and has undeniably been completed today.[107] Under such circumstances, even Justice Story would have agreed that the federal courts would be bound by settled state court decisions on all "substantive" matters not directly controlled by federal law.[108]

As a criticism of *Swift* and as a justification for a change of course, however, the *Erie* opinion was an intellectual disaster. Justice Brandeis had cited

---

remove such a case. *See* 28 U.S.C. § 1441(b). However, a noncitizen defendant may remove on the basis of diversity alone. *See id.* The Court did not consider the problem of the plaintiff who is a citizen of the state in which the action is brought who picks a federal court in the state based on a desire to obtain a more favorable substantive law, even though such a plaintiff could forum shop in the same offensive way as a noncitizen defendant under the *Swift* doctrine. Indeed, in such a case, the plaintiff must have some motive for picking the federal court other than fear of discrimination against noncitizens that might occur in the state courts.

105. *See id.* at 77-78, 58 S. Ct. at 822, 82 L. Ed. at 1195.

106. The jurisprudential developments that resulted in this view were complex and cannot be described fully here. For good descriptions of those developments, see WILLIAM L. TWINING, KARL LLEWELLYN AND THE REALIST MOVEMENT (1973); G. Edward White, *From Sociological Jurisprudence to Realism: Jurisprudence and Social Change in Early Twentieth-Century America, in* PATTERNS OF AMERICAN LEGAL THOUGHT 99 (1978); *see also* JEROME FRANK, LAW AND THE MODERN MIND (1930); KARL N. LLEWELLYN, THE COMMON LAW TRADITION: DECIDING APPEALS (1960); Patrick J. Borchers, *The Origins of Diversity Jurisdiction: The Rise of Legal Positivism, and a Brave New World for* Erie *and* Klaxon, 72 TEX. L. REV. 79, 115-117 (1993); Karl N. Llewellyn, *A Realistic Jurisprudence–The Next Step*, 30 COLUM. L. REV. 431 (1930).

107. It has often been argued that *Erie's* rejection of *Swift* was the result of the rejection of *Swift's* philosophy of law and the acceptance of the philosophy of legal positivism. *See, e.g.,* Bradford R. Clark, *Ascertaining the Laws of the Several States: Positivism and Judicial Federalism After* Erie, 145 U. PA. L. REV. 1459 (1997). For a dissenting view, see Jack Goldsmith & Steven Walt, Erie *and the Irrelevance of Legal Positivism*, 84 VA. L. REV. 673 (1998).

108. *Cf.* RANDALL BRIDWELL & RALPH U. WHITTEN, THE CONSTITUTION AND THE COMMON LAW: THE DECLINE OF THE DOCTRINES OF SEPARATION OF POWERS AND FEDERALISM xiv, 2, 4, 11, 136-37 (1977).

the "recent research of a competent scholar" to the effect that Justice Story's interpretation of the Rules of Decision Act in *Swift* was incorrect. The research referred to was that of Professor Charles Warren, who had discovered an original draft of the Judiciary Act of 1789, in which the Rules of Decision Act originally read:

> And be it further enacted, that the statute law of the several states in force for the time being and their unwritten or common law now in use, whether by adoption from the common law of England, the ancient statutes of the same or otherwise, except where the constitution, treaties or statutes of the United States shall otherwise require or provide, shall be regarded as rules of decision in the trials at common law in the courts of the United States in cases where they apply.[109]

In the final version of the Act, the phrase "the laws of the several states" was substituted for "the statute law of the several states in force for the time being and their unwritten or common law now in use, whether by adoption from the common law of England, the current statutes of the same or otherwise." Professor Warren concluded that the change was intended to be stylistic only and that, as a consequence, decisions of state tribunals on common-law matters were intended to be included within the word "laws."[110]

Professor Warren's interpretation of the Rules of Decision Act has been criticized.[111] For present purposes, it is sufficient to note that Warren simply assumed that expressions such as "unwritten or common law" were the equivalent of "court decisions" in the minds of those who drafted and enacted the original Rules of Decision Act. As the discussion of the *Swift* doctrine in the last section indicated, however, in the late eighteenth and early nineteenth century, "common law" and "judicial decisions," or "law" and "decisions of courts," were simply not equivalent expressions.[112] Thus, it is quite plausible to believe

---

109. Charles Warren, *New Light on the History of the Federal Judiciary Act of 1789*, 37 HARV. L. REV. 49, 86 (1923).

110. *See id.*

111. *See* WILFRED J. RITZ, REWRITING THE JUDICIARY ACT OF 1789, at 165-179 (Wythe Holt & L.H. LaRue eds. 1989); 2 WILLIAM W. CROSSKEY, POLITICS AND THE CONSTITUTION IN THE HISTORY OF THE UNITED STATES 866-867 (1953); HENRY J. FRIENDLY, IN PRAISE OF Erie AND THE NEW FEDERAL COMMON LAW 383, 389-91 (1964); Patrick J. Borchers, *The Origins of Diversity Jurisdiction: The Rise of Legal Positivism, and a Brave New World for* Erie *and* Klaxon, 72 TEX. L. REV. 79, 103-06 (1993). As Professor Crosskey pointed out, one is immediately impressed with the similarity in wording between the original draft that Warren found and the wording of the provision of the First Process Act that established a "static conformity" to state law in matters of procedure. *See* Chapter 1(E)(5) ("The Development of Federal Procedure and the Federal Rules of Civil Procedure") for a description of the First Process Act and static conformity. Thus, if the change were merely stylistic, as Warren contended, then the more plausible interpretation of the Act would be that it was intended to establish a "static conformity" to state law as that law existed in 1789. For a theory of how this static conformity would have made sense, see 2 WILLIAM W. CROSSKEY, POLITICS AND THE CONSTITUTION IN THE HISTORY OF THE UNITED STATES (1953), whose conclusions, however, have been widely rejected.

112. *Cf.* WILFRED J. RITZ, REWRITING THE JUDICIARY ACT OF 1789, at 28-30 (Wythe Holt & L.H. LaRue eds., 1989) (discussing the eighteenth century view that law was "found" rather than "made"); *see also* Patrick J. Borchers, *The Origins of Diversity Jurisdiction: The Rise of Legal Positivism, and a Brave New World for* Erie *and* Klaxon, 72 TEX. L. REV. 79, 111-15 (1993).

that the drafters of the First Judiciary Act intended to require the federal courts to adhere to state common-law rules in the absence of controlling federal statutory, treaty, or constitutional provisions. However, the weight to be given to state decisions interpreting that common law was to be determined in light of the traditional common-law doctrine of stare decisis.

Furthermore, Warren's interpretation does not solve the dilemma of a federal court faced with the kind of problem involved in *Swift*. Even if one assumes that the federal courts are obligated to follow settled[113] state decisions, what were those courts to do when given contradictory commands by the decisions, as New York had given in *Swift*? Recall that New York had indicated that it wished to follow the general commercial law, but its conclusion about the content of that law was at odds with the view of the federal courts and other states. Which New York "decision" was the U.S. Supreme Court supposed to follow, the decision of New York to follow the general commercial law or New York's decision about that law's content? As noted in the last section, the resolution of this problem for those who understand the relative importance of each of New York's "decisions" in the jurisprudence of the time was easy. Only a perverse refusal to understand that jurisprudence could result in the conclusion that New York's decision on the content of commercial law should be treated as more important than the decision to follow the general commercial law and, therefore, as controlling in the federal courts and the courts of other states.

In addition to Justice Brandeis' mistaken reliance upon Professor Warren's conclusions, there were other problems with the opinion in *Erie*. For one, Brandeis indicated that the practice of the federal courts under *Swift* had been unconstitutional because Congress had no power to enact the kinds of rules involved in *Swift* and *Erie* and the Constitution gave the courts no greater powers than Congress. This approach treated the *Swift-Erie* problem simply as one of federalism. If Congress has the power to enact a rule into law, then the federal courts can make up a rule to govern diversity actions within the same area. If Congress does not have such power, then the federal courts do not have law-making power either. This view is flatly wrong. In the first place, Congress did have the power to enact both the rule in *Swift* and the rule in *Erie*. The matter at issue in *Swift* concerned a bill of exchange negotiated between citizens of different states. The matter in *Erie* involved the tort obligations of an interstate railroad. Justice Brandeis failed to explain why Article I, § 8 of the Constitution (the Commerce Clause) does not give Congress power to enact rules of decision to regulate both these subjects.[114]

---

113. Presumably even Professor Warren would have agreed that the federal courts would have to have some powers of independent judgment when state decisions were unsettled or contradictory or rendered by a state court of less than final authority.

114. *See* RANDALL BRIDWELL & RALPH U. WHITTEN, THE CONSTITUTION AND THE COMMON LAW: THE DECLINE OF THE DOCTRINES OF SEPARATION OF POWERS AND FEDERALISM 3 (1977); CHARLES A. WRIGHT, THE LAW OF FEDERAL COURTS § 56, at 384 n.17 (5th ed. 1994). One need not resort to the more troublesome proposition advanced by Justice Reed in concurrence in *Erie* that Article III plus the necessary and proper clause may authorize Congress to provide substantive rules of decision to govern diversity actions. *See Erie*, 304 U.S. at 92, 58 S. Ct. at 828, 82 L. Ed. at 1201-02.

Additionally, Justice Brandeis' willingness to equate the lawmaking power of Congress and the lawmaking power of the courts ignores potential separation-of-powers restrictions on the ability of the courts to create law. In fact, if the powers that the federal courts assumed in the name of the *Swift* doctrine were to be held unconstitutional, a far better ground for so holding is separation of powers, rather than federalism. The notion that the federal courts have lawmaking powers as broad as those of Congress had been rejected long before *Erie*, at least as early as the common law of crimes cases discussed in the preceding section. When the federal courts expanded the coverage of "general law" into areas in which there was no international or interstate body of customary law to which the states were attempting to adhere—*i.e.*, into areas that were purely local—the federal courts arguably were exceeding their proper lawmaking grasp. Although, as observed in the last section, a federalism violation was also produced, it was not because Congress lacked the power to regulate some of the matters being dealt with by the federal courts. It was because the Constitution delegates primary lawmaking responsibility to Congress. Congress' decision to leave areas within its lawmaking authority unregulated should ordinarily mean that the state lawmaking will control those areas.[115] Thus, separation-of-powers restrictions on court lawmaking, operating through political processes that restrict the willingness of Congress to supplant state authority, actually afford valuable federalism protections to the states.[116]

Finally, Justice Brandeis stated in *Erie* that "[t]here is no *federal* general common law."[117] This statement implies that under the *Swift* doctrine, there was such law. But the use of the adjective "federal" was clearly improper, either to describe the law being applied in *Swift*, or to describe the illegitimate general law rules that were applied after *Swift* had been expanded in the latter part of the nineteenth and early twentieth centuries. For, although the federal courts disregarded state court decisions on general law matters—legitimately in *Swift* and illegitimately under the later decisions—the state courts were not bound to follow

---

115. The notion that separation-of-powers restrictions on judicial lawmaking afford protections to the states occurs in numerous areas in constitutional law. *See* 1 LAURENCE H. TRIBE, AMERICAN CONSTITUTIONAL LAW § 2-3, at 126 (3d ed. 2000).

116. *See* Henry J. Friendly, *In Praise of Erie and the New Federal Common Law*, 39 N.Y.U. L. REV. 383, 392-98 (1964). Perhaps Justice Brandeis' seeming equation of congressional and judicial lawmaking powers had another, more legitimate meaning than the one discussed in the text. Perhaps Brandeis was saying that if Congress wishes to act within its delegated powers, it must do so in an accepted "legislative" manner. It is not acceptable "legislation" to provide rules of decision whose applicability become apparent only when parties whose conduct the rules govern find out in which court they have been sued. Thus, an implicit separation-of-powers restriction on Congress' ability to enact statutes within its expressly delegated powers is that Congress must provide rules of decision whose operation on primary conduct does not depend upon fortuitous or arbitrary facts such as the plaintiff's choice of courts. Such a restriction would, at least, have respectable antecedents in due process restrictions on retroactive legislation. *See generally* JOHN E. NOWAK & RONALD D. ROTUNDA, CONSTITUTIONAL LAW § 11.9(a) (5th ed. 1995). Indeed, the retroactivity limitation of the Due Process Clauses appears to be rooted in a separation-of-powers function of those clauses as applied to legislative action. *See generally* Ralph U. Whitten, *The Constitutional Limitations on State Choice of Law: Due Process*, 9 HAST. CONST. L.Q. 851 (1982). The idea that valid legislation must operate in this manner is suggested by a close reading of Friendly, *supra*, though Judge Friendly's article does not elaborate the idea in precisely the manner done here.

117. *Erie*, 304 U.S. at 78, 58 S. Ct. at 822, 82 L. Ed. at 1194.

the general law decisions of the U.S. Supreme Court. The proof that the federal courts' decisions under the *Swift* doctrine cannot be properly characterized as decisions on matters of "federal" law is that the Court consistently refused to entertain appeals from the state courts when those courts rendered decisions that conflicted with the Supreme Court's general law pronouncements. Such appeals could not be heard by the Court because no "federal" question existed in the case.[118]

2. The *Erie* Doctrine Applied to Conflict-of-Laws Issues

(a) The Klaxon *Decision*

As discussed in the preceding section, under *Swift v. Tyson*, the federal courts in diversity cases made conflict-of-laws decisions independent of the state courts. The "in cases where they apply" language of the Rules of Decision Act dictated this result. In *Erie*, the Court seemed to assume that the New York federal court would apply Pennsylvania law in the case. However, the Court's opinion was unclear whether (1) the federal courts continued to have independent choice-of-law authority and should exercise it in favor of Pennsylvania law or (2) after *Erie*, the federal courts had to follow the conflict-of-laws doctrine of the states in which they were sitting and New York would apply Pennsylvania law.[119]

In *Klaxon Co. v. Stentor Electric Manufacturing Co.*,[120] the Court held that *Erie* required federal courts in diversity cases to follow the conflict-of-laws

---

118. *See, e.g.*, New York Life Ins. Co. v. Hendren, 92 U.S. 286, 286-87, 23 L. Ed. 709, 709-10 (1876); Rockhold v. Rockhold, 92 U.S. 129, 130, 23 L. Ed. 507, 507 (1876); Tarver v. Keach, 82 U.S. (15 Wall.) 67, 67-68, 21 L. Ed. 82, 82 (1873); Bethell v. Demaret, 77 U.S. (10 Wall.) 537, 540, 19 L. Ed. 1007, 1008 (1871); *see also* Ralph U. Whitten, *The Constitutional Limitations on State-Court Jurisdiction—A Historical-Interpretative Reexamination of the Full Faith and Credit and Due Process Clauses (Part One)*, 14 CREIGHTON L. REV. 499, 597-98 (1981). It has been commonplace to characterize what was going on in *Swift* as the development of "federal common law." For example, consider the following passage from Professor Chemerinsky's treatise:

> In *Swift v. Tyson*, in 1842, the Supreme Court held that in diversity cases, in the absence of a state statutory or constitutional provision, or a particular local interest, federal courts should fashion federal common law. . . .
>
> . . . Story, writing for the Court in *Swift* . . . concluded that the Rules of Decision Act only required federal courts to apply state constitutional and statutory provisions, not state common law.

ERWIN CHEMERINSKY, FEDERAL JURISDICTION § 5.3.5, at 308-09 (3d ed. 1999). The quoted passage is, like many other current descriptions of the *Swift* doctrine, a curious mixture of accuracy and inaccuracy. The use of the expression "particular local interest" is especially curious, as it seems to represent a recognition that the federal courts would feel bound to follow "state common law" in some instances. But the expression is not explained and is contracted by the other flat statements that the federal courts would not feel bound to follow state common law. As the discussion of *Swift* in section C *supra* should have indicated, however, the federal courts *were* following state common law in cases like *Swift* by adhering to the decision made by the state to follow the general commercial law or not to follow it. The difference between general commercial law and local law was in the degree of deference that the federal courts would pay to state precedents constituting the content of these respective areas of law. However, it is clear that in no realistic sense were the federal courts fashioning "federal" common law. How can common law be deemed "federal" when ultimate control over whether to follow the law remains with the state?

119. *See* CHARLES A. WRIGHT, THE LAW OF FEDERAL COURTS § 57, at 386 (5th ed. 1994).

120. 313 U.S. 487, 61 S. Ct. 1020, 85 L. Ed. 1477 (1941).

rules prevailing in the states in which the courts sit. The purpose, said the Court, was to prevent "the accident of diversity of citizenship" from disturbing the "equal administration of justice in coordinate state and federal courts sitting side by side."[121] The *Klaxon* decision flatly disregarded a clear and direct congressional command embodied in the Act. The "in cases where they apply" language of the Act was uniformly interpreted under *Swift* as a directive to the federal courts to make judgments on matters of conflict of laws independent of the state courts' decisions on the same matters.[122] The power to make independent conflict-of-laws decisions was a valuable protection against biased law application afforded by the diversity jurisdiction under the *Swift* doctrine. The result in *Klaxon* eliminated much of the utility of the diversity jurisdiction to litigants.[123]

The substance-procedure distinction of *Erie* can interact in some tricky ways with *Klaxon's* requirement that federal courts apply the conflict-of-laws doctrine of the state in which they are sitting. Sometimes, evaluation of a state rule will indicate that it is "substantive" for *Erie* purposes, but the rule will be treated as "procedural" for purposes of a state's conflict-of-laws doctrine.[124] If a state classifies an issue as procedural, it will apply its own law to resolve the issue under traditional conflicts practice.[125] In this situation, if the issue is characterized as substantive for purposes of *Erie*, the federal court must apply state law regardless of the state's characterization of the issue. Conversely, a state may treat a particular issue as substantive under its conflict-of-laws doctrine. Thus, the state may or may not apply its own law, depending upon what its conflict-of-laws doctrine tells it to do. In this situation, there is a question posed for a federal court exercising diversity jurisdiction. Should the federal court ask first how the issue is characterized for *Erie* purposes and only then, if *Erie* requires the application of state law, ask which state's law the forum's conflict-of-

---

121. 313 U.S. at 496, 61 S. Ct. at 1021, 85 L. Ed. at 1480; *see also* Day & Zimmermann, Inc. v. Challoner, 423 U.S. 3, 96 S. Ct. 167, 46 L. Ed. 2d 3 (1975); Griffin v. McCoach, 313 U.S. 498, 61 S. Ct. 1023, 85 L. Ed. 1481 (1941).

122. *See* RANDALL BRIDWELL & RALPH U. WHITTEN, THE CONSTITUTION AND THE COMMON LAW: THE DECLINE OF THE DOCTRINES OF SEPARATION OF POWERS AND FEDERALISM 110-11 (1977); 2 WILLIAM W. CROSSKEY, POLITICS AND THE CONSTITUTION IN THE HISTORY OF THE UNITED STATES 832-34, 867 (1953); William F. Baxter, *Choice of Law and the Federal System*, 16 STAN. L. REV. 1, 41 (1963).

123. *See* RANDALL BRIDWELL & RALPH U. WHITTEN, THE CONSTITUTION AND THE COMMON LAW: THE DECLINE OF THE DOCTRINES OF SEPARATION OF POWERS AND FEDERALISM 135 (1977); *see also* CHARLES A. WRIGHT, THE LAW OF FEDERAL COURTS § 57, at 391 (5th ed. 1994) (discussing criticisms of *Klaxon* on the grounds that the federal courts are in a "uniquely favorable position to develop a rational body" of conflicts law); Patrick J. Borchers, *The Origins of Diversity Jurisdiction: The Rise of Legal Positivism, and a Brave New World for* Erie *and* Klaxon, 72 TEX. L. REV. 79, 124-33 (1993) (advocating the development of independent choice-of-law rules in diversity cases); Scott Fruehwald, *Choice of Law in Federal Courts: A Reevaluation*, 37 BRANDEIS J. FAM. L. 212 (1998-99) (arguing that *Klaxon* should be overruled and a federal choice-of-law method substituted that would first determine which states have created legal relations applicable to the controversy and then select the applicable law on the basis of which state has the closest connection to the controversy).

124. This kind of result can occur because "substance" and "procedure" are defined in different ways for purposes of state conflicts doctrine and the *Erie* policies against forum shopping and discrimination against citizens of the forum state. *See* section E *infra* (discussing the evolution of the *Erie* substance-procedure distinction).

125. *See, e.g.,* LUTHER L. MCDOUGAL III ET AL., AMERICAN CONFLICTS LAW ch. 13 (5th ed. 2000) (discussing, *inter alia*, the characterization of matters as substantive or procedural for conflict-of-laws purposes).

laws rule requires the federal court to apply? Alternatively, should the court ask the state conflicts question first, and then make the substance-procedure classification based on the law that would be applied by the forum state? A few courts have adopted the first of these approaches.[126] With respect to the courts reaching this result, however, it is clearly incorrect. As will be shown in sections E and F, below, a federal court cannot determine for *Erie* purposes whether a matter is substantive or procedural until it knows the content of the state law it is being asked to apply. Therefore, it is clear that federal diversity courts should ask the state conflicts question first and the *Erie* categorization question second.

(b) Special Erie Doctrine Problems in Cases of Transfer Under 28 U.S.C. § 1404(a)

The *Klaxon* rule has produced difficulties when more than one federal court deals with a single case. The most important example of these difficulties occurs when a transfer of venue is made for the convenience of parties and witnesses and in the interests of justice from one federal court to another under 28 U.S.C. § 1404(a).[127] The Supreme Court first considered this issue in the context of a defendant's motion to transfer the action. In *Van Dusen v. Barrack*,[128] the Court held that the court to which the action was transferred (transferee court) must apply the same substantive law that would have been applied by the court that transferred the action (transferor court). The Court reached this result to prevent the defendant from moving for the transfer of venue in order to obtain a different applicable law, as opposed to simply a more convenient venue.[129] The Court stated that the result in *Van Dusen* "fully accords with and is supported by the policy underlying *Erie [Railroad] v. Tompkins.*"[130] The *Erie* policy "should ensure that the 'accident' of federal diversity jurisdiction does not enable a party to utilize a transfer to achieve a result in federal court which could not have been achieved in the courts of the State where the action was filed."[131]

---

126. *See* Servicios Commerciales Andinos, S.A. v. General Elec. Del Caribe, Inc., 145 F.3d 463 (1st Cir. 1998) (first determine whether matter is substantive or procedural for *Erie* purposes; then ask which law the forum state would apply under its conflicts rule); *see also* Boyd Rosene & Assocs. v. Kansas Mun. Gas Agency, 174 F.3d 1115 (10th Cir. 1999) (following *Servicios*).

127. *See* Chapter 4(D) ("Forum Non Conveniens and Change of Venue") *supra*.

128. 376 U.S. 612, 84 S. Ct. 805, 11 L. Ed. 2d 945 (1964).

129. The situation is actually more complicated. In determining whether to transfer, the district court must consider the applicable law as well as other factors bearing on the convenience of the transferee forum. If the court decides that the conflict-of-laws rule of the state in which it sits would select the substantive law of the transferee state, then that is one factor favoring the transfer. On the other hand, if the conflict-of-laws rule of the transferor state would result in the application of the substantive law of the transferor state under *Klaxon*, then that is one reason not to transfer, because upon transfer (under the *Van Dusen* rule) the transferee district court would have to apply the transferor state's law, with which it is less familiar. Thus, the choice-of-law decision under *Klaxon* and § 1404(a) has become an integral part of the decision whether to transfer, along with all other factors bearing on the convenience of the transfer. *See Van Dusen*, 376 U.S. at 643-46, 84 S. Ct. at 823-24, 11 L. Ed. 2d at 965-67.

130. 376 U.S. at 637, 84 S. Ct. at 820, 11 L. Ed. 2d at 961.

131. *Id.* at 638, 84 S. Ct. at 820, 11 L. Ed. 2d at 962 (citing Guaranty Trust v. York, 326 U.S. 99, 65 S. Ct. 1464, 89 L. Ed. 2d 2079 (1945), discussed in section E(1) *infra*).

Illustration 5-8. *A*, a citizen of State *X*, sues *B Corp.*, a corporation incorporated and with its principal place of business in State *Y*. *A* seeks $500,000 for the wrongful death of *A's* spouse received in an automobile accident in State *Y*. The action is brought in the U.S. District Court for State *X*. *B* is subject to personal jurisdiction in State *X* because *B* does extensive business there. Thus, venue is also proper under 28 U.S.C. § 1391(a)(1) and (c). *B* moves for a transfer of venue under 28 U.S.C. § 1404(a) to State *Y*, where the accident occurred. *B's* motion is granted. Assume that State *X* would apply its own law to determine the amount of any wrongful death recovery to which *A* is entitled and that State *X* law permits unlimited damages to be recovered for wrongful death. On the other hand, State *Y* limits the amount of damages that can be recovered for wrongful death to $100,000. If the action had been commenced in a State *Y* court, the State *Y* wrongful death limit would have been applied under State *Y* conflict-of-laws rules. Under the *Klaxon* decision, if the action had not been transferred, the U.S. District Court in State *X* would have been obligated to apply State *X* conflict-of-laws rules to determine the applicable law, and those rules would have required the application of the State *X* unlimited recovery rule in the federal diversity action. Under the *Van Dusen* rule, the U.S. District Court in State *Y* must apply the same law that would have been applied had there been no transfer. Thus, the State *X* unlimited recovery rule would have to be applied after transfer to the State *Y* federal district court.

* * * * *

After *Van Dusen*, it was still possible to argue that if a transfer was made on the motion of the plaintiff, the transferee court should apply the law that it would have applied under *Klaxon* if the action had been commenced originally in the transferee court. When the plaintiff is seeking the transfer, it is arguably improper to give the plaintiff a choice-of-law advantage resulting from the plaintiff's initial choice of a forum that the plaintiff is, in the transfer motion, arguing to be inconvenient.[132] The Supreme Court rejected this seemingly sensible rule in *Ferens v. John Deere Co.*[133] In *Ferens*, the plaintiffs filed a tort action in Mississippi to obtain the benefit of the Mississippi statute of limitations. The plaintiffs then moved to transfer the action under § 1404(a) to the Western District of Pennsylvania, where the accident had occurred and where a related breach of contract and warranty action was pending. The district court granted the motion to transfer to the Western District of Pennsylvania. However, the Pennsylvania federal district court held that the *Van Dusen* rule did not apply when the action was transferred on the plaintiff's motion. The Pennsylvania federal court dismissed the tort action under the Pennsylvania statute of limitations. The Third Circuit affirmed. The U.S. Supreme Court granted certiorari and reversed.

In *Ferens*, the Court stated that the advantages the defendant would lose by applying the *Van Dusen* rule to plaintiff's transfer cases would be slight, while applying the transferee state's law would undermine the *Erie* rule in a serious way

---

132. *See* ALI STUDY OF THE DIVISION OF JURISDICTION BETWEEN STATE AND FEDERAL COURTS 155 (1969) (comment to § 1306(c)).

133. 494 U.S. 516, 110 S. Ct. 1274, 108 L. Ed. 2d 443 (1990).

by allowing the initiation of a transfer to result in a change of law. The Court further reasoned that the contrary rule would simply cause plaintiffs either not to sue defendants when they would have no choice but to litigate in an inconvenient forum, or to sue them and hope that the defendants would move to transfer. The Court also felt that the opportunities for forum shopping that the *Van Dusen* rule sought to avoid would not be enhanced by the application of that rule to plaintiffs' transfer motions. Because the plaintiffs would have been able to forum shop in the state courts in any event, the diversity jurisdiction and the application of the transferor state's law merely duplicated the results of that forum shopping.[134] The Court was also concerned that if the applicable law were to change following a transfer, the district court might be reluctant to grant a transfer motion that would disadvantage defendants. Such a disadvantage could occur because plaintiffs might find as many ways to exploit application of the transferee state's law as they would the transferor state's law.[135] In any event, the transferor court would have to make complex inquiries to assure that prejudice did not occur to the defendant. Finally, the Court noted that punishing the plaintiffs for their choice of forum would be improper because § 1404(a) was not only for the benefit of the moving party, but also for the benefit of the witnesses and the interests of justice.[136]

Numerous problems exist with the Court's reasoning in *Ferens*, but the most serious is the Court's failure to appreciate that its holding will encourage an abuse of the federal diversity jurisdiction that is similar to the kind *Erie* sought to eliminate. Under the Court's holding in *Ferens*, a plaintiff faced with a choice of a federal or state court in a state like Mississippi will always pick the federal court. While the state court will apply its longer statute of limitations to the action, it would not transfer the case on the motion of the plaintiff because no transfer mechanism exists between state courts.[137] Thus, unless the action could be dismissed under the doctrine of forum non conveniens on the motion of the

---

134. *See id.* at 525-26, 110 S. Ct. at 1280-81, 108 L. Ed. 2d at 454-55. The Court also expressed the fear that if the transferee state's law were applied on plaintiffs' transfer motions, many states would enact long statutes of limitation like Mississippi's statute. Why? Because if the transferee state law were applied, plaintiffs would not move for transfer, and thus the states, knowing this rule, would enact long statutes of limitation in the hope of getting tort business for their lawyers. *See id.* at 528, 110 S. Ct. at 1282, 108 L. Ed. 2d at 456. It is, of course, just as likely that if all or lots of states enacted long statutes of limitation, then plaintiffs would not have to shop for a forum with a long statute because they would likely have one in their home states.

135. *Id.* at 529, 110 S. Ct. at 1283, 108 L. Ed. 2d at 457. But why wouldn't the plaintiff just file in the transferee state in the first place if its law were more favorable and it was also more convenient?

136. *Id.*

137. This situation may be about to change. Recall from Chapter 4(D)(1)*(b)* (''The Uniform Transfer of Litigation Act''), *supra*, that the National Conference of Commissioners on Uniform State Law has recommended the adoption by the states of the Uniform Transfer of Litigation Act. If this act is widely adopted, the state courts would be able to transfer litigation such as that involved in *Ferens* to another state. Furthermore, § 209 of the Uniform Act provides that a receiving court cannot dismiss an action based on statute of limitations if the matter would not be barred by limitations in the transferring state, provided the transferring state had subject-matter and personal jurisdiction over the action. *See id.* This section would not necessarily place the state and federal law of transfer in parity, however, because a receiving court can refuse a transfer for any reason under § 204 of the Uniform Act. *See id.* Thus, a receiving court that believed that the plaintiff had inappropriately engaged in forum shopping for a longer statute of limitations could presumably refuse to accept a transfer for that reason.

plaintiff, a possibility that seems unlikely in the extreme, the action would remain in the state, with whatever inconveniences that might entail to the plaintiff. However, the option of federal court under the rule in *Ferens* offers the possibility of a favorable applicable law *and* a more convenient place for the litigation. Had the Court instead held that the transferee state's law would be applicable when a case is transferred on the plaintiff's motion, the plaintiff would have no similar incentive to pick a federal court over a state court, because no advantage would be gained by choosing a federal forum. Thus, the rule in *Ferens* encourages abuse of the diversity jurisdiction and the federal transfer mechanism with no seeming gain to the goals of *Erie*.

The Court in *Ferens* indicated that the *Van Dusen* rule would be applied to all sorts of transfers under § 1404(a), including cases that were not before the Court for decision.[138] However, open questions still exist. For one, the *Van Dusen-Ferens* rule should not control transfers under 28 U.S.C. § 1406(a), when plaintiff initially commences the action in the wrong venue. "[W]henever the original venue is improper, so that transfer is under § 1406(a), the transferee court should apply whatever law it would have applied had the action been properly commenced there."[139] The same is arguably true when the transfer is from a district where venue is proper, but personal jurisdiction cannot be obtained over the defendant, regardless of whether the transfer is under § 1404(a) or § 1406(a).[140]

In addition to these obvious questions, litigation in the lower federal courts continues to produce other difficult administrative problems with § 1404(a). For example, in *Boardman Petroleum, Inc. v. Federated Mutual Insurance Co.*,[141] an insurance company instituted a diversity action in a U.S.

---

138. Thus, the Court indicated that the same rule would be applied when (1) both plaintiff and defendant move for a transfer, (2) the court transfers on its own motion, (3) a plaintiff moves for a transfer after a removed action, (4) only one of several plaintiffs moves for transfer, or (5) the circumstances change through no fault of the plaintiff, making a transfer desirable. *See Ferens*, 494 U.S. at 529, 110 S. Ct. at 1283, 108 L. Ed. 2d at 457.

139. 15 CHARLES A. WRIGHT ET AL., FEDERAL PRACTICE AND PROCEDURE: JURISDICTION AND RELATED MATTERS § 3827, at 267 (2d ed. 1986); *see, e.g.,* Adam v. J.B. Hunt Transport, Inc., 130 F.3d 219, 230 (6th Cir. 1997) (transferee state's law applies after transfer under § 1406); Wesland v. Admiral Beverage Corp., 119 F.3d 733 (8th Cir. 1997), *cert. denied*, 522 U.S. 1112, 118 S. Ct. 1043, 140 L. Ed. 2d 108 (1998) (same).

140. *See* 15 CHARLES A. WRIGHT ET AL., FEDERAL PRACTICE AND PROCEDURE: JURISDICTION AND RELATED MATTERS § 3827, at 267 (2d ed. 1986). Recall from Chapter 4 that when venue is proper, but personal jurisdiction cannot be obtained over the defendant, the cases are divided over whether transfer should be made under § 1404(a) or § 1406(a). *See* Chapter 4(D) ("Forum Non Conveniens and Change of Venue") *supra*; *see also* 15 CHARLES A. WRIGHT ET AL., FEDERAL PRACTICE AND PROCEDURE: JURISDICTION AND RELATED MATTERS § 3827, at 262-66 (2d ed. 1986). The *Klaxon* decision also creates problems in areas other than transfers of venue. For example, Rule 501 of the Federal Rules of Evidence provides that the privilege of a witness in a civil action in which state law provides the rule of decision must be determined in accordance with state law. This means that a federal diversity court must generally apply the privilege law of the state in which it is sitting. However, it is possible for a federal action to be pending in one district based on an event occurring in another district and a deposition in the action may be taken in still another district, with perhaps the parties raising the privilege claim having a more substantial relationship to still a fourth district than they have with any of the first three. For a discussion of how the cases have addressed the problem of what state's privilege law to apply in such situations, see 23 CHARLES A. WRIGHT & KENNETH W. GRAHAM, JR., FEDERAL PRACTICE AND PROCEDURE: EVIDENCE § 5435 (1980).

141. 135 F.3d 750 (11th Cir. 1998).

District Court to obtain a declaratory judgment that a policy issued to the insured did not cover a particular occurrence. The insured commenced a separate diversity action in another district to recover under the policy. The insurer's action was transferred under § 1404(a) to the district where the insured's action was pending. The conflict-of-laws rules of the transferor and transferee states pointed to a different applicable substantive law for each action. In this situation, it is obvious that the choice-of-law problem cannot be solved by applying a different state's substantive law to each case, because both cases involve the same issue. The Eleventh Circuit, in effect, applied an independent federal conflict of laws approach to resolve the problem, *Klaxon, Van Dusen*, and *Ferens* notwithstanding. Under this approach, the court balanced the interests of the concerned states in having their law applied and applied the law of the state that, in the court's view, had the greater interest. In contrast, the U.S. District Court for the Eastern District of Pennsylvania, in a similar case, applied the law of the transferor state to both actions, although the court had some misgivings about this approach because the action in the transferree district had been commenced first. However, the court ultimately concluded that the substantive law of all the concerned states was the same, making the choice-of-law decision irrelevant to the result.[142] Other alternatives available to courts in these situations might include (1) the court in the second-filed action deferring to the first filed action, instead of transferring and consolidating the suits;[143] (2) the court in the declaratory judgment action exercising its discretion to defer to the damage action;[144] and (3) one of the courts enjoining the defendant from proceeding as a plaintiff in the other action, as discussed in Chapter 4.[145]

Another problem under 28 U.S.C. § 1404(a) concerns the effect of state law on a forum selection clause relied on by a party seeking transfer. In Chapter 4(D)(2)*(a)*, above, it was observed that the Supreme Court has established that a forum selection clause would not absolutely control the question of transfer under 28 U.S.C. § 1404(a), but would be weighed in the balance along with all other factors bearing on the convenience of the parties and witnesses and the interests of justice. This was the holding of *Stewart Organization, Inc. v. Ricoh Corp.*[146] However, in *Stewart Organization*, the forum selection clause in question would not have been enforceable under the applicable state law controlling the contract between the parties. As the dissent pointed out, there was no apparent reason to have the question of the validity of the forum selection clause controlled by

---

142. Computer Aid, Inc. v. Hewlett-Packard Co., 56 F. Supp. 2d 526 (E.D. Pa. 1999).

143. *See* Kerotest Mfg. Co. v. C-O-Two Fire Equip. Co., 342 U.S. 180, 72 S. Ct. 219, 96 L. Ed. 2d 200 (1952).

144. *See id.*; *see also* Wilton v. Steven Falls Co., 515 U.S. 277, 115 S. Ct. 2137, 132 L. Ed. 2d 214 (1995) (discussing the discretion of federal courts to defer to pending state actions in declaratory judgment suits).

145. *See* Chapter 4(E) ("Injunctions Against Extrastate Litigation and Other Devices for Controlling the Location of Suit") *supra*; *see also* International Bus. Machs. Corp. v. Bajorek, 191 F.3d 1033 (9th Cir. 1999) ("substantive" action commenced in New York federal court and transferred to California, where declaratory judgment action pending; district court dismisses "substantive" action; court of appeals refuses to resolve whether district court must exercise its discretion to dismiss earlier filed declaratory judgment action in favor of "substantive" action because parties agree that New York and California would apply same conflict-of-laws rule to case).

146. 487 U.S. 22, 108 S. Ct. 2239, 101 L. Ed. 2d 22 (1988).

federal law rather than state law, which would control all other issues of the validity of the contract.[147] Certainly, there is nothing in the language, history, or purposes of 28 U.S.C. § 1404(a) that would indicate that federal law was designed to control such an issue under the statute.[148] Additionally, the application of a federal judge-made rule, rather than state law, to determine the validity of the forum selection clause would produce both forum shopping by the party seeking to rely on the clause and discrimination against a citizen of the forum state who is deprived of the benefit of a valuable rule of law that would be applied by the state courts.[149] The majority's only response in *Stewart Organization* to these serious difficulties was to state that the dissent's analysis "makes the applicability of a federal statute depend upon the content of state law."[150] However, it is quite common for the application of federal statutes to depend on the operation of state law. For example, in determining whether the jurisdictional amount requirement of 28 U.S.C. § 1332 is satisfied, it must always be determined whether state law will permit a recovery of more than $75,000.[151]

In addition to the question of whether federal or state law should control the validity of the forum selection clause in *Stewart Organization*, the majority also did not explain why 28 U.S.C. § 1404(a) rather than § 1406 was the controlling federal statute. At the district court level, the defendant had moved in the alternative to transfer under § 1404(a) or to dismiss under § 1406.[152] However, the Supreme Court did not provide an adequate explanation why § 1404(a), which controls transfers of venue when an action is commenced in a correct venue, should govern the case rather than § 1406, which controls dismissal and transfer when an action is commenced in an incorrect venue.[153] Indeed, it has been persuasively argued that there was no reason for the Supreme Court to pick either § 1404(a) or § 1406 as applicable to the problem before it, as opposed to deciding the case under the general *Erie* doctrine discussed in the next section.[154]

---

147. *See* 487 U.S. at 33-38, 108 S. Ct at 2246-48, 101 L. Ed. 2d at 33-39 (Scalia, J., dissenting).

148. As discussed in section F *infra*, the first obligation of a federal court faced with a contention that a federal statute or Federal Rule of Civil Procedure controls a case is to determine whether the statute or rule is broad enough to cover the question in issue. *See also* 487 U.S. at 34, 108 S. Ct. at 2246, 101 L. Ed. 2d at 34 (Scalia, J., dissenting). However, it has been persuasively argued that if a statute such as § 1404(a) is not "plainly on point," the federal courts should disregard the statute and decide the case under the general *Erie* doctrine discussed in section E *infra*. *See* Richard D. Freer, Erie's *Mid-Life Crisis*, 63 TUL. L. REV. 1087, 1117-20 (1989).

149. *See* 487 U.S. at 38-41, 108 S. Ct. at 2248-50, 101 L. Ed. 2d at 37-39 (Scalia, J., dissenting). As discussed in the next section, forum shopping and discrimination against citizens of the forum state are important factors in judging the validity of "federal common-law rules of practice and procedure" under the *Erie* doctrine.

150. *See id.* at 31 n.10, 108 S. Ct. at 2244 n.10, 101 L. Ed. 2d at 32 n.10.

151. *See* Chapter 2(C)(3)*(e)* ("Amount-in-Controversy Requirement") *supra*.

152. *See id.* at 24, 108 S. Ct at 2241, 101 L. Ed. 2d at 28.

153. *See* Allan R. Stein, Erie *and Court Access*, 100 YALE L.J. 1935, 1961-64 (1991).

154. *See* Richard D. Freer, Erie's *Mid-Life Crisis*, 63 TUL. L. REV. 1087, 1117-21 (1989); *see also* Amermed Corp. v. Disetronic Holding AG, 6 F. Supp. 2d 1371 (N.D. Ga. 1998) (holding federal provisions governing improper venue were silent as to dismissal on any ground other than statutorily deficient venue and, therefore, unlike *Stewart Organization*, there was no controlling federal statute or Federal Rule of Civil Procedure to dictate the result in a case involving a permissive forum selection clause); Walter L. Heiser, *Forum*

SECTION E. THE EVOLUTION OF THE *ERIE* DOCTRINE: APPLICABILITY OF STATE "SUBSTANTIVE LAW" UNDER THE RULES OF DECISION ACT

The decisions developing the *Erie* doctrine group themselves into two separate categories. One category of cases involves actual or potential conflicts between state law and Federal Rules of Civil or Appellate Procedure created under the Rules Enabling Act, 28 U.S.C. § 2072. The second category of cases involves the Rules of Decision Act, 28 U.S.C. § 1652, under which *Swift* and *Erie* were decided. These categories must be examined separately because different considerations ultimately determine whether the conflict should be resolved in favor of state law or federal law under each statute. This section examines the problems involved in Rules of Decision Act cases, but a caveat is in order before examining the cases. Differentiating the decided cases on the basis of whether they are controlled by the Rules of Enabling Act or the Rules of Decision Act is analytically proper. However, as demonstrated in the next section, it was not always clear that the cases under the two statutes should be analyzed under different standards. In the early days of the *Erie* doctrine, the Supreme Court appeared to use the same standard under both statutes. Thus, until the case of *Hanna v. Plumer*,[155] discussed in the next section, the Court did not make it clear that the validity of Federal Rules of Civil Procedure were to be judged differently than general *Erie* problems under the Rules of Decision Act.

In *Erie*, the U.S. Supreme Court indicated that the Rules of Decision Act required the federal courts to follow state court decisions on matters of substantive law.[156] Implicit in the Court's description of the obligations of the federal courts was the suggestion that they were *not* bound to follow state law on matters of procedure.[157] Neither the language of the Rules of Decision Act nor the jurisprudence of the *Swift* doctrine distinguished "substantive" matters from "procedural" matters.[158] Under the Conformity Acts,[159] federal courts generally followed the procedural rules of the state in which they were sitting in common-law actions.[160] In 1938, when the Federal Rules of Civil Procedure became

---

Selection Clauses in Federal Courts: Limitations on Enforcement After Stewart Organization *and* Carnival Cruise, 45 FLA. L. REV. 553, 590-95 (1993); Allen R. Stein, Erie *and Court Access*, 100 YALE L.J. 1935, 1961-65 (1991).

155. 380 U.S. 460, 85 S. Ct. 1136, 14 L. Ed. 2d 8 (1965).

156. *See* Erie R.R. Co. v. Tompkins, 304 U.S. 64, 78, 58 S. Ct. 817, 822, 82 L. Ed. 1188, 1194 (1938) (stating that "Congress has no power to declare substantive rules of common law applicable in a State").

157. *See* ERWIN CHEMERINSKY, FEDERAL JURISDICTION § 5.3.5, at 314-15 (3d ed. 1999); CHARLES A. WRIGHT, THE LAW OF FEDERAL COURTS § 55, at 376, 378 (5th ed. 1994); Ralph U. Whitten, Erie *and the Federal Rules: A Review and Reappraisal After* Burlington Northern Railroad v. Woods, 21 CREIGHTON L. REV. 1, 3-4 (1987).

158. *See* Ralph U. Whitten, Erie *and the Federal Rules: A Review and Reappraisal After* Burlington Northern Railroad v. Woods, 21 CREIGHTON L. REV. 1, 3 (1987).

159. The Conformity Acts are discussed in Chapter 1(E)(5) ("Development of Federal Procedure and the Federal Rules of Civil Procedure") *supra*; *see also* Ralph U. Whitten, Erie *and the Federal Rules: A Review and Reappraisal After* Burlington Northern Railroad v. Woods, 21 CREIGHTON L. REV. 1, 3 n.13 (1987).

160. *See* Ralph U. Whitten, Erie *and the Federal Rules: A Review and Reappraisal After* Burlington Northern Railroad v. Woods, 21 CREIGHTON L. REV. 1, 3 (1987).

effective, this pattern changed. Federal courts now had their own uniform procedure. Thus, when *Erie* stated that the federal courts were obligated to follow state law on substantive matters under the Rules of Decision Act, it seemed that a dichotomy had been established between substance and procedure that would have the effect of allowing the federal courts to have their own uniform procedural system.[161]

However, the Federal Rules of Civil Procedure and the Federal Rules of Appellate Procedure do not cover all matters of federal practice and procedure. Numerous issues that can, in some sense, be described as "procedural" are simply not dealt with by the Federal Rules.[162] Furthermore, even before the Federal Rules, a considerable amount of case law had built up a body of independent federal procedural rules and practices, mainly in equity actions in which the federal courts were not obliged by the Conformity Acts to follow state procedural law.[163] One question after *Erie* was whether the federal courts would be able to continue to apply this body of independent "common law"[164] rules of practice and procedure, in the face of conflicting state law.

1. The *Guaranty Trust* Case: Independent Federal Equity Powers and the "Outcome Determinative" Test

The Court first addressed this question in the case of *Guaranty Trust Co. v. York*.[165] A federal class action was brought against Guaranty Trust for breach of trust. The district court granted summary judgment in favor of the defendant. However, that judgment was reversed by the court of appeals. The court of appeals held that in a suit brought on the equity side of a federal court, the court was not obliged to apply the statute of limitations that would govern in the state courts of the same state, even though federal jurisdiction was based exclusively on diversity of citizenship.[166] The U.S. Supreme Court granted certiorari and reversed. In an opinion by Justice Frankfurter, the Court held that the *Erie*

---

161. *See id.* at 1-4.

162. For example, while some issues concerning the effect to be given to federal judgments are covered by the Federal Rules, *see* FED. R. CIV. P. 13(a), 41(b), most such issues are governed by common-law rules. *See* RESTATEMENT (SECOND) OF JUDGMENTS § 87 (1982); *see also* Chapter 13 ("Finality in Litigation") *infra*.

163. *See* Ralph U. Whitten, Erie *and the Federal Rules: A Review and Reappraisal After* Burlington Northern Railroad v. Woods, 21 CREIGHTON L. REV. 1, 8 (1987). The independent equity power of the federal courts is described in Chapter 1(E)(5) ("Development of Federal Procedure and the Federal Rules of Civil Procedure") *supra*. In addition to the independent federal equity practice, federal judge-made rules of practice also grew up in common-law actions because of a requirement in the 1872 Conformity Act that the federal courts only conform "as near as may be" to state procedural law. "Partly in reliance on this latter phrase and partly by a restrictive interpretation of the three categories of 'practice, pleadings, and forms and modes of proceedings', the Court withdrew from the operation of the [Conformity] Act a wide area of particularly important matters affecting the administration of federal justice." RICHARD H. FALLON ET AL., HART & WECHSLER'S THE FEDERAL COURTS AND THE FEDERAL SYSTEM 663 (4th ed. 1996).

164. The expression "common law" is used hereafter to include rules drawn from equity that are not embodied in the Federal Rules of Civil Procedure.

165. 326 U.S. 99, 65 S. Ct. 1464, 89 L. Ed. 2079 (1945).

166. *See id.* at 100-01, 65 S. Ct. at 1465, 89 L. Ed. at 2081.

doctrine required the application of the state statute of limitations even in an "equity" action.[167]

In deciding that *Erie* required the application of state law on the facts of *Guaranty Trust*, the Court had to address both the substance-procedure distinction and the question of whether the federal courts possessed an independent equity power after *Erie*. On the question of independent federal equity power, Justice Frankfurter's opinion was not clear. First, Frankfurter stated correctly[168] that "[i]n giving federal courts 'cognizance' of equity suits in cases of diversity jurisdiction, Congress never gave, nor did the federal courts ever claim, the power to deny substantive rights denied by State law."[169] However, Justice Frankfurter then suggested that there might be some room left for independent equity power after *Erie*. His opinion stated that (1) the federal courts were obligated to follow explicit restrictions placed on their equity powers by Congress and the Constitution; (2) the federal courts were not obligated to give "whatever equitable remedy is available in a State court"; and (3) the federal courts might give an equitable remedy for the violation of a state substantive right, even though the state courts could not give the remedy.[170]

No difficulty exists with the observation that federal courts must abide by explicit congressional restrictions on equity powers. When Congress acts within its delegated powers to restrict the jurisdiction or remedial authority of the federal courts, the congressionally mandated restrictions must be obeyed. Likewise, explicit constitutional commands applicable to the federal courts, such as the Seventh Amendment right to a trial by jury, must also be obeyed. However, the remainder of the Court's discussion of federal equitable power is much more troublesome.

In observing that federal equity was subject to restrictions that might not apply to the states, the Court stated that federal "suits must be within the traditional scope of equity as historically evolved in the English Court of Chancery."[171] This statement suggests that a historical test will be applied to determine whether a federal court in diversity can hear an action that would be adjudicated by the courts of the state in which the federal court is sitting. In some ways, this suggestion is unexceptional. For example, a state might authorize its courts to give advisory opinions on pending legislation, a kind of case that would

---

167. Of course, by the time *Guaranty Trust* had been decided, law and equity had been merged in the federal courts by the Federal Rules of Civil Procedure. *See* FED. R. CIV. P. 2. However, the Rules of Decision Act still applied only to "common-law" actions; it was not amended to apply to all civil actions until the 1948 revision of the judicial code. *See* 28 U.S.C. § 1652 reviser's note. Neither of these facts seemed to affect the Court's decision in *Guaranty Trust*.

168. See the discussion of the independent federal equity power under *Swift* in section C *supra*.

169. *Guaranty Trust*, 326 U.S. at 105, 65 S. Ct. at 1468, 89 L. Ed. at 2084. This statement appears at the end of a lengthy passage in which Frankfurter recounted the history of federal equity. That history is, in all essential respects, in agreement with the history of federal equity under the *Swift* doctrine set out in section C(2)(e) *supra*.

170. *See id.* at 105-06, 65 S. Ct. at 1468-69, 89 L. Ed. at 2084-85.

171. *See id.* at 105, 65 S. Ct. at 1468, 89 L. Ed. at 2084.

not be justiciable under the requirements of Article III of the Constitution.[172] Certainly a federal court sitting in diversity could not entertain such a proceeding. However, to require that a justiciable case within one of the Article III categories (here, the diversity category) also conform to historic equitable forms is unjustifiable. It would presumably mean that if new remedies were authorized at the state level and labeled "equitable," the federal courts could not hear cases in which those remedies were requested if the remedies were not within the historic scope of equity on the date the Constitution was formed. If this conclusion is correct, however, Congress also could not authorize new remedies unknown to the categories "Law" and "Equity" described in Article III. Statutes such as the federal Declaratory Judgment Act would be unconstitutional because they create a remedy that was, strictly speaking, known neither to law or equity at the time the Constitution was formed.[173] The terms "Law" and "Equity" are more reasonably interpreted as encompassing all judicial actions that otherwise fall within the justiciability and category requirements of Article III.[174]

---

172. *See* U.S. CONST. art. III, § 2; Hayburn's Case, 2 U.S. (2 Dall.) 409, 1 L. Ed. 436 (1792); RICHARD H. FALLON ET AL., HART & WECHSLER'S THE FEDERAL COURTS AND THE FEDERAL SYSTEM 92 (4th ed. 1996) (describing the correspondence of the Justices).

173. *See* 28 U.S.C. §§ 2201-02.

> Although it is sometimes said that an action for a declaratory judgment is "equitable in nature," other cases have spoken of an action for a declaratory judgment as "essentially legal." The truth is that "a declaratory judgment action is a statutory creation, and by its nature is neither fish nor fowl, neither legal nor equitable." The new remedy may be sought both in cases that historically would have been legal and those that historically would have been equitable.

CHARLES A. WRIGHT, THE LAW OF FEDERAL COURTS § 100, at 717-18 (5th ed. 1994).

174. In *Guaranty Trust*, the Court did cite cases that seemed to support a historical limit on the equity powers of federal courts in diversity actions. *See, e.g.*, Pusey & Jones Co. v. Hanssen, 261 U.S. 491, 43 S. Ct. 454, 67 L. Ed. 763 (1923); Payne v. Hook, 74 U.S. (7 Wall.) 425, 19 L. Ed. 260 (1869). However, the doctrines announced in those cases should have become obsolete with the change in context brought about by the merger of law and equity by the Federal Rules of Civil Procedure and the decision in *Erie. See, e.g.*, Sprague v. Ticonic Nat'l Bank, 307 U.S. 161, 169-70, 59 S. Ct. 777, 781-82, 83 L. Ed. 1184, 1188-89 (1939) (the new Federal Rules of Civil Procedure have rendered anachronistic the technical niceties pertaining to terms of court as to both law and equity, but the ruling of the district court was made prior to the operation of the new rules). Certainly, the Court's later discussion in *Guaranty Trust* of the standard for resolving conflicts between state and federal law under the *Erie* doctrine seems inconsistent with the older "independent equity" authorities cited by the Court in its opinion. Furthermore, there has been no case after *Guaranty Trust* decided by the Court in which the historic forms of equity jurisprudence have prevented a federal diversity court from adjudicating an action that would be heard by the state courts. *But cf.* Grupo Mexicano de Desarrollo S.A. v. Alliance Bond Fund, Inc., 527 U.S. 308, 119 S. Ct. 1961, 144 L. Ed. 2d 319 (1999), in which the Supreme Court held that U.S. District Courts do not have the power under Federal Rule 65 to issue preliminary injunctions to prevent defendants from disposing of their assets before the plaintiff has obtained a judgment from the defendant "fixing the debt" owed. The court reasoned that such power was not part of the power possessed by equity at the time the federal courts first obtained jurisdiction over equity cases in the Judiciary Act of 1789. The merger of law and equity by the Federal Rules of Civil Procedure pursuant to the Rules Enabling Act, *see* section F *infra*, had not expanded federal equity power because (1) the historic restriction on equity's power to issue this type of injunction, while partly procedural, was also partly substantive and (2) the Rules Enabling Act preserved substantive rights from abridgement or enlargement by the Federal Rules. However, the Court indicated that Congress could give the federal courts this power. Because the argument was not properly raised in the lower courts, the Supreme Court refused to consider whether, if the forum state's law permitted such injunctions, *Erie* would require that the power to issue the remedy be determined by state law. *See* 527 U.S. at __ n.3, 119 S. Ct. at 1968 n.3, 144 L. Ed. 2d at 330 n.3. *Grupo* is discussed further in Chapter 6(F)(4)*(a)*, *infra*. *But cf.* United States *ex rel.* Rahman v. Oncology Assocs., P.C., 198 F.3d 489 (4th Cir. 1999) (*Grupo* does not prevent equitable order freezing assets in a case in which final relief requested is partly equitable, but Federal Rule 64 adopts state law permitting such

In addition to suggesting that historic equity forms might confine the powers of federal diversity courts to follow state law, the Court also suggested that federal courts might still be able to give equitable remedies that were not available under state law.[175] Like the Court's discussion of the confining power of historic equity forms, this discussion also seems erroneous after *Erie*. Besides being infected by a view of independent federal equity power that should have become obsolete after *Erie*, this suggestion by the Court was supported by an erroneous view of the nature of remedies. The modern thinking about remedies is that "remedies are the means of carrying into effect the substantive right."[176] Thus, subject to some qualifications, "the remedy should reflect the right or the policy behind that right as precisely as possible."[177] If this approach is proper—and it seems analytically irrefutable—it is difficult to see how the federal courts could give a remedy for the violation of a state right that the state courts would not give. Likewise, it is hard to see how a federal court could justifiably deny a remedy authorized by the state for the violation of a state right, assuming that neither Congress nor the Constitution has forbidden the grant of the remedy.[178] Even if the policies of the *Erie* doctrine do not forbid the federal denial of a remedy the state courts would give, the policies supporting the diversity jurisdiction would be undermined by such a denial. Plaintiffs needing the remedy would be forced to abandon the possibility of suing in a diversity action and sue in state court to have any possibility of obtaining the remedy.[179]

Illustration 5-9. *M Corp.* is incorporated with its principal place of business in State *X*. *M* does extensive business in State *Y*. *M* sues *B*, a citizen of State *Y* who is also the attorney general of State *Y*, in a U.S. District Court in State *Y*. *M* seeks an injunction to prevent *B* from enforcing a State *Y* statute against *M* that *M* contends is unconstitutional under the State *Y* constitution. Assume that under the traditional equity principles followed by the federal courts, an injunction would be justified, but that under the equity principles followed by the State *Y* courts no injunction would be permissible. It is difficult to imagine a federal interest that would justify the federal court granting an injunction to

---

an order in any event). *See also* Cendant Corp. v. Forbes, 70 F. Supp. 2d 339 (S.D.N.Y. 1999) (there may be settings in which equitable remedial rights doctrine can still be applied, but when it conflicts with *Erie*, *Erie* must prevail).

175. *See Guaranty Trust*, 326 U.S. at 106, 65 S. Ct. at 1468-69, 89 L. Ed. at 2084-85.

176. DAN B. DOBBS, LAW OF REMEDIES § 1.7, at 22 (2d student ed. 1993).

177. *Id.*

178. Perhaps one circumstance which could cause a federal district court to consider not giving a remedy authorized by a state might be when such relief would "unduly" strain the resources of the federal district court. For example, a federal district court might have such a concern when a state would provide injunctive relief that would require extensive, detailed, time-consuming, and continuing "supervisory" regulation. *Cf.* DAN B. DOBBS, LAW OF REMEDIES: DAMAGES—EQUITY—RESTITUTION § 2.9(1), at 164 (2d student ed. 1993) (describing "structural injunctions" that "are typically complex and invasive [and] are likely to involve the judge in tasks traditionally considered to be non-judicial, that is, less about rights and duties and more about management"). However, if a federal court dismissed a diversity action on such a ground, the dismissal would surely have to be without prejudice to a future action in state court. *See* Chapter 13(B)(2) *infra* (discussing the effect of dismissals "on the merits").

179. No Supreme Court decision since *Guaranty Trust* has approved of a federal diversity court granting a remedy the state courts would deny or denying a remedy the state courts would grant in the absence of a statute or a Federal Rule of Civil Procedure dictating the result.

enforce state rights when the state courts would not grant the injunction under similar circumstances.[180] If the courts did grant such an injunction, it would encourage plaintiffs such as *M* to forum shop for federal courts to obtain a different result than could be obtained under state law, and this consequence would seem to run counter to the *Erie* policies.

Illustration 5-10. Assume the same facts as in *Illustration 5-9*, except that traditional federal equitable principles would not permit the award of an injunction, while State *X* principles would permit the injunction. In this situation, denial of the injunction by the federal courts will not encourage the noncitizen plaintiff to forum shop for a different result because the federal result would disfavor the plaintiff. Likewise, if the plaintiff brings the action in state court, the defendant cannot remove the action (and thus forum shop for a different result) because a citizen of the forum state cannot remove an action based solely on diversity of citizenship.[181] If these are the only policies supporting the *Erie* doctrine, that doctrine might not be violated by a refusal of the federal injunction. Nevertheless, the federal court should not refuse an injunction in this situation, because to do so would undermine the policies supporting the diversity jurisdiction. To refuse injunctions under these circumstances would cause plaintiffs such as *M* to abandon their congressionally granted privilege of resorting to the diversity jurisdiction and sue in state court. In the state court, the plaintiffs might be subjected to the very kind of fact-finding bias and prejudice that the diversity jurisdiction was designed to guard against. Therefore, even if the *Erie* doctrine does not compel the duplication of the result that would be reached by the state courts, the policies supporting the diversity jurisdiction require the federal court to grant the injunction on these facts.

* * * * *

The major contribution of *Guaranty Trust* to the *Erie* jurisprudence was the enunciation of a new test to deal with the substance-procedure dichotomy. Justice Frankfurter observed for the Court that "substance" and "procedure" are not mutually exclusive categories. They vary in content depending upon the purpose for which they are being used. As far as the *Erie* doctrine is concerned, the important question is not whether a state statute of limitations can be considered a matter of procedure in some sense—for example, for purposes of conflict-of-laws doctrine. Rather, the important question is whether disregard of the state statute in federal court would significantly affect the result of the litigation.[182] This so-called "outcome determinative test"[183] of *Guaranty Trust*, far from alleviating all problems of distinguishing between substantive and procedural matters, created substantial problems of its own. "[A]lmost every procedural rule

---

180. *But cf.* Beal v. Missouri Pac. R.R., 312 U.S. 45, 61 S. Ct. 418, 85 L. Ed. 577 (1941) (Supreme Court appeared to decide case under federal equitable principles without any reference to what rules of decision existed under state law).

181. *See* 28 U.S.C. § 1441(b).

182. *See Guaranty Trust*, 326 U.S. at 108-09, 65 S. Ct. at 1469-70, 89 L. Ed. at 2085-86.

183. "In essence, the intent of [*Erie*] was to insure that, in all cases where a federal court is exercising jurisdiction solely because of the diversity of citizenship of the parties, the outcome of the litigation in the federal court should be substantially the same, so far as legal rules determine the outcome of a litigation, as it would be if tried in a State court." *Id.* at 109, 65 S. Ct. at 1470, 89 L. Ed. at 2086.

may have a substantial effect on the outcome of a case," but "[i]f the test was not to be carried to its literal limits, . . . there was confusion as to how far it was to go."[184] As discussed in the next section, the main difficulty presented by the test was that it was believed to be applicable to conflicts between Federal Rules of Civil Procedure and state law, with the possibility that many of the Federal Rules would be held invalid because they substantially affect the outcome of cases.[185] However, even as applied to conflicts between federal common-law rules of practice or procedure and state law, the test was, on its face, too extreme.[186]

Nevertheless, the results produced by the outcome determinative test were eminently justifiable. In *Woods v. Interstate Realty Co.*,[187] the Supreme Court considered whether a federal court sitting in diversity was required to apply a Mississippi statute that closed the doors of the state's courts to foreign corporations that failed to qualify under state law to do business within the state. A pre-*Erie* decision had indicated that such statutes did not apply in federal court because it was impermissible for the states to prescribe the qualifications of suitors in federal courts.[188] In *Woods*, the Court held that *Erie* and *Guaranty Trust* now required the application of such door-closing statutes.

After *Woods*, fear was expressed that application of state door-closing statutes in diversity cases may frustrate "the full exercise of [the federal courts'] congressionally invested diversity jurisdiction."[189] This fear is misplaced. If diversity jurisdiction is only designed to prevent bias from operating against out-of-state citizens in state courts, a conclusion that *Erie* seems to mandate, then closing the doors of both the state and federal courts within a state to a litigant will not undermine the diversity policies. Under such circumstances, no out-of-stater will be forced into a state court within the state. If the plaintiff can obtain personal jurisdiction over the defendant in another state, then both the federal and state courts in that state will be available to the out-of-state citizen. If personal jurisdiction cannot be obtained over the defendant in another state and the plaintiff is the out-of-stater, the plaintiff may be effectively deprived of a right of action. Nevertheless, this result is not a concern of the policies supporting the diversity jurisdiction after *Erie* and *Guaranty Trust*. The deprivation of the plaintiff's right of action has occurred as the result of the operation of state law. It has not occurred as the result of bias operating through the state-court system, which is the only concern of the general grant of diversity jurisdiction after

---

184. CHARLES A. WRIGHT, THE LAW OF FEDERAL COURTS § 55, at 379 (5th ed. 1994).

185. *See id.*; John H. Ely, *The Irrepressible Myth of* Erie, 87 HARV. L. REV. 693, 727-28 (1974).

186. *See* Charles E. Clark, *Federal Procedural Reform and States' Rights; to a More Perfect Union*, 40 TEX. L. REV. 211, 220 (1961).

187. 337 U.S. 535, 69 S. Ct. 1235, 93 L. Ed. 1524 (1949).

188. *See* David Lupton's Sons Co. v. Automobile Club of Am., 225 U.S. 489, 500, 32 S. Ct. 711, 714, 56 L. Ed. 1177, 1181-82 (1912). The Court did seem to recognize that if the state law was interpreted as one that voided the contract altogether, rather than simply preventing suit on the contract in the state's courts, it would be enforced. *See id.* at 495-500, 32 S. Ct. at 712-15, 56 L. Ed. at 1179-82.

189. *See* Martin H. Redish & Carter G. Phillips, Erie *and the Rules of Decision Act: In Search of the Appropriate Dilemma*, 91 HARV. L. REV. 356, 378 (1977).

Erie.[190] Thus, given the premises of *Erie* and *Guaranty Trust*, the decision in *Woods* is correct.

2. The *Byrd* Decision: Categorization of State Rules and Balancing

The U.S. Supreme Court mitigated the effect of the *Guaranty Trust* outcome determinative test in *Byrd v. Blue Ridge Rural Electric Cooperative, Inc.*[191] In *Byrd*, a state common-law rule required that, in a personal injury action, the affirmative defense that the plaintiff was an employee of the defendant for purposes of the state worker's compensation statute should be submitted for resolution to the judge. A federal common-law rule of procedure required submission of the defense to the jury. The Court held that the federal practice should govern in diversity actions.[192]

In reasoning that the federal practice should prevail, the Court divided the universe of state laws into the following three categories: (1) rules defining state rights and obligations;[193] (2) rules "bound up" with state-created rights and obligations;[194] and (3) rules of "form and mode."[195] If a state rule either defines state rights and obligations or is bound up with state-created rights and obligations, the federal courts must apply the state rule.[196] However, if the state rule is classified as one of "form and mode," its application by the federal courts is not absolutely mandated. Instead, the state rule of form and mode must be applied only when failing to do so would produce a substantial likelihood of different outcomes in the state and federal courts.[197] Furthermore, even if there is a substantial likelihood of a different outcome if the state rule is disregarded, the federal courts do not have to apply the state rule if federal countervailing considerations exist that are sufficient to outweigh the general *Erie* policies of

---

190. *See* Ralph U. Whitten, Erie *and the Federal Rules: A Review and Reappraisal After* Burlington Northern Railroad v. Woods, 21 CREIGHTON L. REV. 1, 40 n.181 (1987).

191. 356 U.S. 525, 78 S. Ct. 893, 2 L. Ed. 2d 953 (1958).

192. For an excellent criticism of the Court's holding that the federal courts were obligated to submit the issue in *Byrd* to the jury, see Peter Westen & Jeffrey S. Lehman, *Is There Life for* Erie *After the Death of Diversity*, 78 MICH. L. REV. 311, 344-52 (1980).

193. *See Byrd*, 356 U.S. at 535, 78 S. Ct. at 899-900, 2 L. Ed. 2d at 961-62. The Court stated that "[i]t was decided in *Erie [Railroad] v. Tompkins* that the federal courts in diversity cases must respect the definition of state-created rights and obligations by the state courts." *Id.*

194. The Court stated: "We must, therefore, first examine the rule in *Adams v. Davison-Paxon Co.* to determine whether it is bound up with these state rights and obligations in such a way that its application in the federal court is required." *Id.*

195. *See id.* at 536-37, 78 S. Ct. at 900, 2 L. Ed. 2d at 962-63.

196. This conventional interpretation of *Byrd* conforms to the structure of the Court's opinion better than any other interpretation. *See* Szantay v. Beech Aircraft Corp., 349 F.2d 60, 63-64 (4th Cir. 1965); Ralph U. Whitten, Erie *and the Federal Rules: A Review and Reappraisal After* Burlington Northern Railroad v. Woods, 21 CREIGHTON L. REV. 1, 35 (1987). However, it cannot be pretended that all the case law conforms to this interpretation. *See* Martin H. Redish & Carter G. Phillips, Erie *and the Rules of Decision Act: In Search of the Appropriate Dilemma*, 91 HARV L. REV. 356, 364-66 (1977) (discussing other interpretations of *Byrd*). Because the interpretation in the text conforms best to the structure of the Court's opinion, it will be assumed to be correct for purposes of further discussion.

197. 356 U.S. at 537, 78 S. Ct. at 900, 2 L. Ed. 2d at 962.

duplicate outcomes between state and federal actions.[198] In *Byrd* itself, the Court felt that the need to duplicate the outcome between state and federal court was outweighed by federal countervailing considerations in the form of a "strong federal policy against allowing state rules to disrupt the judge-jury relationship in the federal courts."[199]

In applying the *Byrd* decision to new facts, classifying the state rule in the first instance is important. Rules defining state rights and obligations are easy to identify. These are the "purely substantive" rules like the ones involved in *Swift* and *Erie*. The federal courts are not given the discretion to balance federal countervailing considerations against the need to apply these rules. Given that the federal countervailing policies that would be balanced against the application of the state rule will always be procedural policies, the Court wisely established a flat prohibition against application of federal law.[200]

Rules "bound up" with the definition of state rights and obligations are more difficult. The Court cited *Cities Service Oil Co. v. Dunlap*[201] as an example of a case involving a rule bound up with the definition of state rights and obligations. In *Cities Service*, a lower federal court disregarded a settled state burden-of-proof rule and instead applied what it deemed to be a better rule, reasoning that the suit was in equity and the burden of proof was a matter of practice and procedure not governed by *Erie*. The Supreme Court reversed, holding that the federal courts must apply the state burden-of-proof rule.

Although the citation to *Cities Service* in *Byrd* may appear to establish that state burden-of-proof rules are bound up with the definition of state rights and obligations in a way that requires the federal courts to enforce them, this conclusion may not always be correct.[202] This possible uncertainty disappears, however, when the burden-of-proof rule in *Cities Service* is examined closely. The rule required that on an issue of bona fide purchase for value without notice, the person attacking the legal title to land and asserting a superior equity must bear the burden of proof.[203] As to this issue, the Court stated that the state rule was more than simply a rule of practice in courts of equity. Rather, it constituted a valuable assurance to the recorded title holder of state land.[204] This description of the burden-of-proof rule in *Cities Service* suggests a workable distinction between rules bound up with the definition of state rights and obligations and state rules of form and mode. Rules bound up with the definition of state rights and obligations are procedural rules supported by specific policies designed to

---

198. *See id.*; *see also* Szantay v. Beech Aircraft Corp., 349 F.2d 60, 64 (4th Cir. 1965).

199. *Byrd*, 356 U.S. at 538, 78 S. Ct. at 901, 2 L. Ed. 2d at 963.

200. It must be remembered that here only conflicts between state law and federal procedural law are being discussed. In section I ("Federal Common Law") *infra*, it will be seen that the federal courts after *Erie* do have the power to supplant state substantive law rules with substantive federal common-law rules in appropriate cases.

201. 308 U.S. 208, 60 S. Ct. 201, 84 L. Ed. 196 (1939).

202. The uncertainty is created by the failure of *Byrd* to cite Palmer v. Hoffman, 318 U.S. 109, 63 S. Ct. 477, 87 L. Ed. 645 (1943). The *Palmer* case involved, in part, a holding that the question of the burden of establishing contributory negligence is a matter of local law on which the federal courts are bound to follow state practice under *Erie*. *See id.* at 117-19, 63 S. Ct. at 482-83, 87 L. Ed. at 651-53. However, *Palmer* involved a general burden-of-proof rule not specifically designed to "affect decision of the issue."

203. *See Cities Service*, 308 U.S. at 210, 60 S. Ct. at 202, 84 L. Ed. at 197.

204. *See id.* at 212, 60 S. Ct. at 203, 84 L. Ed. at 198.

advance the purposes of the substantive rights to which the "bound up" rules are linked. Rules of form and mode are procedural rules that might dramatically affect the enforcement of substantive rights, but which cannot be seen to be supported by specific policies designed to advance the purposes of the substantive right in question.[205]

Burden-of-proof rules offer good examples of these different kinds of rules. Some burden-of-proof rules, such as the one at issue in *Cities Service*, are designed "to affect decision of the issue rather than to regulate the conduct of the trial."[206] When federal courts are confronted with the latter sort of rule, they should be forbidden from identifying and balancing federal countervailing considerations against the need to duplicate the result that would be reached in state court. Such rules are so closely related to the substantive rights at issue in the case as to be virtually identical to those substantive rights for purposes of the policies of the *Erie* doctrine. The strength of the *Erie* policy is as great in this category of cases as it would be in a case in which a rule defining state rights and obligations is directly involved (as in *Erie* itself). Therefore, *Byrd* should be viewed as holding that no federal countervailing policies ever exist that would justify disregarding this kind of state rule.[207]

If the state burden-of-proof rule is concerned solely with matters of trial administration, the situation is different. Under such circumstances, applying the outcome determinative test of *Guaranty Trust* will protect the *Erie* policies. However, because both state and litigant interests are of lesser strength when rules of trial administration are at issue, *Byrd* allows the identification and weighing of appropriate federal interests against the outcome determinative policy. The reason that such rules are of lesser strength from the standpoint of litigants is that they are less likely than "bound up" rules to be taken into account at the planning stage of activity, as opposed to the litigational stage. The reason that rules of "form and mode" are of lesser strength from the standpoint of the states is that their main utility is in litigation in the state's own courts. When the litigation is in federal court, the states do not have the same interest in enforcing their own views of what rules are best to promote the interests of efficient trial administration as they do when the action is in their own courts. Still, in such circumstances, the *Erie* policy remains strong enough to justify some deference to the state rules, subject to the *Byrd* balancing test.[208]

---

205. *Cf.* S.A. Healy Co. v. Milwaukee Metro. Sewerage Dist., 60 F.3d 305, 310 (7th Cir. 1995) (stating that state procedural rules that are limited to particular substantive areas are "substantive" for *Erie* purposes).

206. RESTATEMENT (SECOND) OF CONFLICT OF LAWS §§ 133-134 (1971).

207. If federal countervailing considerations of sufficient strength to outweigh the need to duplicate the outcome in state court do exist in this situation, they are probably of sufficient strength to justify the creation of a preemptive, substantive federal common-law rule of the sort discussed in section I ("Federal Common Law") *infra.*

208. The *Erie* policies will be protected by this process in most instances because there simply will be no federal countervailing interests to balance against the need to duplicate the outcome. For example, in burden-of-proof cases, the Court has never identified any such policies. This fact does not mean that there are no problems with the balancing portion of *Byrd*, however. The balancing test invites abuse through the identification of spurious federal interests, as discussed *infra.*

In addition to the cryptic nature of the state-rule categories discussed in *Byrd*, the opinion contained other difficulties. For one, neither *Byrd* nor *Guaranty Trust* clearly state what kind of outcome difference ought to be taken into account by the federal courts when they are trying to decide whether to apply a state rule of form and mode or a conflicting federal common-law rule of practice or procedure. Both *Guaranty Trust*, which involved a statute-of-limitations issue, and *Byrd*, which involved a question of judge-jury relations, spoke in terms of ultimate differences in outcome on the merits of the case.[209] However, the Court has never addressed whether outcome differences of a lesser nature than an outcome difference on the ultimate merits of the case will invoke the outcome determinative test. An argument that such lesser differences will justify application of the outcome rule can be derived from *Woods v. Interstate Realty Co.*,[210] discussed above. Recall that *Woods* held that the federal courts were obligated to apply state door-closing statutes that prohibit suits from being brought by certain categories of litigants in the state courts. If a plaintiff barred from the courts of a state by such a statute can obtain personal jurisdiction over the defendant in another state, the plaintiff may still be able to win a judgment on the merits. The *Woods* holding thus seems to indicate that outcome differences of less than an ultimate difference on the merits can be considered by the federal courts in administering the *Guaranty Trust-Byrd* rule.[211]

This interpretation was reinforced by the later decision of the Court in *Hanna v. Plumer*.[212] In *Hanna*, a conflict existed between a Federal Rule of Civil Procedure and state law. Therefore, this decision will be discussed more fully in the next section. In the process of deciding the issue before it, however, the Court in an extended dictum provided some additional guidance on the administration of the outcome determinative test. According to the Court, not just any difference in outcome would produce the obligation to apply state law under

---

209. In *Byrd*, the Court stated as follows: "It may well be that in the instant personal-injury case the outcome would be substantially affected by whether the issue of immunity is decided by a judge or jury." *Byrd*, 356 U.S. at 537, 78 S. Ct. at 900, 2 L. Ed. 2d at 962.

210. 337 U.S. 535, 69 S. Ct. 1235, 93 L. Ed. 1524 (1949).

211. In *Woods*, the Court considered the case controlled by *Guaranty Trust*. *See id.* at 538, 69 S. Ct. at 1237, 93 L. Ed. at 1527. The Court did not discuss whether it would have been possible for the corporate plaintiff to obtain personal jurisdiction over the defendant in another state, though it was clear that the court of appeals had held that the state door-closing statute did not void the contract on which the action was brought, but simply deprived the plaintiff of the benefits of the state's courts. *See id.* at 536, 69 S. Ct. at 1236, 93 L. Ed. at 1525-26. The Supreme Court did not question that part of the court of appeals' holding.

Another problem with *Woods* after *Byrd* is determining how the state door-closing statute should be classified. The statute was not tied to any specific substantive right. Rather, it was a general statute depriving corporate plaintiffs who failed to designate an agent for service of process of the benefits of the state's courts. Thus, it does not seem to be a rule "bound up" with the definition of state rights and obligations in the sense meant by *Byrd*. It does not seem exactly aimed at trial administration either, however. Nevertheless, it is probably best categorized as a rule of "form and mode" because it seems aimed at assuring that resident plaintiffs will be able to sue foreign corporations in the state's courts and removing the privilege of the foreign corporation to sue in the state's courts when such a suit is not possible—*i.e.*, when the foreign corporation has not appointed the statutorily required agent.

212. 380 U.S. 460, 85 S. Ct. 1136, 14 L. Ed. 2d 8 (1965).

Guaranty Trust. Rather, only outcome differences that cause "forum shopping" or "inequitable administration of the laws" are prohibited.[213]

  Hanna's elaboration of the outcome determinative test requires a further inquiry in each instance where a state rule of form and mode is involved in a case. To determine whether a court must apply a state rule of form and mode, one must now ask whether failure to apply the state rule in federal court would cause someone to choose a federal court over a state court or would result in unfair discrimination against a citizen of the forum state by depriving the citizen of the benefit of a valuable rule of law that would be applied in the state court. Since many rules might have either one of these effects but would not necessarily produce a difference in outcome on the merits, the outcome determinative test would seem to extend to lesser outcome differences.

  Illustration 5-11. A, a citizen of Ireland, sues *B*, a citizen of State *X*, U.S.A., in a federal court in State *X*. *B* moves to dismiss the action under the doctrine of forum non conveniens,[214] on the ground that Ireland is a more convenient forum. The State *X* Supreme Court has interpreted a State *X* constitutional provision as forbidding the State *X* courts from applying a doctrine of forum non conveniens. Therefore, if suit were in State *X* court, *B's* motion would be denied. If the State *X* rule defines state rights and obligations or is a rule bound up with state rights and obligations, the federal courts must apply it.[215] If the state rule is one of "form and mode," the federal court may consider whether the action should be dismissed under the federal doctrine of forum non conveniens or whether such a dismissal will offend the *Erie* policies. The plaintiff certainly would not commence suit in federal court to obtain the benefit of the federal doctrine of forum non conveniens. Such action could only result in dismissal of the action and trial in a location that the plaintiff does not prefer (Ireland). Similarly, if the action had been filed in a State *X* court, the defendant would not have been able to forum shop for a federal forum because a citizen of the state in which the action is brought may not remove an action in which jurisdiction is based solely on diversity of citizenship. Therefore, disregard of the state rule could not result in forum shopping by either the plaintiff or the

---

213. *See id.* at 468, 85 S. Ct. at 1142, 14 L. Ed. 2d at 15. In a footnote, the Court added:

> *Erie* and its progeny make clear that when a federal court sitting in a diversity case is faced with a question of whether or not to apply state law, the importance of a state rule is . . . relevant . . . only in the context of asking whether application of the rule would make so important a difference to the character or result of the litigation that failure to enforce it would unfairly discriminate against citizens of the forum State, or whether application of the rule would have so important an effect upon the fortunes of one or both of the litigants that failure to enforce it would be likely to cause a plaintiff to choose the federal court.

Id. n.9, 85 S. Ct. at 1142 n.9, 14 L. Ed. 2d at 15 n.9.

214. *See* Chapter 4(D) ("Forum Non Conveniens and Change of Venue") *supra*.

215. It is possible that such a rule may define state rights and obligations if the constitutional provision in question is interpreted to be a guarantee to both residents and nonresidents of access to a forum for reasons of substantive constitutional policy. The fact that a rule appears procedural in form should not result in automatic classification as a "bound up" rule or a "form and mode" rule. Some such rules can confer valuable rights on residents and nonresidents alike. *See* Ralph U. Whitten, Erie *and the Federal Rules: A Review and Reappraisal After* Burlington Northern Railroad v. Woods, 21 CREIGHTON L. REV. 1, 36 (1987).

defendant. Nor will disregard of the state rule result in discrimination against citizens of the forum state. It is *B*, the citizen of the forum state, who is asking for the state rule to be disregarded. Therefore, none of the *Erie* policies, as redefined through *Hanna*, will be offended by application of the federal doctrine of forum non conveniens. For the *Erie* policies to be offended in the situation described in this illustration, they would have to be more broadly defined. The policies would have to be redefined to include discrimination against *noncitizens* by application of a different law than would be applied in state court.[216]

Illustration 5-12. Although the Court's currently defined *Erie* policies do not preclude dismissal under the federal doctrine of forum non conveniens in *Illustration 5-11*, other federal policies may nevertheless prevent dismissal. The effect of dismissing actions such as the one described in *Illustration 5-11* will be to drive plaintiffs who want to resort to the alienage jurisdiction out of federal court into state court, where no dismissal will be possible. As a result, a federal forum non conveniens dismissal would be improper in the situation described. Forum non conveniens is a federal common-law procedural doctrine that is less important than the subject-matter jurisdiction policies supporting the alienage jurisdiction.

Illustration 5-13. Assume that the citizenship of the parties in *Illustration 5-11* is reversed. Thus, *A* is a citizen of State *X*, and *B* is a citizen of Ireland. In this situation, a federal forum non conveniens dismissal would clearly produce the sort of outcome difference with which *Erie* was concerned. While *A* would still not choose a federal court in State *X* to get the benefit of a doctrine that would result in dismissal of the action, *B* might well remove the action to get the benefit of that doctrine if *A* commenced the action in a State *X* court. Thus, disregard of the state rule might cause forum shopping by the noncitizen defendant.[217] In addition, dismissal of the action would deprive *A* of a valuable rule that would be applied to prevent dismissal in the State *X* courts, resulting in discrimination against a citizen of the forum state. The question whether the federal doctrine of forum non conveniens could be applied, therefore, would depend on whether the policies supporting that doctrine outweighed the *Erie* policies favoring duplication

---

216. The situation described in *Illustration 5-11* will not necessarily result in an ultimate outcome difference because the plaintiff might win a judgment either in Ireland or in State *X*. However, there may nonetheless be ultimate outcome-difference implications. The plaintiff may have chosen an American court to get the benefit of the applicable substantive law in State *X*. If so, and if a dismissal will result in a change in that substantive law to the disadvantage of the plaintiff, an outcome difference that favors the defendant may become more likely. Piper Aircraft Co. v. Reyno, 454 U.S. 235, 102 S. Ct. 252, 70 L. Ed. 2d 419 (1981), cited and discussed in Chapter 4(D)1*(a) supra*, allows a forum non conveniens dismissal even in the face of such a possibility, but *Piper* reserved judgment on whether state law must control the question of forum non conveniens dismissals in diversity actions where it differs from federal law. *See id.* at 248 n.13, 102 S. Ct. at 262 n.13, 70 L. Ed. 2d at 431 n.13; *see also* Koster v. Lumbermens Mut. Cas. Co., 330 U.S. 518, 529, 67 S. Ct. 828, 834, 91 L. Ed. 1067, 1076-77 (1947); Gulf Oil Corp. v. Gilbert, 330 U.S. 501, 509, 67 S. Ct. 839, 843, 91 L. Ed. 1055, 1062-63 (1947); Williams v. Green Bay & W.R.R., 326 U.S. 549, 558-59, 66 S. Ct. 284, 288-89, 90 L. Ed. 311, 317-18 (1946).

217. Although the Court from *Erie* to present has phrased the forum shopping policy in terms of plaintiff forum shopping, there is no apparent policy reason to exclude defendant forum shopping from the *Erie* prohibitions. *But see* Ashley S. Deeks, Comment, *Raising the Cost of Lying: Rethinking* Erie *for Judicial Estoppel,* 64 U. CHI. L. REV. 873, 887 (1997).

of outcomes between state and federal courts. The policies supporting the federal forum non conveniens doctrine are to prevent the vexation of defendants that would result from litigation in an inconvenient forum and to prevent the burden on the federal court system that would result from imposing litigation unrelated to the forum on that system.[218] Because the Supreme Court has never indicated how to attach weight to federal countervailing interests, it is unclear whether these policies would outweigh the outcome determinative policies.

* * * * *

Another problem with the *Byrd* opinion is the vagueness of the Court's balancing test when state rules of "form and mode" are involved. The Court gave the lower courts no guidance on how to identify legitimate federal countervailing considerations.[219] Nor, as indicated in *Illustration 5-13*, did the Court state how to attach weight to such considerations once they had been properly identified. The predictable result was that some lower federal courts recognized demonstrably spurious federal interests and attached substantial weight to interests that should have received little, if any, consideration.[220]

Illustration 5-14. In *Szantay v. Beech Aircraft Corp.*,[221] a Beech aircraft was purchased in Nebraska. It was flown to Miami, Florida and then to Columbia, South Carolina, where Dixie Aviation Co. serviced the aircraft. It then left Columbia bound for Chicago, Illinois, but crashed en route in Tennessee. All of its occupants were killed. The decedents were all Illinois citizens. Their personal representatives commenced a diversity action in South Carolina federal court against Dixie Aviation, a South Carolina corporation, and Beech Aircraft, which is a Delaware corporation with its principal place of business in Kansas. Beech moved to be dismissed from the suit on the ground that the South Carolina door-closing statute prohibited an action against it in the state. The door-closing statute forbade actions against foreign corporations by nonresident plaintiffs unless the cause of action arose in South Carolina. The district court denied Beech's motion. Beech appealed to the Fourth Circuit Court of Appeals. That court held the South Carolina door-closing statute inapplicable under the *Byrd* analysis.

In applying the *Byrd* test to the action,[222] the Fourth Circuit identified "explicit and numerous" countervailing federal interests.[223] First, the court

---

218. *See* Chapter 4(D)(1)*(a)* ("Forum Non Conveniens") *supra*.

219. *Cf.* 19 CHARLES A. WRIGHT ET AL., FEDERAL PRACTICE AND PROCEDURE: JURISDICTION AND RELATED MATTERS (ERIE DOCTRINE) § 4504, at 36-38 (2d ed. 1996) (discussing the ambiguity in the way the Court derived the federal interests in *Byrd*); *see also* ERWIN CHEMERINSKY, FEDERAL JURISDICTION § 5.3.5, at 322-23 (3d ed. 1999).

220. *See* CHARLES A. WRIGHT, THE LAW OF FEDERAL COURTS § 59, at 403-04 (5th ed. 1994).

221. 349 F.2d 60 (4th Cir. 1965).

222. The court identified the door-closing statute as one of form and mode. *See id.* at 64. It then concluded that no citizen of the forum state would be discriminated against if the state statute were not applied. *See id.* However, the court did not evaluate whether forum shopping would occur if the statute were not applied by the federal courts. This failure was a clear error because plaintiffs would be encouraged to forum shop if the state statute is applied by state, but not federal, courts. *See id.*

223. *Id.* at 65. The court apparently thought *Byrd* required it to balance the federal considerations against the state policies involved in the door-closing statute. This conclusion was incorrect because, as demonstrated in the text above, *Byrd* requires that the countervailing federal considerations be balanced against the *Erie* policy of duplicate outcomes between state and federal courts. However, even on its own terms, the court did not give the state interests all they were due. The court interpreted the state statute as a statutory formulation of the argued that applying the door-closing statute would undermine the constitutional grant of diversity jurisdiction to the federal courts.[224] However, no one would have been deprived of the benefits of the diversity jurisdiction in *Szantay* if the South Carolina federal court had dismissed Beech from the action under the state door-closing statute. The Illinois plaintiffs could have sued Dixie Aviation in South Carolina federal court and Beech in a federal court elsewhere—for example, in Kansas, where Beech had its principal place of business. Although this might have been less convenient for, or tactically disadvantageous to, the plaintiffs, it would not deprive the plaintiffs of the benefits of the diversity jurisdiction.

Second, the court argued that the Full Faith and Credit Clause of the Constitution expressed a "national interest 'looking toward maximum enforcement in each state of the obligations or rights created or recognized by the statutes of sister states.' "[225] This federal countervailing consideration was also spurious. As the court itself acknowledged, applying the South Carolina door-closing statute would not violate the Full Faith and Credit Clause.[226] It is difficult to see how a constitutional clause that concededly permits the application of a statute can be the source of a "policy" that prohibits the application of the statute.

Third, the court stated that a federal policy encouraging "efficient joinder in multi-party actions" existed under statutes like the federal interpleader statute and the Federal Rules of Civil Procedure governing joinder of multiple claims and parties.[227] Nevertheless, the federal interpleader statute and most of the federal multiparty joinder rules cited by the court were inapplicable to the case before it. Certain other rules, particularly Federal Rule 20, which permitted joinder of multiple defendants in *Szantay*, were applicable to the case. However, those rules were not designed specifically to override state door-closing statutes. Furthermore, while the Federal Rules governing joinder of multiple claims and parties express important federal efficiency policies, these policies only operate when the federal courts have before them cases which are otherwise within the proper scope of their authority. When a case is outside the subject-matter jurisdiction of the federal courts or when the courts are deprived of power to act by other

---

doctrine of forum non conveniens, which would not be undermined by disregard of the statute by the federal courts. *See id.* at 65. Given the structure of the statute, this conclusion is not persuasive. Beech's argument seems much more plausible. Beech argued that the statute was designed to encourage foreign corporations to do business in the state by freeing them of the fear that they would be sued in the state by nonresidents on causes of action having nothing to do with the state. *See* Arrowsmith v. United Press Int'l, 320 F.2d 219, 226 (2d Cir. 1963) ("State statutes determining what foreign corporations may be sued, for what, and by whom, are not mere whimsy; like most legislation they represent a balancing of various considerations—for example, affording a forum for wrongs connected with the state and conveniencing resident plaintiffs, while avoiding the discouragement of activity within the state by foreign corporations"). In addition, if the policies supporting the state statute in *Szantay* were unclear, as the court supposed, *see Szantay*, 349 F.2d at 65, it would seem more in accord with the *Erie* policies to assume a significant state policy rather than a less significant one. *Cf.* Martin H. Redish & Carter G. Phillips, Erie *and the Rules of Decision Act: In Search of the Appropriate Dilemma*, 91 HARV. L. REV. 356, 395-96 (1977) (arguing that when legislative history is absent, the federal courts should assume the existence of some state interest).

    224. *See* 349 F.2d at 65.

    225. *Id.* at 65.

    226. *See id.* at 65-66.

    227. *Id.* at 66 & n.12.

fundamental doctrines that govern the relationship between state and federal courts, such as the *Erie* doctrine, the policies supporting the Federal Rules surely cannot "outweigh" the more fundamental doctrines.[228]

3. Subsequent Developments: Imprecision and Confusion

For many years after the *Hanna* dictum discussed in the previous subsection, the Supreme Court did not address the problem of conflicts between federal common-law rules of procedure and state law.[229] In the 1990's, the Court twice considered such conflicts in *Chambers v. NASCO, Inc.*[230] and *Gasperini v. Center for Humanities, Inc.*[231] Far from clarifying the analytical structure that its previous decisions seemed to establish, the Court's opinions in *Chambers* and *Gasperini* ignored key steps in and distinctions established by earlier precedents. The result is an intensification of the confusion about how the *Erie* analysis should be conducted, a confusion that has infected the operation of the doctrine in the lower federal courts.[232]

In *Chambers*, a federal diversity action was brought to obtain specific performance of a contract. The defendant engaged in a substantial amount of bad-faith conduct before and during the course of the litigation, some of which was sanctionable under Federal Rule 11 and some of which was not. For the conduct not sanctionable under Rule 11, the district court imposed a substantial sanction against the defendant under the court's "inherent powers." The court of appeals affirmed this use of inherent powers to impose sanctions. The court of appeals rejected the argument that a federal court sitting in diversity must look to state law to determine the circumstances under which sanctions may be assessed.[233] The Supreme Court granted certiorari and affirmed.

The Court rejected the argument that federal statutes and rules of procedure had displaced the inherent power of the district court to impose sanctions.[234] The Court then confirmed that, under the dictum in *Hanna*, "the 'outcome determinative' test of *Erie* and *Guaranty Trust* . . . 'cannot be read without reference to the twin aims of the *Erie* rule: discouragement of forum shopping and avoidance of inequitable administration of the law.' "[235] There

---

228. *Cf.* FED. R. CIV. P. 82. The multiparty joinder policy was the only basis that the court found to distinguish *Woods v. Interstate Realty Co.*, discussed above, in which the Supreme Court had required the application of a state door-closing statute.

229. *See* Ralph U. Whitten, *Developments in the* Erie *Doctrine: 1991*, 40 AM. J. COMP. L. 967, 970 (1992).

230. 501 U.S. 32, 111 S. Ct. 2123, 115 L. Ed. 2d 27 (1991).

231. 518 U.S. 415, 116 S. Ct. 2211, 135 L. Ed. 2d 659 (1996).

232. *See* section G ("The *Erie* Doctrine in the Lower Federal Courts") *infra.*

233. *See Chambers*, 501 U.S. at 43, 111 S. Ct. at 2131, 115 L. Ed. 2d at 43.

234. *See* 501 U.S. at 42-50, 111 S. Ct. at 2131-36, 115 L. Ed. 2d at 43-49. The Court also rejected the argument that its decision in Alyeska Pipeline Service Co. v. Wilderness Society, 421 U.S. 240, 95 S. Ct. 1612, 44 L. Ed. 2d 141 (1975), prohibited a federal court sitting in diversity from awarding attorney's fees as a sanction. The Court held that *Alyeska* only applies to fee-shifting rules "that embody a substantive policy, such as a statute which permits a prevailing party in certain classes of litigation to recover fees." 501 U.S. at 52, 111 S. Ct. at 2136, 115 L. Ed. 2d at 49-50.

235. 501 U.S. at 52, 111 S. Ct. at 2137, 115 L. Ed. 2d at 50.

existed no danger of forum shopping because the imposition of sanctions under the district court's inherent power does not depend upon who wins the litigation, but "on how the parties conduct themselves during the litigation."[236] This conclusion was correct. A party will not be able to shop for a federal court to obtain a different applicable rule of law unless the party not only is aware of a different federal rule, but can anticipate its application. Normally, this will not be possible if the conduct giving rise to the application of the rule cannot occur until after litigation has been commenced.[237] However, the Court's reference to rules that affect "which party wins the lawsuit"[238] could be read as a requirement that only outcome differences on the ultimate merits of the case are prohibited by *Erie*. This interpretation would be unfortunate. As discussed in the preceding subsection, there exist differences between federal and state procedures that will produce forum shopping, but not necessarily a difference on the ultimate merits of the case. These differences seem serious enough to be included within the policy of the outcome determinative rule. Therefore, the holding of *Chambers* should be limited to rules that apply to behavior of the parties after commencement of the action.

The Court also held that inequitable administration of the law was not involved in the case because it is not inequitable to utilize inherent sanctioning power to impose sanctions on "citizens and noncitizens alike, when the party, by controlling his or her conduct in litigation, has the power to determine whether sanctions will be assessed."[239] This part of the Court's opinion is unclear. The "inequitable administration of the law" factor evolved from that part of *Erie* objecting to *Swift v. Tyson* on the ground that *Swift* produced discrimination against citizens of the forum state. This discrimination occurred because in diversity actions the federal courts sometimes applied different substantive rules than would have been applied in the state courts, and the noncitizen plaintiff or defendant was in control of the choice of forum under the rules of subject-matter jurisdiction.

However, *Guaranty Trust* and *Byrd* extended the *Erie* doctrine beyond pure substantive rules to rules of "form and mode." After those decisions, as elaborated in the *Hanna* opinion, it appeared that the inequitable administration of the law factor would be implicated by a federal court's refusal to apply any state rule of law that would confer valuable benefits on a litigant if the action were in state court. This description seems to fit the rule in *Chambers*. A state law that refuses to recognize a bad-faith exception to the traditional rule against fee shifting would certainly have produced valuable benefits to the defendant in

---

236. *Id.* at 53, 111 S. Ct. at 2137, 115 L. Ed. 2d at 50.

237. It is, of course, possible for a plaintiff to anticipate that a defendant will engage in sanctionable conduct during litigation that has not yet been commenced. Such a plaintiff might find a federal diversity court more attractive than a state court that could not levy sanctions for the conduct anticipated. However, to the extent that such "forum shopping" occurs, it does not rise in seriousness to the level of forum shopping for a federal court to obtain the benefit of highly predictable results based on preexisting rules of law. Many differences in procedure exist between federal and state courts that may make the federal courts more attractive in the same way.

238. *See* 501 U.S. at 53, 111 S. Ct. at 2137, 115 L. Ed. 2d at 50.

239. *Id.*

the case. *Chambers* can, therefore, be read as a rejection of the view that disregard of any law conferring a valuable benefit on a litigant will produce inequitable administration of the laws. In fact, the Court's opinion can be read as saying that inequitable administration of the law is never involved when a federal rule applies equally to both citizens and noncitizens alike, a reading with potentially far-reaching effects.

Nevertheless, it would seem safer to interpret *Chambers* more narrowly. In addition to emphasizing that the federal sanctioning power was applicable to citizens and noncitizens alike, the Court also observed that every litigant could avoid the application of sanctions by adopting appropriate behavior during the litigation. Thus, the case should probably be read as holding only that application of independent federal rules to post-commencement behavior does not violate the *Erie* doctrine. The flaw in *Swift* was the ability of the noncitizen to control the application of rules of law to the disadvantage of the citizen of the forum. Post-commencement rules that allow all parties to control the application of legal rules by adopting appropriate litigation behavior are not similarly flawed. Thus, in the case of post-commencement rules, the forum shopping and inequitable administration of the laws factors seem to coincide, with neither factor being applicable under the *Erie* policies.

A final, and potentially more serious, difficulty with *Chambers* was the Court's failure to discuss why the state rule in the case should be considered a rule of form and mode subject to the outcome determinative test. The district court had awarded sanctions in part for conduct by the defendant that had occurred outside the formal confines of the litigation, but which clearly affected it. The dissenting Justices in *Chambers* argued that such an award constituted an expansion of the scope of the remedy for breach of contract that would have existed in state court.[240] The majority's only response was conclusory: the defendant was not sanctioned for breach of contract, but in order to vindicate judicial authority.[241] However, if the dissenters' argument is correct, the state rule in *Chambers* would appear to be a rule ''bound up'' with state rights and obligations. As demonstrated in the previous subsection, state rules ''bound up'' with the definition of state rights and obligations are rules that are specifically linked with particular substantive rights or obligations and designed to support their policies. Remedies rules often fall within this description. If the state rule in question was really a rule prescribing the remedies for breach of contract, it would be plausible to consider it a rule ''bound up'' and, therefore, obligatory on the federal courts. Thus, it would have been preferable for the majority to address directly the question of the state rule's characterization in order to dispel the dissenters' arguments.

Nevertheless, the majority's classification appears to have been correct. The state rule in question was the traditional American rule against fee shifting. The state simply did not recognize an exception to this rule for bad faith conduct

---

240. *See* 501 U.S. at 58-60, 111 S. Ct. at 2140-41, 115 L. Ed. 2d at 53-55 (Scalia, J., dissenting); 501 U.S. at 75-76, 111 S. Ct. at 2148-49, 115 L. Ed. 2d at 64-65 (Kennedy, J., with whom Rehnquist, C.J., and Souter, J., joined, dissenting).

241. *See id.* at 54-55, 111 S. Ct. at 2138, 115 L. Ed. 2d at 52.

on the part of the defendant during the course of litigation. The traditional American rule is not a rule linked to specific substantive rights or obligations. Rather, it is a rule that cuts across all substantive categories and operates unless there is a specific exception to the rule.[242] Therefore, it cannot plausibly be classified as a rule "bound up" with the definition of state substantive rights. Other remedies rules will have to be evaluated on a case-by-case basis to determine whether they are sufficiently linked to state substantive rights or obligations so as to be considered "bound up" with those rights and obligations.

Illustration 5-15. In *Illustration 5-9*, traditional federal equity principles were assumed to justify an injunction for the threatened violation of a state right, while state equity principles would forbid the injunction. If the state rule is linked to the specific kind of case brought by the plaintiff—for example, if a state statute forbids injunctions against state officers—the rule should probably be considered bound up with state substantive rights and obligations and thus obligatory on the federal courts. On the other hand, if the state rule is a general rule of equity jurisprudence applicable to any kind of case brought for an injunction, it should probably be classified as a rule of form and mode.[243] If the rule is a rule of form and mode, federal disregard of it will produce forum shopping by plaintiffs for a federal court, as discussed in *Illustration 5-9*. As stated in that illustration, no apparent federal countervailing interest seems to exist that would justify granting an injunction for the threatened violation of state rights that state law would deny.

Illustration 5-16. *A*, a citizen of State *X*, sues *B Corp.*, a corporation incorporated and with its principal place of business in State *Y*, in a U.S. District Court in State *X*. *A's* claim is based on an insurance policy issued by *B* to *A*. *A* allegedly incurred a loss covered by the policy that *B* refuses to pay. *A* seeks the amount of the covered loss plus attorney's fees from *B* as damages. By statute, State *X* provides that in any case in which an insurer denies payment of a claim under a policy and the insured successfully sues to recover for the loss, the insurer must pay the insured's reasonable attorney's fees in the action. The State *X* rule prescribing payment of attorney's fees is specifically linked to state substantive rights in insurance cases. Therefore, it is a rule "bound up" with the definition of state rights and obligations and obligatory on the U.S. District Court in State *X*.

* * * * *

---

242. As discussed *supra* in subsection (1), remedies rules are closely linked to substantive rights. However, the traditional American rule, because of its peculiar history may not qualify as "substantive" in the same way as other remedies. *See* DAN B. DOBBS, LAW OF REMEDIES § 3.10, at 277 (2d student ed. 1993).

243. An example of such a rule might be the traditional inadequate-remedy-at-law rule, which must, in theory, be satisfied in any case in which the plaintiff requests an injunction. The inadequate-remedy-at-law rule, although still applied after the merger of law and equity, is a rule that is historically linked with the existence of separate law and equity courts. Its retention in modern merged systems of law and equity is a product of both inertia and the failure of the legislatures that enacted merger statutes to instruct the courts what rule to apply in its place. *See* Ralph U. Whitten, *Federal Declaratory and Injunctive Interference With State Court Proceedings: The Supreme Court and the Limits of Judicial Discretion*, 53 N.C. L. REV. 591, 600-04, 611-16 (1975).

Gasperini v. Center for Humanities, Inc.[244] is the Supreme Court's latest pronouncement on the *Erie* doctrine. In *Gasperini*, the plaintiff, a photographer who was a citizen of California, commenced an action in the U.S. District Court for the Southern District of New York to recover damages from the defendant, a New York corporation. The plaintiff's claims were for breach of contract, conversion, and negligence resulting from the loss by the defendant of certain slides that the plaintiff had supplied to the defendant for use in an educational videotape. After a trial, a jury awarded the plaintiff $450,000 in compensatory damages, which represented $1,500 for each of 300 slides. The district court denied the defendant's motion for a new trial without comment. The Court of Appeals for the Second Circuit vacated the judgment as excessive, applying a New York statute that required trial and appellate courts in the state to determine whether verdicts "materially deviate from what is reasonable compensation."[245] The Second Circuit applied the New York statute because the action was a diversity action in which New York substantive law governed the controversy. However, in both state and federal courts, the standard which had controlled prior to the statute was whether the verdict was so exorbitant that it shocked the conscience of the court.[246] The statute thus called for closer supervision of jury verdicts by both trial and appellate courts in New York. Thus, the question was raised whether application of the New York statute at the federal appellate level "would be out of sync with the federal system's division of trial and appellate court functions, an allocation weighted by the Seventh Amendment."[247]

In considering this question, the Supreme Court, in an opinion written by Justice Ginsburg, found Rule 59 of the Federal Rules of Civil Procedure, which generally governs the granting of new trials in federal court, inapplicable to the issue before it.[248] Thus, the issue was whether the Court's precedents under the Rules of Decision Act compelled the application of the New York statute. A majority of the Court found that disregarding the "deviates materially" standard of the statute would violate the policies of the *Erie* doctrine. First, the Court held that if federal courts were to ignore the statutory standard and apply instead the "shock the conscience test" applied before the statute was enacted, substantial variations between state and federal money judgments would result—with the federal judgments being larger because of the lesser scrutiny that would be given to such judgments. This variation, the Court stated, implicated the *Erie* prohibitions against forum shopping and inequitable administration of the laws.[249]

The Court then examined whether application of the state statute would be inconsistent with the Seventh Amendment. On this issue, the Court held that nothing in the Seventh Amendment absolutely precludes appellate review of a

---

244. 518 U.S. 415, 116 S. Ct. 2211, 135 L. Ed. 2d 659 (1996).

245. *See* N.Y. C.P.L.R. § 5501(c) (McKinney 1995).

246. *See* 518 U.S. at 422, 116 S. Ct. at 2217, 135 L. Ed. 2d at 670.

247. *Id.* at 426, 116 S. Ct. at 2219, 135 L. Ed. 2d at 673.

248. *See id.* at 437 n.22, 116 S. Ct. at 2224 n.22, 135 L. Ed. 2d at 680 n.22. This aspect of the case is discussed in section F ("The Evolution of the *Erie* Doctrine: Conflicts Between State Law and Federal Rules of Civil Procedure") *infra.*

249. *See* 518 U.S. at 429-31, 116 S. Ct. at 2220-21, 135 L. Ed. 2d at 675-76.

district court's denial of a motion to set aside a jury verdict as excessive.[250] Nevertheless, the question remained whether application of the New York statute would, in the *Byrd* sense, unduly disrupt the proper relationship between the federal trial and appellate courts. In applying an apparent variation of the *Byrd* balancing test, the Court found that New York's "dominant" substantive interest could be respected without disrupting the federal court system by requiring the district courts to follow the New York statute, but subjecting the district court's decisions to appellate review under the abuse of discretion standard applied throughout the U.S. Courts of Appeals.[251]

There are numerous problems with the *Gasperini* opinion. First, the Court paid no attention to the *Byrd* categorization process. The New York statute applied to review of money judgments in which an itemized verdict was required by another New York statute.[252] The latter provision requires itemized verdicts in tort actions of particular sorts, and it was part of a general reform effort to control the level of damages awarded in tort cases by juries.[253] Thus, the statute appears to be the kind of provision that the *Byrd* opinion would treat as "bound up" with state substantive rights, in that it is designed to affect the decision of the damages issue in specific kinds of substantive cases only. Nevertheless, the Court never considered whether the statute was a rule "bound up" with substantive rights or a rule of form and mode. It simply applied the outcome determinative test to determine whether the federal courts were obligated to apply the rule.

The Court's failure in both *Chambers* and *Gasperini* to consider the proper categorization of the state rule may mean that the *Byrd* categorization

---

250. *See id.* at 431-36, 116 S. Ct. at 2221-24, 135 L. Ed. 2d at 676-79.

251. *See id.* at 436-39, 116 S. Ct. at 2224-25, 135 L. Ed. 2d at 679-81. Justice Stevens dissented. While Justice Stevens agreed that the Seventh Amendment does not limit the power of federal appellate courts in diversity cases to decide whether a verdict exceeds the limits established by state law, he disagreed that *Byrd* required the court of appeals to apply a different damage control standard than the district courts. *See id.* at 439-48, 116 S. Ct. at 2225-30, 135 L. Ed. 2d at 681-87. Justice Scalia, with whom the Chief Justice and Justice Thomas joined, also dissented. In part, Justice Scalia's dissent was based on the view that the Seventh Amendment's re-examination clause prevented the kind of appellate review of which the majority approved. *See id.* at 448-61, 116 S. Ct. at 2230-36, 135 L. Ed. 2d at 688-95. However, Justice Scalia also disagreed with the majority's *Erie* analysis. He was of the opinion that Rule 59 of the Federal Rules of Civil Procedure governed the standard for granting new trials in federal court, a conclusion that is discussed in section F ("The Evolution of the *Erie* Doctrine: Conflicts Between State Law and Federal Rules of Civil Procedure") *infra*. However, he also disagreed with the majority's general *Erie* analysis, finding that "[t]he Court commits the classic *Erie* mistake of regarding whatever changes the outcome as substantive." *Id.* at 465, 116 S. Ct. at 2238, 135 L. Ed. 2d at 697. Rather, he stated, "the Court exaggerates the difference that the state standard will make" at the trial when compared with the standard actually used by the federal courts, and he was of the opinion that forum shopping was much more likely to be encouraged by "the consistent difference between the state and federal appellate standards," a conclusion that seems unlikely in the extreme, given that litigants are not likely to plan litigation on the basis that a federal appellate court will sustain an excessive verdict in their favor that has not been overturned by a federal trial court. *See id.* at 465-67, 116 S. Ct. at 2238-39, 135 L. Ed. 2d at 697. Finally, Justice Scalia appeared to argue that the *Byrd* countervailing considerations test required application of a federal standard at the trial level rather than the New York statute to prevent destruction of the uniformity of federal practice. *See id.* at 467, 116 S. Ct. at 2239, 135 L. Ed. 2d at 698.

252. *See* N.Y. C.P.L.R. § 4111(d) (McKinney 1992).

253. *See id.* §§ 4111(d) (itemized verdict required in medical, dental, or podiatric malpractice actions), 4111(e) (itemized verdict required in certain actions against public employees for personal injury and wrongful death), 4111(f) (itemized verdict required in actions for personal injury, injury to property, or wrongful death).

process is no longer viable and that the outcome determinative test applies both to rules previously denominated as "bound up" with state substantive rights and to rules of "form and mode."[254] If so, the Court's failure to explain why the treatment of the two kinds of rules is to be the same is disturbing. As discussed earlier,[255] a close evaluation of "bound up" rule indicates that they are of the same quality and strength as rules defining state rights and obligations, which are, and should be, absolutely obligatory on the federal courts unless the interests of the federal government in the issue are strong enough to justify the creation of substantive federal common law.[256] Alternatively, the Court could simply have considered it obvious that the state rules in *Chambers* and *Gasperini* were rules of "form and mode" governed by the outcome determinative test. However, given the nature of the state statute in *Gasperini*, this approach is hardly more satisfactory. If the "bound up" category of rules is to survive, it is not appropriate for the Court to refuse to reveal the kinds of cases that it covers.

Worse than the Court's failure to address the *Byrd* categorization process was its application of the outcome determinative test. Although, as indicated above, the majority stated that failure to apply the state rule would violate the "twin aims" of *Erie* to prevent forum shopping and inequitable administration of the law, the opinion did not address some potential problems with this conclusion. The majority's notion was that failure to apply the state statute would result in higher verdicts in federal court than in state court because of the lesser scrutiny that "excessive" verdicts would receive from federal judges after they were rendered. To reach this conclusion, one must reason that plaintiffs, who would be the category of litigants to shop for a federal forum to obtain the higher verdicts, are motivated to forum shop by the vision of obtaining an "excessive" verdict that the federal courts would not set aside after it is rendered, but which the state courts would set aside. However, if Justice Scalia is correct that the majority was exaggerating the difference that the federal and state standards governing excessive verdicts would make to outcomes,[257] it is a proposition that is at least worth more discussion than the majority gave it. It is true that, in *Gasperini* itself, the defendant citizen of the forum state would have been deprived of a rule of law valuable to it in the particular case if the state statute had been disregarded. Therefore, the "inequitable administration of the laws" policy of the *Erie* doctrine may have been violated by disregard of the state statute on the facts of the case. However, this conclusion again depends on the degree of difference that the state and federal standards actually make to the outcome of the particular case, as well as the meaning of "inequitable administration of the laws," which the Court has never extensively addressed.

---

254. *But cf.* Kampa v. White Consol. Indus., Inc., 115 F.3d 585 (8th Cir. 1997) (state law provided that certain claims were to be decided by a judge without a jury; court examines this law to determine whether it is bound up with the substantive rights being enforced as *Byrd* requires; held: law not bound up with substantive rights, but Seventh Amendment requires jury trial in any event); Cendant Corp. v. Forbes, 70 F. Supp. 2d 339 (S.D.N.Y. 1999) (state statutory equitable rule must be applied in diversity action because it is both bound up with the rights of parties and potentially outcome determinative).

255. *See* subsection E(2) *supra.*

256. *See* section I ("Federal Common Law") *infra.*

257. *See* 518 U.S. at 465-66, 116 S. Ct. at 2238-39, 135 L. Ed. 2d at 697-98 (Scalia, J., dissenting).

Finally, while both the majority and dissent considered the *Byrd* ''federal countervailing considerations'' test, the treatment of that test by both sides creates more uncertainty in its application than ever before. It is not clear whether the majority was saying that federal countervailing considerations *required* a less stringent standard of appellate review of district court decisions on excessive verdict issues, or whether the majority avoided the issue altogether by ''accommodating'' state and federal interests in the case. If it is the latter, the majority's approach represents a potentially far-reaching modification of the test. As observed earlier,[258] the *Byrd* opinion indicated that federal countervailing considerations, when present, should be balanced against the outcome determinative policies of the general *Erie* doctrine. The ''accommodationist'' approach of the majority seems to suggest that federal countervailing considerations can be balanced against state interests, a notion that seems likely to assure that the federal interests will virtually always win. In addition, the notion of accommodating state and federal interests may be even fuzzier that the notion of balancing federal countervailing policies against outcome determinative policies, creating further, unnecessary uncertainty in the administration of the *Erie* doctrine.

Nor was the dissent's approach to the countervailing considerations question much better. Justice Scalia indicated that federal countervailing considerations of the same strength as in the *Byrd* case were present.[259] However, in *Byrd* the question was whether shifting a question from the jury to the judge altogether would unduly disrupt the federal judge-jury relationship. In *Gasperini*, the question was whether requiring the judge to review a jury's verdict by a more stringent standard would unduly disrupt that relationship. It is questionable whether the latter practice would produce the same degree of disruption as the former. More importantly, neither Justice Scalia's opinion, nor the majority's, discussed how federal countervailing considerations may legitimately be derived and how they should be weighted once they are identified. For all that can be determined under Justice Scalia's opinion, *any* effect of a state law on the judge-jury relationship will be sufficient to outweigh outcome determinative policies.[260]

---

258. *See* subsection E(2) *supra*.

259. *See* 518 U.S. at 467, 116 S. Ct at 2239, 135 L. Ed. 2d at 698 (Scalia, J., dissenting).

260. For decisions explicitly applying *Gasperini*, see Continental Trend Resources, Inc. v. OXY USA, Inc., 101 F.3d 634 (10th Cir. 1996) (*Gasperini* applies to punitive damage awards), *cert. denied*, 520 U.S. 1241, 117 S. Ct. 1846, 137 L. Ed. 2d 1049 (1997); Medcom Holding Co. v. Baxter Travenol Lab., Inc., 100 F.3d 1241 (7th Cir. 1996) (state law governs substantive assessment of whether the evidence supports the damages award when liability based on state law); *see also* Central Office Tel. v. American Tel. & Tel. Co., 108 F.3d 981 (9th Cir. 1997) (state law determines whether evidence supports plaintiff's claim); Acme Inv., Inc. v. Southwest Tracor, Inc., 105 F.3d 412 (8th Cir. 1997) (federal court with diversity jurisdiction should, in a specific performance action, apply the de novo standard of appellate review that would be applied by Nebraska state courts because it is an issue of substantive rather than procedural law, comparable to the standard for reviewing the sufficiency of evidence to support a jury verdict); *cf.* Miskis v. Howard, 106 F.3d 754 (7th Cir. 1997) (federal standards used to determine excessiveness of verdict in a diversity case); Torres v. Wendco, Inc., Civil No. 95-1544 (CCC) JA, 1997 WL 135682 (D.P.R. Jan. 15, 1997) (in the absence of a state statute governing awards that ''materially deviate'' from awards in similar cases, Puerto Rico has no substantive law governing limitations on jury awards and federal case law provides guidance). For an example of a federal district court case attempting to apply the New York statute involved in *Gasperini*, see Geressy v. Digital Equip. Co., 950 F. Supp. 519 (E.D.N.Y. 1997).

On the whole, the Supreme Court's jurisprudence under the *Erie* doctrine leaves much to be desired. The Court has failed to pay attention to the distinctions that its own opinions suggest should be drawn between different kinds of cases. The Court also has demonstrated a general lack of attention to how the standards that it has articulated should operate. As a result, the Court has created much confusion in the lower federal courts.[261] The Court's latest excursion into *Erie* jurisprudence in the *Gasperini* case is particularly disturbing.[262] The Court seldom addresses *Erie* questions. It would not seem too much to ask that when it does, it not create more confusion than it dispels. *Gasperini* does not meet this standard.[263]

SECTION F. THE EVOLUTION OF THE *ERIE* DOCTRINE: CONFLICTS BETWEEN STATE LAW AND FEDERAL RULES OF CIVIL PROCEDURE

The Rules of Decision Act governed all the cases discussed in the preceding section. However, when dealing with conflicts between Federal Rules of Civil Procedure and state law, the relevant statute is not the Rules of Decision Act, but the Rules Enabling Act, 28 U.S.C. § 2072. The Rules Enabling Act gives the Federal Rules of Civil Procedure the force and effect of statutory law. Because state law is not to apply in the face of a controlling federal statute, valid Federal Rules control any case to which they apply even if contrary state law exists. This conclusion, however, simply pushes the inquiry to a different level. In each case, it must be determined (1) whether a Federal Rule exists which is applicable to the case; (2) if so, whether the Federal Rule is valid under the Rules

---

261. The operation of the general *Erie* doctrine in the lower federal courts will be explored in section G *infra*.

262. For an excellent critique of *Gasperini*, raising many of the same issues as the text, *supra*, see C. Douglas Floyd, Erie *Awry: A Comment on* Gasperini v. Center for Humanities, Inc., 1997 B.Y.U. L. REV. 267; *see also* Richard D. Freer, *Some Thoughts on the State of* Erie *After* Gasperini, 76 TEX. L. REV. 1637 (1998); J. Benjamin King, Note, *Clarification and Disruption: The Effect of* Gasperini v. Center for Humanities, Inc., *on the* Erie *Doctrine,* 83 CORNELL L. REV. 161, 183 (1997); Eva Madison, *The Supreme Court Sets New Standards of Review for Excessive Verdicts,* 50 ARK. L. REV. 591 (1997). For an article defending (for the most part) the Court's *Erie* jurisprudence, see Thomas D. Rowe, Jr., *Not Bad For Government Work: Does Anyone Else Think the Supreme Court is Doing a Halfway Decent Job in Its* Erie-Hanna *Jurisprudence,* 73 NOTRE DAME L. REV. 963 (1998).

263. It has recently been argued that *Erie* cases should be treated like "classic federal common-law cases" and, therefore, that courts should ask (1) whether a source of common-law authority exists that will justify the creation of a federal common-law procedural rule and (2) if so, whether the national interest requires a federal rule or the need for uniformity outweighs the need for uniformity within a state. *See* Wendy Collins Perdue, *The Sources and Scope of Federal Procedural Common Law: Some Reflections on* Erie *and* Gasperini, 46 U. KAN. L. REV. 751 (1998). The problem with this suggestion is that there are two kinds of cases on the Rules of Decision Act "side" of the *Erie* doctrine. In one kind of case, an affirmative "federal common-law procedural rule" or "practice" exists (or someone is asking the federal courts to create one). This kind of case is the sort Professor Perdue's suggestion addresses. However, the other kind of case is one in which there is no federal common-law procedural rule (and no one is asking the federal courts to create one), but one of the litigants is simply arguing that a state law should be disregarded because it is "procedural" in the *Erie* sense. As cases discussed in previous subsections have demonstrated, the policies supporting *Erie* can be offended as much by disregard of state law in the latter kind of case as in the former. Professor Perdue's recommendation, however, does not seem to address the second kind of case.

Enabling Act; and (3) if so, whether the Federal Rule is constitutional. This section considers the standards that govern these issues.

The Rules Enabling Act was enacted in 1934. Under the authority of the Act, the Federal Rules of Civil Procedure became effective in 1938.[264] When the Supreme Court promulgated the Federal Rules, law and equity were merged. The preexisting requirement of conformity to state procedure was also ended in areas covered by the Federal Rules. However, Congress did not delegate the power to promulgate rules of procedure under the Rules Enabling Act to the Supreme Court without restriction. The Act provided that the rules promulgated "shall neither abridge, enlarge, nor modify the substantive rights of any litigant."[265] This restriction has given rise to serious problems of interpretation.

The best examination of the legislative history of the Rules Enabling Act is by Professor Stephen Burbank.[266] Professor Burbank concludes that the "substantive rights" restriction was designed to allocate regulatory power over procedure between Congress and the Supreme Court in such a way that the Supreme Court would not be able to exercise "legislative power."[267] The "substantive rights" restriction, in this sense, merely restated limitations on the Court's rulemaking power embodied in the basic delegation by the first sentence of the Rules Enabling Act. That sentence authorizes the Court to make only rules governing "the forms of process, writs, pleadings, and motions, and the practice and procedure in civil actions."[268] The objective of the Act was thus to prevent the Court's rulemaking power from extending to " 'matters involving substantive legal and remedial rights affected by considerations of public policy.' "[269] In light of the matters later discussed in this section, it is interesting to note that among the kinds of rules *excluded* from the Supreme Court's rulemaking power were rules governing the admissibility of evidence and discovery rules providing for the compulsion of physical and mental examinations by the imposition of contempt sanctions.[270]

1. The *Sibbach* Decision

The U.S. Supreme Court first construed the Rules Enabling Act in *Sibbach v. Wilson & Co.*[271] Mrs. Sibbach instituted an action in the U.S. District Court for the Northern District of Illinois. She sought to recover damages for personal injuries suffered in an accident in Indiana. The district court ordered Mrs. Sibbach to undergo a physical examination under Rule 35 of the Federal Rules of Civil Procedure to determine the nature and extent of her injuries. When

---

264. *See* Chapter 1(E)(5) ("The Development of Federal Procedure and the Federal Rules of Civil Procedure") *supra*.

265. The current version of the Act is worded similarly. *See* 28 U.S.C. § 2072(b); *see also* Chapter 1(E)(5) ("The Development of Federal Procedure and the Federal Rules of Civil Procedure") *supra*.

266. Stephen B. Burbank, *The Rules Enabling Act of 1934*, 130 U. PA. L. REV. 1015 (1982).

267. *See id.* at 1106.

268. *See id.* at 1107.

269. *Id.* at 1121 (quoting S. REP. NO. 1174, 69th Cong., 1st Sess. 9 (1926)).

270. *See id.* at 1129-30, 1137-43, 1176-84.

271. 312 U.S. 1, 61 S. Ct. 422, 85 L. Ed. 479 (1941).

she refused to obey this order, the district court found her in contempt and directed that she be imprisoned until she complied with the order. On appeal, the court of appeals affirmed. The Supreme Court granted certiorari and reversed.

Mrs. Sibbach argued that Rule 35, which authorizes physical examinations, and Rule 37, which deals with sanctions for failure to obey discovery orders, were invalid under the substantive rights restriction of the Rules Enabling Act. Ultimately, the Supreme Court found that the lower courts had erred in interpreting Rule 37 as authorizing the imposition of contempt for failure to comply with an order to submit to a physical examination.[272] However, the Court rejected Mrs. Sibbach's argument that the rules were invalid under the Rules Enabling Act. In so doing, the Court opted for an interpretation of the substantive rights restriction that treated "substantive" and "procedural" matters as entirely distinct. Substantive rights were held to include "rights conferred by law to be protected and enforced by the adjective law of judicial procedure."[273] However, the Court rebuffed Mrs. Sibbach's argument that "substantive rights" within the meaning of the Rules Enabling Act included "important and substantial rights theretofore recognized."[274] "The test," stated the Court, "must be whether a rule really regulates procedure—the judicial process for enforcing rights and duties recognized by substantive law and for justly administering remedy and redress for disregard or infraction of them."[275]

The Court's references to "rights conferred by law to be protected and enforced in accordance with the adjective law of judicial procedure" and to procedure as "judicial process for enforcing rights and duties recognized by substantive law" strongly suggest that the Rules Enabling Act divided the legal universe into two parts: (1) rules of decision found in areas such as contracts, torts, and property that would be deemed purely substantive by anyone's definition; and (2) all other rules, which would be considered procedural, even if they had some effect on the enforcement of pure substantive rules. This bifurcation was reinforced by an example of "substantive rights" given by the Court: "the right not to be injured in one's person by another's negligence."[276]

This view, which treated substance and procedure as mutually exclusive categories, seemed to contradict the structure of the Rules Enabling Act. The Act first authorized the Supreme Court to "prescribe by general rules the forms of

---

272. *See id.* at 16, 61 S. Ct. at 427-28, 85 L. Ed. at 486. Rule 37(b)(2)(iv), which is today Rule 37(b)(2)(D), specifically exempted failures to comply with physical or mental examinations from the contempt sanction, although other substantial sanctions can be imposed for such a failure under Rule 37(b)(2).

273. *See* 312 U.S. at 13, 61 S. Ct. at 426, 85 L. Ed at 484.

274. *See id.* at 13-14, 61 S. Ct. at 426, 85 L. Ed. at 484-85.

275. *Id.* at 14, 61 S. Ct. at 426, 85 L. Ed. at 485. In a cryptic portion of its opinion, the Court had also indicated that there were other restrictions on the rulemaking power of the courts: "There are other limitations upon the authority to prescribe rules which might have been, but were not, mentioned in the Act; for instance, the inability of a court, by rule, to extend or restrict the jurisdiction conferred by a statute." *Id.* at 10, 61 S. Ct. at 424-25, 85 L. Ed. at 483. This language seems to refer to separation-of-powers restrictions on the rulemaking authority, but without elaboration by the Court, the kind of restrictions it had in mind cannot be precisely determined. Potential separation-of-powers restrictions on the rulemaking power are discussed in subsection 6 *infra. See generally* Ralph U. Whitten, *Separation of Powers Restrictions on Judicial Rulemaking: A Case Study of Federal Rule 4*, 40 ME. L. REV. 41 (1988).

276. *Sibbach*, 312 U.S. at 13, 61 S. Ct. at 426, 85 L. Ed. at 485.

process, writs, pleadings, and motions and the practice and procedure of the district courts and courts of appeals of the United States in civil actions.''[277] The Act then provided that ''[s]aid rules shall neither abridge, enlarge, nor modify the substantive rights of any litigant.''[278] On the face of the Act, the expressions ''rules of practice and procedure'' and ''substantive rights'' were apparently not mutually exclusive. Had they been so intended, both clauses of the Act would not have been necessary. Instead, Congress might simply have authorized the Court to regulate the practice and procedure of the district courts without any reference to substantive rights. The mutual exclusivity of substance and procedure would have assured that the Court would not have the power to create substantive rules. By using two expressions, Congress suggested that procedure and substance were overlapping categories and that there are procedural rules within the meaning of the statute that could affect substantive rights. A plausible facial interpretation of the Act was, therefore, that the Court might prescribe uniform procedural rules for the lower federal courts. However, in applying those rules, the courts should take care not to abridge, enlarge, or modify substantive rights.[279]

   Mrs. Sibbach, in fact, argued before the Supreme Court that ''[i]f rules of 'procedure' could not be construed to involve 'substantive rights,' the second sentence in the Act would be surplusage.''[280] Some commentators have likewise concluded that the substantive rights restriction of the Act should be given a meaning different, and more restrictive, than the phrase ''practice and procedure'' in the first sentence of the Act.[281] Nevertheless, Professor Stephen Burbank's research into the legislative history of the Act has indicated that the substantive rights restriction was indeed designed only to emphasize a limitation inherent in the use of the words ''practice and procedure'' in the first sentence of the Act.[282] However, as discussed below, the real problem with the Court's interpretation of the Rules Enabling Act in *Sibbach* and later cases is that it recognizes virtually no restrictions on the rulemaking authority at all. This interpretation is the one that would seem wholly implausible under either the language or history of the Act.[283]

   Sibbach's view of the Enabling Act was followed five years later in *Mississippi Publishing Corp. v. Murphree.*[284] In *Murphree*, the defendant

---

   277. *See* Act of June 19, 1934, ch. 651, 48 Stat. 1064 (codified as amended at 28 U.S.C. § 2072(a)). The current version of the Act simply authorizes the Supreme Court to prescribe ''rules of practice and procedure and rules of evidence.'' *See* 28 U.S.C. § 2072(a). In addition, the Judicial Improvements Act of 1990 added a new subsection (c) to 28 U.S.C. § 2072: ''Such rules may define when a ruling of a district court is final for purposes of appeal under section 1291 of this title.'' Pub. L. No. 101-650, § 315, 104 Stat. 5089, 5115 (codified at 28 U.S.C. § 2072(c)).

   278. Act of June 19, 1934, ch. 651, 48 Stat. 1064 (codified as amended at 28 U.S.C. § 2072(b)).

   279. *See* Ralph U. Whitten, Erie *and the Federal Rules: A Review and Reappraisal After* Burlington Northern Railroad v. Woods, 21 CREIGHTON L. REV. 1, 5 (1987).

   280. *Sibbach*, 312 U.S. at 3 (argument of petitioner).

   281. *See* John H. Ely, *The Irrepressible Myth of* Erie, 87 HARV. L. REV. 693, 718-40 (1974).

   282. *See* Stephen B. Burbank, *The Rules Enabling Act of 1934*, 130 U. PA. L. REV. 1015, 1107-08 (1982).

   283. Professor Burbank, for example, argues that the restrictions of the Act were designed to allocate lawmaking power between the Supreme Court and Congress. *See id.* at 1106.

   284. 326 U.S. 438, 66 S. Ct. 242, 90 L. Ed. 185 (1946).

challenged the validity of Rule 4(f) of the Federal Rules of Civil Procedure. Prior to the promulgation of Rule 4(f), the personal-jurisdiction reach of the federal district courts was limited to the territorial limits of the district. Rule 4(f) permitted a district court in a multidistrict state to summon a defendant from anywhere within a state. In evaluating the validity of Rule 4(f), the Court confirmed *Sibbach's* interpretation of the substance-procedure dichotomy of the Act. Congress, stated the Court, did not aim the substantive rights restriction of the Rules Enabling Act at "such incidental effects as necessarily attend the adoption of the prescribed new rules of procedure upon the rights of litigants who, agreeably to rules of practice and procedure, have been brought before a court authorized to determine their rights."[285] Rule 4(f) would operate to affect the rights of the defendant by subjecting those rights to adjudication by the district court for the Northern District of Mississippi, rather than the district court for the Southern District of Mississippi. However, the rule would "not operate to abridge, enlarge, or modify the rules of decision by which [the district court] will adjudicate its rights."[286] Consequently, the rule related only to the manner and means by which a right to recover was enforced.[287]

2. The Outcome Determinative Test and the Federal Rules of Civil Procedure

After *Erie* but before *Sibbach*, the Supreme Court held that the lower federal courts could not, under the guise of *Erie's* substance-procedure distinction, apply burden-of-proof rules that state courts would not apply in a similar case.[288] Then, in *Guaranty Trust*, the Court established the outcome determinative test to govern when the federal courts had to follow state rules that were in some sense classified as "procedural."[289] In retrospect, it probably should have been clear that the outcome determinative test did not apply to determine the validity of Federal Rules of Civil Procedure under the Enabling Act. Nevertheless, later events made *Guaranty Trust* appear to govern conflicts between state law and Federal Rules of Civil Procedure. The main difficulty was that the Court itself seemed to think that *Guaranty Trust* governed such conflicts.[290]

---

285. *Id.* at 445, 66 S. Ct. at 246, 90 L. Ed. at 191.

286. *Id.* at 446, 66 S. Ct. at 246, 90 L. Ed. at 192.

287. *Id.*

288. *See* Palmer v. Hoffman, 318 U.S. 109, 117, 63 S. Ct. 477, 482, 87 L. Ed. 645, 651 (1943); Cities Serv. Oil Co. v. Dunlap, 308 U.S. 208, 210-12, 60 S. Ct. 201, 202-03, 84 L. Ed. 196, 197-98 (1939).

289. *Guaranty Trust* is discussed in section E(1) ("The *Guaranty Trust* Case: Independent Equity Powers and the 'Outcome Determinative' Test") *supra.*

290. One reason may have been that the Court had by "essentially obliterating the Enabling Act in *Sibbach* . . . created a need for limits on the Rules." John H. Ely, *The Irrepressible Myth of Erie*, 87 HARV. L. REV. 693, 698 (1974). Another reason was that, despite being warned by Justice Frankfurter that the terms "substantive" and "procedural" were not words of unvarying content, the temptation to treat them the same for purposes of both the Rules of Decision Act and the Rules Enabling Act proved too great even for the Court. *See* Guaranty Trust Co. v. York, 326 U.S. 99, 108, 65 S. Ct. 1464, 1469, 89 L. Ed. 2079, 2085 (1945); *see also* WALTER W. COOK, THE LOGICAL AND LEGAL BASES OF THE CONFLICT OF LAWS ch. VI (1942).

In *Murphree*, the Court cited *Guaranty Trust* as authority for sustaining Federal Rule 4(f) under the Enabling Act.[291] In *Ragan v. Merchants Transfer & Warehouse Co.*,[292] an apparent conflict existed between Federal Rule 3, which provides that an action is commenced by filing a complaint with the court,[293] and a Kansas provision that required commencement by service of a summons in order to toll the running of the statute of limitations.[294] The Court held that the Kansas method of commencement by service had to be applied in a federal diversity action. Throughout the *Ragan* opinion, the Court employed the *Erie-Guaranty Trust* line of decisions to analyze the issue before it,[295] even though the argument was explicitly made that Rule 3 governed commencement for purposes of the Kansas statute.[296] One cannot read *Ragan* without concluding that the Court believed *Erie* required the application of state law because of a conflict between Rule 3 and the Kansas statute.[297] The Court did not cite *Sibbach* in its opinion.[298]

In *Cohen v. Beneficial Industrial Loan Corp.*,[299] the Court held that a federal court sitting in diversity had to apply a state statute governing shareholder derivative actions. The statute required that a plaintiff owning less than 5% of the par value of the corporation's outstanding shares had to provide security for the reasonable expenses, including attorney's fees, that the corporation might incur in its successful defense of the derivative action.[300] In considering the applicability of Rule 23 of the Federal Rules of Civil Procedure, which governed derivative actions in federal district court,[301] the Court explicitly stated that the provisions of Rule 23 did not conflict with the state statute.[302] However, the dissenters considered Rule 23 applicable and, like the majority, seemed to consider *Erie* and *Guaranty Trust* to be the only relevant precedents.[303]

Ragan and *Cohen* were widely interpreted to mean that the *Guaranty Trust* outcome determinative test governed the validity of Federal Rules of Civil

---

291. *See Murphree*, 326 U.S. at 446, 66 S. Ct. at 246, 90 L. Ed. at 192.

292. 337 U.S. 530, 69 S. Ct. 1233, 93 L. Ed. 1520 (1949).

293. *See* FED. R. CIV. P. 3.

294. *See Ragan*, 337 U.S. at 531 n.4, 69 S. Ct. at 1234 n.4, 93 L. Ed. at 1522 n.4.

295. *See id.* at 532-34, 69 S. Ct. at 1234-35, 93 L. Ed. at 1522-24.

296. *See id.* at 532-33, 69 S. Ct. at 1234-35, 93 L. Ed. at 1522-23.

297. *See id.* at 532-34, 69 S. Ct. at 1234-35, 93 L. Ed. at 1522-24.

298. *See id.* at 531-34, 69 S. Ct. at 1234-35, 93 L. Ed. at 1521-24.

299. 337 U.S. 541, 69 S. Ct. 1221, 93 L. Ed. 1528 (1949).

300. *Id.* at 544 n.1, 69 S. Ct. at 1224 n.1, 93 L. Ed. at 1535 n.1.

301. The Rules were amended in 1966, and today derivative actions are governed by Rule 23.1 of the Federal Rules of Civil Procedure.

302. *See Cohen*, 337 U.S. at 556, 69 S. Ct. at 1230, 93 L. Ed. at 1541-42.

303. *See id.* at 557, 69 S. Ct. at 1230-31, 93 L. Ed. at 1542 (Douglas, J. & Frankfurter, J., dissenting); *id.* at 558-61, 69 S. Ct. at 1231-32, 93 L. Ed. at 1542-44 (Rutledge, J., dissenting). In Woods v. Interstate Realty Co., 337 U.S. 535, 69 S. Ct. 1235, 93 L. Ed. 1524 (1949), discussed in the preceding section of this chapter, the Court confronted the question whether a federal diversity court was required to apply a Mississippi door-closing statute. The Court held that *Erie* required application of the state statute. Although the Court did not consider any potential conflict between the state law and a Federal Rule of Civil Procedure, others have observed that Federal Rule 17(b), governing capacity to sue and be sued in federal court, may have been applicable to the case. *See* John H. Ely, *The Irrepressible Myth of* Erie, 87 HARV. L. REV. 693, 727-28 (1974).

Procedure.[304] Thus, when the Court decided *Byrd v. Blue Ridge Rural Electric Cooperative Inc.*,[305] discussed in the preceding section of this chapter, it appeared to open an escape valve that might save the Federal Rules: the *Byrd* balancing test might allow the "interest of the federal system in having a uniform procedure in its courts"[306] to outweigh the need to duplicate the outcome between state and federal courts. However, *Byrd* did not turn out to be the savior of the Federal Rules. That role was to be played by the Court's decision in *Hanna v. Plumer*.[307]

3. The *Hanna* Decision: Return to the *Sibbach* Test

In *Hanna*, the issue was a potential conflict between Rule 4(d)(1)[308] of the Federal Rules of Civil Procedure and a state statute. Rule 4(d)(1) provided for service of process upon competent, adult individuals by leaving a copy of the summons and complaint at their home with someone of suitable age and discretion. The state statute required in-hand service under the circumstances of the case. Service had been made in accord with Rule 4(d)(1) rather than the state statute. The defendant thus apparently received actual notice of the action within the limitations period.[309] Nevertheless, in-hand service had not been made within the period required by the state statute of limitations. Therefore, if the state method of service had to be employed in federal court to toll the statute of limitations, the statute would have expired. The district court granted summary judgment for the defendant on the authority of *Guaranty Trust* and *Ragan*. The court of appeals affirmed.[310] The Supreme Court granted certiorari and reversed.

The defendant–plausibly given the history of the Court's decisions dealing with Federal Rule-state law conflicts–argued that the *Guaranty Trust* outcome determinative test required the federal courts to apply the state rule.[311] As noted in section E(2), above, the Court first analyzed the case as if Federal Rule 4(d)(1) were a federal common-law rule of practice or procedure. The Court rejected the argument that, under such a supposition, *Guaranty Trust* required application of the conflicting state rule.[312] However, the Court then held that the *Erie-Guaranty Trust-Byrd* line of cases did not apply to conflicts between Federal Rules of Civil Procedure and state law. Instead, the Court pointed to a separate line of cases, beginning with *Sibbach*, involving the validity of Federal Rules under the Enabling Act. The Court stated that it was this line of cases that had to be consulted when the validity of a Federal Rule of Civil Procedure is questioned.

---

304. *See* Charles A. Wright, The Law of Federal Courts § 55, at 357, § 59, at 402-03 (5th ed. 1994).

305. 356 U.S. 525, 78 S. Ct. 893, 2 L. Ed. 2d 953 (1958).

306. Charles A. Wright, The Law of Federal Courts § 59, at 403 (5th ed. 1994).

307. 380 U.S. 460, 85 S. Ct. 1136, 14 L. Ed. 2d 8 (1965).

308. The provisions of Rule 4(d)(1) in effect at the time *Hanna* was decided are now found in Federal Rule 4(e)(2).

309. *See* 380 U.S. at 463 n.1, 85 S. Ct. at 1139 n.1, 14 L. Ed. 2d at 12 n.1.

310. *See id.* at 462-63, 85 S. Ct. at 1138-39, 14 L. Ed. 2d at 11-12.

311. *See id.* at 465, 85 S. Ct. at 1140-41, 14 L. Ed. 2d at 13.

312. *See id.* at 466-69, 85 S. Ct. at 1141-43, 14 L. Ed. 2d at 13-16.

The Court interpreted *Ragan* and *Cohen* as holding only that the Federal Rules in question were not broad enough to cover the case before the federal court. Under such circumstances, of course, no conflict between federal and state law existed. Thus, both could be applied to the case within their respective spheres.[313]

Hanna clarified the analysis used to determine the validity of Federal Rules. The Court's reinterpretation of *Ragan* and *Cohen* indicated that the first step in any analysis of a Federal Rule-state law conflict is to (1) determine whether the Federal Rule in question is broad enough to cover the issue in the case and (2) when possible, avoid the conflict. In addition, by making it clear that the generalized *Erie* analysis does not apply to issues of Federal Rules validity, the Court focused the lower federal courts on the proper source of statutory authority with which to determine Rule validity: the Rules Enabling Act rather than the Rules of Decision Act.[314]

Nevertheless, *Hanna* contained significant flaws. In *Hanna* itself, the Court missed an opportunity to avoid the conflict between federal and state law. At one point in the decision, the Court stated as follows: "Here, of course, the clash [between state law and the Federal Rule of Civil Procedure] is unavoidable. Rule 4(d)(1) states . . . that in-hand service is not required in federal courts."[315] Earlier, however, the Court had observed that the state statute's purpose was to insure that executors would receive actual notice of claims, which was also the purpose of Federal Rule 4(d)(1). The Federal Rule simply reflected a determination that this purpose could be accomplished by a "less cumbersome" method than prescribed by the state statute. Importantly, the Court noted that the purposes of both the Federal Rule and the state statute had apparently been accomplished because the defendant did not contend that actual notice of the action had not been received.[316] If the purposes of the state statute had indeed been fully achieved by applying the Federal Rule, no real conflict existed in the case.[317]

The Court also might have enhanced the conflict-avoidance process for future cases by discussing the need to evaluate the scope of state law. Conflicts between state law and Federal Rules of Civil Procedure can be avoided if either the Federal Rule or the state law does not apply to the case before the federal court. Some state laws are limited by their terms, policies, or purposes to enforcement only in state courts. Such laws cannot be said to conflict with Federal Rules because the states have limited the operation of their laws to their own judicial systems. Furthermore, it would be inappropriate for a federal court to invalidate a Federal Rule of Civil Procedure that conflicted with state

---

313. *See id.* at 470, 85 S. Ct. at 1143, 14 L. Ed. 2d at 16.

314. *See* Ralph U. Whitten, Erie *and the Federal Rules: A Review and Reappraisal After* Burlington Northern Railroad v. Woods, 21 CREIGHTON L. REV. 1, 13-14 (1987).

315. 380 U.S. at 470, 85 S. Ct. at 1143, 14 L. Ed. 2d at 16.

316. *See id.* at 462 n.1, 85 S. Ct. at 1139 n.1, 14 L. Ed. 2d at 12 n.1.

317. *See* Ralph U. Whitten, Erie *and the Federal Rules: A Review and Reappraisal After* Burlington Northern Railroad v. Woods, 21 CREIGHTON L. REV. 1, 15 (1987).

substantive policies if the state substantive policies supported a rule applicable only in the state's own courts.[318]

Illustration 5-17. Assume that a state rule sets the time limits within which pleadings must be filed. Such a rule should not be interpreted as in conflict with the time limit provisions of Federal Rule 12(a) because the state rule is designed to prescribe time limits only for actions in the state courts. A state statute or rule whose policies or purposes extend only to actions in the state's own courts is, for purpose of conflict-avoidance analysis, essentially no different than a statute that does not apply to the factual occurrences in the case. It is never appropriate for a federal court to apply such a state statute or rule in a federal action when a Federal Rule of Civil Procedure governs the issue.

* * * * *

The most serious difficulty with the *Hanna* opinion was the Court's failure to give content to the substantive rights restriction of the Rules Enabling Act. As Professor Ely has observed, "the text of the opinion did little more, so far as the interpretation of the Enabling Act was concerned, than point to *Sibbach*."[319] As noted above, *Sibbach* suggested that the Enabling Act's restrictions prohibit only Federal Rules that are purely substantive by anyone's definition, an interpretation that is not supported by either the language, the structure, or the legislative history of the Act.[320] Worse, taken together, the

---

318. The failure of the Court in *Hanna* to point this out was, however, much more justifiable than its failure to avoid the conflict in the case by acknowledging that service pursuant to the Federal Rule had satisfied the purposes of the state statute. The underlying policy of the state service provision in *Hanna—i.e.*, the achievement of actual notice within the statutory period—was clearly applicable to the case before the Court. *See* Ralph U. Whitten, Erie *and the Federal Rules: A Review and Reappraisal After* Burlington Northern Railroad v. Woods, 21 CREIGHTON L. REV. 1, 16 (1987).

The form of conflict avoidance discussed in the text—*i.e.*, conflict avoidance by determining that the policies of the state rule are applicable only in state-court actions—is inappropriate under the general *Erie* analysis. For example, if a state has a policy supporting its door-closing statute that indicates that the statute is applicable only in actions brought in the state's own courts, the federal courts under the *Erie-Guaranty Trust-Byrd* analysis must still apply the statute. Under the Rules of Decision Act, failure to do so would violate the policies against forum shopping and inequitable administration of the law. Thus, all the federal court can do by way of conflict avoidance with state law under the general *Erie* analysis is to determine whether the state rule is applicable to the facts of the case before the court. If it is, then the court must apply the general *Erie* analysis to determine whether the state law can be disregarded. Thus, Justice Jackson was incorrect in his dissent in Woods v. Interstate Realty Co., 337 U.S. 535, 539, 69 S. Ct. 1235, 1237-38, 93 L. Ed. 1524, 1527-28 (1949), in taking the majority of the Court to task for failure to observe that the state door-closing statute in that case appeared to be limited in its applicability to actions in the state's own courts. Once it has been determined that a Federal Rule of Civil Procedure is applicable to the case, however, a federal court should examine whether the policies supporting the state rule are, even if "substantive" in some sense, applicable only in the state's own courts in order to avoid the conflict with the Federal Rule.

319. John H. Ely, *The Irrepressible Myth of* Erie, 87 HARV. L. REV. 693, 720 (1974).

320. The Court did state that "in measuring a Federal Rule against the standards contained in the Enabling Act and the constitution" a court "need not wholly blind itself to the degree to which the Rule makes the character and result of the litigation stray from the course it would follow in state courts." 380 U.S. at 473, 85 S. Ct. at 1145, 14 L. Ed. 2d at 18. Given the Court's other remarks in the opinion, this statement cannot seriously be interpreted as designed to import an outcome determinative test of the *Guaranty Trust* variety into the Enabling Act. But if this is not the purpose of the statement, it is not clear what the Court had in mind. The Court's citation at this point to a portion of the *Sibbach* opinion, 312 U.S. 1, 13-14, 61 S. Ct. 422, 426-27, 85 L. Ed. 479, 484-85 (1941), is mystifying. Professor Wright's assessment of the decision seems most accurate: *Hanna* "provides the [Federal] Rules with a presumptive validity if not quite an automatic seal of approval." CHARLES A. WRIGHT, THE LAW OF FEDERAL COURTS § 59, at 405 (5th ed. 1994).

Sibbach and *Hanna* opinions suggest that the power delegated to the Court in the Enabling Act is the whole power of Congress to regulate the practice and procedure of the federal courts.[321] However, as discussed below, some procedural matters are so fundamental that they should be beyond the power of Congress to delegate to the Court. In addition, the Court cannot exercise some fundamental procedural powers that, while they are delegable, are beyond the rulemaking power in the face of an active policy by Congress regulating the procedural matter in question.[322]

4. The *Burlington Northern* Decision: Establishing Content for the Substantive Rights Restriction

After *Hanna*, no significant decision addressed a Federal Rule-state law conflict until 1987.[323] In that year, the Court decided *Burlington Northern Railroad v. Woods*.[324] In *Burlington Northern*, the issue was the applicability in federal diversity actions of an Alabama statute imposing a fixed 10% penalty on appellants who obtain stays of damage judgments pending unsuccessful appeals. A personal injury action was brought against the railroad in Alabama state court and removed to the U.S. District Court in Alabama. The action resulted in a judgment for damages in favor of the plaintiffs. The railroad posted bond to stay the judgment pending appeal, but the judgment was affirmed without modification by the court of appeals. Upon motion of the plaintiffs-appellees, the court of appeals imposed a 10% penalty under the Alabama statute. The U.S. Supreme Court granted certiorari and reversed.

The Court held that the Alabama statute conflicted with Rule 38 of the Federal Rules of Appellate Procedure. Rule 38 provides that "[i]f a court of appeals shall determine that an appeal is frivolous, it may award just damages and single or double costs to the appellee." The Court also held that under the *Hanna*

---

321. In *Sibbach*, the Court at one point stated: "Congress has undoubted power to regulate the practice and procedure of federal courts, and may exercise that power by delegating to this or other federal courts authority to make rules not inconsistent with the statutes or constitution of the United States . . . ." 312 U.S. at 9-10, 61 S. Ct. at 424-25, 85 L. Ed. at 482-83. The Court's citations of authority for this statement indicate that by its references to the constitutional limits on the rulemaking power, it may have had in mind separation-of-powers limitations, but this conclusion is uncertain. *See id.* nn.6-7, 61 S. Ct. at 424 nn.6-7, 85 L. Ed. at 483 nn.6-7; *see also* Ralph U. Whitten, *Separation of Powers Restrictions on Judicial Rulemaking: A Case Study of Federal Rule 4*, 40 ME. L. REV. 41, 51-53 (1988). However, *Hanna's* statements indicating that Congress had delegated all of its rulemaking power to the Court seemed to be more unqualified. *See Hanna*, 380 U.S. at 472-74, 85 S. Ct. at 1144-45, 14 L. Ed. 2d at 17-18. The startling feature of the statements in *Hanna* is that there is no distinction drawn between the power of Congress to regulate procedure directly and the power that Congress has delegated to the Court to regulated procedure in the Enabling Act, suggesting that Congress has delegated all the rulemaking power it can exercise.

322. *See generally* Ralph U. Whitten, *Separation of Powers Restrictions on Judicial Rulemaking: A Case Study of Rule 4*, 40 ME. L. REV. 41 (1988).

323. In 1980, the Court decided Walker v. Armco Steel Corp., 446 U.S. 740, 100 S. Ct. 1978, 64 L. Ed. 2d 659 (1980), in which it reaffirmed the *Hanna* interpretation of *Ragan*—i.e., that the scope of Rule 3 of the Federal Rules of Civil Procedure is not broad enough to cover problems of commencement of an action for purposes of state statutes of limitations. That holding made it unnecessary for the Court to discuss the restrictions of the Enabling Act, and it did not do so. *See id.* at 752 n.14, 100 S. Ct. at 1986 n.14, 64 L. Ed. 2d at 669 n.14.

324. 480 U.S. 1, 107 S. Ct. 967, 94 L. Ed. 2d 1 (1987).

analysis, the Alabama statute had to give way to the Federal Rule. According to the Court, a Federal Rule that conflicts with state law is valid if it comports with both the constitutional restrictions on Congress' rulemaking power and the "substantive rights" restriction of the Rules Enabling Act.[325] In the Court's view, the constitutional limitations "define a test of reasonableness." "Rules regulating matters indisputably procedural are *a priori* constitutional. Rules regulating matters 'which, though falling within the uncertain area between substance and procedure, are rationally capable of classification as either,' also satisfy this constitutional standard."[326] The substantive rights restriction of the Rules Enabling Act is not violated by "[r]ules which incidentally affect litigants' substantive rights," as long as the rules are "reasonably necessary to maintain the integrity" of the "uniform and consistent system of rules governing federal practice and procedure."[327] Furthermore, "the study and approval given each proposed rule by the Advisory Committee, the Judicial Conference, and this Court, and the statutory requirement that the Rule be reported to Congress for a period of review before taking effect . . . give the Rules presumptive validity under both the constitutional and statutory constraints."[328]

Applying these standards, the Court concluded simply that "Federal [Appellate] Rule 38 regulates matters which can reasonably be classified as procedural, thereby satisfying the constitutional standard for validity."[329] The Court also found that the "displacement of the Alabama statute" by Appellate Rule 38 satisfied the statutory limits of the Rules Enabling Act because the selection "of a discretionary procedure" for penalizing unsuccessful litigants under Appellate Rule 38 "affects only the process of enforcing litigants' rights and not the rights themselves."[330]

The Court's opinion in *Burlington Northern* was flawed in many respects. It will suffice here to discuss two problems with the opinion.[331] First, the Court should have construed Federal Appellate Rule 38 as inapplicable to the case before it. Second, in evaluating Rule 38's validity under the Enabling Act, the Court's analysis was entirely conclusory. The analysis failed to (1) examine the Alabama statute carefully to determine whether it created a "substantive" right, (2) examine the impact of Rule 38 carefully to determine whether its impact was more than "incidental," and (3) evaluate whether Rule 38 was "reasonably necessary" to the integrity of the uniform scheme of procedure that is the purpose of the Rules Enabling Act.

---

325. *See id.* at 5, 107 S. Ct. at 969-70, 94 L. Ed. 2d at 7.
326. *Id.* (quoting *Hanna*, 380 U.S. at 472, 85 S. Ct. at 1144, 14 L. Ed. 2d at 17).
327. *Id.*
328. *Id.* at 6, 107 S. Ct. at 970, 94 L. Ed. 2d at 7-8.
329. *Id.* at 8, 107 S. Ct. at 971, 94 L. Ed. 2d at 9.
330. *Id.*
331. For a more complete critical evaluation of *Burlington Northern*, see Ralph U. Whitten, Erie *and the Federal Rules: A Review and Reappraisal After* Burlington Northern Railroad v. Woods, 21 CREIGHTON L. REV. 1 (1987).

Although the Court correctly addressed the interpretation of Appellate Rule 38 as the first analytical step in the case,[332] the Court incorrectly interpreted Rule 38. In discussing the Rule's applicability, the Court observed that it was discretionary, rather than mandatory, in nature and that it only authorized the courts of appeals to penalize frivolous appeals and appeals interposed for delay, rather than all unsuccessful appeals.[333] From these correct observations, however, the Court proceeded to conclude that the Rule was broad enough to cover the case before it and conflicted with the Alabama statute. The Court observed that the "discretionary mode of operation [of Rule 38] unmistakably conflicts with the mandatory provision of Alabama's affirmance penalty statute."[334] Even though the Court was aware that Alabama possessed a rule allowing an appellate court the discretion to penalize frivolous appeals,[335] it nevertheless concluded that the discretion afforded under Rule 38 would be impaired if the federal court was obliged to follow the Alabama statute.[336]

The problem with the Court's analysis was that Federal Appellate Rule 38, by the Court's own admission, only applies to frivolous appeals. Rule 38 does not apply to unsuccessful, but nonfrivolous appeals. In the latter kind of case, Rule 38 confers no discretion at all on the courts of appeals. Therefore, it cannot confer any discretion with which the Alabama statute would interfere. Thus, if the Court felt that the Alabama statute interfered with the discretion afforded the courts of appeals to penalize frivolous appeals, the Court should have directed that the statute could not be applied in cases in which a frivolous appeal is taken. The case then should have been remanded for a determination whether the appeal in *Burlington Northern* was frivolous.[337]

The Court could only have concluded that the Alabama statute interfered with the operation of Rule 38 by interpreting Rule 38 as an implied negation of any other authority to levy penalties in cases of unsuccessful appeals in federal courts. But the Court did not construe Rule 38 in this manner. The Court's discussion was limited to the discretionary mode of the Rule's operation and its purpose to penalize only frivolous appeals.[338] Furthermore, had the Court

---

332. *See id.* at 4-5, 107 S. Ct. at 969-70, 94 L. Ed. 2d at 6-7. The Court was correct to interpret the Rule first, rather than state law, because the interpretation of the Federal Rule will determine the next appropriate analytical step in the case. If the Rule is determined to be inapplicable, the case must be analyzed under the *Erie-Guaranty Trust-Byrd* line of cases. If the Rule is determined to be applicable, the next step is to determine whether there is a conflict between the Rule and state law by interpreting the state law; if there is a conflict, the validity of the Rule under constitutional and statutory standards must be determined. Thus, in any case involving a potential Federal Rule-state law conflict, the interpretation of the Federal Rule is analytically prior to all other steps.

333. *Id.* at 6-7, 107 S. Ct. at 970, 94 L. Ed. 2d at 7-8.

334. *Id.* at 7, 107 S. Ct. at 970-71, 94 L. Ed. 2d at 8-9.

335. *See id.* Rule 38 of the Alabama Rules of Appellate Procedure provides: "In civil cases, if the appellate court shall determine on motion or ex mero motu that an appeal is frivolous, it may award just damages and single or double costs to the appellee." ALA. R. APP. P. 38.

336. *See id.* at 7-8, 107 S. Ct. at 970-71, 94 L. Ed. 2d at 8-9.

337. *See* Ralph U. Whitten, *Erie and the Federal Rules: A Review and Reappraisal After* Burlington Northern Railroad v. Woods, 21 CREIGHTON L. REV. 1, 22 (1987).

338. *See* 480 U.S. at 6-8, 107 S. Ct. at 969-71, 94 L. Ed. 2d at 7-9. The Court had, correctly, interpreted the Alabama statute as having (1) the purpose of penalizing frivolous appeals and appeals taken for purposes of delay and (2) providing additional damages as compensation to appellees for having to suffer the ordeal of construed the Rule as an implied negation of all other authority to impose penalties for unsuccessful appeals, it would have had to contend with its prior decision in *Cohen v. Beneficial Industrial Loan Corp.*[339] Recall that in *Cohen* the Court dealt with a potential conflict between Rule 23 of the Federal Rules of Civil Procedure and a state security-for-expenses statute. The Court held that the state statute had to be applied in federal diversity actions, finding that the statute did not conflict with the Rule 23.[340] Despite the fact that Rule 23 said nothing about security for expenses, the Court did not interpret it as an implied negation of additional requirements for derivative actions that might be imposed by state law. If Rule 38 were to be interpreted as an implied negation of power to impose penalties under other sources of law, the Court would need to distinguish *Cohen* in some reasoned fashion. No such reasoned distinction was provided by the Court.[341]

Even if Court's conclusions about the meaning of Federal Appellate Rule 38 had been correct, the Court's reasoning concerning its validity under the Rules Enabling Act was flawed. The Court explicitly acknowledged that the substantive rights restriction of the Act imposes "an additional requirement" over and above the constitutional test of whether a rule "falling within the uncertain area between substance and procedure, [is] rationally capable of classification as either."[342] Furthermore, the Court stated that the substantive rights restriction does not invalidate rules that "incidentally affect litigant's substantive rights . . . if [the rules are] reasonably necessary to maintain the integrity of [the uniform and consistent system of federal rules that it was the purpose of Congress to authorize

---

defending the judgments on appeal. It attempted to buttress its conclusion about the coextensive purposes of Rule 38 and the Alabama statute by pointing to Rule 37 of the Federal Rules of Appellate Procedure, which provides for an award of post-judgment interest to successful appellees, and 28 U.S.C. § 1961, which does likewise. The Court's conclusion was that these provisions operated to provide the compensation to the victorious appellee that was the second objective of the Alabama statute. *See* 480 U.S. at 7 n.5, 107 S. Ct. at 971 n.5, 94 L. Ed. 2d at 8 n.5. However, this conclusion neglected the fact that Alabama also possesses a rule of appellate procedure authorizing an award of post-judgment interest on money judgments that are successfully affirmed, as well as a separate rule providing for discretionary penalties for frivolous appeals. *See* ALA. R. APP. P. 37, 38. Thus, the structure of Alabama law provided for post-judgment interest, penalties for frivolous appeals that might be imposed in addition to the 10% affirmance penalty under the statute, and the 10% penalty, which could all operate in the same case. *See* McAnnally v. Levco, Inc., 456 So. 2d 66 (Ala. 1984). Given these additional Alabama laws, it is impossible to see how the Supreme Court could have interpreted the purposes of Rule 38 and Alabama law to be coextensive. And if the Court was interpreting Rule 37 and 28 U.S.C. § 1961 to be implied negations of power to compensate for unsuccessful appeals drawn from other sources, its reasoning was as flawed as its reasoning about the scope of Federal Rule 38. *See* Ralph U. Whitten, Erie *and the Federal Rules: A Review and Reappraisal After* Burlington Northern Railroad v. Woods, 21 CREIGHTON L. REV. 1, 23-25 (1987).

339. 337 U.S. 541, 69 S. Ct. 1221, 93 L. Ed. 1528 (1949).

340. *Id.* at 556, 69 S. Ct. at 1230, 93 L. Ed. at 1541-42. Recall, also, that in *Hanna* the Court interpreted *Cohen* as a case in which the Federal Rule involved was not broad enough to cover the issue in the case. *See* Hanna v. Plumer, 380 U.S. 460, 470 n.12, 85 S. Ct. 1136, 1143 n.12, 14 L. Ed. 2d 8, 16 n.12 (1965); *see also* Kamen v. Kemper Fin. Servs., Inc., 500 U.S. 90, 111 S. Ct. 1711, 114 L. Ed. 2d 152 (1991) (holding, in part, that Federal Rule 23.1 is not broad enough to control the content of the demand requirement in shareholder derivative actions).

341. *See* Ralph U. Whitten, Erie *and the Federal Rules: A Review and Reappraisal After* Burlington Northern Railroad v. Woods, 21 CREIGHTON L. REV. 1, 25 (1987).

342. 480 U.S. at 5, 107 S. Ct. at 969-70, 94 L. Ed. 2d at 7.

under the Act]."[343] The standard articulated by the Court thus focuses in part on the state rules and in part on the extent to which a Federal Rule affects the operation of the state rule. Federal Rules may wholly supplant state procedural "rights" or rules. However, a Federal Rule can only "incidentally" affect state substantive rights, and even then such an incidental effect can only be justified if the Federal Rule in question is reasonably necessary to maintain the integrity of the uniform system of procedure that is the purpose of the Rules Enabling Act.

Under this standard, the Court incorrectly concluded that the application of Federal Appellate Rule 38 did not abridge, enlarge, or modify any substantive right within the meaning of the Enabling Act. By the Court's own admission, the Alabama statute was designed in part to provide additional damages as compensation for the appellee's ordeal of having to successfully defend an appeal. This provision is best characterized as creating a claim for relief for perceived harm done to the appellee by appellate litigation—harm that the state deems significant enough to justify relief. So viewed, the state's policies obviously extend beyond the usual procedural policies that exist for supplementing an appellee's damage award—*i.e.*, the policies of penalizing frivolous appeals and of compensating the appellee for loss of use of the judgment proceeds during the appeal through an award of post-judgment interest. Thus, even though the Alabama statute was aimed at a party's unsuccessful resort to a procedure, it was, like most other remedies, created for a seemingly substantive reason—compensation for harm thought to be significant by the state.

Furthermore, Federal Appellate Rule 38, as interpreted by the Court, did not have a mere "incidental effect" on the right created by the Alabama statute. It obliterated the right in all federal actions. It is difficult to see how a rule that altogether prevents a damage recovery allowed by state law can be described as only "incidentally" affecting the right that the recovery aims at vindicating. Nor is it apparent how a rule that effectively negates a right to the remedy of money damages in the circumstances covered by the Alabama statute is necessary to the integrity of the uniform system of federal procedure that the Enabling Act sought to insure. The system of federal procedure could operate both effectively and uniformly if discretion were afforded to the federal courts to impose penalties in whatever amounts are deemed desirable, but only in cases in which appeals are found to be frivolous.[344]

5. Further Confusion: *Business Guides* and *Gasperini*

Since *Burlington Northern*, discussed in the preceding subsection, the Supreme Court has decided only two additional significant cases concerning the validity of a Federal Rule: *Business Guides, Inc. v. Chromatic Communications*

---

343. *Id.*; *see also* Mississippi Publ'g Corp. v. Murphree, 326 U.S. 438, 445-46, 66 S. Ct. 242, 246-47, 90 L. Ed. 185, 191-92 (1946).

344. *See* Ralph U. Whitten, Erie *and the Federal Rules: A Review and Reappraisal After* Burlington Northern Railroad v. Woods, 21 CREIGHTON L. REV. 1, 30-35 (1987). The *Burlington Northern* test is applied in later chapters to specific Federal Rules. *See, e.g.*, Chapter 6(D)(5)*(b)* ("Relation Back of Amendments Changing a Claim or Defense") *infra*.

Enterprises, Inc.[345] and *Gasperini v. Center for Humanities, Inc.*[346] Neither case provides much guidance about how the Rules Enabling Act branch of the *Erie* doctrine should operate. Furthermore, the *Gasperini* case creates more confusion about the proper method of conflict avoidance in cases in which Federal Rules potentially conflict with state law.

In *Business Guides*, the Court considered a challenge to Rule 11 of the Federal Rules of Civil Procedure as applied to a represented party who had signed a document in violation of the rule, but in good faith.[347] The Court upheld the validity of Rule 11 under the Rules Enabling Act. In *Business Guides*, the president and director of research of the plaintiff corporation signed an application for a temporary restraining order and an affidavit in support of the application, both of which contained false information. The Corporate plaintiff and the law firm representing the plaintiff were sanctioned by the district court for violating Rule 11. The sanctions were upheld by the Court of Appeals for the Ninth Circuit, and the Supreme Court affirmed. The Court held that Rule 11's objective standard of reasonable inquiry into the facts applied to represented parties as well as attorneys. The plaintiff argued that imposing sanctions on represented parties who had not acted in bad faith violated the Rules Enabling Act in two ways: (1) by authorizing fee shifting in a manner not approved by Congress; and (2) by creating a federal tort of malicious prosecution that encroached on various state causes of action. The Supreme Court rejected both of these arguments.

Following its previous decision in *Cooter & Gell v. Hartmarx Corp.*,[348] the Court held that Rule 11 of the Federal Rules of Civil Procedure did not constitute an impermissible shifting rule or effectively create a federal tort of malicious prosecution. In its Rules Enabling Act analysis, the Court repeated a statement it had first made in *Hanna v. Plumer* that the Federal Rules are to be judged as "prima facie" valid because of the participation by the Supreme Court, Congress, and the Advisory Committee in the rulemaking process.[349] To over-

---

345. 498 U.S. 533, 111 S. Ct. 922, 112 L. Ed. 2d 1140 (1991); *see also* Kamen v. Kemper Fin. Servs., Inc., 500 U.S. 90, 111 S. Ct. 1711, 114 L. Ed. 2d 152 (1991) (holding that Federal Rule 23.1, governing derivative actions in federal court, is not broad enough to control the content of the demand requirement in such actions and, therefore, that state law controls the content of the demand requirement in actions under the Investment Company Act of 1940). *See generally* Ralph U. Whitten, *Developments in the* Erie *Doctrine: 1991*, 40 AM. J. COMP. L. 967 (1992).

346. 518 U.S. 415, 116 S. Ct. 2211, 135 L. Ed. 2d 659 (1996). The Rules of Decision Act part of *Gasperini* was discussed in section E(3), *supra*.

347. Federal Rule 11 is discussed in Chapter 6(E)(2) ("Good Faith Pleading: Rule 11") *infra*.

348. 496 U.S. 384, 110 S. Ct. 2447, 110 L. Ed. 2d 359 (1990).

349. *See* 498 U.S. at 552, 111 S. Ct. at 933, 112 L. Ed. 2d at 1159. However, there exist the most serious possible reasons to question whether the participation by these groups in the rulemaking process assure rule validity. For a statement that the Court does not engage in meaningful independent review of the rules, see 146 F.R.D. 501-06 (1993) (statement of Justice White made upon the Court's promulgation of the 1993 amendments to the Federal Rules). For evidence supporting the Court's inattention to the rules, see Gene R. Shreve, *Eighteen Feet of Clay: Thoughts on Phantom Rule 4(m)*, 67 IND. L.J. 85 (1991). Furthermore, Justice Frankfurter warned years ago that the participation by Congress in the rulemaking process cannot be given significant weight in determining rule validity. "Plainly," wrote Frankfurter, "the rules are not acts of Congress and can not be treated as such. Having due regard to the mechanics of legislation and the practical conditions surrounding the business of Congress . . . to draw any inference of tacit approval from non-action by Congress is to appeal to unreality." Sibbach v. Wilson & Co., Inc., 312 U.S. 1, 18, 61 S. Ct. 422, 428, 85 L. Ed. 479, 487 (1941). For documentation of confusion on the part of the Advisory Committee on the limits of the rulemaking power under come the "presumptive validity" that this process establishes for rules promulgated under the Enabling Act,[350] litigants must establish that the *Burlington Northern* test, discussed in the preceding subsection, has been violated. In applying this test in *Business Guides*, the Court stated that "[t]here is little doubt that Rule 11 is reasonably necessary to maintain the integrity of the system of federal practice and procedure and that any effect on substantive rights is incidental."[351] The Court concluded that Rule 11 did not inappropriately shift fees because (1) Rule 11 sanctions are not keyed to the outcome of litigation, but to specific filings within the litigation; (2) Rule 11 sanctions do not shift the entire cost of litigation, but only the cost of a discrete event; and (3) Rule 11 only mandates an "appropriate sanction," not necessarily attorney's fees.[352] Likewise, the Court held that Rule 11 did not impermissibly create a federal tort of malicious prosecution because the main objective of the rule is not to reward parties who are victimized by litigation, but to deter baseless filings and curb abuses. "Imposing monetary sanctions on parties that violated the Rule may confer a benefit on other litigants, but the Rules Enabling Act is not violated by such incidental effects on substantive rights."[353]

Justices Kennedy, Marshall, Stevens, and Scalia dissented. However, only the first three of these Justices felt that a Rules Enabling Act question was raised by the majority's interpretation of Rule 11. The dissenters stated that the majority's interpretation of Rule 11 raised "troubling concerns with respect to both separation of powers and federalism."[354] The dissenters argued that the majority's distinction between fee shifting and Rule 11 sanctions for "discrete events" within the litigation was improper where the "discrete event" was the filing of a lawsuit and the "appropriate sanction" was the payment of the opposing party's attorney's fees.[355] In addition, the dissenters argued that the majority's interpretation of Rule 11 did indeed create a federal tort of "negligent prosecution" or "accidental abuse of process" by placing duties on represented parties who sign papers under the rule that exceeded the duties imposed by state tort law.[356] However, the dissenters were reluctant to draw the conclusion that the flaws in the majority's reasoning actually produced a Rules Enabling Act Violation. Rather, they argued that the Rules Enabling Act concerns raised by the plaintiff counseled strongly against an interpretation of Rule 11 that would avoid questions of validity.[357]

---

the Rules Enabling Act, see Stephen Burbank, *The Rules Enabling Act of 1934*, 130 U. PA. L. REV. 1015, 1027, 1135-37 (1982); Ralph U. Whitten, *Separation of Powers Restrictions on Judicial Rulemaking: A Case Study of Federal Rule 4*, 40 ME. L. REV. 41, 73-81 (1988). On the whole, therefore, whatever the "presumption of validity" means, it would seem to be unjustified.

350. *See* Burlington N.R.R. v. Woods, 480 U.S. 1, 6, 107 S. Ct. 967, 970, 94 L. Ed. 2d at 7-8 (1987).

351. 498 U.S. at 552, 111 S. Ct. at 934, 112 L. Ed. 2d at 1160.

352. *See id.* at 553, 111 S. Ct at 934, 112 L. Ed. 2d at 1160.

353. *Id.*

354. *Id.* at 565, 111 S. Ct. at 940, 112 L. Ed. 2d at 1168.

355. *See id.* at 566, 111 S. Ct. at 940, 112 L. Ed. 2d at 1168.

356. *See id.* at 567, 111 S. Ct. at 941, 112 L. Ed. 2d 1169.

357. *See id.* at 568, 111 S. Ct. at 942, 112 L. Ed. 2d at 1170.

Business Guides provides little additional instruction about how to determine the validity of Federal Rules of Civil Procedure under the *Burlington Northern* test. For example, the decision does not indicate how to determine whether a Federal Rule impacts on a state right that is considered "substantive,"[358] or how large an impact a Federal Rule may have on such substantive rights before the impact is considered "substantial" rather than "incidental." Nor did the decision indicate how to determine when a Federal Rule is or is not "reasonably necessary to the uniform system of federal practice and procedure." The Court did not even provide guidance on the most general elements of the test. For example, what does it mean to say that the Federal Rules have "presumptive validity"? Clearly, this presumptive validity is not a factual presumption of the sort that normally aids a litigant in meeting its burden of proof at trial.[359] Yet, if it is not an ordinary "evidentiary presumption," it is unclear what it is. Given the Court's refusal *ever* to invalidate a Federal Rule under the Rules Enabling Act, the "presumption of validity" would seem to be simply a truism. The Federal Rules are not subject to successful attack under the Rules Enabling Act.[360]

As discussed in section E(3), above, the *Gasperini* case was decided under the Rules of Decision Act. However, to reach the Rules of Decision Act question, the Court had to determine whether Rule 59 of the Federal Rules of Civil Procedure, which governs the granting of new trials in federal court, was applicable to the case. The Court determined that Rule 59 did not apply to the case. Although conceding that one ground for a new trial under Rule 59 is that the damages awarded are excessive, the majority stated that "[w]hether damages are excessive for the claim-in-suit must be governed by some law. And there is no candidate for that governance other than the law that gives rise to the claim for relief here, the law of New York."[361] In other words, because Rule 59 did not provide a standard for determining whether damages were excessive, the case was thrown to the Rules of Decision Act side of the *Erie* doctrine, where the question was whether the federal courts could disregard the applicable state statute under that doctrine.

The Court's interpretation of Rule 59 was sensible, though it is not entirely free from doubt. Rule 59 states that new trials may be granted when a jury has returned a verdict "for any of the reasons for which new trials have

---

358. For example, when the Federal Rule conflicts with a state rule, does the state rule itself have to embody a "right" that can somehow be classified as "substantive"? Alternatively, does the Federal Rule impact on state substantive rights even if the state rule with which it conflicts is purely procedural, if application of the Federal Rule instead of the state rule would expand or contract a state right in some more general sense, as long as the expanded or contracted right could somehow be classified as "substantive"? For example, if a state rule governing relation back of amendments to avoid the bar of the statute of limitations is supported by purely procedural policies, but would bar relation back, would application of Rule 15(c) of the Federal Rules of Civil Procedure to allow relation back impact on a state substantive right because it would allow a claim to be prosecuted in federal court that would be barred in state court? *See* Chapter 6(D)(5)*(d)* ("Rules Enabling Act Issues") *infra*.

359. For a discussion of evidentiary presumptions, see Chapter 11(H)(3) ("Presumptions") *infra*.

360. However, for additional discussion of how *Business Guides* might be interpreted, see Chapter 7(F)(3) ("Rules Enabling Act Issues Under Rule 13") *infra*.

361. *Gasperini*, 518 U.S. at 437 n.22, 116 S. Ct. at 2224 n.22, 135 L. Ed. 2d at 680 n.22.

heretofore been granted in actions at law in the Courts of the United States."[362] This provision can be interpreted as incorporating the traditional reasons used by the federal courts for determining whether new trials should be granted because the damages awarded were excessive.[363] However, it is also plausible to read the rule as not listing the content of the grounds for which a new trial can be granted.[364] In choosing between the two interpretations, however, the method of conflict avoidance that the Court had established since *Hanna* is relevant, and that method has been employed by the Court inconsistently.

As discussed in subsections 3 & 4, above, in *Hanna* and *Burlington Northern*, the Court gave excessively broad interpretations to Federal Rules of Civil and Appellate Procedure, producing conflicts with state law when narrower, and arguably more plausible, interpretations would have avoided the conflicts. However, in the *Ragan* and *Cohen* cases, discussed in subsection 2, above, the Court had given narrow interpretations to Federal Rules of Civil Procedure that avoided conflicts between the rules and state law.[365] Furthermore, after *Hanna*, a case identical to *Ragan* arose involving a potential conflict between the provision in Federal Rule 3 that an action is commenced by filing a complaint with the court and a state rule that required commencement by service of process to toll the running of the state statute of limitations. In *Walker v. Armco Steel Corp.*,[366] the Court followed the *Ragan* approach to Federal Rule interpretation rather than that in *Hanna* and *Burlington Northern* and held that Rule 3 was not broad enough to cover commencement for purposes of the state statute of limitations. Curiously, in *Gasperini* the Court cited *Hanna*, *Burlington Northern*, and *Walker* all in the same footnote as if they were consistent with each other. After citing *Hanna* and *Burlington Northern* for the proposition that when a Federal Rule is in point and is "consonant" with the Rules Enabling Act and the Constitution, it "applies regardless of contrary state law,"[367] the Court then cited *Walker* for the proposition that "[f]ederal courts have interpreted the Federal Rules . . . with sensitivity to important state interests and regulatory policies."[368]

The Court's overall approach to rule interpretation in *Gasperini*, together with its citation to its former cases employing incompatible methods of Rule interpretation, clouds the manner in which the lower federal courts should

---

362. FED. R. CIV. P. 59(a).

363. This was, in effect, the way that Justice Scalia interpreted the rule. *See* 518 U.S. at 467-68, 116 S. Ct. at 2239, 135 L. Ed. 2d at 698-99 (Scalia, J., dissenting).

364. *Cf.* CHARLES A. WRIGHT, LAW OF FEDERAL COURTS § 95, at 676-77 (5th ed. 1994) (Rule 59 does not list grounds for new trial, but only states that the usual grounds, including excessive damages, are permissible).

365. At least, this was Court's own view of what it had been doing when it viewed the *Ragan* and *Cohen* cases in retrospect in *Hanna*. *See* subsection 3 *supra*.

366. 446 U.S. 740, 100 S. Ct. 1978, 64 L. Ed. 2d 659 (1980); *see also* Habermehl v. Potter, 153 F.3d 1137 (10th Cir. 1998) (state law provided that filing a complaint with the court would toll the statute of limitations, but only if process served within 60 days after commencement; this was argued to conflict with 120-day period for service in Federal Rule 4(m); holding that Rule 4(m) and state law do not conflict and state law must be used to determine whether the limitations period had run).

367. 518 U.S. at 427 n.7, 116 S. Ct. at 2219 n.7, 135 L. Ed. 2d at 674 n.7.

368. *Id.*

approach potential conflicts between Federal Rules and state law.[369] It may be that the Court's citation to *Walker* was a signal to the lower courts that the "more sensitive" method of interpretation is now back in vogue. Such a change would certainly be desirable. However, it would have been preferable for the Court to acknowledge the inconsistency in its past interpretive methodology and clearly mark the path to a new way. In the absence of such a straightforward rejection of the method used in cases like *Hanna* and *Burlington Northern*, inconsistency in the conflict-avoidance method of the lower federal courts is bound to persist.[370]

6. Separation-of-Powers Restrictions on Judicial Rulemaking

In addition to the restrictions on the rulemaking power that may exist under the Rules Enabling Act, separation-of-powers restrictions may exist on the Supreme Court's authority to make even purely procedural rules under certain circumstances. The Court has seldom addressed the separation-of-powers restrictions that may exist on judicial rulemaking. However, one important early decision, *Wayman v. Southard,*[371] did address these restrictions. The Process Act of 1789[372] established a static conformity to state law on procedural matters. The Process Act of 1792[373] continued this static conformity, but provided power in the federal courts to make "such alterations and additions" as the courts would "deem expedient." It also gave the Supreme Court power to prescribe supervisory rules for the lower federal courts.[374] In *Wayman*, the Supreme Court addressed the validity of this congressional delegation of rulemaking power as applied to a rule made by a lower federal court:

> It will not be pretended that Congress can delegate to the Courts, or to any other tribunals, powers which are strictly and

---

369. Apparently, the *Gasperini* decision has created more confusion than even suggested in the text. On remand in *Gasperini*, the district court stated:

> The Supreme Court decision in this case represents an extension of *Erie* . . . or more likely a reversion by the Supreme Court to prior *Erie* doctrine since abandoned, of which *Guaranty Trust* . . . is the outstanding example. The Supreme Court in *Guaranty Trust* and again in *Gasperini* seems to have endorsed the outcome determinative test to determine whether a disputed point of law is procedural, and therefore governed by the Federal Rules of Civil Procedure, or substantive so as to be governed by state law.

Gasperini v. Center for Humanities, Inc., 972 F. Supp. 765, 767 (S.D.N.Y. 1997). Not in the wildest dreams of the authors of this treatise would they read *Gasperini* as holding that the outcome determinative test governs the applicability or validity of a Federal Rule of Civil Procedure.

370. *See generally* Joseph P. Bauer, *The* Erie *Doctrine Revisited: How a Conflicts Perspective Can Aid the Analysis,* 74 N.D. L. REV. 1235, 1264-65 (1999) (arguing, *inter alia*, that the process of distinguishing true from false conflicts used in the area of conflict of laws could be useful in determining when Federal Rules really conflict with state law).

371. 23 U.S. (10 Wheat.) 1, 6 L. Ed. 253 (1825).

372. ch. 21, § 2, 1 Stat. 93, 93-94; *see* Chapter 1(E)(5) ("The Development of Federal Procedure and the Federal Rules of Civil Procedure") *supra.*

373. ch. 36, § 2, 1 Stat. 275, 276; *see* Chapter 1(E)(5) ("The Development of Federal Procedure and the Federal Rules of Civil Procedure") *supra.*

374. *See* Process Act of 1792, ch. 36, § 2, 1 Stat. 275, 276.

exclusively legislative. But Congress may certainly delegate to others, powers which the legislature may rightfully exercise itself. . . . The Courts . . . may make rules directing the returning of writs and processes, the filing of declarations and other pleadings, and other things of the same description. It will not be contended, that these things might not be done by the legislature, without the intervention of the Courts; yet it is not alleged that the power may not be conferred on the judicial department.

The line has not been exactly drawn which separates those important subjects, which must be entirely regulated by the legislature itself, from those of less interest, in which a general provision may be made, and power given to those [persons] who are to act under such provisions to fill up the details. . . .

. . . .

. . . The power given to the Court to vary the mode of proceeding in this particular [*i.e.*, to regulate whether the officer proceeding under a writ of execution shall leave the property taken by the officer in the hands of the debtor until the day of the sale], is a power to vary minor regulations, which are within the great outlines marked out by the legislature in directing the execution. To vary the terms on which a sale is to be made, and declare whether it shall be on credit, or for ready money, is certainly a more important exercise of the power of regulating the conduct of the officer, but is one of the same principle. It is, in all its parts, the regulation of the conduct of the officer of the Court in giving effect to its judgments. A general superintendence over this subject seems to be properly within the judicial province, and has always been so considered.[375]

Several important principles can be derived from this passage. First, Congress has the power to regulate the procedure of the federal courts. Second, Congress may delegate some of its power to regulate procedure to the federal courts. Third, Congress may not delegate any power to regulate procedure that is ''strictly and exclusively legislative.'' Fourth, the line between procedural regulations that are within the exclusive power of Congress and regulations that Congress may delegate the power to the courts to make is not precisely drawn by the Constitution. However, the line should be drawn by separating ''important subjects'' from those of ''less interest,'' which involve only the ''details'' of procedure. Fifth, it is relevant in drawing the line between important matters and matters of detail to determine whether a ''general superintendence'' over the subject has traditionally been considered ''properly within the judicial province.''[376]

---

376. *Wayman*, 23 U.S. (10 Wheat.) at 42-45, 6 L. Ed. at 262-63.

376. *See* Ralph U. Whitten, *Separation of Powers Restrictions on Judicial Rulemaking: A Case Study of Federal Rule 4*, 40 ME. L. REV. 41, 52 (1988); *cf.* Leslie M. Kelleher, *Taking ''Substantive Rights'' (In the Rules Enabling Act) More Seriously*, 74 NOTRE DAME L. REV. 47 (1998) (reviewing the constitutional and statutory allocation of rulemaking authority between Congress and the Supreme Court and proposing a

The Supreme Court has never materially clarified the boundaries between those procedural matters that only Congress can regulate and those which Congress can delegate to the courts.[377] Nevertheless, several factors can be identified that should be taken into account in determining whether a delegation of rulemaking power to the courts is valid. First of all, it is relevant to determine whether Congress has legislated within a procedural area. If it has not done so, and if it has given general rulemaking power to the courts, there will be greater power in the courts to regulate the area than if Congress has extensively dealt with a procedural matter.[378] Nevertheless, some procedural matters are so fundamental that they must be dealt with by Congress.

Illustration 5-18. Assume that Congress establishes a Supreme Court and delegates to it the following rulemaking authority: "The Supreme Court shall have the power by rule to ordain and establish courts inferior to itself and to define the subject-matter jurisdiction that such courts shall exercise within the limits of Article III, § 2 of the Constitution." Such a delegation of rulemaking authority would be unconstitutional because it would contravene the express language of Article III, § 1, which provides that the "judicial power of the United States, shall be vested . . . in such inferior courts as the Congress may from time to time ordain and establish." The constitutional language implies that only Congress can determine whether there will be inferior federal courts, and this reading is supported by the historic compromise that led to the establishment of § 1 in the Constitutional Convention. Thus, both the text and the history of Article III reveal that the decision whether to create inferior federal courts cannot be delegated, even when Congress has not previously legislated to create such courts.[379]

* * * * *

A more difficult problem, but one of greater relevance to today's statutory context, is what separation-of-powers restrictions exist on the rulemaking power of the courts when Congress *has* extensively regulated a procedural area, but also delegated rulemaking authority to the courts of such a general nature as also to encompass the area, with an additional proviso that any court rules made within the delegated authority shall supersede inconsistent statutes.[380] As long as Congress has delegated none of its fundamental powers to the courts, any court rule made within the delegated powers might seem to be valid, even if the rule supersedes an inconsistent statute. However, this approach is too simplistic. Even when Congress has delegated general rulemaking authority to the courts with the power to supersede inconsistent statutes, Congress may wish to exercise exclusive control over certain areas. These areas might not be so fundamental that Congress

---

multifactor analysis for the Court and the Advisory Committee to use when evaluating the validity of rules created under the Rules Enabling Act).

377. The other early decisions cast little light on the separation-of-powers restrictions because they were based on existing statutory restrictions on judicial rulemaking, rather than on constitutional limits. *See* Ralph U. Whitten, *Separation of Powers Restrictions on Judicial Rulemaking: A Case Study of Federal Rule 4*, 40 ME. L. REV. 41, 52-53 (1988).

378. *See generally id.* at 54-60.

379. *See id.* at 54 and authorities there cited. *See also id.* at 55-60.

380. The Rules Enabling Act contains such a proviso. *See* 28 U.S.C. § 2072(b).

could not delegate them to the courts if it explicitly chose to do so. However, the areas may traditionally have been of great concern to the legislative branch, and Congress may have consistently exercised legislative control over the areas. To paraphrase *Wayman v. Southard*, such areas would *not* be ones in which general superintendence over the subject has been considered properly within the judicial province.

Under these circumstances, to determine whether court rules created pursuant to a general delegation of rulemaking authority, such as the Rules Enabling Act, are valid, several factors should be evaluated: (1) the detail with which Congress has regulated the area; (2) the length of time that Congress has exercised exclusive control over the area before the courts make a rule within the area; (3) the apparent importance of the statutory policies prescribed by Congress within the area to both Congress and litigants; (4) the timing and purpose of the delegation of general rulemaking power to the courts in relation to the statutory scheme; (5) the extent to which the court-made rules will impact on the statutory scheme; and (6) the extent to which a court-made rule will support or protect statutory policies that are more important than the statutory policies replaced or affected by the court rule.[381]

Illustration 5-19. An example of a valid court-made rule under this analysis is original Rule 4(f) of the Federal Rules of Civil Procedure. Rule 4(f) expanded the personal jurisdiction authority of the U.S. District Courts from the limits of the district to the limits of the state in which the federal district court sits. Before Rule 4(f) became effective in 1938, a federal district court sitting in one district of a state could not summon a defendant residing in another district of the same state to defend an action in the district in which the court was sitting. After the effective date of Rule 4(f), however, a district court in one district could summon a defendant anywhere within the state to defend an action in the district. Rule 4(f) thus expanded the territorial power of the district courts. At the time Rule 4(f) was promulgated, Congress had long regulated the personal jurisdiction authority of the district courts in some detail. It had not only limited that authority to the limits of the districts as a general matter, but had paid close attention to matters of personal jurisdiction by expanding the authority of the district courts itself when it thought such an expansion was necessary. In addition, this detailed regulation of federal personal jurisdiction dated from 1789. Thus, the specificity and duration of the congressional regulation of jurisdiction both weighed against the validity of Rule 4(f). Furthermore, although personal jurisdiction is not one of those matters that is so fundamental that power may not be delegated to the Court to affect it, it is not far removed in importance from those fundamental matters and has been treated as of great importance by Congress. In addition, because personal jurisdiction affects the location of suit, it is also of substantial importance to litigants, especially to defendants, though the slight expansion of personal jurisdiction accomplished by Rule 4(f) is not as burdensome as other possible modifications might be. Also weighing against the

---

381. *See* Ralph U. Whitten, *Separation of Powers Restrictions on Judicial Rulemaking: A Case Study of Rule 4*, 40 ME. L. REV. 41, 60-66 (1988).

validity of Rule 4(f) is the fact that the Supreme Court never exercised its rule-making power under the original Conformity Acts to affect personal jurisdiction. The purpose of the delegation of rulemaking authority to the Court in the Enabling Act—to end conformity to state law and establish a uniform system of procedure for the federal courts—could have been fulfilled completely without any regulation of personal jurisdiction.

Nevertheless, favoring the validity of Rule 4(f) are two factors (in addition to the fact, mentioned above, that the burdens of the expansion of personal jurisdiction on litigants are slight). One is the fact that Rule 4(f) only ex-panded the jurisdiction of the district courts to the limits of the state in which they are sitting. Rule 4(f) did not, therefore, encroach on the power, long and exclusively exercised by Congress, to choose when to create federal interstate long-arm jurisdiction. More importantly, the factor that tips the balance in favor of the Rule's validity is that it prevents the defeat of federal subject-matter jurisdiction policies in an important way. The inability to assert personal jurisdiction over defendants located in different districts in the same state prior to Rule 4(f) meant that plaintiffs seeking to sue such defendants might have to sue them in state, rather than federal court, to obtain personal jurisdiction over them. For example, a plaintiff residing in the northern district of a state seeking to sue a nonresident defendant over whom personal jurisdiction could be obtained only in the southern district of the state would either have to go to the de-fendant's state and district of permanent residence and sue the defendant there, where personal jurisdiction would exist *and* venue would be proper, or sue in a state court in the northern or southern district of the state which had the capacity to obtain personal jurisdiction over the defendant. The inconvenience of suing in the defendant's home state would often mean that the plaintiff would abandon the federal courts for the state courts, thus relinquishing the privilege of suing in federal court that had been granted by the subject-matter jurisdiction statutes. Because subject-matter jurisdiction policies are among the most important to the operation of the federal courts, the validity of Rule 4(f) is sustained by the fact that it prevents the defeat of these policies.[382]

Illustration 5-20. Suppose, however, that the Supreme Court had promulgated a rule expanding the venue of the federal courts to allow actions to be brought in either district of a state by multiple plaintiffs residing in different districts in that state. The rationale of such a rule might be similar to that of Rule 4(f)—multiple plaintiffs unable to join in a federal action in their home state because of federal venue restrictions might decide to sue in a state court within the state instead of suing the defendant in the defendant's state of residence, thus abandoning their congressionally granted privilege of resorting to the diversity jurisdiction. Nevertheless, such a modification of the venue statutes by rule would be invalid. Although venue and personal jurisdiction are similar, in that they both govern the location of the action, Congress has regulated general venue in the judicial code in much more detail than it has regulated general intrastate personal jurisdiction for the federal courts. Personal jurisdiction restrictions in existence at

---

382. *See id.* at 86-92.

the time Rule 4(f) was promulgated under the Enabling Act generally limited process to the limits of the district in which the district court sat. However, venue was regulated separately for diversity and all other actions, for actions against multiple defendants residing in different districts in the same state and residing in different divisions in the same district, for local actions, and others. Thus, the detail with which Congress has addressed venue in the Judicial Code would make it improper for the courts to address the question by rule, even to remove obstacles to federal subject-matter jurisdiction.[383]

Illustration 5-21. Not all modifications of federal personal jurisdiction authority would be valid under the analysis described above. For example, Federal Rule 4(k)(2) provides nationwide long-arm jurisdiction for the federal courts in a small category of cases. As amended in 1993, Rule 4(k)(2) authorizes the federal courts to assert personal jurisdiction over defendants in cases arising under federal law whenever the defendants are not subject to the courts of general jurisdiction of any state.[384] This amendment was designed to "correct a gap" in the enforcement of federal law in cases where a defendant has contacts with the United States sufficient to justify the assertion of jurisdiction over the defendant under the Due Process Clause of the Fifth Amendment, but insufficient contacts with any state to permit the assertion of jurisdiction under state law.[385] However, this amendment to Rule 4 raises serious separation-of-powers questions. The detail with which Congress has regulated federal long-arm jurisdiction parallels the detail with which it has regulated federal venue. Establishing nationwide or international long-arm jurisdiction independent of the states has, therefore, not traditionally been considered a matter fit for the general superintendence of the judiciary through court rulemaking. In addition, Rule 4(k)(2) cannot be justified as necessary to prevent the defeat of federal subject-matter jurisdiction policies.[386] The amended rule does not eliminate a discrepancy between the personal jurisdiction authority of the federal and state courts that would encourage litigants to abandon their federally granted privilege of resorting to federal court. On the contrary, it creates a discrepancy between the personal jurisdiction authority of state and federal courts that will encourage litigants to forum shop for federal courts to obtain the benefit of long-arm jurisdiction that does not exist at the state level. An effect of this sort arguably involves a policy judgment that only Congress can make in the absence of an explicit grant of rulemaking authority to the courts over the subject. Balanced against these considerations are the facts that the extension of jurisdiction by Rule 4(k) is small and that the

---

383. *See id.* at 92-93. It may be no accident, therefore, that Federal Rule 82 forbids a construction of the Federal Rules of Civil Procedure that would extend or limit the venue of the district courts. *See* FED. R. CIV. P. 82. Rule 82 also prohibits constructions that extend or limit "jurisdiction," but this reference has always been understood to be limited to subject-matter jurisdiction. *See* Ralph U. Whitten, *Separation of Powers Restrictions on Judicial Rulemaking: A Case Study of Rule 4*, 40 ME. L. REV. 41, 73 (1988).

384. *See* FED. R. CIV. P. 4(k)(2); *see also* Chapter 3(L) ("Special Problems of Amenability to Process in Federal Court") *supra.*

385. *See* FED. R. CIV. P. 4(k)(2) advisory committee's note to the 1993 amendment.

386. *See* Ralph U. Whitten, *Separation of Powers Restrictions on Judicial Rulemaking: A Case Study of Rule 4*, 40 ME. L. REV. 41, 103-06 (1988); *see also id.* at 93-103; *see also* JACK B. WEINSTEIN, REFORM OF COURT RULE-MAKING PROCEDURES 4-5 (1977) (comparing the processes of adjudication and rulemaking).

extension allows litigants in some federal claims cases to sue in federal court within the United States, rather than suing in the courts of a foreign nation. Whether these considerations are sufficient to save the constitutionality of the new rule is questionable.

* * * * *

In *Sibbach*, the Supreme Court stated that "[t]here are other limitations upon the authority to prescribe rules which might have been, but were not, mentioned in the [Rules Enabling] Act; for instance, the inability of a court, by rule, to extend or restrict the jurisdiction conferred by a statute."[387] This statement, in combination with the Court's discussion of the limits on judicial rulemaking in *Wayman*, suggest that one of the "important" subjects reserved for Congress may be the subject of jurisdiction—presumably meaning "subject-matter jurisdiction." As *Illustration 5-18*, above, suggests, surely the Supreme Court could not be given the entire power to define the subject-matter jurisdiction that the federal courts will exercise within the limits of Article III. Such a power would involve policy decisions that the language and history of Article III, fairly construed, reserve to Congress. The question remains, however, whether lesser judicial rulemaking power over subject-matter jurisdiction would be permissible.

In 1992, Congress delegated to the Supreme Court the power to provide for interlocutory appeals from the U.S. District Courts to the U.S. Courts of Appeals in cases not otherwise provided for in 28 U.S.C. § 1292, the statute that currently authorizes appeals from interlocutory orders.[388] In 1998, the Supreme Court exercised this power by creating a new Rule 23(f) under the Rules Enabling Act. Rule 23(f) authorizes the courts of appeals, in their discretion, to permit an appeal from an order of a district court granting or denying class action certification under Rule 23.[389] Rule 23(f) is a clear regulation of appellate subject-matter jurisdiction under a delegation of authority from Congress. It thus squarely raises the separation-of-powers issue posed by *Sibbach* and *Wayman*.

In the language of *Wayman*, Rule 23(f) concerns a matter—subject-matter jurisdiction—whose "general superintendence" has *not* traditionally been considered "properly within the judicial province." Similarly, in the language of *Sibbach*, Rule 23(f) certainly appears to be an "extension" of "jurisdiction" by "rule." Under existing 28 U.S.C. § 1292(b), an interlocutory appeal can be taken from a district court to a court of appeals only (1) if the district court certifies (2) that an order otherwise not appealable involves "a controlling question of law as to which there is substantial ground for difference of opinion and that an immediate appeal from the order may materially advance the ultimate termination of the litigation," and (3) the court of appeals, in its discretion, permits the

---

387. *Sibbach*, 312 U.S. at 10, 61 S. Ct. at 422, 85 L. Ed. at 483.

388. *See* 28 U.S.C. § 1292(e). Congress added subsection (e) to § 1292 in 1992. *See* Federal Courts Administration Act of 1992, Pub. L. No. 102-572, § 101, 106 Stat. 4506, 4506. This enactment had been recommended by the Federal Courts Study Committee, along with a recommendation concerning rulemaking power to define what constitutes a final judgment under 28 U.S.C. § 1291. The Committee recommended that the Court be permitted "to add to—but not subtract from—the list of categories of interlocutory appeal permitted . . . in 28 U.S.C. § 1292. REPORT OF THE FEDERAL COURTS STUDY COMMITTEE 96 (1990). Section 1292(e) conforms to this recommendation.

389. *See* FED. R. CIV. P. 23(f).

appeal. By removing the first two requirements of § 1292(b), Rule 23(f) seems clearly to expand the appellate jurisdiction over class action certification orders.[390] The Advisory Committee suggested that "[t]he expansion of appeal opportunities effected by subdivision (f) is modest."[391] Perhaps the limited nature of the expansion saves the validity of the rule on the theory that it amounts only to a regulation of procedural detail and is, therefore, one of those subjects of "less interest" that *Wayman* suggested was properly within the judicial rulemaking authority. Nevertheless, § 1292(e) and Rule 23(f) raise troubling questions about the ability of Congress validly to delegate its authority over fundamental questions of judicial power to the courts.[392]

SECTION G. THE *ERIE* DOCTRINE IN THE LOWER FEDERAL COURTS

Given the lack of clarity in both the Rules of Decision Act and the Rules Enabling Act branches of the *Erie* doctrine, it is not surprising to find that the lower federal courts have taken different approaches to the application of state law in federal courts. *Erie* issues are numerous in diversity actions because of the wide range of matters upon which Federal Rules of Civil Procedure can potentially conflict with state procedural law, and also because of the abundance of state laws that can be argued to have outcome determinative consequences that violate the *Erie* policies under the Rules of Decision Act. All of the situations in which Rules Enabling Act or Rules of Decision Act issues arise cannot be examined in this section. Instead, a few prominent examples will be taken up here to illustrate the kinds of difficulties that the Supreme Court's *Erie* decisions pose for the lower federal courts. Other issues will be examined in later chapters as they arise in conjunction with the procedural topics there discussed.

As a general, though not universal, proposition, it can be said that issues in which conflicts arise between Federal Rules of Civil Procedure and state law tend to be resolved in favor of the Federal Rules, either because the rules in question are found not to conflict with state law,[393] or because, when they do, the lower federal courts find the Federal Rules valid under the Rules Enabling Act and Constitution. Given the discussion of the Supreme Court's approach to Federal Rule validity in section F, above, such results are not surprising. In cases in which no Federal Rule is applicable and the lower federal courts must decide the case under the Rules of Decision Act branch of *Erie*, state law is more often found applicable. However, the tendency to honor state law is not universal.

---

390. *See* Advisory Committee Note to Proposed Rule 23(f), 167 F.R.D. at 565 (1996).

391. *Id.* at 566; *see also* David L. Shapiro, *Federal Diversity Jurisdiction: A Survey and Proposal*, 91 HARV. L. REV. 317, 346-47 (1977) (arguing for the validity of judicial regulation of subject-matter jurisdiction under a properly circumscribed grant of power from Congress).

392. *See also* 28 U.S.C. § 2072(c) (authorizing the Supreme Court to define by procedural rule "when a ruling of a district court is final for the purposes of appeal under [28 U.S.C. § 1291]."

393. *See, e.g.*, Wade v. Danek Med., Inc., 182 F.3d 281 (4th Cir. 1999) (Rule 23 does not incorporate an equitable tolling rule; state tolling rule applies); Vaught v. Showa Denko, K.K., 107 F.3d 1137 (5th Cir.), *cert. denied*, 522 U.S. 817, 118 S. Ct. 67, 139 L. Ed. 2d 29 (1999) (same).

Furthermore, in both Rules Enabling Act and Rules of Decision Act cases, the approach of the lower federal courts is often not sophisticated, and is, indeed, frequently confused about the proper analysis to be used. Such results are also not surprising, however, given the lack of clarity in the Supreme Court's decisions under the two acts, as well as the tendency of the Court to ignore both branches of the *Erie* doctrine for long periods of time.

One illustrative line of cases that may offer the Supreme Court the opportunity to clarify the workings of one or both branches of the doctrine arises out of state tort reform efforts. As the *Gasperini* case, discussed in section E, above, indicated, the states sometimes tend to curb litigation abuses in the tort area by adopting procedural rules that are designed to create barriers of one sort or another to plaintiffs without altogether precluding recovery or limiting the amount that can be recovered. Thus, some states have imposed requirements that plaintiffs seeking to recover in certain kinds of tort actions supply expert affidavits to demonstrate a factual basis for their suits, or have introduced special pleading requirements that require the plaintiff to demonstrate a factual basis for certain kinds of tort claims without first being able to obtain discovery from defendants on the claims.

In federal diversity actions, these kinds of provisions raise the issue whether the state laws in question conflict with the pleading provisions of Federal Rules 8 and 9 (governing pleading), Federal Rule 11 (governing the standard of factual and legal investigation that plaintiffs must conduct before bringing a federal action), and Federal Rules 26-37 (governing discovery). For example, Florida has provided that when a plaintiff seeks punitive damages, "no claim for punitive damages shall be permitted unless there is a reasonable showing by evidence in the record or proffered by the claimant which would provide a reasonable basis for recovery of such damages."[394] Although the statute also provides that the claimant can move to amend the complaint to assert a claim for punitive damages, and that the rules of civil procedure should be liberally construed to allow the claimant discovery of evidence "which appears reasonably calculated to lead to admissible evidence on the issue of punitive damages," it also provides that no discovery of the defendant's financial worth can be allowed until "after the pleading concerning punitive damages is permitted."[395] The U.S. District Courts in Florida have split on the question whether this statute is applicable in federal diversity actions.

In *Neill v. Gulf Stream Coach, Inc.,*[396] the U.S. District Court for the Middle District of Florida found that the statute did not conflict with any Federal Rule of Civil Procedure and that failure to apply the statute in a federal diversity action would create forum shopping and inequitable administration of the law in violation of the Rules of Decision Act. In an extensive opinion, the court concluded that it was possible to give both Federal Rule 8(a), which establishes

---

394. Fla. Stat. Ann. § 768.72 (West Supp. 1999).

395. *Id.*

396. 966 F. Supp. 1149 (M.D. Fla. 1997); *see also* Teel v. United Techs. Pratt & Whitney, 953 F. Supp. 1534 (S.D. Fla. 1997) (applying same analysis as *Neill*).

a liberal notice pleading standard for the federal courts,[397] and the Florida statute their full field of operation.[398] In the court's view, Federal Rule 8(a) contained no requirement that all claims be pleaded in the first complaint on pain of being lost forever if they are not; rather, Rule 8(a) only provides that when claims are pleaded, the pleading in which they are contained need only contain a short and plain statement showing that the pleader is entitled to relief.[399] Thus, Rule 8(a) and the Florida statute could both be applied, because once the plaintiff made the showing required, the complaint could be amended to add claims for punitive damages that comported in form to Rule 8(a).[400] In addition, the court pointed out that even if Rule 8(a)(2) was "understood as governing when the pleading of certain matters is to occur," it would not conflict with the state statute, because

> [a] "claim" showing that the pleader is entitled to relief—within the meaning of the rule—refers to the pleader's cause of action or legal theory of recovery, as opposed to a specific component of the relief that may be available should the claim be proved. Thus, there can be no such thing as a free standing "claim" for punitive damages. . . . As such . . . the only basis for conflict would be Rule 8(a)(3)'s requirement that the pleading contain a demand for judgment for the relief the pleader seeks.[401]

The court also held that the Florida statute did not conflict with Federal Rule 9(g), which requires that when special damages are claimed, they shall be specifically stated in the pleading in which they are claimed.[402] In the court's view, Rule 9(g) says nothing about when items of special damage may be pleaded, but only requires that when they are pleaded they be stated with specificity. In contrast, the Florida statute has nothing to say about the content of a pleading concerning punitive damages, but speaks only to when an entitlement to such damages can be pleaded. Each provision could thus operate side-by-side and be given its intended sphere of operation.[403]

Turning to the Rules of Decision Act side of the *Erie* doctrine, the court concluded that the failure to apply the Florida statute would cause inequitable administration of the law because the statute was part of a tort reform effort that was designed to "create a positive legal right on the part of those sued in tort under Florida law to be free from punitive damages claims absent a threshold judicial determination of a reasonable basis for their assertion."[404] As such, the

---

397. *See* Chapter 6(D)(2)*(b)* *infra* (discussing federal notice pleading).

398. *See Neill*, 966 F. Supp. at 1153-54.

399. *See id.* at 1153.

400. *See id.* at 1154.

401. *Id.* at 1153 n.8. However, the court did not point out why this conflict with Rule 8(a)(3) would not produce a Rules Enabling Act issue. In Cohen v. Office Depot, Inc., 184 F.3d 1292 (11th Cir. 1999), the court of appeals found a conflict between the Federal Rules of Civil Procedure and the Florida statute on this basis. *Cohen* is discussed in the text, *infra*.

402. *See* Chapter 6(D)(2)*(e)(iii)* *infra* (discussing the requirements of Rule 9(g)).

403. *See id.* at 1154. The court did not discuss possible conflicts between the Florida statute and Federal Rule 11 or the provisions of the Federal Rules governing discovery.

404. *Id.*

statute "represents a means of achieving a substantive legislative goal."[405] Thus, to deny a federal defendant its protection in federal court would be "to thwart one of the twin aims of *Erie*, namely, the avoidance of inequitable administration of the laws."[406] In addition, the court found that the plaintiff's incentive to shop for a federal forum would "increase significantly" if the federal courts disregarded the Florida statute, thus producing the forum shopping that *Erie* sought to avoid.

Other Florida federal courts have reached different results. For example, in *Tutor Time Child Care Systems, Inc. v. Franks Investment Group, Inc.,*[407] the U.S. District Court for the Southern District of Florida disagreed with *Neill*. Essentially, the court's view of the statute was that it required "satellite pleading"[408] in cases in which the plaintiff wishes to claim punitive damages. This satellite-pleading requirement conflicted with both Rules 8(a) and 9(g), which contain no such requirement.[409] Having found a conflict between the state statute and the Federal Rules, the court concluded summarily that the conflict should be resolved in favor of the Federal Rules, which had been "constitutionally promulgated pursuant to the Rules Enabling Act."[410] Similarly, in *Alexander v. University/Gainesville Healthcare Center, Inc.,*[411] the U.S. District Court for the Northern District of Florida concluded that to apply the Florida statute in federal court would be to "convert the pleading of punitive damages from the requirement of mere notice to a quasi-adjudication of plaintiff's claim, requiring evidentiary inquiry and discovery, argumentation of counsel, and a judicial ruling. Such an application would subvert not only the intent of Rule 8, but the entire system of the Federal Rules."[412] Furthermore, the court construed the Florida statute as not having created any new substantive rights (contrary to *Neill*), but as having merely added a pleading requirement.[413] Thus, the application of the Federal Rules instead of the state statute did not violate the Constitution or the Rules Enabling Act.[414]

In *Cohen v. Office Depot, Inc.,*[415] the Eleventh Circuit Court of Appeals adopted the view of the Florida district courts that had found the Florida statute in conflict with the Federal Rules of Civil Procedure and, therefore, inapplicable in federal diversity actions. *Cohen* found the statute in conflict with Federal Rule 8(a)(3) on two grounds. First, the court held that under Rule 8(a)(3), a pleading that sets forth a claim for relief must contain a request for a remedy. Because the Florida statute prohibits a request for punitive damages, the court held that it

---

405. *Id.* at 1155.
406. *Id.* at 1156.
407. 966 F. Supp. 1188 (S.D. Fla. 1997).
408. *See id.* at 1191, 1192.
409. *See also* Primerica Fin. Servs., Inc. v. Mitchell, 48 F. Supp. 2d 1363 (S.D. Fla. 1999) (following *Tutor Time*).
410. 966 F. Supp. at 1193.
411. 17 F. Supp.2d 1291 (N.D. Fla. 1998).
412. *Id.* at 1292.
413. *See id.* at 1293.
414. *See id.*
415. 184 F.3d 1292 (11th Cir. 1999).

conflicted with Rule 8(a)(3). Alternatively,[416] the court held that even if Rule 8(a)(3) does not require that the complaint request a remedy, it permits the complaint to do so. Thus, the Florida statute conflicted with the rule by forbidding the complaint from containing a demand for punitive damages. However, after finding a conflict between Rule 8(a)(3) and the Florida statute, the court's analysis of whether the Rules Enabling Act was violated by Rule 8(a)(3) was purely conclusory. The court relied on the statement in *Sibbach* that Federal Rules are valid if they "really regulate procedure" and a statement from *Mississippi Publishing Corp. v. Murphree* that "incidental effects" by Federal Rules on substantive rights do not violate the Act.[417]

Cohen notwithstanding, even brief reflection on the standards discussed in previous sections will illustrate how difficult it is to determine which of the above approaches is correct. For example, section F(5), above, observed that the Supreme Court's approach to the problem of avoiding conflicts between Federal Rules of Civil Procedure and state law has varied. The Court's latest interpretation of a Federal Rule in the *Gasperini* case may indicate that the Court is now following an approach that is more sensitive to "important state interests and regulatory policies."[418] If so, the approach taken in *Neill* may be correct. Certainly, neither Rule 8(a) nor 9(g) explicitly negate other requirements that may exist under state law for asserting a particular kind of claim, although it would have been desirable if the court had considered possible conflicts with Rule 11 and the federal discovery rules as well as Rules 8 and 9.

Nevertheless, it is also possible to sympathize with the courts in *Tutor Time* and *Alexander* that application of the state statute would create satellite pleading and a mini-adjudication requirement for punitive damages claims, neither of which exists under the Federal Rules. Treating punitive damages in this way would undoubtedly violate the spirit of the liberal notice pleading philosophy of Rule 8(a). If the *Burlington Northern* method of Federal Rule interpretation, discussed in section F(4) and (5), above, is correct, the Florida statute should surely be interpreted as in conflict with Federal Rules 8(a) & 9(g). However, even if the rules are in conflict with state law, the courts' approach to the Rules Enabling Act problem was inadequate in *Tutor Time*, *Alexander*, and *Cohen*. The court in *Neill* had the better case that the state statute embodied "substantive rights." *Tutor Time, Alexander,* and *Cohen* did not examine this issue adequately, much less determine in anything more than a conclusory fashion whether the application of the Federal Rules instead of the state law would abridge the statutory rights more than "incidentally."

---

416. The defendant argued that there was no real conflict between Rule 8(a)(3) and the Florida statute because Rule 8(a)(3) was effectively rendered a nullity by Rule 54(c), which states that, except in the case of default judgments, "every final judgment shall grant the relief to which the party in whose favor it is rendered is entitled, even if the party has not demanded such relief in the party's pleadings." The court did not view Rule 54(c) as nullifying Rule 8(a)(3), and, in fact, viewed the provision of Rule 54(c) dealing with default judgments as reinforcing Rule 8(a)(3)'s direction that a pleading stating a claim include a demand for relief. That part of Rule 54(c) states that the relief awarded in the case of a default judgment "shall not be different in kind from or exceed in amount that prayed for in the demand for judgment" *See* 184 F.3d at 1298.

417. *See id.* at 1299.

418. *See Gasperini*, 518 U.S. at 427 n.7, 116 S. Ct. at 2219 n.7, 135 L. Ed. 2d at n.7.

If the court was correct in *Neill* that there is no conflict between a Federal Rule of Civil Procedure and state law, it was undoubtedly also correct that disregard of the state statute would create forum shopping and inequitable administration of the law. There seems to be no question that defendants would be deprived of valuable benefits that they would enjoy in state court if federal courts disregard the state statute in diversity actions. Moreover, as the court pointed out in *Neill*, plaintiffs will surely shop for a federal forum if the federal courts disregard the requirements of the state statute in diversity cases. On the other hand, the court failed to consider whether federal countervailing considerations existed that might outweigh the outcome determinative policies.[419]

One of the problems in the Florida cases discussed above is that the state legislature may have been framing a procedural restriction for substantive policy purposes. When legislatures act in this way, as they often seem to do, the task of a federal court in determining the purposes of the state laws in order to perform the *Hanna* conflict avoidance analysis becomes more complicated. In addition, the problem of determining whether the state laws should be considered "substantive" for Rules Enabling Act purposes is also enormously complicated. Nevertheless, even when state laws are cast in a procedural form, they are sometimes more clearly substantive that the Florida punitive damages restriction discussed above. As state laws progress toward the substantive end of the substance-procedure spectrum, the federal courts tend to apply them in spite of potentially conflicting federal procedural law.

Good examples of procedural restrictions with a substantive purpose are state "seat-belt statutes." These statutes prohibit the introduction of evidence that a plaintiff in an automobile accident case was not wearing a seat belt in order to prove the plaintiff was contributorily negligent. Although such statutes are framed as rules of evidence, they are actually provisions designed to eliminate the

---

419. *See generally* Jeffrey A. Parness et al., *The Substantive Elements in the New Special Pleading Laws*, 78 NEB. L. REV. 412, 428-38 (1999); Rhett Traband, *An* Erie *Decision: Should State Statutes Prohibiting the Pleading of Punitive Damages Claims be Applied in Federal Diversity Actions*, 26 STETSON L. REV. 225 (1996); *see also* Clark v. Sarasota County Pub. Hosp. Bd., 65 F. Supp. 2d 1308 (M.D. Fla. 1999) (federal diversity court must apply Florida medical malpractice mediation requirements; those requirements do not conflict with Federal Rule 8 and disregard of them would violate the twin aims of *Erie*); Baird v. Celis, 41 F. Supp.2d 1358 (N.D. Ga. 1999) (Georgia expert affidavit requirement conflicts with notice pleading standards in federal court and is, therefore, inapplicable in federal diversity action); McKenzie v. Hawaii Permanente Med. Group, Inc., 29 F. Supp.2d 1174 (D. Hawaii 1998) (state medical claims conciliation procedure, which must be pursued before a state medical malpractice action may be filed, is "procedural" for *Erie* purposes; thus, plaintiff need not pursue the procedure before commencing a federal diversity action); Oakes v. Halvorsen Marine, Ltd., 179 F.R.D. 281 (C.D. Cal. 1998) (California statute establishing procedures for pleading exemplary or punitive damages and obtaining information relevant to such claims is inapplicable because it is "procedural" law that conflicts with Federal Rules); RTC Mortgage Trust 1994 N-1 v. Fidelity Nat'l Title Ins. Co., 981 F. Supp. 334 (D.N.J. 1997) (New Jersey affidavit-of-merit statute does not conflict with any Federal Rule of Civil Procedure or notice pleading policies and must be applied by federal courts in diversity actions because it is outcome determinative and there are no federal countervailing considerations); Robert K. Harris, Brown v. Nichols: *The Eleventh Circuit Refuses to Play the* Erie *Game With Georgia's Expert Affidavit Requirement*, 29 GA. L. REV. 291 (1994); Note, *Tort Law–Products Liability–Illinois Imposes Certificate of Merit Requirement on Products Liability Actions–Civil Justice Reform Amendments of 1995, Pub. Act 89-7, sec. 15, § 2-623, 1995 Ill. Legis. Serv. 224, 229-30 (West) (to be codified at Ill. Comp. Stat. ch. 735, § 5/2-623*, 109 HARV. L. REV. 705, 708 (1996). For a general discussion of certificate-of-merit laws, see Jeffrey A. Parness & Amy Leonetti, *Expert Opinion Pleading: Any Merit to Special Certificates of Merit?* 1997 B.Y.U. L. REV. 537.

defense of contributory negligence under state law for the particular omission covered by the statutes. Nothing could be more substantive. In cases in which defendants have argued that seat-belt laws are inconsistent with the Federal Rules of Evidence[420] governing relevant evidence, the federal courts have universally recognized the substantive character of the laws and held them applicable in federal diversity actions.[421]

Occasionally, in applying a state law to comply with the general *Erie* policies, a federal court will dismiss a diversity action, not seeing that it may be undermining the policies that support the diversity jurisdiction.[422] For example, Illinois has a statute that, at least in the absence of special circumstances, requires dismissal of actions in favor of prior pending actions between the same parties on the same claim. Some Illinois federal decisions have held that *Erie* requires the application of this statute in diversity actions to produce dismissal in favor of prior pending actions commenced in other courts, including Illinois courts and the courts of other states and nations.[423] The problem with this view is that it may represent an abdication of the federal courts' responsibilities to provide an unbiased forum in diversity actions.

Illustration 5-10 in section E(1), above, stated that it would be improper for a federal diversity court to refuse the plaintiff a remedy that would be given by a state court in the same state, because to do so would be literally to drive the plaintiff out of federal court into a state court to obtain the remedy. When the plaintiff is a noncitizen of the forum, this problem is particularly serious because

---

420. The Federal Rules of Evidence were originally promulgated by the Supreme Court under the Rules Enabling Act, but, due to objections to certain of the rules, Congress prevented them from going into effect and later enacted them in revised form as statutes. *See* Chapter 11(I) ("Evidence") *infra*. Thus potential conflicts between the rules and state substantive law raise the issue of the power of Congress to override state substantive provisions.

421. *See, e.g.,* Gardner *ex rel.* Gardner v. Chrysler Corp., 89 F.3d 729 (10th Cir. 1996) (state rule is substantive and must be excluded to prove contributory negligence of plaintiff or failure to mitigate damages, but may be admitted for other purposes permitted by state law); Dillinger v. Caterpillar, Inc., 959 F.2d 430 (3d Cir. 1992) (evidence of failure to use seat belt must be excluded under state law); Barron v. Ford Motor Co. of Can., 965 F.2d 195 (7th Cir. 1992), *cert. denied*, 506 U.S. 1001, 113 S. Ct. 605, 121 L. Ed. 2d 541 (1992) (state law precluding admissibility of failure to use seat belt is substantive and cannot be admitted to show contributory negligence); Potts v. Benjamin, 882 F.2d 1320 (8th Cir. 1989) (state law precluding evidence of failure to use seat belt is substantive and must be applied by federal court in diversity case); Morton v. Brockman, 184 F.R.D. 211 (D. Me. 1999) (state statute excluding evidence of failure to wear seat belt is substantive and must be applied in federal diversity action); *see also* Fitzgerald, P.P.A. v. Expressway Sewerage Constr., Inc., 71 F.3d 177 (1st Cir. 1999) (state law called the "collateral source rule" provided that compensation received from a third party, such as plaintiff's insurance company, will not diminish the plaintiff's recovery from a tortfeasor; this gave rise to a corresponding state rule that evidence of collateral source payments are inadmissible for purpose of reducing damages; held, state law controlled the admissibility of evidence for the purposes of reducing damages, but Federal Rules of Evidence controlled whether evidence was unduly prejudicial when admitted for other purposes).

422. *See* section E, *Illustration 5-10, supra.*

423. *See, e.g.,* Praxair, Inc. v. Slifka, 61 F. Supp. 2d 753 (N.D. Ill. 1999) (following earlier decisions holding the Illinois statute to be "substantive" for *Erie* purposes); Brach & Broch Confections, Inc. v. Redmond, 988 F. Supp. 1106 (N.D. Ill. 1997) (*Erie* requires dismissal under statute because of prior pending action in California state court, subsequently removed to California federal court on basis of diversity); Northbrook Property & Cas. Ins. Co. v. Allendale Mut. Ins. Co., 887 F. Supp. 173 (N.D. Ill. 1995) (statute must be applied in diversity cases and requires dismissal in favor of prior pending Canadian action); *cf.* Locke v. Bonello, 965 F.2d 534, 538 n.3 (7th Cir. 1992) (suggesting that the statute must be applied in federal courts to require dismissal in favor of prior pending actions in Illinois courts).

the plaintiff might encounter in the state court the very bias in fact-finding that the diversity jurisdiction is designed to eliminate. The cases applying the Illinois prior pending action statute do not undermine the diversity policy as seriously as refusal of a remedy in *Illustration 5-10*, however, because even if a federal court refuses to dismiss a case in favor a prior pending state action, a parallel action will still be pending in state court in which state fact-finding bias could potentially operate against the noncitizen. Furthermore, if the state action reaches judgment before the federal action, the state judgment will be res judicata.[424]

However, the application of the state statute is also not as clearly demanded under *Erie* as the state statute in the *Woods* case, also discussed in section E(1), above. In *Woods*, the Supreme Court held that *Erie* required application of state "door-closing" statutes in federal diversity actions. However, in the door-closing situation, dismissal of the federal diversity action will not result in a state action in the same state because the doors of the state courts are also closed to the action. Because the diversity jurisdiction is designed to provide an alternative, unbiased tribunal to a state court, the absence of the possibility of a state action eliminates any danger that subject-matter jurisdiction policies will be undermined. There can be no room for bias to operate in state court if the state courts are closed to the action.

Thus, the Illinois prior-pending action statute represents an intermediate situation, in which, no matter what result the federal court reaches, important federal policies will be undermined. If the federal court refuses to dismiss under the state statute, plaintiffs will surely forum shop for a federal court to obtain whatever procedural advantages the second action will afford them, and defendants will be deprived of the valuable benefit, which would be available in an Illinois state court, of avoiding duplicative litigation. Retention of the case will thus undermine the *Erie* policies. On the other hand, dismissal of diversity actions will deprive noncitizens of the benefit of a presumptively unbiased tribunal in those cases in which the federal court would reach judgment first and thus control the outcome of both actions through the doctrine of res judicata.[425] On balance, the courts should probably resolve the issue in favor of retention rather than dismissal. *Erie* should be viewed as a subordinate policy to subject-matter jurisdiction policies. Therefore, when *Erie* and subject-matter jurisdiction policies cannot both be vindicated in an action, subject-matter policies should control. The question in this situation is a close one, however, and the Illinois federal courts cannot be seriously faulted for reaching the opposite result.

Numerous other problems exist with the administration of the *Erie* doctrine in the lower federal courts. A few courts do not understand *Hanna's* message that the validity and applicability of Federal Rules of Civil Procedure do not depend on whether the general *Erie* policies of forum shopping and inequitable administration of the laws would be violated.[426] Such decisions are

---

424. *See* Chapter 13(F)(1) ("Enforcement of State Judgments") *infra*.

425. *See* Chapter 13(F)(2) ("Enforcement of Federal Judgments") *infra*.

426. *See, e.g.,* Wester v. Crown Controls Corp., 974 F. Supp. 1284 (D. Ariz. 1996) (Federal Rule 26(a) applicable, constitutional, and valid under the Rules Enabling Act, but state rule should be applied because otherwise forum shopping and discrimination against citizens of the forum state would result).

inexcusable. However, other problems of administering the *Erie* doctrine are the byproduct of the Supreme Court's failure to clarify the operation of the doctrine. For example, forum shopping for a federal diversity court can be encouraged by refusals to apply state laws that will not necessarily produce an ultimate outcome difference on the merits, as opposed to some "lesser" outcome difference. The failure of the Supreme Court to clarify whether such "lesser" outcome differences count under *Erie* has led the federal courts to different results. In the Illinois cases discussed above, retention of federal diversity actions rather than dismissal on prior pending action grounds will not necessarily produce an ultimate difference on the merits of the case, but the Illinois federal courts have applied the *Erie* doctrine to require dismissal anyway.

Other courts seem to require an ultimate difference on the merits before a state law may be classified as "substantive" for *Erie* purposes, even though disregard of the law will clearly cause forum shopping or inequitable administration of the law. Thus, in *McKenzie v. Hawaii Permanente Medical Group, Inc.*,[427] the court considered whether plaintiffs were required to proceed through a medical claim conciliation requirement before commencing a federal diversity action, as they would have to do before commencing a state action on the claim. The court held that the state requirement was "procedural" for *Erie* purposes and not obligatory in federal court, despite the fact that plaintiffs will clearly go to federal court to avoid the medical conciliation procedure when they wish, for any reason, to commence an action immediately. The court stated:

> [T]he [medical claim conciliation] requirement is procedural and not substantive, because it does not "materially [affect] the character or result of a litigation.". . . [T]he requirement "does not affect the merits of the parties' positions under state law, and . . . imposes no additional method for parties in state court to have their cases conclusively adjudicated."[428]

Other issues concerning the administration and application of the *Erie* doctrine in the lower federal courts will be discussed in later chapters as they become pertinent to the topics there examined.

SECTION H. DETERMINATION OF STATE LAW

Under the *Swift* doctrine, federal courts had to follow state-court decisions interpreting state constitutions and statutes and articulating state rules of decision on "local" matters. Under *Erie*, federal courts are obligated to follow state decisions on all matters of state law, when state law provides the rule of decision. Because of this broadened obligation, it is important to understand how the federal courts are to determine state law.

Early in the history of the *Erie* doctrine, the federal courts appeared to be obligated to follow even the decisions of lower state courts in the absence of other evidence of what state common law would be—even though the lower state

---

427. 29 F. Supp. 2d 1174 (D. Haw. 1998).

428. *Id.* at 1177, *quoting* Hum v. Dericks, 162 F.R.D. 628 (D. Haw. 1995).

court decisions would not have been binding on another court of the same state in a similar case.[429] The Supreme Court has since retreated from this inflexible doctrine.[430] As Professors Wright, Miller, and Cooper have observed, this retreat was essential if the *Erie* doctrine was not to substitute one kind of forum shopping for another. State precedents that might not be followed by the state's highest court would, under the earlier practice, be binding in federal court, tempting litigants who would be favored by the precedents to pick a federal forum. The federal courts, in turn, would be unable to assure that the outcome in federal diversity actions would be the same as in the state courts.[431]

Under the accepted practice today, a federal court determining state law can use any available sources to predict how the state's highest court would decide a case.[432] Such sources include, but are not limited to, lower state-court decisions, which constitute persuasive, but not binding, authority in federal diversity actions. Similarly, if no state judicial precedents exist with which to predict how the state's highest court will decide a case, the federal courts can look to persuasive authorities from other states on the same issue, scholarly works, and other similar sources, just as lawyers within the state would do. Old decisions of the state's highest court are binding in diversity actions if no evidence exists that they have been undermined by later cases. When confronted with such precedents, the federal courts will examine them to determine whether "clear evidence" exists that they would no longer be followed. In the absence of such evidence, however, the old precedents will be followed.[433]

---

429. *See, e.g.,* Fidelity Union Trust Co. v. Field, 311 U.S. 169, 61 S. Ct. 176, 85 L. Ed. 109 (1940).

430. *See* Commissioner v. Estate of Bosch, 387 U.S. 456, 87 S. Ct. 1776, 18 L. Ed. 2d 886 (1967); Bernhardt v. Polygraphic Co. of Am., 350 U.S. 198, 76 S. Ct. 273, 100 L. Ed. 199 (1956); King v. Order of United Commercial Travelers of Am., 333 U.S. 153, 68 S. Ct. 488, 92 L. Ed. 608 (1948); Weber v. GAF Corp., 15 F.3d 35, 37 (3d Cir. 1994) (refusing to rely on lower state court decision ont he grounds that the plain language of the law dictated a contrary result and it was not persuaded by the lower state decision; ERWIN CHEMERINSKY, FEDERAL JURISDICTION § 5.3.5, at 323-25 (3d ed. 1999); *but cf.* Kurczi v. Eli Lilly & Co., 113 F.3d 1426 (6th Cir. 1997) (decision of state intermediate court of appeals constitutes datum from which state law can be determined and is not to be disregarded by federal court in the absence of other persuasive evidence that the state's highest court would decide otherwise). It has been held that if a federal court of appeals has rendered a decision on a state issue, but the state's highest court has not, a district court should follow the court of appeals decision rather than the decision of a state intermediate court of appeals. *See* FDIC v. Abraham, 137 F.3d 264 (5th Cir. 1998) (*Erie* does not require abandonment of a federal court of appeals decision in deference to a subsequent holding by a state intermediate court of appeals); Perez v. Brown & Williamson Tobacco Corp., 967 F. Supp. 920 (S.D. Tex. 1997) (district court must follow federal court of appeals decision). For an excellent article discussing the problems with the attempts by the lower federal courts to "predict" what rule the highest court of a state would adopt if a question were before it, see Bradford R. Clark, *Ascertaining the Laws of the Several States: Positivism and Judicial Federalism After* Erie, 145 U. PA. L. REV. 1459 (1997); *see also* Michael C. Dorf, *Prediction and the Rule of Law*, 42 UCLA L. REV. 651, 695-715 (1995) (discussing, *inter alia,* the "radical realist roots" of *Erie* as a source of the "prediction model" of determining state law in diversity cases).

431. *See* 19 CHARLES A. WRIGHT ET AL., FEDERAL PRACTICE AND PROCEDURE: JURISDICTION AND RELATED MATTERS (ERIE DOCTRINE) § 4507, at 140-41 (2d ed. 1996) (footnotes omitted); *see also* ERWIN CHEMERINSKY, FEDERAL JURISDICTION § 5.3.5, at 325 (3d ed. 1999).

432. *See* ERWIN CHEMERINSKY, FEDERAL JURISDICTION § 5.3.5, at 325 (3d ed. 1999).

433. *See, e.g.,* Gilstrap v. Amtrak, 998 F.2d 559 (8th Cir. 1993); *see also* Data Specialties, Inc. v. Transcontinental Ins. Co., 125 F.3d 909 (5th Cir. 1997) (relying on dicta in Texas Supreme Court and Court of Appeals decisions, decisions from other states, and commentary in treatises and law reviews).

Illustration 5-22. *A*, a citizen of State *X*, was travelling on a train operated by *B Railroad*, a corporation incorporated with its principal place of business in State *Y*. *A* was assaulted by *C*, an employee of *B*, who was not acting within the scope of *C's* employment by *B* at the time of the assault. *A* sues *B* and *C* in a U.S. District Court for State *X*. *C* defaults, and a judgment is rendered against *C*. *B* defends on the ground that it is not liable for the intentional torts of an employee who is not acting within the scope of employment when the assault is committed. The U.S. District Court determines that under the *Klaxon* doctrine, State *X* would apply the substantive law of State *Y* to resolve the dispute. Under the State *Y* precedents, a sixty-year-old decision holds that because of the special relationship between a common carrier, such as *B*, and its passengers, carriers are liable for the intentional torts of their employees committed against passengers, even if the employees are not acting within the scope of their employment. *B* offers several more recent State *Y* precedents indicating that employers are not liable for the intentional torts of their employees acting outside the course of their employment. However, these precedents do not involve torts committed by the employees of common carriers against passengers of the carriers. The federal court should follow the sixty-year-old decision under these circumstances, unless there is other evidence that the State *Y* Supreme Court would no longer follow the decision. The old decision was a case specially predicated on the relationship between common carriers and their passengers. The newer decisions do not involve common carrier cases. Therefore, the newer decisions are not on point and do not indicate that the old case is obsolete.[434]

Illustration 5-23. *A*, a citizen of State *X*, sues *B*, a citizen of State *Y*, in a U.S. District Court in State *Y*. *A* seeks $500,000 for breach of contract. The district court grants a motion to dismiss *A's* complaint on the ground that contracts of the kind in question are invalid in State *Y*. This decision is based on a decision of the State *Y* Supreme Court in existence at the time the district court rules on the motion. *A* appeals to the court of appeals. While the case is on appeal, the State *Y* Supreme court overrules the decision relied on by the district court and holds contracts of the kind between *A* and *B* valid and enforceable in State *Y*. The court of appeals must apply the later State *Y* Supreme Court decision because it represents the most accurate picture of State *Y* law at the time the court of appeals must make its decision.[435]

* * * * *

---

434. *See* Gilstrap v. Amtrak, 998 F.2d 559 (8th Cir. 1993)

435. *See* Vandenbark v. Owens-Illinois Glass Co., 311 U.S. 538, 61 S. Ct. 347, 85 L. Ed. 327 (1941). *But cf.* Cincinnati Ins. Co. v. Flanders Elec. Motor Serv., Inc., 131 F.3d 625 (7th Cir. 1997) (appellant moved to stay proceedings before court of appeals until state supreme court decided a case involving the identical issue in the federal action; court of appeals denied stay and affirmed district court; a year and a half later, state supreme court decision indicated that court of appeal's decision of state issue was incorrect; appellant's motion for relief under Federal Rule 60(b) denied by district court; court of appeals affirms denial on the ground that use of Rule 60(b) to obtain relief from erroneous interpretations of state law in diversity cases would unduly undermine the principle of finality in litigation); *see also* Willis v. Roche Biomedical Labs., Inc., 21 F.3d 1368, 1372-75 (5th Cir. 1994), *withdrawn after decision of the highest state court and new opinion substituted*, 61 F.3d 313 (5th Cir. 1995) (relying on intermediate state court of appeals decisions even though state's highest court had granted review and correcting decision after highest court ruled).

Ordinarily, federal courts must decide questions of state law themselves, without seeking answers directly from the state courts. However, some states have adopted a procedure called *certification*, whereby federal courts may obtain answers to unsettled questions of state law from the state's highest court. The U.S. Supreme Court has approved of the use of these certification procedures by the federal courts in diversity cases when the procedures exist.[436] However, certification is discretionary with the federal court. The possibility that certification will produce significant delay, the difficulty of certifying a question to the state court in a manner that will result in an authoritative answer, the sensitivity or importance of the question to the state, and the danger of abdicating the federal judicial function all are taken into account in determining whether to certify.[437] When a question is certified to the highest court of a state, the proceedings after certification are governed by the statutes and rules of the state court to which the certification is made.[438]

An additional device for obtaining answers to unsettled state-law questions is the doctrine of *abstention*. In reality, several different doctrines of abstention exist, all of which are complicated subjects reserved for treatment in treatises on Federal Courts.[439] For present purposes, it is only relevant to determine whether a federal court sitting in diversity may abstain from making a decision to obtain an answer to an unsettled question of law from a state court. If abstention is proper in these circumstances, the federal court would postpone decision of the diversity action until such time as the parties had commenced and

---

436. *See* Lehman Bros. v. Schein, 416 U.S. 386, 94 S. Ct. 1741, 40 L. Ed. 2d 215 (1974); *see also* UNIF. CERTIFICATION OF QUESTIONS OF LAW ACT (1995), 12 U.L.A. 64 (1996). For a discussion of certification as a means of making the determination of state law required by *Erie*, see Bradford R. Clark, *Ascertaining the Laws of the Several States: Positivism and Judicial Federalism After* Erie, 145 U. PA. L. REV. 1459, 1544-63 (1997); Larry M. Roth, *Certified Questions From the Federal Courts: Review and Re-Proposal*, 34 U. MIAMI L. REV. 1 (1979); *see also* Stanton S. Kaplan, *Certification of Questions From Federal Appellate Courts to the Florida Supreme Court and Its Impact on the Abstention Doctrine*, 16 U. MIAMI L. REV. 413 (1962); Vincent L. McKuzick, *Certification: A Procedure for Cooperation Between State and Federal Courts*, 16 ME. L. REV. 33 (1964).

437. *See* City of Houston v. Hill, 482 U.S. 451, 470-71, 107 S.Ct. 2502, 2514-15, 96 L. Ed. 2d 398, 417-18 (1987); Florida *ex rel.* Shevin v. Exxon Corp., 526 F.2d 266, 274-75 (5th Cir.), *cert. denied*, 429 U.S. 829, 97 S. Ct. 88, 50 L. Ed. 2d 92 (1976); Barnes v. Atlantic & Pac. Life Ins. Co. of Am., 514 F.2d 704, 705 n.4 (5th Cir. 1975); 17A CHARLES A. WRIGHT ET AL., FEDERAL PRACTICE AND PROCEDURE: JURISDICTION AND RELATED MATTERS § 4248, at 166 (2d ed. 1988); *cf.* Arizonans for Official English v. Arizona, 520 U.S. 43, 117 S. Ct. 1055, 137 L. Ed. 2d 170 (1997) (lower federal courts should have used Arizona's certification procedure to obtain a state-court interpretation of a novel state constitutional question in order possibly to avoid a federal constitutional question concerning the validity of the state constitutional provision). For a questionable use of the certification procedure, see Prodigy Ctrs./Atlanta No. 1 L.P. v. T-C Assocs., Ltd., 127 F.3d 1021 (11th Cir. 1997), in which the court of appeals certified a question of Georgia law to the Georgia Supreme Court concerning whether a partnership interest in a limited partnership constituted a "chose in action." The court of appeals considered Georgia law ambiguous on the issue because of uncertainty about whether this question had been before the Georgia Supreme Court in a prior case in which the latter court had relied on Georgia chose in action law in considering whether a judgement lien attached to a partnership interest sold to a good faith purchaser. However, the court of appeals did not consider factors such as how important the question was in Georgia law in determining whether to certify.

438. *See, e.g.*, NEB. REV. STAT. § 24-224 (1995) (providing for an expedited briefing and hearing procedure so that the certified question can be answered promptly).

439. *See, e.g.*, ERWIN CHEMERINSKY, FEDERAL JURISDICTION §§ 12.1-14.4 (3d ed. 1999); CHARLES A. WRIGHT, THE LAW OF FEDERAL COURTS § 52 (5th ed. 1994).

completed state litigation to obtain an answer to the state-law question. However, the Supreme Court disapproved of abstention for these purposes in *Meredith v. City of Winter Haven*,[440] a case which the Court has subsequently cited with approval.[441] Thus, while *certification* may be available in an ordinary diversity action to obtain an answer to an unsettled issue of state law, *abstention* is improper in such a case in the absence of special factors making one of the other (nondiversity) abstention doctrines proper.[442]

Traditionally, determinations of issues of state law by U.S. District Courts have been paid great deference when diversity cases are appealed to the U.S. Courts of Appeals.[443] However, in *Salve Regina College v. Russell*,[444] the Supreme Court held, contrary to a majority of the courts of appeals, that litigants in diversity actions are entitled to plenary appellate review of matters of state law. In *Salve Regina College*, the plaintiff was asked to withdraw from a nursing program because she was excessively obese. After completing her education at another institution, she filed a federal diversity action against the college from which she was forced to withdraw, asserting claims for intentional infliction of emotional distress, invasion of privacy, and breach of contract. After the close of the plaintiff's case, the district court directed a verdict against the plaintiff on all claims except the breach of contract claim. The refusal to direct a verdict on the latter claim was based on the district court's "intuition" that the Rhode Island Supreme Court would recognize the doctrine of substantial performance in the academic context, even though it had theretofore been limited to commercial contexts. The jury returned a verdict for the plaintiff on the breach of contract claim, and the defendant appealed. In affirming, the court of appeals deferred to the district court's determination of state law rather than exercising an independent judgment about the content of that law. The Supreme Court granted certiorari and reversed.

The Court held that "[n]othing about the exercise of diversity jurisdiction . . . warrants the departure from a rule of independent appellate review."[445] The Court held that deferential appellate review was inconsistent with the aims of the *Erie* doctrine, in that it invited divergent development of state law among the federal courts within a single state and created a dual system of enforcement of state-created rights in which the substantive rule applied to a dispute might depend upon the choice of a federal or state court.[446]

Salve Regina College presented a strong case for requiring independent appellate review. The district court's determination that state law was not

---

440. 320 U.S. 228, 64 S. Ct. 7, 88 L. Ed. 9 (1943).

441. *See* Colorado River Water Conservation Dist. v. United States, 424 U.S. 800, 816, 96 S. Ct. 1236, 1245-46, 47 L. Ed. 2d 483, 497 (1976).

442. *See* 17A CHARLES A. WRIGHT ET AL., FEDERAL PRACTICE AND PROCEDURE: JURISDICTION AND RELATED MATTERS (FEDERAL AND STATE COURTS) § 4246, at 106-07 (2d ed. 1988).

443. *See* 19 CHARLES A. WRIGHT ET AL., FEDERAL PRACTICE AND PROCEDURE: JURISDICTION AND RELATED MATTERS (ERIE DOCTRINE) § 4507, at 211 (2d ed. 1996).

444. 499 U.S. 225, 111 S. Ct. 1217, 113 L. Ed. 2d 190 (1991). *See generally* Ralph U. Whitten, *Developments in the* Erie *Doctrine: 1991*, 40 AM. J. COMP. L. 967, 973-75 (1992).

445. 499 U.S. at 233-34, 111 S. Ct. at 1222, 113 L. Ed. 2d at 199.

446. *See id.* at 234, 111 S. Ct. at 1222, 113 L. Ed. 2d at 200.

grounded in existing state supreme court decisions or other authoritative sources, but was based on the district judge's lengthy experience as a state trial judge and his "feel" for what the state supreme court would do based on that experience. A majority of the Supreme Court seemed to find this intuitive approach to state law distasteful.[447] However, the Court might better have established a requirement of nondeferential appellate review only for cases in which the district court's determination of state law was based on no traditional, preexisting legal sources, but merely, as in *Salve Regina College*, on raw intuition. Such cases present a peculiar danger of arbitrariness by the district courts, justifying a heightened standard of appellate review. In other cases, requiring the parsing of traditional legal materials, a deferential standard of appellate review might have been approved based on the presumptively greater familiarity of the district judge with state law. It is possible to reason otherwise, as did the dissenters in *Salve Regina College*, who concluded that in the face of unsettled state law, the "insights" of an experienced district judge might be deemed particularly valuable in predicting how the state supreme court would resolve the issue in question.[448] Nevertheless, it seems more appropriate to recognize that traditional legal authorities, where they exist, confine the ability of district judges acting in good faith to depart from the likely outcome that would be reached by the state courts. A more deferential standard of review that focuses on the reasonableness of the district court's interpretation of existing authorities seems appropriate in cases where authority exists. When the district court does not rely on preexisting authority, but on raw intuition, heightened appellate scrutiny is called for to assure that the result is based on a good faith attempt to interpret state law, rather than the individual policy predilections of the district judge.[449]

An interesting question that has arisen in recent years is what effect a federal court within one federal circuit should give to a precedent from a federal

---

447. [T]he proposition that a district judge is better able to "intuit" the answer to an unsettled question of state law is foreclosed by our holding in *Erie* doctrine is that the bases of state law are presumed to be communicable by the parties to a federal judge no less than to a state judge. . . . Similarly, the bases of state law are as equally communicable to the appellate judges as they are to the district judge. To the extent that the available state law on a controlling issue is so unsettled as to admit of no reasoned divination, we can see no sense in which a district judge's prior exposure or nonexposure to the state judiciary can be said to facilitate the rule of reason.

Id. at 238-39, 111 S. Ct. at 1225, 113 L. Ed. 2d at 202-03.

448. *See id.* at 240-43, 111 S. Ct. at 1225-27, 113 L. Ed. at 204 (Rehnquist, C.J., with whom White, J., and Stevens, J., join, dissenting).

449. It has been argued that predictive precedents by the courts of appeals on state issues should be presumptively binding on the district courts, but that a litigant should be able to overcome such precedents with substantial evidence of a change in state law. *See* Jed I. Bergman, Note, *Putting Precedent in Its Place: Stare Decisis and Federal Predictions of State Law*, 96 COLUM. L. REV. 969 (1996). This approach seems consistent with the dual obligations of the district courts to *Erie* and court of appeals precedents. However, the argument that district courts are under *no* statutory or constitutional obligation to follow "outrageously wrong" court of appeals decisions and treat court of appeals decisions as, at most, persuasive authority, goes too far. *See* Nififoros Mathews, *Circuit Court* Erie*-Errors and the District Court's Dilemma: From* Roto-Lith *and the Mirror Image Rule to* Octagon Gas *and Asset Securitization*, 17 CARDOZO L. REV. 739 (1996). The latter argument gives too little weight to the position and function of the courts of appeals and the district courts in the federal hierarchy. Indeed, it could be equally applied to U.S. Supreme Court decisions on matters of state law that are "outrageously wrong."

court of appeals of another circuit on a question of state law arising within the latter circuit. This issue was presented for decision in *Factors Etc., Inc. v. Pro Arts, Inc.*[450] *Factors* was a diversity action in a New York federal district court in which Factors sought to prevent Pro Arts and others from making any use of Elvis Presley's name or likeness. Factors contended that it had the exclusive right to use Presley's name and likeness under a grant of authority from Boxcar Enterprises, a Tennessee corporation formed by Presley before his death, to which Presley had assigned the exclusive ownership rights to his persona. Pro Arts argued that a decision of the Sixth Circuit Court of Appeals holding that Presley's right of publicity was not descendible was binding on the New York federal court. This argument was rejected by the district court. The case was ultimately appealed to the U.S. Court of Appeals for the Second Circuit. The issue posed by the Second Circuit for decision was whether the federal courts of one circuit are bound to follow the decisions of the federal courts of appeals of another circuit on a question of state law arising from a state within the latter circuit.

The Second Circuit first reasoned that under the *Erie-Klaxon* doctrine, the courts of New York would apply the law of Tennessee to determine whether Presley's right of publicity was descendible. Then the court reasoned that although the courts of appeals are not absolutely bound to follow the decisions of the courts of appeals of other circuits on matters of state law within the other circuit, they should nevertheless do so in the absence of a clear basis in the law of the pertinent state for predicting that the relevant state courts would reach a different result. The court stated that this approach should be followed in order to prevent diversity actions from disrupting the orderly development of state law. The court's fear was that such disruption would be more likely if there existed divergent federal decisions on the same issue of state law in different circuits.[451]

As the dissent pointed out, however, it seems curious to follow the Sixth Circuit's view of Tennessee law when, as in *Factors*, that view is based on raw speculation, or, perhaps more accurately, was based on the Sixth Circuit's view of what Tennessee law *should* be. Likewise, there is not as much reason for deferring to a court of appeals' view of state law as there is for deferring to the opinion of a district court sitting in the state whose law is at issue, especially where the court of appeals' view is at odds with the view of the district court, as it was in *Factors*.[452] Furthermore, after the *Salve Regina College* decision, discussed above, the rule announced in *Factors* seems even more suspect. If a court of appeals cannot defer to the decisions of the U.S. District Courts on matters of state law, it is difficult to see the justification for allowing them to defer to the judgments of other courts of appeals.[453]

---

450. 652 F.2d 278 (2d Cir. 1981), *cert. denied*, 456 U.S. 927, 102 S. Ct. 1973, 72 L. Ed. 2d 442 (1982); *see* James Balog, Note, Factors etc., Inc. v. Pro Arts, Inc.: *Deference to Circuit Court Rulings on State Law*, 15 J. MARSHALL L. REV. 499 (1982); Note, Factors etc. v. Pro Arts, Inc., 16 SUFFOLK U. L. REV. 787 (1982).

451. *See* 652 F.2d at 282-83.

452. *See* 652 F.2d at 284-85 (Mansfield, J., dissenting); *see also* Northwest Forest Resource Council v. Dombeck, 107 F.3d 897 (D.C. Cir. 1997) (error to give stare decisis effect to a decision of a district court in another circuit on an issue of *federal law*).

453. *Cf.* State v. Greger, 1997 S.D. 14, 559 N.W.2d 854 (state's highest court not bound by decision of federal court of appeals covering the state on an issue of *federal law*).

It has also been suggested that "the critical question that should be asked in a case like *Factors* "is what weight New York's highest court would have given to the Sixth Circuit's construction of Tennessee common law."[454] This view assumes that the *Erie-Klaxon* doctrine requires federal courts to adhere not only to the conflict-of-laws rules or approach of the state in which they are sitting, but also to parrot the forum's understanding of the content of the law of the other state. This approach carries *Klaxon* too far. It is one thing to hold that federal courts must defer to the courts of the states in which they sit to determine whether the forum state's law or some other state's law is applicable to the dispute. It is quite another to hold that litigants in federal courts do not even have the right to an independent judgment about the content of another state's law. The courts of the state in which a federal court is sitting are in no better position to determine the content of another state's law than are the federal courts. The *Klaxon* decision did not hold that federal courts must duplicate the view of the forum state about the content of the law of another state, and there is no apparent reason to impose such a requirement on the speculation that doing so will prevent forum shopping for a federal court. Therefore, once it has been determined that the forum state has effectively disclaimed any sovereign interest in applying its own substantive law to the dispute, the federal courts should feel free to determine for themselves the content of the relevant state's law, including the proper weight to give different kinds of precedents interpreting state law.

SECTION I. FEDERAL COMMON LAW

Well, one thing is for sure. The Court in *Erie* definitely decided that there is no substantive federal common law, right? Wrong. On the same day it decided *Erie*, the Court held in another case that "federal common law" governed the question whether the water of an interstate stream must be apportioned between two states.[455] This section is devoted to an examination of how this "new federal common law" works.[456] However, it is important to remember that the federal common law discussed in this section differs from the federal common law discussed in section E, above. Section E discussed the circumstances in which it is justifiable under the Rules of Decision Act for the federal courts to apply

---

454. 19 CHARLES A. WRIGHT ET AL., FEDERAL PRACTICE AND PROCEDURE: JURISDICTION AND RELATED MATTERS (ERIE DOCTRINE) § 4507, at 220 (2d ed. 1996).

455. *See* Hinderlider v. La Plata River & Cherry Creek Ditch Co., 304 U.S. 92, 58 S. Ct. 803, 82 L. Ed. 1202 (1938).

456. *See* Henry J. Friendly, *In Praise of* Erie—*And of the New Federal Common Law*, 39 N.Y.U. L. REV. 383 (1964). Useful discussions of federal common law include Bradford R. Clark, *Federal Common Law: A Structural Reinterpretation*, 144 U. PA. L. REV. 1245 (1996); Martha Field, *Sources of Law: The Scope of Federal Common Law*, 99 HARV. L. REV. 881 (1986); Stewart Jay, *Origins of Federal Common Law* (pts. 1 & 2), 133 U. PA. L. REV. 1003, 1231 (1985); Thomas W. Merrill, *The Common Law Powers of Federal Courts*, 52 U. CHI. L. REV. 1 (1985); Martin H. Redish, *Federal Common Law, Political Legitimacy, and the Interpretive Process: An "Institutionalist" Perspective*, 83 NW. U. L. REV. 761 (1989); *see also* Martin H. Redish, *Federal Common Law and American Political Theory: A Response to Professor Weinberg*, 83 NW. U. L. REV. 853 (1989); Louise Weinberg, *Federal Common Law*, 83 NW. U. L. REV. 853 (1989); Louise Weinberg, *The Curious Nation That the Rule of Decision Act Blocks Supreme Federal Common Law*, 83 NW. U. L. REV. 860 (1989).

federal common-law rules of practice and procedure. This section discusses when it is appropriate for the federal courts to create and apply substantive federal common-law rules. As section E demonstrated, even the power to apply federal common law rules of procedure is restricted under the *Erie* doctrine. Because of both separation of powers and federalism restrictions, the justifiability of federal courts creating substantive federal common-law rules is even more controversial.

In addition to distinguishing federal substantive common law from the federal procedural common law discussed in section E, two features of the "new federal common law" should be distinguished from the general law applied by the Supreme Court in *Swift v. Tyson*.[457] First, if the plaintiff possesses a claim for relief under the "new federal common law," that claim is one arising under federal law for purposes of the federal-question jurisdiction.[458] Recall from the discussion of the *Swift* doctrine in section C, however, that the general commercial law enforced in that case was not "federal" law that would provide a basis for federal-question jurisdiction.[459] Second, when it is created, the "new" substantive federal common law controls the disputes it covers in both federal and state courts.[460] Under the *Swift* doctrine, federal and state courts were each entitled to their own view of the content of the general commercial law. In addition, the states had the right to localize the rule of decision in the general commercial law area and to control decisions in both state and federal courts with the local rule.[461]

1. A Conceptual Framework for Evaluating Federal Common-Law Decisions

The Rules of Decision Act provides that state law shall be the rule of decision except where the Constitution, treaties, or Acts of Congress otherwise require or provide.[462] The Act does not mention "federal common law." Under a literal interpretation of the provision, therefore, it would seem inappropriate for

---

457. *See* section C ("The Doctrine of *Swift v. Tyson*") *supra*.

458. *See* Illinois v. City of Milwaukee, 406 U.S. 91, 92 S. Ct. 1385, 31 L. Ed. 2d 712 (1972).

459. Derivation of subject-matter jurisdiction from general common-law rules would probably have been considered a separation-of-powers violation in its own right under the *Swift* doctrine. For there existed at that time a concept that distinguished between the common law as a source of judicial power and the common law as a means of exercising judicial power conferred by other sources. The idea was that the courts had "jurisdiction of the common law," but could not obtain "jurisdiction from the common law." *See* RANDALL BRIDWELL & RALPH U. WHITTEN, THE CONSTITUTION AND THE COMMON LAW: THE DECLINE OF THE DOCTRINES OF SEPARATION OF POWERS AND FEDERALISM 31-33, 46 (1977). Modern commentators have had difficulty understanding this phraseology. *See, e.g.*, Note, Swift v. Tyson *Exhumed*, 79 YALE L.J. 284, 297-98 (1969).

460. *See, e.g.*, Hinderlider v. La Plata River & Cherry Creek Ditch Co., 304 U.S. 92, 58 S. Ct. 803, 82 L. Ed. 1202 (1938); *see also* Dice v. Akron, Canton & Youngstown R.R. Co., 342 U.S. 359, 72 S. Ct. 312, 96 L. Ed. 398 (1952); Brown v. Western Ry., 338 U.S. 294, 70 S. Ct. 105, 94 L. Ed. 100 (1949).

461. *See* section C ("The Doctrine of *Swift v. Tyson*") *supra*.

462. 28 U.S.C. § 1652.

the federal courts to create "federal common law."[463] As noted in section A, however, it is inevitable that judges will engage in lawmaking when they articulate the rules of decision applicable to a dispute before them—even when the judges are interpreting a statutory or constitutional provision. It is widely believed today that no bright line exists between statutory and constitutional interpretation on the one hand and common-law decision making on the other. Thus, "[a]s specific evidence of legislative purpose to the issue at hand attenuates, interpretation shades into judicial lawmaking on a spectrum."[464]

Nevertheless, from the terms of the Rules of Decision Act and from the general separation-of-powers obligation of the judges to make law only "interstitially," the creation of federal common law decreases in justifiability as the judges move away from the process of interpreting the will of Congress or the framers and ratifiers of the Constitution toward the promulgation of rules of decision that have only the barest support in any articulated, nonjudicially created policy. The following discussion illustrates the general nature of the problems involved.

(a) "Interpretation"

At the most basic level, judges perform activities that are classified under the labels "statutory interpretation" or "statutory construction." However, different sorts of interpretive activity raise different separation of powers issues. Suppose, first, that the problem confronting a federal court is one of determining the meaning of a particular word or words in a statute or constitutional provision. In other words, the court is attempting in good faith to determine what Congress or the Framers of the Constitution meant when they used a word or phrase and will follow the communicated meaning once it has been determined. This kind of problem has been traditionally defined as one of statutory or constitutional interpretation. The court simply is trying to understand a formal communication made to it by a superior lawmaking institution. The court may do a poor job of determining meaning, because the judges are stupid, lazy, or careless, or because the form of expression chosen by Congress or the Framers was so poor that the meaning is indecipherable. Nevertheless, the performance of the task of interpretation is appropriate for the judges and raises no separation-of-powers problems unless the judges insincerely read their own personal predilections into the words of the statute instead of trying to determine the meaning communicated by the lawmakers.

One step removed from the task of determining statutory meaning is the more creative task of filling in gaps left in a statute or constitutional provision when the court believes Congress or the framers meant a certain rule of decision

---

463. *See* ERWIN CHEMERINSKY, FEDERAL JURISDICTION § 6.1, at 350 (3d ed. 1999); MARTIN A. REDISH, FEDERAL JURISDICTION: TENSIONS IN THE ALLOCATION OF JUDICIAL POWER 127 (2d ed. 1990). *But see* Louise Weinberg, *The Curious Notion That the Rules of Decision Act Blocks Supreme Federal Common Law*, 83 NW. U. L. REV. 860 (1989).

464. RICHARD H. FALLON ET AL., HART & WECHSLER'S THE FEDERAL COURTS AND THE FEDERAL SYSTEM 755 (4th ed. 1996).

to be included within a provision but, for some reason, did not put the rule of decision explicitly into the statutory or constitutional text. This task raises no serious separation-of-powers problems as long as it is done sincerely–*i.e.*, if the court simply is attempting to discern and enforce the will of Congress or the framers, not making up law according to its own policy preferences–and, in the case of statutory gaps, so long also as the gaps left by Congress are not so broad as to involve an unconstitutional delegation of legislative power to the courts. Separation-of-powers difficulties are created when Congress delegates lawmaking authority to the courts in a wholesale manner, not because the courts are usurping functions given to Congress that Congress wishes to retain, but because Congress itself is attempting to give away more of its legislative authority than the Constitution permits.

(b) "Supplementation"

More serious separation-of-powers difficulties exist in what might be called statutory or constitutional "supplementation" cases. Such cases exist when the courts create rules of decision not explicitly found in statutory or constitutional provisions and which the courts cannot sincerely say that Congress or the framers meant, though inadvertently failed, to create explicitly. Sometimes, the courts will create rules of decision in such cases to prevent unforeseen circumstances from undermining the principal purposes of a statute or constitutional provision.[465] This situation is the most justifiable of the supplementation cases, but separation-of-powers dangers exist here nevertheless.

A court appropriately may create supplementary rules of decision that will prevent the main objects of Congress or the framers from being defeated, on the reasonable assumption that those lawmaking bodies would have approved of the creation of the supplementary law so that their legislative acts would not be exercises in futility. However, the courts may go only so far as they think the superior lawmaking institutions would have gone in preserving the statutory or constitutional scheme. Otherwise, the judges effectively elevate themselves into legislators by choosing to vindicate policies that the legislators might have rejected.[466] In addition, the courts must be on guard, in the process of protecting statutory purposes, not to indirectly accept delegations of lawmaking authority that more appropriately belong to Congress.

A second "supplementation" case, distinguishable from the example discussed above, occurs when the judges seek not to prevent the objectives of a statutory or constitutional provision from being undermined, but to further the purposes of a statutory or constitutional scheme by creating rules of decision that the judges deem to be a desirable *extension* of the policies supporting the law. The distinction between this case and the first "supplementation" case is that here the rules created by the judges are not essential to protect the objectives of

---

465. *See* ERWIN CHEMERINSKY, FEDERAL JURISDICTION § 6.3.1 (3d ed. 1999).

466. *See* Learned Hand, *Is a Judge Free in Rendering a Decision? in* THE SPIRIT OF LIBERTY 103, 109 (3d ed. 1974).

Congress or the framers. Rather, they are rules that the courts themselves deem to be desirable extensions of the law. The separation-of-powers problems with this kind of judicial activity are severe. In the process of extending the policies of a law to situations that the creators of the law did not extend them, the courts may go beyond the legislators' policy choices and make the policy choices themselves. Thus, there is a danger that the lawmaking in which the judges are engaging will not be merely "interstitial" in nature.

(c) "Policy Making"

The final category of problems concerns cases in which the courts create rules of decision based on policies identified or created by the judges themselves. Here, some distant statutory or constitutional provision exists, but the articulated congressional or constitutional policies are remote from the immediate issues under litigation. The justifiability of federal court lawmaking in this category of cases depends on the reality and strength of the national policies identified by the courts compared with the strength of any existing state interests in controlling the issues with state law. The stronger the national interest in controlling the case with uniform national law, the more justifiable is the creation of "federal common law" to govern the case.[467]

2. Examples of Federal Common-Law Decisions

The federal courts have actually created "federal common law" in all of the ways described in the preceding subsection, but not always justifiably. Professors Wright, Miller, and Cooper have identified three categories of cases that are "neither exhaustive nor analytically precise" in which federal common law has been developed. Each of these categories can involve "interpretation," "supplementation," or "policy making": (1) cases involving significant conflict between a federal policy or interest and state law in which a federal rule of decision is required to protect federal interests; (2) cases in which legal policy is so dominated by federal statutory or constitutional provisions that it may be inferred that federal courts should provide rules of decision to govern issues not explicitly controlled by the statutory or constitutional provisions; and (3) cases in which there is a strong national concern with an area, and state law would not be sufficiently sensitive to federal concerns, would not be uniform, and would develop at various rates of speed.[468]

The best-known example of the first category of cases described by Professors Wright, Miller, and Cooper is *Clearfield Trust Co. v. United States*.[469] In *Clearfield*, a check issued by the United States was stolen and cashed by the thief. The United States sued a bank that had guaranteed all prior

---

467. *See generally* ERWIN CHEMERINSKY, FEDERAL JURISDICTION § 6.2 (3d ed. 1999).

468. *See* 19 CHARLES A. WRIGHT ET AL., FEDERAL PRACTICE AND PROCEDURE: JURISDICTION AND RELATED MATTERS (ERIE DOCTRINE) § 4514, at 463-73 (2d ed. 1996); *see also* ERWIN CHEMERINSKY, FEDERAL JURISDICTION §§ 6.1-6.3 (3d ed. 1999).

469. 318 U.S. 363, 63 S. Ct. 573, 87 L. Ed. 838 (1943).

endorsements on the check when it presented the check for payment. Under the law of Pennsylvania where the federal district court was sitting, the delay of the United States in notifying the bank that the endorsement was a forgery would have prevented recovery. The U.S. Supreme Court, however, held that federal common law governs the rights and duties of the United States on its commercial paper. The Court's decision was based on the fact that when the United States disburses funds or pays its debts, it exercises a constitutional function, which is not dependent on the laws of any state. Therefore, the Court believed that even in the absence of a controlling federal statute, it was the federal courts' obligation to formulate the governing rule of decision according to their own standards.[470] In the *Clearfield* category of cases, it is the extent to which the rights and liabilities of the United States are implicated in the action that justifies the creation of federal common law, not simply the fact that the United States is a party to the action.[471]

The second category of cases described by Professors Wright, Miller, and Cooper is one in which the federal courts are filling in the gaps ''of a pervasively federal framework'' with federal common law.[472] This situation generally occurs when the courts are filling in the gaps of a federal statutory scheme, but it is obvious that gaps can be lesser or greater depending upon whether the courts are attempting to construe the terms of a statute or to exercise wholesale lawmaking power under a broad delegation of authority from Congress.[473] As noted in subsection (1)*(b)*, above, the former situation presents an ordinary problem of statutory supplementation that the courts are perfectly suited to perform, while the latter presents an extremely serious separation-of-powers problem.

An example of justifiable federal common-law creation in the second category of cases is *Wilson v. Garcia*,[474] in which the Supreme Court held that in actions brought under 42 U.S.C. § 1983 (the Civil Rights Act of 1871), the federal courts should apply the state statute of limitations applicable to personal injury actions to determine whether the actions are time barred. Thus, the Court established a relatively simple, uniform rule of for all § 1983 actions that assures that the limitations period cannot be fixed in a way that discriminates against federal law.[475] *Wilson* constitutes a justifiable case of supplementation because Congress failed to provide a federal limitations period for § 1983 actions, and a period of limitations obviously had to be supplied by the courts.

Perhaps the classic example of a separation-of-powers violation occurring in the second category of federal common law cases occurred in *Textile Workers*

---

470. *See* 318 U.S. at 366-67, 63 S. Ct. at 574-76, 87 L. Ed. at 841-42.

471. *See* 19 CHARLES A. WRIGHT ET AL., FEDERAL PRACTICE AND PROCEDURE: JURISDICTION AND RELATED MATTERS (ERIE DOCTRINE) § 4515, at 485-95 (2d ed. 1996).

472. *See id.* § 4516, at 500.

473. *See id.* at 500-02.

474. 471 U.S. 261, 105 S. Ct. 1938, 85 L. Ed. 2d 254 (1985).

475. *See id.* at 279, 105 S. Ct. at 1949, 85 L. Ed. 2d at 269. For a discussion of the cases after *Wilson* dealing with the appropriate limitations period when a state has one statute of limitations for personal injury actions resulting from intentional torts and another for negligent torts, see 19 CHARLES A. WRIGHT ET AL., FEDERAL PRACTICE AND PROCEDURE: JURISDICTION AND RELATED MATTERS (ERIE DOCTRINE) § 4519, at 610-15 (2d ed. 1996).

Union of America v. Lincoln Mills.[476] *Lincoln Mills* is an excellent example of improper "supplementation" because it involves the acceptance by the Supreme Court of an overbroad delegation of lawmaking authority by Congress. In *Lincoln Mills*, Congress had given the federal courts jurisdiction to determine disputes between employers and labor organizations representing employees in industries affecting commerce.[477] However, Congress had not provided any substantive rules for the determination of the disputes that would arise within the jurisdictional grant. The Supreme Court concluded that the jurisdictional grant authorized the federal courts to create a federal common law of labor-management contracts. The Court's decision has been criticized as essentially unreasoned.[478] Worse than the unreasoned nature of the Court's opinion, however, was the violation of the separation-of-powers doctrine that resulted from the decision. As observed by Justice Frankfurter in dissent, when Congress casts "upon the federal courts, with no guides except 'judicial inventiveness,' the task of applying a whole industrial code that is as yet in the bosom of the judiciary," the courts cannot perform their job by using the ordinary process of interpretation. "For the vice of the statute here lies in the impossibility of ascertaining, by any reasonable test, that the legislature meant one thing rather than another. . . ."[479]

Among other kinds of cases, the third category described by Professors Wright, Miller, and Cooper involves the derivation from federal statutes and constitutional provisions of private rights of action that help to effectively implement the statutes and constitutional provisions.[480] The most important factor in this area, especially as it concerns the derivation of federal common-law rules from statutes, is some indication that Congress would desire the federal courts to fashion such rules. The Supreme Court has vacillated over the years in its willingness to permit the creation of private rights of action from silent federal statutes.[481] The Court's current approach is to allow the creation of a private right of action only when there is "affirmative evidence that Congress intended to create a private right of action."[482] This approach seems to be based on the

---

476. 353 U.S. 448, 77 S. Ct. 912, 1 L. Ed. 2d 972 (1957).

477. *See* 29 U.S.C. § 185(a).

478. *See* Alexander M. Bickel & Harry H. Wellington, *Legislative Purpose and the Judicial Process: The Lincoln Mills Case*, 71 HARV. L. REV. 1, 35-37 (1957).

479. 353 U.S. at 464-65, 77 S. Ct. at 925, 1 L. Ed. 2d at 985 (Frankfurter, J., dissenting); *see* RANDALL BRIDWELL & RALPH U. WHITTEN, THE CONSTITUTION AND THE COMMON LAW: THE DECLINE OF THE DOCTRINES OF SEPARATION OF POWERS AND FEDERALISM 133-34 (1977) (comparing the *Lincoln Mills* approach to the approach of the Court in the common law of crimes cases, discussed in section C(2)*(c)* ("Separation of Powers") *supra*).

480. *See* 19 CHARLES A. WRIGHT ET AL., FEDERAL PRACTICE AND PROCEDURE: JURISDICTION AND RELATED MATTERS (ERIE DOCTRINE) § 4517, at 538 (2d ed. 1996).

481. *Compare* J.I. Case Co. v. Borak, 377 U.S. 426, 84 S. Ct. 1555, 12 L. Ed. 2d 423 (1964) *with* Cort v. Ash, 422 U.S. 66, 95 S. Ct. 2080, 45 L. Ed. 2d 26 (1975) *and* Touche Ross & Co. v. Redington, 442 U.S. 560, 99 S. Ct. 2479, 61 L. Ed. 2d 82 (1979). For an excellent discussion of this area, see ERWIN CHEMERINSKY, FEDERAL JURISDICTION § 6.3.3 (3d ed. 1999).

482. ERWIN CHEMERINSKY, FEDERAL JURISDICTION § 6.3.3, at 382 (3d ed. 1999). *See, e.g.,* Herman & MacLean v. Huddleston, 459 U.S. 375, 103 S. Ct. 683, 74 L. Ed. 2d 548 (1983); Merrill Lynch, Pierce, Fenner & Smith, Inc. v. Curran, 456 U.S. 353, 102 S. Ct. 1825, 72 L. Ed. 2d 182 (1982); Texas Indus., Inc. v. Radcliff Materials, Inc., 451 U.S. 630, 101 S. Ct. 2061, 68 L. Ed. 2d 500 (1981); Northwest Airlines, Inc. v. Transport Workers Union of Am., 451 U.S. 77, 101 S. Ct. 1571, 67 L. Ed. 2d 750 (1981); Transamerica Mortgage theory that the separation-of-powers doctrine vests the primary policy-making role in Congress, not the courts, and that the courts are unsuited for the resolution of complex policy issues.[483]

As noted in the discussion of *Wilson v. Garcia*, above, when federal courts have the power to create federal common law, they sometimes adopt state law as the rule of decision. State law is adopted not because *Erie* or the Constitution requires the federal courts to do so, but as a matter of the courts' discretion in determining the content of federal rules of decision.[484] In cases like *Wilson*, it is easy to understand how federal common law can adopt state law and still be "federal." Congress has left a gap in a statutory scheme that must be filled, and state law is the natural and most available source of law with which to fill the gap. Nevertheless, the controlling principle is still "federal" because it is clearly a federal rule of decision that tells the courts which state limitations period controls the federal right of action. However, in other situations, saying that state law is being adopted as federal common-law is curious. When federal common law can appropriately control an area, but state law is adopted as the federal common law, what is the significance of calling the law "federal"?

It is clear, of course, that the Court will not adopt state law as federal law unless there is little or no need for a uniform federal rule in a category of cases.[485] But this statement does not tell us why, when state law is adopted, it is appropriate to say that "federal" law controls the area. It is also true that state law will not be adopted if it is hostile to federal interests or otherwise inconsistent with federal law.[486] But this statement, again, does not tell us the significance of saying that federal common law controls an area when the law adopted *is* state

---

Advisors, Inc. v. Lewis, 444 U.S. 11, 100 S. Ct. 242, 62 L. Ed. 2d 146 (1979); Touche Ross & Co. v. Redington, 442 U.S. 560, 99 S. Ct. 2479, 61 L. Ed. 2d 82 (1979).

483. *See* Texas Indus., Inc. v. Radcliff Materials, Inc., 451 U.S. 630, 101 S. Ct. 2061, 68 L. Ed. 2d 500 (1981); Northwest Airlines, Inc. v. Transport Workers Union of Am., 451 U.S. 77, 101 S. Ct. 1571, 67 L. Ed. 2d 750 (1981); *see also* 19 CHARLES A. WRIGHT ET AL., FEDERAL PRACTICE AND PROCEDURE: JURISDICTION AND RELATED MATTERS (ERIE DOCTRINE) § 4517, at 547 (2d ed. 1996). For a recent debate concerning the question whether customary international law should have the status of federal common law, see Curtis A. Bradley & Jack L. Goldsmith, *Federal Courts and the Incorporation of International Law*, 111 HARV. L. REV. 2260 (1998); Curtis A. Bradley & Jack L. Goldsmith, *Customary International Law as Federal Common Law: A Critique*, 110 HARV. L. REV. 815 (1997); Curtis A. Bradley, *The Status of Customary International Law in U.S. Courts–Before and After* Erie, 26 DEN. J. INT'L L. & POLICY 807 (1988); *but see* F. Giba-Matthews, *Customary International Law Acts as Federal Common Law in U.S. Courts*, 20 FORD. INT'L. L.J. 1839 (1997); Harold Hongju Koh, *Is International Law Really State Law?* 111 HARV. L. REV. 1824 (1998); Beth Stephens, *The Law of Our Land: Customary International Law as Federal Law After* Erie, 66 FORD. L. REV. 393 (1997); *see also* Hans Smit, *Federalizing International Civil Litigation in the United States: A Modest Proposal*, 8 TRANSNAT'L L. & CONTEMP. PROBS. 57 (1998) (arguing for wholesale overruling of *Erie*, but, in any event, for overruling *Erie* insofar as it requires application of state law in conflicts cases with international aspects) (modest?); William H. Theis, *United States Admiralty Law as an Enclave of Federal Common Law*, 23 TOL. MAR. L.J. 73 (1998).

484. 19 CHARLES A. WRIGHT ET AL., FEDERAL PRACTICE AND PROCEDURE: JURISDICTION AND RELATED MATTERS (ERIE DOCTRINE) § 4518, at 566-67 (2d ed. 1996). *See, e.g.*, United States v. Kimbell Foods, Inc., 440 U.S. 715, 99 S. Ct. 1448, 59 L. Ed. 2d 711 (1979).

485. *See, e.g.*, Wilson v. Omaha Indian Tribe, 442 U.S. 653, 673, 99 S. Ct. 2529, 61 L. Ed. 2d 153, 170 (1979); United States v. Kimbell Foods, Inc., 440 U.S. 715, 728, 99 S. Ct. 1448, 1458, 59 L. Ed. 2d 711, 723-24 (1979).

486. *See, e.g.*, United States v. Little Lake Misere Land Co., 412 U.S. 580, 93 S. Ct. 2389, 37 L. Ed. 2d 187 (1973).

law. It may be that the Court will someday reject the *Klaxon* approach (in cases in which federal law adopts state law) and apply an independent federal conflict-of-laws rule to determine which state's law will be adopted.[487] But this possibility, too, does not tell us the significance of saying that federal law controls when the law ultimately selected by the federal conflict of laws rule is state law. After all, federal courts exercised independent conflict-of-laws authority under *Swift*, but the applicable law was never characterized as "federal" when they did so. A federal court might feel free to reject state precedents interpreting the state law adopted as federal law, but this would raise the question whether the federal court was, in any realistic sense, adopting "state" law at all.

The most plausible explanation for the Court's way of expressing doctrine in this area is as follows: When federal law controls an area, but state law is adopted as federal law, the Court is simply saying that federal interests are sufficient to allow the creation of federal law in an area if state law is in any way insufficient. In addition, when the law in question creates a claim for relief on behalf of the plaintiff, the case is appropriate for federal question jurisdiction. In all other respects, the law in question is state law, and state precedents defining the content of that law should be followed unless and until they become inconsistent with the federal interests in the area. In the latter eventuality, federal courts should develop independent federal common-law rules to govern the issue.

3. Federal Procedural Common Law in State Courts

As noted in Chapter 2, most of the federal question jurisdiction conferred upon the U.S. District Courts is concurrent with the state courts. When the state courts are adjudicating federal claims within their concurrent jurisdiction, the Supreme Court has sometimes denied them the right to use procedures that they would employ in similar actions under state law. In effect, this requires the state courts to follow the procedures that would exist if the plaintiff had sued on the federal claim in federal court.

Illustration 5-24. *A* sues *B Railroad* in a state court of State *X* in an action under the Federal Employers Liability Act (F.E.L.A.). *B* defends on the ground that *A* had released all claims that *A* possessed against *B*. *A* contends that the release is void because it was procured by fraud. If the action had been brought in federal court, the issue of whether the release is fraudulent would have been tried to a jury. The practice in the courts of State *X* is to split the issue of fraud in parts, with the judge trying some parts and the jury trying others. *A* contends that it is impermissible for State *X* to split the fraud issue in this manner in an F.E.L.A. action. In these circumstances, the Supreme Court held in *Dice v. Akron, Canton & Youngstown Railroad Co.*,[488] that federal common law controls the validity of the release *and* that the fraud issue must be submitted

---

487. *See* International Union, United Auto. Workers v. Hoosier Cardinal Corp., 383 U.S. 696, 705 n.8, 86 S. Ct. 1107, 113 n.8, 16 L. Ed. 2d 192, 199 n.8 (1966).
488. *See* 342 U.S. 359, 72 S. Ct. 312, 96 L. Ed. 398 (1952).

entirely to the jury, because jury trial is part and parcel of the remedy afforded under the F.E.L.A.

    Illustration 5-25. *A* sues *B* railroad in a state court of State *X* under the F.E.L.A. *B* demurs to *A's* complaint under state rules of procedure on the grounds that the complaint fails to state facts sufficient to constitute a cause of action. The State *X* court in which the action is pending sustains the demurrer and dismisses the action, despite *A's* contention that it is impermissible for State *X* to use its strict local pleading rules in F.E.L.A. actions. *A* contends that a more liberal "notice pleading" approach, such as that employed under the Federal Rules of Civil Procedure, should be used by the State *X* courts. Under these circumstances, the Supreme Court held in *Brown v. Western Ry.*,[489] that the strict local pleading rules unnecessarily burdened the federal right of action and could not be used by the state courts in the F.E.L.A. action.

* * * * *

    The principle of these decisions does not require the state courts to abandon their own rules of procedure across the board when adjudicating federal claims. Rather, only state procedures that interfere with the policy embodied in the federal statute being enforced must be discarded. This will occur in cases such as *Illustration 5-24* when Congress has embodied procedural rights in a statute conferring a federal right of action. It will occur in cases such as *Illustration 5-25* when state procedures unnecessarily burden the adjudication of the federal claim. This last proposition has been most recently illustrated by the Supreme Court's decision in *Felder v. Casey.*[490] In *Felder*, a state "notice of claim" statute provided that plaintiffs wishing to sue state or local governments or their officers had to notify the defendant of the claim and the intent to hold the defendant liable for it. The notice had to be provided within 120 days after the occurrence of the event giving rise to the claim or the claim would be barred, unless the defendant had actual notice of the claim and the plaintiff could show that the defendant was not prejudiced by failure to provide the notice. After notification, the plaintiff had to refrain from suing for 120 days in order to give the defendant a chance to consider the relief requested. Failure to comply with the statute constituted grounds for dismissing an action based on the claim. The plaintiff commenced an action in state court under 42 U.S.C. § 1983 (the Civil Rights Act of 1871) against a city and certain of its police officers. The action was dismissed for failure to comply with the notice of claim statute. The state's highest court held the statute applicable to cases in which the plaintiff was asserting federal civil rights claims. The Supreme Court held the statute preempted in federal civil rights actions because it unnecessarily burdened the right of recovery afforded by federal law.[491]

---

    489. *See* 338 U.S. 294, 298-99, 70 S. Ct. 105, 108, 94 L. Ed. 100, 104 (1949).

    490. 487 U.S. 131, 108 S. Ct. 2302, 101 L. Ed. 2d 123 (1988); *cf.* Hardy v. New York City Health & Hosps. Corp., 164 F.3d 789 (2d Cir. 1999) (New York notice of claims statute applicable to federal claim under the Emergency Medical Treatment and Active Labor Act, 42 U.S.C. § 1395dd, because of language in Act indicating that notice of claim provision should be considered as part of the applicable law of the state under the Act).

    491. *See* 487 U.S. at 150-51, 108 S. Ct. at 2313, 101 L. Ed. 2d at 145-46 (alternative holding).

In *Johnson v. Fankell*,[492] the Supreme Court held that in civil rights actions under 42 U.S.C. § 1983, state courts are not obligated to provide interlocutory appeals from denials of defendants' motions to dismiss on the basis of "qualified immunity," even though immediate appeals from such denials are available in federal court.[493] The Court interpreted *Brown* and *Felder* as cases in which the ultimate outcome of the state case would have been affected adversely by the application of the state procedures in question. The Court interpreted *Dice* as a case in which the jury trial procedure was a statutory right of plaintiffs suing on claims under the F.E.L.A. This may mean that states can use their own procedures when adjudicating federal claims as long as the procedures will not necessarily affect the outcome of the action or Congress has not mandated an alternative procedure. However, it may also be significant that *Fankell* involved a procedure for adjudicating a federal defense to a federal claim, while all the other cases involved procedures that directly burdened the claims themselves. State procedural burdens on federal claims may represent a more serious encroachment on federal interests than state procedural burdens on federal defenses to federal claims. This may especially be true in cases like *Fankell*, where state officials are likely to be the defendants in civil rights actions under § 1983. There is little danger that the states will not be vigilant in protecting the ability of such parties to assert federal defenses through adequate state procedures.

Even if the *Dice, Brown*, and *Felder* line of cases is narrow, it can be criticized. When Congress provides plaintiffs access to either federal or state courts for the adjudication of federal claims, it is arguable that plaintiffs should have to take the state courts as they find them, as long as the state courts do not discriminate against federal rights. If a plaintiff believes the procedures in state court are unreasonably restrictive or burdensome, the plaintiff should bring the action in federal court. This approach would accommodate both the interests of the federal government in providing for adjudication of federal claims without unnecessary restrictions or burdens on the plaintiff, as well as the interests of the states in providing uniform, nondiscriminatory procedures for all actions in their courts.

---

492. 520 U.S. 911, 117 S. Ct. 1800, 138 L. Ed. 2d 108 (1997).
493. *See* Chapter 12(B)(3)*(d)* ("The Collateral Order Rule") *infra.*

Chapter 6

PLEADING AND RELATED MATTERS

Pleading is the "branch of legal science . . . governing the formal written statements made to the court by the parties to a suit of their respective claims and defenses."[1] Because modern pleading is strongly influenced by its historical antecedents, this chapter begins by reviewing common-law pleading. It then examines the reforms embodied in code pleading and the Federal Rules of Civil Procedure. It also discusses verification and good faith pleading. Lastly, it examines remedies available at the outset of a lawsuit—called "provisional remedies."

SECTION A. COMMON-LAW PLEADING

1. Commencing the Action

A plaintiff commenced a common-law action by obtaining an original writ. This writ ordered the sheriff to compel the defendant to appear. It also gave the court subject-matter jurisdiction over the suit and determined the nature of the action (trespass, case, debt, etc.).[2]

2. Stating the Plaintiff's Claim in the Declaration

After the defendant had appeared, the plaintiff had to state the claim in more detail in the *declaration*.[3] The declaration was a formal specification of the facts and circumstances on which the plaintiff's action was based. Some declarations, such as ones based on trespasses, set forth the events in a relatively direct and straightforward manner. Others reflected elaborate fictions developed in certain common-law actions, such as ejectment.[4] General assumpsit developed standard, generalized allegations known as *common counts*.[5]

---

1. CHARLES E. CLARK, HANDBOOK OF THE LAW OF CODE PLEADING § 1, at 1 (2d ed. 1947).

2. *See* Chapter 1(E)(1)*(b)* ("Issuance of Writs by the Chancellor and the Initial Development of the Forms of Action") *supra*.

3. Originally, the plaintiff or someone on the plaintiff's behalf would orally state the factual basis of the action, and the court would call for the defendant's response. A change to formal, written pleadings began in the late thirteenth century and extended into the second half of the sixteenth century. *See* EDMUND M. MORGAN & FRANCIS DWYER, INTRODUCTION TO THE STUDY OF LAW 116-17 (2d ed. 1948).

4. *See* Chapter 1(E)(1)*(c)(iv)* ("Ejectment") *supra*.

5. *See* Chapter 1(E)(1)*(c)(ii)* ("Assumpsit") *supra*. Provided the declaration showed that the "debt" owed to the plaintiff was not one under seal or on a record, the courts permitted the plaintiff to make a generalized statement of the claim. *See generally* 1 DAN B. DOBBS, LAW OF REMEDIES § 4.2(3), at 581-84 (2d practitioner ed. 1993); JOSEPH H. KOFFLER & ALISON REPPY, HANDBOOK OF COMMON LAW PLEADING § 176, at 347-60 (1969).

Illustration 6-1. The common count for *money had and received* was available (1) when the defendant obtained the plaintiff's money or goods by fraud, duress, or another tort and then converted the money or the proceeds to the defendant's use; (2) when the plaintiff paid money to the defendant by mistake believing it was due, but in fact it was not; or (3) when the plaintiff paid money for a consideration that failed, such as when the seller refused to deliver the bargained-for goods.[6]

* * * * *

Other important common counts were *quantum meruit* (used when the plaintiff performed services in consideration for the defendant's "promise" to pay so much as the plaintiff deserved); *quantum valebant* (used when the plaintiff sold goods in consideration for a "promise" to pay so much as the goods were worth); goods sold and delivered;[7] work, labor, and services;[8] board and lodging;[9] and use and occupation of land.[10]

Common-law pleading required the parties, through a series of pleadings, to disclose the issues between them. The final result was a *single issue* of law or fact. By means of several restrictive pleading rules, the parties often had to elect a set of facts and a legal theory at the outset of the action and had to plead with certainty. The plaintiff could not plead alternatively ("either-or"). Nor was hypothetical pleading ("if-then") permitted. Common-law pleading also prohibited duplicity: stating different grounds to enforce a single right of recovery.[11]

Illustration 6-2. Assume that the plaintiff alleged as follows: "On [date], in a [named] public highway, defendant C.D. or defendant E.F. or both C.D. and

---

6. *See* JOSEPH H. KOFFLER & ALISON REPPY, HANDBOOK OF COMMON LAW PLEADING § 176, at 351-53 (1969). Money had and received was known as a money count. Other money common counts included (1) money paid to the defendant's use (available when the plaintiff became a surety for the defendant's debt at the defendant's request and was subsequently compelled to pay the debt, or when the plaintiff discharged a legal obligation of the defendant based upon an express or implied request of the defendant to make the payment for defendant); (2) money lent (used when the plaintiff loaned money to the defendant); and (3) money due on an account stated (used when the plaintiff and defendant had transactions resulting in matured debts, the parties by agreement had computed a balance that the defendant promised to pay, and the plaintiff agreed to accept in full payment for the items covered by the account). *See id.* at 349.

7. The common count for goods sold and delivered was used when goods had been actually or constructively delivered to the defendant and the defendant refused to pay. *Id.* at 357-58.

8. The common count for work, labor, and services was used when the plaintiff performed services for the defendant under such circumstances that the law would imply a promise to pay what they were worth, or when the plaintiff fully performed services pursuant to a contract with the defendant, who did not compensate the plaintiff for them. Originally, the common counts for work, labor, and services and for goods sold and delivered (unlike the value counts of quantum meruit and quantum valebant) could not be used when the sum claimed was of an uncertain amount. As the law developed, however, these counts could be used when the evidence would reduce an uncertain sum to a certainty; they thus became concurrent with the value counts. *See id.* at 359.

9. The common count for board and lodging was used when the plaintiff furnished the defendant board, lodging, or other "necessaries" at the defendant's special request. *See id.* at 357.

10. The common count for use and occupation of land was used when the defendant (tenant) in possession of land agreed to pay the plaintiff (landlord) either a reasonable sum or fixed sum of money for use and occupation of the land. This action was not available against a trespasser. *Id.* at 354-55; *see also* 1 DAN B. DOBBS, LAW OF REMEDIES § 4.2(3), at 582, § 5.9, at 801-03 (2d practitioner ed. 1993) (citing a few cases that now allow an assumpsit measure of recovery for trespasses that involve actual use and occupation of land).

11. *See generally* BENJAMIN J. SHIPMAN, HANDBOOK OF COMMON-LAW PLEADING §§ 294-327 (3d ed. 1923); HENRY J. STEPHEN, PRINCIPLES OF PLEADING IN CIVIL ACTIONS 434-35 (2d ed. 1901).

E.F. willfully or recklessly or negligently drove or caused to be driven a motor vehicle against plaintiff who was then crossing said highway." This allegation would violate the rule against pleading in the alternative. It would also be considered to be duplicitous because it raised different grounds (willfulness, recklessness, or negligence) to enforce a single right of recovery.[12]

* * * * *

If the declaration contained internally inconsistent or unintelligible allegations, it could be challenged, respectively, as repugnant or insensible. Allegations had to be positive and not by way of recital.[13]

Illustration 6-3. Assume that the plaintiff alleged: "*A*, as agent of *B*, . . ." This allegation would be a prohibited recital. To cure this defect, the plaintiff should use positive terms: "*A* was *B's* agent."[14]

Illustration 6-4. Assume that the plaintiff alleged the following in a declaration: "By written agreement dated [date], plaintiff and defendant agreed to plaintiff's occupancy and cultivation of [certain described lands], for a term of twenty years, commencing [date]. As a result, defendant granted plaintiff a freehold interest in said lands. . . ." The plaintiff has alleged a lease for a specific term, followed by the conclusion that the defendant granted the plaintiff a "freehold interest" in the lands. This pleading would be repugnant (internally inconsistent) because it was legally impossible to obtain a freehold interest (a fee simple or a life estate) from such a lease.[15]

* * * * *

At common law, plaintiffs could not anticipate in the declaration defenses that the adversary might raise. Any such allegations were regarded as immaterial. Fraud, mistake, and the performance of conditions precedent (acts that must be performed before an agreement becomes effective) had to be pleaded with particularity.[16] Furthermore, the common law required the pleading of jurisdictional facts supporting a prior judgment regardless of the type of judgment.[17]

3. Challenges to the Declaration

(a) General Demurrers

A party could challenge a declaration by contending that the alleged facts did not constitute a legally recognized obligation even if they could be proved. This objection was raised by a *general demurrer*. The decision on the demurrer terminated the action: either the demurrer was sustained and the plaintiff's action

---

12. *See* CHARLES E. CLARK, HANDBOOK OF THE LAW OF CODE PLEADING § 42 (2d ed. 1947).

13. *See* JOSEPH H. KOFFLER & ALISON REPPY, HANDBOOK OF COMMON LAW PLEADING § 55, at 130 (1969).

14. *See* FLEMING JAMES, JR. & GEOFFREY C. HAZARD, JR., CIVIL PROCEDURE § 3.12, at 155 (3d ed. 1985).

15. *See* JOSEPH H. KOFFLER & ALISON REPPY, HANDBOOK OF COMMON LAW PLEADING § 69, at 145 (1969).

16. CHARLES E. CLARK, HANDBOOK OF THE LAW OF CODE PLEADING § 45, at 280, § 48, at 312 (2d ed. 1947).

17. 5 CHARLES A. WRIGHT & ARTHUR R. MILLER, FEDERAL PRACTICE AND PROCEDURE: CIVIL § 1306, at 690 (2d ed. 1990).

was dismissed or the demurrer was overruled and judgment was entered against the defendant based on the defendant's admission of the facts. The defendant could not later challenge the truth of the allegations. Nor did the plaintiff have the right to amend the declaration except to correct formal defects and errors of oversight.[18]

(b) Special Demurrers

A *special demurrer* raised formal defects in a party's pleading. At common law, all special demurrers were also general demurrers. Thus, special demurrers also raised defects in substance.

(c) Dilatory Pleas

If the defendant did not file a general or special demurrer, the defendant could enter a *plea*. One type of plea was a *dilatory plea*. It objected to the venue or to the court's jurisdiction over the person or the subject-matter of the suit. A defendant could also use a dilatory plea to raise other objections: nonjoinder or misjoinder of parties, defects in the original writ, misnomer of the defendant, lack of capacity to sue or be sued, prematurity of bringing the action, and the pendency of another action for the same cause.[19] A dilatory plea sought to delay or defeat the particular suit without destroying the plaintiff's right to sue elsewhere. Such a plea had to be presented before the defendant pleaded to the merits (such as by denying the plaintiff's allegations).[20]

The common law rigidly prescribed the order of pleading. For example, the defendant had to make a plea to the jurisdiction over the person before the defendant demurred or offered any other plea. Otherwise, the defendant was deemed to have submitted to the court's jurisdiction.[21] The parties waived defects of form unless the parties raised them by special demurrer.

(d) Traverses

Assuming that the defendant did not file a dilatory plea, the defendant could deny the allegations of the declaration by means of a *traverse*. A traverse had to be directed to an essential element of the plaintiff's claim. It had to be specific. It could not be *argumentative*.

Illustration 6-5. Assume that P, the plaintiff, alleged that D, the defendant, was in State X on a particular day. Assume that D traversed by alleging that D was in State Y on that day. D's traverse is argumentative and would have been

---

18. *See* 5A *id.* § 1355, at 292.

19. These pleas were called dilatory pleas in abatement. *See* BENJAMIN J. SHIPMAN, HANDBOOK OF COMMON-LAW PLEADING § 225 (3d ed. 1923).

20. *See id.* at § 220, at 382-83; JOSEPH H. KOFFLER & ALISON REPPY, HANDBOOK OF COMMON LAW PLEADING §§ 203-206, at 410-20 (1969).

21. *See* JOSEPH H. KOFFLER & ALISON REPPY, HANDBOOK OF COMMON LAW PLEADING § 204, at 411 (1969).

improper. The proper form of pleading would be to deny that *D* was in State *X* on that day.[22]

* * * * *

A traverse could not contain a *negative pregnant*. A negative pregnant was a negative expression that implied an affirmative. It could result from framing the denial in the exact language of the opposing party's averment.

Illustration 6-6. Assume *A* alleged that *B* hit *A* over the head with a lead pipe. If *B* traversed by alleging that ''*B* did not hit *A* over the head with a lead pipe,'' the traverse would contain a negative pregnant. Did *B* intend to deny that *B* had not hit *A* at all or to admit that *B* did hit *A*, but not with a lead pipe? *B's* response would be taken to have admitted the battery.[23]

(e) Pleas in Confession and Avoidance

If the defendant chose not to demur generally or traverse an allegation of fact in the declaration, the defendant could enter a *plea in confession and avoidance*. Such a plea admitted the allegations of the prior pleading and presented new matter to avoid the legal effect of those allegations (for example, self-defense). The defendant had to choose.[24] The defendant could not deny an allegation of the declaration or demur generally and at the same time raise new matters of defense.[25]

(f) The General Issue

The defendant had the alternative of denying the legal conclusion sought to be drawn from the declaration by means of the *general issue*. The form of the general issue varied according to the form of action —''not guilty'' in trespass, case, and trover and ''nil debet'' in debt. The general issue enabled the defendant to contest most of the plaintiff's factual allegations and, in some actions, to raise various defenses. The defendant could also raise some affirmative defenses under the general issue.[26]

(g) Bills of Particulars

If a pleader showed by affidavit that a pleader was not fairly informed of the details of the opposing party's claim, the court frequently granted a bill of

---

22. *See id.* § 230, at 467-69.

23. *See id.* § 221, at 445; 5 CHARLES A. WRIGHT & ARTHUR R. MILLER, FEDERAL PRACTICE AND PROCEDURE: CIVIL § 1267, at 406-07 (2d ed. 1990).

24. The rule requiring the defendant to rely on only a single matter of defense was first evaded by fictitious pleading (''express color'') and eventually changed by statute, which allowed defendants to plead as many defenses as they had. *See* 4 & 5 Anne, ch. 16, § 4 (1705); CHARLES E. CLARK, HANDBOOK OF THE LAW OF CODE PLEADING § 91, at 576 & nn.3-4 (2d ed. 1947).

25. *See* JOSEPH H. KOFFLER & ALISON REPPY, HANDBOOK OF COMMON LAW PLEADING §§ 215, 225-226 (1969).

26. *See id.* § 224; BENJAMIN J. SHIPMAN, HANDBOOK OF COMMON-LAW PLEADING §§ 169, 189 (3d ed. 1923).

particulars. It required a pleader to make a general allegation more specific, especially when the plaintiff had used a common count in general assumpsit in the declaration.[27]

4. Subsequent Pleading

If the defendant demurred generally, traversed, or responded by pleading the general issue, the pleadings were complete because a single issue had been produced. On the other hand, if the defendant entered a plea of confession and avoidance, no issue was produced, and the plaintiff had to respond. If the plaintiff believed the plea was insufficient as a matter of law, the plaintiff would demur to the plea. If not, the plaintiff filed a *replication* either (1) traversing a material allegation in the plea or (2) admitting the truth of the plea and raising a new matter of confession and avoidance. If the plaintiff raised a new matter of confession and avoidance in the replication, the defendant had to either demur or file a *rejoinder* containing either a traverse or a new matter of confession and avoidance. This process continued until a single issue of law or fact was reached when one side traversed or demurred.[28]

During this pleading process, the parties had several opportunities to demur. Whenever a party demurred, it had the effect of "opening up" or *searching the record*. Thus, a demurrer tested not only the legal sufficiency of the pleading to which it was addressed, but also the legal sufficiency of all prior pleadings.

Illustration 6-7. Assume that the defendant demurred to the plaintiff's replication. In addition to considering the legal sufficiency of the replication, the court would examine the legal sufficiency of the plaintiff's declaration and the defendant's plea.[29]

5. Amendments, "Pleading Over," and Pleas
Puis Darrein Continuance

When oral pleading prevailed, courts allowed parties to correct and adjust their pleadings.[30] As written pleadings replaced oral pleadings, formalism increased. Courts began to reject pleadings containing minor errors of form and to arrest and reverse judgments on this basis.[31] Beginning in 1340, Statutes of Jeofails permitted the parties to amend their pleadings to correct formal defects

---

27. *See* CHARLES E. CLARK, HANDBOOK OF THE LAW OF CODE PLEADING § 54, at 338 (2d ed. 1947); JOSEPH H. KOFFLER & ALISON REPPY, HANDBOOK OF COMMON LAW PLEADING § 372 (1969).

28. *See* BERNARD C. GAVIT, CASES AND MATERIAL ON AN INTRODUCTION TO LAW AND THE JUDICIAL PROCESS 10 (1936). Assuming that matters of confession and avoidance were raised each time, the subsequent pleadings were called a surrejoinder, a rebutter, and a surrebutter. *See* JOSEPH H. KOFFLER & ALISON REPPY, HANDBOOK OF COMMON LAW PLEADING § 191, at 380 (1969).

29. *See* CHARLES E. CLARK, HANDBOOK OF THE LAW OF CODE PLEADING § 83, at 524-25 (2d ed. 1947).

30. BENJAMIN J. SHIPMAN, HANDBOOK OF COMMON-LAW PLEADING § 163, at 294 (3d ed. 1923).

31. CHARLES E. CLARK, HANDBOOK OF THE LAW OF CODE PLEADING § 114, at 703-04 (2d ed. 1947); *see also* Chapter 12(A) *infra* (discussing post-trial motions in common-law practice).

and errors of oversight.[32] However, a party could not change the form of action by an amendment (for example, from trespass to case or covenant to assumpsit).[33] Substantive defects might be "aided by pleading over," (*i.e.*, by supplying the omitted allegation in a subsequent pleading).

Illustration 6-8. If the defendant, rather than demurring, pleaded facts by way of confession and avoidance that supplied an omission in the declaration, the defect in the declaration would be cured.[34]

* * * * *

The defendant also had the opportunity to enter a *plea puis darrein continuance.* This plea raised a new matter of defense that arose during a continuance *after* the defendant had entered a plea.[35]

6. Relation of Pleading to Proof at Trial

If the evidence at trial disclosed a valid claim covered by another form of action, the plaintiff could not recover. The allegations in the pleadings were ordinarily "material" and the evidence had to *conform to the pleadings.* Otherwise, a fatal *variance* occurred. Even minor variances could be fatal.

Illustration 6-9. In one case, a fatal variance occurred when the note received in evidence was a half cent larger than the amount alleged in the declaration. In an assumpsit action based on a note allegedly signed by "William Becker," a fatal variance occurred when the note introduced in evidence showed it was signed by "Wilhelm Becker."[36]

* * * * *

Common-law pleading also required certainty in pleading time and place. Matters laid under a *videlicet* ("to wit" or "viz."), however, did not give rise to fatal error if the evidence varied from the stated facts under it.[37] In other respects, a pleader who alleged immaterial facts was ordinarily compelled to prove them literally, even though it was unnecessary to set them out.[38]

SECTION B. PLEADING IN EQUITY

A plaintiff commenced an equity action by filing a bill of complaint with the court. The bill, which originally simply stated the grievance, was also the first

---

32. Benjamin J. Shipman, Handbook of Common-Law Pleading § 163, at 294-95 (3d ed. 1923) (the term "jeofails" was derived from the expression "*J'ai failé*"; early pleaders used this expression when they "perceived a slip in [their] proceedings."); 1 William S. Holdsworth, A History of English Law 223 (6th ed. 1938) ("if the pleader saw and acknowledged the error (J'ai failé), [the pleader] was allowed to amend.").

33. Joseph H. Koffler & Alison Reppy, Handbook of Common Law Pleading § 301, at 559 (1969).

34. *See id.* § 298.

35. Benjamin J. Shipman, Handbook of Common-Law Pleading § 208 (3d ed. 1923).

36. Joseph H. Koffler & Alison Reppy, Handbook of Common Law Pleading § 68, at 145 (1969).

37. Parties frequently used videlicets to detail time, place, or manner that they had previously stated in general language (for example, "on a certain day, *viz.*, September 1, [year]"). Furthermore, common-law courts held that the allegations of place for purposes of venue were not material in transitory actions. *See* Chapter 4(A) ("Transitory and Local Actions") *supra.*

38. Joseph H. Koffler & Alison Reppy, Handbook of Common Law Pleading § 68, at 144 (1969).

pleading in equity. In contrast, pleading in common-law actions did not occur until after the original writ had been issued. The nature of equity jurisdiction explains this difference. The bill petitioned the chancellor for relief when legal remedies were inadequate or nonexistent. The chancellor did not act automatically in such cases, unlike the common-law courts, in which the original writ was issued according to established methods to vindicate settled legal rights. Relief was in the discretion of the chancellor. Therefore, the plaintiff had to make it apparent at the outset that grounds for the relief existed. The bill enabled the chancellor to make this determination before the chancellor compelled the defendant to appear by means of a subpoena.[39]

By the sixteenth century, bills had become more stylistically intricate. Typically, they consisted of three parts: (1) the stating part (stating the grounds for relief), (2) the charging part (stating the evidence in detail), and (3) the interrogative part (propounding interrogatories designed to obtain admissions and discover evidence from the opposing party).[40] After the defendant appeared, the chancellor required the defendant to answer the bill. The evidence was largely documentary, contained in or attached to the pleadings. Pleading in equity cases never achieved the rigidity of common-law pleading. Nor did it embrace the fictions embodied in common-law pleading.

In equity, the plaintiff could file a pleading called a *supplemental bill* in addition to the original bill. A supplemental bill remedied either some defect or omission in the original bill or introduced related matters happening since the commencement of the suit.[41]

SECTION C. CODE PLEADING

In 1848, the Field Code abolished the forms of action in New York. In their place, the Field Code established a single form of action known as the *civil action*. Code pleading reforms quickly followed in many states.[42]

1. Commencing the Action

Section 106 of the original Field Code of New York provided that "[c]ivil actions in the courts of record in this state, shall be commenced by the service of a summons."[43] Other sections prescribed the content of the summons and required a copy of the complaint to be served with the summons in most cases.[44]

---

39. *See* Chapter 1(E)(2) ("Equity Jurisdiction and Procedure") *supra*.

40. *See* Chapter 9(A) ("Development of Modern Discovery") *infra*.

41. BENJAMIN A. SHIPMAN, HANDBOOK OF THE LAW OF EQUITY PLEADING 290 (1897).

42. *See* Chapter 1(E)(4)("The Field Code and the Reform of Procedure in the States") *supra*.

43. Act of Apr. 12, 1848, ch. 379, § 106, 1848 N.Y. Laws 497, 518.

44. *See id.* §§ 107-109, 1848 N.Y. Laws 497, 518. Not all code-pleading systems, however, required a copy of the complaint to be served with the summons. *See, e.g.*, S.C. CODE ANN. §§ 15-9-10 to 15-9-40 (Law. Coop. 1976) (summons only) (repealed 1985) (complaint is now served with the summons in South Carolina); CHARLES E. CLARK, HANDBOOK OF THE LAW OF CODE PLEADING § 14, at 76 (2d ed. 1947). In systems that

2. The Code Complaint

The Field Code, as amended in 1851, required the plaintiff to file a complaint—called a "petition" in some code states. This initial pleading had to contain (1) a formal introductory part or "caption" that specified the names of the parties and the court, (2) "[a] plain and concise statement of the facts constituting a cause of action without unnecessary repetition," and (3) a demand for the judgment.[45] If the plaintiff demanded monetary relief, the plaintiff had to state the amount.[46] Furthermore, the codes required plaintiffs to include in the complaint only those matters on which they would have the initial burden of production of proof at trial, which constituted the prima facie case or cause of action.[47]

(a) Pleading "Facts"

By requiring a plain and concise statement of "facts" constituting a "cause of action,"[48] the codes produced a requirement that plaintiffs should state "ultimate facts" in the complaint, avoiding conclusions of law and evidentiary facts.[49] This requirement posed several difficulties.

---

served only the summons, it could be quite difficult for a layperson to determine the nature of the suit or what action to take. *See, e.g.*, Jolley v. Jolly, 265 S.C. 594, 220 S.E.2d 882 (1975).

45. Act of July 10, 1851, ch. 479, § 142, 1851 N.Y. Laws 876, 887. Originally, the Field Code had provided that the plaintiff's complaint had to contain, *inter alia*, "[a] statement of the facts constituting the cause of action, in ordinary and concise language, without repetition, and in such a manner as to enable a person of common understanding to know what is intended." Act of Apr. 12, 1848, ch. 379, § 120, 1848 N.Y. Laws 497, 521. The thrust of both the original 1848 provision and the amended 1851 provision was to insure that all the elements of the cause of action would be pleaded as clearly and concisely as possible. However, the first version of the Code appeared to require that pleadings be intelligible to the ordinary layperson. The second version eliminated this requirement. It was probably recognized that it was impractical to require both that a cause of action be stated in all its possible technical detail and that the complaint still be intelligible to a layperson. The second version thus simply required as concise, clear, and short a statement of the cause of action as possible.

46. Act of Apr. 12, 1848, ch. 379, § 120, 1848 N.Y. Laws 497, 521.

47. It has been aptly pointed out that "the allocation of an element to the plaintiff's case or to the defendant's affirmative pleading is not determined by abstract logic. There is no logic, for instance, why a plaintiff should not be compelled as an element of his case to establish that he was free of contributory negligence or did not induce a particular contract by fraud; or that an assertedly subsisting claim has not been paid or released. Considerations of fairness and convenience, of the ease or difficulty of making proof, of the comparative likelihood that a particular defensive situation may exist in a reasonable proportion of the cases presented to the court, and even of handicapping disfavored contentions, have contributed to the" allocation of the burden of pleading. *See* Greathouse v. Charter Nat'l Bank-S.W., 851 S.W.2d 173, 175-76 (Tex. 1992); *see also* Chapter 11(H) ("Involuntary Dismissals, Directed Verdicts, Burden of Proof, and Presumptions") *infra*; *see generally* Edward W. Cleary, *Presuming and Pleading: An Essay on Juristic Immaturity*, 12 STAN. L. REV. 5 (1959).

48. The Field Code did not define "cause of action." Three general views reflect varying shades of meaning. First, some courts defined a cause of action as simply a right of action, referring to the legal right of the plaintiff. Second, some courts defined a cause of action as a group of facts relied on by the litigant as entitling the litigant to relief. Third, some courts defined a cause of action as a group of facts entitling the litigant to relief, but limited as a layperson would to a single occurrence or affair, without particular reference to the resulting legal right or rights. CHARLES E. CLARK, HANDBOOK OF THE LAW OF CODE PLEADING § 19, at 129-30 (2d ed. 1947).

49. *See id.* § 38, at 225.

Illustration 6-10. Assume that the plaintiff alleged in a complaint in a code-pleading jurisdiction that the plaintiff was "entitled to possession" of specific property. This allegation could be challenged on the ground that the plaintiff had pleaded a conclusion of law. On the other hand, assume that the plaintiff alleged that "the defendants [had] agreed to convey realty to the plaintiff, that the defendants delivered the deed to the plaintiff, and that the defendants now refuse to deliver possession to the plaintiff." This allegation could be challenged on the ground that the plaintiff was pleading evidence rather than the ultimate facts of ownership and right to possession.[50]

Illustration 6-11. Assume that the plaintiff alleges that "*B* is the wife of *A*."[51] Is this allegation a conclusion of law, an ultimate fact, or an evidentiary fact? Professor Clark has suggested that the particularity of an allegation should vary with the question at issue. The allegation would probably suffice in a suit for personal injuries to one of the persons (either the husband or the wife). However, suppose *B* is claiming an individual statutory share of *A's* estate on the ground that *B* is *A's* common-law wife. *B's* allegation would probably be insufficient.[52]

* * * * *

The availability of challenges to pleading evidence and conclusions of law led to wasteful litigation. This problem was exacerbated by the tendency of pleaders to try to conceal information. It was also exacerbated by the possible lack of information about the facts at the time of pleading.[53] As Clark has pointed out, the codifiers' "ideal of pleading [ultimate] facts, as it has been worked out, has proved probably the most unsatisfactory part of their reform."[54] Clark attributes this result to (1) the reality that the distinction between fact, law, and evidence, "if existent at all, is not clear-cut and obvious," (2) the codifiers "attempt[ed] to apply rigid rules to a matter in which flexibility is a necessity," and (3) the "inherent difficulties" of this general problem.[55]

The common counts at common law were generalized statements of the claim.[56] Even though (1) code pleading required the allegation of "facts" and (2) § 118 of the Field Code specifically provided that "[a]ll the forms of pleading

---

50. *See id.* § 38, at 229. *Compare* Sheridan v. Jackson, 72 N.Y. 170 (1878) *with* McCaughey v. Schuette, 117 Cal. 223, 46 P. 666 (1896). A similar problem arose concerning the allegation of consideration for a contractual promise. Some courts regarded the simple allegation of a "valuable consideration" to be a legal conclusion. These courts wanted the consideration exactly specified as at common law. CHARLES E. CLARK, HANDBOOK OF THE LAW OF CODE PLEADING § 45, at 279-80 (2d ed. 1947).

51. *See* CHARLES E. CLARK, HANDBOOK OF THE LAW OF CODE PLEADING § 38, at 232 (2d ed. 1947) (providing this example).

52. *Id. See generally* Walter W. Cook, *"Facts" and "Statements of Facts,"* 4 U. CHI. L. REV. 233 (1937); Bernard C. Gavit, *Legal Conclusions*, 16 MINN. L. REV. 378 (1932); Nathan Isaacs, *The Law and the Facts*, 22 COLUM. L. REV. 1 (1922); Clarence Morris, *Law and Fact*, 55 HARV. L. REV. 1303 (1942); Carl C. Wheaton, *Manner of Stating Cause of Action*, 20 CORN. L.Q. 185 (1935).

53. *See* CHARLES E. CLARK, HANDBOOK OF THE LAW OF CODE PLEADING § 38, at 226-27 (2d ed. 1947).

54. *Id.* at 226.

55. *Id.*; *see also* Walter W. Cook, *"Facts" and "Statements of Fact,"* 4 U. CHI. L. REV. 233 (1937); Clarence Morris, *Law and Fact*, 55 HARV. L. REV. 1303 (1942).

56. *See* section A(2) ("Stating the Plaintiff's Claim in the Declaration") *supra.*

heretofore existing, inconsistent with the provisions of this act, are abolished,''[57] courts accepted the common counts as proper under code pleading.[58]

(b) *Alternative, Hypothetical, and Inconsistent Pleading*

Code practice generally continued the common-law pleading prohibition on pleading facts in the alternative or hypothetically. However, recognizing that "pleader[s] often cannot know, and cannot reasonably be expected to know, which of two or more alternatives is the correct one" at the time of pleading, several states modified this rule.[59] Traditional code practice also continued to condemn inconsistency.[60]

(c) *Anticipating Defenses*

Under the codes, plaintiffs did not have to anticipate in the complaint defenses that the adversary would raise. Indeed, as at common law, the plaintiff could not do so because the courts regarded any such allegations to be immaterial.[61] Some codes, however, allowed plaintiffs to anticipate defenses in the complaint if the complaint contained matter answering the anticipated defense.[62]

(d) *Pleading Special Matters*

Like the common law,[63] the codes required fraud and mistake to be pleaded with particularity.[64] In some code states, corporate existence had to be alleged. In many code states, however, no such allegation was necessary.[65] If the caption of the complaint clearly identified the capacity in which they were suing, many (but not all) code states did not require fiduciary plaintiffs acting as administrators, executors, guardians, or receivers to allege their appointment.[66] In the absence of an express code provision to the contrary, courts interpreted the codes as continuing the common-law requirement that the performance of conditions precedent had to be alleged with particularity.[67] However, many codes

---

57. Act of Apr. 12, 1848, ch. 379, § 118, 1848 N.Y. Laws 497, 521.

58. *See, e.g.*, Abadie v. Carrillo, 32 Cal. 172, 176 (1867).

59. *See* CHARLES E. CLARK, HANDBOOK OF THE LAW OF CODE PLEADING § 42, at 255 (2d ed. 1947) (allowing allegations in the alternative is "one of the most simple, desirable, and effective improvements upon the common-law rules").

60. *See id.* § 43; 5 CHARLES A. WRIGHT & ARTHUR R. MILLER, FEDERAL PRACTICE AND PROCEDURE: CIVIL § 1282, at 525, § 1283, at 533 (2d ed. 1990); Gregory Hankin, *Alternative and Hypothetical Pleadings*, 33 YALE L.J. 365 (1924); *see also* section A(2) ("Stating the Plaintiff's Claim in the Declaration") *supra*.

61. *See* section A(2) ("Stating the Plaintiff's Claim in the Declaration") *supra*.

62. CHARLES E. CLARK, HANDBOOK OF THE LAW OF CODE PLEADING § 82, at 524 (2d ed. 1947); *see also id.* § 40, at 250-52 (indicating that there was a conflict among the courts whether allegations anticipating defenses should be considered to be immaterial or should be considered a proper part of the complaint).

63. *See* section A(2) ("Stating the Plaintiff's Claim in the Declaration") *supra*.

64. CHARLES E. CLARK, HANDBOOK OF THE LAW OF CODE PLEADING § 48, at 312 (2d ed. 1947).

65. *Id.* § 50, at 323. Apparently, at common law, no such allegation was necessary. *Id.*

66. *Id.* at 324-26.

67. *Id.* § 45, at 280 (2d ed. 1947); *see* section A(2) ("Stating the Plaintiff's Claim in the Declaration") *supra*.

did contain specific provisions permitting a general allegation of performance of conditions precedent.[68] Many code states also eliminated the common-law requirement of pleading jurisdictional facts supporting a prior judgment regardless of the type of judgment.[69]

3. Responding to the Complaint

(a) Motions for More Definite Statements and Bills of Particulars

Assuming that the defendant did not default, the defendant had to prepare some type of defense. In doing so, the defendant could face a real difficulty: the complaint might be so vague or ambiguous that the defendant could not reasonably be expected to respond. The Field Code provided that the defendant could present a motion to require the plaintiff to make the complaint "more definite and certain." Frequently, the codes also required an affidavit specifying the allegations in question.[70]

A similar request, known as a *bill of particulars*, was utilized for a different purpose: to determine the particulars of an opposing party's claim so that the moving party could prepare for trial. It was also used to prevent surprise and limit issues. Several codes, however, limited the use of bills of particulars to actions of account or contract claims for damages. In some states, motions to make more definite and certain and bills of particulars became interchangeable.[71]

(b) Demurrers

The codes continued the common-law practice of using a demurrer to challenge the legal sufficiency of a pleading.[72] The codes also allowed a party to use a demurrer to raise other matters formerly raised by common-law dilatory pleas.[73] Such matters, however, could be raised by demurrer only when they appeared on the face of the complaint.[74] Specifically, the Field Code provided for demurrers on six grounds if they appeared on the face of the complaint: (1) the complaint failed to state sufficient facts to constitute a cause of action; (2) the court did not have (a) personal jurisdiction over the defendant or (b) subject-matter jurisdiction; (3) the plaintiff lacked the legal capacity to sue; (4) a defect

---

68. 5 CHARLES A. WRIGHT & ARTHUR R. MILLER, FEDERAL PRACTICE AND PROCEDURE: CIVIL § 1302, at 679 (2d ed. 1990).

69. *Id.* § 1306, at 690 (1990).

70. CHARLES E. CLARK, HANDBOOK OF THE LAW OF CODE PLEADING § 87, at 548 (2d ed. 1947).

71. *See id.* §§ 54, 87; *see also* section A(3)*(g)* ("Bills of Particulars") *supra.*

72. At common law, a general demurrer put in issue the legal sufficiency of the declaration. *See* section A(3)*(a)* ("General Demurrers") *supra.*

73. *See* section A(3)*(c)* ("Dilatory Pleas") *supra.*

74. A defense appears on the face of a complaint when it is possible to read the complaint alone and determine that the defense exists. This, of course, assumes that the reader of the complaint has a complete knowledge of the substantive law. Thus, the reader perceives the facts alleged in the complaint, compares the fact to the situations in which the substantive law provides for relief (or remedies), and judges whether a cause of action or defense exists.

of parties, either plaintiff or defendant, existed; (5) the plaintiff had improperly united several causes of action; and (6) another action was pending between the parties for the same cause.[75] These grounds were "repeated in practically all codes . . . in most cases with no additions."[76] Some codes later permitted these objections to be raised by a motion to dismiss.[77] Improper venue was often handled by a motion to transfer.[78] The codes also provided that "[s]ham, irrelevant, or frivolous demurrers, may on motion be stricken out."[79]

In some code states, a defendant could use a demurrer to challenge the complaint's failure to use a consistent theory in stating the facts.[80] Most code states repudiated this "theory-of-the-pleadings" doctrine as "inconsistent with the code plan of pleading facts only, leaving the legal conclusions to be drawn by the court."[81]

(c) The Code Answer

The defendant had to raise defenses and objections not appearing on the face of the complaint in the answer. For example, the defendant had to raise the following objections in the answer (rather than by demurrer) when those objections did not appear on the face of the complaint: an objection to improper service, a challenge to the recitals in the officer's return of service, or a question of the plaintiff's lack of capacity to sue.[82]

The codes carried forward the common-law traverse and general issue[83] in the form of the specific denial and the general denial. The typical code provision stated that the answer must contain "[a] general or specific denial of each material allegation of the complaint controverted by the defendant, or of any knowledge or information thereof sufficient to form a belief."[84] In addition, the codes typically required the answer to contain "[a] statement of any new matter constituting a defense or counterclaim, in ordinary and concise language without repetition."[85] The codes usually continued by stating that the "defendant may set forth in [the] answer as many defenses or counterclaims, or both, as [the

---

75. Act of Apr. 12, 1848, ch. 379, § 122, 1848 N.Y. Laws 497, 521.

76. CHARLES E. CLARK, HANDBOOK OF THE LAW OF CODE PLEADING § 79, at 505 (2d ed. 1947). Some codes included misjoinder of parties as a separate ground. *Id.*

77. *Id.*

78. *See, e.g.,* SMITH-HURD ILL. COMP. STAT. ANN. ch. 735, § 5/2-104 (West 1992).

79. CHARLES E. CLARK, HANDBOOK OF THE LAW OF CODE PLEADING § 87, at 551 (2d ed. 1947).

80. This approach is called the "theory-of-the-pleadings" doctrine:

> [A] complaint in the first instance and where challenged by demurrer, may [not] be uncertain and ambulatory, purposely so made, now presenting one face to the court and now another, at the mere will of the pleader, so that it may be regarded as one in tort, or one in contract, or equity as he is pleased to name it and the necessities of argument require.

Supervisors of Kewaunee County v. Decker, 30 Wis. 624, 629 (1872) (Dixon, C.J.).

81. CHARLES E. CLARK, HANDBOOK OF THE LAW OF CODE PLEADING § 43, at 259 (2d ed. 1947).

82. *Id.* at § 81, at 517, § 95, at 601-04.

83. *See* section A(3)*(d)* ("Traverses") and section A(3)*(f)* ("The General Issue") *supra*.

84. CHARLES E. CLARK, HANDBOOK OF THE LAW OF CODE PLEADING § 91, at 577 (2d ed. 1947).

85. *Id.*

defendant] has.''[86] Several codes added a list of defenses that the defendant had to raise affirmatively by specific averment in the answer. Difficult questions often arose whether the defendant had to raise a particular defense (1) affirmatively as a "new matter" in the answer or (2) by way of a denial of the plaintiff's allegations.[87]

Illustration 6-12. Assume that *A* sued *B* for breach of contract. *B* answered by denying the contract. The code states were "thoroughly divided" on the question whether *B's* denial was sufficient to allow *B* to assert that the contract violated the statute of frauds. Some states held that the defendant had to raise this defense by pleading it affirmatively in the answer.[88]

(d) *Waiver of Defenses*

As noted in subsection *(b)*, above, the codes utilized demurrers as the means for challenging certain enumerated defenses that appeared on the face of the complaint (*i.e.*, failure to state sufficient facts to constitute a cause of action, lack of personal jurisdiction, lack of subject-matter jurisdiction, lack of capacity to sue, defects of parties, improperly joined causes of action, and prior pending action). Failure to raise "such an objection" by demurrer resulted in a waiver of the objection.[89] However, the codes provided two exceptions to this rule. First, failure to state facts sufficient to constitute a cause of action could be made at trial.[90] Furthermore, as at common law, defects of substance could be cured by supplying the omitted fact in a subsequent pleading.[91] Second, lack of subject-matter jurisdiction could be raised for the first time as late as the appellate stage.[92]

Illustration 6-13. Assume that the plaintiff's lack of capacity to sue is apparent on the face of the complaint (*e.g.*, the complaint indicates that the plaintiff is twelve years old and the plaintiff has sued in the plaintiff's name alone). Virtually all codes permitted the defendant to raise this defense by demurrer.[93] The defendant waived this defense if the defendant failed to demur before answering the complaint.

Illustration 6-14. Assume that the defendant failed to demur to the complaint on the ground the plaintiff had omitted an essential allegation from the complaint. The defendant did not waive this defense. The defendant could raise

---

86. *Id.* at 578. In some states, however, the courts interpreted the codes to prohibit the defendant from denying matter alleged in the complaint and at the time inconsistently making the same matter part of an affirmative defense. 5 CHARLES A. WRIGHT & ARTHUR R. MILLER, FEDERAL PRACTICE AND PROCEDURE: CIVIL § 1270, at 411-12 (2d ed. 1990).

87. *See* CHARLES E. CLARK, HANDBOOK OF THE LAW OF CODE PLEADING §§ 96-97 (2d ed. 1947).

88. *Id.* § 97, at 613 (citing cases and noting that conflicts also existed as to contributory negligence, assumption of risk, and inherent illegality).

89. *Id.* § 86, at 532.

90. *Id.* at 532-33.

91. *See* section A(5) ("Amendments, 'Pleading Over,' and Pleas Puis Darrein Continuance") *supra*.

92. *See* CHARLES E. CLARK, HANDBOOK OF THE LAW OF CODE PLEADING § 85, at 532-33 (2d ed. 1947).

93. *See* subsection *(b)* ("Demurrers") *supra*.

this defense as late as the trial stage. After trial, however, the defendant waived the defense.

* * * * *

As noted in subsection *(c)*, above, the defendant had to raise defenses and objections not appearing on the face of the complaint in the answer. Failure to include "such an objection" in the answer was deemed to waive the objection. Again, however, objections to the lack of subject-matter jurisdiction could be raised for the first time on appeal.[94]

Illustration 6-15. Assume the facts of *Illustration 6-13*, except that the lack of capacity to sue did *not* appear on the face of the complaint (*e.g.*, the allegations of the complaint did not indicate that the plaintiff was a minor). Instead, the defendant had personal knowledge that the plaintiff was twelve years old and thus lacked the legal capacity to sue. The defendant could not raise this defense by demurrer because it did not appear on the face of the complaint. Assuming that the burden of pleading was on the defendant in this situation, the proper method for the defendant to raise lack of capacity would be an affirmative defense in the answer.[95] If the defendant failed to do so, the defense would be waived—unless the court permitted the defendant to amend the answer later to add the defense.[96] However, one caveat is in order. If the state placed the burden of pleading capacity on the plaintiff, the absence of an allegation of capacity would make the complaint subject to demurrer for legal insufficiency. In theory, the same could be true for many issues that are normally considered affirmative defenses, such as contributory negligence. Thus, one would always need to know where the burden of pleading resided on an issue before it would be possible to determine whether defendant should raise the matter by demurrer or affirmative defense *if the matter were omitted from a pleading altogether.*[97]

Illustration 6-16. Assume that *A* loaned *B* $50,000. *A* sued *B* for repayment of the loan. *B* maintained that *A* had released *B* from the obligation to repay the loan. *B* could not raise this defense (release) by demurrer because it was not a defense that the codes permitted to be raised in that manner. Instead, the proper method of raising this defense was as an affirmative defense in *B's* answer. If the defendant failed to do so, the defense would be waived—unless the court permitted the defendant to amend the answer later to add the defense.

4. The Plaintiff's Reply

Many codes required a reply to any "new matter" contained in the answer. If there was no reply, the new matter would be taken as admitted.[98]

---

94. CHARLES E. CLARK, HANDBOOK OF THE LAW OF CODE PLEADING § 85, at 532-33 (2d ed. 1947).

95. *See id.* § 97, at 616. Under the codes, issues such as the statutes of limitations, accord and satisfaction, payment, release, estoppel, conditions subsequent, truth, and justification could generally be raised only by affirmative plea by the defendant). *Id.*

96. *See* subsection 5 ("Amendments and Supplemental Pleadings") *infra.*

97. *See also Illustration 6-17, infra.*

98. CHARLES E. CLARK, HANDBOOK OF THE LAW OF CODE PLEADING §§ 107-09 (2d ed. 1947).

However, code practice typically permitted a party to demur to a defense in an answer (or reply).[99] The reply ended the pleading process.

Illustration 6-17. Assume that the defendant alleges in the answer that the plaintiff's negligence contributed to an accident. Under the applicable substantive law, the plaintiff's contributory negligence would bar the plaintiff's recovery for injuries sustained in the accident. The plaintiff would have to reply if this allegation is "new matter." Whether something is "new matter" depends on who has the burden of pleading *and* on what appears in the complaint. This allegation would be a new matter if the jurisdiction places the burden of pleading contributory negligence on the defendant. Thus, if the answer contains matter raising the issue of contributory negligence, a reply would be required. On the other hand, some jurisdictions require the plaintiff to plead freedom from contributory negligence. In these jurisdictions, the absence of such an allegation in the complaint is demurrable. However, if the plaintiff pleads freedom from contributory negligence, the defendant's response negating that allegation in the complaint is a denial, not "new matter." Thus, a reply is not necessary.

5. Amendments and Supplemental Pleadings

The codes provided for amendment of pleadings without leave of court within a certain time and for amendments with leave of court thereafter. Generally, a pleading could be amended once as a matter of course (1) at any time before the defendant served a demurrer or answer or (2) within twenty days after demurrer and before determination of the issue raised by the demurrer. The amended pleading simply was filed and served on the opposing party. The opposing party then typically had twenty days to answer, reply, or demur to the amended pleading.[100] After the time allowed for amendments as a matter of course, the court could permit an amendment in its discretion "in furtherance of justice" and "on such terms as may be proper."[101]

Illustration 6-18. Assume that before the defendant responded to the complaint, the plaintiff wanted to amend the complaint to correct a mistake in the name of a party. This amendment would be permitted without leave of court.

Illustration 6-19. Assume that after the defendant served a demurrer on the ground that the complaint failed to state a cause of action, the plaintiff served an amended complaint curing the defect—for example, alleging consideration for the contract set forth in the initial pleading. This amendment would be permitted. If the amendment was timely (usually within 20 days after the demurrer) and the court had not held a hearing on the issues raised by the demurrer, the plaintiff could serve the amendment without leave of court. Thereafter, the plaintiff had to seek leave of court.

* * * * *

---

99. *Id.* § 79, at 509.
100. *Id.* § 115, at 708-09.
101. *Id.* at 710.

Either by explicit provisions or by judicial decision, the codes originally did not permit amendments "changing the cause of action." However, most code states eventually eliminated this restriction. Furthermore, from the outset, the courts in code-pleading states appear to have taken a liberal approach in permitting defendants to raise new defenses by amendments of their answers.[102] When amendments were permitted, courts allowed them to "relate back" for purposes of satisfying the statute of limitations.

Illustration 6-20. Assume that before the defendant responded, the plaintiff wanted to amend the complaint to allege that the defendant negligently, rather than intentionally, drove a vehicle against the plaintiff. A traditional code-pleading state would not permit this amendment because it changed the cause of action from battery to negligence. The plaintiff would have to take a voluntary dismissal and commence a new action.

* * * * *

The codes also permitted *supplemental pleadings*. Most codes, however, limited such pleadings to "a supplemental complaint, answer or reply, alleging facts material to the case occurring *after* the filing of the former complaint, answer or reply."[103] When a party was ignorant of certain facts at the time of the filing of an earlier pleading, a few codes permitted the supplemental pleading of those facts.[104] The codes did not permit supplemental pleadings to cure defects such as prematurity of the claim.[105]

6. Code Motions to Expunge or Strike

A party could use the code motion to expunge to strike out irrelevant, immaterial, redundant, impertinent, or scandalous matter. When the entire pleading or an entire claim in a pleading was a sham, irrelevant, or frivolous, a code motion to strike was proper.[106]

SECTION D. FEDERAL RULES PLEADING

The Federal Rules of Civil Procedure apply to practice in the federal district courts. Many states have also adopted the Federal Rules.[107] They have been described as "one of the greatest contributions to the free and unhampered administration of law and justice ever struck off . . . since the dawn of civilized

---

102. *Id.* § 116.

103. *Id.* § 121, at 741 (emphasis added).

104. *Id.* at 742.

105. *Id.* § 121, at 743.

106. *Id.* § 87, at 550-52.

107. For a comprehensive survey of the extent to which the states have adopted the Federal Rules of Civil Procedure, including federal "notice pleading," see John B. Oakley & Arthur F. Coon, *The Federal Rules in State Courts: A Survey of State Court Systems of Civil Procedure*, 61 WASH. L. REV. 1367 (1986).

law.''[108] Not everyone, however, is convinced that all aspects of the Federal Rules represent a panacea.[109]

1. Commencing the Action

Federal Rule 3 provides that ''[a] civil action is commenced by filing a complaint with the court.''[110] The mechanics of filing a complaint are simple. Rule 5(e) defines filing with the court as filing with the clerk of the court[111] unless the judge permits the papers to be filed with the judge.[112]

2. The Federal Rules Complaint

Federal Rule 8(a) provides that the plaintiff's initial pleading in federal court is a *complaint*. In setting forth a claim for relief, Rule 8(a) indicates that the complaint must contain three basic items. First, the plaintiff must provide ''a short and plain statement of the grounds upon which the court's jurisdiction depends, unless the court already has jurisdiction and the claim needs no new grounds of jurisdiction to support it.''[113] Second, the plaintiff must provide ''a short and plain statement of the claim showing that the pleader is entitled to

---

108. B.H. Cary, *In Favor of Uniformity*, 3 F.R.D. 505, 507 (1943).

109. *See, e.g.*, Maurice Rosenberg, *The Federal Civil Rules After Half a Century*, 36 ME. L. REV. 243 (1984); Stephen N. Subrin, *Fireworks on the Fiftieth Anniversary of the Federal Rules of Civil Procedure*, 73 JUDICATURE 4 (1989); Symposium, *The Fiftieth Anniversary of the Federal Rules of Civil Procedure*, 63 NOTRE DAME L. REV. 597 (1988); Symposium, *The Fiftieth Anniversary of the Federal Rules of Civil Procedure*, 62 ST. JOHN'S L. REV. 399 (1988); Symposium, *The 50th Anniversary of the Federal Rules of Civil Procedure, 1938-1988*, 137 U. PA. L. REV. 1873 (1989); Symposium, The Future of Federal Litigation, 50 U. PITT. L. REV. 701 (1989); Symposium, *Issues in Civil Procedure: Advancing the Dialogue*, 69 B.U. L. REV. 467 (1989); Symposium, *Modern Civil Procedure: Issues in Controversy*, 54 LAW & CONTEMP. PROBS., Summer 1991, at 1.

110. FED. R. CIV. P. 3. After the complaint has been filed, service of process occurs pursuant to Rule 4. *See* Chapter 3(K) (''Service of Process'') *supra*.

111. FED. R. CIV. P. 5(e). Upon receiving the complaint, the clerk ''time-dates'' it. The party instituting a civil action in federal court must pay a $150 filing fee. *See* 28 U.S.C. § 1914(a). In addition, a civil cover sheet must be filed. This cover sheet identifies, *inter alia*, the names of the plaintiff and the defendant, their residences, the names of the attorneys, the basis of jurisdiction, the nature of suit, and the relief requested.

112. If the complaint or other papers are filed with the judge, the judge is required to note thereon the filing date and transmit them to the clerk's office. FED. R. CIV. P. 5(e).

113. FED. R. CIV. P. 8(a)(1). Pleading jurisdiction is simple. Assume, for example, that *A*, a citizen of California, sues *B*, a citizen of Texas. To demonstrate subject-matter jurisdiction based upon diversity, *A* would allege in the complaint: ''Plaintiff is a citizen of California and defendant is a citizen of Texas.'' Official Form 2 illustrates how *A* would plead the jurisdictional amount: ''The matter in controversy exceeds, exclusive of interest and costs, the sum of seventy-five thousand dollars.'' In diversity actions, Form 2 suggests that the plaintiff should allege the state in which the defendant is incorporated but need only allege that the corporation's principal place of business is in a state other than the plaintiff's state of citizenship. *See* Form 2 in the Appendix of Forms following the Federal Rules of Civil Procedure. The reason for this approach is that the plaintiff may have difficulty ascertaining the location of the defendant's principal place of business. *See* 5 CHARLES A. WRIGHT & ARTHUR R. MILLER, FEDERAL PRACTICE AND PROCEDURE: CIVIL § 1208, at 106-07 (2d ed. 1990). No overlap can exist between the plaintiff's citizenship and that of the corporation (determined by both its state of incorporation and its principal place of business). *See* Chapter 2(C)(3)*(c)* (''Citizenship of Corporations and Associations'') and *Illustration 2-41 supra*. Parts (b) and (c) of Form 2 illustrate how federal question jurisdiction is pleaded.

relief."[114] Third, the plaintiff must make "a demand for judgment for the relief the pleader seeks."[115] Rule 8(e)(1) adds that each averment in the pleading should be "simple, concise, and direct."[116]

(a) Captions, Numbered Paragraphs, Separate Counts, and Incorporation by Reference

All pleadings, motions, and other papers filed in a federal court must have a caption. The caption consists of the name of the court, the title of the action, the names of all the parties, the file number, and a designation of the type of document (*i.e.,* "Summons," "Complaint," "Answer," etc.)[117] In subsequent pleadings and other documents served after the complaint, only the name of the first party on each side is required.[118] The clerk supplies the file number of the complaint when the plaintiff commences the action.[119]

When a party makes a claim (or defense) in a federal pleading, the pleader must use numbered paragraphs. Each paragraph should be "limited as far as practicable to a statement of a single set of circumstances."[120] The requirement of numbered paragraphs provides "an easy mode of identification for referring to a particular paragraph in a prior pleading or for cross-referencing within a single pleading."[121]

Rule 10(b) provides that "[e]ach claim founded upon a separate transaction or occurrence . . . shall be stated in a separate count . . . whenever a separation facilitates the clear presentation of the matters set forth."[122] As Professors Wright and Miller point out, however, "[d]espite the express language of Rule 10(b) that more than one transaction must be involved before separate statements of claims are necessary, the federal courts have consistently required separate statements when separate claims are pleaded, notwithstanding the fact

---

114. FED. R. CIV. P. 8(a)(2). Several forms in the Appendix of Forms following the Federal Rules of Civil Procedure illustrate such statements. *See, e.g.,* Form 3 ("Complaint on a Promissory Note"); Form 9 ("Complaint for Negligence"); Form 10 ("Complaint for Negligence Where the Plaintiff Is Unable to Determine Definitely Whether the Person Responsible Is C. D. or E. F. or Whether Both Are Responsible and Where [the Plaintiff's] Evidence May Justify a Finding of Wilfulness or of Recklessness or of Negligence"); Form 11 ("Complaint for Conversion"); Form 12 ("Complaint for Specific Performance of Contract to Convey Land"); Form 13 ("Complaint on Claim for Debt and to Set Aside Fraudulent Conveyance Under Rule 18(b)"); Form 18 ("Complaint for Interpleader and Declaratory Relief") in the Appendix of Forms following the Federal Rules of Civil Procedure.

115. FED. R. CIV. P. 8(a)(3). The official forms give some illustrations of such demands. *See, e.g.,* Form 3 (damages), Form 12 (specific performance and damages), Form 13 (damages and to set aside fraudulent conveyance), Forms 16 and 17 (injunction, accounting, and other remedies), and Form 18 (declaratory relief) in the Appendix of Forms following the Federal Rules of Civil Procedure.

116. FED. R. CIV. P. 8(e)(1).

117. *See* FED. R. CIV. P. 4(b), 7(b)(2) & 10(a); *see also* FED. R. CIV. P. 7(a) (listing the names of the pleadings permitted in federal court).

118. FED. R. CIV. P. 10(a).

119. *See* FED. R. CIV. P. 79(a).

120. FED. R. CIV. P. 10(b); *see also* Forms 3 and 12 in the Appendix of Forms following the Federal Rules of Civil Procedure.

121. 5 CHARLES A. WRIGHT & ARTHUR R. MILLER, FEDERAL PRACTICE AND PROCEDURE: CIVIL § 1323, at 735 (2d ed. 1990).

122. FED. R. CIV. P. 10(b).

that the claims arose from a single transaction."[123] Rule 10(c) permits a party to "adopt by reference" (or "incorporate by reference") prior allegations.[124] Parties may raise defects of form by motion.[125]

(b) "Notice" Pleading

Rule 8(a)(2) omits the code requirement that the complaint state the "facts" constituting the "cause of action." In this way, it avoids the distinctions between factual and legal conclusions and the specificity requirements of code pleading.[126] In *Conley v. Gibson*,[127] the U.S. Supreme Court described the simplified pleading permitted by the Federal Rules:

> The respondents also argue that the complaint failed to set forth specific facts to support its general allegations of discrimination. . . . The decisive answer to this is that the Federal Rules of Civil Procedure do not require a claimant to set out in detail the facts upon which [the pleader] bases [the] claim. To the contrary, all the Rules require is "a short and plain statement of the claim" that will give the defendant *fair notice* of what the plaintiff's claim is and the grounds upon which it rests. The illustrative forms appended to the Rules plainly demonstrate this. Such simplified "notice pleading" is made possible by the liberal opportunity for discovery and the other pretrial procedures established by the Rules to disclose more precisely the basis of both claim and defense and to define more narrowly the disputed facts and issues. Following the simple guide of Rule 8(f) that "all pleadings shall be so construed as to do substantial justice," we have no doubt that petitioners' complaint adequately set forth a claim and gave the respondents fair notice of its basis. The

123. 5 CHARLES A. WRIGHT & ARTHUR R. MILLER, FEDERAL PRACTICE AND PROCEDURE: CIVIL § 1324, at 743 (2d ed. 1990). *But see* Form 17 in the Appendix of Forms following the Federal Rules of Civil Procedure (claims for copyright infringement and unfair competition stated in a single count).

124. FED. R. CIV. P. 10(c). Incorporation by reference was permitted in common-law pleading with respect to allegations in separate counts of the same pleading, but not to allegations in separate pleadings (or motions) as Rule 10(c) permits. 5 CHARLES A. WRIGHT & ARTHUR R. MILLER, FEDERAL PRACTICE AND PROCEDURE: CIVIL § 1326, at 755-56 (2d ed. 1990). Many code states likewise permit incorporation by reference. CHARLES A. CLARK, HANDBOOK OF THE LAW OF CODE PLEADING § 37, at 223-24 (2d ed. 1947).

125. At common law, formal defects in a party's pleading could be challenged by a special demurrer. All special demurrers were general demurrers and thus would also raise defects in substance. In code and federal practice, courts traditionally have entertained motions to correct defects of form, even though the codes or the Federal Rules may not authorize such motions specifically. Such motions are permitted on the ground that they are necessary to effectuate specific provisions of the rules. For example, motions have been used as a means of making the pleadings conform to the formal requirements of Federal Rule 10 (caption, names of parties, paragraphs, etc.). *See* 5A CHARLES A. WRIGHT & ARTHUR R. MILLER, FEDERAL PRACTICE AND PROCEDURE: CIVIL § 1360 (2d ed. 1990).

126. Pleading facts constituting a cause of action in a code-pleading system contrasts with pleading facts and circumstances on which the claim is based in sufficient detail to give notice of the claim, but not necessarily alleging a specific fact to cover every substantive element of the claim. *See* section C(2)*(a)* ("Pleading 'Facts' ") *supra*.

127. 355 U.S. 41, 78 S. Ct. 99, 2 L. Ed. 2d 80 (1957).

Federal Rules reject the approach that pleading is a game of skill in which one misstep by counsel may be decisive to the outcome and accept the principle that the purpose of pleading is to facilitate a proper decision on the merits.[128]

Despite the "fair notice" philosophy stated in *Conley*, lower courts have sometimes attempted to develop stricter pleading requirements for certain cases.[129] The Supreme Court has consistently rejected these attempts.[130] Most recently, in *Leatherman v. Tarrant County Narcotics Intelligence & Coordination Unit*,[131] the Court unanimously rejected a heightened pleading requirement for civil rights cases alleging municipal liability under section 1983 of Title 42.[132] In reaffirming *Conley v. Gibson*, the Court emphasized "that it is not possible to square the heightened pleading standard applied in this case with the liberal system of 'notice pleading' set up by the Federal Rules."[133] The Court pointed out that the Federal Rules do provide exceptions to the liberal pleading requirement in Rule 8(a)(2).[134] Specifically, Rule 9(b) requires pleaders to state with

---

128. *Id.* at 47-48, 78 S. Ct. at 103, 2 L. Ed. 2d at 85-86 (emphasis added) (footnotes omitted); *see also, e.g.*, Rannels v. S.E. Nichols, Inc., 591 F.2d 242, 245 (3d Cir. 1979) (rejecting the infusion of the technical requirements of code pleading into pleading under the Federal Rules). The counter argument against notice pleading focuses on practical implications of the differences between pleading facts under the codes and providing notice of the claim under the Federal Rules:

> When only notice pleading is required, reputedly, practicing lawyers often complain that they do not become fully aware of the issue in many cases until after prolonged discovery. This results in increased costs to the litigants and untoward delay in cases reaching the trial stage. Under code pleading, if the pleadings are properly prepared, the issues are apparent immediately upon the filing of a petition and the filing of an answer. If either a petition or an answer does not clearly set forth a litigant's issues, sustaining a motion to make more definite and certain will expeditiously clarify the issues, save the litigants unwarranted expense, promote judicial economy, and avoid unnecessary delay in a case reaching the trial stage.

Christianson v. Educational Serv. Unit No. 16, 243 Neb. 553, 560, 501 N.W.2d 281, 287-88 (1993).

129. *See* Richard L. Marcus, *The Revival of Fact Pleading Under the Federal Rules of Civil Procedure*, 86 COLUM. L. REV. 433 (1986) (pointing out that fact pleading was "enjoying a revival" in several areas, such as securities fraud and civil rights cases); *see also* Douglas A. Blaze, *Presumed Frivolous: Application of Stringent Pleading Requirements in Civil Rights Litigation*, 31 WM. & MARY L. REV. 935 (1990); C. Keith Wingate, *A Special Pleading Rule for Civil Rights Complaints: A Step Forward or A Step Back?* 49 MO. L. REV. 677 (1984).

130. *See, e.g.*, Hospital Bldg. Co. v. Trustees of Rex Hosp., 425 U.S. 738, 96 S. Ct. 1848, 48 L. Ed. 2d 338 (1976); Conley v. Gibson, 355 U.S. 41, 78 S. Ct. 99, 2 L. Ed. 2d 80 (1957).

131. 507 U.S. 163, 113 S. Ct. 1160, 122 L. Ed. 2d 517 (1993).

132. The defendants argued that a municipality's freedom from *respondeat superior* liability necessarily included immunity from suit. Thus, the more relaxed pleading standard of the Federal Rule 8(a)(2) "would subject municipalities to expensive and time consuming discovery in every § 1983 case, eviscerating their immunity from suit and disrupting municipal functions." *Id.* at 166, 113 S. Ct. at 1162, 122 L. Ed. 2d at 523. The Court rejected this argument, refusing to equate freedom from liability with immunity from suit. According to the Court, municipalities, unlike various government officials, are not immune from suit. "[A] *municipality* can be sued under § 1983, but it cannot be held liable unless a municipal policy or custom caused the constitutional injury." *Id.* (emphasis added). The Court did not "consider whether [its] qualified immunity jurisprudence require a heightened pleading in cases involving *individual* government officials" who are sometimes immune from suit. *Id.* (emphasis added). The federal courts of appeals are now divided on whether to follow *Leatherman* in suits against individuals. *See* Gary T. Lester, Case Comment, 37 S. TEX. L. REV. 413, 439-41 (1996).

133. *Id.* at 168, 113 S. Ct. at 1160, 122 L. Ed. 2d at 523.

134. *Id.* at 168, 113 S. Ct. at 1160, 122 L. Ed. 2d at 524.

particularity the circumstances constituting fraud or mistake.[135] Relying on the traditional maxim in which the expression of one exception to the general rule excludes other unspecified exceptions, the Court refused to create an exception by judicial interpretation.[136]

The Federal Rules also have rejected the theory-of-the-pleadings doctrine prevailing in some code-pleading systems.[137] The frequently stated test for granting a challenge to defective statements of the claim in federal court is contained in a statement by the Supreme Court in *Conley*:

> In appraising the [legal] sufficiency of the complaint we follow, of course, the accepted rule that a complaint should not be dismissed for a failure to state a cause of action unless it appears beyond doubt that the plaintiff can prove no set of facts in support of [the plaintiff's] claim which would entitle [the plaintiff] to relief.[138]

This statement cannot, of course, be taken literally. Otherwise, a complaint stating only that the "defendant is legally liable to the plaintiff" would be legally sufficient because it does not appear beyond doubt that the plaintiff can prove no set of facts in support of the claim that would entitle the plaintiff to

---

135. *See* subsection 2*(e)(i)* ("Fraud and Mistake") *infra* (discussing special pleading requirements imposed by Federal Rule 9).

136. "[T]he Federal Rules do address in Rule 9(b) the question of the need for greater particularity in pleading certain actions, but do not include among the enumerated actions any reference to complaints alleging municipal liability under § 1983. *Expressio unius est exclusio alterius.*" *Id.* at 168, 113 S. Ct. at 1163, 122 L. Ed. 2d at 524. However, it is likely that lower courts will continue to seek more detailed pleading. *See, e.g.,* Ersek v. Township of Springfield, 822 F. Supp. 218 (E.D. Pa. 1993) (requiring the defendant to file a more definite statement to plaintiff's claims for conspiracy, defamation, false light, and § 1983 and attempting to distinguish *Leatherman* on the ground that the redrafting of the complaint ordered in *Ersek* was not designed to preempt any potential defenses or to require plaintiff to plead with any special care because this action involved § 1983; a more definite statement was ordered "to make the claims in a straightforward way because the complaint is rife with unsupportable generalizations"); Paul J. McCardle, *A Short and Plain Statement: The Significance of* Leatherman v. Tarrant County, 72 U. DET. MERCY L. REV. 19, 38-42 (1994) (discussing lower court cases responding to *Leatherman*); Richard L. Marcus, *The Puzzling Persistence of Pleading Practice,* 76 TEX. L. REV. 1749 (1998) (discussing the persistence of traditional pleading practice in spite of the notice pleading philosophy of the Federal Rules and cases like *Leatherman*).

Furthermore, in Schultea v. Wood, 47 F.3d 1427 (5th Cir. 1995), the Fifth Circuit held that, *Leatherman* notwithstanding, Federal Rule 7(a) can be used to order a plaintiff to reply to a defendant's affirmative defense of limited immunity. To the extent that the defendant has pleaded factual details in the defense, the plaintiff can be required to plead details in the reply on the ground that notice pleading under Federal Rule 8(a) applies only to complaints; according to the court, the only rule governing the content of a Rule 7 reply is Federal Rule 8(e)(1), which requires pleadings to be "simple, concise, and direct"; Rule 8(e)(1) would not prohibit a detailed court-ordered reply. However, the Fifth Circuit failed to consider whether Federal Rules 8(b) ("Defenses; Form of Denials") and (c) ("Affirmative Defenses") applied to the plaintiff's reply if it asserted denials and defenses to the defendant's immunity defense. These provisions are worded generally to apply to defenses asserted in all pleadings, and Rules 8(b) and (c) embody the notice pleading standards of the Federal Rules. *See* 5 CHARLES A. WRIGHT ET AL., FEDERAL PRACTICE AND PROCEDURE: CIVIL § 1261, at 384-85, § 1274, at 455 (2d ed. 1990). Nevertheless, Rule 8(b) requires that denials must "fairly meet the substance of the averments denied," and this provision may sometimes produce the result that the Fifth Circuit wants when the defense is pleaded properly. *See* sections D(3)*(f)(ii)* ("Admissions and Denials") & D(4) ("The Plaintiff's Reply and Motions to Strike an Insufficient Defense") *infra*.

137. *See, e.g.,* FED. R. CIV. P. 8(e), 15(b), 54(c); *see also* section C(3)*(b) supra*.

138. *Conley,* 355 U.S. at 45-46, 78 S. Ct. at 102, 2 L. Ed. 2d at 84.

relief.''[139] Rather, the statement must be read in conjunction with the earlier description of the ''fair notice'' philosophy of pleading in *Conley*. Thus, for example, Federal Forms 4 through 8 contain language similar to the old common counts.[140] Federal Rule 84 states that ''[t]he forms contained in the Appendix of Forms are sufficient under the rules. . . . '' On this basis, one can conclude that the common counts meet the ''fair notice'' pleading requirements of Rule 8(a)(2), as interpreted in *Conley*.[141]

(c) Alternative, Hypothetical, and Inconsistent Pleading

Common-law pleading requirements forced a party to elect a set of facts and a legal theory at the outset of the action and to plead them with certainty.[142] In contrast, Federal Rule 8(e)(2) expressly permits a plaintiff to set forth two or more statements of a claim alternatively or hypothetically, either in one count or in separate counts. A plaintiff may also set forth claims inconsistently.

Illustration 6-21. The Federal Rules would permit the alternative and hypothetical allegations in *Illustration 6-2*.[143]

(d) Anticipating Defenses

The Federal Rules do not require the plaintiff to anticipate defenses. If the plaintiff does anticipate a defense, the plaintiff should be permitted to do so—particularly when the plaintiff offers a justification for a defense appearing on the face of the complaint.[144] However, the plaintiff cannot use such an anticipation to satisfy federal jurisdiction.[145]

Illustration 6-22. Assume that the dates alleged in *A's* complaint appear to indicate that the applicable statute of limitations has run on *A's* claim. *A* can anticipate the statute of limitations defense by alleging information demonstrating a recognized basis for tolling the statute (*e.g.*, *A's* mental incompetency or fraudulent concealment of a conspiracy that prevented its discovery).

---

139. *See* FLEMING JAMES, JR. ET AL., CIVIL PROCEDURE § 3.7, at 151 (4th ed. 1992).

140. *See* section A(2) (''Stating the Plaintiff's Claim in the Declaration'') *supra*.

141. The common counts give the general quality of notice necessary to enable the defendant to answer the complaint and proceed to the discovery stage of the litigation. However, Federal Rule 9 may impose further requirements. For example, Form 7 (''Complaint for Money Paid by Mistake'') requires the circumstances to be stated with particularity, in compliance with Rule 9(b). *See* subsection *(e)(i)* (''Fraud and Mistake'') *infra*. *See generally* 5 CHARLES A. WRIGHT & ARTHUR R. MILLER, FEDERAL PRACTICE AND PROCEDURE: CIVIL § 1222 (2d ed. 1990). The common counts also met the requirements of code pleading. *See* section (C)(2)*(a)* (''Pleading 'Facts' '') *supra*.

142. The prohibition against pleading in the alternative at common law was eventually circumvented by using different counts to state the same cause of action in alternative ways. *See* CHARLES E. CLARK, HANDBOOK OF THE LAW OF CODE PLEADING § 70, at 459-60 (2d ed. 1947).

143. The allegation tracks the allegation in Federal Form 10.

144. The fact that no reply is permitted in federal court points in favor of allowing anticipation.

145. *See, e.g.*, Louisville & Nashville R.R. Co. v. Mottley, 211 U.S. 149, 29 S. Ct. 42, 53 L. Ed. 126 (1908); Chapter 2(C)(1)*(b)(ii)* (''The Well-Pleaded Complaint Rule''); *Illustration 2-25, supra*.

(e) Pleading Special Matters

Historically, several pleading problems have been dealt with in special ways. The Federal Rules of Civil Procedure have addressed these matters by a series of special pleading provisions. In certain instances, these provisions preserve common-law and code-pleading requirements.

(i) Fraud and Mistake

Like the common law and codes, Federal Rule 9(b) requires that ''in all averments of fraud or mistake, the circumstances constituting fraud or mistake shall be stated with particularity.''[146]

Illustration 6-23. Assume that *A* sued *B* based upon certain fraudulent misrepresentations made to induce *A* to purchase a tract of land. To satisfy the pleading requirements of Rule 9(b), *A* could allege the following ''circumstances'': (1) time, (2) place, (3) content of the false representations, (4) identity

---

146. FED. R. CIV. P. 9(b); *see also* Form 7 (''Complaint for Money Paid by Mistake'') and Form 13 (''Complaint on Claim for Debt and to Set Aside Fraudulent Conveyance Under Rule 18(b)'') in the Appendix of Forms following the Federal Rules of Civil Procedure. *See generally* Barney J. Finberg, Annotation, *Construction and Application of Provision of Rule 9(b), Federal Rules of Civil Procedure, That Circumstances Constituting Fraud or Mistake Be Stated with Particularity*, 27 A.L.R. FED. 407 (1976). The following reasons have been advanced in support of the requirement of pleading fraud and mistake with particularity:

> [T]he requirement is necessary to safeguard potential defendants from lightly made claims charging commission of acts that involve some degree of moral turpitude. Allegations of fraud or mistake frequently are advanced only for their nuisance or settlement value and with little hope that they will be successful. Further, since assertions of fraud or mistake often are involved in attempts to reopen completed transactions or set aside previously issued judicial orders, courts are unwilling to entertain charges of this type unless they are based on allegations that are sufficient to show whether the alleged injustice is severe enough to warrant the risks and difficulties inherent in a re-examination of old and settled matters. Also, fraud and mistake embrace such a wide variety of potential conduct that a defendant needs a substantial amount of particularized information about plaintiff's claim in order to enable him to understand it and effectively prepare his response. Finally, as has been pointed out by the commentators, the old cliche that actions or defenses based upon fraud are disfavored and are scrutinized by the courts with great care because they often form the basis of ''strike suits'' still retains considerable vitality.

5 CHARLES A. WRIGHT & ARTHUR R. MILLER, FEDERAL PRACTICE AND PROCEDURE: CIVIL § 1296, at 577-81 (2d ed. 1990) (footnotes omitted). Nevertheless, it is doubtful whether these reasons are sufficient to support a specialized pleading requirement today. Other types of allegations, such as assault and battery, involve moral turpitude, but no specialized pleading rule applies to them. In any event, this rationale can, at best, apply to fraud, but certainly not to mistake. Negligence allegations are often ''advanced only for their nuisance or settlement value,'' but no specialized pleading requirement applies to them. Negligence also embraces a wide variety of conduct, but the defendant is not thought to need particularized information from the plaintiff at the pleading stage to prepare a response to an allegation of negligence. Old and settled matters will not have to be reopened if there is no evidence to justify reopening them, but this does not provide a persuasive reason for a particularized *pleading* requirement. Finally, there is no justifiable reason for a Federal Rule to ''disfavor'' any particular kind of action or defense. Indeed, that would seem to be a ''substantive'' matter from which the rulemakers are prohibited under 28 U.S.C. § 2072. Similarly, ''strike suits'' can be dealt with under Federal Rule 11. *See* section E(2) (''Good Faith Pleading: Rule 11'') *infra*.

of the person making the representations, and (5) what was obtained thereby (reliance).[147]

* * * * *

The Private Securities Litigation Reform Act of 1995 imposed additional requirements for pleading fraud and fraudulent intent in investor securities litigation.[148]

(ii) Conditions of the Mind

Federal Rule 9(b) permits "[m]alice, intent, knowledge, and other condition of [the] mind of a person" to be "averred generally."[149] Detailed descriptions of such conditions of mind would be prolix and unworkable. Also, no need exists for more detailed descriptions in light of the general goal of providing notice.[150] However, in investor securities litigation involving fraudulent intent, the Private Securities Litigation Reform Act of 1995 imposes more stringent standards.[151]

---

147. *See id.* § 1297, at 590; Williams v. WMX Techns., 112 F.3d 175 (5th Cir.), *cert. denied*, 522 U.S. 966, 118 S. Ct. 412, 139 L. Ed. 2d 315 (1997) (holding that to plead fraud with particularity, the plaintiff must specify the statements that were fraudulent and why they were fraudulent, identify who made the statements, identify when the statements were made, and identify where the statements were made; furthermore, all this must be done before the plaintiff has access to discovery). *But cf.* Form 13 in the Appendix of Forms following the Federal Rules of Civil Procedure (specificity of allegations will vary depending on circumstances).

148. *See* Pub. L. No. 104-67, 109 Stat. 737 (codified at 15 U.S.C. § 78u-4 *et seq.*). If the plaintiff alleges that (a) the defendant made an untrue statement of a material fact or (b) failed to state a material fact necessary to make the statements not misleading under the circumstances, the Act requires that the complaint "specify each statement alleged to have been misleading, the reason or reasons why the statement is misleading, and, if an allegation regarding the statement or omission is made on information and belief, the complaint shall state with particularity all facts on which that belief is formed." *Id.* § 101(b), Pub. L. No. 104-67, 109 Stat. 737, 747. In addition, with regard to the defendant's fraudulent intent, the Act requires that the complaint, "with respect to each act or omission alleged to violate this title, state with particularity facts giving rise to a *strong inference* that the defendant acted with the required state of mind." *Id.* (emphasis added). *Compare In re* Advanta Corp. Sec. Litig., 180 F.3d 525 (3d Cir. 1999) (Private Securities Litigation Reform Act's requirement for pleading scienter can be satisfied by alleging with particularity facts establishing motive and opportunity to commit fraud or facts constituting circumstantial evidence of reckless or conscious behavior that raise a strong inference of fraudulent intent) *and* Press v. Chemical Inv. Servs. Corp., 166 F.3d 529 (2d Cir. 1999) (same) *with* Bryant v. Avado Brands, Inc., 187 F.3d 1271 (11th Cir. 1999) (allegations of motive and opportunity insufficient to allege scienter) *and In re* Comshare, Inc. Sec. Litig., 183 F.3d 542 (6th Cir. 1999) (same) *and In re* Silicon Graphics Inc. Sec. Litig., 183 F.3d 970 (9th Cir. 1999) (same). *See generally* Patricia J. Meyer, *What Congress Said About the Heightened Pleading Standard: A Proposed Solution to the Securities Fraud Pleading Confusion,* 66 FORD. L. REV. 2517 (1998).

149. FED. R. CIV. P. 9(b).

150. An interesting comparison can be drawn between the Federal Rules and current English practice, which requires the particulars of the facts for malice, fraudulent intention, or other conditions of the mind. *See* 5 CHARLES A. WRIGHT & ARTHUR R. MILLER, FEDERAL PRACTICE AND PROCEDURE: CIVIL § 1296, at 577 n.2 (2d ed. 1990) (citing English Order 18, Rule 12).

151. *See* Pub. L. No. 104-67, 109 Stat. 737. The Act goes beyond Rule 9(b) by introducing the *standard* by which the allegation should be judged: "with respect to each act or omission alleged to violate this title, [the pleader must] state with particularity facts giving rise to a *strong inference* that the defendant acted with the required state of mind." *Id.* § 101(b), Pub. L. No. 104-67, 109 Stat. 737, 747 (emphasis added). This standard surely overrides the provision in Rule 9(b) allowing knowledge and intent to be pleaded generally.

(iii) Special Damages

Like the common-law and code-pleading systems, the Federal Rules require *special damages* to be alleged specifically.[152] The courts have divided damages into two basic categories: (1) *general damages*, which are presumed to flow in the natural course of events from the specific injuries alleged; and (2) *special damages*, which are unusual or peculiar and are not presumed to have occurred.[153] Court decisions over a long period established the dividing line between special damages and general damages. To some extent, this division is an arbitrary classification. Furthermore, the courts are not always completely in accord on how a particular item of damage should be classified.

General damages often are based on either of the following: (1) market measures, such as the difference between the contract price and the market price; or (2) naturally expected consequences, such as pain and suffering resulting from injuries in an automobile accident. General damages need not be alleged at all, except to the extent that damages (actual injury) are part of the statement of a cause of action, as in a negligence claim. On the other hand, special damages must be specifically stated and must be proved at trial with reasonable certainty. Examples include the loss of profits resulting from a contract breach, expenses incurred in pursuing converted property in order to recover it, and statutory double or treble damages.[154]

(iv) Conditions Precedent

Unlike the common law, Federal Rule 9(c) permits a general allegation of performance of conditions precedent.[155] This approach is justified because

---

152. *See* Fed. R. Civ. P. 9(g); Charles E. Clark, Handbook of the Law of Code Pleading § 51 (2d ed. 1947); Joseph H. Koffler & Alison Reppy, Handbook of Common Law Pleading § 54, at 129 (1969).

153. *See* Cotton Bros. Baking Co. v. Industrial Risk Insurers, 102 F.R.D. 964, 965-67 (W.D. La. 1984) (discussing the definitions of general and special damages) (claims for interest due on loans taken out as the result of fire and for loss of sales and accelerated equipment usage were not claims for special damages that had to be alleged specifically).

154. *See* Dan B. Dobbs, The Law of Remedies § 3.2 (2d student ed. 1993); *see also* Fowler v. Curtis Publ'g Co., 182 F.2d 377 (D.C. Cir. 1950) (disparagement claim) (when special damage is part of the substantive claim, a specific statement is required, such as the loss of particular customers by name or a general diminution of business if specific customers can not be alleged; it is not sufficient to allege that the plaintiff has suffered special damages or that the party has been put to great costs and expenses); Irizarry v. Ennia, 678 F. Supp. 957, 959 (D.P.R. 1988) (purpose of requiring that special damages be specifically pleaded is to notify the defendant that damages other than those that are presumed to exist are going to be sought; no requirement that special damages must be pleaded with the same level of particularity as fraud or mistake); Lebeda v. A.H. Robins Co., 101 F.R.D. 689, 690 (D. Me. 1984) (although great particularity is not required in pleading special damages, a specific statement is required). *Compare* Comeau v. Rupp, 762 F. Supp. 1434, 1449 (D. Kan. 1991), Citron v. Armstrong World Indus., Inc., 721 F. Supp. 1259, 1261 (S.D. Fla. 1989) *and* Barton v. Barnett, 226 F. Supp. 375, 378 (N.D. Miss. 1964) (punitive damages are special damages that must be pleaded specially under Rule 9(g)) *with* American Sur. Co. v. Franciscus, 127 F.2d 810 (8th Cir. 1942) *and* Nelson v. G.C. Murphy Co., 245 F. Supp. 846, 847 (N.D. Ala. 1965) (punitive damages are not special damages and need not be specially stated). *See generally* Note, *The Definition and Pleading of Special Damage Under the Federal Rules of Civil Procedure*, 55 Va. L. Rev. 542 (1969).

155. 5 Charles A. Wright & Arthur R. Miller, Federal Practice and Procedure: Civil § 1302, at 679 (2d ed. 1990).

the satisfaction of conditions precedent is usually not an issue.[156] However, if conditions precedent are not usually at issue, perhaps the Federal Rules should not have required any allegation of their performance. The Federal Rules take this approach with regard to other types of allegations, such as capacity to sue or be sued.[157] The probable explanation for treating conditions precedent and capacity differently is the existence of a strong pleading custom in contract cases.

(v) *Official Documents, Official Acts, and Judgments*

Federal Rule 9(d) provides that "[i]n pleading an official document or official act it is sufficient to aver that the document was issued or the act done in compliance with [the] law."[158] Like prior code practice, Rule 9(e) permits a general averment of any judicial or quasi-judicial judgment or decision "without setting forth matter showing jurisdiction to render it."[159] In an action to recover on the judgment of a domestic court of record at common law,[160] the plaintiff did not have to allege facts demonstrating that the court rendering the judgment had jurisdiction. However, the contrary was true when the action was based on a judgment of a domestic court of limited or inferior jurisdiction or a judgment of a foreign court.

(vi) *Capacity of a Party to Sue or Be Sued*

Federal Rule 9(a) provides that a pleader does not have "to aver the capacity of a party to sue or be sued or the authority of a party to sue or be sued in representative capacity or the legal existence of an organized association of persons that is made a party, except to the extent required to show the jurisdiction of the court."[161] In proposing Rule 9(a), the Advisory Committee thought that capacity was rarely in issue.[162]

(vii) *Time and Place*

Unlike the common law, Federal Rule 9(f) provides that "[f]or the purpose of testing the sufficiency of a pleading, averments of time and place are material and shall be considered like all other averments of material matter."[163] Rule 9(f) does not address whether specific allegations of time and place have to

---

156. Professors Wright and Miller aptly point out that "it seems doubtful that even the usually perfunctory allegation of performance . . . serves any significantly useful function." *See id.* at 680.

157. *See* subsection *(vi)* ("Capacity of a Party to Sue or Be Sued") *infra*.

158. FED. R. CIV. P. 9(d). With respect to pleading official documents or acts, see Form 16 and paragraph 4 of Form 17 in the Appendix of Forms following the Federal Rules of Civil Procedure.

159. FED. R. CIV. P. 9(e).

160. *See* Chapter 1(E)(1)*(b)(ii)* ("*Ex Contractu* Personal Actions") *supra*; *Illustration 3-1* in Chapter 3(A)(1) ("Personal Jurisdiction Restrictions Prior to the Fourteenth Amendment") *supra*.

161. FED. R. CIV. P. 9(a).

162. *See* 5 CHARLES A. WRIGHT & ARTHUR R. MILLER, FEDERAL PRACTICE AND PROCEDURE: CIVIL § 1292 (2d ed. 1990).

163. FED. R. CIV. P. 9(f).

be alleged at all, but merely their significance when alleged.[164] Making allegations of time and place material helps to identify the particular occurrence or transaction at issue for purposes of providing the opposing party with notice. It also may facilitate early adjudication of statute of limitation defenses.[165]

(viii) Nonjoinder of Certain Parties

Rule 19(c) requires a pleader to state the names, if known, of any persons who ought to have been made parties pursuant to Rule 19(a)(1)-(2), but who were not. The pleader must also state the reason or reasons for not joining such parties.[166] As demonstrated in Chapter 8, Rule 19(a) requires certain kinds of parties to be joined. If Rule 19(a) parties are not joined, there must be an adequate reason for their nonjoinder. In addition, a specialized inquiry must be made under Rule 19(b) to determine whether the action can continue without the nonjoined parties, or whether they must be classified as "indispensable" and the action dismissed.[167]

3. Responding to the Complaint

(a) Default

After being notified of the lawsuit, the defendant is required to respond. If the defendant fails to respond, "judgment by default will be taken against [the defendant] for the relief demanded in the complaint."[168]

(b) Motions for More Definite Statements and Bills of Particulars

Federal Rule 12(e) provides for a "Motion for More Definite Statement." Rule 12(e) requires that the motion identify "the defects complained of and the details desired."[169] A motion for a *more definite statement* under the Federal Rules deals with the problem of the moving party's inability to frame a

---

164. 5 CHARLES A. WRIGHT & ARTHUR R. MILLER, FEDERAL PRACTICE AND PROCEDURE: CIVIL § 1309, at 696 (2d ed. 1990).

165. *Id.* § 1308, at 693-94; Kincheloe v. Farmer, 214 F.2d 604 (7th Cir. 1954), *cert. denied*, 348 U.S. 920, 75 S. Ct. 306, 99 L. Ed. 721 (1955) (reason for making time and place averments material is to help determine whether the statute of limitations bars an action). Courts have allowed the statute of limitations defense to be raised through a preanswer motion under Rule 12(b)(6) or a motion for judgment on the pleadings under Rule 12(c) if the complaint demonstrates on its face that the action is time-barred. *See* subsection 3*(d)* ("Motions to Dismiss") & Chapter 10(B) ("Judgment on the Pleadings") *infra*; *see also* subsection 2*(d)* ("Anticipating Defenses") *supra*.

166. FED. R. CIV. P. 19(c). Form 26 illustrates how this allegation should be made: "John Doe named in the complaint is not made a party to this action [because he is not subject to the jurisdiction of this court] [because he cannot be made a party to the action without depriving this court of jurisdiction]."

167. *See* Chapter 8(C)(3) ("Joinder of Persons Needed for Just Adjudication") *infra*.

168. Form 1 ("Summons") in the Appendix of Forms following the Federal Rules of Civil Procedure. *See* Chapter 10(A) ("Default Judgment") *infra*.

169. FED. R. CIV. P. 12(e). The general nature of motions in federal court is described in Federal Rule 7(b).

responsive pleading.[170] The original version of Rule 12(e) also permitted bills of particulars.[171] In 1948, Rule 12(e) was amended to eliminate the bill of particulars from federal practice. The Advisory Committee noted that Rule 12(e) ''as originally drawn has been the subject of more judicial rulings than any other part of the rules, and has been much criticized by commentators, judges and members of the bar.''[172]

Given the general notice pleading philosophy of the Federal Rules, it will seldom be the case that a complaint that states a claim upon which relief may be granted will be so vague that a Rule 12(e) motion is appropriate. As long as the complaint is sufficiently definite to allow the defendant to prepare a responsive pleading, a Rule 12(e) motion is improper. Given the options available to the defendant under Rule 8(b), therefore, there should seldom be an occasion to use Rule 12(e).

(c) Motions to Strike

Rule 12(f) permits motions to strike redundant, immaterial, impertinent, or scandalous matter. Rule 12(f) performs the same function as the code motion to expunge.[173] Under Federal Rule 12(f), a motion to strike must be made before responding to a pleading (for example, before serving an answer to the complaint) or within 20 days after service of the pleading if no responsive pleading is permitted (for example, to attack a scandalous answer).

Illustration 6-24. Assume that *D* wants the court to strike out certain scandalous allegations in *P's* complaint prior to filing an answer. *D* can use a motion to strike under Rule 12(f) for this purpose.[174]

---

170. Under the codes, a motion to make more definite and certain deals with this problem. *See* section C(3)*(a)* (''Motions for More Definite Statements and Bills of Particulars'') *supra.*

171. *See* sections A(3)*(g)* (''Bills of Particulars'') & C(3)*(a)* (''Motions for More Definite Statements and Bills of Particulars'') *supra.*

172. The Advisory Committee set forth the reasons for this change:

> Rule 12(e) . . . . The tendency of some courts freely to grant extended bills of particulars has served to neutralize any helpful benefits derived from Rule 8, and has overlooked the intended use of the rules on depositions and discovery. [Original Rule 12(e) provided that ''a party may move for a more definite statement or for a bill of particulars of any matter which is not averred with sufficient definiteness or particularity to enable [the pleader] properly to prepare [a] responsive pleading or to prepare for trial.''] The words ''or to prepare for trial'' . . . have sometimes been seized upon as grounds for compulsory statement in the opposing pleading of all the details which the movant would have to meet at trial.

FED. R. CIV. P. 12(e) advisory committee's note to the 1946 Amendment. The principal reasons for its excessive use appeared to be delay, harassment, and an attempt to put a burden on the plaintiff. *See* CHARLES E. CLARK, HANDBOOK OF THE LAW OF CODE PLEADING § 40, at 250-52 (2d ed. 1947); 5A CHARLES A. WRIGHT & ARTHUR R. MILLER, FEDERAL PRACTICE AND PROCEDURE: CIVIL § 1376 (2d ed. 1990). *See generally* Stefan F. Tucker, Comment, *Federal Rule 12(e): Motion for More Definite Statement–History, Operation and Efficacy*, 61 MICH. L. REV. 1126 (1963).

173. CHARLES E. CLARK, HANDBOOK OF THE LAW OF CODE PLEADING § 87, at 550-52 (2d ed. 1947); *see also* section C(6) (''Code Motions to Expunge or Strike'') *supra.*

174. If the motion is denied, Rule 12(a)(4)(A) states that the responsive pleading shall be served within ten days after notice of the court's action. If the motion is granted, Rule 12(a)(4) does not specifically provide a time period for serving the answer. Technically, the defendant would be in default if the defendant did not serve the answer within twenty days after the complaint was filed. This apparent result may reflect defective drafting

Illustration 6-25. *D* denies the allegations of the complaint in the answer. *D* then moves to strike scandalous matter from the complaint. Rule 12(f) technically bars the motion because *D* has already answered. The court, however, may strike the matter on its own initiative.

(d) Motions to Dismiss

The defendant can move to dismiss an action prior to filing an answer. Rule 12(b) provides seven grounds for such motions: (1) lack of subject-matter jurisdiction; (2) lack of personal jurisdiction; (3) improper venue; (4) insufficiency of process (failure to conform the contents of the summons to the requirements of Rule 4(a) regulating that content); (5) insufficiency of service of process (use of an improper manner of service or the failure to deliver the summons at all); (6) failure to state a claim upon which relief can be granted; and (7) failure to join an indispensable party (as defined by Rule 19).[175] Misjoinder of parties is not a ground for dismissal of the action.[176]

Illustration 6-26. Assume that *P* has served a complaint alleging certain facts. *D* believes that the facts stated, assuming that they could be proved, do not give rise to a recognized legal obligation. At common law and under the Field Code, *D* raised this defense by a demurrer.[177] The Federal Rules have abolished demurrers.[178] The equivalent challenge to the legal sufficiency of the complaint under the Federal Rules is a Rule 12(b)(6) defense of ''failure to state a claim upon which relief may be granted.''[179] Like common-law pleading and the codes, the Federal Rules assume for purposes of this motion that all well-pleaded

---

in Rule 12(a)(4). However, the theory could be that there is no need to delay the answer to obtain the result of a Rule 12(f) motion. *See* 5A CHARLES A. WRIGHT & ARTHUR R. MILLER, FEDERAL PRACTICE AND PROCEDURE: CIVIL § 1346, at 181-82 (2d ed. 1990).

175. FED. R. CIV. P. 12(b).

176. *See* FED. R. CIV. P. 21. Federal Rule 12 does not require that the objection appear on the face of the complaint and it does not list lack of capacity to sue as a matter that can be raised by pre-answer motion. *See* FED. R. CIV. P. 12(b). As noted in subsection D(2)*(e)(vi)* (''Capacity of a Party to Sue or Be Sued''), *supra* Federal Rule 9(a) does not require a plaintiff to plead capacity to sue. The federal rule is in contrast to the practice in some code states, which requires allegations of the legal existence of a corporate plaintiff. Rule 9(a) further provides that

> [w]hen a party desires to raise an issue as to the legal existence of any party or the capacity of any party to sue or be sued or the authority of a party to sue or be sued in a representative capacity, the party desiring to raise the issue shall do so by specific negative averment, which shall include such supporting particulars as are peculiarly within the pleader's knowledge.

FED. R. CIV. P. 9(a). Despite this express language, some federal courts have permitted defendants to raise this objection in a Rule 12(b)(6) motion (failure to state a claim upon which relief can be granted) when the defect appears on the face of the complaint. 5A CHARLES A. WRIGHT & ARTHUR R. MILLER, FEDERAL PRACTICE AND PROCEDURE: CIVIL § 1360, at 432, 434 (2d ed. 1990). In federal court, the pendency of another action between the same parties for the same cause and the prematurity of bringing the action must be raised by answer. 5 *id.* § 1271, at 429; *see* FED. R. CIV. P. 8(c).

177. *See* section A(3)*(a)* (''General Demurrers''); section C(3)*(b)* (''Demurrers'') *supra.*

178. FED. R. CIV. P. 7(c).

179. FED. R. CIV. P. 12(b)(6).

facts in the complaint are admitted.[180] In ruling on the motion, the court may not consider matters outside the complaint, except matters of public record, court orders, items present in the record, and exhibits attached to the complaint.[181]

Illustration 6-27. Assume that *P* serves a summons and complaint on *D*. *D* believes that *P* failed to serve process properly, that venue is improper, and that the court lacks subject-matter jurisdiction of the *P's* action. Rule 12(b) permits *D* to raise all of these defenses in a preanswer motion to dismiss.[182]

(e) The Mechanics of Motion Practice

Federal Rule 5 governs service of papers after original service of process on the defendant, including service of motions.[183] Rule 5(a) states "every written motion other than one which may be heard ex parte . . . shall be served upon each of the parties."[184] Rule 5(b) states that a party who is represented by an attorney is served by serving the attorney. Service upon attorneys or parties may be made by (1) delivering a copy to them or (2) mailing a copy to them. Service is complete upon mailing.[185] Rule 5(b) specifies that delivery may be made by (1) handing a copy to the party to be served, (2) leaving the copy at their office with a clerk or other person in charge, or (3) if no one is in charge, leaving it in a conspicuous place therein. The motion must also be filed with the court.[186]

---

180. Recall that at common law, a decision on the demurrer terminated the action: either the demurrer was sustained and judgment was entered against the plaintiff, or the demurrer was overruled and judgment was entered against the defendant. The defendant did not have an opportunity to challenge the truth of the allegations subsequently, nor did the plaintiff have the right to amend the declaration except to correct formal defects and errors of oversight. *See* 5A CHARLES A. WRIGHT & ARTHUR R. MILLER, FEDERAL PRACTICE AND PROCEDURE: CIVIL § 1355, at 292-93 (2d ed. 1990). Code and federal practice allow further pleading and amendments. *See, e.g.,* NEB. REV. STAT. §§ 25-811, 25-812 (1995); S.C. CODE § 15-13-340 (Law. Coop. 1976) (pleading after demurrer permitted) (repealed 1985); FED. R. CIV. P. 12(a) & 15(a).

181. Breliant v. Preferred Equities Corp., 109 Nev. 842, 858 P.2d 1258 (1993); *see also* Berk v. Ascoll Inv. Corp., 759 F. Supp. 245, 249 (E.D. Pa. 1991) (documents incorporated by reference into the complaint considered); Hollymatic Corp. v. Holly Sys., Inc., 620 F. Supp. 1366, 1367 (N.D. Ill. 1985) (contract attached to complaint and admissions in answer and in reply to counterclaim considered).

182. *See, e.g.,* Form 19 ("Motion to Dismiss, Presenting Defenses of Failure to State a Claim, of Lack of Service of Process, of Improper Venue, and of Lack of Jurisdiction Under Rule 12(b)") in the Appendix of Forms following the Federal Rules of Civil Procedure. As noted in Chapter 2 *supra* and more fully discussed in subsection *(g)(ii)* ("Waiver") *infra*, a subject-matter jurisdiction objection may be made subsequently, for example, at trial or even thereafter.

183. As amended in 1993, Rule 4 governs service of the summons. Rule 4.1 governs the service of other process. *See* FED. R. CIV. P. 4, 4.1 & advisory committee's note accompanying the 1993 amendments.

184. FED. R. CIV. P. 5(a).

185. FED. R. CIV. P. 5(b); *see* Greene v. WCI Holdings Corp., 136 F.3d 313 (2d Cir. 1998) ("mailing" occurs when placed the mail box, not when postmarked).

186. FED. R. CIV. P. 5(b), (d). If the office is closed or the person to be served has no office, the copy may be left at the person's dwelling house or usual place of abode with some person of suitable age and discretion residing there. Rule 5(d) provides that "[a]ll papers after the complaint required to be served upon a party, together with a certificate of service, shall be filed with the court within a reasonable time after service." Rule 5(e) provides that filing the motion with the clerk of the court is "filing with the court." Filing with the court can also be accomplished by filing the motion with the judge if the judge permits the filing. When the filing is with the judge, the judge is directed to note on the motion the filing date and "forthwith" transmit the documents to the office of the clerk. Filing by facsimile or other electronic means may be authorized by local rule. FED. R. CIV. P. 5(e).

At the hearing on the motion, the judge will listen to the arguments of counsel.[187] An oral hearing may be dispensed with as provided in Rule 78. The judge will then issue an order ruling on the motion. If the court denies the motion or postpones its disposition until trial, Rule 12(a)(4) requires the responsive pleading (answer) be served within ten days after notice of the court's action.[188] If a motion for a more definite statement is granted, the responsive pleading (answer) must be served within ten days after the service of the more definite statement.[189] Rule 6(a) provides the exact method for calculating time periods.[190] Rule 6(e) adds three additional days when service is made by mail.[191]

Illustration 6-28. Assume that *P* serves an unintelligible complaint. If *D* can show that *P's* complaint "is so vague or ambiguous that a party cannot reasonably be expected to frame a responsive pleading [*i.e.*, the answer], the court would grant *D's* motion for a more definite statement under Rule 12(e).[192] If the motion for a more definite statement is granted, Rule 12(a)(4)(B) states that the answer must be served within ten days after the service of the more definite statement. On the other hand, if the motion for a more definite statement has been denied, Rule 12(a)(4)(A) states that the answer must be served within ten days after notice of the court's action.[193]

(f) The Federal Rules Answer

Assuming that the action is not dismissed or the defendant's obligation to respond is not otherwise suspended pursuant to a preanswer motion,[194] the defendant must serve an answer within twenty days.[195] However, if service of the summons has been waived pursuant to Rule 4(d), the defendant must serve an answer within sixty days after the date when the request for waiver was sent (or ninety days after that date if the defendant was addressed outside any judicial district of the United States).[196] The answer in federal practice functions as the means of setting forth the defendant's position—the defendant "shall state in short

---

187. Rule 6(d) provides a five-day time period as a minimum between service of a motion and notice of the hearing and the date of the hearing. Rule 6(e) provides an additional three days when service has been made by mail. Rule 78 provides for a motion day. *See* FED. R. CIV. P. 6(d), 6(e), 78. In general, local rules should be consulted to determine how and when the motion will be heard or whether oral argument is permitted at all. *See, e.g.*, NEB. LOCAL R. 7(e) (oral argument permitted only on order of the court).

188. FED. R. CIV. P. 12(a)(4) (unless a different time is fixed by court order).

189. *Id.*

190. FED. R. CIV. P. 6(a).

191. FED. R. CIV. P. 6(e).

192. FED. R. CIV. P. 12(e).

193. FED. R. CIV. P. 12(a)(4)(A) (unless a different time is fixed by court order).

194. A partial motion to dismiss some, but not all, of the claims of the plaintiff extends the time for answering. *See* Oil Express Nat'l Inc. v. D'Alessandro, 173 F.R.D. 219 (N.D. Ill. 1997).

195. FED. R. CIV. P. 12(1)(A) (unless a different time is fixed by court order). *See generally* Chapter 3(K) ("Service of Process") *supra*.

196. FED. R. CIV. P. 12(a)(1)(B) (unless a different time is fixed by court order). The United States and its officers and agencies have sixty days to respond. FED. R. CIV. P. 12(a)(3). *See generally* Chapter 3(K) ("Service of Process") *supra*.

and plain terms the party's defenses to each claim asserted and shall admit or deny the averments upon which the adverse party relies.''[197]

(i) Defenses that Could Have Been Raised by Preanswer Motions But Were Not

Rule 12(b) gives the defendant two options at the pleading stage: (1) to raise certain objections by motion prior to serving an answer or (2) to raise the objections as defenses in the defendant's answer.[198]

Illustration 6-29. Assume that the defendant has all the defenses listed in *Illustration 6-27*. If the defendant does not want to serve a preanswer motion, Federal Rule 12 permits the defendant to raise these defenses in the answer.[199]

(ii) Admissions and Denials

Federal Rule 8(b) requires that a party "shall admit or deny the averments upon which the adverse party relies."[200] The denials must "fairly meet the substance of the averments denied," and "[w]hen a pleader intends in good faith to deny only a part or a qualification of an averment, the pleader shall specify so much of it as is true and material and shall deny only the remainder."[201]

Illustration 6-30. Assume that *A* has alleged in the complaint that *B's* negligent conduct caused *A* injury. *B*, however, wants to show that *B* was somewhere other than where the accident happened. *B* would raise this defense by a denial. The denial should be specific.[202] Thus, it should specify that *B* was not negligent and did not cause the accident because *B* was not present at the time and place of the collision.[203]

Illustration 6-31. Assume that *A* alleges that *B* converted *A's* car. *A* alleges that the car has a value that exceeds $60,000. *B* responds that the car "does not have a value that exceeds $60,000." Under the traditional "negative pregnant" doctrine,[204] *B* has technically denied the immaterial word "exceeds" but has admitted that the car is worth at least $60,000.[205] Rule 8(f) requires that

---

197. FED. R. CIV. P. 8(b).

198. *See, e.g.,* the first ground listed in Form 19 (Motion to Dismiss) and the first defense in Form 20 (Answer) in the Appendix of Forms following the Federal Rules of Civil Procedure. Later, it will be explained how these objections may also be made subsequently, for example, at trial. *See* Chapters 10 ("Disposition of the Action Without Trial") & 11 ("Trial") *infra*.

199. *See, e.g.,* Form 20 ("Answer Presenting Defenses Under Rule 12(b)") in the Appendix of Forms following the Federal Rules of Civil Procedure.

200. FED. R. CIV. P. 8(b).

201. *Id.*

202. At common law, a traverse raised this defense. *See* section A(3)*(d)* ("Traverses") *supra*. Under the codes, it would be raised by a denial. *See* section C(3)*(c)* ("The Code Answer") *supra*.

203. At common law, such a "specific denial" would have been improper because it was argumentative. *See* section A(3)*(d)* ("Traverses"), *Illustration 6-5, supra*.

204. *See* section A(3)*(d)* ("Traverses") and *Illustration 6-6 supra*.

205. *See* Freedom Nat'l Bank v. Northern Ill. Corp., 202 F.2d 601, 605 (7th Cir. 1953); 5 CHARLES A. WRIGHT & ARTHUR R. MILLER, FEDERAL PRACTICE AND PROCEDURE: CIVIL § 1207 (2d ed. 1990).

the pleadings be construed to do substantial justice. Similarly, Rule 1 requires that the Federal Rules of Civil Procedure be construed to secure the just, speedy, and inexpensive determination of every action. Rule 8(f) and Rule 1 would thus probably eliminate the technical objections to the phraseology that caused the negative pregnant to be an ineffective denial at common law. However, Rule 8(b) requires denials to fairly meet the substance of the averments denied. Likewise, Rule 8(b) states that when a pleader intends in good faith to deny only a part or qualification of an averment, the pleader must specify so much of it as is true and material and must deny only the remainder. Thus, it is arguable that a negative pregnant would be effective under these rules only if the pleader intended to deny all aspects of the averments, Rule 8(f) and Rule 1 notwithstanding.[206] The better practice is to avoid the negative pregnant by specifying the truth or falsity of each allegation, as Rule 8(b) requires.

* * * * *

Federal Rule 8(b) further provides, as did the practice under many codes, that when a pleader "is without knowledge or information sufficient to form a belief as to the truth of an averment, the party shall so state and this has the effect of a denial."[207]

Illustration 6-32. Assume that *D* is considering answering the following allegations on the ground that the pleader is without knowledge or information sufficient to form a belief as to the truth of an averment: (1) that *D* was negligent; (2) that *D* is married; (3) that the plaintiff foreign corporation has qualified to do business in the state by registration; or (4) that a street became a one-way street in a certain direction at a particular time of day. In general, one's own conduct and matters of public record are presumed to be within the knowledge of the pleader. Thus, whether the pleader was negligent, whether the pleader is married, or whether the plaintiff is qualified to do business would be matters to which *D* would not normally be able to respond with the "without knowledge" response. Under some circumstances, however, such a response would be appropriate, *e.g.*, lapse of memory or destroyed records.[208] The one-way street allegation may be a matter of general knowledge in the community, but even if it is not, it may be a matter of law under a city ordinance.

* * * * *

Averments not denied (other than those as to the amount of damages) are taken as admitted.[209] Federal Rule 8(b) also permits a general denial: "Defendant denies each and every allegation of the complaint." However, Rule 8(b) states that a general denial may not be used unless the pleader intends to

---

206. *See* 5 CHARLES A. WRIGHT & ARTHUR R. MILLER, FEDERAL PRACTICE AND PROCEDURE: CIVIL § 1207 (2d ed. 1990).

207. FED. R. CIV. P. 8(b). See the denials set forth in the Third Defense of Form 20 and the First Defense of Form 24 in the Appendix of Forms following the Federal Rules of Civil Procedure.

208. *See* 5 CHARLES A. WRIGHT & ARTHUR R. MILLER, FEDERAL PRACTICE AND PROCEDURE: CIVIL § 1263 (2d ed. 1990). The same results would occur under the codes. The codes required an affidavit in support of such a response. CHARLES E. CLARK, HANDBOOK OF THE LAW OF CODE PLEADING § 93, at 596 (2d ed. 1947).

209. FED. R. CIV. P. 8(d).

controvert the entire complaint, "including the averments of the grounds upon which the court's jurisdiction depends."[210]

Illustration 6-33. Assume that *A* has served a complaint on *B* similar to Federal Form 13 in federal court. *A's* complaint contains (1) an allegation of subject-matter jurisdiction. *A* alleges that (2) "Defendant *B*, on or about [date], executed and delivered to plaintiff a promissory note, a copy of which is annexed as Exhibit A, whereby *B* promised to pay plaintiff or order on [date] the sum of one hundred thousand dollars with interest thereon at the rate of six percent per annum." *A* also alleges that (3) "Defendant *B* owes to plaintiff the amount of said note and interest." *A* then alleges that (4) "Defendant *B*, on or about [date], conveyed all of *B's* real property to defendant *C* for the purpose of defrauding plaintiff and hindering and delaying the collection of the indebtedness evidenced by the above referenced note."[211] *B* serves an answer denying the allegation that *B* owes *A* the amount of the note. *B's* answer also admits that *B* conveyed property to *C*. However, *B* denies that the conveyance was fraudulent. Because *B* has denied paragraphs 3 and 4, they are in dispute. Because *B* was required to respond to the complaint, the allegations in paragraphs 1 and 2 are admitted because *B* made no response to them.[212]

(iii) Affirmative Defenses

Rather than generally stating that "new matters constituting a defense" have to be alleged, Federal Rule 8(c) lists nineteen defenses that must be set forth affirmatively: accord and satisfaction, arbitration and award, assumption of risk, contributory negligence, discharge in bankruptcy, duress, estoppel, failure of consideration, fraud, illegality, injury by fellow servant, laches, license, payment, release, res judicata, statute of frauds, statute of limitations, and waiver. Rule 8(c) adds, however, that a party also must set forth affirmatively "any other matter constituting an avoidance or affirmative defense."[213] Federal Rule 8(e)(2) permits a party to set forth defenses alternatively or hypothetically, regardless of their consistency.[214]

Illustration 6-34. Assume that *B* wants to bring forward facts to show that the *A* is an infant and thus lacks capacity to sue. *B* also wants the action dismissed because another action is pending between the same parties for the same cause. Even though lack of capacity and prior pending action are not listed as affirmative defenses in Rule 8(c), they would be "matter[s] constituting

---

210. Fed. R. Civ. P. 8(b); *see* 5 Charles A. Wright & Arthur R. Miller, Federal Practice and Procedure: Civil § 1265 (2d ed. 1990).

211. *See* Form 13 in the Appendix of Forms following the Federal Rules of Civil Procedure.

212. Rule 8(d) provides that "[a]verments in a pleading to which a responsive pleading is required, other than those as to the amount of damages, are admitted when not denied in the responsive pleading." Fed. R. Civ. P. 8(d).

213. Fed. R. Civ. P. 8(c). See the illustration of how to plead an affirmative defense, given in the Fourth Defense in Form 20 in the Appendix of Forms following the Federal Rules of Civil Procedure.

214. Fed. R. Civ. P. 8(e)(2); *see, e.g.,* Little v. Texaco, Inc., 456 F.2d 219, 220 (10th Cir. 1972) (answer may contain inconsistent defenses; defendant can deny and at the same time advance an affirmative defense; parties fail to plead inconsistent defenses at their peril).

avoidance." *B* would have to raise these defenses affirmatively in the answer.[215] Furthermore, Rule 9(a) requires that lack of capacity be raised by specific negative averment. *B* would have to include "such supporting particulars as are peculiarly within the pleader's knowledge."[216]

(iv) Counterclaims and Cross-Claims

A defendant may want to assert a claim against the plaintiff. At common law and in equity, the defendant could do so in certain limited situations by means of *recoupment* or *set-off*. Like the codes, the federal rules permit *counterclaims* and *cross-claims*.[217] Generally, a counterclaim is asserted when a party serves a pleading against an opposing party and possesses a claim for relief against that party. Cross-claims are asserted against coparties. Counterclaims and cross-claims appear in pleadings served after the complaint. They are pleaded just like original claims for relief. However, new jurisdictional allegations may not be required. Recoupment, set-offs, counterclaims, and cross-claims are discussed in detail in the next chapter.

(g) Consolidation and Waiver of Defenses

(i) Consolidation

If the defendant decides to make a preanswer motion rather than waiting to raise all defenses in the answer, Federal Rule 12(g) requires the defendant to consolidate the defenses listed in Rule 12(b) in one motion. If the defendant moves in a preanswer motion on any of the grounds provided in Rule 12 which are then available, the defendant may not make a second preanswer motion based upon any grounds omitted from the motion. This consolidation requirement is subject to the following exception: Rule 12(h)(3) provides that lack of subject-matter jurisdiction may be suggested at any time.[218]

Illustration 6-35. A sues *B* in federal court for personal injuries received in an automobile accident. *B* moves to dismiss *A*'s action on the ground that venue is improper. The court denies the motion. *B* may not raise by preanswer motion any of the other grounds provided in Rule 12 that were available at the time the first motion was served, except lack of subject-matter jurisdiction.

---

215. *See* 5 CHARLES A. WRIGHT & ARTHUR R. MILLER, FEDERAL PRACTICE AND PROCEDURE: CIVIL § 1271 (2d ed. 1990).

216. FED. R. CIV. P. 9(a). At common law, lack of capacity to sue would have been raised by a dilatory plea in abatement. *See* section A(3)*(c)* ("Dilatory Pleas") *supra*. Under the codes, it would be raised as an affirmative defense in the answer (assuming that the matter did not appear on the face of the complaint). *See* section C(3)*(c)* ("The Code Answer") *supra*.

217. *See* Form 20 in the Appendix of Forms following the Federal Rules of Civil Procedure.

218. In this regard, Rule 12(g) is worded in a misleading manner. Rule 12(g) states that if a party makes a motion under Rule 12 and omits any defense that Rule 12 allows to be made by motion, the party may not thereafter make another motion under Rule 12 based on the omitted defenses *except* a motion under Rule 12(h)(2) on the grounds there stated. However, Rule 12(h)(2) says nothing about motions based on subject-matter jurisdiction. The reason the defendant may make the second motion is that Rule 12(h)(3), which reflects statutory subject-matter policies, overrides Rule 12(g).

Illustration 6-36. B moves for a more definite statement of the claim. The motion is granted. *A* then serves an amended complaint containing a more definite statement, showing for the first time possible grounds for a challenge that the complaint fails to state a claim upon which relief may be granted. *B* then moves under Rule 12(b)(6) to dismiss. This motion would be proper because the Rule 12(b)(6) objection was not "available" at the time of the first motion. It only became available when *A* amended the complaint.[219]

(ii) Waiver

Rule 12(h) keys waiver to the consolidation requirement in Rule 12(g), discussed in the preceding subsection. If the "available" defense omitted from a preanswer motion is lack of personal jurisdiction, improper venue, insufficiency of process, or insufficiency of service of process, Rule 12(h)(1)(A) provides that the omitted defense or defenses are waived.[220] Even if they are not waived in this manner, Rule 12(h)(1)(B) provides that these same defenses will be waived if they are not included in the defendant's answer or in an amendment permitted by Rule 15(a) as a matter of course.[221] Rule 15(a) provides, in effect, that the defendant may amend the answer once without the court's permission within 20 days after the defendant has served it if the action has not been placed on the trial calendar.[222]

Illustration 6-37. On the facts of *Illustration 6-35, B* waived any personal jurisdiction defense that *B* possessed at the time *B* moved to dismiss for improper venue because *B* failed to include the personal jurisdiction objection in the motion. *B* may not raise the personal jurisdiction objection in *B's* answer. The interaction of Rules 12(g) and (h)(1) produces waiver of the personal jurisdiction objection by *B's* failure to consolidate it with the improper venue defense in the first motion.

Illustration 6-38. A sues *B* in federal court for breach of contract. *B* does not serve a preanswer motion under Rule 12. Instead, *B* serves an answer containing only admissions and denials of *A's* allegations. *B* waives the defenses of lack of personal jurisdiction, improper venue, insufficiency of process, and insufficiency of service of process by failing to include them in *B's* answer—unless *B* serves an amended answer containing these defenses within the time permitted for amending as a matter of course by Rule 15(a). Waiver here is not produced by failure to raise the objection in a preanswer motion. Rule 12 does not require waivable objections to be raised by preanswer motion *unless* the defendant chooses to make such a motion and omits a waivable objection from the motion. Instead, Rule 12 gives the defendant an option to raise certain defenses by motion or answer. If, as in this illustration, the defendant chooses not to make a preanswer motion, waiver will only occur if the defendant fails to

---

219. *See* FED. R. CIV. P. 12(g).
220. FED. R. CIV. P. 12(b)(1)(A).
221. *See* FED. R. CIV. P. 12(h)(1)(B).
222. *See* section 5 ("Amendments Before Trial") *infra.*

include waivable defenses in the answer and does not discover the error until the time for amendment as a matter of course has expired under Rule 15(a).[223]

Illustration 6-39. B moves to strike redundant and impertinent matter from *A's* complaint. The court grants this motion. *B* then answers challenging venue and personal jurisdiction. *B* has waived any existing venue and personal jurisdiction objections. Rule 12(g) provides that "[i]f a party who makes a motion *under this rule* [*e.g.*, a motion to strike under Rule 12(f)] but omits therefrom any defense or objection then available to the party which this rule permits to be raised by motion, the party shall not thereafter make a motion based on the defense or objection so omitted . . . ."[224] Rule 12(h)(1)(A) thus produces waiver in such circumstances.

Illustration 6-40. D moves before answering to drop a misjoined party. The court grants this motion. *D* then moves to dismiss the complaint on the ground that the court lacks personal jurisdiction over *D*. In this situation, the first motion is "under" Rule 21, not Rule 12. Thus, under the terms of Rule 12(g), the second motion is proper and *D* has not waived the personal jurisdiction objection under Rule 12(h).

* * * * *

Rule 12(g) and (h)(1) are confusingly worded and can trap the unwary litigant. However, the policy of making personal jurisdiction, venue, and process objections waivable at an early stage is sound. These objections primarily involve the personal convenience of the defendant. If the defendant does not care sufficiently about the defenses to raise them promptly, it is appropriate that they be waived. Other defenses, however, involve institutional considerations or the interests of third parties. Thus, Rule 12(h)(2) and (3) appropriately preserve them from waiver. For example, the defense of failure to state a claim upon which relief may be granted and the defense of failure to join an indispensable party are not waived by omitting them from a pre-answer motion or the answer. They may be presented later, including at the trial on the merits. Thereafter, however, these defenses are waived.[225] Lack of subject-matter jurisdiction may be raised even after the conclusion of the trial.[226] Omitting affirmative defenses such as those listed in Rule 8(c) can produce waiver after the time for serving amendments as a matter "of course" under Rule 15(a) expires. However, after that, the defendant may still seek the permission of the court ("leave of court") to add such a defense. The court will usually freely grant permission to amend.

Illustration 6-41. On the facts of *Illustration 6-38*, B still may raise at trial the failure to join an indispensable party.[227]

---

223. *See* section 5 ("Amendments Before Trial") *infra.*

224. FED. R. CIV. P. 12(g) (emphasis added).

225. *See* FED. R. CIV. P. 12(h)(2).

226. *See* FED. R. CIV. P. 12(h)(3); Chapter 2(A)(2) ("The 'No-Waiver, No-Consent' Rule") *supra.*

227. A Rule 12(b)(7) objection of "failure to join a party under Rule 19" is, despite the discrepancy in language, the same as "failure to join a party indispensable under Rule 19" in Rule 12(h)(2). The difference in language might be thought to preserve from waiver only those Rule 19 objections that ultimately result in the conclusion that the absent party is "indispensable." But this interpretation would be improper, since nothing in Rule 12(h)(1) affirmatively produces waiver of "lesser" Rule 19 objections. The objection can be the subject of a motion for judgment on the pleadings or a motion as late as trial under Rule 12(h)(2). *See* 5A CHARLES

Illustration 6-42. On the facts of *Illustration 6-38*, *B* has waived the affirmative defenses of failure of consideration, release, and accord and satisfaction, unless the court permits *B* to amend the answer to include those defenses.

* * * * *

Although Rule 12 specifies the circumstances under which waiver of defenses will take place, some courts have recognized waiver of defenses by the defendants' "conduct" of the litigation, such a failure to press for a ruling on an otherwise properly raised defense of lack of personal jurisdiction.[228] These decisions are questionable. Waiver is a serious matter. It should not be produced without a clear textual basis in the governing rules or statutes. Waiver by conduct has no textual basis in the rules. Nor do the rules provide for waiver for seeking court-approved extensions of time or responding on the merits to motions for preliminary injunctions prior to answering. Although waiver should perhaps be recognized in clear cases of abuse as a matter of policy, the policy should be articulated by Congress or the proper rulemaking authority, not on a case-by-case basis.

4. The Plaintiff's Reply and Motions to Strike an Insufficient Defense

The principal function of common-law pleading was to reach a single issue, either of law or fact. The process of pleading continued until the parties reached such an issue.[229] In contrast, the codes and the Federal Rules of Civil Procedure do not attempt to force the definition of a single issue. In federal court, pleading ceases after the defendant serves an answer unless (1) the defendant includes a counterclaim in the answer or (2) the court orders a reply.[230]

A. WRIGHT & ARTHUR R. MILLER, FEDERAL PRACTICE AND PROCEDURE: CIVIL § 1392, at 758-59 (2d ed. 1990).

228. *See, e.g.,* Continental Bank, N.A. v. Meyer, 10 F.3d 1293 (7th Cir. 1998) (holding that although the defendants had properly raised their objection to personal jurisdiction in their answer, they had waived it by participating in the action for over two and one-half years without actively contesting jurisdiction); Yeldell v. Tutt, 913 F.2d 533, 539 (8th Cir. 1990) (holding that the defendants failed to "comply with the spirit of Rule 12" when they included a personal jurisdiction defense in their answer but failed to reassert the issue until appeal); Network Prof'ls, Inc. v. Network Int'l Ltd., 146 F.R.D. 179 (D. Minn. 1993) (the court considered raising lack of personal jurisdiction to be part of a "calculated strategy of delay and deception" which "violated the spirit of Rule 12"; the court concluded that "defendants have waived their personal jurisdiction defense by raising it again after the Court considered the merits or quasi-merits of the case in the preliminary injunction motion and more than one year after the action commenced); Marquest Med. Prods., Inc. v. EMDE Corp., 496 F. Supp. 1242 (D. Colo. 1980) (waiver held to occur because the defendants requested extensions of time to answer and to respond to discovery as well as entered into stipulation granting preliminary injunctive relief before raising lack of personal jurisdiction and venue).

229. *See* section A(2) ("Stating the Plaintiff's Claim in the Declaration") *supra.*

230. *See* FED. R. CIV. P. 7(a), 12(a). The court may order a reply to an answer or a reply to a third-party answer. FED. R. CIV. P. 7(a). In common-law pleading, the parties had several opportunities to demur. Whenever a party generally demurred, the demurrer had the effect of opening-up or "searching the record"; it thus tested not only the legal sufficiency of the pleading to which it was addressed, but also all prior pleadings. *See* section A(4) ("Subsequent Pleading") *supra; Illustration 6-7.* The codes generally applied a similar rule to code demurrers. For example, the plaintiff's demurrer to the defendant's answer would "search the record" and would test

Although a reply is not ordinarily used in federal court, Federal Rule 12(f) allows the plaintiff to move to strike a defense in an answer as "insufficient." This motion is a partial analogue of a Rule 12(b)(6) motion (failure to state a claim upon which relief may be granted) directed to the complaint.

   Illustration 6-43. Assume that *A* sues *B* in federal court. *A* asserts *B's* negligence. *B's* answer denies *B's* negligence, asserts *A's* contributory negligence, and "counterclaims" for damages that *B* suffered in the accident.[231] Federal Rule 12(a)(2) requires *A* to serve a reply to the counterclaim within twenty days after service of the answer.[232] *A* has three additional days to file the reply if *B* serves the answer by mail.[233]

   Illustration 6-44. On the facts of *Illustration 6-43*, assume that *B* is obviously attempting to set forth a counterclaim but fails to label it a counterclaim. Under these circumstances, *A* does not have to reply. A reply is due only when the counterclaim is "denominated as such."[234]

   Illustration 6-45. On the facts of *Illustration 6-43*, assume that *B* also asserts as an affirmative defense that *A* released the claim on the promissory note for a valuable consideration. *A* is not required or permitted to reply in the absence of a court order. Rule 8(d) provides that "[a]verments in a pleading to which no responsive pleading is required or permitted shall be taken as denied or avoided." Thus, the affirmative defense is taken as denied or avoided. *A* would thus be allowed to take any one of several positions at trial with respect to *B's* affirmative defense. For example, *A* may (1) deny there was such a release or (2) assert an affirmative defense, *e.g.*, fraud in securing the release. A court-ordered reply would be useful under these circumstances if a reply would enable the court to dispose of the action on the pleadings. For example, *A* may not be able to deny or otherwise defend against the affirmative defense.[235]

5. Amendments Before Trial

(a) Amendments as a Matter of Course and with Leave of Court

   Federal Rule 15(a) permits a party to "amend the party's pleading once as a matter of course at any time before a responsive pleading is served."[236]

---

the legal sufficiency of the complaint. CHARLES E. CLARK, HANDBOOK OF THE LAW OF CODE PLEADING § 83, at 524-25 (2d ed. 1947). The Federal Rules have abolished demurrers and have limited the pleadings. Thus, the concept of searching the record is not relevant in federal practice except in certain limited circumstances involving judgment on the pleadings under Federal Rule 12(c). *See* Chapter 10(B) ("Judgment on the Pleadings") *infra*.

   231. *See* Form 20 in the Appendix of Forms following the Federal Rules of Civil Procedure (stating that under the heading "Counterclaim" the pleader would "set forth any claim as a counterclaim in the manner in which a claim is pleaded in a complaint" and noting that "[n]o statement of the grounds on which the court's jurisdiction depends need be made unless the counterclaim requires independent grounds of jurisdiction").

   232. FED. R. CIV. P. 12(a)(2).

   233. *See* FED. R. CIV. P. 6(e).

   234. *See* FED. R. CIV. P. 7(a).

   235. *See* CHARLES E. CLARK, HANDBOOK OF THE LAW OF CODE PLEADING § 108, at 692 (2d ed. 1947).

   236. FED. R. CIV. P. 15(a).

When "the pleading is one to which no responsive pleading is permitted and the action has not been placed upon the trial calendar, the party may so amend it at any time within 20 days after it is served."[237] To amend thereafter, a party must obtain leave of court (or the written consent of the adverse party). The court, however, is directed to permit amendments freely "when justice so requires."[238] Rule 15(a) does not specify the procedure for obtaining leave to amend. Ordinarily, leave to amend is sought by motion pursuant to Rule 7(b). To satisfy the requirements of Rule 7(b), the moving party should submit the proposed amendment with the motion.[239]

(b) Relation Back of Amendments Changing a Claim or Defense

Rule 15(c)(1) allows an amendment to relate back to the date of the original pleading when the law providing the statute of limitations permits relation back. Thus, if state law provides the statute of limitations in a diversity action, a claim *not* arising from the same facts as the claim in the original pleading can relate back if state law so provides.

Rule 15(c)(2) also allows relation back of pleadings changing a claim or defense, but not a party, when the claim or defense in the amended pleading arose out of the same transaction or occurrence as the claim or defense in the original pleading. The "same transaction or occurrence" rule governing relation back of amendments changing claims and defenses reflects the underlying policy of the Federal Rules to provide maximum opportunity for each claim to be decided on its merits rather than on the basis of procedural technicalities.[240] The rule also reflects the limited role of the pleadings under the Federal Rules—the role of providing notice rather than fact revelation or issue formation, which are functions now handled by the discovery process.[241] The assumption is that when an amended claim or defense arises out of the same transaction or occurrence as an original claim or defense, the party opposing the amendment cannot be unfairly surprised or prejudiced. Rather, a party should always be prepared to

---

237. *Id.*

238. *Id. See generally* Annotation, *Timeliness of Amendments to Pleading Made by Leave of Court Under Federal Rule of Civil Procedure 15(a)*, 4 A.L.R. FED. 123 (1970). Time limits for serving amendments under Rule 15(a) can be fixed by a scheduling order under Federal Rule 16(b)(1). If amendments are not made within the time specified in the scheduling order, permission to amend thereafter can be denied. *See* Wildauer v. Frederick County, 993 F.2d 369 (4th Cir. 1993).

239. 6 CHARLES A. WRIGHT & ARTHUR R. MILLER, FEDERAL PRACTICE AND PROCEDURE: CIVIL § 1485 (2d ed. 1990).

240. Professors Wright and Miller point out that

> [t]his is demonstrated by the emphasis Rule 15 places on the permissive approach that the district courts are to take to amendment requests, no matter what their character may be; the rule is in sharp contrast to the common law and code restriction that amendments could not change the original cause of action. No longer is a party to be irrevocably bound to the legal or factual theory of his first pleading. The thrust of the rule also is reinforced by the elimination of the wooden cause of action test for determining whether an amended pleading should relate back.

6 CHARLES A. WRIGHT & ARTHUR R. MILLER, FEDERAL PRACTICE AND PROCEDURE: CIVIL § 1471, at 506-07 (2d ed. 1990) (footnotes omitted).

241. *See id.*

meet as many claims or defenses as may arise from a single set of facts. Nor can a party reasonably rely on a repose policy supporting the statute of limitations. As long as the party is sued on a claim arising from a particular set of facts before the statute runs and the amended claim arises out of those same facts, relation back will not violate the repose policies of the statute of limitations.[242]

(c) Relation Back of Amendments Changing Parties

A specific provision governing amendments changing parties was added to Rule 15(c) in 1966.[243] Under this provision, when an amendment changed the party against whom a claim was asserted, the amendment would relate back if it arose from the same transaction or occurrence as the original claim and certain other requirements were satisfied. The party to be brought in by amendment had to receive "such notice of the institution of the action that the party would not be prejudiced in maintaining a defense on the merits." This notice had to be received "within the period provided by law for commencing the action against the party to be brought in by amendment." Finally, it had to be shown that the party brought in "knew or should have known that, but for a mistake concerning the identity of the proper party, the action would have been brought against the party." The additional requirements that must be met before amendments changing parties will relate back reflect the policies of statutes of limitations.[244] Those policies are twofold: (1) a desire to protect the courts and parties from the danger of inaccurate determination of claims based on stale evidence;[245] and (2) the assurance of a period of repose that will benefit parties in ordering their affairs free from the fear that claims arising from long-past events may be asserted against them.[246] By requiring that a defending party receive a quality of notice that would prevent the party from being prejudiced in defending the claim on the merits, the drafters of the 1966 amendment addressed the policies against stale claims. By requiring that the defending party receive the notice within the period provided by law for commencing the action against the party, the drafters also addressed the policies of repose.

(i) Schiavone v. Fortune

In 1986, the U.S. Supreme Court construed the "change of parties" provisions of Federal Rule 15(c). In *Schiavone v. Fortune*,[247] the plaintiff

---

242. The policies supporting statutes of limitation are discussed more fully below in conjunction with amendments changing parties.

243. Before 1966, amendments changing parties were governed by the same test that governed relation back of amendments changing claims only, the same transaction or occurrence test.

244. The Advisory Committee's note to the 1966 amendment to Rule 15(c) stated that "[r]elation back is intimately connected with the policy of the statute of limitations." *See* FED. R. CIV. P. 15(c) advisory committee's note to the 1966 amendment.

245. *See* RESTATEMENT (SECOND) OF CONFLICT OF LAWS § 142 cmt. f (Supp. 1989).

246. *See, e.g.*, John Hart Ely, *The Irrepressible Myth of Erie*, 87 HARV. L. REV. 693, 726 (1974); *see also In re* Sharps Run Assocs., L.P., 157 B.R. 766, 775 (D.N.J. 1993).

247. 477 U.S. 21, 106 S. Ct. 2379, 91 L. Ed. 2d 18 (1986).

commenced a diversity action on May 9, 1983. The plaintiff named "Fortune" magazine as the defendant. However, "Fortune" is only a trademark of Time, Inc. Thus, the plaintiff should have sued Time. The statute of limitations ran on May 19th, and Time was served with process after this date. Time refused service because it was not properly named as the defendant in the action. The plaintiff then amended the complaint to name Time as the defendant and effectuated new service of process on July 21, 1983. The Supreme Court held that the one-year statute of limitations applicable to the action had run. Thus, the amendment to the complaint did not relate back. According to the Court, although Time had received notice of the action within the 120 day period for serving process prescribed by Rule 4, the party to be brought in had to receive notice of the action within the limitations period, not simply within the period for service of process.[248]

Commentators strongly criticized the Court's interpretation of Rule 15(c) in *Schiavone*.[249] If Time had been properly named in the complaint and had been served after the one-year period had run, the action would have been timely. Yet, under such circumstances, Time would still not have received notice of the action within the limitations period. Furthermore, when Time did receive notice of the action, it understood perfectly that the plaintiff had made a mistake in naming the defendant and that it was the defendant who should have been sued. Under these circumstances, it is difficult to understand how the policies of the statute of limitations would have been undermined if the amended complaint had been allowed to relate back.[250]

(ii) The 1991 Amendment to Rule 15(c)

In 1991, Rule 15(c) was amended to overrule *Schiavone*.[251] Revised Rule 15(c) allows amendments to relate back under three circumstances: (1) when relation back is permitted by the law that provides the statute of limitations applicable to the action;[252] "*or*" (2) when the claim or defense asserted in the

---

248. *See* Schiavone v. Fortune, 477 U.S. 21, 106 S. Ct. 2379, 91 L. Ed. 2d 18 (1986). Prior to the Supreme Court's decision in *Schiavone*, the courts were split on this issue. *Compare, e.g.*, Hendrix v. Memorial Hosp., 776 F.2d 1255 (5th Cir. 1985) (action had to be filed within the statutory limitations period and notice given within the time for service) *with* Weisgal v. Smith, 774 F.2d 1277 (4th Cir. 1985) (notice had to be received before the statute of limitations had run).

249. *See, e.g.*, Joseph P. Bauer, Schiavone*: An Un-*Fortune-*ate Illustration of the Supreme Court's Role as Interpreter of the Federal Rules of Civil Procedure*, 63 NOTRE DAME L. REV. 720 (1988); Robert D. Brussack, *Outrageous* Fortune*: The Case for Amending Rule 15(c) Again*, 61 S. CAL. L. REV. 671 (1988); Lawrence A. Epter, *An Un-*Fortune-*Ate Decision: The Aftermath of the Supreme Court's Eradication of the Relation-Back Doctrine*, 17 FLA. ST. U. L. REV. 713 (1990); Laurie Helzick, Note, *Looking Forward: A Fairer Application of the Relation Back Provisions of Federal Rule of Civil Procedure 15(c)*, 63 N.Y.U. L. REV. 131 (1988). .

250. Some state courts have not followed the *Schiavone* reasoning. See, e.g., West v. Buchanan, 981 P.2d 1065 (Alaska 1999) (rejecting *Schiavone* and holding that the words "within the period provided by law for commencing the action" encompass the reasonable time for service of process when the complaint is timely filed); Hughes v. Water World Slide, Inc., 314 S.C. 211, 442 S.E.2d 584 (1994); Ritchie v. Grand Canyon Scenic Rides, 165 Ariz. 460, 799 P.2d 801 (1990).

251. *See* FED. R. CIV. P. 15(c) advisory committee's note to the 1991 amendment.

252. *See* FED. R. CIV. P. 15(c)(1).

amended pleading arises out of the same transaction or occurrence as the claim or defense in the original pleading;[253] *"or"* (3) when the amendment changes the party or the naming of the party against whom a claim is asserted and (a) the same transaction or occurrence test of Rule 15(c)(2) is satisfied, (b) the party to be brought in by amendment receives notice within the 120 day period for service of process provided in Rule 4, (c) the notice is sufficient to prevent the party from being prejudiced in maintaining a defense on the merits, and (d) the party knew or should have known that, but for a mistake concerning the identity of the proper party, the action would have been brought against the party.[254]

(iii) Relationship Between Amended Rule 15(c)(1) and (3)

The structure of the 1991 amendments to Rule 15(c) has given rise to several problems of interpretation.[255] Rule 15(c)(1) provides that relation back will occur when allowed by the law providing the statute of limitations. Should Rule 15(c)(1) be applied to amendments changing parties because the rule's language is, on its face, applicable to all amendments and such an application would not render any other provision of Rule 15(c) superfluous? Alternatively, should Rule 15(c)(1) be deemed inapplicable to amendments changing parties because it does not specifically state that it is applicable to such amendments and Rule 15(c)(3) does specifically deal with them?

The Advisory Committee apparently intended for Rule 15(c)(1) to apply to amendments changing parties. The Advisory Committee's note to the 1991 amendment states that "[w]hatever may be the controlling body of limitations law, if that law affords a more forgiving principle of relation back than the one provided in this rule, it should be available to save the claim. . . ." In addition, the Advisory Committee stated that "[i]f *Schiavone v. Fortune* . . . implies the contrary, this paragraph is intended to make a material change in the rule."[256] Nevertheless, there is some danger that the courts will not interpret the rule in this fashion. Since the 1991 amendment, courts have interpreted the rule on numerous occasions. A substantial number of courts have applied Rule 15(c)(3) to amendments changing parties without first inquiring whether Rule 15(c)(1) would provide relation back. It is difficult to determine whether these courts consider the provisions of Rule 15(c)(1) inapplicable to amendments changing parties. The

---

253. *See* FED. R. CIV. P. 15(c)(2).

254. *See* FED. R. CIV. P. 15(c)(3).

255. In addition to the problem discussed in the text, a less significant question of the proper relationship between Rule 15(c)(2) and (3) exists. The provisions of Rule 15(c)(3) are clearly designed to apply to amendments changing parties to the action because Rule 15(c)(3) specifically addresses the problem of amendments changing parties. Just as clearly, the same transaction or occurrence test of Rule 15(c)(2), standing alone, is not designed to apply to amendments changing parties. Although each of the subdivisions are worded in the alternative ("or"), it would be unreasonable to interpret Rule 15(c)(2) to allow an amendment changing parties to relate back just because the amendment arises out of the same transaction or occurrence as the original claim. Rule 15(c)(3) specifically incorporates the same transaction or occurrence test as one of several conditions that must be met before an amendment changing parties may relate back. Thus, Rule 15(c)(3) would be rendered superfluous if an amendment changing a party could relate back merely by satisfying the same transaction or occurrence test of Rule 15(c)(2).

256. *See* FED. R. CIV. P. 15(c)(1) advisory committee's note to the 1991 amendment.

courts in question may have considered Rule 15(c)(1) and determined it to be inapplicable without specifically stating as such in their opinions. Alternatively, some other explanation may exist for their failure to address Rule 15(c)(1). However, because many of the cases dealing specifically with Rule 15(c)(3) *deny* relation back, it strongly appears that the courts, in those cases at least, believe Rule 15(c)(1) to be inapplicable to amendments changing parties. Otherwise, when the courts find relation back inappropriate under Rule 15(c)(3), they would consider the applicability of Rule 15(c)(1).[257]

Fortunately, however, a number of decisions also hold that amendments changing parties may relate back if either Rule 15(c)(1) or Rule 15(c)(3) is satisfied. These decisions generally recognized that the Advisory Committee intended relation back to occur under either provision of the rule.[258] This position is better reasoned and should ultimately prevail.[259]

Illustration 6-46. *A*, a citizen of State *X*, sues *B*, a citizen of State *Y*, on January 1st in federal court. *A* asserts a claim for relief for $80,000 arising out of an automobile accident. On February 1st, *A* amends the complaint to add a claim for relief based on a contract that is factually and legally unrelated to *A's* automobile accident claim. The state contract statute of limitations applicable to the latter claim expired on January 15th. Under these circumstances, Rule 15(c)(2) does not provide for relation back of the contract claim. The claim does not arise out of the same transaction or occurrence as the automobile accident claim.

---

257. *See, e.g.*, Whittaker v. United Airlines, Inc., No. 94-1262, 1995 WL 309022 (10th Cir. May 18, 1995) (unpublished opinion); Barrow v. Wethersfield Police Dep't, 66 F.3d 466 (2d Cir. 1995); Worthington v. Wilson, 8 F.3d 1253 (7th Cir. 1993) (no relation back under Rule 15(c)(3); Rule 15(c)(1) not mentioned); Woods v. Indiana Univ.-Purdue Univ., 996 F.2d 880 (7th Cir. 1993) (remanded for reconsideration under Rule 15(c)(3); Rule 15(c)(1) not mentioned); Burgin v. La Pointe Mach. Tool Co., 161 F.R.D. 44 (D.S.C. 1995); Richardson v. John F. Kennedy Mem'l Hosp., 838 F. Supp. 979 (E.D. Pa. 1993) (no relation back under Rule 15(c)(3); Rule 15(c)(1) not mentioned); Hunt v. Department of Air Force, 149 F.R.D. 657 (M.D. Fla. 1993) (same; alternative holding); LaRue v. Missaukee County Sheriff's Dep't, No. 1:91-CV-469, 1993 U.S. Dist. LEXIS 7716 (W.D. Mich. Apr. 22, 1993) (relation back to correct misnomer permitted under Rule 15(c)(3)); Gardner *ex. rel.* Gardner v. Toyota Motor Sales, Inc., 793 F. Supp. 287 (D. Kan. 1992) (no relation back under Rule 15(c)(3)); *cf.* Desanctis v. Hastings, No. 95-2403, 1997 WL 9765 (4th Cir. Jan. 13, 1997) (unpublished opinion) (holding that Rule 15(c)(3) controlled and prohibited the substitution of the estate of a defendant who had died unknown to the plaintiff before the action was commenced; the court seemed to acknowledge that state law would have provided for relation back, but did not consider the possible effect of Rule 15(c)(1)).

258. *See, e.g.*, Lundy v. Adamar, Inc., 34 F.3d 1173 (3d Cir. 1994); Lovelace v. O'Hara, 985 F.2d 847 (6th Cir. 1993); Cruz v. City of Camden, 898 F. Supp. 1100 (D.N.J. 1995); Bryan v. Associated Container Transp., 837 F. Supp. 633 (D.N.J. 1993); Jones v. Wysinger, 815 F. Supp. 1127 (N.D. Ill. 1993); Rae v. Klusak, 810 F. Supp. 983 (N.D. Ill. 1993); Bordner v. FDIC, 145 F.R.D. 13 (D.N.H. 1992); Crowe v. Mullin, 797 F. Supp. 930 (N.D. Ala. 1992); Jordan v. Tapper, 143 F.R.D. 575 (D.N.J. 1992); Wilson v. City of Atlantic City, 142 F.R.D. 603 (D.N.J. 1992). *Compare* Ortiz v. Lebron, 146 F.R.D. 34 (D.P.R. 1992) (Rules 15(c)(1) & (3) both applicable to amendments changing parties; however, court suggests that Rule 15(c)(1) should only be used when Rule 15(c)(3) is inapplicable) *with* Rosario v. Lebron, 144 F.R.D. 14 (D.P.R. 1992) (no relation back under Rule 15(c)(3); Rule 15(c)(1) not mentioned).

259. When a federal statute provides the limitations period applicable to the action, a relation back period will seldom be built into the federal statute. Therefore, Federal Rule 15(c)(1) will not operate, and Federal Rule 15(c)(3) will govern by default. *See* Hamm v. Frank, 985 F.2d 563 (7th Cir. 1993); Skoczylas v. Federal Bureau of Prisons, 961 F.2d 543 (5th Cir. 1992); Hill v. United States Postal Serv., 961 F.2d 153 (11th Cir. 1992); *In re* Convertible Rowing Exerciser Patent Litig., 817 F. Supp. 434 (D. Del. 1993); Hottinger v. Amcoal Energy Corp., No. 89 Civ. 6391 (LMM), 1992 WL 349951, 1992 U.S. Dist. LEXIS 17197 (S.D.N.Y. Nov. 10, 1992); Fenelon v. United States, Nos. 91-810, 91-1011, 91-1012 & 91-1159, 1992 WL 6283, 1992 U.S. Dist. LEXIS 136 (E.D. La. Jan. 3, 1992).

Nevertheless, if the law of the state that provides the contract statute of limitations would allow relation back under these circumstances, the court should permit relation back under Rule 15(c)(1).

 Illustration 6-47. *A*, a citizen of State *X*, wishes to sue *B-1*, a citizen of State *Y*, for personal injuries received in an accident suffered on property owned by *B-1* in State *Y*. *A* commences an action in the U.S. District Court in State *Y*, but mistakenly names *B-2* as the defendant in the action. *B-2* is served with process in the action within the 120 day period provided in Rule 4(m). However, *B-1* receives no notice of the action within the 120 day period. After the 120 day period under Rule 4(m) expires and the state statute of limitations applicable to *A's* claim has run, *A* discovers that *A* has mistakenly named and served *B-2* instead of *B-1* as the defendant in the action. *A* moves to amend the complaint to drop *B-2* from the action and name *B-1* as the defendant. Under these circumstances, Rule 15(c)(3) would not permit the amendment to relate back. *B-1* did not receive any notice of the action within the 120 day time period provided under Rule 4(m). Nevertheless, if the law of the state that provides the statute of limitations applicable to *A's* claim would allow relation back, Rule 15(c)(1) permits relation back.

(iv) Nature, Quality, and Timing of Notice

 Rule 15(c)(3) permits an amendment changing a party or the naming of a party to relate back only when the party to be brought in has received "such notice of the institution of the action" that the party will not be prejudiced in maintaining a defense on the merits. This language was originally added to the rule by the 1966 amendments to Rule 15(c). As indicated above, the language is obviously designed to support the policy of the statute of limitations to protect a party from inaccurate determination of stale claims. The Advisory Committee's note to the amendment stated that "the notice need not be formal."[260] Clearly, therefore, the notice provided does not have to be by service of process, although this method of notice will often be used after the plaintiff has discovered a mistake in the party named as defendant. The question is, what sort of "informal notice" should suffice? The cases do not give a consistent answer to this question.[261]

 One approach allows relation back when the quality of notice assures that the party to be brought in will not be prejudiced in maintaining a defense on the merits. This situation will sometimes occur when the party is aware of the incident giving rise to the claim, even if the party is not aware that the plaintiff has mistakenly commenced an action against another defendant based on the incident. However, this standard is concededly contrary to the literal wording of Rule 15(c)(3). Subdivision (3) requires the party to be brought in to have notice

---

260. *See* FED. R. CIV. P. 15(c) advisory committee's note to the 1966 amendment.

261. *See* 6A CHARLES A. WRIGHT ET AL., FEDERAL PRACTICE AND PROCEDURE: CIVIL § 1498, at 116-26 (2d ed. 1990).

"of the institution of the action."[262] The better approach would be to ask directly whether the notice received by the party is of the sort that would enable the party to maintain a defense on the merits. The key is that the party to be brought in must be given sufficient notice of the circumstances. This notice must alert the party that a defense on the merits of the plaintiff's claim will ultimately be necessary.[263]

A separate problem concerning the notice requirement of Rule 15(c)(3) involves the time period for giving notice. Prior to the 1991 amendment, the rule required that a defendant receive the requisite quality of notice "within the period provided by law for commencing the action."[264] The amended language of the rule now provides that the notice must be received "within the period provided by Rule 4(m) for service of the summons and complaint."[265] Rule 4(m) provides for dismissal of an action if the summons and complaint are not served within "120 days after the filing of the complaint," unless the court extends the time limit.[266] This linkage of relation back to the Rule 4(m) time period has created a significant ambiguity in the operation of the rule. The question is how the 120 day time period should be measured in different factual circumstances.

One interpretation of the language would be that relation back is impermissible after 120 days has expired from commencement of the action, even if the statute of limitations of the state has not yet run at that time.[267] Literally, this is what the rule says, but this would seem to be the least justifiable interpretation of the 1991 amendment. Relation back is a concept that only applies after a pertinent limitations period has expired. If the pertinent limitations period has not yet run, relation back is irrelevant. In addition, this interpretation would effectively create an independent federal statute of limitations that would bar the assertion of a claim against a new defendant even if the claim would be permitted under state law. It is difficult to see how Rule 15(c)(3) could withstand a Rules Enabling Act challenge under these circumstances.[268]

A second interpretation is that the defendant to be brought into the action must receive the required notice within 120 days after the running of the statute

---

262. *See* FED. R. CIV. P. 15(c)(3). For a complete discussion of the cases, see 6A CHARLES A. WRIGHT ET AL., FEDERAL PRACTICE AND PROCEDURE: CIVIL § 1498, 116-26 (2d ed. 1990).

263. *See* 6A CHARLES A. WRIGHT ET AL., FEDERAL PRACTICE AND PROCEDURE: CIVIL § 1498, at 116-26 (2d ed. 1990). Professors Wright, Miller, and Kane suggest also that the notice provision of Rule 15(c)(3) will interact with the provision requiring the party to realize that, but for a mistake, the party would have been sued originally. Obviously, if the quality of the notice is such that the party understands that the party should have been made a defendant in a civil action based on a particular incident, the party cannot complain that the notice was insufficient to allow the party to maintain a defense on the merits. *Cf. id.* at 123.

264. *See* FED. R. CIV. P. 15(c)(2) (1966 amendment).

265. *See* FED. R. CIV. P. 15(c)(3).

266. *See* FED. R. CIV. P. 4(m).

267. *See* Cruz v. City of Camden, 898 F. Supp. 1100, 1110 (D.N.J. 1995) (seeming to interpret the rule in this fashion). In Cruz, the court had previously interpreted Rule 15(c)(1) as not permitting relation back because state law did not do so. *See id.* at 1107-10. Thus, the interpretation of Rule 15(c)(3) by the court did no harm in the actual case. However, under the court's apparent reading of the rule, Rule 15(c)(3) might prohibit an amendment changing defendants before relation back even becomes relevant under state law—*i.e.,* prior to the running of the statute of limitations. *See also* Aslanidis v. United States Lines, Inc., 7 F.3d 1067, 1075 (2d Cir. 1993) (reading the rule in a similar fashion).

268. *See* section D(5)*(d) infra* (discussing Rules Enabling Act problems with Rule 15(c)).

of limitations, even if the action has been commenced long prior to that time.[269] For example, if the statute of limitations runs six months after the federal action is commenced, this reading would allow relation back if the defendant to be brought in by amendment received the required notice within 120 days after the statute of limitations runs, even though this might be, *e.g.*, ten months after commencement. This interpretation also seems off the mark, as it ignores the limiting language of Rule 4(m), which keys the 120 day time period to the filing of the complaint. Although the reference in Rule 15(c)(3) to Rule 4(m) could be interpreted to exclude the reference to filing, there seems to be no reason to do so. In addition, reading the reference to Rule 4(m) to exclude filing runs the risk of unduly extending state statutes of limitations in diversity cases long beyond their expiration date, a questionable result under the Rules Enabling Act.

A third interpretation has occurred in factual contexts similar to the *Schiavone* case. In that case, the statute of limitations had not run at the time the action was commenced, but ran shortly thereafter and before the defendant to be brought in had received the notice required by the rule. However, the defendant did receive notice within the 120 day limit for serving process under Rule 4. Under the amended rule, the notice would be timely received in the *Schiavone* case, and the amendment would relate back. Some courts have interpreted the Rule 15(c)(3) time limit as providing for relation back in this situation.[270] This result is justifiable, and it suggests an interpretation of the rule that will avoid the pitfalls of the other interpretations discussed above.

The ambiguities in the rule can be resolved by adhering closely to the purpose of the 1991 amendment to overrule *Schiavone*, and also by exercising a little common sense. First, relation back should never be permitted when the statute of limitations has run against the defendant to be brought in prior to the commencement of the action.[271] Under these circumstances, even if the defendant had been joined in the original complaint, the action would not have been deemed timely, and thus there should also be no relation back, even if the defendant receives the requisite notice within 120 days of commencement. Second, if the statute of limitations has not run at the time of the amendment, relation back should be deemed irrelevant, and Rule 15(c)(3) should not preclude the amendment just because it is made more than 120 days after commencement.[272] As discussed above, relation back is a concept that is only relevant when a limitations period has run at the time an amendment is sought. When the appropriate limitations period has not run, relation back has no pertinence. Thus, Rule 15(c)(3) relation back should be limited to situations in which the statute of limitations applicable to the defendant to be brought in runs after the federal

---

269. *See* Colbert v. City of Philadelphia, 931 F. Supp. 389, 392 (E.D. Pa. 1996).

270. *See* Lundy v. Adamar, Inc., 34 F.3d 1173, 1181-82 (3d Cir. 1993) (holding the notice timely where the defendant to be brought in received the notice after commencement and after the statute of limitations, but within the 120 day period, but also holding the quality of the notice inadequate).

271. *See* Jermosen v. Coughlin, No. 89 Civ. 1866 (RJW), 1992 WL 131786 n.9 (S.D.N.Y. June 3, 1992) (relation back if required notice received within the statute of limitations or within 120 days after filing, whichever is longer).

272. This statement assumes that the action is commenced by the method provided for in the state statute of limitations in a diversity action, as required by the *Ragan* case, discussed in Chapter 5(F)(2), *supra*.

complaint has been filed but before 120 days from the filing of the complaint has expired—the *Schiavone* situation. Under these circumstances if the defendant to be brought in has received the necessary quality of notice, either before the statute runs, or after it runs but before 120 days from the filing of the complaint has expired, the amendment should relate back, but not otherwise.[273]

(v) *Mistake and Knowledge Requirements*

Rule 15(c)(3) permits an amendment changing a party or the naming of a party only when the party to be brought in "knew or should have known that, but for a mistake concerning the identity of the proper party, the action would have been brought against the party." This language contains at least two requirements. First, it requires that the plaintiff has made a "mistake." Second, it requires that the party to be added know that the party would have been sued in the absence of the mistake.

Many courts have read this language literally and prohibited relation back when the plaintiff's failure to name a defendant in the action was not based on a "mistake." Thus, when the plaintiff knew the identity of the defendant to be added, but did not join the defendant originally, courts have denied relation back on the ground that this mistake was not the kind of mistake within the rule.[274] Furthermore, when the plaintiff simply lacked knowledge of the identity of certain defendants and, therefore, omitted them in the original complaint, many courts have denied relation back.[275] Sometimes, plaintiffs have attempted to deal with this lack of knowledge by using fictitious names for the unknown defendants before the statute of limitations runs; the courts have then refused to allow the plaintiff to amend the complaint to insert the actual names after the statute has

---

273. Obviously, a full 120 days should not be tacked onto the limitations period when it runs after the complaint is filed, as in the second interpretation discussed in the text, *supra*. *See also* Yanez v. Columbia Costal Transp., Inc., 68 F. Supp. 2d 489 (D.N.J. 1999) (discussing the various interpretations in the decided cases).

274. *See, e.g.*, Powers v. Graff, 148 F.3d 1223 (11th Cir. 1998) (relation back not applicable under Rule 15(c)(3) when plaintiff made a deliberate decision not to sue a defendant in the original complaint); Whittaker v. United Airlines, Inc., No. 94-1262, 1995 WL 309022 (10th Cir. May 18, 1995) (unpublished opinion) (tactical decision not to join defendant initially is not a mistake); Gardner *ex rel.* Gardner v. Toyota Motor Sales, Inc., 793 F. Supp. 287 (D. Kan. 1992).

275. *See, e.g.*, Baskin v. City of Des Plaines, 138 F.3d 701 (7th Cir. 1998) (no mistake where plaintiff did not know identity of added defendant); Jacobsen v. Osborne, 133 F.3d 315 (5th Cir. 1998) (no mistake where defendant did not know identity of added defendant); Worthington v. Wilson, 8 F.3d 1253 (7th Cir. 1993); Sealey v. Fishkin, No. 96 CV 6303 (RR), 1998 WL 1021470, 1998 U.S. Dist. LEXIS 20142 (E.D.N.Y. Dec. 2, 1998) (either a mistake of fact or law will suffice under Rule 15(c)(3), but a plaintiff's lack of knowledge of the identity of a defendant cannot constitute a mistake); Rennie v. Omniflight Helicopters, Inc., 165 F.3d 19 (4th Cir. 1998) (plaintiff added Omniflight as a defendant by amendment after the statute of limitations had run; the court of appeals held that the amendment did not relate back, because the plaintiff, rather than making a mistake about the identity of the proper party, lacked knowledge about who the proper party to sue was, and Rule 15 did not cover this kind of mistake). *But see* Brink v. First Credit Resources, 57 F. Supp. 2d 848 (D. Ariz. 1999) (mistake requirement satisfied when plaintiff did not know at time complaint was filed the names of the defendants he later sought to add by amendment and had to obtain the names during discovery; named defendant resisted discovery of names of later-added defendants because named defendant knew they would be added to the action, and this knowledge was imputed to added defendants).

run.[276] In addition, some courts have refused to allow the plaintiff to change the capacity in which the defendant has been sued on the ground that no mistake has been made.[277]

These applications of the "mistake" language may be incorrect. The language of Rule 15(c)(3) seems to be aimed at assuring that the party brought in by amendment has knowledge that the party could, or should, have been sued based on a particular event to (1) protect the party from prejudice in maintaining a defense on the merits and (2) satisfy the repose policies of the statute of limitations. The "mistake" language should arguably be administered in this light. Thus, courts should allow relation back whenever the defendant to be added will not be prejudiced in maintaining a defense and it would have been unreasonable for the defendant to rely on the statute of limitations for repose. Often, this interpretation will also satisfy the second requirement of Rule 15(c)(3)—the requirement that the added defendant have knowledge that the defendant would have been sued "but for" the mistake. As long as the party to be brought in is aware that the party could have been sued based on a set of events, the party's knowledge will often be sufficient to allow the preparation of a defense on the merits. Frequently, the party will also have sufficient knowledge of the probability of an action to make it unreasonable to rely on the statute of limitations for repose.

Cases refusing relation back on the "no mistake" ground often seem to be based on the notion that the plaintiff has been at fault for failure to join the party originally.[278] However, if the plaintiff is somehow at fault for failing to join the defendant originally, the best remedy is to deny permission to amend in the court's discretion under Rule 15(a), rather than to pervert the objectives of Rule 15(c)(3).[279] When administering Rule 15(c)(3), it is preferable to maintain

---

276. *See, e.g.,* Barrow v. Wethersfield Police Dep't, 74 F.3d 1366 (2d Cir. 1996), *modifying,* 66 F.3d 466 (2d Cir. 1995) (initial complaint named some John Doe defendants because plaintiff did not know the identities of all the parties; not a mistake within Rule 15(c)(3)); Bauer v. Ohio Adult Parole Auth., 173 F.3d (6th Cir. 1999) (substitution of named defendants for John Doe defendants is an amendment changing parties and does not relate back because there was no mistake); *see also* Steven S. Sparling, *Relation Back of "John Doe" Complaints in Federal Court: What You Don't Know Can Hurt You,* 19 CARDOZO L. REV. 1235 (1997); Carol M. Rice, *Meet John Doe: It Is Time for Federal Civil Procedure to Recognize John Doe Parties,* 52 U. PITT. L. REV. 883 (1996).

277. *See, e.g.,* Lovelace v. O'Hara, 985 F.2d 847 (6th Cir. 1993) (refusing to allow relation back when the complaint was amended to assert claims against police officers in their individual rather than their official capacity). *But see* Brown v. Shaner, 172 F.3d 927 (6th Cir. 1999) (permitting relation back of an amendment suing officers in their individual capacities; unlike *Lovelace,* the initial complaint named the officers as defendants but did not specify the capacity in which they were being sued; the amended complaint did so specify; the court held that a reading of the complaint indicated that the defendants could not be sued in their official capacities which satisfied the mistake and knowledge requirements of Rule 15(c)(3)).

278. *See, e.g.,* Eison v. McCoy, 146 F.3d 468 (7th Cir. 1998) (the plaintiff's original civil rights complaint identified defendant police officers only by their nicknames; the amended complaint identified them by their correct names; the court held that the amendments were not mere corrections of "misnomers" that were not subject to Rule 15(c)(3), but were amendments changing parties; thus, the amendment did not relate back because the rule only allowed amendments to relate back when there is a mistake about the identity of the proper party and the mistake is chargeable to that party).

279. *Cf.* 6A CHARLES A. WRIGHT ET AL., FEDERAL PRACTICE AND PROCEDURE: CIVIL § 1498, at 142-143 (2d ed. 1990).

a tight focus on the policies of the statute of limitations to assure that those policies are not undermined.

Illustration 6-48. *A* sues the United States for the death of *A*'s spouse in the midair collision of two aircraft. At the time the action was commenced, *A* was unaware that the aircraft owned by the United States was being piloted by an employee of *C*. Therefore, *A* did not join *C* as a defendant. *C* became aware of *A*'s claim when it was required to participate in an administrative proceeding brought to investigate the accident shortly after it occurred. During this administrative proceeding, it was necessary for *C* to prepare evidence to defend the conduct of *C*'s employee in piloting the aircraft. After the statute of limitations and the 120 day period for service of process under Rule 4(m) expired, *A* moved to amend the complaint to add *C* as a defendant to the action. The court should grant *A*'s motion. The amendment should relate back to the commencement of the action. *A*'s "mistake" appears to be due to *A*'s lack of knowledge that *C*'s employee was piloting the aircraft. Nevertheless, the real reason the amendment should be allowed is that the policies of the statute of limitations are satisfied by the quality of notice that *C* possessed concerning the events giving rise to the suit and *A*'s claim. The administrative proceeding alerted *C* to the need to prepare a defense on the merits and, indeed, involved the actual preparation of such a defense. In addition, given *C*'s knowledge of the events and *A*'s claim gained through the administrative proceeding, it would be unreasonable for *C* to rely on the statute of limitations for repose.[280]

Illustration 6-49. *A* sued *B* for the death of *A*'s spouse, who was piloting an aircraft at the time that it crashed. *A*'s claim was based on manufacturing defects in certain equipment made by *B* and used in landing the aircraft. *A* did not name *C*, one of the other manufacturers of the equipment, as a defendant. *C* was aware of the incident giving rise to *A*'s suit because *C* conducted an investigation shortly after the crash in order to prepare a defense to another action brought by a person injured in the crash. However, *C* was not aware of *A*'s action against *B*. After the statute of limitations and the 120 day period for service of process under Rule 4(m) expired, *A* moved to amend the complaint and add *C* as a party defendant. Whether or not there has been a "mistake" on *A*'s part in failing to name *C* originally, the amendment should not relate back because the requirements of Rule 15(c)(3) have not been fulfilled. Preparation by *C* to defend a claim by a party injured in the crash would not necessarily include the preparation necessary to defend a claim for the death of the pilot. Thus, *C*'s knowledge of the event did not necessarily provide *C* with the ability to maintain a defense on the merits. Furthermore, knowledge that a party injured in the crash had decided to sue *B* would not necessarily produce knowledge that the representative of the pilot would also choose to sue *C*. Thus, *C* could reasonably rely on the repose policies

---

280. *See* Graham v. Gendex Med. X-Ray, Inc., 176 F.R.D. 288 (N.D. Ill. 1997) (fact that defendant was a party to an administrative proceeding preceding law suit should have alerted it to the fact that it would have been sued but for a mistake concerning the identity of the proper party); Meredith v. United Air Lines, 41 F.R.D. 34 (S.D. Cal. 1966); *see also* 6A CHARLES A. WRIGHT ET AL., FEDERAL PRACTICE AND PROCEDURE: CIVIL § 1498, at 123-24 (2d ed. 1990) (discussing *Meredith*).

of the statute of limitations with regard to the claim by the pilot's representative.[281]

(vi) Amendments Changing Plaintiffs

Rule 15(c)(3) does not specifically apply to amendments changing *plaintiffs*. Literally, the rule only applies to amendments changing the party or the naming of a party "against whom a claim is asserted." This language was added in 1966. At that time, the Advisory Committee observed that, while the rule did not literally apply to amendments changing plaintiffs, the policies articulated in Rule 15 "toward change of defendants extends by analogy to amendments changing plaintiffs."[282] Based on this comment, many courts have applied the changing parties provisions of Rule 15(c) to plaintiffs.[283] Nevertheless, as discussed below, while some amendments changing plaintiffs should clearly be allowed to relate back, relation back of other such amendments would violate the policies of the statute of limitations. A close application of the criteria of Rule 15(c)(3) is necessary to assure that this does not occur.

When Rule 15(c)(3) is applied "by analogy" to an amendment changing a plaintiff, caution must be exercised. There are certainly circumstances in which allowing relation back of amendments changing plaintiffs is appropriate. For example, when an action is not brought in the name of the real party in interest and an amendment is necessary to substitute the real party in interest for the originally named plaintiff, relation back is permissible. Indeed, the language of Rule 17(a) would seem to compel this result.[284] Furthermore, no discernable prejudice to the defendant or offense to the repose policies of the statute of limitations would seem to be involved in such a case. Similarly, when a plaintiff

---

281. *See* Craig v. United States, 413 F.2d 854 (9th Cir.), *cert. denied*, 396 U.S. 987, 90 S. Ct. 483, 24 L. Ed. 2d 451 (1969); *see also* 6A CHARLES A. WRIGHT ET AL., FEDERAL PRACTICE AND PROCEDURE: CIVIL § 1498, at 124-26 (2d ed. 1990) (discussing *Craig*).

282. *See* FED. R. CIV. P. 15(c) advisory committee's note to the 1966 amendment.

283. *See* 6A CHARLES A. WRIGHT ET AL., FEDERAL PRACTICE AND PROCEDURE: CIVIL § 1501 (2d ed. 1990); *see also* Jerald J. Director, *Amendment of Pleading to Add, Substitute, or Change Capacity of, Party Plaintiff as Relating Back to Date of Original Pleading, Under Rule 15(c) of Federal Rules of Civil Procedure, So as to Avoid Bar of Limitations*, 12 A.L.R. FED. 233 (1972). After the 1991 amendments to Rule 15(c), it will also be possible to rely on the provisions of Rule 15(c)(1) to allow relation back of amendments changing or adding plaintiffs whenever the law that provides the statute of limitations would permit relation back. Unlike the language of Rule 15(c)(3), the language of Rule 15(c)(1) literally applies to all amendments and is not restricted to amendments changing parties against whom claims are asserted. The language of Rule 15(c)(2) would also literally allow an amendment changing plaintiffs to relate back if the claim asserted by the plaintiff brought into the action arises from the same transaction or occurrence set forth in the original complaint. However, for the same reasons that it would be inappropriate to allow an amendment changing a defendant solely on the basis that the claim satisfied the same transaction or occurrence test, it would also be inappropriate to allow an amendment changing a plaintiff for that reason. *See* subsection *(iii)* ("Relationship Between Amended Rule 15(c)(1) and (3)") *supra*.

284. *See* FED. R. CIV. P. 17(a); Advanced Magnetics, Inc. v. Bayfront Partners, Inc., 106 F.3d 11 (2d Cir. 1997) (holding an amendment substituting shareholders as the real parties in interest in an action related back under Rule 17, independently of Rule 15(c)); Schuefler v. General Host Corp., 126 F.3d. 1261 (10th Cir. 1997); Beal v. City of Seattle, 134 Wash. 2d 769, 954 P.2d 237 (1998) (amendment substituting real party in interest related back under state equivalent of Rules 15(c) & 17(a)); *see also* 6A CHARLES A. WRIGHT ET AL., FEDERAL PRACTICE AND PROCEDURE: CIVIL § 1501, at 157-59 (2d ed. 1990).

suing in an individual capacity seeks to add a claim in a representative capacity, or when a plaintiff suing in a representative capacity seeks to add a claim in an individual capacity, the amendment should be allowed to relate back for the same reasons.[285]

However, it is highly questionable whether the policies of the statute of limitations will always be satisfied when one plaintiff sues a defendant and another plaintiff seeks to be added to the action by amendment after the running of the statute of limitations.[286] A danger of prejudice to the defendant exists in such circumstances because the defendant may not be able to maintain an adequate defense on the merits against the new plaintiff if the defendant has not been alerted to the claim and preserved evidence necessary to defend against it. Even if this situation has not occurred, however, allowing amendments adding plaintiffs in these circumstances risks undermining the repose policies supporting the statute of limitations. As *Illustration 6-49*, above, indicates, a defendant sued by one plaintiff should not, without more, necessarily be expected to realize that another plaintiff will also choose to sue the defendant based on the same incident after the statute of limitations has run. Furthermore, if the courts rigidly enforce the requirement that there be a "mistake" by the plaintiff who did not sue within the limitations period, amendments adding plaintiffs after the statute of limitations will seldom be allowed.[287]

Illustration 6-50. A, B, and *C* are involved in a three car collision. Presuit investigation by all three parties indicates that *B* and *C* were driving in excess of the speed limit. *A* sues *B* for personal injuries resulting from the automobile accident. After the statute of limitations and the 120 day period for service of process under Rule 4(m) expire, *A* moves to amend the complaint to add *C* as a plaintiff. The amendment should not relate back to avoid the bar of the statute of limitations. Preparation to defend an action by *A* would not necessarily lead *B* to prepare for an action by *C*. Therefore, "by analogy" to amendments changing parties against whom claims are asserted under Rule 15(c)(3), the amendment should not relate back because the quality of notice possessed by *B* would not prevent prejudice in maintaining a defense on the merits against *C's* claim. Furthermore, knowledge of the event and of the action by *A* would not necessarily alert *B* that *C* also intends to sue. "By analogy" to amendments adding defendants under Rule 15(c)(3), *B* did not know, nor should *B* have known, that *C* would have sued *B* "but for a mistake" in the identity of the proper party. Therefore, *B* should reasonably be able to rely on the repose policies of the statute of limitations. Furthermore, there does not appear to have been a

---

285. *See* 6A CHARLES A. WRIGHT ET AL., FEDERAL PRACTICE AND PROCEDURE: CIVIL § 1501, at 159-62 (2d ed. 1990) and authorities there cited.

286. *See* Fleck v. Cablevision VII, Inc., 807 F. Supp. 824 (D.D.C. 1992); Dayton Monetary Assocs. v. Donaldson, Lufkin, & Jenrette Sec. Corp., No. 91 Civ. 2050 (LLS), 1992 WL 204374, 1992 U.S. Dist. LEXIS 12283 (S.D.N.Y. Aug. 11, 1992).

287. *See* Dayton Monetary Assocs. v. Donaldson, Lufkin, Jenrette Sec. Corp., No. 91 Civ. 2050 (LLS), 1992 WL 204374, 1992 U.S. Dist. LEXIS 12283 (S.D.N.Y. Aug. 11, 1992).

"mistake" in the identity of the proper party in the first place. *C* simply failed to bring the action in a timely fashion.[288]

(d) Rules Enabling Act Issues with Rule 15(c)

The application of Rule 15(c)(1) or (2) in the face of conflicting state relations back law can sometimes raise problems of rule validity under the Rules Enabling Act.[289] As yet, the Supreme Court has never addressed these problems.[290] However, the 1991 amendments to Rule 15(c) have solved half the validity problems that previously existed. Formerly, a conflict between Rule 15(c) and state relations back doctrine could occur in two situations: (1) Rule 15(c) might deny relation back when it was permitted by state law; or (2) Rule 15(c) might permit relation back when it was denied by state law. Under the 1991 amendments, Rule 15(c)(1) now provides for relation back whenever it is permitted by the law that furnishes the statute of limitations. Thus, there should no longer be a conflict between Rule 15(c) and state relations back law when state law permits relation back.

When state law denies relation back, however, relation back in some cases may still be permitted under Rules 15(c)(2) and (3). In such circumstances, the question is whether a Federal Rule of Civil Procedure can validly allow an action to continue that would be barred by the state relations back doctrine. Under the *Burlington Northern* decision, discussed in Chapter 5,[291] Rule 15(c) can validly operate in this way only if it has no more than an incidental impact on state substantive rights and it is reasonably necessary to the operation of the uniform scheme of procedure that it was the purpose of Congress to establish under the Rules Enabling Act.

The Supreme Court has not indicated how to determine whether a Federal Rule impacts on a state "substantive right." However, in the case of Rule 15(c),

---

288. It should be added that there is a more fundamental argument against allowing amendments adding plaintiffs. The drafters of Rule 15 did not textually provide for such amendments except in Rule 15(c)(1). As noted in the text, *supra*, the Advisory Committee's notes to the 1966 amendments suggested that such amendment would be appropriate "by analogy" to amendments changing defendants, which were textually provided for. It is highly questionable whether the Advisory Committee should be able to bring into existence a rule through its notes that it is unwilling to write into textual form. Scrutiny of such extra-textual rules under the process prescribed by the Rules Enabling Act may not be the same as scrutiny of the text of rule amendments. Moreover, if the Supreme Court and Congress find the text of an amendment acceptable, those institutions may not, given the time-consuming nature of the amendment process, be willing to send a rule back to the Advisory Committee for revision of its notes. Finally, to the extent that the Supreme Court adopts a "plain language" interpretation of the civil rules, such textual notes may be ineffective in any event. *See, e.g.*, Delta Air Lines v. August, 450 U.S. 346, 101 S. Ct. 1146, 67 L. Ed. 2d 287 (1981). *But see* Karen N. Moore, *The Supreme Court's Role in Interpreting the Federal Rules of Civil Procedure*, 44 HAST. L.J. 1039 (1993) (arguing against the plain meaning rule).

289. For a discussion of problems of rule validity under the Rules Enabling Act, 28 U.S.C. § 2072, see Chapter 5(F) ("The Evolution of the *Erie* Doctrine: Conflicts Between State Laws and Federal Rules of Civil Procedure") *supra*.

290. *See* CHARLES A. WRIGHT, THE LAW OF FEDERAL COURTS 384 (4th ed. 1983); Harold S. Lewis, Jr., *The Excessive History of Federal Rule 15(c) and its Lessons for Civil Rules Revision*, 85 MICH. L. REV. 1507, 1554 (1987).

291. See Chapter 5(F)(4) ("The *Burlington Northern* Decision: Establishing Content for the Substantive Rights Restriction") *supra*.

there are at least two possible ways in which an impact on substantive rights might occur. First, a state statute of limitations might be supported by policies of repose designed to allow parties to order their affairs free from the fear that claims arising from long past events may be asserted against them. Repose policies are universally viewed as substantive and usually support state statutes of limitations, perhaps among other policies.[292] Therefore, if Rule 15(c) permits relation back when a state statute supported by repose policies would not, the rule would arguably conflict with a state substantive right. Second, Rule 15(c) might conflict with a state substantive right by allowing an action to continue that would be precluded by state law—*i.e.,* by producing a different outcome on the ultimate merits of the case than would state law. It seems clear that Rule 15(c) will at least impact on state substantive rights in the latter way, and it may in a given case impact on state substantive rights in both ways. Therefore, the question remains whether the rule will impact on state substantive rights more than "incidentally" within the meaning of *Burlington Northern.*

The Supreme Court has also not made it clear how to evaluate when the impact of a Federal Rule on substantive rights is "incidental" or "substantial." One view might be that an impact is substantial whenever a Federal Rule (1) entirely forecloses an action that would be permitted under state law or (2) permits an action that would entirely be foreclosed under state law. If this view is correct, Rule 15(c) could not validly allow an action to continue that would be barred by state relations back doctrine. Alternatively, the Court might take the view that a Federal Rule has only an incidental impact on state substantive rights (1) if the Federal Rule does not conflict with state law in a significant number of cases or (2) if the differences between the operation of the Federal Rule and state law result in only a short extension of the state limitations period. If one of these views of "incidental impact" is taken, the first part of the *Burlington Northern* test will be satisfied by allowing relation back under Rule 15(c) when state law does not.

Under the second part of the *Burlington Northern* test, Federal Rule 15(c) must be reasonably necessary to the uniform scheme of procedure that it was the purpose of Congress to establish under the Rules Enabling Act. Providing a more liberal relation back doctrine under Rule 15(c) than would be provided by state law is important to the uniform operation of the Federal Rules of Civil Procedure. The liberal notice pleading philosophy of the Federal Rules requires an amendment policy of equivalent liberality. Otherwise, a party pleading a claim for relief would be required to observe all the pleading niceties that might exist under state law in order to avoid the operation of a harsh state amendment policy. Thus, if Rule 15(c) passes the first part of the *Burlington Northern* test, it will easily pass the second.

---

292. *See, e.g.,* Neuner v. C.G. Realty Capital Ventures, 157 B.R. 766, 775 (D.N.J. 1993); John Hart Ely, *The Irrepressible Myth of* Erie, 87 HARV. L. REV. 693, 726 (1974); RESTATEMENT (SECOND) OF CONFLICT OF LAWS § 142 cmt f. (Supp. 1989). "The periods chosen for different kinds of claims reflect judgments as to the relative difficulties of litigation when time has passed, the importance of repose, and the value of enforcing a particular type of right." ALI COMPLEX LITIGATION: STATUTORY RECOMMENDATIONS AND ANALYSIS WITH REPORTER'S STUDY § 6.04 cmt. a, at 384 (1994).

Illustration 6-51. *A*, a citizen of State *X*, sues *B*, a citizen of State *Y*, in a U.S. District Court for State *Y*. *A* seeks to recover $100,000 for personal injuries received by *A* from a product manufactured by *B*. *A's* original complaint asserts a claim based on strict liability. After the State *Y* statute of limitations expires, *A* moves to amend the complaint to change the claim for relief to a claim based on *B's* negligence in manufacturing the product. Under the law of State *Y*, such an amendment would not be permitted and, therefore, would not relate back because it changes the cause of action.[293] Under Rule 15(c)(2), the amendment would relate back because the claim in the amended complaint arises from the same transaction or occurrence as the claim in the original complaint. It is unclear whether the Supreme Court would take the view that Rule 15(c)(2) has more than an incidental impact on state substantive rights in these circumstances. If the rule's impact on substantive rights *is* more than incidental, it is invalid under the *Burlington Northern* test. However, if the impact of the rule on state substantive rights is no more than incidental, the rule is reasonably necessary to the uniform operation of the Federal Rules of Civil Procedure. *A's* original complaint gave *B* adequate notice that *A* was claiming damages for injuries received from a product manufactured by *B*. If, during discovery or otherwise, *A* learns of a basis for a claim based on an additional or different theory, the liberal amendment policies of Rule 15(a) allow *A* to amend the complaint to assert claims based on the theory. Thus, the liberal pleading, discovery, and amendment policies of the Federal Rules would be undermined if *A's* amendment could not relate back to the date of the original complaint.

6. Supplemental Pleadings

Upon a proper motion, Federal Rule 15(d) permits "supplemental pleadings." As under most codes, such pleadings must be directed toward transac-

---

293. Chapter 5(F) ("The Evolution of the *Erie* Doctrine: Conflicts Between State Laws and Federal Rules of Civil Procedure"), *supra*, discusses the conflict-avoidance policy that must be applied when a potential conflict between a Federal Rule of Civil Procedure and state law is present in a case. Under that process, the first step is to determine whether the Federal Rule in question is broad enough to apply to the issue before the court. It might be possible to interpret Rule 15(c) as inapplicable to relation back when state law provides an inconsistent rule, just as Rule 3 has been held not to provide for commencement for purposes of state statutes of limitations. *See* Harold S. Lewis, Jr., *The Excessive History of Federal Rule 15(c) and its Lessons for Civil Rules Revision*, 85 MICH. L. REV. 1507, 1554 (1987). However, given the presence of Rule 15(c)(1) in the rule after 1991, this is more difficult to do than it formerly would have been. If the drafters of Rule 15(c) did not wish for relation back when it would not be permitted by the law providing the statute of limitations, they could have included a provision that so stated, just as they did in Rule 15(c)(1) when they wanted to codify the opposite policy. Nevertheless, Chapter 5(F) suggested that it is legitimate in the conflict-avoidance process also to ask whether the state rule is one that the state would want applied outside its court system. Although the Supreme Court's existing decisions do not authorize such a step at this time, it is arguably proper whenever a Federal Rule of Civil Procedure has been found applicable to a case and potentially conflicts with state law. See Chapter 5(F)(3) ("The *Hanna* Decision: Return to the *Sibbach* Test") *supra*. In this illustration, it may be possible to interpret the state rule as inapplicable. The rule appears to be a typical code state relation back rule, which is based on an interpretation of the strict code pleading and amendment provisions disallowing amendments that change the cause of action. *See* section C(5) ("Amendments and Supplemental Pleadings") *supra*. It may well be that the state has no interest in applying its relation back rule in a system of procedure governed by a more liberal pleading and amendment policy.

tions, occurrences, or events that have happened after the date of the pleading sought to be supplemented.[294] Unlike the codes, the Federal Rules also permit supplemental pleadings to cure defects such as prematurity of the claim. However, an amendment, not a supplemental complaint, should be used to raise matters that the pleader was ignorant of at the time of pleading.

Illustration 6-52. Examples of proper matters for supplemental pleading include (1) new defenses, *e.g.*, res judicata arising after commencement of the action, or (2) new damages, *e.g.*, additional breaches of a contract occurring after commencement. An example of a matter that is appropriate for an amended pleading, but not a supplemental pleading, is a mature claim omitted from the plaintiff's complaint.

SECTION E. VERIFICATION AND GOOD FAITH PLEADING

1. Verification

Verification is a statement under oath that a pleading is true.[295] The Field Code introduced the requirement that the complaint, answer, and reply must be *verified* in most circumstances.[296] A year later, the Field Code was amended to give the plaintiff the option of verifying and to give any party the authority, by verifying a pleading, to force the verification of subsequent pleadings subject to certain exceptions.[297] Other code states adopted various versions of these two New York Code provisions. When verification is required, unverified pleadings may be treated as a nullity.[298]

---

294. *See* FED. R. CIV. P. 15(d). If the defendant engages in new actionable conduct after the lawsuit has been commenced, however, the plaintiff is not obligated to add such conduct to the action by a supplemental pleading to prevent the new conduct from being barred by the doctrine of claim preclusion even though the new actionable conduct is part of the same transaction or occurrence as the conduct for which the original action was brought. *See* SEC v. First Jersey Sec., Inc., 101 F.3d 1450 (2d Cir. 1996), *cert. denied*, 522 U.S. 812, 118 S. Ct. 57, 139 L. Ed. 2d 21 (1997); *see also* Chapter 13(B) ("Claim Preclusion") *infra*. *See generally* Annotation, *Construction and Application of Rule 15(d) of Federal Rules of Civil Procedure Providing for Allowance of Supplemental Pleadings Setting Forth Transactions, Occurrences, or Events Subsequent to Original Pleadings*, 28 A.L.R. FED. 129 (1976).

295. *See In re* Doe, 91 Haw. 166, 981 P.2d 723 (Ct. App. 1999) (holding a requirement that a petition be verified satisfied by a declaration under penalty of perjury that the matters therein were "true" and "correct" based on the swearer's "knowledge, information and belief.").

296. Act of Apr. 12, 1848, ch. 379, § 133, 1848 N.Y. Laws 497, 523. The pleadings also had to be signed by the attorney.

297. Act of Apr. 11, 1849, ch. 438, § 157, 1849 N.Y. Laws 613, 648. Verification of a pleading can also have other effects, depending on the state in question. *See In re* Marriage of O'Brien, 247 Ill. App. 3d 745, 617 N.E.2d 873 (1993) (verified pleading remains part of the record upon the filing of an amended pleading, and any admissions in the verified pleading which were not the product of mistake or inadvertence remain binding after amendment; however, verified statements in a pleading in one case are ordinary statements against interest when used in another case and may be controverted).

298. CHARLES E. CLARK, HANDBOOK OF THE LAW OF CODE PLEADING § 36, at 216-20 (2d ed. 1947). A typical verification states that "I am the plaintiff in the above-entitled action; I have read the foregoing Complaint and know the contents thereof; the same is true to my own knowledge, except as to those matters which are therein stated upon my information or belief, and as to those matters, I believe them to be true." It is signed by the party and then acknowledged, signed, and sealed by a notary public. In many states, a signed

In federal practice, verification is the exception rather than the rule. Federal Rule 11 provides that verification by a party is not required except when a Federal Rule or statute specifically mandates it.[299] Federal Rules that require verification are Rule 23.1 ("derivative" actions by shareholders), Rule 27(a), (b) (petitions to perpetuate testimony before an action is commenced), Rule 65 (ex parte request for a temporary restraining order), and Rule 66 (appointment of receivers).[300]

2. Good Faith Pleading: Rule 11

Federal Rule 11 is the primary source of sanctions for abuses of the litigation process in federal court and states operating under the Federal Rules of Civil Procedure. Defects in the operation of Rule 11 before 1983 produced certain amendments designed to deter and sanction abuses of the litigation process more effectively.[301] Additional dissatisfaction with the rule after 1983 produced further amendments in 1993. The 1983 and 1993 amendments will be discussed separately below. One should keep in mind that the rule as amended in 1983 may remain in force, at least for a time, in many states, even though the rule as amended in 1993 will govern proceedings in the federal courts. In addition, the 1993 amendments to Rule 11 do not change all the results that occurred under the

---

and dated declaration (for example, "I declare under penalty of perjury that the foregoing is true and correct.") may be used in lieu of a sworn affidavit. When a complaint has been verified, a number of states prohibit a general denial. *Id.* § 92, at 582-83.

299. FED. R. CIV. P. 11.

300. *See* FED. R. CIV. P. 23.1, 27(a), (b), 65 & 66 (by inference). Federal statutes that require verification include 28 U.S.C. § 1734(b) (replacement of lost or destroyed court records), 28 U.S.C. § 1915 (proceedings in forma pauperis), and 28 U.S.C. § 1924 (bill of costs); *see also* 28 U.S.C. § 1746 (form of the verification).

301. The amendments were circulated to the bench and bar in June 1981 by the Committee on Rules of Practice and Procedure of the Judicial Conference of the United States. *See* Preliminary Draft of Proposed Amendments to the Federal Rules of Civil Procedure, 90 F.R.D. 451, 462 (1981). After public hearings and comments from the legal profession, Rule 11 was modified. *See* 97 F.R.D. at 190-94 (explaining the modifications). The Supreme Court then promulgated the amendments under the Rules Enabling Act, 28 U.S.C. § 2072 on April 28, 1983. The amendments became effective on August 1, 1983. The literature on the rule as amended in 1983 is voluminous. In addition to commentary cited in conjunction with textual material presented below, some of the most important literature is as follows: Roger M. Baron, *Stepping Aboard the Rule 11 Bandwagon*, 35 CLEV. ST. L. REV. 249 (1987); Richard H. Battey & John S. Dorsey, *Rule 11 Sanctions: Some Current Observations*, 33 S. DAK. L. REV. 207 (1988); Adam H. Bloomenstein, *Developing Standards for the Imposition of Sanctions Under Rule 11 of the Federal Rules of Civil Procedure*, 21 AKRON L. REV. 289 (1988); Stephen B. Burbank, *The Report of the Third Circuit Task Force on Federal Rule of Civil Procedure 11: An Update*, 19 SETON HALL L. REV. 511 (1989); Mark S. Cady, *Curbing Litigation Abuse and Misuse: A Judicial Approach*, 36 DRAKE L. REV. 483 (1986-87); John M. Johnson & G. Edward Cassady III, *Frivolous Lawsuits and Defensive Responses to Them—What Relief is Available*, 36 ALA. L. REV. 927 (1985); William W. Schwarzer, *Rule 11 Revisited*, 101 HARV. L. REV. 1013 (1988); Georgene M. Vairo, *Rule 11: A Critical Analysis*, 118 F.R.D. 189 (1988); Kim M. Rubin, Note, *Has a "Kafkaesque Dream" Come True? Federal Rule of Civil Procedure 11: Time for Another Amendment*, 67 B.U. L. REV. 1019 (1987); Allan E. Untereiner, Note, *A Uniform Approach to Rule 11 Sanctions*, 97 YALE L.J. 901 (1988); Kathleen M. Dorr, Annotation, *Comment Note—General Principles Regarding Imposition of Sanctions Under Rule 11, Federal Rules of Civil Procedure*, 95 A.L.R. FED. 107 (1989). Additional literature, including studies of the operation of Rule 11, are cited and discussed in 5A CHARLES A. WRIGHT & ARTHUR R. MILLER, FEDERAL PRACTICE AND PROCEDURE: CIVIL § 1332 (2d ed. 1990).

1983 version of the rule. Therefore, even in the federal courts, some of the pre-1993 decisions interpreting the rule will remain good authority.

(a) Background: Original Rule 11

In form, original Rule 11 applied when an attorney or party signed a "pleading." It required that all pleadings be signed by an attorney representing a party or, in the case of *pro se* litigants, by the party acting *pro se*. It also provided that the signature of an attorney constituted a certificate that the attorney had read the pleading, that to the best of the attorney's knowledge, information, and belief there was good ground to support it, and that it was not interposed for delay. The rule further provided if the pleading was not signed, or was signed with the intent to defeat the purposes of the rule, the pleading could be stricken as a sham or false. If an attorney "willfully" violated the rule, the attorney could be subjected to "appropriate" disciplinary action. Similar action was possible if "scandalous" or "indecent" matter were inserted in a pleading. The rule then provided for sanctions when pleadings, motions, or other papers were not signed, or when they were signed in violation of the standards imposed by the rule.

(b) Background: The 1983 Amendments to Rule 11

One problem with original Rule 11 was that its terms applied only to pleadings, leading to confusion about the applicability of the rule to motions and other papers.[302] The 1983 amendments explicitly extended the certification requirement to motions and other papers, as well as to pleadings.[303]

Another problem with original Rule 11 was that the terms of the rule made the certification requirement applicable only to attorneys, not to parties unrepresented by attorneys. The 1983 amendments required parties not represented by an attorney to sign all pleadings, motions, and other papers. This requirement made the certification requirements of the rule explicitly applicable to unrepresented parties.[304]

---

302. *Cf.* 5A CHARLES A. WRIGHT & ARTHUR R. MILLER, FEDERAL PRACTICE AND PROCEDURE: CIVIL § 1331, at 21 (2d ed. 1990).

303. *See* FED. R. CIV. P. 11, 97 F.R.D. at 196 (1983) (containing 1983 amendments and original text of rule). Technically, the standards of Rule 11 were always applicable to motions and other papers. FED. R. CIV. P. 7(b)(2) provided, prior to 1983, that the rules applicable to captions, signing, and other matters of the form of pleadings applied to all motions and other papers provided for by the rules. This provision made the standards of Rule 11 applicable to motions and other papers, such as discovery papers. *See* FED. R. CIV. P. 7 advisory committee's note to the 1983 amendment. However, because Rule 11 itself only mentioned pleadings, some confusion arose about the propriety of sanctions in cases of improper motion practice. To eliminate this confusion, Rule 11 was amended to apply explicitly to motions and other papers. In addition, Rule 7(b) was amended to add the following subsection (3): "All motions shall be signed in accordance with Rule 11." *See id.* The reference to "other papers" in amended Rule 11 literally included discovery papers, but the certification requirements applicable to discovery papers are governed by a new Federal Rule 26(g), also added in 1983. *See* FED. R. CIV. P. 11 & 26(g) advisory committee's notes to the 1983 amendments.

304. *See* 5A CHARLES A. WRIGHT & ARTHUR R. MILLER, FEDERAL PRACTICE AND PROCEDURE: CIVIL § 1331, at 21 (2d ed. 1990). However, in determining whether an unrepresented party has violated the certification standard, the court has discretion to take account of the problems that may confront an unrepresented subscribing party. *See* FED. R. CIV. P. 11 advisory committee's note to the 1983 amendment.

With regard to the certification aspect of original Rule 11, the "good ground to support" standard was unclear—for example, was there a duty to investigate the facts and the law before signing a pleading and, if so, what quality of investigation was required?[305] Under the 1983 amendments, the signature of an attorney or party constituted a certificate that to the best of the signer's "knowledge, information, and belief formed after reasonable inquiry" the pleading, motion, or other paper "is well grounded in fact and is warranted by existing law or a good faith argument for the extension, modification, or reversal of existing law" and that the pleading, motion, or other paper "is not interposed for any improper purpose, such as to harass or to cause unnecessary delay or needless increase in the cost of litigation."[306] This new standard made it clear that the signing party had an affirmative duty to investigate the facts and the law before filing a pleading, motion, or other paper. "The standard is one of reasonableness under the circumstances."[307]

In addition to imposing a reasonable duty of investigation upon a person signing a litigation paper, the 1983 amendments provided that a person's signature constituted a certificate that the paper was not interposed for any improper purpose. The rule then gave three examples of such a purpose: delay (which was included in the original Rule 11), harassment, and needless increase in the cost of litigation. The wording of the rule was open-ended. Thus, the courts had the power to identify improper purposes other than the specific examples.

The 1983 amendments removed the provision in original Rule 11 that a pleading might be stricken as sham or false if the pleading was not signed, or was signed with the intent to defeat the purposes of the rule. The provision was removed because it was rarely used and the decisions under the provision tended to confuse the issue of attorney honesty with the merits of the action. Thus, it was felt that the issues that arose under the old provision could better be dealt with under other rules, such as the general rules governing pleading (Rule 8) and summary judgment (Rule 56).[308] The 1983 amendments provided that if a litigation paper was not signed, it should be stricken unless signed promptly after the omission was called to the attention of the person filing the paper.

---

305. The original rule simply required that an attorney not act in bad faith when signing a pleading. This old "bad faith" standard did not necessarily involve any affirmative duty of investigation. *See* Nemeroff v. Abelson, 620 F.2d 339 (2d Cir. 1980).

306. *See* FED. R. CIV. P. 11 advisory committee's note to the 1983 amendment.

307. However, although the new standard could be triggered by a greater range of circumstances than the old one, the Advisory Committee's note to the amended rule made it clear that the standard was not designed "to chill an attorney's enthusiasm in pursuing factual or legal theories."

> The court is expected to avoid using the wisdom of hindsight and should test the signer's conduct by inquiring what was reasonable to believe at the time the pleading, motion, or other paper was submitted. Thus, what constitutes a reasonable inquiry may depend on such factors as how much time for investigation was available to the signer; whether he had to rely on a client for information as to the facts underlying the pleading, motion, or other paper; whether the pleading, motion, or other paper was based on a plausible view of the law; or whether he depended on forwarding counsel or another member of the bar.

See FED. R. CIV. P. 11 advisory committee's note to the 1983 amendment.

308. *See id.*

The reference in original Rule 11 to scandalous and indecent matter was also removed from the amended rule because the reference was unnecessary. Rule 12(f) already provided for a motion to strike scandalous or indecent matter. However, as the Advisory Committee's note to the amended rule indicated, the presence of scandalous or indecent matter in a litigation paper is a strong indication that it has been interposed for an improper purpose.[309]

One of the most important revisions to Rule 11 in 1983 was the amendment setting out the sanctions that could be imposed on an attorney or party for violating the rule. The amendment provided that if a litigation paper were signed in violation of the rule, the court, upon motion or its own initiative, had to impose upon the person who signed it, a represented party, or both, an appropriate sanction. That sanction could include an order to pay to the opposing party the reasonable expenses incurred because of the filing of the paper, including a reasonable attorney's fee. The 1983 amendments thus required the imposition of a sanction if the rule were violated, though the nature of the sanction, as well as on whom it would be imposed, was left to the discretion of the court. Although the reference to the willfulness of an attorney's conduct was removed from the amended rule, the court could still take willfulness into account in determining upon whom the sanction should be imposed and how severe it should be.[310] The specific mention of the costs and fees sanction explicitly encouraged the use of this sanction for violations of the rule, although other sanctions also remained proper.[311] The time when sanctions should be imposed was left to the discretion of the district judge, but "it is anticipated that in the case of pleadings the sanctions issue under Rule 11 normally will be determined at the end of the litigation, and in the case of motions at the time when the motion is decided or shortly thereafter."[312] The procedure utilized in imposing sanctions was also left to the discretion of the trial judge. Obviously, the procedure utilized had to comport with due process, but the particular format to be followed depended upon the circumstances of the particular case.[313] The judge's participation in the proceedings would often provide full knowledge of the relevant facts "and little further inquiry [would] be necessary."[314]

Under the amended rule, fewer decisions imposed sanctions for failure to make a reasonable factual investigation than for failure to investigate the applicable law. The reasons for this result are several. When the Federal Rules were promulgated and became effective in 1938, one of their primary purposes was to institute a system of simplified "notice pleading."[315] The idea was, partly, that the pleading stage of the litigation should be deemphasized as a means of exchanging factual information between the parties about the details of the case

---

309. See id.

310. See id.

311. See 5A CHARLES A. WRIGHT & ARTHUR R. MILLER, FEDERAL PRACTICE AND PROCEDURE: CIVIL § 1336, at 117-18 (2d ed. 1990).

312. See FED. R. CIV. P. 11 advisory committee's note to the 1983 amendment.

313. See generally Kathleen M. Dorr, Annotation, Comment Note–Procedural Requirements for Imposition of Sanction Under Rule 11, Federal Rules of Civil Procedure, 100 A.L.R. FED. 556 (1990).

314. See FED. R. CIV. P. 11 advisory committee's note to the 1983 amendment.

315. See section D(2) ("The Federal Rules Complaint") supra.

because discovery could do this job much more efficiently and effectively. One aspect of this idea, as applied to plaintiffs, was that there would be situations in which the plaintiff and the plaintiff's attorney would have a good faith belief that a valid claim for relief existed based on the facts in their possession before the commencement of the litigation. However, they could not be certain because essential facts necessary to determine the validity of the claim would be in the possession of the defendant. Therefore, the Federal Rules allow plaintiffs to institute actions and proceed to the discovery stage of the litigation to develop the details of their claims as long as they are doing the best that they can under the circumstances to investigate the facts of the claim.

Nothing in the 1983 amendments to Rule 11 altered this notice pleading philosophy of the Federal Rules. Thus, the reasonable pre-filing investigation requirement of the amended rule had to be interpreted in light of the overall pleading philosophy of the Rules. Rule 11 could not realistically mandate a factual investigation that would, in all cases, require the plaintiff's attorney to confirm absolutely the existence of all the facts necessary to prove the claim before commencing the action. At least in situations in which critical information was in the exclusive possession of the defendant, the overall philosophy of the Federal Rules dictated that no sanctions be imposed for merely filing a complaint that turned out to be factually unmeritorious. In addition, other situations exist in which an attorney who signs a pleading should not be sanctioned for filing a factually unmeritorious pleading. The most common situation arises when the attorney must rely on information provided by the attorney's client that turns out to be erroneous.[316]

Nevertheless, courts can and did impose sanctions for failure to make the reasonable factual investigation required by Rule 11.

Illustration 6-53. Sanctions were approved for failure to make a factual investigation that would have indicated that the action was barred by the statute of limitations,[317] for failure to inquire into facts that would have indicated that the plaintiffs lacked standing for much of the relief that they requested in the action,[318] and for failure to make a reasonable investigation into the facts or the law supporting the exercise of personal jurisdiction over the defendant.[319]

* * * * *

Failure to make a reasonable investigation into the applicable law violated Rule 11, and sanctions were often imposed upon an attorney representing a party for this kind of failure.

Illustration 6-54. Attorneys have been sanctioned for failing to investigate the limitations law applicable to plaintiff's claims;[320] for failing to make a "minimal effort" to discover the law on claims of bad faith, intentional infliction

---

316. *See* FED. R. CIV. P. 11 advisory committee's note to the 1983 amendment.

317. *See, e.g.,* Aetna Cas. & Sur. Co. v. Fernandez, 830 F.2d 952 (8th Cir. 1987); Van Berkel v. Fox Farm & Road Mach., 581 F. Supp. 1248 (D. Minn. 1984); Fisher v. CPC Int'l, Inc., 591 F. Supp. 228 (W.D. Mo. 1984).

318. *See* Baker v. Citizens State Bank, 661 F. Supp. 1196 (D. Minn. 1987).

319. *See* Hasty v. PACCAR, Inc., 583 F. Supp. 1577 (E.D. Mo. 1984).

320. *See* Baker v. Citizens State Bank, 661 F. Supp. 1196 (D. Minn. 1987).

of mental distress, and punitive damages asserted against an insurance company;[321] for filing a frivolous motion to dismiss the plaintiff's complaint on grounds of failure to state a claim upon which relief can be granted, lack of proper jurisdictional amount in controversy, improper venue, lack of personal jurisdiction, and forum non conveniens;[322] for failing to make a proper pre-filing inquiry as to whether venue would be proper in the district in which the action was filed;[323] and for attempting to base subject-matter jurisdiction on the existence of diversity of citizenship when the jurisdictional statement in the plaintiff's complaint alleged that both plaintiffs and two defendants were citizens of New York.[324]

* * * * *

In contrast to the objective requirement of a reasonable pre-filing investigation into the facts and the law, amended Rule 11's requirement that a pleading, motion, or other paper not be interposed ''for any improper purpose'' focused on the signer's subjective intent. Most cases involving an improper purpose also seemed to involve violations of the reasonable investigation requirement of the rule. Nevertheless, the rule clearly made the improper purpose requirement an independent basis for sanctions, which could theoretically result in liability even when a litigation paper was well grounded in fact and law.[325]

Illustration 6-55. One court imposed sanctions on the plaintiff and the plaintiff's attorney for filing a motion to amend the complaint with the intention of withdrawing the motion if the defendant opposed it. The court classified this action as an improper purpose, even though the court recognized that there was a legal basis for the claim asserted in the amended complaint.[326] In another case, the court sanctioned both the defendant and the defendant's counsel for filing an answer in which the defendant attempted to delay the disposition of the action. The answer did not respond to the jurisdictional allegations of the complaint in order to conceal the absence of diversity of citizenship from the court and the plaintiff.[327]

* * * * *

As stated earlier, amended Rule 11 gave the court discretion to impose sanctions upon either a party or the attorney representing a party or both. This discretion included authorization to impose sanctions on *pro se* litigants when

---

321. *See* Glenn v. Farmers & Merchants Ins. Co., 649 F. Supp. 1447 (W.D. Ark. 1986).

322. *See* Lucha, Inc. v. Goeglein, 575 F. Supp. 785 (E.D. Mo. 1983).

323. *See* Saturn Sys., Inc. v. Saturn Corp., 659 F. Supp. 868 (D. Minn. 1987).

324. *See* Solloway v. Ellenbogen, 121 F.R.D. 29 (S.D.N.Y. 1988).

325. As noted earlier, the language of amended Rule 11 was open-ended. Any improper purpose could be the basis for sanctions. However, the text of the amended rule gave harassment, delay, and needless increase in the cost of litigation as specific examples of improper purposes for which a pleading, motion, or other paper could not be filed. Numerous cases involve sanctions for these improper purposes. *See, e.g., In re* TCI, Ltd., 769 F.2d 441 (7th Cir. 1985) (increase in costs); Miller v. Affiliated Fin. Corp., 600 F. Supp. 987 (N.D. Ill. 1984) (delay); United States v. Allen L. Wright Dev. Corp., 667 F. Supp. 1218 (N.D. Ill. 1987) (delay).

326. *See* Cohen v. Virginia Elec. & Power Co., 788 F.2d 247 (4th Cir. 1986).

327. *See* Itel Containers Int'l Corp. v. Puerto Rico Marine Management, Inc., 108 F.R.D. 96 (D.N.J. 1985).

appropriate. Numerous cases imposed sanctions on these categories of persons.[328] Subsequently, however, in *Pavelic & LeFlore v. Marvel Entertainment Group*, the Supreme Court held that sanctions could only be imposed upon the attorney who signs the paper that violates Rule 11, not the law firm in which the attorney is a partner.[329]

(c) The 1993 Amendments to Rule 11

Amended Rule 11 gave rise to a substantial amount of litigation over the question whether sanctions should be imposed for filing meritless papers and, if so, what quality of sanctions was justified. This increased use of the rule prompted criticism on numerous grounds.[330] It will suffice to mention here only two of the most important criticisms. First, Professor Burbank suggested that Rule 11 might violate the Rules Enabling Act, 28 U.S.C. § 2072, because (1) it mandated sanctions, contrary to traditional equitable doctrines allowing the award of attorney's fees in the discretion of the court and (2) it allowed the award of attorney's fees for nonwillful violations of the rule, contrary to the policy judgment made by Congress in 28 U.S.C. § 1927 that such sanctions should be awarded only for willful conduct.[331] Second, it was argued that the federal courts applied amended Rule 11 so broadly that they undermined the liberal pleading system established by the Federal Rules of Civil Procedure.[332] Because of these and other criticisms, the Advisory Committee proposed, and the Supreme

---

328. Sanctions on parties: *See, e.g.,* Ident Corp. of Am. v. Wendt, 638 F. Supp. 116 (E.D. Mo. 1986). Sanctions on attorneys: *See, e.g.,* Baker v. Citizens State Bank, 661 F. Supp. 1196 (D. Minn. 1987); Glenn v. Farmers & Merchants Ins. Co., 649 F. Supp. 1447 (W.D. Ark. 1986); Hasty v. PACCAR, Inc., 583 F. Supp. 1577 (E.D. Mo. 1984); Hearld v. Barnes & Spectrum Emergency Care, 107 F.R.D. 17 (E.D. Tex. 1985). Sanctions on both parties and attorneys: *See, e.g.,* Bastien v. R. Rowland & Co., 116 F.R.D. 619 (E.D. Mo. 1987); Deretich v. City of St. Francis, 650 F. Supp. 645 (D. Minn. 1986); Itel Containers Int'l Corp. v. Puerto Rico Marine Management, Inc., 108 F.R.D. 96 (D.N.J. 1985). Sanctions on pro se litigants: *See, e.g.,* Kurkowski v. Volcker, 819 F.2d 201 (8th Cir. 1987); Mullen v. Galati, 843 F.2d 293 (8th Cir. 1988); Bigalk v. Federal Land Bank Ass'n, 107 F.R.D. 210 (D. Minn. 1985) (sanctions not imposed on pro se litigant who was "sincere"); Eckert v. Lane, 678 F. Supp. 773 (W.D. Ark. 1988); Miller v. United States, 604 F. Supp. 804 (E.D. Mo. 1985).

329. *See* Pavelic & LeFlore v. Marvel Entertainment Group, 493 U.S. 120, 110 S. Ct. 456, 107 L. Ed. 2d 438 (1989); *see also* Cooter & Gell v. Hartmarx Corp., 496 U.S. 384, 110 S. Ct. 2447, 110 L. Ed. 2d 359 (1990) (holding that a voluntary dismissal of the action by the plaintiff did not deprive the district court of jurisdiction to levy Rule 11 sanctions).

330. The criticisms are surveyed and discussed thoroughly in 5A CHARLES A. WRIGHT & ARTHUR R. MILLER, FEDERAL PRACTICE AND PROCEDURE: CIVIL § 1332 (2d ed. 1990). For a useful survey of the impact of the 1983 amendments on the practice of lawyers and on particular kinds of cases, see Lawrence C. Marshall et al., *The Use and Impact of Rule 11,* 86 NW. U. L. REV. 943 (1992).

331. *See* Stephen B. Burbank, *Sanctions in the Proposed Amendments to the Federal Rules of Civil Procedure: Some Questions About Power,* 11 HOFSTRA L. REV. 997, 1001-04, 1008-11 (1983). However, the Supreme Court held that Rule 11 permitted the imposition of a fee-shifting sanction on a represented party who signed a paper in violation of Rule 11's objective standard of reasonable investigation. As so interpreted, the Court held that Rule 11 was valid under the Rules Enabling Act. *See* Business Guides, Inc. v. Chromatic Communications Enters., Inc., 498 U.S. 533, 111 S. Ct. 922, 112 L. Ed. 2d 1140 (1991).

332. *See* Note, *Plausible Pleadings: Developing Standards for Rule 11 Sanctions,* 100 HARV. L. REV. 630, 632-44 (1987).

Court adopted, additional amendments to Rule 11 in 1993.[333] These amendments aroused a great deal of controversy.[334]

The 1993 amendments to Rule 11 made extensive changes in the practice under the rule.[335] The changes render some of the case law developed under the 1983 amendment irrelevant, while other decisions remain good authority under the amended rule. This subsection discusses the changes made by the 1993 amendments and their effect on the prior operation of the rule.

The 1993 amendments divide Rule 11 into four subsections. Rule 11(a) requires that litigation papers be signed and dictates the effect of a failure to sign. Rule 11(b) contains the provisions that determine when violations of the rule have occurred. Rule 11(c) provides for the sanctions that may be imposed for violating Rule 11(b), including how imposition of sanctions may be initiated and the nature and limitations that are imposed on sanctions under the amended rule. Rule 11(d) provides for the inapplicability of Rule 11 to discovery matters.

(i) Signature Requirements

Rule 11(a) retains, with changes in language, the requirement that an attorney or an unrepresented party must sign litigation papers. Added to the rule is a requirement that all litigation papers must state the signer's address and telephone number, "if any."[336] The Advisory Committee's notes accompanying the amendment to Rule 11(a) state that the district courts can require by local rule that additional information be provided, "such as telephone numbers to facilitate facsimile transmissions."[337] Rule 11(a) also retains the requirement that an unsigned paper "shall be stricken" unless the omission of the signature is promptly corrected after it is called to the attention of the party who should have signed the paper.[338] The sentence in former Rule 11 providing that signing a litigation paper constituted a certificate that the signer had read the paper was eliminated from Rule 11(a). The certification requirements are now contained in Rule 11(b), and the provisions of that portion of the rule "obviously require that

---

333. These amendments took effect on December 1, 1993; they govern proceedings after that date in the U.S. District Courts and in states which adopted this amendment.

334. When the Supreme Court promulgated the amendments to Rule 11 under the Rules Enabling Act, two Justices dissented. *See* 146 F.R.D. at 507-10 (1993) (dissenting opinion of Justice Scalia, with whom Justice Thomas joined); *see also* James R. Simpson, Note, *Why Change Rule 11? Ramifications of the 1992 Amendment Proposal*, 29 CAL. W.L. REV. 495 (1993); Kimberly A. Stott, *Proposed Amendments to Federal Rule of Civil Procedure 11: New, but Not Necessarily Improved*, 21 FLA. ST. L. REV. 111 (1993); Comment, *Practice and Procedure: The "Safe Harbor" Amendment to Rule 11 . . . Any Port in a Storm*, 47 OKLA. L. REV. 319 (1994).

335. *See* Ridder v. City of Springfield, 109 F.3d 288 (6th Cir. 1997) (discussing the history of the 1993 amendments to Rule 11).

336. *See* FED. R. CIV. P. 11(a).

337. *See* FED. R. CIV. P. 11(a) advisory committee's note to the 1993 amendment.

338. *See* FED. R. CIV. P. 11(a). The former rule stated: "The rule in equity that the averments of an answer under oath must be overcome by the testimony of two witnesses or of one witness sustained by corroborating circumstances is abolished." This provision was repealed by the 1993 amendments. According to the Advisory Committee, the sentence was no longer needed. *See* FED. R. CIV. P. 11(a) advisory committee's note to the 1993 amendment.

pleading, written motion, or other paper be read before it is filed or submitted to the court.''[339]

(ii) Certification Requirements

The 1993 amendments to Rule 11(b) have substantially altered the certification requirements of the prior rule. Rule 11(b) now provides that an attorney or unrepresented party certifies certain matters to the court by ''presenting to the court (whether by signing, filing, submitting, or later advocating) a pleading, written motion, or other paper.'' Formerly, the rule only provided that certification occurred when a litigation paper was signed. Therefore, the 1993 amendments have expanded the responsibilities that attorneys and unrepresented parties have to the court.[340] The certification now applies not only to initial factual and legal contentions, but also imposes a continuing duty not to insist upon a contention after it has become untenable.[341]

Illustration 6-56. A's attorney commences an action against *B* in a U.S. District Court. At the time the attorney files the complaint, good ground exists to believe that factual allegations in the complaint will have evidentiary support after a reasonable opportunity is given to the plaintiff to engage in discovery from the defendant. However, after discovery has been completed, no evidentiary support for the allegations is developed. Nevertheless, at a pretrial conference, *A's* attorney continues to advocate the validity of the claim. The attorney has ''presented to the court'' the now untenable factual contentions within the meaning of Rule 11(b).[342]

Illustration 6-57. A's attorney commences an action against *B* in a state court. There is no basis in existing law for a claim for relief based on the factual allegations in the complaint and no nonfrivolous argument that can be made for the extension, modification, or reversal of existing law or the establishment of new law that would make the complaint nonfrivolous. *B* validly removes the action to a U.S. District Court and moves to dismiss the complaint for failure to state a claim upon which relief can be granted. If *A's* attorney resists the motion to dismiss—for example, by filing a brief in opposition—the attorney has ''presented to the court'' the frivolous legal contentions within the meaning of Rule 11(b).[343]

* * * * *

Under the 1993 amendments, an attorney or party presenting a pleading, written motion, or other paper to the court certifies four things. First, under Rule 11(b)(1), the attorney or party certifies that the paper ''is not being presented for any improper purpose, such as to harass or to cause unnecessary delay or needless increase in the cost of litigation.'' This provision retains the identical requirement of former Rule 11 but, of course, expands the requirement to papers presented to

---

339. *See* FED. R. CIV. P. 11(a) advisory committee's note to the 1993 amendment.
340. *See id.*
341. *See id.*
342. *See id.*
343. *See id.*

the court, as opposed to papers merely signed by the party. Thus, the cases under the 1983 version of Rule 11 determining what constitutes an "improper purpose" will still be good authority under the new rule.

Second, under Rule 11(b)(2), the attorney or party also certifies that "the claims, defenses, and other legal contentions" in the paper presented "are warranted by existing law or by a nonfrivolous argument for the extension, modification, or reversal of existing law or the establishment of new law." The certification of former Rule 11 literally applied only to "pleadings, motions, and other papers," while the language of the amended rule applies to "claims, defenses, and other legal contentions." Under the former rule, some courts had held that an entire litigation paper, as opposed to only a portion of the paper, had to be frivolous to violate Rule 11.[344] The language of the amended rule makes it clear that presenting even one frivolous claim or defense violates the rule, even if the pleading, written motion, or other paper contains other nonfrivolous contentions.[345] However, the 1993 amendments added language to Rule 11(b)(2) that allows a legal contention to be based on a nonfrivolous argument for the establishment of new law, as well as arguments for the extension, modification, or reversal of existing law, which had been allowed by the former rule.

Third, under Rule 11(b)(3), an attorney or party presenting a paper to the court certifies that "the allegations and other factual contentions have evidentiary support or, if specifically so identified, are likely to have evidentiary support after a reasonable opportunity for further investigation or discovery." As with legal contentions under Rule 11(b)(2), this certification requirement applies to all factual contentions. Thus, if a pleading contains some factual allegations that comply with the certification requirement and some that do not, the pleading violates Rule 11.[346]

Former Rule 11 provided that the signer of a litigation paper certified that, based on a reasonable investigation, the paper was, to the best of the signer's knowledge, "well grounded in fact." The certification requirement of Rule 11(b)(3) was revised to make it clear that a party may have good ground to believe that an allegation is true, but may need discovery to "gather and confirm" the evidentiary basis for the allegation.[347] However, the 1993 revisions are not intended to relieve an attorney or party from the duty to conduct a factual investigation that is reasonable under the circumstances before making an allegation. Furthermore, if evidentiary support is not acquired after further opportunity for investigation and discovery, the attorney or party may not persist in advocating the contention.[348] In addition, the text of the rule clearly states that a party basing an allegation on a good faith belief of its truth, but without

---

344. *See, e.g.,* Golden Eagle Distrib. Corp. v. Burroughs Corp., 801 F.2d 1531 (9th Cir. 1986).

345. *See* Letter to the Honorable Robert E. Keeton, Chairman of the Standing Committee on Rules of Practice and Procedure of the Judicial Conference of the United States from Sam C. Pointer, Jr., Chairman of the Advisory Committee on the Civil Rules, Attachment B, 146 F.R.D. 521, 524 (1993).

346. *See id.*

347. *See* FED. R. CIV. P. 11(b)(3) advisory committee's note to the 1993 amendment.

348. *See id.* The party need not formally amend the pleadings to withdraw the allegation, as long as the party does not further advocate an allegation that turns out after discovery to be untenable. *See id.*

evidentiary support, must so state in the party's pleading or a violation of the certification requirement will occur.

Illustration 6-58. *A* sues *B* in a federal district court. *A* alleges in the complaint that *B* negligently ran *A* down with a motor vehicle while *A* was crossing a specific street. At the time *A* files the complaint, *A's* investigation of the facts has not produced any evidence of *B's* negligence because *A* has, despite reasonable efforts, been unable to interview *C*, who was a witness to the accident. *A's* complaint does not specifically identify the allegation of negligence as one that is dependent upon further investigation or discovery. Under these circumstances, the allegation violates the certification requirement of Rule 11(b)(3).

Illustration 6-59. *A* sues *B* in a federal district court. *A* alleges that *B* slandered *A* in certain remarks made to *C*. *A* specifically identifies the allegation of slander as one that is dependent upon further investigation and discovery for confirmation. *A* is given a reasonable opportunity for further investigation and discovery, during which *A* takes the depositions of *B* and *C*. *B's* deposition states that *B* never made slanderous remarks to *C*. *C's* deposition states that *B* never made slanderous remarks to *C*. *B* and *C* are the only possible witnesses to the slanderous remarks. *B* moves for summary judgment against *A*, supporting the motion with the depositions of *B* and *C*. *A* resists the motion for summary judgment by arguing that *B* and *C* are lying. *A* wants to place *B* and *C* on the stand at trial, cross-examine them, and ask the trier of fact to disbelieve their denials that the slanderous utterances were made. Parties bearing the burden of proof on an issue may not ordinarily satisfy that burden of proof by impeachment evidence alone. Thus, if *A* attempted to satisfy the burden of proof on slander by impeaching *B* and *C* at trial, the court would be obligated to grant a judgment as a matter of law against *A*. On this state of the evidence before trial, *B* is entitled to summary judgment against *A*.[349] Therefore, the court grants *B's* motion for summary judgment. *A* has violated the certification requirement of Rule 11(b)(3). The mere fact that a motion for summary judgment is granted against a party does not mean that there is no evidence for the party's position.[350] However, *A* has been given a reasonable opportunity to support the factual allegations of slander and has been unable to do so with evidence that would allow *A* to win the summary judgment motion. Thus, *A's* resistance of the summary judgment motion violated *A's* duty under Rule 11(b)(3) not to persist with unsupportable contentions.

* * * * *

Fourth, under Rule 11(b)(4), an attorney or a party denying factual allegations certifies that "the denials . . . are warranted on the evidence or, if specifically so identified, are reasonably based on a lack of information or belief." The Advisory Committee noted that denials of factual allegations must be treated more leniently under Rule 11(b)(4) than the allegations themselves are treated under Rule 11(b)(3).[351] Denials can be based on evidence that affirma-

---

349. *See* Chapter 10(C)(2) ("Applying the Summary Judgment Standard") & *Illustration 10-12 infra.*
350. *See* FED. R. CIV. P. 11(b)(3) advisory committee's note to the 1993 amendment.
351. *See id.*

tively contradicts the allegations. However, denials may also permissibly be based on an absence of information, or reasonable doubts about the credibility of the evidence supporting the allegations. Of course, a reasonable investigation must be made to determine whether there is support for a denial. In addition, a party may not deny an allegation the party knows to be true. Nevertheless, a party is not required to admit an allegation simply because the party lacks evidence to contradict the allegation.[352] As with allegations and other factual contentions under Rule 11(b)(3), when a denial is based on a lack of information or belief, the party must specifically identify it as such. This requirement appears to force a party who denies a factual allegation on the basis that the evidence supporting the allegation is not credible to state specifically the lack of credibility as the basis of the denial. Failure to do so will apparently constitute a violation of Rule 11(b)(4). Furthermore, if a denial later proves to be untenable after further investigation or discovery, the denying party may not continue to insist on the denial.[353]

Illustration 6-60. *A* sues *B* in federal district court. *A* alleges that *B* made slanderous remarks about *A* to *C*. *B* tells *B's* attorney that *B* never made any such remarks. Furthermore, *B* tells the attorney that *A* and *C* are *B's* lifelong enemies. *B* thinks *A* and *C* are conspiring against *B* to bring the slander claim. *B* provides information to the attorney that will allow *A* and *C* to be impeached effectively at trial if they falsely testify that *B* made the slanderous remarks. *B's* attorney denies in the answer that *B* made the remarks, but without specifying that the denial is based on lack of belief. No violation of Rule 11(b)(4) has occurred. *B's* testimony at trial that *B* never made the slanderous remarks is affirmative contradictory evidence to the allegations that makes a specification under Rule 11(b)(4) unnecessary.

Illustration 6-61. *A* sues *B* in federal district court. *A* alleges that *C*, *B's* employee, negligently ran *A* down with a motor vehicle while *A* was crossing a highway. Shortly after the alleged accident, *C* was killed in a motor vehicle crash with another party. There is no witness to the accident other than *A*. *B* has no evidence that would indicate whether *C* ran *A* down. However, *B* does provide *B's* attorney with information indicating that *A* is not a credible witness and can be effectively impeached at trial. Based on this information, *B's* attorney denies the allegation that *C* ran *A* down, but does not specify in the answer that this denial is based on a lack of "belief." The denial apparently violates Rule 11(b)(4) because of the failure to specify that it is based on a lack of belief.

Illustration 6-62. On the facts of *Illustration 6-61*, assume that *B's* attorney specified in the answer that the denial was based on a lack of belief. Subsequently, however, the attorney's investigation turns up a neutral witness who witnessed *A* being run down by *C*. Thereafter, the attorney may not continue to insist on the denial without violating Rule 11(b)(4). It is not necessary that the attorney amend *B's* answer to eliminate the denial in order to avoid a violation of the rule, as long as the attorney does not continue to insist on the denial.

---

352. *See id.*
353. *See id.*

However, amendment of the answer to withdraw the allegation might be helpful to avoid any implication that the attorney is continuing to rely on the denial.[354]

Illustration 6-63. *A* sues *B* and *C's* estate. *A* alleges in the alternative that either *B* or *C* was driving a motor vehicle that ran *A* down as *A* was crossing a highway. *B* tells *B's* attorney that *B*, not *C*, was driving the motor vehicle, but *B* does not think that *A* can prove who was driving because *B* and *C* were the only witnesses to the accident, and *C* is dead. Under the circumstances, if *B's* attorney denies in the answer that *B* was driving the motor vehicle, Rule 11(c)(4) is violated. It is not permissible in a civil action to deny a fact the party knows to be true on the basis that the other party has the burden of proof and cannot meet it.

(iii) Sanctions and the "Safe Harbor" Provision

Rule 11(c) contains the most important part of the 1993 amendments to Rule 11. Rule 11(c) sets out the circumstances in which sanctions may be imposed for a violation of Rule 11(b). Rule 11(c) also clarifies the philosophy of sanctions and provides for important limitations on the imposition of sanctions.

Initially, Rule 11(c) provides that an alleged violator of the rule must be given notice and a reasonable opportunity to respond to the allegation of violations. After notice and an opportunity to respond have been given, the rule provides that the court "may, subject to the conditions stated [in Rule 11(c)(1) and (2)], impose an appropriate sanction upon the attorneys, law firms, or parties that have violated subdivision (b) or are responsible for the violation."[355] The provision allowing the imposition of sanctions upon law firms overrules the Supreme Court's decision in *Pavelic & LeFlore v. Marvel Entertainment Group*.[356] As noted in the preceding subsection, *Pavelic* interpreted prior Rule 11 to preclude the imposition of sanctions on a law firm for the violation of the rule by one of its attorneys. This alteration of the rule was thought justifiable because of the so-called "safe harbor" provisions of Rule 11(c)(1), discussed below.[357] More importantly, the use of the word "may" in the initial paragraph of Rule 11(c) eliminates the former provision of Rule 11 mandating sanctions for

---

354. *See id.*

355. FED. R. CIV. P. 11(c)(3); *see* Jeffrey A. Parness, *Sanctioning Legal Organizations Under the New Federal Rule 11: Radical Changes Loosen More Unforeseeable Forces*, 14 REV. OF LITIG. 63 (1994). Rule 11(c)(3) provides that when the court imposes sanctions it must describe the conduct determined to constitute a violation of the rule and explain the basis of the sanction imposed. However, when the court denies sanctions, "it should ordinarily not have to explain its denial." *See* FED. R. CIV. P. 11(c)(3) advisory committee's note to the 1993 amendment. *See also* Nuwesra v. Merrill Lynch, Fenner & Smith, Inc., 174 F.3d 87 (2d Cir. 1999) (district court's orders must apprise party of the specific conduct alleged to be sanctionable to give party adequate notice and opportunity to defend); L.B. Foster Co. v. America Piles, Inc., 138 F.3d 81 (2d Cir. 1998) (court must enter an order to show cause or otherwise give notice to attorney as to whether he is being sanctioned under Rule 11 or § 1927); Thornton v. General Motors Corp., 136 F.3d 450 (5th Cir. 1998) (court's order indicated that the attorney was to produce evidence supporting claim, but did not give notice that the court was contemplating sanctions under the pre-filing investigation standard of the rule).

356. 493 U.S. 120, 110 S. Ct. 456, 107 L. Ed. 2d 438 (1989).

357. *See* FED. R. CIV. P. 11(c) advisory committee's note to the 1993 amendment. The last sentence of Rule 11(c)(1) also states that "[a]bsent exceptional circumstances, a law firm shall be held jointly responsible for violations committed by its partners, associates, and employees."

a violation of the rule. In addition, the nature of any sanction imposed also remains discretionary with the court, subject to the limitations imposed by Rule 11(c)(2).[358]

Rule 11(c)(1)(A) contains the so-called "safe harbor" provisions of the rule. Rule 11(c)(1)(A) provides that a motion for sanctions under the rule shall be made separately from other motions or requests and must describe the specific conduct that is alleged to violate Rule 11(b). The motion must be served as provided in Rule 5, but cannot "be filed with or presented to the court unless, within 21 days after service of the motion (or such other period as the court may prescribe), the challenged paper, claim, defense, contention, allegation, or denial is not withdrawn or appropriately corrected."[359] The rule also provides that the court may award to the prevailing party the reasonable expenses incurred in presenting or opposing the motion, including reasonable attorney's fees.

Under the "safe harbor" provisions of Rule 11(c)(1)(A), a party may no longer be sanctioned unless the party insists on relying on matter that violates the rule after the violation has been called to the party's attention. The Advisory Committee observed that under the prior rule parties were sometimes reluctant to abandon matter that violated the rule for fear that the abandonment would itself be considered evidence of a violation.[360] There will no longer be justification for such a fear under the amended rule. The safe harbor period runs from the time that service of the motion for sanctions is made. Nevertheless, the Advisory Committee opined that "[i]n most cases . . . counsel should be expected to give informal notice to the other party, whether in person or by a telephone call or letter, of a potential violation before proceeding to prepare and serve a Rule 11 motion."[361] However, the Advisory Committee did not say what should happen to an attorney or party who fails to give such informal notice. Presumably, the court may take into account such a failure in determining whether to award sanctions for a violation, the severity of the sanctions to be awarded, or whether to award expenses to the moving party who prevailed on the Rule 11 motion.

Whatever difficulties may be involved with the "safe harbor" provision, it has solved one difficult conceptual problem that existed under the prior rule. When a "waivable" matter was involved in a case, it was not clear how the 1983 version of Rule 11 should have been applied. For example, if a plaintiff brought an action in a place where personal jurisdiction or venue was clearly improper, there was a real sense in which the action did not violate Rule 11. Personal jurisdiction and venue will be proper anywhere if they are not raised in accord with the procedures prescribed in Rule 12. In other words, the defendant can waive such defenses. Thus, it was arguably proper for the plaintiff to bring the

---

358. *See id.*

359. *See* FED. R. CIV. P. 11(c) advisory committee's note to the 1993 amendment. *See also, e.g.,* Barber v. Miller, 146 F.3d 707 (9th Cir. 1998) (safe harbor provision precludes a motion for sanctions after dismissal of the complaint, because the plaintiff has no opportunity to withdraw the complaint voluntarily; however, court can award sanctions on its own motion after judgment); Morganroth & Morganroth v. DeLorean, 123 F.3d 374 (6th Cir. 1997) (safe harbor provision prohibits imposition of sanctions pursuant to a motion raised after verdict, even if lawsuit clearly frivolous), *cert. denied*, 523 U.S. 1049, 118 S. Ct. 1561, 140 L. Ed. 2d 793 (1998).

360. *See id.*

361. *See id.*

action in a location where personal jurisdiction and venue were clearly improper and wait to see whether the defendant would raise the defenses. Similar considerations were involved when the plaintiff asserted claims as to which there were clear affirmative defenses, such as the statute of limitations. The "safe harbor" provision solves the conceptual dilemma of the waivable defense. The plaintiff can now commence an action in which personal jurisdiction or venue is clearly improper, or which is clearly precluded by an affirmative defense, and rely on the safe harbor provision for protection from sanctions.

Rule 11(c)(1)(B) provides that the court may, on its own initiative, enter an order describing specific conduct that appears to violate Rule 11(b). The order must direct the attorney, law firm, or party to show cause why it has not violated Rule 11(b) as described in the order. Unlike Rule 11(c)(1)(A), Rule 11(c)(1)(B) does not contain a "safe harbor" provision. Thus, withdrawal of a contention that violates Rule 11(b) will not automatically insulate a violator from sanctions imposed by the court on its own motion. Nevertheless, the Advisory Committee stated that "corrective action" by a violator "should be taken into account in deciding what, if any, sanction to impose," if the court concludes that a violation has occurred after considering the alleged violator's response to the "show cause" order.[362]

Rule 11(c)(2) provides the nature of and limitations on the sanctions that may be imposed for a violation of Rule 11(b). The first sentence of Rule 11(c)(2) emphasizes that sanctions under the rule are designed to deter repetition of the violator's conduct or the conduct of those similarly situated. To this end, the rule prescribes that the sanction imposed shall be limited to what is sufficient for these deterrent purposes. Furthermore, subject to certain limitations imposed by Rule 11(c)(2)(A) and (B), the rule provides that the sanctions may "consist of or include, directives of a nonmonetary nature, an order to pay a penalty into court, or, if imposed on motion and warranted for effective deterrence, an order directing payment to the movant of some or all of the reasonable attorney's fees and other expenses incurred as a direct result of the violation."

Rule 11(c)(2) is designed to work a major change in the way that Rule 11 operated under the 1983 amendments. As indicated in the preceding subsection, former Rule 11 specifically attempted to encourage the imposition of expenses and attorney's fees as a sanction. The encouragement was successful. An award of costs and attorney's fees became by far the most frequently awarded sanction by the courts. However, this result was criticized on the grounds that the costs and expenses sanction was too frequently selected, led to excessively large sanction awards, and created the incentive for many unnecessary Rule 11 motions.[363] The amendments to Rule 11(c)(2) are designed to make it clear that monetary sanctions imposed by the court should "ordinarily be paid into court as a penalty."[364] Nevertheless, the language of the rule specifically recognizes

---

362. *See* FED. R. CIV. P. 11(c)(1)(B) advisory committee's note to the 1993 amendment.

363. *See* Letter to the Honorable Robert E. Keeton, Chairman of the Standing Committee on Rules of Practice and Procedure of the Judicial Conference of the United States from Sam C. Pointer, Jr., Chairman of the Advisory Committee on the Civil Rules, Attachment B, 146 F.R.D. at 524 (1993).

364. *See* FED. R. CIV. P. 11(c)(2) advisory committee's note to the 1993 amendment.

that it will still be appropriate, albeit under fewer circumstances, to award expenses and fees to the moving party. The Advisory Committee stated that an award of fees and expenses would be particularly appropriate for violations of Rule 11(b)(1) when a paper has been presented for an improper purpose, such as harassment or delay.[365] When expenses and fees are awarded, they should not exceed the amount ''directly and unavoidably caused by the violation of the certification requirement.''[366] Likewise, the award should not provide compensation for services that could have been avoided by an earlier ''disclosure of evidence or an earlier challenge to the groundless claims or defenses.''[367] Special rules, however, apply to private securities litigation.[368]

Illustration 6-64. A files and serves a two-count complaint against B. One count of the complaint contains allegations with specific evidentiary support. The other count contains allegations that violate Rule 11(b)(3) because A has no evidentiary support for the allegations and does not specify that the allegations are likely to have support after further investigation or discovery. After further investigation and discovery, A still has no support for the allegations. After informally notifying A of the Rule 11 violation with no results, B serves a motion for sanctions on A pursuant to Rule 11(c)(1)(A). A refuses to withdraw the offending allegations within the time prescribed in the rule. B files the motion with the court. If the court concludes that a violation has occurred and that it is appropriate to impose sanctions on A in the form of a fees and expenses award to B, the court should award fees and expenses only for the costs and services that B has incurred with regard to the count of the complaint that violated the certification requirement of Rule 11. The court should not award fees and expenses for services attributable to responding to the non-violating count. In determining the appropriate amount to award, the court can consider whether earlier notice by B to A about the violation would have avoided some of the fees

---

365. *See id.*

366. *See id.*

367. *See id.* For a discussion of the problems involved with this aspect of the rule, see Jeffrey A. Parness, *Fines Under New Federal Civil Rule 11: The New Monetary Sanctions for the ''Stop-and-Think-Again'' Rule,* 1993 B.Y.U. L. Rev. 879.

368. The Private Securities Litigation Reform Act of 1995, Pub. L. No. 104-67, 109 Stat. 737, *inter alia,* added § 27(c) to the 1993 Securities Act and § 21D(c) to the 1934 Securities Exchange Act. Pursuant to these sections, upon final adjudication of the action, courts in private securities litigation shall include in the record specific findings regarding compliance by each party and each attorney representing any party with each requirement of Rule 11(b) as to any complaint, responsive pleading, or dispositive motion. These sections also establish a presumption that the appropriate sanction for filing a complaint in violation of Rule 11(b) is an award to the opposing party of the reasonable attorneys' fees and other expenses incurred in the action. This presumption can be rebutted only upon proof that the award of attorney's fees and other expenses will impose an unreasonable burden on that party or attorney and would be unjust, and the failure to make such an award would not impose a greater burden on the party in whose favor sanctions are to be imposed. The presumption can also be rebutted by showing that the violation was de minimis. If the presumption is successfully overcome, the court is directed to award sanctions that the court deems appropriate pursuant to Federal Rule 11. *Id.* § 101(a), 109 Stat. 737, 742, 747-48.

and expenses.[369] Of course, under Rule 11(c)(1)(A), the court can also award *B* the fees and expenses involved in presenting the Rule 11 motion.[370]

* * * * *

Rule 11(c)(2)(A) provides that monetary sanctions may not be awarded against a represented party for a violation of Rule 11(b)(2), which involves frivolous legal contentions. The obvious rationale of this limitation is that monetary sanctions for frivolous legal contentions are "more properly placed solely on the party's attorneys." However, the court may impose nonmonetary sanctions, such as dismissal, that have "collateral financial consequences" to a party.[371]

Rule 11(c)(2)(B) provides that the court may not impose monetary sanctions on its own initiative unless the court issues its order to show cause before a voluntary dismissal or settlement of the claims "by or against the party which is, or whose attorneys are, to be sanctioned." This provision is designed to prevent parties who voluntarily dismiss or settle an action from being unexpectedly faced with sanctions that might have affected their willingness to settle or dismiss.[372]

(iv) Rule 11 Inapplicable to Discovery

Rule 11(d) provides that Rule 11 does not apply to "disclosures and discovery requests, responses, objections, and motions that are subject to the provisions of Rules 26 through 37." Rules 26(g) and 37 provide the certification standards and sanctions applicable to discovery matters.[373]

3. Section 1927 and the Court's Inherent Power to Sanction

Section 1927 of Title 28 provides that district courts may impose sanctions upon attorneys who multiply "the proceedings in any case unreasonably

---

369. There are substantial doubts about the effect that delay will have on the availability of sanctions under the new rule. The Advisory Committee's note states that "[o]rdinarily the motion should be served promptly after the inappropriate paper is filed, and, if delayed too long, may be viewed as untimely." *See* FED. R. CIV. P. 11 advisory committee's note to the 1993 amendment. Thus, on the facts of this illustration, *B's* motion might conceivably be held untimely, because *B* waited until after discovery was complete to serve the motion. *B* may be able to justify this delay if it is necessary to wait for discovery in order to see that *A* had no evidentiary support for the second count in the complaint. The Advisory Committee's note also states that "[i]n other circumstances, it should not be served until the other party has had a reasonable opportunity for discovery." *Id.* However, the Advisory Committee does not state what should be done when a violation of the "specification requirement" occurs upon the filing of a litigation paper and the motion is served after discovery is complete. Under such circumstances, the violation may not be apparent to the moving party until both parties have completed discovery.

370. The Advisory Committee also stated, however, that a partial award of expenses and fees may suffice to deter persons of "modest financial resources," suggesting that even when fees and expenses are awarded to a moving party, the primary, if not exclusive, consideration should be deterrence, rather than compensation. *See id.*

371. *See id.*

372. *See id.* This provision overrules the Supreme Court's decision in Cooter & Gell v. Hartmarx Corp., 496 U.S. 384, 110 S. Ct. 2447, 110 L. Ed. 2d 359 (1990).

373. *See* FED. R. CIV. P. 11(d) advisory committee's note to the 1993 amendment.

and vexatiously." The sanctions authorized are the payment of "the excess costs, expenses, and attorneys' fees reasonably incurred" because of the offending attorney's conduct.[374] In addition, the federal courts have "inherent power" to impose sanctions on litigants for bad faith conduct.[375] These two sources of authority can cover the same conduct as Rule 11 and can potentially conflict with each other.[376] For example, if a party violating Rule 11 withdraws the offending allegations or defenses during the safe harbor period of Rule 11, can sanctions nonetheless be imposed by the court under § 1927 or its inherent power? Some courts have taken the position that they have the power to impose sanctions even when the safe harbor provision has been utilized.[377]

SECTION F. PROVISIONAL REMEDIES

This section concerns special procedures called *provisional remedies* that are sometimes important at the outset of litigation. The purpose of provisional remedies is to preserve the status quo pending the court's determination of the parties' rights or to insure that sufficient resources will be available to satisfy the plaintiff's claim if the plaintiff ultimately prevails. If such remedies—attachment, garnishment, sequestration, replevin, temporary restraining orders, preliminary injunctions, civil arrest—were not available, the litigation process could be substantially undermined.[378]

---

374. 28 U.S.C. § 1927. *See generally* Debra T. Landis, Annotation, *What Constitutes Multiplying Proceedings Unreasonably and Vexatiously so as to Warrant Imposition of Liability on Counsel under 28 U.S.C. § 1927 for Excess Costs, Expenses, and Attorney Fees*, 81 A.L.R. FED. 36 (1987).

375. *See* the discussion of the *Chambers* case in Chapter 5(E)(3) *supra*. *See generally* William A. Harrington, Annotation, *Award of Council Fees to Prevailing Party Based on Adversary's Bad Faith, Obduracy, or Other Misconduct*, 31 A.L.R. FED. 833 (1977).

376. Note that § 2072 of Title 28 provides that "[a]ll laws in conflict with [the Federal Rules of Civil Procedure] shall be of no further force or effect after such rules have taken effect." *See* 28 U.S.C. § 2072(b).

377. *See* Edward D. Cavanagh, *Rule 11 of the Federal Rules of Civil Procedure: The Case Against Turning Back the Clock*, 162 F.R.D. 383, 399-400 (1995) (citing an example from the Northern District of New York relying on the court's inherent powers to impose sanctions and concluding that "any attempts to manipulate the safe harbor provisions to the detriment of a rival litigant [are] amply dealt with in complementary sanction provisions under federal law). In Ridder v. City of Springfield, 109 F.3d 288 (6th Cir. 1997), *cert. denied*, 522 U.S. 1046, 118 S. Ct. 687, 139 L. Ed. 2d 634 (1998), the court held that the safe harbor requirement had not been complied with, so Rule 11 could not be the basis of sanctions. However, the court ordered the plaintiff's attorney sanctioned under § 1927. Nevertheless, the court noted that if an attorney is only guilty of inadvertence or negligence that frustrates the trial judge, a sanction is not appropriate under § 1927. In Corley v. Rosewood Care Center, Inc., 142 F.3d 1041 (7th Cir. 1998), sanctions were held improper under Rule 11 where the separate motion and safe harbor periods were not complied with; furthermore, sanctions were held improper under the court's inherent power because the district court did not make a finding of bad faith or explain why Rule 11 was inadequate to serve the court's purposes. *See also* Primus Automotive Fin. Servs., Inc. v. Batarse, 115 F.3d 644 (9th Cir. 1997) (sanctions requested under § 1927 and Rule 11; sanctions imposed on both attorney and client without allocating responsibility between them; totality of sanctions fell outside § 1927 and Rule 11, but were appropriate under the court's inherent power; however, sanctions required a finding of bad faith to be sustainable under inherent power); Trulis v. Barton, 107 F.3d 685 (9th Cir. 1997) (attempted bribery not sanctionable under Rule 11 but can be sanctioned under district court's inherent powers). *See generally* Ted Lapidus, S.A. v. Vann, 112 F.3d 91 (2d Cir. 1997) (discussing the differences in § 1927 and Rule 11); Robert G. Bone, *Modeling Frivolous Suits*, U. PA. L. REV. 519 (1997).

378. In addition to the provisional remedies listed in the text, receivership is also considered a provisional remedy. Receivership is the appointment of a neutral third party to manage property that is the subject of the action in order to prevent it from ruin or dissipation by the parties to the action. *See, e.g.*, FED. R. CIV. P. 66.

In federal court, "legal" provisional remedies, such as attachment, garnishment, and replevin, are controlled by the law of the state in which the district court is sitting. Rule 64 of the Federal Rules of Civil Procedure states that "all remedies providing for seizure of person or property for the purpose of securing satisfaction of the judgment ultimately to be entered in the action are available under the circumstances and in the manner provided by the law of the state in which the district court is held, existing at the time the remedy is sought."[379] In contrast, federal district courts have independent equitable power, regulated by Federal Rule 65, to issue temporary restraining orders and preliminary injunctions. The difference in approaches under Rules 64 and 65 is attributable to the historical differences in the procedures followed by the federal courts in common law and equity actions before the Federal Rules of Civil Procedure were adopted. In common-law actions, the federal courts were governed by the conformity acts and generally followed the procedures under state law.[380] In equity cases, the federal courts possessed an independent equity power and were governed by federal equity rules.[381] The Federal Rules of Civil Procedure generally preserve this pattern,[382] with Rule 65 constituting a codification of the pre-Rules equity practice.[383]

1. Attachment and Garnishment

Assume that a defendant has been served with process in an action for money damages. What is to prevent the defendant from withdrawing money from the bank or selling assets and going to Las Vegas on a weekend fling? Or hiding the money? Or removing property from the state where the action is pending to another state or to a Swiss bank? Provisional remedies, such as attachment and garnishment, are designed to protect a plaintiff from these hazards. Attachment is the seizure of the defendant's property in advance of judgment, while garnishment makes an obligation owed by a third person to the defendant subject to the plaintiff's claim.

Statutes establish and regulate the right to attach or garnish property. The statutory grounds for attachment and garnishment usually focus on defendants who abscond, hide or convey assets, or leave the jurisdiction with the intent to defraud creditors.[384] The plaintiff must show that a proposed attachment or garnishment is based upon an appropriate statutory ground and that other statutory prerequisites have been met—for example, the action is one in which attachment is permitted, the property is not exempt from attachment, the plaintiff has posted

---

379. FED. R. CIV. P. 64.

380. For a discussion of the conformity acts, see Chapter 1(E)(5) ("Development of Federal Procedure and the Federal Rules of Civil Procedure") & Chapter 5(C)(2)(e) ("Equity and Admiralty Cases") *supra.*

381. *See* Chapter 5(C)(2)(e) ("Equity and Admiralty Cases") *supra* (discussing the federal equity power).

382. *See* 11A CHARLES A. WRIGHT & ARTHUR R. MILLER, FEDERAL PRACTICE AND PROCEDURE: CIVIL §§ 2931, 2941 (2d ed. 1995).

383. *See id.* § 2943, at 79. *But see, e.g.,* United States *ex rel.* Rahman v. Oncology Assocs., P.C., 198 F.3d 489 (4th Cir. 1999) (Rule 64 authorizes the use of state equitable remedies permitting seizures).

384. *See, e.g.,* NEB. REV. STAT. § 25-1001 (1995).

a bond (undertaking) to cover the defendant's damages if the attachment is found to be improper, etc. If the plaintiff makes such a showing in support of an attachment, the court will order the sheriff (or some other officer) to seize a certain amount of the defendant's property. If the plaintiff makes such a showing in support of a garnishment, the court will order the sheriff (or some other officer) to serve the holder of the property owned by the defendant (for example, a bank) with notice not to pay the defendant (for example, not allow the defendant to withdraw funds from the defendant's account).

Illustration 6-65. *A* sues *B* in a state court. *A* seeks to recover $20,000 for personal injuries received in an automobile accident. Before the action, *A* and *B* had been involved in negotiations directed at settling the claim, but the negotiations broke down. *A* received reliable information that *B* was removing *B's* property from the jurisdiction in anticipation of an action by *A*. Upon commencing the action, *A* may proceed under the state attachment statute by having the sheriff seize an amount of *B's* property in *B's* possession that will satisfy *A's* claim against *B* if *A* wins the action.

Illustration 6-66. On the facts of *Illustration 6-65*, if *B* possesses bank accounts in the state where the action is commenced, *A* may proceed under the state garnishment statute to garnish the accounts. Under the garnishment statute, an order would issue from the court in which the action is pending to the bank where *B* had accounts, directing the bank to hold the money in the accounts secure for the further order of the court and to not pay the money to *B*. If the bank violates the order, the bank, as garnishee, can be held liable to *A* for the amount of the accounts.

* * * * *

Attachment and garnishment procedures (as well as those governing other provisional remedies) must afford the defendant due process. In general, the defendant must be served with notice of the proposed attachment or garnishment and be given the right to challenge the attachment or garnishment before it is ordered. However, in many situations, the nature of the grounds for attachment or garnishment are such that a prior notice and hearing would frustrate the purpose of these procedures. In such "emergency" situations, an ex parte order and writ may be issued, provided the defendant is given a *prompt* post-seizure opportunity to challenge the order and writ, to substitute a bond (undertaking) for the property attached or garnished, and to challenge the amount or sufficiency of the plaintiff's bond.[385]

Illustration 6-67. On the facts of *Illustrations 6-65* and *6-66*, the state attachment and garnishment statutes would normally provide for issuance of attachment and garnishment orders without a prior notice and an opportunity to be heard upon a proper showing by *A* that *B* was removing *B's* property from the state to avoid execution of a potential judgment against *B*. The statutes would usually also provide for a prompt postseizure hearing at *B's* request, in which *A* would have the burden of proving the existence of grounds for the provisional

---

385. *See* subsection 5 for a full discussion of the constitutional limitations on the operation of provisional remedies *infra*.

remedy issued. *A* would normally also have to post a bond sufficient to indemnify *B* for any economic losses *B* might suffer if the provisional remedy is eventually shown to have been erroneously issued. *B* would also have an opportunity to challenge the sufficiency of the bond after the provisional remedy is issued.

2. Sequestration and Replevin

The writ of sequestration was used in English chancery actions as a provisional remedy to compel an answer to a bill and as a method of enforcing the final decree. As a provisional remedy today, it is employed primarily to preserve specific property from disposition pending the outcome of litigation. It was adopted by several states, but in many instances it has now been limited or abrogated by statute or court rule. It is directed generally at property or funds that are the subject of conflicting claims of ownership or liens. Sequestration also has been used to restore property that forcibly and unlawfully has been taken from a party. This use of sequestration is very similar to replevin.

As discussed in Chapter 1,[386] replevin as a form of action at common law covered the wrongful seizure of chattels. Today in the United States, the replevin procedure (also called in some states by other names, such as "claim and delivery") is regulated by statute but remains similar to the common-law practice. By claiming the right to immediate possession, the plaintiff can have the property returned to the plaintiff pending a trial on the merits. The plaintiff is required to post a bond to provide security to reimburse the defendant for damages if it is ultimately determined that the defendant is entitled to the property. Before the property is returned to the plaintiff, the defendant is given an opportunity to object to the bond's adequacy. Most states provide for a "re-delivery bond" or "counter bond," which provides security to protect the plaintiff. Such a bond permits a defendant to retain possession of the property until the final determination of the action.[387]

In addition to statutory replevin discussed above, many states have recognized "equitable replevin." Equitable replevin is accomplished by a mandatory injunction ordering the defendant to return property to the plaintiff. It is used when the statutory replevin procedure (the remedy at law) is inadequate for some reason. Often, the property that is the subject of the action is unique or irreplaceable. Under these circumstances, there is danger that the statutory replevin procedure will not produce a return of the property in specie because the defendant is able to post a redelivery bond. The redelivery bond will, by definition, be inadequate to protect the plaintiff because it will only substitute money for the unique or irreplaceable property.[388]

Both statutory and equitable replevin differ from attachment and garnishment in the extent to which the plaintiff is claiming an interest in the property seized. When a plaintiff utilizes attachment and garnishment, the plaintiff

---

386. *See* Chapter 1(E)(1)*(b)(iii)* ("*Ex Delicto* Personal Actions") *supra.*
387. DAN B. DOBBS, LAW OF REMEDIES § 5.17(2), at 583-84 (2d student ed. 1993).
388. *See generally id.* § 5.17(3), at 586.

is simply attempting to seize general assets of the defendant in order to secure a potential judgment. The plaintiff is not claiming any property interest in the assets seized. In contrast, replevin is a provisional remedy used when the plaintiff is claiming an interest in specific personal property that is in the possession of the defendant.

Illustration 6-68. *A*, a merchant, sells a refrigerator to *B* under a contract requiring *B* to make installment payments for 24 months until the price of the refrigerator is paid. Under the contract, *A* retains ownership of the refrigerator as security that the payments will be made. If *B* does not make the payments required by the contract, *A* is entitled to repossess the refrigerator. After a time, *B* ceases making the payments required by the contract. *A* commences an action to obtain a judgment for the payments. Under these circumstances, many states would allow *A* to employ the provisional remedy of replevin to seize the refrigerator pending the outcome of the litigation with *B*. The contract gives *A* a right to a return of the security if *B* does not make the payments. This interest makes the provisional remedy of replevin appropriate. By statute, *B* will usually have the right to post a redelivery bond to obtain the return of the refrigerator during the litigation with *A*.

Illustration 6-69. *A* claims ownership of an irreplaceable work of art. *A* asserts that *A* loaned the work of art to *B* and that *B* refuses to return the work of art. *A* sues *B* to obtain return of the work of art. Under these circumstances, the provisional remedy of equitable replevin may be available to *A* to obtain return of the work of art during the pendency of the litigation with *B*. The irreplaceable nature of the work of art arguably makes *A's* "remedy at law" in the form of statutory replevin inadequate because statutory replevin would allow *B* to obtain its return after seizure by posting a redelivery bond. Thus, equitable replevin will be the only provisional remedy that will assure *A* that the work of art will not be destroyed, sold, or removed from the jurisdiction by *B*.

3. Civil Arrest and Ne Exeat

The provisional remedies discussed in the preceding subsections are directed at the seizure of property as a means of securing the plaintiff's claim if the plaintiff ultimately should be successful. There are also provisional remedies directed at the seizure of the defendant for the same purpose: civil arrest and the writ of ne exeat. As noted in Chapter 3, certain actions at common law were commenced by *capias ad respondendum*. This writ directed the sheriff to arrest the defendant for the purpose of securing the defendant's court appearance on a certain day. A defendant could post security and thus secure release.[389] In most states, the use of civil arrest has been abolished or limited by state constitutional

---

389. *See* Chapter 3(K)(1) ("Service of Process in English and Early United States Practice") *supra.*

provisions prohibiting imprisonment for debt. However, it remains a proper provisional remedy in some states.[390]

The writ of ne exeat is similar to civil arrest. It was used in equity to restrain the impending departure of a defendant from the jurisdiction of the court with the intent to evade its jurisdiction or to defraud the plaintiff. The defendant could gain release by posting a bond or equitable bail securing the defendant's appearance and performance of the court's decree. While still available as a remedy in some states to secure equitable claims, it is rarely used, except in matrimonial actions. In many states, it has been abolished.[391]

4. Temporary Restraining Orders and Preliminary Injunctions

(a) The Nature of Temporary Restraining Orders and Preliminary Injunctions

The development of equity as a separate system complementary to the common-law courts was described in Chapter 1.[392] As noted there, the development of equity has had a substantial impact on modern substantive law, procedures, and remedies, including limitations on the jurisdiction of the federal courts to issue particular types of relief. For example, in *Grupo Mexicano de Desarrollo, S.A. v. Alliance Bond Fund, Inc.*,[393] the Supreme Court held that the U.S. District Courts lack authority under Rule 65 to issue preliminary injunctions preventing defendants from disposing of their assets pending adjudication of claims for money damages in cases in which there has been no prior judgment fixing the amount of the debt. A majority of the Court agreed that the jurisdiction conferred by the Judiciary Act of 1789 over "all suits . . . in equity" gave the federal courts only the authority to administer in equity suits the "principles of the system of judicial remedies which had been devised and was being administered by the English Court of Chancery at the time of the separation of the two countries."[394] That power did not include the authority to issue the kind of preliminary injunction in question. This power was not altered by the merger of law and equity by the Federal Rules of Civil Procedure pursuant to the Rules Enabling Act, because "the rule requiring a judgment [fixing the amount of the debt before a preliminary injunction could issue] was historically regarded as serving, not merely the procedural end of assuring exhaustion of legal remedies

---

390. *See* 5 AM. JUR. 2D *Arrest* §§ 73-91 (1995); *see also* Eugene J. Morris & Hilton M. Wiener, *Civil Arrest: A Medieval Anachronism*, 43 BROOKLYN L. REV. 383 (1977). Curiously, arrest is still indirectly sanctioned in federal court under 28 U.S.C. § 1693, a statute preserved in the modern Judicial Code that traces its origins back to the Judiciary Act of 1789. For a discussion of the history of § 1693, see Ralph U. Whitten, *Separation of Powers Restrictions on Judicial Rulemaking: A Case Study of Federal Rule 4*, 40 ME. L. REV. 41, 71-72 (1988).

391. *See* 57 AM. JUR. 2D *Ne Exeat* §§ 1-34 (1988).

392. *See* Chapter 1(E)(2) ("Equity Jurisdiction and Procedure") *supra*.

393. 527 U.S. 308, 119 S. Ct. 1961, 144 L. Ed. 2d 319 (1999).

394. *Id.* at __, 119 S. Ct. at 1968, 144 L. Ed. 2d at 330.

(which the merger of law and equity could render irrelevant), but also the substantive end of giving the creditor an interest in the property which equity could then act upon."[395] Interestingly, however, the majority indicated that "[t]he debate concerning this formidable power over debtors should be conducted and resolved where such issues belong in our democracy: in the Congress."[396] This implies that Congress could legislate to override state substantive rights with a remedial rule applicable only in federal courts without violating the constitutional restrictions on Congress's power potentially imposed by the *Erie* decision. However, in another part of its opinion, the Court also explicitly reserved judgment (because the parties had not raised the issue) as to whether, if state courts could issue the remedy in question, federal courts would be obliged to do so.[397] The Court also observed that no one in the case had raised the applicability of Federal Rule 18(b), which provides that multiple claims can be joined in an action even when one of them has been "heretofore cognizable" after the other has been prosecuted to a conclusion, but that the court can grant relief in the action only in accord with the "relative substantive rights of the parties." The Court also noted that Rule 18 says nothing about preliminary relief and specifically reserves substantive rights, as does the Rules Enabling Act.[398]

Equity courts usually act through personal orders to the defendant to do or refrain from doing some act. "Injunctive" orders and decrees for specific performance are enforced by contempt proceedings.[399] In the context of provisional remedies, such actions have taken the form of "temporary restraining orders" and "preliminary injunctions." Temporary restraining orders and preliminary injunctions are designed to preserve the status quo until final determination of the action. The primary difference between a temporary restraining order and a preliminary injunction is that the latter is granted only after a hearing while the former can be granted ex parte. In theory, a temporary restraining order should preserve the status quo only until there can be a hearing on a preliminary injunction, while the preliminary injunction is designed to remain in effect until the final determination of the action. Federal Rule 65 sets out a uniform procedure for granting these two equitable remedies in federal court and in states that have adopted the Federal Rules. Rule 65 thus constitutes a useful example of how temporary restraining orders and preliminary injunctions are generally administered.

Temporary restraining orders are granted only in "emergency" situations. They are issued only when it clearly appears from a verified complaint, or from

---

395. *Id.* at __, 119 S. Ct. at 1970, 144 L. Ed. 2d at 333-34.

396. *Id.* at __, 119 S. Ct. at 1975, 144 L. Ed. 2d at 339.

397. *See id.* at __, n.3, 119 S. Ct. at 1968, n.3, 144 L. Ed. 2d at 330, n.3.

398. *See id.* at __, 119 S. Ct. at 1970, 144 L. Ed. 2d at 334; *cf.* United States *ex rel.* Rahman v. Oncology Assocs., P.C., 198 F.3d 489 (4th Cir. 1999) (holding it permissible for a federal court to issue an equitable order freezing assets when part of the final relief requested is also equitable; alternatively, Rule 64 allows federal courts to employ equitable orders freezing assets if state law so permits); *see also* Mary A. Nation, Comment, *Granting a Preliminary Injunction Freezing Assets Not Part of the Pending Litigation: Abuse of Discretion Or an Important Advance in Creditors' Rights?* 7 TUL. J. INT'L & COMP. L. 367 (1999).

399. *See* DAN B. DOBBS, LAW OF REMEDIES §§ 2.8(2)-2.8(7) (2d student ed. 1993) (discussing the differences between civil and criminal contempt).

specific facts shown by affidavit, that the applicant will suffer "immediate and irreparable injury, loss, or damage" before notice can be served and a hearing can be held on a motion for preliminary injunction.[400] The steps that the applicant's attorney has taken (if any) to give notice must be specified and the reasons why notice should not be required also must be stated.[401] Local court rules often require specific efforts to give notice, such as telephoning the adverse party to inform that party of the facts and that an application for a temporary restraining order is being made so that oral counter-arguments might be made.[402] The applicant also must post security to indemnify the opposing party against economic harm that may occur due to an erroneous issuance of an order.[403] Rule 65(b) provides that a temporary restraining order shall "expire by its terms within such time after entry, not to exceed 10 days, as the court fixes, unless within the time so fixed, the order, for good cause shown, is extended for a like period" or the party being restrained consents to a longer extension. Ideally, within this time period, a hearing will be held to determine whether a preliminary injunction will be issued.

     Illustration 6-70. *A* awakens one morning to find *B Co.* present on *A's* property about to bulldoze a large number of ancient, ornamental trees. *B's* employees tell *A* that they are about to grade the land for the construction of an amusement park. Despite *A's* best attempts to convince the employees that they are in the wrong location, they persist in making preparations to destroy the trees. Under these circumstances, *A* should be able to obtain a temporary restraining order to prevent *B* from trespassing on the land and destroying the trees. *A* is faced with an emergency situation in which there is no time to provide notice and an opportunity to be heard to *B* before the order issues. Monetary damages will not adequately compensate *A* because of the age and ornamental character of the trees. Thus, *A* is threatened with "irreparable injury."[404]

* * * * *

     Assume that a court has granted a temporary restraining order and a hearing is being held on the question of whether a preliminary injunction should be granted. What standard should the court use to decide this question? Rule 65 does not state a standard. Furthermore, the federal and state courts are not in full agreement on the proper standard. In general, courts take into account four factors: (1) the injury that will result to the applicant if the preliminary injunction is denied; (2) the likelihood of the applicant's success on the merits; (3) whether the threatened injury to the applicant outweighs the possible injury to the

---

400. *See* FED. R. CIV. P. 65(b).

401. *Id.*

402. SHEPARD'S MANUAL OF FEDERAL PRACTICE 584 (2d ed. 1979).

403. *See* FED. R. CIV. P. 65(c). However, it has been held that the bond requirement is not a jurisdictional prerequisite to the validity of a preliminary injunction. Popular Bank v. Banco Popular de P.R., 180 F.R.D. 461 (S.D. Fla. 1998). *See generally* F.M. English, Annotation, *Furnishing of Bond as Prerequisite to Issuance of Temporary Restraining Order,* 73 A.L.R.2D 854 (1960).

404. *See* DAN B. DOBBS, LAW OF REMEDIES § 2.11(2), at 193-94 (2d student ed. 1993).

opposing party; and (4) whether the public interest would be harmed by issuance of a preliminary injunction.[405]

Illustration 6-71. *A* owns property that *A* uses as a residence. *A's* property is adjacent to property owned by *B*, which *B* uses as a manufacturing plant. *B's* operations produce a small amount of pollution that is affecting the paint on *A's* house, causing it to deteriorate more rapidly than it would under natural conditions. *A* sues *B* for a preliminary injunction to stop *B* from emitting the pollution from *B's* plant. The only way to prevent the pollution over the short run is to close down the plant, which will throw 5,000 employees out of work and severely affect the economy of the local community in which the plant is located. Under these circumstances, it is unlikely that *A* will be able to obtain a preliminary injunction. The injury to *A's* house is minor compared to the effects on *B* and the public interest of granting the injunction. Indeed, the injury can probably be compensated adequately in damages. A full exploration of the merits may reveal some way that the pollution can be eliminated or diminished. Thus, the temporary harm to *A* does not justify the possibly massive harm to *B* and third parties that issuing the injunction would cause.

(b) Contempt

Temporary restraining orders and preliminary injunctions are enforced by means of the contempt sanction. There are two kinds of contempt: *civil contempt* and *criminal contempt*.[406] Violation of a temporary restraining order or preliminary injunction can result in the imposition of *both* civil and criminal contempt sanctions. Criminal contempt sanctions are imposed to punish someone for violating a court decree in order to vindicate the court's authority.[407] To this end, criminal contempt sanctions involve fixed fines or fixed jail sentences.[408] In contrast, civil contempt sanctions are designed to coerce compliance with the court's decree in the future.[409] Thus, a civil contempt fine will be assessed at a certain amount per day until the contemnor complies with the order, or a jail sentence of an indefinite term will be imposed until the contemnor agrees to comply with the court's order.[410] The nature and purpose of the sanction imposed, therefore, determines the kind of contempt involved in the case.[411]

When criminal contempt sanctions are imposed, the protections of a criminal trial must be afforded to the contemnor. For example, the criminal burden of proof applies in criminal contempt proceedings, and when "serious" penalties are imposed for criminal contempt, there is a constitutional right to a

---

405. SHEPARD'S FEDERAL PRACTICE MANUAL 583 (2d ed. 1979). *See generally* DAN B. DOBBS, LAW OF REMEDIES § 2.11(2) (2d student ed. 1993); 11 CHARLES A. WRIGHT & ARTHUR R. MILLER, FEDERAL PRACTICE AND PROCEDURE: CIVIL § 2948, at 430-31 (1973).

406. For a useful discussion of the differences between civil and criminal contempt see Lawrence N. Gray, *Criminal and Civil Contempt: Some Sense of a Hodgepodge,* 72 ST. JOHNS L. REV. 337 (1998).

407. *See* DAN B. DOBBS, LAW OF REMEDIES § 2.8(3), at 139 (2d student ed. 1993).

408. *See id.*

409. *See id.*

410. *See id.*

411. *See id.* at 138.

trial by jury.[412] In contrast, civil contempt sanctions do not ordinarily require the protections of a criminal proceeding and are not subject to the Sixth Amendment requirement of jury trials for criminal proceedings.[413]

Illustration 6-72. *A* sues *B* for specific performance of a contract to convey land. The court issues a decree of specific performance against *B*. *B* refuses to comply with the decree. The court holds *B* in contempt in a proceeding that did not afford *B* the ordinary protections available in a criminal proceeding. The court sentences *B* to remain in jail until *B* agrees to execute a deed of the land covered by the contract and decree of specific performance. The court's action is valid. The sanction imposed on *B* is designed to coerce compliance with the court's decree, not to punish *B* for past violation of the decree. As a result, it is a civil contempt sanction that does not have to be accompanied by the protections of a criminal trial.

* * * * *

Traditionally, a party has been required to obey an injunctive order until it is overturned. Thus, a party can be punished for criminal contempt for disobeying a temporary restraining order or preliminary injunction, even if the order is ultimately reversed on appeal.[414] The ability to impose criminal contempt sanctions for violation of an erroneous order may depend on the availability to the defendant of adequate procedures to challenge the order before the time for disobedience to it arrives. If such procedures do not exist, a defendant may be able to violate the order and effectively challenge it on appeal from a criminal contempt conviction.[415] Nevertheless, it would take a bold lawyer to advise a client to disobey an injunctive order because the order is erroneous and might be reversed on appeal from a criminal contempt conviction. In addition to the fact that the state of the law in this area is unsettled, there is always the possibility that the order will be held correct, rather than erroneous, and the criminal contempt sentence upheld as a result.

There is also a potential escape from criminal contempt sanctions if an order is ultimately found to be "void," as opposed to only "erroneous." Void orders are ones issued without personal or subject-matter jurisdiction over the defendant.[416] However, the "void order" exception is itself subject to an important exception. When a defendant raises a challenge to jurisdiction, the challenge must be determined by the court. This may require time, and the court may deem it proper to issue a temporary restraining order to preserve the status quo during the period of time necessary to determine the jurisdictional issue. It is said that a court always has jurisdiction to determine its own jurisdiction. Thus,

---

412. *See id.* § 2.8(4), at 145-47.

413. There have been recent examples of cases in which the courts have held that it is possible for coercive sanctions imposed for civil contempt to become "criminal" in nature. *See id.* § 2.8(3), at 140-45. The alternative view is that the nature of the sanction should be measured at the time it is imposed. If it is civil then, it cannot become criminal. *Cf. id.* at 145.

414. *See id.* § 2.8(6), at 153. Obviously, however, a court cannot impose civil contempt sanctions on a person in violation of an order that is ultimately held to be in error. Once the order is held erroneous, there is nothing left with which a civil contempt sanction can coerce compliance.

415. *See id.* at 154-55.

416. *See id.*

if the defendant violates the temporary restraining order while the court is trying to determine whether it has ultimate jurisdiction over the action or the defendant's person, the defendant can be punished for criminal contempt even if the court ultimately holds that it lacks jurisdiction over the subject matter or the parties. The court's jurisdiction to determine jurisdiction gives it the power to enter an order that must be obeyed until the ultimate jurisdictional determination is made, at least if the jurisdictional issue is substantial and not frivolous.[417]

Illustration 6-73. B wants to conduct a civil rights march on Easter Sunday. A, a public official, obtains a temporary restraining order to prevent the march. B possesses notice of the order several days before the march, but does nothing to try to get the order overturned under the procedures available in the court that issued the order or the appellate courts of the state. Instead, when Easter Sunday arrives, B conducts the march in violation of the order. B attempts to defend a criminal contempt proceeding brought against B on the ground that the order violated B's First Amendment rights. Even if the order violates the First Amendment, B can be punished for criminal contempt. The order is only "erroneous," albeit constitutionally erroneous, and not "void." B did not attempt to get the order overturned, even though B had the time to do so and procedures were available to B to have the order reviewed by the court that issued it and the appellate courts of the state.[418]

Illustration 6-74. B *Labor Union* engaged in a strike during wartime when the government was operating the industry in which B's members worked. The government sought an injunction to prohibit the strike. B contended that the courts had no jurisdiction to issue injunctions in strike disputes. The court issued a temporary restraining order against B to prevent the strike during the period of time necessary to determine this jurisdictional issue. B violated the order. If the jurisdictional issue under the statute is substantial rather than frivolous, B can be punished for criminal contempt for violating the order, even if the courts ultimately hold that they have no jurisdiction to issue injunctions against strikes. The court's jurisdiction to determine jurisdiction gives it the power to issue a temporary restraining order to allow it to resolve the jurisdictional question.[419]

(c) The Bond Requirement

Ordinarily, temporary restraining orders and preliminary injunctions–as well as most other provisional remedies–cannot be issued without the plaintiff first providing security to protect the defendant from harm that may accrue if the provisional remedy is erroneously issued. This security is often provided in the form of a bond. The bond is quite important to the defendant. The predominant view is that, in the absence of security, the defendant cannot recover anything from the plaintiff for economic harm suffered as the result of an erroneous

---

417. *See id.* at 155-56.
418. *Cf.* Walker v. City of Birmingham, 388 U.S. 307, 87 S. Ct. 1824, 18 L. Ed. 2d 1210 (1967).
419. *See* United States v. United Mine Workers, 330 U.S. 258, 67 S. Ct. 677, 91 L. Ed. 884 (1947).

provisional order.[420] Furthermore, damages can normally be recovered under the bond only for economic losses actually incurred by the defendant as a result of the erroneous issuance of the order.[421] Depending upon the procedure in effect in the jurisdiction where recovery on the bond is sought, the injured party may have to proceed by independent action or may be allowed to recover against the surety on motion.[422]

5. Constitutional Limitations on Provisional Remedies

The procedures governing all provisional remedies presuppose circumstances under which the defendant will not receive notice and an opportunity to be heard in defense before the remedy issues. For example, the rules governing temporary restraining orders envision that such orders can be issued without notice to the adverse party under limited circumstances.[423] It is obvious, however, that the availability of such remedies without prior notice and hearing can be the source of abuse. Abuse of the remedies has led the Supreme Court to place due process restrictions on availability of provisional remedies without prior notice and hearing. The Court's modern decisions have indicated the safeguards that a state's provisional-remedy scheme must have in order to meet constitutional standards. However, the Court's decisions have not yet completely clarified all of the elements of the constitutional test.

The Court's earliest modern decision was *Sniadach v. Family Finance Corp.*[424] In *Sniadach*, the Court invalidated Wisconsin's garnishment procedure under the Due Process Clause of the Fourteenth Amendment because it did not provide for notice and an opportunity to be heard before seizure. The property seized in *Sniadach* was wages, and the Court's opinion implied that wages deserved special protection under the Constitution.[425] However, this view was rejected in the Court's next decision, *Fuentes v. Shevin.*[426] In *Fuentes*, the Court invalidated Florida's replevin procedure under circumstances where a creditor had utilized it to repossess consumer goods from a consumer who had stopped making payments on the goods.[427] The writ of replevin was issued on the ex parte

---

420. *See* DAN B. DOBBS, LAW OF REMEDIES § 2.11(3), at 197 (2d student ed. 1993). Sometimes a plaintiff may be sanctionable under a rule, such as Federal Rule 11, for bringing a frivolous claim, and, rarely, the issuance of a provisional order may give rise to a claim for malicious abuse of civil process or restitution. *See id.* at 199. In addition, some courts have held that it is permissible to impose a condition on the provisional order that the plaintiff be personally liable to the defendant for economic harm suffered as a result of the order. *See id.* at 198. However, in the absence of such circumstances or conditions, the defendant must look to the bond as the sole source of compensation for economic harm suffered as a result of an erroneous provisional remedy.

421. *See id.* at 203-04.

422. *See* FED. R. CIV. P. 65.1. For a complete discussion of the security requirement, including questions such as the court's discretion to dispense with the bond, what will trigger the bond liability, and the measurement of damages recoverable, see DAN B. DOBBS, LAW OF REMEDIES § 2.11(3) (2d student ed. 1993).

423. *See, e.g.,* FED. R. CIV. P. 65(b).

424. 395 U.S. 337, 89 S. Ct. 1820, 23 L. Ed. 2d 349 (1969).

425. *See id.* at 340, 89 S. Ct. at 1822, 23 L. Ed. 2d at 353.

426. 407 U.S. 67, 92 S. Ct. 1983, 32 L. Ed. 2d 556 (1972).

427. The creditor had retained title to the goods as security for payment.

application of the plaintiff, who was also required to file a bond in an amount double the value of the property. The Court recognized that extraordinary situations exist in which no notice or opportunity to be heard need be provided before a provisional remedy issues against a defendant. However, the Court held that the situations in which it had allowed postponement of notice and an opportunity to be heard shared certain common characteristics. In each case, (1) seizure was "directly necessary" to secure an important governmental or general public interest; (2) there was a "special need" for very prompt action; and (3) the state kept strict control over the seizure by requiring a government official to determine, "under the standards of a narrowly drawn statute" that the seizure was necessary under the circumstances of the case.[428]

In cases after *Fuentes*, the constitutional requirements for state provisional remedy statutes evolved into a more precise form. The Court's next two decisions, taken together, seemed to establish that a state provisional remedy statute would meet due process requirements if (1) it requires a factual affidavit or other sworn statement by someone with personal knowledge showing that the grounds for issuing the remedy exist; (2) a judge has to scrutinize the application to determine whether the remedy may properly issue; and (3) a prompt postseizure hearing is available in which the plaintiff has the burden of demonstrating the existence of the grounds for issuing the remedy. Furthermore, the constitutionality of an ex parte provisional remedy will be more secure if (1) it is sought for the seizure of property in which the plaintiff has a preexisting interest and (2) the plaintiff's claim is subject to documentary proof, rather than being dependent upon the testimony of witnesses about (perhaps complex) past events.[429]

In 1991, the Supreme Court clarified that the constitutionality of state provisional remedy schemes is to be determined by a balancing test. In *Connecticut v. Doehr*,[430] the Court held that due process validity of a provisional remedy depends upon a "threefold inquiry," requiring consideration of (1) the private interest that will be affected by the issuance of the provisional remedy; (2) the risk of an erroneous deprivation through the procedures under attack and the probable value of additional or alternative safeguards; and (3) the interest of the party seeking the provisional remedy with due regard for any ancillary interest the government may have in providing the procedure used or forgoing the added

---

428. *See* 407 U.S. at 90-92, 92 S. Ct. at 1999-2000, 32 L. Ed. 2d at 575-77.

429. *See* North Ga. Finishing, Inc. v. Di-Chem, Inc., 419 U.S. 601, 95 S. Ct. 719, 42 L. Ed. 2d 751 (1975); Mitchell v. W.T. Grant Co., 416 U.S. 600, 94 S. Ct. 1895, 40 L. Ed. 2d 406 (1974). In *Mitchell*, the Court upheld Louisiana's sequestration procedures, which had the safeguards described in the text. In addition, the sequestration procedure was used by a creditor to repossess consumer goods in which the creditor had a vendor's lien, and the creditor's claim was simple and could be resolved primarily on the basis of documentary proof. In *Di-Chem*, the provisional remedy was issued by the clerk based on a conclusionary affidavit by the plaintiff, and no way existed to dissolve the remedy except by the defendant filing a bond. In addition, the plaintiff garnished the defendant's bank account, in which the plaintiff had no preexisting interest. *Mitchell* is the only modern decision in which the Court has upheld a state provisional remedy statute against a challenge under the Due Process Clause of the Fourteenth Amendment. *But cf.* Matthews v. Eldridge, 424 U.S. 319, 96 S. Ct. 893, 47 L. Ed. 2d 18 (1976) (administrative procedures for terminating social security disability benefits constitutional, despite the fact that no evidentiary hearing was provided prior to termination).

430. 501 U.S. 1, 111 S. Ct. 2105, 115 L. Ed. 2d 1 (1991).

burden of providing greater protections.[431] Under this test, the Court found Connecticut's attachment statute unconstitutional. The statute allowed attachment of the defendant's real property without prior notice and an opportunity to be heard, but without a requirement that "exigent circumstances" exist for the attachment or that the plaintiff post a bond.[432] The Court held the statute invalid because it permitted ex parte seizure without a showing of exigent circumstances.[433] Four members of the Court also were of the opinion that a bond is an indispensable constitutional requirement, but the majority did not reach this issue.[434]

Nothing in *Doehr* suggested that the result of the case was affected by the fact that real property was the subject of the attachment. However, a subsequent decision of the Court under the Due Process Clause of the Fifth Amendment has suggested that the prejudgment seizure of real property may be more restricted than the seizure of personalty. In *United States v. James Daniel Good Real Property*,[435] the Court invalidated an ex parte prejudgment seizure of the defendant's real property in a proceeding brought to forfeit the property because it had been used to facilitate the commission of a federal drug offense. Applying the *Doehr* balancing test, the Court found that the defendant's interests and the risk of erroneous deprivation outweighed the interests of the government in prejudgment seizure without additional safeguards.[436] The fact that real property "cannot abscond" impaired the government's ability to demonstrate the need for prompt action to seize the property.[437] In addition, the Court emphasized that

---

431. *See id.* at 10, 111 S. Ct. at 2112, 115 L. Ed. 2d at 13.

432. The application for attachment had to be made upon verified affidavit of the plaintiff or some other "competent affiant" that there was probable cause to sustain the validity of the plaintiff's claims. Based on this affidavit, a judge could issue the writ of attachment. The attachment notice had to inform the defendant that a right to a hearing existed in which the defendant could (1) litigate whether probable cause existed for the claim, (2) request that the attachment be vacated, modified, or that a bond be substituted, or (3) claim that the property was exempt from execution. The affidavit and notice complied with these requirements. *See id.* at 5-6, 111 S. Ct. at 2109-10, 115 L. Ed. 2d at 10.

433. The Court found that (1) the private interests affected by the seizure were significant, given the effects that attachment could have on the property owner; (2) the risk of erroneous deprivation was too great, given the highly fact-dependent nature of the plaintiff's claim and the lack of additional adequate safeguards under the statute; and (3) the plaintiff's interests in ex parte attachment were weak in the absence of a showing of exigent circumstances or a preexisting interest in the property on the part of the plaintiff. *See id.* at 11-17, 111 S. Ct. at 2112-15, 115 L. Ed. 2d at 14-16.

434. *See id.* at 18-24, 111 S. Ct. at 2116-19, 115 L. Ed. 2d at 18-21 (Justice White, with whom Justices Marshall, Stevens, and O'Connor joined). The Justices emphasized, however, that a bond requirement would not excuse the absence of exigent circumstances, a prompt post-seizure hearing, or other safeguards. *See id.* at 22-23, 111 S. Ct. at 2118-19, 115 L. Ed. 2d at 20-21.

435. 510 U.S. 43, 114 S. Ct. 492, 126 L. Ed. 2d 490 (1993).

436. *See id.* at 62, 114 S. Ct. at 505, 126 L. Ed. 2d at 508-09.

437. *See id.* at 57, 114 S. Ct. at 502-03, 126 L. Ed. 2d at 505. The Court observed that a notice of lis pendens could be filed under state law when the government commences the forfeiture proceedings. *See id.* at 58, 114 S. Ct. at 503, 126 L. Ed. 2d at 506. Lis pendens is a notice filed on public records for the purpose of warning all persons that the title to certain property is in litigation and that they are in danger of being bound by an adverse judgment. Its purpose is to preserve rights pending litigation. However, lis pendens will often involve the same kind of interference with property rights that the Court previously found objectionable in *Doehr*. For example, lis pendens effectively clouds title and prevents the sale of the property until the action is resolved. Apparently, however, the Court is suggesting that this sort of interference with property rights would be legitimate. In addition, the Court stated that "[i]f there is evidence, in a particular case, that an owner is likely to destroy" the property "when advised of the pending action, the government may obtain an *ex parte* "[i]ndividual freedom finds tangible expression in property rights," and that "security and privacy of the home and those who take shelter within it" are at stake when real property is seized.[438] These statements suggest that real property may receive an extra measure of protection from prejudgment seizure under the Due Process Clauses of the Constitution.

Based on the Court's decisions from *Sniadach* through *Good*, it is possible to summarize the elements that are indispensable to a state provisional remedy scheme in order for the scheme to meet constitutional requirements. In addition, it is possible to extrapolate at least one other likely requirement that the Court may add to the list of indispensable elements in the future. Finally, it is possible to point to certain other factors that will weigh heavily in the balance in determining whether a provisional remedy statute can be validly applied in specific cases.

To meet constitutional standards, a provisional remedy statute must contain at least four elements: (1) "exigent circumstances" must exist that somehow threaten to make the plaintiff's action an exercise in futility;[439] (2) the plaintiff must provide facts through an affidavit or other sworn statement by someone with personal knowledge showing that the grounds for issuing the provisional remedy exist; (3) a judge must examine the application to determine that the grounds for issuing the provisional remedy exist; and (4) a prompt postseizure hearing must be available in which the plaintiff bears the burden of proving that the grounds for the provisional remedy exist.

In addition to these four "indispensable" elements of constitutionality, at least one other element will likely be considered indispensable to the validity of a provisional remedy statute. The plaintiff should have to demonstrate a possibility of success on the merits to the judge examining the application. Thus, it should not be possible, even on a showing of exigent circumstances, to obtain a provisional remedy unless the complaint demonstrates that the plaintiff possesses a claim upon which relief can be granted. No justification would exist for depriving the defendant of liberty or property, even temporarily, if the plaintiff cannot present a minimal case on paper that a judgment will ultimately be rendered against the defendant. Even a bond requirement would not suffice as

---

restraining order, or other appropriate relief, upon a proper showing in district court." *Id.* However, it may be difficult to obtain affirmative evidence that an owner intends to destroy property. The Court's pronouncement on this aspect of the case may have been affected by the fact that the government left the defendant's tenants in possession of the property. "The government's policy of leaving occupants in possession of real property under an occupancy agreement . . . demonstrates that there is no serious concern about destruction in the ordinary case." *Id.* Finally, the Court stated that the government could prevent the property from being used for further illegal activity "with search and arrest warrants obtained in the ordinary course." *Id.* at 59, 114 S. Ct. at 504, 126 L. Ed. 2d at 507. Again, this pronouncement may have been based on the four-year passage of time between the defendant's conviction and the commencement of the forfeiture action, as well as the fact that the defendant was not personally occupying the property.

438. *See id.* at 61, 114 S. Ct. at 505, 126 L. Ed. 2d at 508.

439. In the case of provisional remedies such as attachment or garnishment, the exigent circumstances will ordinarily be a tangible threat that the defendant is going to remove assets from the reach of the court's power of execution. In the case of temporary restraining orders, the threat will ordinarily be that the defendant is about to engage in action—*e.g.*, bulldozing ornamental trees on the plaintiff's property—that cannot be effectively remedied by a later damages judgment.

an adequate substitute for such a showing, since the amount of the bond would be set initially in an ex parte proceeding and might not be sufficient to compensate the defendant for losses that would result from issuance of the provisional remedy.

It is more difficult to assess whether the Court will ultimately require a bond or other security as an indispensable constitutional requirement for the issuance of a provisional remedy. Four Justices made strong arguments in *Doehr* that a bond should be a constitutional requirement.[440] Nevertheless, it is far from certain that a bond will be held indispensable to the validity of a provisional remedy statute. One argument against a mandatory bond requirement is that it would often place an insurmountable obstacle in the path of an impecunious plaintiff's ability to obtain a provisional remedy, even when strong grounds exist for issuing the remedy. In addition, adequate substitutes for a bond may readily be imagined. For example, a state might provide a statutory cause of action that would allow a defendant to recover damages for the economic losses caused by a provisional remedy if the plaintiff's claim ultimately failed.[441] However, even if a bond is not held indispensable to the constitutionality of a provisional remedy, the bond is an important safeguard that could likely tip the balance in favor of validity in marginal cases.[442]

Two other factors will also weigh heavily in determining the validity of a provisional remedy when they are present in a particular case. First, when the plaintiff possesses an interest in the property seized, that interest will weigh in favor of the validity of seizure of the property without prior notice and an opportunity to be heard. The preexisting interest of the plaintiff bears on the existence of exigent circumstances. To leave the defendant in possession of property in which the plaintiff has an interest risks deterioration of the value of the property through the defendant's use, even when there is no additional risk that the defendant will transfer or destroy the property. However, a preexisting property interest cannot be considered an indispensable prerequisite to the validity of a provisional remedy. If it were, attachment or garnishment of the defendant's general assets when the defendant is removing them from the reach of a potential judgment would be impossible. Nothing in the Court's decisions suggests that attachment and garnishment are per se invalid.

---

440. *See Doehr*, 501 U.S. at 18-21, 111 S. Ct. at 2116-18, 115 L. Ed. 2d at 20 (Justice White, with whom Justices Marshall, Stevens, and O'Connor joined).

441. Connecticut provided such a procedure in *Doehr*, although it was hedged with restrictions and defenses that rendered it an inadequate substitute for a preseizure bond. *See id.* at 20-21, 111 S. Ct. at 2117-18, 115 L. Ed. 2d at 19-20.

442. *Cf.* McLaughlin v. Weathers, 170 F.3d 577 (6th Cir. 1999) (Tennessee statute differs from one in Connecticut and is constitutional; statute requires bond, provides for exigent circumstances, and defendant failed to take advantage of opportunities under state law to challenge the seizure in state court). Most states require a bond before issuance of a provisional remedy. *See* 501 U.S. at 24, 111 S. Ct. at 2119-20, 115 L. Ed. 2d at 22-23 (Appendix). It seems highly doubtful that the Court would ever hold that a *redelivery bond* is a mandatory constitutional requirement in every provisional remedy case. Such a requirement would render per se invalid the provisional remedy of equitable replevin, discussed in section F(2), *Illustration 6-69, supra.* Nevertheless, a redelivery bond requirement might also provide an additional safeguard to protect the defendant's interests in a particular case.

Second, *Doehr* and *Good* taken together indicate that when seizure of real property is involved in an action, the plaintiff will have a more difficult time making a case for prejudgment seizure of the property. When real property is the subject of the seizure, it will be more difficult to demonstrate the necessary exigent circumstances because the property cannot be removed from the court's jurisdiction. In addition, the security and privacy values associated with realty will cause the Court to scrutinize real property cases carefully to determine whether less restrictive means of protecting the plaintiff's interests are available, as well as to assure that adequate safeguards are provided to protect the defendant's interests.[443]

---

443. For example, in a marginal case of prejudgment seizure of realty, the presence of an adequate bond requirement might tip the balance in favor of validity.

Chapter 7

JOINDER OF CLAIMS

SECTION A. JOINDER OF CLAIMS BY PLAINTIFFS AT COMMON LAW AND IN EQUITY

The common law restricted the joinder of claims by plaintiffs. The general rule allowed a plaintiff to join all claims within the same form of action. It made no difference that the claims were factually unrelated. Thus, a plaintiff could join a trespass claim with other unrelated trespass claims. Likewise, a plaintiff could join trespass-on-the-case claims with other unrelated trespass-on-the-case claims. However, a plaintiff could not join a trespass claim with a factually related trespass-on-the-case claim.[1]

Illustration 7-1. Assume that *A* wanted to sue *B* in a common-law court for damages, joining two counts. One count alleged an assault and battery. The other count alleged a breach of contract. *A* could not join these two causes of action because they did not fall within the same form of action.

Illustration 7-2. Suppose that *A* wanted to sue *B* in a common-law court for damages, joining two counts. One count alleged property damage due to *B's* negligence in colliding with *A's* wagon. The other count alleged an assault and battery committed by *B* against *A* on a wholly different occasion. Superficially, these causes of action appear to be unjoinable because the first arose in trespass on the case and the second arose in trespass. However, this illustration is unlike *Illustration 7-1.* As discussed in Chapter 1, the plaintiff had an option in negligent collision situations. The plaintiff could sue in trespass on the case, treating the defendant's negligence as the wrong; or instead, the plaintiff could sue in trespass, treating the immediate crash of the wagons as the wrong.[2] Thus, by electing this latter alternative, the plaintiff could join the two causes of action.

Illustration 7-3. Assume that *A* wanted to sue *B* in a common-law court for damages, joining three counts. One count alleges property damage due to *B's* negligence in colliding with *A* in *A's* wagon. The second count alleged an assault and battery occurring immediately after the collision when *B* jumped from the wagon and punched *A* in the nose. The third count alleged slander when, on the

---

1. *See* BENJAMIN J. SHIPMAN, HANDBOOK OF COMMON-LAW PLEADING § 80 (1923). Some exceptions to this rule existed. For example, a cause of action in debt could be joined with an unrelated cause of action in detinue. The reason was that

> anciently both were regarded as actions of debt and were found embodied in the same writ in the register of writs. Notwithstanding the modification and modern use of detinue, which relegates it to the classification of actions ex delicto [founded on tort], the courts have unaccountably continued the ancient practice of permitting its joinder with debt.

ALEXANDER MARTIN, CIVIL PROCEDURE AT COMMON LAW 184 (1905). Similarly, a cause of action for trespass on the case could be joined with a cause of action in trover, because a trover action was "in its nature a species of trespass on the case." *Id.*; *see also* Chapter 1(E)(1)*(c)(iii)* ("Trover") *supra.*

2. *See* Chapter 1(E)(1)*(c)(i)* ("Trespass on the Case") & *Illustration 1-28 supra.*

same occasion, *B* accused *A* of being a drunkard. *A* could not join *all* of these causes of action. Unlike *Illustration 7-2*, *A's* range of options was not broad enough to permit joinder of all three causes of action. As indicated in Chapter 1, the cause of action for assault and battery fell only within trespass, while the cause of action for slander fell only within trespass on the case.[3] *A* could join the cause of action for the damage to the wagon with either of these. However, *A* could not join all three causes of action together.

* * * * *

In addition to these joinder limitations, all the causes of action had to exist in favor of the plaintiff *in the same right* and against the defendant *in the same capacity* before the plaintiff could join them together. This requirement meant, for example, that a plaintiff could not join a claim brought as an individual with another claim brought as an executor. Nor could a defendant be sued in the same action on a claim against the defendant as an individual and on a claim against the defendant as a representative. Likewise, a *joint* claim on behalf of two plaintiffs could not be joined with a *several* claim on behalf of one of them. Furthermore, two plaintiffs could not join claims setting up separate rights against the same defendant.[4] A single plaintiff could not join different causes of action against different defendants. Nor could the plaintiff join a cause of action asserting the joint liability of two or more defendants with causes of action alleging the several liability of any or all the defendants.[5]

The plaintiff could include multiple statements of the same cause of action in the declaration, each of which represented the facts in a different way. Thus, when the plaintiff was uncertain whether one of the statements was legally sufficient or when the plaintiff feared that proof of one of the statements might fail, the plaintiff could plead the cause of action in a different way in separate counts in the declaration. In effect, this approach relaxed the rule against duplicity in pleadings.[6] However, the plaintiff still had to exercise care. As with so many situations at common law, the plaintiff could evade the rule against duplicity, but could not directly violate it. The plaintiff had to make each of the counts appear as if it actually stated an entirely different cause of action.[7]

Illustration 7-4. Assume that *B* entered into a bond with *A*. *B* promised in the bond to pay a penalty if *B* failed to pay a sum of money on the first of September and another sum on the first of October. If the defendant did not pay on both dates, either failure would entitle *A* to recover the penalty. If *A* stated both defaults in a single count, the declaration would be duplicitous. However, *A* could state each of the defaults in a separate count, prove a failure to pay on *either* date, and still win the penalty. To do this, *A* had to allege the penal bond

---

3. *See* Chapter 1(E)(1)*(b)(iii)* ("*Ex Delicto* Personal Actions") & Chapter 1(E)(1)*(c)(i)* ("Trespass on the Case") *supra.*

4. *Cf. Illustration 7-8 infra.*

5. *See* ALEXANDER MARTIN, CIVIL PROCEDURE AT COMMON LAW 184 (1905); BENJAMIN J. SHIPMAN, HANDBOOK OF COMMON-LAW PLEADING § 80 (1923); Edson R. Sunderland, *Joinder of Actions*, 18 MICH. L. REV. 571, 582-83 (1920).

6. The rule prohibiting duplicity in pleadings is discussed in Chapter 6(A)(2) ("Stating the Plaintiff's Claim in the Declaration") *supra.*

7. *See* BENJAMIN J. SHIPMAN, HANDBOOK OF COMMON-LAW PLEADING § 81 (1923).

and a failure to pay on September 1st in the first count. *A* could then plead the same bond, describing it as "a certain other bond" in the second count. *B* then could allege a failure to pay on October 1st. This form of statement evaded the rule against duplicity. It thus allowed *A* to recover the penalty by proving failure of payment on either date.[8]

* * * * *

A plaintiff could use this same technique in other situations when possible variations in proof at trial clouded how a transaction or an event should be described in the complaint. Of course, when the plaintiff pleaded a single cause of action in different ways, the plaintiff could recover only once.

Illustration 7-5. Assume that *B* stole *A's* valuable work of art. *A* wanted to sue *B* for the value of the work of art in an action of assumpsit, but was uncertain whether *B* had sold the work of art to a third party or still had it. If the work of art had not been sold, the proper common count was goods sold and delivered. If *B* had sold the work of art and *A* wanted to recover the amount *B* received on the sale, the proper common count was money had and received.[9] If *A* selected goods sold and delivered and the work of art had been sold for an amount greater than its value, *A* would not be able to recover the greater amount from *B* at trial. On the other hand, if *A* selected money had and received and *B* had not sold the work of art, *A's* cause of action might fail altogether. To avoid this problem, *A* could plead the cause of action in different ways in different counts. Of course, *A* could recover only once.[10]

* * * * *

The consequences of misjoining causes of action at common law were serious. Misjoinder impeached the validity of the entire declaration. The defendant could raise this defect by a general demurrer,[11] a motion in arrest of judgment, or a writ of error.[12] When the plaintiff correctly joined several counts, depending on the nature of the defense, the defendant could demur to all of them, plead to all, demur to one count and plead to another, or plead differently to each count.[13]

Equity was more flexible on matters of joinder than common law. The objective of equity was to determine in a single action as many controversies concerning the subject matter as was convenient.[14] The defendant could demur to a bill in equity as *multifarious.* However, this objection was unavailable unless the joined matters arose out of different transactions or occurrences *and* each matter constituted a complete cause of action in itself sufficient to sustain a bill in equity.[15] "Indeed, the objection of multifariousness, and the circumstances under which it [would] be allowed to prevail, or not, [was] in many cases, a

---

8. *See id.*

9. *See* Chapter 6(A)(2) ("Stating the Plaintiff's Claim in the Declaration") & *Illustration 6-1, supra.*

10. *See* BENJAMIN J. SHIPMAN, HANDBOOK OF COMMON-LAW PLEADING § 81 (1923).

11. *See* Chapter 6(A)(3)*(a)* ("General Demurrers") *supra.*

12. *See* Chapter 12(A) ("Post-Trial Motions") *infra.*

13. *See* ALEXANDER MARTIN, CIVIL PROCEDURE AT COMMON LAW § 229 (1905).

14. *See* HENRY L. McCLINTOCK, HANDBOOK OF EQUITY § 9 (2d ed. 1948).

15. *See* BENJAMIN J. SHIPMAN, HANDBOOK OF THE LAW OF EQUITY PLEADING 340 (1897).

matter of discretion, and no general rule can be laid down on the subject."[16] Equity also enforced a rule with the opposite effect of multifariousness: a plaintiff could not split a single cause of action into separate elements and thus unnecessarily multiply the number of suits. In such a situation, the court would force the plaintiff to join the omitted matter.[17]

Generally, a legal claim could not be joined with an equitable claim in an equity court. In certain cases, however, the *"clean-up doctrine"* allowed an equity court to grant its unique brand of relief and also award common-law damages, thus preventing a multiplicity of suits. In applicable cases, this doctrine had the practical effect of permitting the joinder of legal and equitable claims for relief.[18]

Illustration 7-6. Assume that *A* sued to enjoin *B* from repeatedly trespassing on *A's* land. The only dispute was whether the alleged trespasses were taking place. Under these circumstances, an equity court would take jurisdiction based on the request for an injunction and give damages for the past trespasses under the clean-up doctrine. However, if *B* defended by disputing *A's* title to the land, the equity court would not take the case under any doctrine. Equity would not try the title to land. As a result, there would have to be two actions. The first action would be in a common-law court to settle the title issue. If *A* was successful in that action, the second action would be in equity to obtain an injunction.[19]

SECTION B. JOINDER OF CLAIMS BY PLAINTIFFS UNDER THE CODES

One of the most important reforms instituted by the Field Code was the liberalization of claim joinder. The Code, however, did not permit unlimited joinder. The reformers believed some limitations on the scope of a lawsuit were necessary. As a result, they permitted joinder of claims that arose within limited categories.[20] Thus, a plaintiff could join all contract claims (express and

---

16. JOSEPH STORY, COMMENTARIES ON EQUITY PLEADINGS § 284 (9th ed. 1879).

17. *See id.* § 287.

18. *See* DAN B. DOBBS, THE LAW OF REMEDIES § 2.6(4), at 117 (2d student ed. 1993); *see* Chapter 1(E)(2) ("Equity Jurisdiction and Procedure") *supra*; Chapter 11(E) ("The Right to Trial by Jury in a Merged System: Operation of the Historical and Modern Federal Approaches") *infra*.

19. *See* 1 DAN B. DOBBS, LAW OF REMEDIES § 2.7, at 180-81 (2d practitioner ed. 1993).

20. Section 143 of the 1848 Field Code provided as follows:
> The plaintiff may unite several causes of action in the same complaint, where they all arise out of,
>> 1. Contract, express or implied; or
>> 2. Injuries by force, to person or property; or
>> 3. Injuries without force to person or property; or
>> 4. Injuries to character; or
>> 5. Claims to recover real property; with or without damages, for the withholding thereof; or,
>> 6. Claims to recover personal property, with or without damages for the withholding thereof; or,
>> 7. Claims against a trustee by virtue of a contract or by operation of law.

implied). Likewise, a plaintiff could join all claims arising out of injuries by force to persons or property (such as trespass, false imprisonment, or assault and battery). However, the plaintiff could not join factually related contract and tort claims because torts and contracts were in different categories.

The joinder of claims provision in the 1848 Field Code demonstrated a curious ambivalence. The Code followed the common-law pattern of allowing joinder of the causes of action that were thought to be similar in nature and did not require a factual relationship between the claims within a category. However, the Code contained an overriding restriction: the causes of action joined had to "equally affect" all the parties to the action and not require different places of trial.[21]

In 1852, the New York Legislature substantially liberalized claim joinder (§ 167). The amended joinder provision followed the former equity practice by permitting joinder of claims based on their factual relationship ("same transaction clause") (§ 167(1)). However, the amended section retained all the other joinder categories, which required no factual relationship between the claims (§ 167(2)-(7)).[22] The same transaction clauses of the codes have been subject to widely varying interpretations.[23]

Illustration 7-7. Assume that *A* assaulted and slandered *B* on the same occasion. Some courts held there were multiple causes of action, not joinable, arising out of different transactions. Some held that there were joinable multiple causes of action arising out of the same transaction. Some held there was only a single cause of action.[24] Obviously, the language of the same transaction clauses required some factual relationship between the causes of action joined. After the minimal factual relationship existed to satisfy the face of the statute, litigational

---

But the causes of action, so united, must all belong to one only of these classes, and must equally affect all the parties to the action, and not require different places of trial.
Act of Apr. 12, 1848, ch. 379, § 143, 1848 N.Y. Laws 497, 525.

21. *See id.*

22. The 1852 amendment (§ 167) to the Field Code provided:

The plaintiff may unite in the same complaint several causes of action, whether they be such as have been heretofore denominated legal or equitable, or both, where they all arise out of,

1. The same transaction, or transactions connected with the same subject of action;
2. Contract, express or implied; or
3. Injuries with or without force, to person and property, or either; or
4. Injuries to character; or
5. Claims to recover real property, with or without damages, for withholding thereof, and the rents and profits of the same; or
6. Claims to recover personal property, with or without damages for the withholding thereof; or
7. Claims against a trustee, by virtue of a contract, or by operation of law.

But the causes of action, so united must all belong to one of these classes, and must affect all the parties to the action, and not require different places of trial, and must be separately stated.

Act of Apr. 16, 1852, ch. 392, § 167, 1852 N.Y. Laws 651, 655; *see also* CHARLES E. CLARK, HANDBOOK OF THE LAW OF CODE PLEADING § 67, at 437-38 (2d ed. 1947).

23. *See* CHARLES E. CLARK, HANDBOOK OF THE LAW OF CODE PLEADING § 69, at 452 (2d ed. 1947).

24. *See id.* at 454 and authorities there cited.

efficiency should have determined whether the causes of action were properly joined.[25]

* * * * *

The 1852 amendment to the Field Code also retained the restriction that joined claims had to ''affect'' all parties to the suit and could not require different places of trial. However, the amendment altered the restriction so the claims no longer had to affect all parties ''equally.''[26]

Illustration 7-8. Assume that *A* and *B*, husband and wife, sued the *C Motel* for damages for being wrongfully ejected from the motel on the ground that they were not married. *A* and *B* attempted to join their individual claims in the same action under a joinder provision identical to § 167, as amended in 1852. The claims were improperly joined. Although both parties' causes of action arose out of the same transaction, the causes of action were ''several,'' not joint. Thus, they did not ''affect'' all the parties to the action. In other words, under the substantive law, the husband ''owned'' his cause of action and the wife ''owned'' hers. Neither was entitled to share in the other's recovery.[27]

* * * * *

When claims were factually unrelated, they could still be joined, provided they all fit within a single category of the joinder provision. The result was a rather fortuitous joinder scheme, unrelated to any apparent considerations of litigational convenience.

Illustration 7-9. Assume that *A* sued *B* for damages. *A* joined in the complaint two causes of action. One was based on an automobile accident, in which *B* negligently collided with *A*. The other was based on an assault and battery committed by *B* against *A* on a wholly separate occasion. These causes of action could be joined under § 167(3) of the New York Code of 1852. That section provided for joinder of multiple causes of action when they all arose out of ''injuries with or without force, to person or property or either.'' Assume that *A* also possessed a slander claim against *B* because *B* stated that *A* was an alcoholic immediately after the automobile accident. That claim could not be joined with the other two claims. Even if the slander and negligence claims arose from the same transaction or occurrence under § 167(1), the assault and battery arose from a different factual occurrence. Thus, all three causes of action did not fit within § 167(1). Likewise, the slander claim could not be joined with the other two under § 167(3), because it was not a cause of action for injuries ''to person or property or either.'' Rather, the slander cause of action fell within § 167(4), because it was an injury ''to character.'' The other two causes of action did not fit within that section.

* * * * *

Measured by standards of practical convenience, this pattern was not well thought out.[28] Moreover, when the claim joinder sections were considered

---

25. *Cf. id.* at 455-56.
26. *Id.*
27. *See* Ryder v. Jefferson Hotel Co., 121 S.C. 72, 113 S.E. 474 (1922).
28. *See* CHARLES E. CLARK, HANDBOOK OF THE LAW OF CODE PLEADING § 69, at 455-56 (2d ed. 1947).

together with the party joinder provisions of the codes, joinder was further restricted in multiparty cases, discussed in the next chapter.

Illustration 7-10. A sued *B Bus Co.* for punitive damages for personal injuries received in an accident due to *B's* reckless conduct. *A* joined a cause of action against *I, B's* insurer, to recover compensatory damages for injuries negligently inflicted by *B* in the same accident. These causes of action were improperly joined. Although they both arose from the same transaction or occurrence, the cause of action against *B* did not affect *I*. Thus, both causes of action do not affect all the parties to the action.[29]

SECTION C. JOINDER OF CLAIMS BY PLAINTIFFS UNDER THE FEDERAL RULES

1. Application of Federal Rule 18

Rule 18 of the Federal Rules of Civil Procedure vastly simplified the joinder of claims and remedies. Rule 18(a) allows a party to join as many claims as the party has against an opposing party, regardless of the relationship between the claims. Rule 18 permits unlimited joinder of claims at the pleading stage on the theory that any harm caused by joinder of unrelated claims occurs only at the trial stage.[30] If such harm exists, it can be eliminated in the discretion of the trial court under Rule 42(b), which permits severance and separate trial of joined claims in the interests of expedition and economy.[31]

Federal Rule 18 was derived from former Equity Rule 26. The original version of Rule 18(a) attempted to liberalize former Equity Rule 26[32] by extending unlimited claim joinder to cases involving multiple parties.[33] Unfortunately, the lower federal courts restrictively interpreted the original version of Rule 18(a). Because the original version of Rule 18(a) referred to Rules 19, 20, and 22, the limitations on party joinder in those rules were read into Rule 18 as

---

29. *See* Piper v. American Fidelity & Cas. Co., 157 S.C. 106, 154 S.E. 106 (1930).

30. *See* Edson R. Sunderland, *The New Federal Rules*, 45 W. VA. L.Q. 5, 13 (1938).

31. *See* FED. R. CIV. P. 18 advisory committee's note to the 1966 amendment.

32. Equity Rule 26 provided as follows:

> The plaintiff may join in one bill as many causes of action, cognizable in equity, as [the plaintiff] may have against the defendant. But when there is more than one plaintiff, the causes of action joined must be joint, and if there be more than one defendant the liability must be one asserted against all of the material defendants, or sufficient grounds must appear for uniting the causes of action in order to promote the convenient administration of justice. If it appear that any such causes of action cannot be conveniently disposed of together, the court may order separate trials.

226 U.S. at 655-56 (1912).

33. Original Rule 18(a) stated that

> [t]he plaintiff in his complaint or in a reply setting forth a counterclaim may join either as independent or as alternate claims as many claims either legal or equitable or both as he may have against an opposing party. There may be a like joinder of claims when there are multiple parties if the requirements of Rules 19, 20 and 22 are satisfied.

See FED. R. CIV. P. 18 advisory committee's note 2.

restrictions on claim joinder.[34] Rule 18(a) was amended in 1966 to clarify that this restrictive interpretation was incorrect.[35]

Illustration 7-11. Assume that *A* sues *B* and *C*. *A* asserts alternative claims for relief against *B* and *C* arising out of an automobile accident. Under Rule 18, *A* may join a claim against *B* alone for breach of contract arising out of a wholly separate event. As discussed in the next chapter, Rule 20 is satisfied in this situation because (a) a claim for relief arising out of the same occurrence is asserted against all the defendants and (b) questions of law or fact common to all the defendants will exist in the action. Because Rule 20 is satisfied, *A* may join any other claims that *A* possesses against *B* or *C* by virtue of Rule 18.

* * * * *

Rule 18(b) allows a party to join two claims, even if one of them is contingent on the successful prosecution of the other to conclusion. The second sentence of Rule 18(b), allowing joinder of a claim for money and a claim to set aside a fraudulent conveyance, is merely an example of joinder of this sort.[36] Rule 18(b), in fact, applies to all sorts of contingent or conditional claims.[37]

Rule 18 is permissive. It does not compel a party to join all claims that the party possesses against an opposing party. It merely allows joinder of the claims.

2. Problems of Subject-Matter Jurisdiction, Venue, and Personal Jurisdiction Under Rule 18

The requirements of federal subject-matter jurisdiction, venue, and personal jurisdiction qualify the unlimited joinder of claims permitted by Rule 18.

(a) Subject-Matter-Jurisdiction Restrictions on Joinder

Subject-matter-jurisdiction restrictions on joinder depend both on the general statutes conferring jurisdiction on the lower federal courts, such as 28 U.S.C. §§ 1331 and 1332, and also on the scope of the supplemental jurisdiction conferred by 28 U.S.C. § 1367.

Illustration 7-12. *A*, a citizen of Sweden, sues *B*, a citizen of State *X*, in a U.S. District Court in State *X*. *A* asserts two claims against *B* arising under state law: a tort claim for $33,000 and a wholly unrelated contract claim for $33,000. Although Rule 18 does not restrict *A*'s ability to join the tort and contract claims,

---

34. For example, suppose a plaintiff properly joined two defendants under Rule 20 by asserting against them claims arising out of the same transaction or occurrence and raising common questions of law or fact. The plaintiff was not permitted to join an additional factually unrelated claim against one of the defendants. *See, e.g.,* Federal Hous. Adm'r v. Christianson, 26 F. Supp. 419 (D. Conn. 1939).

35. *See* FED. R. CIV. P. 18 advisory committee's notes to 1966 amendment.

36. *See* FED. R. CIV. P. 18(b).

37. *See generally* E.H. Schopler, Annotation, *Construction, Application, and Effect of Federal Rule of Civil Procedure 18(b) and Like State Rules or Statutes Pertaining to Joinder in a Single Action of Two Claims Although One Was Previously Cognizable Only After the Other Had Been Prosecuted to a Conclusion*, 61 A.L.R.2D 688 (1958).

the requirements of federal subject-matter jurisdiction are not satisfied because the two claims together do not meet the amount-in-controversy requirement.[38]

Illustration 7-13. If, on the facts of *Illustration 7-12,* *A* asserted a $33,000 claim arising under federal law and a totally unrelated state claim for $33,000, the federal court could entertain the federal claim, but probably could not entertain the state claim. Again, Rule 18 does not restrict joinder. The federal court would possess subject-matter jurisdiction over the federal claim because 28 U.S.C. § 1331 (the general federal question jurisdiction statute) does not contain an amount-in-controversy requirement. Before 1990, the district court clearly did not possess subject-matter jurisdiction over the state-law claim because (1) the jurisdictional amount requirement of 28 U.S.C. § 1332 was not satisfied[39] and (2) the state claim did not arise out of the same facts as the federal claim, which would have been necessary to bring the state claim within the pendent jurisdiction of the district court. The 1990 enactment of 28 U.S.C. § 1367 has created doubt as to whether the state claim can be entertained today. Recall from the discussion in Chapter 2 that § 1367 extends the ''supplemental jurisdiction'' of the district courts to all claims that form part of the same constitutional case or controversy as a civil action over which the district courts have original jurisdiction. Recall, also, that a strong argument can be made that Congress has the power under Article III of the Constitution to extend the jurisdiction of the federal courts to factually unrelated state claims joined with federal claims over which the district courts have original jurisdiction.[40] If Article III is interpreted in this fashion, and if § 1367 is interpreted to mean what it says, jurisdiction will exist today over the state claim. However, if, as argued in Chapter 2,[41] § 1367 is construed to limit the ''supplemental jurisdiction'' of the district courts to state claims that arise from the same facts as federal claims over which the district courts have original jurisdiction, there will be no jurisdiction over the state claim.

Illustration 7-14. In *Illustration 7-13,* if *A* 's federal and state claims had arisen out of the same facts, the federal district court, both before 1990 and today, would have jurisdiction over the state claim. Before 1990, this case would have been an appropriate one for pendent jurisdiction over the state claim under 28 U.S.C. § 1331.[42] The codification of the doctrine of ''pendent claim jurisdiction'' in 28 U.S.C. § 1367 would give the federal district court supplemental jurisdiction over the state claim today.[43]

(b) Venue Restrictions on Joinder

Venue restrictions depend not only on the operation of the general and special venue statutes in Title 28 of the *United States Code,* but also on whether

---

38. *See* 28 U.S.C. § 1332; Chapter 2(C)(3)*(e)(i)* (''Single Plaintiff with a Single Claim or Multiple Claims Against a Single Defendant'') *supra.*

39. *See id.*

40. *See* Chapter 2(C)(4)*(b)* (''The Constitutional Basis of Pendent and Ancillary Jurisdiction'') *supra.*

41. *See* Chapter 2(C)(4)*(d)(i)* (''The Scope of Supplemental Jurisdiction: Section 1367(a)'') *supra.*

42. *See* Chapter 2(C)(4)*(a)* (''The General Nature of Pendent and Ancillary Jurisdiction'') *supra.*

43. *See* Chapter 2(C)(4)*(d)(i)* (''The Scope of Supplemental Jurisdiction: Section 1367(a)'') *supra.*

the federal courts may, in some cases, exercise "pendent" or "supplemental" venue.

Illustration 7-15. On the facts of *Illustration 7-14*, if *A* had sued *B* in a U.S. District Court in State *Y* and the facts giving rise to *A's* claims had occurred entirely in State *X*, Rule 18 would permit joinder of the federal and state claims and the requirements of federal subject-matter jurisdiction would be satisfied (before 1990 under the doctrine of "pendent jurisdiction" and today under the doctrine of "supplemental jurisdiction"). However, venue would be improper under 28 U.S.C. § 1391(b). Under this venue section, venue in cases in which jurisdiction is based even partly on the existence of a federal claim is proper only in a judicial district in which (1) the defendant resides, (2) a substantial part of the events or omissions giving rise to the claim occurred, or (3) any defendant may be found, if there is no district in which the action may otherwise be brought.[44] The defendant resides in State *X*, and all of the events giving rise to the claims occurred there. Consequently, even if the defendant can be "found" in State *Y*, venue is improper there, because another district (in State *X*) exists where the action may be brought.

*   *   *   *   *

Occasionally, a case arises in which venue is proper for one claim under a special federal venue statute, but not as to a claim over which the U.S. District Court has supplemental jurisdiction. These cases raise the question whether the district courts may hear the supplemental claim under a doctrine of "pendent" or "supplemental" venue. Some courts have recognized the validity of such a doctrine,[45] while others have rejected it.[46] The venue question cannot be automatically decided on the basis that the requirements of subject-matter jurisdiction have been satisfied. The policies supporting supplemental jurisdiction are concerned with the scope of an Article III case or controversy and the statutory policies supporting grants of jurisdiction to the U.S. District Courts.[47] Satisfaction of these policies will not necessarily satisfy the policies of the federal venue statutes, which focus on the convenience of the particular location in which a suit is brought. If "supplemental venue" is a viable concept at all, therefore, it should only be exercised under narrow circumstances. It would seem justifiable for the district courts to exercise supplemental venue if it is necessary to do so in order to prevent the policies supporting a particular grant of subject-matter

---

44. *See* 28 U.S.C. § 1391(b); *see also* Chapter 4(C) ("Venue in Federal Courts") *supra*.

45. *See, e.g.,* Travis v. Anthes Imperial, Ltd., 473 F.2d 515 (1973); *see also* 15 CHARLES A. WRIGHT ET AL, FEDERAL PRACTICE AND PROCEDURE: JURISDICTION AND RELATED MATTERS § 3808, at 82 n.8 (2d ed. 1986) (citing additional cases); Note, *Ancillary Process and Venue in the Federal Courts,* 73 HARV. L. REV. 1164, 1175-78 (1960).

46. *See, e.g.,* Reuber v. United States, 750 F.2d 1039 (D.C. Cir. 1984); Network Sys. Corp. v. Masstor Sys. Corp., 612 F. Supp. 438 (D. Minn. 1984); *see also* Berger Instruments, Inc. v. Northwest Instruments, Inc., No. 96 C 8393, 1999 WL 159377 (N.D. Ill. Mar. 28, 1997) (must be an independent basis of venue for each claim in the complaint); 15 CHARLES A. WRIGHT ET AL., FEDERAL PRACTICE AND PROCEDURE: JURISDICTION AND RELATED MATTERS § 3808, at 82-83 n.8 (2d ed. 1986) (citing additional cases); *cf.* Geneva Furniture Mfg. Co. v. S. Karpen & Bros, 238 U.S. 254, 35 S. Ct. 788, 59 L. Ed. 1295 (1915) (holding venue proper as to some claims and improper as to other claims arising out of the same events).

47. *See* Chapter 2(C)(4)*(b)-(c) supra* (discussing the constitutional and statutory bases of pendent and ancillary jurisdiction).

jurisdiction from being undermined.[48] Subject-matter-jurisdiction policies are higher-order policies than venue policies, and it is justifiable for the latter to give way in preference to the former in cases of conflict. If an exercise of supplemental venue is not necessary to support subject-matter-jurisdiction policies, a district court should only exercise supplemental venue after assuring that the location of the suit on the supplemental claim will not be materially more burdensome to the defendant than a district where venue would be proper over the claim.[49] In addition, even if the forum would not be materially more burdensome than a proper venue, the court should not exercise supplemental venue if it determines that Congress has made a deliberate policy decision to limit venue over certain kinds of claims, of which the supplemental claim is one, to particular districts.[50]

It should also be noted that supplemental venue should be much harder to establish under the above criteria with regard to claims that are factually unrelated to the freestanding, or jurisdiction-conferring, claim in the action. Supplemental jurisdiction over such claims has traditionally not existed in federal practice and may not exist in the future. However, as discussed above and in Chapter 2, the extension of supplemental jurisdiction to the full limits of Article III by 28 U.S.C. § 1367(a) holds the possibility that factually unrelated federal and nonfederal claims existing between the same parties will someday be found to be within the scope of the same Article III case.[51] In that eventuality, if the events giving rise to the unrelated supplemental claim occurred in a district other than the forum, it would be difficult to imagine how the forum would not be a materially more burdensome place to litigate than a district where venue would be proper over the claim.

(c) Personal Jurisdiction Restrictions on Joinder

Personal jurisdiction requirements must normally be satisfied with regard to each claim joined in an action. However, some courts have also held that it is possible to exercise "pendent" or "supplemental" personal jurisdiction over defendants on claims that fall within the supplemental jurisdiction of the U.S. District Courts. Such cases have sometimes arisen when a federal long-arm statute allows the district courts to exercise personal jurisdiction over a defendant for purposes of a federal claim, but the state where the action is brought would not allow an assertion of personal jurisdiction over the defendant for purposes of a

---

48. In particular, if the plaintiff in a federal question case would be deterred from resorting to federal court by having to adjudicate federal and state claims in different locations, it may be necessary to exercise supplemental venue in order to support the policies of the particular subject-matter jurisdiction grant in question. *See* Chapter 2(C)(4)*(c) supra* (discussing, *inter alia*, the statutory policies supporting the doctrine of pendent jurisdiction).

49. *Cf.* Note, *Ancillary Process and Venue in the Federal Courts,* 73 HARV. L. REV. 1164, 1176 (1960) (additional inquiry beyond satisfaction of pendent jurisdiction policies requires balancing of the factors favoring retention of a claim against the added inconvenience to the defendant in defending against it).

50. *See, e.g.,* Bartel v. FAA, 617 F. Supp. 190, 198 n.33 (D.D.C. 1985) (no pendent venue because Congress has made deliberate decision to limit venue where Title VII claims may be brought).

51. *See* Chapter 2(C)(4)*(b) supra* (discussing the constitutional bases of pendent and ancillary jurisdiction).

supplemental state claim joined in the action.[52] Today, such a case might also arise under the 1993 amendments to Rule 4(k)(2), if a plaintiff sues a defendant on a federal claim and a closely related nonfederal claim in a federal court and the defendant is not subject to personal jurisdiction on the federal claim in any state court of general jurisdiction.[53] As discussed in *Illustration 7-16*, below, it may have been the intent of the drafters of Rule 4(k)(2) to confer supplemental personal jurisdiction over the nonfederal claim under these circumstances.

The federal courts should not assume supplemental personal jurisdiction over a defendant simply based on the fact that subject-matter-jurisdiction requirements have been satisfied. As with venue, the policies supporting supplemental subject-matter jurisdiction are not the same as the policies motivating a grant or denial of long-arm jurisdiction over particular claims. Contrary to the case of venue, however, subject-matter-jurisdiction policies are not always higher-order policies than policies supporting personal jurisdiction. When personal jurisdiction restrictions are based on the Due Process Clauses of the Fifth or Fourteenth Amendments, statutory subject-matter-jurisdiction policies should be considered subordinate to them. Therefore, it would only seem to be justified for the courts to assume supplemental personal jurisdiction to prevent the policies of a subject-matter-jurisdiction grant from being seriously undermined when the personal jurisdiction restrictions on adjudicating the supplemental claim are based on statutory limits. As was the case with supplemental venue, if no subject-matter jurisdiction policy would be undermined by refusing supplemental personal jurisdiction, it would seem justifiable for the courts to assume supplemental personal jurisdiction over a defendant for purposes of the claim only when the burdens of suit in the forum would not be substantially greater than in another location where personal jurisdiction would be proper over the defendant. Finally, the courts should take care to scrutinize the reasons why state law has effectively immunized the defendant from suit in the forum in cases where the supplemental claim is a state claim. It would seem improper for the courts to assert supplemental personal jurisdiction over the defendant for purposes of adjudicating a state claim when the forum has made a conscious policy decision to immunize the defendant from suit on the claim within the state. On the other hand, if the inapplicability of a state long-arm statute results from an apparently inadvertent gap in the statute as opposed to a conscious policy decision, the inability to assert jurisdiction under state law can safely be disregarded.

Supplemental personal jurisdiction should be a doctrine that the federal courts rarely have occasion to use. Given the tendency of the state courts to extend their long-arm statutes as far as the Due Process Clause of the Fourteenth Amendment will permit, there should be few cases in which personal jurisdiction

---

52. *See, e.g.,* Robinson v. Penn Cent. Co., 484 F.2d 553 (3d Cir. 1973) (long-arm jurisdiction over federal securities claim under securities long-arm statute and pendent personal jurisdiction exercised over pendent state claim over which securities long-arm statute does not authorize jurisdiction); *see also* 6A CHARLES A. WRIGHT ET AL, FEDERAL PRACTICE AND PROCEDURE: CIVIL § 1588, at 555-56 (2d ed. 1990); James S. Cochran, *Personal Jurisdiction and the Joinder of Claims in the Federal Courts,* 64 TEX. L. REV. 1463 (1986); Note, *Ancillary Process and Venue in the Federal Courts,* 73 HARV. L. REV. 1164 (1960).

53. *See* Chapter 3(K)(2)(*f*) *supra* (discussing Rule 4(k)(2)).

does not exist over factually related federal and state claims under state law, as well as under any federal long-arm statute that applies to the federal claim. However, as observed in Chapter 3,[54] it is possible that the Supreme Court will someday hold that the same due process standards do not govern Congress and the states in creating long-arm jurisdiction. If so, the federal courts may be able to assert jurisdiction over federal claims under federal long-arm statutes when the forum state's courts could not constitutionally exercise personal jurisdiction over the defendant for purposes of state or foreign claims joined within the supplemental subject-matter jurisdiction of the federal courts.

For example, Congress may be able to extend the jurisdiction of the federal courts to adjudicate federal claims nationwide, without regard to the relationship, or lack of relationship, between the defendant, the claims, and the forum. Such an extension would allow the federal courts to exercise jurisdiction over federal claims that have no relationship to the state in which the action is brought. Furthermore, supplemental state claims lacking any relationship with the state might be joined with the federal claims under Rule 18. Under these circumstances, the federal courts should probably not exercise supplemental personal jurisdiction over the state claims at all if the forum state's courts would be precluded from adjudicating them by Fourteenth Amendment limits. Congress may have power to extend federal long-arm jurisdiction to the state claims as well as the federal claims under such circumstances. However, if suit were in a state court, the defendant's lack of contacts with the state would result in litigational burdens so great as to violate the Due Process Clause of the Fourteenth Amendment. This fact should counsel the federal courts that the decision to extend personal jurisdiction over the claims is a major policy question that should only be decided by Congress itself.

For the same reasons given in the discussion of supplemental venue, extending supplemental personal jurisdiction to factually unrelated nonfederal claims should be difficult, if not impossible. If the supplemental jurisdiction statute, 28 U.S.C. § 1367(a), is some day interpreted to allow supplemental subject-matter jurisdiction over state claims that are factually unrelated to the freestanding, or jurisdiction-conferring, claims in the action, the same problems would exist with extending supplemental personal jurisdiction over the state claims as existed with extending supplemental venue over them. These problems should be resolved in the same manner. In the case of personal jurisdiction, however, the problems may be more serious because of the presence of due process considerations. If supplemental personal jurisdiction were to be asserted over a state claim which has no factual connection with the forum state, and which is also factually unrelated to the federal claim that confers subject-matter jurisdiction over the action, the burdens on the defendant of litigating the claim in the forum might be so substantial as to produce a due process violation if the suit were in a state court. Even if Congress could hypothetically create long-arm jurisdiction over the claim without violating the Fifth Amendment, the Fourteenth

---

54. *See* Chapter 3(L)(1) ("The Constitutional Standard Under Federal Long-Arm Statutes and Rules") *supra.*

Amendment due process considerations should counsel against the courts themselves extending supplemental personal jurisdiction over the defendant for purposes of adjudicating the claim.

Illustration 7-16. *A*, a citizen of State *X*, sues *B*, a citizen of Sweden, in a U.S. District Court in State *X*. *A* asserts a claim under a federal statute against *B* and joins a claim under Swedish law that is factually related to the federal claim against *B*. The events giving rise to both claims occurred in Sweden. Subject-matter jurisdiction is satisfied over the federal statutory claim under 28 U.S.C. § 1331 (the general federal question jurisdiction statute) and over the state claim by 28 U.S.C. § 1367(a) (the supplemental jurisdiction statute). Venue is proper in State *X* under 28 U.S.C. 1391(d), which provides that an alien can be sued in any district. *B* does not have sufficient contacts with any state to satisfy the Due Process Clause of the Fourteenth Amendment, but *B* does have sufficient contacts with the United States to satisfy the Due Process Clause of the Fifth Amendment. Because of the lack of minimum contacts with a state, personal jurisdiction cannot be asserted pursuant to Federal Rule 4(k)(1)(A), because *B* cannot be subjected to the jurisdiction of a court of general jurisdiction in any state, including State *X*. No federal long-arm statute authorizes the district court to assert personal jurisdiction over *B*. Therefore, personal jurisdiction cannot be asserted pursuant to Federal Rule 4(k)(1)(D). The district court can assert personal jurisdiction over the federal claim under Rule 4(k)(2) because of *B's* minimum contacts with the United States. The language of Rule 4(k)(2) only authorizes the district court to assert personal jurisdiction over *B* for purposes of adjudicating the federal claim,[55] but the Advisory Committee Note to the rule makes a cryptic reference to cases in which supplemental subject-matter jurisdiction may be asserted over state or foreign claims.[56] This reference may mean that it was the intent of the drafters of Rule 4(k)(2) to confer supplemental personal jurisdiction over related state or foreign claims. If so, however, the jurisdictional conferral, like that of supplemental subject-matter jurisdiction, should be deemed to be discretionary. If substantial burdens would be imposed on *B* by having to litigate the Swedish claim in State *X*, the court should decline to exercise that jurisdiction in this case. If Rule 4(k)(2) does not specifically confer supplemental personal jurisdiction over the Swedish claim, the court should be reluctant to exercise that jurisdiction on its own for the same reason.[57]

---

55. *See* Chapter 3(K)(2)*(f)* *supra* (discussing Rule 4(k)(2)).

56. This narrow extension of the federal reach applies only if a claim is made against the defendant under federal law. It does not establish personal jurisdiction if the only claims are those arising under state law or the law of another country, even though there might be diversity or alienage subject matter jurisdiction as to such claims. If, however, personal jurisdiction is established under this paragraph with respect to a federal claim, then 28 U.S.C. § 1367(a) provides supplemental jurisdiction over related claims against that defendant, subject to the court's discretion to decline exercise of that jurisdiction under 28 U.S.C. § 1367(c).

Advisory Committee Note to the 1993 Amendment of Rule 4(k)(2).

57. Recall from Chapter 5 that there are also substantial separation-of-powers questions about the power of the Supreme Court to create Rule 4(k)(2) under the Rules Enabling Act. *See* Chapter 5(F)(6), *Illustration 5-21, supra.*

3. Rules Enabling Act Problems Under Rule 18

Potential Rules Enabling Act problems with joinder of multiple claims sometimes occur when a plaintiff suing an insured party also attempts to join the party's insurer as a defendant in the action. State statutes often authorize an injured party to bring suit against a defendant's insurer, but only after obtaining a judgment against the defendant. Similarly, contracts of insurance often contain clauses precluding a suit directly against the insurer until a judgment is obtained against the insured. In contrast, Rule 18 on its face seems to authorize joinder of an insurer in both of these situations: "Whenever a claim is one heretofore cognizable only after another claim has been prosecuted to a conclusion, the two claims may be joined in a single action; but the court shall grant relief in that action only in accordance with the relative substantive rights of the parties."[58] Some federal courts have held that these statutes and contract clauses are designed to protect "substantive rights" and that Rule 18 cannot authorize joinder of an insurance company in contravention of them.[59] However, many of these cases were decided prior to the Supreme Court's development of standards under the Rules Enabling Act that distinguished problems of the validity of the Federal Rules from general *Erie* doctrine problems under the Rules of Decision Act.[60] Other cases holding that Rule 18 cannot authorize joinder of an insurance company in these circumstances seem to violate Justice Frankfurter's admonition in *Guaranty Trust v. York* that substance and procedure do not mean the same thing everywhere the terms are used.[61] These cases sometimes confuse classifications of state joinder statutes as "substantive" for one purpose, such as conflict-of-laws doctrine, with classifications of the statutes as "substantive" for *Erie* or Rules Enabling Act purposes.[62]

It has been argued that the application of Rule 18 in the situation described above is valid because the rule only permits a federal court to render judgment in accordance with the substantive rights of the parties. That is, because the insured must be found liable before a judgment can be entered against the

---

58. FED. R. CIV. P. 18(b).

59. *See* 6A CHARLES A. WRIGHT ET AL, FEDERAL PRACTICE AND PROCEDURE: CIVIL § 1594, at 574 n.5 (2d ed. 1990) (citing contract cases).

60. *See, e.g.,* Headrick v. Smoky Mountain Stages, Inc., 11 F.R.D. 205 (E.D. Tenn. 1950) (Rule 18 inapplicable to joinder of different parties; to read it as authorizing joinder of insurer with insured would be to deprive insurer of a substantive right under its contract of insurance); *see also* Chapter 5(F) *supra* (discussing the Court's evolution of the Rules Enabling Act standards).

61. *See Guaranty Trust,* 326 U.S. at 108-09, 65 S. Ct. at 1469-70, 89 L. Ed. at 2085-86; *see also* Chapter 5(E)(1) *supra* (discussing Justice Frankfurter's opinion in *Guaranty Trust*).

62. For example, in Richards v. Select Insurance Co., 40 F. Supp. 2d 163, 167 (S.D.N.Y. 1999), the court held that New York's "limited direct action statute," which authorized suits directly against insurers only after a judgment against the insured, was "substantive" and had to be applied in a federal diversity action in which the injured party was seeking a declaratory judgment against the insurer and the insured prior to judgment against the insured. However, the court relied in part on cases evaluating similar statutes as "substantive" for non-*Erie* purposes. *See, e.g.,* State Trading Corp. of India, Ltd. v. Skuld, 921 F.2d 409 (1990) (holding Connecticut's limited direct action statute substantive for conflict-of-laws purposes).

insurer, the ultimate substantive rights of the parties are preserved by Rule 18.[63] Under the *Burlington Northern* standard discussed in Chapter 5,[64] it is arguable that this is correct because any infringement of substantive rights, either under the states' limited direct action statutes or under the "no-joinder" contract clauses described above, would be no more than "incidental."

If the state limited direct action statutes are designed to confer substantive rights of action against insurers only when judgments have been obtained against insured parties, these rights are protected fully as long as an insurer is not held liable until the insured has previously been found liable. The express language of Rule 18(b) assures that this relationship will be preserved. On the other hand, if the state statutes in question are designed to confer procedural protections on insurers by limiting their joinder in an action to prevent prejudice against them, the federal courts are arguably entitled to make their own judgments about the likelihood of prejudice and to use their own devices for assuring that the insurers are protected from the prejudice rather than the state device of limited joinder.[65]

As far as "no-joinder" contract clauses are concerned, it is arguable that the insurer has not, in these clauses, contracted for substantive rights at all, but for a kind of procedural protection. If this is an accurate way to view the clauses, allowing joinder of the insurer, but employing other means of protecting it from prejudice, would not impact on substantive rights, but on procedural ones. However, there is a broader sense in which substantive rights may be affected by disregarding the contract clauses in question. To the extent that the states allow the insurers to contract for procedural protections, they are following the traditional substantive contract policy of freedom of contract and enforceability of contractual arrangements. If a federal court overrides the no-joinder clauses by permitting joinder under Rule 18, it is arguably abridging this broader substantive right of freedom of contract, even though the insurer has employed the right to obtain a kind of procedural protection. Nevertheless, even if this is an accurate way to view what is happening, it is not clear that application of Rule 18 would be invalid. Under these circumstances, the validity of the Rule 18 will depend upon what the Supreme Court meant in *Burlington Northern* by "impact" on "substantive rights," something that the Court has yet to make clear. It will also depend on whether, if there is an impact on substantive rights, the impact is only "incidental" or more than incidental, something that the Court has also yet to clarify. Thus, if the Court holds either that the Rules Enabling Act does not protect this kind of substantive right, or that it does, but the impact of Rule 18

---

63. *See* 6A CHARLES A. WRIGHT ET AL., FEDERAL PRACTICE AND PROCEDURE: CIVIL § 1594, at 575-77 (2d ed. 1990) (discussing the purposes of the state statutes and contract clauses in question and describing why Rule 18(b) preserves the parties' substantive rights given these purposes).

64. *See* Chapter 5(F)(4) *supra* (discussing the *Burlington Northern* decision).

65. *See* 6A CHARLES A. WRIGHT ET AL., FEDERAL PRACTICE AND PROCEDURE: CIVIL § 1594, at 576-77 (2d ed. 1990) (describing the likelihood of prejudice against the insurer and the devices available in federal court to prevent it).

on the right is only incidental, Rule 18 may be validly applied in contravention of the no-joinder clauses.[66]

SECTION D. JOINDER OF CLAIMS BY DEFENDANTS AT COMMON LAW AND IN EQUITY

In many instances, a defendant will possess an affirmative claim for relief against the plaintiff. Such a claim may either arise out of the same transaction or occurrence as the plaintiff's claim against the defendant or a separate transaction or occurrence. Should the defendant be permitted or required to assert this kind of claim against the plaintiff in the plaintiff's action? Today, *counterclaim* rules answer this question. At common law, nothing precisely like the modern counterclaim existed. Nevertheless, defendants used two devices, *recoupment* and *set-off*, to assert claims for relief against plaintiffs in certain cases. Equity also permitted defendants to use *cross-bills* to assert claims.

1. Recoupment

Recoupment allowed a defendant to assert a claim arising out of the same transaction or occurrence as the plaintiff's claim as a way to diminish or defeat the plaintiff's recovery. Thus, if the same transaction or occurrence rule were satisfied, a defendant could assert a contract claim against a plaintiff's tort claim. However, the defendant could only use the claim defensively. In other words, the claim could only diminish or defeat the plaintiff's claim, but no judgment for the surplus could be rendered in the defendant's favor when the defendant's claim exceeded that of the plaintiff. The claim did not have to be liquidated.[67]

Illustration 7-17. A sued B for $5,000 to recover for personal injuries incurred when *B's* automobile collided with *A*. *B* possesses a claim for $10,000 against *A* for an assault and battery occurring on the same occasion. At common law, *B* could assert this claim in *A's* action only through recoupment. The same transaction or occurrence rule was satisfied. The claim was not liquidated, but it did not have to be. However, the claim could be asserted only to the extent of $5,000. Recoupment only permitted the defendant's claim to diminish the plaintiff's award. The common-law courts would not allow an affirmative judgment for the surplus.

---

66. Thus, it might be reasoned that the kinds of rights referred to in *Burlington Northern* as "substantive" are only the actual rights embodied in the provision with which a Federal Rule of Civil Procedure conflicts. In the contract cases, this would be the right not to be joined. This right, in turn, might not be considered "substantive" because it involves only guarantees pertaining to the configuration of litigation, as opposed to guarantees such as indemnity, assumption of the burdens and cost of defense, and so forth. In addition, even if freedom of contract and enforceability of contractual arrangements are included in the "substantive rights" referred to in *Burlington Northern*, the impact on that right might still be considered only incidental, on the theory that the impact only occurs in a narrow category of cases in which the federal courts employ Rule 18 to override anti-joinder clauses in insurance contracts. For the impact to be substantial, the rule would have to override freedom of contract in a much broader fashion, or in many more kinds of cases.

67. *See generally* BENJAMIN J. SHIPMAN, HANDBOOK OF COMMON-LAW PLEADING §§ 209-210, at 365 (1923).

2. Set-Off

Originally, the common-law courts did not recognize set-off. However, equity courts permitted a defendant to set off a claim arising out of a different transaction or occurrence than the plaintiff's claim under certain circumstances. When set-off was available, the defendant obtained an affirmative judgment for the amount by which the defendant's claim exceeded the plaintiff's claim. By statute, the device of set-off was extended to the common-law courts.[68] After the passage of the set-off statutes, equity restricted set-off to cases in which some special equitable ground of relief was shown, or in which the claims, if they had been legal, could have been set off under the statutes and one of the claims provided a ground for equitable jurisdiction.[69] Normally, statutes restricted set-off to claims that were liquidated. Practically speaking, this restriction meant that set-off was unavailable in causes of action falling within case, trespass, and replevin, among others.[70]

Illustration 7-18. A sued B for nonpayment of a $5,000 debt. B possessed a claim against A for nonpayment of a wholly separate debt of $10,000. At common law, B could assert the claim against A only by set-off (or a separate action). Here both claims are liquidated. Because set-off permitted the defendant to obtain an affirmative judgment, B could not only diminish A's $5,000 claim to zero, but could also obtain an affirmative judgment for the $5,000 surplus.[71]

* * * * *

The English set-off statutes required that the defendant's claim be for a liquidated amount. Set-off was unavailable when a jury had to ascertain the damages.[72] In the United States, set-off statutes usually followed the English pattern.[73] However, some state statutes allowed unliquidated *contract* damages to be set off.[74]

The ability to set-off an unliquidated contract claim gave rise to the option of using *either* recoupment or set-off in a particular case, as a litigant desired. When set-off was available, it was ordinarily used because it did not, as recoupment did, require the litigant to grapple with the same transaction or occurrence rule, and set-off also allowed the litigant to obtain an affirmative judg-

---

68. *See* 4 & 5 Ann. ch. 4 (1705); 2 Geo. II, ch. 22, § 13 (1729), *as amended*, 8 Geo. II, ch. 24 (1735).

69. *See* Charles E. Clark, Handbook of the Law of Code Pleading § 100, at 636 (1947); 3 Joseph Story, Commentaries on Equity Jurisprudence §§ 1865-1876 (14th ed. 1886).

70. *See generally* 2 Theodore Sedgwick, A Treatise on the Measure of Damages 265-270 (7th ed. 1880).

71. Because the same transaction or occurrence rule was not satisfied, recoupment would not have been proper. *See* subsection D(1) ("Recoupment") *supra.*

72. *See* Morley v. Ingles, 132 Eng. Rep. 711, 713-14 (C.P. 1837); Hardcastle v. Netherwood, 106 Eng. Rep. 1127 (K.B. 1821).

73. *See* William H. Loyd, *The Development of Set-Off,* 64 U. Pa. L. Rev. 541, 561-63 (1916).

74. *See, e.g.,* Johnston v. Niemeyer, 10 Ind. 350, 351 (1858); Stevens v. Able, 15 Kan. 584, 586 (1875); Baltimore Ins. Co. v. M'Fadon, 4 H. & J. 31, 41-48 (Md. 1815); Raymond Bros. v. Green & Co., 12 Neb. 215, 10 N.W. 709 (1881); Gelhaus v. Allemania Loan & Bldg. Ass'n, 6 Ohio. Dec. 443 (Super. Ct. 1897); Braden v. Gulf Coast Lumber Co., 89 Okla. 215, 215 P. 202 (1923); Fessler v. Love & Powell, 43 Pa. 313 (1862); Hubbard v. Fisher, 25 Vt. 539, 541 (1853).

ment. Nevertheless, some courts permitted either set-off or recoupment to be used in an appropriate case.[75]

Illustration 7-19. In a suit on a promissory note given for goods sold to the defendant, the defendant might set-off a breach of warranty claim, even though the damages were unliquidated, when the set-off statute permitted unliquidated contract claims to be asserted.[76] Recoupment also would be appropriate in such a case: the same transaction or occurrence rule is satisfied and the breach of warranty would not produce damages in excess of the contract price.

3. Cross-Bills

Equity permitted cross-bills. A cross-bill allowed the defendant to assert a claim against the plaintiff or against codefendants. The cross-bill was treated as an auxiliary or dependent suit growing out of the original bill. Generally, it was available for the following purposes: (1) to obtain discovery of facts necessary to determine the action; (2) to obtain full relief for all parties to the action (as when a controversy arose between two defendants); (3) to bring a new matter before the court in aid of a defense that could not be raised by answer; and (4) to obtain affirmative relief against the plaintiff. When a cross-bill sought affirmative relief, the relief had to be within the jurisdiction of an equity court.[77]

Illustration 7-20. *A* sued *B* in an equity court for specific performance of a contract to convey land. *A* had taken possession of the land, but *B* refused to convey on the ground that *A* procured the contract by fraud. Under these circumstances, *B* could *not* assert a cross-bill against *A* to recover possession from *A*. Because the cross-bill would seek affirmative relief, it would have to be within the jurisdiction of an equity court. However, because ejectment was an adequate legal remedy for *B*, there would have been no "equity jurisdiction." *B* possessed the legal title and could demonstrate it in an ejectment action. *B* could, of course, defend the equitable action on the ground of fraud.[78]

SECTION E. COUNTERCLAIMS AND CROSS-CLAIMS UNDER THE CODES

The original Field Code of 1848 did not contain a provision for counterclaims.[79] An 1852 amendment established the first counterclaim provi-

---

75. *See* Davenport v. Hubbard, 46 Vt. 200, 207 (1873); *see also* Lehman v. Austin, 195 Ala. 244, 70 So. 653 (1915).

76. *See* Steigleman v. Jeffries, 1 Serg. & Rawle 477 (Pa. 1815).

77. *See generally* BENJAMIN J. SHIPMAN, HANDBOOK OF THE LAW OF EQUITY PLEADING 303-308 (1897).

78. *See* JOSEPH STORY, COMMENTARIES ON EQUITY PLEADINGS § 398, at 345 (9th ed. 1879).

79. *See* Act of Apr. 12, 1848, ch. 379, § 128, 1848 N.Y. Laws 497, 522 (contents of the defendant's answer).

sion.[80] This amendment considerably liberalized the former practice. While including both recoupment and set-off, the counterclaim was broader than recoupment because it permitted an affirmative recovery by the defendant and broader than set-off because the defendant's claim did not have to be liquidated.[81] However, as with joinder of plaintiffs' claims, the drafters of the Code restricted the ability to assert counterclaims in order to limit the scope of the action. A counterclaim had to arise out of the same transaction as the plaintiff's claim. If it did not but was asserted in an action of contract, the counterclaim had to be based on a contract theory. This latter provision was designed to continue the former practice of allowing set-off in cases in which the claim arose from a separate transaction.[82] Although the codes liberalized both recoupment and set-off, it is unclear why the drafters did not go further and allow joinder of any counterclaim, however unrelated to the plaintiff's cause of action. Such a step probably appeared too radical an expansion of the scope of the civil action. In any case, the modern codes following the Field Code pattern usually contain no separate provision for set-offs because the "contracts clause" eliminates the need for such a provision.[83]

Even though code provisions commonly declare that the defendant "must" or "shall" include a counterclaim in the action, the provisions are not read as compulsory unless a separate statute so provides.[84] Thus, the code counterclaim may, but need not, be included in the defendant's answer. If the defendant so chooses, it may be the subject of an entirely separate proceeding.[85]

The language of the code counterclaim provisions and the influence of the former common-law practice, produced some unfortunate interpretations.

---

80. The 1852 amendment provided as follows:

§ 149. The answer of the defendant must contain:

. . . .

2. A statement of any new matter constituting a defense or counterclaim, in ordinary and concise language without repetition.

§ 150. The counterclaim mentioned in the last section, must be one existing in favor of a defendant, and against a plaintiff, between whom a several judgment might be had in the action, and arising out of one of the following causes of action:

1. A cause of action arising out of the contract or transaction set forth in the complaint, as the foundation of the plaintiff's claim, or connected with the subject of the action;

2. In an action arising on contract, any other cause of action arising also on contract, and existing at the commencement of the action;

The defendant may set forth by answer, as many defenses and counterclaims as he may have, whether they be such as have been heretofore denominated legal or equitable, or both. They must be separately stated. . . .

Act of Apr. 16, 1852, ch. 392, §§ 149-150, 1852 N.Y. Laws 651, 654; *see also id.* § 153, 1852 N.Y. Laws 651, 654-55 (allowing the plaintiff, within twenty days, to reply to an answer containing a counterclaim by denial, affirmative defense, or demurrer).

81. *See* CHARLES E. CLARK, HANDBOOK OF THE LAW OF CODE PLEADING § 100, at 637 (2d ed. 1947).

82. *See id.*; BENJAMIN J. SHIPMAN, HANDBOOK OF COMMON-LAW PLEADING § 210, at 364 (1923). As a practical matter, the restrictions on set-offs limited them to contract cases.

83. *See* CHARLES E. CLARK, HANDBOOK OF THE LAW OF CODE PLEADING § 101, at 642-43 (2d ed. 1947). Some modern codes eliminate the contract clause and separately provide for set-offs. *See, e.g.*, NEB. REV. STAT. §§ 25-811, 25-813, 25-816 (1995).

84. *See* CHARLES E. CLARK, HANDBOOK OF THE LAW OF CODE PLEADING § 101, at 646-47 (2d ed. 1947).

85. *See, e.g.*, NEB. REV. STAT. § 25-814 (1995).

Illustration 7-21. Assume that *A* contracted to sell land to *B*. *B* went into possession of the land under the contract. *A* then sued to eject *B* from the land. *A* alleged that *B* had forfeited the right to purchase because of a breach. *B* contended that *B* fully complied with the contract and counterclaimed for damages resulting from *A's* fraud in the sale. Some courts held that *B's* counterclaim was improperly joined under provisions like the amended Field Code. The courts reasoned that the transaction involved in the claim for ejectment was the plaintiff's right to possession. According to those courts, that right had nothing to do with the subject of the defendant's counterclaim–the alleged fraud of the plaintiff.[86] Clearly, however, the defendant's counterclaim arose out of the same basic factual occurrence as the plaintiff's claim and could be efficiently tried in the same action.[87]

Illustration 7-22. Assume that *A* sued *B* for damages for breach of contract. *B* counterclaims for damages that occurred when *A* converted *B's* property and sold it to *C*. *B's* counterclaim might be held proper under the "contracts" clauses of the code counterclaim provisions. At common law, *B* could "waive the tort" of conversion and sue in assumpsit for money had and received. Assumpsit would be classified as a contract action.[88] However, the "contract" involved in the old assumpsit action for money had and received was often purely fictional. Such fictions should have no place in modern joinder.

* * * * *

In addition to counterclaims against the plaintiff, modern codes often provide for cross-claims or cross-actions against co-parties.[89] Typically, such provisions require that the cross-claim arise out of the same transaction or occurrence as the plaintiff's claim.[90]

SECTION F. COUNTERCLAIMS AND CROSS-CLAIMS UNDER THE FEDERAL RULES

1. Application of Rule 13

(a) Counterclaims

Rule 13 of the Federal Rules of Civil Procedure provides for counterclaims. Federal Rule 13 was derived from former federal Equity Rule 30.[91]

---

86. *See* Zettle v. Gillmeister, 64 Cal. App. 669, 222 P. 645 (1923).

87. *See* CHARLES E. CLARK, HANDBOOK OF THE LAW OF CODE PLEADING § 102, at 658 (2d ed. 1947), and authorities there cited; *see also Illustration 7-7 supra.*

88. *See* CHARLES E. CLARK, HANDBOOK OF THE LAW OF CODE PLEADING § 103, at 660-62 (2d ed. 1947); *see also* Chapter 1(E)(1)*(c)(iii)* ("Trover") *supra.*

89. *See, e.g.,* NEB. REV. STAT. § 25-812 (1995).

90. *See id.* § 25-813. Some codes restrict cross-claim provisions even further. *See id.*

91. As applied to counterclaims, Equity Rule 30 stated:

> [t]he answer must state in short and simple form any counter-claim arising out of the transaction which is the subject matter of the suit, and may, without cross-bill, set out any set-off or counter-claim against the plaintiff which might be the subject of an independent suit in equity against him, and such set-off or counter-claim, so set up, shall have the

However, Federal Rule 13 considerably broadens the counterclaim practice from its scope under Equity Rule 30. Under Rule 13, a counterclaim may be either a legal or an equitable claim.[92] In addition, Rule 13 allows any pleader, not just a defendant serving an answer, to counterclaim against an opposing party.[93]

Rule 13 divides counterclaims into two general categories: *compulsory* counterclaims and *permissive* counterclaims. Rule 13(a) provides for compulsory counterclaims. Generally, a compulsory counterclaim arises out of the same transaction or occurrence as the opposing party's claim. A compulsory counterclaim must be asserted by the party possessing it if that party serves a pleading on the opposing party. It may not be the subject of an independent action.[94] The philosophy of the compulsory counterclaim rule is that all closely related claims should be settled in a single action, so multiple litigation over the same basic dispute can be avoided.[95]

Illustration 7-23. A sued B in a U.S. District Court. B did not appear or defend the action. The court then entered judgment by default for A. Subsequently, B sued A. B asserted a claim against A arising out of the same transaction or occurrence as the claim A had asserted against B in the previous lawsuit. A objected that this claim was a compulsory counterclaim in the first action and that the failure to assert it should preclude B from asserting it in a separate action. A's objection is unsound. B never served a pleading on A in the first action. Rule 13(a) only operates when a party serves a pleading on an opposing party.[96] The same result would follow if B had appeared in the action and moved to dismiss A's complaint for failure to state a claim on which relief can be granted under Federal Rule 12(b)(6). If the court dismisses the complaint, B can bring a later action on the claim that B possessed against A. A motion is not a pleading.[97] Thus, B never served a pleading in the action by A against B.

Illustration 7-24. A sued B in a U.S. District Court for damages resulting from an automobile accident. B's answer contained a permissive counterclaim for an assault and battery arising out of a wholly separate factual occurrence from A's claim. A's reply denied the allegations of the counterclaim and asserted certain affirmative defenses to the counterclaim, but omitted a claim that A possesses for assault and battery arising out of the same events as B's counterclaim. A may not

---

same effect as a cross-suit, so as to enable the court to pronounce a final judgment in the same suit both on the original and cross-claims.
226 U.S. 657 (1912).

92. *See* 6 CHARLES A. WRIGHT ET AL., FEDERAL PRACTICE AND PROCEDURE: CIVIL § 1401, at 12 (2d ed. 1990).

93. *See id.*

94. *See* Robin C. Miller, Annotation, *Effect of Filing Separate Federal Action Claim that Would Be Compulsory Counterclaim in Pending Federal Action*, 81 A.L.R. FED. 240 (1987); Annotation, *Failure to Assert Matter as Counterclaim as Precluding Assertion Thereof in Subsequent Action, Under Federal Rules or Similar State Rules or Statutes*, 22 A.L.R.2D 621 (1952).

95. *See* 6 CHARLES A. WRIGHT ET AL., FEDERAL PRACTICE AND PROCEDURE: CIVIL § 1403, at 15 (2d ed. 1990).

96. Under certain rare circumstances, the doctrine of res judicata may prohibit a party from asserting a claim in a subsequent action, even if the compulsory counterclaim rule does not operate. *See* Chapter 13(B)(4)*(c)* ("Jurisdictions Without a Compulsory Counterclaim Rule") *infra.*

97. *See* FED. R. CIV. P. 7(a).

assert the assault and battery counterclaim in a separate action. In the first action, *A* served a reply on *B*. The reply is a pleading.[98] Therefore, the terms of Rule 13(a) obligate *A* to assert any claim arising out of the transaction or occurrence as *B's* counterclaim against *A*. The failure to do so precludes *A* from asserting the claim in a separate suit.

* * * * *

Rule 13 contains certain exceptions to the compulsory counterclaim requirement. An otherwise compulsory counterclaim does not have to be asserted if it requires "for its adjudication the presence of third parties" over whom the court cannot acquire jurisdiction. Likewise, a party serving a pleading on an opposing party does not have to include a counterclaim arising out of the same transaction or occurrence as the opposing party's claim if, at the time the action was commenced, the counterclaim was the subject of another pending action.[99] In addition, an otherwise compulsory counterclaim does not have to be asserted if (1) the opposing party brought suit by attachment "or other process" by which the court did not acquire jurisdiction to render a personal judgment on the claim and (2) the pleader is not asserting any other counterclaim under Rule 13.[100] Finally, a counterclaim that is not mature at the time a pleading is served need not be asserted, even if it arises out of the same transaction or occurrence as an opposing party's claim.[101]

Federal Rule 13(b) defines permissive counterclaims as claims that do not arise out of the same transaction or occurrence as the opposing party's claim. A pleader may assert permissive counterclaims, but the failure to assert a permissive counterclaim will not bar the pleader from asserting it in a separate action. The philosophy supporting permissive counterclaim rules is that it may be convenient for the parties to resolve all the claims that exist between them, however unrelated, in a single action.[102] Nevertheless, because of the unrelated nature of the claim, a party might be seriously prejudiced if the party were forced to assert it in an action. Furthermore, the consequences to the efficiency of the judicial system are less serious when a party fails to assert a counterclaim that is unrelated

---

98. *See* FED. R. CIV. P. 7(a).

99. *See* FED. R. CIV. P. 13(a)(1).

100. This provision was placed in the rule prior to the Supreme Court's decision in the case of *Shaffer v. Heitner,* discussed in Chapter 3(E)(1) ("Quasi In Rem and Related Jurisdictional Doctrines") *supra.* After *Shaffer* invalidated quasi in rem jurisdiction, the exception appears not to be necessary. *See* 6 CHARLES A. WRIGHT ET AL., FEDERAL PRACTICE AND PROCEDURE: CIVIL § 1411, at 89-90 (2d ed. 1990). *But cf.* FED. R. CIV. P. 4(n) (providing that upon a showing that personal jurisdiction cannot be obtained over a defendant the court may assert jurisdiction over the defendant's assets in the district by seizing them under the circumstances and in the manner provided by the law of the state in which the district court is located); Chapter 3(K)(2)(*i*) *supra* (discussing Rule 4(n)).

101. *See* 6 CHARLES A. WRIGHT ET AL., FEDERAL PRACTICE AND PROCEDURE: CIVIL § 1411, at 80-81 (2d ed. 1990). Counterclaims maturing after a pleading is served may be added to the action with the permission of the court by supplemental pleading under Rule 13(e). Supplemental pleadings are discussed in Chapter 6(D)(6) ("Supplemental Pleadings") *supra*. However, courts have held counterclaims to be altogether improper under Rule 13 when they do not mature until the outcome of the principal action is known. This problem is discussed further below. *See also* Allison v. Long, 336 Ark. 432, 985 S.W.2d 314 (1999) (compulsory counterclaim omitted from answer but asserted in supplemental pleading not precluded).

102. *See generally* 6 CHARLES A. WRIGHT ET AL, FEDERAL PRACTICE AND PROCEDURE: CIVIL § 1420 (2d ed. 1990).

to an opposing party's claim, as opposed to a counterclaim that is closely related. Therefore, Rule 13(b) was drafted to give a party a choice whether to assert unrelated counterclaims on the assumption that this approach would best suit the convenience of the parties and the judicial system. For both compulsory and permissive counterclaims, Federal Rule 13(i) permits the court to order separate trials of the counterclaim under Rule 42(b). This approach reflects the general philosophy of federal claims joinder that inconvenience or prejudice does not result from the joinder of claims at the pleading stage of the litigation, but only, sometimes, by the trial of such claims together.[103]

The federal counterclaim rule encompasses the former procedures of recoupment and set-off. Thus, a counterclaim under Rule 13 "may or may not diminish or defeat the recovery sought by the opposing party." It also "may claim relief exceeding in amount or different in kind" from that sought by the opposing party.[104] Federal Rule 13(h) provides that additional persons may be made parties to the action in accordance with Rules 19 and 20 for purposes of adjudicating a counterclaim.[105]

(b) Cross-Claims

In addition to counterclaims, Federal Rule 13 authorizes cross-claims against coparties.[106] A cross-claim must arise out of the transaction or occurrence that is the subject matter either of the original action or a counterclaim therein.[107] Otherwise, there are no limits on the kind of claims that may be asserted as cross-claims. Rule 13(h) provides that parties may be added to the action for purposes of a cross-claim. Rule 13(i) permits severance and separate trial of cross-claims. The policy of federal cross-claim practice is similar to general federal joinder of claims policy: to settle as many related claims as possible in a single action, and thus avoid a multiplicity of suits.[108]

Cross-claims are *not compulsory*. Even though a party possesses a cross-claim arising out of the transaction or occurrence that is the subject matter of the action, the party may assert the cross-claim in a separate action. The decision not to make cross-claims compulsory was based on considerations similar to those bearing on the decision not to make all counterclaims compulsory. The possible prejudice to the parties resulting from a compulsory cross-claim rule, coupled with diminished consequences of failure to plead a cross-claim to the efficiency of the judicial system, dictated that the parties should be able to choose in the first instance whether to assert such claims. Moreover, the possibility that a party might be able to unduly complicate matters for other parties by adding

---

103. *See* section C ("Joinder of Claims by Plaintiffs Under the Federal Rules") *supra*.

104. FED. R. CIV. P. 13(c).

105. FED. R. CIV. P. 13(h); *see also* FED. R. CIV. P. 13(e)-(f).

106. A cross-claim, of course, must be asserted in a "pleading." *See* Smith v. Eighth Judicial Dist. Court, 113 Nev. 1343, 950 P.2d 280 (1997) (defendant improperly filed and served a document labeled a "cross-claim" and a separate document called an "answer"; a cross-claim is not a pleading).

107. FED. R. CIV. P. 13(g).

108. *See* 6 CHARLES A. WRIGHT ET AL., FEDERAL PRACTICE AND PROCEDURE: CIVIL § 1431, at 229 (2d ed. 1990).

claims collateral to the purposes of the suit dictated that cross-claims could not be joined unless factually related to the other claims in the action.

Under Rule 13(g), a cross-claim may only be asserted against a "co-party." Indeed, for purposes of counterclaim and cross-claim practice, Rule 13 appears to divide the universe of parties into "opposing parties" and "co-parties." A litigant is an "opposing party" if the litigant has previously asserted a claim against the pleader, as in *Illustration 7-24*, where *A* was obligated by Rule 13(a) to assert a counterclaim against *B* in *A's* reply to *B's* permissive counterclaim against *A*. Co-parties are normally thought of as litigants who are aligned on the same side of an action against a common opposing party. Thus, if *A* sues *B* and *C*, *B* and *C* are thought of as co-parties, although as soon as either *B* or *C* asserts a claim against the other, they also become opposing parties for purposes of administering the counterclaim provisions of Rule 13.[109]

The "opposing party" and "co-party" provisions of Rule 13 can sometimes cause confusion. For example, assume that *A* sues *B* and *C*. *B* then "impleads" *D* for indemnity against *A's* claim under Rule 14.[110] Assume further that *D* wishes to assert a claim against *C* arising out of the same facts as *A's* claims against *B* and *C*. The term "opposing party" does not describe the relationship between *D* and *C*, because neither *D* nor *C* has asserted a claim against the other. Thus, *D's* claim is not a counterclaim under Rule 13(a) or (b). However, the term "co-party" does not seem to describe the relations between *D* and *C* either, because they are not aligned against a common "opposing party." It is possible to reason that *D's* claim is simply an "original claim" possessed by *D* against *C* which *D* should be allowed to assert, but this classification would raise troublesome problems in cases in which parties such as *D* possess claims against other parties that are factually unrelated to the principal action. To avoid complicating the other parties' cases unjustifiably by joinder of such factually unrelated claims, it is preferable to limit joinder by the same transaction or occurrence rule that is applied to cross-claims. Some federal courts, administering joinder practice in a practical, common-sense manner, have recognized that parties like *D* should be allowed to assert factually related claims against parties like *C*, even if the terms used by Rule 13 do not exactly fit.[111]

(c) Administration of the Same Transaction or Occurrence Test

Determining whether a claim arises out of the "same transaction or occurrence" as another party's claim is a frequent problem under Rule 13.[112]

---

109. *See Illustration 7-30*, section F(1)(d), *infra*.

110. *See* Chapter 8(D)(1) *infra* (discussing Rule 14 impleader).

111. *See, e.g.*, Thomas v. Barton Lodge II, Ltd., 174 F.3d 636, 652 (5th Cir. 1999) (third-party defendants do not have to file an original complaint against an original defendant and move for consolidation, but may file a cross-claim against the defendant even if it would be inappropriate to characterize the third-party defendant as a co-party of the original defendant).

112. *See generally* Mary Kay Kane, *Original Sin and the Transaction in Federal Civil Procedure*, 76 TEX. L. REV. 1723 (1998) (discussing the different interpretations that the "same transaction test" does and should receive in the various places where it appears in the Federal Rules).

Though this determination must be made in several situations, two are of critical importance. One occurs when a defendant pleads a counterclaim for which no independent jurisdictional basis exists in federal court. As indicated below, if a court determines that the counterclaim is compulsory, it falls within the supplemental (ancillary) jurisdiction of the federal court. However, if a court determines that the counterclaim is permissive, the court will dismiss it for lack of jurisdiction. The issue of compulsoriness also can arise when a defendant fails to assert a counterclaim in a pending action and then later files suit independently on the claim. In that sort of case, if the counterclaim is compulsory, the party who failed to assert it will be barred from suing on the claim in the later action. A determination that it is permissive will allow the subsequently filed action to continue.

The courts have suggested four tests to determine when a counterclaim arises out of the "same transaction or occurrence" as the opposing party's claim. First, the claim and counterclaim are sometimes said to arise out of the same transaction or occurrence when they raise substantially the same issues of fact and law. Second, if the doctrine of res judicata would bar a subsequent suit on defendant's claim in the absence of a compulsory counterclaim rule, the counterclaim is sometimes said to be compulsory.[113] Third, if substantially the same evidence will support or refute both the claim and the counterclaim, some courts have held the counterclaim compulsory. Finally, a substantial number of decisions hold that if the claim and counterclaim are "logically related," the counterclaim is compulsory.[114] Each of these four tests can be criticized.[115] However, the "logical relationship" test is the most widely accepted of the four tests, despite its uncertainty.[116]

A better understanding of how the popular "logical relationship" test works can be attained by examining the different contexts in which the test is administered. Professor Wright has noted that very few cases exist in which a party has been barred from asserting a claim on the ground that it was a compulsory counterclaim that should have been pleaded in a prior action.[117] However, many cases hold counterclaims to be compulsory under Rule 13.[118] Although these assertions appear inconsistent, the inconsistency disappears when it is recognized that most of the cases holding counterclaims to be compulsory deal with the issue of "supplemental jurisdiction" (formerly ancillary jurisdiction).[119] In the supplemental (ancillary) jurisdiction context, the courts must determine that the counterclaim in question is sufficiently related to the principal claim to satisfy constitutional and statutory subject-matter jurisdiction requirements. Thus, the consequence of concluding that a particular claim is compulsory

---

113. *See* Chapter 13 ("Finality in Litigation") *infra*.

114. *See* 6 CHARLES A. WRIGHT ET AL, FEDERAL PRACTICE AND PROCEDURE: CIVIL § 1410 at 52-55 (2d ed. 1990) and authorities there cited.

115. *See id.* 58-65.

116. *See id.* at 65.

117. *See* CHARLES A. WRIGHT, THE LAW OF FEDERAL COURTS § 79, at 568 (5th ed. 1994).

118. *See* 6 CHARLES A. WRIGHT ET AL., FEDERAL PRACTICE AND PROCEDURE: CIVIL § 1410, at 61-63 (2d ed. 1990) and authorities there cited.

119. *See id.*; *see also id.* § 1414.

in the jurisdictional context is to allow the federal courts to hear the claim. Although an erroneous decision in favor of hearing such a claim may undermine important policies pertaining to the constitutional and statutory limits on federal subject-matter jurisdiction, safeguards protect against wholesale evasions of jurisdictional requirements. In addition to the safeguard of appeal, the heavy caseload faced by the federal district courts assures that the judges will not cavalierly assume power over counterclaims that bear little relationship to the claim that provides the basis for federal jurisdiction.

On the other hand, when the issue concerns whether a party should be barred from asserting a claim on the ground that it should have been pleaded in a prior action, the courts will, correctly, be reluctant to apply the logical relationship test to produce the conclusion that the claim was a compulsory counterclaim. The severe consequences of such a conclusion dictate that the courts should label the claim a compulsory counterclaim in only the clearest cases of abuse, when the omitted claim obviously should have been raised in the first action.[120] Furthermore, because Federal Rule 13 allows a party to plead *any* counterclaim that the party possesses, "the careful attorney can and will plead all [the] client's claims as counterclaims if there is any reason at all to think that they may be compulsory."[121] This cautious and pragmatic approach further assures that there will be relatively few occasions in which the courts must invoke the bar of Rule 13 against a party, and the cases in which the rule is invoked will usually involve malpractice in the first action.

In sum, the "same transaction or occurrence test" appears in numerous procedural contexts, including compulsory counterclaim rules such as Rule 13(a). However, its proper operation cannot be determined without judging in each context the consequences that flow from the test and the policies supporting the procedural rule that the test is designed to implement.

Illustration 7-25. *W* sued *H* for separate maintenance. *H's* answer contained a counterclaim for divorce on the ground of adultery, in which *H* named *A* as a coparty under a rule identical to Federal Rule 13(h). *W* and *A* replied by denying the allegations of adultery. Subsequently, *A* filed a separate action against *H* for defamation. *A* alleged that *H's* false allegations of adultery in the counterclaim for divorce were defamatory. *H* asserts that *A's* claim was a compulsory counterclaim in the divorce action because it arose from the same transaction or occurrence as *H's* counterclaim for divorce. Assume that the jurisdiction in question has a rule identical to Federal Rule 13(a). Thus, when *A* served the reply to the counterclaim for divorce, *H* claims that *A* should have asserted the defamation claim in that reply. *H's* defense is valid if *A's* defamation claim arose out of the same transaction or occurrence as *H's* counterclaim for divorce. In *Williams v. Robinson*,[122] the court considering *H's* defense held that *A's* counterclaim did not arise out of the same transaction or occurrence as *H's*

---

120. This factor appears to be the primary motivating reason for the paucity of decisions holding a party barred by Federal Rule 13. *See id.* at 78-79; *see also* Michael D. Conway, *Narrowing the Scope of Rule 13(a)*, 60 U. CHI. L. REV. 141 (1993).

121. CHARLES A. WRIGHT, THE LAW OF FEDERAL COURTS § 79, at 568 (5th ed. 1994).

122. 1 F.R.D. 211 (D.D.C. 1940).

counterclaim. The court stated that the same evidence would not support or refute the opposing claims.[123] This conclusion is demonstrably false. If *W* and *A* were guilty of adultery, *H's* divorce claim is valid. Likewise, if *W* and *A* were guilty of adultery, *A's* claim for defamation must fail, because truth is a defense. Conversely, if the allegation of adultery is false, the claim for divorce will fail and the claim of defamation will succeed. Therefore, both the claim for divorce and the claim for defamation turn on the truth of the allegation of adultery. The real reason that *A's* claim should not be considered a compulsory counterclaim to *H's* counterclaim for divorce is that omission of the counterclaim from *A's* reply is not a clear enough case of abuse on *A's* part to justify imposing the severe consequences of the compulsory counterclaim rule on *A*. Ordinarily, a lawyer preparing a reply to a divorce claim will not consider a claim for defamation to be a compulsory counterclaim to the divorce claim. A more technical reason would be that the adultery, if any, occurred at a time before the serving of the pleading that allegedly defamed *A*. Therefore, the separation of the liability-producing events in time could also produce the conclusion that they are part of different transactions and occurrences.[124]

Illustration 7-26. On the facts of *Illustration 7-25*, assume that (1) *A* had attempted to assert the counterclaim for defamation in the action for maintenance and divorce and (2) the issue was whether the counterclaim was sufficiently related to the opposing party's claim to be within the supplemental jurisdiction of the court. In such a situation, the same transaction or occurrence test should be considered to be satisfied. The overlap between the facts necessary to establish *H's* counterclaim for divorce and *A's* counterclaim for defamation would probably be sufficient to place the two counterclaims within the same case or controversy for purposes of a supplemental jurisdiction statute, despite the time gap between the events giving rise to the two claims.[125] Therefore, even though the same transaction or occurrence test should not be considered satisfied for purposes of the compulsory counterclaim rule, the altered context of the supplemental jurisdiction inquiry should produce the conclusion that the test is satisfied in the latter context.

Illustration 7-27. *A* sues *B* in a U.S. District Court. *A* asserts a claim under a federal statute and a related claim for unfair competition under state law. Various amendments to *A's* complaint and other extensions of time delay *B* from serving an answer for over two years from the date the action was commenced.

---

123. *See id.* at 213.

124. *See also* United-Bilt Homes, Inc. v. Sampson, 315 Ark. 156, 864 S.W.2d 861 (1993) (claim for foreclosure of mortgage not a compulsory counterclaim to third-party claim for wrongful refusal of mortgagee to release insurance proceeds to contractor who repaired mortgagor's house after a fire); Rebecca D. Hattabaugh, *United-Bilt Homes, Inc. v. Sampson: A New Standard for Compulsory Counterclaims*, 48 ARK. L. REV. 1009, 1024-25 (1995) (concluding that *Sampson* abandoned the "logical relationship test" for a version of the "same evidence test"); *cf.* Davis v. Lowery, 228 Ill. App. 3d 660, 592 N.E.2d 1203 (1992) (third-party defendant impleaded for contribution in automobile accident case failed to assert counterclaim against third-party plaintiff for damages to the third-party defendant's vehicle; counterclaim was not precluded; even though it arose from the same accident as opposing party's claim, subject matter of first suit was damage to plaintiff's truck, while second suit involved claim for damage to third-party defendant's trailer; plaintiffs in both suits were different!).

125. *See* Chapter 2(C)(4)*(d)(i)* ("The Scope of Supplemental Jurisdiction: Section 1367(a)") *supra*.

B's answer contains a counterclaim for defamation. *B's* counterclaim alleges that the original complaint and certain statements made by *A* on the date the complaint was filed were libelous. *A's* reply to the counterclaim asserts the affirmative defense that the statute of limitations had run on the defamation claim. Assume on these facts that the U.S. District Court certifies the following question to the state's highest court: "Does the filing of a complaint suspend the running of the statute of limitations against permissive counterclaims which are pleaded in the answer under Federal Rule 13(b), and which accrued at the time of the filing of the complaint or thereafter, but before the answer was filed?"[126] In classifying the counterclaim as "permissive," the district court relied on the case whose facts form the basis of *Illustration 7-25*.[127] The certified question was improperly worded. There was no reason to classify the counterclaim as either compulsory or permissive under Rule 13. The issue does not concern the policies of the compulsory counterclaim rule, but the policies of the state statute of limitations applicable to defamation claims. It would have been sufficient to describe the circumstances of the plaintiff's claims and the counterclaim. That approach would have focused the state court on the relevant statute-of-limitations policy.

Illustration 7-28. *I*, an insurance company, sues *A*, its insured party, and *B*, a person injured by *A* in an automobile accident. *I* seeks a declaratory judgment of nonliability on the ground that the terms of the insurance policy issued to *A* do not cover the accident between *A* and *B*. *B's* answer contains a cross-claim against *A* under a rule identical to Federal Rule 13(g). The cross-claim seeks to recover for personal injuries received in the accident and allegedly inflicted by *A's* negligence. *B* should not be allowed to assert the cross-claim because the same transaction or occurrence requirement of the cross-claim rule has not been satisfied. Under Rule 13(g), the same transaction or occurrence requirement operates as a restriction on joinder to protect the plaintiff from having claims added to the action that are too remote from the plaintiff's claim. The factual inquiries involved in the plaintiff's claim and *B's* cross-claim are too dissimilar here to be conveniently litigated in the same action. Therefore, to protect *I*, the same transaction or occurrence requirement should not be deemed satisfied.[128]

Illustration 7-29. On the facts of *Illustration 7-28*, assume that *I's* action is for a declaratory judgment that *I* is not liable to *A* under the policy because the car was not under *A's* control at the time of the accident. Assume further that *A* also asserts as a defense to *B's* cross-claim that the car was not under *A's* control at the time of the accident. Now the overlap between the plaintiff's claim and the cross-claim is sufficient to conclude that no harm will result to *I* from the

126. Certification is described in Chapter 5(H) ("Determination of State Law") *supra.*

127. *See* Bose Corp. v. Consumers Union, 384 F. Supp. 600 (D. Mass. 1974).

128. *See* Allstate Ins. Co. v. Daniels, 87 F.R.D. 1 (W.D. Okla. 1978); *see also* 6 CHARLES A. WRIGHT ET AL., FEDERAL PRACTICE AND PROCEDURE: CIVIL § 1432, at 244-47 (2d ed. 1990).

addition of the cross-claim to the action. Therefore, the same transaction or occurrence test should be deemed satisfied.[129]

(d) *Additional Problems of Administration Under Rule 13*

Apart from the administration of the same transaction or occurrence test, relatively few difficulties exist in administering Federal Rule 13.[130] In some situations, however, the language of Rule 13 has produced problems of interpretation that have yet to be entirely resolved. For example, counterclaims under Rule 13(a) and (b) can only be asserted against "opposing parties."[131] Furthermore, they must be "mature" at the time the party serves the pleading that should contain the counterclaim.

Illustration 7-30. H and W are husband and wife. During an automobile trip in which H was driving and W was riding as a passenger, they are involved in an automobile accident with D. W is killed in the accident. H is appointed administrator of W's estate. Acting in the capacity as administrator of the estate, H sues D for the wrongful death of W. D's answer contains a counterclaim against H for personal injuries D received in the accident as the result of H's alleged negligence. When someone acting in a representative capacity, such as H, brings an action, the defendant in the action generally may not assert a counterclaim against the plaintiff as an individual because the counterclaim would not be asserted against an "opposing party."[132] However, if W had been driving the automobile at the time of the accident, D could then have asserted the counterclaim in an attempt to recover against W's estate. H would have been an opposing party in the latter situation because H, as administrator, is the representative of W's estate.[133]

Illustration 7-31. I, an insurance company, sues D, a party who has been insured by I. I seeks to obtain a declaratory judgment that the policy issued by I to D does not cover a certain loss. D's answer contains a counterclaim against

---

129. *See* Collier v. Harvey, 179 F.2d 664 (10th Cir. 1949); *see also* 6 CHARLES A. WRIGHT ET AL., FEDERAL PRACTICE AND PROCEDURE: CIVIL § 1432, at 248 (2d ed. 1990). In both *Illustration 7-28* and *Illustration 7-29*, if the question is whether the cross-claims are sufficiently related to the main claim to justify an assertion of supplemental jurisdiction under Article III of the Constitution or 28 U.S.C. § 1367, the answer is clearly yes.

130. *See, e.g.,* Annotation, *Claims as to Which Right to Demand Arbitration Exists as Subject of Compulsory Counterclaim Under Federal Rules of Civil Procedure 13(a),* 2 A.L.R. FED. 1051 (1969).

131. *See* Annotation, *Who Is an "Opposing Party" Against Whom a Counterclaim Can Be Filed Under Federal Civil Procedure Rule 13(a) or (b),* 1 A.L.R. FED. 815 (1969) (discussing "opposing party" status of stakeholders in interpleader suits, plaintiff stockholders in derivative actions, employee-beneficiary in Fair Labor Standards Act litigation, informers in qui tam actions, trustees, assignees, plaintiffs in third-party proceedings, and other persons).

132. *See* 6 CHARLES A. WRIGHT ET AL., FEDERAL PRACTICE AND PROCEDURE: CIVIL § 1404, at 19 (2d ed. 1990).

133. *See also* Fielder v. Credit Acceptance Corp., 175 F.R.D. 313 (W.D. Mo. 1997) (compulsory counterclaim rule not applicable in class actions; absent class members not opposing parties). *Contra* Channel v. Citicorp Nat'l Servs., Inc., 89 F.3d 379 (7th Cir. 1996) (counterclaims against class members permissible); *Ex parte* Water Works & Sewer Bd., 738 So. 2d 783 (Ala. 1998) (defendant not precluded from asserting compulsory counterclaims in class action).

I based on a state statute that allows insured parties to recover the expenses of successfully defending actions brought by insurance companies for declarations of nonliability. In this situation, it is arguable that *D's* counterclaim is premature and, therefore, improper under Rule 13. Courts have interpreted Rule 13 as precluding counterclaims that depend upon the outcome of the plaintiff's claim for their validity. The language of Rule 13 lends some validity to this result. Rule 13(a) requires a pleader to assert any claim that the pleader "has" against an opposing party when it arises out of the same transaction or occurrence. Therefore, if *D* omitted the above described counterclaim from the answer, *D* should not be barred by the compulsory counterclaim rule from asserting it in a separate proceeding. The counterclaim arguably arises out of a different transaction or occurrence than *I's* claim, *i.e.*, the lawsuit rather than the event giving rise to the lawsuit. Furthermore, because the counterclaim has not matured, the pleader does not "have" it at the time of serving the pleading.[134] Rule 13(b) does not use the word "has." Instead, it speaks only of a "pleading" that states "as a counterclaim any claim against an opposing party" which does not arise out of the same transaction or occurrence that is the subject of the opposing party's claim. Therefore, the most sensible way to read Rule 13 is to conclude that counterclaims contingent on the outcome of the main action are permissive counterclaims. However, the courts considering this kind of question have not drawn this conclusion. Rather, they have simply held unmatured counterclaims to be altogether improper under the Rule.[135] One argument in favor of this result is the absence in Rule 13 of a provision equivalent to Rule 18(b). Rule 18(b) allows a party to join a claim that is contingent upon the party prosecuting another claim in the action to a successful conclusion.[136]

---

134. *See* Burlington N.R.R. v. Strong, 907 F.2d 707 (7th Cir. 1990); Allstate Ins. Co. v. Valdez, 29 F.R.D. 479 (E.D. Mich. 1962). Rule 13(e) allows a party, with the permission of the court, to assert by supplemental pleading a counterclaim that matures after the party serves a pleading. However, a motion to assert a counterclaim in a supplemental pleading after the main action has terminated in the defendant's favor might be denied by the court as untimely. *But cf.* Ohio Cellular Prods. Corp. v. Adams USA, Inc., 175 F.3d 1343 (Fed. Cir. 1999) (third-party complaint may be amended after judgment to add new third-party defendant who is liable for judgment).

135. *See* Slaff v. Slaff, 151 F. Supp. 124 (S.D.N.Y. 1957); Union Nat'l Bank v. Universal-Cyclops Steel Corp., 103 F. Supp. 719 (W.D. Pa. 1952); Mennen Co. v. Krauss Co., 37 F. Supp. 161 (E.D. La. 1941), *rev'd on other grounds*, 134 F.2d 348 (5th Cir. 1943); Goodyear Tire & Rubber Co. v. Marbon Corp., 32 F. Supp. 279 (D. Del. 1940); Tenneco Oil Co. v. Templin, 201 Ga. App. 30, 410 S.E.2d 154 (1991) (claim for contribution did not accrue until after judgment; therefore, it did not exist when defendant served answer).

136. *See* section C ("Joinder of Claims by Plaintiffs under the Federal Rules") *supra*. Rule 18 itself is no help to a party trying to assert an unmatured counterclaim. Although Rule 18(a) speaks of a party asserting a claim to relief "as an original claim, counterclaim," etc., it applies only to situations in which a party is attempting to join two or more claims against an opposing party. Thus, a defendant asserting a compulsory counterclaim against a plaintiff is authorized by Rule 18(a) to join with that counterclaim any other counterclaim the defendant has against the plaintiff. Rule 18(b) similarly applies to situations in which a party is attempting to join a matured claim with an unmatured claim. Where, as in this illustration, the defendant is not joining two counterclaims, but simply attempting to assert a single unmatured counterclaim, Rule 18 has no application. *Cf.* Glaziers & Glass Workers Union Local 252 Annuity Fund v. Newbridge Sec., Inc., 823 F. Supp. 1188 (E.D. Pa. 1993) (language of Rule 13(g) allowing cross-claims to be asserted against party who "is or may be liable to the cross-claimant" permits the assertion of cross-claims that are not yet mature).

2. Problems of Subject-Matter Jurisdiction, Venue, and Personal Jurisdiction Under Rule 13

(a) Supplemental (Ancillary) Subject-Matter Jurisdiction Over Counterclaims and Cross-Claims

Like joinder of claims by plaintiffs, federal counterclaims and cross-claims must satisfy federal subject-matter jurisdiction, venue, and personal jurisdiction requirements. However, "ancillary jurisdiction" has always facilitated subject-matter jurisdiction over counterclaims and cross-claims. As discussed in Chapter 2, the doctrine of "ancillary jurisdiction" was, along with the doctrine of "pendent jurisdiction," codified by Congress in 1990 under the label "supplemental jurisdiction."[137] Before the codification, ancillary jurisdiction existed over compulsory counterclaims, but not over permissive counterclaims.[138] After the codification, 28 U.S.C. § 1367(a) still allows supplemental jurisdiction to be asserted over compulsory counterclaims.[139] However, as noted in Chapter 2, a question exists whether the language of 28 U.S.C. § 1367 may result in the extension of supplemental jurisdiction to permissive counterclaims.[140] Section 1367(a) extends supplemental jurisdiction to claims that are so related to claims over which the district courts possess original jurisdiction "that they form part of the same case or controversy under Article III of the United States Constitution."[141] As argued in Chapter 2, the scope of an Article III case or controversy may be broad enough to allow the joinder of completely unrelated claims.[142] However, if 28 U.S.C. § 1367(a) is construed as Chapter 2 argued it should be, "supplemental jurisdiction" will be limited to claims that arise out of the same general facts as the claim over which the district courts have original jurisdic-

---

137. *See* Judicial Improvements Act of 1990, Pub. L. No. 101-650, § 310, 104 Stat. 5089, 5113-14 (codified at 28 U.S.C. § 1367); Chapter 2(C)(4)*(d)* ("The Codification of Pendent and Ancillary Jurisdiction") *supra*.

138. *See* Chapter 2(C)(4)*(c)* ("The Statutory Basis of Pendent and Ancillary Jurisdiction") *supra*.

139. *See, e.g.*, Greisbach Invs., Ltd. v. Compania Dominicana de Aviacion, C. Por. A., No. 90-CV-1931 (DHR), 1992 WL 390242, 1992 U.S. Dist. LEXIS 19078 (E.D.N.Y. Dec. 10, 1992) (factually related counterclaims adding additional parties are within the supplemental jurisdiction conferred by 28 U.S.C. § 1367); *see* Chapter 2(C)(4)*(d) supra* ("The Codification of Pendent and Ancillary Jurisdiction"). *But see* Hot Springs Assocs., Inc. v. Kiesler, No. 90-0032-C, 1992 WL 88644, 1992 U.S. Dist. LEXIS 6042 (W.D. Va. Apr. 27,, 1992), in which the court held that supplemental jurisdiction did not exist over factually related counterclaims adding additional parties, because the additional parties were added pursuant to Rules 19 and 20. The *Kiesler* decision is clearly incorrect. *See* Denis F. McLaughlin, *The Federal Supplemental Jurisdiction Statute—A Constitutional and Statutory Analysis*, 24 ARIZ. ST. L.J. 849, 931-32 (1992). Rules 19 or 20 must always be complied with when parties are added to a counterclaim under Rule 13(h). However, § 1367(b) only prohibits claims *by plaintiffs* against persons made parties under Rules 19 or 20 and claims by persons proposed to be joined *as plaintiffs* under Rule 19. *See* 28 U.S.C. § 1367(b).

140. *See* Chapter 2(C)(4)*(d)(i)* ("The Scope of Supplemental Jurisdiction: Section 1367(a)") *supra*.

141. 28 U.S.C. § 1367(a); *see* Chapter 2(C)(4)*(d)* ("The Codification of Pendent and Ancillary Jurisdiction") *supra*.

142. *See* Chapter 2(C)(4)*(b)* ("The Constitutional Basis of Pendent and Ancillary Jurisdiction") *supra*.

tion.[143] In that event, permissive counterclaims will still have to independently satisfy all federal jurisdictional requirements.[144]

Generally, it can be said that § 1367(a) has been interpreted as described in the preceding paragraph. However, in *Channell v. Citicorp National Services, Inc.,*[145] the Seventh Circuit Court of Appeals held that the distinction between compulsory and permissive counterclaims had been rendered irrelevant by § 1367(a), and that the federal courts should today "use the language of the statute to define the extent of their powers."[146] However, although the court sustained supplemental jurisdiction over the defendant's counterclaims in the action, the counterclaims clearly arose out of the same facts as the plaintiff's claims and were, therefore, unquestionably a part of the same Article III case or controversy as those claims. The plaintiff's claims were class action claims alleging violation by the defendant of the federal Consumer Leasing Act. The defendant's counterclaims were claims seeking unpaid amounts under the very consumer leases that were the bases of the class action. In *Rothman v. Emory University,*[147] the Seventh Circuit was confronted with an action by a former law student against Emory University for violation of the Americans with Disabilities Act, a federal statute. The University asserted a counterclaim for the unpaid balance of student loans owed by the student, and the court, following *Channel,* upheld supplemental jurisdiction over the University's counterclaim. The court stated that "Emory's counterclaim, whether compulsory or permissive, was 'so related to' [the student's] original claims that they form the same case or controversy."[148]

The primary difference between *Channell* and *Rothman* is in the degree of relationship that existed between the original claims and counterclaims in both actions. In *Channell,* the original claims and counterclaims both arose out of the leases between the class members and the defendant. However, in *Rothman,* the original claim and counterclaim had in common only that they arose out of the same university-student relationship. Nevertheless, as discussed in Chapter 2, the

---

143. *See* Chapter 2(C)(4)*(d)(i)* ("The Scope of Supplemental Jurisdiction: Section 1367(a)") *supra.*

144. The majority of cases considering this question after the enactment of § 1367 have held that permissive counterclaims require an independent basis of jurisdiction. *See* Cameco Indus., Inc. v. Louisiana Cane Mfg., Inc., No. 92-3158 Section "D"(3), 1993 WL 62420, 1993 U.S. Dist. LEXIS 2686 (E.D. La. Mar. 3, 1993); Koprowski v. Wistar Inst. of Anatomy & Biology, No. 92-1132, 1992 WL 151302, 1992 U.S. Dist. LEXIS 9706 (E.D. Pa. June 17, 1992); Shamblin v. City of Colchester, 793 F. Supp. 831 (C.D. Ill. 1992); *see also* Unique Concepts, Inc. v. Manuel, 930 F.2d 573, 574 (7th Cir. 1991) (dictum). Only one case seems to have considered a permissive counterclaim to be within the supplemental jurisdiction conferred by § 1367. *See* Wesley v. General Motors Acceptance Corp., No. 91 C 3368, 1991 WL 169204, 1991 U.S. Dist. LEXIS 11745 (N.D. Ill. Aug. 20, 1991). The court in *Wesley* stated that the counterclaim was not compulsory in the sense that, had it been omitted from the action, it would have been precluded in a subsequent action by force of Rule 13(a). However, the court correctly recognized that this did not resolve the supplemental jurisdiction issue. That issue depended upon whether the counterclaim was sufficiently related to the plaintiff's claim to satisfy the policies of the supplemental jurisdiction statute. There seems no question that the counterclaim was sufficiently related to the plaintiff's claim for that purpose. Thus, at this writing, no case has clearly held a completely unrelated counterclaim to be within § 1367(a).

145. 89 F.3d 379 (7th Cir. 1996).

146. *Id.* at 385.

147. 123 F.3d 446 (7th Cir. 1997).

148. *Id.* at 454.

claim and counterclaim in *Rothman* arose out of the same "loose factual relationship," which is probably sufficient to make the claims part of the same Article III case or controversy.[149] Thus, even though both cases discarded the distinction between compulsory and permissive counterclaims in making the jurisdictional determination, the actual factual relationship required for supplemental jurisdiction under § 1367(a) in the cases was actually no different than the relationship required for ancillary jurisdiction prior to the enactment of § 1367(a). Indeed, as discussed in section F(1)*(c)*, above, an actual examination of the contexts in which the same transaction or occurrence test has been administered in the past indicates that it has always varied in content depending upon the issue being considered in the particular case. Therefore, the Seventh Circuit's refusal to apply the unrevealing "compulsory" and "permissive" labels to determine jurisdiction under § 1367(a) is arguably a healthy development.[150]

A separate issue concerning the application of § 1367 in Rule 13 cases involves additional parties to compulsory counterclaims under Rule 13(h). Specifically, the question is whether, if a defendant asserts a compulsory counterclaim against the plaintiff and joins an additional nondiverse party to the counterclaim under Rule 13(h), 28 U.S.C. § 1367(b) applies to defeat supplemental jurisdiction over the added party. The correct result is that § 1367(b) should not defeat jurisdiction over the additional party. The language of the statute applies only to defeat "claims by plaintiffs" that violate the policies of 28 U.S.C. § 1332 (the diversity jurisdiction statute). In addition, § 1367(b) nowhere lists Rule 13 among the Federal Rules of Civil Procedure to which the subsection applies. To the extent that authority exists on this issue, it generally agrees that supplemental jurisdiction exists over the additional party under § 1367(a) and that the jurisdiction is not defeated by § 1367(b).[151]

---

149. *See* Chapter 2(C)(4)*(d)(i)*, *Illustrations 2-87* and *2-88, supra,* and accompanying text. However, it should be noted that the student argued in defense to the counterclaims that the university's violation of the ADA constituted a breach of contract that entitled him not to repay the loans. *See* 123 F.3d at 454-55. This argument was unsuccessful.

150. *But cf.* Iglesias v. Mutual Life Ins. Co., 156 F.3d 237 (1st Cir. 1998) (holding that the former distinction between compulsory and permissive counterclaims survives the enactment of § 1367 and denying supplemental jurisdiction over an employer's counterclaim for restitution of money that the employee obtained by submitting overstated expense reports in an action by the employee for discrimination and breach of contract; the court held that despite the fact that the counterclaim arose during the same period as the employee's claims, the original claims and counterclaim rested on different sets of facts). *See also* Blue Dane Simmental Corp. v. American Simmental Ass'n, 952 F. Supp. 1399 (D. Neb. 1997) (holding that supplemental jurisdiction did not exist over a counterclaim when the claim and the counterclaim had only a single factual issue in common). Note that the Seventh Circuit cases described in the text and the cases cited in this note differ primarily in their interpretation of the relationship between the claim and the counterclaim necessary to satisfy Article III of the Constitution. The disagreement over whether the test for Article III is the same as the test for compulsoriness under Rule 13(a) is a separate issue.

151. *See* United Capitol Ins. Co. v. Kapiloff, 155 F.3d 488 (4th Cir. 1998) (§ 1367(b) only limits jurisdiction over plaintiffs' efforts to join nondiverse parties, not over defendants' efforts to join nondiverse parties to a counterclaim under Rule 13(h)); Greisbach Invs., Ltd. v. Compania Dominicana de Aviacion, C. Par. A, No. 90-CV-1931 (DHR), 1992 WL 390242, 1992 U.S. Dist. LEXIS 19078 (E.D.N.Y. Dec. 10, 1992) (factually related counterclaim adding additional parties is within supplemental jurisdiction). *Contra* Hot Springs Assocs., Inc. v. Kiesler, No. 90-0082-C, 1992 WL 88644, 1992 U.S. Dist. LEXIS 6042 (W.D. Va. Apr. 27, 1992) (no supplemental jurisdiction over factually related counterclaims adding additional parties). *See also* Denis F. McLaughlin, *The Federal Supplemental Jurisdiction Statute—A Constitutional and Statutory Analysis,*

Illustration 7-32. B injured A in an automobile accident as a result of B's negligence. A, a citizen of State X, sued B, a citizen of State Y, in a U.S. District Court in State Y for $100,000 in damages. B's answer (1) denied negligence, (2) asserted the affirmative defense of contributory negligence, and (3) pleaded a counterclaim against A for $5,000 in property damage to B's automobile received in the same accident. Even though the amount of the counterclaim is less than the jurisdictional amount prescribed by 28 U.S.C. § 1332, the federal court has supplemental (ancillary) jurisdiction because the counterclaim arose out of the same facts as A's claim against B. If the accident had been a three-car collision in which C, a citizen of State Y, had also been involved, and if B had joined C as a party to the counterclaim against A under Rule 13(h), supplemental jurisdiction would also exist over the claim against C for the same reason.

Illustration 7-33. Assume the same facts as in *Illustration 7-32*, except that B's $5,000 counterclaim is for breach of a contract wholly unrelated to A's tort claim. Before 1990, the federal district courts did not have jurisdiction over this kind of counterclaim because it was not related closely enough to the tort claim to be within the ancillary jurisdiction of the district courts. B's counterclaim was clearly permissive. As such, the counterclaim had to meet all requirements of federal jurisdiction independently, but it fails to do so because the counterclaim is for less than the jurisdictional amount prescribed by 28 U.S.C. § 1332. After 1990, if 28 U.S.C. § 1367(a) is construed to permit supplemental jurisdiction over any counterclaim that is so related to the plaintiff's claim as to be within the same constitutional case or controversy, this kind of counterclaim may be within the jurisdiction of the district courts. This construction depends on whether Article III is interpreted to allow wholly unrelated claims to fit within the same case or controversy, as Chapter 2 argued that it should be.[152] However, as Chapter 2 also argued, the better result would be for the courts to interpret the scope of an Article III case or controversy as broad enough to encompass factually unrelated claims, but to interpret 28 U.S.C. §1367(a) as authorizing supplemental jurisdiction only over claims that arise out of the same transaction or occurrence as the claim over which the district courts have original jurisdiction.[153] If that interpretation of § 1367(a) is adopted, there will still be no jurisdiction over the counterclaim described in this illustration. Thus, even if the enactment of § 1367(a) justifies the courts in discarding the former distinctions between compulsory and permissive counterclaims as a means of determining whether supplemental jurisdiction exists, the factual relationship necessary to justify supplemental jurisdiction should remain the same as it was prior to the enactment of § 1367.

Illustration 7-34. A, a citizen of State X, sues B, a citizen of State Y, and C, also a citizen of State Y, in a U.S. District Court in State Y. A seeks $100,000 in damages for personal injuries received in an automobile accident. B's answer contains a cross-claim against C for $5,000 for personal injuries received in the

---

24 ARIZ. ST. L.J. 849, 931-32 (1992).

152. *See* Chapter 2(C)(4)*(b)* ("The Constitutional Basis of Pendent and Ancillary Jurisdiction") *supra.*

153. *See* Chapter 2(C)(4)*(d)(i)* ("The Scope of Supplemental Jurisdiction: Section 1367(a)") *supra.*

same accident. No diversity of citizenship exists between *B* and *C*. Also, *B's* cross-claim is for less than the jurisdictional amount prescribed by 28 U.S.C. § 1332. Nevertheless, before 1990, the cross-claim was within the ancillary jurisdiction of the district court because of its close factual relationship to the original claim in the action. After 1990, the cross-claim is still within the "supplemental jurisdiction" of the district court under 28 U.S.C. § 1367.

(b) Supplemental (Ancillary) Venue and Personal Jurisdiction Over Counterclaims and Cross-Claims

When the federal courts have ancillary subject-matter jurisdiction over a counterclaim or cross-claim, the question arises whether supplemental (or ancillary) venue and personal jurisdiction should also exist. This question is easily answered when the issue concerns cross-claims. "[T]he venue statute is designed to test the appropriateness of the forum at the institution of a suit by the original plaintiff so that . . . the cross-claim . . . does not have to satisfy the statutory [venue] prerequisites."[154] Likewise, because (1) cross-claims are asserted between coparties to an action, such as codefendants who are already properly before the court, and (2) cross-claims must also arise out of the same facts as the original action, there ordinarily can be no personal jurisdiction questions about such claims.[155]

The same basic reasons normally support the conclusion that a plaintiff may not make venue or personal jurisdiction objections when a compulsory counterclaim is asserted against the plaintiff under Rule 13(a).[156] The exception is a case in which a third party is added under Rule 13(h) for purposes of a compulsory counterclaim under Rule 13(a). Rule 13(a) explicitly excludes from the compulsory category claims that require the presence of third parties over whom the court cannot acquire jurisdiction. This provision thus apparently preserves the third party's right to object to personal jurisdiction.[157] Indeed, even if Rule 13(a) did not explicitly preserve the third party's right to object, the Constitution might require that the personal jurisdiction objection be preserved in cases in which the third party added to the counterclaim does not have minimum contacts with the state where the action is brought.[158]

Illustration 7-35. A, a citizen of State *X*, sues *B*, a citizen of State *Y*, in a U.S. District Court for the District of State *Y*. *A* seeks $100,000 in damages for personal injuries received in an automobile accident in State *X*. *B's* answer contains a counterclaim for $250,000 for *B's* own personal injuries received in the same accident. *B* joins *C*, a citizen of State *X*, as a party on this counterclaim. *B* asserts in the alternative that either the negligence of *A*, or that of *C*, or both,

---

154. 6 Charles A. Wright et al., Federal Practice and Procedure: Civil § 1433, at 261 (2d ed. 1990).

155. *See id.*

156. *See id.* § 1416, at 123.

157. *See id.* § 1411, at 84-85, § 1416 at 124.

158. *See id.* § 1414, at 109; *see also* Chapter 3 ("Personal Jurisdiction and Service of Process") *supra.*

caused *B's* injuries. *C* has no contacts with State *Y*. Under the language of Rule 13(a), *C* appears to have the right to object to the personal jurisdiction of the State *Y* district court over *C*.[159] However, even if the language of Rule 13(a) does not preserve this right, the Constitution may require that *C* be permitted to raise a personal jurisdiction objection based on the absence of contacts between *C* and the claim, on the one hand, and State *Y*, on the other. Clearly though, *A* has submitted to the jurisdiction of the State *Y* court for purposes of counterclaims arising from the same transaction or occurrence as *A's* claim against *B*.

* * * * *

As a general proposition, courts have also held that a plaintiff cannot raise venue and personal jurisdiction objections when a defendant asserts a permissive counterclaim.[160] This result may be sound as an interpretation of the federal venue statutes.[161] However, to conclude that a plaintiff, by filing an action in a particular forum, ''waives'' all personal jurisdiction objections to whatever claims a defendant may possess against the plaintiff raises constitutional questions in some cases. The questions occur when the events giving rise to a permissive counterclaim occur outside the forum state and trial of the counterclaim in the forum would impose severe burdens on the plaintiff because of a lack of contact between the plaintiff and claim on the one hand, and the forum state, on the other.

Illustration 7-36. A, a citizen of State *X*, sued *B*, a citizen of State *Y*, in a U.S. District Court in State *Y*. *A* sought $250,000 in damages for breach of a contract made and to be performed in State *Y*. *B's* answer contained a permissive counterclaim in which *B* sought $400,000 in damages for personal injuries received in an automobile accident in State *Z*. The accident occurred while the parties were vacationing together in State *Z*. Under these circumstances, to conclude that *A* waived personal jurisdiction objections *A* would have otherwise possessed against a suit on *B's* tort claim in State *Y* raises serious constitutional questions. Although State *Y* seems to be the most appropriate place for suit on *A's* contract claim, no relationship exists between State *Y* and *B's* tort claim. If, under the minimum contacts test, it would be unconstitutional for a State *Y* federal court to assert jurisdiction over *A* in an original action on *B's* tort, *A* should be able to object on the same grounds to jurisdiction over *A* for purposes of the permissive counterclaim. This conclusion may have to be qualified in one respect. Recall from Chapter 3 that the U.S. Supreme Court sustained the validity of transient presence jurisdiction in *Burnham v. Superior Court*.[162] If the commencement of an action in a state is a sufficient relationship under *Burnham* to sustain jurisdiction over the plaintiff on a claim arising outside the state, then plaintiffs will not be able to successfully object to permissive counterclaims asserted against them on minimum contacts grounds. The plaintiff will be protected only if the

---

159. *See* Fed. R. Civ. P. 13(a).

160. *See* 6 Charles A. Wright et al., Federal Practice and Procedure: Civil § 1424, at 182-83 (2d ed. 1990).

161. *See id.*

162. *See* 495 U.S. 604, 110 S. Ct. 2105, 109 L. Ed. 2d 631 (1990); Chapter 3(E)(2) (''Transient Presence Jurisdiction'') *supra*.

state possesses an immunity rule that is broad enough in scope to insulate the plaintiff from the permissive counterclaim. However, the existence of such protection is highly unlikely.[163]

(c) *Waiver by the Defendant of Venue or Personal Jurisdiction Objections when the Defendant Asserts a Compulsory or Permissive Counterclaim*

A separate question in some federal actions is whether a defendant waives any venue and personal jurisdiction objections that the defendant possesses by asserting a compulsory or permissive counterclaim in the action. There is authority that waiver occurs by asserting either a compulsory or a permissive counterclaim in an action.[164] These cases rely on the idea that a defendant possessing a counterclaim and a personal jurisdiction or venue objection should make a preanswer motion under Federal Rule 12(b) to challenge jurisdiction or venue rather than consolidating the venue or personal jurisdiction objections with a counterclaim in the answer.[165] This result is incorrect when applied to compulsory counterclaims. The defendant must plead such counterclaims or lose them. Furthermore, Federal Rule 12(h)(1) explicitly provides that venue and personal jurisdiction are waived only by omitting them from a preanswer motion or failing to include them in a responsive pleading.[166] Therefore, the better view, at least as to compulsory counterclaims, is that no waiver is produced by their consolidation with venue or personal jurisdiction objections in the answer.[167]

Some authorities have argued, however, that the assertion of a permissive counterclaim should produce waiver of venue and personal jurisdiction objections. This argument is supported by the theory that the defendant need not assert the permissive counterclaim. Thus, the defendant "is actually indicating a desire to use the forum for [the defendant's] own objectives" and "should not be able to object simultaneously to the inconvenience of that forum for purposes of defending against a claim by [the plaintiff]."[168] This view is also incorrect.

---

163. The immunity rules discussed in Chapter 3(B)(2)*(a)* ("Immunity From Service of Process") *supra* do not operate to immunize a party participating in litigation from the assertion of claims or counterclaims within the litigation. Rather, they insulate the party from separate litigation instituted by third parties. Thus, the states would have to expand their immunity rules considerably to encompass the kind of case described in this illustration.

164. *See* 6 CHARLES A. WRIGHT ET AL., FEDERAL PRACTICE AND PROCEDURE: CIVIL § 1416, at 124-28, § 1424, at 185-86 (2d ed. 1990), and cases there cited; *Comment Note—What Conduct Constitutes Waiver of Venue Privilege—Federal Cases*, 5 L. Ed. 2d 1056 (1960).

165. *See* 6 CHARLES A. WRIGHT ET AL., FEDERAL PRACTICE AND PROCEDURE: CIVIL § 1416, at 126-27 (2d ed. 1990), and authorities there cited.

166. *See id.* at 127.

167. *See, e.g.*, Dragor Shipping Corp. v. Union Tank Car Co., 378 F.2d 241, 244 (9th Cir. 1967); *see also* 6 CHARLES A. WRIGHT ET AL., FEDERAL PRACTICE AND PROCEDURE: CIVIL § 1416, at 128-29 (2d ed. 1990). *See generally* Jean F. Rydstrom, Annotation, *Joinder of Counterclaim Under Rule 13(a) or 13(b) of Federal Rules of Civil Procedure With Jurisdictional Defense Under Rule 12(b), as Waiver of Such Defense*, 17 A.L.R. FED. 388 (1973).

168. 6 CHARLES A. WRIGHT ET AL., FEDERAL PRACTICE AND PROCEDURE: CIVIL § 1424, at 186 (2d ed. 1990).

Federal Rule 12(h) lists the circumstances under which waiver of venue and personal jurisdiction objections will occur. Waiver by assertion of a counterclaim is not among those circumstances. It is clearly contrary to the spirit of the Federal Rules to produce waiver by an action—*i.e.*, consolidation of venue or personal jurisdiction defenses with a permissive counterclaim in the answer—that is not listed in Rule 12(h) as one that will produce waiver. On the contrary, the Rule implicitly appears to permit such an action.

In addition, the view that waiver of venue and personal jurisdiction objections occurs by asserting a permissive counterclaim stems from an apparent inconsistency. It is regarded as inconsistent for a defendant to object to the forum based wholly or partly on the ground of inconvenience while simultaneously asserting a claim that the party does not have to assert, indicating that the forum is convenient. The answer to this argument is that there is no necessary inconsistency in objecting that the forum is inconvenient for purposes of the plaintiff's claim, but not for the permissive counterclaim. The relationship between the forum and the plaintiff's claim might well be so attenuated that it would impose a significant burden on the defendant to litigate the claim there. However, it also might be the case that the relationship between the parties, the permissive counterclaim, and the forum are substantial. Furthermore, the defendant's assertion of the permissive counterclaim may be viewed as conditional. If the defendant's venue and personal jurisdiction objections are overruled, thereby forcing the defendant to litigate the plaintiff's claim in the forum, *then* the defendant would find it convenient to litigate all the claims existing between the parties in the same proceeding, but not otherwise.[169]

If the defendant can bring a separate action in the forum on the claim that is the subject of the permissive counterclaim, it accomplishes little to force the defendant to make the claims the subject of an independent action rather than allowing assertion of the claim as a permissive counterclaim. Yet this result will be the practical consequence of a doctrine that produces waiver of personal jurisdiction and venue objections through the assertion of permissive counterclaims. If the claim can be litigated in the forum in any event, then no good reason exists to deter the defendant from litigating it as part of the existing action with the plaintiff, subject always to the power of the district court to order a separate trial of the counterclaim under Federal Rules 13(i) and 42(b) to prevent inconvenience.

Illustration 7-37. *A*, a citizen of State *X*, sues *B*, a citizen of State *Y*, in a U.S. District Court in State *X*. *A* seeks $400,000 in damages for personal injuries received in an automobile accident in State *Z*. The accident occurred

---

169. *But cf.* Peterson v. Highland Music, Inc., 140 F.3d 1313 (9th Cir. 1998), *cert. denied*, 525 U.S. 983, 119 S. Ct. 446, 142 L. Ed. 2d 401 (1998) (making a timely Rule 12 motion is sufficient to preserve personal jurisdiction objection after it was denied, even though defendant failed to raise issue further; other waiver by conduct cases in courts of appeals involved factors militating in favor of a waiver finding that are not present in this case); Continental Bank, N.A. v. Meyer, 10 F.3d 1293 (7th Cir. 1993) (although defendants had raised personal jurisdiction defense properly in answer, they waived it by participating in the action for over 2 1/2 years without actively contesting jurisdiction); Yeldell v. Tutt, 913 F.2d 533 (8th Cir. 1990) (although defendants literally complied with Rule 12 by including personal jurisdiction defense in their answer, they violated spirit of rule by failing to reassert defense until appeal).

while the parties were vacationing together in State *Z*. *B's* answer contains (1) an objection to venue; (2) an objection on minimum contacts grounds to the jurisdiction of the State *X* district court over *B*; and (3) a permissive counterclaim for $100,000 based on an alleged breach by *A* of a contract that was made and to be performed in State *X*. *B* should be able to object to venue and to the assertion of personal jurisdiction over *B* on the tort claim, while also asserting the permissive counterclaim without fear of waiver. Venue of the action is improper over the tort claim in State *X* under 28 U.S.C. § 1391(a). Moreover, the connection between *B* and the tort claim on the one hand, and State *X*, on the other, is attenuated, while the connection between the contract claim, the parties, and State *X* is substantial. Consequently, there is no inconsistency in *B* objecting to venue or personal jurisdiction in State *X* for purposes of the tort claim, while arguing that State *X* is a convenient place for litigation of the contract claim. *B* clearly could bring an independent action on the contract claim in State *X*, and there seems no reason under the Federal Rules or otherwise to deter *B* from asserting the claim as a permissive counterclaim in *A's* action by the imposition of a waiver rule.

Illustration 7-38. The only question that might legitimately arise in *Illustration 7-37* today would concern the effect of a dismissal of the tort claim on venue and personal jurisdiction grounds, but a retention of the contract counterclaim for adjudication in State *X* at *B's* request. If, after dismissal of the plaintiff's claim, *B* requests that the contract counterclaim be retained for adjudication, *B* is realistically in no different position than if *B* had commenced an original action on the contract claim against *A* in a State *X* federal court. However, suppose, as hypothesized in *Illustration 7-36*, it would be held under the *Burnham* decision that the assertion of an original claim within a state is sufficient to allow an assertion of personal jurisdiction over *B* on claims arising outside the state. Under those circumstances, *A* would be able to assert *A's* tort claim as a permissive counterclaim in an original action by *B* on the contract in State *X*. *B* would have no valid venue objection. As discussed in the text, the venue statutes only apply to original claims, not to counterclaims. *B* would also have no valid personal jurisdiction objection because of the effect of *Burnham*. Therefore, if *B* requests the federal district court to retain the contract counterclaim, and if *Burnham* would have the effect hypothesized above in an original action, it seems unfair to preclude *A* from asserting the tort claim. Instead, to avoid waiver, *B* should have to specify that the permissive counterclaim should be dismissed if *A's* tort claim is dismissed on venue or personal jurisdiction grounds.

(d) Effect of a Counterclaim on the Amount in Controversy

Another jurisdictional question concerning federal counterclaims arises because of a peculiar Supreme Court decision concerning the amount in controversy requirement of 28 U.S.C. § 1332. If the plaintiff asserts a claim for less than the jurisdictional amount requirement and the defendant asserts a compulsory counterclaim that is for more than $75,000, can the counterclaim be considered in determining whether federal jurisdiction exists? In *Horton v. Liberty Mutual Insurance Co.*,[170] the plaintiff asserted a worker's compensation claim for $14,035 before the Texas Industrial Accident Board. The Board awarded the plaintiff $1,050. Under Texas law, either party could sue to set aside the award. In the action to set aside the award, the issues would be tried de novo. On the day the award was made, Liberty Mutual commenced a federal diversity action to set aside the $1,050 award. Liberty Mutual asserted that Horton's $14,035 claim was the amount in controversy.[171] (At that time, the jurisdictional amount requirement of 28 U.S.C. § 1332 was $10,000.) In fact, one week later, Horton, commenced an action in state court to set aside the $1,050 award and recover $14,035.

In the federal action, Horton moved to dismiss Liberty Mutual's claim. Horton argued that it did not satisfy the jurisdictional amount requirement. Horton also counterclaimed for $14,035, subject to this motion to dismiss.[172] The U.S. Supreme Court held that Liberty Mutual's action satisfied the amount-in-controversy requirement.[173] As Professors Wright, Miller, and Kane have observed, this holding results in the somewhat startling conclusion that "the amount[-]in[-]controversy requirement may be satisfied by the plaintiff simply alleging that the defendant will interpose a counterclaim at a time when the defendant has not asserted it!"[174]

The most logical explanation of the *Horton* result is that the procedure for setting aside the worker's compensation award under Texas law appears to make the action similar to one for declaratory relief.[175] Because the Texas procedure provided for complete relitigation of the issues that were before the Texas Industrial Accident Board in a suit to set aside the Board's award, Liberty Mutual's action can be viewed as a request for a declaration of nonliability in which the opposing party was claiming the right to $14,035. In declaratory judgment actions, the amount that would be in controversy in any possible action for nondeclaratory relief determines the amount in controversy for purposes of the declaratory action.[176] In this case, Horton was the party who was seeking nondeclaratory relief, and he claimed $14,035. So viewed, *Horton* was not essentially different from a declaratory proceeding brought by the party who would have been the defendant in a nondeclaratory action in which the amount-in-controversy requirement would have been satisfied. Therefore, the *Horton* case probably should not be read to permit satisfaction of the amount-in-controversy requirement in any case in which the plaintiff anticipates that the defendant will assert a compulsory counterclaim for more than $75,000.

---

170. 367 U.S. 348, 81 S. Ct. 1570, 6 L. Ed. 2d 890 (1961).

171. Liberty Mutual, of course, asserted that Horton was entitled to nothing.

172. *Id.* at 349-50, 81 S. Ct. at 1571-72, 6 L. Ed. 2d at 892.

173. *Id.* at 350-55, 81 S. Ct. at 1572-74, 6 L. Ed. 2d at 893-95.

174. 6 CHARLES A. WRIGHT ET AL., FEDERAL PRACTICE AND PROCEDURE: CIVIL § 1415, at 120 (2d ed. 1990).

175. *See id.* at 121-22.

176. *See id.* at 122.

Illustration 7-39. *A*, a citizen of State *X*, sued *B*, a citizen of State *Y*, in a U.S. District Court in State *Y*, for $1,000 in property damages received in an automobile accident in State *Y*. *A* alleged in the complaint that *B* would counterclaim for $400,000 in damages for personal injuries received in the same accident. In addition to an objection to subject-matter jurisdiction based on the absence of the proper jurisdictional amount, *B's* answer asserted a compulsory counterclaim for $400,000 for personal injuries. Unless the *Horton* case is extended beyond its facts to include anticipation of all compulsory counterclaims, *A's* action should be dismissed for want of subject-matter jurisdiction.

3. Rules Enabling Act Issues Under Rule 13

Potential Rules Enabling Act issues can arise under Rule 13 when state courts do not possess compulsory counterclaim rules patterned after Rule 13(a) and federal courts are faced with the question whether to enforce the state rules or to preclude an omitted counterclaim in a prior federal diversity action under Rule 13. They can also arise when the state courts would either allow the assertion of a counterclaim in the initial action that Rule 13 would not permit to be joined or would preclude a counterclaim that Rule 13 would allow. Fortunately, however, at both a conceptual level and under the Supreme Court's authorities under the Rules Enabling Act examined in Chapter 5, the issues of validity in applying Rule 13 are easily resolved in favor of the rule.

In cases where the state procedure does not contain a compulsory counterclaim rule, courts should not hesitate to apply Rule 13(a) in appropriate cases to preclude assertion of a compulsory counterclaim omitted from a prior federal action. As argued in Chapter 5, there is no conflict between a Federal Rule of Civil Procedure and state law in either of two circumstances: (1) when the Federal Rule in question is not broad enough to apply to the case before the federal court; or (2) when the state rule in question was designed exclusively for use in the state's own court system.[177] Whenever a counterclaim arises out of the same transaction or occurrence as an opposing party's claim in a way that makes the counterclaim compulsory, as described in section F(1)*(c)*, above, it cannot be argued that Federal Rule 13(a) is inapplicable to the case. However, it can virtually always be argued that the state rule in question is designed for operation exclusively in the courts of the state in which the action is brought. For example, if the state has a code system of the sort described in section E, above, it cannot seriously be argued that the counterclaim rules of the system are designed to operate in courts other than those of the state itself. Therefore, it seems clear that in virtually every case involving a difference between Rule 13(a) and state permissive counterclaim practice, there will be no real conflict between the federal and state rules.

Even if such a conflict could be identified, however, the Supreme Court authorities discussed in Chapter 5 would validate Rule 13(a). In particular, the

---

177. *See* Chapter 5(F)(3), *Illustration 5-17* and accompanying text, *supra*.

case of *Business Guides, Inc. v. Chromatic Communications Enterprises, Inc.,*[178] discussed in Chapter 5(f)(5), above, would validate the application of Rule 13(a) even in a case of assumed conflict with state law. In *Business Guides*, the Supreme Court validated the application of Rule 11 of the Federal Rules to a represented party who had signed a document in violation of the rule, but in good faith. As discussed in Chapter 5, the Court rejected arguments that Rule 11 involved impermissible fee shifting by observing, among other things, that the operation of the rule was not keyed to the ultimate outcome of the litigation, but to specific events within the litigation.[179] In addition, the Court observed that "[i]mposing monetary sanctions on parties that violated the Rule may confer a benefit on other litigants, but the Rules Enabling Act is not violated by such incidental effects on substantive rights."[180]

Business Guides* assures that Rule 13(a) can be validly applied in any case of conflict with state rules that do not provide for compulsory counterclaims. This is so not simply because of what the Court said in the case, which, as indicated in Chapter 5, is ambiguous.[181] It is also true because of the configuration of the case and the resemblance of the Rule 11 problem in *Business Guides* to the compulsory counterclaim problem under Rule 13(a). Rule 11 does not directly affect the validity on the merits of a claim or defense in an action, but requires that the parties and their attorneys make reasonable investigations of the facts and the law before taking positions on those claims or defenses.[182] The application of Rule 13(a) to preclude a counterclaim that was omitted from a prior action will, indeed, affect the merits of a second action. However, it is clear that the party possessing the counterclaim can avoid the operation of Rule 13(a) by pleading the counterclaim in the initial proceeding. In this respect, Rule 13 is like Rule 11, in that the adverse effects of the rules can be avoided by compliance with the rules. In contrast, Rule 15(c) governing relation back of amendments, which was examined in Chapter 6(D)(5), above, can produce an adverse effect on a defendant's ability to win on the merits regardless of anything that the defendant does in the case. An amendment that relates back under Rule 15(c) that would not relate back under state law can cause a defendant to lose a case on the merits that the defendant would otherwise have won, and no post-commencement behavior by the defendant can affect this possibility. Thus, as seen in Chapter 6, Rule 15(c) presents much greater Rules Enabling Act problems than does either Rule 11 or Rule 13(a).[183]

Potential conflicts can also exist between Rule 13(a) and state law when state law would permit the assertion of a counterclaim that Rule 13 does not allow to be joined or would preclude the assertion of a counterclaim that Rule 13 would permit. For example, assume that under a state counterclaim rule, a party may assert a "contingent" counterclaim that will not mature until after judgment

---

178. 498 U.S. 533, 111 S. Ct. 922, 112 L. Ed.2d 1140 (1991).

179. *See id.* at 553, 111 S. Ct. at 934, 112 L. Ed.2d at 1160.

180. *Id.* at 553, 111 S. Ct. at 934, 112 L. Ed.2d at 1160.

181. *See* Chapter 5(F)(5) *supra* (discussing *Business Guides*).

182. *See* Chapter 6(E)(2) *supra* (discussing Rule 11).

183. *See* Chapter 6(D)(5)*(d) supra* (discussing the Rules Enabling Act issues with Rule 15(c)).

is rendered on the opposing party's claim, while under Federal Rule 13 this may not be done.[184] As with the problem discussed above where the state has no compulsory counterclaim rule, it does not seem appropriate to view this as a real case of conflict, because the state practice is highly likely to be designed only to operate in the state's own courts.

Even if this hypothetical situation is viewed as a case of conflict between the state rule and Rule 13, however, Rule 13 can be validly applied. At worst, the counterclaim would have to be asserted in an independent action due to the limitations in Rule 13, while under state law it could be joined in the initial action. This kind of difference, while perhaps producing procedural inconvenience to a federal litigant, will not necessarily affect substantive rights at all, and if any effect on substantive rights does exist, that effect will surely be only "incidental." General policies of efficient judicial administration arguably also support the rule against nonjoinder of premature counterclaims and assure that Rule 13 is reasonably necessary to the uniform scheme of procedure that it was the purpose of Congress to establish when it enacted the Rules Enabling Act. Thus, the nonexistent or incidental effect of Rule 13(a) on substantive rights, when coupled with the efficiency concerns described, should validate the rule as applied to this situation.[185]

A situation in which state law prohibits joinder of a counterclaim that Rule 13 would permit is illustrated by *Com/Tech Communication Technologies, Inc. v. Wireless Data Systems, Inc.*[186] In *Com/Tech*, New York had established a summary procedure applicable to actions based upon instruments "for the payment of money only or upon any judgment." Under this procedure, the plaintiff could file an appropriate action and serve the defendant with a motion for summary judgment and supporting papers in lieu of a complaint, and the defendant could not assert counterclaims against the plaintiff in the action.[187] The plaintiff commenced such an action on four notes totalling $150,000 in New York state court, and the defendant removed the action to federal court. However, when the defendant attempted to assert counterclaims against the plaintiff in the federal action, the district judge refused to entertain the counterclaims on the grounds that they were inconsistent with the New York summary procedure. The Second Circuit Court of Appeals vacated the district court's judgment and remanded the case, holding that it had to be conducted in accord with the Federal Rules, including Rule 13, which would permit the assertion of counterclaims by the defendant. The Second Circuit stated that the New York statute in question was only a procedural rule, which did not govern in the federal courts.[188]

Although the court's analysis of the case was unrevealing, the result was entirely correct. As with the other issues discussed above, it appears that there was no real conflict between the state procedure and Rule 13, because the state

---

184. *See* section F(1)*(d) supra* (discussing this problem).

185. *See* Chapter 5(F)(4) *supra* (describing the *Burlington Northern* test for Federal Rule validity under the Rules Enabling Act).

186. 163 F.3d 149 (2d Cir. 1998).

187. *See id.* at 150.

188. *See id.* at 151.

procedure was probably designed to operate only in the courts of New York. Even if it was intended to operate in other courts, however, it is difficult to see how the application of Rule 13 could affect the substantive rights of the parties. At best, Rule 13 would allow adjudication of the defendant's counterclaims in the same action with the plaintiff's claims, while the state procedure would require the adjudication of the defendant's claims in a separate proceeding. Thus, it might impose procedural burdens on the plaintiff in federal court that would not exist in state court, but it is difficult to see how it would affect the outcome on the merits of either the plaintiff's claims or the defendant's counterclaims. Therefore, in the absence of any indication that the New York law itself was supported by substantive policies—for example, such as those involved in the state tort reform effort in the *Gasperini* case, discussed in Chapter 5(F)(5), above—there was no reason for Rule 13 to give way to the state procedure.

Chapter 8

JOINDER OF PARTIES

SECTION A. BASIC JOINDER OF PARTIES
RULES IN COMMON-LAW AND EQUITY ACTIONS

In modern procedural systems, rules on "real parties in interest" and "capacity to sue or be sued" govern who may sue as a plaintiff or be sued as a defendant. Rules on "permissive joinder of parties" and "joinder of persons needed for just adjudication" govern who may and must be joined with other parties in an action.[1] Like other modern procedural rules, these rules have antecedents in common law and equity practice. Typically, the common-law rules governing joinder tended to be rigid, while equity practice was more flexible. The more flexible equity practice provided the basis for modern codes and systems based on the Federal Rules of Civil Procedure.

1. Basic Joinder Rules in Common-Law Actions

The common law developed highly technical and restrictive rules governing joinder of parties.[2] In general, the plaintiff in a common-law action had to be a person who possessed the entire legal right or title involved in the action. Multiple plaintiffs each had to be equally entitled to the recovery before they could join in the suit. Multiple defendants had to be equally subject to a common liability. Even if it was possible to render a separate verdict against each defendant, a single judgment had to be rendered against all the defendants jointly. Otherwise, they could not be joined in the same action.[3]

2. Joinder of Parties in Equity

Compared to joinder rules in common-law actions, the joinder rules in equity cases were more flexible and reflected considerations of practical convenience to the parties. Two general principles governed equity proceedings. First, the real party in interest had to prosecute the suit, although other persons might join as plaintiffs if they had an interest in the subject matter or in obtaining the relief demanded. Second, all persons whose presence was necessary for a

---

1. *See, e.g.,* FED. R. CIV. P. 17, 19 & 20.

2. *See generally* ALEXANDER MARTIN, CIVIL PROCEDURE AT COMMON LAW §§ 181-225 (1904).

3. *See* JOHN N. POMEROY, CODE REMEDIES 77 (1904). The specific application of these common-law joinder rules differed depending upon whether the action was a personal action *ex contractu*, a personal action *ex delicto*, or a real action. *See* Chapter 1(E)(1)*(b)(i)-(iii) supra* (discussing these basic categories of common-law actions).

complete determination of the dispute had to be made parties to prevent a multiplicity of suits.[4]

Parties in equity were classified either as *necessary* (indispensable) or as *proper* (but not indispensable) parties. A person might be a necessary party either because the disposition of the lawsuit would affect the person's interests or because the person's absence might prevent final relief.[5]

Illustration 8-1. In a suit to rescind a contract between several persons, all parties to the contract were necessary parties to the action. A decree of rescission rendered against some, but not all, of the contracting parties would either destroy the absent persons' rights or leave the contract in effect as to the absentees and rescinded as to the parties joined in the action. If the decree would destroy the absentees' rights, the action would affect those rights without giving the absentees an opportunity to be heard. If the decree would leave the contract in effect as to the absentees and rescinded as to the parties to the action, complete relief—rescission as to all parties—would not be afforded to the parties joined in the action.[6]

* * * * *

In some situations, all persons who were necessary parties could not be brought before the court. For example, when it was impossible to obtain jurisdiction over the absent persons, the court would determine whether a decree could be rendered without harming the absent parties. If it could, the action would proceed without them.[7] Such persons were not technically necessary (or indispensable) parties at all. Instead, they were "proper" parties whose interests were deemed to be "separable."[8] For example, in a suit to foreclose a mortgage, persons with liens on the property subordinate to the mortgage would be considered proper, but not indispensable, parties.[9] Another type of proper party was a "formal" party—a person who had a general interest in the subject matter that could be settled conveniently in the suit, but who had no interest in the particular question being litigated. Formal parties did not have to be joined in an action, though they could be.[10]

Illustration 8-2. Assume that *B* mortgaged property to *C*. Subsequently, *C* assigned the debt and mortgage to *A*. If the debt was not paid and *A* sued the mortgagor to foreclose the mortgage, *C*, the mortgagee-assignor, did not have to be joined in the proceeding. By assigning the debt and mortgage, *C* divested *C's* interest absolutely and unconditionally. However, if *A* joined *C* in the action for some reason—for example, to obtain an admission in *C's* answer that the mortgage

---

4. *See generally* BENJAMIN SHIPMAN, HANDBOOK OF THE LAW OF EQUITY PLEADING 13-19 (1897).

5. A necessary party possessed an interest in the dispute of such a nature that the final decree could not be made without affecting that interest or leaving the suit in such a condition that it could not be settled equitably. *See id.* at 19-21.

6. *See id.* at 21-22.

7. *See id.* 24-25.

8. *See id.* at 36.

9. *Id.* at 40.

10. *See id.* 36, 37, n.3.

had been assigned—it would not be error. The mortgagee was a formal, proper party, but not a necessary (or indispensable) one.[11]

* * * * *

In both common-law and equity actions, all persons who had joint interests had to be joined in the suit. At common law, however, if a person possessed a joint interest with another and refused to join as a plaintiff, nothing could be done. In contrast, in equity, the party who refused to join as a plaintiff could be joined as a defendant.[12]

Illustration 8-3. Assume that *C* repeatedly trespassed on land that *A* and *B* owned as joint tenants. *A* wants to sue for an injunction to prevent *C's* trespasses. *B*, the other joint tenant, refuses to join as a plaintiff. Under these circumstances, *A* could bring the action. *B* would be joined as a defendant with the trespasser.

* * * * *

At common law, parties with separate interests had to sue separately. In equity, such persons could join as plaintiffs if they all had an interest in the suit and in obtaining the relief demanded.[13]

Illustration 8-4. Owners of separate parcels of property could join as plaintiffs in an equity action to abate a nuisance affecting their parcels. The parties had separate interests because of their separate ownership of the different parcels. However, all the parties had an interest in the action and in obtaining an abatement of the nuisance.[14]

* * * * *

Joinder of defendants in equity was based on similar standards. As at common law, all persons who had ''joint interests'' had to be joined as defendants. Such persons were ''necessary'' parties. In addition, any person who had an interest in the controversy or whose presence would enable the court to determine the dispute in its entirety could be made a defendant in equity.[15] This kind of joinder was in accord with the rules governing necessary and proper parties. An equity bill could be objectionable on grounds of *multifariousness* if one or more of the defendants had no interest in a matter involved in the suit.[16]

Illustration 8-5. Assume a lease contract stipulates that each of two tenants is liable for payment of only one-half of the rent. Two sureties join in the contract, each guaranteeing payment of only one tenant's portion of the rent. In such a case, joinder of the sureties in an action for the rent would be improper because each surety does not have an interest in the entire subject matter of the suit.[17]

Illustration 8-6. Assume that *A* sued to rescind contracts that *A* made with two defendants, *B* and *C*, on separate occasions. If each contract was

---

11. *See* Merrill v. Bischoff, 3 A.D. 361, 38 N.Y.S. 194 (1896).

12. *See* BENJAMIN SHIPMAN, HANDBOOK OF THE LAW OF EQUITY PLEADING 49-50 (1897).

13. *Id.* at 51.

14. *See id.* at 52.

15. *See id.* at 56.

16. *See id.* at 57.

17. *Id.* at 58, n.8.

induced by a separate and unrelated act of fraud, the bill would be multifarious. Neither of the defendants has any interest in the claim for rescission asserted against the other.[18]

SECTION B. BASIC PARTY JOINDER PROVISIONS OF THE CODES

The New York Field Code adopted the more flexible equity approach to joinder of parties. Section 91 provided that "[e]very action must be prosecuted in the name of the real party in interest, except as otherwise provided in [§] 93."[19] Section 93 stated that "[a]n executor or administrator, a trustee of an express trust, or a person expressly authorized by statute, may sue without joining with him the persons for whose benefit the suit is prosecuted."[20] In addition, § 97 of the Field Code provided that "[a]ll persons having an interest in the subject of the action, and in obtaining the relief demanded, may be joined as plaintiffs, except as otherwise provided in this title."[21] Section 98 stated that "[a]ny person may be made a party defendant, who has an interest in the controversy, adverse to the plaintiff."[22] Section 99 added that persons who were "united in interest must be joined as plaintiffs or defendants; but if the consent of any one, who should have been joined as plaintiff, cannot be obtained, [that person] may be made a defendant."[23] Finally, § 102 provided that "[w]hen a complete determination of the controversy cannot be had without the presence of other parties, the court may order them to be brought in, by an amendment of the complaint, or by a supplemental complaint, and a new summons."[24]

These changes removed many of the technical common-law restrictions on party joinder. For example, in a common-law action, an assignor was merely a nominal plaintiff. The assignee had to sue in the assignor's name to enforce the assignee's right of action, but the assignor was otherwise unimportant. When the codes merged law and equity, the substantive rights of the parties remained unchanged. The assignee still possessed the substantive right of action. However, the assignee now could sue in assignee's own name whether the assignee sought legal or equitable relief. Similarly, the equity rules on compulsory and permissive

---

18. *See* Woodruff v. Young, 43 Mich. 548, 6 N.W. 85 (1880).

19. Act of Apr. 12, 1848, ch. 379, § 91, 1848 N.Y. Laws 497, 515.

20. *Id.* § 93, 1848 N.Y. Laws 497, 515.

21. *Id.* § 97, 1848 N.Y. Laws 497, 516.

22. *Id.* § 98, 1848 N.Y. Laws 497, 516.

23. *Id.* § 99, 1848 N.Y. Laws 497, 516.

24. *Id.* § 102, 1848 N.Y. Laws 497, 516. The Commissioners explained the purpose of these party provisions as follows:

> The rules respecting parties in the courts of law, differ from those in courts of equity. The blending of the jurisdiction makes it necessary to revise these rules, to some extent. In doing so, we have had a three-fold purpose in view: first, to do away with artificial distinctions existing in the courts of law, and to require the real party in interest to appear in court as such[;] second, to require the presence of such parties as are necessary to make an end of the controversy[;] and third, to allow otherwise great latitude in respect to the number of parties who may be brought in.

First Report of the Commissioners on Practice and Pleadings of New York 123 (1848).

joinder applied to actions for legal or equitable relief under the codes, though the substantive rights of the parties remained the same.[25]

Some joinder problems remained, however. One problem concerned the ability to join parties in the alternative. Such alternative joinder had sometimes been permitted in equity, but not at common law. In the absence of a special statutory authorization, the courts often interpreted the codes to prohibit the joinder of defendants in the alternative. For example, assume that a complaint alleged that either one or the other of two defendants, but not both, was liable to the plaintiff. Such a complaint was considered defective because the plaintiff had to state facts which constituted a cause of action against each defendant.[26] Thus, unless the plaintiff could allege a joint liability, the plaintiff had to sue the defendants separately. Separate suits produced a wasteful duplication of proceedings and a danger of losing both actions.[27]

Illustration 8-7. Assume that *A* was injured by the tortious behavior of *B* or *C*, but *A* did not know which one was responsible. It would be convenient to join both *B* and *C* in *A's* action, alleging their liability in the alternative. However, unless specially permitted by statute, courts often prohibited such joinder under the codes.[28]

* * * * *

Another joinder problem was produced by the requirement that all persons joined as plaintiffs had to have an interest in the subject of the action "*and*" in obtaining the relief demanded.[29] The use of the word "and" led some courts to restrict joinder of plaintiffs to situations in which each plaintiff was interested in *all* of the relief demanded. This interpretation contradicted the intent of the Field Code drafters, whose stated purpose was to employ equitable principles of joinder in the new statutes.[30] This restrictive interpretation disallowed joinder of parties who were interested in the same subject matter, but who did not benefit from all the relief demanded.

Illustration 8-8. Assume that an insurance policy designated *A* and *B* as beneficiaries. If each were to receive a separate amount under the policy, *A* and *B* might not be permitted to join as plaintiffs in a suit to recover the policy proceeds.[31] Some courts, however, "realizing that a multiplicity of suits may be avoided without inconvenience at trial or prejudice to the defendant, . . . allowed joinder in this situation, stressing that a lump sum recovery [was] sought."[32]

* * * * *

---

25. *See* CHARLES E. CLARK, HANDBOOK OF THE LAW OF CODE PLEADING § 22, at 161 (2d ed. 1947).

26. Both defendants could admit the allegations and "still the court could not order judgment on the pleadings against either defendant." Casey Pure Milk Co. v. Booth Fisheries Co., 124 Minn. 117, 118, 144 N.W. 450, 451 (1913).

27. *See* CHARLES E. CLARK, HANDBOOK OF THE LAW OF CODE PLEADING § 62, at 393-96 (2d ed. 1947).

28. *See* Casey Pure Milk Co. v. Booth Fisheries Co., 124 Minn. 117, 144 N.W. 450 (1913); CHARLES E. CLARK, HANDBOOK OF THE LAW OF CODE PLEADING § 62, at 393-94 (2d ed. 1947).

29. *See* Act of Apr. 12, 1848, ch. 379, § 97, 1848 N.Y. Laws 497, 516; *see also* NEB. REV. STAT. § 25-311 (1995).

30. FIRST REPORT OF THE COMMISSIONERS ON PRACTICE AND PLEADING OF NEW YORK 123-24 (1848).

31. *See* Keary v. Mutual Reserve Fund Life Ass'n, 30 F. 359 (C.C.E.D. Mo. 1887).

32. CHARLES E. CLARK, HANDBOOK OF THE LAW OF CODE PLEADING § 57, at 366 (2d ed. 1947).

Even after statutes liberalized the party joinder rules in some states, the interaction between the party joinder and claim joinder provisions produced a serious joinder problem. The claim joinder provisions did not distinguish between single and multiple party cases. The courts should have interpreted the liberalized party joinder provisions as overriding the claim joinder sections in multiple party situations, but they did not always do so. When both sets of joinder requirements had to be satisfied, the liberal party joinder sections had no practical effect.[33]

Illustration 8-9. At one time, § 211 of the New York Civil Practice Act provided that "[a]ll persons may be joined as defendants against whom the right to any relief is alleged to exist, whether jointly, severally or in the alternative; and judgment may be given against such one or more of the defendants as may be found to be liable, according to their respective liabilities."[34] In addition, § 212 of the Civil Practice Act stated that "[i]t shall not be necessary that each defendant shall be interested as to all the relief prayed for, or as to every cause of action included in any proceeding against him."[35] However, § 258(9) (the joinder of claims section of the New York Civil Practice Act) provided that the plaintiff might unite in a single complaint two or more causes of action when they were brought to recover "[u]pon claims arising out of the same transaction, or transactions connected with the same subject of action . . . ."[36] In *Ader v. Blau,*[37] the plaintiff sued two defendants for the wrongful death of a child. The plaintiff alleged that one of the defendants negligently maintained a picket fence that caused the death of the child. The plaintiff alleged in the alternative that the other defendant, a doctor, negligently treated the child, which caused the child's death. The New York Court of Appeals held that even if the party joinder provisions, standing alone, would permit joinder of the defendants, the claims joinder section prohibited the joinder because the causes of action asserted against the defendants did not arise out of the same transaction or transactions connected with the same subject of action.[38]

SECTION C. BASIC PARTY JOINDER PROVISIONS OF THE FEDERAL RULES

The basic party joinder provisions of the Federal Rules of Civil Procedure are found in Rule 17 (real party in interest and capacity to sue and be sued), Rule 19 (joinder of persons needed for just adjudication), and Rule 20 (permissive joinder of parties). Generally, the Federal Rules adopted the best features of party joinder under the codes, while avoiding the difficulties experienced under the code provisions.

---

33. *See id.* at 438-39.
34. *See* Ader v. Blau, 241 N.Y. 7, 13, 148 N.E. 771, 772 (1925).
35. *See id.*
36. *See id.* at 14, 148 N.E. at 773.
37. 241 N.Y. 7, 148 N.E. 771 (1925).
38. *See id.* at 16-21, 148 N.E. at 774-75.

1. Real Party in Interest

(a) In General

Federal Rule 17(a) requires that actions be prosecuted in the name of the real party in interest.[39] This rule was derived from former Equity Rule 37. The equity rule, in turn, was derived from real-party-in-interest provisions under the codes. Before 1966, Rule 17(a) stated:

> Every action shall be prosecuted in the name of the real party in interest; *but* an executor, administrator, guardian, trustee of an express trust, a party with whom or in whose name a contract has been made for the benefit of another, or a party authorized by statute may sue in his own name without joining with him the party for whose benefit the action is brought . . . .[40]

The use of the word "but" in original Rule 17(a) to introduce the enumeration of specific instances gave rise to the interpretation that the specific instances were exceptions to the basic real-party-in-interest rule. In 1966, Rule 17(a) was amended to clarify that the specific instances set forth in the text of the rule were not exceptions to, but illustrations of, the rule.[41] The last sentence of Rule 17(a) provides that an action may not be dismissed on the ground that it is not prosecuted in the name of the real party in interest until a reasonable time has been allowed after objection to cure the defect. This sentence was also added in 1966 to insure that an honest mistake in choosing the real party in interest will not result in dismissal of the action until a reasonable time has been given to correct the mistake.

Illustration 8-10. If *A Insurance Co.* pays its insured, *B*, for a loss in full, the substantive law of most states provides that *A* becomes subrogated to *B's* claim. *A* is the party that has the right to bring and control the action. If *A* mistakenly files suit in *B's* name and then seeks to correct its mistake by amendment, the court should permit *A* to do so under the last sentence of Rule 17(a).[42]

* * * * *

The real-party-in-interest rule has come under vigorous criticism in recent years.[43] It has been persuasively argued that Federal Rule 17(a) should be

---

39. FED. R. CIV. P. 17(a).

40. 308 U.S. 645, 685 (1937) (emphasis added).

41. *See* FED. R. CIV. P. 17(a) advisory committee's note to the 1966 amendment.

42. *See* Link Aviation, Inc. v. Downs, 325 F.2d 613 (D.C. Cir. 1963); *see also* Krueger v. Cartwright, 996 F.2d 928, 931-32 (7th Cir. 1993) (insurance company that pays entire claim is real party in interest; when insurance company pays part of claim, it is only partly subrogated and both insured and company own part of the claim); IHP Indus., Inc. v. PermAlert, ESP, 178 F.R.D. 483 (S.D. Miss. 1997) (insurer is real party in interest when insured gives its right to recover damages to insurer, but retains right to share in any recovery by the insurer).

43. An analysis and criticism of this rule appears in the excellent article by Professor June F. Entman, *More Reasons for Abolishing Federal Rule of Civil Procedure 17(a): The Problem of the Proper Plaintiff and Insurance Subrogation*, 68 N.C. L. REV. 893 (1990); *see also* Thomas E. Atkinson, *The Real Party in Interest Rule: A Plea for Its Abolition*, 32 N.Y.U. L. REV. 926 (1957); John E. Kennedy, *Federal Rule 17(a): Will the Real Party in Interest Please Stand?* 51 MINN. L. REV. 675 (1967); Lewis M. Simes, *The Real Party in Interest*, 10 KY. L.J. 60 (1922).

abolished because other procedural devices are available to resolve the issues that arise under that rule.[44] Specifically, a motion to dismiss for failure to state a claim upon which relief can be granted under Rule 12(b)(6), a motion to join a party needed for just adjudication under Rule 19(a), or a motion to dismiss for failure to join an indispensable party under Rule 12(b)(7)[45] can be used to deal with all situations in which proper plaintiff issues are present in an action.[46] Indeed, although proper application of Rule 17(a) "produces results that are consistent with principles of diversity jurisdiction,"[47] manipulation of Rule 17(a) or confusion produced by its overlap with other rules can result in evasion of jurisdictional requirements.

Illustration 8-11. In *Virginia Electric & Power Co. v. Westinghouse Electric Corp.*,[48] an insurance company paid all but $150,000 of a $2,200,000 loss. The insured brought a diversity action on its own behalf and to recover for the amount paid by the insurer. The insurer provided counsel and had exclusive control over the action. No diversity of citizenship existed between the insurance company and the defendant. The Fourth Circuit held that both Rule 17(a) and Rule 19 were satisfied because the action was brought in the name of the insured. However, with regard to subject-matter jurisdiction, the traditional rule is that it is the citizenship of the real party in interest that counts in determining diversity. In *Virginia Electric*, the court did not consider whether the application of this principle should have required that the citizenship of the company be taken into account in determining whether jurisdiction existed.[49]

* * * * *

To avoid misapplication of Rule 17(a) to jurisdictional and other questions, the proper inquiry under the rule is whether the named plaintiff is the person upon whom the applicable substantive law confers the right to bring and control an action.[50] If so, the named plaintiff is the real party in interest. If not, the named plaintiff is not the real party in interest. This issue is not necessarily

---

44. *See generally* June F. Entman, *More Reasons for Abolishing Federal Rule of Civil Procedure 17(a): The Problem of the Proper Plaintiff and Insurance Subrogation*, 68 N.C. L. REV. 893 (1990).

45. Rule 19 objections are discussed in section C(3) of this chapter *infra*.

46. *See* June F. Entman, *More Reasons for Abolishing Federal Rule of Civil Procedure 17(a): The Problem of the Proper Plaintiff and Insurance Subrogation*, 68 N.C. L. REV. 893, 895-96 (1990).

47. *Id.* at 947.

48. 485 F.2d 78 (4th Cir. 1973), *cert. denied*, 415 U.S. 935, 94 S. Ct. 1450, 39 L. Ed. 2d 493 (1974). The *Virginia Electric* case is discussed in June F. Entman, *More Reasons for Abolishing Federal Rule of Civil Procedure 17(a): The Problem of the Proper Plaintiff and Insurance Subrogation*, 68 N.C. L. REV. 893, 947-48 (1990).

49. As Professor Entman states:

   [A] misapplication of Rule 17(a) allowed the litigation in federal court of a . . . claim between nondiverse parties on the basis of the citizenship of a merely nominal representative. This was a complete abrogation of principles of diversity jurisdiction . . . which might not have occurred if there were no Rule 17(a). Without the real party in interest rule, the court might have been forced to respond to the defendant's assertion that the insurer's interest defeated diversity by proceeding directly to the jurisdictional policies that ought to have governed.

See June F. Entman, *More Reasons for Abolishing Federal Rule of Civil Procedure 17(a): The Problem of the Proper Plaintiff and Insurance Subrogation*, 68 N.C. L. REV. 893, 948 (1990) (footnotes omitted).

50. *See id.* at 923-25.

resolved in federal diversity actions by state statutes that give one person, such as an insurer, the right to sue in the name of another, such as an insured. Such provisions are usually considered "procedural" and do not really address the question of who has the right to bring and control an action.[51] Nevertheless, state statutory provisions like these may complicate a federal court's task.[52]

The rule that an action should be brought in the name of the real party in interest should be distinguished from rules governing "standing" and "capacity to sue" (discussed below). A "real party in interest" is the person to whom the substantive law gives the right to bring and control the action.[53] "Standing" is a concept in the area of public law that serves a function similar to the real-party-in-interest requirement. When a person challenges governmental action on constitutional or other grounds, the doctrine of standing is used to determine the proper party to raise the challenge. Standing resembles real party in interest to the extent that standing requires a person challenging government action to be injured by that action. However, standing is a much broader concept than real party in interest. The standing requirement is an element of the "case or controversy" requirement of Article III of the Constitution and thus acts as a limitation on federal subject-matter jurisdiction. In addition to this constitutionally compelled component of the standing doctrine, which differs little, if at all, from the real-party-in-interest requirement, the Supreme Court has developed certain discretionary rules of standing to ensure that its exercise of the power of judicial review will be confined to proper cases. The result of these developments is that standing has become a complicated specialty of federal jurisdiction, whose examination is reserved for treatises on Administrative Law, Constitutional Law, and Federal Courts.[54]

---

51. *See* subsection (c) *infra* (discussing the Rules Enabling Act issues raised by the interaction of provisions like these with Rule 17(a)).

52.   [B]ecause of these provisions, it may be difficult to find state law decisions addressing the substantive rights of the insured and insurer to sue a third party. Insurers permitted to sue in the name of their insureds will do so; thus, there may be no decisions analyzing whether an insurer may enforce its claim directly against the third party. Similarly, unless some conflict between insured and insurer has been litigated, there might be no decisions discussing whether the insured may enforce the entire claim.

June F. Entman, *More Reasons for Abolishing Federal Rule of Civil Procedure 17(a): The Problem of the Proper Plaintiff and Insurance Subrogation*, 68 N.C. L. REV. 893, 923 (1990) (footnotes omitted). Because Rule 17(a) requires every action to be prosecuted in the name of the real party in interest, the rule might seem to prohibit suit by the plaintiff in a fictitious name. However, federal courts allow "John Doe" suits when necessary to protect plaintiffs from serious harm. *See* Doe v. Blue Cross & Blue Shield United, 112 F.3d 869 (7th Cir. 1997) (fictitious names are allowed when necessary to protect privacy of children, rape victims, and other potentially vulnerable parties, but not simply when a case involves a medical issue); *cf.* K.F.P. v. Dane County, 110 F.3d 516 (7th Cir. 1997) (plaintiff permitted to name Doe defendants because she was at a disadvantage in obtaining information about identity; however, when plaintiff failed to isolate the individuals who were liable, summary judgment granted for defendants). *See generally* Carol M. Rice, *Meet John Doe: It Is Time for Federal Civil Procedure to Recognize John Doe Parties*, 52 U. PITT. L. REV. 883 (1996).

53. *See* Lewis M. Simes, *The Real Party in Interest*, 10 KY. L.J. 60, 61 (1922).

54. *See generally* 6A CHARLES A. WRIGHT ET AL., FEDERAL PRACTICE AND PROCEDURE: CIVIL § 1542, at 329-33 (2d ed. 1990).

(b) Subject-Matter Jurisdiction Problems in Administering Rule 17(a)

As observed in *Illustration 8-11* in the preceding subsection, Rule 17(a) sometimes obscures important subject-matter jurisdiction issues. In addition, it should be remembered that federal subject-matter jurisdiction in diversity actions can be affected by 28 U.S.C. § 1332(c)(2), discussed in Chapter 2.[55] For example, even though the representative of the estate of a decedent is the real party in interest, the citizenship of the decedent will be attributed to the representative for purposes of determining whether diversity jurisdiction exists. Also, when an assignee brings suit, 28 U.S.C. § 1359 must be taken into account in determining whether diversity of citizenship has been ''improperly'' or ''collusively'' created by the assignment.[56] In other words, even though the assignee may be the owner of the substantive right in question and, therefore, the real party in interest, a federal court may dismiss the action for lack of diversity jurisdiction if the assignment creates diversity in violation of the prohibition of § 1359.

(c) Rules Enabling Act Problems in Administering Rule 17(a)

Rules Enabling Act issues can arise in administering Rule 17(a) if state law provides that the real party in interest can bring an action in the name of someone else.[57] These problems are sometimes dealt with by the observation that, under the circumstances described, ''the federal court will allow the claim to be asserted by plaintiff since [the plaintiff] has a right under state law, which makes [the plaintiff] the real party in interest for purposes of Rule 17(a),'' and ''the question of in whose name the action should be brought is a procedural one and should be governed by the federal rules.''[58] This seems correct.

For example, suppose under state law that an insurer has become completely subrogated to the claim of an insured against the defendant, but that a state statute allows the insurer to bring the action in the name of the insured. In Chapter 7,[59] a similar problem was discussed concerning joinder of claims *against* insurers, where state law prohibited the joinder of such claims prior to obtaining a judgment against an insured and Rule 18 on its face allowed such joinder. Even in the face of such statutes, it was argued that Rule 18 could be validly applied, and the problem here is much simpler to resolve. There is only one conceivable purpose in allowing an insurer who is the real party in interest to sue in the name of an insured. That purpose is to prevent litigational prejudice

---

55. *See* Chapter 2(C)(3)*(f) supra* (discussing § 1332(c)(2)).

56. *See id.* (discussing § 1359).

57. *See* 6A CHARLES A. WRIGHT ET AL., FEDERAL PRACTICE AND PROCEDURE: CIVIL § 1544, at 345 (2d ed. 1990).

58. *See id.*

59. *See* Chapter 7(C)(3) *supra* (discussing Rules Enabling Act problems with joinder of claims under Rule 18).

that might occur to the insurer in the form of jury bias. The prejudice is avoided under the state law by making it appear that the action is brought by an individual rather than an insurance company. However, this objective is arguably a purely procedural one, because it focuses on the fairness and accuracy of the litigational process. Therefore, for two reasons, Rule 17 can be enforced without fear that any substantive rights of the insurer will be abridged. First, the state law in question neither embodies any "substantive" rights nor is supported by any substantive policies, and thus applying Rule 17(a) instead of the state law will not impinge on anything substantive contained in the state statute itself. However, in Chapter 7, it was also observed that substantive rights could be impacted in the Rule 18 joinder situation if the insurer lost a case on the merits that it would otherwise win by virtue of a federal court's disregard of state procedural law. Nevertheless, to the extent that the federal courts apply their own measures for protecting against biased jury determinations rather than the measures provided for in state law, the ultimate substantive rights of the insured on the merits of the case will arguably be fully protected. Thus, it cannot be said that the application of Rule 17(a) will affect those ultimate substantive rights more than "incidentally," if at all.[60]

2. Capacity to Sue and Be Sued

(a) In General

"Capacity" rules determine the ability of persons to sue and be sued. For example, a person may possess the right to be enforced in the action and may be injured sufficiently and otherwise qualified to possess standing to sue, but may lack the "capacity to sue" because of age, mental deficiency, or other impediments. The capacity requirement extends to both plaintiffs and defendants, unlike the real-party-in-interest rule, which restricts only plaintiffs.

Federal Rule 17(b) provides the basic standards for determining capacity to sue or be sued in federal court. The rule is unusual because it provides a federal-level, choice-of-law standard for determining capacity in several situations. The first sentence of the rule provides that the capacity of an individual not acting in a representative capacity shall be determined by the law of the individual's domicile. The second sentence provides that the capacity of a corporation shall be determined by the law under which it was organized. The third sentence of the rule states that in all other cases, capacity to sue or be sued shall be determined by the law of the state in which the district court is sitting. However, a partnership or unincorporated association that has no capacity to sue or be sued under the law of the state where the district court is sitting may sue or be sued in its common name when a federal substantive right is being enforced by or

---

60. *See* Chapter 5(F)(4) *supra* (discussing the *Burlington Northern* test for rule validity under the Enabling Act, which includes a determination of whether a Federal Rule impacts more than "incidentally" on state substantive rights).

against it. The third sentence also provides that federal law governs the capacity of a federal receiver.

Illustration 8-12. *R Corp.* is a bank incorporated in and has its principal place of business in State *X,* under which it has the capacity to sue. *R* is appointed the representative of *A's* estate. (*A* had been a citizen of State *X.*) *R* sues *B,* a citizen of State *Y,* in a U.S. District Court in State *Y* to recover $500,000 in damages for the wrongful death of *A.* Under the law of State *Y, R* does not have the capacity to sue. Rule 17 states that the capacity of a corporation to sue shall be determined by the law under which it is organized. However, Rule 17 also provides that the capacity of a representative to sue shall be determined by the law of the state in which the district court is held. Thus, Rule 17 appears to contain conflicting provisions about *R's* capacity to sue in this situation. Because there appears to be no reason to treat corporate representatives differently from individual representatives under Rule 17, this conflict should be resolved by applying the provisions governing representatives.[61] Thus, *R* will lack the capacity to sue *B* in State *Y* based on the law of State *Y,* where the district court is sitting.

* * * * *

Rule 17(c) outlines special rules governing the capacity of infants and incompetent persons to sue or be sued. If an infant or incompetent person has a representative, the representative may sue or defend on behalf of the infant or incompetent person. If the infant or incompetent person has no appointed representative, the second sentence of Rule 17(c) provides that the action may be brought by the infant or incompetent's next friend or by a guardian ad litem–a guardian appointed by the court for purposes of the suit. The third sentence of Rule 17(c) expressly authorizes the court to appoint a guardian ad litem or take any other action the court deems proper to protect an infant or incompetent person.

Illustration 8-13. *A* is an infant who is a citizen of State *X. A* was injured in an automobile accident with *B,* a citizen of State *Y. R,* a citizen of State *X,* is appointed to represent *A* in an action for personal injuries against *B. R* has capacity to sue under the law of State *X,* but not under the law of State *Y.* Rule 17(b) provides that the capacity of a representative shall be determined by the law of the state in which the district court is held. Rule 17(c) appears to state that the representative of an infant shall be able to sue for the infant in federal court. If *R* sues *B* on *A's* behalf in a U.S. District Court in State *Y,* there would be an apparent conflict between Rules 17(b) and (c). This conflict should be resolved by applying the capacity provisions of Rule 17(b). There is no apparent reason to allow the appointment of a representative for an infant who does not have capacity to sue under the relevant law designated by Rule 17(b).[62]

---

61. *See* 6A CHARLES A. WRIGHT ET AL., FEDERAL PRACTICE AND PROCEDURE: CIVIL § 1561, at 451 (2d ed. 1990).

62. *See* 6A CHARLES A. WRIGHT ET AL., FEDERAL PRACTICE AND PROCEDURE: CIVIL § 1571, at 510 (2d ed. 1990).

(b) Subject-Matter Jurisdiction Problems
in Administering Rule 17(b)

As noted in section C(1)*(a)*, above, the citizenship of the real party in interest is what counts in determining whether diversity jurisdiction exists.[63] When infants or incompetents do not have the capacity to sue, a representative must sue for them. In such circumstances, the substantive law gives the representative the right to bring the action, and the representative is the real party in interest. Prior to the enactment of § 1332(c)(2), this meant it was the citizenship of the representative that mattered in determining diversity, at least in the absence of any issue about whether the representative was "improperly" or "collusively" appointed to create diversity in contravention of 28 U.S.C. § 1359.[64] However, as observed above,[65] after the enactment of § 1332(c)(2), the citizenship of the infant or incompetent is attributed to the representative for purposes of determining diversity, which also eliminates any issues under § 1359. Nevertheless, one question that remains after the enactment of § 1332(c)(2) is whether the representative of an incompetent has the power to change the citizenship of the incompetent in a way that creates diversity of citizenship that would not otherwise exist.

In *Rishell v. Jane Phillips Episcopal Memorial Medical Center,*[66] the Tenth Circuit held that, under appropriate circumstances, the representative of a mentally incompetent person could, indeed, change the incompetent's domicile in a way that would create diversity jurisdiction. In *Rishell,* Ms. Lacey was hospitalized in the defendant institution when she attempted to commit suicide. As a consequence of the attempted suicide, she existed thereafter in a permanent vegetative state and was unable to make even basic life decisions for herself. Her domicile at the time she became incompetent was Oklahoma. She was then moved to Louisiana. In a court proceeding there, her brother-in-law was appointed as her guardian. Subsequently, the guardian commenced an action against the defendant in an Oklahoma federal court to recover damages from the defendant for negligence in allowing Ms. Lacey to receive the injuries leading to her incompetence. The defendant moved to dismiss on the ground of lack of jurisdiction. The defendant argued that Ms. Lacey was still domiciled in Oklahoma and, therefore, diversity of citizenship did not exist between the parties. The guardian contended that Ms. Lacey's domicile had been changed to Louisiana because she was under the jurisdiction of a Louisiana court and because the guardian and Ms. Lacey's husband, who was a kind of "co-guardian" (called an undercurator under Louisiana law), both intended Louisiana to be her permanent home.

---

63. *See also, e.g.,* Certain Interested Underwriters at Lloyd's London, England v. Layne, 26 F.3d 39 (6th Cir. 1994).

64. *See* Chapter 2(C)(3)*(f) supra* (discussing §§ 1332(c)(2) & 1359).

65. *See* section C(1)*(b), supra.*

66. 12 F.3d 171 (10th Cir. 1993).

The district court dismissed the action for lack of jurisdiction, and the plaintiff appealed.[67] The Tenth Circuit reversed, holding that, under appropriate circumstances, the domicile of an incompetent could be change by the incompetent's guardian:

> If the best evidence available shows the incompetent likely will never be restored to reason, the law must allow another, vested with legal authority, to determine domicile for the best interests of that person. To prohibit such determinations is to leave the incompetent in a never-ending limbo where the presumption against changing domicile becomes more important than the interests of the person the presumption was designed to protect.
>
> This case presents a situation ripe for consideration of that principle. Plaintiff alleges Ms. Lacey's present condition is permanent, which defendant apparently concedes. It is the expressed intent of both her husband and brother-in-law that Ms. Lacey's current hospitalization be permanent and that Ms. Lacey remain in Louisiana so she may obtain benefits from that state. Nothing in the record suggests that Ms. Lacey will ever return to Oklahoma, nor has defendant produced any evidence implying Ms. Lacey was moved to Louisiana simply to create diversity of citizenship.[68]

However, the Tenth Circuit remanded for a full evidentiary hearing in which it directed the district court to examine whether Ms. Lacey's domicile was changed in her best interests.[69]

In *Long v. Sasser,*[70] the Fourth Circuit rejected the holding in *Rishell.* The Fourth Circuit concluded that if the incompetent does not possess the capacity to effectuate a change of domicile, domicile remains the same for purposes of diversity jurisdiction regardless of where the guardian may move the incompetent:

> Jurisdictional rules should above all be clear. They are meant to guide parties to their proper forums with a minimum of fuss. While close cases may arise . . . regarding whether the ward possessed the necessary capacity to effect a change of domicile, *Rishell* requires a more speculative inquiry as to whether the

---

67. After the dismissal, the plaintiff applied for an order from the Louisiana court that Ms. Lacey was domiciled there and received the order. The plaintiff then moved for reconsideration on the basis of the order, but the district court refused to take it into account. *See* 12 F.3d at 172.

68. *Id.* at 174.

69. *See id.* at 174. The court also directed the district court to determine whether Ms. Lacey's domicile was changed by operation of the Louisiana Code when the guardian was appointed for her by the Louisiana court. This ruling seems clearly wrong. As the court recognized earlier in its opinion, the question of domicile for purposes of diversity is controlled by federal principles, *see id.* at 172-73, and it is inconsistent to allow the issue to be controlled absolutely by operation of state law. Such an approach would give the persons in control of the incompetent a weapon with which to create diversity illegitimately simply by obtaining a state-court order.

70. 91 F.3d 645 (4th Cir. 1996).

ward will remain incompetent in the future, as well as inviting litigation over the "best interests" of the ward. . . .

Inquiring whether the "best interests" of the ward are served by a guardian's attempt to effect a change in domicile to secure a federal forum strikes us as singularly unproductive. . . . We note, for example, that this case does not raise the primary concern addressed by diversity jurisdiction—fear of local bias against litigants from out of state. This is essentially a local dispute . . . .[71]

Of the two cases, *Long* is the more persuasive. Even if it is necessary for a guardian to change the residence of an incompetent person for purposes of care and medical treatment, there is no reason to allow the change of residence, even if permanent, to affect the determination of domicile for purposes of diversity jurisdiction. No apparent policy of the jurisdictional grant will be served by doing so in cases like *Rishell* and *Long*. Furthermore, as observed in the latter case, the *Rishell* inquiry will simply complicate the jurisdictional question unnecessarily.[72]

The *Rishell-Long* problem is not limited to incompetents. Section 1332(c)(2) also attributes the citizenship of an infant to the "legal representative" of the infant. However, the problem of determining the domicile of an infant will usually be easier to solve than that of an incompetent. Ordinarily, a child's domicile is the domicile of the parent with whom the child lives.[73] As a result, the child's domicile can be changed by the custodial parent, but this change can only be done by the parent changing his or her own domicile. The inquiry therefore will focus on the intent of the parent to make a new state a permanent home, and this inquiry is no more complicated than the one involved in any ordinary diversity action involving an issue of the domicile of a competent, adult individual. More complicated problems of determining the domicile of a child will only occur when the child does not live with the person who is the child's guardian.[74] These kinds of cases can present problems similar to those in *Rishell* and *Long* and should probably be handled in the same manner—*i.e.,* the guardian should not be allowed to change the domicile of the child for purposes of the diversity jurisdiction by moving the child's residence.

---

71. *Id.* at 647-48.

72. *See also* McEachron v. Glans, 983 F. Supp. 330 (N.D.N.Y. 1997), in which the court agreed with *Rishell* that a guardian could change the domicile of an incompetent in the best interests of the incompetent. However, on the facts of the case, the incompetent had been transferred to an institution in another state and was undergoing short-term therapy to determine the best long-term treatment that he should receive. When the long-term therapy issue was resolved, the incompetent might be transferred to an institution in another state. Therefore, the court concluded that the requisite permanent intent to establish a new domicile was not present.

73. *See* RESTATEMENT (SECOND) OF CONFLICT OF LAWS § 22 (1971). The issue should be resolved in the same way when the child's parents are dead or the child is otherwise in the custody of someone else standing *in loco parentis*, such as a grandparent. *See id.* cmt. i.

74. *Cf. id.* cmt. h (discussing the problems of changing a child's domicile when the child does not live with the guardian).

(c) *Rules Enabling Act Problems in the Administration of Rule 17(b)*

Rules Enabling Act problems potentially exist with Rule 17(b) because it is an independent federal conflict-of-laws rule that may differ from the conflict-of-laws rule governing capacity in the courts of the forum state. The most general problem is whether it is legitimate for the Supreme Court to create a conflict-of-laws rule under the Enabling Act to govern any kind of issue. There may have been a time when conflicts issues were regarded as "procedural" in nature, but surely that view is outmoded today. Modern conflict-of-laws systems focus on the policies and purposes of the laws of the concerned states and the contacts of those states with the parties and the events giving rise to suit.[75] To the extent that a state's conflict-of-laws approach involves policy determinations of significance to a state that transcend actions in the courts of the state, it is questionable whether it is wise for the Supreme Court to override those considerations with Federal Rules of Civil Procedure, even if the particular issue in question can be characterized as "procedural" in some sense.

Focusing particularly on the issue of capacity to sue, the issue under the Rules Enabling Act today is whether the application of Rule 17(b) can ever impact on state substantive rights more than incidentally and whether the rule is reasonably necessary to the uniform scheme of procedure it was the intent of Congress to establish under the Act.[76] As discussed earlier, a Federal Rule may impact on state "substantive" rights in two ways.[77] First, the rule may conflict with a state law that is configured as a procedural rule, but which is supported by discernable "substantive" policies–*i.e.,* policies that do not concern the efficiency or accuracy of the litigational process, but are aimed at achieving purposes outside that process or affecting the primary (nonlitigational) behavior of parties. Second, even if a Federal Rule of Civil Procedure does not conflict with a state rule supported by specific substantive policies, the Federal Rule may impact substantive rights in a broader sense by affecting the outcome of the case. (Although the Supreme Court made it clear in the *Hanna* case that Rules Enabling Act issues are not to be resolved under the general *Erie* outcome determinative test evolved under the Rules of Decision Act, the Court also indicated that the extent to which a Federal Rule of Civil Procedure affects the outcome of the case may be relevant to its validity under the Enabling Act.[78]) Because the Court has not indicated which of these kinds of impacts on

---

75. *See, e.g.,* RESTATEMENT (SECOND) OF CONFLICT OF LAWS § 6 (1971); LUTHER L. MCDOUGAL III ET AL., AMERICAN CONFLICTS LAW ch. 10 (5th ed. 2000) (describing traditional and modern conflicts theories); RUSSELL J. WEINTRAUB, COMMENTARY ON THE CONFLICT OF LAWS § 1.5 (3d ed. 1986) (describing a number of modern conflicts theories).

76. This inquiry is the one now demanded by the *Burlington Northern* case examined in Chapter 5(F)(4), *supra.*

77. *See* Chapter 5(F)(5) *supra* (discussing the *Business Guides* case; Chapter 6(D)(5)*(d) supra* (discussing Rules Enabling Act problems with Federal Rule 15(c); Chapter 7(C)(3) *supra* (discussing Rules Enabling Act problems with joinder under Federal Rule 18); section (C)(1)*(c) supra* (discussing Rules Enabling Act problems under Rule 17(a)).

78. *See* Chapter 5(F)(3) *supra* (discussing the *Hanna* case).

substantive rights is relevant under the Rules Enabling Act, it is necessary to examine Rule 17(b) under both kinds of impacts.

When Rule 17(b) conflicts with a capacity rule of the forum state, it will often be difficult to determine whether the state rule is supported by substantive or only procedural policies. For example, Rule 17(b) provides that the capacity of an individual not acting in a representative capacity is determined by the law of the individual's domicile. Thus, if the individual possesses capacity under the law of that individual's domicile, but lacks capacity under the law of the forum state, a potential conflict exists. As a general matter, rules of capacity are aimed at protecting the parties and the court system in the conduct of litigation. When the capacity of a plaintiff is at issue, a state has an interest in assuring that the plaintiff has the ability to participate in and conduct litigation in a prudent and efficient fashion so as not to lose rights the plaintiff validly possesses through poor judgment or to burden the court system with unwarranted litigation. Rules governing plaintiffs' capacity may also be designed to protect the defendant by assuring that the plaintiff can make prudent decisions about whether to litigate at all as well as decisions about the conduct of the litigation, such as whether to accept reasonable settlement offers, etc. Rules governing defendants' capacity may serve similar purposes, but will surely also be designed to assure that the defendant has sufficient maturity and mental capacity to protect the defendant's rights in the litigation. These policies seem to be a mixture of efficiency concerns and more serious party-protection goals that might legitimately be characterized as "substantive" in nature.

Thus, if a plaintiff is entitled to sue under the law of the plaintiff's domicile, but would, because of age, be considered an infant not entitled to sue under forum law, there could be an impact on a state substantive "right" in the first sense discussed above if the state rule is identified as being supported by plaintiff-protection or defendant-protection policies, as opposed to only litigational efficiency policies. Nevertheless, it is arguable that Rule 17(b) can be validly applied because a federal diversity court can take other procedural steps to protect parties other than disqualifying the plaintiff from suing (or requiring the plaintiff to sue by representation, as would probably be permitted under state law). For this reason, Rule 17(b) might be said to only "incidentally" affect state substantive rights, if it affects them at all.

A more serious question about the validity of Rule 17(b) may be whether the rule is reasonably necessary to the uniform scheme of procedure it was the intent of Congress to establish under the Rules Enabling Act. An inquiry into the reasonable necessity of the rule to the uniform scheme of rules is theoretically necessary any time a conflict is identified between Rule 17(b) and a forum's "substantively based" capacity rule of the sort discussed above, even if the impact of Rule 17 on the state rule is only "incidental." Unlike rules such as Rule 15(c), discussed in Chapter 6,[79] it is difficult to see how a rule like Rule 17(b) contributes to the uniformity of practice in federal court or to the effectiveness of the general scheme of Federal Rules. There would appear to be

---

79. *See* Chapter 6(D)(5)*(d) supra* (discussing Rules Enabling Act problems with Rule 15(c)).

no loss to uniformity of federal practice if capacity issues were governed by the conflict-of-laws rules of the forum instead of by the independent choice-of-law rules contained in Rule 17(b). In either case, there will be disuniformity in determining the capacity of certain litigants to sue or be sued, because the domiciles of individual litigants will inevitably contain as many different capacity rules as will the states in which federal diversity courts are sitting. Furthermore, Rule 17(b) does not seem to contribute in any way to the effective operation of any other Federal Rule of Civil Procedure, or to the efficient or effective operation of the general scheme of Federal Rules. Therefore, if the Supreme Court is serious about this part of the Rules Enabling Act inquiry (always a question about the tests that the Court articulates), Rule 17(b) may be invalid.

Assuming that conflict between Rule 17(b) and ''substantively-based'' state capacity rules is no problem, there remains the question whether Rule 17(b) might impact on substantive rights in the broader, ''outcome determinative,'' sense described earlier in this subsection. Such an impact seems unlikely. Even if forum state law would deprive an individual of capacity to sue or be sued contrary to the law of the individual's domicile, it is improbable that forum law would altogether preclude the assertion of a claim by or against the individual. Rather, it is far more likely that the forum state's law will allow suit if a representative or guardian is appointed to prosecute or defend against a claim for the individual. Under both Rule 17(b) and state law, therefore, suit will be permitted. The difference between the two sets of rules will simply be in the procedure required to maintain the suit. Thus, it seems likely that any effect on the ultimate outcome on the merits of the case by virtue of the application of Rule 17(b) rather than state law is unlikely.

Similar problems of Rule validity may exist in determining the capacity of corporations to be sued under Rule 17(b). However, there has been much unnecessary confusion about the corporate capacity issue because of a question about how to classify state ''door-closing'' statutes. The Supreme Court held in *Woods v. Interstate Realty Co.*[80] that a state statute closing the doors of the forum state's courts to corporate plaintiffs which had not qualified to do business in the state was applicable in federal diversity actions under the Rules of Decision Act.[81] There has been some tendency to view the *Woods* problem as involving an issue of capacity to sue that should have been governed by Rule 17(b).[82] There is support for this view in the history of Rule 17(b).[83] The drafters of Rule 17(b) relied upon an old pre-Rules case, *David Lupton & Sons Co. v. Automobile Club of Am.*,[84] in which the Supreme Court held that a state statute precluding a nonregistering foreign corporation from suing in New York could

---

80. 337 U.S. 535, 69 S. Ct. 1235, 93 L. Ed. 1524 (1949).

81. *See* Chapter 5(E)(1) *supra* (discussing *Woods* and other decisions).

82. *See* 6A CHARLES A. WRIGHT ET AL., FEDERAL PRACTICE AND PROCEDURE: CIVIL § 1569 (2d ed. 1990); John H. Ely, *The Irrepressible Myth of* Erie, 87 HARV. L. REV. 693, 727-28 (1974).

83. *See, e.g.,* PROCEEDINGS OF THE INSTITUTE ON FEDERAL RULES, CLEVELAND OHIO, JULY 21, 22, 23, 1938 at 258 (William W. Dawson, ed., 1938) (statement of Charles Clark on Rule 17(b)).

84. 225 U.S. 489, 32 S. Ct. 711, 56 L. Ed. 1177 (1912).

not be applied in a federal diversity action because the states could not prescribe the qualifications of suitors in the courts of the United States.

However, *David Lupton* was a pre-*Erie* case that did not mention "capacity to sue," but was based on the notion that "despite its transaction of business without authority, the foreign corporation could sue upon its contracts in any court of competent jurisdiction other than a court of the state of New York," including a federal court.[85] As Chapter 5 demonstrated, this view became obsolete with *Erie*, which established that federal diversity courts are not independent of the state court systems on matters of state substantive law. Although the general *Erie* test under the Rules of Decision Act does not determine the validity of Federal Rules of Civil Procedure, *Erie* nevertheless changed the legal context in which federal diversity actions are conducted in ways that cannot be ignored in construing Federal Rules of Civil Procedure. As *Woods* indicated, after *Erie* state door-closing statutes cannot simply be viewed as "procedural" measures immune from application by federal diversity courts, even if other state courts would not apply the provisions as a matter of their conflict-of-laws doctrine.[86] Rather, door closing statutes are, while procedurally configured, designed to effectuate the enacting state's substantive regulation of the activities of foreign corporations. Thus, after *Erie*, which the drafters of the Federal Rules had probably not fully absorbed when they created Rule 17(b),[87] the *David Lupton* view—that state-door closing statutes are simply regulations of practice in the forum state's courts and are not obligatory in federal diversity cases—cannot be justified. Therefore, if the *David Lupton* holding is applied to Rule 17(b), the rule is arguably invalid because it has a significant impact on state substantive policy.

However, there was considerable confusion and inaccuracy in the way in which the drafters of the Federal Rules viewed the interaction of the concept of capacity and the incorporation of the *David Lupton* holding into Rule 17(b). The drafters seemed to view capacity as the general ability to sue and be sued,[88] and

---

85. *Id.* at 499, 32 S. Ct. at 714, 56 L. Ed. at 1181.

86. The *Klaxon* branch of *Erie* also significantly changed the viewpoint that was employed in *David Lupton*. In the latter case, the Court, in discussing a New Jersey case that had held the New York door closing statute inapplicable in a New Jersey proceeding to enforce a New York contract, stated:

> The court conceded the general rule both in New Jersey and New York to be that a contract void by the law of the state where made would not be enforced in the state of the forum. But it was held that the New York statute did not in terms declare the contract void; it provided that no such action should be maintained in that state.

See David Lupton, 225 U.S. at 499, 32 S. Ct at 714, 56 L. Ed. at 1181. However, after *Klaxon* established that federal courts are obligated to apply the conflict-of-laws rules of the state in which they are sitting, the fact that the courts of *another state* could disregard a statute of the forum under their conflicts rule became irrelevant. *Klaxon* is discussed in Chapter 5(D)(2)*(a), supra*.

87. Recall from Chapter 5 that *Erie* was decided and the Federal Rules came into existence in 1938. However, the Rules Enabling Act was enacted in 1934, and the Advisory Committee on the Federal Rules had been working on the rules long prior to the time *Erie* was decided.

88. *See* PROCEEDINGS OF THE INSTITUTE ON FEDERAL RULES, CLEVELAND OHIO, JULY 21, 22, 23, 1938 at 258 (William W. Dawson, ed., 1938):

> The next sentence is: "The capacity of a corporation to sue or be sued shall be determined by the law under which it was organized." Some objectors asserted that that would give the state of incorporation the right of limiting the suability of a corporation

this view seems unquestionably correct. However, they viewed *David Lupton* as a case "holding that a state was not entitled to interfere with substantive rights of action against a corporation, once it had allowed the corporation to come within the borders of the state to do business,"[89] and also viewed it as a capacity decision.[90] Thus, they viewed *David Lupton* as being incorporated within Rule 17(b) as a statement of existing practice.[91] However, if capacity is merely the general ability to sue and be sued, it is hard to see how the state door-closing statutes in *David Lupton* and *Woods* had anything to do with the concept. There is no question that the corporations in both cases had the general ability to sue and be sued. The state door-closing statutes involved in the cases were not in any way designed to affect that general capacity. Rather, they were designed to effectuate the state's substantive regulatory power over foreign corporations that omitted to register in the state. Therefore, it was erroneous for the advisory committee to view *David Lupton* as involving a capacity problem in the first place, and certainly improper for it to attempt to incorporate the holding of the case in Rule 17(b) by indirection—*i.e.*, through the advisory committee notes to the rule.[92]

The best way to avoid the dilemma created by the advisory committee's confusion is to disregard its reliance on *David Lupton* and treat "capacity" in Rule 17(b) as involving only the general authority to sue and be sued, and not

---

in all other states. We felt clearly that that was a misuse of the term "capacity," that capacity dealt merely with suability, and that once a corporation was endowed with the general character of the corporate entity, such as we know it, that then it could not be provided that it was not subject to the liabilities of a corporation.

89. *Id.*

90. *See id.*

91. *See also Hearings Before the Committee on the Judiciary, House of Representatives, Seventy-Fifth Congress, 3d Sess., With Regard to The "Rules of Civil Procedure for the District Courts of the United States," Adopted by the Supreme Court of the United States Pursuant to the Act of June 19, 1934 (48 Stat. 1064) and on H.R. 8892, A Bill to Change and Modify the Rules of Procedure for the District Courts of the United States, Pursuant to the Act of June 19, 1934, Chapter 651, by Amending Sections 412 and 724 of Title 28 of the Code of Laws of the United States of American and by Adding Thereto Sections 430B, 430C, and 430D, Pertaining to Pleadings and Practice in the District Courts of the United States, Who May Sue and Be Sued, the Selection of Jurors, the Appointment of Court Stenographers, and For Other Purposes* at 10 (1938) (statement of Charles Clark):

> Mr. Clark. I wanted to call the attention of the committee to the case in the Supreme Court of *David Lupton's Sons Co.*, which is a case in which the Court held that when a corporation goes into another State to do business it cannot be prevented by the law of that State from suing. The State may prevent its doing business within the State except on the compliance with certain conditions; but if the State permits the corporation to do business it then cannot take away the right of suit, as a penalty when the corporation has done something that the State feels should not be permitted. That case is a decision of the Supreme Court, cited in the notes of the advisory committee as being stated in this section of the rules. It seems to me that this is a statement of the rule as it is worked out in that case. . . .
>
> It seems to me, therefore, in the light of that leading case by the Supreme Court, that the rule just states the existing practice.

Among other curious things, it is hard to understand how a state can prevent a corporation from doing business in the state without complying with the conditions that the state puts on it unless the state can impose a penalty on the corporation, such as depriving it of the right to sue, if it does not comply with those conditions.

92. *See* advisory committee note to original Rule 17(b) (citing *David Lupton* as an example of corporate capacity).

any particular disqualification imposed by state law that depends on the primary behavior of the corporation. *Woods* is authority for this interpretation because it treated the state-door closing statute involved in the case as presenting a Rules of Decision Act question rather than a Rules Enabling Act issue. Other federal courts have also interpreted Rule 17(b) in this fashion.[93] Furthermore, the interpretation will avoid all problems of rule invalidity that would otherwise occur due to conflict between Rule 17(b) and state statutes limiting the right of foreign corporations to sue in order to enforce substantive regulatory statutes of the state. Of course, the question whether Rule 17(b), as a general conflicts rule, is reasonably necessary to the uniform scheme of federal procedure exists as strongly here as it does in the case of individual capacity. However, the possibility of a clash between state rules governing general corporate capacity and Rule 17(b) will be limited, if not altogether eliminated, if the interpretation recommended above is followed, and in the absence of a conflict between Rule 17(b) and state law, the federal courts will not be confronted with any issue of Rules Enabling Act validity.

3. Joinder of Persons Needed for Just Adjudication

(a) History of Rule 19

The principles governing compulsory joinder of parties in the federal courts are found in Federal Rule 19. Existing Rule 19 is a model of outstanding drafting. Perhaps better than any other rule, it reflects the policies of practicality and convenience that should govern actions in a modern procedural system. However, Rule 19 has not always existed in its present form. It is a product of an evolutionary process having its roots in the principles of joinder developed in equity practice.

Much of the history of compulsory joinder in the federal courts is rooted in the case of *Shields v. Barrow*,[94] decided by the U.S. Supreme Court in 1854. In 1836, Barrow sold plantations located in Louisiana to Shields. Barrow and Shields were both citizens of Louisiana. The sale price of the plantations was to be paid in installments evidenced by notes. Each note was indorsed by six persons, two of whom were citizens of Mississippi and four of whom were citizens of Louisiana. After payment of $107,000 in installments, Shields defaulted on the remainder of the purchase price. A compromise was subsequently entered into whereby Shields and the six indorsers agreed to return the plantations to Barrow; the indorsers executed new notes in varying amounts to Barrow totalling $32,000, and Barrow retained the $107,000 already paid. In return,

---

93. *See, e.g.,* Joseph Muller Corp. Zurich v. Societe Anonyme De Gerance Et D'Armement, 314 F. Supp. 439 (S.D.N.Y. 1970) (restrictions on location of suit imposed by the nation under whose law the corporation is organized do not involve capacity; capacity is only general capacity to sue or be sued).

94. 58 U.S. (17 How.) 130, 15 L. Ed. 158 (1855). For the manner in which equitable practice evolved—in an unfortunate way—and was incorporated into American Practice, see Geoffrey C. Hayard, Jr., *Indispensable Party: The Historical Origin of Procedural Phantom*, 61 COLUM. L. REV. 1254, 1256-71 (1961).

Barrow released Shields and the indorsers from their prior liabilities and discontinued the state-court litigation commenced against them.

Barrow subsequently sought to rescind this compromise agreement in a federal diversity action commenced in the U.S. Circuit Court for the Eastern District of Louisiana against the two Mississippi indorsers. The Supreme Court ultimately held that Shields and the four Louisiana indorsers were "indispensable parties," who had to be joined in the action. Because their joinder would destroy diversity of citizenship, the suit had to be dismissed. The Court explained that there were three classes of parties to a bill in equity: (1) formal parties; (2) persons interested in the controversy who ought to be made parties so that the court can determine the entire controversy by "adjusting all the rights in it"; and (3) persons who have an interest in the controversy of such a nature that a final decree cannot be made without affecting their interest or leaving the controversy in such a condition that its final determination would be "wholly inconsistent with equity and good conscience." *Shields* was an example of a controversy in which the parties were of the third class. If only some of the persons interested in the controversy were before the court, a decree of rescission would either destroy the rights of those who were absent or leave the contract in full force with respect to the absentees and set aside as to the parties before the court. The latter result could only be permitted in cases in which the rights of the parties before the court were completely "separable" from the rights of the absentees. *Shields* was not such a case. Thus, the absent parties were classified as indispensable.[95]

The Equity Rules of 1912 generally preserved the distinctions made by the *Shields* case.[96] When original Rule 19 was promulgated in 1938, the distinctions were carried forward again.[97] Under the old equity rules and *Shields*

---

95. *See* 58 U.S. (17 How.) at 139-40, 15 L. Ed. at 160. Nevertheless, the result in *Shields* was highly questionable even as of the time it was decided. The court was correct to be concerned about the absence of the Louisiana indorsers and Shields in the action. *See Illustration 8-14 infra.* However, the Court, even in the legal context of the time, should not have classified the absentees as indispensable parties. The Equity Rules of 1842 provided:

> In all cases where it shall appear to the court, that persons who might otherwise be deemed necessary or proper parties to the suit, cannot be made parties by reason of their being out of the jurisdiction of the court, or incapable of otherwise being made parties, or because their joinder would oust the jurisdiction of the court as to the parties before the court, the court may in their discretion proceed in the cause without making such persons parties; and in such cases the decree shall be without prejudice to the rights of the absent parties.

42 U.S. (1 How.) at lv (1842). The Court declared this rule to be declaratory of an act of Congress, Act of Feb. 28, 1839, ch. 36, § 1, 5 Stat. 321, 321-22, which clearly applied only to problems of personal jurisdiction. However, this view is, equally clearly, contrary to the plain language of Equity Rule 47. The language of Rule 47 stating "or because their joinder would oust the jurisdiction of the court as to the parties before the court" is clearly a reference to subject-matter jurisdiction. Joinder of absent parties never ousts the court of personal jurisdiction over parties who are present; it only ousts the court of diversity jurisdiction. Thus, Equity Rule 47 arguably provided a basis upon which the court could have resolved the case short of dismissal.

96. *See* Rules 25, 36 & 39, 226 U.S. at 655, 658-59 (1912).

97.   (a) Necessary Joinder. Subject to the provisions of Rule 23 and of subdivision (b) of this rule, persons having a joint interest shall be made parties and be joined on the same side as plaintiffs or defendants. When a person who should join as a plaintiff refuses to do so, he may be made a defendant or, in proper cases, an involuntary plaintiff.

(b) Effect of Failure to Join. When persons who are not indispensable, but who ought to be made parties if complete relief is to be accorded between those already parties, have *v. Barrow*, the courts attempted to determine whether rights were "joint," "common," or "separable," and whether parties were "united in interest," as a means of determining whether an absentee was "indispensable" to the action. Original Rule 19 could be read as preserving the notion that persons holding "joint" rights are indispensable parties. The result was sometimes a rather difficult and narrow application of the concepts of "joint" and "separable" interests to determine questions of compulsory joinder. Criticism of this approach centered on the fact that the courts under original Rule 19 tended to decide joinder questions thoughtlessly on the basis of labels rather than by pragmatically analyzing who, if anyone, would be harmed by nonjoinder of a party and whether the harm could be prevented by some means short of dismissal.[98]

The 1966 amendments to Rule 19 were designed to eliminate these problems. The amendments were structured to focus the decisionmaking process on the practical factors that should determine whether an action should be permitted to continue in the absence of a party. Not all courts had ignored these factors, either under original Rule 19 or the prior equity practice. The 1966 amendments to Rule 19 were designed to preserve the approach of these courts while eliminating the results sometimes produced by use of such terms as "joint interest" in the original rule.[99]

(b) Application of Rule 19

Rule 19(a) lists three categories of persons who must be joined in an action if possible: (1) persons whose absence would prevent relief from being accorded among those already parties;[100] (2) persons who claim an interest in the subject of the action and are so situated that disposition of the action in their absence may, as a practical matter, impair or impede their ability to protect their interests;[101] and (3) persons who claim an interest in the subject of the action and are so situated that disposition of the action, in their absence, will leave any of the persons already parties subject to a substantial risk of incurring double, multiple, or otherwise inconsistent obligations by reason of the interest claimed

---

not been made parties and are subject to the jurisdiction of the court as to both service of process and venue and can be made parties without depriving the court of jurisdiction of the parties before it, the court shall order them summoned to appear in the action. The court in its discretion may proceed in the action without making such persons parties, if its jurisdiction over them as to either service of process or venue can be acquired only by their consent or voluntary appearance or if, though they are subject to its jurisdiction, their joinder would deprive the court of jurisdiction of the parties before it, but the judgment rendered therein does not affect the rights or liabilities of absent persons.

(c) Same: Names of Omitted Persons and Reasons for Non-joinder to be Pleaded. In any pleading in which relief is asked, the pleader shall set forth the names, if known to him, of persons who ought to be parties if complete relief is to be accorded between those already parties, but who are not joined, and shall state why they are omitted.

308 U.S. at 687 (1938).

98. *See, e.g.,* John W. Reed, *Compulsory Joinder of Parties in Civil Actions,* 55 MICH. L. REV. 327, 483 (1957).

99. *See* FED. R. CIV. P. 19 advisory committee's note to the 1966 amendment.

100. FED. R. CIV. P. 19(a)(1).

101. FED. R. CIV. P. 19(a)(2)(i).

by the absent parties.[102] If any such persons exist, Rule 19(a) directs that they should be joined, if possible.[103]

Joinder of the absentees may not be possible in some cases because of limitations on the court's power to obtain personal jurisdiction over them, or because of rules limiting the subject-matter jurisdiction of the court or the venue of the action. When joinder is impossible for one of these reasons, Rule 19(b) directs the court to determine whether the action may continue without the absent person. Rule 19(b) lists a number of factors that the court must consider in determining whether the action may go forward: (1) the extent to which a judgment rendered in the absence of a person might be prejudicial to the absent person or to those already parties; (2) the extent to which, by protective provisions in the judgment, by the shaping of relief, or by other measures, any prejudice can be lessened or avoided; (3) whether a judgment rendered in the absence of a person will be adequate; and (4) whether the plaintiff will have an adequate remedy if the action is dismissed for nonjoinder. These factors are not exhaustive. The court may also take into account other factors. Only after it is clear that (1) an absentee fits within one of the categories in Rule 19(a), (2) joinder of the absentee is impossible, *and* (3) no means are available under Rule 19(b) to protect against the harm caused by the party's absence should the court classify the absent party as ''indispensable'' and dismiss the action.

Illustration 8-14. Reconsider the facts of *Shields v. Barrow*, discussed in the previous subsection. How would the absent indorsers have been classified under Rule 19? Would the action be allowed to continue without them today? The absent indorsers do not appear to be Rule 19(a)(1) parties. Complete relief could be granted between the original parties in their absence. Barrow sought rescission plus recovery on the original notes, which all the indorsers had signed. Thus, each indorser was liable for the entire amount of each note. The Mississippi indorsers who were joined in the action could have paid the entire amount of the notes and had the plantations returned. Similarly, the absent indorsers were probably not Rule 19(a)(2)(i) parties. There would probably be no way that the federal action could practically affect the absent indorsers' interests. Barrow could not sue the absentees on the notes if the Mississippi indorsers paid them because Barrow would be forced to surrender the notes in return for payment. The federal judgment would not bind the absentees. Thus, if the absent indorsers were sued by the Mississippi indorsers for contribution, they would have available all defenses they would possess in an action against Barrow. Consequently, it is doubtful that the possibility of a suit by the Mississippi indorsers constitutes the kind of practical effect envisioned by Rule 19(a)(2)(i). However, the absent indorsers are clearly Rule 19(a)(2)(ii) parties. The Mississippi indorsers may incur inconsistent obligations unless the absentees are joined in the action. If the

---

102. FED. R. CIV. P. 19(a)(2)(ii).

103. A Rule 19 objection is raised by a Rule 12(b)(7) defense in a preanswer motion or the defendant's answer. A Rule 12(b)(7) defense is, however, preserved from waiver through trial. *See* FED. R. CIV. P. 12(h)(2). *But cf.* Fireman's Fund Ins. Co. v. National Bank of Coops., 103 F.3d 888 (9th Cir. 1996) (Rule 12(b)(7) motion's timeliness within discretion of district courts and court may take into account whether defendant is interposing objection to protect absent party or protect defendant's own interests).

Mississippi indorsers lose the federal action, they would have to sue for contribution from the absent indorsers and Shields. In that action, they would have to establish the facts necessary to justify rescission and payment of the original notes again, with the danger that the facts found in favor of Barrow might be found against them. These are the kind of "inconsistent obligations" that Rule 19 seeks to prevent. Nevertheless, the absent indorsers probably would not be classified as "indispensable parties" today. The federal court in which the action is pending could withhold judgment until Barrow sued the absent Louisiana indorsers and Shields in state court for the same relief he sought in federal court. If Barrow loses against the state-court defendants, the federal court could refuse judgment in his favor in the action under the doctrine of res judicata.[104] If Barrow wins against the state-court defendants, the Mississippi defendants in the federal action could be made to pay their pro rata share. Thus, Rule 19(b) could be utilized to avoid dismissal of the action today.[105]

* * * * *

The proper analysis of joinder questions under Rule 19 is illustrated by the U.S. Supreme Court's decision in *Provident Tradesmens Bank & Trust Co. v. Patterson*.[106] The dispute in *Provident Tradesmens* arose out of an automobile accident. Dutcher owned an automobile, which he lent to Cionci. While driving the automobile with Lynch and Harris as passengers, Cionci collided with a truck driven by Smith. Cionci, Lynch, and Smith were killed, and Harris was injured. Several state and federal actions arose out of this incident. Lynch's estate sued Cionci's estate in a federal diversity action. This action was settled for $50,000, but the $50,000 was not paid because Cionci's estate had no assets. Smith's estate and Harris each sued Cionci's estate, Dutcher, and Lynch's estate in state court, but those actions never went to trial. Dutcher, the owner of the automobile, had a $100,000 insurance policy with Lumbermen's Mutual Casualty Company that covered Dutcher's liability as Cionci's principal and the liability of anyone driving the car with Dutcher's permission. However, Lumbermen's Mutual refused to defend the federal diversity action for Cionci's estate on the ground that Cionci was driving without permission.[107] Lynch's estate brought another federal diversity action against Cionci's estate and Lumbermen's Mutual for a declaratory judgment that Cionci had been driving with Dutcher's permission. Smith's estate and Harris were joined as plaintiffs in this action. Dutcher was not

---

104. *See* Chapter 13(D) ("Parties Bound by Judgments") *infra*.

105. In contrast to joint contract obligors, the United States Supreme Court has held that joint tortfeasors are not Rule 19(a) parties, much less indispensable parties. *See* Temple v. Synthes, Ltd., 498 U.S. 5, 111 S. Ct. 315, 112 L. Ed.2d 263 (1990). However, the Court did not parse the categories in Rule 19(a) to determine whether any of them fit the situation of joint tortfeasors. It relied instead on the historical fact that defendants have not been allowed to compel the joinder of joint tortfeasors and the fact that the advisory committee's note to the 1966 amendment to Rule 19(a) states that the revisions to the rule in that year were not designed to change this traditional rule. *See* W. PAGE KEETON ET AL., PROSSER AND KEETON ON TORTS § 47, at 327 (5th ed. 1984); 7 CHARLES A. WRIGHT ET AL., FEDERAL PRACTICE AND PROCEDURE: CIVIL § 1623, at 342 (2d ed. 1986).

106. 390 U.S. 102, 88 S. Ct. 733, 19 L. Ed. 2d 936 (1968).

107. The insurance company's position was based on the fact that while Dutcher had loaned his automobile to Cionci, Cionci had deviated from the errand for which Dutcher had allowed the automobile to be taken. *See id.* at 105, 88 S. Ct. at 735, 19 L. Ed. 2d at 942.

joined, however, because he was a citizen of Pennsylvania, as were all the plaintiffs.

The district court granted directed verdicts in favor of the two estate plaintiffs, on the ground that under the applicable state law the automobile was presumed to have been driven with permission. This presumption could not be rebutted as to the two estate plaintiffs because of the state "Dead Man Rule." This rule prevented Dutcher from testifying against the estates if he had an adverse interest to them. The district court found such an adverse interest because Dutcher might have to use the $100,000 insurance fund to pay judgments against him. Thus, he had an interest in seeing that the fund was not exhausted by the payment of claims against Cionci. Dutcher was allowed to testify against Harris, however, and the jury still returned a verdict that the automobile had been driven with Dutcher's permission. The court of appeals reversed the judgment of the district court on the ground that Rule 19 required Dutcher's joinder in the action. The court of appeals raised this Rule 19 objection on its own motion. The court based its decision on its view that Dutcher's right to be joined was a substantive right that could not be affected by the Federal Rules. In the court of appeal's view, the right to be joined existed because of the same adverse interests on the part of Dutcher that caused the state "Dead Man Rule" to be applicable. The Supreme Court granted certiorari and reversed.

The Court assumed that Dutcher was a person who should be joined if feasible under Rule 19(a). Because Dutcher could not be joined without destroying diversity jurisdiction, Rule 19(b) required that the court determine whether the action should be dismissed or proceed without him. However, the Rule 19 issue had been raised for the first time on appeal. Therefore, the court of appeals should have considered the effect of the parties' failure to raise the objection at the trial level, as well as the fact that a judgment binding on all the other parties, but not Dutcher, had already been entered after extensive litigation.[108]

The Court identified four interests that had to be considered under Rule 19(b) in determining whether the action could go on without Dutcher: (1) the plaintiff's interest in having a forum; (2) the defendant's interest in avoiding multiple litigation, inconsistent relief, or sole liability that the defendant actually shares with another; (3) the interest of the nonjoined party; and (4) the interests of the courts and the public in the complete, consistent, and efficient settlement of controversies.[109]

As to the strength of the plaintiffs' interest in a forum, the Court observed that, before trial, the plaintiff's interest depends upon whether a "satisfactory" alternative forum exists. However, if the plaintiff wins, the judgment is appealed, and the joinder question is raised for the first time on appeal, the plaintiff has a strong additional interest in preserving the judgment.[110] While the Court was unable to determine whether the plaintiffs could have brought the same action

---

108. *See id.* at 109, 88 S. Ct. at 737, 19 L. Ed. 2d at 942.

109. *See id.* at 109-11, 88 S. Ct. at 737-39, 19 L. Ed. 2d at 944-46.

110. *See id.* at 109-10, 88 S. Ct. at 738-39, 19 L. Ed. 2d at 945-46.

against the same defendants plus Dutcher in a state court, this possibility was less adequate from the plaintiff's point of view after winning a successful judgment.[111] "[The plaintiffs'] interest in preserving a fully litigated judgment should be overborne only by rather greater opposing considerations than would be required at an earlier stage when the plaintiffs' only concern was for a federal rather than a state forum."[112] The countervailing interests were not sufficient to outweigh the plaintiffs' interest on the facts of the case.

As to the defendants' interests, they were foreclosed by the failure of the defendants to raise them at the trial level.[113] The Court found Dutcher's interest "more difficult to reckon."[114] Importantly, Dutcher's interest was not eliminated by the fact that any judgment rendered in Dutcher's absence would not be res judicata. Rather, Rule 19(a) requires the court to consider the practical effects that the judgment may have on the nonparty. The Supreme Court held that an appellate court should raise the joinder issue on its own motion if necessary to protect the interests of the nonparty.[115] Nevertheless, on the facts of the case, the Court considered that the adverse interest possessed by Dutcher against the plaintiffs was not enough to outweigh the interests of the plaintiffs in preserving the judgment.

> Dutcher had an "adverse" interest (sufficient to invoke the Dead Man Rule) because he would have been *benefited* by a ruling *in favor of* the insurance company; the question before the Court of Appeals . . . was whether Dutcher was *harmed* by the judgment *against* the insurance company.
>
> The two questions are not the same. If the three plaintiffs had lost to the insurance company on the permission issue, that loss would have ended the matter favorably to Dutcher. If, as has happened, the three plaintiffs obtain a judgment against the insurance company on the permission issue, Dutcher may still claim that as a nonparty he is not estopped by that judgment from relitigating the issue. At that point it might be argued that Dutcher should be bound by the previous decision because, although technically a nonparty, he had purposely bypassed an adequate opportunity to intervene . . . . If, however, Dutcher is properly foreclosed by his failure to intervene in the present litigation, then the joinder issue

---

111. It has been held that the availability or unavailability of an alternative forum in the Rule 19 inquiry is primarily of negative significance. That is, the absence of an alternative forum is weighed heavily in favor of a classification of nonindispensability (and nondismissal), while the existence of an alternative forum does not have as significant an impact in favor of a classification of indispensability (and therefore in favor of dismissal). *See* Rishell v. Jane Phillips Episcopal Mem'l Med. Ctr., 94 F.3d 1407, 1413 (10th Cir. 1996), *cert. denied*, 520 U.S. 1166, 117 S. Ct. 1427, 137 L. Ed. 2d 536 (1997).

112. *Id.* at 112, 88 S. Ct. at 739, 19 L. Ed. 2d at 946.

113. *See id.* at 109-10, 112, 88 S. Ct. at 737-39, 19 L. Ed. 2d at 945-46. The Court added that the insurance company would have the ability to litigate each claim against the fund in any event, and its only concern with the absence of Dutcher was to obtain a windfall escape from its defeat at trial. *See id.* at 112, 88 S. Ct. at 739, 19 L. Ed. 2d at 946.

114. *See id.* at 113, 88 S. Ct. at 739, 19 L. Ed. 2d at 947.

115. *See id.* at 110-11, 88 S. Ct. at 738-39, 19 L. Ed. 2d at 945-46.

considered in the Court of Appeals vanishes, for any rights of Dutcher's have been lost by his own inaction.

If Dutcher is not foreclosed by his failure to intervene below, then he is not "bound" by the judgment against the insurance company . . . . There remains, however, the practical question whether Dutcher is likely to have any need, and if so will have any opportunity to relitigate. The only possible threat to him is that if the fund is used to pay judgments against Cionci the money may in fact have disappeared before Dutcher has an opportunity to assert his interest. Upon examination, we find this supposed threat neither large nor unavoidable.[116]

As for the interest of the courts and the public in efficient resolution of controversies, the Court stated that it might have been preferable at the trial level to dismiss the action and force the plaintiffs to sue elsewhere.[117] Nevertheless, there was no reason to disregard the judgment at the court of appeals level just because it did not theoretically settle the entire controversy.[118] Finally, the Court rejected the reasoning of the court of appeals that Dutcher's right to be joined was a "substantive right" that the Federal Rules could not permissibly affect. The court of appeals had reasoned that the substantive law defined the category of persons called indispensable parties and that substantive law could not be modified by rule. It followed that the right of a person falling within the category to participate in litigation was also substantive and absolute. To this reasoning, the Court responded:

> Rule 19 does not prevent the assertion of compelling substantive interests; it merely commands the courts to examine each controversy to make certain that the interests really exist. To say that a court "must" dismiss in the absence of an indispensable party and that it "cannot proceed" without him puts the matter the wrong way around: a court does not know whether a particular person is "indispensable" until it has examined the situation to determine whether it can proceed without him.[119]

Under the *Provident Tradesmens* opinion, few cases should be dismissed on the ground that a party is "indispensable" and, therefore, that the court cannot proceed without that party. The opinion invites—as does the text of Rule 19(b)—both counsel and the federal courts to exercise the utmost ingenuity to pro-

---

116. *Id.* at 114-15, 88 S. Ct. at 740, 19 L. Ed. 2d at 947-48. The Court further explained that the threat to Dutcher was not great because (1) the state court actions against him had lain dormant for years at the pleading stage; (2) Dutcher could defend the state actions in part on the grounds that no permission had been granted to Cionci and that payments made from the insurance fund on Cionci's behalf should be credited against Dutcher's liability; (3) the court of appeals could have phrased the decree so as to avoid any difficulty to Dutcher by ordering payment withheld from the plaintiffs until the state court suits against him were settled; and (4) the plaintiffs had indicated a willingness to accept a limitation on all claims to the amount of the insurance policy. *See id.* at 115-16, 88 S. Ct. at 741, 19 L. Ed. 2d at 948.

117. The Court considered even this possibility to be "highly problematical, however, for the actual threat of relitigation by Dutcher depended on there being judgments against him and on the amount of the fund, which was not revealed to the District Court." *Id.* at 116, 88 S. Ct. at 741, 19 L. Ed. 2d at 948.

118. *See id.*

119. *Id.* at 119, 88 S. Ct. at 743, 19 L. Ed. 2d at 950.

tect the interests described in Rule 19(a) from harm without resorting to the severe action of dismissal. Under this flexible approach, the need to apply the indispensable party label should be rare.[120]

Illustration 8-15. *E*, the executor of a will and a citizen of State *X*, sues the *B* charity, a corporation incorporated and having its sole place of business in State *Y*, in a U.S. District Court in State *Y*. *E* seeks to have the residuary clause of a will declared invalid. Under the residuary clause, *B* would inherit a substantial sum of money. *A*, a citizen of State *X*, stands to lose $100,000 if the residuary clause is declared invalid. *A* is not joined in the action because *A's* joinder would destroy diversity jurisdiction. *A* is a Rule 19(a)(2)(i) party. If the residuary clause under which *A* would inherit is declared void, *A* will have practical difficulty obtaining the inheritance. However, *A* should not be classified as an indispensable party. Under Rule 19(b), the court can create a protective provision in the judgment requiring the executor to retain the amount *A* would inherit to pay any judgment that might go against the executor in a state-court action by *A*.[121]

Illustration 8-16. *A* sues *B* to cancel a mineral lease. *B* counterclaims for a declaration confirming *B's* rights under the lease. If the lease is cancelled, *C* and *D* will lose the royalty interests they possess under the lease. The district court finds the lease invalid and cancels it. On appeal, *B* objects for the first time that *C* and *D* were Rule 19 parties who should have been joined in the action. *C* and *D* are clearly Rule 19(a)(2)(i) parties who should have been joined in the action because the proceeding could adversely affect *C* and *D's* interests. This potential harm justifies allowing the Rule 19 objection to be raised for the first time on appeal, despite Federal Rule 12(h)(2), which appears to preserve the objection only through trial. The parties to an action cannot always be relied on to raise an objection that is aimed at protecting nonparties. Indeed, under *Provident Tradesmens*, it would be justifiable for the court of appeals to raise the Rule 19 objection on its own motion if *B* does not raise it.

Illustration 8-17. Assume on the facts of *Illustration 8-16* that the district court declares the lease valid. Under these circumstances, *Provident Tradesmens* would require the court of appeals to affirm. Although the judgment could have adversely affected the absentees' interest, the judgment that was *actually* rendered did not. Thus, the interest of the plaintiff in preserving a valid judgment that does not adversely affect the interests of the Federal Rule 19 parties must prevail.[122]

Illustration 8-18. *A*, a legatee under a will, sues *B* to set aside gifts made by the decedent to *B*. Other legatees do not join in the suit because their joinder will destroy diversity. *B* objects under Federal Rule 12(b)(7) that the absent

---

120. *See generally* Jean F. Rydstrom, Annotation, *Who Must Be Joined in Action as Person "Needed for Just Adjudication" Under Rule 19(a), Federal Rules of Civil Procedure*, 22 A.L.R. FED. 765 (1975).

121. Note that the possibility of multiple actions here does not make *A* a Rule 19(a)(2)(ii) party. The possibility of a second action here is the possibility of a state-court action against the executor-plaintiff in the federal action. The executor ought to be willing to elect this option over dismissal.

122. In Calcote v. Texas Pac. Coal & Oil Co., 157 F.2d 216 (5th Cir.), *cert. denied*, 329 U.S. 782, 67 S. Ct. 205, 91 L. Ed. 671 (1946), upon which this illustration is based, the court of appeals reversed. This result would not be justifiable after *Provident Tradesmens*.

legatees are Rule 19 parties. The district court overrules this objection and ultimately enters a judgment ordering *B* to pay the sum claimed by *A* to the estate. *B* appeals, raising only the Rule 19 objection on appeal. Despite the fact that the actual judgment entered by the district court did not adversely affect the absentees, the court of appeals should reverse and order the action dismissed. This result is justified in order to force the district courts to obey the requirements of Rule 19.[123]

(c) Problems of Subject-Matter Jurisdiction, Personal Jurisdiction, and Venue Under Rule 19

As noted in the preceding subsection, Rule 19 only permits joinder of absent parties when subject-matter jurisdiction or venue would not be destroyed by the joinder and when personal jurisdiction can be obtained over the absent party. Ordinarily, the court must judge whether subject-matter jurisdiction, venue, and personal jurisdiction would have been proper if the absentee had been originally joined in the action. However, even when joinder of a Rule 19 party would apparently destroy subject-matter jurisdiction, the doctrines of realignment or supplemental jurisdiction may enable the court to avoid dismissal of the action.

Rule 19(a) applies to absent parties who should join as plaintiffs in an action, as well as those who should be joined as defendants. Following the traditional equity practice described in section A(2), above, Rule 19(a) provides that if a person should join as a plaintiff but refuses to do so, that person may be named as a defendant in the action and served with process just like an ordinary defendant. When this action is taken, special problems of federal subject-matter jurisdiction may arise.

Illustration 8-19. *A*, a citizen of State *X*, wishes to sue *B*, a citizen of State *Y*, in a diversity action in federal court. Assume that *C*, who is a citizen of State *X*, is a Rule 19(a) party who should join with A in the suit, but *C* refuses to do so. If *A* joins *B* and *C* as defendants, there will be citizens of State *X* (*A* and *C*) on both sides of the lawsuit. Under the complete diversity of citizenship requirement, the federal court would have no subject-matter jurisdiction over the action—unless the parties are "realigned," as discussed below.

* * * * *

The doctrine of "realignment of parties" ordinarily deals with the problem of federal subject-matter jurisdiction created by overlapping citizenship of the parties discussed in *Illustration 8-19.* The doctrine of realignment is simply that in determining whether diversity of citizenship exists in an action, the court is not bound by the alignment of the parties in the pleadings, but must look beyond the pleadings and arrange the parties according to their true interests in the action.[124] In theory, this rule applies to all diversity actions, even though no question of improper alignment exists in most cases. Because the rule applies to

---

123. *See* Young v. Powell, 179 F.2d 147 (5th Cir.), *cert. denied*, 339 U.S. 948, 70 S. Ct. 804, 94 L. Ed. 1362 (1950).

124. *See* ERWIN CHEMERINSKY, FEDERAL JURISDICTION § 5.3.3, at 299 (3d ed. 1999); CHARLES A. WRIGHT, HANDBOOK OF THE LAW OF FEDERAL COURTS § 30 (5th ed. 1994).

joinder of defendants under Rule 19(a), an assessment of the parties' ultimate interests in the outcome of the action will often result in realignment of a person joined as a defendant under the third sentence of Rule 19(a). Thus, on the facts given in *Illustration 8-19*, C may be realigned with A for purposes of determining whether diversity jurisdiction exists.[125]

The third sentence of Rule 19(a) states that a person who should join as a plaintiff but refuses to do so "may be made a defendant, or, in a proper case, an involuntary plaintiff." The "involuntary plaintiff" provision is designed to ameliorate the situation that occurs when a person who should join as a plaintiff is beyond the reach of service of process. In such circumstances, joining the absentee as a defendant is impossible because the court cannot acquire personal jurisdiction over the absent person. However, for the involuntary plaintiff portion of Rule 19(a) to be available, the plaintiff must notify the absentee of the action and the absentee must refuse to join. Furthermore, Rule 19(a) states that an absentee may be made an involuntary plaintiff only in a "proper case."[126] A "proper case" exists only when the absentee has a duty to allow the plaintiff to use the absentee's name in the action. Consequently, use of the involuntary plaintiff provision has, as a practical matter, been limited to cases in which the exclusive licensees of patents, exclusive licensees of copyrights, or equitable owners of copyrights seek to join the owner of the patent or copyright as a plaintiff.[127]

In 1990, the doctrines of "pendent" and "ancillary" jurisdiction were codified in 28 U.S.C. § 1367 under the label "supplemental jurisdiction."[128] In 28 U.S.C. § 1367(b), Congress sought to preserve the jurisdictional requirements of 28 U.S.C. § 1332 from impairment. Section 1367(b) limits the ability of parties joined under certain multiple party joinder rules to assert claims, or to have claims asserted against them, that would violate the policies of § 1332. Among other things, § 1367(b) provides that the district courts will not have jurisdiction over claims asserted by plaintiffs against persons made parties under Rule 19

---

125. *See* Maryland Cas. Co. v. W.R. Grace & Co., 4 F.3d 155 (2d Cir. 1993), in which the court applied a "collision of interests" test to refuse realignment that would have defeated diversity. The "collision of interests" test requires an actual, substantial controversy, or a collision of interests, though the conflict may concern an issue other than the primary issue in dispute. *See id.* at 160. In contrast, a test that would require alignment in accord with the parties' positions on the primary issue in dispute would ignore controversies on secondary issues in determining the realignment question. *See also* Hidey v. Waste Sys., Inc., 59 F. Supp. 2d 543 (D. Md. 1999) (after realigning claimants in interpleader to oppose each other in accord with their positions on the "primary issue" in the action—the ownership of interpleaded funds, the court then considers whether the remaining claimant should be considered the defendant for purposes of the removal statute; court holds remaining claimant is defendant within removal statutes because if it had sued as plaintiff it could have sued in federal court and if it had been sued in state court by the other claimant, it could have removed).

126. *See* FED. R. CIV. P. 19(a); *see also* Jean F. Rydstrom, Annotation, *What Constitutes "Proper Case" Within Meaning of Provision of Rule 19(a) of Federal Rules of Civil Procedure That When Person Who Should Join as Plaintiff Refuses to Do So, He May Be Made Involuntary Plaintiff "In a Proper Case,"* 20 A.L.R. FED. 193 (1974).

127. *See* Independent Wireless Tel. Co. v. Radio Corp. of Am., 269 U.S. 459, 46 S. Ct. 166, 70 L. Ed. 357 (1926); FED. R. CIV. P. 19 advisory committee's note to the original rule; 7 CHARLES A. WRIGHT ET AL., FEDERAL PRACTICE PROCEDURE: CIVIL § 1606, at 72-76 (2d ed. 1986).

128. *See* Chapter 2(C)(4)(*d*) ("The Codification of Pendent and Ancillary Jurisdiction") *supra*.

when the claims would violate the restrictions of § 1332.[129] This provision assures that a plaintiff may not fail to join a defendant who should be a party under Rule 19 and later assert a claim against that defendant after joinder of the defendant has been compelled under the rule. However, § 1367(b) also provides that claims may not be asserted *by* "persons proposed to be joined as plaintiffs under Rule 19" when the policies of 28 U.S.C. § 1332 would be violated by the claim.[130] Under the traditional practice described above, persons are technically only "joined as plaintiffs" under the involuntary plaintiff provision of Rule 19. Thus, § 1367(b) might be read only to limit assertion of claims by involuntary plaintiffs, but not by persons joined as defendants under Rule 19 and realigned as plaintiffs for jurisdictional purposes. This interpretation would be unfortunate. As noted in Chapter 2, § 1367(b) was probably just clumsily worded and should be interpreted to apply to persons joined as defendants under Rule 19 and realigned as plaintiffs, as well as to persons joined as involuntary plaintiffs under the rule.[131]

The language in § 1367(b) prohibiting plaintiffs from asserting claims *against* "persons made parties under Rule . . . 19" also produces some interpretive problems. Read literally, the language does not prohibit joinder of a party as a defendant under Rule 19, even when the party, if joined originally in the action, would have destroyed subject-matter jurisdiction. It simply prohibits the plaintiff from asserting a claim against the party once the party has been joined. Persons who contributed to the drafting of the statute have suggested that this language in § 1367(b) purposely authorizes the joinder of Rule 19 defendants to take care of a particular kind of case. The case allegedly occurs when a plaintiff has no claim against a nonjoined party, but the absentee is a Rule 19 party because the absentee's interests could be adversely affected by the suit.[132] Others disagree that there can be a case under § 1367 in which a Rule 19 defendant exists against whom the plaintiff asserts no claim.[133]

Two technical realities support the latter position. First, even if there are defendants who should be joined under Rule 19 because their interests would be adversely affected, but against whom the plaintiff possesses no "claim," these defendants will be bound by the judgment in the action once they have been

---

129. *See* 28 U.S.C. §1367(b).

130. *See id.*

131. *See* Chapter 2(C)(4)*(d)(ii)* ("Exceptions to the Scope of Supplemental Jurisdiction in Diversity Cases: Section 1367(b)") *supra*; *see also* Denis F. McLaughlin, *The Federal Supplemental Jurisdiction Statute–A Constitutional and Statutory Analysis*, 24 ARIZ. ST. L.J. 849, 958 (1992).

132. *See* Thomas D. Rowe, Jr. *et al.*, *Compounding or Creating Confusion About Supplemental Jurisdiction? A Reply to Professor Freer*, 40 EMORY L.J. 943, 957-58 (1991); Thomas D. Rowe, Jr. *et al.*, *A Coda on Supplemental Jurisdiction*, 40 EMORY L.J. 993, 1000-01 (1991); *see also* Denis F. McLaughlin, *The Federal Supplemental Jurisdiction Statute–A Constitutional and Statutory Analysis*, 24 ARIZ. ST. L.J. 849, 954-57 (1992).

133. *See* Thomas C. Arthur & Richard D. Freer, *Grasping at Burnt Straws: The Disaster of the Supplemental Jurisdiction Statute*, 40 EMORY L.J. 963, 966-72 (1991); Thomas C. Arthur & Richard D. Freer, *Close Enough for Government Work: What Happens When Congress Doesn't Do its Job*, 40 EMORY L.J. 1007, 1010-11 (1991); *see also* Wendy Collins Perdue, *The New Supplemental Jurisdiction Statute–Flawed but Fixable*, 41 EMORY L.J. 68, 80 (1992).

joined.[134] Thus, they are, in all significant respects, in the position of persons against whom a "claim" for declaratory relief exists.[135] Second, but more importantly, 28 U.S.C. § 1367(b) is a provision that excludes certain cases from the jurisdiction conferred by § 1367(a). Section 1367(a), however, only confers supplemental jurisdiction over "claims."[136] Therefore, if the plaintiff has no "claim" against a Rule 19 defendant, no provision of the judicial code authorizes jurisdiction to be asserted over the defendant, and § 1367(b) is irrelevant.

In addition, allowing joinder of Rule 19 defendants against whom a plaintiff could assert no claim would produce an anomalous result. A party who is of the same citizenship as the plaintiff could not be originally joined by the plaintiff in the action due to the complete diversity rule of 28 U.S.C. § 1332. However, the nonjoined person could be made a party defendant under Rule 19 on the motion of either the court or the original defendant in the action. Under a literal reading of § 1367(b), there is no restriction placed upon persons "made parties" under Rule 19 that would prevent them from asserting claims against the plaintiff. Thus, after being joined, the party could assert defenses or claims in the action. Under the same literal wording, the plaintiff could not assert claims against the joined party. To avoid this difficulty, as well as the difficulties discussed in the preceding paragraph, the language of § 1367(b) should be interpreted to prohibit joinder of a party as a defendant when that party could not have been originally joined in the action due to the restrictions of 28 U.S.C. § 1332. As discussed below in conjunction with intervention under Rule 24, this interpretation accords with the legislative history of § 1367(b).[137] In the alternative, if § 1367 is interpreted to permit joinder by the plaintiff of Rule 19 defendants against whom no claims exist, the plaintiff should be prohibited from asserting claims against the Rule 19 defendant only as long as the Rule 19 defendant asserts no claims against the plaintiff.

Illustration 8-20. *B*, a citizen of State *Y*, leases store space in a mall to *A*, a citizen of State *X*. The lease agreement provides that *B* will not lease store space in the mall to any of *A's* competitors. Subsequently, *B* leases store space to *C*, a citizen of State *X* who is allegedly a competitor of *A*. *A* sues *B* in a U.S. District Court in State *Y* to enjoin enforcement of the lease between *B* and *C*. *C* is a person whose interests are adversely affected in a manner that appears to justify joinder under Rule 19(a)(2)(i). However, if *C* is joined in the action, citizens of State *X* will be on both sides of the action, thus destroying complete diversity of citizenship. Therefore, unless supplemental jurisdiction exists over *C*, joinder is impermissible. If *A* does not possess a "claim" against *C*, 28 U.S.C.

---

134. *See* Thomas C. Arthur & Richard D. Freer, *Close Enough for Government Work: What Happens When Congress Doesn't Do its Job*, 40 EMORY L.J. 1007, 1010 (1991); Thomas C. Arthur & Richard D. Freer, *Grasping at Burnt Straws: The Disaster of the Supplemental Jurisdiction Statute*, 40 EMORY L.J. 963, 969-70 (1991).

135. *See* Thomas C. Arthur & Richard D. Freer, *Close Enough for Government Work: What Happens When Congress Doesn't Do Its Job*, 40 EMORY L.J. 1007, 1010 (1991).

136. *See* Wendy Collins Perdue, *The New Supplemental Jurisdiction Statute—Flawed but Fixable*, 41 EMORY L.J. 69, 80 (1992).

137. *See* subsection (D)(3) ("Intervention") *infra; see also* Denis F. McLaughlin, *The Federal Supplemental Jurisdiction Statute—A Constitutional and Statutory Analysis*, 24 ARIZ. ST. L.J. 849, 955 (1992).

§ 1367(a) does not permit joinder of *C*. If *A* does possess a ''claim'' against *C*, § 1367(a) permits joinder, but § 1367(b) disallows joinder. If § 1367(a) and (b) are read to permit joinder of *C*, *A* should only be prohibited from asserting a claim against *C* as long as *C* does not assert a claim against *A*. Thus, if after *C* is joined, *C* asserts a counterclaim against *A* for a declaratory judgment that the provision in the lease between *A* and *B* is void, *A* should be able to assert a claim directly against *C* for injunctive or other appropriate relief.[138]

* * * * *

Although there has been a substantial amount of case law concerning supplemental jurisdiction under other multiple party joinder rules (discussed below), there have been few cases examining the application of § 1367(b) to Rule 19 since the enactment of the supplemental jurisdiction statute.[139] What case law exists is not encouraging about the courts' understanding of § 1367(b). For example, in *Butcher v. Hildreth,*[140] the plaintiff's state-court action was removed to federal court on the basis of diversity of citizenship. The defendant's answer contained a compulsory counterclaim. The plaintiff objected under Rule 19 that a person named Barfield should be joined in the action as an indispensable party to the counterclaim. The district court ordered Barfield joined, but then remanded the action because Barfield's joinder had destroyed diversity of citizenship. This decision is clearly wrong. As discussed in Chapter 7 in conjunction with the operation of Rule 13(a), the language of § 1332(b) applies only to claims asserted by plaintiffs, not to claims asserted by defendants.[141] Therefore, if supplemental jurisdiction existed over the counterclaim against the plaintiff and the nondiverse party under § 1367(a), as it surely did, § 1367(b) did not destroy diversity.[142]

Rule 19(a) only provides for joinder of parties who are ''subject to service of process.'' Although service of process and personal jurisdiction are distinct, though related, concepts,[143] it seems clear that Rule 19(a)'s reference to service refers generally to the ability of the court to assert personal jurisdiction

---

138. *See* Helzberg's Diamond Shops, Inc. v. Valley W. Des Moines Shopping Ctr., Inc., 564 F.2d 816 (8th Cir. 1977).

139. *See* Krueger v. Cartwright, 996 F.2d 928, 932-34 (7th Cir. 1993) (refusing to allow joinder of a nondiverse Rule 19 party as a plaintiff, holding the party dispensable and refusing to dismiss the action, but directing parties in the future to consider the jurisdictional limits inherent in Rule 19 and 28 U.S.C. § 1367(b) to avoid jurisdictional anomalies); ZB Holdings, Inc. v. White, 144 F.R.D. 42 (S.D.N.Y. 1992) (holding that a derivative action in which an indispensable, nondiverse corporate defendant was not joined had to be dismissed; court relied exclusively on 28 U.S.C. § 1367(a), reasoning that in the absence of the indispensable party, the court never had the ''original jurisdiction'' over the lawsuit required by that section).

140. 992 F. Supp. 1420 (D. Utah 1998).

141. *See* Chapter 7(F)(2)*(a) supra* (discussing supplemental jurisdiction over additional nondiverse parties added to counterclaims under Rule 13(h)).

142. At one point in its opinion, the court held that § 1367(b) was applicable because the additional party to the counterclaim was joined pursuant to a Rule 19 motion, and Rule 19, in contrast to Rule 13, *is* specifically mentioned in § 1367(b). *See* 992 F. Supp. at 1422. However, the court failed to recognize that § 1367(b)'s reference to Rule 19 was made in conjunction with claims by plaintiffs, and there is no indication in the case that the added party was asserting a claim against the defendants, despite the fact that the court referred to the party as an ''involuntary plaintiff.''

143. As indicated in Chapter 3, the fact that a defendant may be served with process in a manner authorized by an appropriate statute or court rule of a court system does not mean that an assertion of jurisdiction over the defendant under the circumstances will also comply with separate statutory or constitutional requirements.

over the defendant. Thus, the rule itself seems to preserve the ability of a Rule 19(a) party to object to personal jurisdiction. Nevertheless, one must keep in mind that the doctrine of "supplemental" or "pendent" personal jurisdiction approved by some federal courts may provide a basis for asserting personal jurisdiction in some cases of Rule 19(a) joinder. For example, assume that a plaintiff wants to assert both a federal and a state claim against a Rule 19(a) party and that service can be made on the party under a federal long-arm statute for purposes of the federal claim only, but that jurisdiction cannot be asserted under Federal Rule 4(k)(1)(A) because the forum's courts would not have minimum contacts over the defendant for purposes of an assertion of long-arm jurisdiction over the federal or state claims. Under these circumstances, federal courts recognizing the doctrine of "pendent" or "supplemental" personal jurisdiction might hold jurisdiction for purposes of the state claim proper under Federal Rule 4(k)(1)(D).[144]

The problems with "supplemental personal jurisdiction" have been discussed in Chapter 7 in conjunction with joinder of claims under Rule 18.[145] The problems with asserting "supplemental" or "pendent" personal *claim* jurisdiction over Rule 19 parties are even more severe than asserting "supplemental" or "pendent" personal jurisdiction for purposes of multiple claim joinder under Rule 18. The explicit reference in Rule 19(a) to a party's right to assert personal jurisdiction objections seems to require an independent basis of personal jurisdiction over Rule 19 parties.

Rule interpretation aside, however, there will be problems with asserting a kind of "supplemental *party*" or "pendent *party*" personal jurisdiction over Rule 19 parties that are more severe than the problems with asserting "supplemental" or "pendent" *claim* personal jurisdiction for purposes of supplemental claims joined under Rule 18. In the Rule 18 situation, the defendant will always be subject to personal jurisdiction in the forum on one claim (the federal claim) and the only question is whether to allow assertion of an additional, presumably related, state claim against the same defendant. In contrast, "supplemental" or "pendent" personal jurisdiction over a Rule 19 party may not involve a situation in which the party is not independently subject to personal jurisdiction in the forum on any other claim. Rather, the party may be summoned to participate in an action because of the party's relationship to other parties already joined in the case who *are* subject to personal jurisdiction. As discussed in Chapter 2(C)(4)*(c)*, above, the Supreme Court refused to recognize the propriety of "supplemental" or "pendent" *party* subject-matter jurisdiction in the absence of an affirmative grant of authority from Congress. For similar reasons, it would seem appropriate for the courts to exercise restraint in subjecting Rule 19 parties to "supplemental" or "pendent" personal jurisdiction in a forum in which neither Congress nor federal rulemakers have explicitly authorized them to be sued.

---

144. *Cf.* ESAB Group, Inc. v. Centricut, Inc., 126 F.3d 617 (4th Cir. 1997) (holding pendent personal jurisdiction proper over state claim under RICO long-arm statute, even though jurisdiction could not be validly asserted over state claim under South Carolina long-arm statute).

145. *See* Chapter 7(C)(2)*(c)* ("Personal Jurisdiction Restrictions on Joinder") *supra*.

Rule 4(k)(1)(B) provides that service of process on a party joined under Rule 19 "at a place within a judicial district of the United States and not more than 100 miles from the place from which the summons issues" is effective to establish personal jurisdiction over the party. Rule 4(k)(1)(B) is, in effect, a "mini" federal long-arm rule. By hypothesis, Rule 4(k)(1)(B) is not useful unless a defendant is neither subject to personal jurisdiction in a court of general jurisdiction in the state in which the action is pending, nor is subject to jurisdiction under a federal long-arm statute. As discussed in Chapter 3(L)(2)(*d*), above, because Rule 4(k)(1)(B) is an exercise of federal long-arm authority, the constitutionality of asserting personal jurisdiction over a Rule 19 party served within the "100-mile" bulge area will be determined by standards developed under the Fifth Amendment, and it is implausible to suppose that the Fifth Amendment would impose any serious restrictions on asserting jurisdiction over Rule 19 parties under the circumstances described in the rule, at least assuming that the parties could be constitutionally subjected to personal jurisdiction in the forum if there existed a state or federal long-arm statute that applied to them under the circumstances of the case.[146] However, the very existence of Rule 4(k)(1)(B) provides an additional reason to suppose that "supplemental" or "pendent" claim and party jurisdiction over Rule 19 parties is improper. If Congress has not chosen to authorize jurisdiction over Rule 19 parties by statute (which would make jurisdiction over them proper under Rule 4(k)(1)(D)), and if the rulemakers have addressed long-arm jurisdiction over Rule 19 parties under Rule 4(k)(1)(B), but have chosen not to extend jurisdiction over such parties any further than the 100-mile area, it would seem improper for the courts to assert jurisdiction in circumstances not specifically authorized by statute or rule.

Rule 19(a) likewise preserves the right of an added party to object to venue, by stating that "[i]f the joined party objects to venue and joinder of that party would render the venue of the action improper, that party shall be dismissed from the action." Thus, only the joined party, and not the originally joined defendant, has the right to make the venue objection, which may be waived if the party so chooses.[147] As with personal jurisdiction, however, there is the possibility that the federal courts will recognize a doctrine of "supplemental" or "pendent" venue in cases in which supplemental subject-matter jurisdiction exists over the claim against the Rule 19 party. The issues concerning supplemental venue have also been discussed in Chapter 7, and will not be repeated here.[148] However, the language of Rule 19 with regard to the ability of a joined party to object to venue seems even stronger than the language of Rule 19 dealing with

---

146. It is possible that if the Fifth Amendment would preclude direct assertion of personal jurisdiction over the defendant in the forum—*e.g.,* because the defendant does not have "minimum contacts" with the United States—it would also be impermissible to assert jurisdiction over the defendant in the forum by serving the defendant in the 100-mile area. However, this may not be true if the *Burnham* case, discussed in Chapter 3(E)(2), *supra*, also permits personal jurisdiction to be asserted validly under the Fifth Amendment by personal service within the territory of the United States, as seems likely.

147. *See* 7 Charles A. Wright et al., Federal Practice and Procedure: Civil § 1610, at 157-58 (2d ed. 1986).

148. *See* Chapter 7(C)(2)*(b)* ("Venue Restrictions on Joinder") *supra*.

personal jurisdiction. Thus, venue objections should arguably be preserved despite the existence of supplemental subject-matter or personal jurisdiction in a case.[149]

(d) Rules Enabling Act Problems in the Application of Rule 19

There are no serious Rules Enabling Act problems with Rule 19. The interpretation of the rule in the *Provident Tradesmens* case, discussed in subsection 1*(b)*, above, requires the federal courts to refer to state substantive law in order to determine the interests of absentees for purposes of joinder under Rule 19. Therefore, Rule 19 fully preserves the substantive rights of all parties and Rule 19(a) nonparties. The fact that state law would require joinder when a Rule 19 analysis would not does not abridge the substantive rights of either parties or nonparties. A proper Rule 19 analysis assures that the interests of the existing parties to the action will be protected by the federal courts under Rule 19(b) or the case will be dismissed. The fact that the rule permits these interests to be protected by measures short of joinder does not adversely affect substantive rights. The federal courts are entitled to use their own independent procedural methods for preserving the substantive rights of the parties, rather than the procedural methods used by the state courts. In the same way, the rights of absent parties are equally protected by the analysis that federal courts are required to pursue under Rule 19(b).[150] In addition, nonparties are not normally bound by the judgment in a civil action, which provides additional protection for their substantive rights.[151]

4. Permissive Joinder of Parties

(a) Application of Rule 20

Federal Rule 20 governs permissive joinder of parties in federal court. Original Rule 20 was derived from English practice and practice in those code states that had liberalized party joinder to free it from the restrictive interpretation placed on the original Field Code provisions (*i.e.*, the interpretation requiring plaintiffs who joined in an action to be interested in both the subject matter of the suit and all of the relief requested).[152] The Advisory Committee stated that Rule 20 represented ''only a moderate expansion of the present federal equity practice to cover both law and equity actions.''[153]

---

149. *Cf.* 7 CHARLES A. WRIGHT ET AL., FEDERAL PRACTICE AND PROCEDURE: CIVIL § 1610, at 159 (2d ed. 1986) (express recognition of venue defense in Rule 19(a) may act as a restraining influence on the exercise of ancillary venue).

150. *See id.* § 1603.

151. *See id.* at 33; Chapter 13(D) *infra* (discussing the persons who are bound by judgments in civil actions).

152. *See* section B (''Basic Party Joinder Provisions of the Codes'') *supra*.

153. *See* FED. R. CIV. P. 20 advisory committee's note to the 1938 rule; *see also* Rules 26, 37, 40, and 42 of the 1912 Equity Rules, 226 U.S. at 655, 659-660. The 1938 Version of Rule 20(a) was as follows:

(a) Permissive Joinder. All persons may join in one action as plaintiffs if they assert any right to relief jointly, severally, or in the alternative in respect of or arising out of the

Under the original version of Rules 18 and 20, some federal courts had erroneously concluded that Rule 20 was designed to limit joinder of claims under Rule 18. The language that produced this result was found in the second sentence of Rule 18(a) stating that joinder of claims was permitted ''if the requirements of Rules 18, 20 and 22 are satisfied.'' From this language some courts concluded that when a complaint asserted some claims against all defendants and some claims against fewer than all the defendants, the claims could be joined *only* if they *all* arose out of the same transaction or occurrence and presented common questions of law or fact. If the claims arose out of different transactions and were not against all of the defendants, they could not be joined. The 1966 amendments to Rule 18 and 20 were designed to make it clear that this interpretation was erroneous.[154]

Illustration 8-21. Assume that *A* sued *B* and *C* on a claim arising out of a contract made with *B* and *C*. Under the pre-1966 interpretation of Rule 20, *A* could not join a claim arising out of a wholly separate contract made with *C*.[155] The 1966 amendments make it clear that *A* can join the claim against *C*.

* * * * *

Today, the most serious restrictions on joinder of parties in federal court arise because of the requirements of federal subject-matter jurisdiction, venue, and personal jurisdiction explored in Chapters 2-4, and discussed in subsection *(b)*, below. Rule 20 cannot override these restrictions.[156] Consequently, even when Rule 20 is satisfied, restrictions on subject-matter jurisdiction, venue, and personal jurisdiction may operate to prevent joinder. In cases of permissive joinder of parties under Rule 20, the consequences are not as serious as they can sometimes be in cases of compulsory joinder of parties under Rule 19. If a person is an indispensable party under Rule 19 and that person's joinder is impossible because it would destroy federal subject-matter jurisdiction or venue, or because the absentee is not subject to personal jurisdiction, the action must be dismissed. In theory, the plaintiff may be deprived of any effective remedy for the deprivation of the plaintiff's rights because, in certain situations, no court may have authority over all the indispensable parties to an action. Because joinder under Rule 20 is permissive, however, inability to join a party because of subject-matter jurisdiction, venue, or personal jurisdiction restrictions simply means that plaintiffs will have to sue in separate actions, or that defendants will have to be sued separately.

---

same transaction, occurrence, or series of transactions or occurrences and if any question of law or fact common to all of them will arise in the action. All persons may be joined in one action as defendants if there is asserted against them jointly, severally, or in the alternative, any right to relief in respect of or arising out of the same transaction, occurrence, or series of transactions or occurrences and if any question of law or fact common to all of them will arise in the action. A plaintiff or defendant need not be interested in obtaining or defending against all the relief demanded. Judgment may be given for one or more of the plaintiffs according to their respective rights to relief, and against one or more of the defendants according to their respective liabilities.

308 U.S. at 687-88.

154. *See* FED. R. CIV. P. 18, 20 advisory committee's note to the 1966 amendment.

155. *See* Federal Hous. Adm'r v. Christianson, 26 F. Supp. 419 (D. Conn. 1939).

156. *See* FED. R. CIV. P. 82.

Nevertheless, even though the operation of the Federal Rules themselves does not produce harsh consequences in cases of permissive party joinder, the inability to join parties under Rule 20 could have serious consequences for other reasons. For one thing, the inability to join parties in an action may result in multiple litigation over the same basic matter, which duplicates effort and expense. In addition, a party may be caught in a serious tactical bind if that party is unable to join others in the same suit.

Illustration 8-22. Assume that in a tort suit *A* wants to assert claims against *B* and *C* in the alternative. *A* is certain that either *B* or *C* is responsible for *A's* injuries, but is uncertain which one. If *A* is forced to sue each defendant in a separate proceeding, *A* may lose *both* suits because the defendant in each action may be able to convince the trier of fact that the absent defendant was solely responsible for *A's* injuries.

* * * * *

Finally, rules of issue preclusion, which are discussed in detail in Chapter 13,[157] may operate to the serious disadvantage of a party who sues or is sued in separate actions.

Illustration 8-23. Assume that a plaintiff is prevented by rules of subject-matter jurisdiction from joining two defendants in the alternative in a tort suit. The plaintiff sues the two defendants separately. One of the actions proceeds to judgment before the other and the plaintiff loses that action because of a finding of contributory negligence against the plaintiff. If that finding can be used against the plaintiff in the second action against the other defendant, the plaintiff will lose that action as well. This result may or may not be fair, depending on the circumstances surrounding the first suit. A plaintiff who anticipates that an action might be lost for reasons unrelated to the merits, such as the jury's sympathy for a particular defendant, might well decide to bring only one suit against the other defendant. Inability to join both defendants will pose difficult choices for the plaintiff, and, if plaintiff's judgment is wrong, the plaintiff may suffer significant costs. For these reasons, inability to join parties even when joinder is only "permissive" is of potentially great importance to litigants.

* * * * *

Rule 20 contains two restrictions on multiple party joinder. First the claims asserted by or against the multiple parties must arise out of the same transaction or occurrence or series of transactions or occurrences. Second, questions of law or fact common to the multiple plaintiffs or defendants must exist in the action.

Illustration 8-24. *A* sues *B* and *C* in a tort action. *A* alleges that *B* negligently collided with *A* in an automobile, severely injuring *A*. *A* also alleges that *C*, a physician, negligently treated *A* at the emergency room where *A* was taken after the accident thus aggravating *A's* injuries. Rule 20 is satisfied under these circumstances. Although the incidents in which *B* and *C* injured *A* are separated in time, Rule 20 permits joinder not only when the same transaction or occurrence is involved. It also permits joinder when the claims arise out of the

---

157. *See* Chapter 13(C) ("Issue Preclusion") *infra.*

same series of transactions or occurrences, which is the case here. In addition, common questions of fact will arise between the claims against *B* and *C*. The factual issues will concern the extent to which *A's* injuries are attributable to *B's* negligence or *C's* negligence.[158]

Illustration 8-25. *A*, *B*, and *C* sue *D*, a municipality. They seek an order to compel *D* to issue the plaintiffs a license to sell alcoholic beverages in their restaurants. *D* had refused licenses to each plaintiff on the same grounds, but on separate occasions. *A*, *B*, and *C* are not associated in any other way. Rule 20 is not satisfied under these circumstances. A common question of law exists between the claims of the plaintiffs. However, the claims asserted by *A*, *B*, and *C* are not factually connected. Therefore, the same transaction or occurrence or series of transactions or occurrences is not involved.[159]

Illustration 8-26. *A* and *B* were fraudulently induced to invest in a sham corporation by a false prospectus issued by *C*. Even though no relationship exists between *A* and *B* other than the fact that they were induced by the same false prospectus to invest in the sham corporation, *A* and *B* may join in an action against *C* under Rule 20. The common question requirement is satisfied by the question whether the prospectus was false and fraudulent. The same transaction or occurrence requirement is satisfied by the fact that the plaintiffs were defrauded by the same prospectus. Here, unlike the situation in *Illustration 8-25*, a factual connection exists between the plaintiffs claims because the issuance of the prospectus was the "transaction or occurrence" that defrauded them both.

(b) Problems of Subject-Matter Jurisdiction, Personal Jurisdiction, and Venue Under Rule 20

The 1990 codification of the doctrines of "pendent" and "ancillary" jurisdiction in 28 U.S.C. § 1367 has removed one obstacle to Rule 20 joinder in federal question cases that previously existed. In *Finley v. United States,*[160] the Supreme Court drastically limited the ability of the federal courts to exercise so-called "pendent party" jurisdiction (*i.e.,* jurisdiction that allows the plaintiff to join with a federal claim a factually related state claim in which a nondiverse party is a defendant).[161] In effect, the *Finley* case held that pendent party jurisdiction would be prohibited in the absence of an explicit, affirmative grant of authority to the federal courts by Congress.[162] The enactment of 28 U.S.C. § 1367(a) was designed to overrule *Finley*. Thus, today the federal courts may exercise "supplemental jurisdiction" over state claims that arise out of the same transaction or occurrence as federal claims over which the federal courts have

---

158. *See* Lucas v. City of Juneau, 127 F. Supp. 730 (D. Alaska 1955).

159. *See* Erwin v. City of Dallas, 85 F. Supp. 103 (N.D. Tex. 1949).

160. 490 U.S. 545, 109 S. Ct. 2003, 104 L. Ed. 2d 593 (1989); *see also* Aldinger v. Howard, 427 U.S. 1, 96 S. Ct. 2413, 49 L. Ed. 2d 276 (1976).

161. *See* Chapter 2(C)(4)*(c)* ("The Statutory Basis of Pendent and Ancillary Jurisdiction") *supra*.

162. *See id*.

original jurisdiction under 28 U.S.C. § 1331, even if those state claims are asserted entirely against additional nondiverse parties.[163]

Recall, however, that Congress authorized joinder of claims within the supplemental jurisdiction whenever the claims formed a part of the same constitutional case or controversy as claims over which the district courts have original jurisdiction. In Chapter 2(C)(4)*(d)(i)*, above, it was suggested that Article III of the Constitution may permit Congress to treat factually unrelated federal and state claims as part of the "same case or controversy."[164] If so, once the joinder requirements of Rule 20 are satisfied, it might be possible to join an additional factually unrelated claim against a nondiverse defendant who has been brought within the supplemental jurisdiction of the district courts under 28 U.S.C. § 1367(a).

Illustration 8-27. *A*, a citizen of State *X*, sues *B* and *C*, who are also citizens of State *X*, in a U.S. District Court in State *X*. *A* asserts a federal claim against *B* and a factually related state claim against *C*. *A* also joins a factually unrelated state claim against *C*. Rule 20 is satisfied in this situation because the federal claim against *B* and the factually related state claim against *C* arise out of the same transaction or occurrence and involve common questions of fact. Recall from Chapter 7(C)(1), *Illustration 7-11* and section C(4)*(a)*, *Illustration 8-21*, above, that once Rule 20 is satisfied by the presence of any claims against multiple defendants that comply with the same transaction and common question requirements, Rule 18 permits joinder of any other claim, however unrelated, against either of the defendants.[165] If (1) Article III is interpreted to permit factually unrelated state and federal claims to become part of the same case or controversy and (2) 28 U.S.C. § 1367(a) is read to extend the "supplemental jurisdiction" of the federal courts as far as the Constitution permits, jurisdiction would exist over the factually unrelated state claim against *C*. However, as argued in Chapter 2(C)(4)*(d)(i)*, above, while the Constitution should be interpreted flexibly to allow Congress to authorize joinder of factually unrelated state and federal claims, § 1367(a) should be construed to permit joinder only of factually related claims. Under this latter construction, no jurisdiction would exist over *A*'s factually unrelated state claim against *C*.[166]

* * * * *

As discussed in Chapter 2(C)(4)*(d)(ii)*, above, § 1367(b) attempts to preserve the policies of the diversity jurisdiction, including the complete diversity rule of *Strawbridge v. Curtis*,[167] and the rules limiting the ability of plaintiffs to aggregate claims in order to satisfy the jurisdictional amount requirement of

---

163. *See* Chapter 2(C)(4)*(d)* ("The Codification of Pendent and Ancillary Jurisdiction") *supra*; *see also* Arnold v. Kimberly Quality Care Nursing Serv., 762 F. Supp. 1182 (M.D. Pa. 1991) (section 1367 confers supplemental jurisdiction over pendent plaintiffs in federal question case).

164. *See id.*

165. As observed in Chapter 7, the case would not differ if the factually unrelated claim had been joined against *B*, rather than *C*, if the scope of an Article III case or controversy is broad enough to encompass factually unrelated federal and state claims.

166. *See* Denis F. McLaughlin, *The Federal Supplemental Jurisdiction Statute—A Constitutional and Statutory Analysis*, 24 ARIZ. ST. L.J. 849, 940-42 (1992).

167. 7 U.S.(3 Cranch) 267, 2 L. Ed. 435 (1806).

§ 1332.[168] Because of serious drafting problems, however, there is a possibility that § 1367(b) has, in some permissive joinder cases under Rule 20, left some unintentional gaps in the exceptions it attempts to create for diversity claims that fall within the supplemental jurisdiction conferred by § 1367(a). The result is that the combined effect of § 1367(a) & (b) may be to expand the diversity jurisdiction.

The language of § 1367(b) prohibits "claims by plaintiffs against persons made parties under Rule . . . 20 of the Federal Rules of Civil Procedure." As discussed above, Rule 20 allows joinder of multiple defendants when claims are asserted against them that arise out of the same events and raise common questions of law or fact. Likewise, the rule permits joinder of multiple plaintiffs when the plaintiffs assert claims that arise out of the same events and raise common questions of law or fact.[169] The language of § 1367(b) thus preserves the requirement of complete diversity of citizenship when a plaintiff joins multiple defendants in federal court under Rule 20. However, the wording of the statute does not seem to preserve the complete diversity rule when multiple plaintiffs join to sue a single defendant. Thus, the question is raised whether the wording of § 1367 expands diversity jurisdiction beyond its previous boundaries.

Illustration 8-28. A, a citizen of State X, and B, a citizen of State Y, sue C, a citizen of State Y, in a U.S. District Court. A and B each seek damages of $100,000 against C for personal injuries received in an automobile accident. Under the wording of § 1367, this action appears to be within the jurisdiction of the district court. Under the "claim-specific" interpretation of § 1367(a) discussed in Chapter 2 and endorsed by most federal courts,[170] the district court has original jurisdiction over the claim between A and C because diversity of citizenship exists between those parties and the jurisdictional amount is satisfied. Under this same interpretation, § 1367(a) would then provide for supplemental jurisdiction over the claim between B and C. Even though there is no diversity of citizenship between those parties, the claim between B and C arises from the same facts as the claim between A and C and is, therefore, within the same Article III case or controversy. Furthermore, the wording of § 1367(b) does not appear to preclude supplemental jurisdiction over the claim in this situation. Section 1367(b) prohibits claims by plaintiffs *against* persons made parties under Federal Rule of Civil Procedure 20. A and B are plaintiffs asserting claims, but they are the ones who are "made parties" under Rule 20. C, against whom the claims are asserted, is a single defendant and is not, therefore, "made a party" under Rule 20. To preserve the rule of complete diversity in this situation, § 1367(b) would have to prohibit claims by *plaintiffs made parties* under Rule 20, as well as by plaintiffs *against* persons made parties under Rule 20.

Illustration 8-29. A, a citizen of State X, and B, a citizen of State X, sue C, a citizen of State Y, in a U.S. District Court. A seeks $100,000 in damages

---

168. *See* Chapter 2(C)(3)*(e)(ii)* ("Aggregation of Claims with Multiple Parties: The Common and Undivided Interest Test") *supra.*

169. *See* FED. R. CIV. P. 20(a).

170. *See* Chapter 2(C)(4)*(d)(i)* ("The Scope of Supplemental Jurisdiction: Section 1367(a)") *supra.*

from *C* for personal injuries received in an automobile accident. *B* seeks $10,000 from *C* for property damage suffered in the same accident. Under these circumstances, the aggregation rules of 28 U.S.C. § 1332 are not satisfied. Therefore, *B* could not, before the enactment of § 1367, join with *A* in a suit against *C* in federal court because *B's* claim does not satisfy the amount-in-controversy requirement.[171] For the reasons given in *Illustration 8-28*, however, the language of § 1367(a) creates supplemental jurisdiction over *B's* claim, and the language of § 1367(b) does not preclude jurisdiction in this case.

* * * * *

The drafters of § 1367 have acknowledged the potentially serious gap in the language of § 1367(b) in multiple plaintiff actions.[172] Because the "Rule 20 gap" is the product of a drafting mistake, the sensible result is to disregard the gap and interpret § 1367(b) as preserving the complete diversity rule in cases in which multiple plaintiffs join in an action against a single defendant as well as in multiple defendant actions.[173] Such a result would conform to the legislative history of the statute.[174] Thus far, the decisions interpreting § 1367(b) have generally, but not uniformly, interpreted the "Rule 20 gap" away. However, in *Stromberg Metal Works, Inc. v. Press Mechanical, Inc.,*[175] the Seventh Circuit

---

171. *See* Zahn v. International Paper Co., 414 U.S. 291, 94 S. Ct. 505, 38 L. Ed. 2d 511 (1973); Chapter 2(C)(3)*(e)(ii)*, *Illustration 2-59, supra.*

172. *See* Thomas D. Rowe, Jr. *et al.*, *Compounding or Creating Confusion About Supplemental Jurisdiction? A Reply to Professor Freer*, 40 EMORY L.J. 943, 961 n.91 (1991). However, the drafters acknowledge the problem only in cases in which a plaintiff commences an action against a diverse defendant and then by amendment attempts to add a nondiverse plaintiff to the action. In cases in which two plaintiffs sue originally, one of them diverse and one of them nondiverse to the defendant, the drafters state that joinder of the nondiverse plaintiff would be prohibited by the complete diversity rule. *See id.* However, the only way this can be so is if § 1367(a) is interpreted literally to require that the entire "civil action" commenced by the plaintiff or plaintiffs as an original matter be within the original jurisdiction of the district courts. As discussed in Chapter 2(C)(4)*(d)(i)*, however, if this interpretation is correct, it destroys the central purpose of § 1367 to overrule the *Finley* case and authorize pendent party jurisdiction in federal question cases. On the other hand, if the "civil action" language of § 1367(a) is given a "claim-specific" meaning in federal question cases involving pendent parties (as opposed to an "action-specific" meaning), it must be given the same meaning in diversity actions, with the result that the statute provides supplemental jurisdiction over the claim of a nondiverse plaintiff joined originally under Rule 20. At least one district court has read § 1367(b) to be applicable only to nondiverse parties added to the action by amendment after the original action has been commenced. *See* First Nat'l Bancshares v. Geisel, Inc., 853 F. Supp. 1333, 1336 n.5 (D. Kan. 1994). However, this result is clearly contrary to the traditional practice of reassessing federal subject-matter jurisdiction whenever amendments are made and thus seems clearly wrong. *See* Scaccianoce v. Hixon Mfg. & Supply Co., 57 F.3d 582, 584-85 (7th Cir. 1995); Dieter v. MFS Telecom, Inc., 870 F. Supp. 561 (S.D.N.Y. 1994); Arnold v. Kimberly Quality Care Nursing Serv., 762 F. Supp. 1182, 1185 (M.D. Pa. 1991); *see also* Patrick D. Murphy, *A Federal Practitioner's Guide to Supplemental Jurisdiction,* 78 MARQ. L. REV. 973, 1003 (1995); *cf.* Darren J. Gold, *Supplemental Jurisdiction Over Claims by Plaintiffs in Diversity Cases: Making Sense of 28 U.S.C. § 1367(b),* 93 MICH. L. REV. 2133, 2157-69 (1995).

173. *See* Denis F. McLaughlin, *The Federal Supplemental Jurisdiction Statute—A Constitutional and Statutory Analysis,* 24 ARIZ. ST. L.J. 849, 940-42 (1992).

174. The House Report accompanying the statute stated: "This section [§ 1367(b)] is not intended to affect the jurisdictional requirements of 28 U.S.C. § 1332 in diversity-only class actions, as those requirements were interpreted prior to *Finley.*" H.R. REP. NO. 734, 101st Cong., 2d Sess. 29 (1990).

175. 77 F.3d 928 (7th Cir. 1996). *Stromberg* is discussed in Mark C. Cawley, Note, *The Right Result for the Wrong Reasons: Permitting Aggregation of Claims Under 28 U.S.C. § 1367 in Multi-Plaintiff Diversity Litigation,* 73 NOTRE DAME L. REV. 1045 (1998); Heather McDaniel, *Plugging the "Gaping Hole": The Effect of 28 U.S.C. § 1367 on the Complete Diversity Requirement of 28 U.S.C. § 1332,* 49 BAYLOR L. REV. 1069 (1997); Note, *Federal Civil Procedure—Supplemental Jurisdiction—Seventh Circuit Holds that 28 U.S.C. § 1367* held, in a Rule 20 joinder case involving an aggregation question, that § 1367(a) & (b) permit the district courts to entertain claims by plaintiffs that do not meet the amount-in-controversy requirement, but which are factually related to claims that do meet the requirement. *Stromberg* followed the decision of the Fifth Circuit in *Free v. Abbott Laboratories,*[176] a class action case discussed in section D(4)*(c)*, below. However, at least two other courts of appeals have rejected the *Abbott* and *Stromberg* rationale,[177] and the district courts have mostly, but not uniformly, held that the aggregation rules survive the enactment of § 1367.[178]

Personal jurisdiction over each party joined under Rule 20 will ordinarily have to be proper under an applicable long-arm statute and the relevant constitutional standards governing the assertion of jurisdiction—*i.e.,* Fourteenth Amendment standards in the case of a state long-arm statute and Fifth Amendment standards in the case of a federal long-arm statute. Ordinarily, there will be no problem with one defendant being subject to personal jurisdiction while another defendant joined under Rule 20 is not. The fact that the claims against the joined defendants must arise out of the same transaction or occurrence or series of transactions or occurrences will assure that if a long-arm statute is constitutionally applicable to one defendant, it will also be constitutionally applicable to other defendants joined under Rule 20. Nevertheless, it is possible to envision situations in which one defendant may be subject to personal jurisdiction within a state, but

---

Allows Supplemental Jurisdiction Over Permissively Joined Plaintiffs in Diversity Suits—Stromberg Metal Works, Inc. v. Press Mechanical, Inc., 77 F.3d 928 (7th Cir. 1996), 110 HARV. L. REV. 1173 (1997).

176. 51 F.3d 524 (5th Cir. 1995).

177. *See* Meritcare v. St Paul Mercury Ins. Co., 166 F.3d 214 (3d Cir. 1999); Leonhardt v. Western Sugar Co., 160 F.3d 631 (10th Cir. 1998). In one curious case, the Fourth Circuit has held that when multiple claims are joined by a single plaintiff against a single defendant and one of the claims is dismissed on summary judgment, thus reducing the amount requested by the plaintiff to less than the amount-in-controversy requirement, the district court has discretion to retain the other claims in the action. *See* Shanaghan v. Cahill, 58 F.3d 106 (4th Cir. 1995). The court held that the basis for the district court's discretion lies in the model of supplemental jurisdiction under § 1367. The district court should first look to the face of the complaint to determine whether the plaintiff's claims meet the amount requirement. If they do, but some subsequent event, such as dismissal of one of the claims, reduces the amount in controversy below the amount requirement in § 1332, the district court should be guided by the same kinds of factors that inform decisions about whether to dismiss supplemental claims in the court's discretion under § 1367(c). *Shanaghan* is clearly wrong. If the amount-in-controversy requirement is satisfied at the outset of the action, the district court has no discretion to dismiss the claims if a subsequent event reduces the amount below the statutorily required figure. *See* Wolde-Meskel v. Vocational Instruction Project Community Servs., Inc., 166 F.3d 59 (2d Cir. 1999) (rejecting *Shanaghan's* reasoning); Amanda Dalton, Note, Shanaghan v. Cahill: *Supplementing Supplemental Jurisdiction,* 1996 B.Y.U. L. REV. 281.

178. Numerous district court decisions have addressed whether the aggregation rules under § 1332 have survived the enactment of § 1367. *See, e.g.,* Fairchild v State Farm Mut. Auto. Ins. Co., 907 F. Supp. 969 (M.D. La. 1995) (aggregation rules overruled in some cases); Henkel v. ITT Bowest Corp., 872 F. Supp. 872 (D. Kan. 1994) (aggregation rules survive); Lindsay v. Kvortec, 865 F. Supp. 264 (W.D. Pa. 1994) (aggregation rules overruled in some cases); Tokarz v. Texaco Pipeline, Inc., 860 F. Supp. 563 (N.D. Ill. 1994) (aggregation rules survive); Fountain v. Black, 876 F. Supp. 1294 (S.D. Ga. 1994) (aggregation rules survive); Chouest v. American Airlines, Inc., 839 F. Supp. 412 (E.D. La. 1993) (aggregation rules survive); Durrett v. John Deere Co., 150 F.R.D. 555 (N.D. Tex. 1993) (aggregation rules survive); Mayo v. Key Fin. Servs., Inc., 812 F. Supp. 277 (D. Mass. 1993) (aggregation rules survive); Hairston v. Home Loan & Inv. Bank, 814 F. Supp. 180 (D. Mass. 1993) (aggregation rules survive); Averdick v. Republic Fin. Servs., Inc., 803 F. Supp. 37 (E.D. Ky. 1992) (aggregation rules survive); *see also* Congram v. Giella, No. 91 Civ. 1134 (LMM), 1992 WL 349845, 1992 U.S. Dist. LEXIS 17230 (S.D.N.Y. Nov. 10, 1992) (aggregation rules in multiple defendant actions remain the same after enactment of § 1367).

another defendant joined under Rule 20 may not be. For example, a defendant may be subject to personal jurisdiction because the defendant is domiciled within the state, or because the defendant is personally served within the state, even though the claim arises outside the state. Another defendant joined under Rule 20 may not be subject to jurisdiction on the same basis and will also not be subject to long-arm jurisdiction within the state because the claim arose elsewhere and the defendant has no contacts with the state. In these circumstances, the action could not be maintained in the forum, even though the parties would be properly joined in the action. In addition, it should be noted that even if the parties could both be subjected to personal jurisdiction in the forum, venue restrictions (discussed below), would usually prevent the action from being maintained there over the objection of the defendants.

When a federal claim is being asserted against one defendant and a state claim is being asserted against a second, nondiverse defendant within a district court's supplemental jurisdiction, a question arises whether the federal court can assert "supplemental" or "pendent" party personal jurisdiction over the nondiverse defendant, assuming that the defendant against whom the federal claim is asserted is subject to personal jurisdiction under a federal long-arm statute or rule, but the nondiverse defendant is not explicitly subject to personal jurisdiction under any federal or state statute or rule. Although Rule 20, unlike Rule 19,[179] does not contain specific language that preserves a joined party's right to object to personal jurisdiction, the problems with asserting "supplemental" or "pendent" personal jurisdiction over Rule 20 defendants are otherwise similar to those under Rule 19. Indeed, it can be argued that the reasons for not recognizing a doctrine of "supplemental" or "pendent" personal jurisdiction in Rule 20 cases are even stronger than those in Rule 19 cases. If a Rule 19 party cannot be subjected to personal jurisdiction within the forum, and if the party is ultimately held to be "indispensable" under Rule 19(b), the action will have to be dismissed. If there is no forum in which all "indispensable" parties can be subjected to personal jurisdiction, the plaintiff will effectively be precluded from asserting a claim against anyone. Thus, the potential consequences of a lack of personal jurisdiction over a Rule 19 party are severe. However, Rule 20 parties do not all have to be joined for an action to proceed against other parties. Although, as noted in subsection *(a)*, above, a plaintiff can encounter serious tactical problems if the plaintiff is unable to join multiple defendants in some actions, these tactical problems are not as serious as having an action dismissed altogether. Therefore, if, as argued above, the courts should not recognize a doctrine of "supplemental" or "pendent" personal jurisdiction in Rule 19 cases in the absence of explicit statutory or rule authority to do so, it is even more arguable that they should not recognize such a doctrine in Rule 20 cases.

Venue must normally be proper for each defendant joined under Rule 20. Thus, if venue is predicated on defendant's residence, both defendants must reside in the same state or venue is improper under the general venue statutes. Likewise,

---

179. *See* section C(3)*(c) supra* (discussing the possibility of "pendent" or "supplemental" personal jurisdiction over Rule 19 parties).

if venue is predicated on the fact that substantial events giving rise to the claim occurred in the district, it should ordinarily have to be true as to all defendants joined under Rule 20 or venue ought to be held improper. Only when the action cannot be brought in any other district is it possible to predicate venue on the ability to assert personal jurisdiction over only one defendant in the district (in diversity actions) or on the fact that one defendant is "found" in the district (in federal question cases). In the latter cases, difficulties of obtaining personal jurisdiction over Rule 20 defendants who are *not* subject to personal jurisdiction or *not* found in the district will often prevent the plaintiff from maintaining the action there in spite of the fact that venue is proper.

As was the case with Rule 19 joinder,[180] the possibility exists that when a federal claim is asserted against one Rule 20 defendant and a supplemental state claim is asserted against another defendant, a special federal statute may make venue proper for the federal claim, but not for the state claim. In such a case, the question arises whether the federal courts should recognize a kind of "supplemental" or "pendent" party venue over the defendant against whom the supplemental state claim is asserted. Unlike Rule 19, the text of Rule 20 does not seem to provide explicitly that each joined defendant may make a venue objection. However, as was the case with the issue of "pendent" or "supplemental" personal jurisdiction discussed above, it may be unjustifiable to deprive a defendant as to whom venue is not independently proper of a venue objection in the absence of express statutory or rule authority for doing so. The problem of "supplemental" or "pendent" venue in Rule 20 cases differs from the problem of "supplemental" or "pendent" venue in cases of multiple claim joinder under Rule 18, discussed in Chapter 7.[181] As with personal jurisdiction, a defendant against whom multiple federal and state claims are joined under Rule 18 must defend an action in the forum on the federal claim in any event, and it may not be much of a burden to require the defendant to defend an additional, presumably related, state claim in the process. However, that situation may not exist for a defendant joined under Rule 20 as to whom no independent basis for proper venue exists. If a doctrine of "supplemental" or "pendent" party venue is recognized by the federal courts, such a defendant might be subjected to substantial burdens against which the general venue statutes were designed to protect.

(c) Rules Enabling Act Issues in the Administration of Rule 20

There are no serious Rules Enabling Act issues with Rule 20. State laws that permit joinder of multiple defendants when Rule 20 does not, or which restrict joinder when it is permitted under Rule 20, are virtually always supported by different views of efficiency in judicial administration than those which

---

180. *See* section C(2)*(c) supra* (discussing the possibility of "pendent" or "supplemental" venue in Rule 19 cases).

181. *See* Chapter 7(C)(2)*(b) supra* (discussing the possibility of "pendent" or "supplemental" venue in cases of multiple claim joinder under Rule 18).

motivated federal rulemakers. Such differences in viewpoint about efficiency do not result in any abridgement, enlargement, or modification of substantive rights within the meaning of the Rules Enabling Act. As indicated in subsection *(a)*, above, the ability to join multiple parties can result in important tactical advantages, especially to plaintiffs wishing to join multiple defendants in an action. Furthermore, such tactical differences can conceivably produce ultimate differences in the results of cases as between state and federal courts. However, even under such circumstances, it is hard to believe that tactical differences of this sort amount to more than an ''incidental'' effect on the substantive rights of parties. Thus, Rule 20 can validly be administered in the face of conflicting state law.[182] Indeed, as suggested in Chapter 5, state efficiency-based joinder rules should probably not be interpreted as in conflict with Rule 20 in the first place, because such rules are virtually never designed to control party joinder in cases outside the courts of the state that created the rules.[183]

SECTION D. SPECIAL JOINDER DEVICES

In addition to the basic joinder rules discussed in the previous sections, special party joinder devices are found in every jurisdiction. These devices are (1) impleader, or third-party practice,[184] (2) interpleader,[185] (3) intervention,[186] and (4) class actions.[187]

1. Impleader

(a) History of Impleader

Impleader is a procedure that allows a party to bring into an action a new party who is allegedly liable to the original party for all or part of a claim asserted against the original party in the action. In equity actions all persons who were necessary to a complete determination of the proceeding would be joined in order to prevent a multiplicity of suits. The codes generally adhered to this equity practice and even sought to broaden it.[188] However, when joinder was optional with the plaintiff, the plaintiff could not be forced to add a new party to the action. Consequently, a defendant could not insist on joining a person who was obligated to indemnify the defendant for all or a part of the plaintiff's claim against the defendant.

At common law, a procedure known as *vouching to warranty* was the predecessor to modern impleader or third-party practice. In ''vouching to

---

182. *See* Chapter 5(F)(4) *supra* (discussing the *Burlington Northern* test for Rules Enabling Act validity of Federal Rules of Civil Procedure).

183. *See* Chapter 5(F)(3), *Illustration 5-17* & accompanying text, *supra*.

184. *See* FED. R. CIV. P. 14.

185. *See* FED. R. CIV. P. 22.

186. *See* FED. R. CIV. P. 24.

187. *See* FED. R. CIV. P. 23-23.2.

188. *See* sections A and B of this chapter *supra*.

warranty'' situations, a defendant who was sued for the recovery of real property could "vouch in" a person who had given a warranty of title to the defendant. The person "vouched in" then had the opportunity to defend the suit. If the person vouched in refused to defend, and if a judgment ultimately was rendered that the defendant's title was invalid, the defendant could sue the warrantor in a second suit on the warranty. In the second suit, the judgment in the first action would bind the warrantor, provided that the defendant successfully proved the attempt to vouch the warrantor into the first action, the terms of the warranty, and the judgment in the first suit.[189] In nineteenth century England, the "vouching to warranty" practice was expanded to permit a defendant to bring in a third party who was obligated to indemnify the defendant against the plaintiff's claim. Based partly on this expanded procedure, the American states developed their own forms of third-party practice that permitted the joinder of third parties who were obligated to the defendant in whole or in part for the claim being litigated.[190]

The federal courts recognized a right of impleader in admiralty cases in the late nineteenth century.[191] In addition, the federal courts utilized impleader in actions at law prior to 1938 under the Conformity Act whenever the state in which the federal court was sitting had adopted a modern impleader rule.[192] When the Federal Rules of Civil Procedure were adopted in 1938, Rule 14 provided for impleader in appropriate cases brought in the district courts.[193] Rule 14 generally exemplifies modern impleader practice in both the state and federal courts.

(b) Application of Rule 14

Serious problems are posed when a defendant has been held liable on a claim and then must bring a separate suit against a third party who, in theory, is obligated to indemnify the defendant in whole or in part for the amount the defendant must pay under the judgment. The most serious problem is the danger of inconsistent results. Because the indemnitor is not a party to the suit against the defendant, the indemnitor is usually not bound by the judgment in that action. As a result, in the second action against the indemnitor, the defendant in the first action may have to relitigate the issues giving rise to the right of indemnity. Thus, there is a danger that the issues will be determined in a fashion inconsistent with their determination in the first proceeding. Second, even if the issues are determined the same way in both the first and second proceedings, the defendant in the first action is subjected to a useless multiplicity of actions over the same

---

189. *See* 6 CHARLES A. WRIGHT ET AL., FEDERAL PRACTICE AND PROCEDURE: CIVIL § 1441, at 286 (2d ed. 1990); Note, *Developments in the Law—Multiparty Litigation in the Federal Courts*, 71 HARV. L. REV. 874, 907 (1958).

190. *See* 6 CHARLES A. WRIGHT ET AL., FEDERAL PRACTICE AND PROCEDURE: CIVIL § 1441, at 287 (2d ed. 1990).

191. *See* The Hudson, 15 F. 162 (S.D.N.Y. 1883).

192. *See* 6 CHARLES A. WRIGHT ET AL., FEDERAL PRACTICE AND PROCEDURE: CIVIL § 1441, at 287 (2d ed. 1990).

193. *See* 308 U.S. at 681-82 (1938).

basic matter, with the attendant inconvenience and expense that multiple suits involve. Finally, even if the defendant in the first action is successful in the second action and is ultimately indemnified for the amounts that the defendant has been forced to pay under the first judgment, that success may not come until a substantial period of time has passed between payment of the first judgment and victory in the suit for indemnification. Throughout this time, the defendant in the first action will be deprived of the amount that has been paid to satisfy the judgment.[194]

The general purpose of Rule 14 is to eliminate these problems. Rule 14 permits a defending party to bring in the third person who is obligated to indemnify the defendant. Thus, the indemnity claim can be settled in the same action with the claim giving rise to the right of indemnity. Impleader is permissive, not compulsory. Impleader is available to any defending party, even a plaintiff against whom a counterclaim is asserted.[195] The person initiating the impleader is called the third-party plaintiff. Impleader is accomplished by serving a summons and "third-party complaint" on the third party. Before 1963, Rule 14 required a party seeking impleader to obtain leave of court before serving the summons and third-party complaint.[196] Rule 14 was amended in 1963 to permit the third party to be impleaded without leave of court if the third-party complaint is filed within ten days after the third-party plaintiff serves the original answer. However, the question whether a third-party may be impleaded is still discretionary with the court, even if the third-party complaint is filed within the ten-day period.[197] After the ten-day period, leave of court is still required. In exercising discretion under the rule, the courts will generally permit the impleader if it is within the scope of Rule 14 and will not significantly prejudice the plaintiff or the third-party defendant. "Prejudice" may be shown, for example, when the impleader is filed at a late stage of the proceeding and might delay the trial. Prejudice may also be shown when the impleader would introduce issues unrelated to the original claim. Such issues may excessively complicate the action.[198]

To be within the scope of Rule 14, the third-party plaintiff's claim must be that the third-party defendant is liable to the third-party plaintiff for all or part of the claim asserted against the third-party plaintiff. Typical of this type of claim is a claim for indemnity.

Illustration 8-30. Assume that *A* sues *B* for personal injuries received when *C*, *B's* employee operating *B's* car on *B's* business, collided with *A*. Under the substantive law often applicable to this type of case, if *C's* negligence caused the accident, both *C* and *B* are liable to *A*, and *A* can sue either or both of them for damages. If *B* must pay *A* because of *C's* negligence, *B* is entitled to

---

194. *See* 6 Charles A. Wright et al., Federal Practice and Procedure: Civil § 1442 at 289-91 (2d ed. 1990).

195. *See* Fed. R. Civ. P. 14(b).

196. *See* 308 U.S. at 681 (1938).

197. *See* Fed. R. Civ. P. 14 advisory committee's note to the 1963 amendment.

198. *See* 6 Charles A. Wright et al., Federal Practice and Procedure: Civil § 1443, at 304, 308 (2d ed. 1990).

indemnity from *C*. Therefore, if *A* sues only *B* for *A's* personal injuries, *B* may implead *C* on the indemnity claim under Rule 14. Note, however, that if *B's only* claim against *C* is that *C* owes *B* damages for *B's* personal injuries or property damage to *B's* car due to *C's* negligence, Rule 14 impleader is improper. A Rule 14 claim must be dependent on *A's* claim against *B*. A direct claim by *B* against *C* does not meet this requirement.[199]

* * * * *

When a third-party complaint is filed, Federal Rule 5(a) requires that a copy be served on each of the parties to the original action. Rule 14 provides that the third-party defendant shall present any defenses to the third-party plaintiff's claim as provided in Rule 12 and counterclaims against the third-party plaintiff and cross-claims against other third-party defendants as provided in Rule 13. Rule 14 also provides that the third-party defendant may assert any defenses that the third-party defendant has to the plaintiff's claim and also may assert any claims against the plaintiff arising out of the same transaction or occurrence as the principal claim in the action. Rule 14 further permits the plaintiff to assert claims directly against the third-party defendant when the plaintiff's claims arise out of the transaction or occurrence that is the subject-matter of the principal claim in the action. In the latter event, the third-party defendant again must assert any defenses against the plaintiff's claims as provided in Rule 12 and counterclaims and cross-claims as provided in Rule 13. A third-party defendant also may implead persons who are liable for all or part of the claims asserted against the third-party defendant.

Illustration 8-31. On the facts of *Illustration 8-30*, once *B* has impleaded *C* under Rule 14, *A* can amend the complaint to add a claim directly against *C* for *C's* negligence. In addition, *B* can join with the impleader claim a claim against *C* for damages to *B's* car by virtue of Rule 18(a).[200] Under the terms of Rule 14(a), *C* may also assert a claim directly against *A* for personal injuries received in the accident.

(c) Problems of Subject-Matter Jurisdiction, Personal Jurisdiction, and Venue Under Rule 14

Cases involving third-party claims can become complex. These complexities increase when problems of federal subject-matter jurisdiction, venue, and personal jurisdiction are considered.

Illustration 8-32. Assume that *A*, a citizen of State *X*, sues *B*, a citizen of State *Y*. *B* impleads *C*, a citizen of State *Y*, under Federal Rule 14. Under these circumstances, diversity of citizenship exists between the plaintiff, *A*, on the one hand, and *B* and *C*, on the other. However, there is no diversity between the third-party plaintiff, *B*, and the third-party defendant, *C*, because they are both

---

199. *See, e.g.,* Evert v. Finn, No. Civ. A. 98-3293, 1999 WL 397401, 1999 U.S. Dist. LEXIS 9412, (E.D. La. June 15, 1999); Collini v. Wean United, Inc., 101 F.R.D. 408 (W.D. Pa. 1983). As indicated in *Illustration 8-31, infra,* however, if *B* possesses a proper Rule 14 claim, Rule 18 authorizes *B* to join with that Rule 14 claim any other claim that *B* possesses against *C*.

200. *See* Chapter 7(C)(1) ("Application of Rule 18") *supra.*

citizens of State *Y.* Nevertheless, the federal courts have traditionally assumed jurisdiction of the impleader claim under the doctrine of ancillary jurisdiction (today supplemental jurisdiction), discussed in Chapter 2.[201] The concept of ancillary jurisdiction is based on the principle that when a federal court obtains jurisdiction of a case, the court obtains jurisdiction of the entire case, not just that part of the case for which there is a specific grant of subject-matter jurisdiction found in Article III and the judicial code. As this concept is applied to impleader cases, subject-matter jurisdiction over the principal claim between the plaintiff and the defendant (the claim asserted by *A* against *B*) gives a federal court ancillary jurisdiction over an impleader claim between the defendant (third-party plaintiff) and the third-party defendant (the claim asserted by *B* against *C*), because the impleader claim is an incidental part of the same case as the principal claim due to its close factual relationship to the principal claim.

* * * * *

For a claim to be within the ancillary (supplemental) jurisdiction of the federal courts, the claim must not only be a part of the same Article III constitutional case or controversy as a claim over which the federal courts have subject-matter jurisdiction. It also must not offend the *statutory* policies of the grant of subject-matter jurisdiction to the federal courts in Title 28 of the *United States Code.* The courts have assumed rather automatically (perhaps too automatically) that impleader claims meet both the constitutional requirements *and* the statutory policies necessary to sustain ancillary jurisdiction.[202] This assumption, however, is not true for all claims that may be asserted under Rule 14. In addition to authorizing the basic impleader claim, Rule 14 also authorizes the plaintiff to assert claims directly against the third-party defendant if the claims arise out of the same transaction or occurrence as the plaintiff's claim against the defendant.

Illustration 8-33. Assume that *A*, a citizen of State *X*, sues *B*, a citizen of State *Y. B* impleads *C*, a citizen of State *X.* There is diversity between *A*, the plaintiff, and *B*, the defendant. There is also diversity between *B*, the third-party plaintiff, and *C*, the third-party defendant. Therefore, because there is complete diversity between all adverse parties, there is no need to resort to the concept of ancillary jurisdiction. However, assume that *A* asserts a claim directly against *C* arising out of the same transaction or occurrence as *A's* claim against *B.* Such a claim is permitted by Rule 14, but is it permitted by 28 U.S.C. § 1332, given the fact that *A* and *C* are both citizens of State *X*?

* * * * *

In 1978, the U.S. Supreme Court decided *Owen Equipment & Erection Co. v. Kroger,*[203] which held that the diversity statute forbids assertion of the plaintiff's claim under the circumstances described in *Illustration 8-33.* To allow the plaintiff's claim against the third-party defendant would be to circumvent the

---

201. *See* Chapter 2(C)(4)*(a) supra* ("The General Nature of Pendent and Ancillary Jurisdiction") and Chapter 7(F) ("Counterclaims and Cross-Claims Under the Federal Rules").

202. *See generally* 6 CHARLES A. WRIGHT ET AL., FEDERAL PRACTICE AND PROCEDURE: CIVIL § 1444, at 314 (2d ed. 1990).

203. 437 U.S. 365, 98 S. Ct. 2396, 57 L. Ed. 2d 274 (1978).

congressional command embodied in 28 U.S.C. § 1332, as interpreted in *Strawbridge v. Curtiss*.[204] The Court indicated that a close factual relationship between the claim over which there is jurisdiction and the putative ancillary claim satisfies the requirements of Article III of the Constitution, but not necessarily the statutory requirements of Title 28. The Court also emphasized that ancillary jurisdiction "typically involves claims by a defending party haled into court against [that party's] will, or by another person whose rights might be irretrievably lost unless [that person] could assert them in an ongoing action in a federal court."[205] This statement indicates that ancillary jurisdiction would still apply to claims asserted directly against the plaintiff by the third-party defendant, as permitted by Rule 14. It also suggests that ancillary jurisdiction might apply to compulsory counterclaims asserted by the plaintiff against a third-party defendant who, by directly asserting a claim against the plaintiff, has put the plaintiff in a defensive position.[206]

In 1990, Congress codified the doctrines of "ancillary" and "pendent" jurisdiction under the label "supplemental jurisdiction" in 28 U.S.C. § 1367(a).[207] However, in 28 U.S.C. § 1367(b), Congress sought to preserve the jurisdictional restrictions of 28 U.S.C. § 1332 from impairment by certain of the multiple party joinder rules. As applied to Rule 14 cases, § 1367(b) prohibits jurisdiction over claims asserted by plaintiffs against persons made parties under Rule 14 who are citizens of the same state as the plaintiffs.[208] Thus, § 1367(b) codifies the holding of *Owen Equipment & Erection Co. v. Kroger*.[209]

However, the language of § 1367(b) creates several problems that the federal courts will have to address. The statute flatly prohibits claims by plaintiffs

---

204. 7 U.S. (3 Cranch) 267, 2 L. Ed. 435 (1806); *see Kroger*, 437 U.S. at 377, 98 S. Ct. at 2404, 57 L. Ed. 2d at 284; Chapter 2(C)(4) ("Supplemental Jurisdiction") *supra.*

205. *Kroger*, 437 U.S. at 376, 98 S. Ct. at 2404, 57 L. Ed. 2d at 284.

206. The application of ancillary jurisdiction to compulsory counterclaims and cross-claims, as described in Chapter 7(F)(2)*(b)* ("Supplemental (Ancillary) Jurisdiction Over Counterclaims and Cross-Claims") *supra*, satisfies this aspect of *Kroger.*

207. *See* Chapter 2(C)(4)*(d)* ("The Codification of Pendent and Ancillary Jurisdiction") *supra.*

208. *See* 28 U.S.C. § 1367(b).

209. *See, e.g.,* ARE Sikeston Ltd. Partnership v. Weslock Nat'l, Inc., 120 F.3d 820 (8th Cir. 1997). After the enactment of § 1367, several courts have upheld supplemental jurisdiction over third-party claims. *See id.*; Estate of Bruce v. City of Middletown, 781 F. Supp. 1013 (S.D.N.Y. 1992); Whitney Nat'l Bank v. Chatelain, No. 91-2432, 1991 U.S. Dist. LEXIS 15056 n.8 (E.D. La. Oct. 15, 1991) (dictum). However, a few courts have shown a willingness to scrutinize third-party claims more carefully to determine whether they arise from the same facts as the principal claim in the action. *See* Fleming Cos. v. Hope Plaza, Inc., No. 90-6323, 1992 WL 30565, 1992 U.S. Dist. LEXIS 2274 (E.D. Pa. Feb. 12, 1992) (alternative holding; third-party claim was improper under Rule 14 and also did not arise out of a common nucleus of operative fact with the principal claim); *In re* Feifer Indus., 141 B.R. 450 (N.D. Ga. 1991) (third-party claim rejected as not sufficiently related to principal claim); *cf.* Molina v. Mallah Org., Inc., 817 F. Supp. 419 (S.D.N.Y. 1993) (defamation claim joined with third-party claim for contribution; third-party claim improper; defamation claim did not arise out of same transaction or occurrence as principal claim, thus no supplemental jurisdiction under § 1367). *But see* Bank Brussels Lambert v. Credit Lyonnais (Suisse) S.A., No. Civ. 6876 (LMM), 1998 WL 91217, 1998 U.S. Dist. LEXIS 2280 (S.D.N.Y. Mar. 3, 1998) (plaintiff asserts federal claim and supplemental state claim against defendant; defendant impleads third-party defendant for indemnity on state claims and joins other claims against third-party defendant under Rule 18, but which post-date events that are the subject of the main action and the Rule 14 claim; court holds supplemental jurisdiction exists over Rule 14 and Rule 18 claims, but without closely examining the relationship between the Rule 18 claims and either the Rule 14 claims or the plaintiff's federal claim).

against persons "made parties under Rule 14" when the restrictions of 28 U.S.C. § 1332 would be violated.[210] But what if the third-party defendant asserts a claim directly against the plaintiff as permitted by Rule 14?[211] The language of § 1367(b) could be read to prohibit the plaintiff from asserting a factually related counterclaim against the third-party defendant under these circumstances. This reading would be terribly unfair to the plaintiff. The courts might respond to this problem by preventing nondiverse third-party defendants from asserting claims against the plaintiff, but that also seems unfair. After all, the third-party defendant has no choice whether to be in the action. Consequently, there seems to be no reason to inflict dual proceedings on the third-party defendant with regard to factually related claims possessed against the plaintiff.[212] The best result would be to interpret the language of § 1367(b) as preventing claims by the plaintiff against the third-party defendant *only* when the third-party defendant does not assert claims against the plaintiff. This interpretation will assure that the policy of § 1367(b)–to prevent evasion of the requirement of the diversity statute by plaintiffs[213]–will be effectuated, while preventing unfairness to the plaintiff, the defendant, and the third-party defendant.[214]

Illustration 8-34. *A*, a citizen of State *X*, sues *B*, a citizen of State *Y*, in a U.S. District Court in State *Y*. *A* asserts a claim for $500,000 against *B* for personal injuries arising out of an automobile accident occurring in State *Y*. When the accident occurred, *A* was riding as a passenger in a car owned by *A*, but driven by *C*, a citizen of State *X*. *B* impleads *C* in the action under Rule 14. *B* alleges that *C* was negligent and that *C's* negligence contributed to the accident. Under the law of State *Y*, *C* would be liable for all or part of *A's* claim as a joint tortfeasor with *B*. After being impleaded, *C* asserts a claim directly against *A* for personal injuries received in the accident. *C* alleges that *A* negligently maintained the brakes on the automobile in which *A* and *C* were riding. Under these circumstances, *A* should not be prohibited from amending the complaint to assert a claim directly against *C*, even though *A* and *C* are both citizens of State *X*. *A* has been put in a defensive position by *C's* claim. *A* did not assert a claim directly against *C* until *C* first asserted a claim against *A*. Therefore, there is no reason to believe that *A* was attempting to evade the policies of the diversity jurisdiction.

* * * * *

---

210. *See* 28 U.S.C. § 1367(b).

211. Rule 14 provides as follows: "The third-party defendant may also assert any claim against the plaintiff arising out of the transaction or occurrence that is the subject matter of the plaintiff's claim against the third-party plaintiff." FED. R. CIV. P. 14(a).

212. Another alternative, even more unpalatable, would be to prevent joinder of third-party defendants altogether when they are citizens of the same state as the plaintiff. This approach, of course, would produce unfairness to the defendant in the action. Indeed, because complete diversity of citizenship might often exist between the defendant and third-party defendant, it would be anomalous to prevent joinder of the third-party defendant in many cases.

213. *See* H.R. REP. NO. 734, 101st Cong., 2d Sess. 29 (1990).

214. *See* Denis F. McLaughlin, *The Federal Supplemental Jurisdiction Statute–A Constitutional and Statutory Analysis*, 24 ARIZ. ST. L.J. 849, 942-49 (1992), and authorities there cited and discussed.

In addition to the interpretive problems discussed above, at least one court has read § 1367(b) to preclude a plaintiff from impleading a nondiverse third-party defendant to indemnify plaintiff on a counterclaim asserted by the defendant. In *Guaranteed Systems, Inc. v. American National Can Co.,*[215] the plaintiff, a contractor, filed suit against American National Can in a North Carolina state court, alleging that American National had failed to pay it for construction work. American National removed the action to federal court on the basis of diversity and asserted a counterclaim against the plaintiff alleging negligence in the performance of the construction work. The plaintiff impleaded a nondiverse subcontractor under Rule 14, asserting claims for indemnity and contribution for any amount that the plaintiff owed to American National as a result of the counterclaim. The district court dismissed the third-party claim, holding that it was prohibited by the terms of § 1367(b). The court stated that "Guaranteed Systems is clearly a plaintiff in a diversity suit asserting a claim against a non-diverse third-party defendant made a party under Rule 14."[216] The court recognized that, if § 1367(b) had not been enacted, the plaintiff would not have been precluded by the Supreme Court's decision in the *Owen Equipment* case, discussed above, from impleading a nondiverse third-party defendant, because *Owen Equipment* only precluded plaintiffs from asserting claims against such third-party defendants impleaded by defendants.[217] Nevertheless, the court felt bound by the "plain terms" of § 1367(b).[218]

As discussed in Chapter 2,[219] the purposes of § 1367(b) were to preserve the policies of the diversity jurisdiction, not to change the results that would have been achieved in diversity actions had the supplemental jurisdiction statute not been enacted. There is little question that prior to the enactment of § 1367(b), ancillary jurisdiction would have existed over the plaintiff's third-party claim in *Guaranteed Systems*, as the court itself recognized. The correct rule in cases like *Guaranteed Systems* in which plaintiffs or other parties seek to employ Rule 14 impleader is that supplemental jurisdiction exists over the impleader claim as long as jurisdiction exists over the claim upon which impleader depends and the two claims form part of the same Article III case or controversy.

Illustration 8-35. *A*, a citizen of State *X*, sues *B*, a citizen of State *Y*, for $500,000 in a U.S. District Court in State *Y*. *B's* answer contains a permissive counterclaim against *A* for $100,000. *A* wants to implead *C*, a citizen of State *X*, under Rule 14, on the ground that *C* is liable to *A* for half of any amount that *A* must pay to *B* under the permissive counterclaim. The language in § 1367(b) prohibiting plaintiffs from asserting claims "against persons made parties under Rule 14" should not be read as prohibiting supplemental jurisdiction over Rule 14 claims asserted by plaintiffs. Therefore, *A* should be able to implead *C*.

* * * * *

---

215. 842 F. Supp. 855 (M.D.N.C. 1994).

216. *Id.* at 857.

217. *See id.*

218. *See id.*

219. *See* Chapter 2(C)(4)*(d)(ii)* ("Exceptions to the Scope of Supplemental Jurisdiction in Diversity Cases: Section 1367(b)") *supra.*

Earlier sections have examined whether, if "supplemental" or "ancillary" subject-matter jurisdiction is established in an action, the federal courts should also recognize a doctrine of "ancillary" or "supplemental" personal jurisdiction.[220] Those sections concluded that a doctrine of "supplemental" personal jurisdiction would be less justifiable in cases of multiple party joinder than in cases of multiple claim joinder under Rule 18, which was discussed in Chapter 7.[221] The same conclusion is warranted, for the same reasons, in cases of Rule 14 joinder. In fact, in Rule 14 cases, the courts agree that personal jurisdiction must be established independently over third-party defendants.[222]

The result is different with venue, however. "According to the existing case law, the statutory venue limitations have no application to Rule 14 claims even if they would require the third-party action to be heard in another district had it been brought as an independent action."[223] As was the case with cross-claims and counterclaims (examined in Chapter 7), this result seems justifiable as an interpretation of the federal venue statutes, which seem aimed at measuring venue only by reference to original claims in the action.[224]

(d) Rules Enabling Act Problems in the Administration of Rule 14

As with claim joinder under Rule 18[225] and party joinder under the other Federal Rules of Civil Procedure discussed in this chapter, there will be cases in which joinder is possible under Rule 14 in a diversity action, but in which joinder of the third-party defendant would not be possible in the courts of the state in which the federal action is brought, which raises the question whether the application of Rule 14 violates the Rules Enabling Act in such cases.

One typical situation in which the Rules Enabling Act issue exists involves a tort action in which the defendant wishes to implead a joint tortfeasor in a federal diversity action for contribution under Rule 14, but state law would require the defendant to pursue the contribution claim in a separate action after paying the plaintiff more than the defendant's proportionate share of the plaintiff's claim. In this kind of case, it is generally agreed that Rule 14 may be applied notwithstanding the restrictions on joinder existing under state law. The

---

220. *See* sections C(3)*(c) supra* (discussing supplemental personal jurisdiction in Rule 19 cases) & C(4)*(b) supra* (discussing supplemental personal jurisdiction in Rule 20 cases).

221. *See* Chapter 7(C)(2)*(c)* ("Personal Jurisdiction Restrictions on Joinder") *supra.*

222. *See* 6 CHARLES A. WRIGHT ET AL., FEDERAL PRACTICE AND PROCEDURE: CIVIL § 1445, at 346-47 (2d ed. 1990). In addition to the general unjustifiability of creating a doctrine of supplemental personal jurisdiction in Rule 14 cases, it should be noted that, as with Rule 19, Rule 4(k)(1)(B) contains a provision allowing third-party defendants to be subjected to personal jurisdiction when they are served outside a state and district, but within 100 miles of the place where the federal action is pending. As was the case with Rule 19, the existence of this provision, which demonstrates that federal rulemakers have considered the problem of long-arm jurisdiction over third-party defendants and not extended it further than the 100-mile area, militates against a doctrine of supplemental personal jurisdiction in Rule 14 cases.

223. *Id.* at 348.

224. *See* Chapter 7(F)(2)*(b)* ("Supplemental (Ancillary) Venue and Personal Jurisdiction Over Counterclaims and Cross-Claims") *supra.*

225. *See* Chapter 7(C)(3) *supra* ("Rules Enabling Act Problems Under Rule 18").

restriction on joinder under state law is not likely to be based on any particular substantive policies, but instead is probably an outgrowth of the historical reluctance in tort cases to compel the joinder of joint tortfeasors.[226] Thus, in the absence of evidence that a particular state joinder restriction is supported by specific substantive policies, permitting joinder under Rule 14 will not undermine any substantive purpose inherent in the restriction. In addition, the broader substantive rights of the parties are fully protected by joinder under Rule 14, as long as the federal courts do not permit a judgment to be enforced against the third-party defendant for contribution unless the liability of the principal defendant to the plaintiff has been determined.[227] Thus, Rule 14 merely accelerates the determination of the third-party defendant's liability, but does not expand it.[228] As a result, Rule 14 should be immunized from any attack on the ground that it would result in an expansion or contraction of the substantive rights of the parties on the merits of the case.

2. Interpleader

Interpleader allows a person in possession of money or property against which inconsistent claims are asserted to bring all the adverse claimants before a court in a single proceeding to resolve their claims. Like impleader, it is grounded in the policy of preventing a multiplicity of suits over the same subject matter, thus protecting against the attendant inconvenience, expense, and danger of inconsistent results.

(a) History of Interpleader

(i) "Strict" Bills of Interpleader

Interpleader existed at common law in certain kinds of cases to protect a defendant from double liability.[229] Interpleader shifted from the law courts to the equity courts over time, and the remedy ultimately came to be viewed as

---

226. *See* W. PAGE KEETON ET AL., PROSSER AND KEETON ON TORTS § 47, at 327 (5th ed. 1984). However, in cases in which Rule 14 is used to implead an insurer who is obligated under an insurance policy to indemnify the defendant for any amounts the defendant must pay the plaintiff, the same kinds of problems may exist as were discussed in Chapter 7(C)(3), *supra*, with joinder of contingent claims against insurers under Rule 18, when the insurer has contracted with the defendant for immunity from suit until a judgment has been rendered against the defendant, or when a state statute exists that prohibits joinder of the insurer until such time as a judgment has been rendered. In these situations, the Rules Enabling Act problems in Rule 18 cases are identical to those existing under Rule 14. The problems were adequately discussed in Chapter 7.

227. *See, e.g.,* Brown v. Shredex, Inc., 69 F. Supp. 2d 764 (D.S.C. 1999); 6 CHARLES A. WRIGHT ET AL., FEDERAL PRACTICE AND PROCEDURE: CIVIL § 1448, at 388-89 (2d ed. 1990).

228. *See* 6 CHARLES A. WRIGHT ET AL., FEDERAL PRACTICE AND PROCEDURE: CIVIL § 1448, at 388-89 (2d ed. 1990).

229. *See generally* Zechariah Chafee, Jr., *Modernizing Interpleader*, 30 YALE L.J. 814 (1921); Ralph V. Rogers, *Historical Origins of Interpleader*, 51 YALE L.J. 924 (1942).

exclusively equitable.[230] The common-law remedy of interpleader was available only to defendants, but the equitable remedy was also available to plaintiffs beset by multiple claimants.[231] Nevertheless, "strict" technical requirements circumscribed even equitable interpleader and limited its usefulness. The most often quoted summary of these "strict" requirements was made by Professor Pomeroy:

> 1. The same thing, debt, or duty must be claimed by both or all parties against whom the relief is demanded;
> 2. All their adverse titles or claims must be dependent, or be derived from a common source;
> 3. The person asking the relief—the plaintiff—must not have or claim any interest in the subject-matter;
> 4. He must have incurred no independent liability to either of the claimants; that is, he must stand perfectly indifferent between them, in the position merely of a stakeholder.[232]

Illustration 8-36. S, a student, has been eating at a college boarding house. *S* made no express agreement with anyone, but expected to pay the standard rates for the meals consumed. A quarrel breaks out between *C-1*, the cook in the boarding house, and *C-2*, the cook's spouse, about which of them owns the house. *C-1* claims that *S* should pay *C-1* $75.00 for the meals *S* has consumed. *C-2* claims that *S* should pay *C-2* $100.00 for the meals consumed. Under Pomeroy's statement of the requirements for interpleader, *S* could not force *C-1* and *C-2* to interplead because the "same thing, debt, or duty" is not being claimed by all the claimants. *C-1* and *C-2* are claiming different amounts.[233]

Illustration 8-37. S is in possession of land. *C-1* claims title to the land under a deed and claims that *S* owes *C-1* $1,000 as the value of *S's* use and occupation of the land. *C-2* claims title to the same land by adverse possession and also claims that *S* owes *C-2* $1,000 as the value of *S's* use and occupation of the land. Under Pomeroy's statement of the requirements for interpleader, *S* could not force *C-1* and *C-2* to interplead. The titles of the claimants are not derived from a common source. *C-1* claims under a deed. *C-2* claims by virtue of adverse possession.

Illustration 8-38. S Insurance Co. issues a policy of automobile insurance to *A*. Subsequently, *A* is involved in an automobile accident with *C-1* and *C-2*, both of whom are injured in the accident. *C-1* and *C-2* both claim the $100,000 face amount of the insurance policy. *A's* negligence is conceded by everyone, but *S* refuses to pay the $100,000 on the ground that the policy issued to *A* does not cover the accident. *S* also wants to interplead *C-1* and *C-2*, so that *S* will not suffer double liability if *S's* position about the policy's coverage turns out to be

---

230. Professor Chafee stated that the shift of interpleader from the law to the equity courts was produced by the introduction of the jury in the common law courts. The jury "demanded a narrow issue and was unsuited to such old practices as interpleader and prohibition." *See* Zechariah Chafee, Jr., *Modernizing Interpleader*, 30 YALE L.J. 814, 822 (1921). Rogers, however, suggests that the shift may have been due to the fact that interpleader at common law was available only to defendants, not as an affirmative remedy, which was "its great weakness." *See* Ralph V. Rogers, *Historical Origins of Interpleader*, 51 YALE L.J. 924, 947-50 (1942).

231. *See* Ralph V. Rogers, *Historical Origins of Interpleader*, 51 YALE L.J. 924, 947-50 (1942).

232. 4 JOHN N. POMEROY, A TREATISE ON EQUITY JURISPRUDENCE § 1322, at 906 (5th ed. 1941).

233. *See* Zechariah Chafee, *Modernizing Interpleader*, 30 YALE L. REV. 814, 824 (1921).

unfounded. Under Pomeroy's statement of the requirements of interpleader, *S* may not force *C-1* and *C-2* to interplead. The stakeholder (*S*), is claiming an interest in the subject matter. *S* is disputing liability on the policy.

   Illustration 8-39. *S Insurance Co.* issued a policy of fire insurance to *A*. Subsequently, a fire destroyed the insured property. The *C-1* loan company, a mortgagee of the property, claims that *S* should pay *C-1* the proceeds of the policy. *C-1* instituted a suit against *S* to recover the proceeds. *S* settled the suit with *C-1* and agreed to pay the proceeds of the policy to *C-1* provided that *C-1's* action against *S* was dismissed on the merits. *C-2* loan company, a creditor of *A*, then claimed the proceeds of the policy as the result of a bankruptcy proceeding involving *A* prior to *S's* settlement with *C-1*. *S*, which has not yet paid the proceeds to *C-1*, wants to commence an interpleader proceeding against *C-1* and *C-2*. Under Pomeroy's statement of the requirements for interpleader, *S* may not force *C-1* and *C-2* to interplead. *S* is potentially liable independently to *C-1* under the settlement agreement. In addition, the "common source" requirement may be violated because *C-1* is claiming under a mortgage and *C-2* is claiming as a creditor who has received priority in bankruptcy proceedings. The "same debt" requirement may also be violated for this last reason.

(ii) Bills "in the Nature of Interpleader"

   The restrictions summarized by Pomeroy applied to a "strict" bill of interpleader. However, in addition to the strict bill, a bill "in the nature of inter-pleader" existed, which could be used by a "stakeholder" threatened with double liability. The stakeholder had to show an independent basis for equitable jurisdiction—for example, a stakeholder's suit for reformation of a contract. If such an independent basis existed, the requirements of the strict bill were not rigidly enforced. However, a good deal of confusion existed about the difference between a "strict" bill and a "bill in the nature of interpleader." It has been suggested that there was no real difference except as to whether the restrictions of a strict bill would be applied or not.[234] This suggestion was undoubtedly true because even in cases in which a strict bill was appropriate, the courts tended to honor Pomeroy's restrictions "in name only."[235] In addition, it should also be noted that some courts do not insist that the stakeholder be faced with a threat of double liability for interpleader. For example, some courts recognize that so-called "pie-slicing" interpleader is appropriate when the stakeholder seeks to assure that a limited fund (the "pie") is fairly apportioned ("sliced") among multiple claimants.[236]

---

234. *See* Geoffrey C. Hazard & Myron Moskovitz, *An Historical and Critical Analysis of Interpleader*, 52 CAL. L. REV. 706, 745-49 (1964).

   235. *See* 7 CHARLES A. WRIGHT ET AL., FEDERAL PRACTICE AND PROCEDURE: CIVIL § 1701, at 485 (2d ed. 1986).

   236. *See, e.g.,* Lawthorne v. Employers Ins. Co., 343 Md. 111, 680 A.2d 518 (1996) (pie-slicing interpleader proper). However, it would seem that the declaratory judgment procedure, discussed below, would be the preferable procedure to employ in "pie-slicing" cases when it is available. *See* subsection *(h) infra* (discussing the declaratory judgment procedure as an alternative to interpleader).

(iii) Interpleader in the State Courts

In state courts, the action of interpleader is usually provided for by statute or court rule. The Field Code, as amended in 1851, so provided in the second paragraph of § 122.[237] Curiously, the Field Code provision limited interpleader to defendants only, as at common law, while extending the remedy to claims against a fund, as in equity. The section also seemed to require that the claims relate to the same fund or thing.[238] This codification may well have impeded reform of interpleader in the states, because many code states copied the Field Code provision more or less verbatim, and some states still retain the provision more or less in this strict form.[239] Other states have modernized interpleader significantly.[240]

(b) Personal Jurisdiction Problems in Interpleader

The primary difficulty confronting American courts in interpleader cases was their inability to secure personal jurisdiction over adverse claimants to the money or property that was the subject of the dispute. In *New York Life Insurance Co. v. Dunlevy*,[241] the U.S. Supreme Court held that interpleader proceedings were "in personam" in nature and required personal service of process on the adverse claimants within the state. The general effect of *Dunlevy* was that a stakeholder who was subject to personal jurisdiction in a state where one of the claimants resided, but who could not obtain personal jurisdiction over all the other claimants in the state where the property that was the subject of the claims was located, could not escape the threat of double liability. After *Dunlevy*, the property could not be the subject of an in rem proceeding to settle the adverse claims, and the nonresident claimants could not be subjected to personal jurisdiction if they could not be served within the state. However, if the stakeholder was subject to personal jurisdiction in the claimants' home states, the stakeholder could be sued in separate actions and potentially lose all the actions.[242]

---

237.   A defendant, against whom an action is pending upon a contract, or for specific, real, or personal property, may at any time before answer, upon affidavit, that a person not a party to the action, and without collusion with him, makes against him a demand for the same debt, or property, upon due notice to such person, and the adverse party apply to the court for an order to substitute such person in his place, and discharge him from liability to either party on his depositing in court the amount of the debt, or delivering the property, or its value, to such person as the court may direct; and the court may, in its discretion, make the order.

Act of July 10, 1851, ch. 479, § 122, 1851 N.Y. Laws 876, 883.

238. *See* Geoffrey C. Hazard & Myron Moskovitz, *An Historical and Critical Analysis of Interpleader*, 52 CAL. L. REV. 706, 748-49 (1964).

239. *See* NEB. REV. STAT. § 25-325 (1995).

240. *See, e.g.*, CAL. CODE CIV. PROC. § 386 (West Supp. 1999).

241. 241 U.S. 518, 36 S. Ct. 613, 60 L. Ed. 1140 (1916).

242. *See* Chapter 3(B)(1)*(a)* ("Affirmative Principles of In Rem Jurisdiction") (discussing the *Dunlevy* case) *supra*.

It is unlikely that the *Dunlevy* restriction still exists under the "minimum contacts test" of *International Shoe Co. v. Washington*.[243] The modern constitutional test has broadened the authority of the states to subject adverse claimants to personal jurisdiction in the state where the property that is the subject of the claims is located. In such cases, the adverse claimants will usually have minimum contacts with the state in which the action is brought. If they do not, jurisdiction would only exist if the Supreme Court someday approves of "jurisdiction by necessity."[244]

(c) *"Statutory" Interpleader in Federal Courts*

Even before *International Shoe* broadened the ability of the states to assert jurisdiction over nonresidents, Congress had extended the authority of federal courts over interstate interpleader cases to alleviate the *Dunlevy* problem. In response to the problem created by the *Dunlevy* case for multi-state businesses like insurance companies, Congress enacted interpleader statutes in 1917, 1925, 1926, and 1936.[245]

Section 1335 of Title 28 of the *United States Code* confers special subject-matter jurisdiction on federal courts in interpleader actions. A jurisdictional amount in controversy of only $500 must be involved in the action. Furthermore, jurisdiction exists if there are two or more adverse claimants of diverse citizenship as defined in § 1332 of Title 28. Thus, the citizenship of the stakeholder is irrelevant under § 1335. Two or more claimants can be citizens of the same state, as long as one claimant is a citizen of some other state.[246] Section 1335 also eliminates the rigid requirements of a strict bill in interpleader by stating that an action "of interpleader or in the nature of interpleader" may be entertained even though the titles of the claimants do not have a common origin, or are not identical, but are adverse and independent of one another.[247] This language abolishes the "common source" restriction and the "same debt" restriction. Although it is unclear from the wording of the statute, the requirement that the stakeholder be "disinterested" has also been abolished. In part, the section achieves this result by authorizing an action "in the nature of interpleader." Historically, however, a bill in the nature of interpleader required an independent ground of equity jurisdiction. The federal courts have generally eroded this requirement,[248] probably because of the merger of law and equity

---

243. 326 U.S. 310, 66 S. Ct. 154, 90 L. Ed. 95 (1945); *see* Chapter 3(B)(1)*(a)* ("Affirmative Principles of In Rem Jurisdiction") *supra*; Chapter 3(D) ("The Development of Modern Restrictions on State-Court Jurisdiction: The Minimum Contacts Test") *supra*; Chapter 3(E) ("The Status of the Territorial Rules of Jurisdiction After *International Shoe*") *supra*.

244. *See* Chapter 3(I) ("Jurisdiction by Necessity").

245. *See* 7 CHARLES A. WRIGHT ET AL., FEDERAL PRACTICE AND PROCEDURE: CIVIL § 1701, at 486-91 (2d ed. 1986). The current version of these federal interpleader statutes is found in §§ 1335, 1397, and 2361 of Title 28 in the *United States Code*.

246. *See* 28 U.S.C. § 1335(a).

247. *See* 28 U.S.C. § 1335(b).

248. *See* 7 CHARLES A. WRIGHT ET AL., FEDERAL PRACTICE AND PROCEDURE: CIVIL § 1701, at 489-90 (2d ed. 1986).

by the Federal Rules of Civil Procedure. The only traditional restriction that remains in doubt under § 1335 is the requirement that the stakeholder not have incurred any independent liability to one of the claimants. The cases are split on whether this requirement remains under the statute, but the trend is to reject it. The reasoning seems to be that the drafters of the 1936 version of the statute viewed the no-independent-liability requirement as merely a special application of the "common source" rule.[249]

In addition to a special grant of subject-matter jurisdiction, special provisions for venue and service of process for actions brought under § 1335 also exist. Section 1397 of Title 28 provides that venue in an action under § 1335 is proper in any district where one or more of the claimants resides.[250] Section 2361 provides for nationwide service of process on all claimants. It also provides that the district court may restrain the claimants from instituting any proceeding in any state or federal court affecting the property in the interpleader action.[251]

As noted in Chapter 3, the traditional assumption was that Congress had absolute power to give the federal courts nationwide long-arm jurisdiction in any case, without the same kinds of constitutional restrictions that apply to state legislatures under the Fourteenth Amendment.[252] This assumption was based on the territorial power theory of *Pennoyer v. Neff.* The idea was that the power of a state legislature was limited by the territorial boundaries of the state under the Fourteenth Amendment. The power of Congress, however, was limited under the Fifth Amendment only by the territorial boundaries of the United States. When the *International Shoe* line of cases substituted a constitutional test that focused on the burdens of the place of action on the defendant for the territorial power theory of *Pennoyer*, the traditional assumption that applied to Congress' power under the Fifth Amendment became questionable. When confronted with this issue, the Supreme Court could hold that Congress cannot enact nationwide long-arm statutes for the federal courts which impose unreasonable burdens on defendants.[253] If this result occurs, the long-arm jurisdiction provided for under § 2361 will have to be applied with a view to the contacts between the claimants and the location of the action. However, the Supreme Court's decision in *Burnham v. Superior Court*[254] may make it more likely that the traditional view of the power of Congress will prevail. If the Court adopts Justice Scalia's position in *Burnham*, the critical factor may be that the longstanding assumption that Congress' power to confer nationwide jurisdiction on the federal courts is

---

249. *See id.* § 1706, at 519-20.

250. *See* 28 U.S.C. § 1397; *see also* Carolina Cas. Ins. Co. v. Mares, 826 F. Supp. 149 (E.D. Va. 1993) (actions of statutory interpleader need not be brought in a district designated in § 1391(b); section 1391(b) limits venue "except as otherwise provided by law"; in statutory interpleader, § 1391(b) must yield to § 1397).

251. *See* 28 U.S.C. § 2361. *See generally* David B. Levendusky, Annotation, *Federal Interpleader Proceeding as In Rem or In Personam in Context of Problem of Service of Process Upon Particular Claimant*, 17 A.L.R. Fed. 447 (1973).

252. *See* Chapter 3(L) ("Special Problems of Amenability to Process in Federal Court") *supra*.

253. *See id.* (discussing lower federal court decisions which hold that the Fifth Amendment contains standards protecting the defendant from burdensome litigation similar to those imposed by the Fourteenth Amendment on the states).

254. 495 U.S. 604, 110 S. Ct. 2105, 109 L. Ed. 2d 631 (1990). The *Burnham* decision is discussed in detail in Chapter 3(E)(2) ("Transient Presence Jurisdiction") *supra*.

absolute. That traditional assumption is still accepted by many lower courts. Thus, continued acceptance by the courts along with the historical pedigree of the rule may serve to validate it. Even if the Court adopts the minimum contacts analysis advocated in Justice Brennan's opinion, absolute congressional power may still be validated. As noted in Chapter 3, the traditional acceptance of the rule may receive enough weight in the analysis to sustain its validity, or other factors such as the procedural mechanisms available in the federal courts to alleviate the burdens of suit in a particular action may result in its preservation.[255]

Illustration 8-40. *S*, a citizen of State *X*, is in possession of a $100,000 fund of money claimed by *C-1*, a citizen of State *Y*, and *C-2*, a citizen of State *Z*. *S* commences an action of interpleader against *C-1* and *C-2* in a U.S. District Court in State *Y*. *C-1* is personally served with process in State *Y*. *C-2* is served with process in State *Z* pursuant to 28 U.S.C. § 2361. Subject-matter jurisdiction is proper under 28 U.S.C. § 1335, because *C-1* and *C-2* are citizens of different states. Venue is proper under 28 U.S.C. § 1397 because the action was brought in a district where one of the claimants (*C-1*) resides. Statutory personal jurisdiction is proper under 28 U.S.C. § 2361. However, if *C-2* has no contacts, ties, or relations with State *Y*, the constitutional restrictions that exist under the Due Process Clause of the Fifth Amendment on the power of Congress to confer personal jurisdiction on the U.S. District Courts may be violated.[256]

(d) "Rule" Interpleader in Federal Courts

In addition to the special form of "statutory" interpleader provided in §§ 1335, 1397, and 2361 of Title 28 of the *United States Code*, federal "rule" interpleader also exists under Rule 22 of the Federal Rules of Civil Procedure. "Rule" interpleader differs from "statutory" interpleader (under § 1335) in several respects. Subject-matter jurisdiction in actions under Rule 22 must be found in the general grants of subject-matter jurisdiction in Title 28 of the *United States Code*. Thus, a "federal question" under 28 U.S.C. § 1331 or diversity of citizenship under 28 U.S.C. § 1332 usually must be present.[257] When diversity of citizenship is the sole basis of jurisdiction, more than $75,000 must be in controversy. Furthermore, complete diversity of citizenship must exist between the stakeholder on the one hand and all the claimants on the other.[258] In addition, actions under Rule 22 are governed by the general venue provision, 28 U.S.C. § 1391. Thus, venue is proper in a diversity case under § 1332 only in a district where (1) one of the defendants resides, if all defendants reside in the same state,

---

255. *Cf.* Chapter 3(E)(2) ("Transient Presence Jurisdiction") *supra*; Chapter 3(G)(1) ("Cases to Which the Minimum Contact Test Applies") *supra*; Chapter 3(G)(2)*(b)(iv)* ("The Reasonableness Test") *supra*; Chapter 3(L)(1) ("The Constitutional Standard Under Federal Long-Arm Statutes and Rules") *supra*.

256. However, it may be possible, as discussed below, for *S* to commence an action of "rule" interpleader in some other federal court that would satisfy all constitutional requirements.

257. *See* Commercial Union Ins. Co. v. United States, 999 F.2d 581 (D.C. Cir. 1993); *see also* Truck-A-Tune, Inc. v. Re, 23 F.3d 60 (2d Cir. 1994) (statutory interpleader improper because of interaction between "permanent resident alien" language of § 1332(a) and provisions governing representatives of estates in § 1332(c)(2); Rule 22 interpleader proper because complete diversity existed between stakeholder and claimants).

258. *See* Chapter 2(C) ("Subject-Matter Jurisdiction of the Federal Courts") *supra*.

(2) a substantial part of the events or omissions giving rise to the claim occurred, or a substantial part of property that is the subject of the action is situated, or (3) personal jurisdiction may be obtained over all the defendants, if there is no other district in which the action may be brought.[259] Personal jurisdiction in actions under Rule 22 must be acquired in the ordinary fashion provided in Rule 4. When nonresident claimants are involved, the state in which the district court is sitting will usually have to have a long-arm statute of some sort permitting jurisdiction to be asserted over the claimants consistent with the Fourteenth Amendment.[260]

Although the subject-matter jurisdiction, venue, and personal jurisdiction restrictions on statutory interpleader are generally more liberal than the restrictions on rule interpleader, circumstances exist in which rule interpleader is available and statutory interpleader is not. For example, subject-matter jurisdiction is proper in statutory interpleader cases only when two or more claimants are citizens of different states. Thus, if diversity exists between the stakeholder and the claimants, but not between the claimants, only rule interpleader is available. Likewise, if the stakeholder wishes to bring the action in a district where none of the claimants resides—for example, where the events giving rise to the claims occurred—rule interpleader must be used because of the venue restrictions of § 1397.[261] Finally, 28 U.S.C. § 2361 only permits service of the claimants in "the respective districts where the claimants reside or may be found." Therefore, if one or more claimants reside outside the United States and cannot be "found" in a district, § 2361 may not be used to assert personal jurisdiction over the claimant. Rule interpleader might still be available, however, by serving process on the claimant in one of the ways provided in Federal Rule 4.

Illustration 8-41. Assume the same facts as *Illustration 8-40*, with the additional fact that the events giving rise to the claims of *C-1* and *C-2* to the fund of money occurred entirely in State *Q*. If *S* wants to institute an action of federal interpleader in State *Q*, *S* can probably do so, assuming that State *Q* has an appropriate long-arm statute that can be utilized under Rule 4.[262] Subject-matter jurisdiction is proper under 28 U.S.C. § 1332 because complete diversity of citizenship exists between *S*, on the one hand, and all of the claimants, on the other. The jurisdictional amount requirement is satisfied because the amount of the fund is $100,000. Venue is proper under 28 U.S.C. § 1391 because the action is brought in the district where all the events giving rise to the claim occurred. The Fourteenth Amendment restrictions on the authority of State *Q* to assert personal jurisdiction over the claimants are probably satisfied by the fact that the events giving rise to the claim occurred entirely in State *Q*. Therefore, minimum contacts probably exist between the claims and the claimants and State *Q*. *S* may

---

259. *See* Chapter 4(C) ("Venue in Federal Courts") *supra*.

260. *See* Chapter 3(K) ("Service of Process"); Chapter 3(L) ("Special Problems of Amenability to Process in Federal Court") *supra*.

261. *Cf.* Carolina Cas. Ins. Co. v. Mares, 826 F. Supp. 149 (E.D. Va. 1993) (section 1391 must yield to § 1397 in statutory interpleader actions).

262. *S* may be able to commence an action of interpleader in state or federal court in State *Q*. If *S* wants to commence an action of state interpleader, *S* will have to comply with whatever restrictions State *Q* places on the action of interpleader under its own law, and State *Q* will have to have a long-arm statute that applies to the facts of the case.

also be able to maintain an action in the state where *S* resides–State *X*. Although the 1990 amendments to 28 U.S.C. § 1391(a) generally eliminated the ability of a plaintiff to predicate venue in the district where the plaintiff resides,[263] here the property that is the subject of the action is located in State *X*, where *S* lives. Thus, venue is proper under 28 U.S.C. § 1391(a)(2) in the district in State *X* where the fund is located. Furthermore, in Chapter 3, it was observed that while *Shaffer v. Heitner*[264] restricted the ability to assert personal jurisdiction over defendants based on the mere ownership of property within the state, the Supreme Court was careful to preserve the authority of the state where property is located to adjudicate direct claims to the property.[265] Thus, if State *X* possesses an appropriate long-arm statute, the minimum contacts test may well be satisfied by an assertion of personal jurisdiction over *C-1* and *C-2* to settle their claims to the fund in that state.

* * * * *

Like statutory interpleader, Federal Rule 22 abolishes the requirements of the strict bill of interpleader. Rule 22 provides that actions under Rule 22 are not objectionable even though "the claims of the several claimants or the titles on which their claims depend do not have a common origin or are not identical but are adverse to and independent of one another, or that the plaintiff avers that the plaintiff is not liable in whole or part to any or all of the claimants."[266] Thus, this language abolishes the "common-source," "same-debt," and "disinterested stakeholder" requirements. Some courts have held that the language allowing the plaintiff (stakeholder) to aver that there is no liability to one or more of the claimants abolishes the requirement that the stakeholder have incurred no independent liability to any of the claimants.[267] This result seems questionable. The language in Rule 22 seems to be a direct attempt only to abolish the "disinterested stakeholder" requirement. However, as suggested in the discussion of 28 U.S.C. § 1335, above, the no-independent-liability requirement may simply be a special application of the "common-source" requirement. If so, the abolition of the "common-source" restriction by Rule 22 will also have abolished the no-independent-liability requirement.

(e) The Effect of the Supplemental Jurisdiction Statute on Interpleader Jurisdiction

One interesting question is whether the supplemental jurisdiction statute has had any effect on interpleader practice in the federal courts. Considering federal question jurisdiction first, the statute will have no effect on jurisdiction under 28 U.S.C. § 1335 because jurisdiction under that statute is based entirely

---

263. *See* Chapter 4(C)(1) ("Plaintiff's Residence as Proper Venue") *supra*.

264. 433 U.S. 186, 97 S. Ct. 2569, 53 L. Ed. 2d 683 (1977).

265. *See Shaffer*, 433 U.S. at 207-08, 97 S. Ct. at 258-82, 53 L. Ed. 2d at 699-700; *see also* Chapter 4(E)(1) ("Quasi in Rem and Related Jurisdictional Doctrines") *supra*.

266. FED. R. CIV. P. 22.

267. *See* 7 CHARLES A. WRIGHT ET AL., FEDERAL PRACTICE AND PROCEDURE: CIVIL § 1706, at 521 (2d ed. 1986).

on diversity of citizenship. Obviously, if all of the claims to the money or property in question arise under federal law, federal question jurisdiction would exist in a Rule 22 interpleader case without the need to invoke the supplemental jurisdiction statute. Thus, the only situation that could be affected by the supplemental jurisdiction statute is one in which at least one claim to the property arises under federal law and other claims arise under state law, with diversity of citizenship not existing between the parties to the action. Under the claim-specific interpretation of § 1367(a) discussed in Chapter 2(C)(4)*(d)(i)*, above, federal question jurisdiction would exist over the federal claim under § 1331, and supplemental jurisdiction would exist over the state claim by virtue of § 1367.[268]

Turning to interpleader based on diversity jurisdiction, the first point to make is that § 1367(b) does not exclude from the supplemental jurisdiction Rule 22 claims over which supplemental jurisdiction exists under § 1367(a). Unlike the "Rule 20 gap," which was discussed in section C(4)*(b)*, above, and unlike the omission of a reference to Rule 23 from § 1367(b), which is discussed in section D(4)*(c)*, below, the omission of a reference to Rule 22 in § 1367(b) does not seem unintentional. It is likely that the drafters of the statute believed that there would be no consequences from such an omission because of the existence of § 1335, which creates jurisdiction based on incomplete diversity of citizenship between any two claimants. Thus, between Rule 22 interpleader under § 1332 and statutory interpleader under § 1335, all cases of interpleader depending on diversity of citizenship would be covered.

Note, however, that in a case of Rule 22 interpleader, the combined effect of § 1367(a) & (b) under the claim specific interpretation of the statute discussed in Chapter 2 would be to create supplemental jurisdiction over a claim by a nondiverse claimant in a case that also contains a claim by a diverse claimant that exceeds $75,000. Although jurisdiction in such a case would also exist under § 1335, the effect of the supplemental jurisdiction statute in this kind of case would be to broaden the venue in which an interpleader action could be brought. If the action is brought under § 1335, venue would be proper only in a district in which one of the claimants resides. However, the ability to use Rule 22, § 1332, and § 1367(a) to establish subject-matter jurisdiction means that venue would be proper under the general venue statute, 28 U.S.C. § 1391(a). For example, the stakeholder could sue in a district in which the property that is the

---

268. The cases subsequent to § 1367(a) generally support this interpretation, but without citation to the statute itself. *See* Commercial Union Ins. Co. v. United States, 999 F.2d 581 (D.C. Cir. 1993); Blackmon Auctions, Inc. v. Van Buren Truck Ctr., Inc., 901 F. Supp. 287 (W.D. Ark. 1995). Furthermore, it may be that in the absence of § 1367(a) no jurisdiction would exist over the state claim in the example given, because the claim would represent an example of "pendent" or "supplemental" party jurisdiction, which *Finley v. United States*, discussed in Chapter 2(C)(4)*(c)*, held was not permissible under statutes like § 1331 and which § 1367(a) was designed to overrule. Note, however, that for supplemental jurisdiction to exist, the federal and state claims would have to be closely enough related to fall within the same constitutional case or controversy. As noted in the preceding subsection, Rule 22 abolishes the common source requirement for interpleader. It is possible to reason that the relationship between the federal question and state claims might not meet the case or controversy requirement if they do not arise from a common source, because the factual relationship between the claims would not be sufficient. However, the preferable conclusion is that the claims fall within the same constitutional case even if they do not arise from a common source, because they are claims to the same property.

subject of the action is situated, which would be impossible under § 1335 unless that district also happens to be the residence of one of the claimants. Thus, while § 1367 may have no net effect on subject-matter jurisdiction in interpleader actions, it could well broaden the available venues in which interpleader actions can be brought.

Illustration 8-42. *S*, a citizen of State *X*, possesses property located in the District of State *X*, where *S* resides. *C-1*, a citizen of State *Y*, claims the property, as does *C-2*, a citizen of State *X*. The property is worth $100,000. Under these circumstances, *S* can sue in a federal interpleader action under 28 U.S.C. § 1335, because diversity of citizenship exists between the claimants in the action. However, if *S* sues under § 1335, the action will have to be brought either in the district where *C-1* or the district where *C-2* resides. If *S* brings a Rule 22 interpleader action, predicating jurisdiction on §§ 1332 and § 1367(a), with supplemental jurisdiction existing over the claim by *C-2*, the action may be brought under 28 U.S.C. § 1391(a)(2) in the District of State *X* in which *S* resides.[269]

(f) Rules Enabling Act Issues with Rule 22

Federal Rule 22 does not pose any serious issues of rule validity under the Rules Enabling Act. As with Rule 20, the ability to maintain federal interpleader when state law would forbid interpleader, or the inability to maintain interpleader under Rule 22 when state law would allow interpleader, involves no more than differences in procedural philosophy between the federal and state systems. These differences impose only tactical burdens and cannot be said to affect substantive rights seriously.[270]

(g) Interpleader "Stages"

Like state interpleader, federal interpleader is usually a two-stage procedure. In the first stage, the court determines whether the stakeholder has a right to force the claimants to litigate their claims in a single proceeding. Thus, for example, in the first stage of statutory interpleader, the court determines at the first stage whether either rule or statutory interpleader is appropriate, including whether subject-matter jurisdiction, venue, and personal jurisdiction are proper. In order to obtain statutory interpleader, the stakeholder must deposit the money or property that is the subject of the adverse claims into the court or post a bond

---

269. One federal court has held that "28 U.S.C. § 1367 does not apply to interpleader as the language of that statute refers only to 'Rule 14, 19, 20, or 24'" and "28 U.S.C. § 1367 may not be . . . used to limit the scope of Rule 22." *See* Atlas Corp. v. Marine Ins. Co., 155 F.R.D. 454, 465 n.7 (S.D.N.Y. 1994) (dictum; stakeholder was diverse from claimants and jurisdictional amount was satisfied). This statement is incorrect, because the omission of a reference to Rule 22 from § 1367(b) does not limit the scope of Rule 22 interpleader, but expands it. The statement is, however, typical of the confusion that § 1367 has produced.

270. *See* section C(4)*(c) supra* (discussing Rules Enabling Act issues with Rule 20). Note also that a stakeholder threatened by double liability who is sued by one of the claimants in a federal action is a Rule 19(a)(2)(i) & (ii) party who can be protected under that rule. *See* section C(3)*(b) supra* (discussing application of Rule 19).

that will insure that the stakeholder will comply with the judgment of the court.[271] During the first stage of interpleader, the court also determines whether this requirement has been satisfied and will not allow the action to proceed unless it has. Once the court has decided that interpleader is proper, it will enter an order enjoining the claimants from prosecuting any other action concerning the subject matter of the interpleader proceeding.[272] If the stakeholder is disinterested—*i.e.*, if the stakeholder is asserting no personal claim to the fund—the court will discharge the stakeholder. If the court finds interpleader to be improper, it will dismiss the action.

In the second stage of interpleader, the claimants litigate their respective rights to the property. The court's initial order to the claimants may direct them to frame the issues for this second stage in their pleadings. The order also may make other provisions for the conduct of the second stage. Essentially, however, the second stage will proceed just as any other action in the absence of unusual circumstances. Thus, the action may be disposed of on summary judgment or after a trial before a judge or jury, whichever is appropriate. If one of the claimants asserts a counterclaim against the stakeholder for independent liability, that counterclaim, if permitted, may be adjudicated in the second stage. It may also be pushed to a third stage after the relative rights of the claimants to the stake have been determined. Generally, all of the Federal Rules of Civil Procedure governing pleading, claim joinder, and party joinder in ordinary cases apply to the second stage of interpleader.[273]

(h) Declaratory Judgment Actions as a Substitute for Interpleader

When interpleader is not available for some reason—for example, when it is confined by one or more of the traditional equity restrictions in a particular jurisdiction,[274] an action for a declaratory judgment can often be used as a

---

271. *See* 28 U.S.C. § 1335(a)(2); *see also In re* Ambassador Group Litig., 830 F. Supp. 147, 152 (E.D.N.Y. 1993) (to vest court with jurisdiction in a statutory interpleader action, plaintiff must deposit total amount sought by claimants, not what plaintiff views as its maximum liability). *See generally* David B. Levendusky, Annotation, *Availability of Interpleader to Insurance Company for Resolving Dispute as to Insurance Policy Under Federal Interpleader Acts (Presently 28 U.S.C.S. §§ 1335, 1397, 2361) and Rule 22 of Federal Rules of Civil Procedure*, 19 A.L.R. FED. 166 (1974).

272. In statutory interpleader actions, 28 U.S.C. § 2361 authorizes the court to enjoin the claimants from conducting proceedings in any state or federal court concerning the property that is the subject of the action. Section 2361 is an "expressly authorized exception" to the prohibition against state-court proceedings in 28 U.S.C. § 2283. However, § 2361 only applies in statutory interpleader cases, leaving the prohibition banning injunctions against injunctions against state proceedings intact in Rule 22 interpleader cases. It has been argued that injunctions against state proceedings should be available in Rule 22 interpleader cases, on the theory that such injunctions fit within another exception in § 2283 for orders "in aid of" the federal courts' "jurisdiction." *See* 7 CHARLES A. WRIGHT ET AL., FEDERAL PRACTICE AND PROCEDURE: CIVIL § 1717, at 616 (2d ed. 1986). However, given the fact that the "in aid of jurisdiction" exception would not allow an injunction against state proceedings in any other kind of parallel in personam state action, this seems questionable. *See generally* Donald L. Dorenberg, *What's Wrong With This Picture?: Rule Interpleader, the Anti-Injunction Act, In Personam Jurisdiction, and* M.C. Escher, 67 U. COLO. L. REV. 551 (1996).

273. For a detailed discussion of the practice in federal interpleader actions, see 7 CHARLES A. WRIGHT ET AL., FEDERAL PRACTICE AND PROCEDURE: CIVIL §§ 1714-1718 (2d ed. 1986).

274. *See* subsection (a) ("History of Interpleader") *supra*.

substitute. When a person (the stakeholder) is in possession of money or property against which multiple adverse claims are asserted, a live controversy exists that the declaratory judgment remedy will serve a useful purpose in resolving.[275] Thus, a stakeholder faced with an inability to obtain interpleader for any reason should always consider the possibility of a declaratory judgment action against the claimants.

The declaratory judgment remedy is available in federal as well as state court. Therefore, it can also be used as a substitute for the remedies of statutory and rule interpleader discussed in the previous subsection. However, there will seldom be an advantage to substituting a federal declaratory judgment action for an interpleader action. Assuming, as seems probable, that the traditional equity restrictions on interpleader no longer exist under 28 U.S.C. § 1335 and Rule 22, federal interpleader will be as readily available, if not more so, than a declaratory judgment remedy. In a declaratory judgment action, the stakeholder, as plaintiff, will have to satisfy all requirements of federal subject-matter jurisdiction, venue, and personal jurisdiction, just as in any other action.[276]

In fact, certain features of the federal declaratory judgment procedure may make it unavailable in typical interpleader cases, depending on how the federal courts view the requirements of the remedy. State actions are often commenced by the claimants against the stakeholder before a federal interpleader action can be brought. In *Wilton v. Seven Falls Co.*,[277] the Supreme Court held in a non-interpleader case that federal declaratory judgment proceedings are discretionary and that such proceedings should be denied when they will not serve a useful purpose in resolving the dispute or controversy between the parties. One situation in which such a situation will exist is when another action is pending between the same parties that can resolve the entire controversy, even if the action is pending in state court. In *Wilton*, a parallel state proceeding existed, and the Supreme Court expressly declined to answer the question whether a federal court might properly dismiss a declaratory judgment action in the absence of such a proceeding. However, other federal courts have held that the existence of another action is only one of a number of factors to be considered in exercising discretion to hear or decline to hear a federal declaratory judgment action.[278] The question is, how should these authorities be applied in interpleader situations? It is possible to reason that declaratory judgment actions brought as a substitute for interpleader should not be dismissed in preference to prior pending state actions, at least if the state actions exist in the form of multiple proceedings by the claimants. In such a case, the declaratory judgment action will arguably resolve in one proceeding what it will take multiple state actions to resolve and will thus serve a useful purpose in resolving the entire controversy that the state actions cannot serve.

---

275. *See* Chapter 2(C)(1)*(b)(iii)* ("Determining Federal Question Jurisdiction in Declaratory Judgment Actions") *supra; see also* DAN B. DOBBS, LAW OF REMEDIES § 1.1, at 7 (2d student ed. 1993).

276. *See generally* Commercial Union Ins. Co. v. United States, 999 F.2d 581 (D.C. Cir. 1993).

277. 515 U.S. 277, 115 S. Ct. 2137, 132 L. Ed. 2d 214 (1995); *see also* Golden Eagle Ins. Co. v. Travelers Cos., 95 F.3d 807 (9th Cir. 1996).

278. *See* Aetna Cas. & Sur. Co. v. Ind-Com Elec. Co., 139 F.3d 419 (4th Cir. 1998) (district court did not abuse its discretion in declining to hear the action in spite of the fact that no state action was pending).

Nevertheless, at least one case has held that if a declaratory action is brought to determine that the stakeholder has no liability and interpleader is requested in the alternative, the district court may abstain from giving *both* declaratory and interpleader relief under the *Wilton* standard.[279]

3. Intervention

Intervention is a procedure by which a person who is not a party to a pending action, but whose interests are affected by the action, may become a party. Intervention rules generally attempt to protect nonparties without unduly infringing upon the interests of the parties to the action.

(a) History of Intervention

Intervention was derived primarily from civil-law procedure. It was quite familiar in Roman law.[280] However, the common law restricted intervention because of a concern that it would interfere with the plaintiff's ability to control the action.[281] Nevertheless, some narrow procedures for intervention existed in early admiralty, common-law, and equity cases.[282]

Section 122 of the Field Code, as amended in 1851, provided a narrow right of intervention that generally corresponded to the pre-code equity practice.[283] In some code states, this Field Code provision was replaced by more lenient provisions extending the right of intervention to all sorts of civil actions in which a nonparty may have an interest in the subject matter of the suit or in the success or failure of either or both parties to the action.[284]

In the federal courts, intervention was governed by Equity Rule 37 and, in common-law actions, by the Conformity Acts. Rule 37 provided that "[a]nyone claiming an interest in the litigation may at any time be permitted to assert his right by intervention, but the intervention shall be in subordination to, and in recognition of, the propriety of the main proceeding."[285] This provision was replaced in 1938 by Federal Rule 24. Although the Advisory Committee Notes to the 1938 version of Rule 24 stated that it "amplifies and restates the present federal practice at law and in equity," Rule 24 made significant changes in federal practice. For one thing, Rule 24 distinguished intervention of right under Rule 24(a) and permissive intervention under Rule 24(b). This distinction was derived from English practice and had no basis in prior federal equity practice or code procedure. Furthermore, the provision in former Equity Rule 37 that

---

279. *See* National Union Fire Ins. Co. v. Karp, 108 F.3d 17 (2d Cir. 1997).

280. *See* CHARLES E. CLARK, HANDBOOK OF THE LAW OF CODE PLEADING § 65, at 420 (2d ed. 1947).

281. *See* 6 EDWARD J. BRUNET, MOORE'S FEDERAL PRACTICE § 24 App. 101 (3d ed. 1999).

282. *See id.*

283. [W]hen, in an action for the recovery of real or personal property, a person, not a party to the action, but having an interest in the subject thereof, makes application to the court, to be made a party, it may order him to be brought in by the proper amendment.

Act of July 10, 1851, ch. 479, § 122, 1851 N.Y. Laws 876, 883.

284. *See, e.g.,* NEB. REV. STAT. §§ 25-328 to 25-330 (1995).

285. 226 U.S. 627, 659 (1912).

intervention was to be "in subordination to, and in recognition of, the propriety of the main proceeding," was omitted in Rule 24.[286]

(b) Intervention Practice Under Rule 24

Federal Rule 24 exemplifies intervention practice in the federal courts and states that have adopted the Federal Rules model. An examination of Rule 24 will, therefore, provide a good illustration of modern intervention practice.

(i) Intervention as of Right

Federal Rule 24 has been amended several times since 1938. The last and most significant amendment occurred in 1966.[287] Original Rule 24(a) distinguished between persons whose interests were not represented adequately in the action and persons who might be affected adversely by a distribution of property in the action. This distinction was predicated on the two kinds of intervention statutes existing under the Codes.[288] The 1966 amendments to Rule 24(a) abolished this distinction. As the Advisory Committee noted, a nonparty's right to intervene should not have to depend on whether there is a fund to be distributed.[289] Rather, that right ought to depend upon more pragmatic considerations that the 1966 amendments sought to insure.

The 1938 version of Rule 24(a)(2) also required that a nonparty applying to intervene be in a situation such that the nonparty "is or may be bound by the judgment in the action." This language resulted in a Supreme Court holding that intervention of right under Rule 24(a)(2) was possible only when the judgment in the action would *legally bind* the applicant for intervention.[290] Under this holding, it was technically impossible for a nonparty to intervene under Rule 24(a)(2). As the Advisory Committee observed, if a member of a class were represented inadequately in an action, that member could not be bound by the judgment in the action, but if the representation of the member's interest was adequate, intervention under Rule 24(a)(2) was impossible. The 1966 amendment to Rule 24(a) eliminated this requirement and replaced it with a test designed to

---

286. *See generally* 7C CHARLES A. WRIGHT ET AL., FEDERAL PRACTICE AND PROCEDURE: CIVIL § 1903 (2d ed. 1986).

287. Before the 1966 amendment, Rule 24(a) read as follows:

(a) Intervention of right. Upon timely application anyone shall be permitted to intervene in an action: (1) when a statute of the United States confers an unconditional right to intervene; or (2) when the representation of the applicant's interest by existing parties is or may be inadequate and the applicant is or may be bound by a judgment in the action; or (3) when the applicant is so situated as to be adversely affected by a distribution or other disposition of property in the custody of the court or an officer thereof.

308 U.S. at 690-91 (1938).

288. *See* FED. R. CIV. P. 24 advisory committee's note to the 1938 version.

289. *See* FED. R. CIV. P. 24 advisory committee's note to the 1966 amendment.

290. *See* Sam Fox Publ'g Co. v. United States, 366 U.S. 683, 694, 81 S. Ct. 1309, 1315, 6 L. Ed. 2d 604, 612-13 (1961).

make intervention depend upon the practical effect that the judgment in the action might have on the nonparty.

Today, upon timely application,[291] Rule 24(a) provides for intervention of right in two situations. First, intervention of right is available when a statute of the United States confers an unconditional right to intervene.[292] Several situations fall within the first category described in Rule 24(a)(1).[293] However, the most important category of intervention of right cases is described in Rule 24(a)(2). Rule 24(a)(2) provides for intervention of right when the intervenor (1) claims an interest in the subject of the action and (2) is so situated that the disposition of the action may, as a practical matter, impair or impede the intervenor's ability to protect that interest, unless the intervenor's interest is adequately protected by the existing parties to the litigation.[294]

Rule 24(a)(2) imposes three requirements on the would-be intervenor. First, the applicant must claim an interest relating to the property or transaction that is the subject of the action.[295] The key term here is "interest." Before the 1966 amendments, Rule 24(a) had been held to require a substantial, legally protectable interest in the action before intervention would be permitted as a matter of right.[296] Under new Rule 24(a)(2), this same requirement still exists. Thus, for example, the "interest" requirement is satisfied when a nonparty claims ownership of property that is the subject of the litigation or asserts a lien to the property, or when the nonparty would be bound by the judgment.[297]

Illustration 8-43. *A* claims to own certain real property, which is in *B's* possession. *A* sues *B* for trespassing. *I* contends that *I* owns the property and seeks to intervene under Rule 24(a)(2) to resist *A's* claim. *I* also contends that *B* is a trespasser. Whether *A* owns the property depends on a question of law that will ultimately have to be resolved by an appellate court. *I* is claiming the kind of interest that is necessary for intervention under Rule 24(a).

* * * * *

However, several cases have gone further than the pre-1966 standard for determining the quality of interest necessary to satisfy the rule. These cases have focused on the policies underlying Rule 24(a)(2) intervention—to avoid multiple litigation over the same matter while simultaneously preventing a single lawsuit

---

291. *See, e.g.,* Sierra Club v. Espy, 18 F.3d 1202 (5th Cir. 1994) (application for intervention timely even though action pending for eight years before application made; claims that affected applicants' interests not asserted until fourth amended complaint); Annotation, *Timeliness of Application for Intervention as of Right Under Rule 24(a) of Federal Rules of Civil Procedure*, 57 A.L.R. FED. 150 (1982).

292. *See* FED. R. CIV. P. 24(a)(1).

293. *See, e.g.,* 28 U.S.C. § 2403 (intervention by United States or a state in actions involving constitutional questions); *see also* 7C CHARLES A. WRIGHT ET AL., FEDERAL PRACTICE AND PROCEDURE: CIVIL § 1906 (2d ed. 1986).

294. *See* FED. R. CIV. P. 24(a)(2).

295. *See generally* Eunice E. Eichelberger, Annotation, *What Is "Interest" Relating to Property or Transaction Which Is Subject of Action Sufficient to Satisfy That Requirement for Intervention as Matter of Right Under Rule 24(a)(2) of Federal Rules of Civil Procedure*, 73 A.L.R. FED. 448 (1985).

296. *See* 7C CHARLES A. WRIGHT ET AL., FEDERAL PRACTICE AND PROCEDURE: CIVIL § 1908, at 271 (2d ed. 1986).

297. *See id.* at 272-78.

from becoming unnecessarily complex.[298] The cases have indicated that these policies can better be served by relaxing the kind of "interest" that is required to justify intervention and focusing instead on the second and third requirements of Rule 24(a)(2). These requirements are that the action practically affect the applicant's interest and that the existing parties not adequately represent the applicant.

Illustration 8-44. In *Smuck v. Hobson*,[299] the parents of school children were allowed to intervene after judgment in a case when the board of education had decided not to appeal a desegregation order. The parents were perceived to have an interest in the ability of the school board to formulate effective educational policies. This interest would not have justified intervention before 1966, but it was enough to permit the parents to intervene for the limited purpose of attacking those portions of the desegregation order that imposed limitations on the school board's ability to formulate educational policies.

* * * * *

The second requirement of Rule 24(a)(2) is that the applicant be so situated that disposition of the action, as a *practical matter*, might impair or impede the applicant's ability to protect the applicant's interests.[300] This requirement abolishes the pre-1966 rule that the applicant must be legally bound by the judgment in order to intervene. Some decisions under this portion of the rule have gone so far as to indicate that the stare decisis effect of a case on a nonparty's interest may be sufficient to place the nonparty at a practical disadvantage in protecting the nonparty's interest.[301]

The third requirement of Rule 24(a)(2) is that the applicant's interest not be adequately represented by existing parties. Clearly, if the nonparty's interest is not represented at all, no adequate representation is possible. In addition, if a party is on the same side of an issue as the nonparty, but is adverse or hostile to the nonparty, the nonparty's interests are not adequately represented. The best example of a case in which the nonparty's interest is adequately represented is a class action in which all the members of the class have exactly the same interests. Another typical "adequate representation" situation is a case in which the

---

298. *See, e.g.*, Smuck v. Hobson, 408 F.2d 175 (D.C. Cir. 1969); Nuesse v. Camp, 385 F.2d 694 (D.C. Cir. 1967).

299. 408 F.2d 175 (D.C. Cir. 1969).

300. *See generally* Eunice E. Eichelberger, Annotation, *General Considerations in Determining What Constitutes Impairment of Proposed Intervenor's Interest to Support Intervention as Matter of Right Under Rule 24(a)(2) of Federal Rules of Civil Procedure*, 74 A.L.R. FED. 632 (1985); Eunice E. Eichelberger, Annotation, *What Constitutes Impairment of Proposed Intervenor's Interest to Support Intervention as Matter of Right Under Rule 24(a)(2) of Federal Rules of Civil Procedure in Employment Discrimination Actions*, 74 A.L.R. FED. 895 (1985); Eunice E. Eichelberger, Annotation, *What Constitutes Impairment of Proposed Intervenor's Interest to Support Intervention as Matter of Right Under Rule 24(a)(2) of Federal Rules of Civil Procedure in Actions Involving Contracts*, 75 A.L.R. FED. 769 (1985); Eunice E. Eichelberger, Annotation, *What Constitutes Impairment of Proposed Intervenor's Interest to Support Intervention as Matter of Right Under Rule 24(a)(2) of Federal Rules of Civil Procedure in Actions Involving Government-Supported Housing and Welfare Programs*, 75 A.L.R. FED. 570 (1985).

301. *See* Atlantis Dev. Corp. v. United States, 379 F.2d 818, 828 (5th Cir. 1967); *Illustration 8-43, supra.*

interests of the nonparty are represented by a formal representative, such as an executor or administrator.[302]

Illustration 8-45. Assume that an insurance company becomes subrogated to the rights of the insured party after paying a claim under an accident policy. The insurance company then sues the alleged tortfeasor. The insured's interest in recovering damages above the insurance coverage is not represented at all in the action.[303]

Illustration 8-46. On the facts of *Illustration 8-43*, *I*'s interests are not adequately protected by *B* because *I* is claiming that *B* is a trespasser. Therefore, while both *I* and *B* have an interest in resisting *A*'s claim, the adversity between *I* and *B* precludes the assumption that *B* will adequately protect *I*'s interest.[304]

(ii) Permissive Intervention

Rule 24(b) provides for *permissive intervention* (*i.e.*, intervention in the discretion of the court) when any one of three following situations exists: (1) "when a statute of the United States confers a conditional right to intervene" on a nonparty; (2) "when a nonparty's claim or defense and the main action have a question of law or fact in common"; or (3) when a state or federal official charged with administering a state or federal statute or executive order seeks to intervene in an action in which one of the parties relies on the statute or executive order, or on any regulation, order, requirement, or agreement, issued or made pursuant to the statute or executive order.[305]

Several federal statutes confer a conditional right to intervene.[306] Like intervention of right, however, the most important category of permissive intervention cases falls outside the "statutory" or "state or federal official" provisions. Because Rule 24(b)(2) requires only that the intervenor's claim or defense share a common question of law or fact with the main action, it may appear that the intervention would be broadly available.[307] However, interven-

---

302. *See* 7C CHARLES A. WRIGHT ET AL., FEDERAL PRACTICE AND PROCEDURE: CIVIL § 1909, at 324-30 (2d ed. 1986). *See generally* Eunice E. Eichelberger, Annotation, *When Is Interest of Proposed Intervenor Inadequately Represented by Existing Party so as to Satisfy that Requirement for Intervention as of Right Under Rule 24(a)(2) of Federal Rules of Civil Procedure*, 74 A.L.R. FED. 327 (1985).

303. *See* Glens Falls Ins. Co. v. Cook Bros., 23 F.R.D. 269 (S.D. Ind. 1959).

304. *See* Atlantis Dev. Corp. v. United States, 379 F.2d 818 (5th Cir. 1967); *see also* Mille Lacs Band of Chippewa Indians v. Minnesota, 989 F.2d 994 (8th Cir. 1993) (presumption exists that state adequately represents the interests of all its citizens; to overcome presumption, an intervenor must demonstrate an interest not shared by the general citizenry).

305. FED. R. CIV. P. 24(b).

306. *See, e.g.*, 42 U.S.C. §§ 2000a-3(a), 2000-3-5(e) (public accommodations and unlawful employment practices provisions of the Civil Rights Act of 1964); *see also* 7C CHARLES A. WRIGHT ET AL., FEDERAL PRACTICE AND PROCEDURE: CIVIL § 1910 (2d ed. 1986).

307. *See* Solid Waste Agency v. United States Army Corps of Eng'rs, 101 F.3d 503 (7th Cir. 1996) (intervention of right denied because applicant's interest would be adequately protected by existing parties; case remanded for determination of whether permissive intervention appropriate because district court erroneously held that applicants lacked an interest sufficient to justify permissive intervention; Rule 24(b) does not require an "interest," only a common question).

tion under Rule 24(b) is wholly discretionary with the court.[308] The court may deny intervention under Rule 24(b) even when the intervenor's claim and the principal action share a common question of law or fact, if the intervention would unduly delay adjudication of the case or otherwise prejudice the rights of the existing parties.[309]

(c) Subject-Matter Jurisdiction Problems Under Rule 24

As with many other federal party and claim joinder rules, some of the most complicated problems under Rule 24 concern subject-matter-jurisdiction limitations in federal cases. Some of these problems may have been alleviated in 1990 by the addition of 28 U.S.C. § 1367 to the Judicial Code.[310] As discussed in Chapter 2, § 1367 codifies and expands the doctrines of "ancillary" and "pendent" jurisdiction under the label "supplemental jurisdiction."[311] However, while § 1367 may have cured certain problems with the exercise of "ancillary jurisdiction" in intervention cases, it may also have created new difficulties of interpretation.[312]

Before 1966, it was generally held that if intervention was of right, ancillary jurisdiction was available to eliminate the need for independent jurisdictional grounds for intervention. On the other hand, if intervention was permissive, ancillary jurisdiction was not available, and the intervenor had to demonstrate independent jurisdictional grounds before intervention would be permitted.[313] After 1966, the courts continued to hold that ancillary jurisdiction applied to Rule 24(a) intervention, but not to Rule 24(b) intervention.[314] Yet it is clear that the 1966 amendments broadened Rule 24(a), so that some cases that would have qualified for permissive intervention under Rule 24(b) before 1966 would qualify today for intervention as a matter of right under Rule 24(a).[315] Rule 82 states that the Federal Rules of Civil Procedure "shall not be construed to extend or limit the jurisdiction of the [federal] district courts or the venue of actions therein."[316] This provision led some commentators to raise a question about the application of the ancillary jurisdiction doctrine in Rule 24 cases: how could ancillary jurisdiction have been improper before the 1966 amendments over those claims that were appropriate only for permissive intervention under Rule

---

308. *See* 7C CHARLES A. WRIGHT ET AL., FEDERAL PRACTICE AND PROCEDURE: CIVIL § 1913, at 375 (2d ed. 1986).

309. This requirement is imposed by the last sentence of Rule 24(b): "In exercising its discretion the court shall consider whether the intervention will unduly delay or prejudice the adjudication of the rights of the original parties." FED. R. CIV. P. 24(b).

310. *See* Chapter 2(C)(4)*(d)* ("The Codification of Pendent and Ancillary Jurisdiction") *supra*.

311. *See id.*

312. *See generally* Marilyn J. Ireland, *Supplemental Jurisdiction Over Claims in Intervention*, 23 N. MEX. L. REV. 57 (1993).

313. *See* 7C CHARLES A. WRIGHT ET AL., FEDERAL PRACTICE AND PROCEDURE: CIVIL § 1917, at 464-65 (2d ed. 1986).

314. *See id.* at 466-72.

315. *See id.* at 473-74.

316. FED. R. CIV. P. 82.

24(b), but be proper after 1966 over the same claims when they were moved into the intervention of right category?[317]

The answer to this question lies in the nature of ancillary jurisdiction. In determining whether ancillary jurisdiction was appropriate under Rule 24, the key questions should have been (1) whether the intervenor's claim and the principal claim were related sufficiently to be considered a part of the same "case or controversy" within Article III of the Constitution and (2) whether the other policies supporting the specific statutory grant of subject-matter jurisdiction applicable to the case would be served (or harmed) by allowing intervention.[318] Unfortunately, instead of directly asking these questions, the courts sought to decide the ancillary jurisdiction question on the basis of easy labels such as "intervention of right" and "permissive intervention." Had the courts instead focused directly on the bases of the ancillary jurisdiction doctrine, they would have understood that the statutory policies supporting grants of jurisdiction to the federal courts were the most important determinants of whether a case of intervention of right or permissive intervention is appropriate for the application of ancillary jurisdiction.[319] Under these policies, particularly in diversity actions,[320] ancillary jurisdiction was indeed inappropriate in permissive intervention cases. However, as discussed below, it should also have been held inappropriate in intervention of right cases under Rule 24(a)(2).

Illustration 8-47. *A*, a citizen of State *X*, *B*, a citizen of State *Y*, and *I*, a citizen of State *Y*, collide in their automobiles in State *Y*. *A* and *I* are injured. *A* sues *B* in the U.S. District Court for the District of State *Y*. *A* asserts a claim for $500,000 for personal injuries received in the accident. *I*, who also wants to assert a claim against *B* for personal injuries received in the accident, seeks to intervene in the action between *A* and *B*. Intervention is not proper as a matter of right under Rule 24(a)(2). *I* probably does not posses an interest "relating to" the transaction that is the subject of the action between *A* and *B*, even though *I's* claim also arises out of that action. Even if *I's* interest is sufficient under Rule 24(a)(2), however, *I* is not situated so that disposition of the action between *A* and

---

317. *See, e.g.,* 7C CHARLES A. WRIGHT ET AL., FEDERAL PRACTICE AND PROCEDURE: CIVIL § 1917, at 474 (2d ed. 1986).

318. *See* Chapter 2(C)(4)*(a)-(c) supra*.

319. *But see* 7C CHARLES A. WRIGHT ET AL., FEDERAL PRACTICE AND PROCEDURE: CIVIL § 1917, at 474 (2d ed. 1986) (arguing that the pre-1966 test for ancillary jurisdiction should be applied under the amended rule).

320. Chapter 2(C)(4)*(c)* ("The Statutory Basis of Pendent and Ancillary Jurisdiction") and section C(4) ("Permissive Joinder of Parties"), *supra*, discussed the Supreme Court's decision in *Finley v. United States*. *Finley* prohibited pendent party jurisdiction in federal question cases when the statutory grant of federal question jurisdiction being exercised did not affirmatively authorize jurisdiction over pendent parties. *Finley* involved the assertion of a federal question claim against one defendant and the joinder of another nondiverse defendant on a state claim. However, the Supreme Court's opinion in *Finley* was broad enough to encompass the assertion of a federal claim against a defendant by one plaintiff and the assertion of a state claim by a nondiverse plaintiff. *Finley* thus might have precluded intervention of nondiverse defendants who could not have been originally joined by a plaintiff who possessed only state claims against the intervenor. Likewise, *Finley* might have precluded intervention by nondiverse plaintiffs wishing to assert state claims against the defendant in a federal question action. However, the impact of *Finley* on intervention in federal question cases is not as clear as the impact of the *Kroger* decision, discussed below, on intervention in diversity actions. As discussed in Chapter 2(C)(4)*(c)* and section C(4) *supra*, *Finley* has been rendered irrelevant by the enactment of 28 U.S.C. § 1367 in 1990.

B will impair or impede *I*'s ability to protect the interest as a practical matter. *I* cannot be bound by the judgment between *A* and *B*, although *I* might be able to benefit from a judgment against *B* in the action.[321] Nevertheless, because there will be common questions of law and fact between *I*'s claim and the main action, permissive intervention would be appropriate under Rule 24(b). However, ancillary jurisdiction over *I*'s claim would not be appropriate. The close factual relationship between *I*'s claim and the main action is sufficient to satisfy Article III of the Constitution.[322] However, under the policies of 28 U.S.C. § 1332 as interpreted in the *Kroger* case, discussed in section D(1)*(c)*, above, *I* is not a person in a defensive position who has been involuntarily haled into federal court. Allowing *I* to intervene would pose an even greater danger of evading the policies of the diversity jurisdiction than the claim asserted in *Kroger* itself.

Illustration 8-48. On the facts of *Illustration 8-47*, assume that *I* is a citizen of State *X*. Assume further that *B* is asserting that *A* is contributorily negligent. *I* seeks to intervene because *I* anticipates a later suit by *A* against *I* and also wishes to assert that *A* was contributorily negligent. For the reasons given in *Illustration 8-47*, *I*'s defense is not appropriate for intervention of right under Rule 24(a)(2). *I*'s defense presents the kind of common questions of law and fact that would make permissive intervention proper under Rule 24(b). Although Article III of the Constitution would be satisfied by *I*'s application for intervention, the statutory policies of 28 U.S.C. § 1332 would probably still not be satisfied here. In this situation, *I* is in a defensive position, but only potentially. *A* has not yet sued *I*. It is difficult to see how any of *I*'s rights would be irretrievably lost by inability to intervene in the action. Therefore, under the *Kroger* decision, ancillary jurisdiction would not be appropriate over *I*'s application for intervention.

* * * * *

In intervention-of-right cases, Federal Rule 24(a)(2) and Federal Rule 19(a)(2)(i) overlap. A party seeking to intervene under Rule 24(a)(2) is, at least, a person whose joinder is needed for just adjudication under Rule 19(a), and the intervenor may be a person who would be classified as an ''indispensable party'' under Rule 19(b). In either case, how should the ancillary jurisdiction doctrine be applied if the intervenor's joinder as an original matter would have destroyed federal subject-matter jurisdiction? Before 1990, the courts generally held that if the intervenor would have been an indispensable party under Rule 19(b), the doctrine of ancillary jurisdiction would not apply, even though joinder was being effected under Rule 24(a)(2) instead of under Rule 19. Thus, the action had to be dismissed. The purpose of this sensible ''exception'' to the general rule of ancillary jurisdiction was to prevent the evasion of federal subject-matter jurisdiction requirements through the use of Rule 24.[323] However, when the intervenor would not be an ''indispensable'' party under Rule 19(b), but only a party whose

---

321. *See* Chapter 13(D)(1) (''Preclusion of Nonparties'') *infra*.

322. *See* Chapter 2(C)(4)*(b)* (''The Constitutional Basis of Pendent and Ancillary Jurisdiction'') *supra*.

323. *See* 7C CHARLES A. WRIGHT ET AL., FEDERAL PRACTICE AND PROCEDURE: CIVIL § 1917, at 477-79 (2d ed. 1986); *cf. Illustration 8-33 supra*; Owen Equip. & Erection Co. v. Kroger, 437 U.S. 365, 376, 98 S. Ct. 2396, 2404, 57 L. Ed. 2d 274, 284 (1978) (discussed in subsection D(1)*(c) supra*).

joinder was "necessary" for just adjudication under Rule 19(a), but who could be dispensed with, the courts permitted intervention under the doctrine of ancillary jurisdiction. The justification for this result was, apparently, that if it were impossible to use ancillary jurisdiction to permit Rule 19(a) parties to intervene, Rule 24(a)'s usefulness might be impaired.[324] However, it seems curious, especially in the face of Rule 82, that the desire to render a particular rule useful should result in an extension of federal jurisdiction to a claim or defense that could not otherwise be heard by the federal courts.[325] As stated above, a tighter focus on the policies supporting statutory grants of federal subject-matter jurisdiction by the courts would have revealed that Rule 24(a)(2) intervention should have been refused if joinder of the intervenor as an original matter would have made federal subject-matter jurisdiction improper.

After 1990, the problems of determining jurisdiction over applications for intervention will be governed by the codification of the doctrines of "ancillary" and "pendent" jurisdiction in 28 U.S.C. § 1367(a). Section 1367(a) authorizes "supplemental jurisdiction" over claims that are so related to claims over which the federal courts have original jurisdiction as to "form part of the same case or controversy under Article III of the United States Constitution."[326] As discussed in Chapter 2, it is possible both that an Article III case or controversy is broad enough to encompass factually unrelated federal and nonfederal claims and that § 1367(a) will be read as allowing such unrelated claims to be heard within the grant of supplemental jurisdiction to the federal courts.[327] If so, § 1367(a) standing alone[328] would authorize jurisdiction over all claims under both Rules 24(a) and (b). However, as also discussed in Chapter 2,[329] § 1367(a) should probably be read to limit supplemental jurisdiction to claims that arise out of the same transaction or occurrence as claims over which the federal courts have original jurisdiction. Under either interpretation of § 1367(a), the courts should

---

324. *See* 7C CHARLES A. WRIGHT ET AL., FEDERAL PRACTICE AND PROCEDURE: CIVIL § 1917, at 479-80 (2d ed. 1986).

325. Furthermore, the Supreme Court's decision in Owen Equipment & Erection Co. v. Kroger, 437 U.S. 365, 98 S. Ct. 2396, 57 L. Ed. 2d 274 (1978) (discussed in section D(1) *supra*), made it questionable whether the rationale articulated in the text was valid in all cases. In *Kroger*, the Court emphasized that ancillary jurisdiction "typically involves claims by a defending party haled into court against his will, or by another person whose rights might be irretrievably lost unless he could assert them in an ongoing action in a federal court." *Id.* at 376, 98 S. Ct. at 2404, 57 L. Ed. 2d at 284. One of the examples cited by the Supreme Court as an appropriate case for ancillary jurisdiction was a party's intervention to protect that party's interest in a fund or property controlled by federal litigation. *See id.* at 375-76 & n.18, 98 S. Ct. at 2403-04 & n.18, 57 L. Ed. 2d at 283-84 & n.18. Many intervention cases, under Rule 24(a)(2), may, in fact, be similar to this example, in that the intervenor would "irretrievably" lose rights unless permitted to intervene. However, it is doubtful that all intervention cases pose so serious a threat to the intervenor's interest under the practical standard enunciated in Rule 24(a)(2). After *Kroger*, therefore, it was arguable that the federal courts should have examined the facts of each intervention case under Rule 24(a)(2) with care to determine whether the congressional purposes supporting the statutory grant of diversity jurisdiction would be furthered or impaired by allowing intervention of a nondiverse Rule 19(a) party.

326. 28 U.S.C. § 1367(a).

327. *See* Chapter 2(C)(4)*(d)(i)* ("The Scope of Supplemental Jurisdiction: Section 1367(a)") *supra*.

328. As discussed further below, § 1367(b) addresses intervention problems specifically in diversity actions. Thus, the effect of § 1367(b) on those actions must be evaluated separately from the effect of § 1367(a) on the distinction between intervention of right and permissive intervention utilized to determine ancillary jurisdiction.

329. *See* Chapter 2(C)(4)*(d)(i)* ("The Scope of Supplemental Jurisdiction: Section 1367(a)") *supra*.

focus on the newly prescribed test under the statute in all cases of Rule 24 intervention, rather than the old distinction between intervention of right and permissive intervention. Thus, under either interpretation of the statute, it is clear that at least some cases of permissive intervention—for example, the one discussed in *Illustration 8-48*—will fall within the scope of § 1367(a).[330]

Section 1367(b) places special restrictions on the exercise of supplemental jurisdiction when the jurisdiction of the federal courts is based exclusively on diversity of citizenship between the parties.[331] These restrictions operate to prohibit supplemental jurisdiction in certain kinds of cases, even if the test of § 1367(a) is met. As applied to intervention cases, § 1367(b) partly addresses one anomalous result that occurred under prior law, but it creates some additional problems of interpretation. Section 1367(b) partially solves the problem created by the overlap between Rule 24(a)(2) and Rule 19(a)(2)(i). Section 1367(b) provides that in actions based solely on diversity jurisdiction, the district courts will not have supplemental jurisdiction over claims by plaintiffs against "persons made parties under Rule . . . 24" or over "claims by persons proposed to be joined as plaintiffs under Rule 19 . . . or seeking to intervene as plaintiffs under Rule 24."[332] The legislative history of § 1367(b) indicates that it was designed, at least in part, to deal with the overlap between Rules 19 and 24. The House Report stated as follows:

> Subsection (b) makes one small change in pre-*Finley* practice. Anomalously, under current practice, the same party might intervene as of right under Federal Rule of Civil Procedure [24(a)][333] and take advantage of supplemental jurisdiction, but not come within supplemental jurisdiction if parties already in the action sought to effect the joinder under Rule 19. Subsection (b) would eliminate this anomaly, excluding Rule [24(a)] plaintiff-intervenors to the same extent as those sought to be joined as plaintiffs under Rule 19.
>
> If this exclusion threatened unavoidable prejudice to the interests of the prospective intervenor if the action proceeded in its absence, the district court should be more inclined not merely

---

330. In York Research Corp. v. Landgarten, No. 89 Civ. 5556(PNL), 1992 WL 373268, 1992 U.S. Dist. LEXIS 18321 (S.D.N.Y. Dec. 3, 1992), the court exercised supplemental jurisdiction over a defendant permissive intervenor. The court recognized that supplemental jurisdiction was ordinarily improper over applications for permissive intervention, but stated that failure to exercise jurisdiction would impair the intervenor's ability to pursue the claims, cause judicial inconvenience and expense to the parties, and risk inconsistent results. Because the action was commenced prior to the effective date of 28 U.S.C. § 1367, the court recognized that the statute was inapplicable, but stated that its analysis would not differ if it was applicable. However, the court's description of the intervenor's claim looks much like a description of an intervention of right claim under Rule 24(a)(2).

331. *See* 28 U.S.C. § 1367(b).

332. *Id.*; *see* Krueger v. Cartwright, 996 F.2d 928 (7th Cir. 1993) (holding it erroneous to allow intervention of a nondiverse plaintiff under § 1367(b)).

333. The House Report cited Federal Rule 23, but it is clear that the report should have cited Federal Rule 24. For one thing, Rule 23 (a) deals with class action prerequisites and does not speak of intervention. For another, the report cites CHARLES A. WRIGHT ET AL., FEDERAL PRACTICE AND PROCEDURE: CIVIL § 1917, at 472-81 (2d ed. 1986), which deals with the intervention problems discussed in the text.

to deny the intervention but to dismiss the whole action for refiling in state court under the criteria of Rule 19(b).[334]

The language and legislative history of 28 U.S.C. § 1367(b) explicitly address only the problem of claims asserted by intervening *plaintiffs*.[335] On the face of the statute, there is no prohibition against the exercise of supplemental jurisdiction over persons who intervene as defendants under Rule 24(a)(2) and whose presence would destroy subject-matter jurisdiction if they had been joined originally in the action.[336] If it is indeed correct that nondiverse Rule 24(a)(2) defendants can intervene under § 1367, then Congress has only partially solved the problem of overlap between Rules 19(a)(2)(i) and Rule 24(a)(2). Recall from section C(3)*(c)*, however, that this same difficulty existed with the application of § 1367(b) to joinder under Rule 19—the statute seems only to preclude the plaintiff from asserting claims against persons joined as defendants under Rule 19, rather than precluding joinder of those parties altogether when their presence in the action originally would have destroyed subject-matter jurisdiction.[337] In section C(3)*(c)*, it was suggested that this anomaly could be avoided by interpreting the language of § 1367(a) and (b) to forbid joinder of the nondiverse Rule 19 defendant altogether.[338] This same approach also seems to be the best solution in cases of Rule 24(a)(2) intervention. A party intervening as a defendant under Rule 24(a)(2) is, in fact, a Rule 19(a)(2)(i) party who should have been originally joined in the action. Intervention should not be permitted when the intervening defendant could not have been originally joined under 28 U.S.C. § 1332, such as when the citizenship of the intervenor is the same as that of the plaintiff.[339] Alternatively, if nondiverse defendants are permitted to intervene

---

334. H.R. REP. NO. 734, 101st Cong., 2d Sess. 29 (1990). It should be noted that the language recommended by the Federal Courts Study Committee only prohibited supplemental jurisdiction in diversity cases over claims asserted under Rule 24(b), although it prohibited claims asserted both by parties seeking to intervene as plaintiffs and by parties seeking to intervene as defendants. *See* 1 FEDERAL COURTS STUDY COMMITTEE WORKING PAPERS AND SUBCOMMITTEE REPORTS 567-68 (1990).

335. In Meredith v. Schreiner Transp., Inc., 814 F. Supp. 1001 (D. Kan. 1993), the court applied § 1367(b) to refuse jurisdiction over an intervenor's claim under Rule 24(a)(2), where the intervenor was asserting a lien against judgment proceeds. The jurisdictional amount requirement of 28 U.S.C. § 1332 was not satisfied by the intervenor's claim. In Atherton v. Casey, No. 92-1283, 1992 WL 167033, 1992 U.S. Dist. LEXIS 9976 (E.D. La. June 29, 1992), the applicant attempted to intervene as a defendant, but the court realigned the applicant as a plaintiff and held that diversity was destroyed.

336. *See* Denis F. McLaughlin, *The Federal Supplemental Jurisdiction Statute—A Constitutional and Statutory Analysis*, 24 ARIZ. ST. L.J. 849, 958 (1992).

337. *See* subsection C(3)*(c)* ("Problems of Subject-Matter Jurisdiction, Venue, and Personal Jurisdiction Under Rule 19") *supra*.

338. *See id.*

339. *But cf.* Range v. National R.R. Passenger Corp., 176 F.R.D. 85 (W.D.N.Y. 1997) (defendant allowed to intervene under Rule 24(a); however, intervenor's interests appeared to coincide with plaintiff's and court did not state whether intervenor was nondiverse from plaintiff or defendant). The same theoretical problem of the defendant against whom the plaintiff is not asserting a claim exists under Rule 24 and Rule 19. If the plaintiff really has no claim against a nondiverse applicant for intervention, § 1367(a), which provides only for supplemental jurisdiction over claims, would not seem to authorize subject-matter jurisdiction. If the plaintiff does have a claim against the intervenor (*e.g.*, for declaratory relief), then § 1367(b) would seem to disallow intervention. *See* section C(3)*(c)* *supra*. In Colonial Penn Insurance Co. v. American Centennial Ins. Co., No. 92 Civ. 3791 (RPP), 1992 WL 350838, 1992 U.S. Dist. LEXIS 17552 (S.D.N.Y. Nov. 17, 1992), the applicant sought to intervene as a plaintiff, but the court realigned the applicant as a defendant because the court stated that the applicant really wanted to assert a "defensive counterclaim." The plaintiff in the action was suing for under § 1367(b), the plaintiff should only be precluded from asserting claims against the intervenor as long as the intervenor asserts no claims against the plaintiff.[340]

Illustration 8-49. On the facts of *Illustration 8-20*, assume that *C* applies to intervene in order to resist *A's* claim. *C* is both a Rule 24(a)(2) party and a Rule 19 (a)(2)(i) party. For the same reasons that supplemental jurisdiction did not exist over *C* as a Rule 19(a)(2) party in *Illustration 8-20*, supplemental jurisdiction should not exist over *C* as an intervenor under Rule 24(a)(2).

* * * * *

The doctrine of realignment applies to intervening parties under Rule 24, just as it does to problems of Rule 19 joinder.[341] Thus, in determining whether § 1367(b) will preclude supplemental jurisdiction over claims by persons seeking to intervene, the intervenors must first be properly aligned in the action. For example, in *Development Finance Corp. v. Alpha Housing & Health Care, Inc.,*[342] the intervening party in an action for breach of contract wished to challenge certain agreements between the plaintiffs and the defendant on the ground that they were ultra vires, a defense that could not be raised by the defendant under the applicable state law. The intervenor first moved to intervene as a defendant, but the district court denied the motion, and the intervenor did not appeal. The intervenor then sought to intervene as a plaintiff, but this motion was also denied by the district court. On appeal from the denial of the latter motion, the court of appeals considered whether the intervenor should be aligned as a plaintiff or defendant in order to determine whether § 1367(b) would preclude subject-matter jurisdiction over the intervenor's claims.[343] The court aligned the intervenor as a defendant, treating the intervenor's application as raising counterclaims against the plaintiffs and a cross-claim against the defendant. Because the intervenor was a citizen of a different state than the plaintiffs, no problem of diversity jurisdiction was presented by the intervenor's counterclaims. (The intervenor was a co-citizen of the defendant.) In addition, because § 1367(b) does not exclude supplemental jurisdiction of cross-claims under Rule 13(g), the

---

a declaratory judgment to determine rights and obligations pursuant to reinsurance agreements. It seems clear that this claim for declaratory relief would be asserted against the intervenor and that any judgment on the declaratory claim would bind the intervenor. In addition, because the intervenor wanted to assert a counterclaim, that counterclaim would also satisfy § 1367(a). So viewed, however, the court exercised supplemental jurisdiction over the intervenor's claim, construing § 1367(b) as not prohibiting jurisdiction. This result is contrary to the result recommended in the text.

340. *See* section C(2)*(c)* ("Problems of Subject-Matter Jurisdiction, Venue, and Personal Jurisdiction Under Rule 19") *supra.*

341. *See* section C(2)*(c)* *supra* (discussing problems of subject-matter jurisdiction in Rule 19 cases, including problems of realignment); *see also* April N. Everett, United States Fidelity & Guaranty Co. v. A & S Manufacturing Co.: *Realignment of Parties in Diversity Jurisdiction Cases,* 74 N.C. L. REV. 1979 (1996).

342. 54 F.3d 156 (3d Cir. 1995).

343. Interestingly, in *Development Finance,* the court considered the applicability of § 1367(b) without first considering whether the intervenor's claim fit within § 1367(a). This failure to consider § 1367(a) first is a problem with the court's analysis because it was not obvious from the court's opinion what the relationship between the intervenor and the other parties in the action was, and as observed in Chapter 2(C)(4)*(d)(i)*, some federal courts have held that something more than a "loose factual relationship" between the freestanding and supplemental claims is necessary to satisfy the Article III case-or-controversy standard incorporated in § 1367(a).

court held that supplemental jurisdiction existed over the cross-claims against the defendant under the ''plain language'' of the statute.[344]

Section 1367(b) applies not only to intervention under Rule 24(a), but also to intervention under Rule 24(b).[345] As in the case of Rule 24(a)(2), when the Rule 24(b) intervenor seeks to enter the action on the plaintiff's side of the litigation, § 1367(b) specifically prohibits intervention when it would be inconsistent with the restrictions of 28 U.S.C. § 1332.[346] Thus, when a plaintiff intervenor under Rule 24(b) is a citizen of the same state as one of the defendants, as in *Illustration 8-47*, above, § 1367(b) prohibits the exercise of supplemental jurisdiction over the intervenor's claim. When the intervenor seeks to enter the action on the defendant's side of the case, as in *Illustration 8-48*, the same result should follow, even though, as in the case of intervention under Rule 24(a)(2), the language of § 1367(b) does not literally prohibit intervention. The cases under Rule 24(b) generally agree that there is no reason to allow a party to intervene in the action under Rule 24(b) when original joinder of the party would have been prohibited by the restrictions of 28 U.S.C. § 1332.[347] Indeed, as with the similar case discussed under Rule 24(a)(2), intervention under Rule 24(b) in these circumstances would contravene the text of § 1367(b),[348] as well as the reasons that § 1367(b) was enacted.[349] Alternatively, however, if intervention

---

344. *Cf.* American Honda Motor Co. v. Clair Int'l, Inc., No. C.A. 98-1125-MLW, 1999 WL 414323, 1999 U.S. Dist. LEXIS 9281 (D. Mass. Apr. 16, 1999) (party seeks to intervene to assert cross-claim; court concludes that intervenor should be realigned as a plaintiff and denies permission to intervene under § 1367(b), which prohibited intervention because intervenor was not diverse from defendant); *see also* Lennox Indus., Inc. v. Yusti, 172 F.R.D. 617 (D.P.R. 1997) (Rule 24(a) intervenor realigned as a plaintiff and intervention denied under § 1367(b) because diversity did not exist between intervenor and defendant).

345. *See* 28 U.S.C. § 1367(b).

346. This result is produced by the language disallowing supplemental jurisdiction over claims by persons ''seeking to intervene as plaintiffs under Rule 24.'' *See id.* Since there is no point in an intervening plaintiff coming into the action except to assert a claim, this language effectively prohibits intervention.

347. *See, e.g.,* Turner/Ozanne v. Hyman/Power, 111 F.3d 1312, 1319 (7th Cir. 1997) (after enactment of supplemental jurisdiction statute, course previously followed in cases of permissive intervention must continue to be followed); Torres v. Puerto Rico Elec. Power Auth., 164 F.R.D. 307 (D.P.R. 1996) (no supplemental jurisdiction over nondiverse plaintiffs seeking permissive intervention); Hallco Mfg. Co. v. Quaech, 161 F.R.D. 98, 102 (D. Or. 1995) (same).

348. As with Rule 19 joinder and Rule 24(a)(2) joinder, discussed earlier in the text, the language of § 1367(b) prohibits ''claims by plaintiffs against persons made parties under Rule . . . 24.'' This language literally would allow intervention if the requirements of § 1367(a) are satisfied, but would prohibit the plaintiff from asserting claims against, for example, a nondiverse intervenor once the intervenor is in the action (*i.e.*, ''made a party''). Thus, this provision would allow a defendant-intervenor to assert defenses, or perhaps even claims, against the plaintiff, but the language of § 1367(b), read literally, would prevent the plaintiff from asserting claims against the intervenor. However, as noted in the text and notes, *supra*, and in the discussion of joinder of Rule 19 defendants in section C(3)*(c)* if the plaintiff is not asserting a claim against a defendant, § 1367(a) does not authorize supplemental jurisdiction over the intervenor in the first place. If the plaintiff is asserting a claim against the nondiverse intervenor, § 1367(b) prohibits intervention.

349. The House Report accompanying § 1367(b) states:

> In diversity-only actions the district courts may not hear plaintiffs' supplemental claims when exercising supplemental jurisdiction would encourage plaintiffs to evade the jurisdictional requirements of 28 U.S.C. § 1332 by the simple expedient of naming initially only those defendants whose joinder satisfies [§] 1332's requirements and later adding claims not within original federal jurisdiction against other defendants who have intervened or been joined on a supplemental basis.

H.R. Rep. No. 734, 101st Cong., 2d Sess. 29 (1990).

of nondiverse Rule 24(b) defendants is permitted under § 1367, plaintiffs should only be prohibited from asserting claims against the intervenors as long as the intervenors do not directly assert claims against the plaintiffs, as in *Illustration 8-48*.[350]

In summary, supplemental jurisdiction should not be available to nondiverse intervenors in any action in which jurisdiction is solely based on diversity of citizenship. Supplemental jurisdiction should only be available over applications for intervention in federal question cases. Even in such cases, however, the text of § 1367(a) will constitute a barrier to intervention of defendants under Rule 24. Section 1367(a) only confers supplemental jurisdiction over claims. If a Rule 24 intervenor is not asserting a claim and if the plaintiff has no claim against the intervenor, § 1367(a) does not authorize supplemental jurisdiction.[351]

(d) Venue Problems Under Rule 24

Federal venue requirements involve fewer problems under Rule 24 than subject-matter-jurisdiction limitations. Because venue is waivable, intervenors cannot complain that federal venue is improper as to them. By moving to intervene, they waive any venue objection they might have had as an original party.[352] Can other parties object if intervention would render venue improper? It been suggested that the answer should depend on whether ancillary jurisdiction—today, "supplemental jurisdiction"—exists over the case. If supplemental jurisdiction exists, the ordinary venue requirements should be disregarded. If supplemental jurisdiction does not exist, venue objections raised by the principal

---

350. *See* section C(3)*(c)* ("Problems of Subject-Matter Jurisdiction, Venue, and Personal Jurisdiction Under Rule 19") *supra*.

351. *See id.* The result in all the intervention cases differs from the result reached in cases of Rule 14 joinder of third-party defendants. In all cases in which intervention would violate the restrictions of 28 U.S.C. § 1332, the text recommends that intervention be prohibited. (The same was true, of course, of joinder under Rule 19.) However, in section D(1)*(c)*, *supra*, the text did not recommend that joinder of third-party defendants be disallowed under § 1367(b). Rather, it was suggested there that joinder be permitted, but the language of § 1367(b) be construed to limit the assertion of claims by the plaintiff against the third-party defendant only when the third-party defendant did not directly assert claims against the plaintiff. This construction was necessary in order to prevent unfair results from accruing to all the parties in the action—the defendant, the plaintiff, and the third-party defendant. *See* section D(1)*(c)* ("Problems of Subject-Matter Jurisdiction, Venue, and Personal Jurisdiction Under Rule 14") *supra*. However, in cases in which Rule 14 parties are joined, a claim is clearly being asserted against them that satisfies the requirements of § 1367(a). Such a situation may not exist in cases of intervening defendants under Rule 24. Furthermore, no parallel problems of unfairness exist in denying intervention to nondiverse Rule 24 defendants. No unfairness accrues to any of the persons already parties by disallowing intervention under either Rule 24(a)(2) or Rule 24(b). Likewise, no serious unfairness occurs to Rule 24(b) intervenors by disallowing intervention by them, as demonstrated in *Illustrations 8-47* and *8-48 supra*. Only persons seeking to intervene under 24(a)(2), whose interests might be adversely affected by the disposition of the action, could suffer harm of a serious nature by the denial of intervention. However, because these intervenors are also Rule 19(a)(2)(i) parties, the court is obligated either to protect them against that harm by taking appropriate steps under Rule 19(b), or to dismiss the action. *Cf.* H.R. REP. No. 734, 101st Cong., 2d Sess. 29 (1990).

352. *See* 7C CHARLES A. WRIGHT ET AL., FEDERAL PRACTICE AND PROCEDURE: CIVIL § 1918, at 485 (2d ed. 1986).

parties to the action should prevent intervention.[353] However, even if this rule is followed, the question would remain whether to allow the original defendants to raise venue objections when subject-matter jurisdiction would be proper over them without resort to the doctrine of "ancillary" or "supplemental" jurisdiction, but venue would be improper. This situation might occur, for example, when complete diversity exists not only between the plaintiff and the original defendant, but also between the plaintiff and the intervenor, but the intervenor is a nonresident of the state and venue is proper over the original defendants based on their residence in the state.

In fact, there is no reason to allow the original defendants in an action to raise venue objections based on intervention in any case, whether subject-matter jurisdiction would exist if the intervenor is an originally joined party or the supplemental jurisdiction statute must be used to establish jurisdiction. As noted in section D(1)*(c)* and in Chapter 7(F)(2)*(b)*, above, the venue statutes are ordinarily applicable only to original claims in the action. This sensible rule should not be abandoned in intervention cases. Even though Rule 24(a) intervenors will often be Rule 19(a) parties, as previously discussed,[354] Rule 19(a) only preserves the right of the Rule 19 party to make venue objections, not the right of other parties to do so. Therefore, there is no reason to abandon the usual approach to venue because of a Rule 24(a) intervenor's status as a Rule 19 party, and if the Rule 24 intervenor is not a Rule 19 party there is no arguable basis for allowing any venue objection to be made by the original defendants on the intervenor's behalf. As discussed in Chapter 4, even in actions not involving intervention, resident defendants cannot raise venue objections for nonresidents in cases where venue is based on the residence of the defendants in the state.[355] These cases are based on the reasoning that the defense of venue is personal to the party possessing it and can only be raised by that party.[356] There is no reason to reach a different result in intervention cases. If the existing defendants will be subjected to any kind of inconvenience due to the presence of the intervenor, they can move for a transfer of venue under 28 U.S.C. § 1404(a) or a dismissal on grounds of forum non conveniens, whichever is appropriate.[357]

---

353. *See id.* at 485. If the position of this text is adopted, supplemental jurisdiction would not extend to any case of intervention when the basis of jurisdiction is diversity of citizenship. Therefore, a venue standard keyed to supplemental jurisdiction could operate only in federal question cases.

354. *See* section C(3)*(c) supra* (discussing venue in Rule 19 cases).

355. *See* 28 U.S.C. § 1391(a)(1) & (b)(1). In cases in which venue is based on the occurrence of substantial events within the district or the presence of a substantial portion of the property that is the subject of the action within the district, it is difficult to envision cases in which intervention would arguably render venue improper that is otherwise proper under 28 U.S.C. § 1391(a)(2) or (b)(2). In addition, the fallback provisions in § 1391(a)(3) & (b)(3) make venue proper in a district in which "any defendant is subject to personal jurisdiction" or in which "any defendant may be found," respectively. Therefore, if one of the original defendants is subject to personal jurisdiction or found within the district, intervention would not even arguably make venue improper.

356. *See* Chapter 4(C)(2) *supra* (discussing venue based on defendants' residence).

357. *See* Chapter 4(D)(1)*(a)* & (2)*(a) supra* (discussing, respectively, forum non conveniens and transfer under § 1404(a)).

Lesser inconvenience can be dealt with, when appropriate, by conditioning the right to intervene in reasonable ways to avoid the inconvenience.[358]

(e) Personal Jurisdiction Problems Under Rule 24

Like venue objections, the intervenor waives any personal jurisdiction objections that the intervenor might otherwise have asserted in the principal action had the intervenor been originally joined as a defendant, though this result should not necessarily be true of other claims, such as permissive counterclaims, asserted against the intervenor by the original parties after intervention.[359] What of personal jurisdiction over parties against whom claims are asserted by the intervenor? The principal parties to an action will seldom be able to raise effective jurisdictional objections when an intervenor asserts claims against them that are closely related to the original subject matter of the suit. It is conceivable, but unlikely, that a long-arm statute might extend to the original defendant based on actions the defendant has performed in the state, but not to the intervenor's closely related claim against the defendant. Certainly, if a statutory basis of jurisdiction exits, one would not expect minimum-contacts problems with the intervenor's claim when jurisdiction can be constitutionally asserted over a factually-related principal claim. However, the same may not be true of claims wholly unrelated to the main action joined under Rules 18(a) or 13(b). Both statutory and constitutional personal jurisdiction requirements might well exist and have to be satisfied independently over any such claims.[360]

(f) Rules Enabling Act Issues with Rule 24

Federal Rule 24 does not pose any serious Rules Enabling Act issues. The ability to intervene in a federal action when intervention is impossible under state law, or the inability to intervene under Rule 24 when state law would permit

---

358. *See* 7C CHARLES A. WRIGHT ET AL., FEDERAL PRACTICE AND PROCEDURE: CIVIL § 1922 (2d ed. 1986) (discussing cases placing conditions on the right to intervene in both Rule 24(a) and 24(b) cases).

359. *See* Chapter 7(F)(2)*(b)* (''Supplemental (Ancillary) Venue and Personal Jurisdiction Over Counterclaims and Cross-Claims'') *supra.*

360. *Cf.* 7C CHARLES A. WRIGHT ET AL., FEDERAL PRACTICE AND PROCEDURE: CIVIL § 1919 (2d ed. 1986). Again, however, this statement must be qualified in the same way it was in Chapter 7, in which the ability of a plaintiff to object to permissive counterclaims on jurisdictional grounds was discussed. The Supreme Court's decision in the *Burnham* case, discussed in Chapter 3(E)(2), may be interpreted to mean that commencement of an action in a particular location without more is sufficient to permit personal jurisdiction to be asserted over plaintiffs on claims arising outside the state. If so, when a defendant-intervenor asserts an unrelated claim against the plaintiff, the plaintiff would have no effective personal jurisdiction objection. A harder question is whether, if a plaintiff-intervenor joins an unrelated claim against the defendant under Rule 18, *Burnham* might be read to deprive the defendant of personal jurisdiction objections to the unrelated claim. Arguably, *Burnham* should not be read so broadly. When an intervenor comes into an action on the side of the plaintiff, the intervenor should be treated as an original party for purposes of assessing personal jurisdiction objections over claims asserted by the intervenor. If the intervenor could not have obtained personal jurisdiction over the defendant on a claim joined under Rule 18 if the intervenor had been an original plaintiff in the action, the defendant should not be deprived of the personal jurisdiction objection merely because joinder has been achieved under Rule 24 rather than an alternative rule. *See* Chapter 7(C) (''Joinder of Claims by Plaintiffs under the Federal Rules'') *supra.*

intervention, involves no more than differences in procedural philosophy between the federal and state systems. The differences impose nothing more than tactical burdens on parties and intervenors and do not significantly affect substantive rights.

4. Class Actions

The class action procedure allows a suit to be brought by or against a party who is a representative of a large number of persons similarly situated to the representative, but who are not formally joined as parties in the action. Class actions are designed to avoid multiple litigation. In the absence of class actions, a large number of individual actions would often be necessary to settle existing claims. In addition, class actions provide for vindication of individual claims by representation when joinder of multiple parties or assertion of each claim singly is impractical.[361]

(a) History of Class Actions

Nothing like the modern class action existed at common law. In common-law actions, rigid principles governed joinder of parties. The class action developed in equity as the bill of peace, which allowed an equity court to entertain an action by or against representatives of a group when the size of the group was so large as to make joinder of all its members impossible or impractical.[362] All members of the group had to share "a common *right*, a community of interest in the *subject-matter of the controversy*, or a common *title* from which all their separate claims and all the questions at issue arise."[363] The representatives also had to represent the interests of the absent members of the class adequately.[364]

These equity procedures for class suits were adopted by the codes. The Field Code provided that "when the question is one of a common or general interest of many persons, or when the parties are very numerous and it may be impracticable to bring them all before the court, one or more may sue or defend for the benefit of the whole."[365] This provision was duplicated widely and still exists in some states.[366]

---

361. The number of federal class actions reached a high of 3654 filings in 1973. By 1990, the filings had dropped to 922. Nancy Morawetz, *Bargaining, Class Representation, and Fairness*, 54 OHIO ST. L.J. 1, n.2 (1993).

362. *See* ZECHARIAH CHAFEE, JR., SOME PROBLEMS OF EQUITY 149-50, 200-01 (1950); Thomas D. Rowe, *A Distant Mirror: The Bill of Peace in Early American Mass Torts and Its Implications for Modern Class Actions*, 39 ARIZ. L. REV. 711 (1997).

363. 1 JOHN N. POMEROY, A TREATISE ON EQUITY JURISPRUDENCE § 268, at 596 (5th ed. 1941); *see also id.* at §§ 245-246, 269-269a.

364. *See* ZECHARIAH CHAFEE, JR., SOME PROBLEMS OF EQUITY 232 (1950).

365. Act of Apr. 11, 1849, ch. 438, § 119, 1849 N.Y. Laws 613, 639.

366. *See, e.g.*, NEB. REV. STAT. § 25-319 (1995). *See generally* CHARLES E. CLARK, HANDBOOK OF THE LAW OF CODE PLEADING § 63 (2d ed. 1947).

In the federal system, the Federal Equity Rules and the Conformity Acts governed class action practice before 1938. The Federal Equity Rules of 1848 provided for class actions in Rule 48:

> Where the parties on either side are very numerous, and cannot, without manifest inconvenience and oppressive delays in the suit, be all brought before it, the court in its discretion may dispense with making all of them parties, and may proceed in the suit, having sufficient parties before it to represent all the adverse interests of the plaintiffs and the defendants in the suit properly before it. *But in such cases the decree shall be without prejudice to the rights and claims of all the absent parties.*[367]

The last sentence of this rule appeared to state that the judgment in a class action would not bind the members of the class—a rule contrary to the English practice[368] and one that would seriously impair the usefulness of the class action procedure. Cases both invoked and ignored this restriction.[369] Rule 38 of the Equity Rules of 1912 omitted the restriction: "When the question is one of common or general interest to many persons constituting a class so numerous as to make it impracticable to bring them all before the court, one or more may sue or defend for the whole."[370] However, questions continued about the binding effect of a judgment under Rule 38, apparently because of doubts about whether due process would be violated by a judgment that bound absent class members.[371]

When the Federal Rules of Civil Procedure were adopted in 1938, class actions were dealt with in Rule 23. The original rule was said to be "a substantial restatement of former Equity Rule 38"[372] and was applied to both law and equity cases.[373] Rule 23(a) divided class actions into three categories: "true"

---

367. 42 U.S. (1 How.) lvi (1848) (emphasis added).

368. *See* ZECHARIAH CHAFEE, JR., SOME PROBLEMS OF EQUITY 224-25 (1950).

369. *Compare* Smith v. Swormstedt, 57 U.S. (16 How.) 288, 303, 14 L. Ed. 942, 948-49 (1854) *with* Wabash R.R. Co. v. Adelbert College of W. Reserve Univ., 208 U.S. 609, 28 S. Ct. 425, 52 L. Ed. 642 (1908).

370. 226 U.S. 627, 659 (1912). This rule was influenced by the procedure in code class actions, discussed above.

371. *See* 7A CHARLES A. WRIGHT ET AL., FEDERAL PRACTICE AND PROCEDURE: CIVIL § 1751, at 13 (2d ed. 1986). *Compare* Supreme Tribe of Ben-Hur v. Cauble, 255 U.S. 356, 41 S. Ct. 338, 65 L. Ed. 673 (1921) *with* Christopher v. Brusselback, 302 U.S. 500, 58 S. Ct. 350, 82 L. Ed. 388 (1938).

372. *See* FED. R. CIV. P. 23 advisory committee's note to the original rule.

373. Original Rule 23 read as follows:

(a) Representation. If persons constituting a class are so numerous as to make it impracticable to bring them all before the court, such of them, one or more, as will fairly insure the adequate representation of all may, on behalf of all, sue or be sued, when the character of the right sought to be enforced for or against the class is

(1) joint or common, or secondary in the sense that the owner of a primary right refuses to enforce that right and a member of the class thereby becomes entitled to enforce it;

(2) several, and the object of the action is the adjudication of claims which do or may affect specific property involved in the action; or

(3) several, and there is a common question of law or fact affecting the several rights and a common relief is sought.

(b) Secondary Action by Shareholders. In an action brought to enforce a secondary right on the part of one or more shareholders in an association, incorporated or uninclass actions (Rule 23(a)(1) actions); "hybrid" class actions (Rule 23(a)(2) actions); and "spurious" class actions (Rule 23(a)(3) actions).[374] Serious difficulties developed with this tripartite categorization. The "true" class action under Rule 23(a)(1) was one in which the right sought to be enforced was "joint," "common," or "secondary." A judgment in a "true" class action bound the absent members of the class.[375] However, as the Advisory Committee stated in 1966, "[i]n practice the terms 'joint,' 'common,' etc., which were used as the basis of the . . . classification proved obscure and uncertain."[376] The primary difficulty involved the inclusion of the term "common," which traditionally had not been used to govern joinder of parties.[377] It was difficult to distinguish between "common" rights, which made a class suit "true," and "several" rights, which made a class suit either "hybrid" or "spurious" under Rule 23(a)(2) and (3).[378]

All actions that were not "true" class actions had to be either "hybrid" or "spurious."[379] "Hybrid" class actions under Rule 23(a)(2) were actions in which the rights asserted by or against the class were "several" *and* in which the object of the action was the adjudication of claims pertaining to specific property in the action. The judgment in a "hybrid" class action bound the absent members of the class only with regard to their rights in the specific property that was the subject of the action.[380] A "spurious" class action resembled a "hybrid" action in that the rights asserted by or against the class in both were "several."[381] However, a "spurious" action did not adjudicate a claim affecting specific property. Instead, the "spurious" class action involved a common question of law or fact affecting the several rights *and* some common relief sought by or against the members of the class.[382] The judgment in a "spurious" class suit bound

---

corporated, because the association refuses to enforce rights which may properly be asserted by it, the complaint shall be verified by oath and shall aver (1) that the plaintiff was a shareholder at the time of the transaction of which he complains or that his share thereafter devolved on him by operation of law and (2) that the action is not a collusive one to confer on a court of the United States jurisdiction of any action of which it would not otherwise have jurisdiction. The complaint shall also set forth with particularity the efforts of the plaintiff to secure from the managing directors or trustees and, if necessary, from the shareholders such action as he desires, and the reasons for his failure to obtain such action or the reasons for not making such effort.

(c) Dismissal or Compromise. A class action shall not be dismissed or compromised without the approval of the court. If the right sought to be enforced is one defined in paragraph (1) of subdivision (a) of this rule notice of the proposed dismissal or compromise shall be given to all members of the class in such manner as the court directs. If the right is one defined in paragraphs (2) or (3) of subdivision (a) notice shall be given only if the court requires it.

308 U.S. at 689-90 (1938).

374. *See* FED. R. CIV. P. 23 advisory committee's note to the 1966 Amendments.

375. *See id.*

376. *Id.*

377. *See* ZECHARIAH CHAFEE, JR., SOME PROBLEMS OF EQUITY 245-46, 255-57 (1950).

378. *See id.*; FED. R. CIV. P. 23 advisory committee's note to the 1966 Amendments.

379. *See* 7A CHARLES A. WRIGHT ET AL., FEDERAL PRACTICE AND PROCEDURE: CIVIL § 1752, at 27 (2d ed. 1986).

380. *See* FED. R. CIV. P. 23 advisory committee's note to the 1966 Amendments.

381. *See id.*

382. *See id.*

only those members of the class before the court, though courts sometimes held that class members could intervene after a favorable result in order to get the benefit of the judgment in a "spurious" class suit.[383] Obviously, the "spurious" class suit, in the absence of intervention by class members, was little more than a permissive joinder rule.[384]

The 1966 amendments to Rule 23 eliminated the three categories of class actions employed by the original rule. The structure of Rule 23 now requires a two-tiered analysis. First, an action must qualify generally for class action treatment under Rule 23(a). Second, the action must be found to fit within one of the three categories of class actions in Rule 23(b). Rule 23(c) and (d) govern various procedural matters, and Rule 23(e) states the requirements for dismissal or compromise of a class action. Rule 23(f) confers discretion on the courts of appeals to permit appeals from orders granting or denying class certification.[385] In addition, Rules 23.1 and 23.2 were added to the Federal Rules of Civil Procedure in 1966. Rule 23.1 governs derivative actions by shareholders, a particular kind of class action governed by Rule 23(b) before 1966. Rule 23.2 deals with actions brought by or against unincorporated associations. No specific provisions governed such actions prior to Rule 23.2. As a result, actions by or against associations had to qualify under one of the three categories of Rule 23(a) before 1966.

The criticisms of class and derivative actions since the 1966 amendments to Federal Rule 23 have been many and varied. These criticisms generally have focused on the ease with which in mass torts, securities, and some other kinds of litigation plaintiffs can bring "frivolous" actions that impose large defense costs on the party opposing the class. Thus, defendants are often inclined to settle class actions for substantial sums in order to avoid the greater litigational costs and risks associated with a full defense of the action.[386] Numerous reforms to the

---

383. *See id.*; York v. Guaranty Trust Co., 143 F.2d 503, 529 (2d Cir. 1944), *rev'd on other grounds*, 326 U.S. 99, 65 S. Ct. 1464, 89 L. Ed. 2079 (1945).

384. *See* 7A CHARLES A. WRIGHT ET AL., FEDERAL PRACTICE AND PROCEDURE: CIVIL § 1752, at 31 (2d ed. 1986). The Advisory Committee's Note to the 1966 Amendment to Rule 23 stated:

> The "spurious" action envisaged by original Rule 23 was in any event an anomaly because, although denominated a "class" action and pleaded as such, it was supposed not to adjudicate the rights or liabilities of any person not a party. It was believed to be an advantage of the "spurious" category that it would invite decisions that a member of the "class" could, like a member of the class in a "true" or "hybrid" action, intervene on an ancillary basis without being required to show an independent basis of Federal jurisdiction, and have the benefit of the date of the commencement of the action for purposes of the statute of limitations.

FED. R. CIV. P. 23 advisory committee's note to the 1966 Amendments.

385. *See* FED. R. CIV. P. 23(f).

386. *See, e.g.*, Janet Alexander, *Do the Merits Matter? A Study of Settlements in Securities Class Actions*, 43 STAN. L. REV. 497 (1991); John C. Coffee, Jr., *The Regulation of Entrepreneurial Litigation: Balancing Fairness and Efficiency in the Large Class Actions*, 54 U. CHI. L. REV. 877 (1987); John C. Coffee, Jr., *Rethinking the Class Action: A Policy Primer on Reform*, 62 IND. L.J. 625 (1987); John C. Coffee, Jr., *Understanding the Plaintiff's Attorney: The Implications of Economic Theory for Private Enforcement of Law Through Class and Derivative Actions*, 86 COLUM. L. REV. 669 (1986); John C. Coffee, Jr., *The Unfaithful Champion: The Plaintiff as Monitor in Shareholder Litigation*, 48 LAW & CONTEMP. PROBS. 5 (Summer 1985); John C. Coffee, Jr., *Rescuing the Private Attorney General: Why the Model of the Lawyer as Bounty Hunter is Not Working*, 42 MD. L. REV. 215 (1983); Howard M. Downs, *Federal Class Actions: Diminished Protection* class action procedure have been suggested, but few of these reforms have been implemented.[387]

In 1995, however, Congress responded to the criticisms of class actions in the securities area by enacting the Private Securities Litigation Reform Act of 1995.[388] The Act amends the Securities Act of 1933 and the Securities and Exchange Act of 1934 to impose special provisions governing class actions under those statutes. In general, the Act adds procedural provisions to the 1933 and 1934 Acts that are designed to discourage frivolous securities litigation. The Act contains (1) special certification requirements for securities class actions; (2) special notice requirements to the absent class members designed to allow other members to qualify as lead representative of the class; (3) restrictions on how frequently persons can serve as class representatives in securities actions; (4) proportionate per share restrictions on the amount that the class representative can recover; (5) reasonableness restrictions on the amount that attorneys can be paid keyed to the amount of damages and prejudgment interest paid to the class; (6) special regulation of class settlements, including specific statements that must be sent to the class concerning proposed settlements; and (7) regulations designed to assure that attorneys representing the class do not have a conflict of interest. In addition, as noted in Chapter 6, above,[389] the Act alters the provisions of Federal Rule of Civil Procedure 11 as to class and non-class actions brought under the Securities Acts.[390]

Specific problems that have developed in class action practice under Rule 23 will be discussed in later subsections.

---

for the Class and the Case for Reform, 73 NEB. L. REV. 646 (1994); Howard M. Erichson, *Mass Tort Litigation and Inquisitorial Justice,* 87 GEO. L.J. 1983 (1999); Owen M. Fiss, *The Political Theory of the Class Action,* 53 WASH. & LEE L. REV. 9 (1996); Michael H. Pinkerton, Castano v. American Tobacco Company: *American's Nicotine Plaintiffs Have No Class,* 58 LA. L. REV. 647 (1998); George L. Priest, *Procedural Versus Substantive Controls of Mass Tort Class Actions,* 26 J. LEG. STUD. 521 (1997); Symposium, *Summing Up Procedural Justice: Exploring the Tension Between Collective Processes and Individual Rights in the Context of Settlement and Litigating Classes,* 30 U.C. DAVIS L. REV. 785 (1997); Symposium, *The Institute of Judicial Administration Research Conference on Class Actions,* 71 N.Y.U L. REV. 1 (1996); Symposium, *National Mass Tort Conference,* 73 TEX. L. REV. 1523 (1995); Note, *When Should Courts Allow the Settlement of Duty-of-Loyalty Derivative Suits,* 109 HARV. L. REV. 1084 (1996). Professor David Shapiro has recently examined the class action in modern litigation and contrasted the "individual autonomy" model of class actions with the "entity" model, discussing the institutional obstacles created by these models that make it more difficult for the class action to reach its full potential. *See* David L. Shapiro, *Class Actions: The Class as a Party and Client,* 73 NOTRE DAME L. REV. 913 (1998).

387. For example, one suggested reform is "judicial auctioning" of lawsuits as a means of more closely connecting the ownership and control of class actions and derivative litigation. The proceeds from the auction would be distributed among the plaintiff class. The winning bidder would be free to conduct the litigation in any manner the winner believes would be most appropriate. *See* Jonathan R. Macey & Geoffrey P. Miller, *The Plaintiffs' Attorney's Role in Class Action and Derivative Litigation: Economic Analysis and Recommendations for Reform,* 58 U. CHI. L. REV. 1 (1991); Randall S. Thomas & Robert G. Hansen, *Auctioning Class Actions and Derivative Lawsuits: A Critical Analysis,* 87 NW. U. L. REV. 423 (1993); Jonathan R. Macey & Geoffrey P. Miller, *Auctioning Class Actions and Derivative Lawsuits: A Rejoinder,* 87 NW. U. L. REV. 458 (1993).

388. Pub. L. No. 104-67, 109 Stat. 737.

389. *See* Chapter 6(E)(2)*(c)(iii)* ("Sanctions and the 'Safe Harbor' Provision") *supra.*

390. As discussed in Chapter 1(E)(5), *supra,* the Federal Rules of Civil Procedure are supposed to be "transsubstantive" in nature; *i.e.,* they are applicable to all civil actions, regardless of the substantive nature of the action. Obviously, reforms such as those found in the Securities Litigation Reform Act undermine this ideal.

(b) Practice Under Rule 23

Federal Rule 23 governs class action practice in federal court and in states that have adopted the Federal Rules model. Therefore, an examination of practice under Rule 23 will provide a good illustration of modern class action practice in both federal and many state courts.

(i) Requirements for a Class Action

Rule 23(a) imposes four requirements for a valid class action. First, the class must be "so numerous that joinder of all members is impracticable."[391] Second, Rule 23(a)(2) requires that questions of law or fact common to the members of the class exist.[392] Third, Rule 23(a)(3) states that the claims or defenses of the representative parties must be typical of the claims or defenses of the class.[393] Fourth, Rule 23(a)(4) states that the representative parties must "fairly and adequately protect the interests of the class."[394]

Illustration 8-50. R brings suit as the representative of all poor persons within the state against the state board of education. R alleges that the board is denying the members of the class its educational rights on the basis of economic status in violation of the Fourteenth Amendment. The class action is not proper.

---

391. *See* FED. R. CIV. P. 23(a)(1). There is no fixed number of persons that a class must contain to satisfy this "numerosity" requirement. *See, e.g.,* Kelley v. Norfolk & W. Ry. Co., 584 F.2d 34, 35 (4th Cir. 1978); Senter v. General Motors Corp., 532 F.2d 511, 523 n.24 (6th Cir.), *cert. denied*, 429 U.S. 870, 97 S. Ct. 182, 50 L. Ed. 2d 150 (1976); David v. Showtime/Movie Channel, Inc., 697 F. Supp. 752, 756 (S.D.N.Y. 1988). Obviously, however, the larger the class becomes, the more likely it is that joinder of all the class members will be deemed "impracticable."

392. "All that can be divined from the rule itself is that the use of the plural 'questions' suggests that more than one issue of law or fact must be common to members of the class." 7A CHARLES A. WRIGHT ET AL., FEDERAL PRACTICE AND PROCEDURE: CIVIL § 1763, at 198 (2d ed. 1986). Beyond this possible complication, the "common questions" requirement seems straightforward and easy to apply, just as it is in cases of permissive joinder under Rule 20.

393. Courts have taken varying approaches in determining whether this standard has been satisfied. Some courts pay little attention to the requirement, while others seem to view it as a requirement intended to buttress the adequacy of representation requirement of Rule 23(b)(4). Probably the best approach is to consider the requirement satisfied if the claims or defenses of the representative parties and the absent class members arise from a single occurrence or are based on the same legal or remedial theory. *See* Mersay v. First Republic Corp., 43 F.R.D. 465 (S.D.N.Y. 1968); 7A CHARLES A. WRIGHT ET AL., FEDERAL PRACTICE AND PROCEDURE: CIVIL § 1764, at 243 (2d ed. 1986).

394. Adequacy of representation is more critical under new Rule 23 than under the former rule because the judgment in all class actions under the new rule binds the absent members of the class. *See* FED. R. CIV. P. 23 advisory committee's note to the 1966 Amendments. Binding a party who has not had a day in court raises serious due process objections. One means of overcoming these objections is to insure that the interests of the absent members of the class are represented adequately in the action. *See* Hansberry v. Lee, 311 U.S. 32, 44-46, 61 S. Ct. 115, 119-20, 85 L. Ed. 22, 28-29 (1940). There is no fixed standard for determining when representation is adequate, and the determination must be made on a case-by-case basis. Relevant factors include the quality of the legal counsel employed by the representatives; the personal characteristics of the representatives, such as honesty; the extent of the representatives' interests in the action; and the extent to which the representatives' interests are adverse, antagonistic, or conflicting with the interests of members of the class. *See generally* 7A CHARLES A. WRIGHT ET AL., FEDERAL PRACTICE AND PROCEDURE: CIVIL § 1766 (2d ed. 1986); *see also* Marcel Kahan & Linda Silberman, *The Inadequate Search for "Adequacy" in Class Actions: A Critique of* Epstein v. MCA, Inc., 73 N.Y.U. L. REV. 765 (1998).

The designation of the class as "all poor persons within the state" is not adequate under Rule 23(a) because it is too vague.[395]

Illustration 8-51. *R*, a public school student, sued the local board of education. *R* sought an order to compel the board to desegregate the faculties of the public schools. *R* seeks to represent a class comprised of the local public school teachers and principals, whose constitutional rights are allegedly infringed by the segregated system maintained by the board. The class action is not proper under Rule 23(a), because *R* is not a member of the class *R* seeks to represent.[396]

Illustration 8-52. *A* sues *R*, the mayor of *City X*, as the representative of a defendant class comprised of the city council, which is comprised of the mayor and seven city council representatives. *A* seeks to have a city building desegregated. The class action is improper under Rule 23(a)(1), because the class is not so numerous that joinder of all of the class members is impracticable.[397]

Illustration 8-53. *R* sues as the representative of a class comprised of all persons who had been defrauded by *A*. *R* alleges that *A* defrauded some 3,000 persons over two years by making a variety of misrepresentations. The class action is improper under Rule 23(a)(2), because there are no questions of law or fact common to all the class members. The variety of misrepresentations prevents satisfaction of the common question requirement.[398]

Illustration 8-54. *R* sues as the representative of a class of 3,000 persons who were defrauded by *A* over a period of years. *R* purchased a replica of a work of art from *A*. *R* alleges that *A* failed to disclose that the replica of the work of art was made of brass. *R* also alleges that *A* had a duty to disclose this information to potential purchasers. *R* alleges that the other class members were defrauded when *A* told them that replicas of the same work were made of gold, when they were really brass. A class action is not proper under Rule 23(a)(4), because the claim of the class representative, *R*, is not typical of the claims of the members of the class.

Illustration 8-55. *R* sues *A* and *B*. *R* brings the suit on *R's* own behalf and as representative of a class of persons who had signed loan contracts with clauses that permitted the lender to confess judgment in a state court against the borrower without notice to the borrower. *A* and *B* are, respectively, the sheriff and clerk of the state court in question. *R* seeks an order restraining the defendants from entering or executing any judgments by confession. *R's* claim is that the practice is unconstitutional under the Due Process Clause of the Fourteenth Amendment because the class members did not knowingly waive their rights to a hearing when they signed the contracts in question. The class is comprised of about 2,000 persons, four percent of whom have incomes in excess of $50,000 per year and the rest of whom have incomes of less than $10,000 per year. *R's* income exceeds $50,000 per year. A class action is not proper under Rule

---

395. *See* Lopez Tijerina v. Henry, 48 F.R.D. 274 (D.N.M. 1969), *appeal dismissed*, 398 U.S. 922, 90 S. Ct. 1718, 26 L. Ed. 2d 86 (1970).

396. *See* Mapp v. Board of Educ., 319 F.2d 571 (6th Cir. 1963).

397. *See* Thaxton v. Vaughan, 321 F.2d 474 (4th Cir. 1963).

398. *See* Westlake v. Abrams, 98 F.R.D. 1 (N.D. Ga. 1981).

23(a)(4), because *R* is not a proper representative of members of the class making less than $10,000 per year. The members of the class, such as *R*, who have higher incomes are likely more educated. Therefore, such members may be more capable of making an understanding and knowing waiver of their rights than those making lower incomes.[399]

(ii) Categories of Class Actions: Rule 23(b)(1)(A) (Risk of Inconsistent Adjudications) or Rule 23(b)(1)(B) (Impairment of Interests in the Absence of Class Action)

Once Rule 23(a) has been satisfied, the action must fit within one of the three categories of Rule 23(b) in order for the action to proceed as a class action. Rule 23(b)(1) allows an action to be maintained as a class action under two separate circumstances. Subsection (A) of Rule 23(b)(1) provides that the action may be maintained as a class action if "the prosecution of separate actions by or against individual members of the class would create a risk of . . . inconsistent or varying adjudications with respect to individual members of the class which would establish incompatible standards of conduct *for the party opposing the class. . . .*"[400] This subsection requires the court to estimate both whether multiple actions are likely to be brought against the party opposing the class and, if so, whether such actions would result in adjudications that would establish incompatible standards for the party opposing the class.[401]

Illustration 8-56. Assume that separate actions by individuals are commenced against a municipality concerning a bond issue. Some individuals want to invalidate the issue, others want to limit it, and still others want to enforce interest payments under the bonds. Under such circumstances, if one group of plaintiffs succeeded in invalidating the issue and another group succeeded in obtaining judgments ordering the payment of interest, the defendant municipality would be subject to incompatible standards with regard to the bond issue, and the action would be appropriate for class action treatment.[402]

Illustration 8-57. Assume that mass tort has occurred and the defendant might be sued by a number of injured plaintiffs, some of whom might recover judgments against the defendant and some of whom might lose their actions.[403] For the "incompatible standards of conduct" principle to be satisfied, the substantive law applicable to the defendant's conduct must require or entitle the defendant to "pursue a uniform continuing course of conduct" with regard to the subject matter of the action.[404] The standard is thus forward looking and does

---

399. *See* Swarb v. Lennox, 314 F. Supp. 1091 (E.D. Pa. 1970), *aff'd on other grounds*, 405 U.S. 191, 92 S. Ct. 767, 31 L. Ed. 2d 138 (1972).

400. FED. R. CIV. P. 23(b)(1)(A) (emphasis added).

401. *See generally* 7 CHARLES A. WRIGHT ET AL., FEDERAL PRACTICE AND PROCEDURE: CIVIL § 1773 (2d ed. 1986).

402. *See* FED. R. CIV. P. 23(b)(1)(A) advisory committee's note to the 1966 amendment.

403. *See, e.g.*, McDonnell-Douglas Corp. v. United States Dist. Court, 523 F.2d 1083 (9th Cir. 1975), *cert. denied*, 425 U.S. 911, 96 S. Ct. 1506, 47 L. Ed. 2d 761 (1976).

404. *See* 7A CHARLES A. WRIGHT ET AL., FEDERAL PRACTICE AND PROCEDURE: CIVIL § 1773, at 431 (2d ed. 1986); *see also id.* at 433.

not embrace circumstances like the mass tort situation, when the separate adjudications would not result in any inconsistent obligations being imposed on the defendant in the future. Traditionally, such an action would not be appropriate for class action treatment under Rule 23(b)(1)(A)[405]

* * * * *

Subsection (B) of Rule 23(b)(1) allows an action to be maintained as a class action when adjudications with respect to individual members of the class, as a practical matter, would be dispositive of the interests of other members of the class or substantially impair or impede the ability of other members to protect their interests.[406] This standard obviously overlaps with the standard of compulsory joinder articulated in Rule 19(a)(2)(i). Rule 23(b)(1)(B) thus offers an escape from the mandatory joinder requirement of Rule 19(a)(2)(i) when the action can be qualified as a class action.

Illustration 8-58. Assume that some shareholders want to force a corporation to declare a dividend. Success in the action, practically speaking, would be dispositive of all other shareholders' interests and such an action would be appropriate for class treatment under Rule 23(b)(1)(B).[407]

(iii) Categories of Class Actions: Rule 23(b)(2) (Affecting an Entire Class by Acting or Refusing to Act)

Rule 23(b)(2) is the provision most often employed to justify class action treatment when declaratory or injunctive relief is sought. Rule 23(b)(2) permits a class action when the party opposed to the class has acted or refused to act on grounds applicable to the class, thereby making final injunctive or declaratory relief appropriate with respect to the class as a whole.[408] The Advisory Committee explained that "[a]ction or inaction is directed to a class within the meaning of this subdivision even if it has taken effect or is threatened only as to one or a few members of the class, provided it is based on grounds which have general application to the class."[409]

Illustration 8-59. An example of such a case is a civil rights action in which the defendant is charged with unlawful discrimination against a class.[410]

(iv) Categories of Class Actions: Rule 23(b)(3) (Common Questions of Law or Fact)

Rule 23(b)(3) provides for maintenance of an action as a class action when (1) questions of law or fact common to the class exist that predominate over

---

405. *But see* subsection *(vi) infra* (discussing contemporary problems in administering class actions under Rule 23).

406. FED. R. CIV. P. 23(b)(1)(B).

407. *See* FED. R. CIV. P. 23(b)(1)(B) advisory committee's note to the 1966 amendment.

408. FED. R. CIV. P. 23(b)(2); *cf.* David E. Rigney, Annotation, *Permissibility of Action Against a Class of Defendants Under Rule 23(b)(2) of Federal Rules of Civil Procedure*, 85 A.L.R. FED. 263 (1987).

409. FED. R. CIV. P. 23(b)(2) advisory committee's note to the 1966 amendment.

410. *See id.*

individual questions and (2) a class action is superior to other available methods for the fair and efficient adjudication of the controversy.[411] The Advisory Committee stated that the purposes of Rule 23(b)(3) were to achieve economies of time, effort, and expense and the promotion of uniformity of decision as to persons similarly situated without the sacrifice of procedural fairness or the production of other undesirable results.[412]

Illustration 8-60. Assume that a fraud has been perpetrated on numerous persons by similar misrepresentations. This situation would be appropriate for Rule 23(b)(3) treatment, even where separate assessments of the damages suffered by individuals in the class will be necessary.[413]

* * * * *

For an action to qualify under Rule 23(b)(3), the common questions of law or fact must be found to predominate over individual questions. Thus, *existence* of common questions alone is not enough unless they *predominate* over the individual questions.[414] The rule does not state any criteria for determining when common questions should be held to predominate.[415] The best approach is a pragmatic one: when the common questions represent an important aspect of the case and those questions can be resolved for the entire class in a single proceeding, they should be held to predominate even if a significant amount of time also will be spent on individual questions.[416] This approach is in accord with the purposes of Rule 23(b)(3) to achieve economies of time and to promote uniformity of decision as to similarly situated persons.[417]

In determining whether a Rule 23(b)(3) class action represents the superior available method for resolving the dispute, the court must compare the alternatives to the class action. Individual actions are the most likely available alternative to class treatment, and the liberal joinder of claims and parties under the 1966 amendments to the Federal Rules of Civil Procedure may make individual actions a viable alternative in some cases.[418] Rule 23(b)(3) enumerates four factors, which, *inter alia*, are to be taken into account in determining whether the class action is superior to the other available methods for the fair and efficient adjudication of the action: (1) the interests of class members in individually controlling the prosecution or defense of separate actions; (2) the extent and nature of any litigation already commenced by or against members of the class; (3) the desirability or undesirability of concentrating litigation of the claims in the

---

411. *See* FED. R. CIV. P. 23(b)(3).

412. *See* FED. R. CIV. P. 23(b)(3) advisory committee's note to the 1966 amendment.

413. *See id.*

414. *See, e.g.,* Windham v. American Brands, Inc., 565 F.2d 59 (4th Cir. 1977), *cert. denied*, 435 U.S. 968, 98 S. Ct. 1605, 56 L. Ed. 2d 58 (1978); 7A CHARLES A. WRIGHT ET AL., FEDERAL PRACTICE AND PROCEDURE: CIVIL § 1778, at 526 (2d ed. 1986).

415. *See* 7A CHARLES A. WRIGHT ET AL., FEDERAL PRACTICE AND PROCEDURE: CIVIL § 1778, at 525-26 (2d ed. 1986).

416. *Cf. id.* at 528.

417. *See id.*

418. *See* FED. R. CIV. P. 23(b)(3) advisory committee's note to the 1966 amendment.

particular forum; and (4) the difficulties likely to be encountered in the management of a class action.[419]

The first factor—the interest of individual class members in "controlling the prosecution or defense of separate actions"[420]—involves an estimation of the advantages of class action treatment compared with the advantages of individual actions. This factor often weighs in favor of class treatment when the damage claims of individual class members are so small that separate prosecutions are impractical.[421]

The second factor listed in Rule 23(b)(3) is the pendency of any existing actions brought by or against individual class members.[422] The pendency of other actions concerning the same subject matter may destroy the ability to achieve economies of time and uniformity of result.[423] Furthermore, preexisting litigation may reveal that the interests of the individual members of the class in conducting separate lawsuits is so strong that it calls for denial of class action treatment.[424]

The third factor listed in Rule 23(b)(3) directs the court's attention to the advantages of concentrating the litigation in the particular forum.[425] This provision bears primarily on whether the location of witnesses, evidence, and other factors determining the geographical convenience of the lawsuit make it the proper place to settle the claims by or against the class.[426]

The fourth factor listed in Rule 23(b)(3) requires the court to consider the difficulties that are likely to be encountered in managing the action as a class action.[427] In considering this factor, the presence of numerous individual issues, the difficulties involved in providing notice to the absent class members under Rule 23(c)(2), and any other administrative difficulties must be balanced against the benefits of the class action.[428]

The Rule 23(b)(3) class action is the most controversial of the actions provided for in Rule 23. The class in Rule 23(b)(3) actions often will be more loosely knit than in Rule 23(b)(1) and (2) actions. As a consequence, serious due process questions exist about binding the absent members of the class in Rule 23(b)(3) actions. Thus, the problem of adequacy of representation is far more acute in Rule 23(b)(3) actions than in Rule 23(b)(1) and (2) actions.[429] In

---

419. FED. R. CIV. P. 23(b)(3).

420. FED. R. CIV. P. 23(b)(3)(A).

421. *See* FED. R. CIV. P. 23(b)(3) advisory committee's note to the 1966 amendment.

422. FED. R. CIV. P. 23(b)(3)(B).

423. *See* 7A CHARLES A. WRIGHT ET AL., FEDERAL PRACTICE AND PROCEDURE: CIVIL § 1780, at 568-70 (2d ed. 1986).

424. *See* FED. R. CIV. P. 23(b)(3) advisory committee's note to the 1966 amendment.

425. FED. R. CIV. P. 23(b)(3)(C).

426. *See* 7A CHARLES A. WRIGHT ET AL., FEDERAL PRACTICE AND PROCEDURE: CIVIL § 1780, at 572-73 (2d ed. 1986).

427. FED. R. CIV. P. 23(b)(3)(D).

428. *See generally* 7A CHARLES A. WRIGHT ET AL., FEDERAL PRACTICE AND PROCEDURE: CIVIL § 1780, at 576-83 (2d ed. 1986).

429. *See* 7B *id.* § 1786, at 194; *see also* subsection *(vi) infra* (discussing, *inter alia*, cases in which Rule 23(b)(3) overlaps with Rules 23(b)(1) and (2) and certification is sought under the latter sections to avoid the mandatory (c)(2) notice).

addition, to insure the due process validity of Rule 23(b)(3), Rule 23(c)(2) provides for a mandatory notice to be given to the members of the class who can be notified through reasonable effort.[430] The notice must inform class members that the court will exclude them from the class if they so request, that the judgment will bind them unless they request exclusion, and that if they do not request exclusion, they may enter an appearance through counsel.[431] The Supreme Court has held that Rule 23(c)(2) notice *must* be given to each individual member of the class who can be identified, contrary to the holdings of some lower courts that such notice was not required when the claims of the class members were so small that it was unlikely that any of them would opt out to pursue individual actions.[432] In the same case, the Court also held that the plaintiff must pay the cost of the notice in the action, even though the cost, as a practical matter, may result in termination of the suit.[433]

Although Rule 23(c)(1) directs the court to determine whether an action may be maintained as a class action at an early stage of the proceeding, a determination that the action may be so maintained, including a determination that the representation is adequate, may be revised at a later stage.[434] Rule 23(c)(3) provides that the judgment in a Rule 23(b)(1) or (b)(2) class action must include and describe those whom the court finds to be members of the class. Rule 23(c)(3) additionally provides that in Rule 23(b)(3) actions, the judgment must "include and specify or describe" those to whom the Rule 23(c)(2) notice was directed, who have not opted out of the class, and whom the court finds are members of the class.[435]

(v) Court Management of Class Actions and Approval of Settlements

Rule 23(d) authorizes the court in a class action to make appropriate orders for the management of the class action. Such orders include but are not limited to notice to members of the class of various steps in the action, of the extent of the judgment, of the opportunity of the members of the class to indicate whether they consider the representation fair and adequate or whether they want to intervene in the action.[436] Finally, Rule 23(e) provides that a class action may not be dismissed or compromised without the approval of the court or notice to the class members.[437]

---

430. *See* Benjamin Kaplan, *Continuing Work of the Civil Committee: 1966 Amendments of the Federal Rules of Civil Procedure (I)*, 81 HARV. L. REV. 356, 396 (1967). *See generally* Marcia G. Robeson, Annotation, *What Constitutes "Best Notice Practicable" Required by Rule 23(c)(2) of Federal Rules of Civil Procedure, in Class Actions Brought Under Rule 23(b)(3)*, 32 A.L.R. FED. 102 (1977).

431. *See* FED. R. CIV. P. 23(c)(2).

432. *See* Eisen v. Carlisle & Jacquelin, 417 U.S. 156, 94 S. Ct. 2140, 40 L. Ed. 2d 732 (1974).

433. *See id.*

434. *See* FED. R. CIV. P. 23(c)(1) advisory committee's note to the 1966 amendment.

435. *See* FED. R. CIV. P. 23(c)(3).

436. *See* FED. R. CIV. P. 23(d).

437. *See* FED. R. CIV. P. 23(e).; Annotation, *Notice of Proposed Dismissal or Compromise of Class Action to Absent Putative Class Members in Uncertified Class Action Under Rule 23(e) of Federal Rules of Civil Procedure*, 68 A.L.R. FED. 290 (1984); Kevin D. Hart, Annotation, *Propriety of Notice of Voluntary Dismissal or Compromise of Class Action, Pursuant to Rule 23(e) of the Federal Rules of Civil Procedure*, 52 A.L.R. FED.

(vi) Contemporary Issues in the Administration of Rule 23

In recent years, several issues have arisen in the administration of Rule 23 that deserve comment. One issue concerns the application of Rule 23 to mass tort cases. In commenting on the 1966 revisions to Rule 23(b)(3), the Advisory Committee stated that

> [a] "mass accident" resulting in injuries to numerous persons is ordinarily not appropriate for a class action because of the likelihood that significant questions not only of damages but of liability and defenses of liability would be present, affecting the individuals in different ways. In these circumstances an action conducted nominally as a class action would degenerate in practice into multiple lawsuits separately tried.[438]

Despite this statement, the Advisory Committee seemed to concede that certain kinds of "mass tort" cases might be appropriate for class treatment.[439] In fact, federal courts have often certified mass tort cases as appropriate for class treatment under Rule 23(b)(3).[440] Nevertheless, such cases clearly present many kinds of management problems that make class certification difficult, and some federal courts of appeals have begun to scrutinize mass tort class certifications more closely than has been the case in the past.[441] These cases have not settled the question whether mass tort actions are appropriate for class treatment, and the debate over the issue is vigorous.[442] However, the problem of whether mass tort actions should be conducted in class action form is part of a larger concern about

---

457 (1981); *see also* Phillip E. Hassman, Annotation, *Right of Class Member, in Class Action Under Rule 23 of Federal Rules of Civil Procedure, to Appeal from Order Approving Settlement with Class*, 30 A.L.R. FED. 846 (1976).

438. FED. R. CIV. P. 23(b)(3) advisory committee's note to the 1966 amendment.

439. *See id.* (discussing fraud cases in which similar misrepresentations are made to the members of the class and damage claims arising out of concerted antitrust violations).

440. *See, e.g.*, AMERICAN LAW INSTITUTE, COMPLEX LITIGATION: STATUTORY RECOMMENDATIONS AND ANALYSIS WITH REPORTER'S STUDY 27-28 (1994). It may be that the "mass accident" example given by the Advisory Committee represents an especially difficult kind of "mass tort" insofar as class certification is concerned, while other kinds of mass torts present more tractable class certification problems.

441. *See, e.g.*, Castano v. American Tobacco Co., 84 F.3d 734 (5th Cir. 1996) (reversing certification of nicotine class action); *In re* American Med. Sys., 75 F.3d 1069 (6th Cir. 1996) (reversing certification of penile prostheses class action); *In re* Rhone-Poulenc Rorer, Inc., 51 F.3d 1293 (7th Cir. 1995) (reversing certification of class action brought against manufacturers of blood solids on behalf of hemophiliacs infected by the AIDS virus as a consequence of using the defendants' products).

442. *See, e.g.*, John C. Coffee, *Class Wars: The Dilemma of the Mass Tort Class Action*, 95 COLUM. L. REV. 1343 (1995); Paul D. Carrington & Derek P. Apanovitch, *The Constitutional Limits of Judicial Rulemaking: The Illegitimacy of Mass-Tort Settlements Negotiated Under Federal Rule 23*, 39 ARIZ. L. REV. 461 (1997); Mary J. Davis, *Toward the Proper Role for Mass Tort Class Actions*, 77 ORE. L. REV. 157 (1998); Samuel Issacharoff, *Administering Damage Awards in Mass-Tort Litigation*, 10 REV. LITIG. 463 (1991); Barry F. McNeil & Beth L. Fancsali, *Mass Torts and Class Actions: Facing Increased Scrutiny*, 167 F.R.D. 483 (1996); Fred Misko, Jr. & Frank E. Goodrich, *Managing Complex Litigation: Class Actions and Mass Torts*, 48 BAY, L. REV. 1001 (1996); Richard A. Nagareda, *In the Aftermath of the Mass Tort Class Action*, 85 GEO. L.J. 237 (1996).

how complex litigation of all sorts should be conducted.[443] Regardless of the merits of specific recommendations on this question, it seems likely that a comprehensive solution to the problem cannot be worked out by the courts on a case-by-case basis, but will have to be addressed by Congress and state legislatures.

A second question that has arisen under Rule 23 concerns the overlap between Rule 23(b)(1), (2) & (3) that sometimes allows class actions to be certified under multiple parts of the rule. Under such circumstances, the class representative has the obvious incentive to seek certification the action under Rule 23(b)(1) or (2), but not Rule 23(b)(3), because of the mandatory notice and opt-out provisions of subdivision (b)(3) of the rule. However, the mandatory notice and opt-out option required in Rule 23(b)(3) cases may be required as a matter of due process because the class in (b)(3) actions is more loosely knit than in (b)(1) or (b)(2) actions, which arguably requires the additional protection that notice will provide to the individual class members.[444] Thus, if an action is brought primarily for damages, but is certified under Rule 23(b)(1) or (2) because of other relief requested in the action, the question is whether the class must be given notice and an opportunity to opt out either under Rule 23 or as a matter of due process.

In *Ticor Title Insurance Co. v. Brown,*[445] the Supreme Court recognized this issue, but refused to decide it. In *Ticor,* an initial class action was settled under circumstances in which all money damage claims against the defendants were purportedly extinguished while injunctive relief and other nonmonetary relief was granted to the members of the class. The district court certified the class settlement under Rule 23(b)(1)(A) and (b)(2). The court rejected an objection by a member of the class that the action could not be certified under these provisions because the relief requested was primarily monetary in nature. Subsequently, a second class action was commenced on behalf of the class in another federal court, and the court granted summary judgment to the defendants on the ground, in part, that the plaintiffs were bound by the judgment in the prior class action. The court of appeals reversed, holding that it would violate due process to give

---

443. For a comprehensive set of recommendations concerning complex litigation generally, see AMERICAN LAW INSTITUTE, COMPLEX LITIGATION: STATUTORY RECOMMENDATIONS AND ANALYSIS WITH REPORTER'S STUDY (1994); *see also* Francis R. Kirkham, *Complex Litigation—Have Good Intentions Gone Awry?,* 70 F.R.D. 199 (1976); Francis R. Kirkham, *Problems of Complex Litigation,* 83 F.R.D. 497 (1980); Jay Tidmarsh, *Unattainable Justice: The Form of Complex Litigation and the Limit of Judicial Power,* 60 GEO. WASH L. REV. 1683 (1992).

444. As the Advisory Committee explained:

> In the degree that there is cohesiveness or unity in the class and the representation is effective, the need for notice to the class will tend toward a minimum. These indicators suggest that notice under subdivision (d)(2) may be particularly useful and advisable in certain class actions maintained under subdivision (b)(3), for example, to permit members of the class to object to the representation. Indeed, under subdivision (c)(2), notice must be ordered, and is not merely discretionary, to give the members in a subdivision (b)(3) class action an opportunity to secure exclusion from the class. This mandatory notice . . . is designed to fulfill requirements of due process to which the class action procedure is of course subject.

FED. R. CIV. P. 23(d)(2) advisory committee note to the 1966 amendment.

445. 511 U.S. 117, 114 S. Ct. 1359, 128 L. Ed.2d 33 (1994).

a binding effect to the judgment in the original class action that involved money damage claims when the plaintiff bringing the second action had not been permitted to opt out in the first proceeding. The U.S. Supreme Court initially granted certiorari, but ultimately dismissed the writ as improvidently granted. A majority of the Court felt that the due process issue would be of no consequence if Rule 23 itself required notice and an opportunity to opt out of actions brought for damages. However, the Rule 23 issue could not be decided in the case because it was clearly res judicata, having been litigated and determined against the plaintiffs in the prior class action. Therefore, the Court reserved judgment on the question until an appropriate case in which the Rule 23 issue is open for decision.

Although Rule 23(b)(2) is specifically keyed to the propriety of declaratory or injunctive relief, Rule 23(b)(1) is not. Therefore, it would seem that the issue in *Ticor* ought not to depend upon whether the action is primarily for money damages, but on whether the class in the action is the "loosely knit" kind of class that was envisioned for (b)(3) cases or the more "tightly knit" kind of class that the drafters of Rule 23 envisioned as proper for (b)(1) actions.[446] If it is the former, the rule (and due process) should require notice and the opportunity to opt out of the class. If it is the latter, no such notice should be required, even if damages is the primary remedy sought. This conclusion, of course, assumes, as the Advisory Committee did, that adequacy of representation and the other protection of Rule 23(a) would suffice to protect the class in (b)(1) & (b)(2) actions without the need for notice. If this assumption is not true, however, due process may also require notice in the latter kinds of actions and the ability to opt out of the class.[447] Nevertheless, the Advisory Committee seems correct that the cohesivenss of the class will suffice in (b)(1) & (b)(2) actions to assure that due process is satisfied if the Rule 23(a) certification requirements are met.

A final important issue concerns the legitimacy of and protection that is necessary in so-called "settlement" class actions. A settlement class action is one in which the representative parties (or, more accurately, their attorneys) arrive at a settlement with the defendant before the action is commenced. The representative party then commences the class action, and the parties ask the court to certify the class as the parties have defined it. The court reviews the settlement before

---

446. *See also* Steven T.O. Cottreau, *The Due Process Right to Opt Out of Class Actions,* 73 N.Y.U. L. REV. 480 (1998); Patricia Anne Solomon, *Are Mandatory Class Actions Unconstitutional?* 72 N.D. L. REV. 1627 (1997). *Cf.* Lawrence J. Restieri, Jr., *The Class Action Dilemma: The Certification of Classes Seeking Equitable Relief and Monetary Damages After* Ticor Title Insurance Co. v. Brown, 63 FORDHAM L. REV. 1745 (1995) (arguing that it is not the presence of a damage claim that should preclude certification under Rule 23(b)(1) or (b)(2), but whether the class claim requires the court to issue a single decree, even if a damage remedy is part of the relief requested; under this standard, the author argues that the (b)(1) & (b)(2) certification in *Ticor* was improper because individual adjudications would not create inconsistent verdicts or different standards of conduct that the defendant would be unable to satisfy, and the class members did not have an ongoing relationship with one another that deprived the class of unity).

447. *See also* Maximilian A. Grant, *The Right Not to Sue: A First Amendment Rationale for Opting Out of Mandatory Class Actions,* 63 U. CHI. L. REV. 239 (1996) (arguing that a First Amendment right to opt out may be sounder than one based on the Due Process Clause because mandatory class actions compel association with, or financial or other support of, activities with which absent class members may disagree).

certifying the action. If it finds the settlement fair, it will certify the action as a class action for settlement purposes only. Class counsel will then notify the members of the class simultaneously of the commencement of the suit, the class certification, and the settlement. The settlement class action is controversial because there are incentives for the representatives' attorneys[448] and the defendants to settle actions on terms that are not fair to all class members. In addition, many settlement class actions are also mass tort actions, which raise additional problems of whether the actions are proper under Rule 23.[449]

In 1996, the Advisory Committee proposed an amendment to Rule 23 that would have addressed some, but by no means all, of the problems with the settlement class action. The amendment was designed to resolve a conflict in the decisions resulting because some courts refused to certify a class action for settlement purposes unless the action could also be certified for trial.[450] Before this amendment could be adopted, it was rendered moot by the Supreme Court's decision in *Amchem Products, Inc. v. Windsor*.[451] In *Amchem*, the Court held that the adequate representation requirement of Rule 23(a)(4) and the predominance requirement of Rule 23(b)(3) were not satisfied by the settlement class action certified by the district court. The Court held that settlement is relevant to

---

448. For an extensive argument that the problems of improper counsel behavior in the settlement class action context can be solved by suing the class counsel involved, see Susan P. Koniak & George M. Cohen, *Under Cloak of Settlement,* 82 VA. L. REV. 1051 (1996). One court has held that if the settlement of a class action results in a rift in the class, with some members objecting to the settlement, class counsel need not necessarily disqualify herself, but may continue to represent the class members who agree with the settlement. *See* Lazy Oil Co. v. Witco Corp., 166 F.3d 881 (3d Cir. 1999).

449. *See, e.g.,* Roger C. Cramton, *Individualized Justice, Mass Torts, and "Settlement Class Actions": An Introduction,* 80 CORNELL L. REV. 811 (1995); John C. Coffee, *Class Wars: The Dilemma of the Mass Tort Class Action,* 95 COLUM. L. REV. 1343 (1995); James A. Henderson, Jr., Comment, *Settlement Class Actions and the Limits of Adjudication,* 80 CORNELL L. REV. 1014 (1995); Michael L. McCabe, Note, *Class Backwards: Does the Fairness, Adequacy and Reasonableness of a Negotiated Class Action Settlement Really Have Any Effect on Approval?:* General Motors v. Bloyed, 916 S.W.2d 949 (Tex. 1996), 28 TEXAS TECH L. REV. 159 (1997); Pamela M. Madas, *To Settlement Classes and Beyond: A Primer on Proposed Methods for Federalizing Mass Tort Litigation,* 28 SETON HALL L. REV. 540 (1997); Stephen E. Morrissey, Note, *State Settlement Class Actions that Release Exclusive Federal Claims: Developing a Framework for Multi-Jurisdictional Management of Shareholder Litigation,* 95 COLUM . L. REV. 1765 (1995); Richard A. Negareda, *Turning From Tort to Administration,* 94 MICH. L. REV. 899 (1996); William W. Schwarzer, *Structuring Multiclaim Litigation: Should Rule 23 Be Revised?* 94 MICH. L. REV. 1250 (1996); Jack B. Weinstein & Karen S. Schwartz, *Notes From the Cave: Some Problems of Judges in Dealing with Class Action Settlements,* 163 F.R.D. 369 (1995); Note, *Back to the Drawing Board: The Settlement Class Action and the Limits of Rule 23,* 109 HARV. L. REV. 828 (1996); *see also In re* General Motors Corp. Pick-Up Truck Fuel Tank Prods. Liab. Litig., 55 F.3d 768 (3d Cir.), *cert. denied,* 516 U.S. 824, 116 S. Ct. 88, 133 L. Ed.2d 45 (1995); *In re* Asbestos Litig., 90 F.3d 963 (5th Cir. 1996).

450. The proposed amendment would have added a new Rule 23(b)(4): ''(4) the parties to a settlement request certification under subdivision (b)(3) for purposes of settlement even though the requirements of subdivision (b)(3) might not be met for trial.'' 167 F.R.D. 523, 529 (1996). The Advisory Committee recognized that there were both risks and benefits in the settlement class action and stated that the competing forces could be ''reconciled by recognizing the legitimacy of settlement classes but increasing the protection afforded to class members.'' *Id.* at 564. However, the Committee stated that ''[n]otice and the right to opt out provide the central means of protecting settlement class members under subdivision (b)(3),'' but exhorted the courts to do a better job (a) in framing ''clear and succinct'' settlement notices that provide the information necessary to determine whether to object to the settlement and (b) to approach the definition of the class with care, so as not to define the class over broadly and thus, *e.g.,* include within it persons with conflicting interests. *See id.* Note, however, that the Advisory Committee did not write its exhortations into the text of the proposed amendment, which is, to say the least, a questionable way to proceed.

451. 521 U.S. 591, 117 S. Ct. 2231, 138 L. Ed.2d 689 (1997).

the propriety of class certification and that the question whether trial would produce intractable management problems is not a consideration when settlement-only certification is requested. However, the Court found the adequacy of representation and predominance problems overwhelming in the context of the case.[452]

Subsequently, in *Ortiz v. Fibreboard Corp.,*[453] the Court reversed a settlement class action under Rule 23(b)(1)(B). The Court held that in a (b)(1)(B) action involving a fund of money, there must be a demonstration that the fund in question is limited by more than the settlement agreement of the parties and has been allocated to claimants within the class by a process that addresses any conflicting interests of the class members. The Court found that the certification of the class in *Ortiz* failed to demonstrate that the fund was limited except by the agreement of the parties, and the settlement also showed exclusions from the class and allocations of assets at odds with the concept of limited fund treatment and the structural protections of Rule 23(a) explained in *Amchem.*

Amchem and *Ortiz* do not formally preclude settlement class actions. However, taken together, the cases constitute a strong message from the Supreme Court that settlement class actions should receive closer scrutiny from the lower federal courts than they have been given in the past.[454] Nevertheless, it is questionable whether all the problems with settlement class actions can be solved on a case-by-case basis under existing Rule 23. Rather, the problems that have been identified to date with settlement class suits call for more vigorous treatment through the legislative or rulemaking processes.[455] One useful suggestion for reform is that class actions with preclusive effect should not be settled unless the court gives all class members the option to reject the settlement and exclude themselves from the class at the time of settlement.[456]

(c) Subject-Matter Jurisdiction Problems Under Rule 23

Like many other joinder devices, subject-matter jurisdiction problems are most acute in class actions based on diversity jurisdiction. The rule of complete diversity poses no serious problem because only the citizenship of the representa-

---

452. For a suggestion that the Court's interpretation of Rule 23 in *Amchem,* to the extent that it allows certification of a settlement class that could not be certified as a litigation class, does not violate the Rules Enabling Act as currently interpreted, but that it might violate the Act under an expanded interpretation, see Note, *The Rules Enabling Act and the Limits of Rule 23,* 111 HARV. L. REV. 2294 (1998).

453. 527 U.S. 815, 119 S. Ct. 2295, 144 L. Ed. 2d 715 (1999).

454. Mark C. Weber, *Thanks for Not Suing: The Prospects for State Court Class Action Litigation over Tobacco Injuries,* 33 GA. L. REV. 979 (1999); Mark C. Weber, *Mass Jury Trials in Mass Tort Cases: Some Preliminary Issues,* 48 DE PAUL L. REV. 463 (1998); Thomas E. Willgiving, *Mass Torts Problems and Proposals: A Report to the Mass Torts Working Group,* 187 F.R.D. 325, 356-63 (1999) (discussing the limits of settlement class actions after *Amchem*); REPORT OF THE ADVISORY COMMITTEE ON CIVIL RULES AND THE WORKING GROUP ON MASS TORTS TO THE CHIEF JUSTICE OF THE UNITED STATES AND TO THE JUDICIAL CONFERENCE OF THE UNITED STATES, 187 F.R.D. 293 (1999).

455. For an empirical analysis of seventeen issues prevalent in class action litigation that pose potential challenges for the rulemaking process, see Thomas E. Willgiving *et al., An Empirical Analysis of Rule 23 to Address the Rulemaking Challenges,* 71 N.Y.U. L. REV. 74 (1996).

456. *See* Mark C. Weber, *A Consent-Based Approach to Class Action Settlement: Improving* Amchem Products Inc. v. Windsor, 59 OHIO ST. L.J. 1155 (1998).

tive party is considered in determining whether diversity exists under 28 U.S.C. § 1332.[457] Therefore, the fact that some absent members of the class are citizens of the same state as the party opposing the class does not destroy diversity jurisdiction.

In contrast, jurisdictional amount problems can be serious under § 1332. The question is whether the claims of the class members may be aggregated in order to meet the amount-in-controversy requirement of the diversity statute. Recall that the general rule governing aggregation in non-class action party joinder cases is that several plaintiffs may aggregate their claims to meet the jurisdictional amount requirement only when they are suing to enforce a single title or right in which they have a common and undivided interest.[458] As applied to class actions before 1966, plaintiffs could aggregate their claims in "true" class actions, but not in "hybrid" or "spurious" class actions because in both of the latter actions the rights asserted were "several."[459]

There was hope that the 1966 amendments to Rule 23 would change the context in which the jurisdictional amount requirement operated and permit aggregation in all class actions. Because the judgment in all Rule 23 class actions would bind the absent members of the class after 1966, it was hoped that the amount in controversy could be satisfied by the aggregate amount claimed by or against the class.[460] Unfortunately, the Supreme Court has settled the rule to the contrary since 1966. In *Snyder v. Harris*,[461] the Court held that when the claims of the class members are all less than the jurisdictional amount, the claims can be aggregated only when the plaintiffs are attempting to enforce a single title or right in which they share a common and undivided interest. Subsequently, in *Zahn v. International Paper Co.*,[462] the Court held that when the claims of some members of the class meet the jurisdictional amount requirement and others do not, aggregation still is permitted only under the traditional test. Thus, each member of the class not possessing a claim in excess of $75,000 must be dismissed from the action unless the single-title-or-right test is satisfied.

The enactment of 28 U.S.C. § 1367 in 1990 should not alter the results in *Snyder* and *Zahn*. Section 1367(b), which is designed to preserve the policies of the diversity jurisdiction, does not refer to Rule 23, as it does to other federal joinder rules. This omission could be interpreted to mean that § 1367(b) does not

---

457. *See* Supreme Tribe of Ben-Hur v. Cauble, 255 U.S. 356, 41 S. Ct. 338, 65 L. Ed. 673 (1921); *In re* "Agent Orange" Prod. Liab. Litig., 818 F.2d 145, 162 (2d Cir. 1987); *In re* Cement Antitrust Litig., 688 F.2d 1297, 1309 (9th Cir. 1982), *aff'd sub nom.* Arizona v. United States Dist. Court, 459 U.S. 1191, 103 S. Ct. 1173, 75 L. Ed. 2d 425 (1983). *But see* Sherman L. Cohn, *The New Federal Rules of Civil Procedure*, 54 GEO. L.J. 1204, 1219 (1966). One federal court has held that if a representative party adds other representative parties to the action who are not diverse to the plaintiff in order to defeat removal, the district court may not dismiss the added parties as long as it is clear that they are real parties in interest. *See* Garbie v. Chrysler Corp., 8 F. Supp. 2d 814 (N.D. Ill. 1998).

458. *See* Chapter 2(C)(3)*(e)(ii)* ("Aggregation of Claims with Multiple Parties: The 'Common and Undivided' Interest Test") *supra*.

459. *See* 7A CHARLES A. WRIGHT ET AL., FEDERAL PRACTICE AND PROCEDURE: CIVIL § 1756, at 66 (2d ed. 1986).

460. *Cf. id.* at 71.

461. 394 U.S. 332, 89 S. Ct. 1053, 22 L. Ed. 2d 319 (1969).

462. 414 U.S. 291, 94 S. Ct. 505, 38 L. Ed. 2d 511 (1973).

except class actions from the operation of § 1367(a).[463] This reading would effectively overrule *Snyder* and *Zahn*, because the claims of the absent members of a Rule 23 class usually, if not always, will be sufficiently related to the representative's claim to be within the supplemental jurisdiction conferred by § 1367(a). Nevertheless, this reading is incorrect. The House Report accompanying § 1367(b) stated that "[t]he section is not intended to affect the jurisdictional requirements of 28 U.S.C. § 1332 in diversity-only class actions, as those requirements were interpreted prior to *Finley.*"[464] Thus, despite the lack of reference to Rule 23 in § 1367(b), the legislative history of the statute supports retention of the *Snyder-Zahn* aggregation requirements.

Initially, the lower federal court decisions dealing with this issue after the enactment of § 1367 overwhelmingly supported the retention of the pre-1990 aggregation requirements.[465] However, a difference of opinion has now developed among the courts of appeals over whether the omission of a reference to Rule 23 in § 1367(b) overrules *Zahn*. The first decision to hold *Zahn* overruled was the Fifth Circuit's decision in *Free v. Abbott Laboratories.*[466] In *Abbott*, the court of appeals acknowledged the legislative history of § 1367(b), which indicated that it was not the intent of the statute to overrule *Zahn*. Nevertheless, the court held that it was impermissible to consult the legislative history of the statute:

> We cannot search legislative history for congressional intent unless we find the statute unclear or ambiguous. Here, it is neither. The statute's first section vests federal courts with the power to hear supplemental claims generally, subject to limited exceptions set forth in the statute's second section. Class actions are not among the enumerated exceptions.[467]

The court's decision in *Abbott* is clearly wrong, even under the premises upon which the court was operating. The court's mistake was in applying a type of "plain meaning" interpretation to only one-half of § 1367. The court

---

463. *See* Denis F. McLaughlin, *The Federal Supplemental Jurisdiction Statute—A Constitutional and Statutory Analysis*, 24 ARIZ. ST. L.J. 849, 972 (1992).

464. H. REP. NO. 734, 101st Cong., 2d Sess. 29 (1990).

465. Two early cases held that § 1367 overruled the aggregation rules. *See* Garza v. National Am. Ins. Co., 807 F. Supp. 1256 (M.D. La. 1992); Corporate Resources, Inc. v. Southeast Suburban Ambulatory Surgical Ctr., Inc., 774 F. Supp. 503 (N.D. Ill. 1991). However, numerous other early district court decisions held that the pre-1990 aggregation rules survived the enactment of § 1367. *See, e.g.,* Chee Chung Leung v. Checker Motors Corp., No. 93 C 2704, 1993 WL 515470, 1993 U.S. Dist. LEXIS 17174 (N.D. Ill. Dec. 7, 1993); Durrett v. John Deere Co., 150 F.R.D. 555 (N.D. Tex. 1993); Benfield v. Mocatta Metals Corp., No. 91 CIV 8255 (LJF), 1993 WL 148978, 1993 U.S. Dist. LEXIS 5856 (S.D.N.Y. May 5, 1993); Mayo v. Key Fin. Servs., Inc., 812 F. Supp. 277 (D. Mass. 1993); Hairston v. Home Loan & Inv. Bank, 814 F. Supp. 180 (D. Mass. 1993); Averdick v. Republic Fin. Servs., Inc., 803 F. Supp. 37 (E.D. Ky. 1992); Bradbury v. Robertson-Ceco Corp., No. 92 C 3408, 1992 WL 178648, 1992 U.S. Dist. LEXIS 10888 (N.D. Ill. July 22, 1992); Cheramie v. Texaco, Inc., No. 91-3114, 1991 WL 236784, 1991 U.S. Dist. LEXIS 15616 (E.D. La. Oct. 31, 1991); Fink v. Heath, No. 91 C 2982, 1991 WL 127614, 1991 U.S. Dist. LEXIS 15090 (N.D. Ill. Oct. 16, 1991).

466. 51 F.3d 524 (5th Cir. 1995).

467. *Id.* at 528; *see also* Afshin Ashourzadeh, Comment, *Supplemental Jurisdiction in Class Action Lawsuits: Recovering Supplemental Jurisdiction From the Jaws of Aggregation,* 26 SW. U. L. REV. 89 (1996); Sean G. Saxon, Comment, *Civil Procedure—Free v. Abbott Laboratories: Supplemental Jurisdiction for Pendent Plaintiffs Becomes More Affordable,* 27 U. MEM. L. REV. 229 (1996).

considered the language of § 1367(b) to be clear, but in describing § 1367(a), it interpreted that section as vesting federal courts "with the power to hear supplemental *claims* generally."[468] However, as discussed in Chapter 2, a literal reading of § 1367(a) does not justify the conclusion that the statute confers jurisdiction over "claims," although it is clear from the history of the statute that a claim-specific interpretation is correct.[469] Thus, if the court had applied a literal, or "plain meaning," method of interpretation to the entire statute it could not have reached the question whether § 1367(b) overruled *Zahn*, because no jurisdiction over the action would have existed under § 1367(a) in the first place.[470] Alternatively, the court might have recognized that a literal interpretation of the entire statute would be absurd, in which case it would have been justified in consulting the legislative history of the statute, which, as discussed above, indicates that it was not the intent of Congress to overrule *Zahn*.[471]

A far better, though not perfect, interpretation of § 1367(b) was made by the Tenth Circuit in *Leonhardt v. Western Sugar Co.*[472] The Tenth Circuit rejected *Abbott* and held that § 1367(b) did not overrule *Zahn*. The court reasoned:

> In determining that nothing in the language of § 1367 limited the broad grant of authority conferred by § 1367(a) so as to preserve the historical aggregation rules for class actions under § 1332, the Fifth and Seventh Circuits focused only on the absence of Rule 23 from the exceptions enumerated in § 1367(b). . . . Those exceptions, however, concern only the exercise of supplemental jurisdiction over claims against defendants who are made parties to a diversity action under certain rules and claims by plaintiffs who seek to be *added* to an ongoing diversity action. We are concerned, however, with whether Congress intended to change the rules about when a plaintiff can bring an *initial* diversity-based class action under Rule 23, where the court's original jurisdiction is based upon § 1332. The omission of Rule 23 from § 1367(b) has no bearing on that question.

---

468. 51 F.3d at 528 (emphasis supplied).

469. *See* Chapter 2(C)(4)*(d)(i) supra* (discussing the language of § 1367(a) conferring jurisdiction on the lower federal courts only over supplemental claims that are part of a "civil action" over which the federal courts have subject-matter jurisdiction under some statute outside of § 1367).

470. In accord with the literal reading of the statute outlined in Chapter 2(C)(4)*(d)(i), supra,* this would be because § 1367(a) literally requires there to be "original jurisdiction" in a district court over a "civil action" under some provision of Title 28 other than § 1367(a) before it provides "supplemental jurisdiction" over "all other claims that are so related to claims in the action within such original jurisdiction" that they form part of the same case or controversy under Article III." In other words, as observed in Chapter 2(C)(4)*(d)(i),* a literal reading of the statute would only codify the doctrine of ancillary jurisdiction.

471. As of this writing, *Abbott* has been followed by one other court of appeals. *See In re* Brand Name Prescription Drugs Antitrust Litig., 123 F.3d 599 (7th Cir. 1997), *cert. denied,* 522 U.S. 1153, 118 S. Ct. 1178, 140 L. Ed.2d 186 (1998) (if one representative party has a claim that meets the jurisdictional amount, the claims of the other members of the class are within the supplemental jurisdiction conferred by § 1367)

472. 160 F.3d 631 (10th Cir. 1998).

In our view, a literal and textually faithful reading of § 1367(a) leads to the opposite conclusion from that of the Fifth and Seventh Circuits. Section 1367(a) specifically addresses "any civil action of which the district courts have *original jurisdiction.*" (Emphasis added.) It then provides for *supplemental jurisdiction* over transactionally related claims. Section 1332 is what confers original jurisdiction over diversity cases and it expressly requires that the "matter in controversy exceed[] the sum or value of $75,000.". . . Thus, Congress in § 1367(a) expressly excepted claims brought under § 1332 and its well-understood definition of "matter in controversy. . . .

Furthermore, § 1367(b) itself supports this interpretation of § 1367(a). Section 1367(b) sets forth various situations in which a court, sitting in diversity, cannot exercise supplemental jurisdiction where the exercise of such jurisdiction "would be inconsistent with the jurisdictional requirements of § 1332.". . . The fact that § 1367(b) prohibits the addition of claims and parties which would destroy diversity supports our interpretation of § 1367(a) as also fully respecting the rules of diversity in cases invoking the original jurisdiction of the federal courts.

Thus, in our view § 1367(a) and (b) can be read literally, and unambiguously, to require each plaintiff in a class action diversity case to satisfy the *Zahn* definition of "matter in controversy" and to individually meet the $75,000 requirement. However, we recognize that it is difficult to argue persuasively that the statute is truly unambiguous when two circuit courts of appeal have reached the opposite conclusion from us, when a majority of district courts are in agreement with us (although not all for the same reasons) and when commentators are divided. We therefore assume that ambiguity of the statute permits us to examine legislative history.[473]

The Tenth Circuit was correct that a literal reading of § 1367(a) would require the plaintiff to meet the *Zahn* aggregation requirements. However, the court stated that this reinforced a reading of § 1367(b) that would also preserve the requirements. In reality, as observed in Chapter 2(C)(4)*(d)(i)*, a literal reading of § 1367(a) would produce the conclusion that the purpose of the statute was to codify the doctrine of ancillary jurisdiction, and this reading would break down when one reaches § 1367(b). Because the concept of ancillary jurisdiction applies only to claims coming into the action *after* the plaintiff's original claim(s) against the defendant(s),[474] the prohibitions in § 1367(b) on plaintiff's claims that violate the policies of the diversity jurisdiction would make no sense.[475] If § 1367(a) only codified the doctrine of ancillary jurisdiction, it would not create

---

473. 160 F.3d at 639-40. *Accord* Meritcare v. St. Paul Mercury Ins. Co., 166 F.3d 214 (3d Cir. 1999).

474. *See* Chapter 2(C)(4)*(a)* ("The General Nature of Pendent and Ancillary Jurisdiction") *supra.*

475. *See* Chapter 2(C)(4)*(d)(i)* ("The Scope of Supplemental Jurisdiction: Section 1367(a)") & accompanying notes *supra.*

jurisdiction over plaintiff's claims in the first place, and there would be no need for § 1367(b) to create exceptions to § 1367(a) for such claims. Thus, under a literal reading of § 1367(a), § 1367(a) & (b) would not mesh. This is why the statute does not have a "clear" meaning.

Furthermore, the Tenth Circuit did not notice that a literal reading of § 1367(a) would defeat the principal purpose of the statute to overrule the case of *Finley v. United States*. If there must be original jurisdiction over an entire diversity-based "civil action" commenced by the plaintiff under § 1332 in order to satisfy the language of § 1367(a), the same would be true of "civil actions" based on federal question jurisdiction. Thus, in a pendent parties jurisdiction case in which a federal claim is asserted against one party and a related state claim is joined against another, nondiverse party, there would be no original jurisdiction of the resulting "civil action" under § 1331 because the *Finley* restriction attaches to the latter statute.[476] Therefore, because an "action-specific" interpretation of § 1367(a) would cause the statute's main purpose to fail, such an interpretation is inadmissible, as the vast majority of federal courts have concluded.

In the end, the only sensible result is to read § 1367(a) as the Fifth Circuit read it in *Abbott*, but to recognize that such a reading is not a "literal," "plain," or "clear" one, with the result that it is permissible to look to the legislative history of both § 1367(a) & (b) in applying the statute. Thus, § 1367(a) should be interpreted to confer supplemental jurisdiction over claims for less than $75,000 in cases like *Zahn, Abbott,* and *Leonhardt*, but § 1367(b) should be interpreted as taking that jurisdiction away unless the restrictive aggregation rules of *Zahn* are satisfied.[477] The conflict among the lower courts on the *Zahn*-§ 1367 issue will apparently soon be resolved. The U.S. Supreme Court has granted certiorari in the *Abbott* case specifically for the purpose of

---

476. *See* Chapter 2(C)(4)*(d)(i) supra* (discussing this problem).

477. Despite the split in the circuits, most district courts continue to reach this result. *See, e.g.,* Green v. H & R Block, Inc., 981 F. Supp. 951 (D. Md. 1997); Crosby v. America Online, Inc., 967 F. Supp. 257 (N.D. Ohio 1997); Gilmer v. Walt Disney Co., 915 F. Supp. 1001 (W.D. Ark. 1996); Snider v. Stimson Lumber Co., 914 F. Supp. 388 (E.D. Cal. 1996); Rodger v. Electronic Data Sys. Corp., 160 F.R.D. 532 (E.D.N.C. 1995); Shelly v. Southern Bell Tel. & Tel. Co., 873 F. Supp. 613 (M.D. Ala. 1995); *see also* E.R. Squib & Sons v. Accident & Cas. Ins. Co., 160 F.3d 925 (2d Cir.1998) (raising, but not deciding, the question whether *Zahn* had been overruled in a Rule 23.2 class action against an association); Lauchheimer v. Gulf Oil, 6 F. Supp. 2d 339 (D.N.J. 1998) (if neither named plaintiff nor any of the class members have claims meeting the amount requirement, the requirement cannot be met by (a) attributing the total amount of the class attorney's fees to every member of the class; (b) attributing the total amount of the potential punitive damages to every member of the class; or (c) attributing the attorney's fees awarded under statutory authority to the named plaintiff); Sanderson, Thompson, Ratledge & Zimmy v. AWACS, Inc., 958 F. Supp. 947 (D. Del. 1997) (if named plaintiff's claim does not exceed $75,000, subject-matter jurisdiction does not exist, even though claims of some of the absent class members do exceed $75,000); *In re* High Fructose Corn Syrup Antitrust Litig., 936 F. Supp. 530 (C.D. Ill. 1996) (named plaintiff's claim must meet amount requirement); *In re* Amino Acid Lysine Antitrust Litig., 927 F. Supp. 273 (N.D. Ill. 1996) (same); Bishop v. General Motors Corp., 925 F. Supp. 294 (D.N.J. 1996) (same). As one district judge stated, given the specific legislative history indicating that § 1367 was not designed to overrule *Zahn*, to hold the contrary would send the following message from the judicial to the legislative branch: "We know what you meant to say, but you didn't quite say it. So the message from us in the judicial branch to you in the legislative branch is: 'Gotcha! And better luck next time.' " *See* Russ v. State Farm Mut. Auto Ins. Co., 961 F. Supp. 808, 820 (E.D. Pa. 1997).

resolving the question.[478] Regardless of the route taken to reach the correct result, the Court should reject *Abbott* and recognize that *Zahn* has not been legislatively overruled.

(d) *Personal Jurisdiction Problems Under Rule 23*

The most serious personal jurisdiction questions in class actions concern the ability of a court to assert jurisdiction over the absent members of the class. May a state or federal court sitting in a particular state enter a judgment that binds absent members of a plaintiffs' or defendants' class who do not have minimum contacts with the state? The earliest post-*International Shoe* case that offers support for jurisdiction over the absent members of the class is *Mullane v. Central Hanover Bank & Trust Co.*,[479] discussed in Chapter 3. However, the *Mullane* case may have involved a "jurisdiction by necessity" situation that may not exist in all class actions.[480] If New York had not had power to settle the accounts of the fund in *Mullane*, it seems certain that no other state would have the power to do so either. This peculiar situation may not be present in most Rule 23 actions. Particularly in Rule 23(b)(3) actions, when class members are scattered throughout the United States and members within each state might bring individual or class actions against a defendant, it is questionable whether the mere efficiency of bringing a single action to adjudicate the interests of the entire class will be permissible as against class members having no contacts with the forum state.

The one Supreme Court decision bearing directly on this question is *Phillips Petroleum Co. v. Shutts*.[481] In *Phillips*, the Court sustained the constitutionality of a state court's assertion of jurisdiction to bind absent plaintiff class members who had no contacts with the state. However, the *Phillips* case involved a Rule 23(b)(3) class action, in which the absent members of the class received notice of the action and an opportunity to opt out of the class. The protection afforded to the absent class members by this procedure appeared to heavily influence the Court's decision. Therefore, the *Phillips* case offers little support for the validity of jurisdictional assertions over absent class members when the notice and opt-out procedures are not available. The Court in *Phillips* also emphasized that the consequences to the absent class members in a plaintiff's class action were not as serious as they might be in other types of actions—for example, a defendant's class action. Thus, even the notice and opt-out provisions might not

---

478. *See* Free v. Abbott Labs., Inc., 176 F.3d 298 (5th Cir.), *cert. granted*, __ U.S. __, 120 S. Ct. 525, 145 L. Ed. 2d 406 (1999).

479. 339 U.S. 306, 70 S. Ct. 652, 94 L. Ed. 865 (1950).

480. *See* Chapter 3(I) ("Jurisdiction by Necessity") *supra* (discussing whether *Mullane* satisfies the conventional minimum contacts test or is a jurisdiction by necessity case).

481. 472 U.S. 797, 105 S. Ct. 2965, 86 L. Ed. 2d 628 (1985).

validate an assertion of jurisdiction to adjudicate a class action that posed the danger of more serious consequences to the class.[482]

(e) Venue Problems Under Rule 23

Before 1990, only the residence of the representative party was relevant for determining venue in class action cases.[483] Consequently, venue problems were no more substantial in class actions than in any other sort of action. However, now that residence of the plaintiff has been eliminated as a proper venue under 28 U.S.C. § 1391, venue has been accordingly narrowed in class actions, as in all other actions.[484] Residence of the representative party would only confer proper venue today in a "defendant's class action."

(f) Rule Validity Problems Under Rule 23

When state laws restrict class actions more than Federal Rule 23, the basis of the restrictions is not likely to be a "substantive" policy of the state, and the same is true of state differences in class action practice that might be more liberal than Rule 23 in permitting class actions. In addition, permitting a class action in a federal diversity suit that would not be maintainable in state court will not be likely to have more than an "incidental effect" on broader state substantive rights, and the same is true of denying class action treatment to a case that would be maintainable as a class action in state court. It might be argued that the *in terrorem* effect of federal class actions on defendants could effectively produce a victory for members of a class that they could not obtain in individual actions. Thus, if state law would only permit individual actions, and if individual actions would be impractical, the parties' substantive rights would be accordingly affected if Rule 23 allowed class action treatment. However, the fact that Rule 23 makes it practical for class members to assert their claims does not mean that it would be impossible for the class members to assert them individually. Therefore, any effect on substantive rights would not be the kind that existing Supreme Court authorities under the Rules Enabling Act would prohibit.

Even though there are no serious Rules Enabling Act problems with Rule 23, a serious separation-of-powers problem exists with new Rule 23(f). This problem is discussed elsewhere,[485] and will not be repeated here. As of this writing, there is only one court of appeals decision interpreting Rule 23(f). In *Blair v. Equifax Check Services, Inc.,*[486] the Seventh Circuit indicated that

---

482. *See In re* Real Estate Title & Settlement Servs. Antitrust Litig., 869 F.2d 760 (3d Cir.), *cert. denied*, 493 U.S. 821, 110 S. Ct. 77, 107 L. Ed. 2d 44 (1989); *see also* Brown v. Ticor Title Ins. Co., 982 F.2d 386 (9th Cir. 1992) (minimal due process requirement in a class action wholly or predominantly for damages requires that members of plaintiff class be allowed to opt out of the class), *cert. dism'd*, 511 U.S. 117, 114 S. Ct. 1359, 128 L. Ed. 2d 33 (1994).

483. *See, e.g.,* Appleton Elec. Co. v. Advance-United Expressways, 494 F.2d 126, 140 (7th Cir. 1974); *In re* Gap Stores Sec. Litig., 79 F.R.D. 283, 292 n.6 (N.D. Cal. 1978).

484. *See* Chapter 4(C)(1) ("Plaintiff's Residence as Proper Venue") *supra*.

485. *See* Chapter 5(F)(6) *supra*; Chapter 12(B)(3)*(b) infra*.

486. 181 F.3d 832 (7th Cir. 1999).

appeals would be permitted under Rule 23(f) when (1) denial of class action treatment can be demonstrated to be questionable and would sound the death knell of the action; (2) granting of class action status is demonstrably questionable and would, in a large stakes suit, produce a risk of settlement or other disposition that would not reflect the merits of the action; or (3) an appeal would facilitate the development of class action law, whether or not the district judge's ruling can be demonstrated to be questionable. No issue concerning the validity of Rule 23(f) was discussed in *Blair*.

(g) Shareholder Derivative Actions: Rule 23.1

Federal Rule 23.1 provides for a special type of class action known as a *shareholder derivative action*. A derivative action is brought by a stockholder of a corporation or a member of an unincorporated association. The action seeks to enforce a right of action belonging to the corporation or association that those in control of the corporation or association refuse to enforce. Prior to the Federal Rules, shareholder derivative actions in federal court were governed by Equity Rule 27 of the Equity Rules of 1912.[487] Original Rule 23(b) substantially duplicated Equity Rule 27.[488] Rule 23.1 was added to the Federal Rules of Civil Procedure in 1966 as a substitute for original Rule 23(b).

In addition to describing the basic nature of the derivative suit, Rule 23.1 imposes five requirements on the plaintiff.[489] First, the plaintiff must file a verified complaint alleging either that the plaintiff was a shareholder of the corporation or member of the association at the time of the transaction about which the plaintiff complains, or that the plaintiff's share or membership thereafter devolved on the plaintiff by operation of law. Second, the complaint also must allege that the action is not a collusive one to confer jurisdiction on a federal court that it would not otherwise have. Third, the complaint must allege "with particularity" the plaintiff's efforts to obtain the action that the plaintiff desires by those in control of the corporation or association, or, if the plaintiff has made no such effort, why the plaintiff has not done so.[490] Fourth, Rule 23.1 states that the derivative action may not be maintained if it appears that the plaintiff is not an adequate representative of the interests of the other shareholders or members similarly situated.[491] Fifth, Rule 23.1 provides that a derivative

---

487. *See* 226 U.S. 627, 656 (1912).

488. *See* 308 U.S. 645, 690 (1938).

489. *See* FED. R. CIV. P. 23.1.

490. *See, e.g.*, Wesley Kobylak, Annotation, *Application to Derivative Actions for Breach of Fiduciary Duty, Under § 36(b) of Investment Company Act of 1940 (15 U.S.C.S. § 80a-35(b)), of Requirement, Stated in Rule 23.1 of the Federal Rules of Civil Procedure, that Complaint in Derivative Actions Allege What Efforts Were Made by Shareholders to Obtain Desired Action or Reasons for Failure to Do So*, 65 A.L.R. FED. 542 (1983).

491. *See* David B. Levendusky, Annotation, *Requirement of Rule 23.1 of Federal Rules of Civil Procedure that Plaintiff in Shareholder Derivative Action "Fairly and Adequately Represent" Shareholders' Interest in Enforcing Corporation's Right*, 15 A.L.R. FED. 954 (1973).

action may not be dismissed or compromised without the court's permission and after notice to the absent shareholders and members.[492]

A corporation is an indispensable party to a shareholder derivative suit brought on behalf of the corporation, and this raises the question of how the corporation should be aligned for purposes of determining whether diversity jurisdiction exists.[493] Because the plaintiff is asserting a right belonging to the corporation, there is some logic in aligning the corporation as a plaintiff for the purpose of determining whether diversity exists. On the other hand, the corporation is often in the control of persons who are antagonistic to the plaintiff's interests. Frequently, this situation exists because officers or directors of the corporation are defendants in the suit. For this reason, it makes sense to refuse to align the corporation as a plaintiff for jurisdictional purposes, and, in fact, the Supreme Court has held that whenever a corporation opposes the litigation, it is to be aligned as a defendant.[494] Such an alignment will always be appropriate when the plaintiff makes a demand on the corporation to enforce its own rights under Rule 23.1 and the demand is refused.

Two venue provisions are available in derivative actions, the ordinary venue provisions (§ 1391)[495] and a special venue provision (§ 1401), which states that "[a]ny civil action by a stockholder on behalf of his corporation may be prosecuted in any judicial district where the corporation might have sued the same defendants."[496] Thus, in a diversity action, the suit may be brought pursuant to § 1391 in a district where any defendant resides, if the other defendants reside in the same state; in a district where a substantial part of the events or omissions giving rise to the action occurred, or where a substantial part of the property that is the subject of the action is situated; or in a district where personal jurisdiction can be obtained over any defendant, if there is no other district in which the action may be brought.[497]

When the special venue provision of § 1401 is employed, a special service of process provision (28 U.S.C. § 1695) allows process to be served on the corporation in any district where the corporation is organized, licensed to do

---

492. *See* Annotation, *Notice to Shareholders and Court Approval of Dismissal or Compromise of Derivative Actions, Under Rule 23.1 of Federal Rules of Civil Procedure,* 26 A.L.R. FED. 465 (1976).

493. *See, e.g.,* City of Davenport v. Dows, 85 U.S. (18 Wall.) 626, 21 L. Ed. 938 (1874); Tryforos v. Icarian Dev. Co., 518 F.2d 1258, 1264 (7th Cir. 1975), *cert. denied,* 423 U.S. 1091, 96 S. Ct. 887, 47 L. Ed. 2d 103 (1976). The jurisdictional amount requirement in shareholder derivative actions is determined by the damage done to the corporation, rather than the plaintiff's individual financial stake in the action. *See* 7C CHARLES A. WRIGHT ET AL., FEDERAL PRACTICE AND PROCEDURE: CIVIL § 1823, at 24 (2d ed. 1986). Therefore, the aggregation problems that exist with class actions under Rule 23 are not present under Rule 23.1.

494. *See* Smith v. Sperling, 354 U.S. 91, 77 S. Ct. 1112, 1 L. Ed. 2d 1205 (1957); Swanson v. Traer, 354 U.S. 114, 77 S. Ct. 1116, 1 L. Ed. 2d 1221 (1957). The U.S. Supreme Court has held that Rule 23.1 is not broad enough to govern the content of the demand requirement in shareholder derivative actions and that state law controls the content of the demand requirement in actions under the Investment Company Act of 1940. *See* Kamen v. Kemper Fin. Servs., Inc., 500 U.S. 90, 111 S. Ct. 1711, 114 L. Ed. 2d 152 (1991).

495. *See* 28 U.S.C. § 1391.

496. 28 U.S.C. § 1401.

497. Under the amendments to 28 U.S.C. § 1391(c), corporate defendants reside in any judicial district in which personal jurisdiction can be obtained over them at the time the action is commenced. *See* Chapter 4(C)(6) ("Residence of Corporations and Associations") *supra.*

business, or doing business.[498] This provision is useful when the plaintiff sues the real defendants in their state of residence and the corporation has no contacts with that state.[499] When venue is based on § 1391, the ability to obtain jurisdiction over all defendants, including the corporate defendant, is governed by Rule 4, as in other cases.[500]

(h) Actions by or Against Unincorporated Associations: Rule 23.2

Federal Rule 23.2 provides that an action brought by or against the members of an unincorporated association may be brought as a class action by naming as representative parties one or more members of the association who will adequately represent the interests of the association and its members. The provisions of Rule 23(d) and (e) also are made applicable to class suits by or against associations under Rule 23.2.[501]

The significance of Rule 23.2 can be understood by comparing the rule with the other methods by which an association may sue or be sued. These methods include suits against the association as an entity, when such an action is permitted or required under the law governing the association, and suits against the association by joining all of its members.[502] When suit is brought by or against an association as an entity or by joining all of its members, diversity jurisdiction must be determined by reference to the citizenship of all the members.[503] When suit is brought by or against the association as a class, diversity is determined by reference to the citizenship of the representative parties only.[504]

---

498. *See* 28 U.S.C. § 1695.

499. *See* 7C CHARLES A. WRIGHT ET AL., FEDERAL PRACTICE AND PROCEDURE: CIVIL § 1825, at 34 (2d ed. 1986).

500. *See id.* at 35.

501. *See* FED. R. CIV. P. 23.2.

502. For a discussion of the methods of suit by and against associations and the consequences of each in terms of the binding effect of the judgment in the suit, see RESTATEMENT (SECOND) OF JUDGMENTS § 61 cmts. a, b (1982).

503. *See, e.g.,* Arbuthnot v. State Auto. Ins. Ass'n, 264 F.2d 260 (10th Cir. 1959); Lowry v. International Bhd. of Boilermakers of Am., 259 F.2d 568 (5th Cir. 1958).

504. *See* Supreme Tribe of Ben-Hur v. Cauble, 255 U.S. 356, 41 S. Ct. 338, 65 L. Ed. 673 (1921); Kerney v. Fort Griffin Fandangle Ass'n, 624 F.2d 717, 720 (5th Cir. 1980). It has been suggested that "the logic of treating [unincorporated associations] as a class indicates that the common claims of the individual members usually will be allowed to be aggregated to fulfill the . . . jurisdictional amount requirement." 7C CHARLES A. WRIGHT ET AL., FEDERAL PRACTICE AND PROCEDURE: CIVIL § 1861, at 219 (2d ed. 1986). If this suggestion is accepted, the aggregation problems experienced under Rule 23 will not exist under Rule 23.2. However, it is not clear that this view will prevail in the courts. *See* Air Line Dispatchers Ass'n v. California E. Airways, Inc., 127 F. Supp. 521 (N.D. Cal. 1954). Section 1367(b), discussed in conjunction with Rule 23 *supra* subsection *(c)*, makes no reference to Rule 23.2. Therefore, as in the case of Rule 23, § 1367(a) can be read to confer supplemental jurisdiction over the claims of members of the association, and § 1367(b)'s lack of reference to Rule 23.2 can be read as a refusal to exempt the claims from the jurisdiction conferred by § 1367(a). However, as in the case of Rule 23, this runs counter to the legislative history of the statute. Therefore, the best result would seem to be to read § 1367(b) as preserving whatever aggregation rules existed prior to its enactment.

In *Denver & Rio Grande Western Railroad Co. v. Brotherhood of Railroad Trainmen*,[505] the Supreme Court held that unincorporated associations should be analogized to corporations for venue purposes. Extrapolating from this position to the existing provisions governing corporate venue gives the following results. When an unincorporated association is sued as an entity, venue will be proper wherever personal jurisdiction can be obtained over the association.[506] Of course, if the association sues or is sued in class action form, as opposed to suing or being sued as an entity, the corporate analogy is not apt and venue will be determined under 28 U.S.C. § 1391, as in class actions generally.

When all members of an association must be joined as defendants, service of process has to be made and personal jurisdiction obtained over each of them. When an association is sued as an entity, process must be served as prescribed in Federal Rule 4[507] and personal jurisdiction must exist over the entity.[508] When the association is sued as a class, process need be served only on the named representatives and personal jurisdiction obtained over them.[509] This last conclusion, however, must be qualified by the same doubts previously raised regarding personal jurisdiction over absent class members under Rule 23.

---

505. 387 U.S. 556, 87 S. Ct. 1746, 18 L. Ed. 2d 954 (1967).
506. *See* 28 U.S.C. § 1391(c).
507. *See* FED. R. CIV. P. 4(h).
508. *See* FED. R. CIV. P. 4(k).
509. *See generally* 7C CHARLES A. WRIGHT ET AL., FEDERAL PRACTICE AND PROCEDURE: CIVIL § 1861, at 215-16 (2d ed. 1986).

Chapter 9

DISCOVERY AND PRETRIAL CONFERENCES

SECTION A. DEVELOPMENT OF MODERN DISCOVERY

1. Discovery in Common-Law Actions

Common-law procedure relied heavily on the pleadings to narrow the dispute to a single issue. The pleadings also gave advance notice of each party's claims and defenses. In many instances, however, the pleadings became formalized statements of conclusions of law and fact.[1] Furthermore, by pleading the general issue, the defendant often could defer to trial the decision concerning the specific defense that the defendant would use.[2] As a result, the parties frequently had to guess what the opposing party's strategy and proof at trial would be.

Bills of particular satisfied part of the need to acquire information about the opposing party's claim.[3] In addition, through the procedure of *profert* and *oyer*, the parties could force the inspection of contracts under seal, deeds, bonds, and letters of administration when the opposing party's pleading relied upon them. However, a party could not use profert and oyer to inspect other writings, such as written agreements not under seal.[4] In real actions, a defendant could demand a *view* of the disputed land before pleading to determine the specific land the plaintiff sought to recover.[5] These forms of discovery provided only limited assistance to a party preparing for trial in a common-law court.

2. Discovery in Equity Actions

In contrast to the limited discovery in common-law actions, equity developed substantially broader discovery. Equity's discovery devices were principally interrogatories, production and inspection of documents, and depositions. These devices were the precursors of modern discovery practice.

A bill in equity contained, *inter alia*, a "stating" part, a "charging" part, and an "interrogating" part.[6] The stating part set forth the facts and circumstanc-

---

1. *See* Chapter 6(A)(2) ("Stating the Plaintiff's Claim in the Declaration") *supra*.
2. *See* Chapter 6(A)(3)(f) ("The General Issue") *supra*.
3. *See* Chapter 6(A)(3)(g) ("Bills of Particulars") *supra*.
4. JOSEPH H. KOFFLER & ALISON REPPY, HANDBOOK OF COMMON LAW PLEADING § 52, § 184, at 368-69 (1969).
5. *Id.* at 370.
6. *See* JOSEPH STORY, EQUITY PLEADINGS § 26, at 18 (9th ed. 1879) (dividing equity pleadings into nine parts).

es on which the plaintiff based the bill. The charging part detailed the plaintiff's evidence. The charging part allowed the plaintiff to anticipate the defendant's excuses or defenses as well as charge matters that disproved or avoided them. The interrogating part propounded questions to the defendant about prior statements or charges in the bill. In response to the bill, equity required the defendant to answer the plaintiff's allegations and interrogatories under oath.[7] Thus, every bill in equity was, in reality, a bill of discovery.[8]

When the plaintiff sought to discover documents dealing with the plaintiff's case that the defendant possessed or controlled, the plaintiff included a charge and interrogatories in the bill describing the documents. Like other charges and interrogatories in the bill, the defendant had to answer by either admitting or denying the possession or control of the documents. Once the possession or control was admitted and the plaintiff had adequately shown the documents' relevance to the plaintiff's case, the plaintiff could move for production and inspection.[9]

The Court of Chancery also granted discovery in aid of proceedings pending elsewhere. Equity courts permitted a party litigating in a common-law court to file a bill for the discovery of facts or documents. Before securing such a bill, the party had to demonstrate that the requested discovery was necessary to effectively defend or prosecute at trial. The party then could introduce as admissions in the common-law trial the sworn answers to the interrogatories. Thus, to a certain extent, a bill of discovery circumvented two traditional common-law rules: (1) the parties could not be compelled to testify at trial for or against each other and (2) they were incompetent to do so even if they so desired.[10] Equity limited its intervention to the discovery of evidence needed to prove the discovering party's claim or defense at trial. Equity courts did not permit a party to discover what evidence the opposing party would use to prove the opposing party's case at trial.[11]

Equity courts also permitted bills to perpetuate testimony. A party could maintain such bills only when the party could not presently bring an action at law. The party had to demonstrate the necessity for preserving the evidence, such as the impending death or departure from the country of a material witness before the case could be investigated in a court of law. A party could also use a bill to perpetuate testimony of the sole witness to a matter because of the uncertainty of human life. The bill prayed for a subpoena to secure the testimony.[12] Furthermore, equity courts permitted bills to take testimony *de bene esse*. A party could use such a bill in aid of a *pending* common-law action when the witness was old, in ill health, or about to depart the country. A party could use the testimony

---

7. *See id.* §§ 27, 31, 35-39.

8. *Id.* § 311, at 281.

9. *See* HENRY L. MCCLINTOCK, HANDBOOK OF THE PRINCIPLES OF EQUITY § 206, at 547-48 (2d ed. 1948).

10. *See* Robert W. Millar, *The Mechanism of Fact-Discovery: A Study in Comparative Civil Procedure IV*, 32 ILL. L. REV. 424, 440-41 (1937); HENRY L. MCCLINTOCK, HANDBOOK OF THE PRINCIPLES OF EQUITY § 206, at 547-48 (2d ed. 1948); *see also* Chapter 11(I)(1) ("Competency") *infra.*

11. *See* JOSEPH STORY, EQUITY PLEADINGS § 311, § 858 (9th ed. 1879); ROBERT W. MILLAR, CIVIL PROCEDURE OF THE TRIAL COURT IN HISTORICAL PERSPECTIVE 204 (1952).

12. *See* JOSEPH STORY, EQUITY PLEADINGS §§ 300-306 (9th ed. 1879).

obtained through bills to perpetuate testimony or to examine witnesses *de bene esse* only if the witness, in fact, was unavailable.[13]

3. Reform in the United States

Court systems in the United States adopted, with minor variations, the general pattern of discovery developed by the English courts. The common-law courts in the United States permitted virtually no significant discovery. However, the parties could resort to equity courts for some assistance. Because the discovery process was cumbersome, slow, and expensive, several states initiated reforms. Some states permitted the incorporation of interrogatories in the complaint or the separate use of interrogatories in common-law actions without resort to an equity proceeding.[14] Several states also authorized their common-law courts to permit discovery of documents.[15]

The New York Field Code of 1848 permitted pretrial oral depositions.[16] Thus, oral examination of parties before trial replaced the chancery method of discovery by bill and answer.[17] If a party refused to attend and testify at the pretrial examination, the court could punish the party by contempt. The court could also reject the complaint, answer, or reply.[18] The Field Code also allowed either party to apply to the court to depose any witness who resided more than 100 miles from the place where the trial or hearing was to be held.[19] A party could use the deposition at trial if the witness was dead, did not reside within 100 miles of the place of trial, or was otherwise unable to attend.[20]

---

13. *See id.* §§ 307-310. Discovery permitted by equity was enforced principally through the use of the contempt power, supplemented by forfeiture of the recalcitrant party's property. Eventually, equity courts in England were empowered to enter a default judgment against a disobedient defendant as an alternative sanction. *Developments in the Law—Discovery*, 74 HARV. L. REV. 940, 947 (1961).

14. In 1831, for example, Virginia permitted either party to file "interrogatories addressed to the other, and for an order to answer the interrogatories when it had been made to appear 'by oath of the party filing the same or otherwise,' that they were material, pertinent, and such as the interrogated party could be bound to answer on a bill in chancery." ROBERT W. MILLAR, CIVIL PROCEDURE OF THE TRIAL COURT IN HISTORICAL PERSPECTIVE 205 (1952).

15. In 1828, for example, pursuant to a New York statute authorizing rules of court in accord with the principles and practices of chancery courts in compelling discovery, either party could petition for the discovery and production of documents from the other to facilitate the drafting of a party's pleadings or to prepare for trial. *Id.* at 221.

16. Act of Apr. 12, 1848, ch. 379, §§ 345, 346, 354, 1848 N.Y. Laws 497, 559-60. The Field Code, *inter alia*, merged law and equity, simplified pleading, and liberalized traditional rules governing party and claim joinder. *See* Chapter 1(E)(4) ("The Field Code and the Reform of Procedure in the States") *supra*. In 1847, a statute permitted the parties to examine each other as witnesses at trial. The Field Code expanded on the statute by permitting such examinations to take place before trial by commission, before a judge of the court, or before a judge of the county court. FIRST REPORT OF THE COMMISSIONERS ON PRACTICE AND PLEADINGS 244-45 (1848).

17. ROBERT W. MILLAR, CIVIL PROCEDURE OF THE TRIAL COURT IN HISTORICAL PERSPECTIVE 206 (1952).

18. Such a rejection could result in a dismissal or a default judgment. *Id.* at 206-07.

19. The examination was held before the county judge, a justice of the peace, or a referee where the examination was to be conducted. *See* Act of Apr. 12, 1848, ch. 379, § 354, 1848 N.Y. Laws 497, 560.

20. *Id.* § 355, 1848 N.Y. Laws 497, 560. The court, however, could specially order the witness to attend in open court. After such an order was issued, the deposition could not be used. *See id.*

The state reforms of the nineteenth century, in effect, substituted statutory means of obtaining depositions and discovery for separate equity actions. Although the specific means varied from state to state and were not uniformly adopted, three principal devices emerged: (1) written interrogatories directed to adverse parties; (2) depositions of parties; certain categories of witnesses related to the parties, such as their employees; and witnesses who might be unavailable at trial; and (3) production or inspection of documents in a party's possession or control.[21] Even though these devices had the potential for supporting a broad range of discovery, traditional equity restrictions on the use of the devices continued. These restrictions limited discovery to (1) facts pertaining to the case of the party seeking discovery and (2) facts or documents that would be admissible in evidence at trial.[22]

Discovery in federal courts in the United States also reflected the traditional patterns of discovery developed in England. Like traditional equity practice, the Judiciary Act of 1789[23] authorized the use of interrogatories, depositions, and discovery of documents. Parties at law or in equity could take depositions *de bene esse* without leave of court when a witness (1) was old or infirm, (2) lived more than 100 miles from the place of trial, (3) was bound on a sea voyage, (4) intended to leave the United States before trial, or (5) intended to go before trial to a place outside the district that was more than 100 miles from the place of trial. A deposition *in perpetuam rei memoriam* was available in equity to preserve testimony relevant to anticipated litigation.[24]

The Judiciary Act of 1789 did not provide for interrogation of a party at law. Equity courts rarely granted bills of discovery for this purpose because they considered the legal procedures provided at law to be adequate. Similarly, production of documents at law was unavailable before trial. Equity limited the production to documents that the parties could specify. In addition, the parties had to demonstrate the documents were relevant to their claim or defense and not solely to their opponent's claim or defense. When a nonparty gave a deposition, a subpoena duces tecum could force that nonparty to produce documents under the nonparty's control.[25]

The Conformity Act of 1872 did not make available the states' more liberal pretrial discovery devices to litigation at law in federal courts.[26] The courts regarded the specific federal provisions on witness testimony as impliedly excluding state discovery provisions.[27] Some changes in federal discovery

---

21. *See* ROBERT W. MILLAR, CIVIL PROCEDURE OF THE TRIAL COURT IN HISTORICAL PERSPECTIVE 211-28 (1952); Michael E. Wolfson, *Addressing the Adversarial Dilemma of Civil Discovery*, 36 CLEV. ST. L. REV. 17, 25-26 (1988).

22. *See* Michael E. Wolfson, *Addressing the Adversarial Dilemma of Civil Discovery*, 36 CLEV. ST. L. REV. 17, 25-26 (1988).

23. ch. 20, 1 Stat. 73.

24. *See id.* §§ 15, 30, 1 Stat. 73, 82, 88-90; *see also Developments in the Law–Discovery*, 74 HARV. L. REV. 940, 949 & n.54 (1961).

25. *Developments in the Law–Discovery*, 74 HARV. L. REV. 940, 949-50 (1961).

26. *Id.* at 950; *see* Chapter 1(E)(5) ("The Development of Federal Procedure and the Federal Rules of Civil Procedure") *supra*.

27. ROBERT W. MILLAR, CIVIL PROCEDURE OF THE TRIAL COURT IN HISTORICAL PERSPECTIVE 212 (1952).

practice occurred with the adoption of the Federal Equity Rules of 1912.[28] Under these rules, bills no longer contained charges and interrogatories. Instead, they consisted of a narrative statement and a prayer.[29] The Equity Rules provided for separate interrogatories to parties and document discovery.[30] However, the rules did not broaden the bases of discovery, but "served only to streamline the cumbersome procedures on the equity side of the federal courts."[31]

4. Discovery Practice Under the Federal Rules of Civil Procedure

In 1938, the Federal Rules of Civil Procedure introduced a dramatic change in federal discovery practice. The basic philosophy of the rules was to insure that the parties could obtain disclosure of all relevant information in the possession of any person before trial, unless the information was privileged.[32] The Federal Rules provide five principal "instruments" of discovery: (1) depositions (both oral and upon written questions) of parties and witnesses; (2) interrogatories to parties; (3) production of documents and things (including entry upon property to inspect, copy, photograph, or conduct tests); (4) physical or mental examinations of parties or persons in the custody or under the "legal control" of parties; and (5) requests for admission of the genuineness of relevant documents or the truth of any matter within the general scope of discovery.[33] The Federal Rules also provide a range of sanctions to punish unjustified failures to comply with discovery requests.

The Federal Rules of Civil Procedure were amended in 1948 to correct uncertainties that experience with the discovery rules had disclosed. Minor amendments were also made in 1949, 1963, and 1966. In 1970, the discovery rules were rearranged and amended in several significant ways. Pursuant to this rearrangement, Federal Rule 26 governed the scope of discovery, Federal Rules 27 through 36 set forth the discovery devices, and Federal Rule 37 provided sanctions for the failure to make or cooperate in discovery. Minor changes were also made in 1972 and 1975.

---

28. These rules were influenced by reforms that had taken place in England. *Id.*

29. 226 U.S. 627, 655 (1912) (Rule 25).

30. *Id.* at 665-66 (Rule 58).

31. *Developments in the Law–Discovery*, 74 HARV. L. REV. 940, 950 (1961).

32. 8 CHARLES A. WRIGHT ET AL., FEDERAL PRACTICE AND PROCEDURE: CIVIL § 2001, at 41 (2d ed. 1994). In Hickman v. Taylor, 329 U.S. 495, 67 S. Ct. 385, 91 L. Ed. 451 (1947), the U.S. Supreme Court characterized the development of the pretrial deposition-discovery procedure as "one of the most significant innovations of the Federal Rules of Civil Procedure." The Court explained that the Federal Rules "restrict the pleadings to the task of general notice-giving and invest the deposition-discovery process with a vital role in the preparation for trial. The various instruments of discovery now serve (1) as a device, along with the pre-trial hearing under Rule 16, to narrow and clarify the basic issues between two parties, and (2) as a device for ascertaining the facts, or information as to the existence or whereabouts of facts, relative to those issues." The Court concluded that "civil trials in the federal courts no longer need to be carried on in the dark. The way is now clear, consistent with recognized privileges, for the parties to obtain the fullest possible knowledge of the issues and facts before trial." *Id.* at 500-01, 67 S. Ct. at 388-89, 91 L. Ed. at 457.

33. *See* FED. R. CIV. P. 26(a)(5) (discovery methods).

In 1980 and 1983, amendments were again made in response to widespread criticism of "discovery abuse." The general problems were excessive ("over") discovery, withholding information, evasive or misleading responses, delay, harassment, misuse of interrogatories, and discovery requests disproportionate to the amount in controversy.[34] The 1980 and 1983 amendments provided, *inter alia*, for a conference before the court to establish a plan and schedule for discovery and to set possible limits on discovery by the parties.[35] These changes encouraged judges to take a "managerial approach" to discovery and other aspects of the litigation through frequent pretrial conferences.[36]

Despite these changes, concern over the cost of discovery and discovery abuse continued.[37] Influential studies proposed mandatory disclosure to alleviate abuses and hardball tactics at the discovery stage.[38] The Civil Justice Reform Act of 1990 required each federal district court to consider encouraging "cost-effective discovery" through (1) "voluntary exchange of information among litigants and their attorneys" and (2) "the use of cooperative discovery devices."[39] In 1991, the President's Council on Competitiveness recommended disclosure of "core information."[40] Also in 1991, the Advisory Committee on Civil Rules published for comment proposed amendments to the Federal Rules, including mandatory disclosures and other significant changes in discovery.[41]

---

34. *See* Wayne D. Brazil, *Civil Discovery: Lawyer's Views of Its Effectiveness, Its Principal Problems and Abuses*, 1980 AM. B. FOUND. RES. J. 787, 824-25; *see also* Maurice Rosenberg & Warren R. King, *Curbing Discovery Abuse in Civil Litigation: Enough Is Enough*, 1981 B.Y.U. L. REV. 579.

35. *See* section N ("Pretrial Conferences and Orders") *infra*.

36. *See, e.g.*, Wayne D. Brazil, *Improving Judicial Controls Over the Pretrial Development of Civil Actions: Model Rules for Case Management and Sanctions*, 1981 AM. B. FOUND. RES. J. 873, 890-921; Robert F. Peckham, *The Federal Judge as a Case Manager: The New Role in Guiding a Case From Filing to Disposition*, 69 CAL. L. REV. 770 (1981); Robert F. Peckham, *A Judicial Response to the Cost of Litigation: Case Management, Two-Stage Discovery Planning and Alternative Dispute Resolution*, 37 RUTGERS L. REV. 253 (1985).

37. *See, e.g.*, Harris & Associates, Inc., *Judges' Opinions on Procedural Issues: A Survey of State and Federal Trial Judges Who Spent at Least Half of Their Time on General Civil Cases*, 69 B.U. L. REV. 731, 735 (1989) (Harris Poll survey of 200 federal and 800 state judges indicating that (1) 47% regarded discovery abuse as a major cause of delay and (2) 81% thought there were some problems with the discovery process).

38. *See, e.g.*, William W. Schwarzer, *The Federal Rules, the Adversary Process and Discovery Reform*, 50 U. PITT. L. REV. 703 (1989); William W. Schwarzer, *Slaying the Monsters of Cost and Delay: Would Disclosure Be More Effective than Discovery?* 14 JUDICATURE 178 (1991); *see also* Wayne D. Brazil, *The Adversary Character of Civil Discovery: A Critique and Proposals for Change*, 31 VAND. L. REV. 1295 (1978).

39. § 103, 104 Stat. 5089, 5091-92 (codified at 28 U.S.C. § 473(a)(4)).

40. PRESIDENT'S COUNCIL ON COMPETITIVENESS, AGENDA FOR CIVIL JUSTICE REFORM IN AMERICA 16-17 (1991). This Council was created in March, 1989. The Council recommended fifty specific changes in the current system of civil litigation, including such areas as discovery, voluntary dispute resolution, punitive damages, and attorney's fees. Vice President Quayle endorsed the discovery recommendation in a speech at the Annual Meeting of the American Bar Association in August, 1991. *See* Ellen J. Pollock, *Quayle Calls for Changes in Legal System*, WALL ST. J., Aug. 14, 1991, at B6; *Quayle: Are There Too Many Lawyers in America?* N.J. L.J., Aug. 29, 1991, at 15 (reproducing the speech). It was followed by a law review article recommending a major restructuring of the pretrial discovery process. *See* Dan Quayle, *Civil Justice Reform*, 41 AM. U. L. REV. 559, 563-64, 568-69 (1992). For a useful review and critique of the discovery reform proposals of the Council on Competitiveness, see Paul R. Sugarman & Marc G. Perlin, *Proposed Changes to Discovery Rules in Aid of "Tort Reform": Has the Case Been Made?* 42 AM. U. L. REV. 1465 (1993).

41. Committee on Rules of Practice and Procedure of the Judicial Conference of the United States, Preliminary Draft of Proposed Amendments to the Federal Rules of Civil Procedure and Federal Rules of Evidence (Aug. 1991), *reprinted in* 112 S. Ct. 259 (1991). The provisions of this preliminary draft are discussed

The proposed rules evoked a strong negative reaction.[42] The principal criticisms focused on a predicted increase in discovery motions, the overproduction of marginally relevant information, and increased expense.[43] Critics also asserted that automatic disclosure would raise serious ethical concerns, undermine the adversary system, and invade the "work product" of lawyers.[44] After the public hearings in February 1992, the Advisory Committee abandoned the mandatory disclosure proposal.[45]

In April 1992, however, the Advisory Committee unexpectedly revived the proposal.[46] The final recommendation retained mandatory disclosure, but narrowed the disclosure requirement from information that "bears significantly on any claim or defense" to "discoverable information relevant to disputed facts alleged with particularity in the pleadings."[47] In June 1992, the Standing Committee approved the proposed rules. In September 1992, the Judicial Conference forwarded the rules to the U.S. Supreme Court.[48] In April 1993, the Court promulgated the changes in the discovery rules as proposed and submitted them to Congress.[49] Three dissenting Justices described the amended rules as a "radical alteration" and "potentially disastrous."[50] Despite a vigorous effort in

---

in several sources. *See, e.g.*, Thomas M. Mengler, *Eliminating Abusive Discovery Through Disclosure: Is It Again Time for Reform?* 138 F.R.D. 155 (1992); Carl Tobias, *Collision Course in Federal Civil Discovery*, 145 F.R.D. 139, 140-41 (1993); Meade W. Mitchell, Note, *Discovery Abuse and a Proposed Reform: Mandatory Disclosure*, 62 MISS. L.J. 743 (1993).

42. *See, e.g.*, Griffin B. Bell et al., *Automatic Disclosure in Discovery–The Rush to Reform*, 27 GA. L. REV. 1, 28-32 (1992) ("Public Reaction: Opposition from All Quarters"); Carl Tobias, *Collision Course in Federal Civil Discovery*, 145 F.R.D. 139, 140 (1993) (original proposal "proved to be extremely controversial"); Randall Samborn, *U.S. Civil Procedure Revisited*, NAT'L L.J., May 4, 1992, at 1 (largely negative reaction to the proposed rules).

43. *See, e.g.*, Griffin B. Bell et al., *Automatic Disclosure in Discovery–The Rush to Reform*, 27 GA. L. REV. 1, 41-46 (1992) (the authors' work was supported by a grant from the Product Liability Advisory Council Foundation).

44. *See, e.g., id.* at 41, 46-48.

45. Randall Samborn, *U.S. Civil Procedure Revisited*, NAT'L L.J., May 4, 1992, at 1, 12 (reporting the decision to abandon the proposal); Carl Tobias, *Collision Course in Federal Civil Discovery*, 145 F.R.D. 139, 141 (1993) (by abandoning the proposal, the Advisory Committee would be able to capitalize on the experimentation taking place under the Civil Justice Reform Act); *see also* Carl Tobias, *In Defense of Experimentation with Automatic Disclosure*, 27 GA. L. REV. 665 (1993).

46. Griffin B. Bell et al., *Automatic Disclosure in Discovery–The Rush to Reform*, 27 GA. L. REV. 1, 35 (1992). The Advisory Committee submitted its final recommendations on May 1, 1992. *Id.*

47. Carl Tobias, *Collision Course in Federal Civil Discovery*, 145 F.R.D. 139, 141-43 (1993).

48. *See id.* at 143; *see also* Ralph K. Winter, *In Defense of Discovery Reform*, 58 BROOKLYN L. REV. 263 (1992).

49. *See* Statement of Justice White, Amendments to the Federal Rules of Civil Procedure, Apr. 22, 1993, *reprinted in* 146 F.R.D. 501, 505-06 (1993).

50. *See* Dissenting Statement of Justice Scalia, joined by Justice Thomas and Justice Souter, *reprinted in* 146 F.R.D. at 507 (1993) (pointing out the "nearly universal criticism from every conceivable sector of our judicial system, including judges, practitioners, litigants, academics, public interest groups, and national state and local bar and professional associations"); *see also* Memorandum to the Chief Justice of the United States and the Associate Justices of the Supreme Court: Comments on Proposed "Disclosure" Amendment to Federal Rule 26(a)(1), submitted by American Exchange Council, Association of Defense Trial Attorneys, Business Roundtable Lawyers Committee, Chamber of Commerce of the United States, Federation of Insurance and Corporate Counsel, Lawyers for Civil Justice, and Litigation Section of the District of Columbia Bar, Public Citizen Litigation Group (Feb. 10, 1993) (opposing amendments). The amended rules also contained controversial changes in Rule 11. *See* Chapter 6(E) ("Verification and Good Faith Pleading") *supra*.

Congress to stop them, the changes took effect on December 1, 1993.[51] Because federal district courts had been experimenting with delay and cost reduction programs under the Civil Justice Reform Act, many districts chose to continue their own programs rather than to follow the new rules.[52] As a result, discovery has been in a state of flux and has varied from district to district as the courts attempt to facilitate efficient pretrial discovery.[53] However, on September 15, 1999,the Judicial Conference recommended that the Supreme Court eliminate the opt-out provision to impose national uniformity.[54] The Judicial Conference also recommended that the Supreme Court narrow the mandatory disclosure obligation.[55]

The development of liberal discovery in federal courts has had a substantial impact on state-court practice. Most states have adopted the 1970 Federal Rules covering discovery in whole or large part.[56] To date, the states have not embraced the 1993 reforms in large measure.[57] Because of the widespread adoption of the prior federal rules governing discovery that are still currently in effect in many states, this chapter will focus on both the pre-1993 federal discovery procedures as well as the changes made by the 1993 amendments. It will also highlight the proposed changes recommended by the Judicial Conference.

SECTION B. THE GENERAL SCOPE OF DISCOVERY UNDER THE FEDERAL RULES

Before the adoption of the Federal Rules, several restrictions limited the scope of discovery.[58] In contrast, the 1970 reform of Federal Rule 26(b)(1) allows the parties to discover any non-privileged matter ''relevant to the subject matter involved in the pending action.''[59] This standard establishes an exceed-

---

51. *See* Harrison Osborne, *Sweeping Changes for Federal Court Discovery*, LAW. WEEKLY, Dec. 6, 1993, at 1.

52. For example, on the day the new rules went into effect, the Judges of the Southern District of New York suspended the operation of the mandatory disclosure rule for purposes of further study. *See* David D. Siegel, *The Recent (Dec. 1, 1993) Changes in the Federal Rules of Civil Procedure: Background, the Question of Retroactivity, and a Word about Mandatory Disclosure*, 151 F.R.D. 147, 151-52 (1993) (describing the ''opt out'' possibilities under Rule 26(a)(1) concerning mandatory disclosure); *see also* Preliminary Draft of Proposed Amendments to the Federal Rules of Civil Procedure, 181 F.R.D. 18, 71 (1998) (describing wide-spread use of the opt-out provision).

53. Some practical difficulties may exist in determining exactly what procedures are in force in certain districts. *See* Carl Tobias, *Finding the New Federal Civil Procedures*, 151 F.R.D. 177 (1993).

54. *See* 68 U.S.L.W., Sept 28, 1999, at 2168, 2169.

55. *See* 68 U.S.L.W., Sept 28, 1999, at 2168, 2169.

56. Some states, however, have not adopted all the amendments to the Federal Rules of Civil Procedure; in particular, some states have not incorporated the substantial reforms made by the 1970 amendments and later modifications.

57. *See* Harrison Osborne, *Sweeping Changes for Federal Court Discovery*, LAW. WEEKLY, Dec. 6, 1993, at 1, 16.

58. *See* section A (''Development of Modern Discovery'') *supra*.

59. FED. R. CIV. P. 26(b)(1). This provision has been criticized. *See, e.g.*, Arthur L. Liman, *The Quantum of Discovery vs. The Quality of Justice: More Is Less*, LITIG., Fall 1977, at 8; Weyman I. Lundquist & H. Stephen Schechter, *The New Relevancy: An End to Trial by Ordeal*, 64 A.B.A. J. 59 (1978). Other provisions also limit discovery of certain materials prepared by or for a party or that party's representative in anticipation ingly permissive scope for discovery. Clearly, under the standard, discovery is not limited to the "issues" raised by the pleadings. Federal Rule 26(b)(1) refers to the "subject matter" of the pending action, not merely the issues raised by the parties' claims or defenses. Nor is discovery limited to evidence that would be admissible at trial under the Federal Rules of Evidence.[60] To protect against abuse of discovery under the broad relevance standard of Rule 26, the Rule also permits the courts to limit discovery through *protective orders*. Such orders are designed to prevent oppression, undue burden or expense, embarrassment, and harassment.[61]

Illustration 9-1. Assume that *A* and *B* witnessed an auto accident that is the subject of litigation between *P* and *D*. At *A's* deposition, *P's* attorney asks *A*: "Who did *B* say was at fault in the accident?" Assume that *A* indicates that *B* said one or the other of the parties was at fault. *A's* answer would be hearsay and would likely be inadmissible at trial.[62] Nevertheless, *A's* answer is reasonably calculated to lead to the discovery of admissible evidence–the testimony of *B*.[63] Thus, this question would be within the permissible scope of discovery.

* * * * *

On September 15, 1999, the Judicial Conference proposed an amendment to Rule 26(b)(1) that would allow parties to discover any non-privileged matter "relevant to the claim or defense of any party."[64] For "good cause shown," a court could order a wider scope of discovery ("any matter relevant to the subject matter involved in the action").[65] This proposal would obviously narrow the existing relevance standard of Rule 26 and is also designed to involve the court more actively in regulating the breadth of sweeping or contentious discovery.[66]

---

of litigation or for trial. *See* subsection 2 ("Attorney 'Work Product' and Trial Preparation Materials") *infra*.

60. FED. R. CIV. P. 26(b)(1). Rule 26(b)(1) specifically states that "[t]he information sought need not as admissible at trial if the information sought appears reasonably calculated to lead to the discovery of admissible evidence." *Id.*

61. *See* FED. R. CIV. P. 26(c).

62. *See* Chapter 11(I)(3) ("Hearsay") *infra*.

63. Under Federal Rule 26(b)(1), the information sought need not be admissible in evidence as long as it is reasonably calculated to lead to the discovery of evidence that would be admissible. The burden of making this showing is on the party seeking discovery. This burden can be met by articulating a plausible chain of inferences showing how discovery would lead to admissible evidence. *Cf.* Oppenheimer Fund, Inc. v. Sanders, 437 U.S. 340, 98 S. Ct. 2380, 57 L. Ed. 2d 253 (1978) (the plaintiffs' request to require the defendants to compile a list of the names and addresses of the class members was not "relevant to the subject matter involved in the pending action" because the plaintiffs were not seeking information that bears on, or that reasonably could lead to other matters that could bear on, any issue that was or might be in the case); Food Lion, Inc. v. United Food & Commercial Workers Int'l Union, 103 F.3d 1007 (D.C. Cir. 1997) (in an abuse-of-process action, Food Lion sought discovery of documents from a nonparty that had served as a public relations firm to the defendant union; the documents sought related to "corporate campaigns" by other union clients of the public relations firm; discovery was denied on the ground that it was not reasonably likely to lead to the discovery of admissible evidence); Vardon Golf Co. v. BBMG Golf, Ltd., 156 F.R.D. 641 (N.D. Ill. 1994) (burden not satisfied by plaintiff seeking information relating to defendant's settlement negotiations with third-party defendant; that information was inadmissible under Federal Rule of Evidence 408, which makes evidence relating to settlement negotiations inadmissible to prove the validity of a claim or its amount).

64. *See* 68 U.S.L.W., Sept 28, 1999, at 2168, 2169.

65. *See id.* Rule 26(b)(1) would also specifically provide that "*[r]elevant* information need not be admissible at the trial if the discovery appears reasonably calculated to lead to the discovery of admissible evidence." *See id.* (emphasis added).

66. *See id. See generally* Carl Tobias, *Discovery Reform Redux*, 31 CONN. L. REV. 1433 (1999).

The following two subsections discuss two significant limitations on the scope of discovery: (1) privilege and (2) exceptions for attorney "work product" and trial preparation materials.

1. Privilege

Federal Rule 26(b)(1) provides for discovery of matters "not privileged."[67] The usual view is that privilege rules apply to discovery in the same way they apply at trial.[68] The law of evidence determines whether a matter is "privileged."[69] Except for privileges based on federal constitutional grounds, the extent to which particular jurisdictions recognize specific privileges varies. The holder of a privilege may waive the holder's objection to disclosure of the privileged matter. During discovery, such waiver may occur in several ways.[70]

Illustration 9-2. A party may lose a privilege to refuse to produce "confidential" records if the party has answered interrogatories about matters contained in the records.[71] Similarly, if a party voluntarily answers (or permits another to answer) questions during a deposition about part of a privileged communication, that party waives the privilege for the entire communication.[72]

* * * * *

If a party withholds "privileged" materials in response to a discovery request or from a required disclosure under Rule 26, the 1993 amendments require that party to notify other parties.[73] According to the Advisory Committee, "withholding materials without such notice is contrary to the rule, subjects the party to sanctions . . . and may be viewed as a waiver of the privilege or protection."[74] In addition to making the claim of privilege "expressly," the withholding party must "describe the nature of the documents, communications, or things not produced or disclosed in a manner that, without revealing [the privileged] information itself . . . , will enable other parties to assess the applicability of the privilege."[75] In this way, the Advisory Committee envisions that the need for an in camera judicial examination of the materials will be reduced.[76] In addition, before a party moves for an order compelling discovery,

---

67. FED. R. CIV. P. 26(b)(1).

68. 8 CHARLES A. WRIGHT ET AL., FEDERAL PRACTICE AND PROCEDURE: CIVIL § 2016, at 221 (2d ed. 1994).

69. Courts have recognized several privileges: doctor-patient, attorney-client, priest-penitent, journalist-confidential news source, psychotherapist-patient, government-informer, military or state secrets privilege, husband-wife, executive privilege, and a privilege against self-incrimination. Some of these privileges are based on constitutional grounds (*e.g.*, self-incrimination), some on statutory grounds (*e.g.*, journalist-confidential news source), and others on the common law (e.g., attorney-client). *See* Chapter 11(I)(4) ("Privilege") *infra*.

70. *See* Richard L. Marcus, *The Perils of Privilege: Waiver and the Litigator*, 84 MICH. L. REV. 1605 (1986).

71. *See, e.g.*, Munzer v. Swedish Am. Line, 35 F. Supp. 493, 497 (S.D.N.Y. 1940) (hospital records).

72. *See, e.g.*, Daniels v. Hadley Mem. Hosp., 68 F.R.D. 583, 586-87 (D.D.C. 1975).

73. FED. R. CIV. P. 26(b)(5). Required disclosures under Rule 26 are discussed in section C ("Required Disclosures Under the Federal Rules") *infra*.

74. FED. R. CIV. P. 26(b)(5) advisory committee's note to the 1993 amendment.

75. FED. R. CIV. P. 26(b)(5).

76. FED. R. CIV. P. 26(b)(5) advisory committee's note to the 1993 amendment.

the 1993 amendments require that party to attempt in good faith to confer and resolve the matter without judicial intervention.[77]

2. Attorney "Work Product" and Trial Preparation Materials

The broad scope of discovery authorized by the Federal Rules of Civil Procedure creates a special problem. To what extent may a party discover materials obtained or prepared in anticipation of litigation or in preparation for trial? On one hand, federal discovery clears the way, "consistent with recognized privileges, for the parties to obtain the fullest possible knowledge of the issues and the facts before trial."[78] On the other hand, such broad discovery may be disruptive of the adversary process. For example, litigants may decide to "sit back" and let their opponents investigate, analyze, and prepare the case. They then can attempt to take a "free ride" on their adversaries' efforts by obtaining through discovery the materials their adversaries gathered or prepared.[79]

In light of the conflicting decisions on the subject, the Advisory Committee in 1946 proposed an amendment to the Federal Rules of Civil Procedure to protect materials prepared in anticipation of litigation or trial.[80] The Advisory Committee submitted this proposed amendment to the U.S. Supreme Court after the Court had granted certiorari in a case involving the same subject. The Court did not adopt the proposed amendment, but instead attempted to resolve the matter by decision of the pending case, *Hickman v. Taylor.*[81]

The principal issue in the *Hickman* case was whether the contents of witnesses' statements made to a party investigating an accident were discoverable under the Federal Rules. On February 7, 1943, the tug "John M. Taylor" sank while towing a car float. Five of the nine crewmen drowned, including the plaintiff's husband. Three days later, the owners of the tug retained Mr. Fortenbaugh, whose firm regularly had represented the owners for several years. The owners and their insurance carriers requested Mr. Fortenbaugh to defend on their

---

77. *See* FED. R. CIV. P. 37(a)(2)(B).

78. Hickman v. Taylor, 329 U.S. 495, 501, 67 S. Ct. 385, 389, 91 L. Ed. 451, 457 (1947) (footnote omitted).

79. *See* 8 CHARLES A. WRIGHT ET AL., FEDERAL PRACTICE AND PROCEDURE: CIVIL § 2021, at 313-15 (2d ed. 1994) (summarizing the disagreement among the courts concerning the permissible scope of discovery under these circumstances).

80. The Advisory Committee proposed that

> [t]he court shall not order the production or inspection of any writing obtained or prepared by the adverse party, his attorney, surety, indemnitor, or agent in anticipation of litigation or in preparation for trial unless satisfied that denial of production or inspection will unfairly prejudice the party seeking the production or inspection in preparing his claim or defense or will cause him undue hardship or injustice. The court shall not order the production or inspection of any part of the writing that reflects an attorney's mental impressions, conclusions, opinions, or legal theories, or, except as provided in Rule 35 [relating to court-ordered physical and mental examinations], the conclusions of an expert.

5 F.R.D. 433, 456-57 (1946).

81. 329 U.S. 495, 67 S. Ct. 385, 91 L. Ed. 451 (1947); *see* 8 CHARLES A. WRIGHT ET AL., FEDERAL PRACTICE AND PROCEDURE: CIVIL § 2021, at 317 (2d ed. 1994).

behalf whatever litigation arose from the sinking of the tug. Pursuant to these general instructions, Mr. Fortenbaugh privately interviewed the four surviving members of the crew and took their written statements. These statements apparently were made shortly after a United States Steamboat Inspector's public hearing held on March 4th, at which the survivors had appeared and testified. The statements were signed on March 29th. Subsequently, Mr. Fortenbaugh interviewed other persons believed to have knowledge about the accident. In some instances, Mr. Fortenbaugh prepared memoranda reflecting what the witnesses told him.[82]

Approximately eight months after the witnesses' statements had been obtained, the wife of one of the deceased crewmen commenced an action under the Jones Act[83] against the owners of the tug and the owner of the car float to recover for her husband's death. One year later, the plaintiff served thirty-nine interrogatories. One of those interrogatories requested copies of any written statements made by crew members taken in conjunction with the accident. Also requested were any oral statements, which had to be "set forth in detail," including "the exact provisions of any such oral statements."[84] The defendants objected to this and other interrogatories. The defendants argued that the interrogatories called for privileged matter obtained in preparation for litigation and constituted an attempt to indirectly obtain counsel's private files.[85] The district court overruled the defendants' objection.[86] The owners of the tug and their attorney refused to comply with the district court's order. The district court then held them in contempt and ordered them imprisoned until they complied.[87] The Third Circuit Court of Appeals reversed. The U.S. Supreme Court affirmed the Third Circuit.[88]

Although the information was not privileged,[89] the Supreme Court recognized a "qualified" immunity from discovery.[90] *Written* statements "obtained or prepared by an adversary's counsel with an eye toward litigation" could be discovered when "relevant and non-privileged facts remain hidden in an attorney's file and [when] production of those facts is essential to the preparation of one's case."[91] In contrast, with respect to *oral* statements made by witnesses to the investigating attorney (whether presently in the form of the attorney's mental impressions or memoranda), the Court held that no showing of necessity could be made to justify their production under the circumstances of the *Hickman* case. The Court reasoned that requiring lawyers to write out or repeat what

---

82. Hickman v. Taylor, 4 F.R.D. 479, 480-81 (E.D. Pa. 1945).

83. 46 U.S.C. § 688.

84. Supplemental interrogatories requested copies of any other oral or written statements that had been obtained relating to the accident. *See Hickman,* 4 F.R.D. at 480.

85. *Hickman,* 329 U.S. at 498-99, 67 S. Ct. at 387-88, 91 L. Ed. at 455-56 (1947).

86. *Hickman,* 4 F.R.D. at 481-83.

87. *Hickman,* 329 U.S. at 500, 67 S. Ct. at 388, 91 L. Ed. at 456.

88. *Id.* at 500, 514, 67 S. Ct. at 388, 395, 91 L. Ed. at 456, 464.

89. The Supreme Court rejected the Third Circuit's view that the attorney-client privilege applied. *See id.* at 508, 67 S. Ct. at 392, 91 L. Ed. at 461.

90. *See id.* at 510-11, 67 S. Ct. at 393, 91 L. Ed. at 462.

91. *Id.* at 511-12, 67 S. Ct. at 394, 91 L. Ed. at 462-63.

witnesses have told them and to deliver those accounts to their adversaries would give rise to grave dangers of inaccuracy and untrustworthiness.[92]

The lower federal courts disagreed about how to apply the *Hickman* case.[93] A significant part of the 1970 revision of the Federal discovery rules was the addition of Rule 26(b)(3), which was designed to clarify discovery practice concerning work product. Rule 26(b)(3) applies to otherwise discoverable documents and other tangible things created for or by a party or that party's representative in anticipation of litigation or in preparation for trial. Such material may be discovered only upon showing that (1) the party seeking them has a substantial need of the materials in preparation of that party's case and (2) substantially equivalent information cannot be obtained from other sources without undue hardship. It also provides that "[i]n ordering discovery of such materials when the required showing has been made, the court shall protect against disclosure of the mental impressions, conclusions, opinions, or legal theories of an attorney or other representative of a party concerning litigation."[94]

Rule 26(b)(3) also contains special provisions concerning the production of a party's or witness's own statement. Under the rule, a party may obtain as a matter of right ("without [making] the required showing") a statement concerning the action or its subject matter that a party had previously made. The rule defines a "statement previously made" as one adopted or approved by the person making it, whether signed or not. It may be a written statement or in the

---

92. *Id.* at 512-13, 67 S. Ct. at 394, 91 L. Ed. at 463. The Court further noted that such testimony could not qualify as evidence, and using it for impeachment or corroborative purposes would harm the standards of the legal profession. The Court concluded that the denial of discovery would not hinder the plaintiff in the preparation of the plaintiff's case:

> Searching interrogatories directed to Fortenbaugh and the tug owners, production of written documents and statements upon a proper showing and direct interviews with the witnesses themselves all serve to reveal the facts in Fortenbaugh's possession to the fullest possible extent consistent with public policy. Petitioner's counsel frankly admits that he wants the oral statements only to help prepare himself to examine witnesses and to make sure that he has overlooked nothing. That is insufficient under the circumstances to permit him an exception to the policy underlying the privacy of Fortenbaugh's professional activities. If there should be a rare situation justifying production of these matters, petitioner's case is not of that type.

Id. at 513, 67 S. Ct. at 394-95, 91 L. Ed. at 463-64.

93. *See* Jeffrey F. Ghent, Annotation, *Development, Since* Hickman v. Taylor, *of Attorney's "Work Product" Doctrine*, 35 A.L.R.3D 412 (1971). Many of the Court's statements were dicta and the Court's policy of allowing discovery only on a substantial showing of necessity stimulated litigation about the scope and propriety of discovery in particular cases. Many states, otherwise adopting the scheme of federal discovery, adopted specific rules to resolve problems left open by *Hickman*. Often, such provisions were modeled on the 1946 amendment proposed by the Advisory Committee, but not promulgated by the Supreme Court. *See* 8 CHARLES A. WRIGHT ET AL., FEDERAL PRACTICE AND PROCEDURE: CIVIL § 2022, at 324-25 & n.24 (2d ed. 1994) (citing state rules).

94. FED. R. CIV. P. 26(b)(3); *see also* Kevin M. Clermont, *Surveying Work Product*, 68 CORNELL L. REV. 755 (1983); Warren H. Smith, Comment, *The Potential for Discovery of Opinion Work Product Under Rule 26(b)(3)*, 64 IOWA L. REV. 103 (1978); Note, *Protection of Opinion Work Product Under the Federal Rules of Civil Procedure*, 64 VA. L. REV. 333 (1978); John F. Wagner, Jr., Annotation, *Protection From Discovery of Attorney's Opinion Work Product Under Rule 26(b)(3), Federal Rules of Civil Procedure*, 84 A.L.R. FED. 779 (1987); Teresia B. Jovanovic, Annotation, *Fraud Exception to Work Product Privilege in Federal Courts*, 64 A.L.R. FED. 470 (1983); Russell J. Davis, Annotation, *Attorney's Work Product Privilege Under Rule 26(b)(3) of Federal Rules of Civil Procedure, As Applicable to Documents Prepared in Anticipation of Terminated Litigation*, 41 A.L.R. FED. 123 (1979).

form of a "stenographic, mechanical, electrical, or other recording, or a transcription thereof, which is a substantially verbatim recital of an oral statement by the person making it and contemporaneously recorded."[95] Rule 26(b)(3) likewise permits a nonparty witness to obtain a copy of the witness's prior statement concerning the action or its subject matter without any showing.[96]

Rule 26(b)(5) also applies to trial preparation materials.[97] Thus, after the 1993 amendments, the parties must notify other parties if they withhold "trial preparation" materials in response to a discovery request or from a required disclosure under Rule 26.[98] In addition, they must provide a sufficient description and explanation to enable other parties to assess whether the protection applies.[99] Furthermore, before a party moves for an order compelling discovery, the 1993 amendments require the party to attempt in good faith to confer and resolve the matter without court intervention.[100]

SECTION C. REQUIRED DISCLOSURES UNDER THE FEDERAL RULES

The 1993 amendments to Federal Rule 26 impose a duty of disclosure on the parties.[101] The disclosures take place in three phases: (1) early in the case, the parties must exchange basic information about potential witnesses, documentary evidence, damages, and insurance; (2) at an appropriate time during the discovery period, the parties must exchange information about expert witnesses and the details of their possible testimony; and (3) as the trial date approaches, the parties must identify the evidence they may offer at trial.[102]

1. Early Disclosures Concerning Potential Witnesses, Documentary Evidence, Damages, and Insurance

Rule 26(a)(1) requires all parties, without waiting for a discovery request, to provide information to other parties about (1) damages, (2) insurance, and (3) potential witnesses and documentary evidence. Unless the court directs or the

---

95. FED. R. CIV. P. 26(b)(3).

96. *Id.*

97. Required disclosures under Rule 26 are discussed in section C ("Required Disclosures Under the Federal Rules") *infra*.

98. FED. R. CIV. P. 26(b)(5).

99. *Id.*

100. *See* FED. R. CIV. P. 37(a)(2)(B).

101. *See* FED. R. CIV. P. 26(a) ("Required Disclosures"). *See generally* Leslie M. Kelleher, *The December 1993 Amendments to the Federal Rules of Civil Procedure—A Critical Analysis*, 12 TOURO L. REV. 7 (1995); Rogelio A. Lasso, *Gladiators Be Gone: The New Disclosure Rules Compel a Reexamination of the Adversary Process*, 36 B.C. L. REV. 479 (1995); Robert Matthew Lovein, *A Practitioner's Guide: Federal Rule of Civil Procedure 26(a)—Automatic Disclosure*, 47 SYRACUSE L. REV. 191 (1996); Linda S. Mullenix, *Adversarial Justice, Professional Responsibility, and the New Federal Discovery Rules*, 14 REV. LITIG. 13 (1994); Charles W. Sorenson, Jr., *Disclosure Under Federal Rule of Civil Procedure 26(a)—"Much Ado About Nothing,"* 46 HASTINGS L.J. 679 (1995); Lisa J. Trembly, *Mandatory Disclosure: A Historical Review of the Adoption of Rule 26 and an Examination of the Events that Have Transpired Since its Adoption*, 21 SETON H. L.J. 425 (1997).

102. *See* FED. R. CIV. P. 26(a) advisory committee's note to the 1993 amendment.

parties stipulate, these disclosures are to take place within ten days after the parties meet to prepare a discovery plan.[103] This requirement can be altered by stipulation, court order, or local rule.[104]

The specifics concerning the meeting time are left to the parties. However, the meeting must be held at least fourteen days before a scheduling conference or before a scheduling order is due under Rule 16. When no scheduling conference is held, the latest that a meeting could ordinarily be held would be within seventy-five days after the defendant has first appeared in the case. Thus, the initial disclosures would be due no later than eighty-five days after the defendant's first appearance.[105]

Before these initial disclosures, Rule 26(g)(1) requires the parties to conduct a reasonable inquiry into the facts of the case.[106] The Advisory Committee indicates that this rule does not require "an exhaustive investigation."[107] According to the Advisory Committee, "reasonableness" depends on various factors, such as

> the number and complexity of the issues; the location, nature, number, and availability of potentially relevant witnesses and documents; the extent of past working relationships between the attorney and the client, particularly in handling related or similar litigation; and . . . how long the party has to conduct an investigation, either before or after filing the case.[108]

Nevertheless, the timing of the disclosures may result in the parties exerting more effort to prepare facts and information earlier in the litigation than the parties did under the prior discovery practices. Parties must make these disclosures even though (1) their investigation is incomplete or (2) another party has failed to make its disclosures or has made an inadequate disclosure.[109]

Under the proposed amendments recommended by the Judicial Conference on September 15, 1999, the timing of these disclosures would be changed. Under the proposals, the disclosures would have to be made at or within 14 days after the Rule 26(f) conference unless a different time is set by stipulation or court order. A party could object during the conference that initial disclosures are inappropriate under the circumstances of the case and state the objection in the Rule 26(f) discovery plan. In ruling on the objection, the proposed rule directs the

---

103. FED. R. CIV. P. 26(a)(1); *see* section D(1) ("The Parties' Discovery Planning Meeting") *infra*.

104. *See* FED. R. CIV. P. 26(a)(1); *see also id.* advisory committee's note to the 1993 amendment (pointing out that courts by order or local rule can require the parties to disclose additional information without a discovery request as well as exempt particular types of cases).

105. *See* FED. R. CIV. P. 26(a) advisory committee's note to the 1993 amendment; *see also* section N ("Pretrial Conferences and Orders") *infra*.

106. *See* FED. R. CIV. P. 26(g)(1) (specifically requiring that disclosures must be signed and that the signature "constitutes a certification that to the best of the signer's knowledge, information, and belief, formed *after a reasonable inquiry, the disclosure is complete and correct as of the time it is made*") (emphasis added).

107. The Advisory Committee refers to an investigation "that is reasonable under the circumstances, focusing on the facts that are alleged with particularity in the pleadings." *See* FED. R. CIV. P. 26(a)(1) advisory committee's note to the 1993 amendment.

108. *Id.*

109. *See id.*

court to determine what disclosures, if any, are to be made as well as to set the time for any such disclosures.[110]

(a) Damages

Rule 26(a)(1)(C) requires parties to disclose how they calculated "any category of damages."[111] Although the rule technically refers only to "damages," courts should construe the rule to apply to restitutionary claims involving money.[112] In addition, Rule 26(a)(1)(C) functions as the equivalent of a standing request for production for documents.[113] The disclosing party must make available for inspection and copying "the documents or other evidentiary material, not privileged or protected from disclosure, on which such computation is based, including materials bearing on the nature and extent of injuries suffered."[114] The Advisory Committee points out that parties must produce only documents that are "then reasonably available" to them. Furthermore, parties are not expected to provide calculations of damages dependent on information in the possession of other parties.[115]

Illustration 9-3. Assume that *A* sues *B* in federal court. *A's* complaint is similar to Federal Form 9. *A* alleges that on a certain date in a certain location, *B* "negligently drove a motor vehicle against plaintiff who was then crossing said highway." *A* also alleges that "as a result plaintiff was thrown down and had [the plaintiff's] leg broken and was otherwise injured, was prevented from transacting business, suffered great pain of body and mind, and incurred expenses for medical attention and hospitalization" in the sum of $100,000. Pursuant to Rule 26(a)(1)(C), *A* would have to include information concerning *A's* damages as part of *A's* initial disclosures. *A* would have to show how each category of damages (medical and hospital expenses, loss of wages, and pain and suffering) was calculated. *A* would also have to make available for inspection and copying the documents or other evidentiary material, not privileged or protected from disclosure, on which the calculation is based. Because these materials bear "on the nature and extent of injuries suffered," *A* would have to make available medical and hospital bills. *A's* required disclosures would also extend to evidence of loss of earning capacity. Furthermore, if *A* used a formula or some other system for calculating pain and suffering, that information would have to be disclosed.[116]

---

110. *See* 68 U.S.L.W., Sept 28, 1999, at 2168, 2169.

111. FED. R. CIV. P. 26(a)(1)(C).

112. Support for this conclusion is provided in the Advisory Committee Note, which indicates that Rule 26(a)(1)(C) applies to "a party claiming damages *or other monetary relief.*" FED. R. CIV. P. 26(a)(1)(C) advisory committee's note to the 1993 amendment. The term "other monetary relief" could also extend to disclosure of other items, such as attorney's fees and costs.

113. FED. R. CIV. P. 26(a)(1)(C) advisory committee's note to the 1993 amendment.

114. FED. R. CIV. P. 26(a)(1)(C). The inspection and copying would be carried out "as under Rule 34." *See* section H ("Production of Documents, Entries on Land, Testing, and Sampling") *infra*.

115. FED. R. CIV. P. 26(a)(1)(C) advisory committee's note to the 1993 amendment.

116. *See* LARRY L. TEPLY, LEGAL NEGOTIATION IN A NUTSHELL 52-55 (1992) (discussing rules of thumb and formulas as methods for case evaluation).

Illustration 9-4. Assume that *A Co.* sues *B Co.* in federal court for breach of warranty. *A's* complaint asserts that a product with components supplied by *B* is "defective" in some unspecified manner. In addition to seeking damages of $100,000, *A* also asserts a special damage claim for loss of profits of $500,000. Pursuant to Rule 26(a)(1)(C), *A* would have to include information about how *A* calculated damages as part of *A's* initial disclosures. For example, *A* might show that the difference between the contract price and market price for the machine was $100,000. With respect to *A's* special damage claim, *A* would be required to show how *A* calculated the lost profits. However, this calculation would only need to be a reasonable one under the circumstances. If expert testimony or an extensive study will be necessary to demonstrate proof of this loss, the continuing obligation to supplement or correct the initial disclosure would force the party to provide greater details as the information develops.

(b) Insurance

Federal Rule 26(a)(1)(D) requires the parties to disclose "any insurance agreement under which any person carrying on an insurance business may be liable to satisfy part or all of a judgment which may be entered in the action or to indemnify or reimburse for payments made to satisfy the judgment" for purposes of inspection and copying.[117] The mandatory disclosure of insurance replaces Federal Rule 26(b)(2), which previously dealt with this matter.[118] According to the Advisory Committee, a principal purpose of these disclosures is "to accelerate the exchange of basic information about the case and to eliminate the paper work involved in requesting such information."[119]

Illustration 9-5. If the defendants in *Illustrations 9-3* or *9-4* have insurance agreements covering part or all of the potential judgment, they must disclose the existence of that insurance agreement and make it available for inspection and copying.

---

117. FED. R. CIV. P. 26(a)(1)(D). The inspection and copying would be carried out "as under Rule 34." *See* section H ("Production of Documents, Entries on Land, Testing, and Sampling") *infra*. The obligation to disclose does not extend to applications for insurance nor does disclosure make the insurance agreement admissible in evidence. The prior rule covering insurance, Rule 26(b)(2), included specific statements to this effect. These statements were dropped from the new rule as "unnecessary." Their deletion does "not signify any change of law." *See* FED. R. CIV. P. 26(a)(1)(D) advisory committee's note to the 1993 amendment.

118. When insurance would be provable at trial, there is no doubt that a party can discover the facts about insurance; but insurance is irrelevant at trial in determining whether a person acted negligently or otherwise wrongfully. *See* FED. R. EVID. 411. Indeed, the mention of insurance may result in a mistrial. The federal courts and states adopting rules similar to Federal Rule 26(b)(1) were divided sharply on whether disclosure of insurance coverage could be compelled through discovery. *See* Cook v. Welty, 253 F. Supp. 875, 876 (D.D.C. 1966). This division was resolved in 1970 for the federal courts. Federal Rule 26(b)(2) was added to the Federal Rules of Civil Procedure to permit discovery of the existence and contents of liability insurance agreements. This change had a marked influence on state practice even in those states not adopting the 1970 discovery amendments. *See, e.g.*, Walls v. Horbach, 189 Neb. 479, 203 N.W.2d 490 (1973) (allowing discovery, overruling a 1964 decision to the contrary); Cropp v. Woleslagel, 207 Kan. 627, 485 P.2d 1271 (1971) (insurance not discoverable, but the court may require disclosure at a pretrial conference).

119. *See* FED. R. CIV. P. 26(a) advisory committee's note to the 1993 amendment.

(c) Potential Witnesses and Documentary Evidence

Rule 26(a)(1)(A) specifically requires the parties, without waiting for a request, to disclose "the name and, if known, the address and telephone number of individuals likely to have discoverable information relevant to disputed facts alleged with particularity in the pleadings, identifying the subjects of the information."[120] Similarly, Rule 26(a)(1)(B) requires the parties to disclose "a copy of, or a description by category and location of, all documents, data compilations, and tangible things in the possession, custody, or control of the party that are relevant to disputed facts alleged with particularity in the pleadings."[121] These disclosure requirements are, in effect, "the functional equivalent of court-ordered interrogatories."[122]

The required initial disclosure of the names of witnesses and identification of documents and other evidence in the possession, custody, or control of the party are limited to those "relevant to *disputed* facts *alleged with particularity* in the pleadings."[123] The Advisory Committee envisioned a common-sense, sliding scale approach: "[t]he greater the specificity and clarity of the allegations in the pleadings, the more complete should be the listing of potential witnesses and types of documentary evidence."[124] The Advisory Committee also envisioned that this rule should be construed and administered like all other rules: to secure the just, speedy, and inexpensive determination of the action.[125] Furthermore, the Advisory Committee assumed that the parties will clarify the issues as part of the required discovery planning meeting.[126]

Illustration 9-6. In *Illustration 9-4, A* alleged that a product with components supplied by *B* was "defective" in some unspecified manner. That allegation would not impose on the parties the obligation in an initial disclosure to identify all persons possibly involved in or documents relating to the design, manufacture, or assembly of the product because it was not alleged with particularity.[127]

Illustration 9-7. Assume on the facts of *Illustration 9-3* that *B's* answer (1) admits *A's* allegations concerning jurisdiction, (2) denies *B's* negligence, (3) alleges *A's* contributory negligence, and (4) denies *A's* allegation of damages. On these facts, the specific disputed facts alleged with particularity are the auto accident, each party's negligence, and *A's* damages. These disputed facts would trigger the duty to disclose, for example, the names of *C* and *D*, eyewitnesses to the accident. It would also trigger the duty to disclose, for example, the location

---

120. Fed. R. Civ. P. 26(a)(1)(A).

121. Fed. R. Civ. P. 26(a)(1)(B).

122. Fed. R. Civ. P. 26(a)(1) advisory committee's note to the 1993 amendment.

123. Fed. R. Civ. P. 26(a)(1)(A) & (B) (emphasis added).

124. *Id.* advisory committee's note to the 1993 amendment.

125. *Id.* (referring to the principles in Rule 1).

126. *Id.* ("Although [disclosure requirements in the rule] by their terms refer to the factual disputes defined in the pleadings, the rule contemplates that these issues would be informally refined and clarified during the meeting of the parties [concerning the discovery plan] and that the disclosure obligations would be adjusted" accordingly).

127. *Id.*

of the vehicle involved in the accident if it is still in a party's possession, custody, or control. No disclosures would be necessary concerning jurisdiction because *B* did not dispute jurisdiction.

* * * * *

On September 15, 1999, the Judicial Conference recommended that the initial disclosures concerning witnesses and documents be changed. Under the proposal, the disclosure would be limited to "discoverable information that the disclosing party may use to support its claims or defenses, unless solely for impeachment."[128] Thus, the disclosures would be limited to information favorable to the disclosing party. The word "use" in the proposed change covers any intended use at a pretrial conference, to support a motion, at trial, or during discovery, such as use of a document to question a witness during a deposition.[129] A proposed amendment to Rule 5(d) would prohibit filing of disclosures under Rule 26(a)(1) or (2) until they are used in the proceeding or the court orders them filed.[130]

2. Disclosures and Discovery Concerning Experts

Expert testimony is often used at trial. A party may use expert testimony when "scientific, technical, or other specialized knowledge will assist the trier of fact to understand the evidence or to determine a fact in issue."[131] In such circumstances, witnesses qualified as experts based upon their "knowledge, skill, experience, training, or education" may testify.[132]

(a) Discovery Concerning Experts Under the Federal Rules Prior to the 1993 Amendments

Because the selection and use of experts was an integral part of an attorney's trial preparation, the early cases generally refused to allow discovery.[133] The proposed 1946 amendments to the Federal Rules of Civil Procedure on attorney work product included a provision creating an absolute immunity for conclusions of an expert.[134] The Supreme Court did not adopt the proposed

---

128. *See* 68 U.S.L.W., Sept 28, 1999, at 2168, 2169.

129. *See* PROPOSED FED. R. CIV. P. 26(a)(1) advisory committee note. As case preparation continues, a party must supplement its disclosures when it determines that it may use a witness or document that it did not previously intend to use. *Id.* The Rule would also exempt eight specific categories of proceedings from initial disclosure. *See* 68 U.S.L.W., Sept 28, 1999, at 2168, 2169.

130. *See* 68 U.S.L.W., Sept 28, 1999, at 2168, 2169.

131. FED. R. EVID. 702.

132. *Id.*

133. *Id.*

134. "The Court shall not order the production or inspection of any part of [a] writing [obtained or prepared by the adverse party, his attorney, surety, indemnitor, or agent in anticipation of litigation or in preparation for trial] that reflects . . . , except as provided in Rule 35, the conclusions of an expert." 5 F.R.D. 433, 456-57 (1946). Federal Rule 35 permits court-ordered physical or mental examinations of a party or of a person in the custody or under the legal control of a party when that person's physical or mental condition is "in controversy." FED. R. CIV. P. 35(a). Specifically, Rule 35(b) allows the party against whom the order was made to discover the medical report detailing the examining physician's findings. Rule 35(b) further provides

1946 amendments, but instead attempted to deal with the general work-product issue by deciding the case of *Hickman v. Taylor*.[135] After *Hickman*, several courts continued to protect the reports and opinions of experts, but some courts took a liberal approach in allowing discovery. The 1970 amendments to the Federal Rules resolved the division among the lower federal courts.[136] Rule 26(b)(4) recognized three categories of experts: (1) experts to be called at trial; (2) experts retained by counsel, but who will not be called at trial; and (3) experts who were consulted, but not retained.[137]

Under subdivision (A)(i) of Rule 26(b)(4), a party could obtain, by written interrogatories and without any special showing, (1) the names of experts that any other party expects to call as witnesses at trial, (2) the subject on which they will testify, (3) the substance of the facts and opinions to which they are expected to testify, and (4) a summary of the grounds for each of their opinions.[138] The Advisory Committee's principal justification for permitting discovery of this information as a matter of course was to enable opposing counsel to prepare effectively for cross-examination of the expert. The Committee pointed out that lawyers, even with the help of their own experts, frequently could not anticipate the particular approach their adversary's expert would take or the data on which they would base their judgment.[139]

Some courts required a substantial showing of need to obtain "further discovery." For example, in *Wilson v. Resnick*,[140] the court refused discovery of an expert physician's report concerning allegedly negligent medical treatment despite the plaintiff's claim that the summary of the opinions provided in the interrogatories was inadequate. However, most courts freely permitted further discovery from experts.[141]

---

that after delivery of the report, the party who requested the examination is entitled to receive reports of other examinations on the same condition previously or thereafter made. FED. R. CIV. P. 35(b); *see* section I(2) ("The Physician's Report") *infra*.

135. *See* section (B)(2) ("Attorney 'Work Product' and Trial Preparation Materials") *supra*.

136. *See* FED. R. CIV. P. 26(b)(4) advisory committee's note to the 1970 amendment; *see also* Lori J. Henkel, Annotation, *Compelling Testimony of Opponent's Expert in State Court*, 66 A.L.R.4TH 213 (1988).

137. *See* FED. R. CIV. P. 26(b)(4).

138. FED. R. CIV. P. 26(b)(4)(A)(i); *see* Thomas R. Trenkner, Annotation, *Pretrial Discovery of Facts Known and Opinions Held By Opponent's Experts Under Rule 26(b)(4) of Federal Rules of Civil Procedure*, 33 A.L.R. FED. 403 (1977). The effectiveness of using interrogatories to discover an expert's opinion was sharply criticized. As one commentator stated, the use of interrogatories is "a totally unsatisfactory method of providing preparation for cross-examination and rebuttal." Michael G. Graham, *Discovery of Experts Under Rule 26(b)(4) of the Federal Rules of Civil Procedure* (pt.2), 1977 U. ILL. L.F. 169, 172. Subdivision (A)(ii) of Federal Rule 26(b)(4) provided that "[u]pon motion, the court may order further discovery by other means," which presumably might include taking of the expert's deposition or the production of the expert's report. The court can restrict the scope of this further discovery. FED. R. CIV. P. 26(b)(4)(A)(ii). The court could also provide for payment of the expert's time spent in further discovery as well as a fair portion of the fee the opponent has paid to the expert, pursuant to the provisions of Federal Rule 26(b)(4)(C).

139. FED. R. CIV. P. 26(b)(4) advisory committee's note to the 1970 amendment.

140. 51 F.R.D. 510 (E.D. Pa. 1970).

141. For example, in Herbst v. International Telephone & Telegraph Corp., 65 F.R.D. 528 (D. Conn. 1975), the court stated as follows:

> All but experts may be freely deposed before trial in keeping with the liberal spirit that pervades the federal rules. Once the traditional problem of allowing one party to obtain the benefit of another's expert cheaply has been solved, there is no reason to treat an expert differently than any other witness. Thus, the motion to compel oral depositions will

Discovery pursuant to subdivision (A) of Rule 26(b)(4) was limited to those experts who were *expected* to testify.[142] In answering an interrogatory under this subsection, parties did not need to disclose the names of experts who *might* testify.[143] However, if a party decided to call an expert after the party had answered the interrogatory, Rule 26(e)(1) specifically required the party to supplement the response by identifying "each person expected to be called as an expert witness at trial, the subject matter on which the person is expected to testify, and the substance of the person's testimony."[144] In contrast, courts rarely permitted discovery of facts known and opinions held by experts who had been "retained or specially employed by another party in anticipation of litigation or preparation for trial" but who were *not* expected to testify. Subdivision (B) of Rule 26(b)(4) allowed such discovery only as provided by Rule 35 (reports involving court-mandated examinations of physical or mental conditions in controversy) or "upon a showing of exceptional circumstances under which it is [impractical] for the party seeking discovery to obtain facts or opinions on the same subject by other means."[145] The 1993 amendments retained this provision.

Subdivision (B) of Rule 26(b)(4) limited discovery to experts "retained or specially consulted." Rule 26(b)(4) did not provide for discovery against an expert who was informally consulted in preparation for trial, but who was not "retained" or "specially employed." As the Advisory Committee noted, discovery concerning this latter group was entirely "precluded."[146] For this preclusion to apply, the expert information had to be acquired or developed either in anticipation of litigation or in preparation for trial. Thus, when an expert acquires information as "an actor or viewer with respect to transactions or occurrences that are part of the subject matter of the lawsuit," the expert will be treated as an ordinary witness.[147] Similarly, a litigant cannot avoid discovery merely because the litigant is an expert. For example, a doctor defending a

---

be granted. If expenses have been incurred by the plaintiffs in obtaining these experts' opinions, and the parties are unable to agree upon an allocation of these costs, the issue may be submitted to the court on affidavits following the depositions. . . . The defendants shall, in addition, pay these experts a reasonable fee for the time spent in deposition.

Id. at 530-31. Professor Graham likewise concluded that "[i]n practice, full discovery is the rule, and practitioners use all available means of disclosure including both the discovery of expert's reports and depositions." Michael G. Graham, *Discovery of Experts Under Rule 26(b)(4)* (pt. 2), 1977 ILL. L.F. 169, 172. *See generally* Joseph M. McLaughlin, *Discoverability and Admissibility of Expert Testimony*, 63 NOTRE DAME L. REV. 760 (1988); Steven K. Sims, Note, *Treating Experts Like Ordinary Witnesses: Recent Trends in Discovery of Testifying Experts Under Federal Rule of Civil Procedure 26(b)(4)*, 66 WASH. U.L.Q. 787 (1988); David E. Vis, Note, *"Further Discovery" of Testimonial Experts Under Federal Rules of Civil Procedure 26(b)(4)(A)(ii)*, 33 S.D. L. REV. 331 (1988). The 1993 amendments have now conformed to this practice. *See* section C(2)*(b)(iii)* ("Further Discovery Concerning Experts") *infra*.

142. FED. R. CIV. P. 26(b)(4)(A).

143. *See* 8 CHARLES A. WRIGHT ET AL., FEDERAL PRACTICE AND PROCEDURE: CIVIL § 2030 (2d ed. 1994).

144. FED. R. CIV. P. 26(e)(1)(B).

145. *See* FED. R. CIV. P. 26(b)(4)(B).

146. *See* FED. R. CIV. P. 26(b)(4) advisory committee's notes to 1970 amendment.

147. *Id.*

malpractice action "should be subject to discovery with regard both to the facts [the doctor] knows and the opinions [the doctor] holds."[148]

(b) *Disclosures and Discovery Concerning Experts Under the 1993 Amendments*

The 1993 amendments impose a duty to disclose information concerning experts and their likely testimony at trial.[149]

(i) *Who Must Be Identified*

Rule 26(a)(2)(A) requires that the parties disclose to other litigants "the identity of any person who may be used at trial to present evidence under Rules 702, 703, or 705 of the Federal Rules of Evidence."[150] These Rules of Evidence govern testimony involving scientific, technical, and other specialized knowledge.[151]

(ii) *Report Requirement*

Rule 26(a)(2)(B) imposes a duty to prepare a written report on identified experts who (1) are retained or specially employed to provide expert testimony or (2) are employees of a party when they are regularly involved in giving expert testimony.[152] Thus, no written report is required for other experts, such as a treating physician called to testify at trial.[153] When a report is required, the report must provide a "complete statement of all opinions to be expressed" at

---

148. 8 CHARLES A. WRIGHT ET AL., FEDERAL PRACTICE AND PROCEDURE: CIVIL § 2033, at 463 (2d ed. 1994). In Young v. United States, 181 F.R.D. 344 (W.D. Tex. 1997), a medical malpractice case, the plaintiff attempted to designate his treating physicians, who were Navy doctors employed by the defendant, as both fact and expert witnesses. The defendant objected on the grounds that treating physicians are not properly considered experts and that the *Code of Federal Regulations* prohibits such a designation. The court held that private litigants may not compel treating physicians to act as experts, but that a non-expert treating physician can be asked questions implicating his expertise only as long as they relate to his treatment. In addition, the court held that the government could not use the *Code of Federal Regulations* to create a privilege that would allow the defendant to prevent the testimony of the treating physician. On the latter question, the court held both that the *CFR* was not designed to create a privilege of the sort asserted and that Rule 45(c)(3)(B) adequately protected unretained experts from being called as expert witnesses against their will, in that the rule allows the court to quash or modify a subpoena for such a witness in its discretion.

149. FED. R. CIV. P. 26(a)(2).

150. FED. R. CIV. P. 26(a)(2)(A).

151. *See* FED. R. EVID. 702 ("Testimony by Experts") ("If scientific, technical, or other specialized knowledge will assist the trier of fact to understand the evidence or to determine a fact in issue, a witness qualified as an expert by knowledge, skill, experience, training, or education, may testify thereto in the form of an opinion or otherwise"), 703 ("Bases of Opinion Testimony by Experts"), 705 ("Disclosure of Facts or Data Underlying Expert Opinion").

152. FED. R. CIV. P. 26(a)(2)(B). This reporting requirement, however, can be waived for particular experts by local rule, court order, or written stipulation. *Id.* advisory committee's note to the 1993 amendment.

153. FED. R. CIV. P. 26(a)(2)(B) advisory committee's note to the 1993 amendment. However, by local rule, order, or stipulation, this written report requirement can be imposed upon additional persons who will provide opinions under Rule 702. *Id.*

trial and the supporting reasons and grounds.[154] The report must also provide (1) "the data or other information considered by the witness in forming the opinions;" (2) "any exhibits to be used as a summary of or support for the opinions;" (3) "the qualifications of the witness, including a list of all publications authored by the witness within the preceding ten years;" (4) "the compensation to be paid for the study and testimony;" and (5) "a listing of any other cases in which the witness has testified as an expert at trial or by deposition within the preceding four years."[155] As an incentive to the parties to make full disclosure, amended Rule 37(c)(1) provides an "automatic sanction."[156] A party may not use any expert testimony on direct examination that the party has not properly disclosed, unless the party can demonstrate a substantial justification or show that the failure to disclose is harmless.[157]

Rule 26(a)(2)(C) envisions that the court will prescribe a time for these disclosures in a pretrial scheduling order.[158] Ordinarily, the party with the burden of proof on an issue should be required to disclose its expert testimony before other parties are required to make their disclosures on the issue. In absence of a specific time in a scheduling order or a stipulation by the parties, Rule 26(a)(2)(C) requires that these disclosures concerning experts be made by all parties at least ninety days before the trial date or the date by which the case is to be ready for trial. However, the rule allows an additional thirty days after the disclosure has been made by another party if the expert testimony "is intended solely to contradict or rebut evidence on the same subject matter" identified by another party's disclosure under this rule.[159] Rule 26(a)(2)(C) also specifically imposes a duty to supplement the disclosures concerning experts.[160]

(iii) Further Discovery Concerning Experts

Amended Rule 26(b)(4) states that experts who are expected to testify may be deposed before trial.[161] This revision conforms with actual practice in most courts.[162] Depositions of experts who must prepare a report can be taken only after the required report has been provided.[163] However, the detailed reports may eliminate the need for further depositions or at least reduce their

---

154. FED. R. CIV. P. 26(a)(2)(B).

155. *Id.* Given the duty to disclose the data or other information considered by the expert in the report, the Advisory Committee maintains that "litigants should no longer be able to argue that materials furnished to their experts to be used in forming their opinions—whether or not ultimately relied upon by the expert—are privileged or otherwise protected from disclosure when such persons are testifying or being disposed." *Id.* advisory committee's note to the 1993 amendment. Counsel can assist experts in preparing these reports. *Id.* ("Rule 26(a)(2)(B) does not preclude counsel from providing assistance to experts in preparing the reports, and, indeed, with experts such as automobile mechanics, this assistance may be needed").

156. FED. R. CIV. P. 37(c)(1) advisory committee's note to the 1993 amendment.

157. FED. R. CIV. P. 37(c)(1).

158. *See* FED. R. CIV. P. 26(a)(2)(C).

159. FED. R. CIV. P. 26(a)(2)(C) & advisory committee's note to the 1993 amendment.

160. FED. R. CIV. P. 26(a)(2)(C).

161. FED. R. CIV. P. 26(b)(4)(A).

162. FED. R. CIV. P. 26(b)(4) advisory committee's note to the 1993 amendment; *see* section C(2)*(a)* ("Discovery Concerning Experts Under the Federal Rules Prior to the 1993 Amendments") *supra.*

163. FED. R. CIV. P. 26(b)(4).

length.[164] Furthermore, the party taking such depositions will ordinarily have to bear the expert's fees involved in the deposition.[165] The rules continue the prior practice concerning depositions of experts who are specially retained or employed in anticipation of litigation or preparation for trial but who are not expected to testify.[166]

3. Disclosures Identifying Particular Evidence that May Be Offered at Trial

The 1993 amendments also impose a duty to disclose the specific evidence that the parties will offer at trial. These disclosures focus on information customarily needed in final preparation for trial.[167]

(a) Names of Witnesses

Rule 26(a)(3)(A) and (B) require the parties to disclose the witnesses who may present substantive evidence at trial, whether in person or by deposition.[168] The rule does not require disclosure of evidence offered solely for "impeachment" purposes.[169] The parties must separately list the witnesses who will probably be called as well as those who may be called if the need arises.[170]

---

164. FED. R. CIV. P. 26(a)(2) & (b)(4) advisory committee's notes to the 1993 amendment.

165. *See* FED. R. CIV. P. 26(b)(4)(C). Rule 26(b)(4)(C) states that "[u]nless manifest injustice would result, (i) the court shall require the party seeking discovery pay the expert a reasonable fee for time spent in responding to discovery under this subdivision." *Id.* In M.T. McBrian, Inc. v. Liebert Corp., 173 F.R.D. 491 (N.D. Ill. 1997), the defendant took the deposition of the plaintiff's expert at the plaintiff's attorneys' offices in Chicago, to which the defendants' attorneys had to travel from St. Louis. The plaintiff sought an order to have the defendant pay the travel expenses of the expert in coming from Minnesota to Chicago for the deposition. The court refused the order because the plaintiff wanted the deposition taken in Chicago and in the absense of the plaintiff's request, the defendant could have as easily taken it in Minnesota where the expert lived and avoided the claimed travel expenses. The court also denied the plaintiff's request that the defendant reimburse the expert for time spent in preparing for the deposition as well as for time actually spent in giving the deposition. The court observed that this case was not a complex one in which the expert needed preparation time because it had been several months since he prepared his report.

166. *See* FED. R. CIV. P. 26(b)(4)(B); section C(2)*(a)* ("Discovery Concerning Experts Under the Federal Rules Prior to the 1993 Amendments") *supra*; *see also* FED. R. CIV. P. 26(b)(4)(C) (continuing to provide that the party seeking discovery must ordinarily pay a reasonable fee for time spent in responding to this discovery as well as a fair portion of the fees and expenses reasonably incurred by the other party in obtaining facts and opinions from the expert).

167. FED. R. CIV. P. 26(a)(3) ("Pretrial Disclosures") & advisory committee's note to the 1993 amendment. The parties must make these disclosures, without any request, pursuant to a scheduling order adopted by the court or by special order. In absence of such orders, the parties must make these disclosures at least thirty days before the commencement of the trial. FED. R. CIV. P. 26(a)(3) & advisory committee's note to the 1993 amendment.

168. FED. R. CIV. P. 26(a)(3)(A) & (B).

169. *See* FED. R. CIV. P. 26(a)(3); *see* Chapter 11(I)(6) ("Objection, Cross-Examination, and Impeachment") *infra*.

170. FED. R. CIV. P. 26(a)(3)(A). In addition to the names of the witnesses, their addresses and telephone numbers must be listed if the party has not previously provided that information. FED. R. CIV. P. 26(a)(3)(A). Listing a witness does not obligate a party to secure that person's attendance at trial. However, listing a witness should preclude the party from objecting if another party calls the witness to testify without previously listing the witness in a disclosure. *Id.* advisory committee's note to the 1993 amendment.

Witnesses expected to present testimony by deposition must also be designated. Furthermore, if the deposition of the witness is not taken stenographically, a transcript of the pertinent portions of the deposition must be provided to other parties at the time of the disclosure.[171]

As an incentive to provide full disclosure, revised Rule 37(c)(1) prohibits a party from calling any witness at trial who has not been properly disclosed, unless the party can demonstrate a substantial justification or show that the failure is harmless.[172] However, a party may call "an unlisted witness if the need for such testimony is based upon developments during trial that could not reasonably have been anticipated," such as an unexpected change of testimony by another witness.[173]

(b) Identification of Documents or Other Exhibits

Rule 26(a)(3)(C) requires the parties to disclose each document or exhibit, including summaries of other evidence, that may be offered as "substantive" evidence at trial.[174] Disclosure of evidence offered solely for "impeachment" purposes is not required.[175] In making the disclosures, the parties must separate (1) those documents and other exhibits that a party expects to offer from (2) those that the party may offer if the need arises. The Advisory Committee's notes indicate that each document or exhibit should be listed separately. However, the note also states that Rule 26(a)(3)(C) "should permit voluminous items of a similar or standardized character to be described by meaningful categories."[176] To encourage full disclosure, revised Rule 37(c)(1) prohibits a party from offering any document or exhibit at trial that has not been properly disclosed. However, the court may permit a party to offer a nondisclosed document or exhibit if the party can demonstrate a substantial justification or that the failure is harmless.[177]

(c) Objecting to the Disclosures

After receiving these final disclosures, a party has fourteen days to object to the matters disclosed. Specifically, a party must serve and file a list disclosing

---

171. FED. R. CIV. P. 26(a)(3)(B). This disclosure allows other parties to verify the transcript which "is an obvious concern since counsel often utilize their own personnel to prepare transcripts from audio or video tapes." *Id.* advisory committee's notes to the 1993 amendment. By local rule or court order, a court can also require the parties to designate the particular parts of stenographic depositions to be used at trial. *Id.*

172. FED. R. CIV. P. 37(c)(1); *see* FED. R. CIV. P. 37(c)(1) advisory committee's note to the 1993 amendment (noting that the preclusion sanction does not apply to impeachment evidence).

173. FED. R. CIV. P. 26(a)(3)(A) advisory committee's note to the 1993 amendment.

174. FED. R. CIV. P. 26(a)(3)(C).

175. *See* FED. R. CIV. P. 26(a)(3); *see also* FED. R. CIV. P. 37(c)(1) advisory committee's note to the 1993 amendment (noting that preclusion sanctions do not apply to impeachment evidence); Chapter 11(I)(6) ("Objections, Cross-Examination, and Impeachment") *infra.*

176. FED. R. CIV. P. 26(a)(3)(C) advisory committee's note to the 1993 amendment.

177. FED. R. CIV. P. 37(c)(1) ("A party that without substantial justification fails to disclose information required by Rule 26(a) . . . shall not, unless such failure is harmless, be permitted to use as evidence at a trial information . . . not so disclosed"); *see* FED. R. CIV. P. 37(c)(1) advisory committee's note to the 1993 amendment (noting that the preclusion sanction does not apply to impeachment evidence).

any objection to (1) the use of any designated deposition or (2) the admissibility of designated documents or exhibits.[178] Failure to object in this manner waives the objection "unless excused by the court for good cause shown."[179] This waiver provision does not apply to objections under Rule 402 (relevancy) or Rule 403 (exclusion of relevant evidence on grounds of prejudice, confusion, or waste of time) of the Federal Rules of Evidence.[180] However, listing a potential objection does not constitute making that objection.[181]

SECTION D. THE DISCOVERY PLANNING MEETING, TIMING, SEQUENCE, PRIORITY, LIMITS, AND CERTIFICATION

1. The Parties' Discovery Planning Meeting

The 1993 amendments to Rule 26 require the parties to have an early meeting for four principal purposes. First, they are to discuss the nature and basis of their claims and defenses. Second, they are to discuss the possibility of a prompt settlement or resolution of the case. Third, they are to make or arrange for the required initial disclosures. Fourth, they are to develop a proposed discovery plan in addition to the mandatory disclosures.[182] The responsibility for arranging and being present or represented at this meeting rests jointly upon the attorneys of record and all unrepresented parties who have appeared in the action.[183] They also share a joint responsibility for attempting in good faith to agree upon the proposed plan and to submit a written report outlining the plan

---

178. FED. R. CIV. P. 26(a)(3)(C). A court may set an earlier time for disclosures of evidence and provide more time for disclosing potential objections. *Id.* advisory committee's note to the 1993 amendment.

179. FED. R. CIV. P. 26(a)(3)(C).

180. *Id.*; *see* Chapter 11(I) ("Evidence") *infra*.

181. FED. R. CIV. P. 26(a)(3)(C) advisory committee's note to the 1993 amendment. Thus, the court does not have to rule on the objection. Instead, the listing simply preserves a party's right to make the objection during trial. Nevertheless, the court may elect to treat the listing as a motion in limine and rule upon it prior to trial. *Id.*

182. FED. R. CIV. P. 26(f). The forerunner of this type of meeting, an early discovery conference, was added by the 1980 amendments to the Federal Rules of Civil Procedure. Prior to a discovery conference, the Federal Rules envisioned that the parties had made a reasonable effort to reach agreement on four matters: (1) the issues as they then appear; (2) a proposed plan and schedule of discovery; (3) limitations that ought to be placed on discovery; and (4) any other matters governing discovery (that could be controlled by a court order). *Id.* (prior to the 1993 amendment). Each party and their respective attorneys were required to participate in good faith in formulating a discovery plan if such a plan was proposed by an attorney for any party. If an attorney had made a reasonable effort to reach agreement with the opposing attorneys on these matters but had not been able to do so, that party could move the court to conduct such a conference. *Id.* (prior to the 1993 amendment). The notice of the motion set forth the above matters. This notice was served on all parties and objections or additions to the matters raised by the motion had to be served not later than ten days after service of the motion. After the conference, the court is required to "enter an order tentatively identifying the issues for discovery purposes, establishing a plan and schedule for discovery, [and] setting limitations on discovery, if any." *Id.* (prior to the 1993 amendment). The court could also allocate expenses and determine other matters necessary for the proper management of discovery. This discovery order could "be altered or amended whenever justice so require[d]." *Id.* (prior to the 1993 amendment).

183. FED. R. CIV. P. 26(f). The specific timing of this meeting is discussed in section C(1) ("Early Disclosures Concerning Potential Witnesses, Documentary Evidence, Damages, and Insurance") *supra*.

within ten days after the meeting.[184] Failure to participate in good faith in framing the development and submission of a discovery plan may be sanctioned. After an opportunity to be heard, the court may require the party or the attorney to pay to any other party the reasonable expenses, including attorney's fees, caused by the failure.[185]

Illustration 9-8. Federal Form 35 illustrates the type of report that the parties are expected to file. First, the report should state who was present and where and when the meeting took place. Second, the report should state when the parties exchanged or will exchange the initial disclosures required by Rule 26(a)(1) or an applicable local rule. Third, the report should propose a discovery plan that indicates items of disagreement. Fourth, the report should discuss other items relevant to processing the case, such as planned dates for completion of various aspects of the case.[186]

* * * * *

Under the proposed amendments recommended by the Judicial Conference on September 15, 1999, Rule 26(f) would be amended to remove the requirement that the parties have a ''meeting'' before the discovery conference. Instead, the rule would only require that they have a ''conference.'' The time for the conference would be changed to at least 21 days before the Rule 16 pretrial scheduling conference, and the time for the report would be changed to no more than 14 days after the Rule 26(f) conference. The proposed amendments would also remove the current authority to exempt cases by local rule from the discovery conference requirement.[187]

2. The Timing of Discovery

Unless authorized by a specific federal rule,[188] local rule, court order, or agreement of the parties, the 1993 amendments prohibit the parties from seeking discovery from any source before the parties have met and conferred to prepare a discovery plan.[189] This prohibition applies to formal discovery, not to informal interviews with witnesses and other informal means of gathering information.[190] Rule 30(b)(2)(C) allows early depositions of persons who are expected to leave the United States and thus be unavailable for examination in this country.[191] The court may also permit appropriate discovery in certain other circumstances, such as in conjunction with requests for preliminary injunctions or motions challenging personal jurisdiction.[192] Under the proposed amendments

---

184. FED. R. CIV. P. 26(f).

185. FED. R. CIV. P. 37(g).

186. *See* Federal Form 35 in the Appendix of Forms accompanying the Federal Rules of Civil Procedure.

187. *See* 68 U.S.L.W., Sept 28, 1999, at 2168, 2169.

188. *See* FED. R. CIV. P. 27(a) (depositions before commencement of an action to perpetuate testimony), 30(a)(2)(C) (depositions of persons about to leave the country).

189. FED. R. CIV. P. 26(d).

190. FED. R. CIV. P. 26(d) advisory committee's note to the 1993 amendment.

191. *See* FED. R. CIV. P. 30(a)(2)(C) (requiring an appropriate certification in the notice).

192. FED. R. CIV. P. 26(d) advisory committee's note to the 1993 amendment (noting also that a local rule may exempt such situations).

recommended by the Judicial Conference on September 15, 1999, Rule 26(d) would be amended to remove the current authority to exempt cases by local rule from the moratorium on discovery before the Rule 26(f) conference.[193]

The Private Securities Litigation Reform Act of 1995, which was enacted to reform securities class action litigation,[194] provides that "all discovery and other proceedings shall be stayed during the pendency of any motion to dismiss, unless the court finds upon the motion of any party that particularized discovery is necessary to preserve evidence or to prevent undue prejudice to that party."[195] Furthermore, "[d]uring the pendency of any stay of discovery . . . , unless otherwise ordered by the court, any party to the action with actual notice of the allegations contained in the complaint shall treat all documents, data compilations (including electronically recorded or stored data), and tangible objects that are in the custody or control of such person and that are relevant to the allegations, as if they were the subject of a continuing request for production of documents from an opposing party under the Federal Rules of Civil Procedure."[196]

3. Sequence and Priority of Discovery

Federal Rule 26(d) provides that "[u]nless the court, upon motion for the convenience of parties and witnesses and in the interests of justice, orders otherwise, methods of discovery may be used in any sequence," with neither side gaining a priority of discovery.[197] This provision eliminated a "priority" rule that some courts had developed before 1970. Although federal practice has rejected the priority rule, the rule still prevails in some states.[198]

4. Limits on Discovery

Rule 26(b)(2) provides that the court shall limit the frequency or extent of discovery if it finds one of the following. First, if the court finds that the discovery sought is unreasonably cumulative or duplicative, or is obtainable from some other source that is more convenient, less burdensome, or less expensive,

---

193. *See* 68 U.S.L.W., Sept 28, 1999, at 2168, 2169.

194. Pub. L. No. 104-67, 109 Stat. 737. In response to the concern that the cost of discovery resulting from "fishing expedition" lawsuits often forced innocent parties to settle frivolous securities litigation, Congress sought to limit "abusive" discovery in such cases.

195. *Id.* § 101(b)(3)(B), 109 Stat. 737, 747; *see* Powers v. Eichen, 961 F. Supp. 233 (S.D. Cal. 1997) (phrase "during the pendency of any motion to dismiss" in the Private Securities Litigation Reform Act includes the time period during which a court is considering a motion for reconsideration of a dismissal decision); *see also* Paul Tyrell & George de Verges, *A Chilling Effect: The Impact of the Motion to Dismiss Under the Private Securities Litigation Reform Act of 1995,* 173 F.R.D. 556 (1997).

196. Private Securities Litigation Reform Act of 1995, Pub. L. No. 104-67, § 101(b)(3)(C)(i), 109 Stat. 737, 747. Willful violations may be punished by the court through "appropriate sanctions." *Id.* § 101(b)(3)(C)(ii), 109 Stat. 737, 747.

197. FED. R. CIV. P. 26(d). The court has the inherent power to set priority and time periods of discovery. Such is often the case in complex litigation.

198. *See* 8 CHARLES A. WRIGHT ET AL., FEDERAL PRACTICE AND PROCEDURE: CIVIL §§ 2045-2046 (2d ed. 1994).

the court is required to limit the discovery in an appropriate fashion. Second, if the court finds that the party seeking discovery has had ample opportunity to obtain the information sought by discovery in the action, the court must limit discovery. Third, if the burden or expense of the proposed discovery outweighs its likely benefit, the court must limit the discovery.[199]

In determining whether to limit discovery, the court must weigh (1) the needs of the case, (2) the amount in controversy, (3) the parties' resources, (4) the importance of the issues at stake in the litigation, and (5) the importance of the proposed discovery in resolving the issue.[200] Limitations on discovery may be raised by a motion for a protective order under Rule 26(c). In addition, the court may act on its own initiative to limit the frequency or extent of discovery after the court has provided reasonable notice to the parties.[201] The limitation of discovery may be accomplished in conjunction with a discovery conference under Rule 26(f) or some other pretrial conference authorized by the rules.[202]

The 1993 amendments also place presumptive limits on the frequency of certain types of discovery.[203] In absence of a stipulation by the parties in writing,[204] Rules 30(a)(2) and 31(a)(2) limit each side (the plaintiffs, the defendants, and third-party defendants) to a total of ten oral and written depositions.[205] The Advisory Committee expects the parties on each side of a multi-party case to confer and agree upon which depositions are "most needed."

---

199. *See* FED. R. CIV. P. 26(b)(2) (renumbered in 1993 from 26(b)(1) to 26(b)(2)). This restriction was added in 1983 in "an attempt to address the problem of duplicative, redundant, and excessive discovery and reduce it." *Id.* advisory committee's note to the 1983 amendment previously numbered as Rule 26(b)(1). Prior to 1983, the last sentence of Federal Rule 26(a) provided that the frequency of the use of the discovery methods listed in Rule 26(a) was not limited unless the court otherwise ordered. In 1983, this sentence was eliminated and a new paragraph was added to Rule 26(b)(1) to deal with the frequency of discovery under the Federal Rules of Civil Procedure. *See* FED. R. CIV. P. 26 advisory committee's note to the 1983 amendment. The purpose of the amendments to Rule 26(a) and (b)(1) was to deal with problems of excessive discovery that had developed. The Advisory Committee stated that the grounds for limiting discovery listed in the amended rule reflected the existing practice of many federal courts. Nevertheless, because federal district judges on the whole had been reluctant to limit the use of discovery, amendments were considered appropriate in order to prevent redundant or disproportionate discovery. Although the design of the amendments is not "to deprive a party of discovery that is reasonably necessary to afford a fair opportunity to develop and prepare the case," the amendments reflect the reality that more judicial involvement in the discovery process is desirable. *See* FED. R. CIV. P. 26(b)(1) advisory committee's note to the 1983 amendment. *See generally* Randy L. Agnew, Comment, *Recent Changes in the Federal Rules of Civil Procedure: Prescriptions to Ease the Pain?* 15 TEX. TECH. L. REV. 887 (1984); Margaret L. Weissbrod, Note, *Sanctions Under Amended Rule 26–Scalpel or Meat-Ax? The 1983 Amendments to the Federal Rules of Civil Procedure*, 46 OHIO ST. L.J. 183 (1985).

200. *See* FED. R. CIV. P. 26(b)(2). The 1993 revisions to this rule "provide the court with broader discretion to impose additional restriction on the scope and extent of discovery," thus enabling "the court to keep a tighter rein on the extent of discovery." *Id.* advisory committee's note to the 1993 amendment. It "also dispels any doubt as to the power of the court to impose limitations on the length of depositions under Rule 30 or the number of requests for admission under Rule 36." *Id.*

201. *See* FED. R. CIV. P. 26(b)(2).

202. *See* section N ("Pretrial Conferences and Orders") *infra.*

203. FED. R. CIV. P. 26(b) advisory committee's note to the 1993 amendment.

204. Subject to court order or local rules, under the 1993 amendment to Rule 29, the parties can ordinarily modify the limitations on discovery without court approval. *See* FED. R. CIV. P. 29.

205. FED. R. CIV. P. 30(a)(2) & 31(a)(2). A deposition under Federal Rule 30(b)(6) naming as a deponent a public or private corporation, a partnership, an association, or government agency is to be treated as a single deposition even though the organization may designate more than one person to provide testimony. FED. R. CIV. P. 30(a)(2) advisory committee's note to the 1993 amendment.

If the parties cannot agree, the court can be asked to resolve the dispute or to permit additional depositions.[206] The 1993 amendments also limit the number of written interrogatories to a total of twenty-five, counting all discrete subparts.[207]

To take additional depositions or to serve additional interrogatories, a party must obtain leave of court.[208] Leave of court is also required to depose a person more than once in the case.[209] Local rules or court orders may vary the numerical limitations on depositions and interrogatories.[210] In addition, local rules or court orders may limit the length of oral depositions under Rule 30. They also may limit the total number of requests for admissions under Rule 36.[211] However, in a deposition context, the court must allow additional time, if needed, for a fair examination of the deponent. The court must also allow additional time if the deponent or another party delays or otherwise impedes the examination.[212]

Under the proposed amendments recommended by the Judicial Conference in 1999, Rule 30(d) would be amended to establish a presumption that no deposition should last more than one seven-hour day, absent an agreement among the parties or a court order.[213] The proposed amendment would direct courts to allow extra time when it is needed for a fair examination of the deponent or if the deponent or some other person or circumstance delays the examination.[214]

5. Certification of Disclosures, Discovery Requests, Responses, and Objections

In 1983, subdivision (g) was added to Federal Rule 26. This subdivision imposed an affirmative duty to engage in pretrial discovery in a responsible

---

206. FED. R. CIV. P. 30(a) advisory committee's note to the 1993 amendment.

207. FED. R. CIV. P. 33(a).

208. FED. R. CIV. P. 30(a)(2), 31(a)(2), & 33(a).

209. FED. R. CIV. P. 30(a)(2)(B) & 31(a)(2)(B). This requirement does not apply to a deposition that is temporarily recessed to gather additional materials or for the convenience of counsel or the deponent. The Advisory Committee points out that "[i]f significant travel costs would be incurred to resume the deposition, the parties should consider the feasibility of conducting the balance of the examination by telephonic means." FED. R. CIV. P. 30(a)(2) advisory committee's note to the 1993 amendment.

210. FED. R. CIV. P. 26(b)(2). The specific reference to local rules and orders was intended to provide the court with broader discretion to impose additional restrictions on the scope and extent of discovery. It also was intended to authorize courts that develop case tracking systems based on the complexity of cases to increase or decrease the presumptive limits allowed in particular types of cases. *Id.* advisory committee's note to the 1993 amendment.

211. FED. R. CIV. P. 26(b)(2); *see also id.* advisory committee's note to the 1993 amendment (dispelling any doubt about a court's authority to impose such limitations). The Advisory Committee emphasizes that the parties should handle time limits on depositions by agreement. The Committee anticipates that limits on the length of depositions prescribed by local rules would be presumptive only, which could be modified by the court or the parties' agreement. This matter could be covered in the discovery plan and included in the court's scheduling order. FED. R. CIV. P. 30(d) advisory committee's note to the 1993 amendment.

212. FED. R. CIV. P. 30(d)(2).

213. *See* 68 U.S.L.W., Sept 28, 1999, at 2168, 2169.

214. *Id.* The court must also consider the general limitation whether the discovery is unnecessary or unreasonably duplicative or cumulative and whether the burden or expense of the proposed extension outweighs its likely benefit. *See* PROPOSED FED. R. CIV. P. 26(b)(1); FED. R. CIV. P. 26(b)(2)(i)-(iii).

manner.[215] The 1993 amendment extended the provisions of Rule 26(g) to apply to disclosures.[216] Rule 26(g) requires that all disclosures, requests for discovery, responses to discovery requests, and objections to discovery be signed by at least one attorney of record representing a party, or by the party when the party is not represented by an attorney.[217] Rule 26(g) further provides that the signature of an attorney or unrepresented party constitutes a certificate that the signer has read a discovery request, response, or objection, and that to the best of the signer's knowledge, information, and belief formed after a reasonable inquiry, it is: (1) consistent with the rules and warranted by existing law or a good faith argument for the extension, modification, or reversal of existing law; (2) not interposed for any improper purpose, such as harassment, delay, or needless increase in the cost of litigation; and (3) not unreasonably or unduly burdensome or expensive, given the needs of the case, the discovery already had, the amount in controversy, and the importance of the issues at stake in the litigation.[218] The signature on a disclosure "constitutes a certification that to the best of the signer's knowledge, information and belief, formed after a reasonable inquiry, the disclosure is complete and correct as of the time it is made."[219]

If the certification violates Rule 26(g) "without substantial justification," Federal Rule 26(g) requires the court to impose a sanction for the violation on the certifying person, or upon a party represented by an attorney who signed in violation of the rule, or both. The court may act after motion or on its own initiative in imposing the sanction.[220] However, the motion must include a certification that the moving party has in good faith conferred or attempted to confer with the person or party failing to make the disclosure or discovery.[221]

SECTION E. ORAL DEPOSITIONS

1. Commencing the Oral Deposition Process

(a) Notice of the Examination

A party commences the oral deposition process by giving "reasonable notice in writing to every other party to the action."[222] After the 1993 amend-

---

215. FED. R. CIV. P. 26(g) advisory committee's note to the 1983 amendment.

216. FED. R. CIV. P. 26(g) advisory committee's note to the 1993 amendment.

217. FED. R. CIV. P. 26(g)(1) & (2).

218. FED. R. CIV. P. 26(g)(2)(A)-(C); *cf.* FED. R. CIV. P. 11; Chapter 6(E) ("Verification and Good Faith Pleading") *supra.*

219. FED. R. CIV. P. 26(g)(1). An unsigned request, response, or objection must be stricken unless it is promptly signed after the failure to sign is called to the attention of the party or attorney who is obligated to sign. Moreover, a party is not obligated to make any response to an unsigned discovery request, response, or objection. *Id.* 26(g)(2).

220. FED. R. CIV. P. 26(g)(3), 37(a). The sanction may include an order to pay the amount of the reasonable expenses incurred because of the violation, including a reasonable attorney's fee. *Id.*

221. FED. R. CIV. P. 37(a)(2) & (3).

222. FED. R. CIV. P. 30(b)(1). Prior to the 1993 amendments, Federal Rule 30(a) provided that after commencement of an action, "any party may take the testimony of any person, including a party, by deposition upon oral examination." FED. R. CIV. P. 30(a) (prior to the 1993 amendments).

ments, an oral deposition may be taken without leave of court after the parties have met to prepare a discovery plan.[223] However, leave of court to take a deposition must be obtained under certain limited circumstances, such as when the deponent is in prison.[224] The notice of the deposition must state "the time and place for taking the deposition and the name and address of each person to be examined, if known," or if unknown, "a general description sufficient to identify the person or the particular class or group to which the person belongs."[225] The notice also must describe any documents or things the deponent will be required to produce at the deposition pursuant to a subpoena duces tecum.[226] If the "person" to be deposed is a corporation, partnership, association, governmental agency, or other organization, a party may simply name the organization and "describe with reasonable particularity the matters on which examination is requested."[227] Federal Rule 30(b)(6) then requires "the organization so named [to] designate one or more officers, directors, or managing agents, or other persons who consent to testify on its behalf . . . on matters known or reasonably available to the organization."[228]

Under the 1993 amendments, the party taking the deposition must also state the method by which the testimony will be recorded—sound, sound-and-visual, or stenographic means.[229] The party taking the deposition bears the cost of the selected method of recording. Any party may arrange for a transcription

---

223. FED. R. CIV. P. 26(b)(2).

224. *See* FED. R. CIV. P. 30(a)(2). Leave of court is required if a party seeks to take a deposition before the parties have had their discovery planning meeting. An exception is made when a party seeking to take a deposition certifies, with supporting facts, that the person to be examined is expected to leave the United States and will be unavailable for examination in this country unless that person is deposed before leaving. *See* FED. R. CIV. P. 30(a)(2)(C).

225. FED. R. CIV. P. 30(b)(1).

226. *Id.*

227. *Id.*

228. *Id.* This provision allows the organization to designate the particular matters on which each person will testify. *Id.* If it appears during the taking of the deposition that the person designated is unable to testify on the matters specified, the organization is under an immediate duty to designate a new person who will be able to provide that testimony. *See, e.g.,* Marker v. Union Fidelity Life Ins. Co., 125 F.R.D. 121, 126 (M.D.N.C. 1989). *See generally* Marlin M. Volz, *Depositions of Organizations: The Designation Procedure Under the Federal Rules,* 33 S.D. L. REV. 236 (1988).

229. FED. R. CIV. P. 30(b)(2) (unless the court orders otherwise); *see* Riley v. Murdock, 156 F.R.D. 130 (E.D.N.C. 1994) (concluding that a video deposition "is a superior method of conveying to the fact finder the full message of the witness in a manner that assists the fact finder in assessing credibility"). *See generally* Henry H. Perritt, Jr., *Changing Litigation with Science and Technology: Video Depositions, Transcripts and Trials,* 43 EMORY L.J. 1071 (1994). Prior to the 1993 amendment, the parties could stipulate in writing or the court could order that the testimony at the deposition may be recorded by other means, such as a videotape. In such a case, the stipulation or order had to detail the "provisions to assure that the recorded testimony will be accurate and trustworthy." FED. R. CIV. P. 30(b)(4) (prior to the 1993 amendment); *see* John A. Glenn, Annotation, *Recording of Testimony at Deposition by Means Other Than Stenographic Means Under Rule 30(b)(4) of Federal Rules of Civil Procedure,* 16 A.L.R. FED. 969 (1973). These provisions included naming the person before whom the testimony would be taken and prescribing the manner of recording, preserving, and filing the deposition. If a party wanted a stenographic transcription of the testimony, that party could have one made at that party's own expense. FED. R. CIV. P. 30(b)(4) (prior to the 1993 amendment). The parties could also take a deposition by telephone if stipulated in writing or by court order upon motion. For purposes of service of the subpoena under former Rule 45(d) and other provisions of the Federal Rules of Civil Procedure, a deposition taken by telephone was taken in the district and at the place where the deponent was to answer the questions. *See* FED. R. CIV. P. 30(b)(7) (prior to the 1993 amendment).

from the recording of a deposition not taken by stenographic means.[230] Furthermore, with prior notice to the deponent and other parties, any party may arrange for an additional method to record the deponent's testimony. That party bears the expense of making this additional record or transcript.[231]

(b) Subpoena to Compel Attendance

If the person to be deposed is a party, all that is necessary to take that party's deposition is the receipt of written notice of the taking of the deposition under Rule 30(b)(1).[232] When nonparties are involved, Rule 30(a)(1) specifically authorizes the use of a subpoena to compel attendance of witnesses at depositions.[233] Under the 1991 amendments to Rule 45(a), a subpoena for attendance at a deposition must issue from the district court for the district designated in the notice of deposition as the district where the deposition is to be taken.[234] The clerk in the district designated by the deposition notice issues a subpoena for attendance at a deposition.[235] As an officer of the court, an attorney "may also issue and sign a subpoena on behalf of (A) a court in which the attorney is authorized to practice; or (B) a court for a district in which a deposition or production is compelled by the subpoena, if the deposition or production pertains to an action pending in a court in which the attorney is authorized to practice."[236]

After the subpoena has been issued, it must be served on the nonparty who will be deposed. Anyone (other than a party) who is at least eighteen years old may serve the subpoena.[237] Rule 45(b)(1) provides that a subpoena shall be served by (1) delivering a copy of the subpoena to the person named (personal service) and (2) by tendering to that person the fees for one day's attendance and

---

230. FED. R. CIV. P. 30(b)(2).

231. FED. R. CIV. P. 30(b)(2) (unless the court orders otherwise).

232. *See, e.g.*, Collins v. Wayland, 139 F.2d 677 (9th Cir.), *cert. denied*, 322 U.S. 744, 64 S. Ct. 115, 188 L. Ed. 1576 (1944); *see also* FED. R. CIV. P. 37(d) (providing sanctions for the failure of a party to appear for taking of that party's deposition after notice alone); Jeffrey S. Kinsler, *The Proper Location of Party-Depositions Under the Federal Rules of Civil Procedure*, 23 MEM. ST. U. L. REV. 763 (1993).

233. FED. R. CIV. P. 30(a)(1). If a corporation or other organization is named in the subpoena and the designation procedure of Federal Rule 30(b)(6) is to be used, the subpoena must "advise a nonparty organization of its duty to make such a designation." FED. R. CIV. P. 30(b)(6). One advantage of using the notice of the taking of the deposition rather than a subpoena is that the party desiring to take the deposition probably has greater leeway in designating the place for taking it. Because a subpoena is not used, the restrictions set forth in Rule 45 do not apply. Nor is personal service required. It is sufficient to serve the notice on the party's attorney unless service on the party has been ordered previously. *See* FED. R. CIV. P. 5(a), (b). *See generally* M. Minnette Massey, *Depositions of Corporations: Problems and Solutions*, 1986 ARIZ. ST. L.J. 81.

234. FED. R. CIV. P. 45(a)(2). The 1991 amendments to Federal Rule 45 are discussed extensively in David D. Siegel, *Federal Subpoena Practice Under New Rule 45 of the Federal Rules of Civil Procedure*, 139 F.R.D. 197 (1992).

235. FED. R. CIV. P. 45(a)(3). The clerk issues a signed, blank subpoena to the party requesting it. The party then must complete it before service. *Id.*

236. FED. R. CIV. P. 45(a)(3)(A) & (B).

237. FED. R. CIV. P. 45(b)(1). When necessary, proof of service of the notice may be made by filing with the clerk "a copy of the notice" and "a statement of the date and manner of service and of the names of the persons served, certified by the person who made service." FED. R. CIV. P. 45(b)(3).

the mileage allowed by law.[238] Contrary to the procedure in many states, the witness and mileage fees must be tendered for the service to be valid.[239]

The subpoena may be served anywhere within the district of the court by which it was issued. It may also be served outside the district, provided service takes place within 100 miles of the place of the deposition specified in the subpoena. In addition, service may occur at any place within the state if authorized by a state statute or rule applicable to the state courts of general jurisdiction.[240] Furthermore, if a federal statute authorizes such service, the court may, upon proper application, authorize service of the subpoena at any other place.[241]

Illustration 9-9. *A*, a citizen of State *X*, sues *B*, a citizen of State *Y*, for $100,000 in a U.S. District Court for the District of State *Y*. *A* wants to take the deposition of *W*, a citizen and resident of State *Z*, which is 500 miles from State *Y*. *A's* attorney is authorized to practice in the district court in State *Y*, but not in State *Z*. *A's* attorney issues a subpoena for *W* from the U.S. District Court for State *Z* (a single district state). The subpoena is properly served on *W* at *W's* home in State *Z*. It commands *W* to attend a deposition proceeding at a specific time and place in *W's* home town in State *Z*. The subpoena is valid under Rule 45. *A's* attorney was authorized to issue the subpoena because it pertained to an action pending in a court (the State *Y* district court) in which the attorney was authorized to practice. The subpoena was properly issued from the district court in State *Z*, where the deposition is to be taken. The subpoena was served on *W* within the district where the deposition is to be taken. Finally, the subpoena

---

238. *See* FED. R. CIV. P. 45(b)(1). When the subpoena is issued on behalf of the United States or one of its agencies or officers, however, the fees and mileage do not need to be tendered. *Id.* With regard to "delivery" of the subpoena, *compare* Smith v. Midland Brake, Inc., 162 F.R.D. 683 (D. Kan. 1995) (service of a subpoena may not be accomplished by mail), Spencer Sav. Bank, SLA v. Excell Mortgage Co., C.A. No. 91-4909 (JCL), 1996 U.S. Dist. LEXIS 21125 (D.N.J. Feb. 15, 1996) (magistrate's authorization of Federal Express for service of a non-party subpoena held invalid where no signatures or receipts obtained from targets of subpoenas), *and* Agran v. City of New York, No. 95 Civ. 2170(JFK), 1997 WL 107452, 1997 U.S. Dist. LEXIS (S.D.N.Y. Mar. 10, 1997) (service by mail improper) *with* Doe v. Hersemann, 155 F.R.D. 630 (N.D. Ind. 1994) (service of a subpoena for a deposition can be accomplished by certified mail), King v. Crown Plastering Corp., 170 F.R.D. 355 (E.D.N.Y. 1997) (in-hand service not necessary; subpoenas served at place of residence and by mail), *and* Windsor v. Martindale, 175 F.R.D. 665 (D. Colo. 1997) (service by mail improper when attempted by plaintiff, but proper when by certified mail by United States Marshals); *see also* Khachikian v. BASF Corp., No. 91-CV-573, 1994 WL 86702, 1994 U.S. LEXIS 2881 (N.D.N.Y. Mar. 4, 1994) (delivery to attorney invalid); *cf.* Abbott v. Kidder, Peabody, & Co., 1997 WL 337228, 1997 U.S. Dist. LEXIS 8500 (N.D. Ill. June 16, 1997) (process servers made repeated, but unsuccessful efforts to serve witness; service was finally made as witness was driving out of her driveway; she saw process servers, yelled "Go away," and honked her horn, but they placed subpoena and witness fee under her windshield wiper arm; service held proper; Rule 45 does not require in-hand service, but only service that "reasonably" insures actual receipt of the subpoena by the witness").

239. SHEPARD'S MANUAL OF FEDERAL PRACTICE § 7.9, at 505-06 (rev. ed. 1979). Under 28 U.S.C. § 1821, the witness fee is forty dollars per day; the mileage fee is based on the deponent's travel to the place of attendance and return to the deponent's residence. Mileage computations are calculated at the official rate for government employees and are based upon a uniform table of distances adopted by the Attorney General. These tables are available in the U.S. Marshals' offices.

240. FED. R. CIV. P. 45(b)(2).

241. *Id.* A subpoena that is directed to a witness in a foreign country who is a national or resident of the United States is governed by 28 U.S.C. § 1783. *See also* section L ("Depositions in Foreign Countries") *infra.*

commands W to attend the deposition at a place within 100 miles of where W resides.[242]

* * * * *

Both the notice to take the deposition and the subpoena must designate where the deposition will be held. On timely motion, the court by which the subpoena was issued may quash or modify the subpoena if it "requires the deponent who is not a party or officer of a party to travel to a place more than 100 miles from the place where that person resides, is employed, or regularly transacts business in person."[243]

Rule 45(a) permits a command to produce evidence or to permit inspection to be joined with a command to appear at a deposition.[244] Thus, in addition to commanding a person to attend and give testimony, a subpoena may command a person to produce and permit inspection and copying of designated books, documents or tangible things in the possession, custody or control of that person. If a subpoena duces tecum is to be served, the designation of the materials to be produced must be attached to or included in the notice to other parties.[245] The subpoena may also require that person to permit inspection of premises.[246] A command to produce evidence or to permit inspection may also be issued separately.[247] If it is issued separately, a subpoena for production or inspection is issued from the court for the district in which the production or inspection is to be made.[248] However, a person commanded to make separate production does not need to appear in person.[249]

(c) Duty to Avoid Imposing an Undue Burden and the Procedure for Objecting to the Subpoena

A party or an attorney who is responsible for issuing and serving a subpoena is required "to take reasonable steps to avoid imposing undue burden

---

242. For a detailed discussion of the complexities produced by the interaction of Rule 45(a)(2), (b)(2), and (c)(3)(A)(ii), see David D. Siegel, *Federal Subpoena Practice Under the New Rule 45 of the Federal Rules of Civil Procedure*, 139 F.R.D. 197 (1992). For example, on the facts of this illustration, suppose W moves to quash the subpoena on the ground that, while it was served on W within the district and designates W's hometown as the place where the deposition will be taken, W "regularly transacts business" at a place in State Z that is 200 miles from W's home town. W argues that Rule 45(c)(3)(A)(ii) requires the court to quash a subpoena whenever it requires a nonparty to travel to a place that is more than 100 miles from where the nonparty "resides, is employed *or* regularly transacts business in person." The alternative phrasing, W argues, means that a subpoena may not command attendance more than 100 miles from *any* of the listed locations. This interpretation is wrong, but it is nevertheless supported by the language of the rule. *See id.* at 213.

243. FED. R. CIV. P. 45(c)(3)(A)(ii).

244. FED. R. CIV. P. 45(a)(1).

245. FED. R. CIV. P. 30(b)(1).

246. FED. R. CIV. P. 45(a)(1)(C).

247. FED. R. CIV. P. 45(a)(1).

248. FED. R. CIV. P. 45(a)(2). The subpoena for separate production and inspection may be issued by an attorney on behalf of a court in which the attorney is authorized to practice or a court for a district in which the production is compelled by the subpoena, if the production pertains to an action pending in a court in which the attorney is authorized to practice. FED. R. CIV. P. 45(a)(3).

249. FED. R. CIV. P. 45(c)(2)(A).

or expense on the person subject to the subpoena.''[250] This protection is backed by the issuing court's authority to impose ''an appropriate sanction, which may include, but is not limited to, lost earnings and a reasonable attorney's fee.''[251] A person served with a subpoena compelling attendance at a deposition, production, or inspection may wish to object on a number of grounds.

Illustration 9-10. Examples of objections include the following: (1) the subpoena fails to allow a reasonable time for compliance;[252] (2) the subpoena was served by a party or a person under the age of eighteen;[253] (3) the fees were not tendered properly;[254] (4) the subpoena was left at the dwelling of the witness rather than personally served;[255] (5) service was made in a location not permitted by Rule 45;[256] (6) the place designated for the taking of the deposition is in a location not permitted by Rule 45;[257] (7) the person served is not an agent of the corporate deponent; (8) the time or place of the deposition is inconvenient or burdensome;[258] (9) the person does not have possession or control of the subpoenaed documents; and (10) the production of the subpoenaed documents may be too burdensome.[259]

* * * * *

A person who is commanded to produce and permit inspection and copying may serve a written objection on the party or attorney designated in the subpoena. This objection must be made within fourteen days after the subpoena was served or before the time specified for compliance if that time is less than four days after service.[260] If the objection relates to a claim of privilege or protected trial preparation materials, the objecting party must expressly state that objection. To enable the demanding party to contest the claim, the objection must describe the nature of the documents, communications, or things for which protection is sought.[261] Failure to object expressly or to provide adequate information risks waiving the privilege. When such an objection is made, an order from the court issuing the subpoena must be obtained before such inspection or copying can occur. Upon notice to the person commanded to produce, the party serving the subpoena can move at any time for an order to compel production.

---

250. FED. R. CIV. P. 45(c)(1).

251. *Id.*

252. FED. R. CIV. P. 45(c)(3)(A)(i).

253. FED. R. CIV. P. 45(b)(1).

254. FED. R. CIV. P. 45(b)(1).

255. *See id.*

256. *See* FED. R. CIV. P. 45(b)(2).

257. *See* FED. R. CIV. P. 45(c)(3)(A)(ii).

258. *See* FED. R. CIV. P. 45(c)(3)(A)(iv).

259. *Id.*

260. FED. R. CIV. P. 45(c)(2)(B); *see* Concord Boat Corp. v. Brunswick Corp., 169 F.R.D. 44 (S.D.N.Y. 1996) (failure to object in writing within the time limits in Rule 45(c)(2)(B) normally results in waiver, but failure can be excused in unusual circumstances and for good cause).

261. FED. R. CIV. P. 45(d)(2). When a party objects to a subpoena on grounds of privilege, the party does not need to make the objection within the time limits specified in Rule 45(c)(2)(B); instead, Rule 45(d)(2) controls and allows a party claiming privilege to raise the objection at the time compliance with the subpoena is called for. *See* Tuite v. Henry, 98 F.3d 1411 (D.C. Cir. 1996).

If the court compels production, the court must protect any nonparty or officer of a party from significant expense resulting from the inspection and copying.[262]

(d) Failure of a Nonparty to Obey a Subpoena or of a Party to Attend a Deposition After Proper Notice

Federal Rule 45(e) provides that the failure to obey a subpoena "without adequate excuse" may be a contempt of the court from which the subpoena was issued.[263] Rule 45(e) specifically provides that an adequate excuse for failure to obey exists when a person is served with a subpoena purporting to compel attendance or production at an improper location.[264] Other examples of "adequate excuse" may include the inability to comply because the deponent did not have the subpoenaed documents or was too ill to attend the deposition.[265]

Federal Rule 37(d) provides that "[i]f a party or an officer, director, or managing agent of a party or a person designated under Rule 30(b)(6) [which requires a corporation or other organization to make such a designation] to testify on behalf of a party fails . . . to appear before the officer," the court may impose various sanctions for that failure.[266] These sanctions range from an order to pay reasonable expenses to an order striking out that party's pleadings.[267] Thus, parties may not remain completely silent even when they regard a notice to take the deposition as improper or objectionable.[268] As amended in 1993, the last sentence of Rule 37(d) indicates that the party must seek a protective order under Rule 26(c): "The failure to act . . . may not be excused on the ground that the

---

262. FED. R. CIV. P. 45(c)(2)(B). The 1991 amendment to Rule 45 imposed a requirement on nonparties to produce the documents in the manner that are kept in the usual course of business. Otherwise, they must be organized and labelled corresponding with the categories in the subpoena. FED. R. CIV. P. 45(d)(1). This requirement parallels a similar duty imposed on parties. *See* section H(2) ("Responding to Production Requests") *infra*.

263. FED. R. CIV. P. 45(e).

264. FED. R. CIV. P. 45(e). Otherwise, "adequate cause" is undefined. *Id.* advisory committee's note to the 1991 amendment. However, citing Walker v. City of Birmingham, 388 U.S. 307, 87 S. Ct. 1824, 18 L. Ed. 2d 1210 (1967), the Advisory Committee points out that a nonparty may "be guilty of contempt for refusing to obey a subpoena even though the subpoena manifestly overreaches the appropriate limits of the subpoena power." FED. R. CIV. P. 45(e) advisory committee's note to the 1991 amendment; *see* Chapter 6(F)(4)*(b)* ("Contempt") *supra*. At least when a nonparty has failed to obey the subpoena because it commanded attendance at an improper location, this should no longer be true. Rule 45(e) now explicitly provides for disobedience without fear of contempt when the subpoena commands attendance in violation of Rule 45(c)(3)(A), and the Advisory Committee's note seems to confirm that contempt is no longer permissible in this circumstance. *See* FED. R. CIV. P. 45(e) advisory committee's note to the 1991 amendment. More generally, it is arguable that the text of Rule 45(e) abolishes the *Walker* rule in any case in which an "adequate excuse" is found to exist. The *Walker* rule is discussed in Chapter 6(F)(4)*(b)* ("Contempt") *supra*.

265. *See* 9A CHARLES A. WRIGHT & ARTHUR R. MILLER, FEDERAL PRACTICE AND PROCEDURE: CIVIL § 2465, at 85-86 (2d ed. 1994). Some authorities suggest that when service of a subpoena has been improper, the subpoena may be ignored. Under this view, the defense of want of jurisdiction may be raised at the subsequent contempt proceeding. *See, e.g.,* SHEPARD'S FEDERAL PRACTICE § 7.09, at 506 (rev. ed. 1979). On the other hand, Professors Wright and Miller suggest that the "better view is that [a] witness should not be permitted to disregard a subpoena that [the witness] has not challenged by a motion to quash." 9A CHARLES A. WRIGHT & ARTHUR R. MILLER, FEDERAL PRACTICE AND PROCEDURE: CIVIL § 2465, at 84 (2d ed. 1994).

266. FED. R. CIV. P. 37(d).

267. *See* FED. R. CIV. P. 37(b), (d).

268. FED. R. CIV. P. 37(d) advisory committee's note to 1970 amendment.

discovery is objectionable unless the party . . . has a pending motion for a protective order.''[269]

2. Taking the Deposition

(a) The Officer in Charge

Unless the parties have otherwise agreed, Federal Rule 30(b)(4) provides that a deposition must be conducted before an officer appointed or designated under Rule 28.[270] Rule 28(a) designates the persons before whom depositions may be taken within the United States (*i.e.*, "before an officer authorized to administer oaths by the laws of the United States or of the place where the examination is held").[271] In addition, Federal Rule 28(a) permits a deposition to be taken "before a person appointed by the court in which the action is pending."[272] Such an appointment would be necessary when the deposition is to be taken at an isolated place where there may be no one readily available to administer oaths and take testimony.[273] Federal Rule 29 also permits the parties to stipulate in writing "that depositions may be taken before any person, at any time or place, upon any notice, and in any manner" unless otherwise directed by the court.[274]

(b) Beginning the Deposition

Pursuant to the 1993 amendments, the officer before whom the deposition is taken must begin by stating for the record: (1) the officer's name and address; (2) the date, time, and place of the deposition; and (3) the deponent's name. The officer then administers the oath or affirmation and identifies all persons who are present.[275] The parties then proceed to examine and cross-examine the deponent.[276] The officer giving the oath or someone acting under the officer's

---

269. FED. R. CIV. P. 37(d). Prior to the 1993 amendment of this rule, Rule 37(d) stated that "[t]he failure to act . . . may not be excused on the ground that the discovery is objectionable unless the party . . . has *applied* for a protective order." The 1993 amendment clarified that it is the *pendency* of the motion that may be urged as an excuse. "If the party's motion has been denied, the party cannot argue that [the party's] subsequent failure to comply would be justified." *Id.* advisory committee's note to the 1993 amendment.

270. FED. R. CIV. P. 30(b)(4).

271. FED. R. CIV. P. 28(a); *see also* section L ("Depositions in Foreign Countries") *infra*.

272. *Id.*

273. 8 CHARLES A. WRIGHT ET AL., FEDERAL PROCEDURE AND PRACTICE: CIVIL § 2082, at 671 (2d ed. 1994).

274. FED. R. CIV. P. 29.

275. FED. R. CIV. P. 30(b)(4). If the deposition is recorded by nonstenographic means, the officer must state the officer's name and business address, the date, time and place of the deposition, and the name of the deponent must be repeated at the beginning of each unit of recorded tape or other recording medium. *Id.* Federal Rule 30(c) provides a party with the option not to participate in an oral examination, but instead to serve written questions in a sealed envelope on the party taking the deposition, who is required to transmit them to the officer before whom the testimony will be taken. At the deposition, the officer will ask the questions of the deponents. *See* FED. R. CIV. P. 30(c).

276. If a deponent refuses to be sworn or to answer a question after being ordered to do so, the court in which the deposition is being taken may hold the deponent in contempt.

direction records the testimony.[277] Rule 30(b)(4) specifically cautions that the appearance or demeanor of deponents should not be distorted through camera or sound-recording techniques.[278]

(c) Producing Documents and Things

Pursuant to Federal Rule 30(f)(1), documents and things produced during the deposition "shall, upon the request of a party, be marked for identification and annexed to the deposition and may be inspected or copied by any party."[279] Rule 30(f)(1) also provides, however, that a person producing materials at a deposition may instead "offer copies to be marked for identification and annexed to the deposition and to serve thereafter as originals if the person affords to all parties fair opportunity to verify the copies by comparison with the originals."[280] The person producing these items can also "offer the originals to be marked for identification, after giving to each party an opportunity to inspect and copy them, in which event the materials may then be used in the same manner as if annexed to the deposition."[281] Rule 30(f) permits any party to move for an order requiring that the original be annexed to and returned with the deposition, pending final disposition of the action.[282]

(d) Depositions Being Conducted in Bad Faith or in a Harassing Manner

If a deposition "is being conducted in bad faith or in such a manner as to unreasonably annoy, embarrass, or oppress the party or a deponent," Federal Rule 30(d)(3) provides that a party or the deponent, at any time during the taking of the deposition, may seek court protection.[283] The court in which the action is pending or the court in the district where the deposition is being taken may order the officer conducting the examination to cease taking it. Alternatively, it may enter a protective order pursuant to Rule 26(c) limiting the scope or manner of the subsequent continuation of the deposition.[284]

(e) Rules of Evidence and Objections During the Examination

The examination and cross-examination of witnesses proceed as permitted at trial under the Federal Rules of Evidence. However, under the 1993 amend-

---

277. *See id.*

278. FED. R. CIV. P. 30(b)(4).

279. FED. R. CIV. P. 30(f)(1).

280. *Id.*

281. *Id.*

282. *Id.*

283. FED. R. CIV. P. 30(d).

284. *See* FED. R. CIV. P. 26(c); W.J. Dunn, Annotation, *Construction and Effect of Rules 30(b), (d), 31(d) of Federal Rules 30(b), (d), 31(d) of Federal Rules of Civil Procedure, and Similar State Statutes and Rules, Relating to Preventing, Limiting, or Terminating the Taking of Depositions,* 70 A.L.R.2D 685 (1960) (corresponding rules prior to the 1970 amendments).

ments, Rules 103 (dealing with offers of proof and timely objections) and 615 (exclusion of witnesses) do not apply.[285] During the course of the examination, objections may be made on a variety of grounds. The 1993 amendment to Rule 30 requires that any objection to evidence during a deposition "be stated concisely and in a non-argumentative and non-suggestive manner."[286] This amendment reflects the Advisory Committee's concern that some "[d]epositions have been unduly prolonged, if not unfairly frustrated, by lengthy objections and colloquy, often suggesting how the deponent should respond."[287]

Illustration 9-11. For instance, a party may object because the matter may be privileged information outside the scope of discovery permitted by Rule 26(b); the form of the question may be objectionable (*e.g.*, the question is "leading"); the information is inadmissible (*e.g.*, hearsay); or the witness is incompetent or unqualified (*e.g.*, the witness is mentally incompetent or the witness is not an expert).

* * * * *

What happens when an objection is made? The answer depends on the nature of the objection. Previously, if the objection was that the matter asked is outside the scope of discovery, the objecting attorney would state the basis for the objection and direct the deponent not to answer the question. However, a 1993 amendment provides that an attorney may so instruct a deponent only to (1) preserve a privilege, (2) enforce a limitation on evidence directed by the court, or (3) present a motion seeking protection from a deposition being conducted in bad faith or in an unreasonably annoying, embarrassing, or oppressive manner.[288]

When an attorney directs a deponent not to answer, counsel asking the question should be sure that the record indicates that the deponent refused to answer. Often, however, this formal refusal to answer is unnecessary. Counsel frequently stipulate that if an attorney directs a witness not to answer a question, it will be deemed that the officer has directed the witness to answer, but the witness still refuses to answer.[289] When the deponent refuses to answer, the discovering party must seek an order compelling an answer.[290] If the application is for an order to a party, the party seeking the answer should apply to the court

---

285. FED. R. CIV. P. 30(c). The exception in Rule 615 was designed to deal with the question whether other potential deponents could attend a deposition. According to the Advisory Committee, "[t]he revision provides that other witnesses are not automatically excluded from a deposition simply by the request of a party" invoking Rule 615. *Id.* advisory committee's note to the 1993 amendment. A court, however, can order exclusion under Rule 26(c)(5) as well as prevent the excluded witness from reading or otherwise being informed about the testimony given in the deposition. The revision applies only to potential deponents and does not attempt to deal with attendance by members of the public, the press, or other persons. *Id.*

286. FED. R. CIV. P. 30(d)(1).

287. *Id.* advisory committee's note to the 1993 amendment.

288. FED. R. CIV. P. 30(d)(1); *see* Boyd v. University of Md. Med. Sys., 173 F.R.D. 143 (D. Md. 1997) (under Rule 30(d)(1), an attorney may not instruct a witness not to answer a question during a deposition unless to assert a privilege, but must deal with objectionable lines of questions either by seeking a protective order prior to the deposition or discontinuing the deposition and seeking such an order).

289. Guy O. Kornblum, *The Oral Civil Deposition: Preparation and Examination of Witnesses*, 17 PRAC. LAW., May, 1971, at 11, 15, 25-26.

290. *See* FED. R. CIV. P. 30(d)(3); *see also* FED. R. CIV. P. 37(a)(2).

where the action is pending. If the application is for an order to a nonparty, the party seeking the answer should apply to the court in the district where the deposition is being taken.[291] In this way, the parties can obtain a judicial determination of the matter. The party seeking the answer has the option of completing or adjourning the examination before that party moves for such an order.[292] The party applying for the order must provide reasonable notice to other parties and all persons affected by the motion.[293] The court may award expenses pursuant to Federal Rule 37(a)(4)(A).[294] Ordinarily, a party should note other objections—for example, competency or hearsay—on the record and the deponent should answer the question.[295] If a party offers the deposition in evidence at the trial, the court will then rule on the objections.

(f) Effect of Failure to Object During the Examination

What happens if a party fails to object to the manner in which the deposition is taken or to the questions asked? The Federal Rules of Civil Procedure provide several answers, depending on the nature of the objection. The basic rule is that "[e]rrors and irregularities occurring at the oral examination in the manner of taking the deposition, in the form of the questions or answers, in the oath or affirmation, or in the conduct of parties, and errors of any kind which might be obviated, removed or cured if promptly presented, are waived" if they are not noted "seasonably" at the deposition.[296] On the other hand, a party does not waive "[o]bjections to the competency of a witness or to the competency, relevancy, or materiality of testimony . . . by [not] mak[ing] them before or during the . . . deposition, unless the ground of the objection is one which might have been obviated or removed if presented at that time."[297] In order to avoid the risk of waiver of objections, the parties frequently stipulate at the outset of the deposition that "all objections to questions propounded to the witness shall be reserved by each of the parties, save and except any objection to the form of the question."[298] However, this stipulation is both unnecessary and fraught with peril. While "form" of questions and answers are examples of objections which might be "obviated, removed or cured if promptly presented," they do not

---

291. FED. R. CIV. P. 37(a)(1) (as amended in 1993).

292. FED. R. CIV. P. 37(a)(2).

293. FED. R. CIV. P. 37(a).

294. Federal Rule 37(a)(4)(A) provides that if a motion to compel discovery is granted or the requested discovery is provided after the motion was filed, the court can require the party or deponent whose conduct necessitated the motion or the party's attorney advising the conduct to pay the reasonable expenses of the movant in making the motion, including reasonable attorney's fees. An opportunity to be heard must be given if it is shown that the motion was filed without the movant first making a good faith effort to obtain the discovery without court action, or that the deponent's refusal to answer was substantially justified, or that other circumstances make the award unjust. *See* FED. R. CIV. P. 37(a)(4).

295. *See* FED. R. CIV. P. 30(c).

296. FED. R. CIV. P. 32(d)(3)(B).

297. FED. R. CIV. P. 32(d)(3)(A).

298. Guy O. Kornblum, *The Oral Civil Deposition: Preparation and Examination of Witnesses*, 17 PRAC. LAW., May 1971, at 11, 15. The Advisory Committee likewise anticipates that the objections made during the depositions "should ordinarily be limited to those that under Rule 32(d)(3) might be waived if not made at that time." FED. R. CIV. P. 30(d)(1) advisory committee's note to the 1993 amendment.

comprise the entire class of such objections. Foundational objections also may obviated, especially if they relate to expert testimony.[299] More importantly, Rule 1101 of the Federal Rules of Evidence provides that "[t]he rule with respect to privileges applies at all stages of all actions, cases, and proceedings."[300] Unless a witness being deposed not only objects to questions calling for privileged information, but also refuses to answer short of a court order, the privilege will be deemed waived.[301] By stipulating that all objections except to form shall be reserved, the person being deposed may falsely assume that foundational and privilege objections may be asserted at trial. Rather than stipulating that the parties reserve all objections other than form, the parties should simply acknowledge that the deposition is being taken pursuant to the rules of civil procedure.

3. Review by the Witness, Changes, Signing, Certification, and Filing

If the deponent or a party wants the deponent to review the deposition prior to filing, the 1993 amendments require the deponent or the party to request the review before the deposition is completed. In response to that request, the deponent has thirty days to review the transcript or recording after being notified by the officer that it is available.[302] This change reflects an attempt by the Advisory Committee to reduce the problems sometimes encountered when depositions are recorded stenographically. Reporters often had difficulties obtaining signatures and return of the depositions from deponents.[303] If there are changes, the deponent is to sign a statement reciting any changes in form or substance.[304] The officer must then certify that the witness was sworn properly and that the deposition is a true record of the testimony given.[305] The certificate must also

---

299. *See* FED. R. EVID. 705.

300. FED. R. EVID. 1101(c).

301. *See, e.g.*, Daniels v. Hadley Mem. Hosp., 68 F.R.D. 583, 587 (D.D.C. 1975); Rosenfeld v. Ungar, 25 F.R.D. 340, 342 (S.D. Iowa 1960); Perrignon v. Bergen Brunswig Corp., 77 F.R.D. 455, 460-61 (N.D. Cal. 1978).

302. FED. R. CIV. P. 30(e); *see* Innovative Mktg. & Tech. v. Norm Thompson Outfitters, Inc., 171 F.R.D. 203 (W.D. Tex. 1997) (interpreting Rule 30(e) to allow a deponent to make changes that clarify answers, correct misstatements, or correct responses that were incorrect because the deponent did not understand the question).

303. *Id.* advisory committee's notes to the 1993 amendment.

304. FED. R. CIV. P. 30(e). Prior to the 1993 amendment, if one of the parties requested that the deposition be transcribed, the deposition was submitted to the witness for examination. The witness or witnesses then read the transcript. The officer was then to note any changes in form or substance upon the deposition along with the reasons given by the witness for such changes. The witness and the parties could agree to waive this review. After the deposition had been reviewed, the witness signed the deposition, "unless the parties by stipulation waive the signing or the witness is ill or cannot be found or refuses to sign." *Id.* (prior to the 1993 amendment). If the deposition was not signed within thirty days of its submission to the witness, the officer signed it, stating for the record "the fact of the waiver or of the illness or absence of the witness or the fact of the refusal to sign together with the reason, if any, given therefor." *Id.*

305. FED. R. CIV. P. 30(f)(1). This certification must be in writing and must accompany the record of the deposition. *Id.*

indicate whether any review was requested. If so, the changes that are made should be appended.[306]

Unless the court orders otherwise, the officer then seals the transcript securely in an envelope or package indorsed with the title of the action and marked "Deposition of _____."[307] The officer then promptly files it with the court in which the action is pending or sends it to the attorney who arranged for the transcript or recording. That attorney then "must store it under conditions that protect it against loss, destruction, tampering, or deterioration."[308] The officer must also furnish copies of the transcript or other recording of the deposition to any party or the deponent upon payment of a reasonable fee.[309] After the deposition has been filed, the party taking the deposition must give "prompt notice of its filing to all other parties."[310] However, a proposed amendment to Rules 5(d) and 30(f) would prohibit filing of depositions until they are used in the proceeding or the court orders filing.[311]

Federal Rule 32(d)(4) provides that a party waives "[e]rrors and irregularities in the manner in which the testimony is transcribed or the deposition is prepared, signed, certified, sealed, indorsed, filed, or otherwise dealt with by the officer" if those errors or irregularities are not raised with "reasonable promptness after such defect is, or with due diligence might have been, ascertained."[312] The means for raising these defects is a motion to suppress the deposition.[313]

SECTION F. DEPOSITIONS UPON WRITTEN QUESTIONS

Another way in which a party may take a deposition is through the exchange of written questions. Prior to the 1993 amendments, any time after the commencement of an action, a party desiring to take such a deposition of any person, including a party, could serve a set of written questions upon every other party to the action along with a notice of the deposition.[314] After the 1993 amendments, a party may take a deposition upon written questions after the parties have met to prepare a discovery plan, subject to the presumptive limit of ten depositions per side.[315] Like an oral deposition, the notice of a deposition upon written questions may use a general description to identify the proposed deponent of a corporation, partnership, association, or governmental agency pursuant to the provisions of Federal Rule 30(b)(6).[316] The 1993 amendments

---

306. FED. R. CIV. P. 30(e).

307. FED. R. CIV. P. 30(f)(1).

308. *Id.* Rule 30(f)(2) also requires the officer to retain stenographic notes of any deposition taken stenographically or a copy of the recording of any deposition by another method. FED. R. CIV. P. 30(f)(2).

309. FED. R. CIV. P. 30(f)(2).

310. FED. R. CIV. P. 30(f)(3).

311. *See* 68 U.S.L.W., Sept 28, 1999, at 2168, 2169.

312. FED. R. CIV. P. 32(d)(4).

313. FED. R. CIV. P. 32(d)(4).

314. FED. R. CIV. P. 31(a) (prior to the 1993 amendment).

315. FED. R. CIV. P. 26(b)(2) & 31(a)(2)(A).

316. *See* FED. R. CIV. P. 30(b)(6).

have shortened the total time for developing questions for cross-examination, redirect, and recross from fifty days to twenty-eight days.[317] Within fourteen days after the questions and notice have been served, a party may serve cross questions on all other parties. Within seven days after the cross questions have been served, a party may serve redirect questions on all other parties. In turn, a party may serve recross questions within seven days after being served with redirect questions.[318]

The person to be deposed may be compelled to attend the deposition by means of a subpoena.[319] After all questions have been exchanged, the party taking the deposition delivers a copy of the notice and copies of all questions to the officer designated in the notice. The officer then takes the testimony of the witness pursuant to the procedure for oral depositions prescribed by Federal Rule 30(c), (e), and (f) (oath, submission to witnesses, signing, certification, and filing).[320] After the deposition has been filed, the party taking the deposition must promptly give notice of the filing to all other parties.[321]

The same waiver rules described for oral depositions apply to errors and irregularities in the notice of the taking of the deposition, the qualifications of the officer, and the completion and return of the deposition upon written questions.[322] Objections to the form of the written questions submitted "are waived unless such an objection is served in writing upon the party propounding them within the time allowed for serving the next succeeding cross or other questions and within five days after service of the last questions authorized."[323] Like oral depositions, "[o]bjections to the competency of a witness or to the competency, relevance, or materiality of testimony are not waived by failure to make them before . . . the taking of the deposition, unless the ground of the objection is one which might have been obviated or removed if presented at that time."[324]

In practice, depositions upon written questions are rarely used. One study found that they were used in only two percent of the cases surveyed. In contrast, oral depositions were used in forty-nine percent of the cases.[325] The principal advantage of depositions upon written questions is that they usually cost less than oral depositions because counsel's attendance at them is unnecessary. The savings will be even greater when the deponent resides at a substantial distance.[326] Their principal disadvantage stems from their lack of flexibility: all direct, cross,

---

317. FED. R. CIV. P. 31(a)(4).

318. *Id.*

319. FED. R. CIV. P. 45(a)(1). Leave of court must be obtained to depose a person confined in prison or a person who has already been deposed in the action. FED. R. CIV. P. 31(a)(2).

320. FED. R. CIV. P. 31(b); *see* section E(3) ("Review by the Witness, Changes, Signing, Certification, and Filing") *supra*.

321. FED. R. CIV. P. 31(c). However, a proposed amendment to Rules 5(d) would prohibit filing of depositions until they are used in the proceeding or the court orders filing. *See* 68 U.S.L.W., Sept 28, 1999, at 2168, 2169.

322. FED. R. CIV. P. 32(d)(1), (2), (4).

323. FED. R. CIV. P. 32(d)(3)(C).

324. FED. R. CIV. P. 32(d)(3)(A).

325. *See* WILLIAM A. GLASER, PRETRIAL DISCOVERY AND THE ADVERSARY SYSTEM 53 (1968).

326. *See* John R. Schmertz, Jr., *Written Depositions Under Federal and State Rules as Cost-Effective Discovery at Home and Abroad*, 16 VILL. L. REV. 7, 36, 42-43 (1970).

redirect, and recross questions must be prepared before any of the deponent's answers are given.[327] Their effectiveness may also be hindered by the deponent's advance knowledge of the questions in certain instances.[328]

SECTION G. INTERROGATORIES TO PARTIES

1. Serving Interrogatories

Subject to the limitations adopted by the 1993 amendments,[329] Federal Rule 33 provides that any party may serve written interrogatories upon any other party.[330] Unlike depositions, which may be taken of any person, interrogatories cannot be served on nonparties.[331] Compared to depositions, interrogatories are simpler discovery devices. Interrogatories are merely questions directed to another party and thus do not involve complicated details that accompany arrangements for depositions, such as setting the time and place for the examination, obtaining a court reporter, ordering a transcription of the testimony, etc. As a result, interrogatories are ordinarily much less expensive than depositions.[332]

Interrogatories can be very useful for acquiring basic information and simple facts. Furthermore, with respect to corporate entities, interrogatories allow a party "to search the composite knowledge" of the corporate party because Federal Rule 33 requires it to answer on the basis of information "available" to it.[333] Thus, the person answering the interrogatories cannot avoid answering them by claiming ignorance when the information can be obtained from sources under the person's control, including employees or files.[334] On the other hand, interrogatories are not well suited to obtaining spontaneous statements because often the opposing attorney drafts the answers only after careful reflection.[335]

---

327. *See* 8A CHARLES A. WRIGHT ET AL., FEDERAL PRACTICE AND PROCEDURE: CIVIL § 2132, at 149 (2d ed. 1994). The authors suggest, however, that a deposition by telephone pursuant to Rule 30(b)(7) might be a preferable alternative. *See id.* at 149-50.

328. *See, e.g.*, Hamdi & Ibrahim Mango Co. v. Fire Ass'n, 20 F.R.D. 181 (S.D.N.Y. 1957) (deposition upon written questions need not be suppressed merely because counsel reviewed the questions with the deponent and supplied the deponent with a copy of them before the deposition took place).

329. *See* section D(4) ("Limits on Discovery") *supra*.

330. FED. R. CIV. P. 33(a). Prior to the 1993 amendments, interrogatories could be served upon the plaintiff after the commencement of the action without leave of court. They could be served on any other party with or after service of the summons and complaint on that party. *Id.* (prior to the 1993 amendment).

331. *See id. But see* Reed Dairy Farm v. Consumers Power Co., 227 Mich. App. 614, 576 N.W.2d 709 (1998) (provision in Michigan Civil Rules that was the equivalent of pre-1993 Rule 26(b)(4)(A)(iii), allowing the court, upon motion, to order further discovery "by other means," permitted interrogatories to nonparty experts under compelling circumstances); *cf.* FED. R. CIV. P. 26(b)(4)(B).

332. *See* 8A CHARLES A. WRIGHT ET AL., FEDERAL PRACTICE AND PROCEDURE: CIVIL § 2163, at 218 (2d ed. 1994).

333. *See* Donald P. Lay, *Plaintiff's Practical Use of Discovery Techniques*, 9 PRAC. LAW., Dec. 1963, at 43, 48; Iain D. Johnston & Robert G. Johnston, *Contention Interrogatories in Federal Court*, 148 F.R.D. 441 (1993).

334. *See* 8A CHARLES A. WRIGHT ET AL., FEDERAL PRACTICE AND PROCEDURE: CIVIL § 2172, at 284, n.10 (2d ed. 1994) (citing cases). The obligation extends to information in the hands of a subsidiary. *Id.* at 285-86.

335. *Id.* § 2163, at 219.

2. Answering Interrogatories

(a) Time for Response

The party served has thirty days after service of the interrogatories to serve a response, including objections.[336] The court may extend or shorten the time for response.[337] The parties may also agree in writing to a different time without leave of court, unless the agreement interferes with any time set for completion of discovery, for hearing of a motion, or for trial.[338] A proposed amendment to Rule 5(d) would prohibit filing of interrogatories and responses to them until they are used in the proceeding or the court orders filing.[339]

(b) Who Must Answer

Interrogatories are "to be answered by the party served or, if the party is a public or private corporation or a partnership or association or governmental agency, by any officer or agent, who shall furnish such information available to the party."[340] When interrogatories are addressed to a corporate entity, the corporation is entitled to choose the officer or agent who will answer them.[341] Each interrogatory is to "be answered separately and fully in writing under oath," and be signed by the person providing the answers.[342]

(c) Option to Produce Business Records

Rule 33(d) provides a responding party with an option to make business records available to the party seeking the information instead of answering an interrogatory, provided that "the burden of deriving or ascertaining the answer is substantially the same" for both sides.[343] If a party wants to produce business

---

336. FED. R. CIV. P. 30(b)(3). Prior to the 1993 amendment, Rule 33 provided that a defendant could serve the answers or objections within forty-five days after service of the summons and complaint. FED. R. CIV. P. 30(b) (prior to the 1993 amendment). The text of Rule 33 does not specifically address how outstanding interrogatories are to be handled upon removal from state to federal court. The Advisory Committee, however, indicates that the time to answer outstanding interrogatories should be measured from the date of the parties' discovery planning meeting required by Rule 26(f). Furthermore, if the number of outstanding interrogatories exceeds the twenty-five permitted by Rule 33, the interrogating party has three alternatives: (1) the interrogating party can seek leave to allow the additional interrogatories; (2) the interrogating party can simply specify which twenty-five to be answered; or (3) the interrogating party can resubmit interrogatories that comply with the limits set by Rule 33. FED. R. CIV. P. 33(a) advisory committee's note to the 1993 amendment.

337. FED. R. CIV. P. 30(b)(3).

338. *Id.*; FED. R. CIV. P. 29.

339. *See* 68 U.S.L.W., Sept 28, 1999, at 2168, 2169.

340. FED. R. CIV. P. 33(a).

341. 8A CHARLES A. WRIGHT ET AL., FEDERAL PRACTICE AND PROCEDURE: CIVIL § 2172, at 286-88 (2d ed. 1994); *cf.* FED. R. CIV. P. 31 (deposition upon written questions must be answered by the person deposed).

342. FED. R. CIV. P. 33(a)(1) & (2).

343. FED. R. CIV. P. 33(d). Rule 33 adopted this procedure from California practice as a means of relieving the answering party of a burdensome or expensive research into a party's own business records. *See* FED. R. CIV. P. 33(c) advisory committee's note to 1970 amendment to Rule 33(c) (as Federal Rule 33(d) was formerly designated).

records for examination, the party should specify the records from which the answer may be derived or ascertained. Such a specification must "be in sufficient detail to permit the interrogating party to locate and to identify, as readily as can the party served, the records from which the answer may be ascertained."[344]

(d) Objections

A party may base proper objections on a variety of grounds. First, the interrogatory may seek information outside the scope of discovery, as defined by Rule 26(b). Second, the interrogatory may place an undue burden on the answering party. This burden may be a financial one arising from the cost of preparing the answers, or it may be in the form of inconvenience to the answering party. Third, the interrogatory may seek unnecessary or repetitious information. For instance, the information may have been covered by prior interrogatories (or, presumably after 1993, prior disclosures). Fourth, the interrogatory may be so broad that an effective response is impossible. Fifth, the interrogatory may constitute improper harassment. Sixth, the interrogatory may call for legal conclusions or matters of "pure" law.

With respect to the latter objection, Federal Rule 33(c) states that an interrogatory that is "otherwise proper is not necessarily objectionable merely because an answer to the interrogatory involves an opinion or contention that relates to fact or the application of law to fact."[345] This provision, adopted as part of the 1970 amendments, resolved a conflict among the courts about whether interrogatories may elicit opinions, contentions, and legal conclusions. The Advisory Committee explained:

> Rule 33 is amended to provide that an interrogatory is not objectionable merely because it calls for an opinion or contention that relates to fact or the application of law to fact. Efforts to draw sharp lines between facts and opinions have invariably been unsuccessful, and the clear trend of the cases is to permit "factual" opinions. As to requests for opinions or contentions that call for the application of law to fact, they can be most useful in narrowing and sharpening the issues, which is a major purpose of discovery. . . . [U]nder the new language interrogato-

---

344. FED. R. CIV. P. 33(d); *cf.* J. Kraut, Annotation, *Propriety of Answer to Interrogatory Merely Referring to Other Documents or Sources of Information*, 96 A.L.R.2D 598 (1964). This provision was added in 1980 to prevent the answering party from directing the interrogating party to a mass of business records without specifying by category and location where the answer may be found. FED. R. CIV. P. 33(c) advisory committee's note to the 1980 amendment (as Federal Rule 33(d) was formerly designated).

345. FED. R. CIV. P. 33(c) (formerly 33(b)). Some interrogatories seek basic information and facts, such as the names of witnesses or the existence, location, and contents of documents. In contrast, "contention" interrogatories request an opposing party to (a) state what it contends; (b) state whether it makes a specified contention; (c) state all the facts upon which it bases a contention; (d) take a position, and explain or defend that position, with respect to how the law applies to facts; or (e) state the legal or theoretical basis for a contention. *See* B. Braun Med. Inc. v. Abbott Labs., 155 F.R.D. 525, 527 (E.D. Pa. 1994).

ries may not extend to issues of "pure law," *i.e.*, legal issues unrelated to the facts of the case.[346]

Before 1993, if a party objected to an interrogatory, Rule 33(a) provided that "the reasons for objection shall be stated in lieu of an answer."[347] The 1993 amendments now require a specific statement of "*all* grounds for an objection."[348] Furthermore, "[a]ny ground not stated in a timely objection is waived unless the party's failure to object is excused by the court for good cause shown."[349]

Illustration 9-12. Assume that *A* sends *B* an interrogatory requesting information concerning *B's* general pattern of consuming alcoholic beverages. *B* thinks that this interrogatory is intended solely to harass or embarrass *B*. *B* refuses to answer the interrogatory, but fails to state any reason for this objection. *B's* response is improper. Rule 33(b)(4) requires a specific statement of the grounds and "unstated . . . grounds for objection ordinarily are waived."[350]

Illustration 9-13. Assume, on the facts of *Illustration 9-12*, that *B* did object to the interrogatory and stated harassment as the reason. *B* has waived other grounds for objection, such as irrelevancy. In order to belatedly raise irrelevancy or other grounds as additional reasons for objection, *B* would have to convince the court that good cause existed to excuse *B's* failure to raise these reasons in a timely manner.

* * * * *

---

346. FED. R. CIV. P. 33(b) advisory committee's note to 1970 amendment; *see* Ronald G. Baker, Comment, *Civil Procedure—Opinion Interrogatories After the 1970 Amendment to Federal Rule 33(b)*, 53 N.C. L. REV. 695 (1975). Because of notice pleadings, contention interrogatories are considered to be useful in helping an opposing party prepare for trial. With the presumptive limits on interrogatories in federal court, it is unlikely that contention interrogatories will be the source of a major abuse of the discovery process. Courts often defer answers to contention interrogatories until the end of the discovery period. *See, e.g.*, B. Braun Med. Inc. v. Abbott Labs., 155 F.R.D. 525, 527 (E.D. Pa. 1994). As the Advisory Committee stated,

> Since interrogatories involving mixed questions of law and fact may create disputes between the parties which are best resolved after much or all of the other discovery has been completed, the court is expressly authorized to defer an answer. Likewise, the court may delay determination until the pretrial conference, if it believes that the dispute is best resolved in the presence of the judge.

See FED. R. CIV. P. 33 advisory committee note to the 1970 amendment. This approach allows a party to complete the discovery process before a party has to finalize its position. Forcing a party to answer at an early point may later prejudice it. *Cf.* McCarthy v. Paine Webber Group, Inc., 168 F.R.D. 448 (D. Conn. 1996) (motion to compel answers to contention interrogatories denied as premature because of burden it would impose on plaintiffs while discovery is ongoing). However, sometimes, a court will not postpone the answers when they "serve to clarify the issues and narrow the scope of the dispute." *See* B. Braun Med. Inc. v. Abbott Labs., 155 F.R.D. 525, 528 (E.D. Pa. 1994) (refusing to defer the answers to the contention interrogatories dealing with "prior art" because the defendants were apparently familiar with the technology involved and thus should have been prepared to answer; the answers would help define exactly how the invention differed, or did not differ, from the prior art for the purpose of determining whether the plaintiff's combination produced a new or different patentable function; prior art was also directly relevant to defendants' "obviousness" defense, which would defeat the patentability of the plaintiff's product if it could be shown that the invention was "obvious" in light of the prior art).

347. FED. R. CIV. P. 33(a).

348. FED. R. CIV. P. 33(b)(4) (emphasis added).

349. *Id.* Rule 26(g) also requires that a responding party indicate when information is being withheld under a claim of privilege or as trial preparation materials. *See* section B(1) ("Privilege") & B(2) ("Attorney 'Work Product' and Trial Preparation Materials") *supra*.

350. FED. R. CIV. P. 33(b)(4) & advisory committee's note to the 1993 amendment.

The 1993 amendments require the responding party to "answer to the extent the interrogatory is not objectionable."[351] This change emphasizes that the duty to provide full answers to the extent possible.[352] The attorney making the objections must sign them.[353]

Illustration 9-14. Assume that *A* sues *B* in federal court for violation of the federal antitrust laws. *B* manufactures aluminum siding. *A* sends *B* the following two interrogatories: (1) "State the name of all products manufactured from aluminum sheet"; and (2) "State the names of all manufacturers of aluminum sheet products in the United States, the locations of each manufacturer's facility, and the product or products produced at each of those facilities." Assume that these interrogatories are objectionable because of the overbreadth of the request. According to the Advisory Committee, if "an interrogatory seeking information concerning a lesser number of facilities or products would not have been objectionable, the interrogatory should be answered with respect to the latter, even if an objection is raised as to the balance of the facilities or products." Thus, if interrogatories referring only to aluminum siding and aluminum siding manufacturers would have been proper, *B* should answer as to them. Furthermore, even if *B* will need more time to answer some aspects of the questions, *B* must respond to those aspects of the questions that can be answered within the prescribed time.[354]

(e) Compelling an Answer

When a party has objected to an interrogatory or has otherwise failed to answer satisfactorily, the party submitting the interrogatory must apply for a court order to compel an answer.[355] However, before making the motion to compel a response, the 1993 amendments to the Federal Rules require the moving party to make a good faith attempt to confer and resolve the matter without court intervention.[356] Sanctions for an improper objection can be imposed.[357] Similarly, if the responding party has exercised the option to allow inspection of business records instead of answering, but the interrogating party believes that the burden on the requesting party to find the answers from the records is substantially greater than the party making the records available, the interrogating party may move for an order compelling a further answer under Rule 37(a).[358] If the court

---

351. FED. R. CIV. P. 33(b)(1).
352. *Id.* advisory committee's note to the 1993 amendment.
353. *Id.*
354. *See id.*
355. FED. R. CIV. P. 33(a)(5), 37(a).
356. *See* FED. R. CIV. P. 37(a)(2)(B) & 37(d).
357. *See* FED. R. CIV. P. 37(a)(4).
358. *See* 8A CHARLES A. WRIGHT ET AL., FEDERAL PRACTICE AND PROCEDURE: CIVIL § 2178, at 334-35 (2d ed. 1994).

does not find the burden to be substantially the same, the court still may refuse to order an unduly expensive or burdensome answer.[359]

(f) Correcting or Supplementing Responses

The 1993 amendments to Rule 26(e) require a party to correct or supplement a prior response to an interrogatory when the responding "party learns that the response is in some material respect incomplete or incorrect." Such a correction or supplementation is served as an amendment to the response.[360] However, an amendment is unnecessary if the additional or corrective information has otherwise been made known to the other parties during the discovery process or in writing.[361] In addition, under the amendments recommended by the Judicial Conference on September 15, 1999, a party must supplement its disclosures when the party determines that a witness or document may be used if the party previously had thought that the witness or document would not be used.[362]

SECTION H. PRODUCTION OF DOCUMENTS, ENTRIES ON LAND, TESTING, AND SAMPLING

1. Serving Production Requests on Parties

During litigation, a party frequently will want to inspect and copy various written documents, charts, photographs, drawings, records, or other data compilations in the control of another party. Similarly, a party may want to inspect, copy, test, or sample other tangible things in another party's control.[363] Subject to the limitations adopted by the 1993 amendments,[364] Federal Rule 34 allows a party to serve a request for production identifying and describing each item or category of items desired with reasonable particularity.[365] Similarly, as amended in 1991, Rule 45 allows such evidence to be subpoenaed from a

---

359. In such a case, the court, pursuant to Rule 26(c)(2), may require the interrogating party to reimburse the answering party for the expense of assembling the records and making them intelligible. *Id.* at 337 n.30; *see also* 8 *id.* § 2038, at 505.

360. FED. R. CIV. P. 26(e)(2).

361. For a discussion of the pre-1993 duties to supplement a response to an interrogatory, see William R. Slomanson, *Supplementation of Discovery Responses in Federal Civil Procedure*, 17 SAN DIEGO L. REV. 233 (1980).

362. *See* PROPOSED FED. R. CIV. P. 26(a)(1) advisory committee note.

363. *See* FED. R. CIV. P. 34(a).

364. *See* section D(4) ("Limits on Discovery") *supra.*

365. FED. R. CIV. P. 34(b). Prior to the 1970 amendment of Federal Rule 34, a party was required to seek a court order for the production of documents and things for the purpose of inspection, copying, or photocopying. In making such a request, the party was required to show "good cause." The good cause requirement was eliminated in part because the 1970 amendments made special provision for the production of trial preparation materials. Protective orders under Federal Rule 26(c) and the objection process provided by revised Federal Rule 34 were thought sufficient to handle claims of privacy, secrecy, undue burden, or undue expense. *See* FED. R. CIV. P. 34 advisory committee's note to the 1970 amendment.

nonparty in conjunction with or independent of a deposition.[366] In addition, a party may want to enter upon land or other property in the possession or control of another party to inspect, survey, photograph, test, or sample the property or a designated operation or object on the property.[367] The request must specify a reasonable time, place, and manner for the inspection or the performance of related acts, such as testing. As amended in 1991, Rule 45 permits the issuance of a subpoena to compel the inspection of premises in the possession of a nonparty.[368]

2. Responding to Production Requests

(a) Time for Response

The party receiving the request has thirty days after the service of the request to respond. The court may allow a shorter or longer time for response.[369] The parties may also agree in writing to a different time without leave of court.[370] A proposed amendment to Rule 5(d) would prohibit filing of production requests and responses to them until they are used in the proceeding or the court orders filing.[371]

(b) Objections

Rule 34(b) provides that the response must state, with respect to each item or category, that inspection and related activities will be permitted as requested or that an objection is made. A party must state a specific reason for the objection. If the objection extends only to part of an item or category, the party must permit inspection on the remaining part.[372]

Illustration 9-15. Reasons for objection might include that the request is outside the scope of discovery authorized by Federal Rule 26(b); the item is not

---

366. FED. R. CIV. P. 45(a); *see* section E(1)*(b)* ("Subpoena to Compel Attendance") *supra.*

367. FED. R. CIV. P. 34(a). Federal Form 24 illustrates the proper format for a request for production of documents, production of objects, and entry on the property. *See* Federal Form 24 in the Appendix of Forms following the Federal Rules of Civil Procedure; *see also* Annotation, *Propriety of Discovery Order Permitting "Destructive Testing" of Chattel in Civil Case*, 11 A.L.R.4TH 1245 (1982).

368. FED. R. CIV. P. 45(a)(1).

369. *See* FED. R. CIV. P. 34(b). Prior to the 1993 amendments, a defendant had forty-five days to respond after the service of the summons and complaint. *Id.* (prior to the 1993 amendment). *Cf.* Wolford v. JoEllen Smity Psychiatric Hosp., 96-2460 (La. 5/20/97) at *3-*4, 693 So. 2d 1164, 1166-67 (1997) (in a personal injury action, if the plaintiff requests production of any surveillance videotapes the defendant has taken of her, the defendant is entitled to depose the plaintiff about her physical injuries and activities during the time pictured in the videotapes before releasing the tapes).

370. However, the agreement cannot interfere with any time set for completing discovery, for hearing of a motion, or for trial. *See* FED. R. CIV. P. 34(b); FED. R. CIV. P. 29.

371. *See* 68 U.S.L.W., Sept 28, 1999, at 2168, 2169.

372. FED. R. CIV. P. 34(b). Rule 26(g) also requires that a responding party indicate when information is being withheld under a claim of privilege or as trial preparation materials. *See* section B(1) ("Privilege") & B(2) ("Attorney 'Work Product' and Trial Preparation Materials") *supra.*

in a party's possession, custody, or control; the documents are not designated adequately; or the inspection may be unduly expensive or oppressive.

* * * * *

A 1980 amendment required that the documents be produced as they are kept in the usual course of business or organized and labeled to correspond with the categories in the request. This amendment was designed to prevent parties from combining critical documents with others to obscure the critical documents' significance.[373]

(c) Compelling Production

If a party refuses to produce requested documents or permit entry or testing, the party seeking discovery must seek an order compelling discovery pursuant to Federal Rule 37(a).[374] However, before making the motion to compel inspection, the 1993 amendments require the moving party to make a good faith attempt to confer and resolve the matter without court intervention.[375] The successful party may be entitled to receive payment of reasonable expenses in securing the order or opposing the motion unless the party's position was not "substantially justified" or other circumstances make the award of expenses unjust.[376]

(d) Correcting or Supplementing Responses

The 1993 amendments to Rule 26(e) require a party to correct or supplement a prior response to a request for production when the responding "party learns that the response is in some material respect incomplete or incorrect." Supplementation is accomplished by serving an amendment to the response.[377] However, an amendment is unnecessary if the additional or corrective information has otherwise been made known to the other parties during the discovery process or in writing.[378]

SECTION I. COMPULSORY PHYSICAL AND MENTAL EXAMINATIONS

1. Securing Physical or Mental Examinations

A party's physical or mental condition will often be at issue in a lawsuit.

---

373. FED. R. CIV. P. 34(b) advisory committee's note to the 1980 amendment.
374. FED. R. CIV. P. 34(b).
375. *See* FED. R. CIV. P. 37(a)(2)(B) & 37(d).
376. FED. R. CIV. P. 37(a)(4).
377. FED. R. CIV. P. 26(e)(2).
378. For a discussion of the pre-1993 duties to supplement a response to an interrogatory, see William R. Slomanson, *Supplementation of Discovery Responses in Federal Civil Procedure*, 17 SAN DIEGO L. REV. 233 (1980).

Illustration 9-16. For example, did the defendant have defective eyesight? To what extent was the plaintiff injured as a result of a traffic accident?

* * * * *

One useful way of addressing the questions of physical and mental conditions is to force an individual to submit to an examination by a physician. Federal Rule 35 provides for such examinations in limited circumstances. Federal Rule 35 permits an order for a physical or mental examination of a party or of a person in the "custody or the legal control" of a party.[379] This rule requires that the condition examined must be "in controversy," and the party seeking the examination must show "good cause" for the order.[380] The order must specify (1) the time, place, manner, conditions, and scope of the examination and (2) the person(s) who will conduct it.[381]

The leading case construing the meaning of the "in controversy" and "good cause" requirements of Rule 35 is *Schlagenhauf v. Holder*.[382] In *Schlagenhauf*, a negligence action based on diversity of citizenship was brought in federal district court. The action sought damages for personal injuries suffered by passengers of a bus when the bus collided with the rear of a tractor-trailer. The named defendants were the owner of the bus, the bus driver (Schlagenhauf), the owner of the tractor, the driver of the tractor, and the owner of the trailer. Each defendant served an answer denying negligence. The bus owner cross-claimed against the owners of the tractor and trailer for damage to the bus. The bus owner alleged that the collision was due solely to their negligence in that the tractor-trailer was driven at an unreasonably low speed, had not remained in its lane, and was not equipped with proper rear lights. The owner of the tractor filed an answer to this cross-claim denying its negligence and asserting "[t]hat the negligence of the driver of the . . . bus proximately caused and contributed to . . . Greyhound's damages." It also alleged as part of its answer that the bus driver was "not mentally or physically capable of driving a bus at the time of the accident."[383]

The owners of the tractor and trailer then petitioned the district court for an order directing the bus driver to submit to both mental and physical examinations by one specialist in each of the following fields: (1) internal medicine, (2) ophthalmology, (3) neurology, and (4) psychiatry. The petition alleged that the mental and physical condition of bus driver was "in controversy" on the ground that it had been raised by the tractor owner's answer to the bus company's cross-claim. The petitioning parties supported the petition with a brief of legal authorities and an affidavit by the tractor owner's attorney. The affidavit stated that the bus driver had seen red lights ten to fifteen seconds before the accident, that another witness had seen the rear lights of the trailer from a distance of three-quarters to one-half mile, and that the bus driver had been involved in a similar

---

379. Fed. R. Civ. P. 35(a).

380. *Id.*

381. *Id. See generally* Paula M. Becker, Note, *Court-Ordered Mental and Physical Examinations: A Survey of Federal Rule 35 and Illinois Rule 215*, 11 Loy. U. Chi. L.J. 725 (1980).

382. 379 U.S. 104, 85 S. Ct. 234, 13 L. Ed. 2d 152 (1964).

383. *Id.* at 106-07, 85 S. Ct. at 236-37, 13 L. Ed. 2d at 157.

prior accident. While disposition of this petition was pending, the trailer owner filed its answer to the bus company's cross-claim and itself "cross-claimed" against the bus company and the bus driver for damage to its trailer. The answer asserted generally that bus driver's negligence proximately caused the accident. The cross-claim additionally alleged that the bus company and the bus driver were negligent by permitting the bus to be operated when both the bus company and the bus driver knew that the bus driver's eyes and vision were impaired and deficient. The district court ordered the examinations on the basis of the tractor owner's petition and affidavit. The Court of Appeals denied mandamus.[384]

In vacating the judgment of the Court of Appeals and remanding the case for further consideration, the U.S. Supreme Court pointed out that the requirements of Federal Rule 35

> are not met by mere conclusionary allegations of the pleadings—nor by mere relevance to the case—but require an *affirmative showing* by the movant that each condition as to which the examination is sought is really and genuinely in controversy and that good cause exits for ordering each particular examination.[385]

According to the Court, the moving party's burden will sometimes be met by the pleadings alone, such as when the plaintiff's own mental or physical injuries are asserted by the plaintiff as the basis for recovery in a negligence action, or when the defendant's own mental or physical condition is asserted by the defendant as a defense to a claim.[386] The Court emphasized, however, that Schlagenhauf had not asserted his mental or physical condition as a defense. Reviewing the allegations in the pleadings and the affidavit, the Court concluded that the proper showing had not been made:

> Nothing in the pleadings or affidavit would afford a basis for a belief that Schlagenhauf was suffering from a mental or neurological illness warranting wide-ranging neurological examinations. Nor is there anything stated justifying the broad internal medicine examination.
>
> The only specific allegation made in support of the four examinations ordered was that the "eyes and vision" of Schlagenhauf were impaired. Considering this in conjunction with the affidavit, we would be hesitant to set aside a visual examination if it had been the only one ordered. However, as the case must be remanded to the District Court because of the other examinations ordered, it would be appropriate for the District Judge to reconsider also this order. . . .[387]

---

384. *See id.* at 107-09 & n.3, 85 S. Ct. at 237 & n.3, 13 L. Ed. 2d at 157-58 & n.3.

385. *Id.* at 118, 85 S. Ct. at 243, 13 L. Ed. 2d at 164. The Court also noted that "[t]he ability of the movant to obtain the desired information by other means is also relevant." *Id.*

386. *Id.* at 119, 85 S. Ct. at 243, 13 L. Ed. 2d at 164.

387. *Id.* at 120-21, 85 S. Ct. at 244, 13 L. Ed. 2d at 165.

2. The Physician's Report

The party examined or against whom an order is entered is entitled to receive a copy of a detailed written report of the examining physician's findings, diagnoses, and conclusions along with all test results. If the discovering party delivers this report (and any like reports of earlier examinations of the same condition that the discovering party may have), the discovering party becomes entitled, upon request, to receive from the party against whom the order was made copies of reports of any examination, previously or thereafter made, of the same condition (unless in the case of a report of an examination of a non-party such as a person under a party's legal control, the party shows the inability to obtain it).[388] By requesting a copy of the examination or taking the deposition of the examiner, the party examined waives any doctor-patient privilege the party possesses with regard to other physicians who have examined the party for the same condition. The waiver applies in the action in which the examination is sought and in any other action involving the same controversy.[389]

3. Sanctions

The court may impose appropriate sanctions on a party who refuses to submit to an order providing for a physical or mental examination.[390] However, contempt of court is not available as a sanction.[391]

SECTION J. REQUESTS FOR ADMISSION

1. Requesting the Admissions

Subject to the limitations adopted by the 1993 amendments,[392] Federal Rule 36 permits a party to serve on any other party a request to admit (1) the truth of any matter within the scope of Federal Rule 26(b)(1) relating to statements or opinions of fact or the application of law to fact; or (2) the genuineness of any documents described in the request.[393] Copies of the

---

388. FED. R. CIV. P. 35(b)(1).

389. *See* FED. R. CIV. P. 35(b)(2).

390. *See* FED. R. CIV. P. 37(b)(2).

391. FED. R. CIV. P. 37(b)(2)(E).

392. *See* section D(4) ("Limits on Discovery") *supra.* Specifically, requests for admissions may not be served until the parties have conferred under Rule 26(f) to arrange for automatic disclosure and develop a discovery plan. *See* FED. R. CIV. P. 26(d) & 36(a).

393. FED. R. CIV. P. 36(a); *cf.* Russell G. Donaldson, Annotation, *Permissible Scope, Respecting Nature of Inquiry, or Demand for Admission Under Modern State Civil Rules of Procedure,* 42 A.L.R.4TH 489 (1985). Prior to the 1993 amendments, like interrogatories served under Federal Rule 33, requests for admission may be served upon the plaintiff after the commencement of the action without leave of court; they may be served on any other party with or after service of the summons and complaint on that party.

documents must be served with the request unless they have been furnished previously or made available for inspection and copying.[394]

2. Responding to the Request

If no response is made within thirty days, the matter is *admitted*.[395] The court, upon motion, may extend or shorten the time for response.[396] The parties may also agree in writing to a different time without leave of court, unless the agreement would interfere with any time set for completion of discovery, for hearing of a motion, or for trial.[397]

If the party served with a request for admission intends to deny the request, Federal Rule 36(a) requires that the denial be specific and provides that the denial must "fairly meet the substance of the requested admission."[398] Furthermore, if "good faith requires that a party qualify an answer or deny only a part of the requested matter, the party must specify so much of it as true and deny only the remainder."[399] What happens if a party cannot truthfully admit or deny the request? Rule 36(a) permits a party to so state, provided that party sets forth "in detail" the reasons. Lack of information and knowledge, however, is an acceptable reason only when the answering party "states that the party has made reasonable inquiry and that the information known or readily obtainable by the party is insufficient to enable the party to admit or deny" the request.[400] The 1970 amendments added this provision to resolve a sharp split of authority concerning the extent to which an answering party had to seek out additional information before the answering party could base an answer on lack of information. The issue was resolved by establishing a duty to make a "reasonable inquiry" from "readily obtainable" sources.[401]

In addition to specifically admitting or denying a request or stating that the matter cannot be truthfully admitted or denied, a party may object to a request and thus refuse to answer. If an objection is made, Federal Rule 36(a) requires the party to state the reasons for the objection.[402] Such reasons include irrelevancy, privilege, or that the form of the request is so defective that an answer to

---

394. *Id.* Each matter should be set forth separately, as required by Rule 36(a). *See* Federal Form 25 in the Appendix of Forms following the Federal Rules of Civil Procedure ("Request for Admission under Rule 36").

395. FED. R. CIV. P. 36(a). Prior to the 1993 amendments, Rule 36(a) provided a defendant had forty-five days to respond after the service of the summons and complaint before the matter was admitted. *Id.* (prior to the 1993 amendment).

396. *Id.*; *see* Annotation, *Extension of Time for Serving Response to Request for Admissions Under Rule 36(a), as Amended, of Federal Rules of Civil Procedure*, 46 A.L.R. FED. 821 (1980).

397. *Id.*; FED. R. CIV. P. 29. On September 15, 1999, the Judicial Conference recommended an amendment to Rule 5(d) that would prohibit filing of requests for admission and responses to them until they are used in the proceeding or the court orders filing. *See* 68 U.S.L.W., Sept 28, 1999, at 2168, 2169.

398. FED. R. CIV. P. 36(a).

399. *Id.*; *cf.* FED. R. CIV. P. 8(b) (similar requirements for responsive pleading).

400. FED. R. CIV. P. 36(a).

401. *See* FED. R. CIV. P. 36(a) advisory committee note to the 1970 amendment; *see* J.P. Ludington, Annotation, *Party's Duty Under Federal Rule of Civil Procedure 36(a) and Similar State Statutes and Rules, to Respond to Requests for Admission of Facts Not Within His Personal Knowledge*, 20 A.L.R.3D 756 (1968).

402. FED. R. CIV. P. 36(a).

it cannot be made.[403] The 1970 amendment to Rule 36(a) clarified that the answering party cannot object on the ground that the request relates to statements or opinions of fact or of the application of law to fact. An objection is still available when admissions of law unrelated to the facts of the case are requested.[404]

What happens when a party objects to a request or states that the party is unable to admit or deny the request? Currently, Federal Rule 36(a) provides that the party seeking the request "may move to determine the sufficiency of the answers or objections."[405] Thus, the party seeking the admissions has the option of seeking court intervention. This same procedure can be used to challenge "answers that are not in conformity with the requirements of the rule," such as when a denial is not "specific" or when the inability to admit or deny the request has not been explained "in detail," as required by Rule 36(a).[406]

If the court decides that an objection is unjustified, the court will order that an answer be served. If the court decides "that an answer does not comply with the requirements of [Federal Rule 36]," the court "may order either that the matter is admitted or that an amended answer be served."[407] Instead of these orders, the court may postpone ruling on the motion until a pretrial conference or another time before trial.[408]

Assume that a party denies the genuineness of a document or the truth of any matter as requested under Federal Rule 36 and that the requesting party proves the genuineness of the document or the truth of the matter at trial. The requesting party may then apply for a court order requiring the other party to pay that party's reasonable expenses incurred in making that proof, including reasonable attorney's fees. However, such an order would be improper if the court "finds that (1) the request was held objectionable pursuant to Rule 36(a), or (2) the admission sought was of no substantial importance, or (3) the party failing to admit had reasonable ground to believe the party might prevail on the matter, or (4) there was other good reason for the failure to admit."[409]

SECTION K. DISCOVERY BEFORE COMMENCING AN ACTION OR PENDING AN APPEAL

Special rules apply when a person wants to perpetuate testimony, inspect and copy documents or other things, or obtain a physical or mental examination of someone for use in a *future* action. To engage in such discovery, the person

---

403. *See* 8A CHARLES A. WRIGHT ET AL., FEDERAL PRACTICE AND PROCEDURE § 2262, at 562 (2d ed. 1994).

404. *See* FED. R. CIV. P. 36(a) advisory committee's note to the 1970 amendment; *cf.* FED. R. CIV. P. 33(c) (similar provision relating to interrogatories).

405. FED. R. CIV. P. 36(a) & advisory committee's note to the 1970 amendment (noting the elimination of the requirement that the objecting party automatically move for a hearing on the objection); *cf.* Annotation, *Formal Sufficiency of Response to Request for Admissions Under State Discovery Rules*, 8 A.L.R.4TH 728 (1981).

406. FED. R. CIV. P. 36(a).

407. *Id.*

408. *Id.*

409. FED. R. CIV. P. 37(c)(2).

seeking it must file a verified petition in the name of the petitioner that meets the requirements of Rule 27(a)(1).[410] The petition may be filed in any district where any one of the expected adverse parties resides.[411] Notice of when the petition will be heard, as well as the petition itself, must be served upon each person named in the petition pursuant to Federal Rule 4.

If the petitioning party cannot make service on an expected adverse party after a diligent effort, the court may order service by other means. The court may also appoint an attorney to represent adverse parties not served pursuant to Rule 4.[412] Furthermore, if the court "is satisfied that the perpetuation of the testimony may prevent a failure or delay of justice," the court may order discovery "of the character provided for by [Federal] Rules 34 and 35."[413] Similarly, special rules apply to the perpetuation of testimony pending an appeal.[414]

SECTION L. DEPOSITIONS IN FOREIGN COUNTRIES

Rule 28(b) governs depositions taken in foreign countries.[415] Rule 28(b) was amended in 1993 "to make effective use of the Hague Convention on the Taking of Evidence Abroad in Civil or Commercial Matters."[416] As amended, the Federal Rules of Civil Procedure envision four methods for taking depositions

---

410. FED. R. CIV. P. 27(a)(1); *see also* Elaine K. Zipp, Annotation, *Right to Perpetuation of Testimony Under Rule 27 of Federal Rules of Civil Procedure*, 60 A.L.R. FED. 924 (1982). Rule 27(a)(1) requires the following be demonstrated:

> 1, [T]hat the petitioner expects to be a party to an action cognizable in a court of the United States but is presently unable to bring it or cause it to be brought, 2, the subject matter of the expected action and the petitioner's interest therein, 3, the facts which the petitioner desires to establish by the proposed testimony and the reasons for desiring to perpetuate it, 4, the names or a description of the persons the petitioner expects will be adverse parties and their addresses so far as known, and 5, the names and addresses of the persons to be examined and the substance of the testimony which the petitioner expects to elicit from each, and shall ask for an order authorizing the petitioner to take the depositions of the persons to be examined named in the petition, for the purpose of perpetuating their testimony.

FED. R. CIV. P. 27(a)(1). A party seeking to perpetuate testimony need not show that the testimony is unique. *See In re* Bay County Middlegrounds Landfill Site, 171 F.3d 1044, 1047-48 (6th Cir. 1999) (testimony need not be unique, but only relevant). The courts are split whether Rule 27 can be used for the purpose of determining whether the plaintiff has a valid claim against the defendant. *Compare, e.g., In re* Ford, 170 F.R.D. 504 (M.D. Ala. 1997) (no) *with In re* Alpha Indus., Inc., 159 F.R.D. 456 (S.D.N.Y. 1995) (inability to file because plaintiff did not know identity of defendant was sufficient to show that evidence was in danger of being lost).

411. FED. R. CIV. P. 27(a)(1).

412. FED. R. CIV. P. 27(a)(2). In two places, Rule 27 currently refers to service "in the manner provided in Rule 4(d)." *Id.* However, as amended in 1993, Rule 4(d) no longer provides for this manner of service. Instead, Rule 4(d) now contains the provisions governing waiver of service. Thus, until amended to conform with current Rule 4, Rule 27 should be read as if it referred to service "in the manner provided in Rule 4(e)-(j)" and to "parties who have been served in the manner prescribed in Rule 4(e)-(j)."

413. FED. R. CIV. P. 27(a)(3).

414. *See* FED. R. CIV. P. 27(b).

415. FED. R. CIV. P. 28(b).

416. *Id.* advisory committee's note to the 1993 amendment. The Hague Convention procedures are supplementary rather than mandatory replacement of the federal discovery rules. *See* Société Nationale Industrielle Aérocspatiale v. United States Dist. Court, 482 U.S. 522, 529-32, 107 S. Ct. 2542, 2548-50, 96 L. Ed. 2d 461, 474-77 (1987).

in foreign countries: (1) according to any applicable treaty or convention; (2) by sending notice to the other parties of an intention to take a deposition before an officer who is authorized to administer oaths in the foreign country by either its law or the law of the United States; (3) by the court's commissioning of a person to give the oath and take the deposition in the foreign country; and (4) pursuant to a letter of request.[417] However, the party taking the deposition must ordinarily conform to an applicable treaty or convention if an effective deposition can be taken by such internationally approved means.[418]

SECTION M. USE OF DISCOVERY AT TRIAL

1. Rule 36 Admissions

Admissions under Federal Rule 36 are binding unless the court permits a party to withdraw or amend them. In the terms of Rule 36, the matter is "conclusively established."[419]

Illustration 9-17. Assume that a party has admitted the following request: "The defendant's barn is red." For purposes of the litigation, the fact that the barn is red is "conclusively established." It eliminates the issue and makes proof of the matter admitted unnecessary.

2. Answers to Interrogatories

In contrast to a Federal Rule 36 admission, an answer to a Federal Rule 33 interrogatory is not binding on the party.

Illustration 9-18. Assume the defendant responds to an interrogatory by stating that the defendant's barn is red. At trial, the defendant still may offer evidence that the barn is black. Obviously, the prior inconsistent answer weakens the defendant's case. The trier of fact in such an instance must weigh all of the evidence, including the inconsistent answer.[420]

---

417. *See* FED. R. CIV. P. 28(b). The 1993 amendment changed the reference from a "letter rogatory" to a "letter of request" because a letter of request is the primary method provided by the Hague Convention. A letter rogatory is "essentially a form of a letter of request." *Id.* advisory committee's note to the 1993 amendment. Letters rogatory are formal, written communications from a court in which an action is pending to a court or judge in a foreign country. Such letters request a foreign court to use its process to have the testimony of a witness within its jurisdiction taken before it. Ordinarily, letters rogatory are channeled through the U.S. State Department to the foreign country involved. Whether letters rogatory will be honored or not depends entirely on comity or applicable treaties. *See* 8 CHARLES A. WRIGHT ET AL., FEDERAL PRACTICE AND PROCEDURE: CIVIL § 2083, at 674-75 (2d ed. 1994).

418. FED. R. CIV. P. 28(b) advisory committee's note to the 1993 amendment.

419. FED. R. CIV. P. 36(b).

420. *See, e.g.*, Freed v. Erie Lackawanna Ry., 445 F.2d 619 (6th Cir. 1971), *cert. denied*, 404 U.S. 1017, 92 S. Ct. 678, 30 L. Ed. 2d 665 (1972).

3. Depositions

With respect to the use of testimony taken in a deposition, the Federal Rules of Civil Procedure show a clear preference for oral testimony of witnesses in open court.[421] Thus, the rules permit the parties to use depositions under limited circumstances at a hearing or trial. However, such use must be consistent with the Federal Rules of Evidence. A 1993 amendment to Rule 32 added a special restriction when a party has taken a deposition of a person about to leave the country without leave of court. Such a deposition may not be used against a party who receives minimal notice but is unable to obtain a court ruling on a motion for a protective order seeking to delay or change the place of the deposition.[422]

Rule 32 of the Federal Rules of Civil Procedure prescribes three specific situations in which depositions may be used. First, any party may use any deposition to contradict or impeach the testimony of deponent as a witness.[423] Thus, the party would usually use such a deposition to show a prior inconsistent statement for impeachment purposes.

Illustration 9-19. Assume that *W*, an observer of an alleged drag race, testifies at a hearing or trial that *W* believes the vehicles were not drag racing. *W's* contrary statements in a prior deposition can be used to cast doubt on *W's* credibility.[424]

* * * * *

Second, an adverse party may use ''for any purpose'' the deposition of a party or anyone who at the time of taking the deposition was an officer, director, or managing agent, or a person designated under Federal Rule 30(b)(6) or 31(a) to testify on behalf of a public or private corporation, partnership or association or governmental agency that is a party.[425] A party will frequently use such a deposition at trial to prove something the deponent asserted in the deposition that is relevant to the action.

Illustration 9-20. If the defendant (*D*) admitted that *D* was drag racing in *D's* deposition, *P* could introduce *D's* statement in evidence to prove that the defendant was, in fact, drag racing. The plaintiff (*P*) could do so without regard to whether *D* was available to testify. Nor would *P* be limited to introducing the statement for impeachment purposes.[426]

* * * * *

---

421. *See* FED. R. CIV. P. 32(a)(3)(E).

422. FED. R. CIV. P. 32(a); *see also* FED. R. CIV. P. 30(a)(2)(C).

423. FED. R. CIV. P. 32(a)(1).

424. The prior out-of-court statement of an ordinary witness can be used to impeach the testimony of the witness and is not consider hearsay for that purpose because of the theory of impeachment by prior inconsistent statement. Because of the effect of Federal Rule of Evidence 801(d)(1), such a statement would also be admissible as affirmative proof of the matters covered by the statement. Thus, in this situation, there would be some evidence before the jury that the parties were not drag racing based on *W's* testimony at the hearing or trial; there also would be some evidence before the jury that they were drag racing. *See* FED. R. EVID. 801(d)(1)(A); *see* Chapter 11(I)(6) (''Objections, Cross-Examination, and Impeachment'') *infra*.

425. FED. R. CIV. P. 32(a)(2).

426. *See* Chapter 11(I)(3)*(a)* (''Admissions of a Party Opponent'') *infra*.

Third, any party may use the deposition of a witness, whether or not a party, who has died or is unavailable due to another recognized cause.[427]

Illustration 9-21. Assume that *W*, a witness, stated in a deposition that *D's* car was drag racing. If *W* is unavailable, *P* may read the relevant portion of *W's* deposition at the hearing or trial to prove that *D*, in fact, was drag racing.

* * * * *

Unless the court otherwise directs, a party offering a deposition may offer it in a stenographic or nonstenographic form. If a party offers it in a nonstenographic form, the offering party must provide the court with a transcript of the portions offered. Furthermore, on request of any party in a case tried before a jury, deposition testimony offered for purposes other than impeachment must be presented in nonstenographic form, if available. The court may change this requirement if a party shows good cause.[428] If a party introduces part of the deposition into evidence, the adverse party may require the introduction of any other part which, in fairness, ought to be considered with the part introduced. In addition, any party may then offer any other part of the deposition in evidence.[429]

Illustration 9-22. Thus, in *Illustration 9-21, D* may require *P* to introduce the part of *W's* deposition admitting that *W* had consumed a twelve-pack of beer just before *W* observed the "race."

SECTION N. PRETRIAL CONFERENCES AND ORDERS

The original purposes of Federal Rule 16, governing pretrial conferences, were to improve the quality of justice in the federal courts by sharpening the preparation and presentation of cases, to eliminate trial surprise, and to improve and facilitate the settlement process. Rule 16 largely achieved these objectives. However, Rule 16 was not as successful in achieving effective and efficient case management as it might have been. As a consequence, extensive amendments

---

427. FED. R. CIV. P. 32(a)(3). Rule 32(a)(3) permits the deposition to be used if the court finds as follows:
(A) that the witness is dead; or
(B) that the witness is at a greater distance than 100 miles from the place of trial or hearing, or is out of the United States, unless it appears that the absence of the witness was procured by the party offering the deposition; or
(C) that the witness is unable to attend or testify because of age, illness, infirmity, or imprisonment; or
(D) that the party offering the deposition has been unable to procure the attendance of the witness by subpoena; or
(E) upon application and notice, that such exceptional circumstances exist as to make it desirable, in the interest of justice and with due regard to the importance of presenting the testimony of witnesses orally in open court, to allow the deposition to be used.
Id.; see Annotation, *Admissibility of Deposition, Under Rule 32(a)(3)(B) of Federal Rules of Civil Procedure, Where Court Finds That Witness Is More Than 100 Miles from Place of Trial or Hearing,* 71 A.L.R. FED. 382 (1985).
428. FED. R. CIV. P. 32(c).
429. FED. R. CIV. P. 32(a)(4).

were made to the rule in 1983.[430] The 1983 amendments involve the trial judge more actively in the management of the case. The primary focus of the rule shifted from trial preparation to case management, and it specifically recognized settlement as an appropriate goal. Rule 16 was also amended in 1993, primarily to take into account the new disclosure provisions and to emphasize planning for efficient trial of cases.

Rule 16(a) is entitled "Pretrial Conference; Objectives." It gives the court discretion to order the attorneys for the parties and any unrepresented parties to appear for a pretrial conference. The list of purposes in Rule 16(a) includes specific references to the goals of management and control of the pretrial stages of the litigation, including settlement.[431] The provision for facilitating settlement is complemented by Rule 16(a)(1), which states that expediting the disposition of the action is a proper goal of the pretrial conference.[432] Finally, Rule 16(a)(4) includes improving the quality of the trial by more thorough preparation as a proper goal of the conference, a purpose implicit in the provisions of old Rule 16.[433] In short, the goals of the pretrial conference have been revised in such a way as to promote more effectively the objectives of the Federal Rules of Civil Procedure "to secure the just, speedy and inexpensive determination of every action."[434]

1. Scheduling Orders

Federal Rule 16(b), entitled "Scheduling and Planning," contains the heart of the 1983 amendments to Rule 16. The first paragraph of Rule 16(b) provides that a scheduling order *must be entered* in every case that is not a part of a category of actions exempted by local rule from the scheduling-order require-

---

430. *See* FED. R. CIV. P. 16 advisory committee's note to the 1983 amendment. Criticisms of old Federal Rule 16 were severalfold. First, application of the rule sometimes resulted in overregulation of run-of-the-mill cases, which led to a burdensome series of mini-trials that wasted attorneys' time, especially when pretrial proceedings occurred long before trial. Second, because old Federal Rule 16 was discretionary and oriented toward a single conference late in the pretrial process, complex or protracted cases tended to be under-administered due to lack of judicial management at an early stage. Third, pretrial conferences often were seen as mere exchanges of legalistic contentions, without any real analysis of the particular case. Fourth, the result of a pretrial conference often was nothing more than a formal agreement on minutiae. Fifth, the pretrial conferences were unnecessary and time-consuming in the vast majority (over 90%) of cases that were settled before trial. Sixth, pretrial conferences often can be ceremonial and ritualistic, having little effect on the trial and being of minimal value, especially when the attorneys attending the sessions lack authority to make binding stipulations or are not the ones who will try the case. Seventh, when the order was issued far in advance of trial, the issues might not be formulated properly. Eighth, when cautious attorneys often tried to preserve in the order as many issues as possible, the order was unduly complicated and lacked proper focus. Ninth, when the judge who tried the case was not the one who issued the order, the judge sometimes had difficulty determining exactly what was agreed to at the conference. *See id.*

431. *See* FED. R. CIV. P. 16(a)(2), (3), (5). Under old Rule 16, there was substantial disagreement whether promoting settlement was a proper purpose of the pretrial conference. *See* 6 CHARLES A. WRIGHT & ARTHUR R. MILLER, FEDERAL PRACTICE AND PROCEDURE: CIVIL § 1522, at 224-26 (2d ed. 1990).

432. FED. R. CIV. P. 16(a)(1).

433. *See* FED. R. CIV. P. 16(a)(4).

434. FED. R. CIV. P. 1.

ment.[435] The order must be issued "as soon as practicable." The 1993 amendments increased the time for the initial scheduling order. As amended, the rule requires the order be entered (1) within 90 days after the date a defendant first appears or (2) within 120 days after service of the complaint on a defendant.[436] This increase in time was intended to alleviate problems in multi-defendant cases.[437] The district judge must enter the order unless a local rule authorizes a magistrate to do so.[438]

The scheduling order *must* limit the time to join parties and to amend the pleadings.[439] This requirement "assures that at some point both the parties and the pleadings will be fixed."[440] The order also must limit the time for filing motions and for completing discovery.[441] The Advisory Committee stated that the purpose of these requirements is to prevent delays in discovery and stalling through the use of motions.[442] Federal Rule 16(b) provides that a scheduling order *may* include the date or dates for conferences before trial, a final pretrial

---

435. FED. R. CIV. P. 16(b). A matter of importance under Rule 16(b) is what categories of cases will be exempted from the scheduling-order requirement by local rule. The Advisory Committee stated the reasons for this provision as follows:

> Although a mandatory scheduling order encourages the court to become involved in case management early in the litigation, it represents a degree of judicial involvement that is not warranted in many cases. Thus, subdivision (b) permits each district court to promulgate a local rule under Rule 83 exempting certain categories of cases in which the burdens of scheduling orders exceed the administrative efficiencies that would be gained. . . . Logical candidates for this treatment include social security disability matters, habeas corpus petitions, forfeitures, and reviews of certain administrative actions.

FED. R. CIV. P. 16(b) advisory committee's note to the 1983 amendment. Because the effectiveness of the scheduling-order requirement depends in part on how extensively the district courts exempt cases from the requirement, the nature and extent of the exemptions created by each district become critical. Also, because every case not exempted requires a scheduling order, the efficiency of the rule's operation will depend on how well the district courts provide exemptions by local rule for categories of cases not suitable for scheduling orders. Even in categories of cases exempted by local rule, scheduling orders can be issued under Federal Rule 16. The only effect of an exemption is to remove the requirement that scheduling orders be issued in every case within the category.

436. FED. R. CIV. P. 16(b) & advisory committee's note to the 1993 amendment. Prior to the 1993 amendment, the order had to be entered no later than 120 days after the date the complaint was filed.

437. FED. R. CIV. P. 16(b) advisory committee's note to the 1993 amendment.

438. FED. R. CIV. P. 16(b). Federal Rule 16(b) directs that, before entering the order, the judge or magistrate must consult with the attorneys for the parties by (1) a scheduling conference; (2) telephone; (3) mail; or (4) "other suitable means." *Id.* This provision makes it clear that the rule authorizes, but does not require, a scheduling conference. The Advisory Committee stated that the scheduling conference may be requested not only by the district judge or magistrate (where authorized by local rule), but by a party, provided a request is made within 120 days after the complaint is filed. *See* FED. R. CIV. P. 16(b) advisory committee's note to the 1983 amendment. The Advisory Committee's notes to the 1993 amendments indicate that the parties should submit to the court the report concerning their meeting and discovery plan before the scheduling order is entered. FED. R. CIV. P. 16(b) advisory committee's note to the 1993 amendment. However, whether or not a scheduling conference is held, the scheduling order must be entered within the time period, "after some communication with the parties." FED. R. CIV. P. 16(b) advisory committee's note to the 1983 amendment.

439. *See* FED. R. CIV. P. 16(b)(1).

440. FED. R. CIV. P. 16(b)(1) advisory committee's note to 1983 amendment.

441. *See* FED. R. CIV. P. 16(b)(2) & (3).

442. *See* FED. R. CIV. P. 16(b)(2) & (3) advisory committee's note to the 1983 amendment.

conference, and trial.[443] The order may modify the times for disclosures under Rules 26(a) and 26(e)(1) as well as the extent of the discovery permitted.[444] The order may also include "any other matters appropriate in the circumstances of the case."[445]

The final sentence of Federal Rule 16(b) provides that a schedule *shall not* be modified except "upon a showing of good cause and by leave of the district judge" (or magistrate judge, when a magistrate is authorized to act by local rule). The "good cause" standard of Rule 16(b) is less stringent than the "manifest injustice" standard for modification of pretrial orders under Rule 16(e).[446] "Good cause" exists if a schedule cannot be met "despite the diligence of the party seeking [an] extension [of time]."[447] It was feared that a more stringent standard would "encourage counsel to request the longest possible periods for completing pleading, joinder, and discovery."[448]

2. Subjects for Discussion at Pretrial Conferences

The amendments to Federal Rule 16(c) have continually expanded the matters that may be discussed at a pretrial conference if and when such a conference is held. The expansion continues Rule 16's emphasis on judicial management and control.[449]

As amended in 1983, Federal Rule 16(c)(1) provides that the *formulation* as well as the simplification of issues may be discussed.[450] This point is emphasized further by explicit additional authority to eliminate frivolous claims or defenses, without waiting for a formal motion for summary judgment.[451] Federal Rule 16(c)(2) retains the authority given in old Rule 16(2) to consider the necessity and desirability of amendments to the pleadings at a pretrial conference.

---

443. FED. R. CIV. P. 16(b)(5). The court is given discretion whether to include dates of pretrial conferences because such conferences may or may not be desirable in any given case. Complex cases may require multiple pretrial conferences and a more elaborate pretrial structure, but uncomplicated cases may require only one conference and little pretrial structure outside the matters mandated by Rule 16(b)(1)-(3). *See* FED. R. CIV. P. 16(b) advisory committee's notes to the 1983 amendment.

444. FED. R. CIV. P. 16(b)(4).

445. FED. R. CIV. P. 16(b)(6).

446. *See* FED. R. CIV. P. 16(b); *see also* subsection 4 ("Pretrial Orders") discussing the provisions of Federal Rule 16(e) *infra*.

447. *See* FED. R. CIV. P. 16(b) advisory committee's note to the 1983 amendment.

448. *Id.*

449. *See* FED. R. CIV. P. 16(c) advisory committee's note to the 1983 amendment. Rule 16(c) provides that in *any* pretrial conference, at least one of the attorneys for each party must have the authority to enter into stipulations and to make admissions regarding all matters that the participants reasonably may anticipate being discussed. This sentence was added in 1983 to meet the criticism that the pretrial conferences held under old Rule 16 often were ritualistic or ceremonial. The aim is to assure proper preconference preparation, not necessarily to compel stipulations or settlements that the attorneys consider unreasonable, or which concern matters that could not have been anticipated or that normally require prior consultation with the client. *See id.*; *cf.* Russell G. Donaldson, Annotation, *Authority of District Court, Under Rule 16 of Federal Rules of Civil Procedure, to Compel Parties to Agree on Pretrial Stipulations of Facts*, 40 A.L.R. FED. 859 (1978). The 1993 amendments added that the court could require "a party or its representative be present or reasonably [be] available by telephone in order to consider possible settlement of the dispute." *See* FED. R. CIV. P. 16(c).

450. *See* FED. R. CIV. P. 16(c)(1).

451. *See id.*

Federal Rule 16(c)(3) continues the authority of old Rule 16(3) to consider the possibility of obtaining admissions of facts and documents that will avoid unnecessary proof. Added to this authority is the further authority to consider and take action concerning stipulations regarding the authenticity of documents and to obtain advance rulings by the court on the admissibility of evidence.[452]

Federal Rule 16(c)(4) gives the court explicit authority to avoid unnecessary proof, cumulative evidence, and restrictions on expert testimony. Rule 16(c)(5) encourages the use of Rule 56 (summary judgment) to avoid or reduce the scope of the trial. Rule 16(c)(6) focuses on the appropriateness of controlling and scheduling discovery and disclosures. Rule 16(c)(7) deals with identification of witnesses and documents, scheduling an exchange of pretrial briefs, and the dates for further conferences and trial. Rule 16(c)(8) authorizes the court to consider the advisability of reference to a magistrate judge or master, whether or not the case is to be tried to a jury.[453]

Rule 16(c)(9) authorizes the court to consider the possibility of settlement.[454] Rule 16(c)(9) also encourages the use of special procedures to assist in resolving the dispute when a statute or local rule authorizes such procedures.[455] Rule 16(c)(10) explicitly authorizes consideration of and action upon the form and substance of the pretrial order.[456] Rule 16(c)(11) authorizes the court to consider and act upon pending motions. This type of matter always has been within the purview of the pretrial conference under Rule 16. It is simply listed to encourage the court to consider it.[457]

---

452. *See* FED. R. CIV. P. 16(c)(2) & (3).

453. *See* FED. R. CIV. P. 16(c)(4)-(8).

454. *See* FED. R. CIV. P. 16(c)(9). The Advisory Committee stated that it is not the Rule's intention to impose settlement on unwilling litigants. Rather, "it is believed that providing a neutral forum for discussing the subject [of settlement] might foster it." *See* FED. R. CIV. P. 16(c)(7) advisory committee's note to the 1983 amendment (now renumbered as 16(c)(9)). *See generally* Michael R. Hogan, *Judicial Settlement Conference: Empowering the Parties to Decide Through Negotiation*, 27 WILLAMETTE L. REV. 429 (1991); Leonard L. Riskin, *The Represented Client in a Settlement Conference: The Lesson of* G. Heileman Brewing Co. v. Joseph Oat Corp., 69 WASH. U. L.Q. 1059 (1991); Susan K. Antalovich, Note, Heileman Brewing Co., Inc. v. Joseph Oat Corporation*: Defining the Perimeters of Judicial Involvement in the Settlement Process*, 5 OHIO ST. J. ON DISP. RESOL. 115 (1989).

455. This provision was added in 1983 to encourage innovative efforts by the litigants to explore "adjudicatory techniques outside the courthouse" to resolve the dispute. *Id.*; *see* Eric D. Green et al., *Settling Large Case Litigation: An Alternative Approach*, 11 LOY. OF L.A. L. REV. 493, 501-06 (1978) (six weeks of expedited, limited discovery and exchange of position papers and exhibits, followed by nonbinding "mini-trial" before top management executives of opposing companies and a mutually selected neutral adviser; management to meet after mini-trial and attempt to resolve dispute from new perspective gained at mini-trial; neutral adviser to submit written nonbinding opinion discussing strengths and weaknesses of parties' positions and predicting likely outcome of trial, in event management not able to resolve dispute in first meeting). *See* John F. Wagner, Jr., Annotation, *Validity and Effect of Local District Court Rules Providing for Use of Alternative Dispute Resolution Procedures as Pretrial Settlement Mechanisms*, 86 A.L.R. FED. 211 (1988); Chapter 1(D) ("Alternative Dispute Resolution") *supra.*

456. Although pretrial conferences obviously had permitted this type of action under old Rule 16, this subdivision was added in 1983 to encourage judges to consider the subject in order to provide better case management. *See* 6A CHARLES A. WRIGHT & ARTHUR R. MILLER, FEDERAL PRACTICE AND PROCEDURE: CIVIL § 1525, at 248 (2d ed. 1990).

457. *See* FED. R. CIV. P. 16(c)(9) advisory committee's note to the 1983 amendment (now renumbered as 16(c)(11)).

Rule 16(c)(12) authorizes the court to consider and adopt special procedures for managing potentially difficult or protected actions that may involve complex issues, multiple parties, difficult legal questions, or unusual proof problems. Like other subdivisions added in 1983, this subdivision encourages flexible, innovative, and vigorous case management in complex actions.[458]

The 1993 amendments added provisions calling attention to opportunities for structuring the trial. Rule 16(c)(13) authorizes orders for separate trials pursuant to Rule 42. Rule 16(c)(14) authorizes orders that direct a party to present evidence early in the trial on an issue which could be the basis for a judgment as a matter of law under Rule 50(a) or a judgment on partial findings under Rule 52(c).[459] Rule 16(c)(15) supplements the power of the court to limit the extent of evidence offered at trial.[460] The underlying rationale of the Advisory Committee for these limits is to "provide the parties with a better opportunity to determine priorities and exercise selectivity in presenting evidence than when [such] limits are imposed during trial" pursuant to Rules 403 and 611(a) of the Federal Rules of Evidence. The Advisory Committee cautions, however, that "[a]ny such limits must be reasonable under the circumstances, and ordinarily the court should impose them only after receiving appropriate submissions from the parties" concerning expected testimony.[461]

Finally, Rule 16(c)(16) authorizes the court to consider and act on "such other matters as may facilitate the just, speedy, and inexpensive disposition of the action."[462]

3. Final Pretrial Conference

Federal Rule 16(d) provides that the final pretrial conference shall be held as close to trial as is reasonable under the circumstances. At the conference, the participants must formulate a plan for trial, including a program to facilitate the admission of evidence. Unrepresented parties and at least one of the attorneys who will conduct the trial for each party *must* attend the conference. The exact timing of the final conference, if any, is left to the discretion of the court for purposes of flexibility. Ten days to two weeks before trial is an "optimum" time.[463] The purpose of requiring the attendance of at least one attorney for each party who will try the case is to assure adequate structuring of the trial.[464]

---

458. *See* FED. R. CIV. P. 16(c)(10) advisory committee's note to the 1983 amendment (now renumbered as 16(c)(12)).

459. *See* Chapter 11(H)(1) ("Involuntary Dismissals (Judgments on Partial Findings) and Directed Verdicts (Judgments as a Matter of Law)") *infra*.

460. *See* FED. R. CIV. P. 16(c)(13)-(15).

461. *See* FED. R. CIV. P. 16(c) advisory committee's note to the 1993 amendment.

462. FED. R. CIV. P. 16(c)(16).

463. *See* FED. R. CIV. P. 16(d) advisory committee's note to the 1983 amendment.

464. *See id.*

4. Pretrial Orders

Federal Rule 16(e) requires that after *any* pretrial conference, an order must issue reciting the action taken at the conference. The order controls the subsequent course of the action unless a subsequent order modifies it. However, Rule 16(e) goes on to provide that the order following a *final* pretrial conference "shall be modified only to prevent manifest injustice." Thus, a distinction is drawn between pretrial orders and orders following the final pretrial conference. The former may be modified without restriction at subsequent pretrial conferences (or otherwise). The latter may be modified only by meeting a stringent standard; this "manifest injustice" formula was also the formula under old Rule 16 and was retained in part because it was familiar.[465] A stringent standard was retained for the final pretrial order because to allow modification of that order without restriction would defeat its function to structure and control the course of the trial.

Because the pretrial order controls the subsequent course of the litigation, admissions and stipulations embodied in the order will bind the parties and stand "as fully determined as if [the issues] had been adjudicated after the taking of testimony at trial."[466] Likewise, if issues are not preserved for trial in the pretrial order, even if the issues were disputed on the face of the pleadings, the trial court may refuse to allow evidence on the issues at trial or to give instructions on the issue. Federal Rule 16, however, must be read in conjunction with other Federal Rules. Thus, if a party objects to evidence at trial on the grounds that it is beyond the scope of the pretrial order, the trial court may apply the standard in Rule 15(b) and allow amendment of the order if justice would be served.[467] Similarly, the formulation of an issue in the pretrial order does not preclude a court from granting a motion for summary judgment, if the court later determines that no genuine issue of fact exists.[468]

Federal Rule 16(e) does not state who is responsible for preparing the pretrial order. Some local rules make the plaintiff's attorney responsible; others allow the court to appoint any one of the attorneys to prepare the order; and still others leave it to the court.[469] Other suggested methods are (1) for the judge to dictate the order directly into the record at the conference or shortly thereafter, (2) to adopt the minutes of the conference as the pretrial order if minutes are prepared, (3) for counsel to meet within a specified time after the conference and draw up an order for submission to the court, or (4) for the court to submit an order to counsel for their objections.[470]

---

465. *See* FED. R. CIV. P. 16(e) advisory committee's notes to 1983 amendment.

466. *See* 6A CHARLES A. WRIGHT & ARTHUR R. MILLER, FEDERAL PRACTICE AND PROCEDURE: CIVIL § 1527, at 271 (2d ed. 1990).

467. *See id.* at 287-90.

468. *See* Irving Trust Co. v. United States, 221 F.2d 303 (2d Cir. 1955).

469. *See* FED. R. CIV. P. 16(e) advisory committee's note to the 1983 amendment.

470. *See* 5 BENDER'S FEDERAL PRACTICE FORMS at 16-8 (1999).

5. Sanctions

Rule 16(f) provides that sanctions may be imposed on a party or a party's attorney who fails to (1) obey a scheduling or pretrial order, (2) appear at a scheduling or pretrial conference, (3) be substantially prepared to participate in a scheduling or pretrial conference, or (4) participate in good faith in a scheduling or pretrial conference.[471] For any such failure, the judge, upon the judge's own initiative or a party's motion, may "make such orders with regard thereto as are just," including the following:[472] (1) an order refusing to allow the party to support or oppose designated claims or defenses, or prohibiting the party from introducing designated matters in evidence;[473] (2) an order striking out pleadings or parts thereof, or staying further proceedings until the court's orders are obeyed, or dismissing the action or proceeding or part thereof, or rendering a judgment by default against the party;[474] or (3) an order treating as contempt of court the failure to obey a court order (unless the failure to obey is a failure to submit to a physical or mental examination).[475]

Federal Rule 16(f) also provides that in lieu of *or* in addition to any of the other sanctions imposed, the court *must* require the violating party, the party's attorney, or both to pay the reasonable expenses incurred because of any noncompliance with Rule 16, including attorney's fees. However, the court does not have to impose sanctions if it finds that the noncompliance was substantially justified or that other circumstances make an award of expenses unjust. The courts imposed sanctions for failure to comply with old Rule 16 even though the rule did not mention sanctions. Therefore, the explicit provision for sanctions in Rule 16(f) simply confirmed existing practice. The sanctions explicitly listed are found in Rule 37(b)(2). The expense-attorney's fees sanction is *mandated* unless a finding is made that the violation should be excused, thus emphasizing the propriety of imposing the costs of violation upon the violating party or that party's attorney, or both. However, the court may select whatever sanctions are appropriate to the circumstances of the case and will be reversed only for an abuse of discretion.[476]

---

471. FED. R. CIV. P. 16(f).

472. *Id.*

473. *See* FED. R. CIV. P. 37(b)(2)(B).

474. *See* FED. R. CIV. P. 37(b)(2)(C). *See generally* Jodi Golinsky, *The Second Circuit's Imposition of Litigation-Ending Sanctions for Failures to Comply With Discovery Orders: Should Rule 37(b)(2) Defaults and Dismissals be Determined by a Roll of the Dice?* 62 BROOK. L. REV. 585 (1996).

475. *See* FED. R. CIV. P. 37(b)(2)(D).

476. *See* FED. R. CIV. P. 16(f) advisory committee's note to the 1983 amendment.

Chapter 10

DISPOSITION OF THE ACTION
WITHOUT TRIAL

Modern procedural systems provide for disposition of actions without trial in several ways. For example, demurrers and motions to dismiss provide methods of challenging the legal sufficiency of an opposing party's pleading. If successful, such challenges can result in the entry of a judgment in the action.[1] Other formal devices can also be used to dispose of a case without a trial. They include (1) default judgments, (2) motions for judgment on the pleadings, (3) summary judgments, (4) voluntary dismissals, and (5) involuntary dismissals. In addition, statutes or court rules often encourage settlements.[2] When effectuated, a settlement can be embodied in a formal judgment.[3]

SECTION A. DEFAULT JUDGMENT

In a common-law or equity case, the defendant had to appear before the court could adjudicate the action. Thus, the traditional systems developed many sanctions to compel the defendant to appear.[4] In contrast, if the defendant fails to appear or otherwise defend in modern systems, service of process on the defendant, without more, authorizes the court to enter a "default judgment." For example, failing to answer the complaint can result in a default judgment against the defendant.[5]

Rule 55 of the Federal Rules of Civil Procedure is an example of a typical default provision. Rule 55 has its roots in common-law and equity practice. At common law, if a defendant appeared but refused to answer or demur, or if the defendant had pleaded but refused to continue to plead until issue was joined, the court would enter a judgment against the defendant for want of a plea. This judgment was called a *judgment nil dicit*—literally, "he says nothing."[6] In equity, the equivalent of a judgment nil dicit was the *decree pro confesso*. The court entered this decree when the defendant did not answer the plaintiff's bill.[7] Before Federal Rule 55, decrees pro confesso could be entered under the Federal Equity Rules. Judgments nil dicit could be entered in

---

1. *See* Chapter 6(C)(3)*(b)* ("Demurrers"); Chapter 6(D)(3)*(d)* ("Motions to Dismiss") *supra.*

2. *See generally* Stephan M. Bundy, *The Policy in Favor of Settlement in an Adversary System*, 44 HASTINGS L.J. 1 (1992) (surveying procedural innovations and discussing policy implications).

3. *See* section F ("Miscellaneous Methods of Disposing of an Action Without Trial") *infra.*

4. *See* Chapter 3(K)(1) ("Service of Process in English and Early United States Practice") *supra.*

5. *See* Chapter 6(D)(3)*(a)* ("Default") *supra.*

6. *See* ANDREW B. MARTIN, CIVIL PROCEDURE AT COMMON LAW § 375, at 316 (1905).

7. *See* Thomson v. Wooster, 114 U.S. 104, 110-11, 5 S. Ct. 788, 791, 29 L. Ed. 105, 107 (1885).

accordance with state law under the Conformity Acts.[8] Rule 55 itself is based largely on Rules 16 and 17 of the Federal Equity Rules of 1912.[9]

Default under Federal Rule 55 involves a two-step process. First, Rule 55(a) allows the clerk to enter default on the record when a party against whom a judgment for affirmative relief is sought fails to plead or otherwise defend, provided that fact is made to appear by affidavit or otherwise. Second, the clerk or the court, depending on the circumstances, enters the default judgment.[10] Rule 55(b)(1) provides that the clerk, as opposed to the court, may enter a default judgment when (1) the plaintiff's claim is for a sum certain or for a sum that can be made certain by computation. In addition, for the clerk to enter a default judgment, (2) the defendant must have been defaulted for failure to appear and (3) the defaulting defendant must not be an infant or incompetent person.[11] If any of these requirements is not satisfied, only the court can enter a judgment by default under Rule 55(b)(2), discussed below.

Illustration 10-1. A sues B in federal court. B moves to dismiss A's complaint for failure to state a claim upon which relief can be granted under Federal Rule 12(b)(6). The court overrules the motion. B then fails to answer within the time prescribed in Federal Rule 12(a). A files an affidavit making B's failure to answer known to the clerk. The clerk then enters B's default on the record. Under these circumstances, only the court can enter a default judgment against B under Rule 55(b). The motion to dismiss A's complaint constituted an appearance by B.[12] Once a defendant has appeared in an action, only the court can enter a default judgment under Rule 55(b)(2), discussed below.

Illustration 10-2. A sues B in federal court for an injunction. B fails to appear or otherwise defend the action. A files an affidavit making B's failure to appear known to the clerk. The clerk then enters the default on the record. Under these circumstances, only the court can enter a default judgment against B under Rule 55(b)(2). A's claim is for an injunction. Thus, it is not for a sum certain or a sum that can be made certain by computation. Even though B defaulted by failing to appear, only the court can enter judgment against B.

* * * * *

Under Rule 55(b)(2), the court is required to exercise discretion in determining whether to enter the judgment. Rule 55(b)(2) states that if the party against whom the default judgment is sought is an infant or incompetent person, no default judgment may be entered unless the person is represented by a general guardian, committee, conservator, or other representative who has appeared in the action. In other cases, when the party against whom the default judgment is sought has appeared in the action, written notice of the application for judgment

---

8. FED. R. CIV. P. 55 advisory committee's notes to the original rule; *see* Chapter 1(E)(5) ("Development of Federal Procedure and the Federal Rules of Civil Procedure") *supra.*

9. 226 U.S. 649, 653 (1912).

10. FED. R. CIV. P. 55(a), (b).

11. FED. R. CIV. P. 55(b)(1).

12. *See* 10A CHARLES A. WRIGHT ET AL., FEDERAL PRACTICE AND PROCEDURE: CIVIL § 2686 (3d ed. 1998).

must be given to that party at least three days before the hearing of the application.[13] This procedure provides the party time to demonstrate why the court should not enter a default judgment. In addition, Rule 55(b)(2) authorizes, but does not require, the court to hear evidence to determine the truth of allegations made against the defaulting party, to establish the amount of damages, or for other purposes.[14]

Rule 55(c) provides that even after a default has been entered on the record, the court may set it aside for good cause shown. Similarly, if a default judgment has been entered, the court may set it aside in accordance with Rule 60(b).[15] Setting aside the entry of a default or a default judgment is within the

---

13. FED. R. CIV. P. 55(b)(2); *see* Town & Country Kids, Inc. v. Protected Venture Inv. Trust #1, Inc., 178 F.R.D. 453 (E.D. Va. 1998) (holding that a letter from defendants to plaintiff's counsel was not an appearance entitling the defendants to notice of a default judgment hearing under Rule 55(b)(2)); *see also* Annotation, *What Amounts to an "Appearance" Under Rule 55(b)(2) of the Federal Rules of Civil Procedure, Providing that If the Party Against Whom a Judgment by Default is Sought Has "Appeared" in the Action, He Shall Be Served with Written Notice of the Application for Judgment,* 27 A.L.R. FED. 620 (1976); R.D. Hursh, Annotation, *Effect, Under Rule 55(b)(2) of the Federal Rules of Civil Procedure and Similar State Statutes and Rules, of Failure, Prior to Taking Default Judgment Against Party Who Has Appeared, to Serve 3-Day Written Notice of Application for Judgment,* 51 A.L.R.2D 837 (1957); *cf.* Annotation, *What Amounts to "Appearance" Under Statute or Rule Requiring Notice, to Party Who Has "Appeared," of Intention to Take Default Judgment,* 73 A.L.R.3D 1250 (1976); J.R. Kemper, Annotation, *Failure to Give Notice of Application for Default Judgment Where Notice Is Required Only By Custom,* 28 A.L.R.3D 1383 (1969).

14. FED. R. CIV. P. 55(b)(2); *see* Norfolk & W. Ry. v. Central States Trucking Co., No. 97 C 3624, 1998 WL 26175, 1998 U.S. Dist. LEXIS 635 (N.D. Ill. Jan. 15, 1998) (holding that although there is no absolute right to a hearing on damages under Rule 55(b)(2), a hearing should be held unless the available evidence permits the court to establish damages without one, such as where the damages are liquidated or can be ascertained from definite figures contained in documentary evidence or detailed affidavits); *cf.* B. Finberg, Annotation, *Defaulting Defendant's Right to Notice and Hearing as to Determination of Amount of Damages,* 15 A.L.R.3D 586 (1967); B. Finberg, Annotation, *Necessity of Taking Proof as to Liability Against Defaulting Defendant,* 8 A.L.R.3D 1070 (1966). *But see* FED. R. CIV. P. 55(e) ("No judgment by default shall be entered against the United States . . . unless the claimant establishes a claim or right to relief by evidence satisfactory to the court"); Joan Kirshberg, Annotation, *Default Judgments Against the United States Under Rule 55(e) of the Federal Rules of Civil Procedure,* 55 A.L.R. FED. 190 (1981).

15. FED. R. CIV. P. 55(c) & 60(b). In Robb v. Norfolk & Western Railway Co., 122 F.3d 354 (7th Cir. 1997), the plaintiff requested an extension of time from the defendant's attorney within which to file a brief in opposition to the defendant's motion for summary judgment. The defendant's attorney agreed, but the plaintiff did not seek an order of court for such an extension as required by local rule. As a result, the court granted summary judgment against the plaintiff for failure to respond to the motion. The plaintiff moved for relief under Rule 60(b), but the trial court denied it. The trial court felt bound by a Seventh Circuit precedent holding that attorney negligence could not constitute excusable neglect. The Seventh Circuit vacated the judgment and remanded the case. The Seventh Circuit relied on the Supreme Court's decision in Pioneer Investment Services Co. v. Brunswick Associates Ltd. Partnership, 507 U.S. 380, 113 S. Ct. 1489, 123 L. Ed.2d 74 (1993), a case which discussed excusable neglect in the bankruptcy context. The court held that based on *Pioneer*, attorney negligence can sometimes constitute excusable neglect. The court also indicated that the district court could, on remand, take into account that the plaintiff's attorney was one of the most conscientious in the bar in following deadlines in determining whether excusable neglect was present. *Cf.* African Methodist Episcopal Church, Inc. v. Ward, 185 F.3d 1201 (11th Cir. 1999) (district court erred in setting aside default and default judgment when parties, after being served, ignored process on advice of pastor of church and were defaulted as a result). *See generally* William H. Danne, Jr., Annotation, *What Constitutes "Good Cause" Allowing Federal Court to Relieve Party of His Default Under Rule 55(c) of Federal Rules of Civil Procedure,* 29 A.L.R. FED. 7 (1976); A.S. Klein, Annotation, *Opening Default or Default Judgment Claimed to Have Been Obtained Because of Attorney's Mistake as to Time or Place of Appearance, Trial, or Filing of Necessary Papers,* 21 A.L.R.3D 1255 (1968); D.E. Ytreberg, Annotation, *Appealability of Order Setting Aside, or Refusing to Set Aside, Default Judgment,* 8 A.L.R.3D 1272 (1966); J.P. Ludington, Annotation, *Failure of Liability Insurer, After Notification, to Defend Suit Against Insured, as Warranting Opening Default Against Insured on Ground of Inadvertence or* discretion of the court.[16] However, when the court has entered a default judgment, the court's discretion is confined by the requirements of Rule 60(b).[17] In determining whether good cause has been shown to set aside a default under Rule 55(c), the courts often rely on the list of factors listed in Rule 60(b).[18] Often, the courts require a party seeking to set aside the entry of a default or a default judgment to demonstrate that a meritorious defense exists to the opposing party's claim.[19]

SECTION B. JUDGMENT ON THE PLEADINGS

At common law, one party could challenge the legal sufficiency of the opposing party's pleading at any stage of the pleading process by a demurrer.[20] Even though the quest for the single issue ended and the number of pleadings were radically limited in code-pleading states, the demurrer continued to perform this function.[21] In the federal courts and many states, another device to test the legal sufficiency of a party's case after the close of the pleadings is a motion for judgment on the pleadings.[22]

Federal Rule 12(c) allows either party to move for judgment on the pleadings after the pleadings are closed "but within such time as not to delay the trial."[23] A motion for judgment on the pleadings allows a party to dispose of an action without trial when the pleadings demonstrate that the party is entitled to judgment as a matter of law. This motion performs basically the same function as a Rule 12(b)(6) defense, but it performs that function after the close of all the pleadings. Furthermore, it allows a party asserting a claim to challenge the legal sufficiency of the defensive pleading of an opposing party. When a party moves for judgment on the pleadings, all of the well-pleaded facts in the opposing

---

Excusable Neglect, 87 A.L.R.2D 870 (1963); H.S. Warren, Annotation, *Setting Aside Default Judgment for Failure of Statutory Agent on Whom Process Was Served to Notify Defendant*, 20 A.L.R.2D 1179 (1951); C.T. Drechsler, Annotation, *Reliance by Employee Codefendant on Promise or Assumption that Employer Would Defend in Employee's Behalf as Ground for Vacation of Default Judgment*, 16 A.L.R.2D 1139 (1951).

16. *See, e.g.*, Inman v. American Home Furniture Placement, Inc., 120 F.3d 117 (8th Cir. 1997) (default judgment and refusal of relief under Rule 60(b) were not an abuse of discretion where defendant's attorney negligently failed to answer complaint, respond to discovery requests, and appear for a scheduled deposition because attorney was having "personal problems"). *But cf.* Argent v. Office of Personnel Management, 96 CIV. 2516, 1997 WL 278115, 1997 U.S. Dist. LEXIS 7216 (S.D.N.Y. May 22, 1997) (entry of default set aside, even though defendants did not present a meritorious defense, where default was the result of negligence rather than wilfulness and the plaintiff would not be prejudiced).

17. *See* FED. R. CIV. P. 55(c), 60(b); *see also* Chapter 12(F) ("Extraordinary Relief From a Judgment") *infra*.

18. *See, e.g.*, Pretzel & Stouffer v. Imperial Adjusters, Inc., 28 F.3d 42 (7th Cir. 1994); *see also* 10A CHARLES A. WRIGHT ET AL., FEDERAL PRACTICE AND PROCEDURE: CIVIL § 2694, at 116-17 (3d ed. 1998).

19. *See, e.g.*, Park v. Tanaka, 75 Haw. 271, 859 P.2d 917 (1993); *cf.* Phillips & Assocs., Inc. v. E & H Plastic Corp., 217 Wis. 2d 348, 577 N.W.2d 13 (1998) (once a defaulted defendant presents a defense that would be legally sufficient, the court need not require the defendant to demonstrate a likelihood of success on that defense before relieving the defendant from a default judgment).

20. *See* Chapter 6(A) ("Common-Law Pleading") *supra*.

21. *See, e.g.*, NEB. REV. STAT. §§ 25-806, 25-820 (1995).

22. *See* FED. R. CIV. P. 12(c).

23. *Id.*

party's pleading are admitted for purposes of the motion, even if the moving party's own pleading has previously denied those factual allegations.

Illustration 10-3. *A* alleges in a complaint against *B* that *B* was negligent. *B* denies the allegation of negligence in *B's* answer. If *B* moves for judgment on the pleadings, the court will assume that *B* was negligent for purposes of ruling on *B's* motion. In addition to assuming the truth of the opposing party's factual allegations for purposes of the motion, the court will draw all reasonable inferences from these facts in favor of the party opposing the motion. The party does not, however, admit conclusions of law, legally impossible facts, or matters that would be inadmissible at trial.[24]

Illustration 10-4. *A* sues *B*, alleging facts *X*, *Y*, and *Z* in the complaint. These facts state a claim for relief. *B's* answer admits fact *X* but denies facts *Y* and *Z*. *A* moves for judgment on the pleadings. For purposes of ruling on the motion, the court will assume that fact *X* is true because *B's* answer admitted it. The court will assume that facts *Y* and *Z* are false because *B's* answer denied them. *A* will be able to obtain judgment on the pleadings under these circumstances only if fact *X* standing alone states a claim for relief against *B*.

Illustration 10-5. *A* sues *B*, alleging facts *X*, *Y*, and *Z* in the complaint. These facts state a claim for relief. *B's* answer admits facts *X*, *Y*, and *Z*. *B's* answer also alleges fact *Q* as an affirmative defense. *A* moves for judgment on the pleadings. Under these circumstances, the court will assume that facts *X*, *Y*, and *Z* are true because *B's* answer admitted them. In addition, the court will assume that fact *Q* is true because the court will assume that all well-pleaded factual allegations in the opposing party's pleading are true for purposes of ruling on a motion for judgment on the pleadings. *A* will be entitled to judgment on the pleadings only if affirmative defense *Q* is legally insufficient.

Illustration 10-6. On the facts of *Illustration 10-5*, assume that *A's* complaint does not state a claim for relief. However, *B* does not raise a Rule 12(b)(6) defense to the pleading. Instead, *B* admits the facts of the complaint and alleges an affirmative defense. *B's* affirmative defense is also legally insufficient. *A* moves for judgment on the pleadings. Under these circumstances, the court should grant judgment on the pleadings for *B*. Like a demurrer at common law, the motion for judgment on the pleadings "searches the record."[25] Thus, the court will return to the beginning of the pleadings, scrutinize each pleading for legal sufficiency, and rule against the party whose pleading is first legally insufficient. Here, that party is *A* because *A's* complaint does not state a claim for relief.[26]

Illustration 10-7. *A* sues *B*, alleging in the complaint facts *X*, *Y*, and *Z*. *B's* answer denies facts *X*, *Y*, and *Z*. *B's* answer also alleges affirmative defense *Q*. *B* moves for judgment on the pleadings. Under these circumstances, the court

---

24. *See* 5A CHARLES A. WRIGHT & ARTHUR R. MILLER, FEDERAL PRACTICE AND PROCEDURE: CIVIL § 1368, at 523 (2d ed. 1990). *See generally id.* at 520-24.

25. *See* Chapter 6(A)(4) ("Subsequent Pleading") *supra*; City Bank Farmers Trust Co. v. Hoey, 23 F. Supp. 831, 834 (S.D.N.Y. 1938), *aff'd*, 101 F.2d 9 (2d Cir. 1939).

26. *See* E.H. Schopler, Annotation, *Court's Power, on Motion for Judgment on the Pleadings, to Enter Judgment Against Movant*, 48 A.L.R.2D 1175 (1956).

will assume that facts *X*, *Y*, and *Z* are true. The court will disregard the affirmative defense for purposes of ruling on the motion. *B* will be entitled to judgment on the pleadings only if facts *X*, *Y*, and *Z* do not state a claim upon which relief can be granted. Thus, *B's* motion for judgment on the pleadings raises the same defense that *B* could have raised by a preanswer motion to dismiss under Federal Rule 12(b)(6) or a defense in the answer.

    Illustration 10-8. *A* sues *B* in federal court, alleging in the complaint facts *X*, *Y*, and *Z*. *B's* answer denies facts *X*, *Y*, and *Z*. *B's* answer also alleges affirmative defenses *R* and *Q*. If *A* believes that affirmative defense *Q* is legally insufficient, the proper procedural action for *A* to take is a motion to strike the affirmative defense as insufficient under Federal Rule 12(f).[27] *A's* motion for judgment on the pleadings would, technically, be improper because *A* is challenging only one of the defenses as legally insufficient. Under these circumstances, *A* is not entitled to judgment. *A* would only be entitled to judgment (and, therefore, to judgment on the pleadings) if (1) facts *X*, *Y*, and *Z* state a claim for relief; (2) *B* had admitted facts *X*, *Y*, and *Z*;[28] and (3) both affirmative defenses (*R* and *Q*) are legally insufficient.

* * * * *

    Federal Rule 12(c) provides that if a motion for judgment on the pleadings is supplemented by material outside the pleadings that the court does not exclude from consideration, the court should treat the motion as a motion for summary judgment. In that event, the court should dispose of the motion pursuant to Rule 56.[29]

SECTION C. SUMMARY JUDGMENT

    Summary judgment allows a party to demonstrate that the factual disputes in the pleadings are not authentic and that, once the apparent disputes are eliminated, the moving party is entitled to judgment as a matter of law. A motion for summary judgment thus resembles the motion to dismiss for failure to state a claim upon which relief can be granted (in code states, the general demurrer). It challenges the legal sufficiency of the opposing party's case. However, a motion for summary judgment is unique. It allows this legal challenge to be raised in conjunction with a demonstration that the factual disputes on the face of the pleadings are not real and that, as a result, no need exists for a trial.

---

    27. *But see* Moran v. Peralta Community College Dist., 825 F. Supp. 891, 893 (N.D. Cal. 1993) (partial judgments on the pleadings can be granted under Rule 12(c)).

    28. When *B* denies facts *X*, *Y*, and *Z* in the answer, *A* cannot obtain judgment on the pleadings, because for purposes of ruling on the motion made by *A*, *B's* denials must be accepted as representing the actual state of facts, *i.e.*, fact *X*, *Y*, and *Z* must be assumed to be false.

    29. FED. R. CIV. P. 12(c); *see* section C ("Summary Judgment") *infra*; *cf.* J.R. Kemper, Annotation, *What, Other Than Affidavits, Constitutes "Matters Outside the Pleadings," Which May Convert Motion Under Federal Rule of Civil Procedure 12(b), (c), into Motion for Summary Judgment*, 2 A.L.R. FED. 1027 (1969).

The motion for summary judgment originated in English procedure, in which it was first applied only to narrow categories of cases.[30] By the time the Federal Rules of Civil Procedure were adopted in 1938, the English summary judgment procedure had been expanded to cover almost all cases.[31] Several American states also had adopted it.[32] In the Federal Rules, Rule 56 provides for summary judgment.[33] Rule 56 has been copied by many states.[34]

1. Summary Judgment Procedure

Rule 56(a) provides that a party seeking to recover upon a claim, counterclaim, or cross-claim or to obtain a declaratory judgment may move for a summary judgment. Such a party may make the motion, with or without supporting affidavits, (1) at any time after the expiration of twenty days from the commencement of the action or (2) after an adverse party serves a motion for summary judgment, whichever occurs first. Rule 56(b) provides that a party defending against a claim, counterclaim, cross-claim, or declaratory judgment claim may move for summary judgment with or without supporting affidavits at any time. Under Rule 56(c), a motion for summary judgment must be served at least ten days before the time fixed for the hearing on the motion.[35] Both Rule 56(a) and 56(b) authorize a motion for summary judgment on all or any part of a claim (partial summary judgment).[36]

Illustration 10-9. *A* sues *B* for $1,000,000 for personal injuries *A* allegedly received due to *B's* negligence in operating an automobile in violation of the speed limit. *B's* answer denies *B's* negligence and *A's* damages. *A* moves for summary judgment. *A* supports the motion with evidence demonstrating that *B* was convicted of speeding at the time of the accident. *A* has demonstrated *B's* negligence as a matter of law. However, the extent of *A's* damages is still in dispute. Thus, the court should grant partial summary judgment on the issue of liability. The only remaining issue for trial would be *A's* damages.

* * * * *

Because a motion for summary judgment is designed to pierce the allegations in the pleadings, materials outside the pleadings, like those mentioned

---

30. *See generally* John A. Bauman, *The Evolution of Summary Judgment Procedure: An Essay Commemorating the Centennial Anniversary of Keating's Act*, 31 IND. L.J. 329 (1956); Charles E. Clark & Charles U. Samenow, *The Summary Judgment*, 38 YALE L.J. 423 (1929).

31. *See* FED. R. CIV. P. 56 advisory committee's note to the original rule.

32. *See id.*

33. For a study of the operation of Rule 56, see William P. McLauchlan, *An Empirical Study of the Federal Summary Judgment Rule*, 6 J. LEGAL STUD. 427 (1977); *see also* Patricia M. Wald, *Summary Judgment at Sixty*, 76 TEX. L. REV. 1897 (1998).

34. *See, e.g.*, ILL. STAT. ANN. ch. 735, ¶ 5/2-1005 (Smith-Hurd 1992); MASS. R. CIV. P. 56; NEB. REV. STAT. §§ 25-1330 to 25-1336 (1995).

35. FED. R. CIV. P. 56(a)-(c); *see also* FED. R. CIV. P. 6(d); Beth Bates, Annotation, *Necessity of Oral Argument on Motion for Summary Judgment or Judgment on Pleadings in Federal Court*, 105 A.L.R. FED. 755 (1991); Richard Neumeg, Annotation, *Propriety, Under Rule 56(c) of the Federal Rules of Civil Procedure, of Granting Oral Motion for Summary Judgment*, 52 A.L.R. FED. 567 (1981).

36. FED. R. CIV. P. 56(a), (b); *see also* E.H. Schopler, Annotation, *Propriety of Summary Judgment on Part of Single or Multiple Claims*, 75 A.L.R.2D 1201 (1961).

in *Illustration 10-9*, normally accompany the motion in an attempt to demonstrate the absence of a genuine factual dispute. The provisions of Rule 56(a), (b), (c), (e), (f), and (g) provide for the submission of affidavits in support of a motion for summary judgment. Rule 56(c) and (e) also clarify that the motion can be supported by depositions, answers to interrogatories, and admissions.[37] However, Rule 56 does not explicitly require that a motion for summary judgment be supported by material outside the pleadings. If a motion for summary judgment is made on the basis of the pleadings alone, it is the equivalent of a motion to dismiss for failure to state a claim upon which relief can be granted or a motion for judgment on the pleadings.[38] Like judgment on the pleadings, a summary judgment can be granted for the nonmoving party if the record shows that no genuine issue of fact exists and that the nonmoving party is entitled to judgment as a matter of law.[39] In addition, a court can order summary judgment on its own motion. However, before entering judgment, the court must give the parties an adequate opportunity to demonstrate that summary judgment is inappropriate because genuine issues of fact exist.[40]

2. Applying the Summary Judgment Standard

Rule 56(c) provides that a motion for summary judgment should be granted ''forthwith'' if the pleadings and supporting materials demonstrate ''that there is no genuine issue as to any material fact and that the moving party is entitled to a judgment as a matter of law.''[41] Rule 56(e) provides that when a motion is properly made and supported, the party opposing the motion may not rest on the mere allegations or denials of the pleadings. The opposing party must respond with materials outside the pleadings that demonstrate a genuine issue for trial.[42] ''If the adverse party does not so respond, summary judgment, *if appropriate*, shall be entered against the adverse party.''[43] By inserting the qualifying phrase ''if appropriate,'' the drafters of the rule sought to make clear that summary judgment is not to be granted against a party unless the moving party first meets the burden of demonstrating that no genuine factual issue exists. This

---

37. *See* FED. R. CIV. P. 56(a)-(c), (d)-(f); *cf.* Annotation, *Admissibility of Oral Testimony at State Summary Judgment Hearing*, 53 A.L.R.4TH 527 (1987).

38. *See* 10A CHARLES A. WRIGHT ET AL., FEDERAL PRACTICE AND PROCEDURE: CIVIL § 2713, at 222-23 (3d ed. 1998); *cf.* J.C. Vance, Annotation, *Raising Res Judicata by Motion for Summary Judgment Under Federal Rule 56 and Similar State Statutes or Rules*, 95 A.L.R.2D 648 (1964); W.E. Shipley, Annotation, *Comment Note.–Raising Statute of Limitations by Motion for Summary Judgment*, 61 A.L.R.2D 341 (1958).

39. *See* 10A CHARLES A. WRIGHT ET AL., FEDERAL PRACTICE AND PROCEDURE: CIVIL § 2720, at 346-54 (3d ed. 1998); E.H. Schopler, Annotation, *Court's Power, on Motion for Summary Judgment, to Enter Judgment Against Movant*, 48 A.L.R.2D 1188 (1956); *cf.* V. Woerner, Annotation, *Proper Procedure and Course of Action by Trial Court, Where Both Parties Move for Summary Judgment*, 36 A.L.R.2D 881 (1954).

40. *See* 10A CHARLES A. WRIGHT ET AL., FEDERAL PRACTICE AND PROCEDURE: CIVIL § 2720, at 339 (3d ed. 1998).

41. FED. R. CIV. P. 56(c).

42. FED. R. CIV. P. 56(e); *see also* Jean F. Rydstrom, Annotation, *Sufficiency of Showing, Under Rule 56(f) of Federal Rules of Civil Procedure, of Inability to Present by Affidavit Facts Justifying Opposition to Motion for Summary Judgment*, 47 A.L.R. FED. 206 (1980).

43. FED. R. CIV. P. 56(e) (emphasis added).

standard applies even when the nonmoving party does not come forward with materials outside the pleadings to oppose the motion.[44]

Illustration 10-10. In *Adickes v. S.H. Kress & Co.*,[45] the plaintiff was a white school teacher. She was with six black students when they were refused service in the defendant's lunchroom. When they left defendant's store, they were arrested for vagrancy. She then commenced a federal civil rights action. She alleged that the defendant had conspired with a police officer in its store to deprive her of service and arrest her because she was a white accompanied by blacks. The defendant moved for summary judgment on the basis of the deposition of its store manager. The store manager maintained that no communication with the police about the plaintiff had occurred. The store manager also maintained that the plaintiff had been refused lunchroom service because the store manager was afraid there would be a riot in the store. The defendant also submitted affidavits by the chief of police and two arresting officers. These affidavits stated that the store manager had not asked that the plaintiff be arrested. The plaintiff's own deposition admitted that she had no knowledge of any communication between the defendant's employees and the police. Instead, she relied on circumstantial evidence to support her claim of a conspiracy. Even though the plaintiff did not respond to the motion with materials that were acceptable under Rule 56(e),[46] the Supreme Court held that summary judgment against her was improper. The plaintiff was not obligated to submit materials under Rule 56(e) because the defendant had failed to meet its initial burden of demonstrating that no genuine issue of material fact existed in the case. The defendant had failed to meet its burden because it did not "foreclose the possibility that there was a police [officer] in the Kress store while [plaintiff] was awaiting service, and that this police [officer] reached an understanding with some Kress employee that petitioner not be served."[47]

* * * * *

In ruling on a motion for summary judgment, a court is not supposed to try factual disputes.[48] Instead, the court's function is to determine when a "genuine" issue of material fact exists. However, Rule 56 provides no guidance concerning when a factual dispute should be considered "genuine." Courts applying the Rule 56 standard often employ catchy expressions to explain the genuineness standard.[49] Nevertheless, it is doubtful whether such explanations add much to the text of the rule. Furthermore, despite repeated statements to the contrary in the decisions, judges do make credibility determinations and weigh evidence in evaluating the genuineness and materiality of a factual dispute.[50] The

---

44. *See* FED. R. CIV. P. 56 advisory committee's note to the 1963 amendment.

45. 398 U.S. 144, 90 S. Ct. 1598, 26 L. Ed. 2d 142 (1970).

46. *See id.* at 159 & n.19, 90 S. Ct. at 1609 & n.19, 26 L. Ed. 2d at 155 & n.19.

47. *Id.* at 157, 90 S. Ct. at 1608, 26 L. Ed. 2d at 154.

48. *See* 10A CHARLES A. WRIGHT ET AL., FEDERAL PRACTICE AND PROCEDURE: CIVIL § 2712, at 205-06 (3d ed. 1998).

49. *See* 10A *id.* § 2725, at 424-37.

50. *See* the U.S. Supreme Court decisions discussed in *Illustrations 10-11* through *10-13 infra*; *see also* Michael Holley, *Making Credibility Determinations at Summary Judgment: How Judges Broaden Their Discretion While "Playing by the Rules,"* 20 WHITTIER L. REV. 887 (1999).

best that can be said about the proper standard of judicial behavior under Rule 56 is that the judge should try to weed out those cases in which a trial will be useless. In doing so, the judge should take care not to deprive the party opposing the motion of the party's right to a trial—often by a jury—of legitimate factual disputes.

The "genuine issue" standard of Rule 56 is often equated with the standard for a judgment as a matter of law (directed verdict) under Federal Rule 50(a).[51] Under the Rule 50(a) standard, the judge is to direct a verdict when, under the governing law, reasonable minds cannot differ as to the result that must be reached on the existing evidence.[52] Thus, sometimes it is said that summary judgment should be granted when the state of the evidence is such that it would require a judgment as a matter of law (directed verdict) for the moving party.[53] This standard must be applied with an eye toward the burden of proof that would exist at trial on the moving and nonmoving parties.

Illustration 10-11. In *Anderson v. Liberty Lobby, Inc.*,[54] the plaintiffs commenced a diversity libel action against the defendants. The plaintiffs alleged that certain statements and illustrations in three magazine articles were false and derogatory. After discovery, the defendants moved for summary judgment. The defendants contended that the plaintiffs had to show actual malice under the applicable legal standard and that such malice was absent as a matter of law. The defendants' motion was accompanied by the affidavit of an employee of the defendants who had authored two of the articles in question. The affidavit detailed the quality of research and variety of sources used in the articles. Plaintiffs opposed the motion on the grounds that (1) numerous inaccuracies existed in the articles and (2) actual malice was present because several sources upon which the defendants had relied were patently unreliable. The district court granted the motion on the ground that the research and sources detailed by the defendants precluded a finding of actual malice. The court of appeals affirmed as to twenty-one and reversed as to nine of the allegedly libelous statements. In ruling on the summary judgment stage of the litigation, the court of appeals refused to apply the requirement that actual malice had to be proved by clear and convincing evidence. The U.S. Supreme Court disagreed. The Supreme Court held that, in ruling on a motion for summary judgment, the judge must bear in mind the actual quantum and quality of proof necessary to succeed under the applicable burden of proof. As the dissenting justices pointed out, however, it is difficult to square the notion that the judge is to evaluate the evidence according to the burden of proof that would exist on the parties at trial with the notion that the judge is not

---

51. *See* Chapter 11(H) ("Involuntary Dismissals, Directed Verdicts, Burden of Proof, and Presumptions") *infra.*

52. *See* Anderson v. Liberty Lobby, Inc., 477 U.S. 242, 250-51, 106 S. Ct. 2505, 2511, 91 L. Ed. 2d 202, 213 (1986).

53. *See id.* at 251, 106 S. Ct. at 2511, 91 L. Ed. 2d at 213.

54. 477 U.S. 242, 106 S. Ct. 2505, 91 L. Ed. 2d 202 (1986).

to weigh the evidence on a motion for summary judgment, lest the judge encroach on the role of the jury.[55]

Illustration 10-12. In *Celotex Corp. v. Catrett,*[56] the plaintiff brought a wrongful death action. The plaintiff claimed that the death of her husband was the result of exposure to asbestos products manufactured by the defendant. The district court granted the defendant's motion for summary judgment because the plaintiff was unable to produce evidence that the decedent had been exposed to defendant's products. The court of appeals reversed on the ground that defendant's failure to support its motion with materials negating such exposure precluded summary judgment in the defendant's favor. The Supreme Court reversed. The Court held that it was unnecessary for a defending party to come forward with materials outside the pleadings to negate the opponent's claim.[57] Instead, the Court held that a party who bears the burden of proof on an element at trial must, after adequate time for discovery, be able to make a showing sufficient to establish the existence of the element.

* * * * *

It is commonly stated that on a motion for summary judgment, the evidence is viewed in the light most favorable to the nonmoving party and that the nonmoving party is given the benefit of all favorable inferences that can be drawn from it.[58] Nevertheless, some decisions seem to utilize the summary judgment procedure in a more vigorous fashion. For example, the *Anderson* decision discussed in *Illustration 10-11* seemed to involve the judge in the process of weighing evidence that is theoretically reserved for the jury after trial.

Illustration 10-13. In *Matsushita Electric Industrial Co. v. Zenith Radio Corp.,*[59] the plaintiffs brought an antitrust action. The plaintiffs alleged that the defendants had conspired to raise, fix, and maintain artificially high prices for television sets in Japan and to fix artificially low prices for television sets in the United States. After several years of discovery, the defendants moved for summary judgment on all claims. The district court found that the admissible evidence submitted by the plaintiffs to defeat the motion did not raise a genuine issue of material fact and granted the motion. The court of appeals found summary

---

55. *See id.* at 257-58, 106 S. Ct. at 2515, 91 L. Ed. 2d at 217-18 (Brennan, J., dissenting); *id.* at 268-73, 106 S. Ct. at 2520-22, 91 L. Ed. 2d 224-27 (Rehnquist, J., with whom Burger, C.J., joined, dissenting).

56. 477 U.S. 317, 106 S. Ct. 2548, 91 L. Ed. 2d 265 (1986).

57. *See id.* at 323, 106 S. Ct. at 2553, 91 L. Ed. 2d at 274. The Court stated that

> the plain language of Rule 56(c) mandates the entry of summary judgment, after adequate time for discovery and upon motion, against a party who fails to make a showing sufficient to establish the existence of an element essential to that party's case, and on which that party will bear the burden of proof at trial. In such a situation, there can be no "genuine issue as to any material fact," since a complete failure of proof concerning an essential element of the nonmoving party's case necessarily renders all other facts immaterial.

Id. at 322-23, 106 S. Ct. at 2552, 91 L. Ed. 2d at 272-73. More recently, the Court has stated that "[w]hen the nonmoving party bears the burden of proof at trial, summary judgment is warranted if the nonmovant fails to 'make a showing sufficient to establish the existence of an element essential to [its] case.' " Nebraska v. Wyoming, 507 U.S. 584, 589, 113 S. Ct. 1689, 1694, 123 L. Ed. 2d 317, 329 (1993) (citing *Celotex*).

58. *See* 10A CHARLES A. WRIGHT ET AL., FEDERAL PRACTICE AND PROCEDURE: CIVIL § 2727, at 459 (3d ed. 1998).

59. 435 U.S. 574, 106 S. Ct. 1348, 89 L. Ed. 2d 538 (1986).

judgment improper and reversed. The U.S. Supreme Court reversed the court of appeals. While paying lip service to the rule that the evidence is to be viewed in the light most favorable to the nonmoving party,[60] the Court stated that a plaintiff seeking recovery under the antitrust laws must present evidence that tends to show the inference of conspiracy is reasonable in light of the possible competing inferences of (1) independent action by the defendants and (2) collusive action that could not have harmed the plaintiffs.[61] After canvassing the nature of predatory pricing conspiracies and the defendants' behavior over the course of the alleged conspiracy involved in the action, the Court concluded that the defendants had no plausible motive to engage in the conspiracy with which they were charged.[62] The Supreme Court's economic analysis of predatory pricing conspiracies may well have been correct.[63] Nevertheless, it is difficult to disagree with the dissenting Justices, who stated that the majority was evaluating the persuasiveness of the plaintiffs' evidence, a task normally reserved for the jury.[64]

* * * * *

The decisions of the U.S. Supreme Court discussed in the above illustrations seem to encourage the use of the summary judgment motion more than in the past.[65] However, cases clearly exist in which summary judgment will still be inappropriate.

---

60. *See id.* at 587, 106 S. Ct. at 1356, 89 L. Ed. 2d at 552-53.

61. *See id.* at 588, 106 S. Ct. at 1356-57, 89 L. Ed. 2d at 553.

62. The Court concluded that

> the absence of any plausible motive to engage in the conduct charged is highly relevant to whether a "genuine issue for trial" exists within the meaning of Rule 56(e). Lack of motive bears on the range of permissible conclusions that might be drawn from ambiguous evidence: if [defendants] had no rational economic motive to conspire, and if their conduct is consistent with other, equally plausible explanations, the conduct does not give rise to an inference of conspiracy.

Id. at 596-97, 106 S. Ct. at 1361, 89 L. Ed. 2d at 558-59.

63. *See generally* Daniel P. Collins, *Summary Judgment and Circumstantial Evidence*, 40 STANFORD L. REV. 491 (1988); James F. Ponsoldt & Marc J. Lewyn, *Judicial Activism, Economic Theory and the Role of Summary Judgment in Sherman Act Conspiracy Cases: The Illogic of* Matsushita, 33 ANTITRUST BULL. 575 (1988). The U.S. Supreme Court has distinguished *Matsushita*, suggesting that the case does not represent a major expansion of the summary judgment power in antitrust cases. In Eastman Kodak Co. v. Image Technical Services, Inc., 504 U.S. 451, 468-69, 112 S. Ct. 2072, 2083, 119 L. Ed. 2d 265, 285 (1992), the Court stated that *Matsushita* did not "introduce a special burden on plaintiffs facing summary judgment in antitrust cases." Rather, *Matsushita* only held that the plaintiff's economic theory could not be "senseless," because a reasonable jury could not find in the plaintiff's favor on a senseless economic theory. *Id. See generally* William W. Schwarzer & Alan Hirsch, *Summary Judgment After* Eastman Kodak, 45 HASTINGS L.J. 1 (1993).

64. *See* 475 U.S. at 598-607, 106 S. Ct. at 1362-66, 89 L. Ed. 2d at 560-65 (White, J., with whom Brennan, Blackmun, and Stevens joined, dissenting); *cf.* Poller v. CBS, Inc., 368 U.S. 464, 473, 82 S. Ct. 486, 491, 7 L. Ed. 2d 458, 464 (1962) ("We believe that summary procedures should be used sparingly in complex antitrust litigation where motive and intent play leading roles, the proof is largely in the hands of the alleged conspirators, and hostile witnesses thicken the plot").

65. *See* 10A CHARLES A. WRIGHT ET AL., FEDERAL PRACTICE AND PROCEDURE: CIVIL § 2727, at 468 (2d ed. 1998). *See generally* Marcy J. Levine, Comment, *Summary Judgment: The Majority View Undergoes a Complete Reversal in the 1986 Supreme Court*, 37 EMORY L.J. 171 (1988); Robert K. Smith, Comment, *Federal Summary Judgment: The "New" Workhorse for an Overburdened Federal Court System*, 20 U.C. DAVIS L. REV. 955 (1987); Susan L. Watchman, Note, *Summary Judgment in Antitrust Cases—Is the Standard Changing?* 20 ARIZ. ST. L.J. 591 (1988). *But see* Samuel Issacharoff & George Loewenstein, *Second Thoughts About Summary Judgment*, 100 YALE L.J. 73 (1990).

Illustration 10-14. *A*, an employee of *C*, was injured when a tank filled with asphalt materials *A* was heating exploded. The tank was supplied by *B* to *C*. *A* sued *B* for damages suffered in the accident. *B* moved for summary judgment against *A*. Under the applicable substantive law, *B* was not liable to *A* on a strict liability theory. Rather, *B* could only be held liable to *A* on a theory of negligence if *B* owed a duty of care to *A*. Under these circumstances, it would be inappropriate to grant summary judgment in *B's* favor. The question whether *B* owes a duty of care to *A* depends upon whether *B*, in performing services for *C*, should have recognized that the services were necessary for *A's* protection. If so, *B* would be obligated to exercise reasonable care in performing the services. Genuine issues of fact exist on this question because the resolution of the question depends upon the context in which the services were performed. In addition, the question of *B's* negligence—*i.e.*, whether *B* exercised reasonable care in performing the services—will usually also raise genuine issues of fact. Because questions of negligence involve the reasonableness of the party's conduct under the circumstances of the case, it is seldom possible to obtain summary judgment in negligence actions.[66]

SECTION D. VOLUNTARY DISMISSALS

At common law and equity, the courts allowed the plaintiff to dismiss a case voluntarily at any time prior to judgment. Such a voluntary dismissal was not "on the merits." Thus, it did not preclude the plaintiff from recommencing the action at a later time.[67] Under modern codes of civil procedure, voluntary dismissals are still available, but are usually restricted in various ways.[68]

Federal Rule 41(a) provides for voluntary dismissals.[69] The plaintiff may dismiss an action without the court's consent either (1) by filing a notice of dismissal at any time before service of an answer or motion for summary judgment, whichever occurs first, or (2) by filing a stipulation of dismissal signed by all parties who have appeared in the action.[70] A dismissal by either of these methods is without prejudice to the plaintiff's ability to recommence the action

---

66. *See, e.g.*, Saddler v. Alaska Marine Lines, Inc., 856 P.2d 784 (Alaska 1993); *see also* 10A CHARLES A. WRIGHT ET AL., FEDERAL PRACTICE AND PROCEDURE: CIVIL § 2729 (3d ed. 1998).

67. *See* ROBERT W. MILLAR, CIVIL PROCEDURE OF THE TRIAL COURT IN HISTORICAL PERSPECTIVE 253-54 (1952).

68. *See e.g.*, NEB. REV. STAT. §§ 25-601 to 25-603 (1995). *See generally* ROBERT W. MILLAR, CIVIL PROCEDURE OF THE TRIAL COURT IN HISTORICAL PERSPECTIVE 256-58 (1952); Chapter 13(B)(2) ("Judgments 'on the Merits' ") *infra*.

69. FED. R. CIV. P. 41(a); *see also* Chapter 8(D)(4)*(b)(v) supra* (discussing dismissals of class actions).

70. FED. R. CIV. P. 41(a)(1); *see* Finley Lines Joint Protective Bd. Unit 200 v. Norfolk S. Corp., 109 F.3d 993 (4th Cir. 1997) (holding that the plaintiff's right to dismiss voluntarily is not automatically cut off when the defendant files and serves a motion to dismiss under Rule 12(b)(6), accompanied by affidavits); *see also* Wade R. Habeeb, Annotation, *Right to Voluntary Dismissal of Civil Action as Affected by Opponent's Motion for Summary Judgment, Judgment on the Pleadings, or Directed Verdict*, 36 A.L.R.3D 1113 (1971); Milton Roberts, Annotation, *Plaintiff's Right to File Notice of Dismissal Under Rule 41(a)(1)(i) of Federal Rules of Civil Procedure*, 54 A.L.R. FED. 214 (1981); Howard J. Alperin, Annotation, *Propriety of Dismissal Under Federal Civil Procedure Rule 41(a) of Action as Against Less than All of Several Defendants*, 3 A.L.R. FED. 569 (1970); W.W. Allen, Annotation, *What Dismissals Preclude a Further Suit, Under Federal and State Rules Regarding Two Dismissals*, 65 A.L.R.2D 642 (1959).

unless (1) stated to the contrary in the notice of dismissal or stipulation or (2) the plaintiff has previously dismissed the same action in any federal or state court.[71]

Illustration 10-15. *A* sues *B* in a state court. *A* then voluntarily dismisses the action without prejudice under a state rule that allows voluntary dismissals at any time before trial without penalty. Subsequently, *A* sues *B* in a U.S. District Court on the same claim in a diversity action. Before *B* answers, *A* dismisses this action under Rule 41(a)(1)(i) by filing a notice of dismissal. This second dismissal is with prejudice. Rule 41(a) provides that "a notice of dismissal operates as an adjudication upon the merits when filed by a plaintiff who has once dismissed in any court of the United States or of any state an action based on or including the same claim." Under the terms of Rule 41, the prior voluntary dismissal of the claim in state court caused the second dismissal of the claim in federal court to operate as an adjudication upon the merits. Thus, *A* may not bring another action against *B* on the same claim in a federal or state court.

Illustration 10-16. On the facts of *Illustration 10-15*, assume that the first dismissal had been in federal court under Rule 41(a)(1)(i) and the second dismissal had been in state court under a state rule that did not make the second dismissal an adjudication upon the merits. Under these circumstances, *A* could bring a third action against *B* on the claim in a state or federal court. Rule 41 cannot make the second dismissal an adjudication upon the merits unless the rule operates in the court system in which the second dismissal occurs. Thus, the law of the state in which the second dismissal occurred defines the effect of the judgment.[72] That law provides that the dismissal is without prejudice.

* * * * *

Rule 41(a)(2) provides that unless one of the methods described in Rule 41(a)(1) is available, the plaintiff may obtain dismissal only by consent of court and under such terms and conditions as the court deems proper.[73] However, Rule 41(a)(2) also provides that an action may not be dismissed over the defendant's

---

71. FED. R. CIV. P. 41(a)(1). Rule 41(d) provides that if the plaintiff has once dismissed an action and then commences an action in any court based on the same claim against the same defendant, the court may order the payment of costs of the action previously dismissed and may stay the proceedings in the action until the plaintiff has complied with that order. FED. R. CIV. P. 41(d). However, costs under these circumstances do not appear to include attorney's fees. *See* Edward X. Clinton, Jr., *Does Rule 41(d) Authorize an Award of Attorney's Fees,* 71 ST. JOHN'S L. REV. 81 (1997) (most reasonable conclusion is that Rule 41(d) does not authorize attorney's fees).

72. *See* Chapter 13(B)(2) ("Judgments 'on the Merits' ") *infra.*

73. FED. R. CIV. P. 41(a)(2); *see* David J. Comeaux, Comment, *Avoiding Nonjudicious Nonsuits: Hearing the Defendant on Rule 41(A)(2),* 32 HOUS. L. REV. 159 (1995); *see also* Michael A. DiSabatino, Annotation, *Appealability of Order Imposing Conditions upon Grant of Plaintiff's Motion for Dismissal Without Prejudice, Pursuant to Rule 41(a)(2) of the Federal Rules of Civil Procedure,* 75 A.L.R. FED. 505 (1985); *cf.* Debra E. Wax, Annotation, *Construction, as to Terms and Conditions, of State Statute or Rule Providing for Voluntary Dismissal Without Prejudice upon Such Terms and Conditions as State Court Deems Proper,* 34 A.L.R.4TH 778 (1984). *Compare* Ohlander v. Larson, 114 F.3d 1531 (10th Cir. 1997) (district court may not refuse permission to voluntarily dismiss an action on the grounds that the party seeking dismissal has engaged in contemptuous conduct), *cert. denied,* 522 U.S. 1052, 118 S. Ct. 702, 139 L. Ed. 2d 283 (1998) *with* Teck Gen. Partnership v. Crown Cent. Petroleum Corp., 28 F. Supp. 2d 989 (E.D. Va. 1998) (plaintiff violates a discovery scheduling order requiring the plaintiff to make disclosure of expert evidence before a certain date and is sanctioned by having stricken the evidence that was the subject of the order; plaintiff's motion for a voluntary dismissal to avoid the effect of the sanction should not be granted).

objection under certain circumstances. If the defendant has pleaded a counterclaim prior to the service of the plaintiff's motion to dismiss, the court may not dismiss the counterclaim unless the counterclaim can remain pending for independent adjudication. A dismissal under Rule 41(a)(2) is without prejudice, unless the court otherwise specifies in its order.[74]

SECTION E. INVOLUNTARY DISMISSALS

Rule 41(b) provides for involuntary dismissal on several grounds, only two of which are pertinent here.[75] The first sentence of Rule 41(b) states that if the plaintiff fails to prosecute the action, to comply with "these rules," or to obey any order of the court, the defendant may move for dismissal of the action or of any claim asserted against the defendant.[76] The last sentence of Rule 41(b) states that unless the court specifies to the contrary in its order of dismissal, a dismissal under Rule 41(b) and any other dismissal not provided for in Rule 41, with certain exceptions, operates as an adjudication on the merits.[77] The exceptions are dismissals for lack of jurisdiction, for improper venue, or for failure to join a party under Rule 19.[78]

In *Costello v. United States*,[79] the U.S. Supreme Court held that a failure to satisfy a precondition to suit would fit within the exception to Rule 41(b) for dismissals on grounds of lack of jurisdiction. After *Costello*, the question thus becomes, what may properly be considered a "precondition of suit"? The *Costello* interpretation of Rule 41(b) can be confined within reasonable boundaries if it is limited to dismissals that cannot be corrected through the liberal procedures available for the correction of error under the Federal Rules and modern systems of appellate review. *Costello* involved the failure to file an affidavit that was required before the action could be brought. Once the failure to file the affidavit had occurred, it could not be corrected by amendment, appeal, or any other available procedure. In contrast, a dismissal on Rule 12(b)(6) grounds for failure to state a claim upon which relief can be granted should not be considered a failure to satisfy a precondition to suit. The liberal notice pleading philosophy of the Federal Rules makes it easy for the plaintiff to state a claim for relief. In addition, the liberal amendment policies of Rule 15 allow

---

74. FED. R. CIV. P. 41(a)(2).

75. Involuntary dismissal after presentation of the plaintiff's evidence in a trial to the court is discussed in Chapter 11(H) ("Involuntary Dismissals, Directed Verdicts, Burden of Proof, and Presumptions") *infra*.

76. FED. R. CIV. P. 41(b); *see also* Jonathan M. Purver, Annotation, *Propriety of Dismissal for Failure of Prosecution Under Rule 41(b) of Federal Rules of Civil Procedure*, 20 A.L.R. FED. 488 (1974); David B. Levendusky, Annotation, *Propriety of Dismissal of Action with Prejudice, Under Rule 41(b) of Federal Rules of Civil Procedure, upon Ground of Plaintiff's Failure to Comply with Order of Court*, 15 A.L.R. FED. 407 (1973); Jonathan M. Purver, Annotation, *Judicial Qualification of Provision of Rule 41(b) of Federal Rules of Civil Procedure that Dismissal for Failure to Prosecute or to Comply with Federal Rules or Court Order, and Certain Other Dismissals, Operate as Adjudication Upon Merits*, 5 A.L.R. FED. 897 (1970); *cf.* Kathleen M. Dorr, Annotation, *Imposition of Sanctions Under Rule 16(f), Federal Rules of Civil Procedure, for Failing to Obey Scheduling or Pretrial Order*, 90 A.L.R. FED. 157 (1988).

77. FED. R. CIV. P. 41(b).

78. *See id.*; *see also* FED. R. CIV. P. 41(c), (d).

79. 365 U.S. 265, 81 S. Ct. 534, 5 L. Ed. 2d 551 (1961).

the plaintiff to correct any deficiency in stating the claim.[80] Furthermore, error committed by the trial court in concluding that the complaint did not state a claim can be readily corrected by appeal. Therefore, a failure to state a claim dismissal should not be considered a failure to satisfy a precondition of suit within the meaning of *Costello*.[81]

Illustration 10-17. *A* sues *B* in a federal diversity action on January 1. *A's* claim is based on a note that does not mature until December 1. The action is dismissed on the grounds that it is premature. A dismissal on prematurity grounds should fit within the *Costello* interpretation of the jurisdictional exception to Rule 41(b). Once the plaintiff makes the mistake of bringing the action prematurely, no procedural means exist under modern procedural systems, including the Federal Rules, to correct the error. The claim must simply mature. Therefore, the dismissal should be considered a dismissal for failure to satisfy a precondition of suit.

SECTION F. MISCELLANEOUS METHODS OF DISPOSING OF AN ACTION WITHOUT TRIAL

1. Settlement: In General

Obviously, not all cases result in disposition by means of formal procedural devices. Many are settled out of court by the parties.[82] When the parties reach a settlement, they often embody their settlement in a consent judgment to protect against further litigation over the same claim. Consent judgments are both contracts and judgments. The parties control the terms of a consent judgment to the same extent that they control the terms of any other contract.[83]

Some kinds of settlements may not be permissible under the prevailing rules of ethics and public policies of a state. So-called ''Mary Carter agreements''[84] occur when a plaintiff sues multiple defendants and settles with one of the defendants, but the settling defendant remains in the action. For example, such an agreement might provide that if the plaintiff obtains a judgment

---

80. *See* Chapter 6(D) (''Federal Rules Pleading'') *supra* for a discussion of federal pleading and amendment practice; *see* Chapter 12(B) (''Appellate Review'') *infra* for a discussion of the availability of appeal in federal court.

81. *Costello* and the effect of Rule 12(b)(6) dismissals are discussed further in Chapter 13(B)(2) (''Judgments 'On the Merits' '') *infra*.

82. *See* Chapter 1(D) (''Alternative Dispute Resolution'') *supra*.

83. The primary difficulty with consent judgments is that because they do not involve actual litigation of issues of fact or law, they can have a claim preclusion effect, but not an issue preclusion effect. *See* Chapter 13 (''Finality in Litigation'') *infra* for a complete discussion of the doctrines of claim and issue preclusion. However, the contractual nature of consent judgments means that if the parties intend for issue preclusion as well as claim preclusion to apply, the judgment can have both claim and issue preclusion effects. *See generally* 18 CHARLES A. WRIGHT ET AL., FEDERAL PRACTICE AND PROCEDURE: CIVIL § 4443, at 384-88 (1981); RESTATEMENT (SECOND) OF JUDGMENTS § 27 cmt. e (1982).

84. The name is derived from Booth v. Mary Carter Paint Co., 202 So. 2d 8 (Fla. Dist. Ct. App. 1967).

against the nonsettling defendants that exceeds a particular amount, the settling defendant's money may be returned in whole or part. The settling defendant thus continues to exercise influence over the conduct of the action. In effect, the settling defendant combines with the plaintiff against the nonsettling defendants. These kinds of agreements have been criticized as unethical and a perversion of the adversary system.[85] Several courts have held them invalid.[86]

2. Settlement: Rule 68

(a) General Problems in Administering Rule 68

Modern procedural systems often contain rules designed to encourage settlement. For example, Federal Rule 68 provides a procedure whereby a defending party can make an offer to allow judgment to be taken against the party for a certain amount plus costs. If the offer is not accepted and the final judgment obtained by the offeree is not more favorable than the offer, the offeree must pay the costs incurred after the making of the offer. The purpose of Rule 68 is obviously to encourage settlements. Comparable provisions often exist within the states.[87] In *Delta Air Lines, Inc. v. August*,[88] the U.S. Supreme Court held that Federal Rule 68 does not allow costs to be awarded against a plaintiff-offeree when the defendant obtains judgment in the case. Rather, the rule applies only to judgments obtained by plaintiffs in an amount less than the defendant offered.

In *Marek v. Chesny*,[89] a plaintiff in a civil rights action under 42 U.S.C. § 1983 recovered less than the amount offered by the defendant under Rule 68. The plaintiff moved for an award of attorney's fees under 42 U.S.C. § 1988. That section provides that a prevailing plaintiff in an action under 42 U.S.C. § 1983 may recover attorney's fees as part of the costs of the action. The U.S. Supreme Court held, however, that attorney's fees were to be included within the term "costs" in Rule 68 whenever such fees were properly awardable as costs under the applicable substantive statute. Thus, the plaintiff was not entitled to recover attorney's fees as costs under the rule because the defendant had made a proper offer under the rule and the plaintiff had recovered less than the amount offered. Under *Marek*, once the defendant has made a proper Rule 68 offer, a prevailing plaintiff will only be able to recover attorneys' fees as costs if the applicable

---

85. *See* June F. Entman, *Mary Carter Agreements: An Assessment of Attempted Solutions*, 38 U. FLA. L. REV. 521 (1986); *see also* LARRY L. TEPLY, LEGAL NEGOTIATION IN A NUTSHELL 239-42 (1992); Warren Freedman, *The Expected Demise of "Mary Carter": She Never Was Well!* 1975 INS. L.J. 602; John E. Benedict, Note, *Its a Mistake to Tolerate the Mary Carter Agreement*, 87 COLUM. L. REV. 368 (1987); David R. Miller, Comment, *Mary Carter Agreements: Unfair and Unnecessary*, 32 SW. L.J. 779 (1978).

86. *See, e.g.*, Dosdourian v. Carsten, 624 So. 2d 241 (Fla. 1993); Lum v. Stinnett, 87 Nev. 402, 488 P.2d 347 (1971); Elbaor v. Smith, 845 S.W.2d 240 (Tex. 1992); *see also* Christopher Carr, Note, *Sudden Death: The Supreme Court of Texas Kills Mary Carter*, 24 TEX. TECH. L. REV. 1227 (1993) (discussing the *Elbaor* case). *See generally* Frank D. Wagner, Annotation, *Validity and Effect of Agreement with One Cotortfeasor Setting His Maximum Liability and Providing for Reduction or Extinguishment Thereof Relative to Recovery Against Nonagreeing Cotortfeasor*, 65 A.L.R.3D 602 (1975).

87. *See e.g.,* NEB. REV. STAT. §§ 25-901, 25-906 to 25-907 (1995).

88. 450 U.S. 346, 101 S. Ct. 1146, 67 L. Ed. 2d 287 (1981).

89. 473 U.S. 1, 105 S. Ct. 3012, 87 L. Ed. 2d 1 (1985).

substantive law classifies attorney fees as "costs" *and* the plaintiff recovers more than the amount offered.[90]

(b) Rules Enabling Act Problems in Administering Rule 68

With the increased interest in settlement, some states may adopt means of encouraging settlement in ways that potentially conflict with Federal Rule 68.[91] Given the way Rule 68 is currently configured, however, states may be able to avoid a direct confrontation between differing state and federal approaches. For example, a Wisconsin statute provides for double costs when the *plaintiff* obtains a favorable judgment after the defendant's refusal of the plaintiff's settlement demand. In *S.A. Healy Co. v. Milwaukee Metropolitan Sewerage District*,[92] the Seventh Circuit found no direct conflict between the Wisconsin statute because Rule 68 deals only with settlement offers by defendants, not plaintiffs. Finding that, under *Erie*, the statute was "substantive," the court concluded that the statute had to be applied in diversity actions in federal

---

90. *Id.* at 11, 105 S. Ct. at 3017-18, 87 L. Ed. 2d at 11. Rule 68 has received extensive attention from the Advisory Committee and the commentators. In August 1983, the Committee on Rules of Practice and Procedure of the Judicial Conference of the United States submitted to the bench and bar a preliminary draft of proposed amendments to the Federal Rules of Civil Procedure, including the draft of an amendment to Federal Rule 68. *See* 98 F.R.D. 361 (1983). In September 1984, the Committee submitted a substitute for this amendment. *See* 102 F.R.D. 432 (1984). Neither proposed amendment has ever been adopted by the Supreme Court. For a recent proposal to amend Rule 68 to allow plaintiffs to make formal offers of judgment and include attorney's fees as recoverable court costs see Joshua P. Davis, *Toward a Jurisprudence of Trial and Settlement: Allocating Attorney's Fees by Amending Federal Rule of Civil Procedure 68,* 48 ALA. L. REV. 65 (1996). For a general analysis of the interpretation of Rule 68, as well as a critique of various proposals to reform the rule and another proposed amendment, see Lesley S. Bonney et al., *Rule 68: Awakening a Sleeping Giant,* 65 GEO. WASH. L. REV. 379 (1997) (proposing to amend Rule 68 would define costs as including attorney's fees, whether or not such fees are otherwise recoverable). For a criticism of the Committee's 1984 proposal (and implicitly other more recent proposals) on the ground that it exceeds the rulemaking authority of the Supreme Court, see Stephen B. Burbank, *Proposals to Amend Rule 68–Time to Abandon Ship,* 19 U. MICH. J.L. REF. 425 (1986). *See generally* Peter Margulies, *After* Marek*, the Deluge: Harmonizing the Interaction Under Rule 68 of Statutes that Do and Do Not Classify Attorneys' Fees as "Costs,"* 73 IOWA L. REV. 413 (1988); W.W. Schwarzer, *Fee Shifting Offers of Judgment—An Approach to Reducing the Cost of Litigation,* 76 JUDICATURE 147 (1993); Roy D. Simon, Jr., *Rule 68 at the Crossroads: The Relationship Between Offers of Judgment and Statutory Attorney's Fees,* 53 U. CIN. L. REV. 889 (1984); Roy D. Simon, Jr., *The Riddle of Rule 68,* 54 GEO. WASH. L. REV. 1 (1985); Victoria C. Choy, Note, *The Impact of Proposed Rule 68 on Civil Rights Litigation,* 84 COLUM. L. REV. 719 (1984); Thomas L. Cubbage III, Note, *Federal Rule 68 Offers of Judgment and Equitable Relief: Where Angels Fear to Tread,* 70 TEX. L. REV. 465 (1991); Jeffrey J. Rogers, Note, *Rule 68 and Equitable Relief–A Common Sense Solution,* 35 ARIZ. L. REV. 265 (1993); Note, *The Conflict Between Rule 68 and the Civil Rights Attorneys' Fees Statute: Reinterpreting the Rules Enabling Act,* 98 HARV. L. REV. 828 (1985). For a study indicating that Rule 68 could have a significant effect on litigation bargaining in civil rights actions if it is interpreted to include post-offer attorney's fees normally paid by plaintiff under 42 U.S.C. § 1988, see Thomas D. Rowe, Jr. & David A. Anderson, *One-Way Fee Shifting Statutes and Offer of Judgment Rules: An Experiment,* 36 JURIMETRICS J. 255 (1996). For a proposal to abolish Rule 68 and add settlement to Rule 11, see Bruce P. Merenstein, *More Proposals to Amend Rule 68: Time to Sink the Ship Once and For All,* 184 F.R.D. 145 (1999).

91. *See* Michael E. Solimine & Bryan Pacheco, *State Court Regulation of Offers of Judgment and Its Lessons for Federal Practice,* 13 OHIO ST. J. ON DISP. RESOL. 51 (1997).

92. 60 F.3d 305 (7th Cir. 1995).

court.[93] More serious conflicts may arise when the state provisions apply to defendants (in addition to plaintiffs) and shift attorney's fees.[94]

The Seventh Circuit was undoubtedly correct in holding that, if there is no conflict between Rule 68 and the state law, a federal diversity court should be required to apply the state law. However, it is not clear that the court's reasoning was entirely correct. As discussed in Chapter 5, the Supreme Court has consistently phrased the *Erie* policies in terms of forum shopping by plaintiffs and discrimination against citizens of the forum state.[95] However, there would be no plaintiff forum shopping if the federal courts disregarded the kind of state settlement statute involved in *Healy*, because the state statute favored the plaintiff in the case. Furthermore, the defendant was the citizen of the forum in the case and wanted the statute disregarded, so it is hard to see how there could be discrimination against a citizen of the forum state on the actual facts. However, the Seventh Circuit stated correctly that disregard of the state statute would encourage noncitizens to remove diversity actions in appropriate cases.[96] As observed in Chapter 5, the court was probably correct to view defendant forum shopping as within the *Erie* prohibition, because there is no obvious difference between the evils of plaintiff and defendant forum shopping that would call for one to be discouraged and the other permitted.[97] Even if defendant forum shopping is not within the *Erie* prohibitions, however, the state statute ought not to be disregarded. As Chapter 5 also discussed, even when *Erie* is not violated, federal diversity courts should not disregard state law under circumstances that would undermine the policies supporting the diversity jurisdiction by driving non-citizen plaintiffs from the federal courts.[98] This will occur most obviously when a plaintiff would be deprived of a state rule of decision that would cause the plaintiff to lose an action in federal courts on the ultimate merits of the case that the plaintiff would win in state court. However, the state statute in *Healy* also gives the plaintiff substantial advantages. Under the state law, the plaintiff might be able to achieve settlements that would not occur in the absence of the law. Thus, the plaintiff might abandon a diversity action to obtain the benefit of the state settlement procedure if the federal courts were allowed to disregard the state law.[99]

A harder question is whether the Seventh Circuit was correct in concluding that Rule 68 was not broad enough to cover the case before the court because it only dealt with defendant's offers while the state statute included plaintiff's offers. As observed in Chapter 5, the Supreme Court has not applied a consistent methodology in interpreting Federal Rules of Civil Procedure to

---

93. *Id.* at 309-12.

94. *See, e.g.,* FLA. STAT. ANN. § 768.79 (West 1997).

95. *See* Chapter 5(E)(2), *Illustrations 5-11 & 5-13, supra.*

96. *See Healy,* 60 F.3d at 311.

97. *See* Chapter 5(E)(2), *Illustration 5-13, supra.*

98. *See* Chapter 5(E)(2), *Illustration 5-12, supra.*

99. *See also* MRO Communications, Inc. v. American Tel. & Tel. Co., 1999 WL 1132969 (9th Cir. Dec. 13, 1999) (because defendant obtained judgment, Federal Rule 68 is inapplicable; state equivalent of Rule 68, which allows award of attorney's fees to defendant, must be applied to avoid violation of *Erie* policy).

avoid conflicts with state law.[100] The Court's latest decision in the *Gasperini* case may represent a return to an interpretive methodology that is "more sensitive" to state interests.[101] If so, the approach taken to the interpretation of Rule 68 in *Healy* may be correct. However, there is sufficient doubt about this to inquire whether, in a case of conflict between Rule 68 and the state law in *Healy*, Rule 68 would be valid.[102]

The question of validity is determined by the standard articulated in the *Burlington Northern* case, discussed in Chapter 5,[103] to determine whether a Federal Rule "abridges, enlarges, or modifies" substantive rights within the meaning of the Rules Enabling Act. Under that standard, a Federal Rule of Civil Procedure is valid if it does not impact on substantive rights more than incidentally and is reasonably necessary to the uniform scheme of procedure that it was the purpose of Congress to establish when it enacted the Act. However, the Court has not yet described how to determine when a Federal Rule impacts on a state substantive right, when the impact is only incidental or more than incidental, or when a rule should be considered "reasonably necessary" to the uniform scheme of procedure that Congress wanted to establish.

Arguably, a Federal Rule impacts on a state substantive right when (1) the policies supporting the state law with which the Federal Rule conflicts are substantive in the sense that they involve legislative judgments about matters other than efficiency and accuracy in the adjudicative process, or (2) when the operation of the Federal Rule would change the ultimate result of the litigation. Rule 68 would arguably have a "substantive" impact in both of these senses in a case like *Healy*. The Seventh Circuit described the Wisconsin rule as one that "imposes a sanction on defendants for turning down reasonable settlement demands"[104] and as a "rule [that] favors plaintiffs by giving them the option of putting the defendant to the unhappy choice of either settling on terms favorable to the plaintiff or running a substantial risk of increasing the amount of money to which the plaintiff will be entitled if the case is not settled but instead is tried and the plaintiff wins."[105] These are goals that transcend judicial efficiency and accuracy to favor one party in the litigation. Thus, they are rightly considered "substantive."[106] In addition, it seems clear that plaintiffs who have available the leverage of the state law will win favorable settlements on the "merits" more often than plaintiffs who do not. This potential effect on the ultimate result of cases is also appropriately classified as a substantive impact.

---

100. *See* Chapter 5(F)(4) *supra* (discussing the holding in the *Burlington Northern* case that Fed. R. App. P. 38, which governed frivolous appeals, applied to a nonfrivolous appeal).

101. *See* Chapter 5(F)(5) *supra* (discussing, *inter alia*, the *Gasperini* case).

102. Also, as indicated in the text, above, other state settlement statutes may more directly conflict with Rule 68.

103. *See* Chapter 5(F)(4) *supra*.

104. *Healy*, 60 F.3d at 308.

105. *Id.* at 311.

106. The Seventh Circuit clearly considered the state law substantive, but it did so in the context of applying the general *Erie* doctrine rather than the Rules Enabling Act test of *Burlington Northern*. *See id.* at 311-12. Therefore, its classification of the rule, in and of itself, is not direct authority for the analysis in this text. However, the court's description of the purposes of the state law is instructive in applying the Rules Enabling Act test.

Assuming that Rule 68 would impact on a state substantive right within the meaning of the *Burlington Northern* case, it would seem that the impact ought to be classified as more than incidental. The operation of Rule 68, to the extent that it negates the ability of plaintiffs to make settlement offers, obliterates the operation of the state law in diversity actions. The only doubt about this is created by *Burlington Northern* itself, in which the Supreme Court construed Federal Rule of Appellate Procedure 38 as, in effect, an implied negation of any other authority to impose sanctions on defendants who took unsuccessful appeals. This effectively prohibited the operation of a state statute that provided for a 10% affirmance penalty against a defendant who took an unsuccessful appeal of a money judgment.[107] If the impact of a Federal Rule on the state law itself is all that counts in determining the rule's validity, then Rule 68 may have no more than the impact Rule 38 had in *Burlington Northern*. However, it is at least arguable that the operation of Rule 68 would have a more severe operation on the merits of cases than Rule 38, as Rule 68 would negate a state law that operates at the trial level of the litigation to give plaintiffs leverage. In contrast, Rule 38 only operated to negate a state law that would discourage defendants from taking appeals after a plaintiff had already won a verdict. This might cause plaintiffs to win some cases in which defendants appeal a federal diversity judgment that they would not have appealed in state court, but, given the fact that the plaintiff has already won at one level, it seems that Rule 38 would affect the ultimate result on the merits far less often that the operation of Rule 68.

Assuming that Rule 68 has no more than an incidental impact on state substantive rights, is it reasonably necessary to the operation of the uniform scheme of procedure that it was the purpose of Congress to set up under the Rules Enabling Act? The question is a close one. Generally, it seems that rules like Rule 68, which are designed to encourage settlement, are important to the efficient operation of the federal courts. However, this is not the same as saying that the rule contributes to the operation of the rest of the Federal Rules of Civil Procedure in any significant way. Unlike Rule 15(c), which was discussed in Chapter 6,[108] Rule 68 does not interact with other provisions of the Federal Rules, such as the liberal notice pleading provisions, in a manner that contributes to their efficient operation. In fact, it is not clear that the removal of Rule 68 from the Federal Rules would in any way impair the operation of the rest of the rules. Therefore, to the extent that the Supreme Court means to measure the "reasonable necessity" of a Federal Rule by reference to its contribution to the operation of the general scheme of the rules, Rule 68 would not seem necessary. Of course, the Court has been quite cryptic in describing this part of the Rules Enabling Act validity test (as it has with other portions of the test), so a more general test focusing on the efficient operation of the federal courts generally may be what the Court had in mind. If so, Rule 68 will probably meet this part of the *Burlington Northern* test.

---

107. *See* Chapter 5(F)(4) *supra* (discussing *Burlington Northern*).
108. *See* Chapter 6(D)(5)*(d) supra* (discussing potential Rules Enabling Act problems with Rule 15(c)).

Chapter 11

TRIAL

SECTION A. THE TRIAL CALENDAR AND THE TRIAL DATE

Trial calendars are ordinarily divided into two types: (1) those for jury actions and (2) those for actions to be tried to the court without a jury.[1] Statutes, local rules of court, and local custom govern the manner in which cases are placed on the trial calendar and the order in which they will be heard. In some jurisdictions, the clerk will place the case on the appropriate trial calendar on the clerk's own initiative, typically after the pleadings have been closed. In many jurisdictions, however, one of the parties must request that the case be placed on the appropriate trial calendar. In that situation, the requesting party must give notice to the other parties.[2] Courts ordinarily hear cases in the same order that they are placed on the trial calendar.[3] The court sets a case for trial by entering an order fixing a certain date on or after which the court may call the case for trial.[4]

SECTION B. NATURE AND ORDER OF A TRIAL

1. Demanding a Jury Trial

For some types of cases, the state or federal constitution may guarantee a party the right to a jury trial. To exercise that right, a party must demand a jury trial. The following is a typical demand: "The plaintiff [or defendant] demands trial by jury of all issues in the above-entitled action." This demand may be filed separately or endorsed on the party's pleading.[5]

---

1. *See* FED. R. CIV. P. 79(c). Courts maintain several types of calendars.

2. *See* FED. R. CIV. P. 40; *cf.* Michael A. DiSabatino & John E. Theuman, Annotation, *What Constitutes Bringing an Action to Trial or Other Activity in Case Sufficient to Avoid Dismissal Under State Statute or Court Rule Requiring Such Activity Within Stated Time*, 32 A.L.R.4TH 840 (1984).

3. Certain types of cases may be entitled to preferential treatment and thus advancement over others. *See* FED. R. CIV. P. 40. Preferential treatment also may be sought based upon the peculiar circumstances of a case. *See* 9 CORA M. THOMPSON, CYCLOPEDIA OF FEDERAL PROCEDURE § 31.08 (3d rev. ed. 1993).

4. The exact trial date is within the court's discretion and is often the subject of discussion at a pretrial conference. In setting the trial date, the judge will usually make an effort to select a date satisfactory to counsel as well as the court. Frequently, counsel will be required to estimate the time that the trial will take. Thus, prior to the conference, counsel should determine any potential conflicts that counsel may have and the times that clients and principal witnesses will be available for trial. *See* 4 AM. JUR. TRIALS 726 (1966).

5. FED. R. CIV. P. 38(b); *see* Janet B. Jones, Annotation, *Sufficiency of Demand for Jury Trial Under Rule 38(b) of Federal Rules of Civil Procedure*, 73 A.L.R. FED. 698 (1985). Parties may limit their demands for a jury trial to specified issues: "Trial by jury in the above-entitled cause is demanded by the defendant [or plaintiff] of the following issues . . . ." In this situation, Federal Rule 38(c) provides that any other party may

Illustration 11-1. Federal Rule 38 provides that "[a]ny party may demand a trial by jury of any issue triable of right by a jury by serving upon the other parties a [written] demand . . . at any time after the commencement of the action and not later than 10 days after the service of the last pleading directed to such issue" by filing the demand with the court.[6]

* * * * *

Provided all necessary pleadings have been served in an action removed from state court to federal court, a party entitled to trial by jury under Rule 38 may demand one within ten days after the party files the notice of removal. The opposing party also has ten days after receiving notice of removal to demand a jury trial.[7] If the party has demanded a jury trial prior to removal, however, the party does not need to make a new demand after removal.[8]

A demand for a jury trial cannot be withdrawn without the consent of *all* the parties.[9] Ordinarily, in both state and federal practice, a party who fails to demand a jury trial waives that right.[10]

2. Selecting the Jury

In jury trials, the trial begins with selecting the jury from a panel of potential jurors called for jury duty. The particular qualifications for jury duty and the method of assembling lists of potential jurors vary from jurisdiction to jurisdiction.

Illustration 11-2. In federal courts, the names of prospective jurors may be drawn from voter registration lists or from lists of actual voters in the political subdivisions in the district. Federal law also provides that other sources of names must be used, when necessary, to yield a cross-section of the community that

---

serve a demand for a jury trial of any or all other issues of fact in the action. *See* FED. R. CIV. P. 38(c).

6. FED. R. CIV. P. 38(b). Federal Rule 5(d) provides that "[a]ll papers after the complaint required to be served upon a party, together with a certificate of service, shall be filed with the court within a reasonable time after service . . . ." FED. R. CIV. P. 5(d).

7. FED. R. CIV. P. 81(c).

8. *Id.* If applicable state law does not require the parties to make express demands to claim trial by jury, the parties need not make demands after removal unless the court orders them to do so within a specified time to obtain a jury trial. *Id.*

9. FED. R. CIV. P. 38(d).

10. *See, e.g.,* FED. R. CIV. P. 38(d) & 39(b); CAL. CIV. PROC. CODE § 631 (West Supp. 1999); FLA. R. CIV. P. 1.430(b); *see also* Wesley Kobylak, Annotation, *Waiver of Right to Trial by Jury as Affecting Right to Trial by Jury on Subsequent Trial of Same Case in Federal Court,* 66 A.L.R. FED. 859 (1984); Jerald J. Diveeter, Annotation, *Rule 38 of Federal Rules of Civil Procedure: Waived Right to Jury Trial as Revived by Amended or Supplemental Pleadings,* 18 A.L.R. FED. 754 (1974); *cf.* Thomas R. Malia, Annotation, *Jury Trial Waiver as Binding on Later State Civil Trial,* 48 A.L.R.4TH 747 (1986). *See generally* ROBERT W. MILLAR, CIVIL PROCEDURE OF THE TRIAL COURT IN HISTORICAL PERSPECTIVE 260-63 (1952) ("Waiver of Jury Trial"). On contractual agreements providing for waiver of jury trials, see Debra T. Landis, Annotation, *Contractual Jury Trial Waivers in Federal Court,* 92 A.L.R. FED. 688 (1989). Judges often have the power to impanel an advisory jury when there is no right to trial by jury or when it has been waived. *See, e.g.,* FED. R. CIV. P. 39(c); *see also* John D. Perovich, Annotation, *Discretion of District Court Under Rule 39(b) of Federal Rules of Civil Procedure, Authorizing It to Order Jury Trial Notwithstanding Party's Failure to Make Seasonable Demand for Jury,* 6 A.L.R. FED. 217 (1971); *cf.* Romnaldo P. Eclavea, Annotation, *Authority of State Court to Order Jury Trial in Civil Cases Where Jury Has Been Waived or Not Demanded,* 9 A.L.R.4TH 1041 (1981).

reflects the race, color, sex, religion, national origin, and economic status of the citizenry.[11]

(a) Challenges for Cause

When a court orders the selection of a jury panel, summonses are issued for the required number of jurors. The prospective jurors are sworn to answer questions about their fitness to serve in a particular case. The manner of conducting this *voir dire examination* is generally within the court's discretion.[12] In federal courts, this examination is often conducted by the court alone.[13] In some jurisdictions, the parties' attorneys conduct the examination. In others, the attorneys and the court do so.[14] The purpose of the voir dire examination is to identify grounds justifying disqualification of a juror "for cause." The number of challenges for cause is not limited. The challenges may be exercised by the court or by the parties by making a timely objection.

Illustration 11-3. Grounds for challenging jurors *for cause* would include any bias or prejudice a juror might have, such as that produced by a juror's occupation or relationships with the parties or witnesses in the action.[15]

---

11. *See* 28 U.S.C. §§ 1861-1863. A party may challenge the sufficiency of the entire selection process on constitutional or statutory grounds. This type of challenge is called a challenge to the array. *See id.* § 1867. *See generally* Ronald P. Eclavea, Annotation, *Construction and Application of Provisions of Jury Selection and Service Act of 1968 (28 U.S.C.S. §§ 1861-1867) Governing Plans for, and Manner of, Selecting Federal Grand and Petit Jurors,* 17 A.L.R. FED. 590 (1973). The 1968 Act was amended in various ways in 1978. *See* Jury Selection Improvements Act of 1978, Pub. L. No. 95-572, 92 Stat. 2453. Note that even if state law absolutely disqualifies a particular category of persons from serving as jurors in a specific kind of case, it has been held that a federal court sitting with diversity jurisdiction is not compelled to follow that state law. *See* Nathan v. Boeing Co., 116 F.3d 422 (9th Cir. 1997) (federal law, 28 U.S.C. § 1870, is broad enough to cover this case and thus governs this procedural question).

12. *See, e.g.,* FED. R. CIV. P. 47(a).

13. *See* 9 CORA M. THOMPSON, CYCLOPEDIA OF FEDERAL PROCEDURE § 31.33, at 263 (3d rev. ed. 1993); *see also* Donald P. Duffala, Annotation, *Propriety and Prejudicial Effect of Federal Court's Refusal on Voir Dire in Civil Action to Ask or Permit Questions Submitted by Counsel,* 72 A.L.R. FED. 638 (1985).

14. *See* ROBERT W. MILLAR, CIVIL PROCEDURE OF THE TRIAL COURT IN HISTORICAL PERSPECTIVE 293-97 (1952); *see generally* Michael J. Ahlen, *Voir Dire: What Can I Ask and What Can I Say?* 72 N. DAK. L. REV. 631 (1996).

15. *See, e.g.,* Poet v. Traverse City Osteopathic Hosp., 433 Mich. 228, 445 N.W.2d 115 (1989) (holding that the trial court abused its discretion in a medical malpractice action involving prenatal treatment and delivery by not sustaining challenge for cause of a registered nurse who (1) had special skill in reviewing quality-of-care issues in neonatal intensive care cases, (2) was in a close working relationship with the wife of the hospital vice president, (3) was acquainted with the vice-president himself (a witness in the case), and (4) had conceded that she had fairly strong personal feelings about damages). *See generally* Todd R. Smyth, Annotation, *Professional or Business Relations Between Proposed Juror and Attorney as Ground for Challenge for Cause,* 52 A.L.R.4TH 964 (1987); Sheila A. Skojec, Annotation, *Examination and Challenge of Federal Case Jurors on Basis of Attitudes Toward Homosexuality,* 85 A.L.R. FED. 864 (1987); Phillip E. Hassman, Annotation, *Competency of Juror as Affected by His Membership in Co-operative Association Interested in the Case,* 69 A.L.R.3D 1296 (1976); Annotation, *Jury: Membership in Racially Biased or Prejudiced Organization as Proper Subject of Voir Dire Inquiry or Ground for Challenge,* 63 A.L.R.3D 1052 (1967); Annotation, *Social or Business Relationship Between Proposed Juror and Nonparty Witness as Affecting Former's Qualification as Juror,* 11 A.L.R.3D 859 (1967).

(b) Peremptory Challenges

In addition to challenges for cause, parties may make a limited number of *peremptory challenges*, which allow a party to exclude a particular juror without stating a reason. However, peremptory challenges are subject to constitutional restrictions—*e.g.*, restrictions that prohibit exclusion of jurors because of their race or sex.[16] The permitted number of such challenges varies according to the jurisdiction. In federal court, each party is allowed up to three challenges.[17] While the practice varies in state court, multiple defendants or plaintiffs in federal court may be treated as a single party for purposes of making challenges. The court, in its discretion, may allow additional peremptory challenges.[18]

3. Trial Procedure

After the jury has been impaneled (if there is going to be one),[19] the

---

16. In Batson v. Kentucky, 476 U.S. 79, 106 S. Ct. 1712, 90 L. Ed. 2d 69 (1986), the U.S. Supreme Court held that a prosecutor's use of peremptory challenges in a criminal trial to exclude jurors solely because of their race violates the Equal Protection Clause of the Constitution, at least when the defendant and the challenged jurors are of the same race. In 1991, the Supreme Court extended the *Batson* rule to civil jury trials to prohibit private, non-governmental parties from using peremptory challenges to exclude jurors on the basis of race. *See* Edmonson v. Leesville Concrete Co., 500 U.S. 614, 111 S. Ct. 2077, 114 L. Ed. 2d 660 (1991); *see also* J.E.B. v. Alabama *ex rel.* T.B., 511 U.S. 127, 114 S. Ct. 1419, 128 L. Ed. 2d 89 (1994) (extending *Batson* to peremptory jury strikes of all males from a jury in civil action by state to establish paternity and recover child support); Hurd v. Pittsburgh State Univ., 109 F.3d 1540 (10th Cir. 1997) (a party raising a *Batson* challenge to a peremptory challenge bears the burden of showing that a race-neutral, but factually mistaken, reason for the strike is pretextual); People v. Martin, 64 Cal. App. 4th 378, 75 Cal. Rptr. 2d 147 (1998) (holding it constitutional to strike a juror on the basis of religious beliefs that might produce bias). *See generally* Barbara A. Babcock, *A Place in the Palladium: Women's Rights and Jury Service*, 61 U. CIN. L. REV. 1139 (1993) (asserting that peremptory strikes of women because of their gender should be prohibited); Cheryl G. Bader, Batson *Meets the First Amendment: Prohibiting Peremptory Challenges That Violate a Prospective Juror's Speech and Association Rights*, 24 HOFSTRA L. REV. 567 (1996); George P. Fletcher, *Political Correctness in Jury Selection*, 29 SUFFOLK U. L. REV. 1 (1995); Amy B. Gendleman, *The Equal Protection Clause, the Free Exercise Clause, and Religion-Based Peremptory Challenges*, 63 U. CHI. L. REV. 1639 (1996) (arguing that religion-based peremptory challenges are unconstitutional); Lance Koonce, J.E.B. v. Alabama *ex rel.* T.B. *and the Fate of the Peremptory Challenge*, 73 N.C. L. REV. 525 (1995); Nancy S. Marder, *Beyond Gender: Peremptory Challenges and the Roles of the Jury*, 73 TEX. L. REV. 1041 (1995); Edmund L. Quatmann, Jr., J.E.B. v. Alabama *ex rel.* T.B.: *The Extension of the Equal Protection Clause to Gender-Based Peremptory Challenges—Is This the End?* 39 ST. LOUIS U. L.J. 1349 (1995); Andrew Weis, *Peremptory Challenges: The Last Barrier to Jury Service for People With Disabilities*, 33 WILLAMETTE L. REV. 1 (1997); Susan A. Winchurch, J.E.B. v. Alabama *ex rel.* T.B.: *The Supreme Court Moves Closer to Elimination of the Peremptory Challenge*, 54 MD. L. REV. 261 (1995).

17. *See* 28 U.S.C. § 1870; Deborah F. Harris, Annotation, *Distribution and Exercise of Peremptory Challenges in Federal Civil Cases Under 28 U.S.C.S. § 1870*, 50 A.L.R. FED. 350 (1980).

18. 9A CHARLES A. WRIGHT & ARTHUR R. MILLER, FEDERAL PRACTICE AND PROCEDURE: CIVIL § 2483, at 124-26 (2d ed. 1995). *But cf.* Morris B. Hoffman, *Preemptory Challenges Should Be Abolished: A Trial Judge's Perspective,* 64 U. CHI. L. REV. 809 (1997).

19. Prior to 1991, the Federal Rules assumed that all juries would consist of exactly twelve persons—or six persons if local district court rules allowed six. Alternative jurors were seated and heard all the evidence. However, they were excused if all of the regular jurors were able to deliberate. *See* Sheldon R. Shapiro, Annotation, *Alternative Jurors in Federal Trials Under Rule 24(c) of Federal Rules of Criminal Procedure or Rule 47(b) of Federal Rules of Civil Procedure*, 10 A.L.R. FED. 185 (1972). A 1991 amendment abolishes the use of alternate jurors. *See* FED. R. CIV. P. 47(b) advisory committee's note to the 1991 amendment. Under party having the burden of proof on the principal issues, usually the plaintiff, makes an opening statement. Opening statements ordinarily explain the nature of the case and summarize the evidence that will be presented. The opposing party is often given the option to respond with an opening statement at this time, but frequently defers until just before presenting the opposing party's case.

After the opening statements, the party having the burden of proof (hereafter referred to as the plaintiff) then presents the *case in chief* by offering proof. After the plaintiff has presented evidence, the plaintiff *rests*. The opposing party (hereafter referred to as the defendant) then rebuts the plaintiff's initial evidence, offers additional evidence, and presents evidence on defenses and counterclaims. After the defendant has completed the defendant's case in chief, the plaintiff may offer *rebuttal* evidence to counter the defendant's evidence. Thereafter, the defendant may present *surrebuttal* evidence to answer the plaintiff's rebuttal. This process continues until each side rests. A reasonable limit may be placed on the time allowed for presenting evidence.[20]

Ordinarily, the witnesses testify orally in open court.[21] Witnesses may be compelled by subpoena to attend trial.[22] Examination of witnesses follows this pattern: (1) direct examination by the party who called the witness; (2) cross-examination by the opposing party (limited generally to the scope of the direct examination); (3) redirect examination (which is limited generally to matters raised by the cross-examination); (4) recross-examination (limited generally to matters raised by the redirect examination). This process continues until counsel have no further questions for the witness. After these presentations have concluded, *closing arguments* will be made. Usually, the plaintiff proceeds first, followed by the defendant's closing. Then the plaintiff is given the opportunity to make a brief conclusion.

When the case is tried to the court, the trial is completed after all the evidence has been presented and closing arguments have been made. In federal court, the judge will decide the case by entering *findings of fact* and *conclusions of law*.[23] When the case is tried to a jury, the court will *instruct* the jury on the law.[24] The court in some jurisdictions also may comment on the evidence or summarize the evidence. The jury then deliberates and returns its verdict.

Federal Rule 48, the court now determines the exact size of the jury, depending on the particular case, but making certain that there are no more than twelve and no fewer than six jurors available to make the decision. All of the jurors seated participate in the verdict unless they are excused from service. *See* FED. R. CIV. P. 47(c) & 48 (allowing the court to excuse jurors from service during trial or deliberation for good cause). The Advisory Committee cautions that "it will ordinarily be prudent and necessary, in order to provide for sickness or disability among jurors, to seat more than six jurors." *See* FED. R. CIV. P. 48 advisory committee's note to the 1991 amendment; *cf.* Ballew v. Georgia, 435 U.S. 223, 98 S. Ct. 1029, 55 L. Ed. 2d 234 (1978) (criminal conviction by a jury of less than six persons violates due process). Federal Rule 48 provides that the verdict must be unanimous "[u]nless the parties stipulate otherwise." *See* FED. R. CIV. P. 48.

20. *See* FED. R. CIV. P. 16(c)(15) (subjects for consideration at pretrial conference); Patrick E. Longan, *The Shot Clock Comes to Trial: Time Limits for Federal Civil Trials*, 35 ARIZ. L. REV. 663 (1993); Chapter 9(N) ("Pretrial Conferences and Orders") *supra.*

21. *See* FED. R. CIV. P. 43(a).

22. *See* FED. R. CIV. P. 45(a)(2).

23. *See* FED. R. CIV. P. 52(a).

24. *See* section K of this chapter *infra* for a discussion of jury instructions.

SECTION C. TRIAL BY JURY IN
ANGLO-AMERICAN LAW

1. Development of Jury Trials

Chapter 1 explained that the development of the forms of action was strongly influenced by the parties' desire to secure a more rational mode of trial–trial by jury.[25] However, in earlier times, the jury functioned differently than it does today. Unlike today's practice, jurors were chosen because of their knowledge about the facts and circumstances of the dispute. Jurors were drawn from the location where the matters giving rise to the dispute occurred, in the hope that they would be informed about these matters.[26]

Although early juries were required to decide issues of fact, the distinction between law and fact was not sharply defined. Indeed, certain kinds of factual issues were clearly issues of law. For example, when an English jury was asked to determine the custom of a particular place, the jury was being asked to determine the law because the custom and the law were the same.[27] Nevertheless, the modern division of functions between the judge and jury has long been established. The jury decides questions of fact and questions of application of law to fact. For example, a jury determines whether a person who causes an injury exercised the care that a reasonable person under similar circumstances would have exercised. In contrast, a judge decides "pure" questions of law.[28] To be sure, this division of function has been subject to some variation at the margins: at one time an issue might be classified as one of fact for the jury, while at another time it would be committed to the judge.[29] Nevertheless, the general law-fact division has long-standing roots.

The right of trial by jury in Anglo-American law has often been depicted in glowing terms.[30] In recent times, however, this view of the jury has begun to

---

25. *See* Chapter 1(E)(1)*(d)* ("Modes of Trial Under the Writ System") *supra.*

26. *See* ROBERT W. MILLAR, CIVIL PROCEDURE OF THE TRIAL COURT IN HISTORICAL PERSPECTIVE 16, 20-23 (1952); Chapter 4(A) ("Transitory and Local Actions") *supra. See generally* Forum, *The Origins of the Jury,* 17 LAW & HIST. REV. 537 (1999) (discussing the origins of the jury in English law).

27. *Cf.* JAMES B. THAYER, A PRELIMINARY TREATISE ON EVIDENCE AT COMMON LAW 184 (1898).

28. *See, e.g.,* Fleming James, *Functions of Judge and Jury in Negligence Cases,* 58 YALE L.J. 667, 667-76 (1949).

29. *See* Stephen A. Weiner, *The Civil Jury Trial and the Fact-Law Distinction,* 54 CAL. L. REV. 1867, 1871-76, 1896-1902, 1910-18 (1966) (providing examples).

30. Blackstone described it as "the glory of the English law." 3 WILLIAM BLACKSTONE, COMMENTARIES ON THE LAWS OF ENGLAND *379 (Chitty ed. 1826). The U.S. Supreme Court has expansively praised the jury's ability to achieve just results:

> Twelve men of the average of the community, comprising men of education and men of little education, men of learning and men whose learning consists only in what they have themselves seen and heard, the merchant, the mechanic, the farmer, the laborer; these sit together, consult, apply their separate experience of the affairs of life to the facts proven, and draw a unanimous conclusion. This average judgment thus given it is the great effort of the law to obtain. It is assumed that twelve men know more of the common affairs of life than does one man, that they can draw wiser and safer conclusions from admitted facts thus occurring than can a single judge.

Railroad Co. v. Stout, 84 U.S. (17 Wall.) 657, 664, 21 L. Ed. 745, 749 (1874).

disintegrate. Juries in civil cases have been criticized on the grounds that they are incompetent fact finders, that they unnecessarily extend the time required for trial, and that they are anachronistic.[31] As demonstrated in the following sections, the "love-hate" relationship between American judges and lawyers and the civil jury is sometimes reflected in the modern decisions concerning jury trial issues.[32]

2. Methods of Controlling the Jury

With the development of juries in the judicial decision-making process, judges have searched for effective methods of controlling the jury.[33] The modern methods of jury control can be grouped into the following categories: (1) methods of control before trial; (2) methods of control during trial; and (3) methods of control after the verdict. The methods of control before trial generally aim at keeping a case from the jury altogether. These methods include the devices such as (a) demurrers to the pleadings (or motions to dismiss);[34] (b) motions for judgments on the pleadings;[35] and (c) motions for summary judgment.[36] The methods of control during trial include (a) admitting and excluding evidence; (b) directing verdicts against parties who fail to meet their burden of producing

---

31. *See, e.g.*, JEROME FRANK, LAW AND THE MODERN MIND 180-81 (1930); Fleming James, Jr., *Trial by Jury and the New Federal Rules of Civil Procedure*, 45 YALE L.J. 1022, 1026 (1938); David W. Peck, *Do Juries Delay Justice?* 18 F.R.D. 455 (1956). *See generally* Kevin M. Clermont & Theodore Eisenberg, *Trial by Jury or Judge: Transcending Empiricism*, 77 CORNELL L. REV. 1124 (1992) (empirical study of federal trials of cases from 1979 through 1989 in which the parties had the right to a jury; finding that, *inter alia*, proportion of jury trials varied greatly depending on the category of case and that plaintiffs won considerably more often before judges than juries in products liability and medical malpractice trials). Several reforms in the jury system have been proposed, including raising the fees for parties who demand jury trials, streamlining jury trials with a variety of procedural reforms, restructuring the jury by altering its size or composition, constraining jury discretion in a variety of ways, such as by use of special verdict forms, and diverting juries to "non-jury forums." *See* Steven Landsman, *The Civil Jury in America,* 62 LAW & CONTEMP. PROBS. 285 (1999); Peter H. Shuck, *How to Respond to the Problems of the Civil Jury,* 77 JUDICATURE 236 (1994); Symposium: *The American Civil Jury: Illusion and Reality,* 48 DEPAUL L. REV. 197 (1998); *see also* Matthew P. Harrington, *The Law-Finding Function of the American Jury,* 1999 WIS. L. REV. 377.

The viability of jury trial has also been caught up in criticism of the tort liability systems, which has resulted in large damage awards in cases considered to be of marginal, if any, merit by large segments of the public. As a result, it has been suggested that reforms such as "damage caps" would limit the jury's power to render excessive verdicts. Occasionally, it is suggested that such recommendations are beyond the power of Congress because of the limitations imposed by the Seventh Amendment. *See* Paul B. Weiss, *Reforming Tort Reform: Is There Substance to the Seventh Amendment,* 38 CATH. U. L. REV. 737 (1989).

32. For example, courts have often gone to great lengths to prevent the adverse effects on the right to trial by jury that can potentially be produced by the merger of law and equity in modern procedural systems. *See* section E ("The Right to Trial by Jury in a Merged System: Operation of the Historical and Modern Federal Approaches") *infra*. On the other hand, courts have approved attempts to reduce the size of the civil jury from its historically established number (twelve) to a lesser number on the ground that such a reduction does not impair the basic right of jury trial, but merely regulates an "incident" of the right. *See* section F ("Right to Trial by Jury Versus Mere 'Incidents' of the Right") *infra*.

33. In the past, various methods have been used to keep the jury within bounds. These methods have included the now defunct writ of attaint, the early use of fines to punish juries for judicial acts, the previously discussed law-fact distinction, demurrers to the evidence, and motions to arrest judgments. *See* JAMES B. THAYER, A PRELIMINARY TREATISE ON EVIDENCE AT COMMON LAW 137-81, 183-87, 234-38 (1898).

34. *See* Chapter 6(C)(3)*(b)* ("Demurrers") & Chapter 6(D)(3)*(d)* ("Motions to Dismiss") *supra*.

35. *See* Chapter 10(B) ("Judgment on the Pleadings") *supra*.

36. *See* Chapter 10(C) ("Summary Judgment") *supra*.

evidence; (c) instructing the jury; and (d) special verdicts and interrogatories,[37] discussed in later sections of this chapter. The post-verdict methods of control include (a) the motion for judgment notwithstanding the verdict (and its common-law predecessors, the motions in arrest of judgment and for judgment *non obstante verdicto*); and (b) the motion for new trial, discussed in Chapter 12.[38]

3. The Basic Problems in Administering the Constitutional Right

In the United States, state and federal constitutions guarantee the right of jury trial in civil actions. The Seventh Amendment to the U.S. Constitution is typical of constitutional provisions concerning civil juries.[39] Like similar state constitutional provisions, the Seventh Amendment "preserves" the right to trial by jury. Thus, these provisions guarantee a trial by jury for those cases in which a jury trial would have been granted at the time the constitutional provision in question was adopted—1791 in the case of the Seventh Amendment.[40] In general, jury trials were allowed for cases denominated as "law" cases, or "common law" cases. They were not allowed in "equity" or "admiralty" cases.[41]

Jury trials in modern procedural systems pose three major problems. The first problem is determining whether a party has a right to a jury trial. Under the old dual system of law and equity courts, the court in which the action was brought determined the mode of trial. If the action was brought in a common-law court, there would be a right of trial by jury (if the appropriate form of action was chosen). On the other hand, if the action was brought in an equity or admiralty court, no right of trial by jury existed. In modern merged systems, however, both legal and equitable matters can be litigated in the same court in a single action. In such cases, the question is how to determine whether the right

---

37. *See, e.g.,* FED. R. CIV. P. 49.

38. *See* Chapter 12(A) ("Post-Trial Motions") *infra*.

39. The Seventh Amendment provides as follows:

> In suits at common law, where the value in controversy shall exceed twenty dollars, the right of trial by jury shall be preserved, and no fact tried by a jury shall be otherwise re-examined in any Court of the United States, than according to the rules of the common law.

U.S. CONST. amend. VII.

40. With regard to state constitutions, the date is usually when the relevant constitutional provision preserving the right came into existence. *See, e.g.,* Housing Fin. & Dev. Corp. v. Ferguson, 91 Haw. 81, 979 P.2d 1107 (1999) (Seventh Amendment preserves right of jury trial that existed under English common law when Amendment was adopted in 1791, while state constitution preserves the right to jury trial that existed under the common law of the state at the time the Hawaii Constitution went into effect in 1959); Des Marais v. Desjardins, 664 A.2d 840 (Me. 1995) (plaintiff has right to jury trial unless it is affirmatively shown that a jury trial was unavailable in such a case in 1820).

41. *See* section D ("The Right to Trial by Jury in a Merged System: The Basic Approaches") & section E ("The Right to Trial by Jury in a Merged System: Operation of the Historical and Modern Federal Approaches") *infra. But see* Charles Wolfram, *The Constitutional History of the Seventh Amendment,* 57 MINN. L. REV. 730 (1973). Although jury trials are constitutionally guaranteed in only certain kinds of cases, it is universally considered to be a right that the parties may waive. *See* section B(1) ("Demanding a Jury Trial") *supra.*

to a trial by jury exists on issues of fact that are relevant to both the legal and equitable claims or remedies.

The second problem in modern systems is distinguishing between the "right" to a trial by jury and mere "incidents of the right." The distinction has recently become important in evaluating attempts to reduce the size of the jury from its historical number, twelve, to some lesser number. When a jurisdiction reduces jury size, the question arises whether the parties have been deprived of the "right" to trial by jury, or whether the basic right has been preserved while a mere "incident" of the right (the jury's size) has been modified.

The third problem in modern systems is whether jury trials are even feasible in certain kinds of complex cases. It has been claimed that there should be a "complex case" exception to the right to a jury trial, because a jury trial in complex cases deprives the parties of another basic right, the right to an opportunity to be heard in defense before life, liberty, or property can be taken from them—a right guaranteed by the due process clauses of the state and federal constitutions. The following sections explore these problems.

SECTION D. THE RIGHT TO TRIAL BY JURY IN A MERGED SYSTEM: THE BASIC APPROACHES

Section 208 of the Field Code of New York dealt with the problem of trial by jury in merged law and equity systems by providing that when "in an action for the recovery of money only, or of specific real or personal property, there shall be an issue of fact, it must be tried by a jury, unless a jury trial be waived. . . ."[42] Because equity courts had sometimes awarded "money only" or "specific real or personal property" in actions in which there was no right to a jury trial, this provision appeared to extend the right of trial by jury.[43] Indeed, the Commissioners stated that "[w]e propose an extension of the right of trial by jury to many cases, not within the constitutional provision."[44] Despite this expressed intention, the courts in other states adopting the Field Code provision generally construed it to be merely declaratory of the constitutional provision preserving jury trial rights in common-law cases.[45] The result was that courts usually construed the Field Code provision to read like Federal Rule 38(a): "The

---

42. Act of Apr. 12, 1848, ch. 379, § 208, 1848 N.Y. Laws 497, 536. Section 221 of the Field Code provided that a jury trial might be waived by failing to appear at the trial, by written consent in person or by attorney filed with the clerk, or by oral consent in open court. *See* Act of Apr. 12, 1848, ch. 379, § 221, 1848 N.Y. Laws 497, 538. These provisions were copied widely by other earlier codes and still exist in some states. *See* ROBERT W. MILLAR, CIVIL PROCEDURE OF THE TRIAL COURT IN HISTORICAL PERSPECTIVE 261 (1952); Fleming James, Jr., *Right to a Jury Trial in a Civil Action*, 72 YALE L.J. 655, 665-66 (1965); *cf.* NEB. REV. STAT. §§ 25-1104, 25-1126 (1995).

43. *See* Fleming James, Jr., *Right to a Jury Trial in a Civil Action*, 72 YALE L.J. 655, 666 (1965) (suggesting that this provision was unsatisfactory "because it specified the action as the unit to be dealt with rather than the component issues").

44. FIRST REPORT OF THE NEW YORK COMMISSIONERS ON PRACTICE AND PLEADINGS 185 (1848).

45. *See* CHARLES E. CLARK, HANDBOOK OF THE LAW OF CODE PLEADING § 16, at 98-99 (1947); Fleming James, Jr., *Right to a Jury Trial in a Civil Action*, 72 YALE L.J. 655, 667 (1965); Note, *The Right to Jury Trial Under Merged Procedures*, 65 HARV. L. REV. 453, 454 (1952).

right of trial by jury as declared by the Seventh Amendment to the Constitution or as given by a statute of the United States shall be preserved to the parties inviolate.''[46]

The basic problem, then, is to determine how traditional constitutional provisions, exemplified by the Seventh Amendment, should be applied in a merged system. At least four different approaches to this problem have been taken, but only two are of major importance: (1) the ''historical'' or ''analogical'' approach and (2) the ''modern federal'' approach.[47] Many state courts follow the historical or analogical approach. A court using this approach ''attempts to discern how the issues would have been tried before the merger of law and equity and to act accordingly.''[48]

Illustration 11-4. If an action was triable exclusively by an equity court before the merger, there is no jury trial. For example, no jury would be required in a case seeking only the remedy of injunction. On the other hand, if the action was triable exclusively by a common-law court, the right of trial by jury would be preserved. For example, a jury trial would be allowed in a case seeking damages for personal injuries.[49]

* * * * *

The modern federal approach evolved under the leadership of the U.S. Supreme Court in cases determining jury trial rights under the Seventh Amendment and the Federal Rules of Civil Procedure. This approach originated in *Beacon Theatres, Inc. v. Westover.*[50] In *Beacon Theatres*, the plaintiff was the owner of a motion-picture theater. The plaintiff contracted with motion-picture distributors for the exclusive right to show the ''first-run'' of pictures in a designated area. The theater also had a ''clearance'' period during which no other theater in the area could exhibit the same pictures. The plaintiff sought a declaratory judgment against another motion-picture theater in the area. The plaintiff asserted that the distributors' grant of ''clearance'' between the plaintiff and the defendant was reasonable and did not violate the federal antitrust laws.

---

46. *See* FED. R. CIV. P. 38(a).

47. In addition to the ''historical'' and the ''modern federal'' approaches discussed in the text, one approach has been to identify the basic nature of the formulated issue. The federal courts used this approach until the U.S. Supreme Court decided Beacon Theatres, Inc. v. Westover, 359 U.S. 500, 79 S. Ct. 948, 3 L. Ed. 2d 988 (1959), discussed in the text *infra*. Under this approach, if the basic nature of the issue was legal, trial was to a jury, while if the basic nature of the issue was equitable, no jury trial right existed. To put it mildly, this test was unhelpful. The test gave no real guidance on how to determine whether the issue was ''basically'' legal or equitable, and often courts seemed to consider it as merely a version of the historical test, discussed in the text *infra*. *See* 9 CHARLES A. WRIGHT & ARTHUR R. MILLER, FEDERAL PRACTICE AND PROCEDURE: CIVIL § 2302, at 20 (2d ed. 1995). A second approach has been to give the court discretion whether to grant a trial by jury when a case contains factual disputes related to both legal and equitable matters in the case. *See id.* However, numerous difficulties exist with this approach as well. The use of discretion may result in the denial of jury trial rights in cases in which they historically have been guaranteed, it may result in extension of jury trial rights to cases in which they have never been given as a matter of right, and it certainly provides no guidance to courts and litigants as to the categories of cases in which jury trial is appropriate. *See* Fleming James, Jr., *Right to a Jury Trial in Civil Actions*, 72 YALE L.J. 655, 692-93 (1963).

48. *Cf.* DAN B. DOBBS, LAW OF REMEDIES § 2.6(3), at 105-06 (2d student ed. 1993).

49. These examples are, of course, the simplest cases. More difficult issues concerning the historical method are discussed in section E of this chapter *infra*.

50. 359 U.S. 500, 79 S. Ct. 948, 3 L. Ed. 2d 988 (1959).

The plaintiff also sought an injunction to prevent the defendant from instituting any action against the plaintiff and its distributors, pending outcome of the litigation arising out of these contracts.[51]

The defendant served an answer containing a counterclaim against the plaintiff and a cross-claim against a distributor who had intervened. The defendant asserted that substantial competition existed between the plaintiff's and the defendant's theaters and denied any threats of litigation. The defendant also asserted that the clearances were unreasonable and that a conspiracy between the plaintiff and its distributors to manipulate contracts and clearances violated the federal antitrust laws. The defendant sought to recover treble damages as a result of this alleged violation.[52]

The defendant demanded a jury trial of the factual issues involved pursuant to Federal Rule 38(b). The district court, however, rejected this demand, reasoning that the issues raised in the complaint, including the question of competition between the theaters, were "essentially equitable." The judge directed that these issues be tried to the court *before* a jury determined the validity of the defendant's antitrust counterclaim and cross-claim. The defendant petitioned the Ninth Circuit Court of Appeals for a writ of mandamus directing the district court judge to vacate this order. The Ninth Circuit denied the petition.[53]

On certiorari, the U.S. Supreme Court assumed that the complaint could be construed (1) to include a request for an injunction against threats of lawsuits and (2) to allege the kind of harassment by a multiplicity of lawsuits that traditionally would have justified equity to take jurisdiction of the case and settle it in one suit. Nonetheless, the Court held that under the Declaratory Judgment Act and the Federal Rules of Civil Procedure, neither of these assumptions could justify denying the defendant a trial by jury of all the issues in the antitrust controversy.[54] The Court recognized that irreparable harm and inadequacy of legal remedies have always been the basis of injunctive relief in the federal courts. The existence of inadequate remedies and irreparable harm, however, had to be "determined, not by precedents decided under discarded procedures, but in the light of the remedies now made available by the Declaratory Judgment Act and the Federal Rules."[55] This approach is partly historical, in that it still asks

---

51. *Id.* at 502-03, 79 S. Ct. at 952, 3 L. Ed. 2d at 992-93.

52. *Id.* at 503, 79 S. Ct. at 952, 3 L. Ed. 2d at 993.

53. *Id.* at 503-05, 79 S. Ct. at 952-53, 3 L. Ed. 2d at 993-94.

54. *Id.* at 506, 79 S. Ct. at 954, 3 L. Ed. 2d at 994-95.

55. *Id.* at 507, 79 S. Ct. at 955, 3 L. Ed. 2d at 995. The Court explained as follows:
Since in the federal courts equity has always acted only when legal remedies were inadequate, the expansion of adequate legal remedies provided by the Declaratory Judgment Act and the Federal Rules necessarily affects the scope of equity. Thus, the justification for equity's deciding legal issues once it obtains jurisdiction, and refusing to dismiss a case, merely because subsequently a legal remedy becomes available, must be re-evaluated in the light of the liberal joinder provisions of the Federal Rules which allow legal and equitable causes to be brought and resolved in one civil action. Similarly the need for, and therefore, the availability of such equitable remedies as Bills of Peace, Qui Timet and Injunction must be reconsidered in view of the existence of the Declaratory Judgment Act [and] liberal joinder provision of the Rules. . . .

whether an issue would have been triable historically at law or equity. However, because the merger of law and equity has made available in all actions a wide range of procedural advantages that previously were only available in equity, the "legal" remedy has became adequate in many situations in which it formerly would have been inadequate. Thus, the scope of "equity" has been narrowed accordingly. In effect, the *Beacon Theatres* approach results in a greater availability of jury trial than before the merger of law and equity.[56]

A troublesome feature of the *Beacon Theatres* opinion is the Court's conclusion that the Federal Rules of Civil Procedure and the Declaratory Judgment Act had increased the adequacy of *legal* remedies. However, there is no evidence that the Declaratory Judgment Act had such a purpose. Indeed, if the declaratory judgment is to be analogized to remedies prior to merger, it looks much more like an equitable remedy than a legal one.[57] Furthermore, the *Beacon Theatres* reasoning holds the potential for massive expansion of the jury trial right. Declaratory relief may be a potentially adequate alternative almost any time an injunction is requested. If so, the legal remedy will almost always be adequate, and the right to trial by jury will attach.[58]

SECTION E. THE RIGHT TO TRIAL BY JURY IN A MERGED SYSTEM: OPERATION OF THE HISTORICAL AND MODERN FEDERAL APPROACHES

The actual operation of the historical and modern federal approaches to jury trial rights can best be explored through comparison of the way these

---

> If there should be cases [in which] the availability of declaratory judgment or joinder in one suit of legal and equitable causes would not in all respects protect the plaintiff seeking equitable relief from irreparable harm while affording a jury trial in the legal cause, the trial court will necessarily have to use its discretion in deciding whether the legal or equitable cause should be tried first. Since the right to jury trial is a constitutional one, however, while no similar requirement protects trials by the court, that discretion is very narrowly limited and must, wherever possible, be exercised to preserve jury trial. . . . [O]nly under the most imperative circumstances, . . . can the right to a jury trial of legal issues be lost through a prior determination of equitable claims.

Id. at 509-11, 79 S. Ct. at 956-57, 3 L. Ed. 2d at 996-98 (footnotes omitted).

56. *See* 9 CHARLES A. WRIGHT & ARTHUR R. MILLER, FEDERAL PRACTICE AND PROCEDURE: CIVIL § 2302.1, at 24-25 (2d ed. 1995).

57. In dissent, Justices Stewart, Harlan, and Whitaker in *Beacon Theatres* asserted that the Declaratory Judgment Act "merely provided a new statutory remedy, neither legal nor equitable, but available in the areas of both equity and law." 359 U.S. at 515, 79 S. Ct. at 959, 3 L. Ed. 2d at 1000. In addition, the dissenting Justices emphasized that the inadequacy of legal remedy as a condition precedent to equity's assumption of jurisdiction was a principle traditionally used to limit the power of an equity court. The inadequacy doctrine, it was argued, should not be used a basis for any extension of the jury trial right, especially when the original claim was cognizable exclusively in equity. *Id.* at 519, 79 S. Ct. at 961, 3 L. Ed. 2d at 1002.

58. *See* Fleming James, Jr., *Right to a Jury Trial in a Civil Action*, 72 YALE L.J. 655, 685-86 (1965); *cf.* Jean E. Maess, Annotation, *Right to Jury Trial in Action for Declaratory Relief in State Court*, 33 A.L.R.4TH 146 (1984). *See generally* John G. Gibbons, Comment, *From* Beacon Theatres *to* Dairy Queen *to* Ross*: The Seventh Amendment, the Federal Rules and a Receding Law-Equity Dichotomy*, 48 J. URBAN L. 459 (1971); John C. McCoid, *Procedural Reform and the Right to Jury Trial: A Study of* Beacon Theatres, Inc. v. Westover, 116 U. PA. L. REV. 1 (1967); John M. Townsend, Comment, *The Right to Jury Trial in Declaratory Judgment Actions*, 3 CONN. L. REV. 564 (1971).

approaches operate in the following specific circumstances: (1) cases in which only legal or only equitable claims are presented; (2) cases in which, historically, an equity court had to act first; (3) cases in which, historically, a common-law court had to act first; (4) cases in which the plaintiff could sue at either law or equity first; (5) cases in which the plaintiff asserts an equitable defense to a legal claim; (6) cases in which the plaintiff asserts a legal claim by means of a procedure available only in equity; and (7) cases in which a jury trial is sought in statutory or administrative proceedings.

1. Cases in Which Only Legal or Only Equitable Claims Are Presented

The simplest case, already referred to in *Illustration 11-4*, is an action in which the relief sought would have been either exclusively legal or exclusively equitable before the merger of law and equity—in other words, a case in which legal and equitable matters are not mixed. If a case was historically legal, a right of trial by jury exists. If a case was historically equitable, no such right exists.[59]

Illustration 11-5. A suit for an injunction in which no other relief is requested is purely equitable. Under both the historical and modern federal approaches, this type of case is resolved in the same way.[60]

* * * * *

This approach presents the real possibility that jury trial rights may be lost through issue preclusion.[61] If an action is brought on an equitable claim first, the judgment will ordinarily bind the losing party in a subsequent action on a legal claim. Thus, the party's right to a trial by jury in the second action may be lost. For example, in *Parklane Hosiery Co. v. Shore*,[62] the Securities and Exchange Commission sued to enjoin misleading statements being made by Parklane. The statements were found to be misleading and the injunction was granted. Shore had already sued Parklane in a class action to recover damages resulting from the misleading statements, but the SEC's action was adjudicated first. After the injunction had been granted, Shore moved for partial summary judgment on the ground that the doctrine of issue preclusion established that the statements were misleading for purposes of the damage action. Parklane argued that applying issue preclusion in the damage suit would deprive it of its Seventh Amendment right to a jury trial. Ultimately, however, the U.S. Supreme Court held that the doctrine of issue preclusion did apply and that its application did not deprive Parklane of its Seventh Amendment rights.[63]

---

59. *See, e.g., In re* Estate of Howard, 542 So. 2d 395 (Fla. Dist. Ct. App. 1989) (no right to jury trial in probate actions, which do not originate in common-law proceedings); *see also* DAN B. DOBBS, LAW OF REMEDIES § 2.6(3), at 105-06 (2d student ed. 1993).

60. *See* DAN B. DOBBS, LAW OF REMEDIES § 2.6(3), at 106 (2d student ed. 1993);

61. The doctrine of issue preclusion is discussed in Chapter 13(C) ("Issue Preclusion") *infra.*

62. 439 U.S. 322, 99 S. Ct. 645, 58 L. Ed. 2d 552 (1979).

63. *Id.* at 333-37, 99 S. Ct. at 652-55, 58 L. Ed. 2d at 563-66; *accord* Nielson v. Spanaway Gen. Med. Clinic, 135 Wash. 2d 255, 956 P.2d 312 (1998); Van Dissel v. Jersey Cent. Power & Light Co., 194 N.J. Super. 108, 476 A.2d 310 (1984). *Contra* Trapnell v. Sysco Food Servs., Inc., 850 S.W.2d 529 (Tex. Civ. App. 1992),

In federal court, the *Parklane* situation will arise only if equitable and legal claims are properly separated. If, for some reason, the claims are improperly separated, the right to a trial by jury on the legal claim will not be lost. For example, in *Lytle v. Household Mfg., Inc.,*[64] the plaintiff joined legal and equitable claims against the defendant. The district court erroneously dismissed the legal claim. The court then adjudicated the equitable claim, without a jury, in favor of the defendant. The court of appeals affirmed. It held that the plaintiff could not litigate the legal claims, despite their erroneous dismissal. The district court's findings on the common issue of fact between the legal and equitable claims would bind the plaintiff if the case were remanded for a trial on the legal claim. The court of appeals rejected the plaintiff's assertion that this result violated the Seventh Amendment.

The U.S. Supreme Court remanded the case for a retrial before a jury on both the legal and equitable claims. The Court held that *Parklane* does not control when equitable claims are tried first solely because they are erroneously separated. Rather, *Beacon Theatres* and *Dairy Queen, Inc. v. Wood* (discussed in subsection 2*(b)*, below), required a trial by jury on the common issues of fact existing between the legal and equitable claims.[65]

2. Cases in Which the Plaintiff Asserts Both Legal and Equitable Claims

(a) The Historical Approach

(i) Cases in Which, Historically, the Equity Court Had to Act First

In certain actions, the plaintiff may raise some issues that historically were triable only in equity courts and some issues that historically were triable only in law courts. Before the merger of law and equity, a party sometimes had to resort first to an equity court to get any relief at all.

Illustration 11-6. If *A* and *B* entered into a contract which, because of a mutual mistake, did not embody their true agreement, one party might have to sue first in an equity court to obtain reformation of the contract in order to be able subsequently to obtain the legal relief to which that party was entitled under the

---

aff'd on other grounds, 890 S.W.2d 796 (Tex. 1994). *See generally* David L. Shapiro & Daniel R. Coquillette, *The Fetish of Jury Trials in Civil Actions*, 85 HARV. L. REV. 442 (1971).

64. 494 U.S. 545, 110 S. Ct. 1331, 108 L. Ed. 2d 504 (1990).

65. If the plaintiff voluntarily separates the legal and equitable elements of a claim, the modern doctrine of claim preclusion would surely prevent a second action on the legal claim, *Lytle* notwithstanding. *See* Chapter 13(B) ("Claim Preclusion") *infra*. Similarly, if the plaintiff somehow possesses separate legal and equitable claims arising from the same facts, issue preclusion would surely bind the plaintiff if the claims are voluntarily separated and issues are adjudicated against the plaintiff in the equitable proceeding. *See* Chapter 13(C) ("Issue Preclusion") *infra*. Therefore, *Lytle* should only apply to erroneous separation of the claims by the court, rather than the voluntary action of a party. *Cf.* Aufderhar v. Data Dispatch, Inc., 452 N.W.2d 648 (Minn. 1990) (plaintiff who sought arbitration proceeding collaterally estopped in subsequent common-law damage action; right to trial by jury waived).

contract. The equity suit might be required in either of two situations. First, assume that *A* sued *B* for damages at law. Assume also that the contract, as written, gave *A* a right to damages. *B* might contend, however, that a mistake had been made in framing the agreement. Once the mistake was rectified, *A* would not be entitled to relief. Thus, *B* would sue *A* for reformation of the contract in equity. The equity court would enjoin the pending legal action until the question of mistake had been resolved. Second, assume that the party entitled to legal relief recognized at the outset that the parties' agreement was the product of mistake. Unless the agreement was reformed, the party would be unable to obtain legal relief. The party would sue in equity for reformation. If the mistake was found to exist, the equity court would order reformation of the contract. The court would also give the plaintiff the legal relief to which the plaintiff was entitled under the "clean up" doctrine.[66]

* * * * *

In either of the two situations described, no jury trial would take place on the equitable issue of mistake, which would, of necessity, be tried first. Under the historical approach, after the merger of law and equity, a jury trial should be denied. In this situation, courts using the historical approach conclude that equity had the real say. Even though a common-law court might be involved at some level, equity decided the determinative issue in the case first without a jury trial.[67]

(ii) Some Cases in Which, Historically, a Common-Law Court Had to Act First

Before the merger of law and equity, certain cases lent themselves to equitable relief, but an equity court would refuse to act until some issue had been first resolved by a law court.

Illustration 11-7. An example of such a suit would be an action for an injunction to prevent the defendant from trespassing on plaintiff's land but in which the plaintiff's title was disputed. Equity would not try the title to land.[68] Therefore, the title issue had to be resolved by a law court before the equity court would give relief. After the merger of law and equity, under the historical method

---

66. *See* Fleming James, Jr., *Right to a Jury Trial in Civil Actions*, 72 YALE L.J. 655, 658-59, 670 (1963); *see also* Weinisch v. Sawyer, 123 N.J. 333, 587 A.2d 615 (1991) (no right to trial by jury in reformation action). The "clean up" doctrine is discussed in Chapter 7(A) ("Joinder of Claims by the Plaintiff at Common Law and in Equity") and *Illustration 7-6 supra; see also* Chapter 1(E)(2) ("Equity Jurisdiction and Procedure") *supra*; Taylor v. Highland Park Corp., 210 S.C. 254, 42 S.E.2d 335 (1947) (reformation, specific performance, and damages can be ordered in a single action).

67. *See* DAN B. DOBBS, THE LAW OF REMEDIES § 2.6(3), at 117 (2d student ed. 1993).

68. *See, e.g.*, Green v. Cowgill, 30 Del. Ch. 345, 61 A.2d 410 (1948); Nottingham v. Elliott, 209 Ga. 481, 74 S.E.2d 93 (1953); Moore v. McAllister, 216 Md. 497, 141 A.2d 176 (1958); St. Louis Smelting & Ref. Co. v. Hoban, 357 Mo. 436, 209 S.W.2d 119 (1948); Carelli v. Lyter, 430 Pa. 543, 244 A.2d 6 (1968); Frost v. Mischer, 463 S.W.2d 166 (Tex. 1971); Kertesz v. Falgiano, 140 W. Va. 469, 84 S.E.2d 744 (1954).

of determining right to trial by jury, this type of case should be treated as one in which the legal issue predominates and a jury trial should be provided.[69]

(iii) Cases in Which the Plaintiff Could Sue in Either Law or Equity First

In certain kinds of cases before merger of law and equity, the plaintiff could control whether a right of trial by jury existed.

Illustration 11-8. The plaintiff might want to sue the defendant for an injunction to prevent future trespasses on the plaintiff's land and also to obtain damages for past trespasses. If the plaintiff desired, the plaintiff could sue in an equity court for an injunction. The equity court would also award damages under the "clean-up" doctrine without a jury. On the other hand, the plaintiff could first bring suit for damages in a law court and obtain a jury trial. If successful, the plaintiff could then sue in equity for an injunction. The issues decided in the plaintiff's favor in the law action that were also pertinent to the equity suit would be res judicata.

* * * * *

After merger, under the historical approach, the plaintiff could decide to treat the case as one at "law," with a right to jury trial, or as one in "equity," without a jury, at the plaintiff's option.[70]

(b) The Modern Federal Approach

What would be the result in the above cases under the federal approach? Did the "clean-up" doctrine survive *Beacon Theatres*?[71] The U.S. Supreme Court answered this question in *Dairy Queen, Inc. v. Wood.*[72] In *Dairy Queen*, the plaintiff alleged that the defendant breached a trademark licensing agreement by failing to pay the agreed amount for the use of the plaintiff's trademark within a certain territory. The plaintiff further alleged that after it had cancelled the agreement for the material breach, the defendant continued the business. The plaintiff requested (1) temporary and permanent injunctions to restrain the defendant from any future use of or dealing in the franchise or trademark; (2) an accounting to determine the exact amount of money owed by the defendant and a judgment for that amount; and (3) an injunction pending the accounting to prevent the defendant from collecting any money from stores in the territory carrying the trademark.[73]

---

69. *See* Mobile County v. Knapp, 200 Ala. 114, 75 So. 881 (1917); *cf.* I.C. Gas Amcana, Inc. v. Hood, 1992 OK 119, 855 P.2d 597 (equitable quiet title claim no longer the primary issue after reassignment of rights from plaintiff to defendant, rendering defendant's counterclaim for damages predominant and requiring jury trial at request of plaintiff); Fleming James, Jr., *The Right to a Jury Trial in Civil Action*, 72 YALE L.J. 655, 663, 671, 673 (1963).

70. *See* Fleming James, Jr., *The Right to a Jury Trial in Civil Action*, 72 YALE L.J. 655, 672, 675 (1963).

71. The decision in *Beacon Theatres, Inc. v. Westover* is discussed in section D ("The Right to Trial by Jury in a Merged System: The Basic Approaches") *supra.*

72. 369 U.S. 469, 82 S. Ct. 894, 8 L. Ed. 2d 44 (1962).

73. *Id.* at 473-75, 82 S. Ct. at 897-98, 8 L. Ed. 2d at 50.

The defendant's answer raised several defenses, including (1) a denial of any breach of the contract, apparently because the contract allegedly had been orally modified to remove the required minimum annual payment; (2) laches and estoppel arising from the failure to raise the claim promptly; and (3) violations of the federal antitrust laws.[74] The federal district court granted a motion to strike the defendant's demand for a trial by jury in the action on alternative grounds. The court held that either (1) the action was "purely equitable" or (2) if not purely equitable, the legal issues that were raised were "incidental" to the equitable issues. In either case, no right to trial by jury existed. The defendant then sought mandamus in the Court of Appeals for the Third Circuit to compel the district judge to vacate this order. After that court denied the request without opinion, the Supreme Court granted certiorari and reversed.[75]

The Court initially disposed of one of the grounds upon which the trial court acted in striking the demand for trial by jury—that the right may be lost as to legal issues when those issues are characterized as "incidental" to equitable issues. The Court reiterated the view taken in *Beacon Theatres*: when both legal and equitable issues are presented in a single case, the right to a jury trial of the legal issues can be lost through the prior determination of equitable claims only under the most imperative circumstances. The Court stated that this holding applied whether or not the trial judge chose to characterize the legal issues as "incidental" to the equitable issues. The sole question was whether the action contained "legal issues." In resolving this question, the Court emphasized that the complaint requested a money judgment.[76] The Court also rejected the plaintiff's contention that the money claim was purely equitable because it requested an equitable "accounting" rather than "damages." The Court stated:

> [T]he constitutional right to trial by jury cannot be made to depend upon the choice of words used in the pleadings. The necessary prerequisite to the right to maintain a suit for an equitable accounting [is] the absence of an adequate remedy at law. [To] maintain such a suit on a cause of action cognizable at law, as this one is, the plaintiff must be able to show that the "accounts between the parties" are of such a "complicated nature" that only a court of equity can satisfactorily unravel them. [In this case,] a jury, under proper instructions from the court, could readily determine the recovery, if any, to be had here, whether the theory finally settled upon is that of breach of contract, that of trademark infringement, or any combination of the two.[77]

The Court concluded that the district judge erred in refusing to grant defendant's demand for a jury trial on the factual issues related to the factual breach-of-

---

74. *Id.* at 475-76, 82 S. Ct. at 898-99, 8 L. Ed. 2d at 49-50.

75. *Id.* at 470, 82 S. Ct. at 896, 8 L. Ed. 2d at 47.

76. *Id.* at 472-73, 82 S. Ct. at 897, 8 L. Ed. 2d at 48.

77. *Id.* at 477-79, 82 S. Ct. at 900, 8 L. Ed. 2d at 51-52 (footnotes omitted) ("The legal remedy cannot be characterized as inadequate merely because the measure of damages may necessitate a look into petitioner's business records.")

contract issues. Because those issues were common with those upon which the plaintiff's claim to equitable relief was based, the legal claims involved in the action had to be determined before the court decided the outcome of the plaintiff's equitable claims.[78]

Thus, based on *Beacon Theatres* and *Dairy Queen*, a right to trial by jury would exist in all three of the situations discussed in subsections *(a)(i)-(iii)*, above. It is therefore immaterial under the federal approach whether equity had to act first, a common-law court had to act first, or the plaintiff could control which court acted first.[79]

3. Cases in Which the Plaintiff Sues in Equity and the Defendant Asserts a Counterclaim for Legal Relief

Before the merger of law and equity, a plaintiff could sue in an equity court for an equitable remedy. In response, the defendant could assert a claim for legal relief against the plaintiff by cross-bill.[80] The defendant in such an action, however, did not have to assert the legal claim. Instead, the defendant could sue separately on the counterclaim in a law court. Thus, there could be (1) a single proceeding in equity without a jury or (2) two proceedings, one in equity without a jury and one at law, with a jury. When separate proceedings were maintained on the legal and equitable claims, the first proceeding to reach judgment would be res judicata in the other proceeding on the common issues.[81]

Courts following the historical approach after merger have arrived at different solutions in this situation. Some courts have held that no jury trial right exists when the defendant serves a legal counterclaim in an equitable action.[82] Other courts, following the federal approach in *Beacon Theatres*, have required a jury trial when the defendant asserts a compulsory "legal" counterclaim.[83]

---

78. *Id.* at 479-80, 82 S. Ct. at 900-01, 8 L. Ed. 2d at 52 (footnotes omitted).

79. Reception of the *Dairy Queen* approach in the states has been mixed. *See* DAN B. DOBBS, LAW OF REMEDIES § 2.6(4), at 120-21 (2d student ed. 1993); *see also* Fleet v. Sanguine, Ltd., 1993 OK 76, 854 P.2d 892 (when equitable and legal claims arise out of same transaction, the court may decide equity claims but legal issues must be decided by the jury); State v. Crees, 474 N.W.2d 282 (Iowa Ct. App. 1991) (trial court has discretion to try equitable and legal claims separately).

80. The converse was not possible: if the plaintiff sued at common law, the defendant could not counterclaim against the plaintiff for equitable relief. *See* Chapter 7(D) ("Joinder of Claims by Defendants at Common Law and in Equity") *supra*.

81. *See* Fleming James, Jr., *Right to a Jury Trial in Civil Action*, 72 YALE L.J. 655, 681-83 (1963).

82. *See* DAN B. DOBBS, THE LAW OF REMEDIES § 2.6(4), at 122 (2d student ed. 1993); *cf.* Sargent County Bank v. Wentworth, 500 N.W.2d 862 (N.D. 1993) (legal counterclaim in equitable action really raised legal defenses to foreclosure action; therefore, no right to jury trial existed); Adolph Rub Trust v. Rub, 474 N.W.2d 73 (N.D. 1991) (same).

83. *See* DAN B. DOBBS, LAW OF REMEDIES § 2.6(4), at 122 (2d student ed. 1993); *see also* the discussion of *Beacon Theatres* in section D ("The Right to Trial by Jury in a Merged System: The Basic Approaches") *supra*.

Finally, some courts have held that the judge has discretion whether to order a jury trial in this situation.[84]

4. Cases in Which the Defendant Asserts an Equitable Defense to a Legal Claim

At common law, the defendant could not interpose an equitable defense to a legal claim. For example, a defendant possessing a defense of fraud to a contract claim would have to sue in equity to obtain relief from the contract. The equity court would enjoin the plaintiff at law from prosecuting the legal action until the equity suit had been tried. If the equitable "defense" was sustained, the entire suit would effectively be resolved. The equity court would dispose of any residual legal issues under the clean-up doctrine. If the equitable defense failed, the suit in equity would be dismissed and the parties would be left to their legal remedies.[85]

Under the historical approach in a merged system, the defendant simply pleads the equitable defense to the plaintiff's claim. The equitable issue is tried to the court first. If the equitable defense is valid, the entire case is resolved. Over time, however, some defenses that originally were recognized only in equity came to be recognized in law courts. These defenses had "worked over" into law.[86] When this situation occurred, equity regarded the remedy at law to be adequate and refused to act. Thus, before determining whether a jury trial is appropriate, a jurisdiction using the historical test must determine whether the defense in question had "worked over" prior to merger.[87]

Under the federal approach, the ability to raise "equitable defenses" under the Federal Rules of Civil Procedure renders the legal remedies adequate and requires a jury trial of all issues. This conclusion is the inevitable result of the Court's decisions in *Beacon Theatres* and *Dairy Queen*.

5. Cases in Which the Plaintiff Asserts a Legal Claim by Means of a Procedure Available Only in Equity

Before the merger of law and equity, certain procedures were available only in an equity court. For example, class actions were available only in an equity court.[88] When legal claims were asserted using these equitable procedures,

---

84. *See* DAN B. DOBBS, LAW OF REMEDIES § 2.6(4), at 122 (2d student ed. 1993). Such an order is particularly appropriate when the plaintiff sues for equitable relief on the basis of a ground that would be a defense in an action at law and the defendant interposes a legal counterclaim. *See* Fleming James, Jr., *Right to a Jury Trial in a Civil Action*, 72 YALE L.J. 655, 685 (1965).

85. *See* Fleming James, Jr., *Right to a Jury Trial in a Civil Action*, 72 YALE L.J. 655, 679 (1965).

86. *See id.* at 673, 679-80.

87. *See id.* at 679.

88. *See* Chapter 8(D)(4) ("Class Actions") *supra*.

no right of jury trial existed. Thus, under the historical test in a merged system, no right to jury trial would exist in such a case.[89]

The result in the federal courts today is dictated by the decision of *Ross v. Bernhard*.[90] In *Ross*, stockholders brought a derivative suit against the directors of a closed-end investment company and the corporation's brokers. The plaintiffs alleged that the defendant directors had converted assets of the corporation. The plaintiffs also alleged that the defendant brokers had violated the Investment Company Act of 1940 by extracting excessive fees from the corporation.[91] The plaintiffs demanded that the defendants "account for and pay to the Corporation for their profits and gains and its losses."[92]

The plaintiffs requested a jury trial on the corporation's claim. The federal district court denied the defendants' motion to strike the jury trial demand. The Second Circuit, however, reversed. The Second Circuit held that a derivative action was entirely equitable in nature. Thus, a jury was not available to try any part of that action.[93] On certiorari, the U.S. Supreme Court reversed the Second Circuit.[94] The Court concluded that although the stockholders' standing to sue on behalf of the corporation was an equitable matter prior to merger, the underlying corporate "claim is, at least in part, a legal one."[95] The Court pointed out that had the law courts recognized the stockholders' right to sue, the basis for equitable relief would have disappeared. The Court indicated that the merger of law and equity under Federal Rules of Civil Procedure had the same effect. Thus, the Federal Rules of Civil Procedure removed the barrier to a jury trial of the corporate claim after there has been a nonjury adjudication of the stockholders' right to bring the derivative action. Because the case involved two claims, one equitable and one legal, the Court held that the Seventh Amendment required the corporation's claim to be tried by a jury.[96]

---

89. *See* 9 CHARLES A. WRIGHT & ARTHUR R. MILLER, FEDERAL PRACTICE AND PROCEDURE: CIVIL § 2302.1, at 35 (2d ed. 1995).

90. 396 U.S. 531, 90 S. Ct. 733, 24 L. Ed. 2d 729 (1970).

91. *See* Investment Company Act of 1940, Pub. L. No. 76-686, tit. I, 54 Stat. 589 (codified as amended at 15 U.S.C. § 80a-1 to 80a-64).

92. Ross v. Bernhard, 396 U.S. at 531-32, 90 S. Ct. at 734, 24 L. Ed. 2d at 732.

93. Under premerger practice, the corporation's legal claim could have been disposed of by an equity court because the corporation refused to bring the action at law. Without equitable determination of standing, the stockholder could not sue. On this basis, the equity court remedied what would otherwise be irreparable injury.

94. *Id.* at 532, 90 S. Ct. at 735, 24 L. Ed. 2d at 733.

95. *Id.* at 542, 90 S. Ct. at 740, 24 L. Ed. 2d at 738. The Court stated that

> [t]he relief sought is money damages. There are allegations in the complaint of breach of fiduciary duty, but there are also allegations of ordinary breach of contract and gross negligence. The corporation, had it sued on its own behalf, would have been entitled to a jury's determination, at a minimum, of its damages against its broker under the brokerage contract and of its rights against its own directors because of their negligence.

Id.

96. *Id.* at 533-40, 90 S. Ct. at 735-39, 24 L. Ed. 2d at 733-37. In dissent, Justice Stewart, joined by Chief Justice Burger and Justice Harlan, asserted, *inter alia*, that the case differed from *Beacon Theatres* and *Dairy Queen* because those cases dealt with not only claims properly cognizable at law, but also claims triable in equity. In contrast, according to Justice Stewart, the shareholders' derivative suit had always been treated a single cause of action tried exclusively in equity. Thus, Justice Stewart rejected the Court's position that the proceeding to establish standing and the proceeding on the corporation's claim constituted two different elements of the action. *Id.* at 543-51, 90 S. Ct. at 740-45, 24 L. Ed. 2d at 739-43. Note, however, that if the corporation's

6. Right to a Jury Trial in Statutory and Administrative Proceedings

In the leading case of *Curtis v. Loether*,[97] the plaintiff commenced an action under § 812 of the Civil Rights Act of 1968. Section 812 authorized private plaintiffs to bring civil actions to redress fair housing violations. In *Curtis*, the plaintiff alleged that the defendants had refused to rent an apartment to her because of her race. The plaintiff initially sought only injunctive relief and punitive damages. Later, she amended her complaint to include a claim for compensatory damages. The Act provided that "[t]he court may grant as relief, as it deems appropriate, any permanent or temporary injunction, temporary restraining order, or other order, and may award to the plaintiff actual damages and not more than $1,000 punitive damages, together with court costs and reasonable attorney fees . . . ."[98]

The defendants demanded a jury trial. The trial court denied the jury trial request because the Civil Rights Act did not authorize a jury trial and the Seventh Amendment did not require one. The trial court dissolved a preliminary injunction after the plaintiff obtained other housing. At trial, the court found that the defendants had discriminated against the plaintiff because of her race. Although no actual damages were found, the court awarded $250 in punitive damages. The Seventh Circuit reversed on the jury trial issue. On certiorari, the U.S. Supreme Court affirmed the reversal.[99]

After reviewing several cases, the Court recognized that Congress had the "power to entrust enforcement of statutory rights to an administrative process or specialized court of equity free from the strictures of the Seventh Amendment."[100] The Court, however, stated that "when Congress provides for enforcement of statutory rights in an ordinary civil action in the district courts, where there is obviously no functional justification for denying the jury trial right, a jury trial must be available if the action involves rights and remedies of the sort typically enforced in an action at law."[101] With respect to damage actions under § 812, the Court stated that a § 812 damage action

> sounds basically in tort—the statute merely defines a new legal duty, and authorizes the courts to compensate a plaintiff for the injury caused by the defendant's wrongful breach. [Thus,] this cause of action is analogous to a number of tort actions recognized at common law [principally the common-law action against innkeepers who refused temporary lodging to a traveler without

---

claim is equitable, a trial by jury will not be required in a derivative action. *See* Kalish v. Franklin Advisers, Inc., 928 F.2d 590 (2d Cir.), *cert. denied*, 502 U.S. 818, 112 S. Ct. 75, 116 L. Ed. 2d 48 (1991).

97. 415 U.S. 189, 94 S. Ct. 1005, 39 L. Ed. 2d 260 (1974); *see also* Atlas Roofing Co. v. Occupational Safety & Health Review Comm'n, 430 U.S. 442, 97 S. Ct. 1261, 51 L. Ed. 2d 464 (1977); Pernell v. Southall Realty, 416 U.S. 363, 94 S. Ct. 1723, 40 L. Ed. 2d 198 (1974).

98. *Curtis*, 415 U.S. at 189-90, 94 S. Ct. at 1006, 39 L. Ed. 2d at 263-64.

99. *Id.* at 190-91, 94 S. Ct. at 1006-07, 39 L. Ed. 2d at 264-65.

100. *Id.* at 195, 94 S. Ct. at 1009, 39 L. Ed. 2d at 267.

101. *Id.*

justification and dignitary torts]. More important, the relief sought here—actual and punitive damages—is the traditional form of relief offered in the courts of law.[102]

In *Tull v. United States*,[103] the federal government sought injunctive relief and civil penalties against a real estate developer for allegedly violating the Clean Water Act by dumping fill on protected wetlands. The Supreme Court held that the Seventh Amendment guaranteed a jury trial to determine the defendant's liability because the government's suit for civil penalties was most analogous to the eighteenth century common-law action of debt. Thus, a jury trial was guaranteed on the legal claim and all issues common between that claim and the injunctive relief sought.[104] On the other hand, because assessing civil penalties was not one of the fundamental "incidents" of a jury trial, the Court held that the Seventh Amendment did not guarantee a jury determination of the amount of the statutory civil penalties.[105]

In *Feltner v. Columbia Pictures Television, Inc.*,[106] the plaintiff exercised his right to recover statutory damages under § 504 of the Copyright Act instead of actual damages. The district court denied the defendants' request for a jury trial and ultimately awarded plaintiff $8,800,000. The Supreme Court held that the Seventh Amendment guaranteed the defendants a right to jury trial under the circumstances. The Court found that before the Seventh Amendment, damage actions for copyright infringement were tried in courts of law before juries. *Tull* was distinguished on the grounds that there was no indication in that case that juries had historically determined the amount of civil penalties to be paid to the government and because an award of civil penalties could be viewed as analogous to sentencing in a criminal proceeding.[107]

In *City of Monterey v. Del Monte Dunes, Ltd.*,[108] the plaintiff sued under 42 U.S.C. § 1983 to obtain compensation from the city for a regulatory taking of property without compensation. The Supreme Court held that the Seventh Amendment right to jury trial applied on the issue of the plaintiff's regulatory takings claim. The Court reasoned that a suit for just compensation is, like ordinary money damages, a compensatory remedy that was legal in nature.

---

102. *Id.* at 195-96, 94 S. Ct. at 1009, 39 L. Ed. 2d at 267.

103. 481 U.S. 412, 107 S. Ct. 1831, 95 L. Ed. 2d 365 (1987).

104. *Id.* at 417-25, 107 S. Ct. at 1835-39, 95 L. Ed. 2d at 372-78.

105. *Id.* at 425-27, 107 S. Ct. at 1839-40, 95 L. Ed. 2d at 378-79; *see also* Chauffeurs, Teamsters & Helpers Local No. 391 v. Terry, 494 U.S. 558, 110 S. Ct. 1339, 108 L. Ed. 2d 519 (1990) (employees seeking relief in the form of back pay for union's alleged breach of its duty of fair representation have a right to trial by jury); Granfinanciera, S.A. v. Nordberg, 492 U.S. 33, 109 S. Ct. 2782, 106 L. Ed. 2d 26 (1989). If a proceeding cannot be analogized to a proceeding at common law, no right of trial by jury will exist. *See* Vinson v. Hamilton, 854 P.2d 733 (Alaska 1993) (statutory forcible entry and detainer remedy analogized to equitable remedy); County of Sutter v. Davis, 234 Cal. App. 3d 319, 285 Cal. Rptr. 736 (1991) (paternity action; no right to jury trial in this kind of action at common law); Zora v. State Ethics Comm'n, 415 Mass. 640, 615 N.E.2d 180 (1993) (action to determine violations of conflict-of-interest law is sui generis and does not express claim recognized at common law entitling party to jury trial); Department of Revenue v. Jarvenpaa, 404 Mass. 177, 534 N.E.2d 286 (1989) (statutory claim by illegitimate child to establish support rights; no right of trial by jury existed because bastardy actions not tried to juries prior to 1780).

106. 523 U.S. 340, 118 S. Ct. 1279, 140 L. Ed. 2d 438 (1998).

107. *Id.* at 354-55, 118 S. Ct. at 1287-88, 140 L. Ed. 2d at 449-50.

108. 526 U.S. 687, 119 S. Ct. 1624, 143 L. Ed. 2d 882 (1999).

Thus, because the plaintiff's suit sounded in tort and sought legal relief, it was an action at law to which the Seventh Amendment applied, even though there was no equivalent to § 1983 framed in specific terms for "vindicating constitutional rights" at the time the Seventh Amendment was ratified. The Seventh Amendment applies not only to common-law causes of action, but to statutory causes of action that are analogous to common-law causes of action that were ordinarily decided in English common-law courts in the late eighteenth century. The Court rejected the city's argument that it should focus on the nature of the underlying right, a "takings clause" claim, and deny the right to jury trial on the theory that the jury's role in estimating just compensation in condemnation proceedings was inconsistent and unclear at the time the Seventh Amendment was ratified. Among other things, the Court reasoned that condemnation proceedings were not properly analogous to § 1983 actions to redress uncompensated takings because liability is not an issue in condemnation proceedings, but it is in § 1983 actions.[109]

SECTION F. RIGHT TO TRIAL BY JURY VERSUS MERE "INCIDENTS" OF THE RIGHT

The Seventh Amendment and state constitutional provisions preserve the *right* to a jury trial but not mere "incidents" of the right. In the immediately preceding discussion of the *Tull* case, for example, the Court permitted the jury to determine liability, but refused to allow the jury to determine the amount of the civil penalty because the latter function was not a fundamental "incident" of a jury trial.[110]

How does one determine whether a historical practice is an essential part of the right to a jury trial or a mere incident of the right? The Supreme Court has principally explored this issue in the context of attempts to reduce the size of the jury. In *Colgrove v. Battin*,[111] the Court reviewed the validity of a local rule that provided that a jury for the trial of civil cases shall consist of six persons instead of the traditional twelve.[112] When the district court set this case for trial before a jury of only six, the plaintiff sought mandamus from the Court of Appeals for the Ninth Circuit to direct the judge to impanel a twelve-person jury. The plaintiff contended that the local rule violated the Seventh Amendment. The

---

109. *Id.* at __, 119 S. Ct. at 1638-44, 143 L. Ed. 2d at __.

110. *See* Tull v. United States, 481 U.S. 412, 107 S. Ct. 1831, 95 L. Ed. 2d 365 (1987) (discussed in the preceding section); *cf.* Clark v. Container Corp. of Am., 589 So. 2d 184 (Ala. 1991) (statute providing that first $150,000 of future damages not be reduced to present value violates state constitutional right to trial by jury by removing from fact-finding function of jury the ability to determine amount of plaintiff's remedy for personal injuries).

111. 413 U.S. 149, 93 S. Ct. 2448, 37 L. Ed. 2d 522 (1973).

112. Prior to *Colgrove*, in Williams v. Florida, 399 U.S. 78, 90 S. Ct. 1893, 26 L. Ed. 2d 446 (1970), the Court sustained the constitutionality of a Florida statute providing for six-member juries in certain criminal cases. The constitutional challenge rejected in that case relied on the guarantees of jury trial secured the accused by Art. III, § 2, cl. 3, of the Constitution and by the Sixth Amendment. The Court expressly reserved, however, the question whether "additional references to the 'common law' that occur in the [S]eventh [A]mendment might support a different interpretation" with respect to jury trial in civil cases. *Id.* at 92 n.30, 90 S. Ct. at 1901 n.30, 26 L. Ed. 2d at 455-56 n.30.

Court of Appeals found no merit in this contention, sustained the validity of the local rule, and denied the writ.[113]

On certiorari, the Supreme Court affirmed. The Court stated that the language of the Seventh Amendment is not directed to jury characteristics, such as size, but rather defines the kind of cases for which jury trial is preserved. From the Amendment's reference to "suits at common law," the Court concluded that the framers of the Seventh Amendment were concerned with preserving the right of trial by jury in civil cases in which the right existed at common law. However, the Court also concluded that the Seventh Amendment did not bind the courts to the exact procedural incidents or details of jury trial existing at the common law in 1791. The Court pointed out that new devices may be used to adapt the ancient institution to present needs and to make it an efficient instrument in the administration of justice. The Court rejected the notion that the reliability of the jury as a factfinder is a function of its size. The number twelve was not a substantive aspect of the right of trial by jury. Although it expressed no view as to whether any number less than six would suffice, the Court held that a jury of six satisfies the Seventh Amendment's guarantee of jury trial.[114]

SECTION G. THE RIGHT TO TRIAL BY JURY IN COMPLEX CASES

The U.S. Supreme Court stated three criteria to determine the "legal" nature of an issue for purposes of determining a right to a jury trial in a footnote in *Ross v. Bernhard*:[115] "first, the custom [prior to merger] with reference to such questions; second, the remedy sought; and third, the practical abilities and limitations of juries . . . ."[116] The third criterion suggested the Court might restrict the jury trial right in complex cases that are beyond the competence of a jury. To date, the Court has not recognized a "complexity exception."[117] However, several lower courts have considered arguments that such an exception should be recognized.

Illustration 11-9. In the *U.S. Financial Securities* case,[118] a federal district court, on its own motion, struck the demands for a jury trial because of

---

113. Colgrove v. Battin, 413 U.S. at 149-51, 93 S. Ct. at 2449-50, 37 L. Ed. 2d at 525.

114. *Id.* at 151-60, 93 S. Ct. at 2450-54, 37 L. Ed. 2d at 526-31; *see also* Cott v. Peppermint Twist Management Co., 253 Kan. 452, 856 P.2d 906 (1993) (Kansas statute providing for nonunanimous verdict of 10 of 12 jurors in civil action does not violate the Due Process Clause of the U.S. Constitution or the Kansas Constitution). For a reexamination of the empirical evidence on twelve and six member juries and an argument for return of the twelve member jury, see *Developments in the Law—The Civil Jury,* 110 HARV. L. REV. 1411, 1466-89 (1997).

115. 396 U.S. 531, 90 S. Ct. 733, 24 L. Ed. 2d 729 (1970) (involving a right to a jury trial in a derivative action). The *Ross v. Bernhard* decision is discussed in section E(5) *supra.*

116. *Id.* at 538 n.10, 90 S. Ct. at 738 n.10, 24 L. Ed. 2d at 736 n.10.

117. The third criterion listed in the *Ross* footnote was noticeably omitted from discussion in Tull v. United States, 481 U.S. 412, 417, 107 S. Ct. 1831, 1835, 95 L. Ed. 2d 365, 373 (1987), which was discussed in section E(6) ("Right to a Jury Trial in Statutory and Administrative Proceedings") *supra.*

118. *In re* United States Fin. Sec. Litig., 609 F.2d 411 (9th Cir. 1979), *cert. denied,* 446 U.S. 929, 100 S. Ct. 1866, 64 L. Ed. 2d 281 (1980).

the complexity of the issues, the massive amount of evidence, and the expected two-year duration of the trial.[119] On interlocutory appeal, the Ninth Circuit reversed. The court stated that "[w]e do not believe that *Ross* may be read as establishing a new test for determining when the Seventh Amendment applies."[120] The court maintained counsel had a duty to present the legal claims and supporting evidence in a comprehensible manner and concluded that "we do not believe any case is so overwhelmingly complex that it is beyond the abilities of a jury."[121]

Illustration 11-10. In the *Japanese Electronics* case,[122] the Third Circuit agreed with the Ninth Circuit that the Seventh Amendment guaranteed a right to trial by jury in complex cases. However, the Third Circuit concluded that the Due Process Clause of the Fifth Amendment prohibits a trial by jury of a suit that is too complex for a jury to decide it competently. Although the Third Circuit recognized that no specific precedent existed for finding a due process violation in the trial of any case to a jury, it maintained that

> [t]he primary value promoted by due process in factfinding procedures is "to minimize the risk of erroneous decisions." . . .
> A jury that cannot understand the evidence and the legal rules to be applied provides no reliable safeguard against erroneous decisions. . . . Unless the jury can understand the legal rules and evidence, we cannot realistically expect that the jury will rest its decision on them.[123]

In assessing whether a case is too complex for a jury to decide, the court stated that a federal district court should consider three factors:

> [F]irst, the overall size of the suit, the primary indicia of which are the estimated length of trial, the amount of evidence to be introduced and the number of issues that will require individual consideration; second, the conceptual difficulties in the legal issues and the factual predicates to the issues, which are likely to be reflected in the amount of expert testimony to be submitted and the probable length and detail of jury instructions; and third, the difficulty of segregating distinct aspects of the case, as indicated by the number of separately disputed issues related to single transactions or items of proof.[124]

---

119. *Id.* at 413, 416-17.

120. *Id.* at 424. The court added that "it is doubtful that the Supreme Court would attempt to make such a radical departure from its prior interpretation of a constitutional provision in a footnote." *Id.* at 425.

121. *Id.* at 432.

122. *In re* Japanese Elecs. Prods. Antitrust Litig., 631 F.2d 1069 (3d Cir. 1980), *aff'd in part and rev'd in part on other grounds following summary judgment,* 723 F.2d 238, 319 (3d Cir. 1983), *rev'd on other grounds,* 475 U.S. 574, 106 S. Ct. 1348, 89 L. Ed. 2d 538 (1986).

123. 631 F.2d at 1084.

124. *Id.* at 1088-89. Although recognizing a "lack of precision in this standard," *id.* at 1089, the court opined that district judges would apply the standard "with a good faith concern for the general preservation of the right to jury trial." *Id. See generally* George K. Chamberlin, Annotation, *Complexity of Civil Action as Affecting Seventh Amendment Right to Trial by Jury,* 54 A.L.R. FED. 733 (1981); Morris S. Arnold, *A Historical Inquiry into the Right to Trial by Jury in Complex Civil Litigation,* 128 U. PA. L. REV. 829 (1980); James S. Campbell & Nicolas LePoiderin, *Complex Cases and Jury Trials: A Reply to Professor Arnold,* 128 U. PA. L.

SECTION H. INVOLUNTARY DISMISSALS, DIRECTED VERDICTS, BURDEN OF PROOF, AND PRESUMPTIONS

When a case goes to trial, the plaintiff ordinarily presents direct evidence first, followed by the defendant's direct evidence, the plaintiff's rebuttal evidence, the defendant's rebuttal evidence, and so forth until both sides rest.[125] The rules governing burden of proof and presumptions determine how much evidence the parties must produce and which parties must produce evidence. Involuntary dismissals (judgments on partial findings) and directed verdicts (judgments as a matter of law) are the modern procedural means provided in the rules for taking advantage of failures to produce sufficient evidence.

1. Involuntary Dismissals (Judgments on Partial Findings) and Directed Verdicts (Judgments as a Matter of Law)

Historically, the earliest means of withdrawing a case from the jury during the course of a trial was a *demurrer to the evidence* at the close of the plaintiff's case. When the plaintiff had failed to introduce evidence to warrant a favorable verdict, even when the evidence was taken as true and construed as strongly as possible in the plaintiff's favor, a demurrer to the evidence would be sustained. In such circumstances, a judgment was entered in favor of the defendant and a later action on the same claim was barred. On the other hand, if the demurrer was overruled, a judgment was entered in favor of the plaintiff. In either event, the defendant was not allowed to offer evidence or argue that the plaintiff's evidence should not be believed, and the case was not submitted to the jury.[126]

Many American jurisdictions developed the practice of allowing the defendant to move for a *nonsuit*—a compulsory dismissal of the plaintiff's action for failure of proof when the plaintiff rested. If the court granted the motion, the court dismissed the action. However, the dismissal ordinarily did not bar a new

---

REV. 965 (1980); Morris S. Arnold, *A Modest Replication to a Lengthy Discourse*, 128 U. PA. L. REV. 986 (1980); Richard O. Lempert, *Civil Juries and Complex Cases: Let's Not Rush to Judgment*, 80 MICH. L. REV. 68 (1981); Frank M. Loo, *Rationale for an Exception to the Seventh Amendment Right to a Jury Trial:* In re Japanese Electronics Products Antitrust Litigation, 30 CLEV. ST. L. REV. 647 (1981); Joseph A. Miron, Jr., Note, *Constitutionality of a Complexity Exception to the Seventh Amendment*, 73 CHI.-KENT L. REV. 865 (1998); William W. Schwarzer, *Reforming Jury Trials*, 132 F.R.D. 575 (1991). For an examination of the jury's role in complex cases and a proposal that rulemakers adopt reforms which will help judges and attorneys empower juries to perform better in complex cases, see *Developments in the Law—The Civil Jury*, 110 HARV. L. REV. 1411, 1489-1513 (1997).

125. *See* section B(3) ("Trial Procedure") *supra*.

126. As Shipman pointed out, "[t]his step [was] taken only in cases in which it [was] very clear that the evidence ha[d] no tendency to prove the case; and naturally it [was] not often resorted to, for it is generally unsafe for a party to rest [the party's] case solely upon the test of what the evidence tends to prove." BENJAMIN J. SHIPMAN, HANDBOOK OF COMMON-LAW PLEADING §§ 328-329, at 526-27 (3d ed. 1923). *See generally* Charles H. King, Comment, *Trial Practice—Demurrer upon Evidence as a Device for Taking a Case from the Jury*, 44 MICH. L. REV. 468 (1945).

action on the same claim.[127] If the court denied the motion, the defendant could then offer evidence. In some jurisdictions, this motion was called a *motion for involuntary dismissal.*

Another method of preventing a case from reaching the jury that developed in American jurisdictions was the motion for a *directed verdict.* When this motion is granted, the judgment has the same preclusive effect as a jury verdict. It thus bars a second action on the same claim. Traditionally, the defendant could make this motion at (1) the close of the plaintiff's case or (2) the close of all the evidence. The plaintiff could also move for a directed verdict at the close of the defendant's case.[128]

A 1991 amendment to Federal Rule 50(a) redesignates a motion for a directed verdict in federal court as a motion for *judgment as a matter of law.*[129] In contrast to prior practice, in which the motion could not be made before a party had rested its case-in-chief, this motion may now be made as soon as it is apparent that any party is unable to carry a burden of proof of any issue that is essential to that party's case.[130] The latest that such a motion may be made is just before the court submits the case to the jury. The motion must "specify the judgment sought and the law and the facts on which the moving party is entitled to the judgment."[131] One purpose of this requirement is to enable the responding party to correct any overlooked deficiencies in the proof.[132]

As revised in 1993, Rule 50(a)(1) specifies that a motion for judgment as a matter of law should be granted when "there is no legally sufficient evidentiary basis for a reasonable jury to find for that party" on an issue essential to any "claim or defense that cannot under the controlling law be maintained or defeated without a favorable finding on that issue."[133] Before the 1991 amendment, Rule 50 had not stated a standard for granting the motion for a directed verdict. The Advisory Committee indicated that this reasonable jury standard had been "articulated in long standing case law" and "effect[ed] no change in the existing standard."[134] The U.S. Supreme Court, however, has not decided whether this standard can be validly applied in a diversity case when the state court would use a different standard.[135] The lower federal courts disagree on the answer to this

---

127. *See* RESTATEMENT (FIRST) OF JUDGMENTS § 53 (1942).

128. *See* Fleming James, Jr., *Burden of Proof,* 47 VA. L. REV. 51, 56 (1961); *see also* David B. Harrison, Annotation, *Propriety of Direction of Verdict in Favor of Fewer than All Defendants at Close of Plaintiff's Case,* 82 A.L.R.3D 974 (1978).

129. *See* FED. R. CIV. P. 50(a).

130. *See* FED. R. CIV. P. 50(a)(1) advisory committee's note to the 1991 amendment.

131. FED. R. CIV. P. 50(a)(2).

132. *Id.* advisory committee's note; *see also* Chapter 12 ("Post-Trail Motions, Appellate Review, and Extraordinary Relief from Judgments") *infra.*

133. FED. R. CIV. P. 50(a)(1). The 1993 amendment corrected an ambiguity in the text of the 1991 revision of this rule. The 1993 "amendment makes clear that judgments as a matter of law in jury trials may be entered against both plaintiffs and defendants and with respect to issues or defenses that may not be wholly dispositive of a claim or defense." *Id.* advisory committee's note to the 1993 amendment.

134. FED. R. CIV. P. 50(a) advisory committee's note to the 1991 amendment.

135. *See* Mercer v. Theriot, 377 U.S. 152, 84 S. Ct. 1157, 12 L. Ed. 2d 206 (1964) (open question); Dick v. New York Life Ins. Co., 359 U.S. 437, 79 S. Ct. 921, 3 L. Ed. 2d 935 (1959) (same).

question.[136] For example, some states follow the "scintilla rule." This rule requires that the judge deny the motion and submit the case to the jury if any evidence exists on which the jury could find in favor of the nonmoving party.[137] Applying a different standard under Federal Rule 50(a)(1) in a diversity action could affect how an issue is ultimately resolved in a "scintilla state," thus producing a conflict that would have to be resolved under the *Erie* doctrine.

It is unclear whether the Advisory Committee intended to establish a uniform "independent" federal standard for use in every case, or whether the Committee was simply leaving unresolved the question of the appropriate standard in diversity cases. In the *Gasperini* case, discussed in Chapter 5,[138] the Supreme Court seemed to signal that the federal courts should, in interpreting Federal Rules of Civil Procedure, turn back to a method that is more "sensitive" to state interests. If such a method were applied to Rule 50(a)(1), the courts would, of necessity, have to conclude that Rule 50(a)(1) does not incorporate an independent federal standard for determining a motion for a judgment as a matter of law, and thus there could be no conflict between Rule 50(a)(1) and state law.

However, a question would still be left under the Rules of Decision Act: can federal courts apply their own "common law" standard for determining whether the evidence is sufficient to go to the jury, or does *Erie* require that they follow the standard of the state in which they are sitting? *Gasperini* also seems relevant to this inquiry. Recall from Chapter 5 that in *Gasperini* the Court held that Federal Rule 59 was inapplicable to a question whether a new trial could be granted because a jury award on a state claim was excessive. The Court additionally held that *Erie* required that federal district courts follow the state standard for determining the excessiveness of jury awards to avoid forum shopping and inequitable administration of the laws.[139] The issue under Rule

---

136. *Compare, e.g.*, Charleston Area Med. Ctr. v. Blue Cross & Blue Shield Mut., Inc., 6 F.3d 243, 247 (4th Cir. 1993) (sufficiency of evidence to create a jury question resolved on the basis of federal law) *with* Burke v. Deere & Co., 6 F.3d 497, 511 (8th Cir. 1993) (sufficiency of evidence is a matter of state law). Neither court discussed the possible significance of incorporating the test into a Federal Rule of Civil Procedure, which is governed by the standards of the Rules Enabling Act–as opposed to a test based on non-Federal Rule federal practice, which is governed by the Rules of Decision Act. *See* Chapter 5 ("Sources of Law") *supra*. *See generally* 9A CHARLES A. WRIGHT & ARTHUR R. MILLER, FEDERAL PRACTICE AND PROCEDURE: CIVIL § 2525 (2d ed. 1995) (citing cases); Walter W. Jones, Jr., Annotation, *Sufficiency of Evidence as Question of Federal or State Law in Diversity Action*, 10 A.L.R. FED. 451 (1972).

137. *See, e.g.*, Barber v. Stephenson, 260 Ala. 151, 69 So. 2d 251 (1953). Furthermore, a state may make an issue always one for the jury. *See, e.g.*, Herron v. Southern Pac. Co., 283 U.S. 91, 51 S. Ct. 383, 75 L. Ed. 857 (1931) (pre-*Erie* case upholding federal judge's refusal in a diversity case to be bound by Arizona constitutional provision making the jury the sole arbiter of the issue of contributory negligence; the court directed a verdict for defendant when it appeared that the plaintiff was guilty of contributory negligence as a matter of law). In some instances, a state may make an issue one that will never be given to the jury. *Cf.* Byrd v. Blue Ridge Rural Elec. Coop., Inc., 356 U.S. 525, 78 S. Ct. 893, 2 L. Ed. 2d 953 (1958) (proper for a federal court in diversity case to refuse to follow South Carolina state court practice of having the court rather than the jury decide the affirmative defense of immunity concerning the status of an employee; factual issues are for the jury in federal court) (strong federal policy against allowing state rules to disrupt the judge-jury relationship in the federal courts).

138. *See* Chapter 5(F)(5) *supra* (discussing *Gasperini's* statement about rule interpretation).

139. *See* Chapter 5(E)(3) *supra* (discussing the Rules of Decision Act holding of *Gasperini*). Furthermore, if the state standard is one that is "bound up" with state substantive rights, assuming that this is still a relevant inquiry under the Rules of Decision Act, the federal courts would be obligated to apply the standard without

50(a)(1) seems indistinguishable from that in *Gasperini* and would seem to call for the same result. If a more stringent federal standard for submitting a case to the jury were applied than would be applied in the forum state's courts, there would be no plaintiff forum shopping, because the more stringent standard would disadvantage plaintiffs. However, in cases involving nonresident defendants, the defendants would be encouraged to forum shop to obtain the more stringent federal standard, and this would also disadvantage a citizen of the forum state in violation of the *Erie* policies.[140] In addition, application of a more stringent federal standard would discourage noncitizen plaintiffs from invoking the diversity jurisdiction, which would illegitimately undermine the policies of the jurisdictional grant.[141]

If application of an independent federal standard to determine whether a case should be submitted to the jury violates the general *Erie* policies, it would be necessary to inquire whether sufficiently strong federal countervailing considerations are present to outweigh the outcome determinative effects. Analogous to *Byrd*, it might be argued that an independent standard is justifiable to avoid disrupting the judge-jury relationship in federal court.[142] However, granting a directed verdict or a motion for judgment as a matter of law is directly related to whether a party has satisfied the burden of proof applicable to the case. In diversity actions, the Supreme Court has uniformly held that state law controls the burden of proof.[143] Given the burden-of-proof cases, therefore, it would seem unlikely that federal countervailing considerations of the *Byrd* variety could be found that would outweigh the outcome determinative violation that would occur by disregarding the state standard for submitting a case to the jury.

Assuming that Rule 50(a)(1) were held to incorporate an independent federal standard for determining whether a case should be submitted to a jury, there would be conflicts between the Rule and state law in some cases. Under these circumstances, it would be necessary to apply the standard for rule validity articulated in the *Burlington Northern* case discussed in Chapter 5.[144] This requires an inquiry into whether Rule 50(a)(1) would impact on a state substantive right, whether the impact would be "substantial" or only "incidental," and whether Rule 50(a)(1) would be reasonably necessary to the uniform scheme of procedure that it was the intent of Congress to establish under the Rules Enabling Act. Because the standard for submitting a case to the jury is closely linked to the

---

regard to the forum shopping and inequitable administration rationales. *See* Chapter 5(E)(2) *supra* (discussing the *Byrd* "bound up" category of cases); Chapter 5(E)(3) *supra* (suggesting that *Gasperini* may have discarded the "bound up" category of cases *sub silentio*).

140. *See* Chapter 5(E)(2), *Illustrations 5-11 & 5-13 supra* (advocating that defendant forum shopping be included in the *Erie* policies). Of course, if a less stringent standard were applied by federal courts, plaintiff forum shopping would be encouraged in violation of the Supreme Court's stated *Erie* policies, and discrimination against defendants who are citizens of the forum state would also occur.

141. *See* Chapter 5(E)(2), *Illustration 5-13 supra* (arguing that even if the *Erie* policies were inapplicable in the situation described, the policies of the diversity jurisdiction should dictate that the federal courts apply state law).

142. *See* Chapter 5(E)(2) *supra* (discussing this aspect of *Byrd*).

143. *See* Palmer v. Hoffman, 318 U.S. 109, 63 S. Ct. 477, 87 L. Ed. 645 (1943); Cities Serv. Oil Co. v. Dunlap, 308 U.S. 208, 60 S. Ct. 201, 84 L. Ed. 196 (1939).

144. *See* Chapter 5(F)(4) *supra* (discussing the *Burlington Northern* test).

burden of proof, it is possible to argue that an independent federal standard under Rule 50(a)(1) would impact on state substantive rights in cases in which the state standard is supported by policies transcending concerns of efficiency and judicial administration and aimed instead at "affecting the decision of the issue."[145] Under these circumstances, the substantive right upon which Rule 50(a)(1) would impact would be the "right" conferred by the state standard itself. However, even if the state standard is supported only by concerns of judicial administration and efficiency, it is arguable that Rule 50(a)(1) would impact on a state substantive right by producing an ultimate outcome on the merits of the case that would not occur under the state standard. If either one of these impacts on substantive rights results, it would seem difficult to argue that the impact would only be "incidental" within the meaning of the *Burlington Northern* standard. Perhaps if the federal and state standards do not differ substantially in a particular case, the effect of the Rule 50(a)(1) standard might be classified as incidental. However, in all other cases, it would seem that the impact on substantive rights would be substantial, as the Federal Rule would either obliterate the policy of the state rule in all diversity cases in which it would otherwise be applicable or affect the outcome on the merits in such cases or both. Furthermore, even if Rule 50(a)(1) has only an incidental impact on state substantive rights, it is difficult to see how such a rule is reasonably necessary to the uniform operation of the Federal Rules scheme. If it is not necessary to the uniform operation of the Federal Rules to have uniform burden-of-proof rules in the first place, it is difficult to see how it is necessary to have an independent federal standard for determining whether a case should be submitted to the jury or not.

Because it appears that a strong case can be made that an independent federal standard incorporated in Rule 50(a)(1) would make the rule invalid under the Rules Enabling Act, the preferable result is to construe the rule as not incorporating such a standard, as indicated above. This should produce the result that the standards of the forum state should be applied under the general *Erie* doctrine.

Former Federal Rule 41(b) provided for involuntary dismissals at the close of the *plaintiff's* case as a means of terminating a *nonjury* action on the merits when the plaintiff had failed to meet the burden of proof applicable to the plaintiff's claim.[146] Under amendments adopted in 1991, a motion to dismiss under former Rule 41 on the ground that a plaintiff's evidence is legally insufficient is now treated as a *motion for judgment on partial findings* as provided in a new Federal Rule 52(c). Rule 52(c) now authorizes the entry of judgment against the defendant as well as the plaintiff. As revised in 1993, Rule 52(c) specifies that after a party has been fully heard on an issue in a *nonjury* trial, the judge "may enter *judgment as a matter of law* against that party with respect to any claim or defense that cannot under controlling law be maintained or defeated

---

145. *Cf.* RESTATEMENT (SECOND) OF CONFLICT OF LAWS § 133 (1971) (discussing burden-of-proof rules supported by such policies).

146. The basis of the defendant's motion for an involuntary dismissal is that "upon the facts and the law the plaintiff has shown no right to relief." FED. R. CIV. P. 41(b) (before 1991 amendment).

without a favorable finding on that issue."[147] If the court renders such a judgment, it is required to make findings of facts and conclusions of law as provided in Federal Rule 52(a).[148] Because the judge is the trier of fact and thus decides factual issues, a motion for judgment on partial findings may be granted even though the judge would let the case go to the jury if there were one.[149]

2. Burden of Proof

To understand when a case should be prevented from reaching the jury through a directed verdict or a judgment as a matter of law, one must focus on the significance of the *burden of proof*. This term has two meanings: (1) the burden of persuasion; and (2) the burden of production.[150] In civil actions, the burden of persuasion is usually described as a requirement that there must be a *preponderance of evidence*, or that the *greater weight of the evidence* must exist in favor of the party having the burden of persuasion before that party is entitled to a verdict.[151] The burden of persuasion becomes relevant only at the end of the trial, when the trier of fact must decide the case.[152] If the trier of fact is a jury, the jury is told that the party having the burden of persuasion on each issue must have the issue decided against that person if the burden has not been satisfied.[153] Thus, because the burden of persuasion is only allocated at the end of the trial, it does not shift back and forth between the parties during the trial.

In contrast, the burden of production is the duty to produce evidence or to go forward with evidence. Unlike the burden of persuasion, the burden of production can shift back and forth between the parties during the trial.[154] The production burden begins at the outset of the trial. The plaintiff must introduce sufficient evidence on each of the propositions of fact that must be established as part of the plaintiff's case to justify a favorable verdict. The consequence of a failure to produce such evidence is loss of the case by means of a nonsuit,

---

147. FED. R. CIV. P. 52(c) (emphasis added). Like the 1993 amendment of Rule 50(a)(1), the 1993 amendment of the 1991 version of Rule 52(c) clarifies that the court may enter a judgment as a matter of law in a nonjury trial against both plaintiffs and defendants on issues or defenses that may not entirely dispose of a claim or defense. *Id.* advisory committee's note to the 1993 amendment.

148. *See* FED. R. CIV. P. 52(a), (c).

149. *Cf.* J.R. Kemper, Annotation, *Comment Note—Power of Court Sitting as Trier of Fact to Dismiss at Close of Plaintiff's Evidence, Notwithstanding Plaintiff Has Made Out Prima Facie Case*, 55 A.L.R.3D 272 (1974). A judgment on partial findings differs from a summary judgment "in the nature of the evaluation made by the court." Summary judgment is based on facts established because of the absence of contrary evidence or because of presumptions which are, in effect, rulings on questions of law. On the other hand, a judgment on partial findings is made after all the evidence bearing on a crucial issue of fact has been heard. In order to be reversed on appeal, a judgment on partial findings must be found to be "clearly erroneous"; that stringent standard does not apply to summary judgment rulings. FED. R. CIV. P. 50(c) advisory committee's note; *see also* Chapter 12 ("Post-Trial Motions, Appellate Review, and Extraordinary Relief from Judgments") *infra*.

150. *See* JAMES B. THAYER, A PRELIMINARY TREATISE ON EVIDENCE AT THE COMMON LAW 355 (1898); Fleming James, Jr., *Burden of Proof*, 47 VA. L. REV. 51, 51 (1961).

151. Fleming James, Jr., *Burdens of Proof*, 47 VA. L. REV. 51, 51 (1961).

152. *See* JOHN W. STRONG ET AL., MCCORMICK ON EVIDENCE § 336, at 596 (4th student ed. 1992).

153. *See id.* Of course, if the trier of fact is a judge, the judge will simply decide the case in accord with the burden of persuasion.

154. *Id.*

directed verdict, involuntary dismissal, or judgment as a matter of law.[155] Because the judge rules on these motions, the judge allocates the burden of production on each issue and determines whether the evidence is sufficient to meet the burden of production.[156]

Illustration 11-11. A sues *B* for libel, alleging that *B* sent a letter to *C* containing false statements about *A*. At trial, *A* calls *B* as a witness, but *B* denies ever sending the letter. *A* also calls *C* as a witness, but *C* denies ever receiving the letter. *A* has the burden of producing evidence that *B* sent the letter to *C*. On the state of the evidence described above, *A* would not satisfy the burden of production. To satisfy the burden of production, a party must ordinarily introduce some affirmative evidence that the fact in question has occurred. *A* has not done that. *B* and *C* denied the sending and receipt of the letter. *A* cannot ordinarily satisfy the burden of production by arguing that *B* and *C* are liars and the trier of fact should not believe their denials.[157]

* * * * *

Once a party has met the initial burden of going forward with the evidence on which the party has the production burden, the party escapes a nonsuit, directed verdict, involuntary dismissal, or judgment as a matter of law. At that point, the burden of production may or may not shift to the opposing party. If the party having the production burden simply offers enough evidence so that the trier of fact *may* infer the truth of the matter in question, but not so much that, without opposing evidence, the trier of fact will be *compelled* to infer the truth of the matter, the production burden will not shift.[158] Under these circumstances, even if the opposing party offers no evidence on the matter, the case will simply be submitted to the trier of fact and decided in accordance with the burden of persuasion.[159]

However, the party having the production burden may introduce enough evidence on the matter to compel the trier of fact to find for the party in the absence of any contrary evidence. Under these circumstances, if the opposing party fails to offer any evidence to controvert that proof, the initial proponent may be entitled to a directed verdict or judgment as a matter of law (in a jury trial)—if the proponent's evidence "leaves open no question of credibility, of evaluation of conduct, or of choice among competing inferences, about which

---

155. *See* Fleming James, Jr., *Burdens of Proof*, 47 VA. L. REV. 51, 55-57 (1961); *see also* Smith v. Rapid Transit, Inc., 317 Mass. 469, 58 N.E.2d 754 (1945).

156. *See* Fleming James, Jr., *Burdens of Proof*, 47 VA. L. REV. 51, 56 (1961). The burden of production is "a device whereby the court determines whether, if the trial were stopped at any given point, it would send the case to the jury. If not, the court decides the case and the jury has no role to play. If the case is sent to the jury, the production burden drops out of the case and has no role to play. The jury will be concerned only with the persuasion burden." *Id.* at 57; *see also id.* at 58-63 (discussing the bases for allocating the burdens of proof); Edward W. Cleary, *Presuming and Pleading: An Essay on Juristic Immaturity*, 12 STANFORD L. REV. 5, 5-16 (1959).

157. *Cf.* Dyer v. MacDougall, 201 F.2d 265 (2d Cir. 1952).

158. *See generally* JOHN W. STRONG ET AL., MCCORMICK ON EVIDENCE § 338 (4th student ed. 1992).

159. *Cf.* Pan Am. World Airways v. Port Auth., 995 F.2d 5 (2d Cir. 1993) (granting of Rule 50(a) motion by defendant for judgment as a matter of law was erroneous; plaintiff introduced sufficient evidence from which a jury could infer negligence by defendant).

reasonable minds might differ."[160] To prevent a directed verdict or judgment as a matter of law from being entered, the opponent must "offer evidence which either (a) presents a question for the jury, so that the production burden rests on neither party, or (b) is of such compelling force as to shift the production burden back again to the party who bore it at the outset . . . ."[161]

3. Presumptions

Parties may satisfy their respective burdens of production or persuasion in other ways than producing evidence on each issue at trial. As previously discussed, admissions made in the pleadings or during discovery may eliminate issues from trial. Furthermore, when no genuine dispute on an issue exists, partial summary judgment may eliminate it from trial.[162] In addition, a party seeking to establish a fact at trial may benefit from a *presumption*. A presumption is best defined as "a standardized practice, under which certain facts are held to call for uniform treatment with respect to their effect as proof of other facts."[163] Presumptions are either *rebuttable* or *conclusive*. However, it is generally agreed that a conclusive presumption is not a presumption in the true sense at all. Rather, a conclusive presumption, although cast in evidentiary language, is really a rule of substantive law.[164]

Illustration 11-12. *T* dies testate, leaving a life estate in land to *A*, the remainder to *A's* children. If *A* should die without issue, the land is to go to *B*. When *A* is ninety-four years old and after *A* has had a hysterectomy, *B* enters into a contract with *C* to sell *C* a fee simple title in the land, subject to *A's* life estate. When *C* later refuses to perform the contract, *B* sues to compel performance. The court holds that *B* cannot convey marketable title due to a conclusive presumption that men and women are capable of having children until they die.[165] This conclusive presumption is simply a substantive rule that disallows the sale of the property under the circumstances described to increase certainty and security of land titles.

* * * * *

True presumptions are always *rebuttable*.

Illustration 11-13. Assume that a person dies under unexplained circumstances. In general, courts recognize a rebuttable presumption against suicide as the cause of the death. This presumption can be overcome (rebutted)

---

160. *See* Fleming James, Jr., *Burdens of Proof*, 47 VA. L. REV. 51, 57 (1961).

161. *Id.*

162. *See* Chapter 10(C) ("Summary Judgment") *supra*.

163. JOHN W. STRONG ET AL., MCCORMICK ON EVIDENCE § 342, at 578 (4th student ed. 1992). *See generally* Fleming James, Jr., *Burdens of Proof*, 47 VA. L. REV. 51, 63-70 (1961).

164. *See* JOHN W. STRONG ET AL., MCCORMICK ON EVIDENCE § 342, at 579 (4th student ed. 1992).

165. *See, e.g.*, Walton v. Lee, 634 S.W.2d 159, 160-61 (Ky. 1982); Owings v. Owings, 247 S.W.2d 221 (Ky. 1952).

and disappears when either direct or circumstantial evidence is introduced showing suicide was the cause of death.[166]

SECTION I. EVIDENCE

The rules of evidence limit the parties' ability to prove the elements of their claim or defense. The rules are primarily designed to prevent the introduction of untrustworthy evidence and to assure the trial has reasonable boundaries. However, some rules of evidence, notably those conferring various evidentiary privileges, are designed to protect important values extraneous to the litigation at the expense of the search for truth.

The rules of evidence have evolved over centuries through the familiar common-law processes. Consequently, as with other common-law rules, evidence rules reflect the attitudes of common-law judges and lawyers at the time they were developed. From time to time there have been attempts to codify and reform the law of evidence. One such attempt is the recent enactment of the Federal Rules of Evidence.[167] The Federal Rules are typical of evidence rules generally. Therefore, they provide a good basis for a discussion of evidentiary problems.

Before examining particular evidence rules, one should understand certain concepts that operate in the general subject area of evidence. The first concept is *judicial notice*—a method of avoiding proof of certain kinds of facts at trial. When a fact is not subject to reasonable dispute because it is generally known to be true within the community or is subject to "demonstration" by resorting to readily available unimpeachable sources, the judge may take judicial notice of the fact. Judicial notice thus relieves the party who possesses the burden of proof from presenting evidence on undisputable facts. The purpose of judicial notice is

---

166. *See, e.g.*, Breckenridge v. Midlands Roofing Co., 222 Neb. 452, 455, 384 N.W.2d 298, 300 (1986); Annotation, *Comment Note.—Effect of Presumption as Evidence or Upon Burden of Proof, Where Controverting Evidence Is Introduced*, 5 A.L.R.3D 19 (1966). *Illustration 11-13* describes the "bursting bubble" theory of presumptions, which is the most widely accepted theory of the effect of presumptions in civil actions. *See* JOHN W. STRONG ET AL., MCCORMICK ON EVIDENCE § 344, at 582 (4th student ed. 1992). Under the bursting bubble theory, the effect of a presumption is to shift the production burden to the opposing party. Once the opposing party comes forward with evidence to rebut the presumption, it has no further value in the case. *See id.* at 582-83. Some courts give greater effect to presumptions. Especially when the presumptions are created for important policy reasons, courts sometimes place the burden of persuasion on the party opposing the presumption, as well as the production burden, or place a heavier-than-normal production burden on the opponent. *See id.* at 583-84.

167. The U.S. Supreme Court originally promulgated the Federal Rules of Evidence under 28 U.S.C. § 2072. However, because of objections that had been raised to the rules, particularly to the sections governing evidentiary privileges, Congress passed a statute suspending the operation of the rules unless Congress expressly approved them. *See* Act of Mar. 30, 1973, Pub. L. No. 93-12, 87 Stat. 9. After two years of study and changes in the rules, Congress enacted them into law. *See* Act of Jan. 2, 1975, Pub. L. No. 93-595, 88 Stat. 1926. Congress also supplied 28 U.S.C. § 2076, which, within certain limits, permitted the Supreme Court to amend the Federal Rules of Evidence. Section 2076 was repealed in 1988, and the power to prescribe rules of evidence was provided for in 28 U.S.C. §§ 2072-2074. *See generally* 21 CHARLES A. WRIGHT & KENNETH W. GRAHAM, JR., FEDERAL PRACTICE AND PROCEDURE: EVIDENCE § 5006 (1977). The Federal Rules of Evidence have since been adopted in a large number of states. *See* CHRISTOPHER B. MUELLER & LAIRD C. KIRKPATRICK, EVIDENCE § 1.2 n.2 (2d ed. 1999) (As of 1999, 36 states had patterned their rules or codes on the federal model).

obviously to save time and expense at trial when a fact is not reasonably controvertible.[168]

Illustration 11-14. Examples of judicially noticeable facts include historical facts (such as the date that the United States declared war on Japan in World War II), geographic facts (such as the location and name of the counties in the state in which the court is sitting), scientific and technological facts (such as that the speed of light is 186,282 miles per second or that the speed of sound is much slower than the speed of light), and commonly known facts in a community (such as there are no one way streets in a particular community).[169]

* * * * *

Second, several terms should be understood which relate to the different ways that evidence is categorized. All evidence is either *direct* or *circumstantial*. Direct evidence is evidence that tends to show the existence of a fact in issue without the intervention of any other fact.

Illustration 11-15. An example of direct evidence is eyewitness testimony on the occurrence of an event. Admissible direct evidence, such as the testimony of an eyewitness, usually presents no problems other than problems concerning the credibility of the witness—problems concerning whether the witness should be believed or not.

* * * * *

On the other hand, circumstantial evidence is evidence of a fact or circumstance from which the fact to be proved can be inferred.

Illustration 11-16. Suppose a party is trying to prove the color of the barn on April 1st. Testimony of an eyewitness who observed that the barn was red on April 1st would be direct evidence, but testimony by an eyewitness who observed that it was red on March 30th would be circumstantial evidence of its color on April 1st, because the trier of fact must infer that the barn remained red between March 30th and April 1st.

* * * * *

In addition to direct and circumstantial evidence, evidence is divided into *testimonial* and *real* evidence. Testimonial evidence is simply the testimony of a witness in open court. Real evidence is something produced for direct observation by the trier of fact, such as a photograph, a person's body, or a gun. Real evidence must be authenticated before it can be admitted.

Illustration 11-17. A document might be authenticated by the testimony of a person with personal knowledge that the document is what it is claimed to be.[170] The principal purposes of this requirement are to prevent fraud as well as to prevent mistaken attribution of the document to someone who fortuitously happens to possess the same name as the real author of the document.[171]

* * * * *

Testimonial evidence is further divided into evidence of what the witness has observed or ''knows'' (often described as narrative testimony) and opinion

---

168. *See* FED. R. EVID. 201.

169. *See* JOHN W. STRONG ET AL., McCORMICK ON EVIDENCE §§ 329-330 (4th student ed. 1992).

170. *See generally* FED. R. EVID. 901.

171. JOHN W. STRONG ET AL., McCORMICK ON EVIDENCE § 218, at 403 (4th student ed. 1992).

evidence. Opinion evidence is most often encountered in expert testimony. When specialized knowledge will aid the trier of fact, a witness qualified as an expert may provide the specialized knowledge ''in the form of an opinion or otherwise.''[172] Nonexpert witnesses can also give opinion evidence, but a lay witness's opinion testimony is limited to those opinions or inferences which (1) are based rationally on the witness's perceptions and (2) are helpful in giving the trier of fact a clear understanding of that witness's testimony or of a fact in issue.[173] The distinction between opinion testimony and narrative testimony is only a matter of degree.

In evaluating evidence, a discrete division of functions exists between the judge and the jury. The judge determines preliminary questions of admissibility.

Illustration 11-18. In the first instance, the judge determines whether a witness is qualified as an expert or whether real evidence has been authenticated properly.[174] However, the weight to be given to the evidence is generally a matter for the jury. Thus, the question of whether an expert who is allowed to give an opinion should be believed is a jury decision.

* * * * *

An important qualification to this last rule exists. The judge can refuse to allow a case to go to the jury when a party has failed to satisfy that party's burden of producing evidence. As discussed in section H(2), above, this failure can occur when a party produces no evidence at all on an essential element of that party's case. However, the failure can also occur when the party produces evidence from which a reasonable person could not draw an inference of the truth of the fact to be proved. In such a situation, despite the rule that questions of weight and credibility are reserved for the jury, the judge is making a qualitative judgment about the state of the evidence that amounts to the same thing. Judges make similar determinations in connection with post-trial motions.[175] Likewise, a judge makes a related determination in ruling on a motion for summary judgment—that a factual dispute on the face of the pleadings is not *genuine*.[176]

1. Competency

Traditionally, a witness has been allowed to testify only if the witness is *competent*. At common law, a witness could be incompetent for many

---

172. FED R. EVID. 702. A particular problem exists when an expert wants to provide an opinion based on an ''innovative'' scientific or technical theory that is not generally accepted by those in the field. In Daubert v. Merrell Dow Pharmaceuticals, Inc., 509 U.S. 579, 113 S. Ct. 2786, 125 L. Ed. 2d 469 (1993), the Court held that scientific and technical evidence could be admitted only if the trial court found it to be relevant and to rest on a reliable foundation. Thus, the trial court should perform a ''gatekeeper'' function by excluding such expert testimony.

173. *See* FED. R. EVID. 701.

174. *See* FED. R. EVID. 104(a).

175. *See* Chapter 12(A) (''Post-Trial Motions'') *infra*.

176. *See* Chapter 10(C) (''Summary Judgment'') *supra*.

reasons.[177] The most drastic ground of incompetence was embodied in the rule that parties and persons with a direct pecuniary or proprietary interest in the lawsuit could not testify. The party's self-interest in the outcome of the trial was thought to make the party's testimony on the party's own behalf unreliable. This rationale, however, did not explain why parties were given a privilege not to testify against themselves. The rule has been abolished both in this country and in England, but a vestige of the rule remains in some states in the form of *dead man's statutes*. These statutes disqualify a person from testifying concerning controversies over transactions or occurrences when another party to the transaction or occurrence has died. The fear is that "[t]he survivor could testify though the adverse party's lips would be sealed in death," a fear grounded in the theoretical unreliability of an interested party's testimony.[178] The general view today is that dead man's statutes impede justice. No solid reason exists why a survivor's testimony may not be tested by the same means[179] as all other testimony.

Today, under the Federal Rules of Evidence, "[e]very person is competent to be a witness except as otherwise provided in [the] rules."[180] The rules provide very few grounds of incompetence.[181] However, Rule 601 of the Federal Rules of Evidence also provides that "in civil actions and proceedings, with respect to an element of a claim or defense as to which state law supplies the rule of decision, the competency of a witness shall be determined in accordance with state law."[182]

2. Relevancy

To be admissible, all evidence must be *relevant*.[183] Rule 401 of the Federal Rules of Evidence defines relevant evidence as evidence having any tendency to make a fact of consequence more or less probable than it would be

---

177. At common law, the husband or wife of a party was incompetent to testify for or against the party in a civil or criminal case. When this rule continues to exist at all, it has been modified drastically. Spouses usually can testify for or against their husbands or wives in civil cases in most states. This rule of competence should be distinguished from the rule providing a privilege to prevent testimony about confidential communications between husband and wife, which still exists in some states. *See* JOHN W. STRONG ET AL., MCCORMICK ON EVIDENCE §§ 66, 78-86 (4th student ed. 1992). Other grounds of incompetence that still have broad support in most jurisdictions include the incompetence of a judge or juror to testify in the trial of a case in which the judge or juror is participating, *see* FED. R. EVID. 605, 606, incompetence on grounds of immaturity, and incompetence on grounds of mental capacity. *See* JOHN W. STRONG ET AL., MCCORMICK ON EVIDENCE § 62 (4th student ed. 1992). A ground of incompetence recognized at common law was the disqualification of a witness who had been convicted of a crime. This ground also has been abolished virtually everywhere, although conviction of crime can still be used for purposes of impeaching the credibility of a witness under certain circumstances. *See* FED. R. EVID. 609. A party who was unable to take a religious oath at common law also was disqualified from being a witness. This ground of incompetence has been abolished and probably is prohibited by the First and Fourteenth Amendments to the U.S. Constitution. *See* FED. R. EVID. 603, 610.

178. *See* JOHN W. STRONG ET AL., MCCORMICK ON EVIDENCE § 65, at 92 (4th student ed. 1992).

179. *See* subsection 6 ("Objections, Cross-Examination, and Impeachment") *infra*.

180. FED. R. EVID. 601.

181. *See* FED. R. EVID. 605, 606.

182. FED. R. EVID. 601.

183. *See* FED. R. EVID. 401.

without the evidence.[184] This standard simply means that the evidence must have some tendency in logic, however slight, to prove or disprove a fact in issue. Rule 401 encompasses the traditional definition of both relevant and material evidence. Traditionally, evidence was immaterial if it had no bearing on any fact of consequence to the litigation, though it might have a great bearing on some inconsequential fact.

Illustration 11-19. If the fact of consequence is the color of the barn and a party attempts to introduce evidence proving the color of the house, the evidence is immaterial.

* * * * *

Irrelevant evidence, on the other hand, is evidence that is introduced to prove a fact of consequence to the action but has no logical tendency to do so. Obviously, relevance and materiality are closely related.

Illustration 11-20. The evidence described in *Illustration 11-19* bearing on the color of the barn may be described plausibly as either immaterial or irrelevant. To the extent that the party offers the evidence to prove the color of the house, the evidence is immaterial because the party is attempting to prove a fact of no consequence to the action. However, if the party offers evidence on the color of the house to prove the color of the barn, the evidence is irrelevant because it has no apparent logical bearing on the color of the barn.

* * * * *

Sometimes, however, evidence may be relevant only in connection with other evidence not yet offered. In such cases the apparently irrelevant evidence may be "connected up" later.[185]

Illustration 11-21. In the house example given in *Illustration 11-19*, for instance, the color of the house might be admitted conditioned on the subsequent introduction of evidence that the house and the barn were painted the same color.

* * * * *

Just because evidence is relevant does not mean that it is admissible. The Federal Rules of Evidence enumerate several categories of evidence which are inadmissible even if they are relevant. Relevant but inadmissible evidence includes the following: (1) evidence of character to prove that a person acted in conformity with that person's character on a particular occasion;[186] (2) evidence of subsequent remedial measures to prove negligence or culpable conduct;[187] (3) evidence of offers or acceptances of settlement of claims disputed as to validity or amount to prove liability for or invalidity of the claims;[188] (4) evidence of payments or offers to pay medical expenses to prove liability for an injury;[189] (5) evidence of certain pleas or statements made during criminal proceedings;[190]

---

184. *See id.*

185. *See* FED. R. EVID. 104(b).

186. *See* FED. R. EVID. 404.

187. *See* FED. R. EVID. 407.

188. *See* FED. R. EVID. 408. *See generally* Sonja A. Saehnel, Annotation, *Evidence Involving Compromise or Offer of Compromise as Inadmissible Under Rule 408 of Federal Rules of Evidence*, 72 A.L.R. FED. 592 (1985).

189. *See* FED. R. EVID. 409.

190. *See* FED. R. EVID. 410.

(6) evidence that a person possessed liability insurance to prove negligence or wrongful conduct;[191] and (7) evidence of a sex offense victim's past sexual behavior, with certain exceptions.[192]

In addition, Rule 403 provides that the court may exclude otherwise relevant evidence if its probative value is substantially outweighed by the danger of unfair prejudice, confusion of the issues, misleading the jury, or by considerations of undue delay, waste of time, or needless presentation of cumulative evidence.[193]

3. Hearsay

Hearsay is a statement made out of court which is offered in court to prove the truth of the matter contained in the statement.[194]

Illustration 11-22. Suppose the color of the barn is at issue. If a witness takes the stand and testifies, based on personal knowledge, ''The barn is red,'' there is no hearsay. However, if the witness takes the stand and states, ''Farmer *X* told me that the barn was red,'' the testimony is objectionable as hearsay. The witness is attempting to relate an out-of-court statement (the statement of Farmer *X*) about the color of the barn, and the statement is being offered to prove the truth of the matter contained in the statement.

* * * * *

Hearsay is objectionable because the trier of fact cannot properly assess the credibility of the out-of-court declarant. The statement about the color of the barn in *Illustration 11-22* is objectionable because the trier of fact did not have the opportunity to observe Farmer *X* at the time Farmer *X* made the statement, nor was Farmer *X* subject to cross-examination at that time. Stated differently, hearsay statements are objectionable because the number of testimonial difficulties for the trier of fact doubles when hearsay is offered, but the means of dealing with the testimonial difficulties do not increase correspondingly.[195]

Illustration 11-23. When a witness testifies based on personal knowledge that the barn is red, the trier of fact can be said to be faced with four separate testimonial difficulties. First, the trier must determine whether problems of ambiguity exist. For example, when the witness uses the word ''red,'' does the witness have in mind the same color as the trier of fact? Second, the trier must determine whether problems of insincerity exist. Does the witness really believe what is being communicated to the trier? Does the witness have any reason to lie about the color of the barn? Third, even if the trier of fact concludes that the witness believes what the witness is saying, the trier must determine whether problems of false memory exist. Is there reason to believe that the witness'

---

191. *See* FED. R. EVID. 411.

192. *See* FED. R. EVID. 412.

193. *See* FED. R. EVID. 403; *see also* Steven J. Halasz, Annotation, *Propriety Under Rule 403 of the Federal Rules of Evidence, Permitting Exclusion of Relevant Evidence on Grounds of Prejudice, Confusion, or Waste of Time, of Attack on Credibility of Witness for Party*, 48 A.L.R. FED. 390 (1980).

194. *See* FED. R. EVID. 801(c).

195. *See* Laurence H. Tribe, *Triangulating Hearsay*, 87 HARV. L. REV. 957 (1974).

memory about the color of the barn has faltered? Fourth, the trier must determine whether problems of inaccurate perception exist. Did the witness correctly perceive the color of the barn—for example, is the witness color blind? All of these testimonial difficulties can be considered by the trier of fact through the ordinary process of observing the witness' demeanor during cross-examination. When hearsay is involved, however, the number of testimonial difficulties doubles, because the witness is relating a statement made out of court about the color of the barn. The usual four testimonial difficulties discussed above are present with regard to the witness' testimony about the making of the statement, but in addition there exist four identical testimonial difficulties with the contents of the out-of-court statement. These latter difficulties cannot be explored in the same way that they are explored in the case of ordinary testimony. The trier of fact had no opportunity to observe the demeanor of the declarant at the time the declarant made the out-of-court statement, and the declarant, of course, was not subject to cross-examination about the statement at the time the declarant made it.[196]

* * * * *

It should not be assumed that all hearsay is inadmissible. In fact, numerous exceptions to the hearsay rule enormously complicate the operation of the rule. An exception to the hearsay rule is usually supported either by extraordinary guarantees of trustworthiness concerning a hearsay statement (produced by the absence of one or more of the testimonial difficulties described above), or by a special need for the hearsay statement in the trial of a case, or by both.

The exceptions to the hearsay rule in the Federal Rules of Evidence are found in Rules 803 and 804. Rule 803 contains twenty-four exceptions. Rule 804 contains five exceptions. In addition, Rule 801(d) defines hearsay as not including two kinds of statements that often were classified as exceptions to the hearsay rule at common law. An examination of a few of these exceptions will provide some indication of how the hearsay rule and its exceptions operate.

(a) Admissions of a Party Opponent

Rule 801(d)(2) provides the federal version of the traditional rule governing admissions of a party opponent. An out-of-court statement made by a party to the suit or that party's representative and offered by the party's opponent is defined as an admission by a party opponent.[197]

Illustration 11-24. *A* states to *B*, the tax assessor, "That's not my barn. It's not on my property. I don't own it." Later, *A* sues *C* for damages after *C* intentionally sets the barn on fire. *C* can offer the testimony of *B* about *A's* statement as evidence that *A* does not own the barn. The statement is admissible as an admission of a party opponent.

* * * * *

---

196. *See generally id.*
197. *See* FED. R. EVID. 801(d)(2).

The Advisory Committee's Note to Rule 801(d)(2) states that ''[a]dmissions by a party-opponent are excluded from the category of hearsay on the theory that their admissibility in evidence is the result of the adversary system rather than satisfaction of the conditions of the hearsay rule.''[198] The Advisory Committee meant that there are not necessarily any special guarantees of trustworthiness, nor any special need to allow admissions into evidence. Rather, parties against whom admissions are offered should not be heard to complain that they had no opportunity to observe their own demeanor or cross-examine themselves.

(b) Present Sense Impressions and Excited Utterances

Rule 803 provides for a large number of exceptions to the hearsay rule that are available even though the declarant is available as a witness.[199] Two are found in Rule 803(1) and (2) under the heading of *present sense impressions* and *excited utterances*. At common law, both of these exceptions were sometimes lumped together under the label *res gestae*.[200] The exceptions are based upon special guarantees of trustworthiness that are thought to be inherent in these types of out-of-court declarations. A present sense impression is defined as a statement describing or explaining an event or condition made while the declarant is perceiving the event or condition or made immediately thereafter. The theory ''is that substantial contemporaneity of event and statement negative the likelihood of deliberate or conscious misrepresentation.''[201]

Illustration 11-25. In *Makuc v. American Honda Motor Co.,*[202] for example, a products liability action was brought in connection with a motorbike accident. The First Circuit Court of Appeals held that the district court properly admitted under Rule 803(1) the testimony of previous owners of the motorbike repeating statements made to them by a mechanic regarding the cost of repairs necessary to correct damage that had been done to the motorbike by the previous owners' grandsons. The mechanic's description or explanation of the condition of the motorbike at the time he had been engaged in examining it was regarded as a present sense impression.[203]

* * * * *

An excited utterance is defined as a statement relating to a startling event or condition made while the declarant was under the stress of excitement caused by the event or condition.[204] The theory ''is simply that circumstances may

---

198. FED. R. EVID. 801(d)(2) advisory committee's note.

199. *See* FED. R. EVID. 803.

200. *See* JOHN W. STRONG ET AL., MCCORMICK ON EVIDENCE § 268, at 471 (4th student ed. 1992).

201. FED. R. EVID. 803(1) & advisory committee's note. *See generally* Russell J. Davis, Annotation, *When Is Hearsay Statement a ''Present Sense Impression'' Admissible Under Rule 803(1) of the Federal Rules of Evidence*, 60 A.L.R. FED. 524 (1982).

202. 835 F.2d 389 (1st Cir. 1987).

203. *See id.* at 391-92.

204. FED. R. EVID. 803(2). *See generally* Russell J. Davis, Annotation, *When Is Hearsay Statement an ''Excited Utterance'' Admissible Under Rule 803(2)*, 48 A.L.R. FED. 451 (1980).

produce a condition of excitement which temporarily stills the capacity of reflection and produces utterances free of conscious fabrication.''[205]

Illustration 11-26. In *Hilyer v. Howat Concrete Co.*,[206] for example, a wrongful death action was brought when a construction worker was allegedly run over by the defendant's concrete mixer truck. A co-worker of the deceased construction worker told a police officer shortly after the accident that the decedent had moved in front of the truck without looking. The D.C. Circuit held that the district court properly admitted the police officer's testimony relating the statement. The co-worker's statement was an excited utterance relating to a startling event or condition within the meaning of Rule 803(2).[207]

(c) Statements Against Interest

In contrast to Rule 803, Rule 804 provides certain exceptions to the hearsay rule that are available *only* if the declarant is unavailable as a witness.[208] One such exception is a statement against interest. A statement against interest is a statement that was contrary to the declarant's interest at the time it was made. Statements against interest are thought to possess an extra guarantee of trustworthiness because people do not usually make false statements contrary to their own interests. At common law, a statement against interest had to be against the declarant's pecuniary or proprietary interest to be admissible under the exception. Statements that tended to subject a person to civil or criminal liability did not qualify in all jurisdictions.

However, Rule 804(b)(3) of the Federal Rules of Evidence defines a statement against interest to include statements against the declarant's pecuniary or proprietary interest, as well as statements that so tend ''to subject the declarant to civil or criminal liability, or to render invalid a claim by the declarant against another, that a reasonable person in the declarant's position would not have made the statement unless [the declarant] believ[ed] it to be true.''[209] Rule 804(b)(3) thus extends the exception to its logical limit.[210] Statements against interest are sometimes confused with admissions of a party opponent, but there are important differences between the two.

---

205. FED. R. EVID. 803(2) advisory committee's note.

206. 578 F.2d 422 (D.C. Cir. 1978).

207. *See id.* at 424-25.

208. *See* FED. R. EVID. 804(a). The Advisory Committee explained the reason for the requirement of unavailability as follows:

> [H]earsay which admittedly is not equal in quality to testimony of the declarant on the stand may nevertheless be admitted if the declarant is unavailable and if his statement meets a specified standard. The rule expresses preferences: testimony given on the stand in person is preferred over hearsay, and hearsay, if of the specified quality, is preferred over complete loss of the evidence . . . .

FED. R. EVID. 803(2)(b) advisory committee's note.

209. *See* FED. R. EVID. 804(b)(3). *See generally* Marcia C. Robeson, Annotation, *What Constitutes Statement Against Interest Admissible under Rule 804(b)(3) of Federal Rules of Evidence*, 34 A.L.R. FED. 412 (1977).

210. *See* FED. R. EVID. 804(b)(3) advisory committee's note (originally note to 804(b)(4)).

Illustration 11-27. Admissions of a party opponent do not have to be contrary to the party's interest at the time they are made, while statements against interest must be. The statement in *Illustration 11-24* by *A* to the tax assessor might not be against *A's* interest at the time it was made, if *A* was attempting to prevent the collector from assessing *A* taxes on the property. For that reason, if for no other, it could not qualify as a statement against interest, but it would qualify as an admission. In addition, for a statement against interest to be admissible, the declarant must be unavailable as a witness. The admissions rule contains no such requirement.[211]

(d) Dying Declarations

Traditionally, statements made by persons who were under the belief that their own death was imminent and who did, in fact, die were admissible in a criminal prosecution for homicide to prove the cause or circumstances of the person's impending death. Rule 804(b)(2) of the Federal Rules of Evidence extends the effect of this exception to civil actions. Rule 804(a) provides, in effect, that the declarant only need be unavailable as a witness on one of the grounds there listed, so that the declarant need not actually die for the exception to be available. The theory behind the "dying declarations" exception is that there is a strong likelihood that a person who believes death is imminent will tell the truth. Obviously, the basis of this theory is religious.[212]

Illustration 11-28. Assume that *A* was shot in the chest. Believing that death was imminent and that there was no hope of recovery, *A* tells *W* that *A* had been shot by *B*. *W's* testimony concerning *A's* statement is admissible under Rule 804(b)(2).

(e) Hearsay Within Hearsay and Other Problems

There is the possibility of "hearsay within hearsay."[213] Furthermore, even if a hearsay statement falls within an exception, it may be challenged on other grounds.

Illustration 11-29. *C* may attempt to testify that *A* told *C* that *B* told *A* that the barn was red. Under these circumstances, *B's* statement is hearsay and so is *A's*, if they are offered to prove the color of the barn. For multiple hearsay statements to be admissible, each hearsay statement must fall within one of the exceptions to the hearsay rule.

Illustration 11-30. A hearsay declarant ordinarily must have personal knowledge about the matter contained in the statement and the statement must be relevant. If a hearsay statement is admitted, the credibility of the declarant can be attacked in the same way as the credibility of an ordinary witness.[214]

---

211. *Cf.* 5 JOHN H. WIGMORE, WIGMORE ON EVIDENCE § 1464 (J. Chadbourn rev. 1972). *See also* 4 *id.* § 1069.

212. *See* JOHN W. STRONG ET AL., MCCORMICK ON EVIDENCE §§ 309-315 (4th student ed. 1992).

213. *See* FED. R. EVID. 805.

214. *See* FED. R. EVID. 806.

4. Privilege

Rules of privilege exclude otherwise relevant and admissible evidence to attain some socially beneficial goal unrelated to litigational efficiency. Numerous common-law, statutory, and constitutional privileges exist.[215] These rules of privilege are easily confused with rules of competency. However, important differences exist between competency and privilege rules. Rules of competency are designed to safeguard against unreliable evidence by excluding the testimony of persons who are incapable of giving an accurate or reliable account of the transactions or events. Rules of privilege are designed to exclude even reliable testimony to protect "interests and relationships which, rightly or wrongly, are regarded as of sufficient social importance to justify some sacrifice of availability of evidence relevant to the administration of justice."[216] In addition, rules of competency, if violated by a trial court, produce error which is reversible on appeal. If a claim of privilege is erroneously honored at trial, reversible error also is produced. However, if a claim of privilege is erroneously denied and privileged testimony is admitted into evidence, the purpose of privilege is destroyed and cannot be fulfilled by reversal of the trial court's judgment on appeal.

5. The Best Evidence Rule

Traditionally, in proving the terms of a writing, the courts have required that the original writing be produced unless the original is unavailable for some reason other than the fault of the proponent of the evidence.[217] The original writing is the "best evidence" of the content of the writing. In the Federal Rules of Evidence, the best evidence rule is embodied in Rules 1001-1004 and Rule 1007. By these rules, duplicates are admissible under certain circumstances.[218]

6. Objections, Cross-Examination, and Impeachment

To obtain the exclusion of inadmissible evidence, the party opposing the evidence must object as soon as the ground for objection becomes apparent. The

---

215. To list a few of the most important, there are privileges for (1) confidential communications between husband and wife, (2) confidential communications between attorney and client, (3) confidential information secured in the course of the physician-patient relationship, and (4) a privilege against self-incrimination. *See generally* JOHN W. STRONG ET AL., MCCORMICK ON EVIDENCE §§ 72, 76-77 (4th student ed. 1992). Except to the extent that a privilege, such as the privilege against self-incrimination, is constitutionally based, a particular privilege may or may not exist in any given jurisdiction.

216. *Id.* § 72, at 171.

217. *See id.* § 230, at 412.

218. FED. R. EVID. 1001-1004, 1007. *See generally* Robin C. Larner, Annotation, *Admissibility Pursuant to Federal Rules of Evidence: Admissibility, Pursuant to Rule 1004(1), of Other Evidence of Contents of Writing, Recording, or Photograph, Where Originals Were Allegedly Lost or Destroyed*, 83 A.L.R. FED. 554 (1987); Janet B. Jones, Annotation, *Admissibility of Duplicates Under Rules 1001(4) and 1003 of Federal Rules of Evidence*, 72 A.L.R. FED. 732 (1985); Deborah F. Harris, Annotation, *Admissibility of Summaries of Writings, Recordings, or Photographs Under Rule 1006 of the Federal Rules of Evidence*, 50 A.L.R. FED. 319 (1980).

objection also must reasonably specify the grounds for the objection, unless the ground for the objection is apparent from the context. If a party is unable reasonably to object before the objectionable evidence is admitted, an objection must be made promptly after the evidence comes in and the judge must be asked to instruct the jury to disregard the evidence.[219] Failure to abide by this "contemporaneous objection" rule gives the trier of fact discretion to weigh the evidence as it chooses and prevents the party opposing the evidence from complaining about its admission on appeal.

An important qualification of the contemporaneous objection rule is the so-called *plain error rule.* Even without an objection, a trial court judgment may be reversed when admitted evidence was so plainly inadmissible or so taints a trial that it is fundamentally biased.[220] This rule usually is applied to evidence that is constitutionally inadmissible in criminal proceedings and is rarely used in civil actions.[221] Of course, even evidence that is improperly admitted over objection must cause some harm to the opposing party to be the basis for a reversal on appeal.

If evidence is excluded after an objection, the party attempting to introduce the evidence may have to make an *offer of proof* to establish a record for a later appeal.[222] An offer of proof is simply a statement of what the evidence would show had it been admitted. Such an offer should be made outside the hearing of the jury to prevent the jury from being prejudiced by the information. If the parties disagree about whether the evidence will show what its proponent claims, the evidence actually can be heard in the absence of the jury to make a record.[223]

After a witness has testified, the opposing party may cross-examine and attempt to impeach the witness. In most jurisdictions, cross-examination of a witness is limited to the subjects covered in the direct examination and to matters affecting the credibility of the witness.[224] On cross-examination, however, the questioner is permitted to "lead" the witness, whereas such leading usually is not permitted on direct examination.[225] A *leading question* is simply one that suggests the answer to the witness.[226]

A witness may be *impeached* in a variety of ways. On cross-examination, the questioner may ask questions that demonstrate (1) biases, prejudices, or ambiguities in the witness's testimony; (2) the inability of the witness to observe what the witness claims to have seen; or (3) the inability to accurately remember

---

219. *See* FED. R. EVID. 103(a)(1); *see also* Collen R. Courtade, Annotation, *Sufficiency in Federal Court of Motion in Limine to Preserve for Appeal Objection to Evidence Absent Contemporary Objection at Trial,* 76 A.L.R. FED. 619 (1986).

220. *See* FED. R. EVID. 103(d).

221. *See* JOHN W. STRONG ET AL., MCCORMICK ON EVIDENCE § 52, at 78 (4th student ed. 1992).

222. *See* FED. R. EVID. 103(a)(2).

223. *See generally* J.A. Bock, Annotation, *Construction of Provision of Rule 43(c) of Federal Rules of Civil Procedure, and Similar State Provisions, Providing for Entry into Record of Evidence Excluded by Trial Court,* 9 A.L.R.3D 508 (1966).

224. *See, e.g.,* FED. R. EVID. 611(b).

225. *See* FED. R. EVID. 611(c).

226. *See* JOHN W. STRONG ET AL., MCCORMICK ON EVIDENCE § 6, at 9 (4th student ed. 1992).

the facts to which the witness has testified. The testimony of other witnesses giving their opinion of the original witness' character for truthfulness, or who can testify to the original witness' reputation for truthfulness in the community can be used to attack the witness' character.[227] Specific instances of the witness' conduct that bear on the original witness' truthfulness may be inquired into on cross-examination, though they may not be the subject of extrinsic evidence.[228] Evidence that a witness was convicted of a serious crime can be elicited, within certain limits, from the witness or established by public record during cross-examination.[229] Finally, a prior statement of a witness inconsistent with the witness' testimony on the stand can be introduced to impeach the witness.

Traditionally, a party was not permitted to impeach a witness that party had called to the stand. This rule left the party somewhat vulnerable when a witness gave testimony on direct examination that unexpectedly damaged the party. The federal courts and many states have abolished this rule.[230] Even when the rule remains in effect, however, a party can contradict a story told by a witness by calling other witnesses to testify to contrary facts.[231] *Impeachment by contradiction* also is open, of course, to the party opposing a witness' testimony.

Impeachment is simply a device aimed at getting the trier of fact to doubt a witness. When a witness has been impeached by one of the methods described above, the witness' testimony is not excluded from evidence. Since matters of weight and credibility are ordinarily for the trier of fact, whether impeachment is successful or unsuccessful depends upon the impression it makes on the trier.

SECTION J. VARIANCE AND AMENDMENTS AT TRIAL

Evidence proving matters outside the pleadings and not directed to a proposition of consequence in the action could be objected to as "irrelevant." Such evidence produces a "variance" between the issues framed by the pleadings or pretrial order and the proof at trial. A variance at common law was fatal, even though the evidence may have disclosed a meritorious claim outside the pleadings. In 1833, a statute permitted judges at nisi prius (on circuit trying the case) to amend the pleadings at trial when a variance occurred.[232] Previously, such an amendment could not be made during trial because the judges on circuit were only authorized to try issues raised in the pleadings, not to alter the pleadings.[233]

---

227. *See* FED. R. EVID. 608(a).

228. *See* FED. R. EVID. 608(b).

229. *See* FED. R. EVID. 609.

230. *See* FED. R. EVID. 607.

231. *See* JOHN W. STRONG ET AL., MCCORMICK ON EVIDENCE § 38, at 50 (4th student ed. 1992).

232. 3 & 4 Will. IV, ch. 42 (1833).

233. CHARLES E. CLARK, HANDBOOK OF THE LAW OF CODE PLEADING § 114, at 705 (2d ed. 1947).

When the codes were enacted, the drafters provided for liberal amendment of pleadings.[234] Under these general provisions governing amendments, the courts were vested with discretion to deal with variances by ruling on amendments to the pleadings after an objection had occurred. In guiding the courts in using their discretion, most codes directed the court to consider whether the variance was "material."[235] As noted in Chapter 6, however, some codes either explicitly or by interpretation prohibited amendments that "substantially changed the claim," and in those states the court's discretion to permit amendments to cure variances was significantly limited.[236]

Rule 15(b) of the Federal Rules of Civil Procedure provides that when an objection to evidence is made at trial on the grounds that the evidence is not within the issues made by the pleadings, the court may allow an amendment to the pleadings "when the presentation of the merits of the action will be subserved thereby and the objecting party fails to satisfy the court that the admission of such evidence would prejudice the party in maintaining the party's action or defense on the merits."[237] Prejudice to the objecting party might take the form of surprise—that the party is not prepared to meet the unexpected evidence outside the pleadings. This ground for claiming prejudice is undercut, however, by the last sentence of Rule 15(b): "The court may grant a continuance to enable the objecting party to meet such evidence."[238]

In the preceding discussion, it has been assumed that the opposing party objected to the evidence offered and the issue of variance was to be decided by the court's ruling on a subsequent amendment. What happens if the opposing party does not object to the evidence at the time it is offered? At common law, the doctrine of "aider by verdict" would cure variances in some cases. The basic

---

234. Although there were minor differences in wording, most codes provided as follows:

The court may, in furtherance of justice, and on such terms as may be proper, allow a party to amend any pleading or proceeding by adding or striking out the name of any party, or by correcting a mistake in the name of a party, or a mistake in any other respect; and may, upon like terms, enlarge the time for answer or demurrer. The court may likewise, in its discretion, after notice to the adverse party, allow, upon such terms as may be just, an amendment to any pleading or proceeding in other particulars. . . .

Id. § 115, at 710 (quoting CAL. CODE CIV. PROC. § 473 (Deering 1941)).

235. For example, the California Code of Civil Procedure provided as follows:

No variance between the allegation in a pleading and the proof is to be deemed material, unless it has actually misled the adverse party to his prejudice in maintaining his action or defense upon the merits. Whenever it appears that a party has been so misled, the court may order the pleading to be amended upon such terms as may be just.

Where the variance is not material, * * * the court may direct the fact to be found according to the evidence, or may order an immediate amendment, without costs.

Where, however, the allegation of the claim or defense to which the proof is directed, is unproved, not in some particular or particulars only, but in its general scope and meaning, it is not to be deemed a case of variance, * * * but a failure of proof.

Id. § 120, at 739 (quoting CAL. CODE CIV. PROC. §§ 469-471 (Deering 1941)).

236. *Id.* § 115, at 711-12; *see* Chapter 6(C)(5) ("Amendments and Supplemental Pleadings") *supra.*

237. FED. R. CIV. P. 15(b); *see* David B. Levendusky, Annotation, *What Constitutes "Prejudice" to Party Who Objects to Evidence Outside Issues Made by Pleadings so as to Preclude Amendment of Pleading Under Rule 15(b) of Federal Rules of Civil Procedure*, 20 A.L.R. FED. 448 (1974).

238. FED. R. CIV. P. 15(b); *see* Robbins v. Jordan, 181 F.2d 793 (D.C. Cir. 1950). *But see* Moody v. FMC Corp., 995 F.2d 63 (5th Cir. 1993) (permission to amend at trial denied because of delay in requesting permission and prejudice to opposing party).

rule presumed that after the verdict any fact necessary to sustain the verdict was sufficiently proved even if it was ill-pleaded. The common law, however, refused to allow aider by verdict when the declaration contained no averment at all, imperfect or otherwise, of the ultimate fact required to establish the pleader's case. Thus, it was said that "the verdict will supplement an incomplete pleading, but will not supply a total want of averment."[239]

If a party failed to object to evidence that varied from the pleadings in a code-pleading state, the matter might be deemed to have been *tried by consent*. If a matter were tried by consent, a party would be permitted in most code states to amend the pleadings to "conform" to the evidence so that they were consistent with the issues that were actually litigated at trial. Some codes, however, permitted such an amendment only when it did "not change substantially the claim or defense."[240]

Federal Rule 15(b) also envisions that issues may be tried by consent of the parties: "When issues not raised by the pleadings are tried by express or implied consent of the parties, they shall be treated in all respects as if they had been raised in the pleadings."[241] Rule 15(b) directs the court to permit amendments of the pleadings so that they conform to the evidence, even after judgment.[242] Once a court determines that an issue has been tried by consent, the court cannot refuse the amendment. Furthermore, the issue tried by consent must be submitted by the court to the jury (if it is otherwise appropriate for it to do so) or the court in a nonjury trial must make a finding on the issue.[243]

SECTION K. JURY INSTRUCTIONS

At the close of a trial, the court instructs the jury.[244] Instructions state the law that applies to the facts and issues in the case. They also explain the rules regulating how the jury should conduct its deliberations to arrive at a verdict. If a party wants to request that a particular instruction or set of instructions be given, that request must be made at the close of the evidence or at an earlier time when the court reasonably so directs.[245] If no specific requests are made, "the court must nevertheless charge the jury on the broad general fundamental rules applicable to the principal issues of fact in the case [but] in the absence of a

---

239. JOSEPH H. KOFFLER & ALISON REPPY, HANDBOOK OF COMMON LAW PLEADING § 299, at 556-57 (1969).

240. *See, e.g.,* NEB. REV. STAT. § 25-852 (1995); McCook Nat'l Bank v. Myers, 243 Neb. 853, 503 N.W.2d 200 (1993) (amendment cannot substantially change the claim or defense; prejudicial error occurs when amendment changes issues and affects quantum of proof as to any material fact); *see also* CHARLES E. CLARK, HANDBOOK OF THE LAW OF CODE PLEADING § 115, at 711 (2d ed. 1947); Chapter 6(C)(5) ("Amendments and Supplemental Pleadings") *supra*.

241. FED. R. CIV. P. 15(b).

242. *Id.*

243. 6A CHARLES A. WRIGHT ET AL., FEDERAL PRACTICE AND PROCEDURE: CIVIL § 1493, at 43 (2d ed. 1990).

244. FED. R. CIV. P. 51. In 1987, Rule 51 was amended to give federal courts discretion to instruct the jury either before or after closing argument. *See id.*

245. *Id.*

timely request for detailed instructions, counsel must rest content with an accurate general statement of the basic principles of law applicable to the case.''[246] In many jurisdictions, however, each party is required by statute or rule to submit a proposed set of instructions. In federal court, the court is specifically required to inform counsel of its proposed action upon their requests prior to their arguments to the jury.[247] In federal court and in nearly all state courts, if counsel wants to object to the giving or the failure to give an instruction, that objection must be made before the jury retires to consider its verdict. Counsel must state the specific grounds of the objection.[248]

SECTION L. VERDICTS AND FINDINGS BY THE COURT

The most common form of a verdict is the *general verdict*. In a general verdict, the jury simply finds either for the plaintiff and awards a certain dollar amount or finds for the defendant that the plaintiff shall take nothing. No explanation of the verdict is required.[249] In some state jurisdictions, however, *special verdicts*, rather than general verdicts, are routinely used.[250] A special verdict requires the jury to answer interrogatories submitted to it without concluding which party should prevail in the case. In the federal courts, special verdicts are authorized by Federal Rule 49(a), which gives the district judge discretion to require the jury to return a special verdict.[251]

Use of the general verdict accompanied by interrogatories has been described as a "middle course" between use of a general verdict form and use

---

246. 9 Cora M. Thompson, Cyclopedia of Federal Procedure § 31.100, at 568 (3d rev. ed. 1993).

247. Fed. R. Civ. P. 51; *see* W.R. Habeeb, Annotation, *Provision in Federal Rule 51, Federal Rules of Civil Procedure and Similar State Rules and Statutes Requiring Court to Inform Counsel, Prior to Argument to Jury, of Its Proposed Action upon Requests for Instructions*, 91 A.L.R.2d 836 (1963).

248. *See* Annotation, *Construction and Application of Provision of Rule 51 of Federal Rules of Civil Procedure Requiring Party Objecting to Instructions or Failure to Give Instructions to Jury, to State "Distinctly the Matter to Which He Objects and the Grounds for Objections,"* 35 A.L.R. Fed. 727 (1977); D.E. Ytreberg, Annotation, *Construction and Effect of Provision of Rule 51 of Federal Rules of Civil Procedure, and Similar State Rules, that Counsel Be Given Opportunity to Make Objections to Instructions Out of Hearing of Jury*, 1 A.L.R. Fed. 310 (1969).

249. A typical general verdict would be: "We, the jury in the above-entitled and numbered action, find in favor of plaintiff and against defendant, and assess plaintiff's damages at $_____ [or, find in favor of defendant and against plaintiff.]" *See* 23 Am. Jur. Pleading and Practice Forms 560, 562 (rev. ed. 1993) (Forms 289 and 297).

250. *See, e.g.*, Wis. Stat. Ann. § 805.12(1) (West 1994) ("Unless it orders otherwise, the court shall direct the jury to return a special verdict"); *cf.* William V. Dorsaneo, III, *Broad-Form Submission of Jury Questions and the Standard of Review*, 46 SMU L. Rev. 601 (1992) (discussing Texas practice).

251. *See* Fed. R. Civ. P. 49(a); *see also* 9 Bender's Federal Practice Forms 49:1 to 49:11 (1999). Rule 49(a) also provides that if, in submitting the special verdict and instructions to the jury, the court omits any issue of fact raised by the pleadings and evidence, each party waives the right to trial by jury of the omitted issue unless the party demands its submission to the jury before the jury retires. In the absence of such a demand by a party, the court may, in its discretion, make a finding on the omitted issue; but if it fails to do so, the court will be deemed to have made a finding in accord with the judgment on the special verdict. Fed. R. Civ. P. 49(a).

of a special verdict form.[252] The underlying rationale of this middle course is that the jury will be required "to give close attention to the more important issues and their answers serve to check the propriety of the general verdict."[253] When the general verdict and the answers to the interrogatories are harmonious, Rule 49(b) provides that an appropriate judgment shall be entered on the verdict and answers pursuant to Rule 58. When the answers are *consistent with each other*, but one or more answers are inconsistent with the general verdict, Rule 49(b) provides three options: (1) judgment may be entered under Rule 58 in accord with the answers; (2) the court may return the jury for further consideration of its answers and verdict; or (3) the court may order a new trial.[254] However, when the answers to the interrogatories are *inconsistent with each other* and one or more of the answers are inconsistent with the general verdict, Rule 49(b) directs the court either (1) to return the jury for further deliberation of the answers and verdict or (2) to order a new trial. Therefore, the court has no discretion to enter judgment under such circumstances.[255]

The equivalent of a jury verdict in actions tried to the court is findings of fact and conclusions of law by the judge. Some states permit the court to state its findings generally (*i.e.*, for the plaintiff or for the defendant), at least unless the parties request specific findings.[256] More typically, however, the trial court is required to make separate findings of fact and conclusions of law.

Illustration 11-31. Federal Rule 52(a) requires a federal court to "find the facts specially and state separately its conclusions of law thereon, and judgment shall be entered pursuant to Rule 58 . . . ."[257] Rule 52(a) also provides that "[i]t will be sufficient if the findings of fact and conclusions of law are stated orally and recorded in open court following the close of the evidence or appear in an opinion or memorandum of decision filed by the court."[258] Rule 52(a) further admonishes the appellate courts that findings of fact shall not be set aside unless clearly erroneous, with due regard for the trial judge's ability to judge the credibility of witnesses.[259]

SECTION M. JUDGMENT

The culmination of litigation at the trial court level is the *judgment*. A judgment is the decision of the court on the matters subject to litigation.[260] A judgment may be *final* or *interlocutory*, but this section limits the discussion to

---

252. *See* 9A Charles A. Wright & Arthur R. Miller, Federal Practice and Procedure: Civil § 2511, at 217 (2d ed. 1995).

253. *Id.*

254. *See* Fed. R. Civ. P. 49(b).

255. *Id.*; *see also* Toucet v. Maritime Overseas Corp., 991 F.2d 5 (1st Cir. 1993) (failure to object to inconsistency after verdict is read, but before jury is dismissed, waives objection).

256. *See, e.g.*, Neb. Rev. Stat. § 25-1127 (1995).

257. Fed. R. Civ. P. 52(a).

258. *Id.*

259. *Id.*

260. For purposes of the Federal Rules, a judgment is defined to include "a decree or any order from which an appeal lies." Fed. R. Civ. P. 54(a).

final judgments. As discussed in the next two chapters, the final judgment in a civil action has important effects on the ability to appeal and to pursue later litigation on the same subject matter. The entry of the final judgment also brings into play various devices for executing the judgment if it is not voluntarily paid or obeyed, such as an execution sale of defendant's nonexempt assets to satisfy a money judgment in favor of the plaintiff.

A typical provision governing the entry of judgment is Rule 58 of the Federal Rules of Civil Procedure. Rule 58 provides that "upon a general verdict of a jury or a decision by the court that a party shall recover only a sum certain or costs or that all relief shall be denied, the clerk . . . shall forthwith prepare, sign, and enter the judgment without awaiting any direction from the court," unless the court otherwise orders. When the court grants other relief, or after the jury has returned a special verdict or a general verdict accompanied by interrogatories, the court "promptly" must approve the form of judgment.[261] After approval, the court "shall thereupon enter it."[262] Rule 58 also provides that a judgment must be set forth on a separate document. It is effective only when it is entered in the civil docket in accord with Federal Rule 79(a).[263]

When multiple claims or multiple parties are involved, Rule 54(b) allows the court to "direct the entry of a final judgment as to one or more but fewer than all of the claims or parties."[264] Such an entry of judgment, however, is conditioned on "an express determination that there is no just reason for delay and [on] an express direction for the entry of judgment."[265] When the court does not dispose of all the claims, the court may stay the enforcement of a judgment entered pursuant to Rule 54(b) until subsequent judgment or judgments are entered. The court may also prescribe appropriate conditions to secure the benefit of the stayed judgment.[266]

If a money judgment is not paid voluntarily, the defendant's assets can be seized on a writ of execution and sold to satisfy the judgment. Discovery devices available before trial also can be used at this stage of the litigation to locate nonexempt assets of the defendant.[267] Other kinds of judgments may order the defendant to deliver property to the plaintiff, or to do or cease doing other acts found unlawful by the court. The latter form of injunctive "judgments" or orders are enforced, if need be, through the use of contempt sanctions.[268]

---

261. FED. R. CIV. P. 58; *see* Forms 31 ("Judgment on Jury Verdict") and 32 ("Judgment on Decision by the Court") in the Appendix of Forms following the Federal Rules of Civil Procedure. A judgment should not contain a recital of the pleadings, a master's report, or the record of prior proceedings. FED. R. CIV. P. 54(a).

262. FED. R. CIV. P. 58; Walter W. Jones, Jr., Annotation, *What Constitutes "Entry of Judgment" Within Meaning of Rule 58 of Federal Rules of Civil Procedure, as Amended in 1963,* 10 A.L.R. FED. 709 (1972).

263. *See* FED. R. CIV. P. 58; *see also* Deborah F. Harris, Annotation, *Requirement of Rule 58, Federal Rules of Civil Procedure, that Every Judgment Shall Be Set Forth on a Separate Document,* 53 A.L.R. FED. 595 (1981).

264. FED. R. CIV. P. 54(b).

265. *Id.*; *see* Martin J. McMahon, Annotation, *Modern Status of Federal Civil Procedure Rule 54(b) Governing Entry of Judgment on Multiple Claims,* 89 A.L.R. FED. 514 (1988);

266. FED. R. CIV. P. 62(h).

267. *Cf.* FED. R. CIV. P. 69(a).

268. *See* Chapter 6(F) ("Provisional Remedies") *supra.*

Furthermore, as discussed in Chapter 1, the clerk may tax costs pursuant to Rule 54(d)(1).[269] In 1993, a new procedure was established for presenting claims for attorneys' fees and related nontaxable expenses.[270] Rule 54(d)(2) provides that such claims must be presented by motion. The motion must specify (1) the judgment, (2) the statute, rule, or other grounds entitling the moving party to the award, and (3) the amount or a fair estimate of the amount sought. Furthermore, if directed by the court, the motion must also disclose the terms of the fee agreement with the moving party's client.[271] Rule 54(d)(2) establishes a fourteen-day deadline for filing and serving motions for attorneys' fees after the court enters a final judgment, unless the court or a statute specifies otherwise.[272] The purpose of this time limit is to assure that opposing parties are informed of the claim before this time for appeal expires.[273] The rule also assures that the parties have an opportunity to make appropriate presentations concerning any issues regarding the fees or other nontaxable expenses—most likely through an evidentiary hearing. The rule explicitly authorizes the court to determine the liability for fees before receiving submissions bearing on the amount of the award.[274]

---

269. FED. R. CIV. P. 54(d)(1); *see* Chapter 1(C)(4)*(a)* ("Allocating the Direct Costs of Litigation") *supra*.

270. The purpose of this new procedure is "to harmonize and clarify procedures that had developed through case law and local rules." FED. R. CIV. P. 54(d) advisory committee's note to the 1993 amendment. The rule does not apply to fees awarded as sanctions under the Federal Rules nor to fees awarded under 28 U.S.C. § 1927. *Id.*; Debra T. Landis, Annotation, *What Conduct Constitutes Multiplying Proceedings Unreasonably and Vexatiously so as to Warrant Imposition of Liability on Counsel Under 28 USCS § 1927 for Excess Costs, Expenses, and Attorney Fees*, 81 A.L.R. FED. 36 (1987).

271. FED. R. CIV. P. 54(d)(2)(B).

272. FED. R. CIV. P. 54(d)(2)(B). The Advisory Committee pointed out that prior to the adoption of this provision, there was no general time limit on claims for attorneys' fees. *See* White v. New Hampshire Dep't of Employment Sec., 455 U.S. 445, 102 S. Ct. 1162, 71 L. Ed. 2d 325 (1982). However, some statutes establish specific deadlines. *See, e.g.*, Equal Access to Justice Act, 28 U.S.C. § 2412(d)(1)(B) (thirty-day filing period).

273. FED. R. CIV. P. 54(d) advisory committee's note to the 1993 amendment.

274. FED. R. CIV. P. 54(2)(C) & advisory committee's note accompanying the 1993 amendment.

Chapter 12

POST-TRIAL MOTIONS, APPELLATE REVIEW, AND EXTRAORDINARY RELIEF FROM JUDGMENTS

SECTION A. POST-TRIAL MOTIONS

In early English practice, jury trials were often held away from the courts at Westminster.[1] When a verdict had been rendered during a "vacation" of the courts, judgment on the verdict was delayed until after the next term began. At the beginning of the term, the losing party could present motions designed to prevent entry of the judgment. These post-trial motions attempted to point out errors that appeared on the face of the record (which consisted of the process, pleadings, and verdict) or errors that had occurred during the trial.

Illustration 12-1. A defendant who had lost a trial could use a *motion in arrest of judgment* to raise a matter of law appearing on the face of the record, such as a defect in the pleadings. In effect, this motion was "a kind of [d]elayed [d]emurrer."[2] A plaintiff who lost at trial could raise substantive defects by moving for *judgment notwithstanding the verdict (judgment non obstante veredicto)*. This motion was used primarily to test the legal sufficiency of a defense.[3] A motion for a new trial raised errors and irregularities that occurred during the trial.

* * * * *

In modern practice, after the trial has been completed and judgment has been entered, the parties are permitted to make the following post-trial motions: (1) a motion for judgment notwithstanding the verdict (now called a motion for judgment as a matter of law in federal court);[4] (2) a motion for a new trial; and (3) a motion to alter or amend the judgment. They are known in federal practice as *ten-day motions* because they must be made "not later than 10 days after the entry of the judgment."[5] However, as discussed in the following subsections, these motions differ in important ways from their common-law predecessors. In

---

1. *See* Chapter 4(A) ("Transitory and Local Actions") *supra*.

2. JOSEPH H. KOFFLER & ALISON REPPY, HANDBOOK OF COMMON LAW PLEADING § 307, at 571 (1969). To obtain review, the defendant would obtain a "rule" directing the plaintiff to appear before the full court and to show cause why the judgment should not be arrested. If the court decided in the defendant's favor, the rule became absolute. If the court decided in the plaintiff's favor, the rule was discharged or refused. If the judgment was arrested, the plaintiff could commence the action again if the plaintiff believed success was possible.

3. As noted in Chapter 6, common-law pleading required the defendant to "confess" the plaintiff's right before it could be "avoided" by a defense. *See* Chapter 6(A)(3)*(e)* ("Pleas in Confession and Avoidance") *supra*. If the defense was insufficient, the plaintiff was entitled to a judgment because of the defendant's confession. JOSEPH H. KOFFLER & ALISON REPPY, HANDBOOK OF COMMON LAW PLEADING § 308, at 577 (1969).

4. *See* FED. R. CIV. P. 50(a) & advisory committee's note to the 1991 amendment.

5. *See* FED. R. CIV. P. 50(b), 59(b) & (e).

modern practice, post-trial motions are principally used for the following reasons: (1) to correct errors that occurred during the trial; (2) to challenge the sufficiency of the evidence on which the judgment rests; and (3) to rectify improper conduct by the parties, their attorneys, or the jury. Post-trial motions give the trial judge one last opportunity to correct these deficiencies before the complaining party is forced to seek an appeal.

1. Judgment Notwithstanding the Verdict (Judgment as a Matter of Law)

The modern judgment notwithstanding the verdict has its historical origin in the *judgment non obstante veredicto* (judgment n.o.v.). The common-law courts allowed plaintiffs to move for judgment in their favor, despite a jury verdict in favor of the defendant, when the defendant's plea was in proper form but failed to demonstrate any valid defense to the merits of the plaintiff's action. Defendants were later allowed to use this motion when the plaintiff's pleadings were insufficient to support a judgment in the plaintiff's favor.[6]

In the federal courts and states adopting the Federal Rules of Civil Procedure, the motion for judgment notwithstanding the verdict is governed by Rule 50(b). Before 1991, Federal Rule 50(b) provided that a party might move to have a jury verdict and judgment set aside and instead have judgment entered in the moving party's favor. A 1991 amendment to Federal Rule 50(b) redesignates this motion as a motion for *judgment as a matter of law* in federal court.[7] Pursuant to such a motion, the court will disregard a jury determination lacking a legally sufficient evidentiary basis. The court may then decide these issues as a matter of law and enter judgment when either (1) the jury has decided all other material issues based on legally sufficient evidence or (2) the court has decided all other material issues as a matter of law.[8] In federal practice, in order to make a *post-trial* motion for judgment as a matter of law, the same motion must have been made before the case was submitted to the jury.[9] The standard used is the same as the one for a directed verdict (now also called a judgment as a matter of law).[10] Chapter 11 addressed whether a motion for a judgment as a

---

6. *See* JOSEPH H. KOFFLER & ALISON REPPY, HANDBOOK OF COMMON LAW PLEADING § 308, at 577 (1969).

7. FED. R. CIV. P. 50(b). For further discussion of the standards applied in ruling on motions for directed verdicts (judgment as a matter of law), see Chapter 11(H)(1) ("Involuntary Dismissals (Judgments on Partial Findings) and Directed Verdicts (Judgments as a Matter of Law)") *supra*.

8. FED. R. CIV. P. 50(b) advisory committee's note to 1991 amendment.

9. FED. R. CIV. P. 50(b); *see* Chapter 11(H)(1) ("Involuntary Dismissals (Judgments on Partial Findings) and Directed Verdicts (Judgments as a Matter of Law)") *supra*; *see also* Wells v. State Farm Fire & Cas. Co., 993 F.2d 510 (5th Cir. 1993) (motion for judgment as a matter of law made by defendant at close of plaintiff's case denied; defendant and plaintiff then introduced additional evidence; defendant did not renew motion at close of plaintiff's rebuttal evidence, but waited until after jury returned verdict for plaintiff; failure to renew motion at the close of plaintiff's evidence waived right to plenary appellate review of sufficiency of the evidence).

10. FED. R. CIV. P. 50(a)(1) & advisory committee's note to the 1991 amendment; *see also* Chapter 11(H)(1) ("Involuntary Dismissals (Judgments on Partial Findings) and Directed Verdicts (Judgments as a Matter of Law)") *supra*.

matter of law under Rule 50(a) before the verdict in a diversity action should be governed by an independent federal standard, either under Rule 50(a) or under a "federal common law rule of procedure."[11] The issues are the same under Rule 50(b), and, therefore, the discussion of the Rules Enabling Act and Rules of Decision Act questions in Chapter 11 is also pertinent here.

Illustration 12-2. A judgment n.o.v. (or judgment as a matter of law) may be based on a variety of circumstances. Consider the following examples: (1) There was no evidence which, if believed, would authorize a verdict against the defendant; (2) there was no evidence to warrant the submission of the case to the jury; and (3) the verdict which the jury returned was based on speculation and conjecture.[12]

* * * * *

A motion for a new trial may be joined with a motion for judgment notwithstanding the verdict (or judgment as a matter of law).[13] Under Federal Rule 50(c)(1), the court must rule on both motions. In this way, should an appellate court vacate or reverse the judgment as a matter of law, the appellate court will know whether the original judgment should be reinstated or a new trial should be ordered.[14]

2. Motion for a New Trial

Federal Rules 50(a) and 59(a) exemplify how the motion for new trial works in federal court and in states adopting the Federal Rules. Rule 59(a) permits a motion for a new jury trial to be made on any grounds previously recognized "in actions at law in the courts of the United States."[15] In the *Gasperini* case, discussed in Chapter 5, the Supreme Court held that Rule 59 did not incorporate an independent federal standard for granting new trials on the grounds that a jury verdict was excessive. Rather, the issue was governed by the general *Erie* standard under the Rules of Decision Act, which required the federal district court to follow state law on the issue to avoid the *Erie*-prohibited forum shopping and inequitable administration of the laws.[16] Rule 50(a) permits a motion for a new trial in cases tried by a judge without a jury to be made on any

---

11. *See* Chapter 11(H)(1) ("Involuntary Dismissals (Judgments on Partial Findings) and Directed Verdicts (Judgments as a Matter of Law)") *supra.*

12. *See* E.H. Schopler, Annotation, *Practice and Procedure with Respect to Motions for Judgment Notwithstanding or in Default of Verdict Under Federal Rule of Civil Procedure 50(b) or Like State Provisions,* 69 A.L.R.2D 449 (1960). Thus, a sharp distinction exists between the modern motion for judgment notwithstanding the verdict and its common-law predecessor. The modern motion is "actuated by the state of the evidence, instead of the state of the pleadings." ROBERT W. MILLAR, CIVIL PROCEDURE OF THE TRIAL COURT IN HISTORICAL PERSPECTIVE 330 (1952). The motion for judgment notwithstanding the verdict in modern practice is principally used as a device for controlling the jury. *See* Chapter 11(C)(2) ("Methods of Controlling the Jury") *supra.*

13. *See* FED. R. CIV. P. 50(b).

14. *See* FED. R. CIV. P. 50(b) & (c)(1).

15. FED. R. CIV. P. 59(a).

16. *See* Chapter 5(F)(3) *supra* (discussing the Rules of Decision Act aspects of *Gasperini*) & 5(F)(5) *supra* (discussing the interpretation of Rule 59).

grounds previously recognized "in suits in equity in the courts of the United States."[17]

Illustration 12-3. The following are some examples of grounds on which a motion for new trial may be based: (1) The verdict is against the weight of the evidence;[18] (2) newly discovered evidence;[19] and (3) the jury verdict is excessive and appears to have been given under the influence of passion and prejudice.[20]

* * * * *

Furthermore, when the jury renders an unreasonably high verdict, judges have long had the power to condition the denial of the defendant's motion for a new trial on the plaintiff's consent to a *remittitur* (a reduction in the amount of the verdict).[21] However, if the court of appeals orders a remittitur of damages on the ground that the evidence does not support such a large award, the Seventh Amendment requires that the plaintiff be allowed the option of a new trial on the damages issue, rather than forcing the plaintiff to accept a judgment for the lesser amount.[22]

Like a renewed motion for judgment as matter of law (judgment n.o.v.) in federal court, a motion for a new trial must be served not later than ten days after the entry of the judgment. This time limit may not be extended.[23] Unlike a judgment as a matter of law (judgment n.o.v.), the court may order a new trial on its own motion.[24] When the motion for a new trial depends on factual grounds in federal court, the motion should be supported by affidavits filed at the same time as the motion.[25]

3. Motion to Alter or Amend the Judgment

Federal courts and states adopting the Federal Rules recognize another ten-day motion—a motion to alter or amend the judgment.[26] Clerical mistakes,

---

17. *Id.*

18. *See* 11 Charles A. Wright et al., Federal Practice and Procedure: Civil § 2806 (1995).

19. *See id.* § 2808.

20. *See* 11 Bender's Federal Practice Forms 59-19 to 59-20 (1999) (Form 59:1).

21. *See, e.g.,* Atlas Food Sys. & Servs., Inc. v. Crane Nat'l Vendors, Inc., 99 F.3d 587 (4th Cir 1996) (no abuse of discretion for district judge to order new trial after plaintiff refused remittitur of $3,000,000 punitive damage award to $1,000,000). Remittitur should not be used, however, when the verdict was the result of passion and prejudice because prejudice may have affected the determination of liability as well. Under such circumstances, a new trial should be ordered. *See* 11 Charles A. Wright et al., Federal Practice and Procedure: Civil § 2815, at 165 (2d ed. 1995).

22. Hetzel v. Prince William County, 523 U.S. 208, 118 S. Ct. 1210, 140 L. Ed. 2d 336 (1998). In addition, federal courts may not use *additur* to cure an inadequate verdict. Dimick v. Schiedt, 293 U.S. 474, 55 S. Ct. 296, 79 L. Ed. 603 (1935) (5-4 decision) (holding that additur in the federal courts violates the Seventh Amendment).

23. Fed. R. Civ. P. 59(b); *see also* Ethel R. Alston, Annotation, *Motions for New Trial: Time Limitations Under Rule 59(b) of Federal Rules of Civil Procedure,* 45 A.L.R. Fed. 104 (1979).

24. Fed. R. Civ. P. 59(d).

25. Fed. R. Civ. P. 59(c).

26. *See* Fed. R. Civ. P. 59(e).

however, "may be corrected by the court at any time [on] its own initiative or on the motion of any party."[27]

Illustration 12-4. *A* sued *B* in a U.S. District Court. *B* moved for summary judgment, which the district court granted. Two days later, *A* filed a "motion for reconsideration" asserting that *A* had failed to file the deposition of an expert in opposition to the motion for summary judgment. The district court allowed the filing of the deposition but denied the "motion to reconsider." *A* and *B* appealed. *B's* appeal objected to the decision of the court to admit and consider the deposition of the expert. A "motion to reconsider" does not exist under the Federal Rules of Civil Procedure. On similar facts, however, a court of appeals held that the motion could be considered to be a motion to alter or amend the judgment under Rule 59(e) or a motion to reopen the judgment under Rule 60(b). The time when the motion is served determines the classification of the motion. If it is served within ten days of the rendition of the judgment, it is a motion to alter or amend under Rule 59(e). If it is served thereafter, it is a motion to reopen under Rule 60(b). *A's* motion was served two days after the judgment. Therefore, it was a motion to alter or amend. As a motion to alter or amend, it would not be subject to the "exacting substantive standards" of Rule 60(b). Therefore, A would not be required to show that the failure to file the deposition was due to "mistake, inadvertence, surprise, or excusable neglect" as would be required under Rule 60(b). Thus, while the district court was not obligated to consider the deposition, it had discretion to do so under Rule 59(e).[28]

SECTION B. APPELLATE REVIEW

1. The Right to Appeal

Three fundamental rules govern the right to appeal. First, a prevailing party cannot appeal a judgment. Second, a nonparty cannot appeal a judgment in an action between others. Third, a party cannot appeal a judgment against another party.[29] Several other closely related rules preclude parties from appealing based on their behavior in the action or in relation to the judgment.[30]

---

27. *See* FED. R. CIV. P. 60(a) (during the pendency of an appeal, clerical mistakes may be "corrected before the appeal is docketed in the appellate court, and thereafter while the appeal is pending . . . with leave of the appellate court").

28. *See* Lavespere v. Niagara Mach. & Tool Works, Inc., 910 F.2d 167 (5th Cir. 1990).

29. *See, e.g.,* Walker v. Kazi, 316 Ark. 616, 875 S.W.2d 47 (1994) (dismissing appeal because the appellant was the prevailing party and lacked standing to appeal for another party); *see also* Felzen v. Andreas, 134 F.3d 873 (7th Cir. 1998) (nonparties may not appeal from a decision of any kind in a class action); Valley Bank v. Ginsburg, 110 Nev. 440, 874 P.2d 729 (1994) (nonparty shareholders who had never intervened were not parties who had standing to appeal order approving settlement agreement). *But cf.* Rosenbaum v. MacAllister, 64 F.3d 1439 (10th Cir. 1995) (unnamed class member has standing to appeal award of attorney's fees to plaintiff's counsel without intervening). *See generally* 15A CHARLES A. WRIGHT ET AL., FEDERAL PRACTICE AND PROCEDURE: JURISDICTION AND RELATED MATTERS §§ 3902-3902.1 (2d ed. 1992).

30. For example, certain kinds of orders, such as orders voluntarily dismissing claims against the defendant, are not appealable, since they are not considered adverse to the plaintiff and do not have the effect of determining the case against the plaintiff. *See, e.g.,* American Water Dev. v. City of Alamosa, 874 P.2d 352, 374 (Colo.), *cert. denied,* 513 U.S. 1015, 115 S. Ct. 575, 130 L. Ed. 2d 491 (1994). In addition, a party may

Illustration 12-5. *A's* truck was struck from the rear by a car driven by *B-1*. *A* commenced an action for personal injuries against a party designated as "*B*," and served *B-2*, *B-1's* father who lived at the same address as *B-1*. *B-2* served an answer denying that he was the driver of the automobile that hit *A* and asserting that *B-1*, his son, was the driver; *B-2* also filed a motion for summary judgment. The trial court granted *B-2's* motion for summary judgment and also granted a motion by *A* to amend her complaint to name *B-2* as the defendant and allowed this amendment to relate back to the filing of the complaint. An appeal was filed in which the notice of appeal and appellate brief were both in the name of "*B*." If *B-1* is the appellant, the appeal must be dismissed because *B-1* has not had a final, appealable order issued against him.[31] If *B-2* is the appellant, the appeal must also be dismissed. *B-2* is a prevailing party, and prevailing parties cannot appeal. If *B-2* is trying to appeal for *B-1*, he has no right to do so, because a party cannot appeal a judgment against another party.[32]

2. Jurisdiction on Appeal

The two basic functions of appellate courts are to (1) review the trial court record and (2) establish whether or not reversible error has occurred.[33] While the appeal is pending, the trial court has no jurisdiction.[34] The specific methods of obtaining appellate "review" can be divided into the following four basic categories: (1) appeals as a matter of right; (2) discretionary review; (3) certification; and (4) extraordinary writs. Statutory provisions generally determine which appeals are a matter of right and which appeals are within a court's discretion.

(a) Appeals as a Matter of Right

The first level of appeal will ordinarily be an appeal as a matter of right.
Illustration 12-6. An appeal from the final decision of a federal district court to a federal court of appeals is a matter of right.[35]

---

not, pursuant to the doctrine of "invited error," ask the court to make a ruling in its favor and then complain on appeal about the ruling. *See, e.g.,* Security Pac. Hous. Servs., Inc. v. Friddle, 315 Ark. 178, 866 S.W.2d 375 (1993). A party may not accept the benefits of a judgment and then appeal from the judgment. *Cf.* Baker's Supermarkets, Inc. v. Feldman, 243 Neb. 684, 502 N.W.2d 428 (1993). Furthermore, a party who voluntarily complies with a judgment "acquiesces" in it and cannot appeal the judgment. *See, e.g.,* Varner v. Gulf Ins. Co., 254 Kan. 492, 866 P.2d 1044 (1994).

31. *See* section B(3) *supra* (discussing the final judgment rule and its exceptions).

32. *See* Walker v. Kazi, 316 Ark. 616, 875 S.W.2d 47 (1994).

33. *See* DANIEL J. MEADOR & JORDANA S. BERNSTEIN, APPELLATE COURTS IN THE UNITED STATES 55-58 (1994).

34. Miller v. United States, 114 F.2d 267, 269 (7th Cir. 1940).

35. *See* 28 U.S.C. § 1291. The Judiciary Act of 1789 established one federal district court in each state. The states were divided into three circuits. The district courts had only original jurisdiction. In contrast, the circuit courts had both original and appellate jurisdiction. The circuit courts were authorized to hear cases appealed from the district courts if the amount in controversy exceeded fifty dollars (in admiralty cases, three hundred dollars). As originally established, the U.S. Supreme Court had appellate jurisdiction over appeals from the circuit courts when the amount in controversy exceeded two thousand dollars. The Court also had appellate

(b) Discretionary Review

Review of some decisions is at the discretion of the appellate court. In such instances, a party ordinarily must first file a petition, which is usually called a petition for a writ of *certiorari*. In this petition, the party seeking review must persuade the court to hear the appeal. After a petition has been filed, the other party will ordinarily file an opposing brief. Today, virtually all of the cases heard by the U.S. Supreme Court are the result of discretionary review.[36] Several states with intermediate appellate courts also have systems for discretionary review in the highest courts of those states. These systems generally follow the same pattern used in the U.S. Supreme Court.

(c) Certification

Another method of review is *certification*.

Illustration 12-7. A federal court of appeals may certify to the Supreme Court "any question of law in any civil or criminal case as to which instructions are desired."[37] Certification is one exception to the earlier statement that the litigants initiate appellate review. In this instance, a federal court of appeals certifies questions to the Supreme Court when it is in doubt and desires instructions. The Supreme Court has discretion in answering. The use of this procedure is rare. A few states also allow an intermediate appellate court to certify a question before a decision is reached.[38]

* * * * *

Certification of an interlocutory appeal by a federal district court judge under 28 U.S.C. § 1292(b) to a federal court of appeals is more common. Such appeals are permitted when the trial judge certifies (1) the matter "involves a controlling question of law as to which there is a substantial ground for difference of opinion and (2) an immediate appeal from the order may materially advance the ultimate termination of the litigation."[39] The federal court of appeals has discretion to hear the interlocutory appeal.[40] Although the process deviates in

---

jurisdiction over judgments from the highest courts of the states when a federal question was presented. *See* ROBERT L. STERN, APPELLATE PRACTICE IN THE UNITED STATES § 1.3 (2d ed. 1988); 13 CHARLES A. WRIGHT ET AL., FEDERAL PRACTICE AND PROCEDURE: JURISDICTION AND RELATED MATTERS §§ 3503-3504 (2d ed. 1984). In 1891, the Evarts Act repealed the circuit courts' appellate jurisdiction and created the circuit courts of appeals (now called the U.S. Courts of Appeals). Act of Mar. 3, 1891, 26 Stat. 826. Appellate jurisdiction of the state courts is likewise governed by statutory provisions.

36. *See* 28 U.S.C. § 1254 (decisions of federal courts of appeal reviewed by U.S. Supreme Court by writ of certiorari); 28 U.S.C. § 1257 (certain decisions of a highest state court reviewed by U.S. Supreme Court by writ of certiorari). For a long period, part of the appellate jurisdiction of the U.S. Supreme Court was of right. Although it was mandatory that the Court "hear" these appeals, full consideration of the case was often avoided by a summary dismissal of the case for "want of a substantial federal question."

37. 28 U.S.C. § 1254(2).

38. *See generally* ROBERT L. STERN ET AL., SUPREME COURT PRACTICE §§ 9.1-9.4 (7th ed. 1993).

39. 28 U.S.C. § 1292(b).

40. *See generally* MICHAEL E. TIGAR, FEDERAL APPEALS: JURISDICTION AND PRACTICE § 2.14 (1987); 16 CHARLES A. WRIGHT ET AL., FEDERAL PRACTICE AND PROCEDURE: JURISDICTION AND RELATED MATTERS §§ 3929-3931 (2d ed. 1996).

some ways, several states have similar methods of certification for review of interlocutory orders not otherwise appealable.[41]

Courts of *other* jurisdictions may certify questions to state supreme courts when a state has authorized this type of review. About half of the states permit certification from a federal court to their respective state supreme courts. A few states permit appellate courts of other states to do so also.[42] This method of determining state law is particularly useful for the federal courts as a means of fulfilling their obligation under the Rules of Decision Act, which requires federal courts to apply state substantive law in diversity cases.[43]

(d) Extraordinary Writs

A petition for an extraordinary writ technically commences an original action in the appellate court. Such a petition, however, often involves objections arising out of lower court proceedings. One of the principal extraordinary writs is *mandamus*, which has traditionally been issued in response to abuses of judicial power.

Illustration 12-8. When judges refuse to take a required action or take an action that they are not empowered to take, a writ of mandamus may be proper. For example, the Supreme Court has held that mandamus is appropriate when necessary to protect the Seventh Amendment right to a jury trial.[44]

* * * * *

Another extraordinary writ that may be used to "review" judicial proceedings is *prohibition*. Traditionally, a superior court issues this writ to prevent an inferior court from usurping matters not within its jurisdiction. This writ is directed to the judge of the inferior court and to the parties in the action. Still another extraordinary writ is *habeas corpus*, which today is primarily used to test the legality of a prisoner's detention.[45]

Mandamus, habeas corpus, and various other extraordinary writs such as *quo warranto* (traditionally used to determine who has title to a public office) may be directed to public officers other than judges, and original jurisdiction over these actions may be vested in a trial court.[46] These writs are available only in

---

41. *See* ROBERT L. STERN, APPELLATE PRACTICE IN THE UNITED STATES § 4.5(a) & (b) (2d ed. 1988) (discussing similarities between § 1292 and state provisions as well as basic patterns of state deviations).

42. *See* ROBERT L. STERN, APPELLATE PRACTICE IN THE UNITED STATES § 1.3 (2d ed. 1988); *see also* UNIFORM CERTIFICATION OF QUESTIONS OF LAW [ACT] [RULE] (1995), 12 U.L.A. 67 (West 1996).

43. *See* Chapter 5(H) ("Determination of State Law") *supra.*

44. *See* Dairy Queen, Inc. v. Wood, 369 U.S. 469, 472, 82 S. Ct. 894, 8 L. Ed. 2d 44 (1962); Beacon Theatres, Inc. v. Westover, 359 U.S. 500, 511, 79 S. Ct. 948, 3 L. Ed. 2d 988 (1959). *But see* First Nat'l Bank v. Warren, 796 F.2d 999 (7th Cir. 1986) (discussing U.S. Supreme Court decisions on mandamus in jury trial cases and indicating that mandamus is only available when a jury trial issue will not be reviewable on appeal from final judgment).

45. For an example of the use of habeas corpus, see *Illustration 1-4* in Chapter 1 *supra. See generally* ROBERT L. STERN ET AL., SUPREME COURT PRACTICE §§ 11.1-11.8 (7th ed. 1993).

46. *See, e.g.,* 28 U.S.C. § 1361 (jurisdiction vested in federal district court for actions in the nature of mandamus to compel an officer or federal employee to perform a duty owed to the plaintiff). The power of federal courts to issue these extraordinary writs is based upon their inherent power and the "all writs" authority established by § 1651 of Title 28. Section 1651 provides that "[t]he Supreme Court and all lower courts established by Congress may issue all writs necessary or appropriate in aid of their respective jurisdictions and exceptional circumstances, principally when other judicial remedies have failed or are considered inadequate.[47]

3. The Final Judgment Rule and Its Exceptions

(a) The Basic Rule

The common-law rule allowing an appeal only from a final judgment has been generally carried over into modern practice.[48]

Illustration 12-9. Section 1291 of Title 28 of the *United States Code* provides that "[t]he courts of appeals . . . shall have jurisdiction of appeals from all final decisions of the districts courts . . . except where a direct review may be had in the Supreme Court."[49]

* * * * *

A "final judgment"[50] is the order of the court[51] that is controlling and dispositive; it is not one in which the trial court can reserve the ability to make further orders regarding the parties' rights or liabilities.[52]

---

agreeable to the usages and principles of law." 28 U.S.C. § 1651.

47. *See* 16 CHARLES A. WRIGHT ET AL., FEDERAL PRACTICE AND PROCEDURE: JURISDICTION AND RELATED MATTERS § 3932 (2d ed. 1996).

48. *See* Carleton M. Crick, *The Final Judgment as a Basis for Appeal,* 41 YALE L.J. 539, 543-52 (1932).

49. 28 U.S.C. § 1291. *See generally* Martin H. Redish, *The Pragmatic Approach to Appealability in the Federal Courts,* 75 COLUM. L. REV. 89 (1975). Congress has given the power to the Supreme Court to "define when a ruling of a district court is final for purposes of appeal under section 1291 of this title." 28 U.S.C. § 2072(c). Rulemaking power exercised under this provision may present separation of powers problems. These kins of problems were discussed in Chapter 5(F)(6), *supra,* and will be discussed further in subsection *(b), infra,* dealing with a similar grant of rulemaking power to expand jurisdiction over interlocutory appeals in 28 U.S.C. § 1292(e).

50. Annotation, *Formal Requirements of Judgment or Order As Regards Appealability,* 73 A.L.R.2D 250 (1960).

51. Federal Rule 58 requires that "every judgment . . . be set forth on a separate document." FED. R. CIV. P. 58. *See* Walker W. Jones, Jr., Annotation, *What Constitutes "Entry of Judgment" Within Meaning of Rule 58 of Federal Rules of Civil Procedure,* 10 A.L.R. FED. 709 (1972).

52. For example, in WMX Technologies, Inc. v. Miller, 104 F.3d 1133 (9th Cir. 1997), the district court dismissed three of the plaintiff's claims with prejudice and two claims without prejudice. The court gave the plaintiff leave to amend the latter two claims within thirty days. The plaintiff did not either amend or inform the court that it would not amend, but simply appealed. The appellate court dismissed the appeal because no final dismissal order had been entered. In National Distribution Agency v. Nationwide Mutual Insurance Co., 117 F.3d 432 (9th Cir. 1997), the district court dismissed the plaintiff's complaint with the qualification that "[t]he court may amend or amplify this order with a more specific statement of the grounds for its decision." The court of appeals held that this qualification made the order nonfinal and unappealable. The court of appeals also declined to treat the plaintiff's notice of appeals as an expression that the plaintiff would stand on his complaint rather than amend. *See also* Catlin v. United States, 324 U.S. 229, 233, 65 S. Ct. 631, 633, 89 L. Ed. 911, 916 (1945) (a final judgment is an order that "ends the litigation on the merits and leaves nothing for the court to do but execute the judgment"); Kirchner v. Western Mont. Reg'l Community Health Ctr., 261 Mont. 227, 861 P.2d 927 (1993) (any decree that leaves matters undetermined is interlocutory in nature, not an appealable final judgment). *But see* Daniel A. Klein, Annotation, *When Will Premature Notice of Appeal Be Retroactively Validated in Federal Civil Case,* 76 A.L.R. FED. 199 (1966).

Illustration 12-10. In the federal system, an order granting a new trial is not appealable because that order is not a "final judgment."[53]

* * * * *

The final judgment rule serves to unify all issues for appeal and to reduce delay.[54] In a multiple-claim or multiple-party action, Federal Rule 54(b) allows the trial court to "direct the entry of a final judgment as to one or more but fewer than all of the claims or parties . . . upon an express determination that there is no just reason for delay."[55]

(b) Interlocutory Appeals

An interlocutory appeal may be possible even when a final judgment has not been entered. In the federal system, § 1292(a)(1) allows, *inter alia*, appeals as a matter of right from orders of the district courts "granting, continuing, modifying, refusing or dissolving injunctions" or orders "refusing to dissolve or modify injunctions."[56]

Section 1292(b) provides another exception to the final judgment rule in the federal system. This section allows a district court to certify for appeal that (1) an order presents "controlling questions of law" on which a "substantial difference of opinion" exists and that (2) immediate review will "materially advance the ultimate termination of the litigation."[57] After such a certification is made, the party seeking review applies to the appropriate court of appeals for leave to appeal. The court of appeals may grant or deny the appeal in its discretion.[58]

Illustration 12-11. *A* sues *B* in U.S. District Court for personal injuries received in an automobile accident. *B* moves to dismiss the action on the ground

---

53. *See, e.g.,* Taylor v. Washington Terminal Co., 409 F.2d 145, 147 (D.C. Cir.), *cert. denied,* 396 U.S. 835, 90 S. Ct. 93, 24 L. Ed. 2d 85 (1969). If the new trial is granted as an alternative to the granting of a motion for judgment notwithstanding the verdict, then both rulings may be immediately appealed. *See* FED. R. CIV. P. 50(c)(1). *But cf.* Jarrett v. Eichler, 244 Neb. 310, 506 N.W.2d 682 (1993) (order vacating a dismissal for want of jurisdiction was a final order).

54. *See* Note, *Appealability in the Federal Courts,* 75 HARV. L. REV. 351, 351-52 (1961).

55. FED. R. CIV. P. 54(b). In Ebrahimi v. City of Huntsville Board of Education, 114 F.3d 162 (11th Cir. 1997), the plaintiff sued fifteen defendants, alleging multiple civil rights claims against the defendants. The district court dismissed two of the claims and certified them as final under Rule 54(b). The Eleventh Circuit found the certification improper. The district court's conclusion was based on its determination that the dismissed claims should not have been brought by the plaintiff and thus no useful purpose would be served by postponing final disposition of them. However, the court of appeals viewed this as a commonplace reason for dismissal, and held that certification under these circumstances would produce piecemeal appeals. If the district court believed that appellate review of the dismissed claims prior to the trial of the other claims would avoid the necessity of a second trial if the dismissals were held erroneous, an interlocutory appeal under 28 U.S.C. § 1292 (discussed in the next subsection) would be more appropriate.

56. 28 U.S.C. § 1292(a)(1). In Nutrasweet Co. v. Vit-Mar Enterprises, Inc., 112 F.3d 689 (3d Cir. 1997), the court held that a temporary restraining order entered with notice that was continued beyond the period prescribed in Federal Rule 65(b) was the equivalent of a preliminary injunction and appealable under § 1292(a)(1). *See generally* Michael E. Solimine, *Revitalizing Interlocutory Appeals in the Federal Courts,* 58 GEO. WASH. L. REV. 1165 (1990).

57. 28 U.S.C. § 1292(b).

58. *See generally* Note, *Interlocutory Appeals in the Federal Courts Under 28 U.S.C. § 1292(b),* 88 HARV. L. REV. 607 (1975).

that personal jurisdiction is improper under the minimum contacts test of *International Shoe v. Washington*.[59] Assume that the district court denies the motion. However, at *B's* request, the court certifies that the order involves a controlling question of law as to which there is substantial ground for difference of opinion and that an immediate appeal from the order might materially advance the termination of the litigation. Personal jurisdiction issues are appropriate for certification under 28 U.S.C. § 1292(b),[60] as are subject-matter jurisdiction and venue issues.[61] However, in determining whether to accept the appeal, the court of appeals should make sure that the question is a truly difficult one. Otherwise, the final judgment rule of 28 U.S.C. § 1291 may be undermined by frequent interlocutory appeals on jurisdictional questions.

* * * * *

In 1992, Congress added a subsection (e) to § 1292, which authorized the Supreme Court to prescribe rules, in accordance with the Rules Enabling Act, to provide for interlocutory orders of the district courts to the courts of appeals that are not otherwise provide for in § 1292.[62] In 1998, the Supreme Court exercised this new power by creating subsection (f) to Rule 23 of the Federal Rules of Civil Procedure, which authorizes the courts of appeals, in their discretion, to permit an appeal from an order of a district court granting or denying class certification under Rule 23.[63] Rule 23(f) raises troubling separation-of-powers questions under the *Wayman* and *Sibbach* cases, discussed in Chapter 5.[64] The rule constitutes a clear expansion of (appellate) subject-matter jurisdiction,[65] which *Sibbach* suggested would be invalid.[66] In addition, it cannot be said, in the words of *Wayman*, that appellate subject-matter jurisdiction is a matter "whose general superintendence" has traditionally been considered "properly within the judicial province" as a matter of rule making.[67] However, until the Supreme Court speaks, it cannot be determined with any certainty whether Rule 23(f) will be found to deal with what *Wayman* called an "important matter" beyond the

---

59. *See* Chapter 3(D) ("The Development of Modern Restrictions on State Court Jurisdiction: The Minimum Contacts Test") *supra*.

60. *See, e.g.*, Donatelli v. National Hockey League, 893 F.2d 459 (1st Cir. 1990); Burchett v. Bardahl Oil Co., 470 F.2d 793 (10th Cir. 1972); *see also* Alexander & Alexander Servs., Inc. v. Lloyd's Syndicate 317, 925 F.2d 44 (2d Cir. 1991) (difficult interpretation of state long-arm statute).

61. *See* 16 CHARLES A. WRIGHT ET AL., FEDERAL PRACTICE AND PROCEDURE: JURISDICTION AND RELATED MATTERS § 3931, at 453-54 (2d ed. 1996).

62. *See* Pub. L. No. 102-572, § 101, 106 Stat. 4506, 4506.

63. *See* FED. R. CIV. P. 23(F).

64. *See* Chapter 5(F)(6) *supra* (discussing potential separation of powers restrictions on judicial rule making).

65. Prior to Rule 23(f), § 1292(b) required that in all interlocutory appeals not covered by some other specific statutory provision the district court had to certify an issue for interlocutory appeal, and Rule 23(f) requires no such certification. In addition, § 1292(b) requires that an interlocutory order must involve a controlling question of law as to which there is substantial ground for difference of opinion and that an immediate appeal from the order have the potential to materially advance the ultimate termination of the litigation. Rule 23(f) contains no such requirement.

66. *See* Chapter 5(F)(6) *supra* (discussing the statement in *Sibbach* that "[t]here are other limitations on the authority to prescribe rules which might have been, but were not, mentioned in the [Rules Enabling Act]; for instance, the inability of a court, by rule, to extend or restrict the jurisdiction conferred by a statute").

67. *See* Chapter 5(F)(6) *supra* (discussing potential separation of powers restrictions on judicial rule making, including the *Wayman* standard).

legitimate province of judicial rule making, or one that merely concerns the "details" of procedure, which is within the rule making power. Perhaps the validity of Rule 23(f) will be saved by the fact that, in the Advisory Committee's language, "[t]he expansion of appeal opportunities effected by subdivision (f) is modest."[68] This, in the words of the Supreme Court in *Wayman*, may make the expansion of jurisdiction in Rule 23(f) a subject of "less interest" within the judicial rule making authority.[69]

(c) Extraordinary Writs

Another exception to the final judgment rule in the federal system is provided in § 1651(a).[70] This provision allows the court of appeals to issue an extraordinary writ of mandamus, prohibition, or certiorari to review actions taken by the trial court. At one time, it appeared that mandamus might be available in either of two circumstances: (1) when an order may not be easily reparable on appeal; or (2) when mandamus is necessary to achieve supervisory control of the district court.[71] However, there is reason to believe that the supervisory use of mandamus has been limited in later cases to situations in which a district court repeatedly disregards the rules of procedure or other established rules of law.[72] If so, the primary use of mandamus will be to obtain relief from orders that are not easily reparable on appeal.[73]

(d) Collateral Order Rule

The *collateral order* rule is a judicially created exception to the final judgment rule. The collateral order rule makes "final," for purposes of § 1291 (permitting appeals only from "final" judgments) certain orders which do not fully and finally determine the entire controversy between the parties. This rule originated in *Cohen v. Beneficial Industrial Loan Corp.*[74] In *Cohen*, the district court refused to order the plaintiff to post security for costs as required by a New Jersey statute governing stockholder derivative suits. The defendant sought immediate review of this question. In permitting the appeal, the U.S. Supreme Court recognized that there is a "small class" of decisions that "finally determine claims of right separable from, and collateral to, rights asserted in the

---

68. *See* advisory committee note to proposed amendment of Rule 23(f), 167 F.R.D. 565 (1996).

69. *See* Chapter 5(F)(6) *supra* (discussing *Wayman* and other potential separation of powers restrictions on judicial rule making authority); *see also* David L. Shapiro, *Federal Diversity Jurisdiction: A Survey and Proposal,* 91 HARV. L. REV. 317, 346-47 (1977) (arguing that properly circumscribed delegations of rule making power over subject-matter jurisdiction are constitutional).

70. 28 U.S.C. § 1651(a).

71. *See* First Nat'l Bank v. Warren, 796 F.2d 999 (7th Cir. 1986) (Easterbrook, J.) (discussing these two strands of doctrine).

72. *See id.; see also* Will v. United States, 389 U.S. 90, 88 S. Ct. 269, 19 L. Ed. 2d 305 (1967).

73. *See generally* Amy Schmidt Jones, *The Use of Mandamus to Vacate Mass Exposure Tort Class Certification,* 72 N.Y.U. L. REV. 232 (1997); Elizabeth A. Snyder, Comment, *The Use of Extraordinary Writs for Interlocutory Appeals,* 44 TENN. L. REV. 137 (1976).

74. 337 U.S. 541, 69 S. Ct. 1221, 93 L. Ed. 1528 (1949).

action.''[75] These rights are ''too important to be denied review and too independent of the cause itself to require that appellate consideration be deferred until the whole case is adjudicated.''[76]

(e) The Rejected "Death Knell" Doctrine

Several federal courts of appeals recognized another exception to the final judgment rule. This exception was known as the *death knell doctrine*, which allowed a party to appeal a non-final order when the order sounded the "death knell" of the action. Thus, this doctrine treated an order as "final" for purposes of § 1291 (final judgment requirement) when the alternatives were either an appeal or an end to the lawsuit for all practical purposes. However, the U.S. Supreme Court rejected the death knell doctrine in *Coopers & Lybrand v. Livesay*.[77]

(f) Pendent Appellate Jurisdiction

In addition, some federal courts of appeals have recognized the doctrine of "pendent appellate jurisdiction" as a basis for reviewing orders that are not otherwise immediately reviewable when they are "closely related" to an order properly before the appellate court.[78] The courts of appeals have indicated that pendent appellate jurisdiction should be exercised "rarely" and only in "exceptional circumstances."[79] However, the Supreme Court has not yet

---

75. *Id.* at 546, 69 S. Ct. at 1225-26, 93 L. Ed. at 1537.

76. *Id.*; *see* Lloyd C. Anderson, *The Collateral Order Doctrine: A New "Serbonian Bog" and Four Proposals for Reform,* 46 DRAKE L. REV. 539 (1998); Comment, *Collateral Orders and Extraordinary Writs as Exceptions to the Finality Rule,* 51 NW. U. L. REV. 746 (1957). Most orders, however, are not considered to be collateral orders for purposes of appeal. *See, e.g.,* Cunningham v. Hamilton County, 527 U.S. 198, 119 S. Ct. 1915, 144 L. Ed. 2d 184 (1999) (sanction imposed under Rule 37(a)(4) against attorney no longer representing any party in case for failure to comply with discovery orders is not a collateral order; although the order was conclusive, appellate review of a sanctions order cannot remain entirely separate from the merits, it can be reviewed after final judgment, an immediate appeal would frustrate the purpose of Rule 37(a) sanctions, and no special considerations in favor of appeal existed just because the attorney was no longer participating in the case); Digital Equip. Corp. v. Desktop Direct, Inc., 511 U.S. 863, 114 S. Ct. 1992, 128 L. Ed. 2d 842 (1994) (holding that a refusal to enforce a settlement agreement claimed to shelter party from suit altogether not a basis for immediate appeal under collateral order doctrine); Stringfellow v. Concerned Neighbors in Action, 480 U.S. 370, 107 S. Ct. 1177, 94 L. Ed. 2d 389 (1987) (refusing to allow appeal in an intervention context).

77. 437 U.S. 463, 98 S. Ct. 2454, 57 L. Ed. 2d 351 (1978) (involving a district court's determination that an action could not be maintained as a class action). *See generally* Kenneth A. Cohen, *"Not Dead But Only Sleeping": The Rejection of the Death Knell Doctrine and the Survival of Class Actions Denied Certification,* 59 B.U. L. REV. 257 (1979).

78. *See, e.g.,* Rendall-Speranza v. Nassim, 107 F.3d 913 (D.C. Cir. 1997) (a claim of immunity is rejected by the district court by denial of a motion to dismiss; at the same time the district court also denies a motion to dismiss on the basis of the statute of limitations; pendent appellate jurisdiction exists over the limitations issue when immunity ruling is immediately appealable); Freeman v. Complex Computing Co., 119 F.3d. 1044 (2d Cir. 1997) (where issues raised by appeal of an appealable order substantially overlap issues raised by nonappealable order, pendent appellate jurisdiction can be exercised over nonappealable order).

79. *See, e.g.,* Natale v. Town of Ridgefield, 927 F.2d 101 (2d Cir. 1991) (holding pendent party appellate jurisdiction improper on the facts of the case).

indicated whether the doctrine is appropriate at all and, if it is, in what circumstances.[80]

SECTION C. APPELLATE PROCEDURE

A fundamental principle underlying appellate litigation is that at least one of the parties must ordinarily initiate appellate review of a trial court decision. Before the Federal Rules of Civil Procedure were adopted, initiating a federal appeal involved several complicated steps, each of which was considered to be jurisdictional. A failure to take any of the correct steps could result in a dismissal of the appeal. The Federal Rules simplified the appellate process by establishing just one jurisdictional step: the timely filing of a notice of appeal.[81]

To be timely, a party must file a notice of appeal with the district court within thirty days after the entry of the judgment or order from which the party appeals. The United States and its officers or agents are allowed sixty days.[82] The time period for appeal is automatically extended while the court considers post-trial motions (*e.g.*, a motion for a new trial, a motion to alter or amend the judgment, etc.) and disposes of the last such remaining motion.[83] If a notice of appeal is filed while the court is considering such motions, the notice of appeal becomes effective when the order disposing of the last such motion is entered.[84]

A federal district court has limited power to extend the time for filing the notice of appeal. However, the court may do so only when a party has demonstrated good cause or excusable neglect.[85] A motion filed under Federal Rule

---

80. *See* Swint v. Chambers County Comm'n, 514 U.S. 35, 50-51, 115 S. Ct. 1203, 1211, 131 L. Ed. 2d 60, 74 (1995) (refusing to "definitively or preemptively settle here whether or when it may be proper for a court of appeals with jurisdiction over one ruling to review, conjunctively, related rulings that are not themselves independently appealable"). *See generally* Joan Steinman, *The Scope of Appellate Jurisdiction: Pendent Appellate Jurisdiction Before and After* Swint, 49 HAST. L.J. 1337 (1998) (arguing that the existence and scope of pendent appellate jurisdiction do not lie exclusively with the legislature and rule makers, and that the prudent use of pendent appellate jurisdiction is more consistent with the purposes of § 1291 than would be rejection of the doctrine); 16 CHARLES A. WRIGHT ET AL., FEDERAL PRACTICE AND PROCEDURE: JURISDICTION AND RELATED MATTERS § 3937 (2d ed. 1996); Riyaz A. Kanji, *The Proper Scope of Pendent Appellate Jurisdiction in the Collateral Order Context*, 100 YALE L.J. 511 (1990).

81. *See* FED. R. APP. P. 3(a).

82. *See* FED. R. APP. P. 4(a)(1); *see* David A. Johns, Annotation, *Construction of Provision in Rule 4(a) of Federal Rules of Appellate Procedure (Formerly Civil Procedure Rule 73(a)), Making an Exception as to Time for Filing Notice of Appeal from District Court to Court of Appeals in Civil Case "If the United States or an Officer or Agency Thereof" Is a Party*, 9 A.L.R. FED. 611 (1971).

83. *See* FED. R. CIV. P. 4(a)(4)(A); *cf.* Marine Midland Bank v. Slyman, 995 F.2d 362 (2d Cir. 1993) (stipulation signed by parties was functional equivalent of Rule 59(e) motion to amend judgment and extended time for appeal).

84. *See* FED. R. APP. P. 4(a)(4)(B)(i).

85. *See* FED. R. APP. P. 4(a)(5); *see* Paul A. Fischer, Annotation, *What Constitutes "Excusable Neglect" Which Will Permit Federal District Court to Extend Time for Filing Notice of Appeal from Civil Judgement Under Rule 4(a) of Federal Rules of Appellate Procedure and Under Former Rule 73(a) of Federal Rules of Civil Procedure*, 26 A.L.R. FED. 569 (1976); Jean F. Rydstrom, Annotation, *Appellate Review of Order Denying Extension of Time for Filing Notice of Appeal Under Rule 4(a) of Federal Rules of Appellate Procedure*, 39 A.L.R. FED. 829 (1978).

60(b) to reopen a judgment does not extend the time for filing a notice of appeal, unless it is filed no later than ten days after the judgment is entered.[86]

Illustration 12-12. *A* sued *B* in U.S. District Court. After trial on the merits, the jury found in favor of *A* and awarded *A* seven million dollars in damages. The court then entered judgment in favor of *A*. *B* filed a notice of appeal with the district court within forty days after the court entered that judgment. *B's* notice of appeal is untimely because *B* was required to file the notice of appeal within thirty days after the judgment was entered. Assume instead that after judgment was entered, *B* believed that jury verdict was excessive and appeared to have been given under the influence of passion and prejudice. *B* moved for a new trial on this ground pursuant to Rule 59 within ten days after the entry of the judgment (as required by Federal Rule 59(b)). The time period for appeal is automatically extended while the court considers this post-trial motion. Assume that the court denies *B's* motion sixty days later. *B* then has up to thirty days to file a notice of appeal after the entry of the order disposing of *B's* motion for a new trial.

* * * * *

The basic procedure for review in the federal courts of appeals is stated in the Federal Rules of Appellate Procedure.[87] The federal courts of appeals have adopted additional rules governing practice in their respective courts.[88] In general, the notice of appeal must designate the following: (1) the judgment or some portion of the judgment that is being appealed; (2) the appealing party and the parties against whom relief is sought; and (3) the name of the court which may take the appeal.[89] Procedures for initiating appellate review vary in state courts, but they generally follow the same basic steps as appellate review in the federal courts. One variation, however, is that in a few states, the parties first must file with the trial court a *bill of exceptions* in which their objections to a trial judge's rulings or jury instructions are stated for the record.[90]

The appealing party is also required to designate[91] the items to be included in the record on appeal, such as the pleadings, motions, orders, and

---

86. FED. R. APP. P. 4(a)(4)(A)(vi). The ten-day period is computed using the method set out in Federal Rule 6(a). *Id.*

87. Appellate Rules 3 and 4 govern appeals as a matter of right; Rule 5 governs appeals under § 1292(b); Rule 7 governs bonds to cover costs; Rules 10 and 11 govern the record on appeal; Rule 12 governs the docketing of the appeal and filing of the record; Rules 28 and 31 govern the preparation of the briefs; and Rule 30 governs appendices to the briefs and appeals on original records.

88. *See* FED. R. APP. P. 47; 28 U.S.C. § 2071 (individual court rules may be adopted, provided they are not inconsistent with the Federal Rules of Appellate Procedure). Special rules apply for the review of interlocutory (non-final) decisions, such as preliminary injunctions.

89. FED. R. APP. P. 3(c); *see also* R.L. Martyn, Annotation, *Sufficiency of "Designation," Under Federal Appellate Procedure Rule 3(c) or Former Federal Civil Procedure Rule 73(b), of Judgment or Order Appealed from in Civil Case by Notice of Appeal Not Specifically Designating Such Judgment or Order,* 2 A.L.R. FED. 545 (1969).

90. *See* ROBERT L. STERN, APPELLATE PRACTICE IN THE UNITED STATES § 6.7(d)(4), at 162 (2d ed. 1988).

91. This designation process is important because appellate courts normally confine review to matters reflected in the record. *See* DANIEL J. MEADOR & JORDANA S. BERNSTEIN, APPELLATE COURTS IN THE UNITED STATES 55 (1994). Thus, counsel should be sure that the record on appeal enables the court to fully and accurately comprehend the case and issues.

transcripts.[92] The appellees are entitled to cross-designate other matters that they believe should be included in the record on appeal.[93] Typically, thirty to sixty days after the record has been filed, the appellant must then submit a brief.[94] After the appellee submits a brief, the appellant usually has the opportunity to file a reply brief. Oral arguments are then held in most cases.

SECTION D. SCOPE OF REVIEW

The scope of appellate review is generally limited to matters contained in the trial-court record. Thus, even if a question was presented to the trial court and was decided, that question will ordinarily not be subject to review unless the question is reflected in the record.[95] Furthermore, the scope of review is generally limited to matters raised and preserved in the trial court.[96] In other words, alleged errors will be reviewed only if they were earlier presented to the trial court for decision. The delay and expense of an appeal cannot be justified when a matter could have been corrected had it been properly raised during trial. There are, however, several exceptions.

Illustration 12-13. An appeal may be allowed when the error is so great as to render the lower court's judgment void even though the error was not raised until the appeal.[97]

* * * * *

Appellate review is usually limited to examining questions of law or determining whether substantial evidence supports the trial court's factual findings. If the trial was before a jury, the appeal is framed in terms of whether the jury might have reasonably found as it did in light of the evidence. The standard for appellate review in this context is similar to that used for a directed verdict.[98]

In a nonjury trial in federal court, the trial judge's factual findings will be set aside only if they are "clearly erroneous." Furthermore, "due regard" must be "given to the opportunity of the trial court to judge the credibility of the

---

92. In federal courts of appeals, the Federal Rules of Appellate Procedure specify that the original papers and exhibits filed in the district court, a certified copy of the docket entries, and a transcript of the proceedings, if any, constitute the record on appeal. *See* FED. R. APP. P. 10(a); Alan R. Gilbert, Annotation, *Composition of Record on Appeal from District Court Under Rule 10(a) of Federal Rules of Appellate Procedure,* 33 A.L.R. FED. 588 (1977).

93. *See* FED. R. APP. P. 10(b)(3) (designation by appellee); *see also* FED. R. APP. P. 10(d) (agreed statement of the case on appeal in lieu of the record on appeal), 10(e) (correction or modification of the record on appeal); Ronald I. Mirvis, Annotation, *Correction, Modification, or Supplementation of Record on Appeal Under Rule 10(e) of Federal Rules of Appellate Procedure,* 60 A.L.R. FED. 183 (1982).

94. *Id.*

95. *See* DANIEL J. MEADOR & JORDANA S. BERNSTEIN, APPELLATE COURTS IN THE UNITED STATES 55 (1994).

96. *See* FED. R. CIV. P. 46.

97. Likewise, some courts will consider on appeal errors not presented to the trial court when they affect a party's fundamental rights or the public interest. *See* Allan D. Vestal, *Sua Sponte Consideration in Appellate Review,* 27 FORDHAM L. REV. 477 (1958).

98. *See* Chapter 11(H)(1) ("Involuntary Dismissals (Judgments on Partial Findings) and Directed Verdicts (Judgments as a Matter of Law") *supra.*

witnesses.''[99] One question about the ''clearly erroneous'' standard is whether it should be applied to factual findings based entirely on documentary evidence. Most jurisdictions apparently apply the standard in this situation, although some courts take a contrary view.[100] A 1985 amendment of Rule 52(a) resolved this issue for the federal courts by adding the language ''whether based on oral or documentary evidence, shall not be set aside unless clearly erroneous.''[101]

A trial judge often makes several ''discretionary'' determinations.[102] In reviewing these rulings, appellate courts give the trial judge wide latitude. The appellate court will not reverse the trial court unless the appellate court finds that the trial court abused its discretion.[103]

SECTION E. HARMLESS ERROR

The two basic prerequisites for an appellate court to reverse a judgment are (1) error and (2) injury. Error is prejudicial only if the error affects (1) the outcome of the case and (2) a substantial right.[104]

Illustration 12-14. When the plaintiff has been granted all available relief, any error that the plaintiff complains of is harmless. Likewise, prejudicial error may be cured by later proceedings or by a judgment in favor of the complaining party.

* * * * *

In contrast, an error should not be considered to be harmless merely because the verdict finds support in the evidence. When review of the record leaves the appellate court uncertain as to the correctness of the jury findings or judgment, or uncertain whether the jury would have found as it did but for the

---

99. FED. R. CIV. P. 52(a); *see also* United States v. United States Gypsum Co., 333 U.S. 364, 395, 68 S. Ct. 525, 542, 92 L. Ed. 746, 766 (1948) (''A finding is 'clearly erroneous' when although there is evidence to support it, the reviewing court on the entire evidence is left with the definite and firm conviction that a mistake has been committed'').

100. *See* Charles A. Wright, *The Doubtful Omniscience of Appellate Courts,* 41 MINN. L. REV. 751 (1957); *see also* Jean F. Rydstrom, Annotation, *Application of ''Clearly Erroneous'' Test of Rule 52(a) of Federal Rules of Civil Procedure to Trial Court's Findings of Fact Based on Documentary Evidence,* 11 A.L.R. FED. 212 (1967).

101. FED. R. CIV. P. 52(a); *see also* Edward H. Cooper, *Civil Rule 52(a): Rationing and Rationalizing the Resources of Appellate Review,* 63 NOTRE DAME L. REV. 645 (1988).

102. For example, such rulings include the scope of discovery, severance or consolidation of issues for trial, the order in which the evidence is presented, whether the probative value of certain evidence is outweighed by its prejudicial effects, etc.

103. *See* Maurice Rosenberg, *Judicial Discretion of the Trial Court, Viewed from Above,* 22 SYRACUSE L. REV. 635 (1971).

104. *See* 28 U.S.C. § 2111 (''On the hearing of any appeal or writ of certiorari in any case, the court shall give judgment after an examination of the record without regard to errors or defects which do not affect the substantial rights of the parties''); *cf.* FED. R. CIV. P. 61 (''No error in either the admission or the exclusion of evidence and no error or defect in any ruling or order or in anything done or omitted by the court or by any of the parties is ground for granting a new trial or for setting aside a verdict or for vacating, modifying or other disturbing a judgment or order, unless refusal to take such action appears to the court inconsistent with substantial justice. The court at every stage of the proceeding must disregard any error or defect in the proceeding which does not affect the substantial rights of the parties''); FED. R. EVID. 103(a). *See generally* Sheila A. Skojec, Annotation, *Error in Evidentiary Ruling in Federal Civil Case as Harmless or Prejudicial Under Rule 103(a), Federal Rules of Evidence,* 84 A.L.R. FED. 28 (1987).

error, reversal is appropriate. Furthermore, a demonstration of an infringement of a constitutional or statutory right may be the basis for reversal even when it is difficult to show specific injury resulting from that infringement. The cumulative effect of several minor errors, although harmless when independently considered, may also justify reversal when they are considered together.[105]

SECTION F. EXTRAORDINARY RELIEF FROM A JUDGMENT

Parties sometimes seek "extraordinary" relief from a judgment (1) when the time for ordinary post-verdict motions and appeal has expired and (2) when the effect of the judgment is questioned in a later action. Historically, the common-law courts could modify, reopen, or vacate a judgment during the term of the court in which it was rendered. The common-law writ of *error coram nobis*, which was addressed to the rendering court, was available both during and after expiration of the term. This writ was used to set aside a judgment for clerical errors in fact. It was not available for errors of judgment.[106] Another option available to a party to a common-law proceeding was to bring an independent suit in equity if a party had grounds for relief which could not have been pleaded in the action at law, such as fraud or mistake. Equity court decrees were challenged by a bill or petition to reopen the decree. Furthermore, a plea of invalidity could be asserted against a judgment set up by an adverse party in a subsequent action.[107]

Except for an independent suit in equity to set aside a judgment or the attempt to avoid the judgment in a subsequent action,[108] Federal Rule 60(b) supersedes all of these earlier devices for extraordinary relief from a judgment. Rule 60(b) authorizes post-judgment motions addressed to the judgment-rendering court on six grounds:[109]

---

105. *See* 14 DENNIS JENSEN & CORA THOMPSON, CYCLOPEDIA OF FEDERAL PROCEDURE § 68.52 (3d rev. ed. 1991).

106. *See* ROBERT W. MILLAR, CIVIL PROCEDURE OF THE TRIAL COURT IN HISTORICAL PERSPECTIVE 390-95 (1952).

107. *See id.* at 386, 396-401; 11 CHARLES A. WRIGHT ET AL., FEDERAL PRACTICE AND PROCEDURE: CIVIL § 2868 (2d ed. 1995).

108. *See* Deborah F. Harris, Annotation, *Independent Actions to Obtain Relief from Judgments, Order, or Proceedings Under Rule 60(b) of the Federal Rules of Civil Procedure,* 53 A.L.R. FED. 558 (1981). An independent action can be permitted only to prevent a "grave miscarriage of justice." *See* United States v. Beggarly, 524 U.S. 38, 118 S. Ct. 1862, 141 L. Ed. 2d 32 (1998) (not present in this case involving an independent action is brought to vacate a consent decree entered in favor of the government in a previous quiet title action and to recover just compensation for the taking of the plaintiffs' property.) Note that an independent basis of subject-matter jurisdiction need not exist when suit brought in the same court as the original lawsuit. *Id.* ("ancillary jurisdiction" exists over the action).

109. *See generally* Annotation, *Effect of Filing of Notice of Appeal on Motion to Vacate Judgment Under Rule 60(b) of Federal Rules of Civil Procedure,* 62 A.L.R. FED. 165 (1983); Jean F. Rydstrom, Annotation, *Construction and Application of Rule 60(b) of Federal Rules of Civil Procedure Authorizing Relief from Final Judgment or Order for "Any Other Reason,"* 15 A.L.R. FED. 193 (1973); J.M. Purver, Annotation, *Propriety of Conditions Imposed in Granting Relief from Judgment Under Rule of Civil Procedure 60(b),* 3 A.L.R. FED. 956 (1970).

(1) mistake, inadvertence, surprise, or excusable neglect; (2) newly discovered evidence which by due diligence could not have been discovered in time to move for a new trial under Rule 59(b); (3) fraud (whether heretofore denominated intrinsic or extrinsic), misrepresentation, or other misconduct of an adverse party; (4) the judgment is void; (5) the judgment has been satisfied, released, or discharged, or a prior judgment upon which it is based has been reversed or otherwise vacated, or it is no longer equitable that the judgment should have prospective application; or (6) any other reason justifying relief . . . .[110]

Rule 60(b) requires that the motion "be made within a reasonable time, and for reasons (1), (2), (3) no more than one year after the judgment, order, or proceeding was entered or taken."[111]

Recently, the U.S. Supreme Court has indicated that Rule 60(b) may be used to obtain relief from the prospective operation of an injunction by effectuating a change of law, as well as to obtain such relief on the basis of a change of law that had already taken place. In *Aguilar v. Felton*,[112] the Court had held that it was a violation of the Establishment Clause of the First Amendment for the New York school Board to send public school teachers into parochial schools to provide remedial education to disadvantaged children. On remand, the district court issued a permanent injunction against the Board. Twelve years later, the Board moved under Rule 60(b)(5) for relief from the injunction on the grounds that intervening U.S. Supreme Court decisions had undermined the original decision upon which the injunction was based. The district court held that the Board had properly proceeded under Rule 60(b)(5), but denied the motion on the grounds that the Supreme Court decision upon which the original injunction was based had not yet been formally overruled by the Court. The Court of Appeals for the Second Circuit affirmed for the same reasons. The U.S. Supreme Court granted certiorari and reversed.

In *Agostini v. Felton*,[113] the Court held that Rule 60(b) was a proper vehicle with which to seek relief from the injunction, even though the Court recognized that the district court and court of appeals had correctly denied relief because *Aguilar* had not yet been overruled. The Court held that its intervening decisions had indeed undermined *Aguilar* and overruled the decision. The Court's prior decisions had established that Rule 60(b)(5) was a proper vehicle with which to obtain relief from an injunction where decisional law had changed to make legal what the injunction was designed to prevent. However, in *Agostini*, the Court noted that Rule 60(b)(5) was, on the facts of the case, also properly used to effect a change in the law rather than to recognize one that had already taken place. The Court emphasized that petitioners were seeking relief from an injunction that sought prospective relief and that intervening developments in the

---

110. FED. R. CIV. P. 60(b).

111. *Id.*

112. 473 U.S. 402, 105 S. Ct. 3232, 87 L. Ed. 2d 290 (1985).

113. 521 U.S. 203, 117 S. Ct. 1997, 138 L. Ed. 2d 391 (1997).

law by themselves rarely constitute the extraordinary circumstances required for relief under Rule 60(b) from judgments lacking any prospective component. Justice Ginsburg, joined by Justices Stevens, Souter, and Breyer, dissented, arguing that the Court erroneously used Rule 60(b) to effectuate a change in law rather than to recognize one that had already taken place. Justice Ginsburg expressed the opinion that the Court should have waited for a more appropriate case in which to overrule *Aguilar*–*i.e.,* one in which relief was not sought under Rule 60(b).[114]

---

114. *See* 521 U.S. at 259-60, 117 S. Ct. at 2028, 138 L. Ed. 2d at 437 (Ginsburg, J., dissenting); *see also* Michael R. Tucci, *Putting the Cart Before the Horse:* Agostini v. Felton *Blurs the Line Between Res Judicata and Equitable Relief,* 49 CASE W. RES. L. REV. 407 (1999).

Chapter 13

FINALITY IN LITIGATION

SECTION A. INTRODUCTION

Rules of civil procedure attempt to secure the just, speedy, and inexpensive determination of civil actions.[1] To this end, procedural rules attempt to promote an accurate resolution of the merits of a dispute. Modern procedural rules thus aim to enhance the truth-finding capacity of the legal system. Obviously, this truth-finding objective of procedural rules must be qualified to some extent. For example, rules of evidentiary privilege protect socially beneficial interests that might be harmed by the introduction of entirely trustworthy evidence at trial.[2] Thus, the stronger societal policy of protecting privileged information qualifies the aim of securing the accurate determination of the action. The principle of finality in litigation also qualifies this truth-determining goal.

The principle of finality seeks to bring litigation over a particular matter to an end.[3] No matter how sophisticated a procedural system is or how many opportunities for the correction of error the system provides, it will never be possible to say with absolute certainty that the court has accurately resolved a dispute. Consequently, both fairness and efficiency dictate that even if the courts sometimes err, litigation should be brought to a close after a reasonable opportunity to reach a correct result.[4] The principle of finality also reflects other related policy interests: it "relieve[s] parties of the cost and vexation of multiple lawsuits, conserve[s] judicial resources, and, by preventing inconsistent decisions, encourage[s] reliance on adjudication."[5] In addition, preclusion rules also have important indirect effects on the settlement of disputes.[6] In the absence of preclusion rules, the parties would be more likely to extract settlements unrelated to the merits of the dispute through threats of multiple litigation.[7]

---

1. *See* FED. R. CIV. P. 1.

2. *See* Chapter 11(I)(4) (''Privilege'') *supra.*

3. *See, e.g.*, Stark v. Starr, 94 U.S. 477, 485, 24 L. Ed. 276, 278 (1877) ("'[A] party is not at liberty to spit up his demands and prosecute by piecemeal, or present only a portion of the grounds upon which special relief is sought and leave the rest to be presented in a second suit if the first fails. There would be *no end of litigation* if such practice were permissible.") (emphasis added).

4. *See, e.g.*, Thompson v. State Dep't of Licensing, 138 Wash. 2d 783, 795, 982 P.2d 601, 608 (1999) (relieving a party from the issue preclusion effect of a judgment on the ground that it was incorrect as a matter of law would eviscerate the doctrine of issue preclusion).

5. Allen v. McCurry, 449 U.S. 90, 94, 101 S. Ct. 411, 415, 66 L. Ed. 2d 308, 313 (1980); *see also* Edward W. Cleary, *Res Judicata Reexamined*, 57 YALE L.J. 339, 344-49 (1948) (principal justifications for the finality rule are (1) avoiding the danger of double recovery; (2) promoting the desirability of stable judicial determinations; (3) relieving defendants of the expense and vexation of repeated litigation; and (4) economizing judicial resources).

6. *See* Bruce L. Hay, *Some Settlement Effects of Preclusion*, 1993 U. ILL. L. REV. 21.

7. Professor Hay has suggested that although the prevailing view of finality rules is to regulate the litigation of disputes by preventing relitigation, the more important effect of such rules is to encourage the parties to settle their dispute for an amount close to the expected judicial valuation of the plaintiff's claim. *See id.* at 21-41.

The Anglo-American legal system groups the rules embodying the principle of finality under the label *res judicata*.[8] Res judicata literally means "a thing adjudicated."[9] It simply refers to the body of rules that limit a party's opportunity to litigate matters in a second action that were, or could have been, litigated in a prior action.[10] The nature of the procedural system substantially influences when a final judgment in an action will preclude litigation in another proceeding.[11] When a system narrowly confines the ability to plead a claim for relief, to join claims, to amend pleadings, and to correct trial errors by appeal, the rules of res judicata will be narrow in scope.[12] For example, the common-law system had restrictive pleading and joinder rules. Thus, it allowed more matters to be relitigated than modern procedural systems, which have more liberal pleading and joinder rules.[13]

Within the broad category of res judicata, finality rules are grouped under the labels *claim preclusion* and *issue preclusion*. Claim preclusion deals with the effect of a final judgment on the "cause of action" or "claim" involved in an action. Claim preclusion rules prevent a party from litigating in a subsequent action any matter that was a part of the same claim or cause of action adjudicated in a prior action.[14] These rules thus preclude from litigation any part of the claim that *might* have been litigated, even though the matter was *not actually* litigated in the action. In contrast, issue preclusion rules prevent only issues *actually litigated* in an action from being relitigated in a subsequent proceeding.[15]

To avoid confusion, one point concerning terminology should be made about claim and issue preclusion. Some court opinions use the label "res judicata" to refer only to claim preclusion. These opinions label issue preclusion "collateral estoppel."[16] Other opinions use res judicata to include both claim and issue preclusion. These opinions describe specifically which of the two doctrines they are dealing with in a given case. They use the labels "claim preclusion" or "issue preclusion."[17] Obviously, this varying use of terminology creates the potential for confusion. Fortunately, however, as courts recognize the

---

8. *See* RESTATEMENT (SECOND) OF JUDGMENTS ch. 1, at 2 (1982) ("Introduction").

9. The less common spelling of the name of this doctrine is "res adjudicata." For a discussion of the historical origins of claim and issue preclusion as well as a discussion of the civil law on this subject, see Robert W. Millar, *The Historical Relation of Estoppel by Record to Res Judicata*, 35 ILL. L. REV. 41 (1940); Robert W. Millar, *The Premises of the Judgment as Res Judicata in Continental and Anglo-American Law* (pts. 1 & 2), 39 MICH. L. REV. 1, 238 (1940) (pointing out that res judicata entered English law from Roman law; in contrast, nothing in civil law corresponds to the principle of estoppel in English law, which was derived from Germanic law).

10. *See* RESTATEMENT (SECOND) OF JUDGMENTS ch. 1, at 1 (1982) ("Introduction").

11. *See generally id.* at 5-13.

12. *See id.* at 8-9.

13. *See id.* at 7.

14. *See id.* at 6.

15. *See id.*

16. *See* Kaspar Wire Works, Inc. v. Leco Eng'g & Mach., Inc., 575 F.2d 530, 535-36 (5th Cir. 1978). For an example of a case in which this confusion occurred at the trial level, see McCoy v. Cooke, 165 Mich. App. 662, 419 N.W.2d 44, *appeal denied*, 430 Mich. 897 (1988).

17. *See* Migra v. Warren City Sch. Dist. Bd. of Educ., 465 U.S. 75, 77 n.1, 104 S. Ct. 892, 894 n.1, 79 L. Ed. 2d 56, 59 n.1 (1984).

confusion that can result when "res judicata" is used only to refer to claim preclusion, discussions of claim and issue preclusion are becoming more precise. Still, until usage becomes uniform, readers of judicial opinions must examine each case carefully to determine whether claim preclusion or issue preclusion is involved. In this chapter, the expression "res judicata" will be used, as it is in the *Restatement (Second) of Judgments*, to include both claim and issue preclusion. The expressions "claim preclusion" and "issue preclusion" will be used to describe the kind of res judicata rules involved.[18]

The rules of claim and issue preclusion do not prevent continued litigation over a matter in the original action in which a court has rendered judgment. For example, when a party appeals a judgment, res judicata rules do not operate because the appeal is simply a continuation at another level of the original litigation. The rules of res judicata come into play only after a judgment has become final and a second action is brought to litigate a matter that has been, or might have been, litigated in the first proceeding. Often, courts express this difference between the applicability of res judicata in original and subsequent proceedings in terms of *direct attack* versus *collateral attack*. It is often said that res judicata does not apply to "direct attacks" on judgments—attacks designed to correct error in the original proceeding. Rather, res judicata applies only to "collateral attacks" on a judgment—attacks leveled at a judgment in a separate proceeding when the judgment in the original action is brought into issue in the separate (collateral) proceeding.[19]

By definition, the rules of res judicata apply only to *final* judgments.[20] "Final" for purposes of the res judicata rules is not precisely the same as finality for purposes of appellate review.[21] Compared to the requirement of finality for purposes of appellate review, finality for purposes of issue preclusion is treated somewhat less stringently. In a res judicata context, finality means any prior

---

18. *See* RESTATEMENT (SECOND) OF JUDGMENTS ch. 3, at 131 (1982) ("Introductory Note"); Allan D. Vestal, *Res Judicata/Preclusion: Expansion*, 47 S. CAL. L. REV. 357, 359 (1974).

19. *But cf.* Arizona v. California, 460 U.S. 605, 618, 103 S. Ct. 1382, 1391, 75 L. Ed. 2d 318, 332 (1983) (a case within the original jurisdiction of the Supreme Court in which the Court had retained jurisdiction "to correct certain errors, to determine reserved questions, and if necessary, to make modifications in the decree"). The Court refused to "extrapolate" the discretionary doctrine of "law of the case," *see infra* section G, into its original jurisdiction "where jurisdiction to accommodate changed circumstances is often retained," because to do so "would weaken to an intolerable extent the finality of our decrees in original actions." 460 U.S. at 619, 103 S. Ct. at 1391, 75 L. Ed. 2d at 333 (footnote omitted). Rather, the Court applied the principles of res judicata, even though it recognized that those principles were not "strictly applicable" because they "do not apply if a party moves the rendering court in the same proceeding to correct or modify its judgment," as had been done in the case before the Court. *Id.* The same principles of finality underpinning the doctrine of res judicata were found to be strong in the case before the Court, which involved a prior determination of an issue concerning water rights in the Southwest, an adjudication that was calculated to provide assurance to the states and various private interests in the region of the amount of water they could anticipate receiving from the Colorado River system. *Id.* at 620, 103 S. Ct. at 1392, 75 L. Ed. 2d at 334.

20. *See* G. & C. Merriam Co. v. Saalfield, 241 U.S. 22, 28, 36 S. Ct. 477, 480, 60 L. Ed. 868, 872 (1916) ("familiar law that only a final judgment is res judicata").

21. *See* RESTATEMENT (SECOND) OF JUDGMENTS § 13 cmt. b (1982); Bay State HMO Management, Inc. v. Tingley Sys., Inc., 181 F.3d 174, 178 (1st Cir. 1999) (finality for purposes of appeal does not mean final judgment has been rendered for purposes of claim preclusion; consolidated actions in which some "claims" dismissed and others remained for adjudication); *see also* Chapter 12(B)(3) ("The Final Judgment Rule and Its Exceptions") *supra*.

adjudication of an issue in another action that is sufficiently firm to be accorded conclusive effect.[22]

Illustration 13-1. *A* sues *B* for negligence. *B's* answer denies negligence and pleads contributory negligence. The jurisdiction in which the action is filed permits "split" trials–a trial of liability followed by a separate trial on the issue of damages if liability is found. The jury finds *B* liable. Even if *B* cannot appeal this judgment under the rules of finality governing appeals in the jurisdiction, the verdict as to liability may be held conclusive as to the issues of *A's* and *B's* negligence in any separate action between them in which these issues arise.[23]

* * * * *

For a judgment to operate as res judicata, the judgment must be a valid judgment.[24] Mere error does not render a judgment invalid in the sense meant here. For a judgment to be invalid, the court must have rendered it without personal jurisdiction over the defendant or without subject-matter jurisdiction over the action.[25] Traditionally, absence of jurisdiction renders a judgment "void" and subject to collateral attack in a subsequent proceeding. In contrast, nonjurisdictional errors merely render a judgment "voidable" on direct attack. However, these statements should not be accepted uncritically. As discussed in section E, some judgments rendered without subject-matter or personal jurisdiction are immune from collateral attack. Furthermore, in some jurisdictions, violation of rules other than rules of subject-matter and personal jurisdiction may also render a judgment "void" and subject to collateral attack–for example, rules prohibiting the procurement of a judgment by fraud.[26]

SECTION B. CLAIM PRECLUSION

1. "Merger," "Bar," and the Rule Against Splitting a Claim

Traditionally, courts have expressed rules of claim preclusion in terms of *merger* and *bar*.[27] When a court has rendered a valid and final personal judgment in favor of the plaintiff, the plaintiff's claim or cause of action "merges" into the judgment. Thereafter, the plaintiff may not maintain an action

---

22. *See* RESTATEMENT (SECOND) OF JUDGMENTS § 13 cmt. a & g (1982).

23. *See id.* illus. 3; *see also id.* illus. 1 & 2; Fox v. Maulding, 112 F.3d 453 (10th Cir. 1997) (a judgment becomes final for purposes of claim preclusion under Oklahoma law after the time for appeal has expired and no appeal has been taken; judgment becomes final for purposes of issue preclusion as soon as a court has decided an issue of fact or law necessary to its judgment). *But cf.* Mower v. Boyer, 811 S.W.2d 560 (Tex. 1991) (partial summary judgment not sufficiently firm and not subject to appeal; therefore, it had no issue preclusion effect).

24. *See* RESTATEMENT (SECOND) OF JUDGMENTS § 17 (1982).

25. *See id.* § 1.

26. *See* section E ("Claim and Issue Preclusion on Questions of Subject-Matter and Personal Jurisdiction") *infra.*

27. *See, e.g.,* McCoy v. Cooke, 165 Mich. App. 662, 419 N.W.2d 44, *appeal denied*, 430 Mich. 897 (1988) (discussing merger, bar, and the distinction between claim and issue preclusion).

on the original claim or cause of action.[28] The plaintiff may only execute the judgment against the defendant's property or bring a second action on the judgment itself.[29] Similarly, if the plaintiff brings an action on the judgment, the defendant cannot use any defenses that the defendant raised or could have raised in the initial action.[30] On the other hand, if the judgment in the first action is for the defendant, the operative concept is "bar" rather than merger. The rule is, simply, that "[a] valid and final personal judgment rendered in favor of the defendant bars another action by the plaintiff on the same claim."[31]

The rules of merger and bar are actually different components of a single rule: a party may not split a "claim" or "cause of action." This rule obviously makes the "scope" of a claim or cause of action quite important. As noted in section A, above, the rigidity of the common-law system, particularly its limitations on joinder of causes of action,[32] produced a relatively narrow operation of the principle of finality. The narrow operation of the principle of finality continued to be reflected in the traditional definitions of "cause of action" that evolved in the nineteenth century.[33] These definitions often conceptualized the scope of a cause of action in terms of the right being asserted by the plaintiff. Thus, it was common to speak of the plaintiff's "right of action" or "the right which is being enforced." Sometimes, the scope of a cause of action combined "the primary right" of the plaintiff with the "primary duty" of the defendant and the breach of that duty which infringed the plaintiff's right.[34] Another popular definition focused on whether "the evidence needed to sustain the second action would have sustained the first action."[35]

---

28. *See* Robinson v. Buie, 307 Ark. 112, 817 S.W.2d 431 (1991) (plaintiff's second action against principal of business dismissed on basis of claim preclusion, where plaintiff had won prior action against business on same claim; principal in privity with business).

29. If the plaintiff is forced to bring a second action to enforce the judgment, as, for example, when the plaintiff must sue to enforce the judgment in another state, the judgment in the first action is not considered to be merged in any judgment the plaintiff obtains in the second proceeding. The plaintiff will be able to enforce either judgment by execution or otherwise. However, satisfaction of one judgment operates as satisfaction of the other. *See* RESTATEMENT (SECOND) OF JUDGMENTS § 18 cmt. j. (1982).

30. *See id.* § 18.

31. *Id.* § 19.

32. *See* Chapter 7(A) ("Joinder of Claims by the Plaintiff at Common Law and in Equity") *supra.*

33. *See* RESTATEMENT (SECOND) OF JUDGMENTS § 24 cmt. a (1982).

34. *See id.* at 197; CHARLES E. CLARK, HANDBOOK OF THE LAW OF CODE PLEADING § 19, at 130-36 (2d ed. 1947).

35. RESTATEMENT (FIRST) OF JUDGMENTS § 61 (1942). The substantive problems with these definitions of the scope of a cause of action are described by the drafters of the *Restatement (Second) of Judgments*:

"Claim," in the context of res judicata, has never been broader than the transaction to which it related. But in the days when civil procedure still bore the imprint of the forms of action and the division between law and equity, the courts were prone to associate claim with a single theory of recovery, so that, with respect to one transaction, a plaintiff might have as many claims as there were theories of the substantive law upon which he could seek relief against the defendant. Thus, defeated in an action based on one theory, the plaintiff might be able to maintain another action based on a different theory, even though both actions were grounded upon the defendant's identical act or connected acts forming a single life-situation. In those earlier days there was also some adherence to a view that associated claim with the assertion of a single primary right as accorded by the substantive law, so that, if it appeared that the defendant had invaded a number of primary rights conceived to be held by the plaintiff, the plaintiff had the same number of

The modern tendency is to define "claim" or "cause of action" by reference to a factual grouping. A factual grouping includes all events comprising a single transaction or a series of connected transactions.[36] Sections 24 and 25 of the *Restatement (Second) of Judgments* describe the modern rules.[37] Section 24 states that when merger or bar extinguishes a plaintiff's claim, "the claim extinguished includes all rights of the plaintiff to remedies against the defendant with respect to all or any part of the transaction, or series of connected transactions, out of which the action arose."[38] Section 24 indicates that a pragmatic approach should be taken in determining "[w]hat factual grouping constitutes a 'transaction,' and what groupings constitute a 'series' for this purpose." Weight is to be given "to such considerations as whether the facts are related in time, space, origin, or motivation, whether they form a convenient trial unit, and whether their treatment as a unit conforms to the parties' expectations or business understanding or usage." Section 25 states that this rule extinguishing the plaintiff's claim applies even if "the plaintiff is prepared in the second action (1) [t]o present evidence or grounds or theories of the case not presented in the first action, or (2) [t]o seek remedies or forms of relief not demanded in the first action."[39]

---

claims, even though they all sprang from a unitary occurrence. There was difficulty in knowing which rights were primary and what was their extent, but a primary right and the corresponding claim might turn out to be narrow. Thus it was held by some courts that a judgment for or against the plaintiff in an action for personal injuries did not preclude an action by him for property damage occasioned by the same negligent conduct on the part of the defendant—this deriving from the idea that the right to be free of bodily injury was distinct from the property right. Still another view of claim looked to sameness of evidence; a second action was precluded where the evidence to support it was the same as that needed to support the first. Sometimes this was made the sole test of identity of claim; sometimes it figured as a positive but not as a negative test; that is, in certain situations a second action might be precluded although the evidence material to it varied from that in the first action. Even so, claim was not coterminous with the transaction itself.

RESTATEMENT (SECOND) OF JUDGMENTS § 24 cmt. a (1982).

36. *See* RESTATEMENT (SECOND) OF JUDGMENTS § 24 cmt. a (1982). As noted in section A *supra*, this modern trend is based upon the "ample procedural means" provided by modern systems for fully and fairly litigating all matters arising from a common factual basis in a single proceeding.

37. *Id.* § 24 ("Dimensions of 'Claim' for Purposes of Merger or Bar—General Rule Concerning 'Splitting' "), § 25 ("Exemplifications of General Rule Concerning Splitting"). *See generally* John F. Wagner, Jr., Annotation, *Proper Test to Determine Identity of Claims for Purposes of Claim Preclusion by Res Judicata under Federal Law*, 82 A.L.R. FED. 829 (1987). A recurrent question involves the question whether a property damage claim and a personal injury claim resulting from a single tortious act give rise to one or two claims. Most, but not all, jurisdictions today hold that only one claim arises from such an event. However, some jurisdictions that recognize only one claim have a "subrogation exception." An insurer will sometimes require its insured to assign a claim for damage to the insured's automobile to the insurer before it will pay a collision insurance claim to its insured. When a property damage claim has been so assigned and litigated or settled, the insured can still maintain a claim for personal injuries under this exception. *See* Andrea G. Nadel, Annotation, *Simultaneous Injury to Person and Property as Giving Rise to Single Cause of Action—Modern Cases*, 24 A.L.R.4TH 646 (1983) (describing the prevailing views).

38. *See* RESTATEMENT (SECOND) OF JUDGMENTS § 24(1) (1982).

39. *Id.* § 24(2). *See, e.g.,* Powder Basin Psychiatric Assocs., Inc. v. Ullrich, 129 Idaho 658, 931 P.2d 652 (1997) (first suit by employer against former employee for taking and wrongfully withholding office furniture settled and dismissed with prejudice; second action by employer against employee for wrongfully withholding $10,000 for services rendered while he was employed, but which belonged to employer, barred by claim preclusion). *But see* Harborside Refrigerated Servs., Inc. v. Vogel, 959 F.2d 368 (2d Cir. 1992) (exception to

Illustration 13-2. *A* sues *B* for breach of an oral contract for the sale of land. *B* asserts that the statute of frauds makes the contract unenforceable, and *B* wins. *A* then sues *B* for restitution to recover the money paid for the land. Under the modern rule, *A* may not sue for the restitutionary remedy in the second suit (assuming that *A* could have requested it in the first suit).[40] In contrast, under the traditional narrow view of a cause of action, courts would have permitted two separate suits because these two actions involved different ''rights'' and ''wrongs.''[41]

Illustration 13-3. *A* and *B* were involved in an automobile accident due to *B's* negligence. Immediately after the accident *B* jumped from the car, punched *A* in the nose, and falsely stated to a bystander that *A* was an alcoholic. *A* sues *B* for personal injuries received in the automobile accident and recovers a judgment. *A* then sues *B* for the assault and battery occurring immediately after the accident. *A* also sues *B* in a third action for slander. Under the modern rule, *A* may not maintain the second or third actions. The events on which *A's* injuries were based all arose out of the same transaction or series of connected transactions and are considered part of the same claim.[42] In contrast, a system that focused on a traditional definition of the scope of a ''cause of action,'' such as

---

ordinary res judicata principles when prior action is for declaratory judgment because parties may pursue further relief based on declaratory judgment); Carver v. Heikkila, 465 N.W.2d 183 (S.D. 1991) (same); *cf.* Schwartz v. City of Flint, 187 Mich. App. 191, 466 N.W.2d 357, *appeal denied*, 439 Mich. 867 (1991) (property owner precluded from asserting claim for damages by prior declaratory judgment action in which damage claim could have been raised). *See generally* Annotation, *Extent to Which Principles of Res Judicata Are Applicable to Judgments in Actions for Declaratory Relief*, 10 A.L.R.2D 782 (1950).

40. *See* RESTATEMENT (SECOND) OF JUDGMENTS § 25 illus. 15 (1982); *see also* Silcox v. United Trucking Servs., Inc., 687 F.2d 848 (6th Cir. 1982); Plum Creek Dev. Co. v. City of Conway, 334 S.C. 30, 512 S.E.2d 106 (1999) (plaintiff sued for mandamus in first action and was precluded from suing for damages in second action where both actions based on same breach of contract); *cf.* Howard J. Alperin, Annotation, *Decree Allowing or Denying Specific Performance of Contract as Precluding, as a Matter of Res Judicata, Subsequent Action for Money Damages for Breach*, 38 A.L.R.3D 323 (1971).

41. *See* RESTATEMENT (FIRST) OF JUDGMENTS § 65 illus. 7 (1942); Smith v. Kirkpatrick, 305 N.Y. 66, 111 N.E.2d 209 (1953) (second action on a quantum meruit theory after the plaintiff had lost a prior action for the same sum on the ground that the oral contract was unenforceable because it did not comply with the statute of frauds). The *Smith* court stated:

> The two actions involve different ''rights'' and ''wrongs.'' The requisite elements of proof and hence the evidence necessary to sustain recovery vary materially. The causes of action are different and distinct . . . . [T]he rights and interests established by the previous adjudication will not be impaired by a recovery, if that be the outcome, in quantum meruit.

Id. at 72, 111 N.E.2d at 111. The *Smith* case has now been overruled. *See* O'Brien v. City of Syracuse, 54 N.Y.2d 353, 429 N.E.2d 1158, 445 N.Y.S.2d 687 (1981). *See generally* Howard J. Alperin, Annotation, *Judgment in Action on Express Contract for Labor or Services as Precluding, as a Matter of Res Judicata, Subsequent Action on Implied Contract (Quantum Meruit) or Vice Versa*, 35 A.L.R.3D 874 (1971). For a discussion and critique of a New York statute providing that a judgment denying recovery in an action on a written agreement will not preclude a subsequent action for reformation of the agreement, *see* Bernard E. Gegan, *Claim Preclusion and Reformation of Contracts: New York CPLR 3002(d)*, 70 ST. JOHN'S L. REV. 539 (1996); *see also* Walter W. Heiser, *California's Unpredictable Res Judicata (Claim Preclusion) Doctrine*, 35 SAN DIEGO L. REV. 599 (1998) (discussing and critiquing the California ''primary rights'' doctrine).

42. *See* RESTATEMENT (SECOND) OF JUDGMENTS § 24 illus. 6 (1982).

the "primary right" of the plaintiff, may have permitted three separate actions under these circumstances.[43]

Illustration 13-4. *O* leases land to *L* for a two-year period. A dispute arises between *O* and *L* over the amount of land leased. As a result, *L* occupies a larger portion of the land than *L* leased. *O* contends that the fair rental value of this extra land is $1,000 per year. *L* refuses to pay the $1,000 due for either year. *O* sues *L* for the $1,000 owed for the first year, and *O* recovers. *O* then sues *L* for the $1,000 owed for the second year. Under the modern approach, the second action would not be permitted. The lease was a single transaction. Normally, a plaintiff would be expected to sue for the total amount due under that lease at one time. Alternatively, if the claim is not predicated on the lease, but on a restitutionary theory, the same would be true: the plaintiff would be expected to sue at the same time for all amounts due.[44]

Illustration 13-5. *A* pays state income taxes in Year 1 and Year 2. In Year 3, *A* sues the state for a refund of the Year 1 taxes and recovers. *A* then sues the state on the same factual and legal grounds for a refund of the Year 2 taxes. Under the modern transactional rule, these separate actions can be maintained. Each tax year represents a separate claim because of the parties' expectations and how tax years have been traditionally regarded.[45]

2. Judgments "On the Merits"

Traditionally, claim preclusion operated only when the court had rendered a final judgment *on the merits* of an action. Consequently, when the court dismissed a case for some reason not based upon the merits, the doctrine of bar generally did not preclude the plaintiff from bringing a second suit on the same claim or cause of action.[46] One important situation in which this rule operated was when the plaintiff's complaint was dismissed for legal insufficiency—for failure to state facts sufficient to constitute a cause of action (in code language) or failure to state a claim on which relief could be granted (Federal Rules). When such a dismissal occurred, the plaintiff could commence a new action in which the plaintiff cured the insufficiency in the complaint. Even though the plaintiff failed to take advantage of an opportunity to amend in the first action, the judgment in the first action would not be deemed "on the merits." Thus, the plaintiff could bring the second suit.[47]

---

43. *Cf.* RESTATEMENT (FIRST) OF JUDGMENTS § 62 cmt. f (1942) ("Where there are a number of successive acts which are substantially simultaneous . . . [or which] are all substantially *of the same sort,* public convenience and fairness to the defendant may require that they be dealt with in one proceeding. Thus, where in a series of rapidly successive acts a person breaks into the house of another, beats him and takes his chattels, a judgment based upon a claim for any one of these harms is a bar to a subsequent action.") (emphasis added). Note that this comment uses a series of intentional torts rather than a series of causes of action based on different legal theories—*e.g.,* negligence, battery, and slander occurring in succession.

44. *See* RESTATEMENT (SECOND) OF JUDGMENTS § 24(2) cmt. d, illus. 9 & reporter's note at 228 (1982); *cf.* Sutcliffe Storage & Warehouse Co. v. United States, 162 F.2d 849 (1st Cir. 1947).

45. *See* RESTATEMENT (SECOND) OF JUDGMENTS § 24(2) & illus. 9 (1982).

46. *See* RESTATEMENT (FIRST) OF JUDGMENTS § 49 (1942).

47. *See id.* § 50 cmt. c & e.

Illustration 13-6. *A* sued *B* for slander in a state court. *B* filed a demurrer on the ground that *A* did not allege special damages. The court ruled that the complaint failed to allege facts sufficient to constitute a cause of action for slander because an allegation of special damages was lacking, but the court granted *A* leave to amend. *A* did not amend, and a judgment was entered against *A*. *A* did not appeal. Instead, *A* filed a second action in the same court curing the pleading defect that caused the dismissal in the first action. Under the traditional rule reflected in the *Restatement (First)*, the judgment in the first action would not be "on the merits," and the second suit would be permitted.[48]

* * * * *

Assume, however, that after a dismissal of the complaint for insufficiency, the plaintiff tried to bring a new action with a substantially unchanged complaint. The doctrine of *direct estoppel* would bar this new action.[49] Furthermore, when the plaintiff's complaint revealed on its face a defense to the action, the plaintiff was not permitted to bring a second suit, even if the plaintiff's second complaint did not disclose the defense. Similarly, when "an entire failure to state a cause of action" had occurred in the first action, a second action was precluded.[50]

Illustration 13-7. *A* sued *B* for violating *A's* right of privacy. The court sustained *B's* demurrer on the ground that the applicable law afforded no right of action for violation of privacy. Under the traditional rule, *A* could not commence a second action on the same claim against *B*, even if the highest court of the state recognized such a right of action between the first and second suit.[51]

* * * * *

The traditional "on the merits" rule is vulnerable to criticism today. Given the adequacy of modern procedures for (1) stating a claim or cause of action and (2) correcting pleading and other errors by amendment, no justification exists for restricting the scope of claim preclusion to judgments technically "on the merits." Although the plaintiff should always be afforded a reasonable opportunity to present the merits of the case, the rules of claim preclusion should apply when such an opportunity has been provided. Section 19 of the *Restatement (Second) of Judgments* now makes the general rule of bar applicable to a judgment for the defendant on demurrer or motion to dismiss granted due to the insufficiency of the plaintiff's complaint.[52] This rule of bar does not apply when the plaintiff's action is dismissed "for lack of jurisdiction, for improper venue, or for nonjoinder or misjoinder of parties."[53]

---

48. *Id.* cmt. c.

49. *See id.* cmt. d. Direct estoppel thus precludes a party from relitigating issues once litigated and determined against that party in cases in which a second action was based on the *same* claim or cause of action as the party's first action. In contrast, "collateral estoppel," which is discussed in section C *infra*, precluded a party from relitigating issues once litigated and determined against the party when the second action involved a *different* claim or cause of action than the first action (in which the issue was originally adjudicated). *See* Bachman v. Bachman, 997 S.W.2d 23 (Mo. Ct. App. 1999) (example of direct estoppel).

50. *See* RESTATEMENT (FIRST) OF JUDGMENTS § 50 cmt. c (1942).

51. *See id.*

52. *See* RESTATEMENT (SECOND) OF JUDGMENTS § 19 cmt. d (1982).

53. *Id.* § 20(1)(a). *See generally* E.H. Schopler, Annotation, *Res Judicata Effect of Judgment Dismissing Action, or Otherwise Denying Relief, for Lack of Jurisdiction or Venue*, 49 A.L.R.2D 1036 (1956).

Illustration 13-8. *A* sues *B* for personal injuries. The action is dismissed for improper venue. *A* may bring a second action in a court in which venue is proper.[54] On the other hand, assume that *A* commences a second action in the same court. *A* asserts the same claim and alleges that the judge erred in dismissing the first action for improper venue. The rules of issue preclusion (here direct estoppel) will preclude *A* from relitigating the venue issue.

Illustration 13-9. On the facts of *Illustration 13-6*, under the *Restatement (Second)*, *A* would be precluded from bringing the second action.[55] If the action had been brought in a federal court and the dismissal ordered pursuant to Federal Rule 12(b)(6) on the ground the complaint failed to state a claim upon which relief could be granted, Rule 41(b) appears to prescribe the same result—assuming the court did not specify otherwise in its order of dismissal. Rule 41(b) treats dismissals pursuant to Rule 41(b) and any other dismissal not otherwise provided for in Rule 41 as adjudications on the merits. Rule 41 makes an exception for dismissals based on lack of jurisdiction, improper venue, or failure to join a party under Rule 19.[56] However, the U.S. Supreme Court indicated in *Costello v. United States*,[57] that the word "jurisdiction" in Rule 41(b) includes a failure to satisfy a precondition of suit. The dismissal in *Costello* was not a Rule 12(b)(6) dismissal based on a failure to state a claim. Nevertheless, some federal courts have held that Rule 12(b)(6) dismissals fit within the *Costello* rationale.[58] Given the ease of stating a claim for relief, the liberality of amendment under the Federal Rules, and the ability to reverse erroneous dismissals or refusals to allow

---

54. *See* RESTATEMENT (SECOND) OF JUDGMENTS § 20 cmt. b, illus. 1 (1982). This result would follow under the *Restatement (Second)* even if the court erroneously specified the dismissal on venue grounds to be "with prejudice." Rule 41(b) explicitly states that venue dismissals are not on the merits, but even if a rule like Rule 41(b) did not exist, dismissal on venue grounds is so clearly a threshold determination that a "with prejudice" specification should be disregarded as an abuse of discretion. *See id.* § 20, cmt. d. Note that to do otherwise would be to force the plaintiff to appeal a possibly correct determination on the venue question merely in order to reverse the "with prejudice" designation, thus increasing appellate litigation unnecessarily. Such a consequence would run counter to the stated policies of the finality doctrine to hold down the level of litigation. *See also* Kulinski v. Medtronic Bio-Medicus, Inc., 112 F.3d 368 (8th Cir. 1997) (plaintiff files two federal actions, one on a federal claim and the second a diversity action on a state claim, arising from the same facts; the federal-claim action was dismissed for lack of subject-matter jurisdiction "with prejudice;" plea of res judicata in second action denied, the court holding that while the judgment could preclude relitigation of the subject-matter jurisdiction issue, it could not preclude the state claim because it was not "on the merits" despite the "with prejudice" specification).

55. *See* RESTATEMENT (SECOND) OF JUDGMENTS § 19 cmt. d, illus. 1 (1982).

56. FED. R. CIV. P. 41(b).

57. 365 U.S. 265, 81 S. Ct. 534, 5 L. Ed. 2d 551 (1961) (dismissal arising from a failure to file a good cause affidavit within the meaning of the "lack of jurisdiction" exception in Rule 41).

58. *See, e.g.,* Nasser v. Isthmian Lines, 331 F.2d 124, 127 (2d Cir. 1964) (dictum) ("[T]he preclusive effect afforded dismissals by Rule 41(b) was intended to apply only to those situations in which a defendant must incur the inconvenience of preparing to meet the merits of the plaintiff's claims because there is no initial bar to the court's reaching the merits as there would be, for illustrative purposes, *if there were a defect in pleadings* or parties.") (emphasis added); Rambur v. Diehl Lumber Co., 144 Mont. 84, 93, 394 P.2d 745, 750 (1964) ("Rule 41(b) has no application to a motion to dismiss for failure to state a claim under Rule 12(b).").

amendments, however, the better result is that a Rule 12(b)(6) dismissal should be considered on the merits.[59]

* * * * *

This rule of bar also does not apply when the judgment for the defendant "rests on the prematurity of the action or on the plaintiff's failure to satisfy a precondition to suit." Under such circumstances, the judgment "does not bar another action by the plaintiff instituted after the claim has matured, or the precondition has been satisfied, unless a second action is precluded by operation of the substantive law."[60]

Illustration 13-10. In consideration for the payment of $100 by *A*, *B* agrees to deliver certain goods to *A*. On January 1st, *A* sues *B*. *A* alleges that *B* failed to deliver the goods. At the trial, it appears the goods were to be delivered on June 1st. As a result, the court directs a verdict for *B* and enters a judgment on the verdict. If *B* fails to deliver the goods by June 1st, *A* may maintain a second action for breach of contract against *B*. The judgment in the first action was clearly based on the prematurity of the suit.[61]

* * * * *

Likewise, this rule of bar does not apply "when the plaintiff agrees to or elects a nonsuit (or voluntary dismissal) without prejudice or the court directs that the plaintiff be nonsuited (or that the action be otherwise dismissed) without prejudice."[62] Nor does it apply "[w]hen by statute or rule of court the judgment does not operate as a bar to another action on the same claim, or does not so operate unless the court specifies, and no such specification is made."[63] For example, Federal Rule 41(a) provides that a voluntary dismissal by the plaintiff or by stipulation of all the parties is without prejudice (unless it is otherwise stated in the notice of dismissal or the stipulation). Rule 41(a), however, makes a dismissal based on a notice of voluntary dismissal by the plaintiff "an adjudication upon the merits when [such a notice] is filed by a plaintiff who has

---

59. *See, e.g.,* Glick v. Ballentine Produce, Inc., 397 F.2d 590, 592-93 (8th Cir. 1968) (The "distinction between a dismissal on the pleading and a dismissal on the merits is irrelevant . . . because of Rule 41(b)." . . . [A] dismissal for failure to state a cause of action is a final judgment on the merits sufficient to raise the defense of res judicata in a subsequent action between the parties."); *see also* Hall v. Tower Land & Inv. Co., 512 F.2d 481 (5th Cir. 1975); *cf.* Schroeder v. Morton Grove Police Pension Bd., 219 Ill. App. 3d 697, 579 N.E.2d 997, *appeal denied,* 142 Ill. 2d 665, 584 N.E.2d 140 (1991) (prior federal dismissal for failure to exhaust state remedies was not a judgment on the merits); Rinehart v. Locke, 454 F.2d 313, 315 (7th Cir. 1971); Velasquez v. Franz, 123 N.J. 498, 589 A.2d 143 (1991) (Rule 12(b)(6) dismissal on ground of lack of defendant's capacity to be sued is a judgment on the merits under Rule 41(b)). *See generally* Jonathan M. Purver, Annotation, *Judicial Qualification of Provision of Rule 41(b) of Federal Rules of Civil Procedure that Dismissal for Failure to Prosecute or to Comply with Federal Rules or Court Order, and Certain Other Dismissals, Operate as Adjudication Upon Merits,* 5 A.L.R. FED. 897 (1970). *Cf.* Wolford v. Lasater, 126 N.M. 614, 973 P.2d 866 (Ct. App. 1998) (differing federal and state standards for summary judgment would not prevent the operation of claim preclusion).

60. RESTATEMENT (SECOND) OF JUDGMENTS § 20(2) (1982). The drafters did not consider the exceptions in § 20 to be rigid. They stated: "The rule of this [s]ubsection is not an inflexible one. In some instances, the doctrine of estoppel or laches could require the conclusion that it would be plainly unfair to subject the defendant to a second action." *Id.* cmt. n.

61. *See id.* § 20(2) illus. 5.

62. *Id.* § 20(1)(b).

63. *Id.* § 20(1)(c).

once dismissed in any court of the United States or of any state an action based on or including the same claim.''[64]

Illustration 13-11. A sues *B* in federal court. *A* subsequently files a notice of voluntary dismissal pursuant to Federal Rule 41(a). *A* may commence a new action in federal or state court. If the court then grants *A* another voluntary dismissal under a rule identical to Rule 41(a)(1), *A* would be thereafter precluded from commencing a new action on the same claim.

3. General Exceptions

Section 26 of the *Restatement (Second)* recognizes six general exceptions to the rule against splitting a claim.[65] First, the rule against splitting does not apply when ''[t]he parties have agreed in terms or in effect that the plaintiff may split [the plaintiff's] claim, or the defendant has acquiesced therein.''[66]

Illustration 13-12. A and *B* are involved in an automobile accident. *A* files two actions in the same jurisdiction against *B*. One action is for personal injuries resulting from the automobile accident. The other action is for property damage resulting from the accident. *B* could have objected in the second action on the ground that another action was pending concerning the same subject matter. However, *B* did not do so. Had *B* objected, *B* would have been entitled to have the second action consolidated with the first. After a judgment in *A's* favor in the personal injury action, *B* requests dismissal of the second action for property damage. *B* asserts that the judgment in the personal injury action is res judicata. The court should refuse to dismiss the second action because *B* has, in effect, consented to the splitting of the claim.[67] Res judicata is a defense that must be raised, or it is lost.[68]

* * * * *

---

64. FED. R. CIV. P. 41(a)(1); *see also* FED. R. CIV. P. 41(b) (involuntary dismissals). *See generally* Chapter 10(D) (''Voluntary Dismissals'') & 10(E) (''Involuntary Dismissals'') *supra.*

65. RESTATEMENT (SECOND) OF JUDGMENTS § 26 (1982) (''Exceptions to the General Rule Concerning Splitting''). The exceptions recognized in § 26 deal with situations in which there has been ''partial merger or bar''—with the plaintiff losing some of the freedom the plaintiff originally had to present the case. In contrast, the exceptions discussed at the end of the preceding subsection based on § 20 of the *Restatement (Second)* involve situations in which the general rule of bar does not apply at all. Furthermore, § 20 does not deal with situations in which ''policy reasons favoring the maintenance of the second action come to light only after the first action is completed.'' The latter situations are dealt with in § 26. *Id.* § 20 cmt. a.

66. *Id.* § 26(1)(a); *cf.* Bennun v. Rutgers State Univ., 941 F.2d 154 (3d Cir. 1991), *cert. denied*, 502 U.S. 1066, 112 S. Ct. 956, 117 L. Ed. 2d 124 (1992) (prior action to compel arbitration did not preclude second action for employment discrimination when prior action was brought to enforce contractual right to arbitration).

67. *See* RESTATEMENT (SECOND) OF JUDGMENTS § 26(1)(a) cmt. a, illus. 1. (1982).

68. *See* FED. R. CIV. P. 8(c); Lake v. Jones, 89 Md. App. 579, 598 A.2d 858 (1991) (failure to object to splitting of claim constituted waiver of res judicata defense by defendant); Chapter 6(D)(3)*(g)(ii)* (''Waiver'') *supra. But see* Buchanan v. Dain Bosworth, Inc., 469 N.W.2d 508 (Minn. Ct. App. 1991) (defendant must give some positive indication of acquiescence in splitting claim); Dakota Title & Escrow Co. v. World-Wide Steel Sys., Inc., 238 Neb. 519, 471 N.W.2d 430 (1991) (appellate court may raise issue of res judicata sua sponte). *See generally* Joseph E. Edwards, Annotation, *Waiver of, by Failure to Promptly Raise, Objection to Splitting Cause of Action*, 40 A.L.R.3D 108 (1971).

Second, the general rule against splitting a claim does not apply when "[t]he court in the first action has expressly reserved the plaintiff's right to maintain the second action."[69]

Illustration 13-13. On the facts of *Illustration 13-2*, assume that the judgment in the defeated action for breach of contract had expressly reserved to the plaintiff the opportunity to commence a second action for restitution. A court would give effect to such a reservation under this exception.[70]

* * * * *

Third, the general rule against splitting a claim does not apply when "[t]he plaintiff was unable to rely on a certain theory of the case or to seek a certain remedy or form of relief in the first action" arising from either (1) "the limitations on the subject matter jurisdiction of the courts or restrictions on their authority to entertain multiple theories" or (2) "demands for multiple remedies or forms of relief in a single action."[71] Under such circumstances, the plaintiff can rely on that theory or seek that remedy or form of relief in the second action.

Illustration 13-14. *A* suffers personal injuries resulting from *B's* negligence. Under the applicable substantive law, if *A* was *B's* employee at the time of the accident, *A's* sole remedy is under worker's compensation law. If *A* was not an employee, then *A* has only a common-law action for negligence. Assume that *A* files an action before the state worker's compensation commission, but loses because *A* is found not to have been *B's* employee. *A* is not precluded from maintaining a second action for common-law negligence because the workers' compensation and negligence remedies are mutually exclusive and each must be pursued in different forums.[72]

Illustration 13-15. In contrast, assume that *A* sues *B* for negligently causing *A* personal injuries. Instead of suing in a court of general jurisdiction within the state, *A* brings suit in a court that has no jurisdiction to give judgments in excess of $500. At trial, the court assesses *A's* damages at $2,000 and enters judgment for *A* for $500. *A* cannot sue *B* in a second action in a court of general jurisdiction to recover the remainder of the $1,500. The exception does not apply to situations in which a court with broader jurisdiction is available. *A* has to

---

69. RESTATEMENT (SECOND) OF JUDGMENTS § 26(1)(b) (1982); *see* Venuto v. Witco Corp., 117 F.3d 754 (3d Cir. 1997) (court refuses plaintiff's request to amend to add more plaintiffs on defendant's argument that it would be more efficient for those plaintiffs to file a second action; when they did, defendant pleads claim preclusion on theory that they are in privity with plaintiff in first action; res judicata denied because court in first action had reserved right of plaintiffs to bring second action); *cf.* Nutter v. Monongahela Power Co., 4 F.3d 319 (4th Cir. 1993) (holding that district court's findings of federal preemption would have no preclusive effect after remand to state court for lack of removal jurisdiction).

70. *See* RESTATEMENT (SECOND) OF JUDGMENTS § 26(1)(b) cmt. b (1982).

71. *Id.* § 26(1)(b); *see also* Parker v. Blanvelt Volunteer Fire Co., 93 N.Y.2d 343, 712 N.E.2d 647, 690 N.Y.S.2d 478 (1999) (claim preclusion is inapplicable when the plaintiff was unable to seek a certain remedy or form of relief in first action).

72. *See* RESTATEMENT (SECOND) OF JUDGMENTS § 26(1)(b) (1982); *see also id.* § 25 cmt. k, illus. 22; Bates v. Department of Corrections, 774 F. Supp. 536 (E.D. Wis. 1991); Stacks v. Saunders, 812 S.W.2d 587 (Tenn. Ct. App. 1990); Eagle Properties, Ltd. v. Scharbauer, 807 S.W.2d 714 (Tex. 1990).

choose the court with broader jurisdiction or *A* will lose the right to sue for the full amount.[73]

* * * * *

Fourth, the general rule against splitting a claim does not apply when "[t]he judgment in the first action was plainly inconsistent with the fair and equitable implementation of a statutory or constitutional scheme, or it is the sense of the scheme that the plaintiff should be permitted to split [the] claim."[74]

Illustration 13-16. A group of pupils and parents sue the Board of Education to enjoin a state tuition "voucher system." The pupils and parents allege that the law unconstitutionally promotes an establishment of religion. The court holds the law to be constitutional. The plaintiffs do not appeal because existing constitutional precedents do not justify an appeal. Subsequently, the U.S. Supreme Court holds a similar voucher system unconstitutional in another case. The same pupils and parents then commence a second action against the same defendants, asserting the same claim they asserted in the first action. According to the *Restatement (Second)*, this second suit can be maintained because "[i]n a matter of such public importance the policy of nationwide adherence to the authoritative constitutional interpretation overcomes the policies supporting the law of res judicata."[75]

* * * * *

Fifth, the general rule against splitting a claim does not apply when "for reasons of substantive policy in a case involving a continuing or recurrent wrong, the plaintiff is given an option to sue once for the total harm, both past and prospective, or to sue from time to time for the damages incurred to the date of suit, and chooses the latter course."[76]

Illustration 13-17. *A* and *B* enter into a contract under which *A* employs *B*. *B* commits a material breach of the contract. *B* requests that *A* allow the contract to continue. *A* agrees to do so, but demands damages for the breach already committed. *A* sues *B* for the breach and obtains a judgment. Subsequently, *A* sues *B* for a subsequent breach of the contract committed after the first action was commenced. This second action may be maintained. As a matter of substantive policy, a judgment in a breach action does not normally preclude the plaintiff from thereafter maintaining a second action for later breaches occurring after commencement of the first action.[77] An argument can be made against this result in some cases—for example, when, although the first action has been commenced,

---

73. *See* Molovinsky v. Monterey Co-op., Inc., 689 A.2d 531 (D.C. App. 1997); Bagley v. Hughes A. Bagley, Inc., 465 N.W.2d 551 (Iowa Ct. App. 1990). *Compare* RESTATEMENT (SECOND) OF JUDGMENTS § 26(1)(c), cmt. c (1982) *with id.* § 24 cmt. g, illus. 13 *See generally* E.H. Schopler, Annotation, *Res Judicata as Affected by Limitation of Jurisdiction of Court Which Rendered Judgment*, 83 A.L.R.2D 977 (1962).

74. RESTATEMENT (SECOND) OF JUDGMENTS § 26(1)(d) (1982); *see* Carson v. Davidson, 248 Kan. 543, 808 P.2d 1377 (1991) (statute provided that no suit could be brought against an officer, director, or stockholder until a judgment had been obtained against the corporation; therefore, suit against corporation did not preclude action against stockholders).

75. *See* RESTATEMENT (SECOND) OF JUDGMENTS § 26(1)(d), cmt. e, illus. 6 (1982). *But see* Federated Dep't Stores, Inc. v. Moitie, 452 U.S. 394, 101 S. Ct. 2424, 69 L. Ed. 2d 103 (1981).

76. RESTATEMENT (SECOND) OF JUDGMENTS § 26(1)(e) (1982).

77. *Id.* illus. 7.

it has not progressed so far that adding the claim for the second breach by supplemental pleading would be disruptive. The rule is different if the initial breach is accompanied by a repudiation. Repudiation gives rise to a claim for total breach.[78]

* * * * *

Sixth, the general rule against splitting a claim does not apply when "[i]t is clearly and convincingly shown that the policies favoring preclusion of a second action are overcome for an extraordinary reason."[79] Examples of such reasons include "the apparent invalidity of a continuing restraint or condition having a vital relation to personal liberty or the failure of the prior litigation to yield a coherent disposition of the controversy."[80]

Illustration 13-18. *A's* husband, *B*, deserts *A*. *A* sues *B* for separate maintenance and obtains a judgment. Subsequently, *A* sues *B* for a divorce on the same ground (desertion). *A* can maintain this second action. As a matter of policy, *A* should not be forced to demand the most drastic remedy against *B* in the first action. Nor would it be appropriate to deprive *A* of a divorce if *A* is now prepared to make the case for it.[81]

4. Counterclaims

(a) Application of Claim Preclusion Rules to Counterclaims

The rules of merger and bar generally apply to counterclaims interposed by the defendant in the plaintiff's action. If the defendant interposes a counterclaim in an action and the court renders a valid and final personal judgment against the defendant "on the counterclaim, the rules of bar are applicable to the judgment," subject to the exceptions in § 20 and § 26 of the *Restatement (Second)*, discussed above.[82] Likewise, if a defendant interposes a counterclaim and the court renders a judgment in the defendant's favor on the counterclaim, the counterclaim merges in the judgment.[83] Of course, if the defendant is unable to obtain a full recovery in the action because, for example, the court in which the action is brought can render judgments only up to a certain amount and the defendant is unable to remove the case to another court with broader power, merger does not operate.[84]

Illustration 13-19. *A*, a citizen of State *X*, sues *B*, also a citizen of State *X*, in a state court for breach of contract. *B* defends on the ground that the contract is illegal under state and federal antitrust laws. *B* also pleads a

---

78. *See* RESTATEMENT (SECOND) OF CONTRACTS § 236, cmt. b, § 250 (1979); *see* RESTATEMENT (SECOND) OF JUDGMENTS § 26(1)(e) cmt. g, illus. 7 (1982).

79. RESTATEMENT (SECOND) OF JUDGMENTS § 26(1)(f) (1982).

80. *Id.*

81. *Id.* cmt. i, illus. 8; *see also* D.E. Evans, Annotation, *Decree in Suit for "Separation" as Res Judicata in Subsequent Suit for Divorce or Annulment*, 90 A.L.R.2D 745 (1963).

82. RESTATEMENT (SECOND) OF JUDGMENTS § 23 (1982).

83. *See id.* § 21(1).

84. *See id.* § 21(2).

counterclaim under the state antitrust laws against *A*. The court enters judgment in the action for *B* on both *A's* contract claim and *B's* counterclaim. Subsequently, *B* sues *A* in federal court. *B* asserts a claim under the federal antitrust laws for additional relief obtainable only under those laws, a claim over which the federal courts have exclusive jurisdiction. *B* may maintain this second action because (1) *B* could not assert the federal claim as a counterclaim in state court because the federal courts have exclusive jurisdiction over the claim and (2) *B* did not have the option of choosing the forum in the first suit.[85]

(b) Jurisdictions with a Compulsory Counterclaim Rule

When the jurisdiction in question possesses a compulsory counterclaim rule, such as Federal Rule 13, and the counterclaim arises out of the same transaction or occurrence as the opposing party's claim, the compulsory counterclaim rule bars the defendant from asserting an omitted claim in a subsequent proceeding.[86] If the counterclaim is factually unrelated to the opposing party's claim, the counterclaim is "permissive." Under such circumstances, the defendant can make it the subject of a subsequent action.[87]

(c) Jurisdictions Without a Compulsory Counterclaim Rule

When the jurisdiction does not possess a compulsory counterclaim rule, however, the situation becomes more complicated. When the defendant fails to interpose a factually unrelated counterclaim, the result should be the same as described above for permissive counterclaims under Federal Rule 13. On the other hand, if the counterclaim arises out of the same transaction or occurrence as the opposing party's claim, the result may be different. The rules of issue preclusion (discussed in the next section) may prevent the defendant from asserting the counterclaim in a subsequent action if the defendant loses the first action to the plaintiff. Even if the rules of issue preclusion do not prevent litigation of the counterclaim, however, the defendant may be prohibited from asserting the counterclaim in a subsequent action when the counterclaim will "so plainly operate to undermine the initial judgment that the principle of finality requires preclusion of such an action."[88]

Illustration 13-20. *A* commences an action against *B* to quiet title to Blackacre and obtains a judgment by default. *B* then brings an action against *A*

---

85. *Cf. id.* cmt. b, illus. 3. *But cf.* McDaneld v. Lynn Hickey Dodge, Inc., 1999 OK 30, 979 P.2d 252 (when a defendant is sued in a small claims court with a jurisdictional amount limit, the defendant is obligated to plead a compulsory counterclaim even if it exceeds the amount limit and seek removal to a court of general jurisdiction; otherwise the compulsory counterclaim rule will bar assertion of the claim in a separate action).

86. *See, e.g.,* Johnson v. First Carolina Fin. Corp., 200 Ga. App. 340, 408 S.E.2d 151 (1991). Problems involved in determining when a counterclaim arises out of the same transaction or occurrence as an opposing party's claim were fully explored in Chapter 7(F)(1)*(c), supra*.

87. *See* RESTATEMENT (SECOND) OF JUDGMENTS §§ 22(1), 22(2)(a) (1982); *see also* W.R. Habeeb, Annotation, *Failure to Assert Matter as Counterclaim as Precluding Assertion Thereof in Subsequent Action, Under Federal Rules or Similar State Rules or Statutes,* 22 A.L.R.2D 621 (1952).

88. RESTATEMENT (SECOND) OF JUDGMENTS § 22 cmt. f (1982).

to quiet title to the same property. *B* alleges that at the time of the first action *B* had acquired title by adverse possession. If successful, *B's* action will completely undermine the judgment obtained by *A*.[89] For this reason, *B* is precluded from bringing the action even in the absence of a compulsory counterclaim rule.[90]

* * * * *

Ordinarily, the fact that a defendant pleads matter in defense that also might be the subject of a counterclaim will not preclude the defendant from asserting the counterclaim in a subsequent action in the absence of (1) a compulsory counterclaim rule, (2) the operation of issue preclusion against the defendant, or (3) a relationship between the counterclaim and the plaintiff's claim which would nullify the judgment in the first action or impair rights established therein.[91] However, a caveat is in order. A few courts have held that asserting a defense, but not a counterclaim, splits the defendant's cause of action when the facts constituting the defense and counterclaim are substantially the same.[92] Thus, the precedents in a particular state must be carefully examined to determine whether the decision to plead a defense also carries with it the duty to assert a closely related counterclaim.[93]

Illustration 13-21. A sues *B* for personal injuries arising out of an automobile accident. *A* alleges that *B's* negligence caused the accident. *B* wants to deny *B's* own negligence and assert *A's* contributory negligence in the action. However, *B* wants to omit a claim *B* possesses against *A* for personal injuries arising out of the same accident because *B* would prefer to assert that claim in a subsequent action. Assuming that the state in which the action is brought has no compulsory counterclaim rule and *B* fails to plead the counterclaim, *B* may encounter two obstacles: (1) the doctrine of issue preclusion might prevent *B* from asserting the claim in the second proceeding if *B* loses the first proceeding;[94] and (2) the rule in some jurisdictions that raising a defense, but not a counterclaim, based on the same facts may result in a splitting of the claim.

(d) Special Problems Involving Insureds and Their Insurers

In jurisdictions with compulsory counterclaim rules, there can be a conflict between the interests of insured defendants and their insurers who control the defense of actions.

---

89. *See id.* illus. 10.

90. *See id.* § 22(2)(b); *see also* Dakota Title & Escrow Co. v. World-Wide Steel Sys., Inc., 238 Neb. 519, 471 N.W.2d 430 (1991) (action for declaratory judgment was based on a defense that could have been raised in prior action against the declaratory judgment plaintiff; therefore, prior action was res judicata). *See generally* E.H. Schopler, Annotation, *Doctrine of Res Judicata as Applied to Default Judgments*, 77 A.L.R.2D 1410 (1961); J.E. Macy, Annotation, *Default Decree in Divorce Action as Estoppel or Res Judicata with Respect of Marital Property Rights*, 22 A.L.R.2D 724 (1952).

91. RESTATEMENT (SECOND) OF JUDGMENTS § 22 cmt. d (1982).

92. *See, e.g.*, Mitchell v. Federal Intermediate Credit Bank, 165 S.C. 457, 164 S.E. 136 (1932).

93. *Cf.* Fowler v. Vineyard, 261 Ga. 454, 405 S.E.2d 678 (1991) (bus driver asserted against codefendants cross-claims for indemnity and contribution which were later voluntarily dismissed with prejudice; dismissal precluded bus driver from asserting claims for personal injury against codefendants in later action).

94. *See* section C ("Issue Preclusion") *infra*.

Illustration 13-22. *A* and *B* are involved in an automobile accident. *A* sues *B* for personal injuries received in the accident. *A* alleges that *B's* negligence was the sole cause of the accident. *B's* insurer defends the action for *B* by denying *B's* negligence and asserting *A's* contributory negligence. After trial, the court enters judgment for *B*. Subsequently, *B* sues *A* for personal injuries received in the same accident. If the state has a compulsory counterclaim rule identical to Federal Rule 13(b), should *B* be allowed to assert the counterclaim? The insurance company may have little interest in pursuing such a counterclaim on behalf of its insured.[95] On the other hand, it is unfair to *A* to have to defend the second action when the matter could have been effectively handled in the first proceeding. Here, flexibility may be required in order to balance the competing interests.[96]

Illustration 13-23. *A* and *B* set out on a trip in *A's* automobile with *B* driving. While on the trip, they are involved in an accident. Both *A* and *B* are injured. *A* sues *B* for personal injuries received in the accident. *A's* insurance company defends the action in accord with the requirements of a clause in *A's* insurance contract insuring persons who were driving *A's* automobile with *A's* permission. The insurance company notifies *B* to obtain a lawyer because the complaint requests damages in excess of the policy limits. *B* fails to do so. After the close of the pleadings, the insurer settles the action with *A*. A consent judgment is then entered in favor of *B*. Subsequently, *B* sues *A* for *B's* personal injuries received in the same accident. *B* alleges that *A* was negligent when *A* grabbed the steering wheel from *B*. Assuming that the state possesses a compulsory counterclaim rule identical to Federal Rule 13(a), should *B* be

---

95. The stated obligation in the insurance contract is to "defend" against claims, not to assert them, Allen E. Smith, *The Miscegenetic Union of Liability Insurance and Tort Process in the Personal Injury Claims System*, 54 CORNELL L. REV. 645, 658 (1969), and the insurance company itself may not be compelled to interpose counterclaims on the insured's behalf. *See* Reynolds v. Hartford Accident & Idem. Co., 278 F. Supp. 331, 333-34 (S.D.N.Y. 1967) (to imply an obligation on the insurance carrier to bring affirmative claims on behalf of its insured would entail extra expenditures on the part of the carrier and would be manifestly unfair).

96. *Cf.* RESTATEMENT (SECOND) OF JUDGMENTS § 20 cmt. n (1982) (suggesting that the rule of that section is a flexible one). *Compare* Reynolds v. Hartford Accident & Indem. Co., 278 F. Supp. 331 (S.D.N.Y. 1967) (insureds should not be estopped because of a compulsory counterclaim rule from bringing a separate action for injuries suffered in the accident when attorneys retained by insurance carrier refused to assert counterclaims on behalf of the insureds) *and* Suchta v. Robinett, 596 P.2d 1380 (Wyo. 1979) (waiver or estoppel theory applied to compulsory counterclaim rule which, in effect, makes its application dependent upon the conduct of a litigant in failing to pursue the counterclaim) *with* Rothtrock v. Ohio Farmers Ins. Co., 233 Cal. App. 2d 616, 43 Cal. Rptr. 716 (1965) (insurer is liable to its own insured when the insurer knowingly authorized dismissal with prejudice of a municipal court action against its insured for damage to motorist's automobile by paying $250 to the motorist in settlement that as a result barred a pending superior court action by insured of a personal injury claim against the motorist). *See generally* 6 CHARLES A. WRIGHT ET AL., FEDERAL PRACTICE AND PROCEDURE: CIVIL § 1417, at 133 (2d ed. 1990) (focusing on waiver or estoppel by the insured "provides a more apposite and useful approach of the omitted counterclaims than does the doctrine of claim preclusion [because] it affords a means of extricating a defendant who has not knowingly refrained from asserting [a] claim from the rigors of the compulsory counterclaim rule; this type of safety value may be particularly important when an insurance company has controlled the defense of the first action and the actual defendant has not had a realistic opportunity to assert [the omitted] claim"); W.E. Shipley, Annotation, *Liability Insurer's Settlement of Claim Against Insured as Bar to Insured's Tort Action Against Person Receiving Settlement*, 32 A.L.R.2D 937 (1953).

permitted to maintain this action? In *Dindo v. Whitney*,[97] the First Circuit Court of Appeals held on similar facts that a conscious failure to plead the counterclaim precluded the second action.[98] If the counterclaim had been raised in the suit, a serious conflict of interest would have resulted. In effect, the insurer would be on both sides of the suit. On the other hand, if the counterclaim had been pleaded, surely contributory negligence would also have been raised as a defense to the main claim and the counterclaim. In this situation, one of several things might then have occurred: (1) both parties might have been found negligent, in which case the insurance company would not be liable on either claim (in a jurisdiction in which contributory negligence is an absolute defense); (2) both parties might have been found not negligent, in which case, also, the insurance company would not be liable; or (3) one party might have been found negligent and the other not negligent, in which case the insurance company would be liable on one claim only. Thus, the worst that could have happened was *one-claim* liability. By failure to plead the counterclaim, if it can be asserted in a second action, the insurer could be held liable twice, once on the settlement and once in the second suit.

SECTION C. ISSUE PRECLUSION

1. The Basic Rule

A valid and final personal judgment can have a preclusive effect in two ways, either through claim preclusion or issue preclusion. Claim preclusion focuses on what a party ought to have litigated in the first action. Issue preclusion concerns only those issues that were actually litigated and determined in the first action.[99] Section 27 of the *Restatement (Second) of Judgments* states the basic rule of issue preclusion: "When an issue of fact or law is actually litigated and determined by a valid and final judgment, and the determination is essential to the judgment, the determination is conclusive in a subsequent action between the parties, whether on the same or a different claim."[100] Several discrete requirements appear within this rule.

---

97. 451 F.2d 1 (1st Cir. 1971).

98. *Id.* at 3.

99. One example of issue preclusion, described as "direct estoppel," was discussed in section B, *supra*. Direct estoppel results when an issue has actually been litigated and determined and a second action is brought on the same claim. *See* RESTATEMENT (SECOND) OF JUDGMENTS § 27 cmt. b (1982). Direct estoppel is distinguished from "collateral estoppel," in that collateral estoppel applies to issues actually litigated and determined in a first action when a second action is brought on a different claim as to which the earlier determined issues are also relevant. The rules governing when an issue will be precluded from relitigation are otherwise the same for both direct and collateral estoppel. *See id.* This section will deal primarily with issue preclusion in the collateral estoppel context.

100. *Id.* § 27. This rule can produce dramatic consequences. *See, e.g.,* State *ex rel.* West Va. Dep't of Health v. Cline, 185 W. Va. 318, 406 S.E.2d 749 (1991) (paternity issue precluded); *In re* Paternity of J.R.W., 814 P.2d 1256 (Wyo. 1991) (same). *See generally* Donald M. Zupanec, Annotation, *Effect, in Subsequent Proceedings, of Paternity Findings or Implications in Divorce or Annulment Decree or in Support or Custody Order Made Incidental Thereto*, 78 A.L.R.3D 846 (1977); Gregory G. Sarno, Annotation, *Applicability and Effect of Collateral Estoppel Doctrine in Deportation Proceedings*, 91 A.L.R. FED. 764 (1989).

(a) Identity of the Issue

For issue preclusion to apply, the issue litigated in the first and second actions must be the same.[101] This proposition seems straightforward enough, but the matter can become complicated. A party may in successive actions attempt to bring forward different grounds or evidence to support a conclusion the party wishes the trier of fact to reach. A total identity between the matters involved in the two actions may not exist. For example, the events in the suits may be separated in time or different rules of law may apply in the suits.[102] The *Restatement (Second)* does not articulate a fixed rule for resolving these scope-of-issue problems. Instead, the drafters suggest several factors that should be considered in determining whether the issues in the two proceedings are the same: (1) whether substantial overlap exists between the evidence or arguments made in the first and second actions; (2) whether the new evidence or argument involves the same rule of law as that involved in the first proceeding; (3) whether pre-trial preparation and discovery in the first action could reasonably be expected to have embraced the matters presented in the second proceeding; and (4) whether a close relationship exists between the claims in the two proceedings.[103] Two examples drawn from the *Restatement (Second)* demonstrate the difficulties that this "scope of the issue" inquiry poses.

Illustration 13-24. A sues B to recover an installment payment due under an oral contract between A and B. B's only defense is that the contract is unenforceable under the statute of frauds. After trial, the court enters judgment for A based on a specific finding that the oral contract is enforceable. A sues B in a subsequent action to recover a second installment that came due after the first action was brought. B may not raise the statute of frauds as a defense, even if B is prepared to assert arguments about the applicability of the statute that were not made in the first action. The scope of the issue is the same in the first and second actions. However, B may assert that the contract is not enforceable as a matter of law on any other ground.[104] For example, B could assert that the contract violated the state usuary statutes.

Illustration 13-25. A sues B to recover for personal injuries received in an automobile accident. A alleges that B was negligent in driving at an excessive rate of speed. After trial, verdict and judgment are given for B on the ground that B was not negligent. Subsequently, B sues A for personal injuries received in the

---

101. *See, e.g.,* Shoemaker v. Smith, 353 Md. 143, 725 A.2d 549 (1999) (finding of immunity in prior federal § 1983 action does not preclude litigation of immunity under state tort claims act, because federal immunity standard operates more broadly than state standard); Holtman v. 4-G's Plumbing & Heating, Inc., 264 Mont. 432, 872 P.2d 318 (1994) (claim of asbestos contamination in first action alleged an intentional wrongful act and adjudication of that issue did not preclude litigation of a different party's negligence in a subsequent action); Farrell v. Mountain Folk, Inc., 730 A.2d 597 (Vt. 1999) (valuation of corporation in first action did not preclude litigation of issue of misappropriation of corporate funds in subsequent action).

102. *See* Hebden v. Workmen's Compensation Appeal Bd., 534 Pa. 327, 632 A.2d 1302 (1993) (in first worker's compensation action worker was found to suffer irreversible condition; therefore, employer could not seek in second action to show worker was no longer suffering from disability, because in effect that was an attempt to relitigate an issue determined in prior action).

103. *See* RESTATEMENT (SECOND) OF JUDGMENTS § 27 cmt. c (1982).

104. *See id.* § 27 illus. 6.

same accident. *B's* action is permitted because the state in question has no compulsory counterclaim rule. *A* is precluded from defending the second action on the ground that *B* was negligent in failing to keep a proper lookout. According to the *Restatement (Second)*, it is reasonable to require *A* to bring forward all evidence in support of *B's* alleged negligence in the first action.[105]

* * * * *

In *Illustration 13-25*, the drafters of the *Restatement (Second)* consider the issue to be *B's* negligence. However, in *Illustration 13-24*, the drafters considered the issue to be the "statute of frauds." Under the factors suggested by the *Restatement (Second)* for determining the scope of an issue, discussed above, the reasons for treating the scope of the issue differently between the two illustrations is clear. In *Illustration 13-25*, all four of the factors point toward defining the scope of the issue in the first action as "*B's* negligence."[106] However, in *Illustration 13-24*, only two of the factors point toward defining the scope of the issue as the same between the first and second actions.[107]

Nevertheless, the issue in *Illustration 13-24* can be stated at a different level of generality. For example, the issue can be characterized as the "enforceability of the contract." This characterization would preclude asserting any other grounds of unenforceability in an action to recover a second installment. Furthermore, it is difficult, as a matter of policy, to see why the defendant should not be required to bring forward all available grounds of unenforceability in the first action. The possible lack of a solidly grounded policy distinction between the two illustrations should lead the careful attorney to bring forward all available grounds that exist in support of an issue at the time of the first action.

(b) *Actual Litigation Requirement*

Issue preclusion applies only when an issue has actually been litigated and determined in the first action, not to issues which might have been litigated and determined but were not.[108] A party may choose not to raise an issue in a particular action for several reasons: (1) the amount in controversy may be small; (2) the forum may be inconvenient; (3) the timing of the litigation may be bad;

---

105. *See id.* cmt. c, illus. 4.

106. That is, (1) substantial overlap exists between the evidence and arguments between the first and second actions (they both involve the same event and same legal theory); (2) the new evidence involves the same rule of law (negligence) as the one involved in the first proceeding; (3) pre-trial preparation and discovery in the first action could reasonably have been expected to have embraced the matters presented in the second proceeding (the different ways in which *B* might be negligent); and (4) a close relationship exists between the claims in the two proceedings (they both arose out of the same event).

107. That is, pre-trial preparation and discovery in both actions might have been expected to reveal all bases upon which the contract was unenforceable and the claims in both actions are closely related because they both arise out of the same contract.

108. *See, e.g.,* Harris v. Board of Trustees of State Insts. of Higher Learning, 731 So. 2d 588 (Miss. 1999) (lower court erred in concluding that claims dismissed without prejudice were barred by collateral estoppel because claims not actually litigated).

or (4) many other factors may dictate that an issue not be litigated.[109] At the same time, insisting upon preclusion as to issues that might have been litigated could encourage litigation in the first action to the utmost extent to avoid preclusion. Such insistence might decrease economy of litigation by elevating the first action to such importance that it requires more judicial resources than two actions involving the same issue.[110]

An issue need not be disposed of after a full trial to meet the actual litigation requirement. For example, an issue may be litigated on a general demurrer or a motion to dismiss for failure to state a claim, on a motion for judgment on the pleadings, or on a motion for summary judgment.[111] On the other hand, an issue has not actually been litigated when judgment is entered for the plaintiff after the defendant has defaulted for failure to appear.[112] The issue must be actually raised, submitted for determination, and decided.[113]

Illustration 13-26. *A* sues *B* for personal injuries received in an automobile accident. *A* alleges that *B* was negligent. *B* admits negligence in the answer and asserts contributory negligence as a defense. After trial, the court enters judgment for *B* on the ground that *A* was contributorily negligent. Subsequently, *B* sues *A* for personal injuries received in the accident. *B's* action is permitted because the state has no compulsory counterclaim rule. *A* contends that the prior judgment establishes that *B* was negligent. As a result, *A* contends that *B's* suit is barred. However, the issue of *B's* negligence was not actually litigated in the prior action because *B* admitted it in *B's* pleading. Therefore, *A's* contention is not sound, and *B* can maintain the action.[114]

* * * * *

---

109. *See* Cromwell v. County of Sac, 94 U.S. 351, 356, 24 L. Ed. 195, 199 (1877); RESTATEMENT (SECOND) OF JUDGMENTS § 27 cmt. e (1982) ("The interests of conserving judicial resources, of maintaining consistency, and of avoiding oppression or harassment of the adverse party are less compelling when an issue on which preclusion is sought has not actually been litigated before").

110. RESTATEMENT (SECOND) OF JUDGMENTS § 27 cmt. e (1982).

111. *See id.* § 27 cmt. d.

112. *See, e.g.,* Christian v. Sizemore, 185 W. Va. 409, 407 S.E.2d 715 (1991). The rule that a default judgment has no issue preclusion effect is not universally observed. For a discussion of the position of the *Restatement (Second)* and the contrary doctrine, see Jackson v. R.G. Whipple, Inc., 225 Conn. 705, 627 A.2d 374 (1993).

113. *See* RESTATEMENT (SECOND) OF JUDGMENTS § 27 cmt. d (1982); Truck Ins. Exch. v. Ashland Oil, Inc., 951 F.2d 787 (7th Cir. 1992) (issue of successor liability never litigated, even though that was the only basis for joining corporation in first action); Linder v. Missoula County, 251 Mont. 292, 824 P.2d 1004 (1992) (consent judgment based on settlement agreement does not have issue preclusion effect unless parties intend it to have such an effect); Sheldon R. Shapiro, Annotation, *Modern Views of State Courts as to Whether Consent Judgment Is Entitled to Res Judicata or Collateral Estoppel Effect,* 91 A.L.R.3D 1170 (1979); Ernest H. Schopler, Annotation, *Comment Note.–Res Judicata Effect of Federal Consent Decree in Patent Cases,* 4 A.L.R. FED. 214 (1970); *see also* Clayton Act, § 5(a), 15 U.S.C. § 16(a) (government antitrust suits resulting from final judgments or decrees finding that a defendant had violated the antitrust laws are prima facie evidence against the defendant in private antitrust actions, but an express proviso to § 5(a) excludes "consent judgments or decrees entered before any testimony has been taken"); Burbank v. General Elec. Co., 329 F.2d 825, 834-35 (9th Cir. 1964) (no contendere pleas are within consent judgment proviso of § 5(a)); Sun v. State, 830 P.2d 772 (Alaska 1992) (by statute, nolo contendere plea estops defendant from contesting issues in subsequent civil action); David L. Shapiro, *Should a Guilty Plea Have Preclusive Effect?* 70 IOWA L. REV. 27 (1984). For a criticism of California's application of the actual litigation requirement, see Walter W. Heiser, *California's Confusing Collateral Estoppel (Issue Preclusion) Doctrine,* 35 SAN DIEGO L. REV. 509 (1998).

114. *See* RESTATEMENT (SECOND) OF JUDGMENTS § 27 cmt. c (1982).

As observed in section B(2), above, to have a claim-preclusive effect, a judgment traditionally had to be "on the merits." However, even a judgment that is "without prejudice," or "not on the merits," can have an issue preclusion effect.[115] Unfortunately, a substantial number of courts, in stating the requirements for issue preclusion, include the requirement that a judgment must be "on the merits" for issue preclusion to operate.[116] Others correctly recognize that actions dismissed on procedural grounds can have a preclusive effect on the procedural issues actually litigated and determined in the action.[117] The cases stating that a judgment must be rendered "on the merits" before it may have an issue preclusion effect do not really seem to be using the "on the merits" phrase in its traditionally understood sense. Rather, they seem to be using the expression as a substitute for one of the other requirements for issue preclusion, such as the requirement that an issue must actually have been litigated and determined.[118] Thus, the courts seldom, if ever, reach incorrect results due to the misstatement of the issue preclusion requirements. Nevertheless, the courts sometimes give incorrect reasons for correct results,[119] and their incorrect statements of doctrine run the risk of confusing practitioners.

(c) Ability to Identify What Was Decided

The actual litigation requirement depends, of course, on the ability to identify what was decided. It must be possible in the second action to discern what issues were decided and how they were decided in the first proceeding.

Illustration 13-27. *A* sues *B* for negligence. The record reveals that *B's* sole defense to the action is a denial of negligence. Thus, even after a general

---

115. *See* section B(2), *Illustration 13-7* and accompanying text *supra* (discussing the doctrine of direct estoppel).

116. *See, e.g.,* Dorrance v. Lee, 90 Haw. 143, 149, 976 P.2d 904, 910 (1999); Huelsman v. Kansas Dep't of Revenue, 267 Kan. 456, 980 P.2d 1022 (1999); *In re* Raymond W. George Trust, 1999 MT 223, 986 P.2d 427; Stewart v. Hechtman, 254 Neb. 992, 581 N.W.2d 416 (1998); Garganta v. Mobile Village, Inc., 730 A.2d 1 (R.I. 1999); Farrell v. Mountain Folk, Inc., 730 A.2d 597 (Vt. 1999).

117. *See, e.g.,* Pohlmann v. Bil-Jax, Inc., 176 F.3d 1110 (8th Cir. 1999) (issue of personal jurisdiction decided in a prior action precluded: dismissals without prejudice do not have a claim preclusion effect, but do have an issue preclusion effect on identical issues actually litigated and determined); Transaero, Inc. v. La Fuerza Aerea Boliviana, 162 F.3d 724 (2d Cir. 1998) (decision in prior action that party was improperly served has issue preclusion effect); Offshore Sportswear, Inc. v. Vuarnet Int'l, B.V., 114 F.3d 848 (9th Cir. 1997) (dismissal of U.S. District Court action under a forum selection clause; subsequent action commenced in state court and removed to federal court; held: prior dismissal, even though not on the merits, was preclusive on the issue of whether the action had to be litigated in Switzerland under the forum selection clause).

118. In Stewart v. Hechtman, 254 Neb. 992, 581 N.W.2d 416 (1998), the Nebraska Supreme Court listed the "on the merits" requirement as one of the requirements of issue preclusion, but clearly seemed to mean only that the issue must actually have been decided by the court in the prior action. In the actual case, the court indicated that an issue of personal jurisdiction decided in a prior action was not precluded from relitigation because it was not identical with the issue in the second action. The clear implication of the court's opinion was that the issue would have been precluded if it had been identical, but this cannot be so if the judgment of dismissal in the prior action had to be on the merits in order to have an issue preclusion effect.

119. *See* Shahan v. Shahan, 988 S.W.2d 529 (Mo. 1999) (stating, in part, that issue preclusion did not apply to determination of an issue in an action not decided on the merits, when real reason for denying preclusion was that determination of the issue did not support the judgment in the prior action); *see also* subsection *(d) infra*.

jury verdict, it is possible to determine what issue was decided.[120] However, assume that *B* denies negligence and asserts contributory negligence as a defense. If a jury delivers a general verdict in *B*'s favor, there may be no way to tell upon what ground the judgment was based. The jury may have found *B* negligent and *A* contributorily negligent; or the jury may have found *B* not negligent and *A* not contributorily negligent; or the jury may have found *B* not negligent and the jury may never have reached the issue of *A*'s contributory negligence, and so forth. In such a case, the general verdict will not reveal the grounds for the decision and there can be no issue preclusion without resort to extrinsic evidence, as discussed below.[121]

* * * * *

Evidence extrinsic to the record in the first action may be introduced to show what issues were litigated and determined, but even this may not help. Evidence contradicting the record is admissible. However, to be successful, this evidence must prove the extrinsic matter clearly and convincingly.[122] Courts will allow the subsequent testimony of a juror to demonstrate that the jury in a prior action was improperly influenced or prejudiced.[123] Generally, judges are not allowed to testify to explain the basis for a prior judgment.[124] Nevertheless, courts have sometimes allowed judges to testify at a collateral proceeding when

---

120. *See, e.g.,* Dowling v. Finley Assocs., Inc., 248 Conn. 364, 727 A.2d 1245 (1999) (general verdict will not support issue preclusion where there is no way to ascertain the basis of the jury's decision). Kret *ex rel.* Kret v. Brookdale Hosp. Med. Ctr., 93 A.D.2d 449, 462 N.Y.S.2d 896 (1983), *aff'd*, 61 N.Y.2d 861, 462 N.E.2d 147, 473 N.Y.S.2d 970 (1984). In *Kret,* the plaintiff first sued a physician for malpractice. The court submitted a number of interrogatories to the jury, some of which assumed that the physician had failed "to properly" monitor or check the patient's condition. Other interrogatories simply queried whether failure to perform certain actions was malpractice. The jury answered all the interrogatories in the negative. Judgment was entered in favor of the physician. In a second action, plaintiff sued the hospital. The court held that issue preclusion barred the action. In the court's view, the negative answers to the interrogatories in the first action inevitably meant that the patient did not suffer from the condition that allegedly caused the harm. Because of this conclusion, no recovery could be obtained from either the physician or the hospital.

121. *Cf.* Griffin v. Parker, 219 Conn. 363, 593 A.2d 124 (1991) (inconsistent jury verdict on state of mind in prior action makes it impossible to tell what was decided).

122. *See* RESTATEMENT (SECOND) OF JUDGMENTS § 77(2) (1982).

123. *See* FED. R. EVID. 606(b); *see also* Kazan v. Wolinski, 721 F.2d 911 (3d Cir. 1983) (holding the trial judge could consider a mid-deliberation jury note to ascertain the truth of the verdict, but the note could not be used in subsequent proceeding); Ohio-Sealy Mattress Mfg. Co. v. Kaplan, 90 F.R.D. 11 (N.D. Ill. 1980) (holding a juror's notes and affidavit were inadmissible to clarify the general verdict); *cf.* Katz v. Eli Lilly & Co., 84 F.R.D. 378 (E.D.N.Y. 1979) (holding "that, where through permissible investigation apart from the compulsion of any court order a party demonstrates a factual basis for a belief that a judgment asserted against it as collateral estoppel was based on a compromise verdict, further inquiry into the facts by depositions of jurors shown to have information relevant to the issue is warranted").

124. *See, e.g.,* Grip-Pak, Inc. v. Illinois Tool Works, Inc., 694 F.2d 466 (7th Cir. 1982) (holding that the trial judge could not testify to explain verdict because the judgment should be the sole guide in interpreting the trial decision), *cert. denied*, 461 U.S. 958, 103 S. Ct. 2430, 77 L. Ed. 2d 1317 (1983); Eaton v. Weaver Mfg. Co., 582 F.2d 1250 (10th Cir. 1978) (holding that the trial judge's subsequent remarks and the judge's letter to the attorneys in the case were not nunc pro tunc and were inadmissible because the record speaks for itself). Courts frequently cite the parol evidence rule as one justification for not allowing such testimony. *See* Timothy Travers, Annotation, *Judge as Witness in Cause Not on Trial Before Him*, 86 A.L.R.3D 633 (1978); *see also* Emerick v. Emerick, 28 Conn. App. 794, 613 A.2d 1351 (judge's testimony not allowed because the interpretation of the trial court judgment is limited to the express or implied intention within the written document), *appeal denied*, 224 Conn. 915, 617 A.2d 171 (1992).

no other source exists to clarify the judgment.[125] Such testimony, however, can only clarify the judgment and not contradict it.[126] Nor can the judge's mental processes be questioned or cross-examined.[127] Thus, while extrinsic evidence may be admissible, only in compelling circumstances do most courts allow jurors or the judge to testify at collateral proceedings. In the absence of such testimony, determining what issues were decided in a prior action may sometimes be impossible.

(d) Supporting the Judgment in the First Action

Another basic rule also stems from the actual litigation requirement: an issue must support the judgment in the first action before the issue will be precluded in a later proceeding. The reason for this rule is that determinations not essential to the judgment "have the characteristics of dicta, and may not ordinarily be the subject of an appeal by the party against whom they were made."[128] Thus, no full and fair opportunity existed to litigate the finding before a tribunal that gave the issue full consideration in producing a decision.

Illustration 13-28. *A* sues *B* for negligence. *B* denies negligence and pleads contributory negligence as an affirmative defense. After a trial, the jury specifically finds that *B* was negligent and *A* was contributorily negligent. The court enters a judgment on the verdict for *B*. In a subsequent action, the finding of *B's* negligence is not precluded. The finding did not support the judgment in *B's* favor. The judgment in *B's* favor was supported only by the finding that *A* was contributorily negligent. The finding that *B* was negligent did not support the judgement because the finding was adverse to the party (*B*) who won the judgment. Preclusion does not apply because the winning party cannot ordinarily appeal a judgment. Thus, the winning party cannot correct any error that might have infected findings against the party.[129]

---

125. *See, e.g.,* Woodward v. City of Waterbury, 113 Conn. 457, 155 A. 825 (1931).

126. *See, e.g.,* Schumert & Warfield v. Security Brewing Co., 199 F. 358 (D. La. 1912); *see also* Timothy Travers, Annotation, *Judge as Witness in Cause Not on Trial Before Him,* 86 A.L.R.3D 633 (1978).

127. *See* Gold v. Warden, 222 Conn. 312, 610 A.2d 1153, 1156-57 (1992) (allowing testimony but limiting it to facts observed during trial); Brinkerhoff v. Home Trust & Sav. Bank, 109 Kan. 700, 708-09, 205 P. 779, 784 (1921) (a trial judge may testify to clarify the judgment but not about secret or unexpressed reasons for the decision); *cf.* United States v. Morgan, 313 U.S. 409, 61 S. Ct. 999, 85 L. Ed. 1429 (1941).

128. RESTATEMENT (SECOND) OF JUDGMENTS § 27 cmt. h (1982); *see* Dorrance v. Lee, 976 P.2d 904 (Hawaii 1999) (for issue preclusion to apply, the issue determined must be essential to the judgment in the first action).

129. *See* Bannister v. Commonwealth, 411 Mass. 130, 579 N.E.2d 163 (1991) (prior determination of liability made against defendant who obtained a favorable judgment in an action was not precluded in second suit). In Van Dyke v. Boswell, O'Toole, Davis & Pickering, 697 S.W.2d 381 (Tex. 1985), a law firm sued a former client to recover the reasonable value of its services. The client counterclaimed for malpractice. The trial court separated the claim and counterclaim. The court adjudicated the fee claim first. During the trial of that claim, the defendant attempted to meet the law firm's claim for the reasonable value of its services by showing defensively that the firm had committed malpractice. The firm recovered $87,232.91 in fees. The firm then asserted that this judgment precluded the counterclaim for malpractice. First, the Texas Supreme Court held that issue preclusion did not apply because the malpractice issues had not actually been litigated in the fee action. Second, the court stated that even if it could imply a finding of no malpractice from the fact that the firm recovered fees, the issue of malpractice would not be essential to the judgment. The court's first conclusion was slightly off the mark. The defendant had attempted to litigate the malpractice issue defensively. The problem

(e) Alternative Determinations

Traditionally, if a judgment were based upon the determination of two issues ("alternate determinations"), either of which standing alone would suffice to support the judgment, *both* issues were precluded from relitigation. The *Restatement (First) of Judgments* adopted this rule.[130]

Illustration 13-29. Assume in *Illustration 13-28* that the jury specifically had found that *B* was *not* negligent and that *A was* contributorily negligent. Under the traditional rule, both findings would be precluded from relitigation in a second action. Both findings are favorable to the winning party (*B*), and either finding alone would have supported the judgment. The *Restatement (First)* reasoned that "[i]t seems obvious that it should not be held that neither [finding] is material, and hence both should be held to be material."[131]

* * * * *

The *Restatement (Second) of Judgments* takes the opposite approach. If alternative determinations support the judgment in the first action, the judgment is not conclusive as to any of the determinations.[132] The *Restatement (Second)* reasons, first, that neither determination in the alternative may have been considered as carefully or as rigorously as if it were the only determination in support of the judgment. Second, "and of critical importance," the losing party may be dissuaded from appealing because of the likelihood that at least one of the determinations might be upheld. The judgment would thus be sustained against that party and the appeal would be rendered futile even if there was error in the other determination.[133] The reporters of the *Restatement (Second)* concede that the choice between the two approaches to preclusion is a close one. However, they are persuaded by the reasoning of *Halpern v. Schwartz*,[134] which deter-

---

seemed to be that it could not be determined how the issue was decided. The trier of fact could, theoretically, have determined that malpractice existed, but that the reasonable value of the firm's services was nevertheless $87,232.91. Alternatively, the trier of fact could have concluded that malpractice did not exist at all. Without a more intensive inquiry into the record or a resort to extrinsic evidence, it was impossible to tell what, if anything, was decided on the malpractice issue. *See* subsection *(c)* ("Ability to Identify What Was Decided") *supra*; *cf.* Kret *ex rel.* Kret v. Brookdale Hosp. Med. Ctr., 93 A.D.2d 449, 462 N.Y.S.2d 896 (1983), *aff'd*, 61 N.Y.2d 861, 462 N.E.2d 147, 473 N.Y.S.2d 970 (1984) (discussed in a note accompanying *Illustration 13-27* in subsection *(c)*, *supra*). However, the court's second conclusion was simply incorrect. If a finding of no malpractice is implied from the first judgment, it supports the judgment in favor of the firm. Furthermore, if malpractice would wholly defeat the claim for fees, a finding of no malpractice is essential to produce victory for the firm for the fees. Even if malpractice would only partly defeat the claim for fees, a finding of no malpractice would be essential in order to obtain a higher recovery, *e.g.*, +$87,000 rather than $10,000. *See also* Quinney Elec., Inc. v. Kondos Entertainment, Inc., 988 S.W.2d 212 (Tex. 1999) (issue preclusion does not prevent prevailing party from relitigating issue on which party prevailed in prior action).

130. RESTATEMENT (FIRST) OF JUDGMENTS § 68 cmt. n (1942).

131. *Id.*

132. RESTATEMENT (SECOND) OF JUDGMENTS § 27 cmt. i (1982). This situation should be compared to one in which two issues are decided that are both essential to the judgment. *See id.* cmt. g, illus. 12. In the later situation, both issues are precluded in a second action.

133. *See id.*

134. 426 F.2d 102 (2d Cir. 1970); *see* RESTATEMENT (SECOND) OF JUDGMENTS § 27, at 270 (1982) (reporter's note to cmt. i); Jean F. Rydstrom, Annotation, *Collateral Estoppel Effect, in Federal Court, of Judgment Resting on Independent Grounds*, 29 A.L.R. FED. 764 (1976); *cf.* Malloy v. Trombley, 50 N.Y.2d 46, 405 N.E.2d 213, 427 N.Y.S.2d 969 (1980). In *Malloy*, the New York Court of Appeals refused to adopt the flat mined that preclusion should not apply to alternative determinations. If the judgment is appealed and the appellate court upholds one or both determinations, the *Restatement (Second)* reaches the opposite result. In such a case, the judgment is conclusive as to the determinations upheld.[135] The reason seems obvious: the party has not been deterred from appealing and has had a full and fair opportunity to litigate as to all issues.

In addition, the drafters of the *Restatement (Second)* were careful to distinguish the situation in which alternative determinations of two issues were involved from the situation "in which there are *alternative bases* for a determination that is essential to the judgment."[136] When alternative bases are involved, relitigation of the issues determined in the first action is precluded.[137]

Illustration 13-30. Assume that *A* brings an action to recover an installment of interest on a promissory note, the principal not yet being due. *B* defends on two grounds: (1) *B* was induced by fraud to execute the note and (2) *A* gave *B* a binding release of the obligation to pay interest. Findings in favor of *B* on both the fraud and release issues will not preclude *A* from relitigating the fraud issue if *B* raises that issue in a subsequent suit *for the principal of the note.* This situation is simply one of "alternative determinations," either of which standing alone would be sufficient to support the first judgment. On the other hand, the *Restatement (Second)* drafters state that in the above situation, if the second action is *for a second installment of interest*, the principal still not being due, the judgment in the first action is a complete defense to the second because the finding on the fraud and release issues were "alternative bases" for a determination essential to the judgment in the first action (*i.e.*, that no interest is due).[138]

* * * * *

The result in *Illustration 13-30* reflects the emphasis placed by the drafters on the availability of appeal as an important component of an adequate opportunity to be heard. When the second action is for the principal of the note, the fear of the *Restatement (Second)* drafters is that the plaintiff may have been deterred from appealing because one of the determinations could be upheld on appeal, even though the other one was erroneous. The result would be that the judgment would be affirmed. Thus, if the fraud determination happened to be the erroneous one, while the release determination was correct and, therefore, irreversible on appeal, the plaintiff would be deprived of an adequate opportunity

---

rule of the *Restatement (Second)*. Instead, the court adopted a discretionary, case-by-case approach to determining whether alternative findings should be precluded. However, *Malloy* was a particularly strong case for nonpreclusion under the *Restatement (Second)*. In the first action, the issues of negligence and contributory negligence were both adjudicated against the plaintiff. In the second action, the plaintiff sued a different defendant. The finding of no negligence in the first action appeared unassailable, while the finding of contributory negligence appeared to have been thrown in by the trial judge in anticipation of an appeal. Thus, if the plaintiff had appealed, the appeal would likely have failed on the negligence issue. Furthermore, the issue of contributory negligence may well not have been considered as carefully by the trial judge as it would have if the finding of no negligence had not been so solid.

135. *See* RESTATEMENT (SECOND) OF JUDGMENTS § 27 cmt. o (1982).

136. *Id.* § 27 cmt. i (emphasis added).

137. *See id.*

138. *See id.* illus. 15 & 16.

to challenge the fraud determination on appeal. Consequently, the plaintiff should be allowed to relitigate the issue of fraud in the second action to recover the principal.

This rationale is not applicable when the second suit is for a second installment of interest. If either of the determinations in the first action is correct, the inevitable conclusion is that *no interest is due* because both the fraud and release determinations are relevant to a second suit for another installment of interest. Therefore, if either of the determinations is sound, a second suit for interest should not be permitted. If the plaintiff did not appeal because only one of the determinations was correct, logically no second action for the interest should be permitted. If the plaintiff did not appeal because both determinations were correct, the same is true. If both determinations were erroneous, and the plaintiff still did not appeal, the plaintiff cannot be heard to complain about preclusion produced by the plaintiff's own failure to resort to an appeal that would have been successful.

The impossibility of determining from the position of the second action *which* finding is solid and which erroneous, of course, creates the dilemma that makes this distinction necessary. Nevertheless, it is questionable whether the average lawyer or judge will appreciate the distinction. The drafters may well be "creating," rather than "restating," law that is too complex for ordinary practice.

2. Exceptions

Like claim preclusion, numerous exceptions to the basic rule of issue preclusion exit. The exceptions focus upon the ability of a party to have obtained a full and fair adjudication in the first action. The absence of a full and fair opportunity renders the principle of finality inapplicable because that principle is based upon the assumption that a party has had one adequate opportunity to present the merits of the party's case.[139]

(a) Inability to Obtain Review

Issue preclusion does not operate when a party is precluded as a matter of law from obtaining appellate review of a determination made in the first action. The inability to correct error in the judgment renders the opportunity to litigate less than adequate. This exception does not apply, however, when appellate review is available, but not sought by the losing party.[140]

Illustration 13-31. *A* sues *B* for negligence. *A* wins a verdict and judgment for $1,000. If there is a minimum jurisdictional amount in controversy of $2,000 on the state appellate court's jurisdiction, *B* would be precluded from

---

139. *See* section A ("Introduction") *supra*.

140. *See* RESTATEMENT (SECOND) OF JUDGMENTS § 28(1) cmt. a (1982); *see also* Askin v. District of Columbia, 728 A.2d 665 (D.C. 1999) (issue preclusion does not prevent a party from litigating issues when the party could not appeal from non-final and non-appealable orders).

obtaining a reversal of the judgment. Consequently, *B* would not be precluded from relitigating the determination in a subsequent proceeding.[141]

Illustration 13-32. *A* sues *B* for a declaratory judgment that a statute being enforced by *B* against *A* is unconstitutional. The trial court finds the statute constitutional as applied and enters judgment for *B*. *A* appeals, but the appeal is dismissed for mootness because *A* has ceased the activities prohibited by the statute. However, the judgment of the trial court is not vacated. Subsequently, *A* again undertakes the activities prohibited by the statute. *A* sues *B* again for a declaratory judgment that the statute is unconstitutional. The judgment in the first action does not preclude *A* from relitigating the constitutional issue because *A* was unable as a matter of law to obtain appellate review of the first determination.[142]

(b) Issues of Law

Another exception exists in some cases when the issue determined is one of law. Although issue preclusion applies to issues of law as well as to issues of fact, in some circumstances preclusion on an issue of law can operate unfairly. One such circumstance arises when the claims between the parties in the two actions are substantially unrelated. In this situation, it is thought unfair to bind the parties for all time by a rule of law announced in the first action.

Illustration 13-33. *A* sues *City B* for personal injuries allegedly resulting from *B's* negligence. *B* defends on grounds of sovereign immunity, and this defense is sustained. Several years later, *A* sues *B* again for personal injuries inflicted in an unrelated accident occurring after the judgment in the first proceeding. Obviously, it would be unfair to prevent *A*, on the ground that the issue is res judicata, from arguing that the doctrine of sovereign immunity should be abolished, when *B's* other adversaries, who have not been parties to prior litigation, are free to argue that the rule should be overturned.[143]

* * * * *

---

141. RESTATEMENT (SECOND) OF JUDGMENTS § 28(1) cmt. a (1982).

142. *Id.*

143. *See id.* § 28(2) cmt. b, illus. 2; Bingaman v. Department of Treasury, 127 F.3d 1431 (Fed. Cir. 1997) (exception to issue preclusion for changes in the applicable legal context applicable to changes in the interpretation of a statutory standard by an administrative agency); Hackley v. Hackley, 426 Mich. 582, 395 N.W.2d 906 (1986) (issue of paternity is one of fact, not law); *cf.* Elysium Inst., Inc. v. County of Los Angeles, 232 Cal. App. 3d 408, 283 Cal. Rptr. 688 (1991) (county not prevented by issue preclusion from relitigating constitutionality of zoning ordinance pertaining to nudist camps when judgment in prior action arose out of different transaction and different ordinance), *cert. denied*, 502 U.S. 1098, 112 S. Ct. 1180, 117 L. Ed. 2d 424 (1992). With the *Hackley* case, *supra*, compare Dixon v. Pouncy, 979 P.2d 520 (Alaska 1999), in which the court allowed an attack on a paternity determination in a prior action under Alaska's equivalent of Federal Rule 60(b). The court held that Rule 60(b) attacks were "direct" rather than "collateral" attacks on judgments, so issue preclusion did not apply. Of course, one of the grounds for a Rule 60(b) attack must exist, and the dissenters argued that a Rule 60(b) attack was improper in the case because (1) it was foreseeable at the time of the initial proceeding that the party attacking the judgment was not the father and he actually contested the issue; and (2) Rule 60(b)(5) requires a change in either legal or factual conditions, which were not present because there was no change in law and the availability of a DNA test could not be considered a change in facts.

For reasons similar to those given in the *Illustration 13-33*, it may be appropriate to allow relitigation in another situation involving a prior determination of issues of law. Sometimes even when the claims in two actions are substantially related, a new determination of an issue will be necessary to take account of an intervening change of law or to prevent an inequitable administration of the laws.[144]

Illustration 13-34. State *A* sues *B* to enjoin *B* from engaging in certain allegedly illegal business operations. *B* defends on the grounds that the business operations are legal. The court sustains this defense. Subsequently, *State A* sues *C*, a competitor of *B*, to enjoin *C* from engaging in the same kind of business. The highest court of the state holds that the business activities are illegal. The state should not be precluded from suing *B* again. To allow *B* to engage in activities from which *B's* competitors (and others) would be prohibited would be an inequitable administration of the laws as between persons similarly situated.[145]

(c) *"Mediate Data" Versus "Ultimate Facts"*

Traditionally, courts distinguished between the preclusive effect of a determination on matters of "ultimate fact" as opposed to "mediate data." An "ultimate fact" in an action is the logical conclusion that is drawn from the evidence produced. "Mediate data," or "evidentiary facts," are the steps leading to the "ultimate fact."

Illustration 13-35. In an action for personal injuries resulting from an automobile accident, the negligence of the defendant is an "ultimate fact." The evidence that the defendant was driving at an excessive speed is a "mediate datum."

* * * * *

A finding as to an "ultimate fact" could be used in a subsequent action to establish either an "ultimate fact" or a "mediate datum" in that proceeding, but that a finding on a "mediate datum" could not be used at all in a subsequent

---

144. *See* RESTATEMENT (SECOND) OF JUDGMENTS § 28(2) cmt. c (1982). At least one court has held that an exception exists to the doctrine of claim preclusion when there is an intervening change in the law that would validate a claim that has failed under prior law. *See* Statler v. Catalano, 293 Ill. App. 3d 483, 691 N.E.2d 384 (1997). Such a holding is clearly incorrect.

145. *See* RESTATEMENT (SECOND) OF JUDGMENTS § 28(2)(b) cmt. c, illus. 3 (1982). *But see* United States v. Stauffer Chem. Co., 464 U.S. 165, 104 S. Ct. 575, 78 L. Ed. 2d 388 (1984) (mutual defensive issue preclusion applicable against government on issue of law). In addition to the situations discussed in the text, preclusion on issues of law is often limited in successive litigation between the government and different parties for fear that binding the government by issue preclusion would thwart the development of important issues of law by freezing the issue as it was decided in the first case to proceed to judgment. *See* United States v. Mendoza, 464 U.S. 154, 104 S. Ct. 568, 78 L. Ed. 2d 379 (1984); Arcadia Unified Sch. Dist. v. State Dep't of Educ., 2 Cal. 4th 251, 825 P.2d 438, 5 Cal. Rptr. 2d 545 (1992). *See generally* A. Leo Levin & Susan M. Leeson, *Issue Preclusion Against the United States Government*, 70 IOWA L. REV. 113 (1984); Allan D. Vestal, *Relitigation by Federal Agencies: Conflict, Concurrence and Synthesis of Judicial Policies*, 55 N.C. L. REV. 123 (1977); Jean F. Rydstrom, Annotation, *Modern Status of Applicability of Doctrine of Estoppel Against Federal Government and Its Agencies*, 27 A.L.R. FED. 702 (1976).

proceeding.[146] The distinction between "ultimate facts" and "mediate data" was never entirely clear, and the rules really seemed to be directed at assuring that the issue in question was litigated in the first action with a full awareness of its implications for future proceedings. The modern approach, adopted by the *Restatement (Second)*,[147] directly asks whether it was sufficiently foreseeable at the time of the first action that the issue would arise in a subsequent proceeding.[148] If so, one can be relatively assured that the issue was litigated fully in the first proceeding. If not, relitigation of the issue is called for because an adequate opportunity to litigate the issue has not been afforded.[149]

(d) Differences in the Burden of Proof

Another exception to the rule of issue preclusion exists when the party against whom preclusion is sought had a heavier burden of persuasion on the issue in the first action than in the second action. An exception also exists when the adversary has a heavier burden than the party had in the first action.[150] The burden of persuasion has a potentially significant effect on the outcome of an action. When it shifts between two actions, the ordinary rules of issue preclusion should not apply.[151]

Illustration 13-36. A sues B for personal injuries resulting from an automobile accident. A alleges that B was negligent. In the state in which A brings the action, the plaintiff in a negligence suit is required to plead and prove the plaintiff's freedom from contributory negligence. After a trial, the court holds that A has failed to discharge that burden and finds A contributorily negligent. The court enters a judgment for B based on this finding. B then sues A for personal injuries received in the same accident. B's action is permitted because the state has no compulsory counterclaim rule. B contends that the judgment in the first action conclusively establishes A's negligence in the second. B's argu-

---

146. *See* RESTATEMENT (FIRST) OF JUDGMENTS § 68 cmt. p (1948); The Evergreens v. Nunan, 141 F.2d 927 (2d Cir.), *cert. denied*, 323 U.S. 720, 65 S. Ct. 49, 89 L. Ed. 579 (1944). Commentators have criticized the *Evergreens* rule. *See, e.g.,* Maurice Rosenberg, *Collateral Estoppel in New York*, 44 ST. JOHN'S L. REV. 165, 182 (1969); Charles A. Heckman, *Collateral Estoppel as the Answer to Multiple Litigation Problems in Federal Tax Laws: Another View of* Sunnen *and* The Evergreens, 19 CASE W. RES. L. REV. 230 (1968).

147. *See* RESTATEMENT (SECOND) OF JUDGMENTS § 27 cmt. j (1982).

148. *See, e.g.,* Hyman v. Regenstein, 258 F.2d 502, 510-11 (5th Cir. 1958), *cert. denied*, 359 U.S. 913, 79 S. Ct. 589, 3 L. Ed. 2d 575 (1959).

149. *See* RESTATEMENT (SECOND) OF JUDGMENTS § 27 cmt. j, § 28(5)(b) cmt. i (1982).

150. *See id.* § 28(4).

151. *See, e.g.,* United States v. One Assortment of 89 Firearms, 465 U.S. 354, 104 S. Ct. 1099, 79 L. Ed. 2d 361 (1984). *See generally* John H. Derrick, Annotation, *Acquittal or Conviction in Criminal Prosecution as Bar to Particular Actions for Forfeiture of Property or for Statutory Damages or Penalty—Federal Cases*, 79 L. Ed. 2d 960 (1986). A criminal prosecution resulting in a judgment of conviction beyond a reasonable doubt can be used to establish facts essential to the conviction that arises in a later civil proceeding. *See, e.g.,* Doe v. Tobias, 715 N.E.2d 829 (Ind. 1999) (criminal conviction can be used in subsequent civil proceeding as offensive collateral estoppel). This is, of course, the opposite of the situation discussed in the text, because in the criminal proceeding the burden of proof is heavier on the state than it is on the plaintiff in the subsequent civil action. However, in addition, for the criminal conviction to be useful in an issue preclusion sense, the doctrine of mutuality of estoppel discussed in subsection 3, *infra*, must not exist in the judicial system in which the criminal judgment is rendered.

ment is not sound because *A* had a significantly heavier burden of proof in the first action than *A* will have in the second action.[152]

(e) Nature and Quality of the Procedures
in the Original Action

Another exception to issue preclusion occurs when "differences [exist] in the quality or extensiveness of the procedures followed in the two courts or . . . factors [are present] relating to the allocation of jurisdiction between them."[153] Sometimes, the first action is brought in a court without subject-matter jurisdiction to consider claims presented in another court with broader jurisdiction. This factor alone should not prevent issue preclusion from operating. However, the determination in the first proceeding should not be binding in the second action when (1) the procedures available in the first court do not allow a full opportunity to litigate the issue in the action or (2) the legislative allocation of jurisdiction between the courts in the two actions is designed, for policy reasons, to prevent consideration of an issue "directly" by the first court. This exception can operate as between (1) courts of the same state, (2) courts of different states, or (3) courts of a state and a federal court.[154]

Illustration 13-37. *A* sues *B* in a small claims court for property damage arising out of an automobile accident. The small claims court has a jurisdictional ceiling on its competence of $500 and operates informally without pleadings, counsel, or rules of evidence. The court finds that *B* was negligent and enters a judgment for *A*. Subsequently, *B* sues *A* in a state court of general jurisdiction for personal injuries received in the same accident. In the second action, the judgment in the small claims court does not establish conclusively that *B* was contributorily negligent. The quality and extensiveness of the procedures in the first court did not (arguably) give *B* a full and fair opportunity to litigate. This conclusion is based on issue preclusion, not on claim preclusion. It might be argued that if *B* could not counterclaim in action No. 1, *B* should not be precluded in action No. 2. However, this factor is relevant only to *claim* preclusion, *not* to issue preclusion. The doctrines must be analyzed separately. Even if claim preclusion does not apply, issue preclusion may.[155]

(f) Injustice in Particular Cases

Finally, modern practice supports an exception to the rule of issue preclusion anytime the circumstances surrounding the first action did not afford

---

152. *See* RESTATEMENT (SECOND) OF JUDGMENTS § 28(4) cmt. f, illus. 10 (1982).

153. *Id.* § 28(3); *cf.* Hackley v. Hackley, 426 Mich. 582, 395 N.W.2d 906 (1986) (successive actions in *same court*; change in rules of evidence between the two actions; rule existing in prior action did not prevent litigation of issue in question; therefore, issue preclusion operates).

154. *See* RESTATEMENT (SECOND) OF JUDGMENTS § 28(3) cmt. d & e (1982); *see also* section F ("Complications Produced by the Federal System") *infra*.

155. *See* RESTATEMENT (SECOND) OF JUDGMENTS § 28(3) cmt. d, illus. 7 (1982); *cf.* Board of Educ. v. Gray, 806 S.W.2d 400 (Ky. Ct. App. 1991) (procedures in prior unemployment compensation proceeding did not afford full and fair opportunity for defendant to litigate).

"an adequate opportunity or incentive to obtain a full and fair adjudication in the initial action."[156] For example, a party may have been laboring under a physical or mental disability that impeded effective litigation. The jury's verdict may have been the result of compromise in the first action. In addition, the amount in controversy in the first action may have been small in relation to the amount in the second proceeding, which resulted in a lack of incentive to litigate the issue vigorously in the first action.[157]

Illustration 13-38. A sues B for $50.00 in property damage resulting from an automobile accident. A alleges that B was negligent and B denies negligence. After a trial to the court, the court finds B negligent and enters judgment for A. Subsequently, B sues A for $10,000 in damages for personal injuries received in the same accident. B's action is permitted because the jurisdiction does not have a compulsory counterclaim rule. A contends that the judgment in the first action establishes B's negligence conclusively for purposes of the second action. A's argument is not sound. Because of the small amount involved in the first action, B did not have an adequate incentive to litigate fully the issue of B's negligence. This situation should be distinguished from *Illustration 13-37*, above, in which it was specifically stated that the action had been brought in a small claims court. In this illustration, there is no indication that the court in which the first action was brought did not afford the quality or extensiveness of procedures holding preclusion applicable.[158] Therefore, the lack of incentive to litigate in the first action is the only basis for avoiding preclusion.[159]

* * * * *

This general "injustice" exception to the rule of issue preclusion can be criticized. The principle of finality supporting claim and issue preclusion aims at achieving a just and efficient legal order by preventing multiple litigation over the same basic matter. However, if exceptions become too numerous or too broad, the danger is great that this important objective will be undermined. Despite the value of an open-ended standard in preventing injustice in particular cases, such a standard may undermine the effectiveness of the entire doctrine of issue preclusion by encouraging widespread litigation over the preclusive effects of judgments in circumstances too numerous to foresee when the standard was originally adopted. Should this result, greater injustice than justice may flow from the exception.[160]

---

156. RESTATEMENT (SECOND) OF JUDGMENTS § 28(5)(c) (1982).

157. *See id.* cmt. j.

158. *See id.* § 28(5)(c).

159. *See* Hackley v. Hackley, 426 Mich. 582, 395 N.W.2d 906 (1986) (section 28(5)(c) does not create exception unless there is a compelling showing of unfairness in first action; showing not made in paternity action due to restrictive rule of evidence in first action, when the putative father had other means of litigating paternity issue).

160. *Compare* RESTATEMENT (SECOND) OF JUDGMENTS §§ 27-28 (1982) *with* RESTATEMENT (FIRST) OF JUDGMENTS §§ 68-71 (1942). In Faigin v. Kelly, 184 F.3d 67 (1st Cir. 1999), the court indicated substantial doubt whether a Rule 11 hearing in a prior action can ever provide a satisfactory basis for issue preclusion because of the way in which such hearings are circumscribed. In the prior action, the plaintiff had been sanctioned for failure to make an adequate factual investigation of the claim, and the court indicated that this did not mean that no objective facts actually existed to support the claim. However, as the court admitted, this really means the issues are not the same between the first and second actions, which provides an independent

3. Nonmutual Preclusion

(a) The Mutuality of Estoppel Rule and Traditional Exceptions to the Rule

Traditionally, issue preclusion did not operate against a party to a first action when the party sued, or was sued by, a party not involved in the first action.[161] Under this *mutuality of estoppel* rule, all parties to an action had to be bound by the judgment for any to be bound. Because a nonparty cannot ordinarily be bound by a judgment, the mutuality rule prevented a party to the prior action from being bound either. Today, many jurisdictions have abolished this rule.[162]

Illustration 13-39. Suppose a three-car collision occurred between *A*, *B*, and *C*. If *A* sued *B* and recovered based upon *B's* negligence, the finding against *B* would preclude relitigation of *B's* negligence in any subsequent action between *A* and *B*. However, if *C* sued *B*, issue preclusion would not operate against *B*. Both parties to a proceeding had to be bound or neither was bound. *C* would not be bound by the judgment in the first action because *C* was not a party to that proceeding and had no opportunity to litigate the issues raised. As a result, under the mutuality of estoppel rule, *B* also could not be bound by the finding of negligence either, even though *B* had an adequate opportunity to litigate the issues in the first proceeding.[163]

* * * * *

Even when the rule of mutuality of estoppel generally prevailed, exceptions existed. One exception was recognized when an indemnitor-indemnitee relationship existed between the party to be bound and the nonparty.[164]

Illustration 13-40. Suppose that an employee was driving the employer's car on the employer's business when the employee collided with *P*. Under the law ordinarily applicable to this sort of case, if the employee's negligence caused the accident, *P* is entitled to sue (1) the employer alone, (2) the employee alone, or (3) both of them together for *P's* injuries. If *P* sues the employer and recovers, the employer is entitled to be indemnified by the employee for the amount the employer had to pay to *P*. However, if *P* sued the employee first and the employee won, a difficulty was created. If *P* then could sue the employer and win, one of two unacceptable consequences would follow. If the employer could sue the employee for indemnity and recover, the employee would be deprived of the benefit of the judgment the employee won in the suit with *P*. On the other hand, if the employer was not permitted to recover from the employee, the employer would be deprived of the right of indemnity. To avoid this difficulty,

---

basis for refusing preclusion.

161. *See* RESTATEMENT (FIRST) OF JUDGMENTS § 93(b) (1942).

162. But not all. *See, e.g.,* E.C. v. Katz, 731 So. 2d 1268 (Fla. 1999) (mutuality rule exists in Florida; identity of parties is required before issue preclusion can be used defensively against plaintiff in prior action).

163. RESTATEMENT (FIRST) OF JUDGMENTS § 93(b) cmt. d, illus. 7 (1942); *see, e.g.,* Dual & Assocs., Inc. v. Wells, 241 Va. 542, 403 S.E.2d 354 (1991).

164. *See* RESTATEMENT (FIRST) OF JUDGMENTS § 96 (1942).

an exception was created to the mutuality rule to allow an employer to plead the judgment in the employee's favor as res judicata in *P's* suit against the employer.[165] However, this exception did not exist if *P* sued the employer first and the employer won on the ground that there had been no negligence. Because the employer owed no duty of indemnity to the employee, the unacceptable consequences described above were not present when *P* sued the employee in a second suit. Therefore, the mutuality of estoppel rule operated in full force, and *P* was not bound by the finding of no negligence in the first action.[166]

* * * * *

Another exception existed when the plaintiff in the initial action sued for a tort or a breach of contract and lost. If the court found no tort or breach and the plaintiff then sued a second defendant for inducing the tort or breach of contract that was the subject of the first suit, the second defendant could plead judgment in the first action as res judicata in the second proceeding. It was unacceptable to allow the second action to continue when the first proceeding had negated the existence of the tort or breach upon which the second action was based.[167]

(b) Abolition of the Mutuality Rule

Direct challenge to the mutuality of estoppel rule first occurred in *Bernhard v. Bank of America National Trust & Savings Association*.[168] In *Bernhard* and many other cases abolishing the mutuality of estoppel rule, the judgment in the first action was used *defensively* in the second action against the person who was the plaintiff in the first suit.

Illustration 13-41. Suppose that in the first action *A* sues *B*, and *B* wins. In the second action, *A* sues *C*. Abolishing the doctrine of mutuality is easy in this case because the party being bound (*A*) picked the time and court for suit in the first action. The judgment is simply being used to prevent *A* from trying again against a different adversary (*C*).[169]

* * * * *

However, more difficult cases exist.

Illustration 13-42. Suppose instead that *A* sues *B*, and *A* wins. If *B* then sues *C*, a case is presented in which, if mutuality of estoppel is abolished, the judgment in the first action would be used defensively in the second action

---

165. *See id.* § 96 cmt. d, illus. 1; Sullivan v. American Cas. Co., 582 N.E.2d 890 (Ind. Ct. App. 1991) (issue preclusion applied despite mutuality rule when defendant's liability was contractually derivative of liability of defendant in first action who had been found not liable)..

166. *See* RESTATEMENT (FIRST) OF JUDGMENTS § 96 cmt. j, illus. 9 (1942).

167. *See id.* § 99.

168. 19 Cal. 2d 807, 122 P.2d 892 (1942). *See generally* Jean F. Rydstrom, Annotation, *Modern Status of Mutuality of Estoppel Requirement for Application of Doctrine of Collateral Estoppel in Federal Civil Case to Stranger to Prior Judgment*, 58 L. Ed. 2d 938 (1980); E.H. Schopler, Annotation, *Comment Note—Mutuality of Estoppel as Prerequisite of Availability of Doctrine of Collateral Estoppel to A Stranger to the Judgment*, 31 A.L.R.3D 1044 (1970).

169. For a discussion of the application of these rules in a comparative negligence context, see David Polin, Annotation, *Comparative Negligence: Judgment Allocating Fault in Action Against Less Than All Potential Defendants as Precluding Subsequent Action Against Parties Not Sued in Original Action*, 4 A.L.R.5TH 753 (1992).

against *B* (the defendant in the first action). Because *B* did not choose the time or the court for suit in the first action, it might be argued that the judgment should not bind *B*. On the other hand, the judgment still is being used only defensively to prevent the loser in the first action from affirmatively recovering in a second proceeding.

Illustration 13-43. An even harder case is presented when *A* sues *B*, *B* wins, and then *C* sues *A*. The judgment would be used *offensively* if mutuality of estoppel has been abolished. However, the judgment would be used against the plaintiff in the first action (*A*), who picked the time and place of suit. Nevertheless, if *A* knows issue preclusion can be used offensively against *A*, *A* may well be deterred from bringing the first suit. The doctrine of issue preclusion is supposed to cut down the amount of litigation, but not at the expense of discouraging persons from bringing what they believe are otherwise legitimate actions.

Illustration 13-44. The most difficult case of all in which to justify the abolition of the mutuality of estoppel rule is when issue preclusion is used offensively against a defendant in the initial action. Suppose that *A* sues *B*, and *A* wins. *C* then sues *B*. If mutuality of estoppel is abolished, the judgment will be used offensively against one who did not choose the court, time, or place of suit in the first action. This situation arises when a mass disaster occurs—for example, an airline crash, the collapse of a hotel walkway, or a fire. If the defendant loses the first suit and the mutuality rule has been abolished, enormous liability may result from the judgment. "The result is great disparity in litigating risks. A further consequence of this disparity is that it puts great pressure on a defendant who faces multiple claimants to settle with each one rather than risk an adverse determination by going to trial."[170]

(c) Deciding when a Party Has Had a Full and Fair Opportunity to Litigate an Issue

Despite the problems involved with abolishing mutuality of estoppel, the modern tendency, exemplified by § 29 of the *Restatement (Second) of Judgments*, is to eliminate mutuality for all kinds of actions. The central focus is whether the party to be bound by the judgment had a full and fair opportunity to litigate in the first proceeding. Section 29 lists several factors that are used to make this determination. These factors operate in addition to the ordinary exceptions to issue preclusion applicable in subsequent litigation between the same parties.[171]

(i) Ordinary Exceptions Applicable

Recall that a factor listed by § 28 of the *Restatement (Second)* is whether an adequate incentive to litigate existed in the first action.

---

170. FLEMING JAMES, JR. ET AL., CIVIL PROCEDURE § 11.25, at 621-22 (4th ed. 1992).

171. *See* RESTATEMENT (SECOND) OF JUDGMENTS § 29 (1982). Recall that the exceptions to the rule of issue preclusion are found in § 28 of the *Restatement (Second)*; *see* section C(2) for a discussion of exceptions to issue preclusion *supra*.

Illustration 13-45. A sues B in a small claims court for $100 in property damage arising from an automobile accident. After a trial, the court enters judgment for A, specifically finding that B was negligent. Subsequently, C sues B in a court of general jurisdiction in the state. A seeks $50,000 for personal injuries received in the same automobile accident. Even if the rule of mutuality has been abolished, B is not precluded from relitigating the issue of negligence by the judgment in *A v. B.* Issue preclusion would not operate here even if the second action were between A and B. B did not have an adequate incentive to litigate in *A v. B* because of the small amount involved in that action.[172]

(ii) Incompatibility with a Scheme of Remedies

According to § 29 of the *Restatement (Second)*, issue preclusion is inappropriate in subsequent litigation with a third party when "[t]reating [an] issue as conclusively determined [by a prior judgment] would be incompatible with [the] scheme of administering the remedies in the actions involved."[173]

Illustration 13-46. A sues *B Airline* for the wrongful death of *A's* spouse in a crash of one of *B's* airplanes. After trial, the court enters a judgment for A on the grounds that B was negligent and that *B's* negligence caused the fatal crash. Subsequently, C sues B for the wrongful death of *C's* spouse resulting from the same crash. The wrongful death statute applicable to the crash provides that a judgment rendered against a defendant in a mass disaster case shall have no preclusive effect in a subsequent action arising out of the same disaster. B may relitigate the issue of negligence in the action by C, notwithstanding the unfavorable judgment in *A's* action against B.[174]

(iii) Differences in Procedural Opportunities

Issue preclusion should not be applied if the issue determined in the first action would likely be decided differently in the second action because "the forum in the second action affords the party against whom preclusion is asserted procedural opportunities in the presentation and determination of the [case] that were not [present] in the first" action.[175]

Illustration 13-47. A sues B in a summary proceeding to recover on a note executed by B and cosigned by C. B defends on the ground of part payment of the note. A loses on this issue. In a subsequent action by A against C, the fact

---

172. *See Illustration 13-38 supra*; RESTATEMENT (SECOND) OF JUDGMENTS § 28(5)(e) (1982).

173. *See* RESTATEMENT (SECOND) OF JUDGMENTS § 29(1) (1982).

174. *See id.* § 29 cmt. c. *But cf.* Clayton Act § 5(a), 15 U.S.C. § 16(a) (Section 5(a) of the Clayton Act provides that judgments in government antitrust suits are prima facie evidence against the defendant in subsequent suits brought by private parties; however, a 1980 amendment to § 5(a) provides that nothing in this section "shall be construed to impose any limitation on the application of collateral estoppel"). This amendment legislatively overruled Illinois v. General Paving Co., 590 F.2d 680 (7th Cir.), *cert. denied*, 444 U.S. 879, 100 S. Ct. 168, 62 L. Ed. 2d 109 (1979) (holding that original § 5(a) permitted the court to give only prima facie, and not preclusive, effect to an earlier criminal conviction, even thought the case was appropriate for preclusion under the doctrine of offensive collateral estoppel).

175. *See* RESTATEMENT (SECOND) OF JUDGMENTS § 29(2) (1982).

that *A* was compelled to litigate in a summary proceeding may be considered in determining whether *A* should be precluded on the issue of part payment.[176]

(iv) Inconsistency with Another Determination

In determining whether issue preclusion should be applied, it should be considered whether "the determination relied on . . . was itself inconsistent with another determination of the same issue" in an earlier action.[177] This factor affords some protection to the defendant in mass disaster litigation who successfully defends one or more actions with different plaintiffs before losing an action. However, the amount of protection afforded by the factor is questionable, given the strong incentive for the defendant to settle, rather than litigate, and the ability of plaintiffs to select the most appealing case to try first among all the available actions.

Illustration 13-48. After the wreck of a passenger train, *A*, a passenger on the train, sues *B Railroad* for personal injuries. *A* alleges that *B's* negligence caused the accident. After a trial, verdict and judgment are given for *B* on the ground that it was not negligent. Subsequently, *C*, another passenger on the wrecked train, sues *B* for personal injuries alleging negligence. This time, verdict and judgment are given for *C* after a finding that *B* had been negligent. Subsequently, *D*, a third passenger on the train, sues *B* for personal injuries received in the accident. *D* contends that *B's* negligence is conclusively established by the judgment in *C v. B*, the jurisdiction in question having abolished the mutuality rule. *D's* contention is unsound because of the inconsistent findings.[178] However, it may be fortuitous that *D* did not sue first and win, thus giving all others the benefit of issue preclusion. In addition, plaintiffs may sometimes cooperate to bring the action with the most sympathetic plaintiff to trial first. These considerations may indicate that the mutuality rule should be retained in mass disaster litigation.

(v) Ability to Join in the First Action

In determining whether issue preclusion should be applied, it is also relevant to determine whether the person seeking to invoke favorable preclusion or to avoid unfavorable preclusion could have joined the present adversary in the

---

176. *See id.* cmt. d, illus. 1. However, if the general exceptions in § 28(3) or § 28(5)(c) are inapplicable because *A* had a full and fair opportunity to litigate in the action with *B*, there is a strong argument that a "special exception" of this sort should not be recognized just because the second action is with a different party (*C*).

177. *See* RESTATEMENT (SECOND) OF JUDGMENTS § 29(4) (1982).

178. *See id.*; Hoppe v. G.D. Searle & Co., 779 F. Supp. 1425 (S.D.N.Y. 1991) (defendant had won sixteen of twenty prior suits reaching juries).

first action.[179] Professor Hay has argued that this rule has an economic under-pinning.[180]

Illustration 13-49. A is injured in an accident while riding as a passenger in an automobile owned by *B* and driven by *C* during the course of *C's* employment by *D. A* sues *D* for damages. *D* defends on the ground that *C* was not negligent. After trial, *D* wins, the court explicitly finding that *C* was not negligent. Subsequently, *A* sues *B* for damages based on the same event. *A* is precluded by the finding that *C* was not negligent. When "a plaintiff brings a subsequent action involving the same issues against a person whom [the plaintiff] could appropriately have joined as a codefendant in the first action, only strongly compelling circumstances justify withholding preclusion."[181]

---

179. *See* RESTATEMENT (SECOND) OF JUDGMENTS § 29(3) (1982).

180. In absence of this restriction, no plaintiff (except those who have already sued and lost) can be excluded from the fruits of a prior action because the benefits of a favorable judgment under the nonmutuality rule are indivisible. This fact creates an incentive for plaintiffs to try to take a "free ride" on the efforts of others, particularly if effective collective action requires cost sharing by a large number of plaintiffs. The propensity to do so increases as the degree of dispersion of the benefits to noncontributing plaintiffs increases because it is less likely that the marginal gain from contributing will be worth the cost. Furthermore, "by suing separately from the group, the free rider gets two bites at the apple; if the group loses, [the free rider] is not bound by the adverse judgment." Bruce L. Hay, *Some Settlement Effects of Preclusion*, 1993 U. ILL. L. REV. 21, 49. Professor Hay gives the following illustration: "Suppose that claims have an expected judicial valuation of $100 if the plaintiffs sue separately, and $150 if they sue collectively; and assume that a plaintiff's litigation costs are the same whether [the plaintiff] sues alone or in a group. If nonmutual preclusion is available, [the plaintiff] gains little by joining. If others have already banded together, contribution has no point; most of the benefits of collective action probably will be realized whether or not [the plaintiff] contributes, and by holding back [the plaintiff] can get a second bite at the apple if the group loses." *Id.* nn.79-80 (also pointing out, however, that the conduct of prospective free riders is affected by their "place in line." If a plaintiff knows that the plaintiff's case will be tried before those of other plaintiffs, the plaintiff will be better off by contributing to a collective action because the chances of recovering alone are worse than the chances of recovering as a part of the group).

181. *See* RESTATEMENT (SECOND) OF JUDGMENTS § 29(3) cmt. e, illus. 4 (1982); *see also* Hunter v. City of Des Moines, 300 N.W.2d 121 (Iowa 1981) (defendant's motion to consolidate actions by different plaintiffs arising from same facts resisted by plaintiff in second action; issue preclusion denied when defendant loses the first action). *Illustration 13-49* is basically illustration 4 of the *Restatement (Second)*, cited above. Yet, in the *Restatement (Second)'s* illustration, *A* would be bound by issue preclusion without the need to "weigh" the failure to join *C*. In *Hunter*, the plaintiff in the second action resisted consolidation of a separate action by a different plaintiff against the same defendant. It makes sense there to resort to a special exception to issue preclusion to prevent the plaintiff in the second action from obtaining the benefit of a judgment against the defendant in the first action. But how far should this approach extend? If the plaintiff in the second action simply did not join with the plaintiff in the first action, should this fact be given weight? To the drafters of the *Restatement (Second)*, the answer is apparently "yes." *See* RESTATEMENT (SECOND) OF JUDGMENTS § 29(3), illus. 4 (1982). However, if this factor is given substantial weight, it would prevent nonmutual offensive issue preclusion altogether in this and many other situations. Such a widespread application may have desirable economic effects:

> Desirable (from the plaintiffs' standpoint) collective action is therefore less likely to occur under nonmutuality. Because the rule converts favorable judgments into public goods, each plaintiff has an incentive to understate the value . . . of a favorable judgment and to decline to contribute to a collective effort at securing one. Suits will be brought individually even when the group as a whole would profit from a pooling of efforts. Precisely by making the benefits of a favorable judgment available to all, the rule reduces the likelihood that such a judgment will be rendered in the first place.
>
> . . . .
>
> The free-rider problem created by nonmutuality supports the principle, urged by the Second Restatement [in §29(3)] and adopted by the Supreme Court in the *Parklane Hosiery* case, that a plaintiff cannot take advantage of nonmutual preclusion if [the

(vi) Relationships Not Present in the Second Action and Compromise Verdicts

In determining whether issue preclusion should apply, a court may consider whether the determination in the prior action might have been affected by relationships among the parties to the first action that are not present in the second proceeding. An apparent compromise verdict or finding can also be taken into account.[182]

Illustration 13-50. A real estate developer advertises vacation lots for sale. A real estate broker and a retired schoolteacher each contract to buy a lot, but they both subsequently refuse to complete their contracts because the lots are not as advertised. Assume that the real estate developer sues the real estate broker for breach of contract. The broker successfully defends the action on the grounds that the broker reasonably relied on the advertising. Subsequently, the developer sues the schoolteacher for breach of contract. The finding in the action between the developer and the broker that the statements in the advertising were ones on which reliance might reasonably be placed is not binding on the developer in the action with the schoolteacher. The resolution of the issue may have resulted from the knowledge or comparative responsibility of the parties toward one another in the first proceeding.[183]

Illustration 13-51. A and B are killed in the wreck of C's car. A's personal representative sues C for $70,000 for wrongful death. At trial, the evidence of C's negligence is minimal, but the jury returns a verdict in A's favor for $35,000. Subsequently, B's representative sues C for $100,000 for wrongful death. Under these circumstances, the issue of C's negligence should not be deemed precluded by the judgment in A v. C. It looks very much like the judgment in the first action was based on a compromise verdict. The evidence of negligence is weak, and the requested damages are divided in half.[184]

(vii) Inappropriate Foreclosure of the Opportunity to Review of Issues of Law

If the issue determined in the prior action was one of law and treating it as conclusively determined would inappropriately foreclose opportunity for obtaining reconsideration of the legal rule on which it was based, issue preclusion

---

plaintiff] could have joined the earlier action. Though embraced mostly out of concern for fairness to the defendant, this restriction on nonmutual preclusion actually may benefit the plaintiffs as a group—particularly [when] sequential litigation enables the defendant to divide and conquer effectively. If effectively enforced, the restriction should give potential contributors the right incentives: they will join if and only if collective action increases the value of their claims. Without the restriction, these gains from cooperation are more likely to be lost, and the defendant will be better able to extract favorable settlements . . . .

Bruce L. Hay, *Some Settlement Effects of Preclusion*, 1993 U. ILL. L. REV. 21, 49-50 (footnotes omitted).

182. *See* RESTATEMENT (SECOND) OF JUDGMENTS § 29(5) (1982).

183. *Id.* cmt. g, illus. 5.

184. *See id.* illus. 7.

should not operate.[185] However, the usefulness of this factor is highly questionable. There is an exception to issue preclusion even in successive actions between the same two parties when issues of law are involved and the two actions are substantially unrelated or a new determination of the issue is warranted in order to take into account intervening changes in the applicable legal context or otherwise avoid inequitable administration of the law.[186] This exception would also be applicable in subsequent litigation between different parties and would be analytically prior to the application of a special exception for issues of law in nonmutual estoppel situations. However, it is difficult to think of a situation in which an issue of law would be precluded in litigation between the same two parties in spite of the ordinary exception for issues of law applicable to such cases, but would *not* be precluded in litigation between different parties because of the special exception for issues of law in those cases.

Illustration 13-52. *A* sued *B Bank* for damages, alleging that the bank breached a loan contract with *A* by charging a higher annual interest rate than permitted by a state statute, and alleging further that the bank's method of computing interest rates was illegal. The court granted summary judgment against *A* on the grounds that the rates charged by the bank were permissible under the statute and that the bank's method of computing interest was also lawful. Subsequently, *A* sued *C Bank* asserting claims against *C Bank* that are identical to the ones raised by *A* in the prior action against *B Bank*. Under these circumstances, issue preclusion would not apply even if *A's* action had been brought against *B Bank*, if the claims in the two actions are unrelated. The reason is that it would be unfair to preclude *A* from arguing that the issues of law determined in the prior action were determined incorrectly, when all other customers of *B Bank* would be allowed to litigate that issue.[187] If issue preclusion would not operate in an action between the same two parties for this reason, it will also not operate in an action between different parties.[188] Therefore, even

---

185. *See* RESTATEMENT (SECOND) OF JUDGMENTS § 29(7) (1982).

186. *See id.* § 28(2); subsection C(2)*(b)* ("Issues of Law") *supra.*

187. *See* section C(2)*(b)*, *Illustration 13-33, supra.*

188. The *Restatement (Second)* states that a person precluded from litigating with an opposing party is precluded from litigating with others unless one of the special exceptions to nonmutual preclusion found in § 29 is applicable. *See* RESTATEMENT (SECOND) OF JUDGMENTS § 29 (1982). This indicates that the case should first be analyzed under the basic doctrine of issue preclusion applicable to successive actions between the same two parties and the exceptions to that doctrine *before* the special exceptions in § 29 are considered. This means that the exception in § 28(2) for issues of law in actions between the same parties must be applied to determine whether preclusion would exist before determining the applicability of the special exception for issues of law in nonmutual preclusion cases in § 29(7). *See also* Garcia v. General Motors Corp., 294 Ariz. Adv. Rep. 26, 990 P.2d 1069 (Ct. App. 1999). In *Garcia*, the plaintiffs were injured in a single-car accident in Idaho while riding in a General Motors van. One of the plaintiffs sued G.M. in the United States District Court in Idaho and recovered, the court, as required by Idaho law, excluding all evidence that the plaintiff was not wearing a seat belt to prove contributory negligence. Subsequently, other plaintiffs sued G.M. in Arizona state court to recover for their injuries suffered in the accident. G.M. again raised the seat belt defense, invoking Arizona law which permitted the introduction of such evidence to prove contributory negligence, and the plaintiffs argued that the Idaho federal court's ruling on the seat belt defense should have a preclusive effect in the Arizona action. The Arizona Court of Appeals held that issue preclusion did not apply. One reason given by the court was that if it reached a contrary result, one plaintiff in a multiple plaintiff case could bring suit in the forum most likely to make a favorable conflict-of-laws ruling and the other plaintiffs could then use that ruling against the defendant in subsequent actions in different jurisdictions. The court ultimately held that Arizona law applied and though there would also be a special exception in the situation described which would prevent issue preclusion from operating in a nonmutual defensive fashion against *A* in the suit against *C Bank*,[189] it would not be necessary to reach that exception in the case.[190]

(viii) Undesirable Effects on Subsequent Proceedings

A court may also consider whether treating an issue as conclusively determined by a prior action might complicate the determination of issues in the subsequent proceeding or prejudice the interests of a party to the second action.[191] If so, issue preclusion should not be applied.

Illustration 13-53. A is injured in a fight with an employee on the employer's business premises. The employee is tried in a criminal proceeding for assaulting *A*. The employee's defense is self-defense. The employee is convicted. *A* then joins the employee and the employer in an action to recover damages for the injuries *A* received in the assault. In *A's* action, the issue of employee's liability may be relitigated by both the employee and the employer, if it appears that precluding the employee would prejudice the employer's defense. Little will be gained by way of judicial economy in foreclosing the issue against the employee. Much of the evidence that bears on the employee's liability will have to be introduced to determine the employer's liability.[192]

(ix) Other Compelling Circumstances

Finally, § 29(8) of the *Restatement (Second)* provides that issue preclusion should not apply if "other compelling circumstances" dictate that a party be able to relitigate an issue. Like the general exception to the rule of issue preclusion provided whenever a party has not had a full and fair opportunity to litigate,[193] this factor is subject to criticism on the ground that it could potentially undermine the entire doctrine of issue preclusion by encouraging litigation over the question of when "other compelling circumstances" are present.

---

permitted evidence of seat belt nonuse.

   189. *See id.* § 29(7), which would also prevent issue preclusion from operating in a successive action between different parties because it would inappropriately foreclose *A's* opportunity to obtain a reconsideration of the legal rules upon which the prior action was based.

   190. In addition, as noted in section C(2)*(b)*, in footnote accompanying *Illustration 13-34, supra*, preclusion on issues of law is also sometimes limited in successive suits between the government and private parties in order not to thwart the development of important issues of law by freezing them as they were decided in the first case to proceed to judgment. As observed there, the policy of nonpreclusion applies with even more vigor in cases in which nonmutual preclusion is involved. *See also* Note, *Nonmutual Issue Preclusion Against States,* 109 HARV. L. REV. 792 (1997).

   191. *See id.* § 29(6).

   192. *See id.* § 29(6) cmt. h, illus. 8; O'Connor v. O'Leary, 247 Cal. App. 2d 646, 56 Cal. Rptr. 1 (1967).

   193. *See* section C(2)*(f)* ("Injustice in Particular Cases") and accompanying discussion of RESTATEMENT (SECOND) OF JUDGMENTS § 28(5)(c) *supra; see also* Vandenberg v. Superior Court, 21 Cal. 4th 815, 982 P.2d 229, 88 Cal. Rptr. 366 (1999) (collateral estoppel will only apply when it comports with fairness and justice).

SECTION D. PARTIES BOUND BY JUDGMENTS

1. Preclusion of Nonparties

As noted in the previous subsection, res judicata rules ordinarily do not operate *against* nonparties.[194] Due process generally requires that a party have an opportunity to be heard on a claim or issue before being bound by a judgment. However, exceptions exist to this rule. Certain representational relationships as well as certain substantive relationships between parties and nonparties to an action may result in the nonparties being bound by the judgment. These relationships can produce both claim and issue preclusion effects in appropriate cases.

(a) Representational Relations Binding Nonparties

One kind of exception exists when a person's interests are represented by another in an action. For example, a nonparty may be bound by the judgment in a properly constituted class action.[195] Persons also are bound by the judgment in an action to a limited extent when, although they are not parties to the action, they control litigation brought by another or substantially participate in the control of a presentation made on their behalf. In this situation, nonparties are bound by the determination of the issues in the action they control, but not by the doctrine of claim preclusion. Although they have had a fair opportunity to litigate the issues by their control of the action, they, by definition, are not asserting a claim belonging to themselves in the action.[196]

Illustration 13-54. Assume that *A* sues *B* for personal injuries received in an automobile accident. *B's* insurer defends the action on *B's* behalf. In this situation, a judgment favorable to *A* will preclude *B's* insurer from relitigating the issues determined against *B* in a subsequent action in which the company is a

---

194. RESTATEMENT (SECOND) OF JUDGMENTS § 34(3) (1982). *But see* Robert G. Bone, *Rethinking the "Day in Court" Ideal and Nonparty Preclusion*, 67 N.Y.U. L. REV. 193 (1992) (arguing for a broader definition of "participation"; preclusion should vary with the type of case).

195. *See* Chapter 8(D)(4) ("Class Actions") *supra*; Annotation, *Res Judicata Effect of Judgment in Class Action upon Subsequent Action in Federal Court*, 48 A.L.R. FED. 675 (1980); *cf.* Becherer v. Merrill Lynch, Pierce, Fenner & Smith, 131 F.3d 580 (6th Cir. 1997) (holding members of plaintiff class who opted out of a settlement in a federal class action were not precluded from bringing a state-court action because they did not control the federal action, could not hold the plaintiffs in that action accountable for the result in the federal proceeding, and did not acquiesce to being represented in the federal action). Other similar examples include persons represented by a fiduciary, such as the trustee of an estate or an interest of which the persons are beneficiaries, or by an executor, administrator, guardian, or conservator. *See* RESTATEMENT (SECOND) OF JUDGMENTS § 41(1)(a), (c) (1982). Persons also may be bound by representation when they have given another the authority to represent them in an action. *See id.* § 41(1)(b). In addition, public officials or agencies are sometimes authorized to maintain or defend litigation on behalf of others who will be bound by the judgment in an action. In such cases, the authority of the official or agency may or may not preclude the represented individuals from enforcing their own interests. *See id.* § 41(1)(d) cmt. d; *see also* Fournier v. Illinois Cas. Co., 391 N.W.2d 258 (Iowa 1986) (administrator who sought to litigate defendant's obligations to her as administrator and individual in first action was bound by claim preclusion in second action brought in her individual capacity; discussing § 36).

196. *See* RESTATEMENT (SECOND) OF JUDGMENTS § 39 cmt. b (1982).

formal party. However, claim preclusion, even if otherwise appropriate, would not operate against the insurer.[197]

* * * * *

A person who agrees to be bound by the determination of issues in an action between others will be bound by the agreement.[198]

Illustration 13-55. On the facts of *Illustration 13-54*, *B's* insurer could agree to be bound by a judgment in an action against *B*, even when the insurer does not control the defense of that action.

* * * * *

A person who is a "nominal party" to an action also is bound by a judgment in most circumstances. Although an action must be brought in the name of the real party in interest and against the person from whom relief is sought, those parties may not be the persons who control the action. Nevertheless, the persons denominated as plaintiff or defendant usually will be bound by the judgment to the same extent as the persons who control the action, as long as they have put the person controlling the action in a position to denominate them as parties.[199] However, a person who lacks an interest in the action, even if denominated a party, will not be bound by the judgment if the opposing party knows of the nominal party's lack of interest.[200]

Illustration 13-56. Assume that an insurance company pays the loss of an insured party and becomes subrogated to the insured party's claim. The insurer may be permitted under the contract of insurance or the laws of a particular jurisdiction to bring suit on the claim in the name of the insured. In any such action, the insured will be bound by the judgment if the insured engages in conduct that would lead the opposing party to believe the insured owns the claim. This binding effect may result, for example, if the insured signs the complaint or participates in the action and gives no indication that the insured is not the owner of the claim.[201]

* * * * *

Numerous exceptions exist to the general rules of representation that are designed to ensure that a nonparty's interests will be adequately represented in an action before the nonparty is bound.[202]

---

197. *See id.* § 39 illus. 2.

198. *See id.* § 40.

199. *See id.* § 37 cmt. c, illus. 3.

200. *See id.* cmt. f, illus. 8.

201. *See id.* § 37 cmt. c, illus. 3.

202. These rules are summarized in § 42 of the *Restatement (Second) of Judgments*:

§ 42. Exceptions to the General Rule of Representation

(1) A person is not bound by a judgment for or against a party who purports to represent him if:

(a) Notice concerning the representation was required to be given to the represented person, or others who might act to protect his interest, and there was no substantial compliance with the requirement; or

(b) The subject matter of the action was not within the interests of the represented person that the party is responsible for protecting; or

(c) Before rendition of the judgment the party was divested of representative authority with respect to the matters as to which the judgment is subsequently invoked; or

(b) Substantive Relationships Binding Nonparties

A second category of cases in which a nonparty can be bound by a judgment in an action occurs when the applicable substantive law defines the nonparty's legal right in such a manner that a judgment for or against another person will conclude the nonparty's rights. These substantive relationships include (1) family; (2) contract; (3) property; (4) organizational affiliation; and (5) indemnitee and indemnitor.[203] Traditionally, when the substantive law regulates rights in a way that results in nonparties being bound by a judgment, it has been said that the nonparties were in "privity" with the parties in the action.[204] However, the reported decisions use the term "privity" to cover so many different situations that it has little descriptive value.[205] Therefore, in the discussion that follows, the term "privity" will be avoided.

(i) Family Relationships

An example of a situation in which family relationships will result in a judgment binding on a nonparty occurs when a person who is injured in an accident sues for injuries, and then dies from the injuries. A judgment in a personal injury action, whether favorable or unfavorable to the injured party, usually will prevent a wrongful death action by that person's beneficiaries after the injured party's death.[206]

(d) With respect to the representative of a class, there was such a substantial divergence of interest between him and the members of the class, or a group within the class, that he could not fairly represent them with respect to the matters as to which the judgment is subsequently invoked; or

(e) The representative failed to prosecute or defend the action with due diligence and reasonable prudence, and the opposing party was on notice of facts making that failure apparent.

(2) A person who has litigated on his own behalf in a previous action is not bound by or entitled to the benefits of a judgment in a subsequent action concerning the same claim that is brought or defended by a party representing him.

Id. § 42.

203. *See id.* §§ 43-61 (preclusion as a result of a legal relationship).

204. *See, e.g.,* State v. Hale, 978 P.2d 1276 (Alaska 1999) (no issue preclusion against person who was not a party to prior action or in privity with a party); Commercial Union Ins. Co. v. Pelchat, 727 A.2d 676 (R.I. 1999) (issue preclusion does not apply to a nonparty not in privity with a party to the prior action); State *ex rel.* Luedtke v. Bertrand, 226 Wis. 2d 271, 594 N.W.2d 370 (1999) (nonparties not in privity with party to prior action cannot be bound by the judgment).

205. *See* Becherer v. Merrill Lynch, Pierce, Fenner & Smith, Inc., 43 F.3d 1054, 1069-70 (6th Cir. 1995); Huelsman v. Kansas Dep't of Revenue, 267 Kan. 456, 980 P.2d 1022 (1999) (whether a party is in privity with another for purposes of issue preclusion is a question of policy); *see also* Ear, Nose & Throat Group, P.C. v. Stanescu, 46 Conn. Supp. 14, 734 A.2d 152 (Super. Ct. 1999) (when liability of party is derivative of or predicated upon the liability of a primary party, the parties share the same legal right and privity exists; thus, if the primary party is not held liable, the other party is not liable either).

206. *See id.* §§ 45-48 (legal relationships which result in preclusion in personal injury actions); Brown v. Rahman, 231 Cal. App. 3d 1458, 282 Cal. Rptr. 815 (1991) (heirs of decedent in privity with decedent; heirs bound by determination on issue of negligence in favor of defendant in prior action); *see also* Vitauts M. Gulbis, Annotation, *Judgment in Favor of, or Adverse to, Person Injured as Barring Action for His Death,* 26 A.L.R.4TH 1264 (1983); Wayne F. Foster, Annotation, *Judgment in Death Action as Precluding Subsequent Personal Injury Action by Potential Beneficiary of Death Action, or Vice Versa,* 94 A.L.R.3D 676 (1979); *cf.* Jonathan M. Purver, Annotation, *Judgment Against Parents in Action for Loss of Minor's Services as Precluding*

(ii) Contractual Relationships

An example of a situation in which a contractual relationship will result in preclusion against a nonparty occurs when contract rights are assigned. Prior to an assignment, the assignor can sue to enforce the contract. After the assignment, the assignee can sue to enforce the contract. A judgment in favor of or against either the assignor or assignee will usually bind the other party.[207]

(iii) Property Relationships

The classic example of a situation in which a property relationship will result in a judgment binding on a nonparty is when a judgment is rendered against an owner of property which is later transferred. In such circumstances, the judgment binds the successors in ownership to the same extent that it bound the original owner.[208]

Illustration 13-57. Suppose the owner of Blackacre sues the owner of Whiteacre to establish an easement over Whiteacre by virtue of a conveyance by the owner. The court enters judgment for the owner of Whiteacre on the ground that the conveyance did not give the owner of Blackacre an easement. The owner of Blackacre thereafter conveys Blackacre to a third party. The judgment precludes the third party from asserting an easement over Whiteacre on the same basis asserted in the prior litigation.[209]

(iv) Organizational Relationships

Membership in an organization can result in liability to a member of the organization who is not a party to an action. Such liability, however, varies with the characteristics of the organization and its treatment under applicable law. For example, a judgment against a corporation normally will not result in liability to a member of the corporation over and above the diminution in value of the member's share in the organization resulting from the judgment. However, such a judgment otherwise binds the members.[210]

Illustration 13-58. Suppose that *A Corp.* sues *B*, an officer of *A*, for allegedly breaching *B's* fiduciary duty to the corporation. The suit by the

---

Minor's Action for Personal Injuries, 41 A.L.R.3D 536 (1972); E.R. Tan, Annotation, *Judgment in Spouse's Action for Personal Injuries as Binding, as Regards Loss of Consortium and Similar Resulting Damage, Upon Other Spouse Not a Party to the Action*, 12 A.L.R.3D 933 (1967); E.H. Schopler, Annotation, *Judgment Involving Real Property Against One Spouse as Binding Against Other Spouse Not a Party to the Proceeding*, 58 A.L.R.2D 701 (1958); W.E. Shipley, Annotation, *Judgment in Personal Injury Action by One Spouse as Res Judicata Against or for Other Spouse, Where Cause of Action Was Community Property*, 6 A.L.R.2D 472 (1950).

207. *See* RESTATEMENT (SECOND) OF JUDGMENTS § 55 (1982). For another example of the operation of res judicata based on contractual relationships, see C.C. Bjorklund, Annotation, *Judgment in Action Against Seller or Supplier of Product as Res Judicata in Action Against Manufacturer for Injury from Defective Product, or Vice Versa*, 34 A.L.R.3D 518 (1970).

208. *See* RESTATEMENT (SECOND) OF JUDGMENTS §§ 43-44 (1982).

209. *See id.* § 43 illus. 2.

210. *See id.* § 59.

corporation will preclude a subsequent derivative action on the same claim by shareholders.[211]

* * * * *

There are exceptions to the rule against individual liability of corporate members.

Illustration 13-59. Under certain circumstances involving closely held corporations—ones owned by one or a few persons—shareholders can sometimes be held individually liable for the corporation's obligations.[212]

* * * * *

At common law, partnerships were treated as aggregations of individuals rather than entities. The result was that partners were treated as joint obligors and obligees in contract cases, and they all had to join or be joined in contract suits. Similarly, they were regarded as co-owners of partnership property who had to join or be joined in actions concerning the property. However, in tort actions, they were regarded as jointly and severally liable, so that one could be sued without joining the other.[213]

These common-law rules have been reshaped to a large extent by statute. As a result, the effect of a judgment on partners who are nonparties varies considerably. If the applicable rules require all partners to join or be joined in an action, the action, of course, will result in a judgment binding on all of them individually. If the applicable rules allow one partner to sue or defend on behalf of all, the judgment will be binding on the absent partners to the extent of the partnership property, but no further, though the judgment may have evidentiary effect in a subsequent proceeding to establish the partners' individual liability.[214]

When the organization involved is an unincorporated association, the effect of a judgment will depend upon whether the association is given entity treatment by the applicable law. At common law, associations were not treated as entities, with the result that treatment of associations was substantially like that of partnerships, with one important exception. Partners were regarded as agents for other partners, but association members generally had to ratify the acts of other members for individual liability to result. Today, associations often are treated as entities. Thus, a judgment for or against the association has the same effect as a judgment for or against a corporation.[215]

If the association is not given entity treatment, a judgment in an action brought on behalf of the association by representative members will be binding on the members in accord with the rules of representation previously discussed. In suits against the association defended by representatives of the association, liability depends on the kind of suit involved. In property and contract cases, the

---

211. *See id.* § 59(2); Huck *ex rel.* Sea Air Shuttle Corp. v. Dawson, 106 F.3d 45 (3d Cir. 1997) (if corporation brings an action for injunctive relief and loses, a shareholder cannot bring an action for damages based on the same activity, but which accrued after the first action terminated).

212. *See* RESTATEMENT (SECOND) OF JUDGMENTS § 59(3) (1982).

213. *See id.* § 60 cmt. a.

214. *See id.; see also* E.H. Schopler, Annotation, *Judgment for or Against Partner as Res Judicata in Favor of or Against Copartner Not a Party to the Judgment,* 11 A.L.R.2D 847 (1950).

215. *See* RESTATEMENT (SECOND) OF JUDGMENTS § 61(2) (1982).

underlying transaction upon which the action is based virtually always will have been ratified expressly or impliedly by the members, with corresponding individual member liability being the result. In tort cases, however, specific prior authorization of the tort is less likely, and subsequent ratification will require proof that each individual member participated in the wrongful act or approved the act later. Practically speaking, each member of the association to be held liable must be shown to have participated in the tort or to have approved of it for liability to attach, though this may be demonstrated in a suit brought against the association by naming a representative as a defendant. Furthermore, a judgment in favor of the injured party may not be enforced against association property unless all members are found liable. Because this situation is highly unlikely in a tort case, association property will be subject to the judgment only if the interests of liable members can be severed from those of nonliable members. Thus, enforcing a judgment against the association property is difficult or impossible.[216]

(v) Indemnitee-Indemnitor Relationships

Finally, the relationship of indemnitor and indemnitee can result in a judgment binding on a nonparty. Assume that a person or entity such as an insurance company (the indemnitor) is obligated to indemnify another (the indemnitee) for the liability of the indemnitee to an injured party. If the injured party sues the indemnitee, the indemnitee can notify the indemnitor of the pendency of the action and call upon the indemnitor to defend the action. If the indemnitor does so, the indemnitor will be bound under the rule, discussed above, that parties who control an action are bound by the judgment in the action. However, even if the indemnitor does not defend the action, the indemnitor can be precluded from relitigating the issue of the indemnitee's liability to the injured person, though the indemnitor still may contest the obligation to indemnify.[217]

(c) Transformational Effects

One additional effect that a judgment may have on nonparties should be mentioned–what Professors James, Hazard, and Leubsdorf call the ''trans-

---

216. *See id.* cmt. a. For a discussion of the liability of members of an unincorporated association for torts committed by another member against a nonmember, see Ian Davis, *Membership Has Its Privileges: Court Sets Forth the Liability of Individual Members of Unincorporated Associations for Torts Against Third Parties*: Juhl v. Arington, 39 TEX. SUP. CT. J. 830 (June 28, 1996), 28 TEX. TECH. L. REV. 103 (1996).

217. The rules governing preclusion between the indemnitor and indemnitee are somewhat more complex than this simple statement indicates. The full scope of the rules is discussed in the RESTATEMENT (SECOND) OF JUDGMENTS §§ 57-58 (1982). For a complete description and discussion of the rules governing the binding effect of judgments on nonparties, *see id.* §§ 43-63; *see also* E.H. Schopler, Annotation, *Judgment Obtained by Third Person Against Indemnitee as Conclusive Against the Latter, Irrespective of Its Conclusiveness Against Indemnitor, In Indemnitee's Action Against Indemnitor for Amount Paid in Satisfaction of Judgment,* 24 A.L.R.2D 329 (1952).

formational'' effect of a judgment.[218] A judgment can transform relationships in ways that nonparties will be unable to contest.

Illustration 13-60. When a couple is validly divorced, nonparties ordinarily may not dispute the couple's marital status. This result is not derived from the operation of res judicata. Instead, the result reflects the change in the parties' relationship produced by the judgment.[219]

2. Preclusion Between Coparties

Traditionally, the rules of res judicata have applied only to determinations between persons in an adversary relationship.[220] The reason for this limitation is that, normally, only parties aligned on opposite sides of the litigation will have a full and fair opportunity to litigate matters determined in the action. Sometimes, however, coparties may find themselves in an adversary relationship on some issues while remaining aligned against a third party on other issues. This situation always occurs when there are cross-claims, third-party claims, or interpleader claims in the action;[221] but even when no such claims are present, coparties can find themselves in an adversary position.

Illustration 13-61. When a plaintiff sues two defendants in the alternative, each defendant may defend in part by pointing the finger at the other as the sole party responsible to the plaintiff. When such adversary relations arise, coparties have a sufficient opportunity and incentive to litigate the issues between them to bring into play the doctrine of issue preclusion.[222]

SECTION E. CLAIM AND ISSUE PRECLUSION ON QUESTIONS OF SUBJECT-MATTER AND PERSONAL JURISDICTION

As observed in section A, the rules of claim and issue preclusion only operate when a valid judgment—one rendered by a court with subject-matter and personal jurisdiction—has been rendered. However, under certain circumstances, discussed below, a question of subject-matter or personal jurisdiction can be foreclosed by the judgment in a prior action.

Illustration 13-62. Assume that *A*, a citizen of State *X*, sues *B*, a citizen of State *Y*, in a state court of State *X*. If *B* perceives a deficiency in the State *X* court's personal or subject-matter jurisdiction, *B* ordinarily has two options. *B* may refuse to appear and defend the action, in which case a default judgment will

---

218. *See* FLEMING JAMES, JR. ET AL., CIVIL PROCEDURE § 11.24, at 618-19 (4th ed. 1992).

219. *See id.* at 619.

220. *See* RESTATEMENT (SECOND) OF JUDGMENTS § 38 cmt. a (1982).

221. *See* Fowler v. Vineyard, 261 Ga. 454, 405 S.E.2d 678 (1991).

222. *See* RESTATEMENT (SECOND) OF JUDGMENTS § 38 cmt. a (1982). *See generally* V. Woerner, Annotation, *Judgment in Action Against Codefendants for Injury or Death of Person, or for Damage to Property, as Res Judicata in Subsequent Action Between Codefendants as to Their Liability Inter Se*, 24 A.L.R.3D 318 (1969).

be entered against *B*. In the typical course of events, *A* then will attempt to enforce the judgment against *B* in State *Y*, where *B* lives and owns assets that may be used to satisfy the judgment. Traditionally, *A* would have had to enforce the judgment by bringing an independent action on the judgment in a court of State *Y*.[223] When *A* brought this action, *B* would defend on the ground that the judgment was invalid because the judgment was rendered by a court without subject-matter or personal jurisdiction.[224]

* * * * *

However, the procedure described in *Illustration 13-62* entails substantial risks. If *B* is wrong about the jurisdictional objection, *B's* defense in State *Y* will fail. *B* will then be foreclosed from litigating the merits of *A's* claim against *B*. In other words, if *B's* jurisdictional objection is incorrect, the State *X* court will have entered a valid judgment against *B*. *B* will be precluded by res judicata from presenting defenses on the merits that *B* possessed against *A's* claim.[225] Therefore, if *B* has any doubt at all about the validity of the jurisdictional objection, and if *B* also possesses a potentially valid defense on the merits, *B* will not wish to default in the State *X* action.[226]

As noted in Chapter 3, every state now possesses a procedure that will allow *B* to raise jurisdictional objections without submitting to the jurisdiction of the State *X* court.[227] The procedures are either "special appearance" procedures, in which *B* appears only for the purposes of litigating the jurisdictional issue, or a motion procedure such as that described in Federal Rule 12, which accomplishes the same result. Thus, if in *Illustration 13-62,* above, *B* wishes to object to the jurisdiction of the State *X* court over *B*, *B* may employ one of these procedures to do so. If *B* does so and loses, however, the rules of issue preclusion will prevent *B* from relitigating the jurisdictional question in a subsequent proceeding to enforce the judgment against *B* in State *Y*.

Thus, if *B* specially appears in the State *X* proceeding, objects to the court's personal jurisdiction, and wins, *B* has no problems. The action will be dismissed and *A* will have to sue *B* in a court with proper personal jurisdiction, such as a State *Y* court. If *B* loses, however, *B* must pursue whatever avenues State *X* provides for reversing the court's determination. For example, *B* may not lose on the jurisdictional objection at the trial level and then default in the expectation that *B* may relitigate the issue of jurisdiction in a later enforcement

---

223. However, forty-eight jurisdictions have adopted the Uniform Enforcement of Foreign Judgments Act, which provides a more streamlined procedure for enforcing judgments than the traditional common-law procedure. *See* UNIFORM ENFORCEMENT OF FOREIGN JUDGMENTS ACT (1964), 13 U.L.A. 16 (Supp. 1999).

224. *See id.* §§ 1, 81.

225. *See id.* § 18(2).

226. In Dennis M. Garberg & Associates, Inc. v. Pack-Tech International Corp., 115 F.3d 767 (10th Cir. 1997), the court held that a district court should not enter a default judgment without first determining that it has personal jurisdiction. This holding may afford additional protection to nonresident defendants, but it should not be held to preclude relitigation of the jurisdictional question in a subsequent action to enforce the judgment. Under the ordinary rules of issue preclusion, the court's determination would not be binding because there has been no actual litigation of the issue. *See* section C(1)(*b*) *supra* (discussing the actual litigation requirement). Given the tradition under which subject-matter jurisdiction issues must be raised on a court's own motion while personal jurisdiction issues are not raised by the court, the decision seems questionable in any event.

227. *See* Chapter 3(B)(3) ("In Personam Jurisdiction: Consent, Appearance, and Waiver") *supra*.

proceeding in State *Y*. If State *X* requires *B*, after losing on the jurisdictional objection, to litigate the merits of the action and then appeal on the jurisdictional issue (as well as any other errors *B* claims have been committed) after a final judgment has been rendered against *B*, that is what *B* must do. If *B* loses after both trial and appeal, *B* may attempt to obtain direct review of any federal constitutional question concerning the State *X* court's personal jurisdiction in the U.S. Supreme Court. If none of these avenues of relief succeeds, the judgment will bind *B*.[228]

The same result will occur if *B* actually litigates an issue of the State *X* court's subject-matter jurisdiction: issue preclusion will prevent *B* from relitigating the issue in a subsequent proceeding in State *Y*.[229] In addition, even if *B* litigates the merits of the State *X* action without raising a question of the court's subject-matter jurisdiction, *B* ordinarily will be precluded from raising subject-matter jurisdiction by way of collateral attack on the judgment. This result would obviously occur with regard to a personal jurisdiction objection because personal jurisdiction objections not raised in a timely fashion are waived.[230]

It might be thought that the rule on subject-matter jurisdiction should be different because subject-matter jurisdiction objections cannot be waived.[231] However, the rule that subject-matter jurisdiction objections cannot be waived is a rule that applies only to direct attacks on judgments. When a subject-matter jurisdiction objection exists but is not raised in a contested action, the objection is normally foreclosed from litigation on collateral attack by claim preclusion rules. Because subject-matter jurisdiction is ordinarily treated so seriously by the courts, however, some exceptions to this rule exist. Section 12 of the *Restatement (Second) of Judgments* describes these exceptions:

> When a court has rendered a judgment in a contested action, the judgment precludes the parties from litigating the question of the court's subject matter jurisdiction in subsequent litigation except if:
>
> (1) The subject matter of the action was so plainly beyond the court's jurisdiction that its entertaining the action was a manifest abuse of authority; or
>
> (2) Allowing the judgment to stand would substantially infringe the authority of another tribunal or agency of government; or

---

228. *See, e.g.,* Wall v. Stinson, 983 P.2d 736 (Alaska 1999) (Oregon judgment cannot be collaterally attached in Alaska for lack of personal jurisdiction where defendant had vigorously litigated personal jurisdiction issue in Oregon and lost); Williams v. Williams, 997 S.W.2d 80 (Mo. Ct. App. 1999) (burden is on party challenging sister-state judgment to show it is not entitled to full faith and credit; finding by Oklahoma court that it had personal jurisdiction is binding when defendant litigated the issue in Oklahoma and did not show that the opportunity to litigate was inadequate). *But cf.* St. Clair & Assocs. v. Northwest Carpets, Inc., 237 Ga. App. 537, 515 S.E.2d 660 (1999) (no presumption of jurisdiction when a foreign judgment is rendered by default and party seeking to domesticate the judgment bears the burden of negating the defense of lack of jurisdiction).

229. *See* RESTATEMENT (SECOND) OF JUDGMENTS § 12 cmt. c (1982).

230. *See* Chapter 6(D)(3)*(g)(ii)* ("Waiver") *supra; see also* Chapter 3(B)(3) ("In Personam Jurisdiction: Consent, Appearance, and Waiver") *supra.*

231. *See* Chapter 2(A)(2) ("The 'No-Waiver, No-Consent' Rule") *supra* for a discussion of the rule that subject-matter jurisdiction objections cannot ordinarily be waived.

(3) The judgment was rendered by a court lacking capability to make an adequately informed determination of a question concerning its own jurisdiction and as a matter of procedural fairness the party seeking to avoid the judgment should have opportunity belatedly to attack the court's subject-matter jurisdiction.[232]

These rules are the normal rules which govern collateral attack on grounds of lack of subject-matter or personal jurisdiction. There can be variation in the rules because of the combined effect of differences in local practice and 28 U.S.C. § 1738, which requires the courts of one state to give the same effect to judgments of other states that the judgments would be given in the states that rendered them.[233]

Illustration 13-63. If State X provides by its own domestic rules that subject-matter jurisdiction objections litigated and determined against a party can also be raised in subsequent proceedings in the courts of State X, then the objections can also be raised on collateral attack in a subsequent proceeding in State Y. Of course, State X would not be allowed to prescribe rules beyond its domestic competence. Thus, State X could not make default judgments immune from collateral attack in cases beyond its power under the U.S. Constitution. The State Y court would be entitled and, indeed, required to disregard such a rule and permit collateral attack. As to matters within the domestic competence of a state that are not limited by the Constitution, however, the rules can be varied.

* * * * *

In addition, the ordinary rules of issue preclusion apply to questions of personal and subject-matter jurisdiction in the same way that they apply to "substantive" issues. Thus, the rules requiring a determination to support the judgment, and so forth, all apply to questions of personal and subject-matter jurisdiction.

Illustration 13-64. A, a citizen of State X, sues B, a citizen of State Y, in a state court in State X. B specially appears in accord with State X procedure to object to the State X court's personal jurisdiction under the Due Process Clause of the Fourteenth Amendment and its subject-matter jurisdiction under State X law. The State X court holds that it has personal jurisdiction, but that it lacks subject-matter jurisdiction and dismisses the action. Subsequently, A sues B in a State X court of proper subject-matter jurisdiction. B specially appears and objects to personal jurisdiction. B is not precluded from relitigating the issue of personal jurisdiction by the judgment in the first action. The determination in that action that the court had personal jurisdiction over B did not support the judgment of dismissal in B's favor.[234]

---

232. RESTATEMENT (SECOND) OF JUDGMENTS § 12 (1982); *see also* E.H. Schopler, Annotation, *Comment Note.–Fraud as Defense to Action on Judgment of Sister State*, 55 A.L.R.2D 673 (1957).

233. *Cf. id.* §§ 70, 82. Other complications in the enforcement of judgments produced by the federal system are discussed in section F *infra*.

234. *See* section C(1)*(d)*, *Illustration 13-28 supra*.

SECTION F. COMPLICATIONS PRODUCED BY THE FEDERAL SYSTEM

In addition to the subject-matter and personal jurisdiction complications discussed in the preceding section, other problems exist because of (1) the existence of different rules among the fifty states defining the scope and effect of judgments, (2) different rules defining the scope and effect of federal and state-court judgments, and (3) differing approaches to the effect that should be given to the judgments of foreign nations. Each of these problems will be discussed in turn.

1. Enforcement of State Judgments

As noted in section E, above, and in Chapter 3, the U.S. Supreme Court's interpretation of 28 U.S.C. § 1738 requires the courts of each state to give the same effect to the valid judgments of other states as those judgments would receive in the state that rendered the judgments. The Full Faith and Credit Clause of the Constitution provides Congress with the authority to enact this statute: "Full faith and credit shall be given in each state to the public acts, records and judicial proceedings of every other state. And the Congress may by general laws prescribe the manner in which such acts, records and proceedings shall be proved, and the effect thereof."[235] The power to prescribe the effect that the judicial proceedings of one state should have in all others sustains the requirement in 28 U.S.C. § 1738 that the judgments of each state be given the same effect in the courts of other states as those judgments have in the states that render them.[236] In addition to prescribing the effect that state judgments must receive in the courts of other states, 28 U.S.C. § 1738 prescribes that federal courts shall give the same effect to state-court judgments as those judgments would receive in the state where they were rendered.[237]

Section 1738 does not absolutely require that state and federal courts employ the same enforcement mechanisms that would be employed by the courts of the state that rendered a judgment. In *Baker v. General Motors Corp.,*[238] the U.S. Supreme Court placed limits on the obligation of the states to enforce judgments of other states that would interfere with the operation of judicial proceedings in the judgment-enforcing state. In *Baker,* a Michigan court granted an injunction prohibiting a General Motors employee from testifying against G.M. as an expert witness. Subsequently, G.M. was sued by another party in a Missouri

---

235. *U.S. Const.* art. IV, § 1.

236. *See* Chapter 3(A)(1) ("Personal Jurisdiction Restrictions Prior to the Adoption of the Fourteenth Amendment") *supra*.

237. The statute actually states: "Such . . . judicial proceedings . . . shall have the same full faith and credit in every court within the United States and its Territories and Possessions as they have by law or usage in the courts of such State, Territory or Possession from which they are taken." 28 U.S.C. § 1738. *See generally* David H. Bothe, Annotation, *Supreme Court's Views as to Res Judicata or Collateral Estoppel Effect of State Court Judgments on Federal Courts,* 72 L. Ed. 2d 911 (1983).

238. 522 U.S. 222, 118 S. Ct. 657, 139 L. Ed. 2d 580 (1998).

federal court in a wrongful death and products liability action, and the plaintiff sought to depose the employee and use him as a witness. G.M. resisted the employee's appearance on the basis of the Michigan injunction, but the federal district court allowed the employee to testify. Reversing the district court, the Eighth Circuit held that the Missouri court was obligated to give effect to the Michigan injunction. The U.S. Supreme Court reversed the Eighth Circuit and held that Michigan had no power to control courts and parties in other states by precluding them from determining which witnesses may testify.

The *Baker* holding appears to be a narrow one and does not create a broad exception to the general obligation of the states to give the same effect to judgments that the judgments would receive in the state that rendered them. The Court emphasized that it was not creating a "general exception to the full faith and credit command" and that its holding "surely does not permit a State court to refuse to honor a sister state judgment based on the forum's choice of law or policy preferences."[239] Rather, the Court's decision was based on "two critical counter principles to the near-automatic recognition of judgments."[240] The first was that the states need not "adopt the practices of other States regarding the time, manner, and mechanisms for enforcing judgments."[241] The second was that "[o]rders commanding action or inaction have been denied enforcement in a sister State when they purported to accomplish an official act within the exclusive province of that other State or interfered with litigation over which the ordering State had no authority."[242] Indeed, G.M. may simply have mistaken its remedy in the case. The Court itself recognized that the Michigan decree could operate against the employee to preclude him from volunteering his testimony.[243] Thus, G.M. might have sued the employee in a separate proceeding in Missouri to enforce the injunction against him.[244] In addition, it seems clear that G.M. could have enforced the injunction in Michigan by seeking a contempt citation against the employee there.[245]

Apart from the *Baker* "exception" to § 1738, the statute appears to operate more or less absolutely. Nevertheless, several important issues have arisen in recent years concerning the application of § 1738 between different state courts and between state and federal courts. First, does § 1738 *ever* permit a state or federal court to give *less* effect to a state-court judgment than would be given to the judgment by the courts of the judgment-rendering state? Second, does § 1738 permit a state or federal court to give *more* effect to a state-court judgment than the judgment would be given by the judgment-rendering state? Third, does § 1738 require that federal (or state) courts give the same effect to a state-court judgment

---

239. *Id.* at 239, 118 S. Ct. at 667, 139 L. Ed. 2d at 596.
240. Patrick J. Borchers, *Conflict of Laws,* 49 SYRACUSE L. REV. 333, 336 (1999).
241. *Baker*, 522 U.S. at 235, 118 S. Ct. at 665, 139 L. Ed. 2d at 593.
242. *Id.*, 118 S. Ct. at 665, 139 L. Ed. 2d at 593.
243. *See Id.* at 239, 118 S. Ct. at 667, 139 L. Ed. 2d at 595.
244. The Court itself indicated that it had "never placed equity decrees outside the full faith and credit domain." *Baker*, 522 U.S. at 234, 118 S. Ct. at 664, 139 L. Ed. 2d at 593. Coupled with its statement that the Michigan decree would have a preclusive effect against the employee, it appears that it could be enforced against the employee in Missouri.
245. *See* Patrick J. Borchers, *Conflict of Laws,* 49 SYRACUSE L. REV. 333, 337 (1999).

as the judgment would be given by the judgment-rendering state when the judgment determines federal issues?

(a) Giving Less Effect to State Judgments

As interpreted by the U.S. Supreme Court,[246] § 1738 appears to be relatively absolute in its operation. Every state and federal court must give the same effect to judgments of other state courts rendered with jurisdiction as those judgments would receive in the state where they were rendered. Thus, it appears that no *less* effect can ever be given to a state judgment than would be given to the judgment by the court that rendered the judgment. Nevertheless, commentators have expressed doubt whether the statute compels such a result.

> Collectively, [the] cases make it clear that full faith and credit embraces the central doctrines of res judicata. No other result could be tolerated in a federalistic society as mobile and litigious as ours. None of [the] decisions, however, compels the conclusion that full faith and credit incorporates every minute detail of res judicata doctrine. They simply do not address the compelling arguments that can be made for limiting full faith and credit to the rules that support the core values of finality, repose, and reliance, as well as some of the rules that facilitate control by the first court over its own procedure. . . . The essential point is that some aspects of modern preclusion doctrine should fall outside full faith and credit both because they are incidental to the central role of res judicata and because they may intrude on substantial interests of later courts.[247]

When should the policies implicit in § 1738 give way to the interests of "later courts"? Consider the following illustration, which will help indicate the kinds of considerations that might operate to allow a court to give less effect to a state judgment than would be given to it in the judgment-rendering state.

Illustration 13-65. Suppose an airliner operated by *A Airways* crashes in State *X*. *A* is incorporated and has its principal place of business in State *X*. The survivors of one of the deceased passengers, who had resided in State *Y*, bring a wrongful death action in State *Y*. *A* is validly served with process by service on a managing agent in State *Y*, where the airline does a large amount of business.

---

246. *See* Mills v. Duryee, 11 U.S. (7 Cranch) 481, 3 L. Ed. 411 (1813); D'Arcy v. Ketchum, 52 U.S. (11 How.) 165, 13 L. Ed. 648 (1851). These cases are discussed in Chapter 3(A)(1)*(d)* ("The 1790 Implementing Statute") *supra. See also, e.g.,* Holzemer v. Urbanski, 86 Ohio St. 3d 129, 712 N.E.2d 713 (1999) (Ohio courts obligated to give same res judicata effect to probate proceeding in Michigan as that proceeding would have in Michigan). *But cf.* Sheldon R. Sharior, Annotation, *Res Judicata or Collateral Estoppel Effect, in State Where Real Property Is Located, of Foreign Decree Dealing with Such Property*, 32 A.L.R.3D 1330 (1970). Even if § 1738 requires that exactly the same effect be given to state judgments as they would receive in the states that rendered them, the judgment-enforcing state can still enact its own statute prescribing the procedures that must be used in authenticating and enforcing foreign judgments as long as the statute does not detract from the command of § 1738. *See, e.g.,* Conglis v. Radcliffe, 119 N.M. 287, 889 P.2d 1209 (1995).

247. 18 Charles A. Wright et al., Federal Practice and Procedure: Jurisdiction and Related Matters § 4467, at 636 (1981).

The action results in a verdict and judgment for the plaintiff for a substantial amount based on *A's* negligence. Under the rules of issue preclusion in State *Y*, the mutuality rule has been abolished. Thus, the judgment in the action described could be used to establish *A's* negligence in all subsequent actions by the survivors of deceased passengers in State *Y's* courts. Suppose, however, that a second wrongful death action is brought in State *X*, rather than State *Y*. Suppose further that State *X* has retained the mutuality rule in mass accident cases for the express purpose of protecting defendants with close connections to State *X* from ruinous liability based on a single judgment. The plaintiff in the State *X* action seeks to use the State *Y* judgment to establish the negligence of *A*. Does § 1738 compel State *X* to abandon its adherence to the mutuality rule and give the same nonmutual estoppel effect to the State *Y* judgment that it would receive in State *Y*? The answer ought to be "no." State *Y's* abandonment of mutuality is based upon its view that procedural efficiency and fairness will be best preserved, and litigation costs diminished, by nonmutual estoppel. These policies will be preserved substantially if State *Y* is able to enforce its rules of nonmutual preclusion in its own court system. Moreover, to require State *X* to apply nonmutual preclusion in its courts would be to force State *X* to give up a substantively based procedural rule designed to protect defendants with whom State *X* has a close connection in order to enforce a procedural rule of another state designed primarily to achieve litigational efficiency in that other state's courts. Based on the policies embodied in § 1738, State *X* should not be required to give the same effect to the State Y judgment that the judgment would receive in State *Y*.

* * * * *

As interpreted by the Supreme Court, § 1738 seems directed toward achieving nationwide finality and repose in dispute resolution by insisting that most res judicata questions be resolved by reference to the judgment-rendering state's law.[248] However, some state policies are remote from the core concerns of finality and repose that are embodied in the statute.[249] Consequently, when (1) it is possible to see, as in *Illustration 13-64*, that the judgment-rendering state's res judicata rules are based on narrow procedural policies applicable primarily or exclusively to litigation in the state's own courts and (2) these policies are opposed by important substantive concerns of the state where the second action is brought, § 1738 should not be read to require the second state to enforce the res judicata rules of the judgment-rendering state.

---

248. *See id.* at 637.

249. *See id.*

> It is even possible to argue that some preclusion rules are really not attributes of the judgment, or "judicial proceeding," at all. Instead, they are matters of local procedural law that other courts are free to reject in the sweeping freedom that exists in choosing domestic over foreign law outside the realm of judgments.

Id.; *see also* Paul D. Carrington, *Collateral Estoppel and Foreign Judgments*, 24 OHIO ST. L.J. 381 (1963).

(b) Giving More Effect to State Judgments

Superficially, it may appear that if § 1738 *sometimes* permits the courts of a state to give less effect to judgments of other states than the judgments would receive where rendered, the statute should *always* permit a court to give *more* effect to a judgment than would be given in the judgment-rendering state. There is support for such a reading of the statute.[250] However, the wisdom of such a result is questionable.

Illustration 13-66. Assume again the basic facts of *Illustration 13-65* concerning an airline crash in State X and an initial action in State Y. Suppose, however, that State Y adheres to the mutuality rule for no good reason other than inertia, so far as it is possible to tell. Suppose further that State X has abandoned mutuality in all cases, even in mass accident cases. If a judgment is entered in favor of the plaintiff in the State Y action and a subsequent suit based on the same event is brought against the defendant by a different plaintiff in State X, should State X give nonmutual preclusive effect to the State Y judgment even though State Y would not do so? Section 1738 does not *require* State X to give more effect to State Y judgments than would State Y.[251] Moreover, it probably would be unwise for State X to do so. For one thing, the defendant may have relied on the judgment-rendering state's rule in either choosing to litigate rather than settle (because of the limited risks in other litigation that the mutuality rule of State Y afforded), or in litigating less vigorously than it would otherwise have done if nonmutual preclusion had been in effect. Even an examination of the first proceeding under the "full and fair opportunity to litigate" test of the *Restatement (Second) of Judgments* might not reveal the extent of the defendant's reliance after the fact.[252] Consequently, even in a case such as the one posed, when the judgment-rendering state retains the mutuality rule out of inertia, it seems that the policy of nationwide security of judgments supporting § 1738 is implicated sufficiently to require adherence to the judgment-rendering state's rule.[253]

* * * * *

The U.S. Supreme Court has not resolved the question whether a state can *ever* give greater effect to another state's judgments than would be given by the

---

250. *See, e.g.*, Hart v. American Airlines, Inc., 61 Misc. 2d 41, 304 N.Y.S.2d 810 (Sup. Ct. 1969).

251. *See, e.g.*, People *ex rel.* Halvey v. Halvey, 330 U.S. 610, 67 S. Ct. 903, 91 L. Ed. 1133 (1947); Meenach v. General Motors Corp., 891 S.W.2d 398 (Ky. 1995).

252. *Cf.* 18 CHARLES A. WRIGHT ET AL., FEDERAL PRACTICE AND PROCEDURE: JURISDICTION AND RELATED MATTERS § 4467, at 648 (1981). In addition,

> [a]ssertion of nonmutual preclusion in such circumstances would make it impossible for the first court to give effect to policies that may include broad freedom in selecting parties, freedom to litigate a particular case according to its own needs without concern about the impact on other cases, and acceptance of results that seem just between particular parties even though a new trial or directed verdict would be required if the stakes were greater.

Id. § 4465, at 617.

253. The case, of course, would be made much stronger for this result if the judgment-rendering state retained the mutuality rule for substantive policy reasons, such as to protect defendants in whom the state has a legitimate interest from massive liability proceeding from a single judgment.

judgment-rendering state. However, the Court has concluded that in subsequent federal antitrust and civil rights actions, the federal courts may not generally give a greater claim preclusion effect to a state judgment than would be given to the judgment by a state court.[254] These cases support a general interpretation of § 1738 that would forbid a greater effect from ever being given to a judgment than would be given the judgment in the judgment-rendering state.

(c) Giving Effect to State Judgments in Cases Applying Another State's Law or Federal Law

(i) Another State's Law

Section 1738 on its face does not provide for different effects to be given to state judgments depending upon the source of law being employed by the judgment-rendering court. Furthermore, it would be unwise to interpret § 1738 as permitting an exception to the ''same effect'' rule *merely* because the judgment-rendering state applied (or tried to apply) the substantive law of the judgment-enforcing state. Only when the judgment-rendering state's res judicata rules are based on procedural policies applicable exclusively in the courts of the judgment-rendering state, as in *Illustration 13-65*, should an exception be allowed.

Illustration 13-67. It does not matter that an Iowa court is applying (or attempting to apply) Mississippi law when it renders a judgment, nor that Mississippi's highest court would find that the Iowa court erred in determining the content of Mississippi law. The Iowa court's judgment must be given the same effect in Mississippi and all other states as it would be given in Iowa.[255]

(ii) Federal Law

Section 1738 does not provide for any exceptions for cases in which the state courts apply federal law in rendering a judgment. Nevertheless, questions exist in two areas about the extent to which state judgments should be given preclusive effect in subsequent federal actions. One area involves cases in which the first action is adjudicated in a state court and a second action is brought in federal court under a grant of exclusive jurisdiction to the federal courts. The basic question is whether a limited claim or issue preclusion effect should be given to the state judgment because of the policies underlying the grant of exclusive jurisdiction to the federal courts. The second area involves cases in which the first adjudication in the state courts is followed by a second proceeding in federal court under a federal civil rights act, such as 42 U.S.C. § 1983. The question here is whether the policies supporting the various civil rights acts demand that a limited claim or issue preclusion effect be given to the state judgment.

---

254. *See* Marrese v. American Academy of Orthopaedic Surgeons, 470 U.S. 373, 105 S. Ct. 1327, 84 L. Ed. 2d 274 (1985); *cf.* Migra v. Warren City Sch. Dist. Bd. of Educ., 465 U.S. 75, 104 S. Ct. 892, 79 L. Ed. 2d 56 (1984).

255. *See* Fauntleroy v. Lum, 210 U.S. 230, 28 S. Ct. 641, 52 L. Ed. 1039 (1908).

Section 26(1)(c) of the *Restatement (Second) of Judgments* takes the position that if a plaintiff brings a state claim in state court and subsequently sues on a federal claim in federal court over which the federal courts would have exclusive jurisdiction, there would be no claim-preclusion effect, even if the state and federal claims arose out of the same facts.

Illustration 13-68. Suppose that *A* commences an action in state court under the state antitrust laws and loses on the merits. *A* then commences an action in federal court against the same defendant under the federal antitrust laws, an action over which the federal courts have exclusive jurisdiction. Under the approach of the *Restatement (Second)*, even though both the state and federal actions are based on the same events, *A's* federal action is not precluded. The reason is simply that the state court had no subject-matter jurisdiction over the federal antitrust claim. Consequently, the *Restatement (Second)* provides that claim preclusion does not operate in this situation.[256]

* * * * *

In two decisions, the U.S. Supreme Court has cast substantial doubt about whether § 1738 will be interpreted in accord with the *Restatement (Second)'s* position. In *Marrese v. American Academy of Orthopaedic Surgeons,*[257] the Court held that the first inquiry in a case involving a state judgment must be whether state claim preclusion principles would prohibit a second action. Only if state law does prohibit a second action is it necessary to determine whether an exception should be created to § 1738 because a federal claim omitted from the state action was within the exclusive jurisdiction of the federal courts.[258] The Court also stated that once the question of an exception under § 1738 is presented, its answer depends ''on the particular federal statute as well as the nature of the claim or issue involved in the subsequent federal action. Our previous decisions indicate that the primary consideration must be the intent of Congress.''[259]

Subsequently, in *Matsushita Electric Industrial Co. v. Epstein,*[260] the Court was faced with a situation in which a state class action was brought in Delaware asserting state claims arising out of a tender offer made by Matsushita for the common stock of a Delaware Corporation. While the state action was pending, a federal class action was commenced in California under the federal securities laws based on the same facts, an action over which the federal courts had exclusive jurisdiction. The California district court refused to certify the action as a class action and dismissed the case. After the federal plaintiffs had appealed, the state class action in Delaware was settled. As part of the settlement, the class agreed to release all claims arising out of the tender offer, including the federal claims that were being asserted in the California action. Although the class members were given notice of the proposed settlement, they did not opt out of the class or object to the settlement in Delaware. After the settlement, Matsushita

---

256. RESTATEMENT (SECOND) OF JUDGMENTS § 26(1)(c) cmt. (1), illus. 2 (1982).
257. 470 U.S. 373, 105 S. Ct. 1327, 84 L. Ed. 2d 274 (1985).
258. *Id.* at 382-86, 105 S. Ct. at 1332-35, 84 L. Ed. 2d at 282-85.
259. *Id.* at 386, 105 S. Ct. at 1335, 84 L. Ed. 2d at 285.
260. 516 U.S. 367, 116 S. Ct. 873, 134 L. Ed. 2d 6 (1996).

asserted that the Delaware judgment embodying the settlement had a claim preclusive effect on further prosecution of the California action. The Ninth Circuit Court of Appeals rejected Matsushita's argument on the grounds that the preclusive effect of the Delaware judgment under § 1738 was limited to the state claims involved in the action.

The U.S. Supreme Court reversed. Following *Marrese*, the Court held that the first inquiry had to be whether Delaware would give a claim preclusive effect to the judgment that would include the federal claims. The Court indicated, as it had in *Marrese*, that examination of state law would not always give a clear answer to the preclusion question, because state courts will usually not have any occasion to pronounce upon the preclusive effect of a state judgment in a later action that can only be brought in federal court.[261] However, the Court stated that federal courts could obtain guidance from ''general state law on the preclusive force of settlement judgments.''[262] Examining Delaware law, the Court concluded that general Delaware preclusion principles as well as particular Delaware decisions speaking to the preclusive force of class-action settlements in federal court indicated that the state would give a preclusive effect to the judgment in question.[263]

The Court then turned to the question whether the exclusive grant of federal jurisdiction for federal securities claims should be interpreted to create an exception to § 1738. The Court held that for an exception to exist, there must be an irreconcilable conflict between the grant of exclusive jurisdiction and § 1738.[264] The Court found that the federal statutory grant of exclusive jurisdiction did not manifest any congressional intent either to create an exception to § 1738 or to prevent litigants in state court from releasing federal securities claims as part of a settlement within the jurisdiction of the state courts.[265] In addition, the Court found nothing in the legislative history of the grant of exclusive jurisdiction that would justify creating an exception to § 1738.[266] Other parts of the securities acts also suggested to the Court that Congress had contemplated dual litigation in state and federal court, but had, nevertheless, done nothing to ''modify the background rule that where a state-court judgment precedes that of a federal court, the federal court must give full faith and credit to the state judgment.''[267] Finally, the Court invoked its own prior decisions holding that state-court judgments could have an issue preclusion effect in subsequent federal actions and that parties can waive the right to have federal securities claims litigated in federal court by agreeing to arbitrate the claims.[268] Thus, the Court held that the Delaware judgment had to be given a preclusive

---

261. *See id.* at 375, 116 S. Ct. at 878, 134 L. Ed. 2d at 18.
262. *See id.*, 116 S. Ct. at 878, 134 L. Ed. 2d at 18.
263. *See id.* at 376-78, 116 S. Ct. at 879-80, 134 L. Ed 2d at 18-20.
264. *See id.* at 381, 116 S. Ct. at 881, 134 L. Ed 2d at 21.
265. *See id.* at 381-82, 116 S. Ct. at 881-82, 134 L. Ed. 2d at 21-22.
266. *See id.* at 383, 116 S. Ct. at 882, 134 L. Ed. 2d at 23.
267. *Id.* at 383-84, 116 S. Ct. at 882, 134 L. Ed.2d at 23.
268. *See id.* at 384-85, 116 S. Ct. at 882-83, 134 L. Ed. 2d at 23-24.

effect on the federal claims by force of § 1738 and remanded for proceedings consistent with its opinion.[269]

Taken together, *Marrese* and *Matsushita* are strong evidence that the *Restatement (Second)'s* position on preclusion of exclusive federal claims will not prevail in many cases. In the absence of explicit statutory language or legislative history, which is seldom likely to exist,[270] the grant of exclusive jurisdiction is not likely to be read as creating an exception to § 1738.[271] The greatest difficulty that the federal courts will face in these cases is determining whether state claim preclusion principles would encompass federal claims that are omitted from a state action because they are within the exclusive jurisdiction of the federal courts. As *Matsushita* indicated, there will usually be no occasion for the state courts to pronounce upon such a question. However, in the event that the state courts have not explicitly addressed the question, *Matsushita* also indicated that federal courts can rely on general state preclusion principles to determine the question. Some federal courts have done this.[272]

Nevertheless, the question may not be easy to resolve on the basis of a state's general preclusion principles. For example, a state may follow the general position of the *Restatement (Second)* that claim preclusion does not occur when elements of a claim are omitted because they are not within the subject-matter jurisdiction of the court in which the action is brought. However, the state may also follow the rule that if a plaintiff has multiple courts in which to sue and picks a court with narrow subject-matter jurisdiction, the plaintiff should be precluded from later asserting claims arising out of the same facts that could have been joined if the action had been brought in a court of broader subject-matter jurisdiction.[273] Assuming that the plaintiff could have sued on both claims in federal court, joining the state claim within the federal court's supplemental jurisdiction,[274] should the state's general preclusion principles be interpreted to allow or forbid later assertion of the federal claim if the plaintiff chooses to

---

269. On remand, the Ninth Circuit Court of Appeals held that the Delaware judgment had no preclusive effect because the representation of the class members in the state proceeding was inadequate. The court found that the interests of the Delaware counsel were antagonistic to the interests of the class and that counsel had failed to investigate or develop the federal claims, with the result that the Delaware judgment deprived the class members of their right to adequate representation and was not entitled to full faith and credit. *See* Epstein v. MCA, Inc., 126 F.3d 1235 (9th Cir. 1997). For a criticism of *Matsushita*, see Mollie A. Murphy, *The Interstate Class Settlement: Of Comity, Consent, and Collusion,* 47 U. KAN. L. REV. 413 (1999).

270. *See* 18 CHARLES A. WRIGHT ET AL, FEDERAL PRACTICE AND PROCEDURE: JURISDICTION AND RELATED MATTERS § 4470, at 678-89 (1981 & Supp. 1999).

271. *Cf.* Fox v. Maulding, 112 F.3d 453 (10th Cir. 1997) (parties argued that they should not be precluded from asserting their federal RICO claims by a state compulsory counterclaim rule, because at the time of the state action it was not clear that the state courts could adjudicate the claims, so they were omitted; court held that in the absence of clear authority that the state courts could not hear the claims, the parties at least had to try to assert them in the state court).

272. *See* Aquatherm Indus., Inc. v. Florida Power & Light Co., 84 F.3d 1388 (11th Cir. 1996) (Florida follows general rule that splitting of cause of action does not occur when suit is not brought in court that has jurisdiction over all of plaintiff's claims; therefore, claim within exclusive federal jurisdiction not precluded by state judgment); *see also* Gonzales v. Hernandez, 175 F.3d 1202 (10th Cir. 1999) (federal § 1983 action in which state law on the effect of a prior state judgment on vicarious liability was interpreted by relying on a prior state case following § 51(1) of the *Restatement (Second)*).

273. *See* section B(3), *Illustrations 13-14 & 13-15 supra.*

274. *See* Chapter 2(C)(4) ("Supplemental Jurisdiction") *supra.*

litigate in state court instead? Suppose instead that the state has not indicated whether it would follow either of the above rules, but has indicated generally that it follows the *Restatement (Second)'s* approach to preclusion. Under these circumstances, should state law be interpreted as incorporating the rule, approved by the *Restatement (Second)*, that omission from a state action of a claim within the exclusive jurisdiction of the federal courts does not preclude later litigation of the claim in a federal action, even though *Marrese* and *Matsushita* indicate that the *Restatement's* position was not, in fact, a real restatement? These are not easy questions, and it does not seem likely that the answers given to them by federal courts will necessarily be the same as those that would be given by the state courts if they had an opportunity to answer the questions themselves.[275]

Issue preclusion poses similar problems in exclusive jurisdiction situations. However, as indicated above in the discussion of the *Matsushita* case, the Supreme Court has indicated that issue preclusion will be accepted in at least some cases where state courts adjudicate matters that later become relevant in federal actions within the exclusive jurisdiction of the federal courts.[276] However, the problems here are no easier to resolve than in the claim preclusion area.

Illustration 13-69. In a state suit for breach of contract, the defendant may assert that the contract is invalid under the federal antitrust laws. The state court has the authority to decide the federal antitrust issue raised as a defense, even though it would not have jurisdiction over the same issue if asserted as an affirmative claim by a plaintiff. If the state court decides against the defense and the state defendant then sues as a plaintiff in a federal antitrust action, the question is whether the exclusive grant of jurisdiction to federal courts over antitrust claims should be read to create an exception to § 1738 (assuming that the federal antitrust issue would be deemed res judicata in the state courts).

* * * * *

---

275. In fact, it seems that there is likely to be a good bit of confusion, at least for a time, about what it is proper for federal courts to do in these cases. For example, in Rads, P.C. v. Mercy Memorial Hospital, 3 F. Supp. 2d 772 (E.D. Mich. 1998), Rads had asserted state antitrust counterclaims against Mercy in an action in state court, and the state court had dismissed those counterclaims for failure to state a claim upon which relief could be granted. In a separate federal action asserting federal antitrust claims, but commenced before the state action, Rads had not asserted the state claims. The federal district court dismissed the federal action, holding that it was precluded by the dismissal of the state counterclaims. The court looked to state preclusion law and found that the subject matter of the state and federal actions was the same, the parties were the same, and the prior state judgment was on the merits. However, the state court did not have jurisdiction over the federal antitrust claims. The court may have been holding that the claims were split by the assertion of the state claims in state court, but compulsory counterclaim rules also have a preclusive effect in situations where no counterclaim is asserted at all by a defendant. Therefore, it would seem that a failure to assert the state counterclaims in the state action would also have to have a claim preclusive effect in the federal action. However, such an approach would mean that plaintiffs asserting federal claims within the exclusive jurisdiction of the federal courts would always have to join any related state claims that they possess if they are being sued in state court in a related matter. Otherwise, they may be met with a defense of res judicata on the federal claims by virtue of the operation of a state compulsory counterclaim rule. Thus, they would be forced to assert state claims that they do not wish to assert in the federal action in order to prevent preclusion on the federal claims. Such a result, to say the least, would violate the spirit of the doctrine of finality which aims to hold down the level of unnecessary litigation.

276. *See* Becher v. Contoure Labs., Inc., 279 U.S. 388, 49 S. Ct. 356, 73 L. Ed. 752 (1929) (issue preclusion in federal patent infringement action on issue of historical fact determined in prior state action).

State courts also have authority to adjudicate factual issues that later may be relevant in actions within the exclusive jurisdiction of the federal courts.

Illustration 13-70. In a state action on a license agreement, the state court may determine that the agreement terminated as of a particular date. This determination also might be relevant in a later federal action for patent infringement within the exclusive jurisdiction of the federal courts. Again, the issue is whether the exclusive grant of jurisdiction to federal courts over patent infringement suits requires an exception to the ordinary rule of § 1738.

* * * * *

Under the approach taken by § 28(3) of the *Restatement (Second) of Judgments*, "[t]he question in each case would be resolved in the light of the legislative purpose in vesting exclusive jurisdiction in a particular court."[277] Issue preclusion seems to have been accepted most readily in cases in which the state courts have adjudicated issues of historical fact, mixed issues of fact and "legal evaluation," and application of state law to fact.[278]

When the state courts directly adjudicate issues of federal law, however, the proper result is less clear. As was true of the Supreme Court's approach to the problem of claim preclusion in the *Marrese* case, it is easy to state (as the *Restatement (Second)* does regarding issue preclusion) that the reasons for the exclusive grant of jurisdiction to the federal courts should be evaluated in each case and the determination made whether those purposes require an exception to the ordinary rule of preclusion under § 1738. It is quite another matter to find in the federal statutes granting exclusive jurisdiction to the federal courts or the legislative history of those statutes any concrete reasons why the state courts have been excluded from hearing certain kinds of cases.[279] As might be expected under such circumstances, the authorities are split on the correct result.[280] In addition, it seems likely that the first question in the issue preclusion area (as in the claim preclusion area) will be whether state preclusion rules would prohibit relitigation of issues of federal law in a later suit within exclusive federal jurisdiction. It will be no easier to find state precedent directly bearing on this question than it was to find state authority on preclusion of federal claims.

The argument was once made that federal civil rights laws, especially 42 U.S.C. § 1983, justify an exception to the ordinary preclusion rules that operate under § 1738. Basically, the argument was that the civil rights acts embody a congressional policy against final state-court adjudication in the situations to which they apply, thus requiring that the ordinary rules of claim and issue preclusion that the states would apply to their own judgments be superseded, § 1738 notwithstanding.

---

277. RESTATEMENT (SECOND) OF JUDGMENTS § 28(3) cmt. e (1982).

278. *See id.*; Becher v. Contoure Labs., Inc., 279 U.S. 388, 49 S. Ct. 356, 73 L. Ed. 752 (1929); 18 CHARLES A. WRIGHT ET AL., FEDERAL PRACTICE AND PROCEDURE: JURISDICTION AND RELATED MATTERS § 4470, at 680-81 (1981), and authorities there cited.

279. *See* 18 CHARLES A. WRIGHT ET AL., FEDERAL PRACTICE AND PROCEDURE: JURISDICTION AND RELATED MATTERS § 4470, at 678-79 (1981).

280. *See id.* § 4470, at 683-84, and authorities there cited; RESTATEMENT (SECOND) OF JUDGMENTS § 28, reporter's note to subsection (3), at 288 (1982) and authorities there cited; *see also* Turnbow v. Pacific Mut. Life Ins. Co., 934 F.2d 1100 (9th Cir. 1991).

Although some questions remain in this area, the U.S. Supreme Court has thoroughly rejected this line of reasoning. In *Allen v. McCurry*,[281] the Court held that issue preclusion prevented the plaintiff from relitigating a federal constitutional issue in a federal civil rights action under § 1983 when that issue previously had been determined against him in a state criminal proceeding in which he was a defendant. In *Allen*, a criminal defendant had moved in his state trial to suppress evidence seized from him by the state police on the grounds that the search and seizure violated the Fourth and Fourteenth Amendments. The motion to suppress was denied, the defendant was convicted, and his conviction was upheld on appeal. Subsequently, the criminal defendant sued two of the police officers who conducted the search (and whom he had shot), as well as some other defendants, in a federal civil rights action under § 1983, seeking damages for the same unconstitutional search and seizure. The district court granted summary judgment on the grounds that issue preclusion prevented the plaintiff from relitigating the search and seizure question decided against him in the state courts. The Eighth Circuit reversed, holding that issue preclusion inapplicable in the particular case because an action under § 1983 was the only route to a federal forum for the plaintiff's constitutional claim. The Supreme Court granted certiorari and reversed.

The Court held that nothing in the language or legislative history of § 1983 demonstrated any intention to deny the binding effect to a state-court judgment that ordinarily would be required under § 1738. The Court stated that the history of § 1983 might support an exception to § 1738 when "state law did not provide for procedures for the litigation of constitutional claims, or [when] a state court failed to even acknowledge the existence of the constitutional principle on which a litigant based his claim."[282] However, such an exception

> would be essentially the same as the important general limit on rules of preclusion that already exists: collateral estoppel does not apply where the party against whom an earlier court decision is asserted did not have a full and fair opportunity to litigate the claim or issue decided by the first court.[283]

Subsequently, in *Migra v. Warren City School District Board of Education*,[284] the Court considered whether claim preclusion also applied when a state judgment was asserted as res judicata in a subsequent federal action under § 1983.[285] The Court reasoned that nothing in § 1983 would justify drawing a

---

281. 449 U.S. 90, 101 S. Ct. 411, 66 L. Ed. 2d 308 (1980).

282. *Id.* at 101, 101 S. Ct. at 418, 66 L. Ed. 2d at 317.

283. *Id.*

284. 465 U.S. 75, 104 S. Ct. 892, 79 L. Ed. 2d 56 (1984).

285. In *Migra*, the plaintiff first sued the Board of Education and three of its members who had voted not to renew her contract in state court, joining a breach of contract claim and a claim (against the individual Board members) for wrongful interference with her contract of employment. The state court found in plaintiff's favor on the breach of contract claim and ordered her reinstated to her position, awarding compensatory damages. Issues of conspiracy and individual Board member liability were dismissed without prejudice. Subsequently, the plaintiff commenced a federal action under § 1983, alleging that the Board's actions were designed to punish her for the exercise of her First Amendment rights, and that the actions deprived her of property without due process and of equal protection of the law. The district court granted summary judgment on grounds of res judicata, and the Sixth Circuit affirmed. The Supreme Court granted certiorari and ultimately vacated the judgdistinction between issue preclusion and claim preclusion. The Court rejected the argument that giving "state-court judgments full issue preclusive effect but not claim preclusive effect would enable litigants to bring their state claims in state court and their federal claims in federal court, thereby taking advantage of the relative expertise of both forums."[286] The Court stated § 1738 "embodies the view that it is more important to give full faith and credit to state-court judgments than to ensure separate forums for federal and state claims."[287] The Court thus held that the state-court judgment in this litigation has the same claim preclusive effect in federal court that the judgment would have in the state courts.[288]

Subsequent decisions of the Court have expanded the reach of *Allen* to civil rights statutes other than § 1983. In *Kremer v. Chemical Construction Corp.*,[289] the Court held that the Title VII of the Civil Rights Act of 1964[290] does not create an exception to 28 U.S.C. § 1738.[291] On the central question involved in *Kremer*, the Court stated that an exception to § 1738 would not be recognized unless a later statute contained an express or implied partial repeal of the section. Title VII contained no express repeal. The Court found no implied repeal of § 1738 because no irreconcilable conflict existed between the two statutes. Furthermore, Title VII was not intended as a substitute for § 1738.[292]

Recall that in *Allen*, the Court indicated a state judgment would not be given preclusive effect in a subsequent federal action if a full and fair opportunity to litigate the federal issues had not been afforded by the state court. However,

---

ment and remanded the case for further consideration of whether state res judicata rules would preclude the plaintiff's action.

286. *Id.* at 84-85, 104 S. Ct. at 898, 79 L. Ed. 2d at 64.

287. According to the Court, this view reflected "a variety of concerns, including notions of comity, the need to prevent vexatious litigation, and a desire to conserve judicial resources." The Court also pointed out that "[i]n the present litigation, petitioner does not claim that the state court would not have adjudicated her federal claims had she presented them in her original suit in state court. Alternatively, petitioner could have obtained a federal forum for her federal claim by litigating it first in a federal court. Section 1983, however, does not override state preclusion law and guarantee petitioner a right to proceed to judgment in state court on her state claims and then turn to federal court for adjudication of her federal claims." *Id.*

288. *Id.* Because it was unclear whether the district court had applied the Ohio law of preclusion, the court vacated the judgment of the Court of Appeals for further proceedings consistent with the Supreme Court's decision.

289. 456 U.S. 461, 102 S. Ct. 1883, 72 L. Ed. 2d 262 (1982).

290. 42 U.S.C. § 2000e to 2000e-17.

291. In *Kremer*, the plaintiff claimed that he had been discharged discriminatorily on grounds of national origin and religious faith. The plaintiff filed discrimination charges with the Equal Employment Opportunity Commission, which referred them to the New York State Division of Rights as required by Title VII. The state agency found against the plaintiff and he sought review of the administrative decision in the state's courts. This was his fatal mistake. The state courts upheld the agency determination, and the plaintiff brought a federal action under Title VII. The Supreme Court held that while state agency decisions are not given preclusive effect under § 1738, the state court proceedings reviewing the agency action were entitled to such effect under the section. Title VII requires that the EEOC defer action for sixty days while a state agency with jurisdiction over employment discrimination complaints has an opportunity to consider the discrimination charge. However, Title VII does not require the plaintiff to pursue state judicial review of the state agency's action. If the plaintiff does, however, § 1738 applies as it does to all other judicial action. *See Kremer,* 456 U.S. at 463-75, 102 S. Ct. at 1888-94, 72 L. Ed. 2d at 268-76.

292. *See id.* at 468-76, 102 S. Ct. at 1890-95, 72 L. Ed. 2d at 271-77. *See generally* William T. Goglia, Annotation, *Effect of Prior State Court Judgment upon Action in Federal District Court for Unlawful Employment Practices Under Title VII of the Civil Rights Act of 1964 (42 U.S.C.S. §§ 2000e et seq.),* 51 A.L.R. FED. 829 (1981).

the Court did not indicate whether this "full and fair opportunity" exception was a federal or state standard. In other words, it was unclear from *Allen* whether the scope of the full and fair opportunity exception would be defined by state law, as are other questions under § 1738, or whether an independent federal standard would be utilized to measure the fairness of state procedures.[293] Later decisions have addressed this question. These decisions have resolved that the standard will be federal, but the scope of the federal standard is not yet clear.

In *Kremer*, discussed above, the Court seemed to state clearly that the federal standard would be the narrow one of whether the state procedures complied with the Due Process Clause of the Fourteenth Amendment:

> The State must, however, satisfy the applicable requirements of the Due Process Clause. A state may not grant preclusive effect in its own courts to a constitutionally infirm judgment and other state and federal courts are not required to accord full-faith-and-credit to such a judgment. Section 1738 does not suggest otherwise; other state and federal courts would still be providing a state court judgment with the "same" preclusive effect as the courts of the state from which the judgment emerged. In such a case, there could be no constitutionally recognizable preclusion at all.[294]

The apparent clarity of this statement was clouded by the Court's later decision in *Haring v. Prosise.*[295] In *Haring*, the Court, in an extended dictum, suggested that the exceptions to § 1738 may be broader than the due process exception articulated in *Kremer*.

> Title 28 U.S.C. § 1738 generally requires "federal courts to give preclusive effect to state-court judgments whenever the courts of the State from which the judgments emerged would do so" [citing *Allen v. McCurry*]. In federal actions, including § 1983 actions, a state-court judgment will not be given collateral estoppel effect, however, where "the party against whom an earlier court decision is asserted did not have a full and fair opportunity to litigate the claim or issue decided by the first

---

293. *See* 18 CHARLES A. WRIGHT ET AL., FEDERAL PRACTICE AND PROCEDURE: JURISDICTION AND RELATED MATTERS § 4471, at 707 (1981).

294. *Kremer,* 456 U.S. at 483, 102 S. Ct. at 1898, 72 L. Ed. 2d at 281.

295. 462 U.S. 306, 103 S. Ct. 2368, 76 L. Ed. 2d 595 (1983). In *Haring*, a state criminal defendant pleaded guilty to manufacturing a controlled substance. No question of the legality of the search and seizure of the controlled substance that led to the defendant's arrest and conviction was raised in the state proceeding. Subsequently, however, the convicted person sued the police officers who conducted the search in a federal civil rights action under 42 U.S.C. § 1983, seeking damages on the grounds that the search was unconstitutional. The district court granted summary judgment on the grounds that the plaintiff's guilty plea barred the § 1983 claims. The guilty plea was held to be a waiver of the defendant's right to appeal the plea in a subsequent proceeding and an implied admission that the search was legal. The Fourth Circuit reversed and remanded for further proceedings, holding that the case should have been decided on the basis of 28 U.S.C. § 1738 and state preclusion principles. The Supreme Court granted certiorari and affirmed. The Court concluded that state principles of issue preclusion would not prevent the plaintiff from raising the constitutional claim in a later proceeding. This conclusion was all that was necessary to decide the case. *See id.* at 312-17, 103 S. Ct. at 2372-75, 76 L. Ed. 2d at 603-06.

court. . . .'' Moreover, additional exceptions to collateral estoppel may be warranted in § 1983 actions in light of the ''understanding of § 1983'' that ''the federal courts could step in where the state courts were unable to protect federal rights.''[296]

2. Enforcement of Federal Judgments

The language of 28 U.S.C. § 1738 does not require state courts or other federal courts to give any particular effect to the prior judgments of federal courts. Nevertheless, it is settled that federal judgments must be given effect in other courts and that the effect to be given a federal judgment is a ''federal question'' reviewable by the Supreme Court on appeal from a state court.[297] The *Restatement (Second) of Judgments* flatly states this rule as follows: ''Federal law determines the effects under the rules of res judicata of a judgment of a federal court.''[298] The best explanation for *why* federal judgments are binding on state courts and other federal courts is that: (1) Article III of the Constitution limits the ''judicial power'' of the federal courts to cases and controversies; (2) proceedings that do not have at least the potential effect of precluding later relitigation of the same issues would fall outside the proper exercise of the judicial power; and (3) the Supremacy Clause of Article VI mandates that federal judgments be binding on state courts.[299]

When federal courts adjudicate questions of federal law, there is no controversy over the proposition that federal law also defines the res judicata effects of the judgment in subsequent actions in state or federal courts.[300] However, when state law provides the rule of decision, a question still exists whether the law of the state where the federal court sits controls the preclusive effect of the federal judgment.[301] It has been argued that even in cases in which state law provides the rules of decision, the policies favoring determination by a court of its own judgments are so strong as to demand that federal law define the

---

296. *Id.* at 313-14, 103 S. Ct. at 2373, 76 L. Ed. 2d at 603-04 (footnotes omitted). *But see* Bar-Tec, Inc. v. Akrouche, 959 F. Supp. 793 (S.D. Ohio 1997) (state courts afforded plaintiffs due process, and, therefore, the exception to the doctrine of res judicata for the unwillingness or inability of state courts to protect federal rights is inapplicable). *See generally* 18 CHARLES A. WRIGHT ET AL., FEDERAL PRACTICE AND PROCEDURE: JURISDICTION AND RELATED MATTERS § 4471.2, at 692-96 (Supp. 1999); David H. Bathe, Annotation, *Supreme Court's Views as to Res Judicata or Collateral Estoppel Effect of State Court Judgments on Federal Courts*, 72 L. Ed. 2d 911 (1983).

297. *See* PAUL M. BATOR ET AL., HART AND WECHSLER'S THE FEDERAL COURTS AND THE FEDERAL SYSTEM 1603 (3d ed. 1988); 18 CHARLES A. WRIGHT ET AL., FEDERAL PRACTICE AND PROCEDURE: JURISDICTION AND RELATED MATTERS § 4468, at 651 (1981).

298. RESTATEMENT (SECOND) OF JUDGMENTS § 87 (1982); *see* Jean F. Rydstrom, Annotation, *Federal or State Law as Governing in Matters of Res Judicata and Collateral Estoppel in Federal Tort Claims Act Suit*, 49 A.L.R. FED. 326 (1980); Romvaldo P. Eclavea, Annotation, *State or Federal Law as Governing Applicability of Doctrine of Res Judicata or Collateral Estoppel in Federal Court Action*, 19 A.L.R. FED. 709 (1974).

299. *See* CHARLES A. WRIGHT, THE LAW OF FEDERAL COURTS § 100A, at 736-37 (5th ed. 1994). *See generally* Stephen Burbank, *Federal Judgments Law: Sources of Authority and Sources of Rules*, 70 TEX. L. REV. 1551 (1992).

300. *See* CHARLES A. WRIGHT, THE LAW OF FEDERAL COURTS § 100A, at 737 (5th ed. 1994).

301. *See id.* at 737-38.

scope of federal judgments.[302] This view was adopted by § 87 of the *Restatement (Second) of Judgments*, quoted above.

The notion accepted by the *Restatement (Second)* drafters that federal law should always, even in diversity actions, define the scope of a federal judgment is attributable to an influential article written by Professor Ronan Degnan.[303] Among other things, Professor Degnan argued that early decisions of the Court applying state law to define the scope of a federal diversity judgment were the result of the command in the Conformity Acts that federal courts apply state procedural law.[304] Thus, with the advent of the Federal Rules, procedural conformity to state law ended. Furthermore, because res judicata law is so heavily dependent on the applicable procedural context, dependence on state res judicata principles also ended.[305]

There are numerous problems with this view. First, Professor Stephen Burbank's recent examination of the same early decisions discussed by Professor Degnan casts serious doubt upon the proposition that those decisions can be explained by the Conformity Acts.[306] Instead,

> long before *Erie* [*Railroad v. Tompkins*] and the Federal Rules, the Supreme Court had held that federal preclusion law governs at least some questions of the effects to be accorded federal judgments on matters of federal substantive law. During the same period, the Court required that the preclusive effects of federal alienage and diversity judgment on matters of state substantive law follow state law. The Court's articulated concern in both contexts was to protect rights conferred by the substantive law.[307]

Second, although the Supreme Court has firmly accepted the proposition that federal law should define the scope of a federal judgment rendered in a federal question case,[308] the Court has expressly reserved the question of whether the *Erie* doctrine requires state law to be applied to federal scope-of-judgment problems in diversity actions. In *Heiser v. Woodruff*,[309] the Court stated: "We need not consider whether . . . the rule of res judicata applied in the

---

302. *See* Kern v. Hettinger, 303 F.2d 333, 340 (2d Cir. 1962); CHARLES A. WRIGHT, THE LAW OF FEDERAL COURTS § 100A, at 737-38 (5th ed. 1994). *See generally* RICHARD H. FALLON ET AL., HART & WECHSLER'S THE FEDERAL COURTS AND THE FEDERAL SYSTEM 1473-74 (4th ed. 1996).

303. *See* Ronan E. Degnan, *Federalized Res Judicata*, 85 YALE L.J. 741 (1976).

304. The Conformity Acts are discussed in Chapter 1(E)(5), *supra*.

305. *See id.* at 755-71.

306. *See* Stephen B. Burbank, *Interjurisdictional Preclusion, Full Faith and Credit and Federal Common Law: A General Approach*, 71 CORNELL L. REV. 733, 747-53 (1986).

307. *Id.* at 752.

308. *See, e.g.*, Parklane Hosiery Co. v. Shore, 439 U.S. 322, 99 S. Ct. 645, 58 L. Ed. 2d 552 (1979); Blonder-Tongue Labs., Inc. v. University of Ill. Found., 402 U.S. 313, 91 S. Ct. 1434, 28 L. Ed. 2d 788 (1971). *Parklane Hosiery* applied nonmutual offensive issue preclusion even though the defendant had no right to a jury trial in the action in which the first judgment was rendered, but would have had in the second action if issue had not applied. This aspect of the case is discussed in Chapter 11(E)(1) ("Cases in Which Only Legal or Only Equitable Claims Are Presented") *supra*; *cf.* Lytle v. Household Mfg., Inc., 494 U.S. 545, 110 S. Ct. 1331, 108 L. Ed. 2d 504 (1990) (*Parklane* rule not applicable when legal and equitable claims erroneously separated by trial judge in first action).

309. 327 U.S. 726, 66 S. Ct. 853, 90 L. Ed. 970 (1946).

federal courts, in diversity of citizenship cases, under the doctrine of *Erie [Railroad] v. Tompkins* . . . can be other than that of the state in which the federal court sits.''[310]

Finally, a theoretical problem exists with the flat rule of § 87 of the *Restatement (Second)*. The res judicata doctrine receives support from multiple sources. As noted at the beginning of this chapter, the preclusive effects of judgments tend to vary depending on whether the procedural rules of the judgment-rendering court are stringent or liberal. Thus, when it can be seen that the major contributing factors to a preclusion question are the pleading, joinder, and other rules of the federal courts, a strong argument can be made that federal law should define the scope of the judgment independent of state law.

However, res judicata rules also can be dependent upon substantive policies.[311] When state substantive law provides the rule of decision and the state possesses related substantive policies that shape its law of res judicata, a strong argument can be made that independent federal law should not define the scope of the federal judgment.[312] The *Restatement (Second)* takes the position that while federal law always should determine the effect of a federal judgment, federal law sometimes should incorporate state law to protect state substantive policies.[313] However, it is doubtful whether this approach is as faithful to the multiple sources of law that contribute to res judicata doctrine as would be a straightforward application of the *Erie* doctrine to scope-of-judgment problems in federal diversity actions. The *Restatement (Second)* advocates the adoption of state res judicata law as federal law only in areas covered by §§ 43 to 61 of the *Restatement (Second)* (dealing with substantive legal relationships resulting in preclusion), but not in areas governing the basic rules of claim and issue preclusion, which the *Restatement (Second)* drafters seem to assume will be influenced primarily by procedural policies.[314] This position is demonstrably incorrect, however, leading to the conclusion that a careful case-by-case analysis under the *Erie* doctrine will be more faithful to state substantive interests than the approach of the *Restatement (Second)*.[315]

Illustration 13-71. *A* sues *B Airline* in a federal diversity action to recover damages for the wrongful death of *A's* spouse in a crash of one of *B's* aircraft. After a trial, *A* recovers a judgment based on the court's specific finding that *B* had been negligent. The state where the district court was sitting has retained the

---

310. *Id.* at 731-32, 66 S. Ct. at 855, 90 L. Ed. at 975.

311. *See* 18 CHARLES A. WRIGHT ET AL., FEDERAL PRACTICE AND PROCEDURE: JURISDICTION AND RELATED MATTERS § 4472, at 733 (1981).

312. *See id.* at 734.

313. *See* RESTATEMENT (SECOND) OF JUDGMENTS § 87 cmt. b (1982). This position has won the support of a number of commentators. *See, e.g.,* CHARLES A. WRIGHT, THE LAW OF FEDERAL COURTS § 100A, at 696 (4th ed. 1983); 18 CHARLES A. WRIGHT ET AL., FEDERAL PRACTICE AND PROCEDURE: JURISDICTION AND RELATED MATTERS § 4472, at 734 (1981).

314. *See* RESTATEMENT (SECOND) OF JUDGMENTS § 87 cmt. b (1982).

315. Federal lower courts are split on the question whether federal or state law controls the res judicata effect of a federal diversity judgment. *Compare, e.g.,* Hillary v. Trans World Airlines, Inc., 123 F.3d 1041 (8th Cir. 1997) *cert. denied,* 522 U.S. 1090, 118 S. Ct. 881, 139 L. Ed. 2d 870 (1998) (state law) *with* Paramount Aviation Corp. v. Agusta, 178 F.3d 132 (3d Cir. 1999) (federal law) *and* Petromanagement Corp. v. Acme-Thomas Joint Venture, 835 F.2d 1329 (10th Cir. 1988) (federal law).

mutuality rule only in mass disaster cases. The state's expressly stated purpose for retaining the mutuality rule is to prevent massive liability from a single judgment from attaching to defendants in whom the state has an interest. Thus, if *A's* action against *B* had been brought in a state court in the state where the district court was sitting, the judgment rendered in *A's* favor would not be given a nonmutual preclusive effect in a later action. Under § 87 of the *Restatement (Second) of Judgments*, however, this case is not one in which federal law would adopt state res judicata law because the rule in question is a basic rule of issue preclusion. The *Restatement (Second)* drafters assume that such rules will be influenced primarily by procedural policies.

The *Restatement (Second)* drafters are erroneous.[316] Application of the *Erie* doctrine would protect both state and federal interests in the situation described better than the approach of the *Restatement (Second)*. Assume that *C* sues *B* in a later action for the wrongful death of *C's* spouse. If the federal rule employed to define the scope of federal judgments in federal question cases is employed to define the scope of the federal judgment in *A's* action against *B*, a nonmutual preclusive effect would be given to the judgment. *C* could, therefore, bind *B* with the finding of negligence in the prior action.[317] On the other hand, applying the *Erie* doctrine would produce a different result. If the state rule is classified as a rule defining state rights and obligations or a rule bound up with state rights and obligations, then the decision in *Byrd v. Blue Ridge Rural Electric Cooperative, Inc.*, discussed in Chapter 5,[318] will require the application of the rule to define the scope of the federal judgment. If the rule is classified as a rule of form and mode, the application of the state mutuality rule would still be obligatory. The application of the federal rule of nonmutual, offensive preclusion would not cause forum shopping for a federal court. Once it is determined what rule defines the scope of the federal judgment, all courts, state and federal, are obligated to apply that rule in a later action in which the judgment comes into play. *C* would therefore not have any incentive to sue in federal court to get the benefit of the federal rule because the state courts would be obligated to apply the same rule. However, the application of the federal rule would deprive *B* of a valuable benefit that state law would confer if the first action had been in state court. Thus, inequitable administration of the laws in the *Erie* sense would result from the application of the federal rule. Because no apparent countervailing federal substantive or procedural policies would dictate that the federal rule define the scope of the federal judgment instead of the state rule, the *Restatement (Second)* notwithstanding, the policy against inequitable administration of the law dictates that the state rule define the scope of the federal judgment.

* * * * *

---

316. *See* CHARLES A. WRIGHT ET AL., FEDERAL PRACTICE AND PROCEDURE: JURISDICTION AND RELATED MATTERS § 4472, at 734 (1981) (providing other examples of basic rules of claim and issue preclusion supported by substantive policies).

317. *See* Parklane Hosiery Co. v. Shore, 439 U.S. 322, 99 S. Ct. 645, 58 L. Ed. 2d 552 (1979) (Supreme Court approved of nonmutual offensive preclusion against the party who was the defendant in a prior action).

318. *See* Chapter 5(E) ("The Evolution of the *Erie* Doctrine: Applicability of State "Substantive Law" Under the Rules of Decision Act") *supra*.

In addition to conflicts between federal and state common-law res judicata rules, there can also be Rules Enabling Act problems of the sort discussed in Chapter 5 when a Federal Rule of Civil Procedure defines the scope of a federal judgment and conflicts with state law.[319] Some of these problems are easy to resolve. For example, Chapter 7 examined the problems involved in the administration of compulsory counterclaims under Federal Rule 13.[320] Assume that Rule 13 would bar a defendant from asserting a compulsory counterclaim omitted from an initial action, but that under the applicable state law there exists no compulsory counterclaim rule. Under these circumstances, there is no legitimate problem of rule validity. In the first place, it is likely that an accurate analysis of whether Rule 13 conflicts with state law will produce the conclusion that no conflict exists. The state counterclaim rule is likely to be designed for operation only in the state's own courts, thus eliminating any real conflict with Rule 13.[321] Even if a conflict exists between Rule 13 and state law, however, there is no serious question of Rule validity involved. As discussed in Chapter 7, litigants can sometimes avoid any effect on their substantive rights that would be produced by noncompliance with a Federal Rule of Civil Procedure by adopting appropriate post-commencement behavior.[322] Thus, by pleading a compulsory counterclaim under Rule 13, a party can avoid the bar of the rule. Under these circumstances, there can be no serious contention that the operation of the Federal Rule substantially impacts on substantive rights.

More serious problems of rule validity can occur when a Federal Rule defines the scope of a federal judgment regardless of any post-commencement behavior that a litigant may adopt. For example, Rule 41(b), on its face, makes all dismissals not otherwise specified "on the merits" except dismissals for lack of jurisdiction, improper venue, and failure to join a party under Rule 19. This provision effectively imposes the bar of claim preclusion on all such dismissals, even if a similar dismissal under state law would not preclude a subsequent action on the same claim. Sometimes this difference in results between federal and state preclusion can be justified as the byproduct of differences in the structure of the procedural systems of the state and federal courts. Thus, a dismissal under Rule 12(b)(6) grounds is treated as "on the merits" due to the liberality of the federal procedural system, while a similar dismissal under state law for failure to state a cause of action may be without prejudice due to the rigidity of the state system.[323] Under these circumstances, the operation of claim preclusion is simply the byproduct of procedural differences between the two systems that cannot seriously be said to affect substantive rights more than "incidentally."

---

319. *See* Chapter 5(F)(4) *supra* (discussing the test for resolving conflicts between Federal Rules of Civil Procedure and state law under the Rules Enabling Act, 28 U.S.C. § 2072).

320. *See* Chapter 7(F)(3) *supra* (discussing potential Rules Enabling Act problems with Rule 13).

321. *See* Chapter 5(F)(4) *supra* (discussing the desirability of determining whether the state's rule is limited to its own court system in order to avoid a conflict between applicable Federal Rules of Civil Procedure and state law).

322. *See* Chapter 7(F)(3) *supra* (discussing the Supreme Court's decision in the *Business Guides* case).

323. *See* section B(2) *supra* (discussing the operation of claim preclusion in cases involving dismissals for failure to state a claim); Chapter 6(C)(2) & (D)(2) *supra* (discussing the differences between the code and Federal Rules systems of pleading).

However, more difficult problems exist under Rule 41(b). For example, assume that a federal diversity action is dismissed on state statute of limitations grounds and the plaintiff recommences the action in a state with a longer statute of limitations. The traditional conflict-of-laws rule governing statute of limitations dismissals is that such dismissal will preclude a second action in the state where the dismissal occurred, but not in a state with a longer statute of limitations.[324] If the state in which the district court sat in the initial action follows this rule,[325] a potential conflict arises between Rule 41(b), which would seem to make the dismissal on the merits, and state law, which would permit a second action. The lower federal courts overwhelmingly hold in this situation that Rule 41(b) makes such a dismissal on the merits, thus precluding a second action.[326] This can perhaps be justified on the grounds that the plaintiff in such cases can request the dismissal to be "without prejudice" under Rule 41(b), thereby assuring that any adverse effect on substantive rights can be avoided by appropriate action by the party affected. Nevertheless, the Rules Enabling Act issue would still be presented in full force if the district court refuses to specify the dismissal as without prejudice, or if it is held improper for the district court to specify a statute of limitations dismissal as "without prejudice."[327] Under either of the latter circumstances, it is difficult to see how the federal court in the second action could avoid the conclusion that the operation of Rule 41(b) affected substantive rights more than incidentally, thus rendering the Rule invalid as applied to this kind of case. The operation of Rule 41(b) would entirely preclude an action that would be permitted under the law of the state where the dismissal occurred, and it is difficult to see any federal interest that would justify such a result.

3. Enforcement of Foreign Judgments

Neither the full faith and credit clause nor 28 U.S.C. § 1738 applies to the judgments of foreign nations. Consequently, the extent to which the judgment of a court of a foreign nation will be given effect in a state or federal court in the United States is governed by common-law rules. Chapter 3 discussed the

---

324. This result is a byproduct of the traditional classification of statutes of limitation as "procedural" for conflict-of-laws purposes. *See* RESTATEMENT (FIRST) OF JUDGMENTS § 49 cmt. a (1942).

325. It may be quite difficult to determine whether the state where the federal dismissal occurred would consider a dismissal on statute of limitations grounds in its own courts to be "on the merits." The state courts will ordinarily have no occasion ever to consider such a question, because in the nature of things, the issue will only arise in the second action in a different state with a longer statute. Thus, the federal courts in that state may have to derive such general guidance on the issue as they can from the original state's posture on conflict-of-laws issues in other kinds of cases. The problem is similar to that discussed in section F(1), *supra*, when federal courts must determine the content of state res judicata law in the absence of specific authority on point.

326. *See, e.g.,* Murphy v. Klein Tools, Inc., 935 F.2d 1127 (10th Cir. 1991), *cert. denied,* 502 U.S. 952, 112 S. Ct. 407, 116 L. Ed.2d 355 (1992); Shoup v. Bell & Howell Co., 872 F.2d 1178 (4th Cir. 1989); Steven D. Thompson Trucking, Inc. v. Dorsey Trailers, Inc., 870 F.2d 1044 (5th Cir. 1989), *rehearing denied,* 880 F.2d 1044 (1989); PRC Harris, Inc. v. Boeing Co., 700 F.2d 894 (2d Cir. 1983), *cert. denied,* 464 U.S. 936, 104 S. Ct. 344, 78 L. Ed.2d 311 (1983); Nathan v. Rowan, 651 F.2d 1223 (6th Cir. 1981).

327. *Cf.* Sack v. Low, 478 F.2d 360 (2d Cir. 1973) (dismissal of prior diversity action on statute of limitations grounds was specified by dismissing court to be without prejudice; therefore, it was not a dismissal on the merits; court questions whether it was proper for the district court to specify this kind of dismissal as without prejudice).

variations in the rules governing the enforcement of foreign judgments. The traditional rule in the United States was announced by the Supreme Court in the *Hilton v. Guyot.*[328] In *Hilton*, the Court held that the judgments of foreign courts rendered with jurisdiction would be given effect only to the extent that United States judgments would be given effect in the foreign courts. However, the English rule is that the judgments of foreign courts rendered with jurisdiction in the "international sense" are res judicata.[329] Today, most state courts give the same effect to foreign nation judgments as they give to sister-state judgments.[330] However, even though the reciprocity requirement has been widely rejected, it is still necessary for a foreign judgment to comply with the basic requirements of procedural fairness, which includes personal jurisdiction standards similar to those imposed by the Fourteenth Amendment on state courts.[331] In addition, American courts may refuse to enforce a foreign nation's judgment on the grounds that the judgment would violate the strong public policy of the enforcing court,[332] a ground of defense that is impermissible with judgments of sister states.[333]

The serious question today is what law should control the effect to be given a foreign judgment. The United States is not a party to any multilateral treaty providing for the recognition and enforcement of foreign nation judgments, which would effectively make the enforcement of foreign nation judgments a matter of federal law.[334] The prevailing view today is that state law governs the

---

328. 159 U.S. 113, 16 S. Ct. 139, 40 L. Ed. 95 (1895).

329. *See* Chapter 3(A)(1)*(a)* ("The Forms of Action in Suits on Foreign Judgments and the 'International' Rules of Jurisdiction") *supra.*

330. *See* RESTATEMENT (THIRD) OF THE FOREIGN RELATIONS LAW OF THE UNITED STATES § 481 cmt. c & d (1987); Wanda E. Wakefield, Annotation, *Judgment of Court of Foreign Country as Entitled to Enforcement or Extraterritorial Effect in State Court,* 13 A.L.R.4TH 1109 (1982). For an excellent guide to enforcement of foreign judgments in the United States, see Robert E. Lutz, *Enforcement of Foreign Judgments, Part I: A Selected Bibliography of U.S. Enforcement of Judgments Rendered Abroad,* 27 INT'L LAW. 471 (1993). For a discussion of the treatment of U.S. judgments abroad, see Robert E. Lutz, *Enforcement of Foreign Judgments, Part II: A Selected Bibliography on Enforcement of U.S. Judgments in Foreign Countries,* 27 INT'L LAW. 1029 (1993).

331. *See* RESTATEMENT (THIRD) OF THE FOREIGN RELATIONS LAW OF THE UNITED STATES § 482(1) (1987).

332. *See id.* § 483(2)(d).

333. *See* section F(1) *supra* (discussing this rule).

334. The United States is a party to many bilateral treaties of Friendship, Commerce, and Navigation (FCN), and certain clauses in these treaties have been interpreted by some courts to impose an obligation to recognize and enforce the judgments of the other signatory to the treaty. *See* Choi v. Kim, 50 F.3d 244 (3d Cir. 1995) (interpreting the FCN between the U.S. and South Korea as imposing the obligation to treat Korean judgments as sister-state judgments, but applying New Jersey law to control the effect of the judgment in a diversity action); Vagenas v. Continental Gin Co., 988 F.2d 104 (11th Cir.), *cert. denied,* 510 U.S. 947, 114 S. Ct. 389, 126 L. Ed. 2d 337 (1993) (holding the FCN between the U.S. and Greece obligated the states to give the same treatment to a Greek national as would be given to a United States citizen in an action to enforce a judgment). *See generally* Edward A. Liang, *Equal Access/Non-Discrimination and Legitimate Discrimination in International Economic Law,* 14 WIS. INT'L L.J. 246 (1996); Herman Walker, Jr., *Modern Treaties of Friendship, Commerce and Navigation,* 42 MINN. L. REV. 805 (1958); Robert R. Wilson, *Access to Courts Provisions in United States Commercial Treaties,* 47 AM. J. INT'L L. 20 (1953). Currently, the U.S. has proposed a Hague Convention on Jurisdiction and Foreign Judgments in Civil and Commercial Matters, and the American Law Institute has begun an international jurisdiction and judgments project, still in its infancy at this date, to draft implementing legislation for the treaty if it is successfully drafted and implemented. *See* ALI INTERNATIONAL JURISDICTION AND JUDGMENTS PROJECT (Council Memorandum No. 1, Nov. 19, 1999). At this recognition and enforcement of foreign judgments in state courts and, under *Erie*, in federal diversity actions, though federal preclusion law governs in federal question cases.[335] It has been argued that the U.S. Supreme Court should create federal common-law rules to govern the effect of all foreign judgments, due to the difficulties of dealing with such judgments under the "potentially divergent law of fifty states and federal courts" and the fact that "recognition of foreign judgments at least touches concerns of foreign relations in which the national government has paramount interests."[336] However, given the difficulties of negotiating a general treaty on judgments with other countries, it is more plausible to argue that the creation of federal law in this area is beyond the legitimate prerogatives of the Court and should be left to the Executive and Congress.[337]

SECTION G. OTHER PRECLUSION DOCTRINES: STARE DECISIS, LAW OF THE CASE, AND JUDICIAL ESTOPPEL

Three doctrines should be distinguished from the principles of res judicata: stare decisis, the law of the case, and judicial estoppel.

---

time the prospects for the treaty do not seem bright due to the concern by other nations with certain bases of personal jurisdiction used by United States' courts, as well as judgments for excessive and punitive damages rendered by our courts in certain torts cases. For a general discussion of the problems involved with negotiating the treaty, see Symposium, *Enforcing Judgments Abroad: The Global Challenge,* 24 BROOK. J. INT'L L. 1-220 (1998); *see also* Patrick J. Borchers, *Judgments Conventions and Minimum Contacts,* 61 ALBANY L. REV. 1161 (1998); Patrick J. Borchers, *Comparing Personal Jurisdiction in the United States and the European Community: Lessons for American Reform,* 40 AM. J. COMP. L. 121 (1992); Kevin M. Clermont, *Jurisdictional Salvation and the Hague Treaty,* 85 CORNELL L. REV. 89 (1999); Andrew L. Strauss, *Where America Ends and the International Order Begins: Interpreting the Jurisdictional Reach of the U.S. Constitution in Light of A Proposed Hague Convention on Jurisdiction and Satisfaction of Judgments,* 61 ALBANY L. REV. 1237 (1998).

335. *See* RESTATEMENT (THIRD) OF THE FOREIGN RELATIONS LAW OF THE UNITED STATES § 481 cmt. a (1987) (state law controls); Southwest Livestock & Trucking Co. v. Ramon, 169 F.3d 317 (5th Cir. 1999) (*Erie* requires federal diversity courts to follow state law on the recognition of foreign country money judgments); Alfadda v. Fenn, 966 F. Supp. 1317 (S.D.N.Y. 1997) (federal preclusion law gives issue preclusion effect to French judgment in federal question case); Allstate Ins. Co. v. Administratia Asigurarilor de Stat, 962 F. Supp. 420 (S.D.N.Y. 1997) (New York law governs effect of foreign judgment in federal diversity action in New York); Russell J. Weintraub, *How Substantial Is Our Need For A Judgments-Recognition Convention and What Should We Bargain Away to Get It,* 24 BROOK. J. INT'L L. 167, 173-74, 177 (1998) (state law controls in state courts, state law controls in federal diversity and alienage cases, and federal law controls in federal question cases); *see also* Jerome A. Hoffman, *Recognition by Courts in the Eleventh Circuit of Judgments Rendered by Courts of Other Countries,* 29 CUMB. L. REV. 65 (1998-99).

336. 18 CHARLES A. WRIGHT ET AL, FEDERAL PRACTICE AND PROCEDURE: JURISDICTION AND RELATED MATTERS § 4473, at 743 (1981). Federal common law is discussed in Chapter 5(I) *supra*.

337. Thirty states have adopted the UNIFORM FOREIGN MONEY-JUDGMENTS RECOGNITION ACT, 13 U.L.A. 261 (1986). *Id.* at 85 (Supp. 1999). The Act does not require reciprocity in enforcement of U.S. judgments by the foreign country whose judgment is being enforced, although three states, Georgia, Massachusetts, and Texas, added a requirement of reciprocity to their versions of the Act. *See* 13 U.L.A. 269-70. The Act does not provide for separate enforcement procedures for foreign nation judgments, but prescribes that they shall be enforced in the same manner as the judgments of sister states. *See* Don Docksteader Motors Ltd. v. Patal Enters., Ltd., 794 S.W.2d 760 (Tex. 1990) (Act permits enforcement of foreign nation judgment by registration under the Texas Uniform Enforcement of Foreign Judgments Act or by common-law action, just as in the case of state judgments). Certain kinds of judgments are also excluded from the act—judgments for taxes, fines or penalties and for matrimonial or family support, and the Act permits a public policy defense, as well as defenses based on a lack of procedural fairness in the judgment-rendering court.

1. Stare Decisis

Stare decisis is simply the doctrine that when a court has once established a principle of law as applicable to a certain state of facts, the court will follow that principle in all future cases in which the facts are substantially the same. Thus, even if the rules of issue preclusion do not preclude relitigation of an issue of law by a party, relitigation of the issue in a subsequent proceeding may prove futile because of the doctrine of stare decisis.

Stare decisis is based on policies of security and certainty. People rely upon principles of law declared by courts. As a consequence, departure from those principles should not be lightly regarded. Stare decisis, however, is a policy of discretion.[338] Courts can and often do depart from established principles when compelling reasons for doing so are present, and sometimes even when they are not.[339]

2. Law of the Case

The *law-of-the-case* doctrine precludes relitigation of issues of law at successive stages[340] of the same case.[341] This doctrine is designed to maintain consistency, to terminate litigation over particular matters, and to maintain the prestige of courts.[342] Like res judicata, however, the law of the case entails costs. When the doctrine is applied without regard to the correctness of the earlier determination, the values described above are attained at the expense of justice to the parties. This price is a much heavier one to pay within the confines of a

---

338. *See, e.g.*, Lowing v. Allstate Ins. Co., 176 Ariz. 101, 859 P.2d 724 (1993).

339. Stare decisis can operate in cases in which claim and issue preclusion do not operate, or it can operate in addition to claim and issue preclusion. *See* State *ex rel.* Moore v. Molpus, 578 So. 2d 624 (Miss. 1991) (claim preclusion not operative; stare decisis and issue preclusion operative); *cf. In re* PCH Assocs., 949 F.2d 585 (2d Cir. 1991) (law of the case, claim preclusion, and issue preclusion all inoperative); Society of Separationists, Inc. v. Herman, 939 F.2d 1207 (5th Cir. 1991) (stare decisis, claim preclusion, issue preclusion, and law of the case all inapplicable).

340. *See* Allan D. Vestal, *Law of the Case: Single-Suit Preclusion*, 11 UTAH L. REV. 1 (1967). These successive stages include when "(1) [a]n appellate court [rules] on a matter and then the same legal questions [is] raised in the trial court after the case has been remanded to that court for further proceedings"; "(2) [a]n appellate court [rules] on a matter and then the same legal question [is] raised in the same appellate court when the case is appealed a second time"; and "(3) [a] trial court [rules] on a matter and then the same legal question [is] raised a second time in the same trial court . . . before the same judge or before a different judge." *Id.* at 4. Successive stages of litigation also arise in transferred and consolidated cases as well as in multidistrict litigation. For an exhaustive treatment of law-of-the case issues in these latter contexts, see Joan Steinman, *Law of the Case: A Judicial Puzzle in Consolidated and Transferred Cases and in Multidistrict Litigation*, 135 U. PA. L. REV. 1 (1987).

341. The law-of-the-case doctrine "expresses the practice of the courts generally to refuse to reopen what has been decided, not a limit on their power." Messenger v. Anderson, 225 U.S. 436, 444, 32 S. Ct. 739, 740, 56 L. Ed. 1152, 1156 (1912).

342. *See* Allan D. Vestal, *Law of the Case: Single-Suit Preclusion*, 11 UTAH L. REV. 1, 1-4 (1967). *See generally* Martin J. McMahon, Annotation, *Application of Doctrine of Law of the Case to Review by One Federal Court of Appeals of Determination by Another Federal Court of Appeals*, 74 A.L.R. FED. 878 (1985); John A. Glenn, Annotation, *Propriety of Federal District Judge's Overruling or Reconsidering Decision or Order Previously Made in Same Case by Another District Judge*, 20 A.L.R. FED. 13 (1974); E.H. Schopler, Annotation, *Erroneous Decision as Law of the Case on Subsequent Appellate Review*, 87 A.L.R.2D 271 (1963).

single proceeding than it is between different proceedings. Perhaps for this reason, the doctrine is not applied rigidly and seems to be diminishing in importance.[343]

3. Judicial Estoppel

Judicial estoppel is a doctrine that precludes a party from taking inconsistent positions in successive judicial proceedings. The policy supporting judicial estoppel is the protection of the integrity of the judicial processes. The integrity of the judicial process would be undermined if a party could take a position in litigation or administrative proceedings that produces a judgment or award in the party's favor and then take an inconsistent position in later litigation in an attempt to obtain a second favorable judgment.[344] The issue often seems to arise in disability cases in which a party contends in an initial proceeding that the party is disabled and obtains an award of disability benefits, but later commences a second action based on the premise that the party is not disabled. In these cases, the courts have invoked the doctrine of judicial estoppel to preclude the second action.[345] However, the judicial estoppel doctrine is not universal. Some courts have rejected it as inconsistent with modern pleading doctrine, which permits inconsistent and alternative pleading.[346] Others reject

---

343. *See* Allan D. Vestal, *Law of the Case: Single-Suit Preclusion*, 11 UTAH L. REV. 1, 30-31 (1967). *See also* Wilson v. Merrill Dow Pharm., Inc., 160 F.3d 625 (10th Cir. 1998) (law of the case does not preclude a new district judge from granting a motion for summary judgment previously denied twice by former judge when former judge would have had power to reconsider his rulings); Filbatte v. Pennsylvania Truck Lines, Inc., 131 F.3d 21 (1st Cir. 1997) (law of case does not require successor judge to deny a post-verdict motion for judgment as a matter of law when original judge had denied pre-verdict motion for judgment as a matter of law); Hanover Ins. Co. v. American Eng'g Co., 105 F.3d 306 (6th Cir. 1997) (court of appeals language erroneously describing state law was not law of the case, but dicta; even if language was law of the case, it falls within an exception to law of the case which permits departures from prior rulings when they are clearly erroneous and would cause manifest injustice); Tahoe Sierra Preservation Council, Inc. v. Tahoe Reg'l Planning Agency, 992 F. Supp. 1218 (D. Neb. 1998) (law of case does not require district court to follow court of appeals decision on an issue when court of appeals decision is clearly erroneous). For an excellent treatment of law of the case issues in the context of transferred and consolidated cases, see Joan Steinman, *Law of the Case: A Judicial Puzzle in Consolidated and Transferred Cases and in Multidistrict Lit; ation*, 135 U. PA. L. REV. 595 (1987).

344. *See* 18 CHARLES A. WRIGHT ET AL, FEDERAL PRACTICE AND PROCEDURE: JURISDICTION AND RELATED MATTERS § 4477, at 781 (1981). *See generally* Eric A. Schreiber, *The Judiciary Says, You Can't Have it Both Ways: Judicial Estoppel—A Doctrine Precluding Inconsistent Positions*, 30 LOY. L.A. L. REV. 323 (1996).

345. *See, e.g.,* McConathy v. Dr. Pepper/Seven Up Corp., 131 F.3d 558 (5th Cir. 1997) (plaintiff estopped from suing her employer under the Americans with Disabilities Act because of statements she had made in an application for Social Security benefits to the effect that she did not see how she could hold any position even on a part time basis); Simon v. Safelite Glass Corp., 128 F.3d 68 (2d Cir. 1997) (plaintiff estopped from suing his employer under the Age Discrimination in Employment Act due to statements the plaintiff had made under penalty of perjury in an application for Social Security Benefits); Scarano v. Central R.R. Co., 203 F.2d 510 (3d Cir. 1953) (plaintiff precluded from suing his employer for reinstatement to his job because of judgment in prior action in which the plaintiff had obtained jury award for total and permanent disability).

346. *See, e.g.,* Konstantinidis v. Chen, 626 F.2d 933, 938 (D.C. Cir. 1980) (inconsistent with modern rules of pleading). It has been argued that this rationale is not a sound reason for rejecting judicial estoppel, because modern pleading only condones alternative and inconsistent pleading within a single case, while judicial estoppel is designed to prevent inconsistency between different judicial proceedings. *See* Ashley S. Deeks, Comment, *Raising the Cost of Lying: Rethinking* Erie *for Judicial Estoppel*, 64 U. CHI. L. REV. 873, 881 (1997).

the doctrine because they feel it is an excessively costly interference with the truth-finding function of courts.[347]

The U.S. Supreme Court has recently discussed the use of judicial estoppel in cases arising under federal law. In *Cleveland v. Policy Management Systems Corp.,*[348] the Court held that a person who seeks and receives Social Security Disability Insurance (SSDI) benefits cannot automatically be precluded from pursuing a claim against her employer under the Americans with Disabilities Act (ADA). SSDI benefits are only available to people who are unable to engage in any substantial gainful activity by reason of a disability. The ADA prohibits covered employers from discriminating against disabled individuals who can perform the essential functions of their jobs, including those who can do so only with reasonable accommodations. Although it might seem that claims under the two acts will inevitably conflict, the Court held in *Cleveland* that this is not so, because there are situations in which a person may qualify for SSDI benefits and still remain capable of performing the essential functions of her job. Thus, the Court held that judicial estoppel could not be applied to prevent a claimant of SSDI benefits from asserting that she is a qualified individual under the ADA. However, the Court emphasized that its holding did not change the rules of judicial estoppel applicable to directly conflicting statements about purely factual matters. The Court also indicated that in order to avoid summary judgment, the plaintiff in the second action must explain any apparent discrepancies between her SSDI statements that she is totally disabled and her ADA claim that she can perform the essential functions of her job.

The Court has not yet addressed whether the *Erie* doctrine requires federal diversity courts to follow state law on matters of judicial estoppel where it differs from the doctrine that the federal courts would apply in federal question cases.[349] It seems clear that if a federal diversity court either refuses to apply judicial estoppel when a state court would, or applies a less stringent judicial estoppel doctrine than the state courts, forum shopping will occur by plaintiffs in derogation of the *Erie* policies.[350] When the plaintiffs are noncitizens, this will cause the *Erie* prohibited "discrimination against citizens of the forum state."[351] On the other hand, if the federal court applies judicial estoppel when a state court would not, or applies a more stringent judicial estoppel doctrine than the state courts would apply, forum shopping by nonresident defendants will occur in some cases,[352] and in other cases in which resident defendants are

---

347. *See* United States v. 49.01 Acres of Land, 802 F.2d 387, 390 (10th Cir. 1986).

348. 526 U.S. 795, 119 S. Ct. 1597, 143 L. Ed. 2d 966 (1999).

349. *See generally* Ashley S. Deeks, Comment, *Raising the Cost of Lying: Rethinking* Erie *for Judicial Estoppel,* 64 U. CHI. L. REV. 873 (1997) (concluding that federal diversity courts should apply the most aggressive version of judicial estoppel available to them).

350. *See id.* at 889.

351. *See* Chapter 5(E)(2), *Illustration 5-11 supra* (discussing the refinement of *Erie* by *Hanna v. Plumer* and the possibility that discrimination against noncitizens of the forum might also be included within the *Erie* prohibitions).

352. *But see* Ashley S. Deeks, Comment, *Raising the Costs of Lying: Rethinking* Erie *for Judicial Estoppel,* 64 U. CHI. L. REV. 873, 887 (1997), arguing that defendant forum shopping is irrelevant under *Hanna's* twin aims test. *Cf.* Chapter 5(E)(2), *Illustration 5-13 supra* (arguing that forum shopping by nonresident defendants should be included within the *Erie* prohibitions).

involved, nonresident plaintiffs will be driven from federal court to obtain the benefit of the more lenient state rule, thus undermining the policies of the diversity jurisdiction.[353]

Because the policy supporting judicial estoppel is one of protecting the integrity of the judicial system,[354] it is arguable that this policy is a sufficiently strong "federal countervailing consideration" under the *Byrd* decision to justify federal disregard of state judicial estoppel doctrine in diversity cases.[355] However, as noted above, this would, at least in some cases, result in serious frustration of the policies of the diversity jurisdiction when federal courts applied an independent judicial estoppel doctrine that was more aggressive than the doctrine applied by the state courts. Because subject-matter jurisdiction policies are among the strongest policies applicable to litigation in the federal courts, it seems unjustified to elevate the policies of judicial estoppel above them. On balance, therefore, it seems more prudent to apply *Erie* straightforwardly to this issue and require federal diversity courts to duplicate state judicial estoppel doctrines.

On the other hand, the judicial integrity rationale is sufficiently persuasive to counsel state courts to adopt vigorous judicial estoppel doctrines as a matter of their own common law. If this is done, the problem in diversity actions will be eliminated, since both the state and federal courts (the latter by virtue of *Erie*) will apply judicial estoppel aggressively, thus assuring both judicial integrity and sound state-federal relationships.

---

353. *See* Chapter 5(E)(2), *Illustration 5-12 supra* (discussing the problem of federal court application of rules that are more stringent than state rules from the plaintiff's point of view and how such a practice would undermine the policies of the diversity jurisdiction).

354. *See* Ashley S. Deeks, Comment, *Raising the Costs of Lying: Rethinking* Erie *for Judicial Estoppel,* 64 U. CHI. L. REV. 873, 888 (1997).

355. *See id.* at 891-96.

TABLE OF CASES

References are to Pages. Bold page numbers indicate principal textual discussion when multiple pages are listed.

INDEX

References are to Pages.